Farm Holiday Guide
ENGLAND
1986

The best in coast and country accommodation throughout England.

An FHG Publication

Board/Self-Catering   AVON

HOME REARED ROAST BEEF – FARM BAKED BREAD

Churchill Green Farm

CHURCHILL GREEN, CHURCHILL, SOMERSET (AVON)

AA Listed **Licensed**

David and Janet Sacof **Phone Churchill 852438**

This is a charming old 17th century farmhouse, with modern comforts and yet the character has not been spoiled. It commands splendid views of open countryside at the foot of the Mendip Hills, and is an excellent centre for trips to Wells, Bath, Weston-Super-Mare, Cheddar and the varied and beautiful countryside of North Somerset. Golf, fishing, riding, swimming, tennis and many more sporting facilities are available nearby, clay pigeon shooting arranged, or you can spend your day relaxing in the quiet of two acres of garden by the full-sized swimming pool surrounded by over 20 acres of our own farmland, with no nearby main roads to disturb the peace.

This is a working farm and our beef is raised on the farm, we have our own eggs, and most vegetables. Fresh bread is baked daily. The food is excellent and abundant.

The bedrooms have hot and cold water, reading lamps and comfortable beds – two of which are antique and unique Canopy "Tester" beds! Although the house is centrally heated, log fires are lit whenever necessary. The atmosphere at Churchill Green is relaxed and friendly — we have been here for over 20 years. The house is open all year round and visitors from home and overseas are welcome to stay as long as they like. The farm is highly recommended for all times of year. Please write direct or telephone for further details and brochure and tariff, which may vary according to the time of year, with reductions for children, who are most welcome. Pony for small children.

There is now a self-catering cottage in the garden, details are in the "Self-Catering" section of this Guide.

2   **Please mention Farm Guide England when enquiring**

Board   AVON

Good food and a warm friendly welcome await you at
MOORLANDS

An attractive Georgian house, the Holt family's home for the last nineteen years, "Moorlands" stands in extensive grounds with a mature landscaped garden and paddock. The house has central heating throughout. All eight bedrooms have H&C handbasins; one family room has private bath, another has a private shower; there are two ground floor rooms, one with private toilet, and additionally there are two bathrooms and three toilets. Guests enjoy good food in generous variety, and fresh vegetables and fruit from the garden are used whenever possible. Margaret's and David's daughter, Nina, is a trained pâtisserie chef and home baking is a speciality.

There is a happy, friendly atmosphere here and children are especially welcome. The garden offers a playground with a slide and games; pony riding can be arranged, in the paddock. The house is open at all times during the day, and there is always someone available for babysitting by arrangement. There are reduced terms for children, and cots are available.

"Moorlands" is an ideal place for a relaxing holiday; Hutton is a charming village lying below the steep, wooded slopes of the western Mendips, with excellent walking on the hills. It's a good touring centre with broad, sandy beaches nearby, and good golf courses and fishing in the area. The Holts have a temporary-membership arrangement for their guests at a local country club for dancing, swimming, etc., and there's a good sports centre within five miles.

They are members of the West Country Tourist Board, and "Moorlands" has its fire safety certificate.

"Moorlands" is open all the year round. Write or telephone for a brochure.

MARGARET and DAVID HOLT, "MOORLANDS", HUTTON, near WESTON-SUPER-MARE, SOMERSET BS24 9QH.
BLEADON 812283 [STD 0934]

Please mention Farm Guide England when enquiring

Board

AVON

LEMON PARK FARM, Wrington, Avon. Mrs J. Pope
Tel: Wrington (0934) 862571

A modern blending farmhouse set in unspoilt, rural position – a country and conservationists' paradise, yet central for north Somerset and Avon resorts. Good food and a warm welcome await all guests. Two double and one family bedrooms, with washbasins; lounge with colour TV and sun lounge; bathroom, two toilets; diningroom. Heated swimming pool. Children welcome; babysitting by request; reduced rates under 12 years. No pets. Evening Dinner, Bed and Breakfast. SAE, please for terms. Car essential, ample parking. Many tourist attractions in the area.

DORNDEN GUEST HOUSE (AA Listed)
Church Lane, Old Sodbury, Bristol, Avon. Tel. 0454-313325. John & Daphne Paz

Dornden, former vicarage of Old Sodbury, is two miles from junction 18 of M4. The house is surrounded by two acres of beautiful gardens with a grass tennis court enjoying the peace of the countryside and magnificent views to the west. All nine bedrooms (two en suite) have washbasins and razor points. There is a comfortable lounge with colour TV and spacious diningroom. Every room has a view of the garden and countryside beyond. Convenient overnight break to Cornwall and Wales, also central for touring with Bath, Bristol, Cheddar, Longleat and Cotswolds nearby. Good home cooking using own garden produce in season. Reduction for four day breaks and children sharing parents room.

Home Baking
Fresh Vegetables
Jersey Cream
at . . .

POOL FARM, Hewish, nr. Weston-super-Mare, Somerset.
Tel: Yatton (0934) 833138

Let the children sample the excitement of life on a working farm. There are horses, ponies, calves, chickens and ducks to see, and sometimes help to feed, and delicious food to enjoy. Although modernised and centrally heated, the farmhouse retains much of its old world charm. Ingelnook fireplaces, with open fires on chilly days; two spacious lounges, one with colour TV. All bedrooms have washbasins and two are on the ground floor. Five bath/shower rooms, six toilets. Good facilities for children, and someone available for babysitting. Pleasant gardens. The house makes a good base for touring Bath, Wells, Glastonbury, Cheddar, Longleat and Bristol. Weston-super-Mare with its beaches, fine open-air swimming pool, tennis courts, golf course, etc., only four miles distant. Open all year except Christmas and New Year. Dog allowed (owners must bring food).

For more details write or telephone Josephine and Graham Murphy.

Board   CORNWALL

AA ★★   Ashley Courtenay Recommended   RAC ★★

ENJOY A HOLIDAY BY THE SEA
and in the country in the heart of
KING ARTHUR'S KINGDOM
at

BOSSINEY HOUSE HOTEL
Tintagel, Cornwall PL34 0AX

The North Cornish Coastline, particularly around Boscastle and Tintagel, has always appealed to all appreciative of wild cliff scenery, romance and contentment never found in towns. Bossiney House is perched about half a mile from Tintagel on the cliffs overlooking one of the finest stretches of coastline in Great Britain.

There are Three Lounges, Colour Television, Spacious Dining Room and Cocktail Bar. All 20 bedrooms have sea or country views; 17 including the family suite have private facilities, 9 are on the ground floor.

Here emphasis is on fine English cooking with excellent choices and variation of menus and really personal attention by the resident proprietors. They give excellent value for money, and they and their staff work as a dedicated team to make your stay most comfortable.

Outside there are two and a half acres of attractive gardens and lawns, an interesting putting course, ample free parking space and a Scandinavian log chalet contains the heated swimming pool, sauna and solarium. Nearby activities include surfing, horse riding, golf, squash, pony trekking, shark fishing and a host of interesting places to visit.

Open from Easter to early October.
Dinner, Room and Breakfast
£21.75 – £25 daily
£130 – £159 weekly
Room and Breakfast
£15 – £18 daily
£91 – £108 weekly

Attractive reductions for 3, 5 and 14-day stay. Reductions for children according to age.

For more details and full tariff please write mentioning publication or telephone Mr & Mrs John Wrightam, (0840) 770240.

YOUR IDEAL BASE TO AN AREA PACKED WITH INTEREST AND BEAUTY

Board   **CORNWALL**

A warm welcome, excellent varied food and high standards of service and accommodation ensure the perfect holiday at **Rainbow's End**. Ten minutes' walk from both beach and shops, and adjacent to magnificent National Trust cliff walks. **Rainbow's End** has a beautiful garden, and terraces in daylong sunshine. Comfortably furnished bedrooms with washbasins and spring mattresses, including a four-poster room, twin and double rooms, one with en-suite facilities. Colour TV in lounge, separate tables in sunny diningroom. Payphone. Ample parking. Early morning tea, hot bedtime drinks. Regret no children under 10. No pets. Large breakfast. Four-course Evening Dinner — £61-£72 inclusive weekly. Tourist Board approved. RAC listed. Open March to September. Stamp please, for brochure. FHG Diploma Winner.

RAINBOW'S END, Brentfield, Polperro, Cornwall PL13 2JJ
Polperro [0503] 72510 Hugh McKernan

Mrs M. Welsby, Hillcrest, Trevellas, St. Agnes, Cornwall TR5 0XY
(St. Agnes [087-255] 3142)

Hillcrest is situated on the coastal road between Perranporth and St. Agnes. The lovely sea cove of Trevellas Porth one and a quarter miles. All bedrooms are well-appointed and have washbasins; shaver and power points. Large lounge with Colour TV and log fire. Dining room. Central heating. Large car park. Heated outdoor swimming pool; children's play areas and games room. Special reductions Senior Citizens. One child free all season. All children (sharing) FREE, Easter to Whitsun and after 1st September. Holiday cottage in grounds.

DALSWINTON
COUNTRY HOUSE HOTEL

Telephone: St Mawgan (0637) 860385   Visitors (0637) 860695
ST MAWGAN ● Nr. NEWQUAY ● CORNWALL TR8 4EZ

Residential and Restaurant Licence

Ten Bedrooms
Fire Certificate

An old Cornish House, full of character and charm in a beautiful secluded position, standing in 1½ acres of grounds, facing south with panoramic views over the wooded Vale of Lanherne to the sea. Away from the bustle yet only six miles from Newquay, seven miles to Padstow and two miles to the magnificent Atlantic beaches and coastline.

* All bedrooms have H&C, shaver points, radio/baby listening, teasmades available. Five rooms with private bathroom or shower.
* Outdoor heated swimming pool.
* Licensed bar with pool table.
* Good home cooking with choice of five-course Dinner and full English Breakfast.
* A la carte menu for lunches and suppers.
* Reduced rates for children sharing with parents.
* Dogs accepted.
* Full central heating and open wood fires in lounge and bar off season.
* OPEN ALL YEAR. SAE (please) for brochure from resident proprietors Marian and Derrick Molloy.

Terms: Bed & Breakfast £9.50 to £13 per night;
Dinner, Bed and Breakfast £75 to £103 per week (plus VAT).
BARGAIN BREAKS EARLY AND LATE SEASON

Board/Self-Catering **CORNWALL**

A REAL COUNTRY HOUSE HOTEL JUST OUTSIDE OF FALMOUTH

THE HOME
PENJERRICK, FALMOUTH

Telephone: Falmouth (STD 0326) 250427 and 250143

Situated in lovely unspoilt countryside, yet only 2½ miles from Falmouth. Ideal for lovers of the country, yet within 18 minutes' walk of Maenporth Beach.

An Ashley Courtenay Recommended Hotel

Our house, in its large garden, has lovely views over tree-clad countryside to Maenporth and the bay. Close to the Helford River with its beautiful walks and boating facilities. Ideal base for touring.

All bedrooms have H&C, razor points and bedside lights. Our home is graciously furnished and carpeted to a high standard. All beds are modern divans. Partial central heating.

Our elegant dining room has separate tables. Large lounge with colour TV. In addition there is a spacious sun lounge overlooking the garden.

★
GOOD ENCLOSED CAR PARK   BUS SERVICE
★

Mr & Mrs P. Tremayne have welcomed guests to their lovely house for the past 21 years

Dinner, Room and Breakfast from £70 per week, including 15% VAT.
Illustrated brochure from: Mrs. T. P. Tremayne

We are of a farming family and our visitors' book is blushingly complimentary over the home-cooked food and its presentation. This is our home and as such we welcome you to it and hope you will enjoy it as much as we do. Special petrol scheme for regular and new guests for April, May, June and September subject to availability.

Also Self-Catering Furnished Farmhouse and Cottage at Constantine, Falmouth

Please mention Farm Guide England when enquiring

Board/Self-Catering   **CORNWALL**

Crantock Plains Farm

Relax in this charming character farmhouse in peaceful countryside and combine comfort, home cooking and personal service for an enjoyable holiday. Crantock Plains Farm is situated two and a half miles from Newquay and half a mile off the A3075 Newquay — Redruth road. Picturesque village of Crantock with Post Office, village stores, tea rooms, two pubs and beautiful sandy beach is nearby, as are riding stables and many sporting activities. Two doubles, one single, three family (one with bathroom en-suite), shower room, three toilets, sittingroom and diningroom. No pets. Babysitting arranged. B.B. from £48 weekly. B.B. & E.M. from £61 weekly. SAE for brochure.

**Mrs B. Franks, Crantock Plains Farm, Near Newquay, Cornwall.
Tel. Crantock [0637] 830253.**

Picturesque group of 17th century cottages overlooking beautiful National Trust Valley with fabulous views of the sea. All our cottages are individually furnished and equipped to a very high standard. All have colour TV etc. Cottages are warm and comfortable and are open all year. Wonderful walks, peace and quiet and unspoilt beaches are on our doorstep. Our cottages offer you quality and comfort at a reasonable cost. Please write or phone any time for our free colour brochure.

Alan and Beryl Tomkinson, Courtyard Farm, Lesnewth, near Boscastle, Cornwall. Tel: 084-06 256.

---

* Superior S/C Apartments for 2 to 9
* Fully equipped, all electric, Col.TV.
* Own bath/shower and toilet
* Unrivalled views over Bay. Minutes from beach
* Free parking. Coin-op launderette
* Quiet peaceful location
* Well behaved pets welcome
* Low Season from £50 – High from £100 to £230 depending on size of Apartment
* SAE for Brochure and Tariff

**Resident Proprietors:
Kevin & Beryl Dolley**

**PLAIDY BEACH HOLIDAY APARTMENTS,
Dept FG, Plaidy, Looe, Cornwall PL13 1LG.**   **Phone 05036 2044**

Dream old world country cottages. Individual private gardens. Breathtaking views. Roses round the door. Heated pool. Full linen. Delicious home cooked meal service. Furnishings and equipment par excellence – antiques, paintings, wool carpets, washer driers, colour TV's, log fires. Golf, riding, fishing, sea, nearby. Looe 3 miles. Sleeps 2 to 6. Open all year. Well behaved pets welcome. Personal attention and free colour brochure from:

**A. Wright, Treworgey Cottages, Duloe, Liskeard, Cornwall PL14 2PP
Tel. Looe (05036) 2730**

Please mention Farm Guide England when enquiring

Coastal Cottages

LOOE, CORNWALL

On the fringe of Looe, a cluster of beautifully furnished cottages, of **rare and exceptional quality**, only 350 yards from the beach and coastal footpath. Country lanes, riding, fishing and golf.
Colour TV and linen included, with beds made up for your arrival. Electric blankets and comprehensive heating for out of season breaks. Regret no pets.

For colour brochure please telephone
Looe (050 36) 2736

Board　　　　　　　　　　　　　　　　　　　　　　　　　　**CUMBRIA**

THE OAKTHORPE HOTEL

The Hotel can be found in Windermere, the heart of England's Lake District and ideally situated for walking, boating, fishing and golf. Tony and Sue Tasker, the resident proprietors, offer a warm welcome and the guarantee of a relaxing family holiday. The Oakthorpe has a licensed bar, and has 20 bedrooms each with tea and coffee making trays; eight rooms with private facilities; an excellent restaurant serving the best of traditional and continental cooking which caters also for non-residents; and the advantage of being two minutes' walk from Windermere Station, coach and bus stops.

AA　　　　High Street
Windermere, Cumbria LA23 1AF
Telephone: Windermere (09662) 3547　　　RAC

Lane Head Farm

Troutbeck Penrith Cumbria　Threlkeld 220
Proprietors: Christine and Peter Fellows

A charming 17th century farmhouse, set in beautiful gardens overlooking undisturbed views of Lakeland Fells. Midway between Keswick and Penrith. The house has been tastefully decorated throughout with many rooms featuring beams. Three bedrooms have en suite bathrooms, one has a four poster bed, and the others have washbasins and shaver points. A pretty lounge with colour TV and a separate sittingroom, all add to the comfort of our guests. Our main attraction is the high standard of food, a large breakfast and five-course dinner, prepared from local home-fed produce, bring our guests back time after time. Separate dining tables, selected wine list and small well-stocked bar complete our package for relaxation.

We will be happy to supply further details. SAE.

Craigburn Farm

PENTON, CARLISLE CA6 5QP
PHONE NICHOLFOREST
022-877-214

Enjoy the delights of beautiful Cumbrian countryside and life on the farm. Craigburn, under the personal supervision of owners Jack and Jane Lawson offers home cooking, warm hospitality and a variety of facilities within easy reach; heated indoor pool, shooting, fishing. Tennis court at the farm and ponies, children's games. Central heating and H&C in all bedrooms, some with en-suite bathroom. Licensed bar. SAE for details.

With its commanding views of Loughrigg Fell, the Hotel provides the ideal base for your holiday, whether it be one of relaxation or activity. Ambleside is at the heart of the Lake District, with easy access to all areas. There are 16 bedrooms, 13 with private facilities, a comfortable lounge, spacious diningroom, separate TV lounge, garden and ample car parking. Residents' Cocktail Bar and Tannery Bar offer a warm welcome. Friendly atmosphere, excellent food, fine wines, delightful surroundings and the personal attention of BRIAN and KATHLEEN BARTON, provide the makings of a wonderful holiday. Brochure on request.

RAC ★★ **The Fisherbeck Hotel** AA ★★
Lake Road, Ambleside, Cumbria LA22 0DH
Ambleside (0966) 33215

Please mention Farm Guide England when enquiring

Board/Self-Catering   **CUMBRIA**

AWARDED THE BRITISH TOURIST AUTHORITY COMMENDATION
Ashley Courtenay Recommended   RAC*

THE MILL, Mungrisdale, Penrith, Cumbria CA11 0XR
Tel. Threlkeld (059-683) 659

Delightfully situated immediately at the foot of blue/grey crags and soft mountain slopes, in grounds bounded by a stream. This former Mill Cottage (dated 1651) provides eleven comfortable bedrooms, some with private bathrooms and colour TV and all with tea/coffee making facilities. Residential and Restaurant licence. Our reputation is based on our high standard of freshly prepared appetising food and a friendly relaxed atmosphere. Resident proprietors: **Mr and Mrs David Wood.**

THE WHITE HOUSE

A converted 18th century farmhouse brought tastefully up to date. The rooms are large and comfortable throughout with log fire in the lounge and central heating in every room. Set in pleasant gardens, our aim is to help you to unwind and relax in peaceful surroundings, yet there is easy access to the motorway, Penrith, Ullswater and The Lake District. All bedrooms have washbasins, teamakers, central heating and some have private facilities. We like guests to enjoy their holiday in comfortable surroundings with good home cooking, bar and separate lounge, and no restrictions so they are encouraged to come and go as they please.

Jean and Donald Fowler, The White House, Clifton, Penrith, Cumbria CA10 2EL
(Penrith [0768] 65115)

Bessiestown Farm   PENTON, CARLISLE, CUMBRIA CA6 5QP
Tel. Mrs Margaret Sisson, (0228 77) 219. AA & RAC Listed. Residential Licence.

AA AWARD WINNER – 1984
Friendly, relaxing atmosphere combined with delicious home cooking in delightful 10 bedroom — five en-suite — farmhouse overlooking Scottish Borders. Also three self-catering cottages with option of evening meal in farmhouse. Ideal for family holiday, break to and from Scotland, or touring Lake District and South Scotland.
**INDOOR HEATED SWIMMING POOL,
PONY RIDING   GAMES ROOM.**

Esthwaite Farm Holidays, Near Sawrey, Ambleside

Seven holiday flats in traditional farmstead, two for handicapped people. Close to Esthwaite Water and Hill Top (the home of Beatrix Potter). Two miles from Lake Windermere, near Grizedale Forest with its Nature Trails and 'Theatre in the Forest'. Each unit sleeps four adults, furnished and equipped to a comfortable standard with cooking and heating. Six flats have wood burning stoves. Electricity meter. Each flat has livingroom, kitchen, two bedrooms with single beds, shower room with WC and washbasin. TV. Use of washing machine and drying room. Linen not supplied. Coarse fishing on private lakeshore inclusive. Rowing boats available at extra charge. Open all year. Weekly terms from £45 to £150.

Apply to Esthwaite Estates Ltd., Graythwaite Estate Office, Nr. Ulverston, Cumbria LA12 8BA.
Telephone Newby Bridge (0448) 31248.

Self-Catering/Board — **CUMBRIA/DEVON**

Plumgarths Holiday Flats

Between Kendal and Windermere

Open All Year
6 Spacious Flats – Garden Chalet
Sleep 2 – 7
Central Heating, Col.TV.,
3 acres secluded grounds.
**Jonathan and Fidelia Somervell,
Crook, Kendal, Cumbria LA8 8LE
Tel: Staveley (0539) 821345**

For full details see:
Self-Catering Section — Cumbria : Kendal
Founder Member Cumbria and Lakeland
Self-Caterers' Association

- Established 15 years
- Luxury self-contained flats for 2-4 adults
- Open all year round
- AA listed and member Cumbria Tourist Board
- Extensive peaceful lake gardens and woodland
- All electric, TV, fridge, bathroom etc
- Ideal centre lakes and coast
- Out of season breaks from £15/3 nights
- Low season £25/week, high season £75 – £100/week
- Brochure on request, SAE please

**AYNSOME MANOR PARK, CARTMEL, GRANGE-OVER-SANDS, CUMBRIA
LA11 6HH Tel. Cartmel 433 (STD 044 854)**

Raddicombe Lodge
COUNTRY GUEST HOUSE

A.A.   LISTED   R.A.C.

The Lodge lies midway between the picturesque coastal towns of Brixham and Dartmouth, overlooking sea and country, with National Trust land between us and the sea. Reached by a private drive, away from the rush and noise.

The house has a charm and character of its own with open pitched ceilings and lattice windows in many of the bedrooms, which all have hot and cold water, mirror lights, shaver lights, over bed or bedside lights and fitted carpets. The diningroom has separate tables for each party of guests where delicious home cooked country foods are served, which include Brixham crab and fish from the quay. Devon cream, locally-baked crusty bread and fresh produce from our garden as available with a fine selection of wines. Central heating and a comfortable lounge, with colour television, for you to relax after a busy day. We have a large car park where you may leave your car and explore the coast and country lanes of South Devon on foot.

Room, Breakfast & Evening Dinner, £14.10 to £17.45 per night each, to include early morning tea, supper time coffee and VAT at 15%. No service charge. Reduction for children sharing a room with two adults, according to age.

Stamp only for brochure
or telephone:
**Brixham 2125 (STD 08045).
GRAHAM & YVONNE GLASS,
Raddicombe Lodge,
102 Kingswear Road,
Brixham, Devon TQ5 0EX**

Please mention Farm Guide England when enquiring

Seclusion and Peace at
THE COVE GUEST HOUSE, TORCROSS

As the pace of modern life increases so does the need for people to use available holiday periods to get away from it all. Torcross, a small seaside village and The Cove House are a combination which can serve to be one of the most relaxing holidays you have ever had. The only sound you hear will be that of the sea as it kisses the shore only 25 yards from the house. The Cove House is situated in $3\frac{1}{2}$ acres of its own coastline; there can be no better place from which to enjoy the pleasures the sea can give, whether it be fishing, swimming or just strolling along the beach. By night one can indulge in romantic gazes at starlit skies or looking at uninterrupted views of both rises of sun and moon.

Within one hour by car one can visit the following places, Dartmouth, Torquay, Paignton, Plymouth or Dartmoor.

Visitors to The Cove House can be assured of excellent food both in quality and quantity, served in the Diningroom which immediately overlooks the sea. There is an attractive licensed Bar Lounge. The Proprietors and Staff are always on hand and they care about your holiday. Accommodation is excellent. All bedrooms have TV sets installed and basins with hot and cold water. Some have private showers. There is ample free car parking in the grounds. A car is desirable but not essential. A Fire Certificate is held. Children under 8 years of age and pets are not catered for.

The Cove House is open for visitors from March 1st to November 30th offering Dinner, Bed and Breakfast. Price reductions apply during March, April, May and from mid-September to end of November.

Please send postage stamp only for free coloured brochure and tariff to:

**MR & MRS K. SMALL
THE COVE GUEST HOUSE
TORCROSS, NEAR KINGSBRIDGE**
South Devon. Telephone Kingsbridge 580448 (STD 0548)

Board DEVON

Sandy Cove Hotel
THE SEA FOOD HOTEL
Combe Martin Bay, Berrynarbor, Nr. Ilfracombe, Devon. Tel: (0271-88) 2243

RAC**

How would you like to arrive for a week's holiday at a hotel overlooking a beautiful bay, the sea and Exmoor? The first thing you would notice would be the acres of gardens and woods running down to the cliff edge, and the heated swimming pool set in its midst. A warm bath then dinner in the restaurant, an extensive a la carte menu, Caribbean and lobster dishes, a speciality is extra but the table d'hote is excellent. The hot carvery and Swedish Smorgasbord on a Saturday will wet your lips and the barbecues and country and western cabaret – first class (in the height of the season). Dance on a Saturday night until midnight, use the heated outdoor pool (heated in season), putting green, games room, fitness room with gymnasium equipment, sauna and sun bed to your likes. Or relax in the 'Crows Nest' secluded cliff-top Summer House overlooking the bay and the sea. CHILDREN ARE VERY WELCOME AND AT CERTAIN TIMES OF THE YEAR THEY HAVE ABSOLUTELY *FREE* ACCOMMODATION PROVIDING THEY SHARE THEIR PARENTS' ROOM – YOU JUST PAY FOR THEIR MEALS. We are also happy if you bring your pets with you. Baby sitting can be arranged. Invalids catered for. Open all the year – Christmas and mini weekend breaks a speciality. Some four poster bedrooms for romantic honeymoons. Free Golf with some package holidays.

37 Bedrooms, 35 Private Bathrooms. Fully Licensed. Combe Martin 1 mile, Ilfracombe 4 miles
Please write or ring for free colour brochure to:
DAWN & RICHARD GILSON, DEPT. (13), SANDY COVE HOTEL, COMBE MARTIN BAY, BERRYNARBOR, Nr ILFRACOMBE, N. DEVON.

Fun for the family at Leworthy Farm

OPEN ALL YEAR
AA and RAC listed
DCC Fire Certificate
RESIDENTIAL LICENCE

LEWORTHY FARM is an excellent centre for touring Devon and Cornwall. Surrounded by beautiful countryside, it extends to 240 acres and guests will enjoy the farming activities besides all the seaside amenities in the area. Access is easy to the glorious coastline where there is surfing, swimming and fishing, and for walks and picnics on the farm and Dartmoor. Mr Cornish happily combines the double role of farmer and host to guests, while Mrs Cornish a B.Sc.(Dom.Sc.) supervises the catering. The standard of food and comfort is very high – what better proof than the FARM HOLIDAY GUIDE AWARD won by Leworthy Farm in 1976!

Guests are accommodated in three double bedrooms, two single and five family rooms (eight with washbasins), en suite available; two sittingrooms and diningroom with separate tables. There is a provision for children who will glory in the spacious surroundings. Sorry, no pets. Special early season terms for children sharing parents' room. Large farm buildings for indoor recreation such as badminton, skittles, table tennis, snooker. Party evenings with live music. Hay rides, fishing, pony riding, tennis. Car essential. Enjoy *the* holiday with a difference! Good living! Never a dull moment! Have you tried a winter break at Leworthy Farm, complete with inglenook log fires, at out of season rates?

AA Award: UK Farmhouse of the Year 1980 – Send stamp for brochure and tariff to:

**Eric and Marion Cornish,
Leworthy Farm, Holsworthy, Devon (Holsworthy [0409] 253488)**

Please mention Farm Guide England when enquiring

Board DEVON

HAZELDENE, Lee Road, Lynton, Devon EX35 6BP

This family-run guest house provides comfortable, well-appointed accommodation with full central heating making it ideal for early/late holidays. Mouthwatering food, dine by candlelight. Good wine selection. Double and family bedrooms, all with colour televisions and two with en suite bathrooms; pleasant lounge, colour TV. Tea making facilities in bedrooms. Children and pets welcome. Car park. AA/RAC listed. Member of West Country Tourist Board. Open January to November.
ACCESS/VISA CARDS ACCEPTED.

Mrs. H. E. Blight – Lynton (0598) 52364

COMBAS FARM, CROYDE, DEVON

This mixed farm of 140-acres is ¾ mile from sea. The 17th century farmhouse has attractive garden and orchard where children can play. Set in unspoiled valley near excellent beaches. National Trust coastline. Care taken over presentation and variety of menu; own produce. Guests taken on Beer and Skittles outings. Tennis one mile; golf three. Access to house at all times. Sorry, no pets. Cot, high chair, babysitting available. Double and family rooms; bathroom, toilets; sittingroom; diningroom. Evening Dinner, Bed and Breakfast. Rates reduced for children and for senior citizens early/late season.

Tel: Croyde (0271) 890398. Mrs G. M. Adams

Nymet Bridge House
Lapford, Crediton, Devon EX17 6QX

Charming 14th century cottage-style country guest house situated in glorious countryside. Ideal touring centre within easy reach of Exmoor, Dartmoor and Exeter. Golf, fishing, riding and tennis locally.

Terms from £98 per week for Bed, Breakfast and four-course Dinner.

Five bedrooms, three with private bathrooms. Home cooking. Log fires. Private car park. Open all year. Residential Licence. Winter breaks.

Write or telephone (036-35-334) to Mrs B. Cullimore for colour brochure and tariff.

AWARDED A BRITISH TOURIST AUTHORITY COMMENDATION.

RADFORDS
DAWLISH

In beautiful unspoilt countryside not too far from the beach

FOR THE PERFECT FAMILY HOLIDAY

Come and relax at Radfords in one of our chintzy old world lounges, our comfortable bar or our six acres of lovely garden – or come and enjoy an active action-packed holiday swimming in our heated indoor pools, playing badminton outdoors or enjoying a game of table tennis or skittles or one of the many other games in our large indoor games room. Squash, indoor badminton, golf, tennis, fishing and horse riding are all available close by. We have our own solarium for that essential sun tan.

We have family bedrooms or two room family suites available, all with a private bathroom to accommodate a total of about thirty families. All bedrooms have tea/coffee making facilities.

THE CHILDREN will love their special heated indoor pool, the outdoor playground, the freedom of our large gardens and the assorted ponies and dogs there are to talk to. In the evenings they can look forward to a swimming gala, live entertainment, a party and their own cartoon show etc.

THE ADULTS can look forward to superb food lovingly cooked and served and the various entertainments we arrange for them – from skittle tournaments to live entertainers.
We also have a fully equipped laundrette and an evening babysitter to help make your holiday as relaxing as possible. We have a playgroup several mornings a week. Mothers can bring babies and small children here with every confidence.

AA LISTED, MEMBER WEST COUNTRY TOURIST BOARD.
Please telephone or send for an illustrated brochure to:

Mr and Mrs T. C. Crump, MHCI
**RADFORDS, DAWLISH, SOUTH DEVON EX7 0QN
(Dawlish 863322. STD 0626-863322)**

Board   **DEVON**

Poltimore

South Zeal, Okehampton, Devon EX20 2PD
Telephone: Okehampton (0837) 840209

A charming thatched Guest House delightfully situated in the

DARTMOOR NATIONAL PARK

Awarded the British Tourist Authority's Commendation for Outstanding Hospitality

Nothing could be cosier than this old thatched cottage situated on the northern fringe of Dartmoor. Unpretentious, with the kind of warmth and hospitality which gives an instant sense of relaxed well-being, Poltimore is a place to 'come home to' anytime of the year. Blazing log fires whenever it's cool and always superlative home cooking with a Devonshire flavour. An ideal base for touring with all the West country attractions within easy reach. Home grown produce. Licensed bar, Colour TV. Central heating. Dogs welcome. Seven bedrooms, four with private bathroom.

Terms from £17.00 per day or £112.00 per week for room, English breakfast and four course dinner. No children under 12 years.

For the discerning visitor to this beautiful part of Devonshire, there can be no finer combination of situation and value for money.

AA LISTED

**Self-catering accommodation available.
(see colour advertisement)**

For a colour brochure and terms, telephone or write to the
Resident Proprietors: Mr. and Mrs. M. Harbridge.

Please mention Farm Guide England when enquiring   **17**

Self-Catering/Board DEVON

West Ridge, Devon
Seaton EX12 2TA "West Ridge", Harepath Hill, Mrs E. P. Fox (Seaton [0297] 22398).

"*West Ridge*" bungalow stands on elevated ground above the small coastal town of Seaton. It has 1½ acres of lawns and gardens and enjoys wide panoramic views of the beautiful Axe Estuary and the sea. Close by are Axmouth, Beer and Branscombe. The Lyme Bay area is an excellent centre for touring, walking, sailing, fishing, golf etc. This comfortably furnished accommodation (including the spacious kitchen/living room on the right of the picture) is ideally suited for up to 5 people. A cot can be provided. Available March to October. £85 to £195 weekly (fuel charges included). Full gas c/h; Colour TV. AA Listed and Approved. S.A.E. for brochure.

MARSH HALL

A secluded Victorian Country House set in its own grounds with panoramic views. Six luxuriously appointed bedrooms, all en suite with colour TV, direct dial telephone, and lounge area. Activity weekend breaks in Bird Watching and Clay Pigeon Shooting. Stabling available. From £28 per person per night for Bed, Breakfast and 6 course dinner. Christmas breaks also available. Ashley Courtenay Recommended.

SOUTH MOLTON, NORTH DEVON
Telephone (07695) 2666

AA ** RAC

MAELCOMBE HOUSE

A small coastal farm nestling beneath wooded cliffs overlooking Lannacombe Bay. Beach one minute from comfortable farmhouse which is nearly the most southerly in Devon. Choice of family, double or single rooms. Excellent food, much being produced on farm; freshly caught seafood is a speciality. Activities include fishing, bathing, spectacular walking, exploring, climbing or just relaxing in the gardens. Prices from £59.50 per week for Bed & Breakfast or £89.50 for Bed, Breakfast & Evening Meal, with special reductions for children. Also self-catering flat to sleep 6; camping facilities are provided. Telephone or write for colour brochure.

Mr and Mrs C. M. Davies, Maelcombe House, East Prawle, Near Kingsbridge. (Chivelstone [054-851] 300).

MRS JILL BENT, WEST PITT FARM,
Uplowman, Tiverton, Devon EX16 7DU
Tiverton (0884) 820296

Delicious home cooking is our speciality, and every comfort is available at the farmhouse including washbasins in all bedrooms. Ideally situated for all parts of Devon and the West Country. With all LEISURE FACILITIES available, West Pitt offers a unique, relaxing holiday. Also self-catering farm cottage – sleeps 6 plus.

★ HEATED SWIMMING POOL ★ GRASS TENNIS COURT
★ WELL STOCKED COARSE FISHING POOL ★ GAMES ROOM

DEVON

HOPE COVE HOTEL
AND LICENSED BISTRO

is 50 yards from slipway and sandy beaches. Young or old, beginners or experienced – Hope Cove has something for everyone. Sailing, surfing, snorkeling, diving, ski-ing, fishing or just splashing around. Safe for children in the cove, more fun for the experienced outside. Nearby there are plenty of things to do – trekking, shire horses, zoos, theme parks and more. Hope Cove is a sleepy, picturesque fishing village in the middle of National Trust walks. Water sport equipment available for hire, plus lock-up facilities.

Party rates available. Phone David or Avril for details.

Inner Hope, Kingsbridge, Devon TQ7 3HP
Tel. (0548) 561215

THE OLD RECTORY
Michelin   Ashley Courtenay Recommended   RAC*   Country House Hotel   AA*   HBL

Martinhoe, Parracombe (059 83) 368

Tucked in a hollow on the cliffs above Woody Bay, surrounded by gardens of 3 acres, with a lake, stream and putting green, stands an attractive Georgian former rectory, now converted to a comfortable hotel. All rooms en suite and individually decorated with complementary furnishings. High standard of cuisine, prepared and cooked by the proprietors. While secluded, the hotel, is in easy reach of many lovely coast and moor walks. Superb scenery, horse riding, fishing, golf nearby. One of the few hotels to receive the AA's coveted HBL merit award for four consecutive years. Colour brochure by return. See classified section also. Your hosts are **Tony and Elizabeth Pring.**

"COURT BARN"
COUNTRY HOUSE HOTEL

AA RAC**, 2 AA Merit Awards,
British Tourist Authority Commendations,
Ashley Courtenay and ExecHotel recommended**

Keith and Josephine Lax invite you to enjoy the comfort and luxury of their eight bedroomed country house in the heart of beautiful Devonshire. Six bedrooms have either bath or shower and toilet ensuite, all have central heating, wash hand basins, radio alarms and tea/coffee making facilities. An excellent five course dinner with choice of menu is served each evening. Set in approx. 5 acres including croquet lawn and putting green the house is spacious with two lounges, dining room, intimate bar and sun lounge with snooker/pool table. Convenient for fishing, golf, horse riding, tennis, surfing and swimming. Also for exploring Devon and Cornwall.
Please telephone or write for colour brochure and tariff.

**Mr and Mrs F. KEITH LAX
"Court Barn", Clawton, Holsworthy, Devon EX22 6PS
Tel. North Tamerton [040-927] 219.**

DEVON

Wigham
Morchard Bishop, Mid-Devon EX17 6RK.
(Eight miles NW of Crediton)

Centrally situated for Dartmoor, Exmoor, Exeter, Tiverton and Barnstaple with beaches to the north at Croyde, Saunton or Woolacombe, or to the south at Exmouth or Dawlish Warren.

THATCHED DEVON LONGHOUSE with original beams, oak panelling, inglenook fireplaces, roof timbers, underthatch, bread and cream ovens and all situated in quiet, rolling farmland, 1½ miles out of the village. Wigham is run as a guesthouse with an 11-acre smallholding which offers to guests freshly picked fruit and vegetables; honey from our own hives; our own beef and pork; free range eggs; soft and pressed cheeses and, of course, thick Devonshire cream and golden butter! Dinners are prepared daily from fresh ingredients, for example:
Savoury wholemeal pancakes; Pork casseroled in cream and local cider with new potatoes and fresh vegetables; Treacle tart; homemade ice-cream or lemon syllabub; cream; selection of local farm cheeses; biscuits; freshly baked bread; coffee.

We are fully licensed with some 20 excellent wines plus spirits, liqueurs and local matured cider. For your comfort we have a colour TV and video plus teamakers and electric blankets if required. We only have four guestrooms but there are two bathrooms and you are assured of a warm welcome and a memorable holiday or break.

Listed

Dinner, Bed and Breakfast from £18.00.
Telephone or write to Steve or Les Chilcott, Morchard Bishop (036 37) 350.
We regret no dogs, SMALL children or smokers!

Board/Self-Catering **DEVON**

Muddlebridge House, Fremington, Barnstaple, North Devon EX31 2NQ.

This large period country house offers two double bedrooms plus family room with shower/bathroom, central heating, H&C in each room. Food is of the highest quality. For **self-catering**, six superb cottages converted from stone farm buildings, sleeping two to eight persons, set in two-acre plot with formal gardens, heated swimming pool, childrens play area, snooker room, table tennis etc. Close to beaches. Evening meals available. Residents' Bar. SAE or telephone for further details.

Keith & Wendy Le Voir   Tel. (0271) 76073

SMYTHEN FARM LUXURY HOLIDAY COTTAGES

Superior Holiday Cottages to let, all self-contained on this family working farm of 165 acres, mainly sheep, lambs and cattle. Situated on the edge of Exmoor National Park, where you can find wild deer and ponies and the famous Lorna Doone country. Two miles to Olde Worlde Village with village stores, butcher's shop and Olde Worlde Inn. Plenty of sports in the area — surfing, fishing, golf, pony trekking and miles of golden sands. All guests are welcome to free pony and donkey riding, and may enjoy walks over the farm and woods. One, two and three bedroomed cottages to sleep from two to 11 persons. Large picture windows with magnificent sea and coastal views. Modern bathrooms and toilets. Airing cupboard. TV. Fridge, cooker and heaters, all-electric. Fully equipped except linen. SAE, please, for terms and brochure; special out of season rates.

Mrs F. M. Irwin, Smythen Farm, Sterridge Valley, Berrynarbor, Ilfracombe, Devon EX34 9TB
Combe Martin (027-188) 3515

WEST PUSEHILL FARM COTTAGES

Situated in picturesque and peaceful country surroundings one mile from Westward Ho! beach and 2½ miles from the market town of Bideford.

Each of the eleven cottages has been carefully converted, being equipped and furnished to an extremely high standard. Varying in size, they accommodate 2-8 people. Prices from £65 – £370.

Facilities include: heated swimming pool, residents' bar, sauna, solarium, children's play area, pets corner, games room and laundry. For full colour brochure phone anytime or write to John and Gill Violet.

West Pusehill Farm, Westward Ho!, N.Devon
Tel: Bideford (02372) 75638 or 74622

Eight lovely holiday cottages set in peaceful countryside with superb views, four miles from Totnes, eight miles from beaches. Spacious rooms, modern comforts and conveniences. One, two and three bedroomed cottages sleeping two to seven people. Fitted kitchen/diner, electric cooker and fridge, sittingroom, TV; modern bathroom, cot, high chairs available. Car essential – parking. Sorry no pets. No linen. Open all year. SAE please. AA listed. Weekly terms from £50.

Mrs S. C. Hodges, Higher Poulston, Halwell, Totnes, Devon TQ9 7LE
(Harbertonford [080-423] 345)

Please mention Farm Guide England when enquiring

Self-Catering   **DEVON**

Shell Cove House

Spacious luxury holiday flats, Lodge and Cottage in idyllic setting

OPEN ALL YEAR ROUND

UNIQUE POSITION. A beautiful Georgian country house fully furnished and modernised. The highest attainable standards personally maintained by resident proprietors (since 1968), who take pride in a happy family atmosphere. Beautiful views of gardens and sea, ¾ mile from Dawlish, between the coastal road from Exeter to Torquay and the sea. In its own timbered grounds of over six acres with private cliff path to Shell Cove. The Cove has a lovely secluded beach only otherwise readily accessible by boat.

★ Large Heated Swimming and Paddling Pools, open May to September.
★ Croquet and Badminton Lawns
★ Hard Tennis Court
★ Spacious Flats each with own key and private coloured bathroom suite
★ Secluded Sheltered Beach
★ Full Central Heating
★ Colour TV in each flat
★ Bed linen included
★ TV Lounge, Games Room, Laundry Room
★ Mains Gas Cookers, Electric Refrigerators
★ Ample Free Parking, Dinghies Welcome
★ Good facilities and Games for children
★ Occasional Barbecues in the Cove

E.T.B. Category 4 (Top Grade)
✶   ✶   ✶   ✶

SAE. State dates and size of party.

**Mr and Mrs P. J. Jameson
SHELL COVE HOUSE
The Old Teignmouth Road
Dawlish, Devon EX7 0LA
(Dawlish 86/2523)**

DARTMOOR NATIONAL PARK

Delightful Self-catering accommodation in beautiful surroundings for two to six persons

Ideal for dog owners

Situated on the side of a hill amongst gorse and bracken in the grounds of a BTA Commended Country Guest House, the accommodation comprises a 17th century granite barn converted into two apartments each sleeping up to four adults and two children, and an attractive summer chalet for two persons.

The Old Barn: Each apartment has two double bedrooms each with washbasins, electric blankets and duvets and one also with two bunk beds for children. Charming beamed sitting room with dining area. Kitchenette with electric cooker and refrigerator. Bathroom with bath, shower, washbasin and w.c. Fully equipped and furnished throughout including colour TV, electric fires and night store heating. Weekly terms from £35 to £160 according to season. Special terms for long lets in the winter.

The Chalet: One twin-bedded room, sitting/dining room, kitchenette with electric cooker and refrigerator. Shower room with washbasin and w.c. Fully equipped and furnished throughout including colour TV, electric fires and night store heating. The Chalet is available only between April and October and the terms range from £15 to £85 per week.

The Surroundings: An exploration of Dartmoor can begin at the doorstep. Both properties adjoin open common land with woods and the Moor beyond. Ideal for exercising dogs. The area is a delight for walking, riding, fishing (both game and coarse) with swimming, golf and pony-trekking available nearby. There are superb views of the surroundings which form the northern fringe of Dartmoor, and Exmoor can be seen about 50 miles away. Village stores are ½ mile distant.

Whatever you prefer to do on holiday, you will find Poltimore a most convenient spot to be. If you are looking for good holiday accommodation away from the crowds but with all the West Country attractions within easy reach, then write or telephone for further details.

**Mr Harbridge, Poltimore, Ramsley Common, South Zeal, Okehampton, DEVON EX20 2PD
Telephone: Okehampton (0837) 840209.**

Devon

Choose Unspoilt North Devon
and enjoy a change that offers so much more than the rest

With our **Free Colour Guides** and unbiased recommendation and booking service, we can spoil you for choice in the beautiful unspoilt region around Exmoor and the wide sandy beaches and coves of Devon's Golden Coast.

Choose from over **400 selected properties** including thatched cottages, working farms, beachside bungalows with swimming pools, luxury manor houses etc — from only £40 pw in Spring and Autumn.

New colour guide and booking service to **over 100 recommended Hotels and Guest Houses** from peaceful country inns to first class hotels with every amenity you could wish for. Bargain break weekends from £20 pp.

**Free tourist information and Discount Club membership with every booking.
First class value assured.
Tel
(0271) 76322** (24hr. brochure service)
(0271) 44915 (Tourist Information)

North Devon Holiday Centre

48 Boutport Street, Barnstaple, Devon, EX31 1SE,

Self-Catering/Board — **DEVON/DORSET**

LUXURY COUNTRY COTTAGES

4 character cottages, tastefully converted from a stone barn, set in lovely Devon countryside, with farmhouse and cottages grouped round cobbled yard. Cottages face south-west onto their own private patios, sleep 2-8, are beautifully furnished, well equipped. Woodburning fires, heating, colour TV, bed linen, cots, high-chairs are provided, also swimming pool, games room, laundry room, children's play area. Dogs permitted. Contact resident owner: Mrs S. D. Francis, Collacott Farm, King's Nympton, Umberleigh, N. Devon. Tel. South Molton (07695) 2491.

EXMOOR, DARTMOOR & CLOVELLY WITHIN EASY REACH

Self catering at its BEST. Luxury caravans and chalets with hot and cold shower, flush toilet, colour TV, full size cooker and fridge. No dogs, cleanliness assured. Highly recommended, considered the best chalet/caravan park in Westward Ho! 3 miles of golden sand, safe bathing, surfing, fishing, horse riding, golf.
Write or phone now for colour brochure with details of discounts and special offers for two persons and the small family, in chalets and large caravans, some with 3 bedrooms.

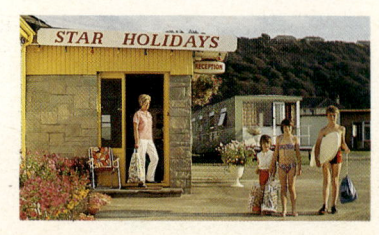

Star Holidays (FG), Westward Ho!, Devon EX39 1HF. Tel. Bideford (023-72) 72238

Large private Country House in own beautifully wooded 600 acre valley with streams and small lake. Nature lovers and children's paradise and for those who want to be off the beaten track though the sea at Beer and Branscombe is 4 miles away and Sidmouth and Seaton 6. Owned and farmed by the family. Also charming old secluded cottage sleeping 8.

Mrs. M. Chichester, Wiscombe Park, Southleigh, Nr. Colyton, Devon. (Farway [040-487] 252/344)

MARSHWOOD MANOR

Near Bridport, Dorset DT6 5NS
Tel. Broadwindsor
(0308) 68442/68825

Comfort and informal atmosphere in 50 acres of the peaceful Marshwood Vale. Excellent food, home made bread, garden produce. Open all year. Children and pets welcome.

For full details see
Board Section – 'Bridport', Dorset

Please mention Farm Guide England when enquiring

Board/Self-Catering **DORSET/HAMPSHIRE/HEREFORD**

MANOR FARM HOLIDAY CENTRE
CHARMOUTH, BRIDPORT, DORSET

AA

Situated in rural valley of outstanding natural beauty, Manor Farm has all the requisite amenities for an exciting yet carefree holiday. Shop, launderette, licensed bar with family room, swimming pool and children's pool, play area. Ten minutes to beach, safe for bathing and famous for its fossils. Golf, riding, tennis, fishing and boating all nearby. Accommodation in 3 bedroomed bungalow, 2 and 3 bedroomed houses, and luxury caravans. All units sleep six, and are equipped with colour TV, fitted carpets and parking/garage.

**SAE to Mr R. B. Loosmore
or Tel. 0297-60226**

THE CLOUD HOTEL

Ideal for a restful and homely holiday with lovely Forest views from public rooms and most bedrooms — a tranquil setting rarely found today. A high standard of real home cuisine is offered by the resident proprietors. Very comfortable surroundings with all facilities for an enjoyable holiday. Four cosy lounges include a TV lounge and bar lounge. All 19 bedrooms have central heating. H&C and radios. Children are welcome at reduced rates. Terms: D.B.&B. from £130 to £151 per week. Ashley Courtenay recommended. Send for colour brochure to:

**Mr and Mrs T. W. Owton, The Cloud Hotel,
Meerut Road, Brockenhurst SO4 7TD
Tel. Lymington [0590] 22165/22254**

Pool House

With its shady lawns and attractive garden this fine country house will please anyone wishing for a quiet, restful holiday. Own fishing and mooring rights on River Severn. Within walking distance of the market town of Upton-upon-Severn and ideal for touring Wye Valley, Cotswolds and Stratford-upon-Avon. Four miles from M5 and M50 motorways. There are six double and three family rooms, four with washbasins and five with en suite facilities. Excellent cuisine. Licensed. Ample car parking. Sorry no pets. Terms on request.

**Mr and Mrs G. B. Webb, Pool House, Hanley Road,
Upton-upon-Severn, Worcester WR8 0PA.
Tel. (068 46) 2151.**

HEREFORDSHIRE FARM COTTAGES

A warm welcome awaits you in our farm cottages. Many of them are tasteful conversions of old farm buildings, full of character but with every modern convenience.
Try a holiday with us and feel the freedom of self catering in our lovely countryside. Situated throughout Herefordshire, near rivers, woods, historical houses and golf courses are our granaries, hop kilns and stables or spacious farm houses.

THE CHOICE IS YOURS!

**SAE to Ashton Court Farm, Ashton, Leominster,
Herefordshire, or Phone 058 472 245.**

Please mention Farm Guide England when enquiring   **25**

Self-Catering/Board   **NORFOLK/SHROPSHIRE/SOMERSET**

HOLIDAY IN OUR ENGLISH COUNTRY GARDEN
2 ACRES IN RURAL NORFOLK WITH RIVER NEARBY.

10 select and spacious family-run bungalows and lovely country farmhouse. Peacefully set in 2 acres of delightful gardens with Games room, Heated pool, Children's play area. Fishing, Boating, Riding and Golf nearby. Only 50 yards from river staithe with access to Broads and well situated for touring. Car essential.

HEDERA HOUSE & Plantation Bungalows

For full details & colour brochure contact:
H. G. Delf, Thurne Cottage, The Staithe, Thurne, Norfolk NR29 3BU. Tel. (0692) 67024 or (0493) 844568.

NORFOLK

Superior two-storey modernised and extended cottage with garage, in excellent condition and available all year for self catering holidays. In quiet rural position with good walking; an ideal base for touring, the house accommodates seven people. Large lounge with wood-burning stove (logs provided); diningroom and fitted kitchen. Colour TV. Downstairs cloakroom and toilet. One double room with bathroom en-suite; two twin bedrooms, one single room and second bathroom with shower. Fitted carpets throughout. Electric heaters (central heating optional). Coin box phone. Children welcome, cot and high chair available. One pet allowed. Linen an optional extra. Metered electricity. Golf, tennis, riding at Ludlow three and a half miles. Weekly terms from £90 to £180.

**Apply to Mrs N. C. Powell, Deepwood Farm, Ludlow, SHROPSHIRE SY8 2JQ.
Tel. Bromfield [058-477] 208.**

DEEPWOOD COTTAGE

BATCH FARM
COUNTRY HOTEL LYMPSHAM, Nr. WESTON-SUPER-MARE SOMERSET

Telephone: Edingworth 371

Fully Licensed Bar   AA**RAC**
Egon Ronay Recommended
W.S.M. Hotels and Restaurants Merit Award

A charming spot in a lovely part of England

There is an air of old world charm that still pervades Batch Farm lending atmosphere to the modern accommodation. Situated midway between the resorts of Weston and Burnham-on-Sea, three miles to sea and sands. Ideal centre for touring. Easy reach of Cheddar Gorge, Wells, Longleat, Bristol and Bath. Hotel surrounded by spacious lawns away from busy main roads and traffic yet only five to ten minutes by car to local resorts. Acres of land for children to play games in safety. Guests have freedom of 150 acres beef working farm. Fishing in River Axe in own grounds. Riding school, swimming, tennis, golf, available locally.

Guests welcome Easter to October. 10 bedrooms, family, doubles, singles, all with vanity units with H&C and shaver sockets, some bedrooms with bathrooms en suite. All bedrooms have panoramic views of countryside and hills. Fully licensed lounge bar also three lounges, one with colour TV and large diningroom with separate tables. Two bathrooms and five toilets.

Traditional home cooking with variation of menus. Home reared beef and local produce used when available. Personal attention by Resident Proprietors and their family combined with their staff whose ambition is to make your holiday a happy one. A large games room with table tennis etc. will please the children. It is regretted dogs not accepted.

Please enclose stamp for colour brochure and terms.

Mr and Mrs D. J. Brown, Batch Farm Country Hotel, Lympsham, Nr. Weston-Super-Mare, Somerset   Phone Edingworth [093472] 371.

Please mention Farm Guide England when enquiring

FOR BETTER HOLIDAYS IN BRITAIN!

The Farm Holiday Guide Diploma

Every year Farm Holiday Guides Ltd award a small number of Diplomas, normally twelve, to advertisers whom our readers have recommended as outstanding holiday hosts. The Diploma is a recognition that the winners have offered service, accommodation and/or catering which readers have found worthy of note.

To date we have never made special mention in print of the winners of our Diploma, mainly because the award is based on the personal experience of a small group of readers, unverified. There are no objective criteria and we all know that personal tastes, likes and dislikes, vary enormously.

However it seems wrong not to give Diploma winners some public acknowledgment and with the clear proviso that no formal recommendation or endorsement by Farm Holiday Guides Ltd is implied, the following were the holiday proprietors who were awarded Diplomas at the beginning of 1985:

Board accommodation (Hotels, farms, guest houses etc.): *Mr and Mrs Allan,* Rockfield, Buckfastleigh, Devon; *Mr McKernan,* Rainbows End, Polperro, Cornwall; *Mr and Mrs Pickering,* Hawthorn Farm, Standlake, Oxon; *Mrs McCormack,* Arran-Emm, Newton Stewart, Wigtownshire; *Mr and Mrs Morrison,* Rose Grove Guest House, Dulnain Bridge, Inverness-shire; *Mr and Mrs Laing,* Atholl House, Dunvegan, Isle of Skye.

Self-catering accommodation: *Mrs Dyke,* The Old Cheese House, Warminster, Wiltshire; *Mr and Mrs MacLennan,* Burn Bank Holiday Homes, Spean Bridge, Inverness-shire; *Mr and Mrs Roberts,* Llys Perran, Llanrwst, Gwynedd.

Caravans/Camping: *Mrs M. Bowen,* Snapdown Farm Caravans, Chittlehamholt, Devon.

WE WELCOME YOUR NOMINATIONS

Comfortable, clean accommodation; wholesome and well-cooked food; courtesy and consideration towards guests; these are the aims of Farm Holiday Guides and our advertisers. When you meet high standards, you can help your holiday host to win our coveted Diploma if you write to us at

FARM HOLIDAY GUIDES LTD, ABBEY MILL BUSINESS CENTRE, SEEDHILL, PAISLEY PA1 1JN.

Your commendation and constructive criticism should encourage the holiday trade in Britain to make sure that it really does offer the good value and warm welcome which we all hope to enjoy on holiday.

Board/Self-Catering   **SOMERSET**

Mr & Mrs J. M. SHOWELL, HARLEY HOUSE HOTEL, IRNHAM ROAD, MINEHEAD, SOMERSET TA24 5DL (MINEHEAD [0643] 2850).

Minehead is the perfect centre for touring the outstanding beauty of Exmoor and for a delightful seaside holiday. The hotel occupies a remarkably open sunny position in a quiet side road just by the town centre and lies in a large walled garden with a croquet lawn and putting green. Ample car parking in forecourt. Six double bedrooms, some en-suite, one single, three family, all with washbasins and gas or electric fires. They overlook the surrounding hills, while the lounge, a particularly peaceful charming room, looks on to the garden. Bathroom, shower room, three toilets. Lounge with TV. Cot. Pets allowed. Breakfast a la carte. The four-course dinner is the best of traditional English cooking, with delicious and unusual sweets a speciality. Evening Dinner, Bed and Breakfast or Bed and Breakfast only. Reductions for children in family rooms and for Senior Citizens out of season. Colour Brochure.

WOODLANDS HOTEL

Woodlands Hotel, a beautiful old house, brick built and ivy clad, has been converted to a hotel which offers every modern comfort yet loses none of its country house atmosphere. Set in its own wooded grounds, it looks out across open country to the Quantock Hills. Secluded gardens provide delightful sun traps. Most bedrooms with private shower and toilet. Real home cooking. Horse riding arranged. Cocktail bar. Heated swimming pool. AA one star. Free holidays offered to those organising parties. Also bargain breaks and special hunting weekends. Livery arranged. Terms on application.

Mr and Mrs Gibson, Woodlands Hotel, Hill Lane, Brent Knoll, Somerset TA9 4DF (Brent Knoll [0278] 760232).

Little Ash Farm Cottage is situated on a 200-acre family run farm between the villages of Winsford and Withypool in the centre of Exmoor National Park. Ideal for touring and exploring, walking, riding, fishing, golf, racing, also swimming and surfing at many local beaches. Places of interest to visit include Dunster Castle, Tarr Steps, Landacre Bridge, Doone Valley and Lynmouth Railway. The south-facing semi-detached cottage sleeps up to eight and is set amidst beautiful scenery. Available from March to November. Extremely comfortable; furnished and equipped to high standard. Most rooms fully carpeted. Linen supplied. Regret no pets. Lawn for children to play and plenty of parking space. Milk and newspapers can be delivered. Near shops and pub. Terms on request.

Mrs Diana Williams, Little Ash Farm, Withypool, Minehead TA24 7RR (Winsford [064-385] 344).

WITHY GROVE FARM
FRIENDLY, COMFORTABLE, LICENSED

A warm welcome awaits you at Withy Grove Farm which adjoins the River Huntspill, famous for its coarse fishing, and which is central to most of Somerset's beauty spots. All bedrooms have wash-basins and tea making facilities; lounge with colour TV and a pleasant dining room where generous helpings of traditional home cooking are served with cream desserts a speciality.

We also have six well equipped self-catering BUNGALOWS and a large BARN FLAT to sleep 5/6 persons.
OUTDOOR HEATED POOL   GAMES ROOM   SKITTLE ALLEY   LICENSED BAR

Details – Mrs Wendy Baker, Withy Grove Farm, Nr. Burnham-on-Sea, Somerset. Phone Burnham-on-Sea (0278) 784471.

BROADWAY HOUSE
CARAVAN AND CAMPING PARK, CHEDDAR
Telephone: Cheddar (0934) 742610

in the heart of Somerset

VIDEO FILM AVAILABLE ON REQUEST

Rose award park — An English Tourist Board

LEISURE FACILITIES
- Heated Swimming Pool
- Amusements
- Marvellous Adventure Playground
- Disabled and Babies Rooms
- Shop

AVAILABLE
- Premier Camping Spots
- Licensed Bar/Family Room
- Barbecues
- 4-8 berth caravans for hire
- Launderette

CHEDDAR GORGE
NEAR WESTON-SUPER-MARE

Proprietors: Mr and Mrs C.K. Neville: Mr and Mrs D.R. Moore

Self-Catering   **SOMERSET/E. SUSSEX**

EXMOOR NATIONAL PARK

TRISCOMBE FARM

Delightful self catering apartments and cottage, sleeps two to nine guests, situated on 50-acre farm. Well appointed kitchens, colour TV, carpeted throughout. Linen, cot and high chair provided if required. Pets welcome. Hard tennis court. Games room. Golf, riding, fishing and sea within easy reach.

Evening Meals are available in Licensed Restaurant in main house.

SAE please, for brochure. Mr & Mrs Sims, Dept. F., Triscombe Farm, Wheddon Cross, Minehead, Somerset TA24 7HA. Telephone: Winsford (064-385) 227.

OLD FARM PLACE

Situated in the hamlet of Henley Down within four miles of the sea at Bexhill amongst unspoilt farmland, a well furnished self contained wing of attractive old farmhouse. Sleeps five with separate front door, car parking and use of small garden. Fortnightly bookings preferred in summer. Rent depending on season. SAE for details.

Mrs G. Malins, Old Farm Place, Catsfield, Battle, East Sussex TN33 9BN Tel. Crowhurst (0424-83) 262

Please note all advertisers in this colour section also have a full review in the classified section under the relevant county.

30   **Please mention Farm Guide England when enquiring**

Spring Time

4½ miles from the City...
alongside the River Ouse...
and right at the heart of
YORKSHIRE – and quiet,
homely and spacious
that's...

THE MANOR
COUNTRY GUEST HOUSE

**ACASTER MALBIS,
YORK YO2 1UL**

Telephone (9 am to 9 pm): York (0904) 706723
(To speak to a guest at The Manor dial 0904 707534;
at Oak Tree, dial 0904 703341)

Peacefully and restfully situated in the countryside amidst 6 acres of delightful grounds and woodland, THE MANOR is away from all main roads; but York is only 12 minutes or so away by car or local bus. Easily reached from York or from the A64 (Leeds – Tadcaster section) via Tadcaster, Copmanthorpe or Bishopthorpe; and from the A64 (York) Ring Road via either Copmanthorpe or Sim Balk Lane and Bishopthorpe.

Part of the Garden

Join us if you like it really quiet!

Lounge has open coal fire. Some rooms have showers. Carport and large car park. Stairlifts to both floors. Unlicensed. Showers in all bathrooms. One ground-floor bedroom with shower – nearby toilet adapted for wheelchair. No service charge and no extras – Closed only during Christmas week. Room and full English buffet breakfast or room, breakfast and cold buffet evening meal.

**Illustrated details, with pleasure from MISS C. P. PEACOCK. Please be sure to send stamp or 9" x 6" SAE and if possible, give full details of requirements.
ENQUIRIES FROM ABROAD, please send *four* International Reply Coupons. (Obtainable from Post Offices).**

Chapel in the Wood

Farm Holiday Guide
ENGLAND
1986

Farm Holiday Guide Publications 1986

Farm Holiday Guide — England
Farm Holiday Guide — Scotland
Farm Holiday Guide — Wales and Ireland
Britain's Best Holidays — A Quick Reference Guide
FHG Self-Catering & Furnished Holidays
England's Best Holidays
Scotland's Best Holidays
Holidays in Wales
Guide to Caravan & Camping Holidays
Bed & Breakfast Stops
Activity Holidays in Britain
Heritage Britain

Cover photograph supplied by Ivan J. Belcher

ISBN 1 85055 020 4 © Farm Holiday Guides Ltd.

No part of this publication may be reproduced by any means or transmitted without the permission of the Publishers.

Typeset by R.D. Composition Ltd., Glasgow.
Printed and bound by Benham's Ltd., Colchester.

Published by Farm Holiday Guides Ltd.,
(Benn Brothers), a member of the Extel Group.
Abbey Mill Business Centre, Seedhill, Paisley PA1 1JN (041-887 0428/9).

Distributed by Ian Allan Ltd., Coombelands House, Addlestone,
Weybridge, KT15 1HY (0932 58511).

Contents

BOARD

AVON 43
BEDFORDSHIRE 47
BERKSHIRE 47
BUCKINGHAMSHIRE 47
CAMBRIDGESHIRE 48
CHESHIRE 49
CORNWALL 52
CUMBRIA "English Lakeland" 87
DERBYSHIRE 114
DEVON 125
DORSET 178
DURHAM 191
ESSEX 193
GLOUCESTERSHIRE 195
HAMPSHIRE 205
HEREFORD & WORCESTER 208
KENT 222
LANCASHIRE 227
LEICESTERSHIRE 229
LINCOLNSHIRE 232
MERSEYSIDE 234
NORFOLK 235
NORTHAMPTONSHIRE 244
NORTHUMBERLAND 245
NOTTINGHAMSHIRE 253
OXFORDSHIRE 254
SHROPSHIRE 257
SOMERSET 264
STAFFORDSHIRE 282
SUFFOLK 288
SURREY 294
SUSSEX (EAST) 295
SUSSEX (WEST) 298
WARWICKSHIRE 302
WILTSHIRE 306
YORKSHIRE 310
ISLE OF WIGHT 334
CHANNEL ISLANDS 337

SELF-CATERING

LONDON 365
AVON 365
BERKSHIRE 368
CHESHIRE 368
CORNWALL 369
CUMBRIA "English Lakeland" 392
DERBYSHIRE 406
DEVON 409
DORSET 439
DURHAM 448
ESSEX 448
GLOUCESTERSHIRE 448
HAMPSHIRE 451
HEREFORD & WORCESTER 452
KENT 460
LANCASHIRE 463
LEICESTERSHIRE 464
LINCOLNSHIRE 465
NORFOLK 465
NORTHUMBERLAND 473
NOTTINGHAMSHIRE 476
OXFORDSHIRE 477
SHROPSHIRE 477
SOMERSET 480
STAFFORDSHIRE 491
SUFFOLK 491
SURREY 492
SUSSEX (EAST) 493
SUSSEX (WEST) 494
WARWICKSHIRE 495
WILTSHIRE 495
YORKSHIRE 497
ISLES OF SCILLY 509
ISLE OF WIGHT 509
CHANNEL ISLANDS 509

VILLAGE INNS 341
ACTIVITY HOLIDAYS 342
CARAVAN AND CAMPING 345

THE BEST OF COAST & COUNTRY HOLIDAYS IN ENGLAND

This 1986 edition of **FARM HOLIDAY GUIDE ENGLAND** continues to offer the wide range of friendly accommodation with which it has long been associated. The freedom and economy of making our own holiday arrangements direct with the proprietors is a particularly British characteristic and survives strongly, in spite of package holidays, computerised central booking and the like.

As you read on, you will find names, addresses and telephone numbers of Board (farms, hotels, guest houses, private houses), Self-Catering and Caravan & Camping accommodation. You will also find small sections for Inns and Activity Holidays. Please bear the following points in mind:

ENQUIRIES AND BOOKINGS. Give full details of dates (with an alternative), numbers and any special requirements. Ask about any points in the holiday description which are not clear and make sure that prices and conditions are clearly explained. You should receive confirmation in writing and a receipt for any deposit or advance payment.

If you book your holiday well in advance, especially self-catering, confirm your arrival details nearer the time.

CANCELLATIONS. A holiday booking is a form of contract with obligations on both sides. If you have to cancel, give as much notice as possible. The longer the notice the better the chance that your host can replace your booking and therefore refund any payments. If the proprietor cancels in such a way that causes serious inconvenience, he may have obligations to you which have not been properly honoured. Take advice if necessary from such organisations as the Citizen's Advice Bureau, Consumer's Association, Trading Standards Office, Local Tourist Office, etc., or your own solicitor.

COMPLAINTS. It's best if any problems can be sorted out at the start of your holiday. You should therefore try to raise any complaints on the spot. If you do not, or if the problem is not solved, you can contact the organisations mentioned above. You can also write to us. We will follow up the complaint with the advertiser – but we cannot act as intermediaries or accept responsibility for holiday arrangements.

Farm Holiday Guides Ltd. do not inspect accommodation and an entry in our guides does not imply a recommendation. However our advertisers have signed their agreement to work for the holidaymaker's best interests and as their customer, you have the right to expect appropriate attention and service.

HOLIDAY INSURANCE. It is possible to insure against holiday cancellation. Brokers and insurance companies can advise you about this.

The Farm Holiday Guide DIPLOMA. Every year we award a small number of diplomas to holiday proprietors whose services have been specially commended by our readers. Please let us know if you have had an outstanding holiday experience so that we can give due recognition.

Holidays in Britain still offer a range and variety which is unrivalled. Foreign visitors appreciate the benefits, and we have one great advantage over them – it's not difficult to get home when the weather turns really nasty! We have it on good authority, however, that the sun will shine this year!

Peter Clark
Publishing Director

ENGLAND – Counties

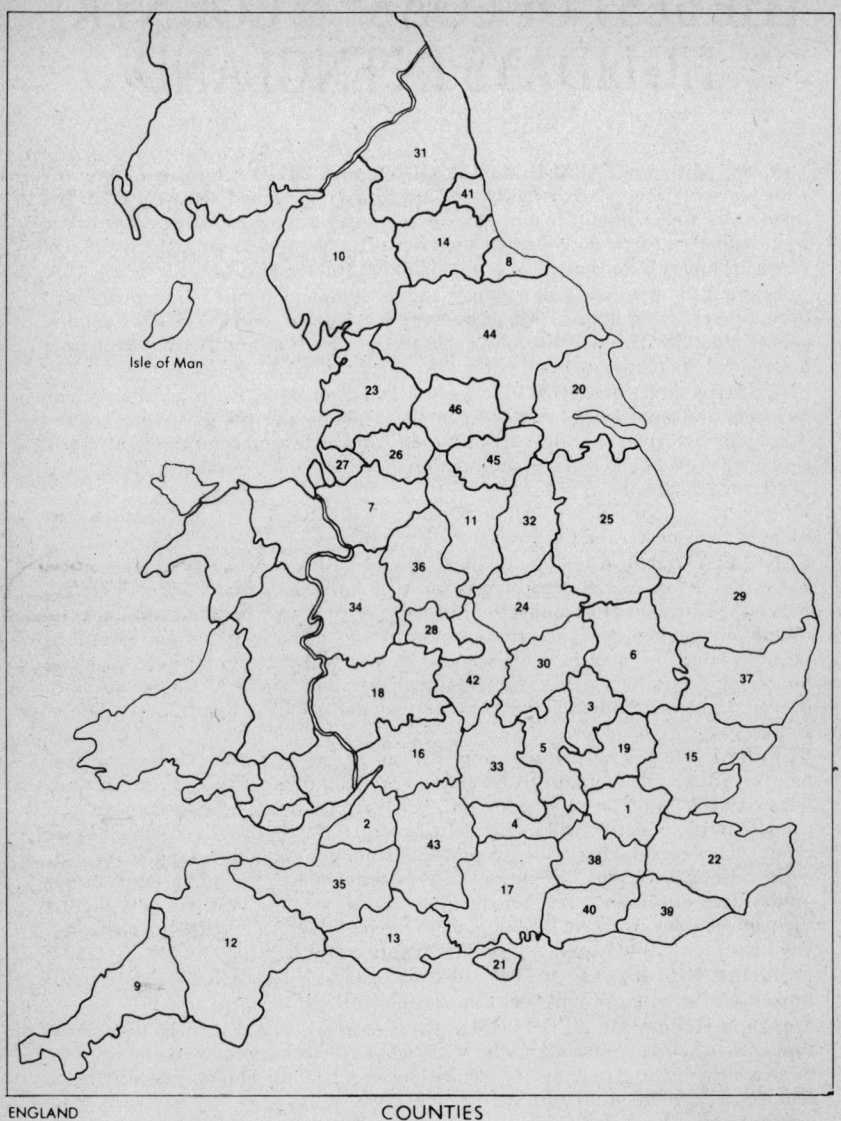

COUNTIES

1. London
2. Avon
3. Bedfordshire
4. Berkshire
5. Buckinghamshire
6. Cambridgeshire
7. Cheshire
8. Cleveland
9. Cornwall
10. Cumbria
11. Derbyshire
12. Devon
13. Dorset
14. Durham
15. Essex
16. Gloucestershire
17. Hampshire
18. Hereford & Worcester
19. Hertfordshire
20. Humberside
21. Isle of Wight
22. Kent
23. Lancashire
24. Leicestershire
25. Lincolnshire
26. Manchester, Greater
27. Merseyside
28. Midlands, West
29. Norfolk
30. Northamptonshire
31. Northumberland
32. Nottinghamshire
33. Oxfordshire
34. Salop
35. Somerset
36. Staffordshire
37. Suffolk
38. Surrey
39. Sussex, East
40. Sussex, West
41. Tyne & Wear
42. Warwickshire
43. Wiltshire
44. Yorkshire, North
45. Yorkshire, South
46. Yorkshire, West

ENGLAND – Towns and Main Roads

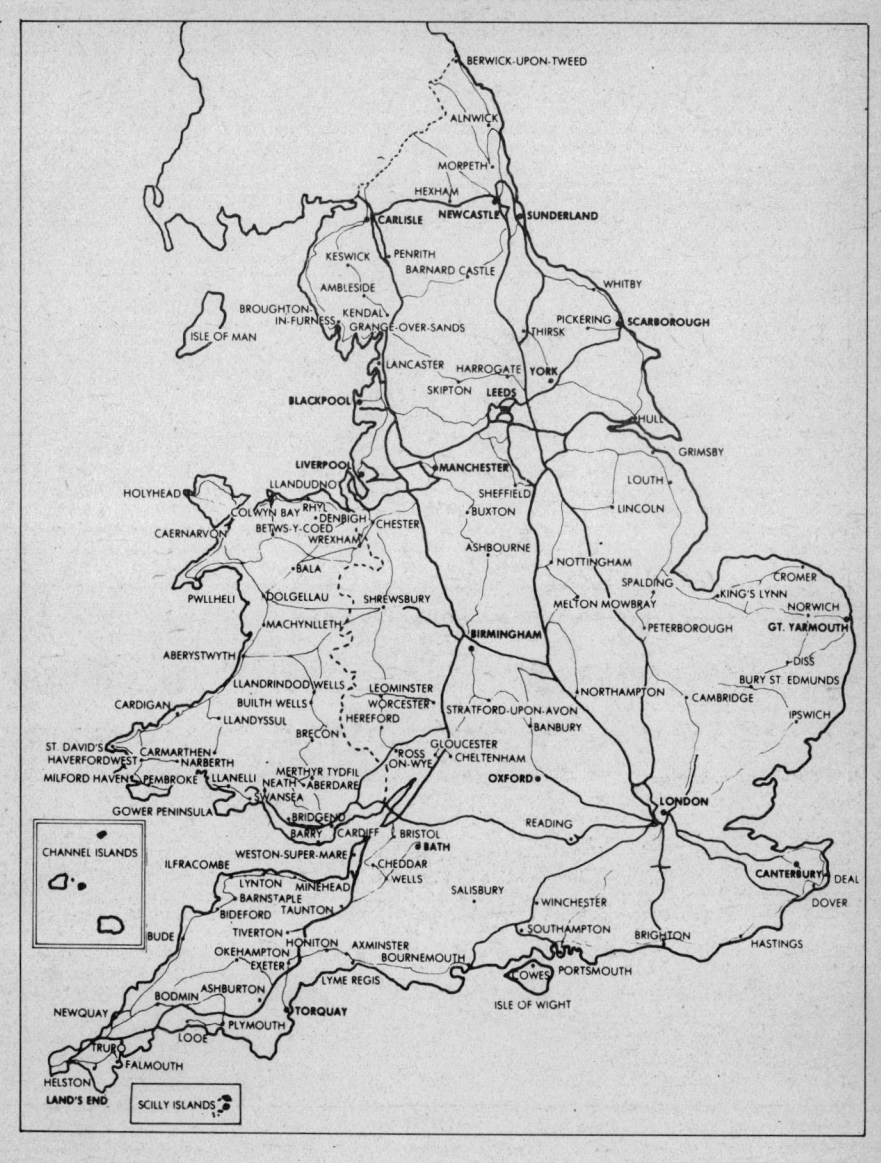

Farm Holiday Guide
ENGLAND
1986
BOARD ACCOMMODATION

AVON

BACKWELL. Mrs Jenny Parsons, The Batch, Brockley Coombe, Backwell, Bristol BS19 3DF (Lulsgate [027-587] 2093). Working farm. This lovely small guest house, set in a beautiful wild garden, is completely hidden from roads and other houses by peaceful, mature woodland. Adjacent to 1,500 acres of forestry, our own 30 acres support sheep and calves, a pony and a Jersey cow. Three delightful rooms, including a superb new bathroom, are set aside for guests at the top of the house. Meals are wholesome and home-grown, and we welcome families with young children (ours — Rachel, Andrew and Timothy — are eight, seven and three) who may use our high chair, cot, tree-house, etc. Babysitting. Your dogs are welcome if they will respect our sheep. Car essential — parking. Situated one mile from the A370, The Batch is open all year for Evening Dinner/Meal, Bed and Breakfast or Bed and Breakfast. Reduced rates for children. No brochure, but please phone for further details.

BATH. Mrs G. Russell, Wallmead Farm, Lippiatt Lane, Timsbury, Bath BA3 1JE (Timsbury [0761] 70326). Working farm. Wallmead Farm is a spacious secluded Georgian farmhouse half mile from the village of Timsbury. All rooms have tea and coffee making facilities and are large and well appointed. There is a comfortable lounge with colour TV, a large garden with ample parking. An ideal centre for touring the Cotswolds, Mendips, Weston-Super-Mare, Wells, Longleat, and many more. Children and pets welcome. Complies with British Tourist Board standards. Bed and full English Breakfast from £8 per person. Open February to end November.

BATH near. THE OLD MALT HOUSE HOTEL, Radford, Timsbury, Near Bath BA3 1QF (Timsbury [0761] 70106). AA and RAC listed, Member of West Country Tourist Board, English Tourist Board Bedroom category 4. Family run hotel in beautiful countryside. Within easy reach by car of Bath, Wells, Cheddar, Mendip Hills. Tastefully converted with all comforts, private bathrooms, lounge, central heating, car park, fire certificate. Residential and Restaurant Licence. Open all year. Well known for good food, full English Breakfast, Evening Dinner optional. Nearby we also keep our Shire Horses and Wheelwright and Carriage Restoration business. Please write/telephone for colour brochure — Miss T. Horler.

BATH. Mr and Mrs John and Daphne Paz, Dornden Guest House, Church Lane, Old Sodbury, Near Bristol BS17 6NB (Chipping Sodbury [0454] 313325). AA listed. Former vicarage two miles from junction 18 off M4, surrounded by two acres of beautiful gardens, with grass tennis court, magnificent views. All nine bedrooms (two en-suite) have washbasins, razor points, lounge with colour TV; spacious diningroom. Central for touring and good overnight stop travelling to Cornwall or Wales. Good home cooking. Reduction for four-day breaks and children sharing parents' room. See also Colour Display Advertisement in this Guide. ✶

BATH. Len and Beryl Willis, Proprietors, Villa Magdala Hotel, Henrietta Road, Bath BA2 6LX (Bath [0225] 25836 or Bath [0225] 66329). An elegant villa quietly situated overlooking Henrietta Park, yet only five minutes' walk from City centre. All bedrooms with private bathrooms or showers en suite, TV and radio, tea and coffee making facilities. Some rooms with period four-poster beds. Colour TV in all rooms and full central heating. The hotel offers an extensive Breakfast Menu of traditional English Fare. There is ample car parking in the grounds. A valid Fire Certificate exists. AA and RAC listed. Open January to December.

BRISTOL near. Mrs Delia Edwards, Brinsea Green Farm, Brinsea Lane, Congresbury, Near Bristol BS19 5JN (Churchill [0934] 852278). Working farm. Comfortable 18th-century farmhouse on a 360-acre working dairy and sheep farm situated one and a half miles from village with views of the Mendip Hills. Easy access from M5 (approximately 12-15 minutes Exit 21), the farm is centrally situated between Bath, Bristol, Weston-super-Mare, Wells, Cheddar Caves and Blagdon Lake (fishing). Sports and Equestrian centres within one mile radius. The village has nine inns, many with eating facilities, post office and small shopping centre. Bed, Breakfast with home-made marmalade and jams, offered to guests all year round. Keeping in character, both the sittingroom and diningroom in the farmhouse have inglenook fireplaces. Three double bedrooms, with hot drinks facilities. Bathroom, plus shower, toilet. Central heating. Children welcome at reduced rates, cot and babysitting. Pets accepted. Car essential — ample parking. Bed and Breakfast.

EXCELLENT HOSPITALITY at COURT FARM

Court farm, situated in a most delightful position on a no-through-road from the village of Marksbury, a short distance off the main A39 Bath to Wells road, is very quiet and peaceful and is an excellent place to relax, enjoy the large gardens or take trips into countryside steeped in history and beauty.

There are two sun patios, beautiful gardens and uninterrupted views across the hills, and the City of Bath lies only five miles from this 260-acre dairy farm. Wells and Cheddar are 30 minutes away by car. Longleat House and Safari Park 45 minutes, while North Somerset coast, North Devon and Wales can be explored on day trips. Fishing in Blagdon Lake (30 minutes) and Chew Valley Lake (20 minutes). Car essential, garage and outside parking. All bedrooms (double, single and family size) have washbasins, and there is ample toilet accommodation; the premises are not suitable for young children or for disabled.

Children over six years welcome. Open from Easter to October for Evening Dinner or Meal, Bed and Breakfast.

There's a warm welcome at Court Farm, excellent food and the hospitality you deserve for a satisfying holiday.

MRS MARY GILES, COURT FARM, MARKSBURY, Nr. BATH BA2 9HR
(Timsbury 70385)

THE OLD INN GUEST HOUSE

The Old Inn Guest House is very attractive, built 1684, and at one time a Coaching Inn, but extensively modernised to offer every comfort, though retaining its charm and character. Stands on the side of a hill overlooking the valley on the edge of Farmborough Village. Attractive landscaped garden. It is highly recommended, and maintains a high standard of home cooked food, a family atmosphere, with personal attention. All bedrooms (doubles, twins, and family size) have H&C. Lounge with TV. Ample parking space. Very central for touring Bath, Wells, Cheddar, Wookey Hole, Longleat, Chew Lake, Wye Valley. Open all the year. Evening Meal, Bed and Breakfast. Full English Breakfast. (Fire certificate held.)

Mrs. B. M. Martin, The Old Inn Guest House, Farmborough, Nr. Bath BA3 1BY — Tel: Timsbury (0761) 70250.

BOARD   Avon   45

BRISTOL near. Mrs I. M. Knight, "Phoenix Lodge", Bye-Pass, Langford, Near Bristol BS18 7JQ (Churchill [0934] 852966). Homely accommodation and good food are provided all year round at "Phoenix Lodge", standing in a pleasant one third of an acre garden overlooking the Mendip Hills, situated on A38 Bristol to Taunton road. The M5 is six miles. Within easy touring distance of Bath, Bristol, Cheddar, Wells, Wookey Hole, Weston-Super-Mare, etc. Nearby activities include pot-holing, caving, swimming, riding, climbing, sailing, walking, golf. Accommodation comprises one double, one twin-bedded and one family bedrooms with washbasins; two bathrooms, three toilets; sittingroom; diningroom. Central heating. Children welcome at reduced rates, babysitting provided. Sorry, no pets. Car essential, parking for four cars. Tea and evening drink available. Please telephone or send SAE for terms for Bed and Breakfast or Evening Dinner, Bed and Breakfast to **Ina Knight.**

BRISTOL near. Mrs J. E. Griffin, Grey Tiles, Winford, Near Bristol BS18 8AN (Lulsgate [027-587] 2532). Six miles south of Bristol, good centre for trout fishing and touring Bath, Wells, Cheddar. Grey Tiles is a superior centrally heated house in half an acre of gardens on the southern slopes of Dundry Hill with views over the Chew Valley. The guest accommodation is a self-contained luxury flat on the first floor, comprising two twin, one single bedrooms. Kitchen, bathroom, large sitting-room with access to sun patio. Children over 12 welcome. Regret, no pets. SAE, please, for Bed and Breakfast or Self-catering terms.

BRISTOL near. Mr and Mrs R. R. Lewis, "Falanda", Bye-Pass, Langford, Near Bristol BS18 7JQ (Churchill [0934] 852021). Within easy reach of the M5, an ideal touring centre for Bath, Bristol, Weston-Super-Mare, Cheddar, Wookey, Taunton, "Falanda" is a modern semi-bunaglow, situated in one third of an acre, and set back from main A38 (Bristol-Taunton) road. Surrounded by beautiful countryside, "Falanda" is open all year round and we offer homely accommodation and good food. One double, one single, one family/twin bedrooms; two bathrooms, two toilets. Sittingroom and diningroom. Central heating. Children welcome, babysitting available. Sorry, no pets. Car essential — ample parking. There are local facilities for fishing, sailing, pot-holing, pony trekking and a Sports Centre. Walking on the Mendips. Please telephone Pauline or Ray Lewis or send SAE for terms — mid week bookings accepted. Reduced rates for children.

BRISTOL near. Mrs Colin Smart, Leigh Farm, Pensford, near Bristol BS18 4BA (Compton Dando [07618] 281). Working farm. Off A37 Bristol/Shepton Wells road. Leigh Farm is a beef and sheep farm enjoying all the advantages of COUNTRY life, yet close to many tourist attractions such as Bath, Bristol, Cheddar, Wells and Glastonbury and the famous Stanton Drew Stone Circles. Excellent trout fishing can be found within a few miles. Breakfasts are served in the farmhouse kitchen complete with its pine dresser, and guests are made to feel at home in their own lounge where log fires burn during cold evenings. Large lawns surround the farmhouse and visitors can relax and enjoy the view and the peaceful surroundings. One double, one single and one family rooms all with washbasins; bathroom, toilet. Car essential – parking. Terms on request. Evening Meal by prior arrangement.

BRISTOL. Mrs J. Hasell, Woodbarn Farm, Denny Lane, Chew Magna, Bristol BS18 8SZ (Chew Magna [0272] 332599). Working farm. Woodbarn Farm is just outside the attractive village of Chew Magna which has a good range of shops, post office and three pubs. It is three minutes' away from the Chew Valley Lake where there are opportunities for trout fishing, birdwatching, walking or watching the sailing boats. Centrally situated for touring Bath, Wells, Bristol, Cheddar etc. Woodbarn is a 75 acre working arable/beef farm with large garden. The house itself has been modernised and has all conveniences. The guests have their own lounge with colour TV and separate diningroom. The bedrooms are comfortably furnished with washbasins and tea making facilities. The atmosphere is friendly and flexible. The guests have access to their rooms at all times. Children are welcome and there is cot and high chair. Car essential — parking ample. Bed and Breakfast from £7.50. Reduced rates for children.

CHURCHILL. David & Jean Sacof, Churchill Green Farm, Churchill Green, Churchill, Avon * **(Churchill [0934] 852438).** Charming old 17th century farmhouse commanding splendid views of open countryside at the foot of the Mendip Hills. Excellent touring centre — Wells, Bath, Weston-super-Mare, Cheddar within easy reach. Many sporting facilities available nearby. Full sized swimming pool, two acres of garden for guests' enjoyment. Central heating and log fires whenever necessary. Open all year. Licensed. Brochure and tariff on request. See also Colour Display Advertisement in this Guide.

WHEN MAKING ENQUIRIES PLEASE MENTION
FARM HOLIDAY GUIDE

Avon BOARD

HEAD FOR THE HILLS

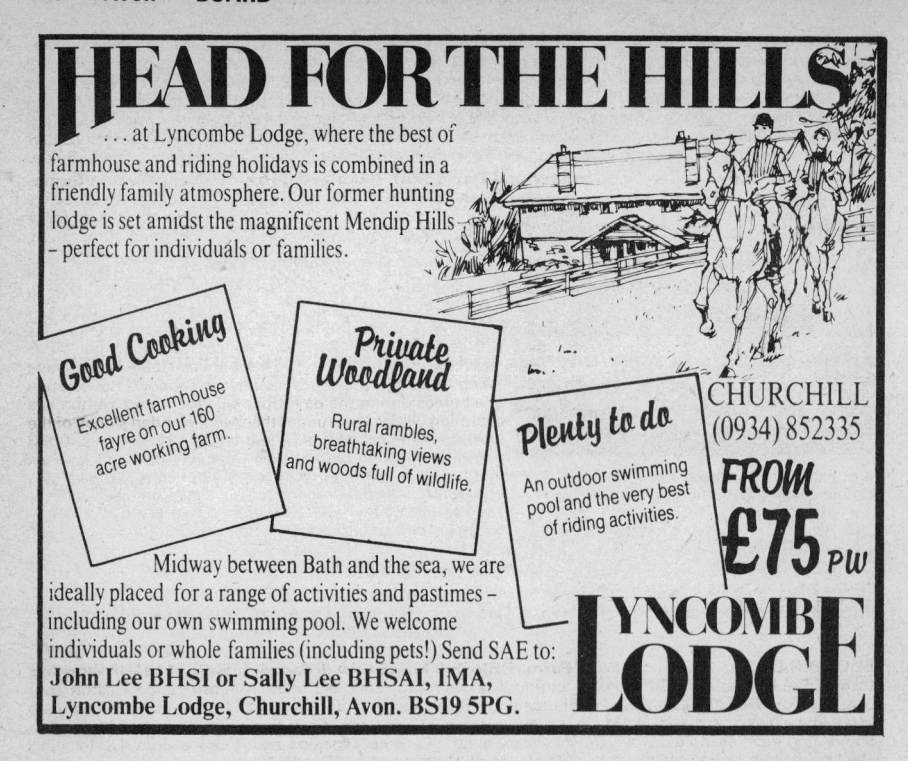

...at Lyncombe Lodge, where the best of farmhouse and riding holidays is combined in a friendly family atmosphere. Our former hunting lodge is set amidst the magnificent Mendip Hills - perfect for individuals or families.

Good Cooking — Excellent farmhouse fayre on our 160 acre working farm.

Private Woodland — Rural rambles, breathtaking views and woods full of wildlife.

Plenty to do — An outdoor swimming pool and the very best of riding activities.

CHURCHILL (0934) 852335

FROM £75 PW

Midway between Bath and the sea, we are ideally placed for a range of activities and pastimes - including our own swimming pool. We welcome individuals or whole families (including pets!) Send SAE to:
John Lee BHSI or Sally Lee BHSAI, IMA, Lyncombe Lodge, Churchill, Avon. BS19 5PG.

LYNCOMBE LODGE

CLEVEDON near. Mrs F. E. Griffin, Elm Cottage, Ham Lane, Kingston Seymour, Near Clevedon (Yatton [0934] 838367). Working farm. One of two houses serving this dairy and sheep farm, Elm Cottage stands hidden near the centre of a peaceful village three miles from M5 (Junction 20 Clevedon). Convenient for Bristol, Bath, Wells, Cheddar, Mendip Hills. Local swimming. Lake fly fishing nearby. Cycles available. Three double, two family, one single bedrooms. Guests' bathroom, sittingroom, diningroom. Garden. Laundry facilities. Cot, high chair, babysitting. Parking. Wood burners, open fires for chilly days. Traditional Farmers' Breakfasts. Evening Meals by arrangement. Also vegetarians, special diets. Leave convenience foods behind and rediscover the taste of garden grown vegetables and fruit, home baking and meat straight from the farm. A warm welcome all year. SAE for terms, please.

UPPER LANGFORD. Mrs Nicky Parsons, Langford Green Farm, Upper Langford, Near Bristol BS18 7DG (Churchill [0934] 852368). Working farm. This delightful farmhouse situated at the foot of the Mendip Hills, at the bottom of Burrington Coombe, is an 84-acre dairy farm. Local amenities include walking, horse riding (own horse welcome), fishing in Blagdon and Chew Valley Lakes, and is only a short distance from Bristol, Bath and Weston Super Mare. Our children Sarah and William, aged seven and six, have a pony, dog and cats, and a safe walled garden to play in. Children's teas, Evening Meals by arrangement. Cot, high chair, babysitting available. No brochure but please phone for details.

✷ WESTON-SUPER-MARE. Mrs J. E. Pope, Lemon Park Farm, Wrington (Wrington [0934] 862571). Working farm. The modern blending farmhouse is set in an unspoilt rural position — a country and conservationists' paradise, yet central for North Somerset and Avon resorts. Good food and a warm welcome awaits all guests. The small farm rears beef cattle and is within easy reach of seaside resorts and other tourist attractions including Cheddar Gorge and caves, Wookey Hole, the Mendip Hills, Wells Cathedral, the floral Roman City of Bath and Glastonbury Abbey. Children are welcome. Babysitting by request. Reduced rates for 12 years and under. Sorry, no pets. Lounge with colour TV and sun lounge. Heated swimming pool. Two double and one family rooms (three with washbasins); bathroom, two toilets; diningroom. Car essential, ample parking. Evening Dinner, Bed and Breakfast. SAE, please, for terms. See also Colour Display Advertisement.

BOARD Avon / Bedfordshire / Berkshire / Buckinghamshire

WESTON-SUPER-MARE near. Mr and Mrs G. & J. Murphy, Pool Farm, Hewish, Near Weston-super-Mare, Somerset BS24 6SG (Yatton [0934] 833138). Working farm. Modernised, centrally heated farmhouse retaining much of its old world charm — inglenook fireplaces, with open fires on chilly days, two spacious lounges, one with colour TV. All bedrooms have washbasins (two on the ground floor). Children will enjoy the excitement of life on a working farm, babysitting available. Ideal centre for touring Bath, Wells, Glastonbury, Cheddar, Longleat, Bristol and Weston-super-Mare with its beaches and holiday amenities four miles. Open all year (except Christmas and New Year). See also Colour Display Advertisement in this Guide. *

WESTON-SUPER-MARE near. Margaret and David Holt, Moorlands, Hutton, Near Weston-Super-Mare BS24 9QH (Bleadon [0934] 812283). An attractive Georgian house in extensive grounds with mature landscaped garden and paddock. Central heating throughout. Good food in generous variety using fresh vegetables and fruit from the garden when possible. Home baking a speciality as the Holts' daughter Nina is a trained patisserie chef. Members of West Country Tourist Board. Fire Certificate held. A happy, friendly atmosphere prevails and families with children are especially welcome. Sorry, no dogs. Reduced terms for children — cots are available — and pony riding for them can be arranged in the paddock. House open at all times during the day. Open all year round. Hutton is a charming village lying under the steep, wooded slopes of the western Mendips, with excellent walking on the hills. Good touring centre. Sandy beaches nearby. Good golf courses and fishing in the area. Membership of Country Club arranged. Sports centre within five miles. See also Colour Display Advertisement. *

BEDFORDSHIRE

PULLOXHILL. Mrs J. Tookey, Pond Farm, Pulloxhill MK45 5HA (Flitwick [0525] 712316). Working farm. Pond Farm is an ideal base for touring Woburn Abbey and Safari Park, Whipsnade Zoo, Luton Zoo, Luton Airport, Dunstable Downs and Shuttleworth Collection of Historic Aircraft. Three double, one single, two family bedrooms; bathroom, toilet; sittingroom, diningroom. Children welcome at reduced rates. Babysitting most evenings. Open from January to 20th December for Bed and Breakfast from £8; Evening Meal on request from £3.50 or Meals at the local inn. Ample parking. Further details on request.

BERKSHIRE

STREATLEY. Mrs P. J. Webber, Bennets Wood Farm, Southridge, Streatley RG8 9ST (Goring-on-Thames [0491] 872377). Working farm. Situated high above the Thames Valley, the farm holds a unique position in peaceful wooded countryside free from noise and traffic. It is a homely farm of 80 acres. Lovely walks include the famous Ridgeway. Boating and fishing may be enjoyed on the Thames. Day trips to Oxford, Windsor and London. The modern farmhouse has every comfort and a traditional English Breakfast is served. One double, one family bedrooms, with washbasins; bathroom, toilets; sitting/diningroom. Children over five welcome. Sorry, no pets. Open from May to September. Car essential, parking. SAE, please, for terms for Bed and Breakfast.

BUCKINGHAMSHIRE

SLOUGH. Mr and Mrs K. J. Willmer, White Close, 59 Montagu Road, Datchet, Slough SL3 9DR (0753-41086). Bed and Breakfast in comfortable family home. Single and double rooms all with washbasins and H&C. Large family room with en-suite bathroom. Adequate bathroom and toilet facilities available. TV lounge. Large garden with car parking. Two miles from Windsor, six miles Heathrow Airport. Few minutes' walk from River Thames for boating, fishing. Fishing facilities also at local reservoir. Ten minutes' walk from main line railway station for London.

Please note that entries marked with an asterisk also have a colour display advert in the colour section in this guide

CAMBRIDGESHIRE

CAMBRIDGE. Mrs M. Quintana, Segovia Lodge, 95 Cherry Hinton Road, Cambridge CB1 4BS (Cambridge [0223] 248213). Comfortable, centrally heated house, open all year for Bed and Breakfast. Situated in a delightful south part of the city. Close to the new Addenbrooke's Hospital, railway station, bus stop, city centre, also very near the M11, A604, A10. The accommodation comprises of three nice bedrooms, family room with private shower; all with TV, washbasin and razor point. Parking space. Children welcome. Sorry, no pets. Registered with the English Tourist Board. From £10 — breakfast included.

CAMBRIDGE near. Mrs Margaret Gilmore, Cintra Lodge, 14 Church Street, Little Shelford, Near Cambridge CB2 5HG (Cambridge [0223] 842374). Large Victorian family house, with garden, overlooking grazing paddock in a quiet, picturesque village five miles south of Cambridge. One-and-a-half hours to London. Convenient for visiting Imperial War Museum at Duxford; two miles from A10 and M11, A45 Felixstowe and A604 Harwich. Two twin-bedded rooms, one double, with hot and cold water; sittingroom with TV. Bed and Breakfast from £9 per night (non-smokers only, please). Good pubs and restaurants nearby.

LYNDEWODE LODGE
Bed and Breakfast

* English breakfast
* Colour TV in all rooms
* H & C and central heating
* Tea and coffee facilities
* Quietly situated
* Close to rail station, city centre, bus stops, laundrette, post office, restaurants and pubs.

Mr & Mrs Greg Pilmer
2 Lyndewode Road
Cambridge
Cambridgeshire
CB1 2HL
(0223-356161)

CAMBRIDGE near. Mrs G. Buckle, St. Andrews, 16 Church Street, Little Shelford, Near Cambridge CB2 5HG (Cambridge [0223] 842254). This is a pleasant house in a quiet picturesque village five miles south of Cambridge, with good pubs/restaurants nearby. Fire Certificate. Full central heating, hot and cold and razor points in all bedrooms. A large family room with a balcony overlooking flower garden and grazing paddock. Large lounge, colour TV. Diningroom, choice of breakfast. Parking. Bed and Breakfast from £9. Children's reductions. Member of English Tourist Board. Three miles from Duxford Imperial War Museum. Two miles from A10 and M11, A45 Felixstowe and A604 Harwich.

ELY. Mrs Jenny Farrow, Laurel Farm House, 8 High Street, Mepal, Ely CB6 2AW (Ely [0353] 778023). Spacious old Georgian farmhouse in small, peaceful Fen village. Excellent food, comfort and personal attention. Ideal for touring the many places of historical interest in East Anglia (brochures provided). Cambridge 15 miles, cathedral city of Ely six miles. Norfolk and Suffolk borders half an hour's drive away. Several National Trust properties in the area. Good fishing locally. Wildfowl Trust and RSPB Reserves nearby. One twin, one double and one single bedrooms. Two bathrooms, toilets; separate sitting and diningroom; TV; central heating. Older children welcome. No pets. Open all year. Car essential. Evening Dinner, Bed and Breakfast or Bed and Breakfast. Reduced weekly rates. SAE, please.

CAMBRIDGESHIRE – FENLANDS AND CHALK HILLS!

Never is it easier to relax than when you are in Cambridgeshire. The flat fens in the north and gentle chalk hills in the south combine to create a unique ambience. Cambridge, a beautiful university town, is the final contribution to this county's perfection. Make sure you visit the twin villages of Hemingford Grey and Hemingford Abbots, Grafham Water, the Ouse Wash Reserves and Wicken Fen.

BOARD   Cambridgeshire / Cheshire   49

HOUGHTON. Mr and Mrs David and Beryl Taylor, Millside Cottage, 9 Mill Street, Houghton PE17 2AZ (St. Ives (Cambs) [0480] 64456). Houghton is a picturesque riverside village south of the A1123 road between Huntingdon and St. Ives. 'Millside Cottage', a licensed Guesthouse, is a Victorian ex-public house extended and modernised without loss of character to provide comfortable accommodation. Your hosts emphasise service and cleanliness, with delicious home cooking, offering guests Bed and Breakfast with Evening Meal optional. Four double, one single, one family bedrooms, all with washbasins. Bathroom, three toilets. Two sittingrooms, diningroom. Children, small dogs welcome. Cot, high chair available. Ample parking. Local features include a watermill museum, river lock and 12th-century church. Cambridge, Ely, Peterborough, Bedford, all within half hour drive. London one hour by car or train. Public footpaths permit walks to numerous local villages of similar charm. Also two twin-bedded caravans, plus twin chalet accommodation (at reduced rates), including breakfast and use of house toilet facilities. Open all year except New Year. SAE, please, or phone for terms.

HUNTINGDON. Mrs B. E. Moir, Hartford Cottage, Longstaff Way, Hartford, Huntingdon PE18 7XT (Huntingdon [0480] 54116). Hartford Cottage is a very spacious, comfortable, detached Edwardian House in lovely gardens of over an acre, situated on A141, in village of Hartford, one mile from Huntingdon. Delightful riverside walks nearby. Cambridge within easy travelling distance (15 miles), historic St Ives three miles. Overnight guests welcome. With Great North Road (A1) only three miles away, this is a convenient place to break a journey. London approximately 65 miles. Open all year except Christmas. Central heating. Ample parking space. Sorry, no pets. Three double rooms, washbasins; ample toilet facilities. Children welcome at reduced rates. Babysitting available. Bed and Breakfast. SAE for terms.

PETERBOROUGH. Mrs S. A. Harris, Lower Lodge Farm, Upton, Wansford, Peterborough PE6 7BA (Castor [073-121] 279). Working farm. Over 200 years old stone and slate farmhouse of 127 acres arable/pigs. Close to A47 and A1 roads. Situated in rural surroundings, easy reach of Stamford, Cambridge, Peterborough, Ely. Visit Rockingham, Belvoir and Nottingham Castles, Burghley and Sandringham Houses. Beautiful thatched cottages in pretty, unspoilt villages. The rivers Nene, Welland and also Eppingham Water provide excellent fishing. My aim is to provide an enjoyable stay, however short. Open March to November for Bed and Breakfast only.

CHESHIRE

CHESHIRE. Shropshire and Cheshire Farm Holidays. Comfortable farmhouse accommodation in the stretch of peaceful countryside between the ancient city of Chester and the birthplace of industry at Ironbridge. For details see Half Page Display under Shropshire (Board) in this publication.

CHESTER. Mrs Nora Evans, Kidnal Grange, Malpas SY14 7DJ (Malpas [0948] 860344). Working farm. This 120-acre mixed farm lies a mile and a half off the A41 road, with fine views of Cheshire and Welsh hills. Malpas, "The Gateway to Wales," is unique in history and architecture and there are many interesting castles within 10 miles. The house stands in wooded lawns, alongside a pool and island which are the homes of a variety of fish and birds. One single, one family and four double bedrooms (three with twin beds); bathroom and toilets; sittingroom and diningroom. Cot, high chair and babysitting by arrangement. There are swings and indoor games for children. Car necessary, parking provided. Pets allowed. Open from April to October. Bed and Breakfast from £8.50 per day. Children under 10 years from £6.50. Ideal spot to break the north/south journey.

CHESTER. Mrs Joan Critchley, Roslyn Guest House, 6 Chester Street, Near Saltney, Chester CH4 8BJ (Chester [0244] 672306). Situated conveniently one-and-a-quarter miles from the centre of Chester, this traditional guest house is bright, clean and comfortable, with personal attention from the owner. Two twin, four double, two single and three family bedrooms, all with hot and cold water, and central heating. Shower and bathroom, three toilets (showers and baths free). Diningroom, sittingroom with colour TV. Home cooked Evening Meals available if booked in advance. Children welcome — cot and high chair. Pets permitted. Open all year, except Christmas season. Car parking. Ideal base for exploring Cheshire, North Wales and Liverpool area. Evening Dinner, Bed and Breakfast from £13, Bed and Breakfast from £8 — including tea making facilities. Reduced rates for children.

stapleford hall

BED AND BREAKFAST
Mrs. Margaret Winward,
Stapleford Hall, Tarvin,
Chester CH3 8HH.
Tel: (0829) 40202

Beautiful Georgian farmhouse only 4 miles from Chester with interesting historical connections. Large gardens in peaceful and attractive countryside. Views of Peckforton and Beeston Castles. Attractively furnished drawing room and dining room. Spacious bedrooms. Within easy reach of North Wales close to A51 and A41 and M56. Several good local inns nearby. On 250 acre working dairy farm.

MALPAS. Mrs Margaret M. Davies, Millhey Farm, Barton, Malpas SY14 7HU (Broxton [082-925] 431). Working farm. Charming black and white half-timbered farmhouse on a 160-acre dairy farm, situated approximately one-and-a-half miles off A41 road to Chester, on the A534 road to Wrexham and North Wales. Bed and Breakfast accommodation provided all year round in one double, one family bedrooms; bathroom, two toilets; sittingroom, diningroom. Children welcome and babysitting arranged. Many interesting places to visit within easy driving distance include Beeston and Peckforton Castles, Erdigg Hall, Chester Zoo, Chondeley Castle and gardens; golf courses and many lovely walks. Excellent centre for touring the Welsh border country and North Wales. Good food served in an interesting country inn just across the road. Bed and Breakfast £7.50. Children £3.50. Car essential — parking.

MALPAS. Mrs Doris Bevin, Pitt's Farm, Malpas SY14 7AJ (Threapwood [094-881] 224). Working farm. Guests can participate in the activities on this 100-acre working dairy farm all year round. Attractive farmhouse with oak beams, open fire and double glazing. Three family, three double and one single bedrooms (two with washbasins); bathroom, two toilets; two sittingrooms, diningroom. Children welcome — cot, high chair, babysitting, reductions 12 years and under. Sorry, no pets. Many interesting places to visit in the vicinity including Chondeley Castle and gardens, Ergidd Hall, Peckforton and Beaston Castles. Golf courses within seven miles and lovely farm walks. City of Chester 16 miles, Llangollen and North Wales 15 miles and interesting country inns within easy reach. Car essential, parking. Full Board £75 per week; Bed, Breakfast and Evening Meal £12.50; Bed and Breakfast £8. Also two self-catering cottages available on farm land.

HELP IMPROVE BRITISH TOURIST STANDARDS

You are choosing holiday accommodation from our very popular FARM HOLIDAY GUIDES. Whether it be a hotel, guest house, farmhouse or self-catering accommodation, we think you will find it hospitable, comfortable and clean, and your host and hostess friendly and helpful.

Why not write and tell us about it?

As a recognition of the generally well-run and excellent holiday accommodation reviewed in our publications, we at FARM HOLIDAY GUIDES LIMITED present a diploma to proprietors who receive the highest recommendation from their guests who are also readers of our Guides. If you care to write to us praising the holiday you have booked through FARM HOLIDAY GUIDES – whether this be board, self-catering accommodation, a sporting or a caravan holiday, the content of your letter will be evaluated and the proprietors who reach our final list will be contacted.

The winning proprietor will receive an attractive framed diploma to display on his premises as recognition of a high standard of comfort, amenity and hospitality. FARM HOLIDAY GUIDES LIMITED offer this diploma as a contribution towards the improvement of standards in tourist accommodation in Britain. Help your excellent host or hostess to win it!

DIPLOMA
AWARDED BY
READERS
of
FARM HOLIDAY GUIDE
PUBLICATIONS LIMITED

TO ....
FOR HOLIDAY ACCOMMODATION
of the HIGHEST STANDARD

AT ....

BOARD   Cheshire   51

Cheshire Farm Holidays

FARMHOUSE ACCOMMODATION

Higher Elms Farm, Minshull Vernon, Crewe. (Mrs M. Charlesworth Tel No: [027071] 252)
Attractive farmhouse and gardens set alongside the Shropshire Union Canal in heart of rolling Cheshire countryside. Woodlands and river for walks and fishing. Children welcome.

Green Farm, Balterley, Crewe. (Tel No: [0270] 820214)
Chris and Geof Hollins offer you a friendly welcome to their home on a 145-acre dairy farm. Situated in quiet and peaceful surroundings. Within easy reach of many places of interest.

Beechwood House, Weaverham, Northwich. (Roger and Janet Kuypers Tel No: [0606] 852123)
Comfort and freedom offered on this 19th century small stock farm. Home cooking, adaptable meal times. Guest dining room/lounge with colour TV. Ideal mid-week business accommodation.

Hardingland Farm, Macclesfield Forest, Macclesfield. (Mrs Anne Read Tel No: [0625] 25759)
Beautiful setting. A warm welcome and good food await you in this 18th Century stone built farmhouse in the Peak District National Park.

Curtis Hulme Farm, Bradwall Road, Middlewich. (Mrs Miriam Williams Tel No: [060 684] 3230)
Spacious 17th Century farmhouse in peaceful surroundings. 3 miles from M6, ideal base for touring, large gardens. B & B.

SELF-SERVICED ACCOMMODATION

Torgate Farm, Macclesfield Forest, Macclesfield. (Mrs S. M. Bowler Tel No: [02605] 2392)
396-acre hill farm with scenic views within the Peak Park. Comfortable self-catering accommodation, also B & B. sleeps 6. Bed linen and electricity included. No pets.

Manor Farm, Peckforton, Tarporley. (Mrs F. Dakin Tel No: [0829] 260353)
A comfortable cottage in a large garden with views of Beeston Castle. Sleeps 5. Electricity and fuel included. Ideal for walking or touring South Cheshire.

CHESHIRE – A COUNTY OF MANY HISTORIC CONNECTIONS AND A WIDE VARIETY OF BEAUTIFUL SCENERY.

MALPAS. Mrs Angela Smith, Mill House, Higher Wych, Malpas SY14 7JR (Redbrook Maelor [094-873] 362). Situated in a peaceful rural valley with the Welsh border running through the grounds, Mill House is ideally placed for touring North Wales and for visiting historic Chester and Shrewsbury. The accommodation is available all year round with central heating for cold weather comfort. Two double bedrooms with washbasins, radio and tea making facilities; TV lounge with open log fire; diningroom. Children welcome, cot and babysitting available. Garden with small stream and walled patio. Car essential; parking. Bed and Breakfast from £8. Evening Meal from £4.

NANTWICH. Mrs G. Fox, Newbridge Farm, Aston, Nantwich CW5 8DU (Nantwich [0270] 780239). Working farm. Accommodation is offered on this 85-acre dairy farm in rural Cheshire, 15 miles off M6 motorway, exit 17N or 16S. Many places of interest within easy reach; Wedgwood pottery, historic houses, old castle ruins, 20 miles to Chester City and North Wales is easily reached. Three local golf courses, two street markets. Farm is on banks of River Weaver. Two family rooms with washbasins; two double rooms; bathroom and showers, two toilets; sitting and diningrooms. Children welcome, also pets. You will enjoy the home cooking; Evening Meal, Bed and Breakfast from just £11; Bed and Breakfast from £7.50. Reductions for children. Car essential — parking. Open all year.

STOCKPORT. Mrs Barbara Susan White, Park Lodge, Park Hall Estate, Little Hayfield, Stockport SK12 5NN (New Mills [0663] 43759). Park Lodge is the east wing of Park Hall, a large country house built in 1812 by Captain John White. It is situated just outside the popular village of Hayfield and the Lodge is set in one-third of an acre of beautiful gardens on a private estate inside the Peak National Park. Access is by a private drive one-third of a mile in length, via the former stables which form a charming Georgian crescent. Walks are easily accessible as the grounds adjoin open countryside and the National Trust Kinder estate. The accommodation comprises two large double bedrooms plus one twin-bedded room with private shower and toilet. Hayfield village is one mile away.

WHITCHURCH. Mrs Anne Huxley, Bell Farm, Tushingham, Whitchurch, Shropshire SY13 4QS (Whitchurch [0948] 2074). Working farm. This farmhouse on the Cheshire/Shropshire border is over 200 years old and stands on a 112-acre dairy farm. Most rooms are oak-beamed. There is accommodation in two double, one single and one family rooms, all with washbasins; bathroom, two toilets; sitting/diningroom. Children are welcome, cot, high chair and babysitting. Sorry, no pets. Open all year with fires. Car essential, parking. Chester 17 miles away, Whitchurch three, Welsh Border five miles, Llangollen 18. The house is opposite a 14th century Black and White Inn. The Llangollen canal is one mile away. For walkers there is the sandstone trail which crosses our land. We are situated 200 yards off the A41 road for Chester. Within easy reach Chester Zoo, Wrexham, Erddig Hall, Ellesmere and the Meres. Evening Meal, Bed and Breakfast from £11; Bed and Breakfast from £7.50. Children under 12 half price.

PLEASE SEND A STAMPED ADDRESSED ENVELOPE WITH ENQUIRIES

CORNWALL

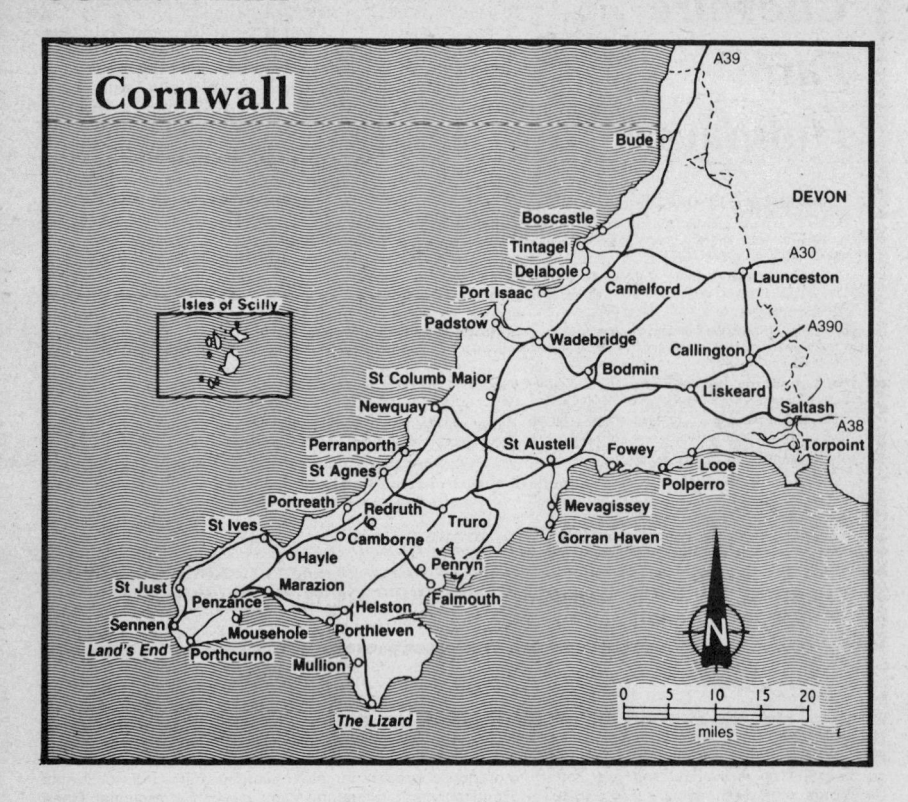

BODMIN. Mr and Mrs R. J. Holser, Lamerton House, St. Kew Highway, Bodmin PL30 3EE (St. Mabyn [020884] 572). Lamerton House is a tastefully converted stone built railway station standing well back from the A39 in one and a half acres of attractive gardens. Acommodation consists of one double bedroom, one family bedroom and three twin-bedded rooms, one of which is situated on the ground floor. Bathroom, toilet; sittingroom with colour TV; diningroom. All bedrooms have washbasins. Open 1st March to 30th November. Central heating. Car is essential, large car park. Children over 10 welcome. Pets allowed. Fresh home grown and locally grown produce used. Welcoming pot of tea on arrival. Fire Certificate held. SAE for colour brochure and terms. Convenient for swimming and surfing, sailing, pony trekking, riding and golf. Warm welcome and personal attention guaranteed by the proprietors. Bed and Breakfast or Evening Meal, Bed and Breakfast.

BODMIN. Mrs Nancy Harris, "Trekelly Meadow", Tremeer Lane, St. Tudy, Bodmin (Bodmin [0208] 850275). Working farm, join in. Trekelly Meadow is a modern bungalow situated on the edge of the pretty village of St. Tudy in the heart of the Cornish countryside, adjoining "Kelly Green Farm", which is and has been farmed by the Harris family since 1900. Guests are welcome to visit the 300-acre farm and watch the 95 cow herd being milked and join in other farm activities. The bungalow is 200 yards from the church and 300 yards from the post office, shops and "The Cornish Arms" pub. We are in easy reach of the North Cornwall coast, Polzeath, Rock, Port Isaac, Tintagel and the moors. Car essential, parking. No pets. Bed and Breakfast. SAE, please, for terms.

BODMIN. Mrs E. Thomas, Kerryn, Lower Kernick, St. Wenn, Bodmin PL30 5PF (Roche [0726] 890339). Modern farm bungalow, ideal for touring, surfing, golf, swimming or cliff walks is open to visitors from May to October. Set in beautiful countryside about one and a half miles from main A30 holiday route. Eight miles Newquay; eight/ten miles from North Cornwall beaches. Good home cooking is provided for Bed and Breakfast with Evening Meal optional. Children welcome and babysitting can be arranged. One double bedroom and one twin-bedded room; separate bathroom and toilet; large lounge/diningroom with colour TV. Car essential — parking. Please phone or write for details and terms which include bedtime drink and reductions for children.

BOARD   Cornwall   53

BODMIN. Mrs Gill Hugo, Bokiddick Farm, Lanivet, Bodmin PL30 3HP (Bodmin [0208] 831481). Working farm. A warm welcome awaits you at Bokiddick Farm, a 120-acre dairy farm in Central Cornwall situated at the base of the picturesque Helman Tors. The farm supports 70 dairy cows, plus followers, also a donkey for children. The farmhouse stands in its own large garden with shrubbery and fish pond. Accommodation comprises two double bedrooms with hot and cold water; large pine bathroom and shower unit. Oak-beamed lounge/diningroom with rustic fireplace leads into conservatory overlooking the garden. Colour TV. Centrally located for both coasts; also river and sea fishing, golf courses, horse riding, tennis and squash courts; beautiful National Trust houses of Lanhydrock and Pencarrow close by. Relax in a friendly family atmosphere with plenty of good farmhouse cooking. Registered with the English and Cornwall Tourist Boards. Also available, furnished bungalow sleeping six. Open April to October. Please phone or send for brochure with SAE.

BODMIN. Mrs Jewell, Trevisquite Bungalow, St. Mabyn, Bodmin PL30 3DF (St. Mabyn [020-884] 331). Ideal for a "get-away-from-it-all" holiday. This country bungalow of Cornish stone, set in quiet location with easy access to North Cornish Coast and moors. Two double bedrooms, one with two single beds, with washbasins; colour TV. Well cooked meals, beef, lamb, pork, Cornish cream, roast duck, fresh home grown vegetables. Port Isaac 20 minutes, unspoilt 17th century fishing village; 20 minutes from Rock with golden sands, surfing, swimming, sailing, water ski-ing, golf. Tintagel 20 minutes. Personal attention guaranteed. Trevisquite has very pleasant garden. Children over nine welcome. Sorry, no pets. Evening Dinner, Bed and Breakfast. Open from May to September. SAE, please.

BODMIN. Mrs Daphne Eddy, Trehannick Farm, St. Teath, Bodmin PL30 3JW (Bodmin [0208] 850312). Working farm. First mentioned in Doomsday in 1086, Trehannick is a 180 acre family farm consisting of dairy cows, beef cattle and cereals. The tastefully and comfortably furnished farmhouse stands in an acre of garden overlooking the beautiful Allen Valley. Safe sandy beaches, sailing, fishing, surfing and golf all within eight miles. One family, three double (one twin-bedded) and one single bedrooms, all but single room with handbasins. Bathroom, two toilets; lounge with colour TV; diningroom with separate tables. Electric blankets. Children welcome. Sorry, no pets. Varied menu of good farmhouse cooking using mainly all home produce including beef, milk and cream. Car essential. Open Easter to October for Bed and Breakfast and Evening Meal, or Bed and Breakfast only. Reductions for children. SAE for terms.

BODMIN. Mrs J. M. Cleave, Tregellist Farm, Tregellist, St. Kew, Bodmin PL30 3HG (Bodmin [0208] 880537). Working farm. Tregellist Farm stands in tiny hamlet with wonderful views of surrounding countryside. A mile away is the 15th century church and village inn at St. Kew. Five miles away from safe, sandy beaches of Daymer Bay, Polzeath, Rock, Port Isaac, all suitable for swimming and surf riding, also close to golf course and a health club. The farm carries beef cattle and a flock of pedigree Dorset Horn sheep. Fully modernised house. Comfortable lounge with colour TV; separate diningroom where home produced beef, pork, lamb and fresh home grown vegetables are served. Bathroom and toilet. One family room and one twin bedded room. Sorry, no pets. Car essential, parking. Cot, high chair available; babysitting on request. Open April to October for Evening Dinner, Bed and Breakfast or Bed and Breakfast. SAE, please, for terms.

BODMIN. Mrs M. J. Jory, Treveighan Farm, St. Teath, Bodmin PL30 3JN (Bodmin [0208] 850286). Working farm, join in. Treveighan is a 175-acre dairy farm with plenty of friendly animals to meet and make friends with. All guests welcomed with a "pot of tea" into a friendly atmosphere. Children welcome at reduced rates; cot and free babysitting available. Two double and one family bedrooms; bathroom, toilet; sittingroom; diningroom. Colour TV. Fully carpeted. No pets please. All home cooking and produce including home produced beef and cream. Ideal centre for touring. Safe bathing six miles; golf, pony trekking and fishing all within easy reach. Open March to October for Bed and Breakfast or Bed, Breakfast and Evening Meal. SAE for brochure and terms. AA listed and Cornwall and English Tourist Authority registered.

BODMIN near. Mrs E. M. Wilton, Greenacres, Wetherham Lane, St. Tudy, Near Bodmin PL30 3NG (Bodmin [0208] 850096). Working farm. Greenacres is a small 25-acre mixed farm situated in a quiet lane on the edge of the unspoilt village of St. Tudy, which has post office, shop, church and pub. The bungalow, open to guests from March to October, enjoys beautiful views and offers a homely atmosphere with plenty of good home cooking. Ideal for touring the north coast (12 miles) with lovely sandy beaches, surfing, sailing, water ski-ing, etc. Many places of interest and sporting amenities within easy reach. Riding stables nearby on edge of Bodmin Moor. One double, one single, one family bedrooms; bathroom, toilet. Sittingroom, diningroom. Children welcome, cot, high chair, babysitting. Accommodation suitable for disabled. Car essential — parking. Sorry, no pets. Evening Meal, Bed and Breakfast from £63 per week; Bed and Breakfast from £42 per week. SAE, please.

54 Cornwall BOARD

BODMIN near. Mrs Joy Rackham, High Cross Farm, Lanivet, Near Bodmin PL30 5JR (Lanivet [0208] 831341). Working farm. High Cross is a 91-acre dairy farm situated in the village of Lanivet which is the geographical centre of Cornwall, and therefore central to beaches and places of interest. A warm welcome awaits visitors all the year round and emphasis is placed on good home-produced farmhouse cooking. The three double bedrooms are centrally heated and have washbasins; TV lounge and separate diningroom. Children are welcome on the farm, babysitting available. Evening Dinner, Bed and Breakfast or Bed and Breakfast only. Reduced rates for children. Special inclusive rates for late autumn to early spring. SAE, please, or telephone.

BOSCASTLE. Mrs M. J. Findlay, Trehane Farm, Trevalga, Boscastle PL35 0EB (Boscastle [084-05] 265). Working farm. Approached by a concrete road, this farmhouse is situated high on a hillside with magnificent view of 30 miles of coastline. There are 190 acres mixed farming land. Plenty to interest the tourist including King Arthur's Castle, Boscastle Harbour and many secluded beaches within easy reach. Comfort and good food assured. Three double rooms, all with washbasins, and one single room; bathroom with toilet and one outside toilet; lounge with colour TV; diningroom. Children welcome at reduced rates if under 10; cot, high chair and babysitting provided by arrangement. Regret no dogs. Car essential, ample parking space. Open Easter to October for Evening Dinner, Bed and Breakfast or Bed and Breakfast only.

BOSCASTLE. Mrs J. Grinsted, Tredole Farm, Trevalga, Boscastle PL35 0ED (Boscastle [08405] 495). Working farm. The farmhouse, part of which is 300-years-old, is situated on the coast in a beautiful valley, and is in an area of outstanding natural beauty. From the farm we run horse and pony trekking, riding out in small groups, receiving personal attention. Tredole Farm is well placed for beaches, touring, walking, fishing and places of interest. Guests served good home cooking using fresh vegetables and dairy produce. We offer a relaxed and informal holiday and guests are welcome to lend a hand with the farm chores, ponies and other farm animals. Tea-making facilities. Shower/bath inclusive. Television/Video lounge. Gardens. Children welcome. Open all year. Bed, Breakfast and Evening Meal.

BUDE near. Mrs J. B. Hale, Lodgeworthy, Bridgerule, Holsworthy, Devon EX22 7EH (Bridgerule [028-881] 351). Working farm. Attractive old Devon Longhouse, within walking distance of the village, offers guests a warm welcome and a secluded, peaceful setting. This is a dairy farm of 150 acres where visitors are welcome to participate in farm activities. Families are very welcome and are accommodated in double, twin, single and family bedrooms, with washbasins; bathroom, toilet. Sittingroom and diningroom. Farmhouse fare is a speciality, with ample portions and mostly home-grown produce. The farm has three-quarter mile of River Tamar on its boundary and fishing is available. Bude and the sea five miles; local facilities for golf, tennis, surfing and many delightful cliff walks. Children welcome, cot, high chair and babysitting available. Sorry, no pets. Car essential — ample parking. Bed, Breakfast and Evening Dinner/Meal — long or short stays. Reduced rates for children. Open Easter to October.

BUDE. Mrs Patricia Nicklen, Creathorne Farm, Bude EX23 0NE (Widemouth Bay [028885] 407). Traditionally built in Cornish style, Creathorne Farm is a family run 185-acre working dairy farm, situated midway between beautiful Widemouth Bay and the scenic village of Marhamchurch. Guests are welcome to wander around the farm or to follow the footpath to the beach. Three spacious bedrooms with sea views and washbasins; bathroom, toilet; diningroom, lounge — all for guests' use only. Warm welcome and good farmhouse cooking using own produce when possible. Children at reduced rates, cot, high chair, babysitting. Pets welcome. Local amenities: surfing, golf, riding, fishing, squash, tennis, coastal walks. Evening Meal, Bed and Breakfast or Bed and Breakfast only. SAE, please, for brochure.

BUDE. Mrs S. J. West, Sharland House, Marhamchurch, Bude EX23 0EN (Widemouth Bay [028 885] 394). Sharland House overlooks the village square of Marhamchurch, two miles from Widemouth Bay and Bude, and affords panoramic views over the rolling countryside to the sea beyond. Guests can be assured of a warm welcome, with tea and scones served on arrival. Good home cooking and all the other ingredients essential for a relaxed and enjoyable holiday are provided. Accommodation for guests is separate from the remainder of the house and comprises three double bedrooms, one single and a family bedroom sleeping two adults and two children. All bedrooms have washbasins and hot and cold water. Children are most welcome and a cot and high chair are available. Babysitting can be arranged. There is an enclosed garden with tables for relaxing and where children can play safely. Ample parking. Open all year. Regret, no pets. Bed and Breakfast or Bed, Breakfast and Evening Meal with reduced rates for children.

BUDE. Mrs V. M. Hale, The Villa, Bridgerule, Holsworthy, Devon EX22 7TA (Bridgerule [028-881] 452). Working farm. An attractive old farmhouse with an acre of gardens plus a safe children's play area and pets' corner. Comfortable rooms. Excellent meals including some regional dishes prepared by qualified cook using fresh home produce. The family run dairy farm is within walking distance. Private fishing is available on one mile of River Tamar. Situated in the picturesque village of Bridgerule which has an Inn, Antique Shop and a General Store. Only five miles from the sandy beaches and surfing of the North Cornwall coast, or the popular market town of Holsworthy; also ideal for touring Dartmoor and Bodmin Moor. One family, one double, one twin and one single bedrooms; bathroom; lounge; diningroom. Attractive rates. Children welcome at reduced rates, cot, high chair and babysitting available. On bus route. Parking. Evening Meal, Bed and Breakfast or Bed and Breakfast only. Further details on request.

BUDE. Mrs M. Trewin, Court Farm, Marhamchurch, Bude EX23 0EN (Widemouth Bay [028-885] 494). Working farm. Court Farm, a stone-built farmhouse set in 200 acres of mixed farmland, is situated in the centre of the very pretty village of Marhamchurch. Small pony available for children to ride and the large gardens have swings and plenty of space for cars. Bude and various other beaches, golf, tennis, etc., nearby. Good central point for touring Devon and Cornwall. Places of interest include Tintagel, King Arthur's Castle, picturesque Clovelly. Surfing and swimming, lovely coastal walks. Guests are assured of a warm welcome, good food and personal attention. Three double and two family bedrooms, with washbasins; bathroom, two toilets; sittingroom, diningroom. Children welcome at reduced rates, cot, high chair, babysitting available. Regret, no pets. Open April to October. Car essential, parking. Evening Dinner, Bed and Breakfast or Bed and Breakfast only. Terms on application.

BUDE. Mrs Sylvia Lucas, Elm Park, Bridgerule, Holsworthy, Devon EX22 7EL (Bridgerule [028-881] 231). Working farm. Elm Park, on 180 acres of mixed and dairy farmland, is a modern pebbledash farmhouse, a quarter of a mile from the village, right on the Devon-Cornwall border, five miles from the surfing beaches of Bude and Widemouth. Guests welcome to wander the farm, see the animals and watch the milking; also a large terraced garden where children can play, and they are welcome to ride our children's pony. Open all year except Christmas. It has three family rooms and one double room, all with washbasins; bathroom, toilets; sitting and diningroom. Cot, high chair and babysitting offered. Mainly roast dishes served, with attractive sweets. Reasonable terms on request. Evening Meal, Bed and Breakfast or Bed and Breakfast. Parking space, car essential. Everyone welcome. Holsworthy four miles. Sorry, no pets. SAE for prompt reply.

BUDE. Mrs Patricia M. Rowland, Quinceborough Farm, Widemouth Bay, Bude EX23 0NA (Widemouth Bay [028-885] 236). Working farm. Quinceborough Farm, mixed farm of 120-acres, occupying magnificent position, sea and country views, approximately three-quarters of a mile from famous surfing beach of Widemouth Bay. Originally a local squire's riding stables, in 1905 converted into large farmhouse. Today guests delighted with comfortable accommodation, friendly atmosphere, peaceful position and proximity of beaches; good, plentiful farmhouse fare, much home produced. Bude, one of the least commercialised resorts in Cornwall, is approximately three and a half miles distant. Golf, tennis, squash, putting, riding, sea and river fishing all available. Guests also invited to use our heated outdoor swimming pool, games room and tennis court. Market towns of Holsworthy and Launceston within easy reach, also Clovelly, Boscastle and Tintagel, etc. Children welcome at reduced rates (cot, high chair and babysitting). Sorry, no pets. Easter to October. Terms on request with SAE, please.

BUDE. Mrs M. N. Boundy, Lopthorne Farm, Morwenstow, Bude EX23 9PJ (Morwenstow [028-883] 226). Working farm. Farmhouse modernised over the years, but still retains its old character with low ceilings downstairs and beams in diningroom. Situated by road in lovely unspoilt area with fine coastal views; scenery, surfing and sandy beaches of Bude and Widemouth Bay are a few miles away; for those who like it quieter small bays and woodland walks nearby; for the energetic badminton and table tennis in barn. Many guests make return visits to enjoy traditional English food, a speciality, much of it being produced on the farm. Fire Certificate held. One double bedroom, one twin-bedded room and two family rooms, all with washbasins; one bathroom, two toilets; sittingroom; diningroom; sun lounge. Children welcome, cot and babysitting. Car essential, parking. Sorry, no pets. Evening Dinner, Bed and Breakfast; Bed and Breakfast only. Rates reduced for children. SAE, please, for brochure.

BUDE. Mrs Monica Heywood, Cornakey Farm, Morwenstow, Bude EX23 9SS (Morwenstow [028-883] 260). Working farm. This is a 220-acre mixed farm on the coast, with lovely views of sea and Lundy Island. Good touring centre, within easy reach of quiet beaches. The farmhouse offers two family bedrooms; bathroom, toilet; sittingroom; diningroom. Children welcome; cot, high chair, babysitting. Good home cooking. Colour TV. Sorry, no pets. Open from Easter to November. Car essential — parking. SAE, please, for terms. Evening Meal, Bed and Breakfast or Bed and Breakfast only. Reduced rates for children and children's pony on farm.

BUDE. Mrs Carol Short, Bagbury Farm, Bude EX23 0LT (Bude [0288] 2740). Working farm, join in. Situated down a quiet country lane, Bagbury overlooks River Neet and Bude Canal. Only one mile from Bude which offers swimming, surfing, tennis, squash, golf, bowls, dry ice skating, cinemas, and coarse and sea fishing. Ideal touring centre for Tintagel, Boscastle, Crackington Haven, Clovelly, Westward Ho!, Bideford and Barnstaple. Accommodation in two family rooms with electric fires; one room has washbasin; bathroom, two toilets; TV lounge; separate diningroom. Access to rooms at all times. Children welcome; cot, high chair, babysitting. Car essential; ample parking. This is a 64-acre dairy farm and guests are welcome to participate in farm activities. Evening Dinner, Bed and Breakfast from £65 per week; Bed and Breakfast from £6.50 per night. Reduced rates for children.

BUDE near. Mrs J. Cholwill, Tackbeare Farm, Marhamchurch, Near Bude EX23 0HH (028-881) 264. Working farm. Tackbeare Farm is our own home and we wish guests to enjoy its peaceful comfortable surroundings. It is ideally situated for touring and within easy reach of sandy beaches, golf and fishing. The 16th-century farmhouse comprises three family bedrooms, two double, one single, hot and cold in all rooms, colour TV in lounge. Good home cooking with fresh farm produce. Bed and Breakfast, and Bed, Breakfast and Evening Meal. Bedtime drinks provided. Visitors are welcome to view any of the farm activities. Children welcome, babysitting, cots, high chairs available. Open all year. Mrs Cholwill assures you of a pleasant and relaxing holiday.

BUDE. Mrs P. J. Metherell, Barne Farm, Kilkhampton, Bude EX23 9RH (Kilkhampton [028-882] 248). Working farm. Barne Farm is an old farmhouse, which has been modernised, tastefully decorated and well furnished. The 170 acre farm has a dairy herd of cows, and various other animals. Situated four miles from Bude where there is tennis, golf, boating and many beautiful beaches. Family, double and single bedrooms; bathroom and separate toilet. Lounge with colour TV; diningroom with separate tables. Children welcome, cot and babysitting available. Open May to October. SAE, please, for terms. Reductions for children.

BUDE. Mrs S. A. Trewin, Lower Northcott Farm, Poughill, Bude EX23 7EL (Bude [0288] 2350). Working farm. Lower Northcott is built of stone in Georgian design, a mile from Bude, set on side of secluded valley with outstanding views of the local rugged coastline. Good farmhouse cooking, with most produce home grown. It is a mile from sandy beaches, all safe for swimming; surfing on larger beaches; Life Guard patrolled. There are 200 dairy cows and a large calf-rearing unit. Visitors welcome to wander about. Ideally situated for either a sightseeing or walking holiday. Three family, one double and one single bedrooms, all with washbasins; bathroom, toilet; sittingroom; diningroom. Children welcome, cot, high chair and babysitting. Sorry no pets. Open April to September. Car not essential but parking available. Evening Meal, Bed and Breakfast or Bed and Breakfast only. Rates reduced for children.

CAMBORNE near. Mrs H. Tyack, Sea View Farm, Troon, Near Camborne TR14 9JH (Praze [0209] 831260). Farmhouse on small horticultural holding. Six double, one single and three family bedrooms, all with individual heating, washbasins etc. Large lounge with colour TV; bathroom, three toilets; two diningrooms. Good home cooking. Well recommended by previous guests. Cot, high chair, babysitting and reduced rates for children. Pets permitted. Panoramic views from some bedrooms. Within easy reach of north and south coasts, being only 15 minutes by car. Open all year round for Evening Meal, Bed and Breakfast from £9 daily — £61 weekly or Bed and Breakfast £6 daily.

CAMELFORD. Mrs S. J. Stephens, Castle Goff Farm, Lanteglos, Camelford PL32 9RQ (Camelford [0840] 213535). Working farm. Castle Goff with historic surroundings and 70 acres of land in quiet wooded river valley, overlooking Lanteglos church, one mile from Camelford, five miles from Trebarwith Strand. Farm comprises herd of pedigree Friesians with their calves. Very large bungalow with lawn, orchard and flower beds, has accommodation in four family bedrooms; two with washbasins; bathroom, two toilets; comfortable lounge, colour TV; diningroom, separate tables; verandah. Cot, high chair, babysitting. Pets allowed. Car essential — ample parking. Good food, fresh vegetables; mealtimes can be altered; door keys provided. Open all year except Christmas. Evening Meal, Bed and Breakfast from £56; Bed and Breakfast from £42. Reductions for Senior Citizens and children.

CAMELFORD. Mrs P. A. Dennis, Bodulgate Farm, Trewalder, Delabole, Camelford PL33 9EY (Camelford [0840] 213792). Working farm. Situated three miles from Camelford, in the midst of the Cornish countryside, Bodulgate Farm makes an ideal centre from which to visit many delightful beaches and quaint villages, as well as Bodmin Moor which is a short car ride. The farm is 178-acre mixed farm and the farmhouse welcomes guests to a happy, friendly atmosphere. Accommodation is offered in two double bedrooms, one single; bathroom, toilet; lounge with TV, diningroom. Children and pets welcome; babysitting. Car essential; parking. Delicious home cooking with fresh home produced vegetables. Evening Meal optional. Reduced rates for children. Very reasonable terms.

FUN FOR ALL THE FAMILY IN CORNWALL

Woolly Monkey Sanctuary, Murrayton, Looe; Padstow Bird & Butterfly Gardens, Fentonluna, Padstow; Bird Paradise, Hayle; Bodmin Farm Park, Fletchers Bridge, Bodmin; Newquay Zoo, Trenance Park, Newquay; Cornish Seal Sanctuary, Gweek, Helston; Mevagissey Model Railway, Mevagissey; The Forest Railroad Park, Dobwalls, near Liskeard; Age of Steam, Crowlas, near Penzance; Lappa Valley Railway, Benny Halt, Newlyn East; Poldark Mining & Wendron Forge, Wendron, near Helston; Cornwall Aero Park, Royal Naval Air Station, Culdrose; Museum of Nautical Art, Chapel Street, Penzance; St. Agnes Leisure Park, St. Agnes.

COVERACK. Mrs Wendy Watters, Boak House, Coverack, Helston TR12 6SH (St. Keverne [0326] 280608). This small guest house has splendid sea views from all of its five bedrooms — one family, three double and one single (three with washbasins); comfortable lounge (with colour TV), diningroom. Guests can go on family fishing trips or enjoy quiet coastal walks, swim in the cove or tour the surrounding glorious countryside. All home cooking with fresh cream and farm produce served daily. Children welcome, cot, high chair, babysitting and reduced rates offered. No objection to pets. Open January to November for Evening Dinner, Bed and Breakfast. Rooms are spacious and well-furnished and the food is good. The hosts' aim is to please all guests producing a relaxing and enjoyable holiday. Moderate terms.

COVERACK. Mr and Mrs N. Parr, The Beach House, Coverack, Near Helston TR12 6TE (St. Keverne [0326] 280621). Charming 17th century fisherman's cottage only 15 feet from the sea in a delightful Cornish village. Ideal for bathing, fishing, painting or just lazing on the sands. The cottage is attractively furnished and equipped to give guests every comfort, and excellent variety of appetising home-cooked food is provided. Home-made bread is always on the menu. For early and late holidaymakers the cottage is heated by a log fire and partial central heating. Two double bedrooms and one single (two with washbasins); one bathroom and two toilets; sitting/diningroom forming lounge. There are parking facilities for three cars. Small well-behaved dogs are allowed. Accommodation not suitable for small children. Open all year for Evening Dinner, Bed and Breakfast, or Bed and Breakfast only. SAE, please, for brochure. Also cottage nearby for self-catering holidays.

Crill House Hotel

Maen Valley, Golden Bank,
Falmouth, Cornwall.
Tel: Fal.(0326) 312994
AA ★★ RAC

ASHLEY COURTENAY RECOMMENDED
AA MERIT AWARDS FOR HOSPITALITY & BEDROOMS

Crill House is tucked away down a country lane in a sheltered valley. All 11 bedrooms have private bathroom, colour TV, radio/intercom, and tea making facilities. The swimming pool is heated from May to September, and there is free tennis and squash at the Falmouth Club. The atmosphere is friendly and informal, and children are welcome. Dinner, room and breakfast from £147 per week. Special Spring & Autumn Holidays visiting local gardens and country houses.
BROCHURE FROM MR & MRS F. H. FENTON

FALMOUTH. Mrs T. P. Tremayne, The Home, Penjerrick, Falmouth TR11 5EE (Falmouth [0326] * 250427 and 250143). An Ashley Courtenay Recommended Hotel. The house, in its large garden, has lovely views over tree-clad countryside to Maenporth and the bay. Close to Helford River with its beautiful walks and boating facilities and an ideal base for touring. All bedrooms have H&C, razor points, bedside lights and modern divan beds. Graciously furnished and carpeted to a high standard. Part central heating. Separate tables in the elegant diningroom. Colour TV in large lounge. Spacious sun lounge overlooking garden. Car park. Good home cooked food, well presented. The Tremaynes welcome guests to their home and hope they enjoy their stay. Special petrol scheme during April, May, June and September, subject to availability. Also self-catering furnished farmhouse and cottage at Constantine, Falmouth. See also colour display advertisement.

FALMOUTH. Mrs John Myers, Dolvean Hotel, 50 Melvill Road, Falmouth TR11 4DQ (Falmouth [0326] 313658). This small family-run hotel faces due south and is only 250 yards from the sea front and sandy Gyllyngvase Beach with safe bathing. The fascinating old town with its fine harbour is within walking distance. Good food, varied menus, table licence, cheerful service assured. Four double, four twin, four single and two family bedrooms, all with washbasins, and some with bathroom en suite, radio-intercom and automatic tea/coffee makers; six bathrooms, eight toilets; diningroom with separate tables; lounge with TV. Fire Certificate granted. Suitable for disabled guests. Children over three welcome (reduced rates if sharing with two adults); car not essential but ample parking. Reduced rates early and late season. Dogs welcome. Easter till October. Evening Dinner, Bed and Breakfast or Bed and Breakfast only. Stamp please, for colour brochure.

Please note that entries marked with an asterisk also have a colour display advert in the colour section in this guide

58 Cornwall BOARD

FALMOUTH near. Mrs C. F. Denton, High Cross Farm, High Cross, Constantine, Near Falmouth TB11 5RE (Falmouth [0326] 40373). In a delightful hill-top position, this seven-acre smallholding is one mile from Constantine village and four miles from the sea. This is a modernised farmhouse with direct access road. One mile from lovely Helford River and boat trips, sailing and fishing. Good food and personal attention given to guests. One single, two double and two family rooms, all with washbasins; bathroom and toilets; lounge and diningroom. Children welcomed at reduced rates. Pets are not allowed in the house. Car essential, parking space. Open all year except Christmas week. Evening Meal, Bed and Breakfast or Bed and Breakfast only. SAE, please, for terms.

FOWEY. Mrs S. C. Dunn, Menabilly Barton, Par PL24 2TN (Par [072-681] 2844). Working farm. MENABILLY BARTON is a secluded farmhouse set in a wooded valley leading to a quiet cove, accessible by footpath, safe for bathing. Farmhouse with spacious diningroom and large lounge with TV, also peaceful garden with view of the sea. Good traditional farmhouse cooking. Nearby local pubs with excellent buffet lunches one mile away. Beach with all amenities one mile. National Trust cliff walks around the coast. Fowey, 10 minutes by road, offers fishing, sailing, quaint shops, etc. Golfing on the coast nearby. North coast about 40 minutes' drive. Land's End two and a half hours. Several National Trust properties in the area. Open January to November with accommodation in three double, one single and two family bedrooms, bathroom, toilet. Cot, high chair, babysitting. Pets allowed. Bed and Full English Breakfast only from £6.50 per adult; reductions for children.

GOONHAVERN. Mrs D. H. Ricketts, Cumbria, Martyns Close, Goonhavern, Truro TR4 9JW (Truro [0872] 572057). Cumbria is a modern attractive, detached house in quiet pleasant surroundings three miles from the coast offering hospitality and superior Bed and Breakfast accommodation with optional Evening Meal. One double room with en-suite shower, toilet and handbasin, additional single bed available to this room for child five/ten years old at reduced rate. One double room with washbasin. Guest bathroom. Heating, alarm radios, tea/coffee making facilities in rooms. Lounge — colour television — own keys. Ample parking. April to October. Regret, no pets. Goonhavern is a pleasant village well placed for touring. Perranporth three miles. Newquay six. Truro seven. Terms from — £45.50 per week Bed and Breakfast or £70 Bed, Breakfast and Evening Meal.

Perhaver

**THE HOUSE ON THE CLIFF
GORRAN HAVEN
(Licensed) AA**

Perhaver is a delightful Guest House where you can relax in a pleasantly informal atmosphere. The house occupies a commanding cliff-top position above the most attractive unspoilt fishing village of Gorran Haven. In an area designated as being of outstanding natural beauty, Perhaver is situated at the end of the cliff road away from all the traffic and stands on a small headland with the sea on two sides and open country at the rear. All the rooms have lovely views of the sea and coastline. The bedrooms have hot and cold running water, shaver points, reading lamps, fitted furniture and fitted carpets and are most attractive and comfortable. The lounge has colour television and is tastefully decorated and furnished. The Residents' bar and the diningroom have the same magnificent views as the lounge. An excellent standard of food is maintained and served at tables for two. Personal attention is given to everyone and you can be assured of absolute comfort.

A small quiet beach below the house is reached by a natural cliff path starting at the stile at the top of the drive and there are other beaches within a few minutes' walk. All are sandy and ideal for sailing, fishing and safe swimming. Fishing trips may be taken from the quay in the summer. Some beautiful walks can be enjoyed and the path over the cliffs to Mevagissey begins at the entrance to Perhaver. This is a perfect place to spend a honeymoon. Parking space for vehicles not exceeding 7' in height. Mr and Mrs Bolt regret they are unable to accommodate persons under 18 years of age or pets. There is no accommodation for single persons. The standards at Perhaver comply with those of the British Travel Association and the Guest House is registered with both the English Tourist Board and Cornwall County Tourist Board and recommended by the Nurses Holiday Association. Mr and Mrs Bolt will be pleased to forward a brochure showing the magnificent position. Please send SAE for reply.

Evening Dinner, Bed and Breakfast from £82 to £85 per person weekly, no VAT. Please confirm price when enquiring as this may alter due to any inflationary increase. Mevagissey 3 miles, St. Austell 10 and Truro 14.

**Mr and Mrs I. W. Bolt (Mevagissey [0726] 842471)
Perhaver Guest House, Perhaver Point, Gorran Haven, Cornwall**

BOARD Cornwall 59

A REAL COUNTRY HOUSE HOTEL JUST OUTSIDE OF FALMOUTH

THE HOME
PENJERRICK, FALMOUTH

Telephone: Falmouth (STD 0326) 250427 and 250143

Situated in lovely unspoilt countryside, yet only 2½ miles from Falmouth. Ideal for lovers of the country, yet within 18 minutes' walk of Maenporth Beach.

An Ashley Courtenay Recommended Hotel

Our house, in its large garden, has lovely views over tree-clad countryside to Maenporth and the bay. Close to the Helford River with its beautiful walks and boating facilities. Ideal base for touring.
All bedrooms have H&C, razor points and bedside lights. Our home is graciously furnished and carpeted to a high standard. All beds are modern divans. Partial central heating.
Our elegant dining room has separate tables. Large lounge with colour TV. In addition there is a spacious sun lounge overlooking the garden.

★
GOOD ENCLOSED CAR PARK   BUS SERVICE
★
Mr & Mrs P. Tremayne have welcomed guests to their lovely house for the past 21 years
★
Dinner, Room and Breakfast from £70 per week, including 15% VAT.
Illustrated brochure from Mrs. T. P. Tremayne

We are of a farming family and our visitors' book is blushingly complimentary over the home-cooked food and its presentation. This is our home and as such we welcome you to it and hope you will enjoy it as much as we do. Special petrol scheme for regular and new guests for April, May, June and September subject to availability.

Also Self-Catering Furnished Farmhouse and Cottage at Constantine, Falmouth

GORRAN HAVEN. Mr and Mrs A. and B. Butterworth, "Mellins Close", Trewollock Lane, Gorran Haven, St. Austell PL26 6NT (Mevagissey [0726] 843318). "Mellins Close" is situated in its own grounds on the edge of the small fishing village of Gorran Haven. Safe, sandy beaches just a few minutes' walk away. Come and relax in pleasant comfortable surroundings. Good food, sea and country views. Ideally situated to explore the beautiful Roseland Peninsula with its many coves, beaches and coastal walks. Three double bedrooms with washbasins; two bathrooms (one with shower). Lounge; diningroom with separate tables. Private parking. Sorry, no pets. Open Easter to October. Bed and Breakfast (Evening Meal optional). SAE for terms, please.

HAYLE. Mrs M. E. Pascoe, Polwhele Farm, 16 Gwinear Lane, Gwinear, Hayle TR27 5LA (Praze [0209] 831371). Traditionally stone-built farmhouse on small mixed farm. It has been extensively modernised and has had an enlarged and spacious sun lounge added. The village is a short walk and the sea four/five miles away. Hayle and Cambourne three miles. Guests are warmly welcomed from May to September and accommodated in two double and two single bedrooms, two of which have washbasins. There is a bathroom, two toilets; sittingroom with TV and diningroom with separate tables. Children welcome at reduced rates; cot available. Car essential; parking provided. Safe bathing in the area. Evening Dinner, Bed and Breakfast. Terms on request.

HELFORD. Mr and Mrs J. J. Pascoe, Trelease Farm, St Keverne, Near Helston TR12 6RF (St Keverne [0326] 280379). Working farm. The farm is situated a mile and a quarter off the Helston to St Keverne B3293 road in a wooded valley enjoying peaceful surroundings away from the traffic noise. Coverack is two and a quarter miles, and several sandy beaches, including those on the Helford River are about four miles away. The 16th century farmhouse has a warmth of character and guests are accommodated in family or double bedrooms (three with washbasins); dining on separate tables; sittingroom with TV and log fire. All meals include home and local produce. Large secluded garden with fishpool. This is a true farm carrying Guernsey cattle and a variety of animals and poultry. Open January to December. Parking for essential cars. The aim of the proprietors is to provide an informal relaxed atmosphere unfettered by rules and regulations. Phone or send SAE please, for terms for Evening Dinner, Bed and Breakfast or Bed and Breakfast only.

HELSTON. Mr and Mrs W. A. Jenkin, Higher Trevurvas, Ashton, Helston TR13 9TZ (Penzance [073676] 3613). Higher Trevurvas is set in a beautiful position with views covering most of Mount's Bay. The beach of Praa Sands is reached in about 10 minutes by a public footpath. It is very central for touring with many places of interest nearby. The house is fully modernised. Lounge/diningroom with separate tables; two double and three family rooms, four with H/C; open all year with central heating. Children over six welcome with reduced rates if sharing parents' room. Excellent food is served — roast beef, pork, chicken, etc. Beef cattle are kept on the eight and a half acre farm. Bed and Breakfast and Evening Meal or Bed and Breakfast only. SAE, please for terms.

HELSTON. Mrs A. Harry, Polhormon Farm, Mullion, Helston TR12 7JE (Mullion [0326] 240304). Polhormon Farm overlooks Poldhu Cove on The Lizard Peninsula and enjoys beautiful sea and country views; five minutes from four sandy beaches, golf course, cliff walks and charming village of Mullion. Character farmhouse separate from farm buildings; large airy room (double, twin, family, single) all with washbasins, traditionally furnished. Access to rooms at all times. Good substantial English Breakfast. Children welcome, cot, high chair, babysitting and reduced rates. Open March to October with electric heating. Pets allowed. Easy parking. Guests very welcome on this 200 acre dairy farm. *On Helston/Lizard road A3083, pass Culdrose Air Station; first right after roundabout (sign for Mullion golf club) through Poldhu Cove up hill and look for our sign on the left.

HELSTON. Mrs P. Roberts, Hendra Farm, Wendron, Helston TR13 0NR (Falmouth [0326] 40470). Working farm. Hendra Farm, just off the main Helston/Falmouth road, is an ideal centre for touring Cornwall; three miles to Helston, eight to both Redruth and Falmouth. Safe sandy beaches within easy reach — five miles to the sea. Beautiful views from the farmhouse of the 60-acre beef farm. Two double, one single, and one family bedrooms; bathroom and toilets; sittingroom and two diningrooms. Cot, babysitting and reduced rates offered for children. No objection to pets. Car necessary, parking space. Enjoy the good cooking with roast beef, pork, lamb, chicken, genuine Cornish pasties, fish and delicious sweets and cream. Open all year except Christmas for Evening Dinner, Bed and Breakfast from £50 per week; Bed and Breakfast from £5.50 per night.

HELSTON. Mrs Maureen Dale, Polgarth Farm, Crowntown, Helston TR13 0AA (Helston [032-65] 2115). Working farm. Polgarth Farm is very central for touring West Cornwall. Situated three miles from the market town of Helston (on the main Helston/Camborne road — B3303). Polgarth is a mixed farm, growing broccoli, cabbage, early potatoes and corn; supporting beef cattle and pigs on its 110 acres. Maureen Dale, having cooked at The London Dairy Show, Ideal Home Exhibition and on TV, takes great pleasure in producing sumptuous meals for all her guests and, with her family, welcomes you to her home. Babysitting available and pets welcome by prior arrangement. Open all year except Christmas. The house has full central heating. Three double and two family bedrooms, with washbasins; bathroom, ample toilets; TV lounge and diningroom. Reductions for children. SAE, please, for terms. Registered with the English and Cornwall Tourist Board.

BOARD   Cornwall   61

HELSTON. Mrs I. E. Johns, Halvanance Farm, Longstone, Sithney, Helston TR13 0HF (Helston [03265] 2375). Working farm. This farm is situated on high ground in a quiet and peaceful area, four miles north east of Helston, with extensive downland views to the coast. Fishing and interesting harbour at Porthleven. Safe, sandy beach at Marazion nine miles. Poldark Mine, Tolgus Tin, Carn Brea Leisure Centre and Aero Park, all within 10 mile radius. Horse riding in area. Two double bedrooms; one double bedroom with bunk beds, if required, sleeping four. All with washbasins. Bathroom/toilet. Sittingroom; diningroom; colour TV. Children welcome, cot, high chair; babysitting by arrangement. Pets accepted (within reason). Open June to September inclusive. Car essential — parking. Evening Dinner/Meal, Bed and Breakfast or Bed and Breakfast only. Terms on application. No VAT chargeable.

HELSTON. Mrs Kathleen Worden, Anhay Farm, Gunwalloe, Helston TR12 7QF (Helston [03265] 2114). Working farm. Anhay consists of 74 acres of dairy farm and market gardening and is situated about five minutes' walk from the sea. Three family rooms and two double all with hot and cold water, diningroom and sittingroom. Gunwalloe is within easy reach of many beauty spots: Church Cove which has an adjoining 18-hole golf course and St. Ives, Land's End, Helford River and The Lizard. Helston is the home of the "Furry Dance" which takes place on the 8th May every year. Bed, Breakfast and Evening Meal or Bed and Breakfast. Children taken. Terms on request. Open Easter to October.

TREGADDRA

Hilary and David Lugg welcome you to their 200 acre working farm set in beautiful surroundings, with views of coast and countryside for 15 miles. Good home cooking and friendly atmosphere bring guests back year after year. All bedrooms with H&C. Lounge with inglenook and colour TV. Games room. Sandy beach 2 miles; Helford River 7 miles; golf 2 miles; pony trekking, tennis and squash available locally. Sorry, no pets. Bed, Breakfast and Evening Meal served every day.
Send for colour brochure. Mrs H. E. Lugg, Tregaddra, Cury, Helston, CORNWALL. Tel. (0326) 240235.

HELSTON. Mr and Mrs Edwin Lawrance, Boscadjack Farm, Coverack Bridges, Helston TR13 0LZ (Helston [032-65] 2086). Working farm. Mr and Mrs Lawrance and family welcome visitors to their modernised farmhouse, which is set in the 92 acres of this dairy farm situated in the Cober Valley amidst delightful unspoilt countryside, two miles from Helston. Car essential. Central for beaches. Cornwall CC registered. RAC and AA listed. Fire Certificate No. 869. Two family bedrooms and two doubles (all with washbasins) available for guests. Modern bathroom, two toilets; comfortable lounge with colour TV, separate diningroom with individual tables. Carpeted and well-furnished. Oil central heating. Children welcome, babysitting. Sorry, no pets. Good home cooking, including roast dishes, varied sweets with Cornish cream, fresh farm eggs and vegetables. Evening Dinner, Bed and Breakfast or Bed and Breakfast only. SAE for terms.

HELSTON. Mrs M. F. Osborne, Polglase Farm, Cury Cross Lanes, Helston TR12 7AY (Mullion [0326] 240469). Polglase is situated just 80 yards off the main Helston/Lizard road, central for beaches. Two miles from Mullion village and golf course, and five miles from the Helford River where boats are available for hire. Excellent farmhouse cooking served, from home produced vegetables and meat. Separate diningroom and lounge with colour TV. Two double, two single, two family bedrooms; bathroom, separate shower, two toilets. Reduced rates for children; cot and occasional babysitting. No pets. Open Easter to October. Car essential — parking. Evening Dinner, Bed and Breakfast. Terms on request.

HELSTON. Mrs G. Hosken, Withan, St. Martin, Helston TR12 6BY (Manaccan [032623] 237). Working farm. Withan Farm is a mixed family farm of 120 acres with footpath through fields and woods to famous Frenchman's Creek. It is three miles from Helford and St. Anthony where there are facilities for boating, sailing and fishing. Within easy driving distance of villages and beaches of the Lizard Peninsula. One double bedroom with bath and handbasin en suite. Two double bedrooms with handbasins. Comfortable lounge with colour TV. Good farmhouse food. Children welcome. Bed and Breakfast, Evening Meal optional. SAE for terms.

Hillsdale Hotel

Comfort and friendly hospitality

* Set in peaceful countryside near several beautiful coves and fishing harbour – convenient for both North and South coasts.
* Residents' bar, television lounge, sun lounge and immaculate dining room.
* Excellent home cooking using local produce, early morning tea and packed lunches available.
* All bedrooms have fitted vanitory units with hot and cold running water, central heating and interior sprung mattresses.
* Children and pets welcome – happy, informal atmosphere – come and go as you please.
* Ample free parking space.
* Fire certificate granted.

The resident proprietors, Norman and Anne Price, offer a warm, friendly welcome and take a personal pleasure in ensuring that your holiday will be happy and memorable.

Send SAE for colour brochure. Terms £65 to £82 inclusive.

HILLSDALE HOTEL, POLLADRAS, Nr. HELSTON. PENZANCE (0736) 763334.

HELSTON near. Mrs M. E. Williams, Clahar Garden Farm, Mullion, Near Helston TR12 7DT (Mullion [0326] 240571). Situated in peaceful valley on its own 53 acres of land, this farmhouse is only two miles from good, sandy beach and lovely harbour; also 18-hole golf course; riding stables nearby. The excellent food served includes home produce and diningroom has separate tables; lounge with colour TV. Three double, one single bedrooms (three with washbasins); bathroom, toilet. Children over seven welcome, reduced rates up to 10 years. Sorry, no pets. Car essential — parking. Central heating. Open Easter to September for Evening Meal, Bed and Breakfast or Bed and Breakfast only. SAE, please, for terms.

HELSTON. Mrs Gillian E. Lawrance, Longstone Farm, Trenear, Helston TR13 0HG (Helston [03265] 2483). Working farm. A warm welcome is extended to guests at this modernised farmhouse situated on a 62 acre dairy farm set in peaceful countryside, ideal for touring and within easy reach of West Cornwall's beautiful beaches. All bedrooms have hot and cold; spring interior mattresses, carpeted throughout. Separate tables in diningroom, colour TV in lounge, large sunlounge provides additional relaxation area, either for reading or games. Good farmhouse fare served, milk and cream produced on farm with Cornish eggs, meat and vegetables. SAE for terms. Fire Certificate. AA listed. Cornish Tourist Board Approved and English Tourist Board Approved. Full electric central heating. Open February to November for Evening Dinner/Meal, Bed and Breakfast or Bed and Breakfast only. Reductions for children and senior citizens. Babysitting by arrangement.

HELSTON. Tim Fraser, Trythance Guest House, The Square, St. Keverne, Helston TR12 6ND (St. Keverne [0326] 280-054). In hub of pleasant village (church, pubs, post office, shops), two miles from beautiful east coast of Lizard Peninsula. Many nearby beauty spots — Porthallow, Coverack, Cadgwith, Kynance, Mullion, lovely Helford River; marvellous walks. Helston 12 miles, Falmouth 24, Penzance 25 and Truro 28. Four family rooms, also let as doubles (washbasins and built in wardrobes); bathroom, toilet, second toilet; diningroom (separate tables); lounge, colour television. Central heating. Fitted carpets. Garden overlooking village square; easy parking. Bed, Breakfast and optional Evening Meal. Reduced rates for pre-teenagers. Regret, no pets. Open all year except Christmas/New Year. SAE, please, for details and rates.

HELSTON. Mrs S. J. Boaden, Skewes Farm, Cury Cross Lanes, Helston TR12 7BD (Mullion [0326] 240374). Working farm. Skewes Farm is five and a half miles from Helston and the Lizard. Poldhu Cove with its sandy beach and adjacent golf course is just two miles away; boating five miles. The Boaden family welcome guests into their home and everyone is free to wander round the farm. Younger children may like to ride the children's pony. Three double, one single, one family bedrooms; bathroom, two toilets; sittingroom; diningroom. Cot, high chair, babysitting by arrangement. Sorry, no pets. Open from Easter to end of September. Car essential — parking. Full English Breakfast served and three-course Evening Meal. SAE, please, for terms. Fire Certificate granted.

PLEASE SEND A STAMPED ADDRESSED ENVELOPE WITH ENQUIRIES

LAUNCESTON. Mrs J. E. Blackmore, Secretary, Launceston and District Publicity Committee, 22 Priory Park Road, Launceston PL15 8JD (Launceston [0566] 2820). Launceston — the Gateway to Cornwall. Historic town with Norman Castle, set amidst the splendour of Bodmin Moor and Dartmoor. Excellent facilities for riding, fishing and golf. Both North and South coasts are within easy reach. Colour Guide, 25p plus postage. Enquiries to above.

LAUNCESTON. Mrs Mary Rich, "Nathania", Altarnun, Launceston PL15 7SL (Pipers Pool [056-686] 426). Open all year, this attractive bungalow, standing on the edge of the moors, lovely walks in the country lanes, is situated approximately one mile from A30 and makes an ideal centre for touring the north and south coast of Cornwall, and the many picturesque areas of Devon, Dartmoor and Bodmin Moor, sandy beaches, many places of historical interest within easy reach. Local facilities include golf, riding and fishing. The accommodation is comfortable and comprises three double bedrooms; bathroom (separate shower), two toilets. Sittingroom, diningroom. Good and plentiful farmhouse cooking. Children welcome, cot and babysitting available. Car essential — ample parking. Evening Meal, Bed and Breakfast from £7; Bed and Breakfast from £5. Also self-catering accommodation and touring caravans for hire.

MRS MARGARET SMITH, HURDON FARM, LAUNCESTON CORNWALL PL15 9LS. LAUNCESTON (0566) 2955

This 400-acre mixed working farm and its gracious 18th century stone farmhouse is situated 1½ miles from the ancient market town of Launceston. Great priority is placed on the use of our own farm and garden produce to create sumptuous dinners, home made rolls, soups and starters. Traditional and original main courses and delicious desserts and to start the day a hearty four course English Breakfast. Washbasins in all bedrooms. Log fires for those colder evenings. Fire Certificate issued. Pony to ride. Reductions for senior citizens and children. Bed and Breakfast or Bed, Breakfast and Evening Meal.

RAC LISTED. REGISTERED WITH ENGLISH TOURIST BOARD. MEMBER OF BRITISH RELAIS ROUTIERS.

LAUNCESTON. Mr and Mrs A. E. Sloman, Carn House, Canworthy Water, Launceston PL15 8UB (Canworthy Water [056-681] 208). Working farm. Carn House is a 220-acre farm with sheep, horses and corn. It offers accommodation to entire families or unaccompanied children — Bed, Breakfast, Evening Meal, residential or packed lunch. Selection of activities on offer: riding, fishing, games room, barbecues, farm walks, kiddies' play area, adventure park, cart rides. Babysitting available. Ideally situated for touring Devon and Cornwall. Other attractions in the area include heated swimming pools, golf and surfing. Car essential — ample parking. SAE, please, or telephone for particulars.

LAUNCESTON. Mrs R. Robbins, Welltown Farm, Launceston PL15 9QU (Lifton [056-684] 259). Working farm. Welltown is a beautifully built house just off the main road, away from noise of traffic. A long established business and everything possible is done to ensure guests have a happy holiday. Rivers Tamar and Carey run through the farmland and the house is surrounded by a large, pretty garden. Ideally situated for touring all Cornwall and Devon. Good and plentiful food is served. The accommodation is modern and comfortable; one double and four family bedrooms, all with washbasins; bathroom; two toilets; sittingroom and diningroom. Log fires. Colour TV. Fire Certificate held. Children welcome, cot and babysitting available. Pets permitted. Open all year. Bed and Breakfast from £7.50 (Dinner from £4.50). One room is suitable for disabled guests. Reduced rates for children. Car essential — parking. Good atmosphere and good value for money.

LAUNCESTON. Mr and Mrs R. P. Irving, The Old Station, Egloskerry, Launceston PL15 8ST (North Petherwin [056-685] 492). Egloskerry was a station on the old North Cornwall Railway in Padstow. The buildings are now an ordinary home, nature has claimed the track and the platforms are part of the quiet garden, which looks south over grazing land. Half an hour's drive away are the splendid North Cornwall coast, Bodmin Moor and Dartmoor. Available are one twin-bedded room, one family room, both with hot and cold, and a ground floor single room; bathroom and shower room, each with WC. Bed and Breakfast £6, Evening Meal optional. Also a 4/5 berth caravan at £3 per night, and room for a touring caravan. Please phone above for further details.

LISKEARD. Mrs Thelma Crabb, Hill Farm, Merrymeet, Liskeard PL14 3LL (Liskeard [0579] 42752). Working farm. This delightfully modernised old farmhouse, situated in the heart of the countryside with picturesque views yet close to many amenities, offers accommodation for up to six people to suit your requirements — double, twin or family bedrooms. Bathroom and separate toilet. Diningroom; lounge with colour TV. It is a 190-acre dairy farm within easy reach of many north and south coast beaches, National Trust properties and sporting activities including riding, fishing, swimming, tennis, squash and golf, and many places of interest. Ideal centre for touring Cornwall and South Devon. Children welcome at reduced rates; cot and babysitting available. Sorry, no pets. Open all year for Bed and Breakfast, with Evening Dinner optional. Really good farmhouse cooking served in friendly atmosphere. Cornwall Tourist Board approved accommodation.

LOWER TRENGALE FARM

Informal and relaxing family holidays are the speciality of our small farm. Situated in lovely countryside, we are within easy reach of many beaches, tourist attractions and Bodmin Moor. There is plenty of fun for children with ponies to ride, animals to watch and a playground. Guests are welcome to explore the farm and fields, watch at milking time, help feed the calves, pigs and lambs, collect the eggs, or relax in the garden. We provide Bed, Breakfast and optional Evening Meal with delicious home cooked food using our own produce when possible. We also do babysitting and packed lunches and have cots, high chairs, TV lounge and a laundry. Well behaved pets are welcome. Self catering cottage also available with evening meals (see self-catering section). Please contact **Mrs Louise Kidd at Lower Trengale Farm, Liskeard, Cornwall PL14 6HF (Liskeard [0579] 21019).**

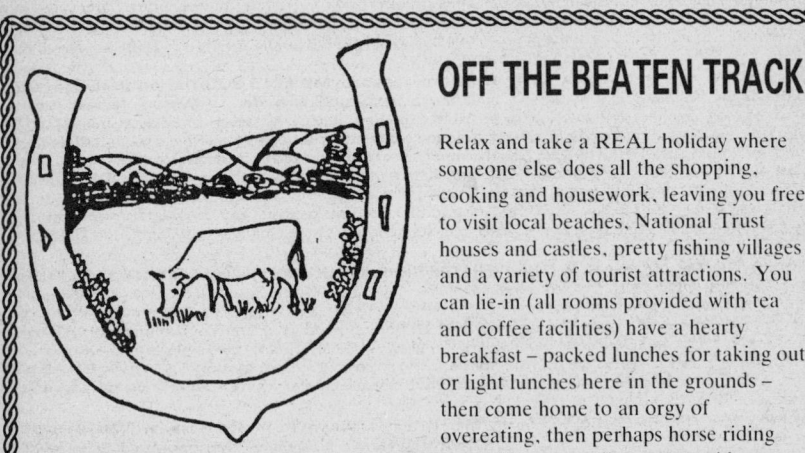

OFF THE BEATEN TRACK

Relax and take a REAL holiday where someone else does all the shopping, cooking and housework, leaving you free to visit local beaches, National Trust houses and castles, pretty fishing villages and a variety of tourist attractions. You can lie-in (all rooms provided with tea and coffee facilities) have a hearty breakfast – packed lunches for taking out or light lunches here in the grounds – then come home to an orgy of overeating, then perhaps horse riding and walking it off afterwards in the beautiful peaceful surrounding countryside. Children are an integral part of the light-hearted informal atmosphere here – we have cots and highchairs, babysitting to enable you to have some time on your own – ponies and bicycles to hire, 30 acres of farm and woodland to explore. We have kittens to cuddle, geese to goggle at, two dogs, Dougal and Becky, a house cow – Celia, chickens to feed and eggs to collect. (Has Dad always wanted to drive a Tractor?) Pets welcome. Luxury self-catering accommodation plus games room, pool, table tennis. For more information write or telephone: **Ian and Anne Beadle, Lee Barton Farm, Herodsfoot, Liskeard, Cornwall. Tel Liskeard 20594.**

BOARD Cornwall 65

LISKEARD. J. M. Dingle, East Quethiock Farm, Quethiock, Liskeard PL14 3SQ (0579-43040). **Working farm.** There is always a warm welcome at East Quethiock Farm, which overlooks the picturesque village of Quethiock. It is a mixed farm with beef cattle, sheep, lambs and young stock. Children welcomed. The farmhouse is registered and recommended by the Cornwall Tourist Board and is fully modernised. Fitted carpets throughout. All bedrooms have H/C with washbasins, divans, shaver points etc. Two family rooms. Lounge with colour TV. Separate diningroom. Good farmhouse meals, of roast beef, lamb, pork, chicken etc. with plenty of home produced vegetables. Parking space ample. You are assured personal attention at all times. There are many places of interest in the area to visit. Evening Meal, Bed and Breakfast or Bed and Breakfast only. Also self-catering caravan on the farm, fully equipped. H/C water, fridge, TV and flush toilet, and a self-catering bungalow at Liskeard.

LISKEARD. Mrs S. Tamblyn, Beara Farm, Herodsfoot, Liskeard PL14 4RB (Liskeard [0579] 20323 or 21063). Working farm. A very peacefully situated farm, short distance from B3359. Excellent walks and lovely countryside views. Mixed farm, with emphasis on dairy, all calves being reared, 200 head of stock. Children made very welcome, cot, high chair and babysitting. Pets welcome. Within easy reach of beaches and moors, National Trust properties. Log fire. H/C in all bedrooms. Excellent home made food, personally supervised. Six guests only. A warm welcome assured. Evening Meal/Dinner, Bed and Breakfast or Bed and Breakfast only. Reduced rates for children.

LISKEARD. Pamela and Tony Miller, Bodmin Moor Nature Observatory, Ninestones Farm, Liskeard PL14 6SD (Liskeard [0579] 20455). Tony and Pamela Miller welcome all country lovers to stay at the Observatory which is an old Cornish longhouse, situated above the Upper Fowey Valley, three miles south of Jamaica Inn. Splendid views down the valley. Guided field trips to habitats of interest on the Moor and coasts. Five double bedrooms and one family room; dormitory for six; sittingroom/diningroom; central heating. Children are welcome, one cot and high chair, babysitting available. Open all year. Car essential, parking. SAE, please, for prospectus, terms and natural history observations.

LISKEARD. Mr and Mrs E. J. & C. H. Sendall, Lanrest Cottage, Horningtops, Liskeard PL14 3QD (Liskeard [0579] 46201). Lanrest Cottage is set amidst beautiful country surroundings offering lovely walks, peace and tranquillity. Three miles from Liskeard and six and a half miles approximately from Looe, Seaton, Downderry and Millendreath beaches. Half-mile from quaint one-track train alternating between Looe, St. Keyne and Liskeard; change train for Plymouth. Good home cooking. Two double and one family bedrooms all with H&C; TV lounge; shower room; bathroom. Full central heating. Lanrest is mentioned in Daphne du Maurier's book "The King's General". Evening Dinner, Bed and Breakfast from £65 per week; Bed and Breakfast from £42 per week. Open all year. Car essential; ample parking. The proprietors make every effort to ensure the comfort of their guests. Special weeks for non-smokers.

LISKEARD. Mr and Mrs B. and P. Bunney, Crylla Farm, Common Moor, Liskeard PL14 6ER (Liskeard [0579] 42473). Working farm. Brian and Pearl welcome you to their 173-acre beef farm overlooking Sibley Black Lake (140 acres) where you can fly fish, sail and windsurf. Crylla Farm is within easy reach of the coast of Cornwall and four and a half miles from the town of Liskeard. There are pleasant walks over the moors to the disused tin mines. Shooting allowed on Crylla Farm. Pony riding adjoining farm. Good food. Homely comforts. TV lounge, diningroom. Six bedrooms, all with washbasins. Children welcome at reduced rates. Pets accepted. CCC registered accommodation. Fire Certificate held. Bed and Breakfast (Evening Meal optional). Hot drinks in the evening. Car essential. Open all year. SAE, please.

LISKEARD. Mrs Lindsay M. Pendray, Caduscott, East Taphouse, Liskeard PL14 4NG (Liskeard [0579] 20262). Working farm. Traditional Bed, Breakfast and Evening Meal in this old farmhouse on a 500-acre mixed dairy farm three quarters of a mile off A390, 10 miles from Looe/Polperro. Well situated for touring or visiting numerous local attractions including miniature railway, monkey sanctuary and National Trust properties. Comfortable accommodation for up to six people to suit your requirements. Double and family bedroom; sitting/diningroom. Children especially welcome, cot, high chair, babysitting and open spaces to play in with swing, climbing frame, table tennis. Central heating and log fires. Sorry, no pets. Open March to November. Please write or phone for terms. Reductions for children.

LISKEARD. Mrs S. M. Wherry, Beneathway Farm, Dobwalls, Liskeard PL14 6JU (Dobwalls [0579] 20231). Working farm, join in. A warm welcome awaits at Beneathway, just off the A38 a few minutes from the village of Dobwalls and within easy reach of Plymouth, north and south coasts. Children will enjoy riding the pony, joining in farm activities; swings and slides too. Three double and one family bedrooms, three with washbasins; bathroom, two toilets; sittingroom with colour TV; diningroom. Cot, high chair, babysitting arranged. Sorry, no pets. Car essential — parking space. Open March to October for Bed and Breakfast. Reductions for children. Fire Certificate held. CTB registered. Farm Holiday Guide Diploma Award 1978. SAE, please, for terms. Also six-berth caravan.

Cornwall BOARD

LISKEARD. Mrs S. R. P. Rowe, Tregondale Farm, Menheniot, Liskeard PL14 3RG (Liskeard [0579] 42407). Working farm, join in. Tregondale is situated in an attractive valley and is set back in a walled garden where there is a swing and see-saw for children. Tregondale is a mixed farm of 180 acres easily located near A38, and includes a resident pony. All rooms are comfortable and attractively furnished. Good Cornish food is served in a house which is fully modernised, yet still retains its character. Within easy reach of many beaches; Looe six miles; Plymouth and the moors close by. Golf, fishing, boating are all obtainable and there is a swimming pool at Liskeard. Much to interest the children, and National Trust properties, villages and model railway within a few miles. Pony trekking. Two double bedrooms, one family room with washbasins; bathroom with toilet; shower with toilet; sitting/diningroom. Cot, high chair, babysitting and reduced rates for children. Sorry, no pets. Car essential — parking. Evening Dinner/Meal, Bed and Breakfast or Bed and Breakfast only. AA listed. Open all year. SAE, please, for brochure.

LISKEARD. Mrs E. R. Elford, Tresulgan Farm, Horningtops, Liskeard PL14 3PU (Widegates [050-34] 268). Working farm. Tresulgan is a 115-acre dairy farm situated on the Plymouth/Liskeard road, set in quiet surroundings. The attractive farmhouse, built in 1700s, still retains its quiet character and original beams. Having been modernised over the past few years, including double glazing, adds to its comfort. The bedrooms, which overlook the large enclosed garden, have picturesque views of the wooded Seaton Valley. Nearest beach at Seaton (four miles), and the popular fishing village of Looe is six miles away (shark fishing and boating). Sailing, golf, riding, Woolly Monkey Sanctuary, Forest Railway, National Trust properties and other attractions within a few miles. Friendly accommodation — two double, one single, one family bedrooms, all with washbasins; bathroom/toilet and shower; separate toilet, shower and washbasin. Colour TV in guests' lounge. Includes cooked Breakfast, three-course Evening Meal and Light Supper. SAE, please, for terms and Brochure.

LISKEARD. Mrs A. R. Hawke, Cartuther Barton, Liskeard (Liskeard [0579] 43244). Cartuther Barton is a pleasant Cornish manor farmhouse, situated one mile from Liskeard on the A38 Plymouth road. Within easy reach of Looe, Polperro and many other coastal resorts. Ideal for touring. Lounge with TV; diningroom with separate tables, and hot and cold water in bedrooms. Ample free parking space. Bed, Breakfast and Evening Dinner. Terms on application.

LISKEARD. Mrs M. Northcott, Pendower, East Taphouse, Liskeard PL14 4NH (Liskeard [0579] 20332). Country guest house, pleasantly situated on main A390 road between Liskeard (five miles) and Lostwithiel. Good views of surrounding countryside, only a few miles from picturesque Looe, Polperro and many other coastal resorts. Ideal centre for touring Cornwall and South Devon. Fishing, horse riding nearby. Two family and four double bedrooms, all with washbasins; bathroom, toilets; lounge with TV; diningrooms. Ground floor self-contained flat, with twin beds, hot and cold water, toilet. Parking. A warm welcome awaits you all year. Excellent food. Fire Certificate. Fowey 13 miles. Looe and Polperro 10. Plymouth and Newquay 20. SAE please, for terms for Evening Meal, Bed and Breakfast, or Bed and Breakfast (reductions for children — moderate terms for senior citizens).

LOOE. Mrs M. L. Gibson, Kellow Cottage, Plaidy, Looe PL13 1LE (Looe [050-36] 2232). Kellow Cottage is part of an old farmhouse, dating back to smuggling days. It provides comfortable accommodation with plenty of good food, own garden produce and eggs. The Smugglers Lane leads to steps down to nearby beach, three minutes' walk, with shop, recreational facilities, cafe, boating, fishing, etc. Two double bedrooms, bathroom with toilet, electricity, free parking for cars. Towels supplied. Evening Dinner, Bed and Breakfast. Reductions for children, open all year round. Looe two miles by road, one mile by pleasant footpath, Polperro six miles, Plymouth 16. SAE, please.

LOOE. Mrs D. Eastley, Bake Farm, Pelynt, Looe PL13 2QQ (Lanreath [0503] 20244). This is an old farmhouse, bearing the Trelawnay Coat of Arms (1610) situated midway between Looe and Fowey. There are three double bedrooms all with washbasins; bathroom, two toilets; combined sitting/diningroom. Children welcome at reduced rates, babysitting available. Sorry, no pets. Open from May to September. Plenty of fresh farm food, a lot of home produce including Cornish clotted cream, an abundance of roasts including home-bred chicken. A car is essential for touring the area, ample parking. There is much to see and do here — horse riding four miles, golf seven. The sea is only five miles away and there is shark fishing at Looe. SAE, please for terms for Evening Meal, Bed and Breakfast. Cleanliness guaranteed.

AA 2-Star

Egon Ronay and
Ashley Courtenay
Recommended

RAC 2-Star

Fully Licensed
Free House

HAVE CHICKEN IN CIDER...
IN AN ANCIENT HOSTELRY

This is an Ancient Hostelry, over 400 years old, situated in a delightful old-world Cornish village. Here is offered excellent modern accommodation for visitors, with the delightful atmosphere of the Country Inn in which the traditional character has been maintained. It is also a grand centre for touring Devon and Cornwall. The Inn has been in turn Courthouse, Coaching Inn and "Smugglers" distribution house and the bars have changed little since smuggling days.

This is the only Inn in Great Britain where the bars as kitchens are licensed. Here you find the "Visitors' Kitchen", "The Farmers' Kitchen" and the "Men's Kitchen". There is also the "Wagon Wheel" Snack Bar. In the "Visitors' Kitchen" you will find the "Lovers' Nook", and in the "Men's Kitchen", "The Priest's Hideout" – all being reminders of days gone by.

Fourteen double bedrooms, three single and two family-sized rooms (all with hot and cold running water). 60 per cent of the bedrooms have private bathrooms and the remainder have one bathroom per two bedrooms. All rooms have tea and coffee making facilities and colour TV. Residents lounge with TV alcove and separate residents' bar. Diningroom, four lock-ups for cars and parking space for fifty cars. Brochure and tariff sent on receipt of SAE. The food served is delicious... Chicken in Cider, Duck in Cherry Wine Sauce, locally-caught Salmon and Trout, local Lamb and of course Cornish Cream. Open from Easter to October. Dogs allowed. Children's summerhouse.

The Inn has now been issued with a Fire Certificate and complies with the latest fire regulations. Plymouth 23 miles, Newquay 33 miles and the sea five miles. SAE will bring full particulars about this OLD-WORLD INN from:

MR T. C. and MRS M. MANSFIELD
The Famous Old Punch Bowl Inn,
Lanreath, By Looe, Cornwall PL13 2NX
Telephone: Lanreath 20218 (STD Code 0503)

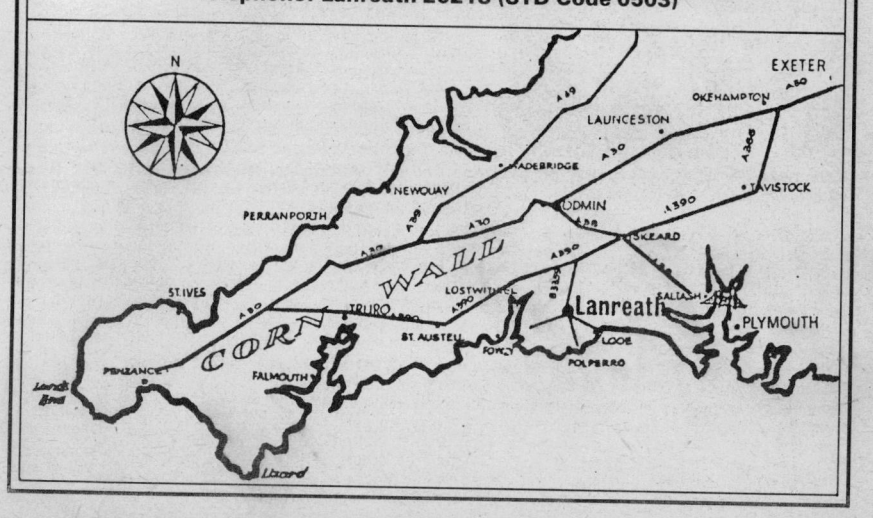

Cornwall BOARD

LOOE. Mr A. F. Tomkinson, Pixies Holt, Shutta, East Looe PL13 1JD (Looe [05036] 2726). Built around 1878, this old world house has been converted into a small, well-appointed, centrally heated hotel, in its own grounds of one-and-a-half acres with private car park, sun patio and lawn, with river, rural and woodland views. A few minutes' walk to the ancient, picturesque fishing port of Looe with all its coastal amenities. Two double bedrooms with bathroom/toilet en-suite; one single, two double and two family bedrooms with washbasins; all rooms have radio, TV and tea-making facilities. Children over five welcome at reduced rates. Sorry, no pets. Comfortable lounge with colour TV; residential licence, light meals available during the evening. Open March to end of October. RAC listed. Bed and Breakfast from £8.00 to £12.50 according to room and season. Access and Visa cards accepted. Write or telephone for brochure now.

Coombe Farm

WIDEGATES, Nr. LOOE, CORNWALL PL13 1QN
Telephone: Widegates (05034) 223

A lovely country house, furnished with antiques, set in ten acres lawns, meadows, woods, streams, and ponds with superb views down wooded valley to sea. Log fires. Delicious home cooking. Candlelit dining. Licensed. Many birds, animals and flowers. Children's paradise. Games include snooker, table tennis, croquet and heated outdoor swimming pool. Nearby golf, fishing, tennis, horse riding, glorious walks and beaches.
The perfect centre for visiting all parts of Cornwall and Devon.
Open March to October.
B&B from £9.00. Four course dinner from £8.50.
Reductions for children, families, half board, etc.
Please send for our free brochure.
A warm welcome is assured by
Alexander and Sally Low.
Listed.
AA "THE BEST BED AND BREAKFAST IN THE WORLD" RAC

WINNER AA GUEST HOUSE OF THE YEAR AWARD WEST OF ENGLAND 1981

LOOE near. Mrs Margaret A. Pearce, Lower Rosecraddoc Farm, Liskeard PL14 5AE (Liskeard [0579] 45272). Working farm. The farmhouse is large and modern with hot and cold in bedrooms; night storage heaters. Two double and one family room. Bed and Breakfast or Bed, Breakfast and Evening Dinner. Terms on request. Reductions for children. The farm of 186 acres in truly unspoilt countryside is peaceful and quiet. Plenty of safe sandy beaches about 20 minutes' drive; also Sibleyback Lake, Caradon Moors, riding stables and Liskeard swimming pool, all within 10 minutes' drive. Really good farmhouse food; genuinely fresh eggs, poultry, milk, cream and vegetables direct from farm. Ample car space. Personal attention. SAE, please, for terms.

LOOE near. Mrs G. Swann, The Old Rectory Country House Hotel, St. Keyne, Liskeard PL14 4RL (Liskeard [0579] 42617). Warm and comfortable, peacefully secluded 16th century former rectory, retaining its original character and charm. Set in three acres of mature grounds and surrounded by farmland. Bath/shower en-suite rooms, tea/coffee facilities and two four-posters. Elegant lounge with quality furnishings, marble fireplace with log fires on cooler evenings. Cosy bar. Separate diningroom. Substantial, freshly cooked five-course Dinner with the very best of food. Dinner, Bed and Breakfast from £20.50 inclusive. Excellent centre; near beaches, moors, quaint old villages, Poldark mine, stone circles, slate caverns, wild life parks and many more interesting places to visit. Open all year.

LOOE near. Mr F. C. J. Leach, "Harescombe Lodge," Watergate, Near Looe PL13 2NE (Looe [050-36] 3158). Harescombe Lodge originally built in 1760 and once the shooting lodge of the Trelawne Estate; now tastefully restored, offers luxury accommodation, all bedrooms being en suite, full central heating and every comfort with the accent being on friendly and informal personal attention. The Lodge is situated in its own gardens with a trout stream running through in the picturesque wooded valley of Watergate, an area of outstanding natural beauty which offers peace and tranquillity, yet is only a few minutes from Looe and Polperro and all the attractions of the south Cornish coast and countryside. We have our own small herd of pedigree goats, a donkey, chickens, etc. Full English breakfast is served and dinner, which is optional, is a meal always freshly prepared using local produce and fish straight from the sea (as available). Regret no children under 12. Dogs by arrangement. OPEN ALL YEAR. Registered with the English Tourist Board, Cornish Tourist Board and Members of the Looe Hotels and Restaurants Association. SAE for brochure and tariff.

LOOE. Mrs E. M. Lee, Trevollard, Lanreath, Looe PL13 2PD (Lanreath [0503] 20206). Working farm. A warm welcome awaits guests at Trevollard Farm situated just one mile from the village of Lanreath on the Bodinnick Ferry Road, and only four miles from the coast across the ferry to Fowey. Looe and Polperro seven miles. The area is well known for its beautiful coastline and sandy beaches. Within easy reach of all recreational facilities and many places of interest, including National Trust Properties. Accommodation offered in the farmhouse includes one family and one double bedroom, both with washbasins; bathroom, shower, two toilets; lounge with TV. Diningroom with separate tables where good home cooking is served. SAE, please, for terms for Evening Meal, Bed and Breakfast or Bed and Breakfast only. Reductions for children. Sorry, no pets. Car essential. Parking.

LOOE. Irvine and Norma Edmondson, Polliscove House, Millendreath, Looe PL13 1NY (Looe [05036] 2388). "The House in the Country by the Sea". A warm welcome awaits you in this Cornish farmhouse, five minutes' walk from the beach and surrounded by beautiful countryside. Looe is two miles by road, one and a half miles by cliff path and one mile along the beach. One family room with shower, one double room with shower and WC (both with sea views). One twin room and one double room, each with washbasin. There is a bathroom with shower and an additional shower room. Imaginative cooking using home grown/local produce. Residential licence. Good children and well-behaved pets are welcome. Ample parking. OPEN ALL YEAR. Bed and Breakfast from £8.50. Optional four-course Evening Meal.

LOOE. Miss V. J. Liddicoat, Keveral Barton, St Martin-by-Looe, Looe PL13 1PA (Downderry [050-35] 619). Working farm. A Norman arch, a walled garden and a duck pond are features of this lovely secluded old farmhouse, four miles from Looe, one mile from Seaton. There is a golf club and horse riding nearby, with facilities for sailing and fishing at Looe. Wholesome, well-cooked food, own milk, butter, cheese, eggs and organically grown vegetables served and diets are catered for. Every comfort and service for a restful holiday is offered. There is a lounge with colour TV and a quiet room. The one double, one single and five family rooms all have washbasins. Bathroom, two toilets; diningroom and sittingroom with open fire. Rates reduced for children; cot, high chair and babysitting. Pets permitted. Open May to October. Car essential. Evening Meal, Bed and Breakfast. Terms £70 weekly.

LOOE. Mrs J. D. Philp, South Much Larnick Farm, Pelynt, Looe PL13 2NP (Lanreath [0503] 20263). Working farm. Traditional farmhouse Breakfast is served at South Much Larnick Farm from May to end September. Stone and slate farmhouse on 191-acre dairy and sheep enterprise farmed by a Cornish family. Looe Bay can be glimpsed from the house where the atmosphere is friendly, the area peaceful and relaxing and good food is served. Safe bathing at Looe, also shark fishing. Coarse fishing at lakes three miles away. Twice-weekly cattle market at Liskeard; theatre, cinemas, museum and all holiday amenities at Plymouth where a visit to the Hoe is "a must". Explore National Trust properties and many places of historical interest in the locality. One double, one family (also used as a double), bedrooms, with washbasins; bathroom, toilet; sittingroom, diningroom. Car essential — parking. Bed and Breakfast from £6.50. Reductions for children. SAE, please, for prompt reply.

MEVAGISSEY. J. B. and B. Wildgoose, Valley Park Private Hotel, Valley Park, Mevagissey PL26 6RS (Mevagissey [072-684] 2347). AA and RAC LISTED. Eight bedrooms. Situated in a delightful sub-tropical garden, only one minute's walk from the old harbour. We offer our guests comfort and attention in a relaxed atmosphere. Within easy reach of several fine beaches and an ideal centre for touring the Cornish Riviera. Day or Evening boat trips and fishing can be arranged with a local fisherman. We are open all the year round. Pleasant gardens. Ample car parking space, television lounge, games room and residential licence. Brochure and terms on request.

MEVAGISSEY. Mrs M. A. Semmens, Trewolla Farm, Gorran, St. Austell PL26 6LR (Mevagissey [0726] 842228). Working farm. Centrally situated for most interests, this stonebuilt farmhouse is set in green fields where a herd of Guernsey cows graze and produce rich Channel Island milk. The 80-acres have a few beef cattle and plenty of scope for free-range hens, which supply fresh eggs for breakfast. Two double and one single bedrooms; bathroom, toilet; sittingroom, diningroom. Children welcome in this home-from-home accommodation (cot available), small dogs allowed. St. Austell is 10 miles away. Mevagissey five, Gorran and the sea one. Car essential, parking available. The house is not suitable for the disabled. Open May to September for Evening Dinner, Bed and Breakfast with reductions for children. Telephone enquiries only.

MEVAGISSEY. Mrs Linda Hennah, Kerry Anna, Treleaven Farm, Mevagissey PL26 6RZ (Mevagissey [0726] 843558). "Kerry Anna" is a licensed Guest House on a dairy farm within easy walking distance of the village and shops. There are many attractions in Mevagissey with its quaint narrow streets and lovely shops. Fishing and boat trips are available and very popular. The Guest House offers a warm and friendly welcome with the accent on good food. A varied menu is served including plenty of fresh local produce. Tastefully furnished throughout with central heating there are three double and two family rooms, with washbasins, some rooms with en-suite facilities; two bathrooms with showers, three toilets; lounge with lovely country views and colour TV, diningroom. Table licence. Sorry, no pets. Children at reduced rates with cot, high chair. Open April to end of September with special prices April, May, June. Evening Dinner, Bed and Breakfast.

MEVAGISSEY. Mrs Ann Pallett, Mount Pleasant House, Gorran High Lanes, Gorran, St. Austell PL26 6LR (Mevagissey [0726] 843351). A modern house on the outskirts of Gorran, within easy distance of safe sandy beaches, Mevagissey five miles, St. Austell nine miles. A market garden producing own vegetables which are used in the high class meals. One family room with double bed and bunks, one twin-bedded room, one single, all with washbasin and shaver points. Bathroom, shower room, toilet. Sitting/diningroom with separate tables. Children welcome at reduced rates. Cot, high chair available. Open May to September. Car essential, ample parking. No pets. Not suitable for the disabled. Evening Dinner, Bed and Breakfast or Bed and Breakfast. Send SAE please, for terms.

Mandalay Hotel

School Hill, Mevagissey, Cornwall
Tel: (0726) 842435

Open all year; Licensed; Family Run. Set in gardens overlooking Valley. Minutes to harbour; 10 minutes to beach. TV lounge; Bar and Sun Lounge; parking. 10 bedrooms some with private shower. Reductions for children; Spring & Autumn Breaks. Bed, Breakfast and Evening Meal £70-£80 (plus VAT). **For colour brochure telephone: Mrs Helen Cosier.**

MEVAGISSEY. Mrs J. Rowe, Rosedale, Valley Park, Mevagissey PL26 6RS (Mevagissey [0726] 842769). This is the beautiful view from the sittingroom of "Rosedale" an attractive modern farmhouse with its own market garden. It is approached by a private road, no sound of passing traffic, and guests are assured of a warm welcome, good food and home produced vegetables and fruit, with strawberries in the summer. Three minutes' walk from shops and picturesque harbour with fine beaches nearby and pleasant walks in the area. Two double bedrooms, one bedroom with twin beds, all with washbasins. Dining/sittingroom with colour TV. Bathroom with shower, two toilets. Children seven years and older welcome, babysitting by arrangement. Sorry, no pets. Ample free parking space at the house. Open Easter to October. Reductions for children under 10 years. Terms on application (SAE, please) for Evening Dinner, Bed and Breakfast or Bed and Breakfast.

MEVAGISSEY. Mrs Anne Hennah, Treleaven Farm, Mevagissey PL26 6RZ (Mevagissey [0726] 842413). Working farm. Treleaven Farm is situated in quiet, pleasant surroundings overlooking the village and the sea. The 200 acre dairy farm is well placed for visitors to enjoy the many attractions in Mevagissey with its quaint narrow streets and lovely shops. Fishing and boat trips are available and very popular. The house offers a warm and friendly welcome with the emphasis on comfort, cleanliness and good food using local produce. A licensed bar and solar heated swimming pool add to your holiday enjoyment. Tastefully furnished throughout, with central heating, there are five double and two family bedrooms, all with washbasins; bathroom, two toilets. Sittingroom and diningroom. Open February to November for Evening Dinner, Bed and Breakfast or Bed and Breakfast. Sorry, no pets. SAE, please, for further particulars, or telephone.

Terms quoted in this publication may be subject to increase if rises in costs necessitate

BOARD   Cornwall   71

MILLBROOK. Mrs Ann Heasman, Venton House, Millbrook PL10 1AW (Plymouth [0752] 823110). A lovely Georgian Manor House set in three acres of grounds on the outskirts of the village. One mile from superb beaches of the unspoilt Rame peninsula. Eight miles from Plymouth by road, one mile by boat. Sailing, fishing, bird-watching. Lovely walks and the beginning of the south Cornwall coastal path. Three double bedrooms with washbasins etc. Full central heating and log fires. Lounge, diningroom. TV room. Bed and Breakfast and Evening Meals by arrangement. Super food. Many pubs and restaurants nearby. Children welcome. Ample car parking. Member English Tourist Board.

MINGOOSE. Valerie J. Maltwood, The Old Inn Cottage, Mingoose, Mount Hawke, Truro TR4 8BX (Porthtowan [0209] 890545). A warm welcome awaits guests at Old Inn Cottage in the tiny hamlet of Mingoose near Chapel Porth and St. Agnes. Ideal for coastal walkers and anyone wishing peace and quiet — nearest beach approximately one mile by car or near footpath through lovely National Trust Valley to Chapel Porth beach. Car parking. Accommodation — diningroom, lounge, two double bedrooms, each with four poster beds, one twin room. Morning Tea. Solarium. Open from Easter to Halloween. Bed and Breakfast from £8.50 per person per night, £8 for two to six nights. Full week £49 per person. Telephone for further details.

MOUSEHOLE. Mrs P. A. Harvey, Raginnis Farm, Mousehole, Penzance TR19 6NJ (Penzance [0736] 731523). Working farm. This Cornish farmhouse is situated on a 100-acre dairy farm about one-third mile from the fishing village of Mousehole, with superb views of Mount's Bay, Lizard Point and Penzance. The farm borders the coastal footpath with many interesting and beautiful coves, villages and beaches close by. One double and one family room for guests; bathroom, toilet; own dining/sittingroom. Children welcome at reduced rates; cot, high chair and babysitting available. Open all year. Electric heating. Pets allowed. Car essential, parking. Bed and Breakfast. Terms on request. SAE, please.

NEWQUAY near. Mr S. B. Brooker, Trewerry Mill Guest House, Trerice, St. Newlyn East, Near Newquay TR8 5HS (Mitchell [087-251] 345). A 16th-century water mill situated in quiet country lanes four miles south of Newquay. Fives acres of pastureland with attractive gardens, flowing stream and resident donkey family. Open Easter to October. Three doubles, one single, one family bedrooms, with washbasins, electric fires and fitted carpets. All beds have spring interior mattresses. Bathroom/shower, two toilets. Charming Mill Room Lounge and separate TV room, diningroom with individual tables where guests can enjoy excellent home cooking with a varied menu. Residential licence. Children welcome, reductions. Pets accommodated in the stable block. Car essential, free parking. Sandy beaches within four miles. Dinner, Bed and Breakfast from £73.50. Send stamp only for brochure.

NEWQUAY. Mr D. J. Sessions, Mitchell Farm, Mitchell, Newquay TR8 5AX (Mitchell [087251] 657). You are welcomed warmly to Mitchell Farm, an attractive 19th century stone built farmhouse enjoying views across open farmland situated in the village of Mitchell on the A30 Penzance road. The farm is within easy reach of the surfing beaches of Newquay and the north coast resorts; the more picturesque south coast and attractive Truro are also easily accessible making Mitchell an ideal base. Warm, friendly atmosphere, good food, comfortable accommodation with full central heating, hot and cold in rooms, lounge with colour TV. There is also self-catering accommodation in a charming converted millhouse in farm grounds. Open all year. Parking. Children welcome, cot, high chair and baby listening offered. Bed and Breakfast or Evening Meal, Bed and Breakfast. Details of both Board and Self Catering accommodation on request.

NEWQUAY. Mrs K. J. A. Woodley, Degembris Farm, St. Newlyn East, Newquay TR8 5HY (Mitchell [087-251] 555). Working farm. Degembris is a small country farmhouse with a recorded history as far back as the 11th century. The house is set on a 165-acre farm overlooking a beautiful wooded valley where pleasant walks in the peace of the countryside may be enjoyed. It is nevertheless within easy reach of the wonderful holiday facilities and beaches of Newquay. Accommodation in double and family rooms, with washbasins; bathroom, two toilets; sittingroom; diningroom. Children are welcome, cot and high chair. Open from May to October. A car is essential and there is parking. Fire Certificate granted. Evening Meal, Bed and Breakfast or Bed and Breakfast only. Rates are reduced for children. SAE, please, for terms and details.

72 Cornwall BOARD

ENJOY YOUR HOLIDAY ON A FARM
RAC LISTED
C.C.C. FIRE CERTIFICATE
HOMESTAKE FARM
BLACKCROSS, NEWQUAY, CORNWALL TR8 4LU
Tel: 0726-860423

An 82 acre working mixed farm having extensive views of the surrounding countryside. Ideally situated for touring and within easy reach of north and south coast beaches. The farmhouse is well appointed. All 8 bedrooms (4 double, 4 family) having H & C. Colour TV lounge, sun diningroom, 2 bathrooms, 3 toilets. Reductions for children sharing parents' bedroom. Cots & high chairs provided.

★ Ample car parking space.
★ Excellent cuisine — home produced meat.
★ Conducted farm tours.
★ Donkey rides for children.
★ Children's play area — well equipped.
★ Open Easter to October.
★ Stables nearby — beginners welcome.
★ Skittles and tennis.
★ Light refreshments provided 9.30 p.m. to 10 p.m.

Terms: Dinner, Bed & Breakfast from £59, incl. of VAT. Brochure on request (SAE please) to
Mrs P. EDWARDS

NEWQUAY. Mr and Mrs R. R. Allen, Trenance Farm House, Trenance, Mawgan Porth, Newquay (St. Mawgan [0637] 860515). Enjoy a short break on your annual holiday at this beautiful 18th-century farmhouse situated on the coastal road between Newquay and Padstow. Adjacent to Mawgan Porth's magnificent sandy beach, ideal for surfing, there are many coastal walks including the famous Bedruthan Steps. The picturesque village of St. Mawgan is two miles inland and Trevose golf course only 10 minutes away. All bedrooms are large and most have sea views, all have washbasins. Two bathrooms, two toilets. The facilities include comfortable lounge with colour TV and log fires in season; spacious diningroom. Children over six years welcome. Sorry, no pets. Ample parking although car is not essential. Bed and Breakfast from £10 (no VAT). Evening Meal optional. Weekly rates on request.

NEWQUAY. Mrs E. Miller, San Felice Guest House, Fraddon, St. Columb TR9 6NR (0726-860534). San Felice, standing in its own grounds and pleasantly situated in the centre of Cornwall, is ideal for touring. Newquay six miles distant. Offering a comfortable carefree holiday with good home cooking, late night drinks available; TV lounge, sun lounge and terrace; diningroom with individual tables; all rooms are centrally heated; bedrooms have hot and cold, razor points, beds fitted with duvets; shower room and toilet; bathroom and toilet. Cornwall Tourist Board registered. Open March to October, Bed, English Breakfast, five-course Dinner, or Bed, English Breakfast (VAT exempt). Stamp for brochure, and terms.

NEWQUAY. Mrs M. Vercoe, Penhale Farm, Fraddon, St Columb TR9 6NA [0726] 860469. Working farm. Welcome to Penhale Farm which is pleasantly situated in the centre of Cornwall. Newquay, with its glorious beaches, is approximately six miles and the whole coast is within easy reach. An ideal touring centre. Guests are welcome to wander round the 86-acre mixed farm and take the children for a ride on the farm pony. Four family bedrooms with washbasins and two double rooms; bathroom, two toilets. TV lounge and diningroom. Children welcome with reduced rates if sharing parents' room. Pets permitted by arrangement. Car essential — parking. Fresh farm produce served and late night drinks available. Full Fire Certificate. Cornwall Tourist Board approved. Donkey for children's entertainment. Terms gladly sent on receipt of SAE for Evening Meal, Bed and Breakfast or Bed and Breakfast.

NEWQUAY. Mrs S. M. Kilker, "Thorn-Lea," 17 East Road, Quintrell Downs, Newquay TR8 4LQ (Newquay [063-73] 5654). Personal service and a warm Cornish welcome awaits you at Thorn-Lea, well recommended by regular visitors who enjoy plenty of good food, served with home grown vegetables from the large garden. Situated in a quiet village, near the sea and lovely countryside, with village shop and inn a few minutes away. Open between May and October with accommodation for guests in two family and one double bedrooms, each with washbasin, also one single room. Separate lounge, large diningroom; bathroom and shower. Two separate toilets. Children very welcome; cot, high chair and babysitting. Play area with swing and slide in garden. Full central heating, colour TV. Car park. Bed and Breakfast from £30 weekly; Bed, Breakfast and Evening Dinner from £49. Reductions for children. SAE, please, or telephone.

NEWQUAY. Mrs J. C. Wilson, Manuels Farm, Newquay TR8 4NY (Newquay [0637] 873577). Working farm. Built in the early 17th century on site mentioned in Doomsday Book, "Manuels" is situated two miles inland from Newquay on the A392. In a sheltered wooded valley it offers peace of the countryside with charm of traditional Cornish farmhouse. Emphasis placed on comfort, good farm-produced food and a friendly relaxed atmosphere. Pony to ride, pets galore and a games room with table tennis, etc. Children especially welcome, free babysitting every night. Two double, one single and two family bedrooms; two bathrooms and toilets; lounge and diningrooms. Cot and high chair available. Open all year except Christmas. Log fires and storage heating. Reduced rates for children. Pets accepted but not in the house. SAE, please, for terms for Evening Meal, Bed and Breakfast. Packed lunches and suppers also available. Farm Cottage for self-catering also available.

NEWQUAY near. Marian and Derrick Molloy, Dalswinton Country House Hotel, St. Mawgan, Near Newquay TR8 4EZ (St. Mawgan [0637] 860385). * Facing south with panoramic views over the wooded Vale of Lanherne to the sea, old Cornish House, full of character and charm welcomes guests all year round. Newquay six miles, Padstow seven and two miles to the magnificent Atlantic beaches and coastline. All bedrooms have H&C, shaver points, radio/baby listening, teasmade available. Some rooms with private bathroom or shower. Outdoor heated swimming pool. Full central heating and open wood fires in lounge and bar off season. Excellent cuisine with home grown or local produce. Reduced rates for children sharing with parents. Dogs accepted. Bed and Breakfast £9.50 to £13; Dinner, Bed and Breakfast £75 to £103 per week (plus VAT). Bargain Breaks early/late season. RAC*/AA*. SAE, please, for brochure. See Full Colour advertisement for details.

NEWQUAY near. Mr and Mrs B. Kellythorn, Belmont Country House Hotel, St Mawgan, Near Newquay TR8 4EU (St Mawgan [0637] 860212). The Belmont is a small family hotel nestling in the hillside overlooking the wooded Vale of Lanherne and the lovely village of St Mawgan — an ideal centre for exploring the delights of Cornwall by car; for walkers wooded paths abound, horse riding in the area. Pleasant and well-stocked bar, food good and plentiful, happy and friendly atmosphere. Five double, two single and four family rooms all with H&C; two bathrooms, five toilets; two sittingrooms and diningroom. Children welcome, cot, high chair and babysitting available. Ample parking space. Bed, Breakfast and Evening Dinner. Open May to October. Reductions for children. Sorry, no pets. For brochure and terms, please send SAE or telephone.

NEWQUAY near. Mrs B. Franks, Crantock Plains Farm, Near Newquay TR8 5PH (Crantock [0637] * **830253).** Charming character farmhouse in peaceful countryside. Comfort, home cooking and personal service combine to make an enjoyable, relaxing holiday. Crantock Plains Farm is situated two and a half miles from Newquay and half a mile off the A3075 Newquay/Redruth Road. One and a half miles to the village of Crantock with post office, village stores, tea rooms, two pubs and beautiful sandy beach. Riding stables and many sporting activities nearby. Choice of double, single and family bedrooms; shower room, three toilets. Sittingroom and diningroom. Babysitting arranged. Sorry, no pets. Bed, Breakfast and Evening Meal from £61 per week; Bed and Breakfast from £48 per week. Brochure on request. SAE, please. See also Colour Display Advertisement.

Please note that entries marked with an asterisk also have a colour display advert in the colour section in this guide

74 Cornwall BOARD

PADSTOW. Mrs Millie Geach, St. Cadoc Farm, Harlyn Bay, Padstow PL28 8SA (Padstow [0841] 520487). St. Cadoc lies in a quiet position overlooking the wide sandy beach at Harlyn and is just two miles from the fishing port of Padstow. The bay, with its excellent facilities for all the family, is only five minutes' walk from the farm, and is renowned for its safe bathing and surfing. There are a wide range of activities in the area including golf, water ski-ing, pony trekking and many beautiful cliff walks. Guests are welcome from April to October for Bed and Breakfast (Evening Meal optional). One double and one family room. Bathroom, toilet. Cot, high chair, babysitting on request. Dining/sittingroom with colour TV. Car essential — parking. Sorry, no pets. SAE, please, for terms.

PADSTOW near. Mrs E. M. Dennis, Tregavone Farm, St. Merryn, Near Padstow PL28 8JZ (Padstow [0841] 520148). Working farm. This 120-acre beef and sheep farm is open for guests from March to October. It is set in peaceful surroundings in an area of great scenic beauty. Situated near the coast road to Treyarnon, Porthcothan, Constantine, Harlyn and Trevose Head. Golf, surfing and sailing can be enjoyed. Shops one mile at St Merryn. One double and two family bedrooms, one bathroom, toilet; sittingroom with colour TV; diningroom. All rooms are carpeted. Children over five welcome at reduced rates. Good home cooking served in friendly atmosphere, with eggs, milk, cream and vegetables fresh from the farm. Car essential, ample parking space. Sorry, no pets. The farm is just two miles from the sea. SAE for terms, please.

PAR. Mrs Rita L. Beeley, Elmswood, 73 Tehidy Road, Tywardreath, Par PL24 2QD (Par [072-681] 4221). AA and RAC listed. Elmswood is a quiet Guest House in the village of Tywardreath, overlooking open farmland and only half-a-mile from Par Beach. Fowey, Polkerris and St Austell are easily accessible, and sports' complex, indoor swimming pool, squash courts, etc., within easy reach; riding stables locally. Guests will appreciate the homelike atmosphere and the good home cooking with vegetables from the garden. Two double, one single and three family rooms, all with washbasins, are available all year. Separate sitting and diningrooms. Table licence. Bathroom, three toilets. Elmswood has its own car park. Children are welcome (reduced rates), a cot is available and babysitting offered. Pets permitted. SAE, please, for terms for Evening Meal, Bed and Breakfast or Bed and Breakfast only. Coach tours from village will pick you up from door; sea fishing trips from Fowey and Mevagissey.

PAR. Mrs R. M. Olford, East Crinnis Farm, Par PL24 2SQ (Par [072-681] 2958) Working farm. East Crinnis is an attractive modern farmhouse on a mixed farm of 168 acres, in pleasant country surroundings. Only half-mile from Carlyon Bay, beach, church and chapel. Guests are assured of good home cooking, using own produce, and are welcome from March to October. Guest accommodation comprises two double and four family bedrooms, all with washbasins; three bathrooms and four toilets; sittingroom, diningroom. Children welcome, cot, high chair and babysitting available. Pets allowed. Car essential — parking. SAE, please, for terms for Evening Dinner, Bed and Breakfast. Reduced rates for children. (Mrs Olford has also a self-catering flat to let furnished for holiday makers who enjoy the freedom a self-catering holiday allows.)

PELYNT. Mr and Mrs P. Carnell, The Towers, Richmond Road, Pelynt (Lanreath [0503] 20442). Pat and Peter Carnell welcome you to their home in Pelynt, a small village between Polperro and Looe. The Towers is luxuriously appointed and has H/C in all bedrooms; central heating in all rooms; twin, double and family rooms available; lounge with colour TV and video; games and books readily available. Access at all times. Parking. Children welcome with cot, high chair and babysitting. Small dogs allowed and also if required small pets can be accommodated. Children under five free of charge. Open all year. The proprietors pride themselves on the food, comfort and service offered to guests at all times. Good country fare with home baking and fresh fruit and vegetables in season. Packed lunches on request. Looe offers good bathing, yachting, river and sea trips and shark fishing; Polperro is all that a Cornish fishing village is said to be. A warm welcome guaranteed at The Towers. Collection from local railway stations if required.

PENZANCE. Mrs J. Blewett, Wellway, Menwidden Farm, Ludgvan, Penzance TR20 8BN (Cockwells [0736] 740300). "Wellway" is a very attractive guest house built on Menwidden Farm with pleasant country views. Good traditional cooking is served and guests are assured of a warm welcome in a homely atmosphere. Three-and-a-half miles from Penzance, St. Ives and within easy reach of many fine beaches. Sailing, water ski-ing, surfing, fishing, tennis, golf, walking and horse riding are among the sporting activities offered. Chrysauster Ancient Village, the Seal Sanctuary at Gweek, Aero Park at Helston and the tin mines at Redruth are among the many attractions for visitors. The picturesque fishing villages of Mousehole and Newlyn are nearby. Two double, one family and one single bedrooms; bathroom, two toilets; sittingroom, diningroom. Children welcome at reduced rates with cot and babysitting available. Pets permitted. Car essential, parking. Open all year. Evening Dinner, Bed and Breakfast or Bed and Breakfast. Reduced rates for Senior Citizens. SAE, please.

PENZANCE. Mary and Dennis Yellop, Tolverth House, Long Rock, Penzance TR20 8JH (Penzance [0736] 710736). Tolverth House is a small Victorian mansion built in 1875 of local granite and is in walled and wooded gardens of approximately two acres. Situated just 250 yards from Long Rock village — Mount's Bay beach and the coastal footpath — midway between Penzance and Marazion. It is an ideal centre from which to explore the many coves and beautiful bays of the Cornish peninsula, and is convenient for travellers to the Isles of Scilly — car parking can be arranged with courtesy transport to the terminals. We have eight bedrooms some of which have showers en suite. All rooms have tea/coffee making facilities and are heated. The residents' lounge is comfortably furnished with log fires when required. Our aim is that you have an enjoyable holiday in a relaxed and homely atmosphere and like many of our guests, will wish to return. Emphasis is on personal service with good food complemented by a carefully chosen wine list.

PENZANCE. Mrs Marion Bailey, Trewellard Manor Farm, Pendeen, Penzance TR19 7SU (0736 788526). Working farm. A friendly and comfortable atmosphere prevails at this farmhouse on 250-acres dairy farm midway between Land's End and St. Ives, 300 yards off St. Ives/St. Just coast road. Pendeen is situated in a superb coastal position and is within easy reach of Sennen Cove and Porthcurno overlooked by the Minack Theatre along with a host of tiny coves. Horse riding available nearby. This is an area of great historic interest. The accommodation is in three double bedrooms with washbasins; bathroom, two toilets. Guests' lounge with colour TV available at all times. Cot, high chair, babysitting and reduced rates for children. Bed and Breakfast. Evening Meal available five nights a week. Further details on request.

PENZANCE. Ronald and Jean Jarratt, Kenython, St. Just, Penzance TR19 7PT (Penzance [0736] 788607). We welcome you to our Guest House, situated in peaceful, large grounds; pool. Guests will find a warm welcome, good home cooking and friendly service. Some en-suite bedrooms; comfortable lounge, diningroom and sun lounge with views over St. Just towards Land's End and to the Isles of Scilly. Kenython makes an ideal base for people of all ages to visit the many and varied attractions of this outstandingly beautiful area, others find it provides peace and quiet to relax and do nothing. Open all year. Central heating. Children welcome, reduced rates, provision made. Also a self-contained bungalow for self-caterers — accommodates six. Dinner available. Ashley Courtenay recommended. Brochures with pleasure.

PENZANCE. Mr & Mrs W. Watts, Doldolphin Cottage, Pengersick Lane, Praa Sands, Penzance TR20 9SL (Penzance [0736] 763480). Open April to October, Goldolphin Cottage is situated approximately half a mile from the lovely beach of Praa Sands. Nine-hole golf course within half a mile open to visitors. Ideal touring centre, within easy reach of many pretty coves and beaches; lovely walks and magnificent coastal scenery. Fishing, riding, surfing and many places of historical interest within easy reach. Good home cooking using fresh garden produce as available. Four double, two single bedrooms (five with washbasins); bathroom, shower room, three toilets. Sittingroom; diningroom. Central heating and wood fires. Children/pets welcome; cot, high chair, babysitting available. Parking. Also self-catering holiday chalets accommodating four/six and six/eight people. Electric cooking/heating. Electricity by slot meter. Everything supplied except linen. Shops half a mile.

PENZANCE. Mrs M. Olds, Mulfra Farm, Newmill, Penzance TR20 8XP (Penzance [0736] 63940). This 20 acre smallholding, situated on Mulfra Hill, offers outstanding rural and sea views. The granite-built character farmhouse, offering a double room and twin or family room with washbasins, bathroom, toilet, colour TV and sun lounge, provides a rare opportunity to stay in an area of great historical and natural beauty, with an inglenook fireplace and Cornish stone oven in the lounge/diner. Good traditional food, warm friendly atmosphere and a variety of animals including cows and calves, horses and dogs, welcome our guests. Children welcome at reduced rates sharing family room. Babysitting available. Sorry no pets. Bed and Breakfast, Evening Meal optional. Three miles Penzance, seven miles St. Ives. Car essential, parking.

CORNWALL – SOMETHING FOR EVERYONE!

Sea, sand, cliffs and quite often the sun, but that's not all you will find in this interesting county. Cornwall has many fascinating places to visit, such as the Charlestown Shipwreck Centre, the Tropical Bird Gardens at Padstow, Cornwall Aeronautical Park near Helston, Botallack Tin Mine, The Cornish Seal Sanctuary, Perranporth and of course, St. Michael's Mount.

Summer Court Cottages

A unique and imaginative service ... A cottage with Meals! The perfect, reasonably priced family holiday for those who desire privacy and comfort.

Summer Court offers you a Guest Cottage with no worries over the meals, as *The Torrances* provide a good breakfast and an excellent three-course dinner with coffee, served at separate tables in the diningroom overlooking the garden of Summer Court itself, which has a Table Licence, and is only seconds away from your cottage. *The Torrances*, who conceived this grand idea wish they could find a similar service when planning their own holiday. The 200-year-old cottages with three foot thick walls have been tastefully modernised and retain the best of their old character.

Another of the pleasant things about Rose Valley, which is just off the St.Ives-Land's End coast road, is its peacefulness and the ideal situation makes it a good spot from which to explore the interesting Land's End peninsula, with all its fabulous beaches, including Portheras, which is close by.

The Guest Cottages are comfortably furnished for four to eight persons, with all necessary utensils, full-size cooker. Modern bathroom, all services; bedside lights, razor points. Bed linen is supplied. Each cottage has a three-channel colour TV. Open air heated swimming pool and sauna. Paddling pool and sandpit for children. Ample parking space. Brochure sent with pleasure on receipt of stamp. Please state number in party for quick reply.

The TORRANCES, "Summer Court," Rose Valley, Morvah, near Penzance TR19 7TS. (STD 0736 788 327)

PENZANCE. Mrs A. R. Blewett, Menwidden Farm, Ludgvan, Penzance TR20 8BN (Cockwells [0736] 740415). Working farm, join in. Mendwidden Farm is centrally situated in west Cornwall four miles from St Ives north coast, and three miles from Marazion (south coast). Within easy reach of Land's End and the Lizard. It is a dairy and market gardening farm of 40 acres. Comfortable bedrooms and good home cooking including Roast Meats, pasties and Cornish Cream. Two double and two family bedrooms, one with washbasin; bathroom, toilet; sittingroom; diningroom. Cot, high chair, reduced rates for children. Pets allowed. Open February to November. Car essential — parking. Lots of interesting places nearby, including many beaches and coves, St. Michael's Mount, Bird Paradise, model village. Fire Certificate held. Evening Meal, Bed and Breakfast or Bed and Breakfast. SAE for terms.

PENZANCE. Mrs P. M. Eddy, Mar-Laree, Cove Road, Sennen, Penzance TR19 7BT (Sennen [073-687] 252). Near Land's End, a comfortable small Guest House situated on the road to Sennen Cove. Hot and cold in all rooms, full central heating and enjoying a magnificent view of sea and coastline towards Cape Cornwall. Near excellent sandy beach, popular for swimming and surfing. Children welcome and guests assured of a happy, friendly and comfortable holiday with traditional English cooking. Sorry, no pets. Open all year, except Christmas, for Bed, Breakfast and Evening Meal, or Bed and Breakfast only. Reduced rates out of season and for children. One double, two family bedrooms, all with washbasins; bathroom, separate shower, two toilets. Sittingroom, diningroom. Terms and further details on request.

PENZANCE. Mrs M. S. Harvey, Bosavern Farm, St Just, Penzance TR19 7RD (Penzance [0736] 788517). Working farm, join in. This is a 40-acre dairy farm in a delightful part of Cornwall. An ideal touring centre. Guests have the freedom of the farm and are welcome to participate in the farm activities. Two double bedrooms and one family room (one double with washbasin); bathroom, toilet; sittingroom; diningroom, colour TV. Children welcome, with reduced rates for those under 12 years; cot and babysitting available. Pets permitted free of charge. Open fires. Open all year round. Car essential; parking. One mile from nearest public transport. Evening Dinner, Bed and Breakfast or Bed and Breakfast only. Good home cooking and fresh farm produce.

The information in the entries in this guide is presented by the publishers in good faith and after the signed acceptance by advertisers that they will uphold the high standards associated with FARM HOLIDAY GUIDES LIMITED. The publishers do not accept responsibility for any inaccuracies or omissions or any results thereof. Before making final holiday arrangements readers should confirm the prices and facilities directly with advertisers.

BOARD   Cornwall   77

PENZANCE. Mrs N. J. White 'Ennys', St. Hilary, Penzance TR20 9BZ (Penzance [0736] 740262). Working farm. Beautiful 16th century manor, on a 50-acre arable beef farm, offering farmhouse accommodation in idyllically peaceful surroundings. Excellent food from our own produce. Comfort guaranteed. Within easy reach of many lovely coves and beaches — St. Michael's Mount (well worth a visit) three miles, and the picturesque town of St. Ives eight miles. Ideal touring centre with scenic drives and many places of interest to visit. Horse riding at centre arranged. Families welcome. Log fires, bread baked daily. Accommodation comprises three double bedrooms, one with en suite facilities, one with four-poster bed. Two bathrooms. Open March – October. Car essential. Dinner, Bed and Breakfast from £17.50; Bed and Breakfast £10.

PERRANPORTH. Mrs Thelma Hawkey, Lambourne Castle Farm, Penhallow, Truro TR4 9LQ (Truro [0872] 572365). Working farm. Lambourne Castle Farmhouse is stone-built and adjoins a tarmacadam council road only 200 yards from the main Newquay to Redruth Road. It is just two miles from the golden sands at Perranporth which is ideal for surfing, also 18 hole golf course, pottery and horse riding. An ideal centre for the whole of Cornwall, there are beautiful local walks. Plenty of good wholesome food much of which is produced on the farm. The comfortable accommodation comprises two double and two family rooms (three with washbasins); bathroom, toilet; sittingroom; diningroom. Children welcome. Regret no dogs. A car is essential — ample parking space. Open Easter to end of October. Fire Certificate held. SAE, please for terms for Evening Dinner, Bed and Breakfast or Bed and Breakfast. Reductions for children sharing parents' room.

PERRANPORTH. Cynthia and Alan Humphries, Perrancourt Hotel, 27 Tywarnhayle Road, Perranporth TR6 0DX (Truro [0872] 572151). This attractive private hotel, quietly situated near beach, shops, cliff walks is open from Easter to October. Residential Licence, RAC Listed, Tourist Boards registered. Well appointed single, double and family rooms all have washbasins (some with private WC and bath/shower), tea-making facilities, radio/intercom/baby listening. Lounge, separate colour TV room, sunbed room, car parking. Children at reduced rates if sharing parents' room. Pets accepted. Central heating. Access at all times. Cynthia and Alan concentrate on personal service, relaxed family atmosphere and exceptionally good value. Evening Dinner, Bed and Breakfast from £53 weekly, Bed and Breakfast from £6 per day. Please write or phone for colour brochure.

POLPERRO. Mr F. A. Crane, Sleepy Hollow Private Hotel, Brentfields, Polperro, Looe PL13 2JJ (Polperro [0503] 72288). "Sleepy Hollow", true to its name, is a relaxing spot amidst beautiful surroundings. Good home cooking served at separate tables in pleasant diningroom. Colour TV in comfortable lounge. Fire Certificate granted. Six doubles, one single, all with hot and cold and shaver points — some with shower/toilet. Special Honeymoon Suite. Ground floor bedrooms open on to terrace overlooking gardens with coastal views of Polperro. The quaint harbour — one of Britain's best known beauty spots — and unspoiled Talland Bay only 10 minutes' walk down lane or along Coastal Path with magnificent views. Regret, no young children or pets. Parking on premises. Open all year. Stamp, please, for brochure and terms.

POLPERRO. Mr Hugh McKernan, Rainbow's End, Brentfield, Polperro PL13 2JJ (Polperro [0503] ✱
72510). A warm welcome, excellent varied food and high standards of service and accommodation ensure the perfect holiday at Rainbow's End. Ten minutes' walk from both beach and shops and adjacent to magnificent National Trust cliff walks. Rainbow's End has a beautiful garden and terraces in daylong sunshine. Comfortably furnished bedrooms with washbasins and spring interior mattresses, including a four-poster room, twin and double rooms, one with en-suite facilities. Colour TV in lounge, separate tables in sunny diningroom. Payphone. Ample parking. Early morning tea, hot bedtime drinks. Regret no children under 10 years. No pets. Large breakfast, four-course Evening Dinner — £61 to £72 inclusive weekly. Tourist Board approved. RAC listed. FHG Diploma Award. Open March–September. Stamp, please, for brochure. See also Colour Display Advertisement in this Guide.

Please note that entries marked with an asterisk also have a colour display advert in the colour section in this guide

Penryn House Hotel
Proprietor Mrs M. K. Wright

THE COOMBES : POLPERRO : CORNWALL

Polperro is a popular fishing village situated on the sheltered south coast of Cornwall. Noted as one of Britain's beauty spots, its quaint streets, harbour, and cliff walks ooze with the essence of traditional Cornwall. The village is further enhanced by its geographical situation, which makes it the perfect spot from which to explore the beautiful surrounding countryside of Cornwall and West Devon. The Penryn House Hotel is a medium sized family run hotel situated in the main street of the village. All bedrooms have washbasins and five are equipped with en-suite facilities. Sittingroom with colour TV; lounge bar; diningroom. The hotel offers a good standard of food and accommodation at reasonable prices. Car not essential, however there is private parking for fifteen cars. Open all year. Midweek bookings accepted. Pets permitted.

AA and RAC listed. E.T.B.

Cornwall registered.

Telephone for reservations.
Open Christmas.
Tel. Polperro (0503) 72157

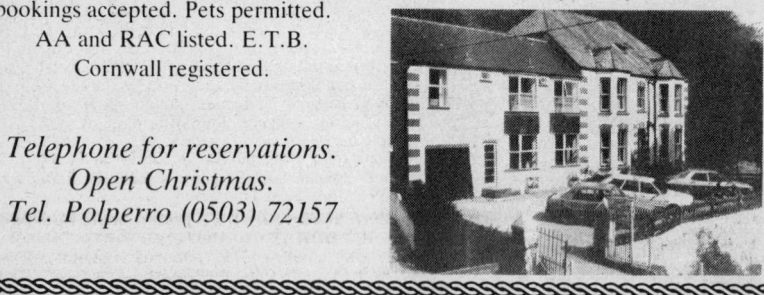

POLZEATH. Mrs P. White, Seaways, Polzeath, Near Wadebridge PL27 6SU (Trebetherick [020886] 2382). Small family Guest House, 250 yards from safe, sandy beach, where good surfing and safe bathing are enjoyed; ideal for outdoor enthusiasts, with riding, sailing, tennis, squash, golf nearby. Accommodation in three double, one with bunk-bedded annexe, one single and one family bedrooms, all with washbasins; bathroom, two toilets; sittingroom, diningroom. Children welcome, cot, high chair and babysitting. Sorry, no pets. Open all year round. Car essential — parking. Lovely cliff walks nearby and Padstow only short distance by ferry. Other places of interest Tintagel, Boscastle, Port Isaac. SAE, please for terms for Evening Meal, Bed and Breakfast or Bed and Breakfast only. (Reduced rates for under 11's).

POLZEATH. Mrs B. Dally, Tredower Barton, St. Minver, Wadebridge PL27 6RG (Wadebridge [020-881] 3501). Working farm. Tredower Farm is situated in pleasant, quiet position, near Rock and Polzeath on the Cornish coast, where there are ample opportunities available for swimming, sailing, surfing, riding, squash and golf; also numerous lovely walks along the golden sandy beaches and the cliff tops. Open moors nearby for rambles and picnics. Nearest town is Wadebridge, three miles. The mixed farm is 120-acres. Tredower Barton has one family room, and one double room. Diningroom/lounge and TV. Children welcome, cot, high chair. Sorry, no pets. Homely atmosphere and good food assured. Open May to October. Car essential, ample parking. Bed, Breakfast and Evening meal (optional). Reductions for children. Terms on request with SAE, please.

PORT ISAAC. Mrs A. Williams, Trewint, Port Quin, Port Isaac, Bodmin PL29 3ST (Port Isaac [020-888] 200). Working farm. Trewint Farm is situated in peaceful surroundings less than a mile from the picturesque bay of Port Quin, and nearby to numerous sandy beaches and coastal walks. Trewint is an attractive farmhouse of character, with original beams and stone fireplace with cloam oven in the diningroom. The mixed farm is 360 acres and visitors are welcome to look around. Trewint has two double rooms, one single and one family room. Two bathrooms, two toilets. Diningroom and lounge with colour TV. Children welcome, cot, high chair. Sorry, no pets. Good home cooking and comfort assured. Open April to October. Car essential — parking. Bed and Breakfast (Evening Meal optional). Reductions for children. Terms on request with SAE, please.

PLEASE SEND A STAMPED ADDRESSED ENVELOPE WITH ENQUIRIES

BOARD Cornwall 79

PORT ISAAC. Tony and Pat Sweett, Trethoway Hotel, Fore Street, Port Isaac PL29 3RF (0208-880214). Trethoway is a small, friendly, licensed hotel, situated in the old fishing village of Port Isaac, with delightful views of the village and sometimes the rough Atlantic Ocean. The Hotel, on the North Cornish Coast between Tintagel and Padstow is ideally positioned for touring Cornwall; for sports enthusiasts there is shark and deep-sea fishing, sailing, surfing, pony trekking and a parachute course, all run from the hotel. Glorious beaches, magnificent cliff walks, many interesting pubs, restaurants and places to visit. Bodmin Moor, superb St. Enodoc golf course nearby. For relaxing there is ample space on the terrace and in the cosy bar. Colour TV lounge. Special attention is given to providing good food, and the proprietors aim to achieve a high standard at all times. Parking available at hotel. Winter breaks (October, November, March, April, two days).

PORT ISAAC. Mrs Pamela Richards, Bodannon Farm, Trewetha, Port Isaac PL29 3RU (Bodmin [0208] 880381). Working farm. Guests are catered for all year round at Bodannon Farm, half-a-mile from the picturesque village of Port Isaac and sea on 100-acre mixed farm. The house has all modern conveniences. Two family and two double bedrooms, all with washbasins; bathroom, two toilets; lounge with TV; diningroom with separate tables. Children welcome — cot available; occasional babysitting. Ample parking space for cars which are necessary here. The menu includes roast chicken, pork, lamb, beef; fresh farm eggs, cream, etc., and home grown vegetables. Pets are permitted. Fire Certificate held. SAE, please, for terms for Evening Dinner, Bed and Breakfast or Bed and Breakfast only.

PORT ISAAC. Mrs D. Phelps, Trewetha Farm, Port Isaac PL29 3RU (Bodmin [0208] 880256). Trewetha Farmhouse is traditionally Cornish, about 150 years old, set in 20 acres of grazing land with superb views of Port Isaac Bay and the countryside. Unlimited parking. Beaches, riding and fishing available locally. Golf, boating at Rock, seven miles away. Three double and one family bedrooms all with washbasins. Diningroom. Separate lounge with colour TV. Open all year. Children welcome, babysitting by arrangement. Tea making facilities. Fire Certificate held. Poultry and miniature Shetland ponies kept. Pets by arrangement. Bed and Full English Breakfast. Vegetarians catered for. Reductions for children. English Tourist Board registered. Also holiday bungalow to let. SAE for terms, please.

PORTSCATHO. Mrs Deidre Hooper, "Thornfield," Trewithian, Portscatho, Near Truro TR2 5EJ (Portscatho [0872-58] 435). Thornfield is an old renovated cottage with splendid country and sea views, set back on the village green in the beautiful Roseland Peninsula which is mainly National Trust property. Safe, sandy beach with good sailing, cliff walks. Ideal touring base. Truro and St. Austell 15 miles. The cottage is of high standard throughout with two double bedrooms (one twin bedded), bathroom, two toilets; lounge with colour TV, sun lounge, diningroom with excellent views. Good quality food with varied menu served in friendly atmosphere. The cottage is centrally heated; ample car space. Attractive gardens. Open May to September. Dinner, Bed and Breakfast or Bed and Breakfast only. Terms on request. No children under 10.

REDRUTH. Mrs Jean Ormandy, San Paula, Tolgus Mount, Redruth TR15 3TA (Redruth [0209] 216986). Working farm. Mrs Ormandy's main aim is to make her guests comfortable and ensure that they have a happy holiday. San Paula is a pleasant farmhouse nicely situated in the quiet hamlet of Tolgus Mount, one mile from Redruth and central for touring Cornwall. Famous houses, fine gardens and castles to visit. Both Cornish Coasts within easy reach. Truro 10 miles; Falmouth nine miles; Land's End 28 miles. Home baking. Spacious lounge/diningroom with ample seating; tastefully furnished, comfortable bedrooms (four double, one with twin beds) all with washbasins. Only six guests are accommodated at the one time so the bedrooms can be let as doubles or singles. Bed and Breakfast or Evening Meal, Bed and Breakfast. Early Morning Tea and late evening snack included. Reductions for children. SAE, please. Farm Holiday Guide Diploma winner.

When you read one you *haven't* read them all —
we have *eleven* other publications

RUAN MINOR. Miss L. J. Bowman, Gwavas Jersey Farm, Ruan Minor (The Lizard [0326] 290577). **Working farm, join in.** Get away from it all and enjoy a relaxing holiday in this historic Cornish farmhouse. The 70-acre dairy farm is situated one mile from the most southerly point in Britain and boasts cliff walks and its own cove for fishing and very safe swimming. Five sandy beaches, surfing, golf course, horse riding, fishing trips, all in a five mile radius. Within easy reach of Helford River for sailing and boating facilities. Farmhouse cooking using our own high quality produce. All bedrooms with hot and cold water; there is a large TV lounge with log fire on chilly evenings and a large diningroom. Free access at all times. Guests may participate in farm activities. Open May to September. Ample parking. Pets allowed. Facilities for children. SAE for terms.

SALTASH. Mrs Queenie Griffin, Heathfield Farm, St. Mellion, Saltash PL12 6RR (0579) 50203. **Working farm.** The first sight of Heathfield Farm is a pleasing one — 300-yard concrete drive leads to the pleasant house of the 296-acre mixed holding, carrying sheep, beef cattle and arable crops. Lawns and flowers surround the house. Half an hour by car to the coast — Plymouth within easy reach. A good variety of food is served at the farm. Three guest bedrooms all with washbasins and shaving points; all modern conveniences; TV in sittingroom; separate diningroom. Ample parking space. Children over 12 years welcome. Regret, no dogs. Open Easter to end September for Evening Meal, Bed and Breakfast and Bed and Breakfast — terms on request. Good golf and country club just a mile away.

SALTASH. Mrs M. G. Gillbard, Treskelly, St. Germans, Saltash PL12 5PE (0503) 30293. Ideal for a family holiday, farmhouse accommodation offering Bed and Breakfast (Evening Meal if required). Four double/family bedrooms (two bedrooms with vanity units); bathroom with shower; drawing room with TV and separate diningroom. Central for touring Cornwall and Devon. Beaches, moors, towns and golf courses and many lovely beauty spots within easy reach. Land's End one-and-a-half hour's drive; shark fishing at Looe (seven miles), horse riding and water sports. Cotehele House, Gardens, Mill and Quay owned by National Trust a delightful attraction for holidaymakers. Bed and Breakfast £7 per person, plus £3.50 Evening Meal for early booking, with a small increase from 16th July inclusive.

ST. AGNES. D. E. Gill-Carey, Penkerris Country Guest House, Penwinnick Road, St. Agnes TR5 0PA (St. Agnes [087-255] 2262). A most attractive Edwardian country house on outskirts of village (near St. Agnes Leisure Park on B3277 road), with fields surrounding the front garden. There is a lawn with peacocks and doves. It is convenient for the beaches of Trevaunance Cove and Chapel Porth (National Trust), swimming, surfing, riding and tennis. Bedrooms have hot and cold, TV and electric kettles. There are two bathrooms and a public shower room. Colour TV in lounge. Ample parking. Dogs accepted. Children welcome. Beautiful rooms and good food. Excellent touring centre. Open all year. AA/RAC listed.

ST. AGNES. Mrs K. B. Blewett, Mount Pleasant Farm Guest House, Rosemundy, St. Agnes TR5 0UD (St. Agnes [087-255] 2387). Mount Pleasant Farm Guest House is set amongst the farm meadows and overlooks the unspoilt village of St. Agnes. For swimming and surfing, the local beach Trevaunance Cove is one of the most safe on the north coast of Cornwall. On either side the beautiful coves of Chapelporth and Trevellas are as they were 100 years ago. Whilst many visitors are quite happy to spend the day locally any part of Cornwall is within easy reach by car. Horse riding, both undercover and outdoors, golf, surfing and beautiful walks can all be found within a radius of seven miles. Double, single and family rooms are offered all on ground level and with washbasins. Reduced rates for children. Bed, Breakfast and Evening Dinner or Bed and Breakfast only. AA and RAC listed.

PLEASE ENCLOSE A STAMPED ADDRESSED ENVELOPE WITH ENQUIRIES

ST. AGNES. Mrs M. Welsby, Hillcrest, Trevellas, St. Agnes TR5 0XY (St. Agnes [087-255] 3142). *
Hillcrest is a large dormer bungalow set in its own grounds, situated on the coastal road between Perranporth (renowned for its miles of sand and surf) and St. Agnes (a delightful unspoilt Cornish village by the sea). The Cathedral City of Truro is eight miles away; the lovely sea cove of Trevellas Porth one and a quarter miles. An ideal base for touring south-west Cornwall. All bedrooms are well appointed and have washbasins, shaver and power points. Four family rooms, one with bathroom en suite, two double rooms, two twin-bedded rooms. Large lounge with colour TV and log fire. Separate diningroom. Central heating all year. Heated outdoor Leisure Pool and Children's Play Area and Games Room. Large car park and gardens. One child free all season. All children (sharing) free, Easter to Whitsun and after 1st September. Bed, Breakfast and Evening Dinner £59.50 to £86.50 per week. Bed and Breakfast £49 to £70 per week. Special rates for senior citizens. No restrictions on access to bedrooms. Facilities for children include cots, babysitting etc. Reduced fees at Perranporth Golf Club. Holiday cottage in grounds. See also Colour Display Advertisement in this Guide.

ST. AUSTELL. Mrs L. Inch, Higher Harros Farm, Roche, St. Austell PL26 8LN (St. Austell [0726] 890318). Working farm. The farm is in a quiet setting a short distance from the main road. Beef cattle, cows, horses, ducks and chickens kept. Farm food served. A home from home welcome awaits all guests. Two double and one family bedrooms; bathroom, toilet; sittingroom; diningroom. Colour TV. Cot and reduced rates for children; babysitting by arrangement. Pets permitted. Open from May to September. Car essential; parking. Mid-week bookings accepted early/late season. Central heating. The farm is central for both coasts and near pubs, shops etc. Terms on request for Evening Meal, Bed and Breakfast or Bed and Breakfast only.

ST COLUMB. Mrs O. B. Dunn, "Heidelberg," Gaverigan, Indian Queens, St Columb TR9 6HE (St Austell [0726] 860392). This small, quiet guest house is just off the A30, a quiet spot but convenient for touring the whole of Cornwall, with numerous beaches nearby and Newquay seven miles. Three double and four family bedrooms with washbasins; TV lounge; diningroom with good varied food; bathroom and shower; two toilets. Children welcome at reduced rates; cot and babysitting. Car essential — good parking. Coarse fishing; riding in the area. Cornwall Tourist Board registered; Fire Certificate. Cheerful service, with every attention to your comforts, will ensure an enjoyable holiday. Evening Dinner, Bed and Breakfast from £38; Bed and Breakfast terms on application. SAE, please.

ST. IVES. Mr and Mrs Coles, Palm Trees, Wheal Whidden, Carbis Bay, St. Ives TR26 2QX (Penzance [0736] 798055). This large detached private residence in quiet surroundings provides accommodation in three double rooms; two bathrooms, two toilets; sittingroom; diningroom. Open all year with electric heating. The house has magnificent views over beach, and sea from balcony and all rooms. There are picturesque coastal and country walks and a glorious safe sandy beach, ideal for swimming, surfing, ski-ing etc. Ample evening entertainment nearby. A car is preferable and there is ample parking. A warm welcome is guaranteed and personal attention at all times. Bed and Breakfast from £6.50, optional Evening Dinner from £3.50.

ST. IVES. Mr and Mrs C. B. Ryley, "Greystones", Pannier Lane, Carbis Bay, St. Ives TR26 2RF (Penzance [0736] 795717). "Greystones", a detached house situated in the midst of glorious country, has a path from the garden which leads directly to the lovely Hain Walk, and thence to Carbis Bay beach (four minutes away), where bathing is always safe. Two hundred feet above sea level, the house commands views of 30 miles of coastline stretching to the Cornish Moors. Guests are given individual attention by the resident proprietors and each of the four double, one single and three family bedrooms are comfortably furnished with interior spring mattresses. The lounge and diningroom overlook the sea and beach and provide a relaxed, friendly atmosphere. Adequate car parking space is available. Children are welcome and rates are reduced if sharing parents' room. Evening Dinner, Bed and Breakfast or Bed and Breakfast only. Pets allowed. SAE for terms and brochure, please.

ST. IVES. Mrs E. Gynn, Boswednack Manor Farm, Zennor, St. Ives TR26 3DD (Penzance [0736] 794183). A farm guest house which overlooks the spectacular Gurnard's Head cliff promontory and the Penwith moors. There is a quiet rocky cove nearby and fine walks with much natural history and archaeological interest all around. Help with the chickens, geese and goats and enjoy our friendly atmosphere. Accommodation in family, double, twin or single rooms. Two bathrooms, diningroom, sittingroom. Six miles from St. Ives and Penzance. Ample parking. Open all year. Bed and Breakfast, optional Evening Meal. Natural History, Birdwatching, Art and Archaeology holidays also available. SAE please, for further details.

ST. IVES. Mrs N. I. Mann, Trewey Farm, Zennor, St Ives TR26 3DA (Penzance [0736] 796936). Working farm. On the main St Ives to Land's End road, this attractive granite-built farmhouse stands among gorse and heather-clad hills, half-a-mile from the sea and five miles from St Ives. The mixed farm covers 300 acres with Guernsey cattle and fine views of the sea; lovely cliff and hill walks. Guests will be warmly welcomed and find a friendly atmosphere. Menus include beef, duck, pork and Cornish cream. Five double, one single and three family bedrooms (three with washbasins); bathroom, toilets; sittingroom, diningroom. Cot, high chair and babysitting available. Pets allowed. Car essential — parking. Open all year. Electric heating. Evening Dinner, Bed and Breakfast or Bed and Breakfast only. SAE for terms, please.

Cornwall BOARD

ST. IVES. Jack and Irene Sykes MHCIMA, The Old Vicarage Hotel, Parc-an-Creet, St. Ives TR26 2ET (Penzance [0736] 796124). Just over half-a-mile from the town centre and beaches, this typical Victorian vicarage lies in wooded ground on the edge of lovely moorlands. The bird life in the surrounding trees is a delight. The house has been extensively modernised but retains all its original features; residential licence; the decor in the bar is Victorian, red velvet, gilt and mahogany, the elegant diningroom is blue and gold. Four family, four double and one single bedrooms, all with washbasins; three rooms with bathroom en suite and two rooms with private shower. Restful lounge with colour TV and stereo record player; central heating; two cots available. Plentiful varied meals are prepared by the proprietrix herself. Evening Dinner, Bed and Breakfast and light supper at no extra charge. Out of doors stables and coach house add to the property's character. Putting green. Large car park in grounds. Stamp, please, for brochure and tariff.

MONOWAI PRIVATE HOTEL
Headland Road, Carbis Bay, St. Ives, Cornwall
Telephone: 0736 795733

Give yourself the holiday you are looking for at our family run hotel with old world charm and breathtaking sea views. Cliff walks directly from landscaped gardens, ample parking space, solar heated swimming pool nestling among palm trees. High standard of home cooked foods with a choice of Evening Dinner. Take your Evening Drink in the bar with its beautiful panoramic view of St. Ives Bay, or lounge in the gardens and watch the sun go down. TV lounge, games room. If you are looking for a quiet, relaxing holiday away from the madding crowd, please write for our colour brochure. Evening Dinner, Bed and Breakfast from £60 weekly inclusive. Reductions for over 60's May, June and September. Under personal supervision of resident proprietors: Mr and Mrs T. Cook. SAE, please. **Hotelier Association – CCC Registered/Conditions – AA Listed – E.T.B. Registered.**

ST. IVES. Mrs A. B. Prowse, Trewey-Vean Farm, Zennor, St. Ives TR26 3DA (Penzance [0736] 796919). Trewey-Vean Farm is on the main St. Ives-Land's End coastal road, five miles from St. Ives and six miles from Penzance. Guests are assured of a warm welcome and home from home atmosphere. Car essential, parking. Fresh farm food and Cornish cream. Lovely hill walks, and the local pub is only two minutes' walk away. Two double and four family-sized bedrooms (three with washbasins); bathroom, toilet; sittingroom, diningroom. Children welcome, cot, high chair, babysitting and reductions for the under 12s. No pets. Sea one mile. Open March to October. Evening Meal, Bed and Breakfast or Bed and Breakfast. SAE, please.

ST. IVES BAY. Audrey and Alan Kay, Cove Bungalow, 33 Riviere Towans, Phillack, Hayle (Hayle [0736] 753673). Cove Bungalow could not be much closer to the sea, our garden extends down to the Cornish Coastal Footpath and just below is a superb beach with three miles of golden sands. From our diningroom you will enjoy lovely views of the Cornish coast from St. Ives Harbour to Godrevy Lighthouse. Cove Bungalow has every comfort, central heating, H and C in bedrooms, colour TV etc. You will enjoy excellent home cooking using fresh local produce whenever possible. Dinner, Bed and Breakfast or Bed and Breakfast only. Also available, self-catering accommodation with the same lovely views.

ST. IVES near. Mrs H. L. Blight, Trencrom Farm, Lelant Downs, Hayle, Near St. Ives TR27 6NU (Cockwells [0736] 740214). Situated half-way between Hayle and St. Ives, Trencrom Farmhouse offers guests a really homely atmosphere, comfortable rooms and excellent home cooking. Commanding magnificent views of Cornwall, the house is open from Easter to end of October. Pony rides available from adjoining stables, many wonderful walks and good, safe sandy beaches abound. St. Ives three miles, Carbis Bay one and a half miles, Lelant one and a half miles and Hayle two miles. Accommodation comprises two double and one family bedrooms, all with washbasins; bathroom and shower, toilet; sittingroom with TV, diningroom with separate tables. Children welcome, cot, high chair and babysitting available. Sorry, no pets. Car essential — parking. Bed and Breakfast or Bed, Breakfast and Evening Meal. Reductions for children sharing parents' room. Reductions for senior citizens (not in high season). Further details on request.

PLEASE SEND A STAMPED ADDRESSED ENVELOPE WITH ENQUIRIES

BOARD   Cornwall   83

ST. MARTIN-BY-LOOE. Mrs B. Baynes-Reid, The Slate House, Bucklawren Farm, St. Martin-by-Looe PL13 1NZ (Widegates [05034] 481). Imagine a small hamlet in the lovely Cornish countryside and there you will find "The Slate House". A mellow old Cornish Farmhouse restored and furnished with care, where you will be assured of a warm welcome, log fires when chilly and a delicious variety of food; a delightful sittingroom is at your disposal and secluded gardens to sit in. It is a beautiful part of the world which we invite you to relax in and enjoy with us. Facilities for golf, riding, fishing, tennis etc. are all close by. Renowned Cornish fishing villages, coves and beauty spots all near. Lovely walks. Light lunches and afternoon teas can be provided, just ask. Plymouth with shops, theatres and cinemas only 16 miles. Bed and Breakfast. Please ring for brochure and rates.

THE LIZARD. Penmenner House Hotel, The Lizard TR12 7NR (The Lizard [0326] 290370). AA and RAC listed. Residential Licence. Marion and Keith Williams invite you to enjoy a stay at their Cornish home. Standing in its own grounds, it has panoramic sea views over Britain's most southerly point. Some rooms have private bathrooms. Tea making in all rooms. Central heating. Children are most welcome. Open Spring, Summer and Autumn. Penmenner is the ideal base to explore the beauty of The Lizard Peninsula.

THE LIZARD. Rod and Nella Weddell, Treglow House, Penmenner Road, The Lizard, Near Helston TR12 7NP (The Lizard [0326] 290472). "Treglow House" being situated south of The Lizard village, and only a few minutes' walk from the coastal path, enjoys superb views of the magnificent coastline around Lizard Head and Kynance Cove. The house has been recently modernised and extended and now offers very comfortable accommodation for a small number of guests. All our bedrooms have sea views with H&C and razor points. The well-furnished lounge with colour TV is open to our guests at all times. Within easy reach of many beautiful bays, coves and places of interest. Car advisable — there is ample free parking. We offer you good food, hospitality and our aim is to make your stay a happy one. Children over seven welcome. Dogs welcome. Fire Certificate / Cornwall Registered Accommodation. Write or phone for brochure, please.

TINTAGEL. Mr and Mrs John Wrightam, Bossiney House Hotel, Tintagel PL34 0AX (Tintagel [0840] 770240). * An ideal base to tour and explore an area packed with interest and beauty. Bossiney House is situated about half a mile from Tintagel on the cliffs overlooking a magnificent stretch of coastline. All 20 bedrooms have sea or country views. Spacious diningroom and cocktail bar; three lounges; colour TV. Good English cooking with excellent choice of menu. Personal attention. Indoor heated pool, sauna, solarium. Nearby activities include surfing, riding, golf, squash, pony trekking and shark fishing. Reductions for children. Open Easter to early October. See also Colour Advertisement in this Guide.

TINTAGEL. Mrs A. Jones, Grange Cottage, Bossiney, Tintagel PL34 0AX (Camelford [0840] 770487). Traditional Cornish cottage catering for a small number of guests. Large comfortable double/family bedrooms with hot and cold washhand basins (electric blankets available for early or late season visitors); single room also available. Lounge with colour TV; diningroom with beamed ceiling and stone fireplace. All home cooking. Almost opposite Grange Cottage is a footpath to the Coastal Path and a short walk takes you to Bossiney Cove with its sandy beach and rock pools or Tintagel Castle. The area is ideal for walkers or for those who just enjoy beautiful scenery. Open April to October for Bed, Breakfast and Evening Meal (daily or weekly terms) or Bed and Breakfast only. Reductions early or late season and for children sharing parents' room. Telephone or SAE, please.

Please note that entries marked with an asterisk also have a colour display advert in the colour section in this guide

Trebrea Lodge
Trenale, Nr. Tintagel, North Cornwall

This grand old Cornish house dates from 1300 AD and is now a small family-run hotel in its own rural setting on the magnificent north coast. Our bedrooms, all with private bathrooms and all with colour TV, look out across fields to the sea as does the first floor drawing room. The bar and Victorian smoking room are for those comfortable cosy evenings. Our reputation, for really good home-made food and a friendly atmosphere, is borne out by previous guests written comments which we'll send you with our brochure. We offer reductions for children, there's a games room in the grounds, and dogs are welcome too.

Phone or write for brochure pack to Ann and Guy Murray. Tel. 0840 (STD) 770410.

TRURO. Mrs Ann Lutey, Cregan Gate Farm, Grampound Road, Truro TR2 4EL (St. Austell [0726] 882884). Working farm, join in. At Cregan Gate our aim is to give a restful holiday away from busy roads and noise. The house is comfortably furnished and there are carpets throughout. Meals consist of roast beef, lamb, pork, chicken, salads and good wholesome sweets. If guests wish to help on the farm in the evenings at hay and corn harvests they are very welcome; or just relax indoors, whatever your personal taste. There are many interesting places to visit in Cornwall and we are central for them all — golfing, riding, surfing, roller skating, swimming, all within 10 miles. Very interesting museum in Truro for a wet day visit. Double, single and family rooms, three with washbasins; bathroom, toilet; sittingroom, diningroom. Children welcome. Cot, high chair and babysitting. Pets allowed. Open Easter to September. Car essential, parking. Evening Dinner, Bed and Breakfast or Bed and Breakfast only. Rates reduced for children.

TRURO. Mrs M. Pearce, Turnpike, Tregony, Truro TR2 5TD (Tregony [087253] 266). Small holding, new bungalow situated at the end of the village overlooking River Fal with lovely views. Approximately three miles from the beach. Village Inn, shops, post office within walking distance. Ideal for touring. Children welcome. Bed and Breakfast, Evening Meal optional. Good home cooking, fresh garden produce. Colour TV, H/C in bedrooms, shower available. Packed lunches provided (extra charge). Terms on application or telephone **Mrs Pearce.**

TRURO. Mrs E. E. Tremayne, Higher Calenick Farm, Kea, Truro TR3 6AH (0872-71189). Working farm. The farm is one mile from the city and market town of Truro and is surrounded by woods and close to the river. Two family bedrooms with washbasins; tea making facilities; bathroom; diningroom; lounge with colour TV. Open April to October with electric heating. Children welcome, cot, high chair and babysitting. Pets are allowed. Car not essential, but there is parking. Good home cooking and a warm welcome. Evening Dinner, Bed and Breakfast from £58 per week. Bed and Breakfast from £6.50 per night. Rates reduced for children.

TRURO. Mrs Christine Toms, Hillside Guest House, 8 The Square, Portscatho, Truro (Portscatho [087258] 523). Hillside Guest House is a family-run guest house in the village square 100 yards from the sea. Porthscatho is a delightful fishing village set among sandy beaches and rocky coves of the beautiful Roseland Peninsula. Safe bathing, ideal for swimming, sunbathing, boating, windsurfing and fishing. Most of the coast is National Trust property and walkers enjoy miles of cliff paths that link picturesque villages with rocky coves. Double, single and family bedrooms; sittingroom; diningroom. Children are welcome and there is cot and high chair. Open all year, Evening Dinner, Bed and Breakfast or Bed and Breakfast only. Reduced rates for children. A warm welcome is assured at Hillside.

TRURO. Mrs Margaret Opie, Kennall Farm, Ponsanooth, Truro TR3 7HL (Stithians [0209] 860315). Working farm. A very warm welcome awaits you at Kennall Farm, a 90-acre beef farm situated in beautiful countryside overlooking a valley of trees and the River Kennall. Within seven miles of many lovely sandy beaches. There are one family and two double rooms, all with washbasins, accommodating six guests only at any one time. Bathroom, two toilets, lounge with colour TV, diningroom with separate tables, every comfort assured. Evening Meal, with home produced beef, pork, poultry and fresh vegetables when possible. Desserts with fresh cream if desired, also a good breakfast. Children under 13 years at reduced prices. Sorry, no pets. Car necessary. Parking. Open May to September. Electric blankets and central heating early and late in season. Evening Meal (bookings only), Bed and Breakfast or Bed and Breakfast only. Terms on request — SAE please.

Mrs Bridget Dymond, Trevispian-Vean, St. Erme, Truro, Cornwall TR4 9BL (Truro [0872] 79514). Trevispian-Vean is beautifully situated seven miles from the coast in the heart of the countryside and winding country lanes. Although secluded, the farm is only half a mile from Trispen Village. Guests are welcome to enjoy looking over the farm – 400 acres (beef, sheep, pigs). There are two double, one single and four family bedrooms, six with washbasins; bathroom, toilet; cot, high chair and babysitting facilities available. Lounge with colour TV and diningroom with separate tables. Good home cooking. Table tennis room. Donkey for children. Open April/September. Electric blankets early/late season. Car essential; parking. Tea making facilities available. SAE for terms and further details. Reduced rates for children. Leave A30 after Mitchell, on to A3076, second left in Trispen, FIRST LEFT – farm on left.

TRURO. Mrs Diane Dymond, Great Hewas Farm, Grampound Road, Truro TR2 4EP (St. Austell [0726] 882218). Working farm. Stone-built farmhouse, completely modernised yet retaining its character, on 160-acre working farm, beef cattle and sheep; numerous pets for children. House is carpeted throughout, shaving lights and sockets, tea making facilities, room heaters and electric blankets early and late season. Hand towels supplied. Modern bathroom with shower. Colour TV. Log fires. Fire Certificate held. Mostly home produced traditional English dishes. The aim of the owners is comfort enhanced by good wholesome food. Very central for touring. Car essential, parking provided. Two double, one single and two family bedrooms, all with washbasins. Children welcome at reduced rates. Guests are welcomed from Easter to October for Evening Dinner, Bed and Breakfast or Bed and Breakfast only. Terms on request.

TRURO. Mrs J. C. Gartner, Laniley House, St. Clement, Near Trispen, Truro TR1 1SZ (Truro [0872] 75201). Laniley House, a Gentleman's Residence, built in 1830 and featured in "Homes and Gardens", stands in two acres of gardens amidst beautiful, unspoilt countryside, yet only two miles from the Cathedral City of Truro. Ideally situated for discovering Cornwall and close to major towns, beaches and National Trust properties. Laniley offers unequalled privacy and peace. Our aim is to make you feel at home, giving each person individual attention; only six guests at any one time. Accommodation consists of three large double bedrooms, two with H/C, one with en-suite bathroom, separate breakfast/dining room, lounge with colour television. All rooms with television and Teasmade. Regret, unable to accommodate children under eighteen years, also no pets. Bed and Breakfast or Bed, Breakfast and Evening Meal. Terms on request with SAE, please. Highly recommended accommodation.

Terms quoted in this publication may be subject to increase if rises in costs necessitate

86 Cornwall BOARD

TRURO. Mrs D. M. Gane, Trewarren Farm, New Mills, Ladock, Truro TR2 4QJ (St. Austell [0726] 882263). Working farm. Trewarren Farm is situated in mid-Cornwall, nine miles from Truro with its interesting cathedral, and St. Austell. Newquay, with its miles of golden sands is within driving distance. The farm entrance is on the A39, but the farmhouse is 600 yards from the main road. A comfortably furnished cottage-type residence, the accommodation comprises double and family bedrooms with washbasins, and a single bedroom. Lounge with colour TV, diningroom with separate tables. Plenty of good food is always served including milk, cream, eggs and home produce. Children welcome, with cot, high chair and babysitting available; also reduced rates. Open from Easter to October for Evening Dinner/Meal, Bed and Breakfast or Bed and Breakfast. Car essential — parking. Reduced rates for Senior Citizens in early and late season.

TRURO. Mrs J. Pearce, North Hill House, The Terrace, Chacewater, Truro TR4 8NW (Truro [0872] 560352). North Hill House is a house of delightful character with most modern comforts, just four and a half miles from Truro and Redruth. Its situation makes it an ideal centre for touring, with any place in Cornwall within two hours' easy driving distance. Every effort is made to give guests an enjoyable stay with a variety of good food. One twin and one double-bedded rooms with washbasins, and one family bedroom, all fully carpeted. Beamed diningroom, colour TV. Garden available for guests' use. Car parking. Open from April to October for Bed and Breakfast from £6.50–£7.50 or Evening Meal, Bed and Breakfast from £9.25–£10. Reduced rates for children. Cornwall Registered Accommodation. Brochure with full details on receipt of SAE.

TRURO. Mr Peter Wright, Trembroath Farm, Stithians, Truro TR3 7DT (Stithians [0209] 860522). Working farm. A house-party atmosphere and friendly reception await all visitors to this Victorian house where only farmhouse cuisine of the very best is served and all meals are taken in the old kitchen around one large table. Very quiet and beautiful surroundings and good area for birdwatching. Quarter-mile from the interesting village of Stithians. Falmouth is six miles away and many beaches can be reached. Two double and two single bedrooms with washbasins; bathroom, shower room, three toilets; sittingroom; diningroom. Solid fuel stoves and full central heating make it ideal for off-season breaks. Pottery and painting can be taught and the barn is used as a studio. Evening Dinner, Bed and Breakfast from £88 per week; Bed and Breakfast from £55 per week.

TRURO near. Mrs P. M. Saint, Laurel Cottage, Trispen, Near Truro TR4 9BJ (Truro [0872] 79632). Laurel Cottage is clean and comfortable and offers a good relaxed holiday, plenty of good food and friendly atmosphere. Within walking distance of pub, so no fear of drinking and driving. One family, one single and three double bedrooms, all with washbasins; bathroom, shower-room; two toilets; sittingroom; diningroom. Cot, babysitting, reduced rates for children. Car essential — parking. Evening Dinner, Bed and Breakfast or Bed and Breakfast only. Open May-September. Coal fire for chilly evenings. Guests enjoy their stay so much that they leave as friends and many return year after year, sometimes booking the next year's holiday before they leave, so be sure to book early for popular dates. Fire Certificate held. RAC and CCC recommended. SAE, please, for terms.

TRURO near. Mrs L. M. and Mrs P. Lyon, Menna House, Grampound Road, Near Truro TR4 4HA (St Austell [0726] 882072). Situated in mid-Cornwall in uninterrupted countryside and on a main road, Menna House has easy access to all beaches and beauty spots, and places of interest in the county. The house has been completely modernised with central heating, washbasins and colour TV installed in the comfortable lounge. Most vegetables and fruit served are grown in the large garden, where there is also a play area for children. Five golf courses within close proximity and a Sports Centre at St Austell. Sailing at St Mawes and Padstow, both easily accessible, and a number of riding schools in the district. Three double bedrooms; bathroom and toilets; sittingroom, diningroom. Children welcome at reduced rates, cot, high chair and babysitting by arrangement. Car essential, parking. Pets by prior arrangement. Open all year. SAE for terms.

WADEBRIDGE. Mrs V. M. Davey, Carns Farm, Trewethern, Amble, Wadebridge PL27 6ER (Port Isaac [020-888] 398). Working farm. A fully-modernised 15th century farmhouse with its original oak beams and open fires situated on a dairy farm. Guests are welcome to explore the farm and watch the milking. Only four miles from the safest beaches in North Cornwall, sailing, fishing, surfing and golf. Lovely walks nearby. Mrs Davey's aim is to give guests a restful holiday and real farmhouse fare, with home-produced eggs, cream, etc. One double, one single and two family bedrooms with washbasins; two bathrooms, two toilets; shower; lounge, diningroom. Cot, high chair available, babysitting on request. Please enquire about pets. Parking for essential car. Open Easter to October. SAE, please, for terms for Evening Dinner/Meal, Bed and Breakfast or Bed and Breakfast only. Reductions for children.

WHITSAND BAY. Mrs V. J. Andrew, Trewickle Farm, Crafthole, Torpoint PL11 3BL (St. Germans [0503] 30333). Working farm. This 360-acre mixed farm is situated on the coast of Whitsand Bay — land runs down to Portwrinkle beach. Mid-way between Plymouth and Looe (about six miles). Good food and cleanliness guaranteed and a home from home atmosphere with freedom to come and go as you please. Two double and three family bedrooms, all with washbasins; one bath/shower room, two toilets; sitting/diningroom; TV. Children welcome at reduced rates — cot, high chair and babysitting available. Pets permitted. Open from April to December. Car essential, parking. Evening Dinner, Bed and Breakfast from £10.50 per night — £72 per week. Bed and Breakfast from £7.50 per night — £45 per week. Hot drinks and sandwiches at night if required. Fire Certificate. Also two fully furnished self-catering farmhouses available.

CUMBRIA — English Lakeland

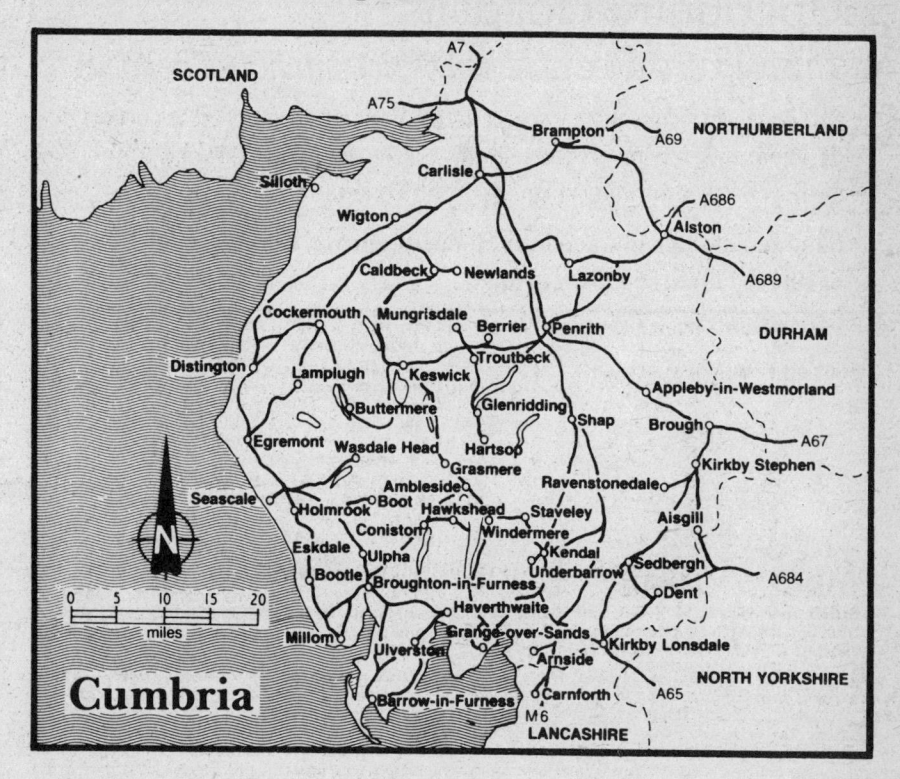

ALSTON. Mrs M. Bell, Hawthorn Garth, Clitheroe, Alston CA9 3TJ (0498) 81664). A very warm welcome awaits you at Hawthorn Garth, built in the late 16th century, standing on main road from Alston to Nenthead with beautiful views of Alston Moors; quarter mile from Alston, 200 yards playground, bowling green, tennis court. Fishing nearby; lovely walks to riverside; miniature railway; golf within easy reach at Hexham and Allendale. Good touring centre — Pennine Way, Hadrian's Wall, Roman camps, lead mine and flour mill to visit. Bed and Breakfast (Breakfast to suit you) provided, with a late cup of tea included, £7; Evening Meal £4. One twin-bedded room (downstairs), one family and one double bedroom. After a good day out come back to good home-cooked meal, open fires, colour TV, small library you can read in own sittingroom. All beds have electric blankets. Children and dogs welcome. Brochure available. Open March-October.

ALSTON. Mrs P. M. Dent, Middle Bayles Farm, Penrith Road, Alston CA9 3BS (Alston [0498] 81383). Working farm. A 300-acre family-run hill farm with cattle and sheep, in Cumbria, on the borders of Northumbria and Durham, an ideal base for walking or touring or just to relax by the lily pond in the garden and admire the breathtaking views across the valley; golf and fishing nearby. One mile from Alston with its cobbled streets, historical buildings, narrow gauge railway. Within easy reach of the Lakes, Hadrian's Wall, Scottish Borders and Kielder Lake. Many historical houses, museums, wildlife parks close at hand. The house is centrally heated with open log fire in the dining/sittingroom early and late season. One double, one family rooms, both with washbasins, electric blankets, cotton sheets. Tourist Board inspected and approved. AA listed. Member of the Farm Holiday Bureau. Many visitors return to our warm welcome and real home cooking. Dinner, Bed and Breakfast £11.50 daily. Good reductions weekly and for children under 14 years. Dog by prior arrangement. SAE for brochure. Advance bookings, November to March. Open all year.

PLEASE SEND A STAMPED ADDRESSED ENVELOPE WITH ENQUIRIES

Upcountry Holidays
The biggest choice of Lake District farmhouse holidays
- Genuinely independent inspection
- Personal advice on your needs
- Informative illustrated brochure
- Convenient central booking
- Big choice of area and price
- North Yorks too

Send two stamps to Upcountry Holidays, Alston, Cumbria CA9 3LG or ring (0498) 81563 (9am to 9pm)

AMBLESIDE. Miss Gillian Fletcher, High Green Gate Guest House, Near Sawrey, Ambleside LA22 0LF (Hawkshead [096 66] 296). The Guest House is a converted 17th-century farmhouse in the quiet hamlet where Beatrix Potter lived and wrote. Her house, owned by the National Trust is close by and open to the public. The area abounds with pleasant easy walks and is a good centre for the Southern Lakes. Open from March till October. Good food and service under the personal attention of the owner. Spacious dining room, lounge and separate TV lounge. All bedrooms have hot and cold water and individual heating in addition to central heating. Reduced rates for children sharing with parents. Cot and highchair are available and babysitting cam be arranged. Dogs welcome. A car is desirable and there is parking for seven cars. Bed and Breakfast from £10 per night; Bed, Breakfast and Evening Meal from £98 per week.

AMBLESIDE. Mrs Rachel Geldard, Highwray Farm, Wray, Ambleside (Ambleside [0966] 32280). Working farm. Highwray Farm is a 260-acre beef and sheep farm specialising in pedigree Poll Charollais cattle, blue-faced Leicester and Charollais sheep, with a picturesque 16th-century farmhouse once owned by Beatrix Potter. It has oak staircase and beams and is set in peaceful surroundings, midway between Ambleside and Hawkshead. Highwray Farm has magnificent views of mountains and Lake Windermere, only minutes away, and is also a central base for touring the Lake District. Highwray offers clean, comfortable Bed and Breakfast £8.00, with option of Evening Meal. The accommodation comprises two double, one family, one single bedrooms; bathroom; sittingroom, diningroom. Reductions for children. Open March to December. SAE, please, for enquiries.

AMBLESIDE. Mrs Lynne Blair, Eversly, Low Gale, Ambleside LA22 0BB (Ambleside [096-63] 3311). Eversly is a family-run guest house situated above the town centre giving good views, yet only a two-minute walk from the shops. There are many short walks close by, together with boating, fishing, swimming, horse riding, etc. All rooms have washbasins and shaver points, tea/coffee making facilities; guests are supplied with room and front door keys for greater freedom. Children are most welcome with reduced rates for sharing parents' room. As we are well served by restaurants in Ambleside, we only serve Breakfast but we feel sure it is large enough to sustain most people until teatime. Open all year round. Bed and Breakfast from £8.

AMBLESIDE. Mrs J. Hancock, Thrang House, Compston Road, Ambleside LA22 9DS (Ambleside [0966] 32112). Thrang House is conveniently situated for many amenities as it overlooks bowling and putting greens, tennis courts, etc. We are open most of the year providing guests with a warm welcome, and to start your day, a sumptuous Cumbrian farmhouse Breakfast. In Ambleside village centre Thrang House is ideally positioned having magnificent views and yet close to shops, buses, boats and local transport. All rooms equipped to a high standard with tea and coffee making facilities available. Private car parking and central heating. Dinner, Bed and Breakfast from £14.50; Bed and Breakfast from £9.00.

AMBLESIDE. Mrs Elizabeth Mallett, Esthwaite How Farmhouse, Near Sawrey, Ambleside LA22 0LB (Hawkshead [09666] 450). A warm and friendly welcome awaits you at Esthwaite How Farmhouse situated in this lovely village where Beatrix Potter wrote her books, with beautiful views of the countryside and nearby lake. Ideal for walking, fishing and touring. Children welcome. Babysitting can be arranged. Open all year. Accommodation comprises one double and one family bedroom; bathroom; dining/sittingroom. Car essential with parking for two cars. Bed and Breakfast from £8, Bed, Breakfast and Evening Meal from £12. Half-price rates fror children.

AMBLESIDE. Mrs Ivy Cain, Oaks Farm Cottage, Loughrigg, Ambleside LA22 9HQ (Langdale [096-67] 348). Oaks Cottage is a country cottage adjoining Oaks Farm, situated in the heart of the Lake District, one mile from Grasmere and Elterwater and within easy reach of Windermere, Hawkshead and Coniston. Ideal for touring or walking. Fishing in Loughrigg Tarn. Accommodation is in two double and one family rooms (one double, one single bed), all with washbasins, TV and tea/coffee making facilities. One bathroom and one shower (water hot at all times). Fully centrally heated and open fire when chilly. Mrs Cain provides a home from home atmosphere and guests are treated as friends. Pets welcome. Car essential — parking available. Bed and Breakfast from £8 with reduced rates for children under 12. Children under three years free. Babysitting if required. Open all year, except for two weeks at Christmas.

BOARD Cumbria 89

AMBLESIDE. Mrs Joan Newby, Kingston, Waterhead, Ambleside LA22 0HA (Ambleside [0966] 33062). A warm welcome awaits guests and overseas visitors at this small comfortable guest house situated at the head of Lake Windermere close to boat and steamer landings. The proprietrix, being local born and bred, has expert knowledge of the history of the area and can advise guests on what to do and where to go. All home cooking a speciality. Open from March to November and situated on a bus route from Windermere to Keswick, the house has two double and one family bedrooms, with washbasins; bathroom and toilet; sittingroom and diningroom. Children welcome, babysitting offered. Suitable for disabled persons. Central heating. Car is not essential, parking provided. Bed and Breakfast from £8; Evening Meal, Bed and Breakfast from £12; rates reduced for children sharing room. SAE for reply, please.

AMBLESIDE. Mr and Mrs G. R. Pickup, The Dower House, Wray Castle, Ambleside LA22 0JA (Ambleside [0966] 33211). Commanding one of the most beautiful views in Lakeland, selected thus by the wealthy builder of Wray Castle, the "Dower House" overlooks Windermere about 300 yards away. Magnificent views of major peaks, the woods at the head of Lake Windermere and the surrounding valleys can be seen from the house, which is in the Wray Castle Park, with direct access to the woodlands and beauty of the lake shore. Three double bedrooms with washbasins; bathroom, two toilets; sittingroom, electric heating. Children over 11 years welcome. Sorry, no pets. A car is essential and there is ample parking. Open Easter to November 1. Every comfort is assured and all modern conveniences. Ambleside three miles. Evening Dinner, Bed and Breakfast. SAE, please, for terms.

AMBLESIDE. Mrs Audrey Whittle, Meadow Bank, Elterwater, Ambleside (Langdale [096-67] 278). Beautifully furnished accommodation with all home comforts. Elterwater, in the magnificent Langdale Valley, is ideally situated for walking and natural history interests as well as for general touring. Within this setting in the Heart of Lakeland we offer a superbly appointed home, centrally heated throughout, with washbasins in all bedrooms and no nylon sheets. High-class home-cooking and a sense of being home from home are the basis of our hospitality. Open all year except Christmas. Six persons. Sorry, no children under 11 or pets. Bed and Breakfast from £8.50. Dinner optional. Also holiday cottage (coastal). SAE, please.

AMBLESIDE. Mr and Mrs A. J. Marsden, Betty Fold, Hawkshead Hill, Ambleside LA22 0PS (Hawkshead [096-66] 611). Betty Fold is a large country house in its own spacious grounds with magnificent views and set in the heart of the Lake District National Park. The quaint village of Hawkshead is nearby and Coniston and Ambleside are within four miles. The beauty spot Tarn Howe is 15 minutes' walk away. The guest house is privately run by the resident owners and offers Bed, Breakfast, Evening Meals and Packed Lunches. All bedrooms are en suite. Children are welcome, cots are available and babysitting can be arranged. Parties are particularly welcome. We regret, no pets in the guest house. See also advertisement in SELF CATERING section of the guide.

AMBLESIDE. Jim and Joyce Ormesher, Rothay House, Rothay Road, Ambleside LA22 0EE (Ambleside [0966] 32434). Rothay House is a modern detached tastefully furnished Guest House, situated just 200 yards from centre of village. There is ample parking, with gardens front and rear. All rooms (double and family), have colour TV, washbasins, tea-making facilities and are centrally heated. We guarantee a warm welcome, friendly service and a comfortable stay. Open all year. Children welcome. Sorry no pets. Car not essential. Bed and Breakfast. Weekend winter breaks available.

AMBLESIDE. Mrs Jennifer Toms, Middlefell Farm, Great Langdale, Ambleside LA22 9JU (09667-684). Owned by the National Trust and beautifully situated on an old pack horse route at the head of Great Langdale Valley. Middlefell is a comfortable 17th century farmhouse full of character and old world charm. It is an excellent base for both touring and fell walking, with such popular walks as the Langdale Pikes, Bowfell and Crinkle Craggs and Scawfell, all starting directly from the farm yard. All rooms are tastefully decorated and spotlessly clean, with excellent views onto surrounding mountains. Ample hot water always available. Guests are welcome to bring their own wines to complement the superb home cooking. Fire Certificate awarded. Tea and coffee facilities available. SAE, please, for colour brochure.

FARM HOLIDAY GUIDES LIMITED publish a large range of well-known accommodation guides. We will be happy to send you details or you can use the order form at the back of this book.

AMBLESIDE. Mrs D. E. Wrathall, The Oaks, Loughrigg, Ambleside LA22 9HQ (Langdale [096-67] 632). Set in the secluded Loughrigg Valley in the heart of the Lake District, this 18th century farmhouse is the property of the National Trust. Fishing is available in nearby Loughrigg Tarn and this is also an ideal centre for many of the popular fell walks. Ambleside three miles, Grasmere two miles. Accommodation is offered in two family and one double bedrooms, with washbasins; bathroom, toilet; sittingroom, diningroom. Central heating in all bedrooms during winter months. Children welcome — cot and high chair provided. Pets accepted. Open fires in lounge except July/September. Good farmhouse fare is served in a friendly atmosphere. Open February to November. Car essential, parking. Reductions for children under ten years. Evening Dinner, Bed and Breakfast. SAE for prompt reply.

AMBLESIDE. Mrs E. Peers, Fisherbeck Farmhouse, Old Lake Road, Ambleside LA22 0DH [0966] 32523]. The charming 16th-century old farmhouse/dairy is situated in quiet side lane at the foot of Wansfell to the south of the village. Warm, comfortable rooms, single, double, twin and family with hot and cold. Lounge with TV. Separate morning/breakfast room, tea/coffee making facilities. Parking no problem, either on own ground or free car park. Car is not essential as village is only five minutes' level walk away; one minute walk to bus stop. SAE, please, for terms and details. Les Relais Routiers recommended.

AMBLESIDE. Mrs Helen Green, "Lyndhurst", Wansfell Road, Ambleside LA22 0EG (Ambleside [0966] 32421]. Quietly situated in its own garden, this Lakeland stone house offers a relaxed and friendly atmosphere with good home cooking. An ideal centre for exploring, touring, walking or relaxing. Private car park. Three double and two family bedrooms, all with washbasins with hot and cold, shaver points, tea and coffee trays. Children are welcome, cot, high chair, babysitting and reduced rates. Open February to December. A warm welcome awaits you.

AMBLESIDE. Mr J. B. Forbes, West Vale Guest House, Far Sawrey, Ambleside LA22 0LQ (Windermere [09662] 2817). Superbly situated in the village of Far Sawrey, West Vale offers you personal service and good food in a warm friendly atmosphere. We are open all year, including Christmas and New Year and have central heating and open fire in lounge. Most bedrooms have private facilities en-suite and all rooms have tea and coffee making facilities. Residential Licence. AA Listed and RAC Listed. We offer special Winter and Spring breaks. For further details, please send for our brochure.

AMBLESIDE. Mr I. Gordon, Brantfell Guest House, Kelsick Road, Ambleside LA22 0JB (0966–32239). Ambleside is the ideal resort for the Lake District holiday and Brantfell Guest House makes the perfect base. A tastefully converted Victorian house, it is centrally situated and convenient for all local amenities including tennis courts and bowling green. There are three double, two single and two family rooms, most of which have views to the fells. Bathroom, two toilets; sittingroom and diningroom. Central heating. Children welcome; cot and high chair available. Sorry, no pets allowed. Parking, though car not essential. Open from 1st March to 30th October for Bed and Breakfast. Terms from £8.50.

AMBLESIDE. Mrs S. Harryman, Fell Foot Farm, Little Langdale, Ambleside LA22 9PE (Langdale [096-67] 294). Working farm. Nestling at the foot of the famous Wrynose Pass a 17th century farmhouse, once a coaching inn, welcomes visitors from Easter to November. Full of charm and character the house, owned by the National Trust, contains fine oak beams and panelling and a log fire blazes on chilly evenings. One mile from the village of Little Langdale, on a 431-acre sheep and beef farm, the house offers comfortable accommodation with beautiful views from all bedrooms and excellent home cooking. Three double bedrooms, all with washbasins; bathroom, two toilets; sitting/diningroom. Tea/coffee making facilities all rooms. Children welcome at reduced rates and babysitting may be arranged. Sorry, no pets. Part central heating. Car essential, parking. Evening Dinner, Bed and Breakfast or Bed and Breakfast. Fishing in Blea Tarn and the coast 20 miles away. SAE, please.

FUN FOR ALL THE FAMILY IN CUMBRIA

Appleby Castle Conservation Centre, Appleby; *Brockhole National Park Visitor Centre*, near Ambleside; *Grizedale Forest Wildlife Centre*, Hawkshead; *Lowther Wildlife Adventure Park*, near Penrith; *Muncaster Castle*, Ravenglass; *Levens Hall*, near Kendal; *Ravenglass & Eskdale Railway*, Ravenglass; *Lakeside & Haverthwaite Railway*, Haverthwaite, near Newby Bridge; *Windermere Steamboat Museum*, Rayrigg Road, near Bowness-on-Windermere; *Fell Foot Park*, Newby Bridge, Lake Windermere.

AMBLESIDE near. David and Jane Vaughan, Ivy House Hotel, Hawkshead, Near Ambleside LA22 0NS (Hawkshead [096-66] 204). Ivy House is a most attractive Georgian residence of character and charm having a lovely entrance hall leading to an unusual cantilever spiral staircase. Situated in a central position for all the lakes in the quaint village of Hawkshead, near lovely Tarn Howes, there are 11 bedrooms of which six are in the house (three of which have private facilities) and the remainder in two motel-type buildings adjacent. One of these is a two bedroomed unit and the other has three bedrooms. All bedrooms have washbasins, razor points, bedside lights and tea-making facilities. Three bathrooms, five toilets, two shower rooms. Central heating. Log fire in lounge early and late season, colour TV; diningroom in which good home cooking is served. AA listed. Restaurant licence. Fire Certificate held. Parking space. Dogs accepted. Evening Dinner, Bed and Breakfast or Bed and Breakfast. Reduced rates for children if sharing parents' room; babysitting. Brochure on request.

AMBLESIDE. B. & K. Barton, Fisherbeck Hotel, Lake Road, Ambleside LA22 0DH (Ambleside [0966] 33215). With its commanding views of Loughrigg Fell, the Hotel provides the ideal base for your holiday, whether it be one of relaxation or activity. Ambleside is at the heart of the Lake District, with easy access to all areas. There are 16 bedrooms, 13 with private facilities, comfortable lounge, spacious diningroom, separate TV lounge, garden and ample car parking. The residents' Cocktail Bar and Tannery Bar offer a warm welcome. Friendly atmosphere, excellent food, fine wines, delightful surroundings and the personal attention of Brian and Kathleen Barton provide the makings of a wonderful holiday. Brochure on request. Children welcome. See also colour display advertisement in this guide.

APPLEBY-IN-WESTMORLAND. Mr D. and Mrs Y. Mawdsley, "Hoff Lodge", Hoff, Appleby-in-Westmorland CA16 6TD (0930-51875). "Hoff Lodge", a former shooting lodge, is situated in six acres with lovely views, three miles from Appleby on the B6260, in the beautiful Eden Valley. The family-run Lodge is quiet, peaceful and good home cooking is a speciality of the proprietors. Table licence. Central heating and log fires. Three double rooms, one family room with washbasins. TV lounge; diningroom. Children welcome, cot available. Pets accepted if kept under strict control. Car essential — ample parking. Excellent base for touring the Lake District, Yorkshire Dales and Scottish Borders. Open all year for Bed and Breakfast or Bed, Breakfast and Evening Meal. Reductions for children sharing parents' room. Also four-berth 24' caravan for hire. SAE for brochure.

APPLEBY-IN-WESTMORLAND. Mrs E. Pigney, Howgill House, Appleby-in-Westmorland CA16 6UW (Appleby [0930] 51574). "Howgill House" lies on the B6542 (old A66) which runs through Appleby, the "gateway to the Lake District." Appleby, a quiet country place on the River Eden, is well-known for its trout fishing. Fine golf courses in lovely surroundings three miles from the house; heated outdoor swimming pool in Appleby. Open Easter to October. Two double and three family bedrooms, all with washbasins; tea-making facilities; bathroom, two toilets; sittingroom and diningroom. Children welcome, cot available. Car essential, parking. Swings for children: Dogs not allowed inside house. Kendal 22 miles; Carlisle 30 and M6 eight miles. Fire Certificate held. Evening Dinner, Bed and Breakfast or Bed and Breakfast. Reductions for children sharing parents' room. SAE brings prompt reply.

BAMPTON. Mrs L. White, Beckfoot Guest House, Helton, Bampton, Near Penrith CA10 2QB (Bampton [093-13] 241). Beautiful Victorian country house, one single, three double, three family rooms, all with private shower/bath and WC, together with tea-making facilities. Ullswater seven miles. Pony trekking, golfing, fishing and swimming available nearby. Cots, high chairs and babysitting available. Dogs permitted by arrangement. Car essential. Open all year. Evening Meal, Bed and Breakfast. Children seven and under free if sharing room. Stamp for brochure.

Terms quoted in this publication may be subject to increase if rises in costs necessitate

Cumbria BOARD

BASSENTHWAITE LAKE. Mr B. W. Patrick, Ouse Bridge Hotel, Dubwath, Bassenthwaite Lake CA13 9YD (Bassenthwaite Lake [059-681] 322). Ouse Bridge Hotel is situated at the North Western end of Bassenthwaite Lake, just off the A66, and overlooking Skiddaw and the Lake. All 10 bedrooms are comfortably furnished and equipped with washbasins, shaver points; some have electric shower units and others private bathrooms. Central heating ensures year round comfort. Elizabeth and Barry Patrick take pride in the food they serve and are known locally for their good home cooking and mouth-watering sweets. We have a well-stocked, fully licensed bar lounge and a comfortable TV lounge with colour TV. Our tariff includes a full English Breakfast and a four-course Dinner, with coffee, priced from £15 per person. Colour brochure available.

BORROWDALE. Mrs S. Bland, Thorneythwaite Farm, Borrowdale, Keswick CA12 5XQ (Borrowdale [059-684] 237. Working farm. Thorneythwaite Farm has the most beautiful, peaceful position in the Borrowdale Valley standing half-mile off the road. The 220-acre sheep farm, with grazing on Glaramara, is some seven miles from Keswick. Half-mile from Seatoller. The 18th century farmhouse has great character inside and out. It has several rooms with oak beams and panelling, furnished to suit. Two double and one family bedrooms all with tea/coffee making facilities. Sittingroom with open or electric fire; diningroom; bathroom and toilet. Cot, high chair, babysitting and reduced rates for children. Sorry, no pets. Open from April to November, mid-week bookings accepted. A perfect base for a honeymoon or for those who like fell walking. Bed and Breakfast from £8.

BOWNESS-ON-WINDERMERE. LANGDALE VIEW GUEST HOUSE, 114 Craig Walk (off Helm Road), Bowness-on-Windermere LA23 3AX (Windermere [09662] 4076). Langdale View Guest House is a family run house five minutes' walk from the lakeside yet in a quiet spot with views over the lake to the mountains. We offer Bed and Breakfast with dinner (optional). There is a guest lounge, toilets and showers, private washbasins, central heating, fire certificate and parking. Canoe available. We will collect you from the station. Our double, twin and family rooms cost from £8 per person per night with reduced rates for weekly, out of season or group bookings. For reservations or brochure please ring or write to Mrs Marilyn Tordoff.

BROUGHTON-IN-FURNESS near. Mrs Jennifer Temple, Longhouse Guest House, Seathwaite, Near Broughton-in-Furness LA20 6EE (Broughton-in-Furness [065-76] 470). Quiet, secluded 17th century farmhouse set in the hills. Ideal for walkers; 14 miles Coniston Lake; 24 miles Windermere; 12 miles Eskdale and Ravenglass railway. Stately homes nearby are Muncaster Castle and gardens; Holker Hall and deer park. Approximately 15 miles to the sea and ideal for quiet peaceful holidays. One double bedroom, one double/twin bedroom and one family bedroom suitable for small children. Two bathrooms; lounge with B/W TV; diningroom. Cot, high chair, babysitting by arrangement. Pets permitted but must sleep in car. Open from February to November; mid-week bookings accepted. Bed and Breakfast from £6. Evening Meal, Bed and Breakfast from £10. Reductions for children. Fire Certificate held.

BROUGHTON-IN-FURNESS. Mr and Mrs D. V. Walker, High Duddon Guest House, Broughton-in-Furness LA20 6ET (Broughton-in-Furness [06576] 279). High Duddon is a residential guest house situated at the foot of the most beautiful valleys in the Lake District near the Lakes. Broughton one-and-a-half miles, Ulverston 13 and Barrow 18. Car essential, parking provided. Open all year. Three double, six family, two single bedrooms with ten washbasins. Four bathrooms, four toilets. Sittingroom, TV, bar and diningroom plus games room. Cot, high chair and babysitting facilities. Reduced rates for under 12s. Fishing, riding, climbing, pony trekking and bathing all in area; three miles from sea. Evening Dinner, Bed and Breakfast. Self catering facilities in two flats also available. SAE, please, for terms.

BROUGHTON-IN-FURNESS. Mr and Mrs J. and M. Atkinson, Fair View, Broughton-in-Furness LA20 6ES (Broughton-in-Furness [065-76] 368). Overlooking the River Duddon, and just off the A595, Fair View occupies an elevated position commanding fine views of the river estuary and moors. There is a wealth of interest for holidaymakers of all ages in the surrounding area. Guests are warmly welcomed and good food is served with a varied menu. Comfortable lounge with colour TV and books; separate diningroom. Three double, one single and one family bedrooms, with washbasins, shaving points, bed lights, spring interior mattresses. Central heating. Cot and babysitting available. Sorry, no pets. Open March to November. Car essential, parking. Evening Dinner, Bed and Breakfast from £10.50, or Bed and Breakfast only from £7.50. Fire Certificate.

PLEASE SEND A STAMPED ADDRESSED ENVELOPE WITH ENQUIRIES

CALDBECK. M. Monkhouse, Denton Guest House, Hesket New Market, Caldbeck CA7 8JC (Caldbeck [06998] 415). Denton Guest House is a large 17th century house modernised to 20th century comforts still retaining character with new extension. Situated in the unspoilt village in Cumbria, it is an ideal base for touring lakes or Scottish borders. Ideal also for walking the Northern Fells. Why not stay overnight when journeying from or to Scotland. Easy access from M6 junction 41. A friendly atmosphere with good home cooking and log fires welcomes everyone. Residential licence. Fire Certificate. Seven bedrooms all with hot and cold. Children welcome at reduced rates, cot, high chair and babysitting. Pets welcome. Open all year. Car essential, parking. SAE, please, for brochure.

CALDBECK. Mrs D. Coulthard, Friar Hall, Caldbeck, Wigton CA7 8DS (Caldbeck [069-98] 633). Working farm. Ideally situated for touring Lakes, Scottish Border, and Roman Wall, Friar Hall, 140-acre dairy and sheep farm lies in Caldbeck village, overlooking the river which runs in front of the house and in which visitors can fish (permit required). Carlisle 13 miles, Keswick and Penrith 14 miles. Tennis half a mile and hill climbing two miles away. The modernised farmhouse has oak beams and open fire. Two double and one family rooms with washbasins; bathroom, toilet; sittingroom and diningroom. Cot, babysitting, high chair and reduced rates offered for children. Well-heated, the house is open from Easter to October for Evening Dinner, Bed and Breakfast or Bed and Breakfast. Car essential — parking. Sorry, no pets. AA listed. SAE, please, for terms and further details.

CARLISLE. Jean and Dennis Martin, The Hill Cottage, Blackford, Carlisle CA6 4DU (Rockcliffe [0228] 74739). Three miles north of Carlisle on A7, one minute from M6/A74 (Junction 44) — 19th century hill cottage, recently modernised and extended, with spacious, centrally heated rooms, high standard of furnishings and decor. Enjoying a peaceful, rural setting in farm country, an ideal base for exploring the Solway coasts, Lakes, Scottish Borders, Hadrian's Wall and historic Carlisle. Golf, fishing, bird watching nearby. Comfortable accommodation in single, twin, double or family rooms with washbasins, shaver points, fitted wardrobes and Yale locks. Bathroom/shower, two toilets. Lounge with colour TV; diningroom. Excellent cuisine. Children welcome, cot, high chair, babysitting, reduced rates. Sorry, no pets. Ample parking, car not essential, convenient public transport. Special weekly terms, out of season bookings etc. ETB registered. Evening Dinner available. SAE for brochure.

CARLISLE. Eric and Joan Harrison, West Highberries, Scaleby, Carlisle CA6 4LD (Kirklinton [022-875] 210). This farmhouse built in 1767 is set in a large garden in peaceful surroundings. It is situated six miles from the M6 and a quarter of a mile off the A6071 between Brampton and Longtown. Accommodation comprises: two double and one twin bedded rooms. Lounge, diningroom, bathroom, shower and toilet. Central heating when season demands. Within easy reach of the Roman Wall, Lake District and South West Scotland. Rates are reduced for children. Car is essential, parking. Sorry, no pets. Fifteen miles from the sea. Open Easter to October. Bed and Breakfast and bedtime snack. Terms on application.

CARLISLE. Mrs Dorothy Nicholson, Willow Grove, Kirklinton, Carlisle CA6 6DD (Kirklinton [022-875] 326). This spacious bungalow is situated on A6071 Longtown to Brampton Road. Central for touring Lakeland, Border towns, Roman Wall, Solway coast, all within easy reach, also ideal for breaking journey to and from Scotland (only four miles from M6). Willow Grove offers friendly welcome to all and being all on ground level is suitable for elderly or disabled guests. Accommodation comprises two double and one family bedrooms; bathroom, toilet; sitting/diningroom. Children welcome at reduced rates and cot, high chair, babysitting available. Car essential — parking. Pets permitted. Open March to November for Evening Dinner/Meal, Bed and Breakfast or Bed and Breakfast. Terms on request with SAE.

CARLISLE. Mrs Elizabeth S. Woodmass, Howard House Farm, Gilsland, Carlisle CA6 7AN (Gilsland [069-72] 285). Working farm. A 300-acre mixed farm with a 19th century stone-built farmhouse situated in a rural area overlooking the Irthing Valley on the Cumbria-Northumbria border. Half-a-mile from Gilsland village and the Roman Wall. Haltwhistle five miles and the M6 at Carlisle 20. Good base for touring — Roman Wall, Lakes and Scottish borders. Trout fishing on farm. Guests' lounge with colour TV where you can relax anytime in comfort. Diningroom. One twin-bedded and one family bedrooms (both with washbasin); bathroom, toilet. Children welcome at reduced rates, cot and babysitting available. Sorry, no pets. Car essential — parking. Open January to December for Bed and Breakfast with Evening Meal optional. SAE or telephone for further details. Also self-catering.

CARLISLE. Mrs Doreen Bell, Glendinning Rigg, Penton, Longtown, Carlisle CA6 5QB (Nicholforest [022-877] 236). This old world farmhouse is pleasantly situated in its own grounds 500 yards away from the road along a tarmac lane. Within easy distance of the Lake District, Roman Wall, Edinburgh, Glasgow and any of the Border towns. Carlisle, a market town, has many interesting features and historical buildings. Kielder Dam 30 miles. Fishing is available, with permission, on the nearby river. A good half-way house to or from Scotland. Excellent home cooking using fresh home produce. One double, one single and one family bedrooms; one bedroom with washbasin; bathroom, two toilets; sittingroom and diningroom. Children welcome, cot and babysitting offered. A car is required and there is parking space. Pets allowed. Open Easter to October for Evening Dinner/Meal, Bed and Breakfast or Bed and Breakfast. Reductions for children. SAE, please, for terms.

CARLISLE. Mr and Mrs Mike and Pat Armstrong, Skitby Farm, (Smithfield), Kirklinton, Carlisle CA6 6DL (Kirklinton [022-875] 241). Working farm. Typical farmhouse built in 1791 with every modern amenity, situated six miles north of Carlisle in the village of Smithfield (shop, post office, garage and village inn), within easy reach of Scottish Borders, Lake District, Roman Wall, Solway Coast. Accommodation comprises one family, one double, one single rooms, bathroom and toilets; two lounges (one with colour TV); diningroom where fine food is a speciality using meat and vegetables produced on the farm. Dinner by prior arrangement, and packed lunches available on request. Children well catered for with reduced rates and babysitting provided. For sports enthusiasts fishing can be arranged, golf courses and swimming pools within easy reach. Sorry, no pets. Open Easter to October for Bed and Breakfast from £7. Car essential — parking.

Eden Valley & Alston Moor Country Holidays in Lakeland

That Other Eden

Eden Valley and Alston Moor Country Holidays offer a warm welcome in farmhouses, smallholdings and country cottages. We can offer country pursuits in the peace and tranquillity of the vast and sometimes wild landscapes that are to be seen all around. There is something to suit everyone. For a wide choice of farmhouse and guesthouse accommodation send a stamped addressed envelope to: Anne Ivinson (FHG), Green View, Welton, Dalston, Carlisle, CUMBRIA. Tel: Raughton Head (06996) 230.
NO AGENTS FEE.

REGISTERED WITH THE ENGLISH TOURIST BOARD   FARM HOLIDAY BUREAU MEMBER

Bessiestown Farm
Penton, Nr. Carlisle

A.A. – R.A.C. Listed Residential Licence

Proprietors: Jackie & Margaret Sisson
Tel. No: Nicholforest [0228-77] 219

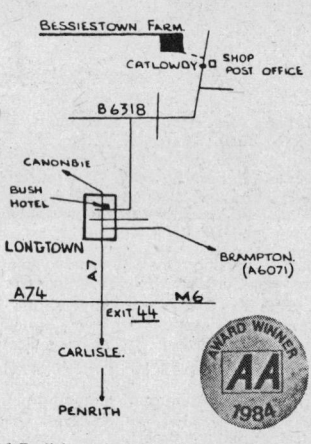

Bed, Breakfast and evening meals are available in the delightful and spacious farmhouse. The house is centrally heated, has guests' diningroom and lounge with colour TV, nine modern comfortable bedrooms – six with en suite bath/shower room. Excellent accommodation, friendly atmosphere and good home cooking. **Heated indoor swimming pool. Open mid-May to mid-September. Riding.** BESSIESTOWN FARM is a small beef/sheep rearing farm situated in a quiet rural area approximately 17 miles north of Carlisle and only 3 miles from the Scottish Border, making it an ideal base for a family/touring holiday or for breaking your journey to and from Scotland. There is a children's play area and games room (pool, table tennis and darts) and many farm animals to interest the children and adults alike. For the tourist it is convenient for the Lake District, Roman Wall, Galloway and Solway Coast or pleasant country walks, shooting, fishing and golf within a 15 mile radius. There are also three self-catering cottages with evening meals in the farmhouse if desired.

AA AWARD WINNER 1984

Peace and Seclusion at the
Fish Hotel

The Fish Hotel, personally run by the proprietors, Jean and John Richardson and open from late March till early November, is ideally situated in one of Lakeland's most beautiful valleys between the two Lakes, Buttermere and Crummock Water (five minutes from each). The delightful village of Buttermere lies at the foot of Honister Pass and Newlands Hause.

The 12 very pleasant rooms all have hot and cold running water and shaving points. Children are welcome and have 30 per cent reduction in rates. Ample bath and toilet accommodation. There are two comfortable lounges. The hotel has recently been made fully centrally heated and modernised but still retains its old charm; there are two bars (*one serving Bar Meals*) and friendly, small cocktail lounge.

The restaurant offers a very high standard of food and cooking with Evening Dinner, Bed and Breakfast costing from £110 weekly; Evening Meal, Bed and Breakfast from £17.00 per night and Bed and Breakfast, £16.00 per person per night. All prices include VAT. 30% off for children. Pets are permitted free of charge and there is parking space for 40 cars.

This is ideal walking and climbing country, where fishing and pony trekking are also readily available.

Mr and Mrs JOHN RICHARDSON, THE FISH HOTEL, BUTTERMERE, via COCKERMOUTH, CUMBRIA CA13 9XA. Tel Buttermere 253.

CARLISLE. Mrs Jane Lawson, Craigburn Farm, Penton, Carlisle CA6 5QP (Nicholforest [022-877] *
214). Working farm. Craigburn Farm, dating back to 1760, is a beef and sheep farm situated near the border forest, in a quiet rural area. Ideal for breaking your journey to and from Scotland, or as a base for touring the Lake District, South Scotland, the Solway coast and Roman Wall. Other facilities within easy reach include fishing, golf, horse riding and beautiful country walks. Good Sports Centre eight miles. Tennis court and snooker/pool table at farm for visitors' use, also ponies for hire. Shooting on the farm by arrangement. Home cooking and homely atmosphere entice visitors year after year and the family is always willing to spend their spare time with guests. Four double, two single, four family bedrooms, all have washbasins and some have bathroom en-suite. Two bath/shower rooms, two toilets; sittingroom; diningroom. Cot, high chair, babysitting. Pets permitted. Car essential — parking. Open all year. Evening Dinner/Meal, Bed and Breakfast or Bed and Breakfast only. Licensed Bar. See also colour advertisement. SAE for details and terms.

Craigburn Farm

CARLISLE. Mrs D. Davidson, Fordlands, Hethersgill, Carlisle CA6 6ET (Kirklinton [022-875] 372). Spacious farmhouse, with a friendly atmosphere and excellent home cooking, makes an ideal centre for touring the Lake District, Roman Wall, Scottish Border and Kielder Dam. Situated 11 miles north east of Carlisle off A6071 Longton to Brampton, it is also a good overnight stop for travellers going to, or returning from Scotland. Clean and comfortable accommodation is provided in two double and one family bedrooms; bathroom, toilet; sittingroom, diningroom. Central heating. Children are welcome with reduced rates under 12 years. Pets accepted free of charge. Open June to September for Full Board; Evening Meal, Bed and Breakfast, or Bed and Breakfast only. Car essential — parking. Public transport one mile.

COCKERMOUTH. Mrs Dorothy E. Richardson, Pardshaw Hall, Cockermouth CA13 0SP (Cockermouth [0900] 822607). Working farm. Pardshaw Hall is pleasantly situated in a small village three-and-a-half miles from Cockermouth and is a listed building. Large garden at the rear where children can play safely. Pardshaw is ideally situated for touring the lakes and there are some really lovely walks. Good home cooking with succulent roast beef, roast lamb, roast chicken and home-made cheesecake and souffles. Accommodation in two double bedrooms, two single and one family rooms, one with washbasin; bathroom, two toilets; sittingroom, diningroom; open fires. Children are welcome and there is cot, high chair and babysitting. Sorry, no pets. Open all year. Car essential, parking. Evening Meal, Bed and Breakfast or Bed and Breakfast only. Rates reduced for children. SAE, please.

COCKERMOUTH. Mrs E. Cameron, Dairy Farm, Greysouthen, Cockermouth CA13 0UN (Cockermouth [0900] 825466). Working farm. Dairy Farm is a pleasant 100-acres mixed farm on the outskirts of the village of Greysouthen. Four miles from Cockermouth, Keswick 17 miles. Easily accessible from the new A66 trunk road. Makes an ideal centre for touring, within easy reach of the West Cumbria coast and Lake District Fells. An 18th-century farmhouse modernised for comfort yet retaining much of the original charm. Two double rooms with washbasins; one double room with private suite; two single rooms; fitted carpets, divan beds, reading lamps all rooms. Guests have exclusive use of the diningroom and sittingroom with TV. Car essential, parking. Open all year. Evening Dinner, Bed and Breakfast or Bed and Breakfast only. Reduced terms for children. Regret, no pets. Open electric fire. SAE for details and price.

CONISTON. Mrs R. Inman, High Ground Farm, Coniston LA21 8AU (Coniston [0966] 41239). High Ground Farm is a family run hill sheep farm. It is situated two miles from Coniston with easy access to Lake Coniston and surrounding fells. Good food can be obtained within one mile radius of the farm. One double and one family room for guests, one with washbasin. Bathroom, toilet, sittingroom, diningroom. Open 1st April to 31st October with electric heating. Car essential, parking. Children are welcome and there is babysitting available. Bed and Breakfast from £7. Reduced rates for children.

CONISTON. Mrs B. E. Nelson, Townson Ground, Coniston LA21 8AA (Coniston [0966] 41272). Townson Ground is a fascinating old house, picturesquely set on the east of the Lake, about one mile from Coniston village. Convenient for bathing, fishing, sailing. "Brantwood", home of John Ruskin, Grizedale Forest, Tarn House, Hawkshead, all an easy drive away. It is an ideal centre for touring or walking. A very high standard of comfort is maintained and all beds have electric blankets. Choice of double, twin, family and single bedrooms, all with washbasins; bathroom, three toilets, shower room. Lounge with TV, games and books. Diningroom. Coal and log fires give the house a cosy atmosphere and the house is open from January to December. Car essential, ample parking. Children over three years welcome, reduced rates. Pets by arrangement. Evening Dinner, Bed and Breakfast or Bed and Breakfast only. Light supper supplied. Terms on request.

CONISTON. Mrs J. Lancaster, Heathwaite Farm, Coniston LA21 8HD (Coniston [0966] 41505). Working farm. Heathwaite Farm, nestled into the foot of Coniston Old Man approximately half-a-mile from the village, has its own metalled road. The traditionally run 160-acre Lakeland hill farm supplies the house with produce for home cooking. The large-roomed 19th century house enjoys peace and tranquillity with excellent views over Coniston Lake where the "Gondola" can be seen steaming past John Ruskin's birthplace, "Brantwood." Two family bedrooms with electric blankets; bathroom; sitting/diningroom with TV. Reduced rates for children, and babysitting offered. Pets free of charge. Open all year. Part central heating and open fire. Car essential — parking. Public transport one mile. Terms on request for Evening Meal, Bed and Breakfast or Bed and Breakfast only.

CONISTON. Mrs M. L. Knipe, Dixon Ground Farm, Coniston LA21 8HQ (Coniston [0966] 41443). Dixon Ground Farm, built in 1762, is a fully modernised 52-acre farm on the main footpath to Coniston Old Man and Copper Mines Valley. Ideal for walking, climbing, sailing or relaxing in the beauty of the countryside. Amenities in nearby village and places of historical interest to visit. Two double bedrooms, two single and one family, all with spring interior mattresses and electric blankets; bathroom, two toilets; sittingroom with colour TV; diningroom. Children welcome at reduced rates. Open fires. Car essential — parking. Dogs permitted. Warm welcome assured. Home cooking and produce. SAE for terms. Evening Dinner, Bed and Breakfast or Bed and Breakfast only.

CONISTON near. Mrs Frances Mayvers, Wilson Cottage, Torver, Near Coniston LA21 8BB (Coniston [096-64] 237). Wilson Cottage is situated in the quiet, picturesque village of Torver, two and a half miles from Coniston. An excellent touring centre for the Lakes, Dales, Borders and coast. The very good walking area includes the Coniston Old Man, Walwa Scar, Don Crags. Good home cooking is served to guests who are welcome all year round. Residential and Restaurant Licence. Accommodation comprises four double, one single, two family bedrooms (five with washbasins); two bathrooms, three toilets; sittingroom and diningroom. Well-behaved children are welcome, high chair and babysitting available. Regret, no pets. Car essential to make the most of the many beauty spots, parking. Public transport 100 yards. Evening Meal, Bed and Breakfast or Bed and Breakfast. Reductions for children. SAE, please, for terms.

The information in the entries in this guide is presented by the publishers in good faith and after the signed acceptance by advertisers that they will uphold the high standards associated with FARM HOLIDAY GUIDES LIMITED. The publishers do not accept responsibility for any inaccuracies or omissions or any results thereof. Before making final holiday arrangements readers should confirm the prices and facilities directly with advertisers.

DENT. Mrs E. Gardner, Bridge Cottage Guest House, Gawthrop, Dent, Near Sedbergh LA10 5TA (Dent [058-75] 240). Bridge Cottage is situated in beautiful Dentdale, which extends from Sedbergh to Newby Head. The old world village of Dent is half a mile away and still retains its cobbled streets and whitewashed stone houses. Birthplace of Adam Sedgewick (18th century geologist). Dentdale is one of the most picturesque and unspoiled of the former Yorkshire Dales (now in Cumbria) with a river running through giving a remarkable variety of scenery. Good centre for touring the Dales and the Lakes. Delicious food served including York ham and eggs. Local steak, home baking. Full central heating. Cosy TV lounge with coal fire to relax by in the evening and personal attention given to guests' comfort. One double and two family bedrooms with washbasins; bathroom, toilet; diningroom. Children welcome — babysitting and reduced rates. No pets. Open March to November. Car essential — parking. Evening Dinner, Bed and Breakfast or Bed and Breakfast only. SAE for terms.

ESKDALE. Mrs A. E. Harrington, Wha House Farm, Boot, Holmrook CA19 1TH (Eskdale [094-03] 212). **Working farm.** This is a hill sheep farm of 157 acres, situated at the bottom of Hardknott Pass where the Roman Fort can be seen. This is an ideal base for walkers, as Wha House Farm is directly opposite the Traverse Route to Scafell and other mountain climbs. The famous Ratty Railway is two miles away. Accommodation consists of two double, one family and one single bedrooms; bathroom, toilet; sittingroom, diningroom. Older children welcome at reduced rates for the under tens. Sorry, no pets. Towels are provided and Mrs Harrington serves excellent farmhouse fare. Car not essential but parking provided. Open March to November for Bed and Breakfast only. Also self-catering flat adjacent to the farmhouse. Terms on request with SAE, please.

ESKDALE. Mrs Gillian Temple, Gill Bank Farm, Boot, Holmrook, Eskdale CA19 1TG (Eskdale [09403] 292). **Working farm.** A secluded National Trust hill farm in upper Eskdale offering many beautiful and varied walks. Local attractions include Boot Mill, the Ravenglass and Eskdale miniature Railway, waterfalls, Scafell, Hardknott Roman Fort and Muncaster Castle. Residents have separate diningroom and lounge with open log fire and TV. A variety of Evening Meals are available locally. Terms: Bed and Breakfast from £7 per person. Reductions for children. Open all year. Welcome afternoon tea on arrival.

ESKDALE. Mr & Mrs R. L. Davis, Brook House Hotel, Boot, Eskdale CA19 1TG (Eskdale [094-03] 288). Situated in the beautiful unspoilt Eskdale Valley, Brook House is an ideal centre for fell walking and touring the Lake District. Local attractions include a Roman fort, an ancient cornmill, dramatic waterfalls and a narrow gauge steam railway. Guided walks, rock climbing, canoeing and wind surfing may be booked at the hotel. The accommodation is comfortable and is fully centrally heated. All bedrooms have television, washbasins and a delightful view. Brook House has a licensed bar and boasts excellent home cooking. Pets and children welcome. Bed and Breakfast from £10, Dinner, Bed and Breakfast from £16 daily, £105 weekly. Prices include VAT. Open January to November.

GRANGE-OVER-SANDS. Mr and Mrs W. J. Whiteside, Hampsfell Hotel, Hampsfell Road, Grange-over-Sands LA11 6BG (Grange-over-Sands [044-84] 2567). Hampsfell Hotel is a small family-run hotel standing in almost two acres of private ground and woodland. A quiet and peaceful setting, yet within a few minutes' walking distance of the shops in the town centre. The hotel is fully centrally heated and there is ample private parking in the grounds. The accommodation consists of four double rooms, three family and one single, some with private bathrooms. There are tea and coffee making facilities in all bedrooms, lounge with colour TV, diningroom with separate tables and cosy bar with log fire (as required). Children welcome at reduced rates. Pets permitted. Open all year for Evening Dinner, Bed and Breakfast from £14 per day; Bed and Breakfast from £10 per day (including VAT). Restaurant and Residential licence. Low Season Bargain Breaks.

GRANGE-OVER-SANDS. Mr D. W. Foster, Craiglands Hotel, Kents Bank Road, Grange-over-Sands LA11 7DP (Grange-over-Sands [04484] 2348). Craiglands is a family-run hotel, situated on the level, overlooking the sea. The hotel has a table licence, central heating throughout, tea and coffee-making facilities, spacious lounge with TV and a sun lounge. The Promenade, open air swimming pool, tennis courts and bowling greens are five minutes' walk away and for those intending to tour, the Lake District National Park is within easy reach. Open March to October. Dinner, Bed and Breakfast or Bed and Breakfast. Weekly rates on request.

GRANGE-OVER-SANDS. Mrs Jean Jackson, Templand Farm, Allithwaite, Grange-over-Sands LA11 7QX (Grange-over-Sands [04484] 3129). **Working farm.** Though built in 1687, Templand offers comfortable and quiet accommodation with all modern conveniences. This 100-acre mixed farm is close to the Grange-over-Sands/Cartmel road and is within easy reach of the Lake District. Under two miles to the sea. Fishing and hill walking, swimming pool, golf and tennis at Grange. Superb 12th century Priory at Cartmel. Two double, one single and one family bedrooms; bathroom, toilet; lounge and diningroom. Children welcome — cot, high chair and babysitting available. Car not essential but parking provided. Open 1st March to 31st October. SAE, please, brings prompt reply for terms for Evening Dinner/Meal, Bed and Breakfast or Bed and Breakfast. Reductions for children. No pets.

GRANGE-OVER-SANDS. Mr & Mrs G. F. B. and K. Symons, Lymehurst Hotel, Kents Bank Road, Grange-over-Sands LA11 7EY (044-84 3076) (F.H.). Lymehurst Hotel is a modern, well-equipped hotel centrally situated in the beautiful, peaceful resort of Grange-over-Sands on the sheltered coast of Morecambe Bay. A warm friendly welcome awaits you at this family-run hotel. Ten, well-appointed bedrooms on the first floor, equipped with spring interior beds, fitted carpets, hot and cold water, shaver points, convector heaters, radios. Eleventh bedroom on the ground floor has private bathroom en-suite. Spacious, comfortable lounge with colour TV; diningroom with separate tables serving the best in home-cooked food. Cosy lounge bar, with dance floor, where evening refreshments are available. Free car park. Mini weekend and special weekday breaks. Dogs welcome. Dinner, Bed and Breakfast £16 (including VAT). Ideal centre for touring the beautiful Lake District. Please write for brochure. Highly recommended.

GRANGE-OVER-SANDS. Mr and Mrs W. N. Watson, "Lightwood Farm", Cartmel Fell, Grange-over-Sands LA11 6NP (Newby Bridge [0448] 31454). Enjoy overnight accommodation, a weekend break, or your annual holiday at this delightful 17th-century farmhouse, with its original oak beams. Set in large gardens, ample parking facilities. Ideally based for walking or windsurfing etc. Lake Windermere two miles, sea and open air swimming pool six miles. Cosy sittingroom with TV and log fire, four bedrooms, two with washbasins, bathroom, shower, razor points, central heating, tea-making facilities. Children welcome, cots and highchair available. Delicious home cooking served, with full English Breakfast. Evening Meal optional. Open all year.

GRANGE-OVER-SANDS. Mrs M. B. Legat, "Milton House", Grange Fell Road, Grange-over-Sands LA11 6DH (Grange-over-Sands [044-84] 3398). Small, well-established Guest House. Comfortably furnished. Central heating throughout. All bedrooms have a washbasin, fitted carpet and new divan beds. The meals are excellent. Bed and Breakfast from ££8.50 per day; Bed, Breakfast and Evening Dinner from £12 per day. We are open from February to November. Situated near woods and fells, within easy reach of Lakeland, the Cumbrian Coast and the Yorkshire Dales, this is an ideal holiday centre for tourists and hikers. The house commands beautiful and extensive views of Morecambe Bay. Two double and one family rooms; sitting/diningroom. Children welcome. Sorry, no pets. Available locally is a swimming pool, two golf courses, tennis and putting, A friendly welcome is assured here. Parking. Registered with the English Tourist Board.

GRASMERE. Edwin and Vera Watson, Titteringdales, Pye Lane, Grasmere LA22 9RQ (Grasmere [09665] 439). Grasmere is the centre of the Lake District, and Titteringdales has, without doubt, the finest views of surrounding fells. Comfort is our boast, the lounge with colour TV opens on to the lawns of two-acre gardens, a truly peaceful setting. Some bedrooms have private facilities, central heating throughout. Two bathrooms, two toilets; sittingroom, diningroom. Pets by arrangement. Parking. Open from March to November for Evening Meal Bed and Breakfast from £19 or Bed and Breakfast from £12. Food is cooked personally by Eddy and Vera Watson. A SAE will, we hope, introduce you to a perfect holiday. AA listed. Restaurant licence. Open fires early and late season. Tea making facilities.

HAWKSHEAD. Linda and Alan Bleasdale, Summer Hill Cottage, Hawkshead Hill, Hawkshead LA22 0PP (Hawkshead [096-66] 311). A family run gentleman's 17th century country house with an olde worlde friendly atmosphere, comfortable accommodation and good home cooking, situated in its own grounds in an area of outstanding natural beauty. Surrounded by fields and fells in secluded and tranquil setting in the heart of the Lake District National Park, yet near the quaint village of Hawkshead and only a short stroll from Tarn Howes. Bed and Breakfast accommodation together with Dinner at peak times. Restaurant licence. Central heating throughout. Guests' lounge with colour TV, books and log fire (in the cooler evenings). En-suite rooms available. Open all year (Christmas and New Year breaks). Fire Certificate. Private parking. Sorry, no pets. A warm welcome assured. SAE for terms.

BOARD Cumbria 99

HAWKSHEAD. Mr and Mrs P. Hart, Bracken Fell, Outgate, Ambleside LA22 0NH (Hawkshead [096-66] 289). Bracken Fell is situated in beautiful open countryside between Ambleside and Hawkshead in the picturesque hamlet of Outgate. Ideally positioned for exploring the Lake District and within easy reach of Coniston, Windermere, Ambleside, Grasmere and Keswick. All major outdoor activities are catered for nearby including sailing, fishing, canoeing, pony trekking etc. All bedrooms possess outstanding views and have washbasins with hot and cold water. The house has central heating throughout, a comfortable lounge and dining room with separate tables. There is ample parking and two acres of gardens. Open all year. Write or 'phone for brochure and tariff.

HOLMROOK. Mrs E. Parr, Carleton Green Guest House, Saltcoats Road, Holmrook CA19 1YX (Holmrook [094-04] 608). Situated between hill and sea, Carleton Green is in a good position for walks in Wasdale (four miles) and Eskdale (four miles), swimming from the sandy beaches of Drigg (two miles) or Seascale (three miles), or bird watching in Ravenglass Nature Reserve (two miles). The miniature train starts from Ravenglass for the journey to Eskdale, and there is a golf course at Seascale for the more energetic. Carleton Green is a quiet and spacious Georgian House with a large and interesting garden supplying fruit and vegetables almost throughout the season. Guests are offered excellent home cooking, comfortable beds, electric blankets, washbasins with hot and cold water, and tea-making equipment in each bedroom. There is full central heating. The chief concern of the proprietors is that each guest should have a truly happy holiday. Terms on application for Evening Dinner, Bed and Breakfast or Bed and Breakfast only. Parking. Reductions for children under 12.

KENDAL. Mrs Beresford, Wattsfield Farm Guest House, Wattsfield Lane, off Wattsfield Road, Kendal (Kendal [0539] 27767). Come and enjoy the peaceful atmosphere of a 17th century farmhouse. Situated in pleasant gardens just one mile from historic Kendal town and castle viewpoint. Wattsfield Farm standing on the banks of the River Kent has been carefully restored by the Beresford family. It was once the home of Simpson, Coach Builder to George III. Useful as an overnight stay en route to Scotland or a pleasant base whilst visiting Lakeland. Candle-lit meals with the family by arrangement. Open all year. Bed and Breakfast from £8.00. Some self-catering available.

KENDAL. Mrs Jean Elliott, Town End, Farleton, Holme, Carnforth LA6 1PB (Crooklands [04487] 255). Town End is a 17th century former farmhouse with oak-beams and staircase. Situated in beautiful country surroundings at the foot of Farleton Fell, canal 200 yards. Is readily accessible from M6 Junction 36. Ideal touring centre Lakes/Yorkshire Dales, Morecambe Bay close by; five miles from Carnforth Steam Town. There are two double bedrooms with washbasins and one single bedroom. There is a shower room and dining and sitting room with TV. Parking space as a car is essential. A garden to enjoy on summer evenings. Evening Meal if required, bedtime drinks. Good home cooking. Sorry no pets. Evening Meal, Bed and Breakfast from £9.75; Bed and Breakfast from £6.50. Reduced rates for children.

KENDAL. Mrs Catherine E. Packham, Docker Hall, Docker, Kendal LA8 0DB (Grayrigg [053-984] 216). Working farm. Docker Hall is a 385-acre dairy and sheep farm situated three-and-a-half miles from M6 (Junction 37); three miles north-east of Kendal and Leisure Centre. Ideal base for touring the Lakes, Dales, Borders and Coast. The farmhouse is set in peaceful countryside with many local walks. Guests are assured of a warm welcome with plenty of home cooking. Accommodation consists of two double and one family bedrooms, all with washbasins; bathroom and toilet. Dining/sittingroom with tea-making facilities. Colour TV. Central heating. Children welcome — cot, high chair and babysitting; reduced rates for children under eight years and for weekly bookings. Parking. Open March to November. SAE, please, for terms for Bed and Breakfast.

KENDAL. Mrs A. M. Harper, Hutton Park, New Hutton, Kendal LA8 0AY (Kendal [0539] 20565). Working farm. Holidays can be enjoyed in a homely atmosphere on this 390-acre mixed farm where plenty of excellent home cooked food is served — beef, lamb, chicken etc., sherry trifle, strawberries and cream when in season. A different set meal each evening. Full English Breakfast. Two double, one family rooms; two bathrooms (one with shower), two toilets. Sittingroom with TV; diningroom. Within easy reach of Lake District, Yorkshire Dales and coast. Numerous castles, Halls and Houses to visit within 20 mile radius. Horse-riding three miles. One and a half miles from M6 Motorway (Junction 37). Bed and Breakfast, Evening Dinner (optional). Regret, no pets. Open March to November. SAE, please.

KENDAL. Mrs E. Robinson, Park End Farm, Brigsteer, Near Kendal LA8 8AS (Sedgwick [0448] 60641). Working farm. 'Park End Farm' is situated amidst beautiful surroundings in an elevated yet sheltered position overlooking the 'Kent Estuary' and the 'Lythe Valley', famous for its damsons; only two-and-a-half miles from Junction 36 and the M6 motorway, an ideal base for touring the 'Lake District' and 'Yorkshire Dales'. This charming 16th century farmhouse is one of the oldest in Westmorland, with oak beams and an attractive open fireplace in the diningroom, where excellent home cooking is served at separate tables: roast beef, lamb, turkey and pork; chocolate gateaux, trifles and fruit pies all served with fresh cream. These are only a few of the delicious meals served by Mrs Robinson and her daughter. Guests return yet again to enjoy the comfortable, relaxed and friendly atmosphere. Lounge with open fires and colour TV. Two double bedrooms and one twin-bedded room, bathroom with toilet. Ample parking space. Special reductions for senior citizens. Awarded the 'Farm Holiday Guides Diploma' for providing holiday accommodation of the highest standard. Highly recommended. Open Easter to end October for Bed and Breakfast only or Evening Dinner, Bed and Breakfast. SAE brings prompt reply.

KENDAL. Mrs Marjorie Hoggarth, Low Hundhowe Farm, Burneside, Kendal LA8 9AB (Kendal [0539] 22060). Working farm. Low Hundhowe Farm, with its comfortable 17th century farmhouse offers a quiet and peaceful holiday. Open all year, the accommodation comprises two double, one twin bedded rooms, all with washbasins, tea making facilities and electric blankets; bathroom and toilet; sittingroom; diningroom with separate tables. Colour TV. Central heating. Children welcome. Sorry, no pets. Car essential; ample parking. Low Hundhowe is a family run 235-acre working farm and the well furnished farmhouse makes an ideal touring base for the Lake District; Kendal four miles; Windermere five miles. SAE, please, for terms for Evening Dinner, Bed and Breakfast from £11 or Bed and Breakfast from £7.50. Packed lunches. Children half price.

KENDAL. Mrs A. E. Bell, Hill Fold Farm, Burneside, Kendal LA8 9AU (Kendal [0539] 22574). Working farm. Hill Fold Farm is situated three miles north of Kendal, close to rolling hills of Potter Fell, with many quiet walks within easy reach of Lakes and sea. Genuine working farm over 200 acres; dairy and sheep. One double and two family rooms with washbasins, heaters and shaving points. Sittingroom; diningroom; bathroom, toilet. Cot and babysitting; reduced rates under 12 years. Wholesome meals served. Evening can be spent enjoying local entertainments, strolling by the river or simply lounging by the cosy log fire and watching colour TV. Car essential, parking. Open January to December. Evening Meal, Bed and Breakfast. Reduced rates for children and Senior Citizens. Sorry, no pets. Comprehensive literature available on the surrounding areas, etc. Terms on request.

KENDAL. Mrs Sylvia Beaty, Garnett House Farm, Burneside, Kendal LA9 5SF (Kendal [0539] 24542). Working farm. An AA and RAC listed 15th-century farmhouse on large dairy/sheep farm situated half a mile from A591 (Kendal/Windermere road). Two doubles, one twin, two family bedrooms with washbasins, shaver points and tea-making facilities. Bathroom, shower room, two toilets; 16th century panelling and four foot thick walls in colour TV lounge. Diningroom with separate tables for full English Breakfast and five-course Dinner using home produced beef, lamb, meringues, trifles, gateaux etc. Child reductions, cot, high chair, babysitting. Parking, but car not essential; walking distance to shops, inn, bus stops and railway station. Fire Certificate. Scrabble players welcome. Open all year for Bed and Breakfast from £7.50; Dinner, Bed and Breakfast from £11.

KENDAL. Mrs Helen Batty, Selside Hall Farm, Selside, Kendal LA8 9LA (Selside [053-983] 228). Working farm. A homely atmosphere exists in this 14th century farmhouse on 250-acre family run mixed farm. Five miles through Kendal on A6 and 10 miles approximately from centre of Lake District. Kendal itself has much to interest the holidaymaker, including the earthworks of the 12th century castle and the Perpendicular Church of Holy Trinity. One double and one family bedroom; bathroom, toilet; sittingroom; diningroom. Children welcome, reduced rates for those under 11 years. Cot available. Sorry, no pets. A car is essential as there is no public transport. Parking for four cars. Open April to September for Evening Meal, Bed and Breakfast from £10; Bed and Breakfast from £7.

KENDAL. Mrs Emma Ladds, Benson Hall Farm, Kendal (Kendal [0539] 21419). Old-world farmhouse, steeped in history, has been modernised for comfort with fitted carpets throughout. A Peel Tower, Priest Hole and a spiral stairway are just a few of the features of interest to visitors. Situated five miles from the M6 at Junction 37, Benson Hall is quiet and secluded with beautiful views of lakes and hills. Close to Yorkshire Dales, Kendal, Windermere and the seaside resort of Morecambe 20 miles. Warm welcome and good food assured. One double, two family and two single rooms; bathroom, two toilets; sittingroom, diningroom. Children welcome. Cot, high chair, babysitting and reduced rates for the under 13's offered. Regret, no dogs. Open May to November. Bed and four-course Breakfast from £6.50. Snack in the evening at no extra charge. Car preferable — ample parking.

BOARD Cumbria

**KENDAL. Mrs Margaret Hodgson, Patton Hall Farm, Kendal LA8 9DT (Kendal [0539] 21590).
Working farm.** Patton Hall is a 200-acre sheep and dairy farm with its own length of river for fishing. Guests are free to wander on the farmland, and to ask questions about farming. A weekly slide show is given of local views and life on the farm. Morecambe is 25 miles away. Windermere 12 miles. The farmhouse is heated by log fires and electric heating in cold weather. Bedrooms comprise one double, one twin and one family (two with washbasins); bathroom, toilet; sitting-room with TV; diningroom. Children are welcome at reduced rates if sharing parents' room. Mrs Hodgson can provide cot and arrange babysitting. Comfort and good food are assured. Bed and Breakfast from £6.75; Dinner, Bed and Breakfast from £10. Bedtime drink for adults. Car essential — parking. Open March to November. SAE, please.

KENDAL. Mrs A. Taylor, Russell Farm, Burton-in-Kendal, Carnforth, Lancs. LA6 1NN (Burton [0524] 781334). Working farm. Why not spend a few days at Russell Farm? The proprietors pride themselves in trying to give guests an enjoyable holiday with good food, friendly atmosphere, relaxing surroundings away from the hustle and bustle. The 150 acre dairy farm is set in a quiet hamlet one mile from the village of Burton in Kendal, and five miles from the old market town of Kirkby Lonsdale. An ideal centre for touring Lakes and Yorkshire dales, or going to the coast. Horse riding is available nearby. Two double, one single and one family bedrooms; bathroom, toilet; sittingroom and diningroom. Children welcome; cot, high chair and babysitting offered. Pets accepted, if well-behaved. Open from February to November (inclusive) for Evening Dinner, Bed and Breakfast or Bed and Breakfast. Reductions for children. Parking for essential car. SAE, please, for terms.

KENDAL near. Mrs Joan E. Salkeld, High Fold Farm, Kentmere, Near Kendal LA8 9JP (Staveley [0539] 821531). Working farm. High Fold is a 17th century farmhouse commanding panoramic views of the secluded Kent Valley and the magnificent Kentmore Fells. The farm has sheep and Friesian cattle, on 560-acres of farmland. Ideal centre for walking, fishing or touring the Lakes. The house has been modernised and has two family bedrooms, one double room; dining/sittingroom; bathroom and toilet. Electric heating. Car essential — parking space. Sorry, no pets. Children welcome. Cot and babysitting. Open from March to October for Evening Meal, Bed and Breakfast from £9; Bed and Breakfast from £7 per person per day. Reductions for children under 12 years. Also furnished cottage to let.

KENDAL near. Mrs Olive M. Knowles, Cragg Farm, New Hutton, Near Kendal LA8 0BA (Kendal [0539] 21760). Working farm. Cragg Farm is a 260-acre farm with cows, sheep, dogs, cats and chickens. It is conveniently situated two-and-a-half miles from M6, junction 37. The 17th century farmhouse is tastefully modernised yet retaining its old world character. Guests return to enjoy comfort, cleanliness and good home cooking. Mrs Knowles serves local farm produce such as roast beef, chicken and pork. Sweets include sherry trifle, chocolate gateaux, cheesecake and fruit pie and cream, all home made. Nearby you can go horse riding, fell walking or visit historic buildings. In Kendal you can enjoy sporting facilities at the Leisure Centre. Car essential, parking. Open April to October. Children welcome, cot and babysitting. Evening Dinner, Bed and Breakfast or Bed and Breakfast only. SAE, please, for particulars. Reduced rates for children. There is also a six-berth holiday caravan to let. Situated on its own site with parking space. Fully equipped, TV, fridge, electricity, water.

KENDAL near. Mrs D. Harrison, South Gateside, Selside, near Kendal LA8 9JX (Selside [053-983] 214). This delightful south facing farmhouse situated 100 yards from the A6 Kendal to Penrith road has magnificent views over the surrounding countryside. Good approach road, ample parking space; a convenient base from which to tour Lakeland. Many guests return year after year to this comfortable house where all are made welcome and good food is served. Two double, two family and one single bedrooms, all have heaters, washbasins, tea/coffee making facilities and shaver sockets. Shower/bathroom, two toilets; sittingroom (TV) and diningroom, both with fires. Reductions for children sharing parents' bedroom; cot, high chair. Open Easter to October. Car essential. No pets. Fire Certificate held. Evening Dinner, Bed and Breakfast or Bed and Breakfast only. SAE, please. Sporting facilities at Kendal, Windermere and Bowness.

KESWICK. Mrs J. M. Davis, The Mount, Portinscale, Keswick CA12 5RD (Keswick [0596] 73070). This Guest House is set in the quiet village of Portinscale and is small but friendly. At the Mount the accommodation for our guests is in one double and one family bedrooms, both with own shower/toilet/washbasins, and one double and one single bedrooms with washbasins. We are open from March to November with full central heating and there are tea-making facilities in all rooms. Children welcome (reduced rates) and pets are allowed. The house has lovely views overlooking Derwentwater. There is a lounge with colour TV and a separate diningroom. Public bathroom and toilet. Car is not essential, but there is a private car park at the rear. Dinner, Bed and Breakfast or Bed and Breakfast only offered. SAE, please, for terms or telephone.

KESWICK. Brian and Marion Watterson, Avondale, 20 Southey Street, Keswick CA12 4EF (Keswick [0596] 72735). Avondale is a small comfortable guest house close to Town Centre, Park, Lake and public transport. A good centre for touring, owners are County Trust and RSPB members, and can offer local knowledge to walkers and bird watchers. Open all year. Good food and a friendly welcome are guaranteed. Double, twin, family and single rooms available. All rooms have central heating, hot and cold, teamakers. Guests have own keys and access at all times. Lounge; separate diningroom. Children and well-behaved dogs welcome. Fire Certificate. Bed, Breakfast and Evening Dinner or Bed and Breakfast. Terms on request.

Cumbria BOARD

KESWICK. Mr and Mrs M. J. Popple, Skiddaw Grove Hotel, Vicarage Hill, Keswick CA12 5QB (Keswick [0596] 73324). Skiddaw Grove is a warm and comfortable family hotel enjoying magnificent views of Skiddaw and the Bassenthwaite Valley. Situated in a quiet location Skiddaw Grove is convenient for all local amenities — the ideal centre from which to walk the fells, sail on the lake, tour the passes, or simply relax by our private swimming pool. All bedrooms, many with private bathrooms, are heated and have hot and cold. Children are welcome and full details of reductions are available on request. Our excellent cuisine is complemented by a good selection of wines and an after-dinner drink may be enjoyed in our cosy bar lounge. Car parking available. Open all year. AA*. Class Winner in the 1984 Keswick Daffodil Festival.

**MR & MRS I. ATKINSON, LYZZICK HALL HOTEL, NEAR KESWICK, CUMBRIA CA12 4PY
Tel: Keswick (0596) 72277**

A charming country house hotel with magnificent panoramic views of the Newlands Valley and Derwent Falls, set in spacious grounds on the southern foot of Skiddaw Mountain. Inside, the charm and character are not lost; there is a large comfortable lounge for peace and quiet, spacious TV lounge and a pleasant, welcoming diningroom. Residential Licence. Below is Cellar Bar with "away from it all" atmosphere. Set well away from road noise with large lawns and an outdoor swimming pool. Ideal for family or quiet holidays. The bedrooms, mostly first floor, are well appointed, with modern divans, washbasins, many with showers. Ample bathroom and toilet facilities. Central heating throughout. Extensive car park. Boating, fishing, golf etc. in the area, plus many pleasant walks. SAE, please, for terms and further details.

KESWICK. Mrs V. A. Trafford, Peter House Farm, Bassenthwaite, Keswick CA12 4QX (Bassenthwaite Lake [059-681] 278). Working farm. Peter House Farm is an ideal centre for touring the Lake District. Built in 1692, the farm is set amidst lovely views of Skiddaw and other fells, woodlands and Bassenthwaite Lake. There are pleasant walks by footpaths and lanes into Bassenthwaite village and into the peaceful recesses of the fells. The superb cascades of Dash Falls are about one and half miles away. Pony trekking is available nearby. Lounge and Dining Room available for guests. Children and pets are welcome. Choice of family or double bedrooms with hot and cold. A warm and personal welcome to this working hill farm is assured by the family. Terms — Bed and Breakfast from £5; reductions for children. Evening Meals by arrangement.

KESWICK. Mr Brian Smith, Kiln Hill Barn, Bassenthwaite, Keswick CA12 4RG (Bassenthwaite Lake [059-681] 454). Accommodation in Lakeland farmhouse, ideal for family holidays in relaxed informal surroundings. Delightful rural situation between Keswick and Cockermouth, just off A591 main road. Enjoying superb views to Skiddaw and Bassenthwaite Lake, the house has central heating and log fire. Games and diningroom in converted barn. Open all year, the accommodation comprises one single, one twin and four family bedrooms, with washbasins; two bathrooms, three toilets; sittingroom, diningroom. Children welcome, cot provided. Sorry, no pets. Car not essential, the house is on a good bus route, but there is ample parking. Walking, fishing and riding nearby. Evening Meal, Bed and Breakfast from £12; Bed and Breakfast from £8.50. Reductions for children.

KESWICK. Mrs Audrey M. Hodgson, Kevley, 10 Southey Street, Keswick CA12 4EF (Keswick [0596] 73455). A small, comfortable guest house where good food and cleanliness are guaranteed. Situated conveniently for shops and parks and 10 minutes' walk from the Lake. All bedrooms heated, have hot and cold water, and all beds with spring interior mattresses and electric blankets. There is colour TV lounge where guests can relax anytime. Packed lunches are available on request. A light supper served at 10.15 pm. Two double bedrooms, one family room, all with washbasins; bathroom, two toilets; sittingroom; diningroom. Sorry, no pets. Car not essential but parking space. Fire Certificate granted. Evening Meal, Bed and Breakfast or Bed and Breakfast only. SAE, please, or telephone for terms.

RICKERBY GRANGE, Portinscale, Keswick CA12 5RH
Tel. 0596 72344

Rickerby Grange is delightfully situated in the quiet village of Portinscale, a fifteen minute scenic stroll to Keswick. It is a licensed residence surrounded by its own pretty gardens with ample private parking. A comfortable home with an enthusiastic family serving imaginative home cooked meals in an attractive but informal diningroom. A cosy bar and TV lounge complete the picture. Guests' rooms with or without private facilities as the budget will allow. Open all year. Special New Year break. AA Listed. E.T.B. & 'Guest-accom' member. Colour brochure sent with pleasure. Tel: Rodney or Margaret Roper. Keswick (0596) 72344.

KESWICK. Mrs Jean Ray, Applethwaite Farm, Applethwaite, Keswick CA12 4PN (Keswick [0596] 72608). The 17th century oak-beamed farmhouse is situated in lovely quiet village at the foot of Skiddaw, one and a half miles from Keswick. Three guest bedrooms all with washbasins and electric blankets when required. Lounge with open fire and TV. Home cooking with local produce. Ample parking space. Ideal centre for touring, walking, pony trekking and all lakeland pursuits. Sorry, no pets. Bed and Breakfast or Bed, Breakfast and Evening Meal. Telephone or SAE for terms and photograph. Open all year.

KESWICK. Mr David A. Davenport, "Greystones", Ambleside Road, Keswick CA12 4DP (Keswick [0596] 73108). "Greystones" is a quietly situated traditional Lakeland house giving excellent views of the Fells, and is within a five minute walk of the Lake, town and parks. All rooms are centrally heated with hot and cold, plus tea making facilities. Some rooms have full en suite showers and WC. We pride ourselves on high quality of fresh home-made food, the preparation and cooking of which is personally supervised. We are ideally situated whatever type of holiday you require, with advice on walks and motoring routes readily available. Greystones is recommended by Hunter Davies in the Good Guide to the Lakes. We are licensed, and supply packed lunches on request.

KESWICK. Mr and Mrs L. & S. A. Duncan, "Dolly Waggon", 17 Helvellyn Street, Keswick (Keswick [0596] 73593). Clean, homely, friendly Guest House, open all day where guests have their own bedroom and front door keys. Good plain traditional cooking, English Tourist Board category 3. Near to town, parks and lake. Central for fell walking, climbing, boating, pony trekking or just a relaxing holiday. Rambling parties made welcome. Drying room for clothes. Spacious accommodation in every room; own table in diningroom; colour TV in lounge. Log fire in winter. Only two minutes' walk from bowling green. Short guided walks undertaken by arrangement. Children welcome. Car not essential, but there is parking. Only 15 minutes to bus station. Evening Dinner/Meal, Bed and Breakfast from £12.50; Bed and Breakfast from £8.50. Reduced rates (half) for children under eight. Reduced rates for pensioners. Open all year.

KESWICK. Mrs H. Scrimgeour, Lonscale Farm, Brundholme, Keswick (Threlkeld [059-683] 603). Working farm. Attractive 19th-century farmhouse built on 1,000 acre working sheep farm. Situated on Skiddaw and commanding beautiful views down the valley. We are under three miles from Keswick with its many amenities. Our local lakes are Derwentwater and Bassenthwaite, and the farm has various delightful hill walks including the Forge Brow. Well located for touring. Accommodation consists of two double bedrooms; bathroom; dining/sittingroom. Bed and Breakfast (reduced weekly rates). Open May-October.

KESWICK. Mrs M. A. Relph, Little Town Farm, Newlands, Keswick CA12 5TU (Braithwaite [059-682] 353). Working farm. Little Town Farm is a 150-acre mixed farm, mainly beef and sheep, standing at the bottom of Catbells. Lots of easy walks or hard fell walking within easy reach. Ideally situated for a holiday in the Lake District, in a nice peaceful part of Newlands Valley, approximately two miles from Derwentwater Lake, five miles Keswick. Farm is mentioned in Beatrix Potter's "Mrs Tiggy Winkle". Open April to end October. Children welcome at reduced rates sharing parents' room. Two double, two family and one twin bedrooms all with radiators; tea-making facilities; four with washbasins; bathroom, toilets; sitting and diningrooms. Evening Dinner, Bed and Breakfast or Bed and Breakfast. Terms on request with SAE, please. Car preferable. Parking.

KESWICK. Mr and Mrs J. W. Bunce, Lynwood, 12 Ambleside Road, Keswick CA12 4DL (Keswick [0596] 72081). Lynwood is a friendly, 130-year-old guest house in the heart of the Lake District, quietly situated five minutes' walk from town centre and 10 minutes' walk from the Lakeside. All our bedrooms have tea/coffee makers, electric blankets, hot and cold water and shaver points. Access at all times. Lynwood has full central heating. Fire Certificate. AA and RAC listed. We have a comfortable colour TV lounge. Home cooking is our speciality and our diningroom has separate tables and a wine licence. Your comfort is our priority. A warm welcome awaits you. Sorry, no pets. Colour brochure, tariff and details on request.

104 Cumbria BOARD

KESWICK. Mrs M. M. Beaty, Birkrigg Farm, Newlands, Keswick CA12 5TS (Braithwaite [0596-82] 278). Working farm. Birkrigg is a dairy cattle and sheep farm pleasantly and peacefully situated in a valley surrounded by mountains. Ideal for walking and climbing. Five miles from Keswick and three from Buttermere. A mini-bus service operates between the two, passing farm several times daily. A car is essential if wishing to tour the many beauty spots. Parking space. Clean, comfortable accommodation comprises one single, two double and two family bedrooms, all with washbasins, shaver points. Bathroom, toilet; sittingroom with colour TV, diningroom. Good meals assured. Children welcome at reduced rates. Bed and Breakfast. Evening dinners available five nights of the week. Evening tea 10 pm. Open late March/early November. Fire Certificate held. Terms on request. SAE, please.

KESWICK. Mr and Mrs L. W. Dickinson, Swinside Lodge, Newlands, Keswick CA12 5UE (Keswick [0596] 72948). Enjoy a break away from the everyday pressures in the relaxed and friendly atmosphere of Swinside Lodge, a Victorian house set in its own grounds at the foot of Catbells. Comfortable accommodation with full central heating, the house offers seven double and one family bedrooms with washbasins, shaver points, bedside lights; two bedrooms en suite. Three bathrooms, three toilets. Lounge with colour TV. Diningroom with separate tables. Excellent home cooking. Log fires. Car essential — ample parking space. An ideal touring and walking centre — three miles from Keswick, five minutes' walk from the shores of Derwentwater. Fire Certificate held. Sorry, no pets. Open January to November for Bed and Breakfast, or Bed, Breakfast and Evening Meal. Reductions for children. Terms and further details on request.

KESWICK. Mrs M. Houldershaw, White Stones, Underskiddaw, Keswick CA12 4QD (Keswick [0596] 72762). Mrs Margaret Houldershaw offers you a warm welcome to this large old country bungalow, set in beautiful gardens with panoramic view of Newlands and Derwent Fells, two and a half miles from Keswick, set back from the main road to Carlisle. We have two double and one family rooms, all with washbasins, shaving points and tea and coffee facilities. One toilet, one bathroom with shower. Spacious dining room, lounge with colour TV. Fully centrally heated. Babysitting available. Flasks filled for walkers; car parking space for tourers and use of the house and gardens for those who just want to relax in quiet surroundings. Open Easter to November. Moderate terms (from £7.00) with reduced rates for children.

KESWICK. Mrs J. Hibbert, Holmwood House, The Heads, Keswick CA12 5ER (Keswick [0596] 73301). HOLMWOOD HOUSE is a well-appointed Guest House offering friendly, personal attention. It is ideally situated in a quiet road and has breathtaking views the length of Lake Derwentwater and the surrounding mountains, yet is only a few minutes' walk from the town centre, parks and lake. Our accommodation comprises two double, two family, two twin-bedded rooms and one single room. Some rooms with private shower. Large lounge with colour TV. Spacious diningroom. Table Licence. Full central heating. You are assured of comfortable rooms and excellent food with generous portions. Children over four years welcome. Regret no pets. Bed and Breakfast. Evening Dinner optional. Brochure and tariff available on request.

KESWICK. Mrs Ruth Edmondson, Stoneycroft, Newlands, Keswick CA12 5TS (Braithwaite [059-682] 240). This converted farmhouse, standing in an elevated, peaceful location and surrounded by superb mountain scenery is reached by taking the A66 to Braithwaite and then the Buttermere via Newlands road. Four double bedrooms, one with private shower; two family bedrooms, two with private bathrooms; one public bathroom; one public toilet; sittingroom and diningroom. Full central heating. Oak beamed lounge, log fire, TV room. Table licence. Children and pets welcome. Car essential; ample parking. Bed and Breakfast from £9.50. Dinner optional. Bargain Breaks. Open March to October. Also two self contained holiday flats. Duvets on all beds but no linen supplied. Slot meter. Good area for walking, touring, fishing, riding. Theatre at Keswick during summer months. Wild life park. SAE, please.

BOARD Cumbria 105

KESWICK near. Mrs Rosalind Hunter, Croft House, Applethwaite, Near Keswick CA12 4PN (Keswick [0596] 73693). Beautifully situated house, enjoying magnificent views of Lakeland mountains, in a lovely quiet village at the foot of Skiddaw, one-and-a-half miles from Keswick. An excellent base for touring all parts of the Lake District, walking, pony trekking and all Lakeland pursuits. A warm welcome is assured and good home cooking a speciality. The comfortable accommodation comprises three double, one single and one family bedrooms, all with washbasins; bathroom, plus shower, two toilets. Sittingroom, diningroom. Children welcome, cot, high chair, babysitting and reduced rates available. Well-behaved pets accepted. Car an advantage — ample parking. SAE, please, or telephone for terms for Bed and Full English Breakfast, or Dinner, Bed and Breakfast. Open all year.

KESWICK near. Ms N. Godfrey-Evans, Coledale Cottage, Braithwaite, Keswick CA12 5TN (Braithwaite [059-682] 475). Enjoy peace and tranquillity in a relaxed atmosphere at this 18th century fellside cottage. Standing in an acre of ground, with superb views in all directions, Coledale is at the edge of Braithwaite village and two-and-a-half miles from Keswick. Three guest rooms (single, twin/double or triple), all with washbasins. Two reception rooms, colour TV, tea and coffee making facilities, log fires. The house and garden are open to visitors all day. Home cooking a speciality. Excellent walking base. Local sightseeing and guided walks available. Parking. Bed and Breakfast from £10. Dinner £6.50. Open all year. Phone or write for brochure.

KESWICK near. Mrs L. C. Edward, The Old Mill, Applethwaite, Near Keswick CA12 4PN (Keswick [0596] 73604). Two miles from Keswick. Magnificent views towards Derwentwater. Elevated charming old house of character set on the slopes of Cumbria's oldest mountain, Skiddaw. The property has been recently renovated to provide an exclusive setting offering comfort and good food in a delightful, peaceful hamlet. The owners have retained the character of the property enhancing it with their tasteful decor. The Old Mill has an open fire in the drawing room complementing the central heating. The delightful fare provided is fast becoming a speciality as both owners are interested in good food. They look forward to meeting you.

KESWICK near. Eleanor and Julian Atkinson, Thornthwaite Hall, Thornthwaite, Near Keswick CA12 5SA (Braithwaite [059-682] 424). Thornthwaite Hall is a traditional 17th century farmhouse modernised and converted into a very comfortable Guest House. It stands in a large garden with a private car park. The quiet and sheltered village is three miles north of Keswick, with wooded fells rising immediately behind, through which there are many walks. Skiddaw rises in full view just across the valley. The house is carpeted and centrally heated throughout. All bedrooms (five double, two single) have washbasins and shaving points. There is a large lounge/diningroom with fine views. Fire Certificate held. Good home cooking with full English breakfast. Evening Dinner, Bed and Breakfast. Open February to November. Brochure and tariff on request.

KESWICK. Mrs P. Fearon, Skelgill Farm, Newlands, Keswick CA12 5UE (Braithwaite [059-682] 367). Working farm. Pleasant farmhouse situated at the foot of Cat-Bells, in an excellent area for walking, has lovely views and is only ten minutes' walk from Lake Derwentwater. The farmhouse is part of 98-acre mixed farm and has three double, one single and one family rooms (three with washbasins); sittingroom; diningroom; bathroom and two toilets. Children welcome and a cot, high chair and babysitting are provided. Pets permitted. Open from April to October the house is heated by electricity and Evening Dinner, Bed and Breakfast or Bed and Breakfast only with reduced rates for children are available. Parking (public transport four miles). SAE, please, for terms.

KESWICK. Mrs D. Cook, Swinside Farm, Newlands, Keswick CA12 5UE (Braithwaite [059-682] 363). Working farm. Swinside Farm is a small dairy and sheep farm with an old world farmhouse completely modernised. Ideally situated at the foot of the Catbells and Causey Pike. Sits on the roadside between Keswick and Newlands Pass, with beautiful views of the surrounding hills. Very good for walking and climbing. Three double bedrooms; dining/sittingroom; bathroom, toilet. Parking space for cars. Children welcome and cot, babysitting and terms according to age. Bed and Breakfast or Bed, Breakfast and Evening Dinner. Open from March to November. Terms on request. Braithwaite and Portinscale two miles; Cockermouth with Wordsworth's birthplace and castle 11 miles; Buttermere five and Borrowdale three; very close to Derwentwater.

PLEASE SEND A STAMPED ADDRESSED ENVELOPE WITH ENQUIRIES

KESWICK. Mrs Jean Tyson, Steps End Farm, Watendlath, Keswick CA12 5UW (Borrowdale [059-684] 245). Working farm. Farmhouse on sheep rearing farm offering holiday accommodation from March to October. Three double bedrooms with washbasins; bathroom, toilet; sittingroom; diningroom. Children welcome, also pets free of charge. Solid fuel and gas heating. Watendlath lies south of Derwentwater, in a picturesque valley, threaded by a beck adjoining the attractive Watendlath tarn, below Armboth Fell (1,588'). Sir Hugh Walpole used the village as a setting in his novel "Rogue Herries". A good touring area and a car is essential. Ample parking. Evening Dinner, Bed and Breakfast or Bed and Breakfast. SAE for terms.

KIRKBY STEPHEN. Mrs J. Atkinson, Augill House Farm, Brough, Kirkby Stephen (Brough [093-04] 305). Working farm. Augill is a 40-acre dairy farm and is ideally situated for the Lakes, Yorkshire Dales, Tees Valley and Hadrian's Wall. The farmhouse is comfortably furnished and is AA recommended. All bedrooms have washbasins, hot and cold water, soap and towels, spring interior mattresses, tea/coffee making facilities. Diningroom; lounge and TV. The house has full central heating — log fire when needed. The food is good and plentiful — beef, lamb, pork and fresh trout are served, and fresh cream desserts. Own milk, cream and eggs (butter and cheese when available); home-made bread. Bed and Breakfast or Bed, Breakfast and five-course Dinner is available. Pets welcome. Ample parking. Open all year except Christmas and New Year. English Tourist Board recommended. Self-catering accommodation also available. Stamp for brochure.

KIRKBY STEPHEN. Mrs C. M. Bainbridge, Bonnygate Farm, Soulby, Kirkby Stephen CA17 4PQ (Kirkby Stephen [0930] 71347). Working farm. Bonnygate Farm is a comfortable spacious old farmhouse on a dairy farm offering Evening Meal, Bed and Breakfast all year round. It is a pleasant place to stay amidst lovely surroundings, near River Eden and within easy reach of the Lake District, Yorkshire Dales and the Pennines. Easy access from M6 and M1. Good walking area, also pony trekking, fishing and golf available. A warm welcome and excellent home cooking awaits all guests. Accommodation in two double and one single bedrooms, all with washbasins; bathroom, two toilets; sittingroom, diningroom. Children welcome at reduced rates. Pets welcome by prior arrangement. SAE, please, or telephone for further details and terms.

Terms quoted in this publication may be subject to increase if rises in costs necessitate

Hollin House Hotel
CHURCH LANE, LORTON, CUMBRIA CA13 9UN
Telephone: Lorton (090-085) 656

Hollin House is a small, friendly, family run licensed hotel set in two acres of wooded grounds on a quiet lane in the beautiful Vale of Lorton, surrounded by the Grasmoor and Loweswater Fells. The Vale leads to the nearby Lakes of Loweswater, Crummock Water and Buttermere. Cockermouth, a quiet market town – the birthplace of William Wordsworth – is three miles away. Hollin House is ideally situated for a walking, fishing, touring or the 'get away from it all' holiday.
A comfortable hotel of character with an enthusiastic family serving a high standard of home cooking – full English breakfast – five course dinner – fine wines – packed lunch if required. Charming and relaxing rooms, fully centrally heated with open fires in the lounge and dining rooms. Variety of bedrooms, including four-poster suite and half-tester suite, most with private bathrooms or shower-rooms, all with washbasins, shaver points and tea making facilities. Drying room. Ample parking. Open March to October inclusive.
Geraldine Hollister and family look forward to welcoming you and making your holiday a happy one. Write or phone for brochure and tariff.

LANGDALE. Mrs M. Wilkinson, Long House, Great Langdale LA22 9JS (Langdale [09667] 222). Traditional Lakeland cottage type house situated in the heart of Lakeland at the foot of the Langdale Pikes and set in lovely, south facing terraced garden of over one acre with direct access on to the fell. Log fires, low beamed ceilings and alcoves with stained glass windows create a cosy atmosphere. Prettily decorated bedrooms with private facilities. Central heating. Reputation for good food, having been previously recommended by Arthur Eperon in "Travellers Britain". Surrounded by many major peaks and lower lying walks and only a short distance to most of Lakeland's lakes and places of interest. No pets or children under nine. SAE, please, for brochure. **Telephone Langdale 09667-222.**

LOWESWATER. Mrs Hayton, Brook Farm, Thackthwaite, Loweswater, Cockermouth CA13 0RP (Lorton [090-085] 606). Working farm. 180-acre stockrearing hill farm. Good centre for walking and touring; Loweswater and Crummock Water two miles; boating, fishing and pony trekking nearby. Guests are assured of a quiet and comfortable holiday, with bedrooms having washbasins, razor points and electric overblankets. Two double rooms, bathroom, toilet; sittingroom. Homely atmosphere and good food. Children welcome at reduced rates. Sorry, no pets. Car essential — parking. Open from May to October for Evening Meal, Bed and Breakfast from £11.50; Bed and Breakfast from £7. Weekly terms Evening Meal, Bed and Breakfast from £77.

MUNGRISDALE. Mr and Mrs David Wood, The Mill, Mungrisdale, Penrith CA11 0XR (Threlkeld * [059-683] 659). Awarded the British Tourist Authority Commendation. AA and RAC listed. Ashley Courtenay recommended. Delightfully situated at the foot of blue/grey crags and soft mountain slopes, in grounds bounded by a stream. This former Mill Cottage (dates 1651) provides 11 comfortable bedrooms, some with private bathrooms and colour TV, and all with tea/coffee making facilities. Residential and Restaurant licence. Our reputation is based on our high standard of freshly prepared appetising food, and a friendly relaxed atmosphere. See also Colour Display Advertisement in this Guide.

MUNGRISDALE. Mrs Ruth Bird, Askew Rigg, Mungrisdale, Penrith CA11 0SZ (Threlkeld [059-683] 638). Working farm. Askew Rigg House, AA Listed, is dated 1649 and has many old oak beams and stone fireplaces with open fires. This listed building is fully modernised yet retains its old world charm. Situated on 200 acre mixed farm where guests are free to participate in farming activities. Approximately half a mile off A66, though in a quiet position with no noise from main road. Penrith 10 miles; Keswick and Ullswater seven. Pony trekking two miles. Children, pets and Senior Citizens very welcome; a warm welcome awaits all. One double, one single and two family bedrooms with tea/coffee-making facilities; bathroom, toilet; sittingroom; diningroom. Cot, high chair and babysitting. Table licence and all home cooking with own produce served. Car essential, parking. Open all year. Evening Meal from £4, Bed and Breakfast only from £6.50. British Routiers Recommended. SAE, please, or telephone for terms.

MUNGRISDALE. Mrs J. M. Tiffin, Wham-Head Farm, Hutton Roof, Mungrisdale, Penrith CA11 0XS (Skelton [085-34] 289). Working farm. Hutton Roof is a peaceful hamlet, half-hour's ride from Lakes and 1,000 feet above sea level. Well-built farmhouse on 126 acre farm, carries Friesian cattle and Swaledale sheep. In John Peel country with easy access to Fells (of special interest to geologists). Golf, pony trekking, heated swimming pool in area. Very warm welcome assured to all guests; good home cooked farmhouse fare, mostly home produced. Children welcome — cot, high chair, babysitting, reduced rates. Pets allowed. Open March-October. Accommodation in two double and two family bedrooms, three with washbasins; bathroom, toilet; sittingroom. Car essential, ample parking. Wham-Head within easy reach of Borders and Scotland. Evening Dinner, Bed and Breakfast from £10.50 daily, £70 weekly; Bed and Breakfast from £7 daily, £45 weekly.

MUNGRISDALE. Mrs O. M. Wilson, High Beckside, Mungrisdale, Penrith CA11 0XR (Threlkeld [059-683] 636). Working farm. A true Cumbrian welcome awaits you at High Beckside Farm, a dairy and hill farm, set in the valley of Mungrisdale by the River Glendermackin, eight miles from Keswick and 10 miles from Penrith. It is ideally situated for touring the Lakes or for a walk in the hills. There is a well furnished comfortable farmhouse where good farmhouse food and home baking is served. One double with washbasin and one family bedrooms, tea and coffee making facilities, bathroom, toilet; sittingroom; diningroom. Children welcome with cot and babysitting offered. Sorry, no pets. Car is essential — parking. Open from May to November with electric heating. Evening Dinner, Bed and Breakfast or Bed and Breakfast only. Reductions for children. SAE, please, for prompt reply.

MUNGRISDALE near. Mrs V. Thompson, 1-2 Town End, Mosedale, Penrith CA11 0XQ (Threlkeld [059-683] 261). Verna and Bryan Thompson welcome you to Mosedale and their country cottage in the hamlet of Mosedale at the foot of Carrock Fell in the secluded Caldew Valley situated within the Lake District National Park. Keswick 12 miles, four miles from A66 road, Ullswater 10 miles. Ideal for walking or touring the Lakes and Border Country. Three double bedrooms with radiators in all rooms. One bathroom, one toilet; sitting/diningroom. Log fires. Excellent home baking, free range eggs and home grown vegetables in season. Tea and cakes served at no extra charge in late evening. Mrs Thompson will also prepare packed lunches on request. Children welcome, cot, high chair and reduced rates for under 10. Pets accepted. Car essential — parking. Open all year for Bed and Breakfast with Evening Meal optional. Mid-week bookings taken. Terms and further details on request. Residential Licence.

PENRITH. Mrs M. R. Taylor, Tymparon Hall, Newbiggin, Stainton, Penrith CA11 0HS (Greystoke [085-33] 236). Working farm. Relax in this charming character farmhouse standing in half-acre of garden on 160-acre mixed farm, combine comfort, home cooking and personal service for an enjoyable holiday. Within easy reach are pony trekking, fell walking, swimming and golf, situated close to M6, Lake Ullswater also Lowther Wild Life Park. Accommodation for guests in two double, two family and one single bedrooms, three have washbasins; two bathrooms, two toilets; sittingroom with colour television; diningroom. Open April/October. Car essential. Evening Dinner, Bed and Breakfast or Bed and Breakfast only.

NUNNERY HOUSE

A wide range of accommodation from luxury rooms en suite to family accommodation, home cooked meals, fully licensed bar, the comfort of open fires, is provided at this 18th century house, built on the site of a Benedictine Nunnery dating from the 12th century, in the lovely Eden Valley. Set in its own grounds at the end of the beautiful Nunnery Walks – two miles of riverside walks along the River Eden, past magnificent waterfalls in the Croglin Gorge. Within easy reach of Lakes, Hadrian's Wall, the Yorkshire Dales. Personal service by the proprietors, in the atmosphere of a country home, make a perfect combination for the ideal holiday. Two sittingrooms; diningroom; bathrooms, toilets. Full central heating. Children and pets welcome. Car essential; ample parking. BARGAIN BREAKS AVAILABLE AUTUMN & SPRING. For brochure and tariff contact JOAN ARMSTRONG, NUNNERY HOUSE, Staffield, Kirkoswald, Penrith, Cumbria CA10 1EU. Tel. Lazonby (076-883) 537.

PENRITH. Mrs Christine Weightman, Near Howe, Mungrisdale, Penrith CA11 0SH (Threlkeld [059-683] 678). Working farm. Farmhouse on 330-acre mixed hill farm, running sheep and beef cattle, overlooking the valley leading to Keswick, nine miles away. One-and-a-half miles off main A66 Keswick road. Golf, bathing, fishing, pony trekking, within easy reach. Three double, three family rooms, with washbasins — two with own shower/toilet/washbasin. Bathroom, two toilets. Sittingroom. Diningroom. Bar (residential licence). Children welcome. Pets allowed. Open all year. Electrically heated. Car essential, parking. Guests are assured of a warm welcome and good food. SAE, please, for terms — Evening Dinner/Meal, Bed and Breakfast or Bed and Breakfast. Reduced rates for children.

PENRITH. Mrs Gillian Dickinson, Seat Farm, Howtown, Penrith CA10 2NA (Pooley Bridge [9936] 208). Lake Ullswater. Seat Farm is a traditional Lakeland hill farm situated beneath Barton Crags and running down to the shores of Ullswater. Bed and Breakfast accommodation in this 18th century farmhouse and tastefully converted granary is comfortably furnished to a high standard with splendid views over the lake, guests' bathroom, oak beams, central heating and TV lounge. We also have for hire modern six-berth caravan with full mains services and uninterrupted views over the lake. Caravan prices from £45 to £90 per week. Bed and Breakfast from £8 (VAT not charged) all of which include access to our private lakeshore.

PENRITH. Mrs Doreen Cameron, Millrigg Farm, Greystoke, Penrith CA11 0UQ (Greystoke [085-33] 336). Working farm. Millrig is a 56-acre farm, having dairy cows, sheep and chickens. Located in a quiet rural setting, the house is about 250 years old with original oak beams in some rooms. A full English Breakfast and a three-course Evening Meal are served with roasts, fruit pies, etc., using a variety of home-produced food. Many sporting facilities within easy reach, a heated swimming pool at Greystoke one-and-a-half miles away; golf, tennis, etc., at Penrith five miles away. The farm is situated four miles from M6 at Penrith and four miles from Ullswater Lake. Accommodation in two family rooms with washbasins; bathroom, toilet; combined sittingroom/diningroom. Facilities for children include cot, high chair and babysitting. Sorry, no pets. Car essential — parking. Open Easter to November for Evening Meal, Bed and Breakfast from £10; Bed and Breakfast from £7 per night. Reductions for children.

BOARD Cumbria 109

PENRITH. Mr D. W. Fowler, The White House, Clifton, Penrith CA10 2EL (Penrith [0768] 65115). *
Set in pleasant gardens, this converted 18th-century farmhouse has spacious rooms, log fire in lounge and central heating throughout. Easy access to the Motorway, Penrith, Ullswater and the Lake District. All bedrooms have washbasins, teamakers, some have private facilities. Good home cooking, bar and separate lounge, guests are encouraged to come and go as they please. See also Colour Display Advertisement in this Guide.

PENRITH. Mrs Mabel Purdham, White House, Blencarn, Penrith CA10 1TX (Culgaith [076888] 682). Once a farmhouse, White House stands in an almost unspoilt farming village, lying under shadow of Cross Fell in wild and beautiful landscape well away from the motorway or trunk road. The house faces south-west towards the Lakes and Cumbrian Mountains with the Pennines in the background. Penrith nine miles; Appleby eight, and the Lakes 12. One family bedroom, with two double beds; bathroom with shower, toilet; combined lounge/diningroom with electric fire and TV. Towels supplied. Parking for cars. Evening Dinner, Bed and Breakfast from £6.

PENRITH. Miss M. E. Miller, Tirril Hall, Tirril, Penrith CA10 2JE (Penrith [0768] 62649). An historic 17th century house conveniently situated about three miles from Ullswater and four miles from the M6. Converted to high standards of comfort (full central and hot and cold in bedrooms), it still retains many original features, stone-mullioned windows, etc. and much of the furniture is antique. Pleasant garden. Tirril is a quiet unspoilt village but a shop, garage and inn cater for most needs. From here the whole of Lakeland can be explored easily and also the Northern Pennines, border country and Roman Wall. Miss Miller welcomes all guests, including overseas visitors. She speaks German and some French. Caravan also available. Terms from £7.50.

Tirril Hall
Penrith 62649

PENRITH. Mr and Mrs P. H. Robinson, Troutbeck Hotel, Troutbeck, Penrith CA11 0SJ (Greystoke [085-33] 243). This small country inn is situated near the junction of the A66-A5091 in the Lake District National Park, ideal for Lake District touring and activities. Pony trekking, boating, fishing, hunting, climbing. A Free House, the inn has a Public Bar offering bar snacks, billiards, etc. Car essential, parking and petrol available. Open all year, central heating, fire certificate. Accommodation comprises two double and three family bedrooms, with washbasins and shower. Tea making equipment offered. Lounge with colour TV. Diningroom, separate tables; bathroom, four toilets. Children welcome, babysitting available. Pets allowed. Bed and Breakfast, Bar Meals. Reductions for children. SAE, please, for terms.

PENRITH near. Mr D. M. Willison, Croft House Farm, Crosby Ravensworth, Near Penrith CA10 3JP (Ravensworth [09315] 286). Small friendly guest house in a small pretty valley on fringe of Lake District and Yorkshire Dales, on the New Westmorland Walk. Six miles from M6. This is a good walking and touring area, ideal for a country holiday. The modernised farmhouse on 100-acre farm offers accommodation with good home cooking all year round. Three double, one single and two family bedrooms; bathroom, two toilets; sittingroom and diningroom. Children are welcome at reduced rates. Pets permitted. A car is essential to make the most of your holiday here and there is ample parking. Evening Dinner/Meal, Bed and Breakfast from £12; Bed and Breakfast from £7.40. SAE, please.

PENRITH via. Mr and Mrs W. A. Leak, Gaisgill Farm, Gaisgill, Tebay, Via Penrith CA10 3UA (Orton [058-74] 634). Working farm. Gaisgill Farm with nine acres pastureland is quietly situated in the small hamlet of Gaisgill yet only one-and-a-quarter miles Exit 38 M6 motorway. The house, dated 1721, has been attractively converted retaining beamed ceiling and mullion windows, and guests are assured of a warm homely atmosphere and Mrs Leak's excellent home cooking. The Howgill Fells await keen walkers but those who prefer to explore by car can find many interesting places in the Lakes, Dales and Borders. Centrally heated and open all year. Three double bedrooms, washbasins; children over seven years. Dogs by arrangement. Parking. SAE please, for terms for Dinner, Bed and Breakfast or Bed and Breakfast only. Reductions for children sharing parents' room.

SATTERTHWAITE. Mrs S. H. Brown, High Dale Park Farm, High Dale Park, Satterthwaite LA12 8LJ (Satterthwaite [022-984] 226). Our farm nestles snugly in the heart of Grizedale Forest situated between Lake Windermere and Coniston Water. Dale Park Beck runs through our long garden which accommodates our hens, geese, etc. Around us is magnificent, deciduous woodland containing a wealth of wildlife: deer, red squirrels, owls and a wide variety of birds. A drive down our lane brings you to Hawkshead, three miles away. In the opposite direction, Cumbria's famous "Theatre in the Forest" is a mere 15 minutes' drive. If you love Lakeland's peace but hate its crowds, you will love our 17th century farmhouse where we do all our own whole food cooking. A paradise in all seasons. Open all year.

SEDBERGH. Mrs Rosemary Harper, Ghyll Farm, Sedbergh LA10 5LJ (Sedbergh [0587] 20528). Working farm. Ghyll Farm is situated in a super elevated position with good views, half mile off the A683 to Kirkby Stephen, one mile from the small market town of Sedbergh. It is a family farm where guests are invited to join the family or can be peaceful in their own sittingroom. Five miles from M6 it is an ideal resting place from North to South or a holiday in general. In easy reach of Lake District, Yorkshire Dales and Morecambe Bay, and excellent for walking. A comfortable bed and excellent breakfast provided in this comfortable and well furnished oak-beamed farmhouse which has one double room and one family room. Children welcome (reduced rates if under eight). Sorry, no pets. Open all year. Car essential, parking. Terms from £6.50 per night which includes light supper of home made scones and cakes. If you are interested just ring, write or call. Warm welcome assured. Also large static caravan for hire.

Please note that entries marked with an asterisk also have a colour display advert in the colour section in this guide

THE FARM HOUSE, CHURCH STILE FARM, NETHER WASDALE, SEASCALE, CUMBRIA CA20 1ET
Mrs R. Knight. Telephone Wasdale (094-06) 252

The farmhouse, being several hundred years old, and of mixed periods, has character and charm as well as being tastefully decorated and centrally heated. All rooms have tea/coffee making facilities. Comfortable seating areas with BW televisions. Towels provided. High class home cooking to complement the attractive surroundings and superb Lakeland views. Excellent area for fell walking and climbing. **Family room with double bed, two single beds and cot; double room and single room.** TOURIST BOARD APPROVED.

SHAP. Mr and Mrs D. L. and M. Brunskill, Brookfield, Shap, Penrith CA10 3PZ (Shap [093-16] 397).

AA listed. Fire Certificate granted. Situated one mile from M6 Motorway (turn off at Shap interchange No. 39), first accommodation off motorway. Excellent position for touring Lakeland, or overnight accommodation for travelling north or south. Central heating throughout, renowned for good food, comfort and personal attention. All bedrooms are well appointed, with washbasins. Diningroom where delicious home cooking is a speciality. Well stocked bar. Residents' lounge (colour TV). Sorry, no pets. Open from February to December. Terms sent on request. Car essential — ample parking.

For the Mutual Guidance of Guest and Host

Farm Holiday Guides Ltd. do not inspect or recommend accommodation but advertisers agree to accept our Farm Holiday Guide standards of comfortable and clean accommodation and wholesome and well-cooked food. Advertisers are also bound by the Trades Description Act.

When accommodation has been booked, deposits sent, and letters of acceptance exchanged, both parties – host and guest – have entered into a binding contract.

Friends and families can easily be upset and much bitterness caused if holiday arrangements are not carefully made. The following points can be of real importance:

Guest When enquiring about accommodation, be as precise as possible. Give exact dates, numbers in your party and the ages of any children. State the number and type of rooms wanted and also what catering you require – bed and breakfast, full board etc. Make sure that the position about evening meals is clear – and about pets, reductions for children or any other special points.

Read our reviews carefully to ensure that the proprietors you are going to contact can supply what you want. Ask for a letter confirming all arrangements, if possible.

Host Give details about your facilities and about any special conditions. Explain your deposit system clearly and arrangements for cancellations, charges etc, and whether or not your terms include VAT.

We regret that Farm Holiday Guides cannot accept responsibility for any errors or omissions in descriptions. Prices in particular should be checked before booking because of the early compilation of the Guides, far ahead of the next holiday season.

THIRLMERE. Mr J. Hodgson, Stybeck Farm, Thirlmere, Keswick CA12 4TN (Keswick [0596] 73232). Working farm. This farm is situated in the beautiful Thirlmere valley at the foot of the Helvellyn Range of mountains. It is both central for touring and walking. A warm welcome awaits you with good farmhouse food on this hill farm. Three double, one single and one family bedrooms (three with washbasins); two bathrooms, two toilets; sittingroom and diningroom. Children welcome at reduced rates. Sorry, no pets. Open from January to December; mid-week bookings accepted. Car essential — parking. SAE, please, for Tariff. Evening Dinner (optional), Bed and Breakfast. Flasks filled and wet clothes dried. British Relais Routiers recommended.

TROUTBECK. Mrs C. S. Fellows, Lane Head Farm, Troutbeck, Penrith CA11 0SY (Threlkeld ✻ [059-683] 220). Working farm. Charming 17th century, typical Lakeland farmhouse situated 250 yards from main A66 midway between Penrith and Keswick. Outstanding panoramic views of Lakeland countryside with an attractive garden. The house has been tastefully decorated throughout but retaining its old-world character. Attractive lounge with colour TV and a separate sittingroom. Large diningroom where an extremely high standard of cuisine is maintained — large Breakfast and five-course Evening Dinner, prepared from local home-fed produce. Selected wine list and small well-stocked bar will add to your enjoyment and relaxation. Choice of bedrooms (three en suite, one with four-poster bed), all have washbasins and shaver points. Central heating. Car essential — ample parking. Children welcome at reduced rates, cot, high chair. Open March to November. See also Colour Display Advertisement in this Guide.

TROUTBECK (Windermere). Mrs M. Tyson, Troutbeck Park, Troutbeck, Windermere LA23 1PS (Ambleside [0966] 33398). This 2574-acre hill farm, one mile off the main road, situated at the head of the Troutbeck Valley, was once owned and farmed by Beatrix Potter who bequeathed it to the National Trust. A beautiful place with an abundance of wild life, flowers, plants and a large selection of animals. A very peaceful and relaxing place for a holiday yet within easy reach of all amenities. Trout and salmon fishing in season. Pony trekking one-and-a-half miles away. A family room with two double and one single beds available. Bathroom, toilet; combined sitting/diningroom. Children welcome at reduced rates; cot provided and babysitting whenever possible. Sorry, no pets. Open from Easter to November. Car essential — parking. SAE, please, for terms for Bed and Breakfast.

ULVERSTON near. Mrs M. Irving, Riddingside Farm, Colton, Greenodd, Near Ulverston LA12 8HF (Greenodd [022-986] 336). Working farm. Riddingside Farm is pleasantly situated in the Rusland Valley only five miles from the sea. It is a 110-acre mixed dairy farm with Friesian cows and sheep. Ideally situated for touring the Lakes, being six miles from Windermere and seven from Coniston. Your every comfort is assured in the farmhouse which has three double and one family bedrooms; bathroom and toilet; dining and sittingroom. Colour TV. Children welcome, cot, high chair, babysitting. Sorry, no pets. Open Easter to October. Car essential, parking. Ulverston swimming pool four miles. Plentiful food. Evening Dinner, Bed and Breakfast or Bed and Breakfast only. SAE, please, for terms. Reductions for children under 14.

WINDERMERE. Mrs Eileen Tuer, Common Farm, Windermere LA23 1JQ (Windermere [096-62] 3433). Working farm. Common Farm is a 160-acre dairy farm, with its picturesque 17th-century farmhouse, set in peaceful surroundings, a short distance from the main road (A591), with Windermere village just three-quarters of a mile away, and offers clean comfortable accommodation and good home cooking. With its superb views of the Langdale Pikes and Orrest Head, it is an ideal base for touring the Lake District. Accommodation comprises two double and one family bedrooms (all with washbasins); bathroom/shower, toilet. Sittingroom with tea-making facilities. Colour TV. Central heating. Sorry, no pets. Parking. Reduced rates for children sharing parents' room. Open March to December. Bed and Breakfast. Special weekly terms £50 per person. SAE, please.

WINDERMERE. Mr and Mrs Hartley, South View, Cross Street, Windermere LA23 1AE (Windermere [096 62] 2951). Noted for good food and friendly service, South View is central for all facilities but also very quiet. Comfortable lounge. Colour TV. Full central heating. Tea/coffee making facilities in all bedrooms, some with private facilities. No hidden extras. Personal attention ensured. Ideal for access to the rest of the Lake District.

The information in the entries in this guide is presented by the publishers in good faith and after the signed acceptance by advertisers that they will uphold the high standards associated with FARM HOLIDAY GUIDES LIMITED. The publishers do not accept responsibility for any inaccuracies or omissions or any results thereof. Before making final holiday arrangements readers should confirm the prices and facilities directly with advertisers.

Boston House

RAC Listed
A Lakeland Guest House

This attractive, tastefully furnished Victorian Guest House, listed as being of architectural interest, occupies an elevated position on the edge of Windermere village with views of surrounding hills. There are six bedrooms, all heated and with tea and coffee making facilities, three with private showers. The sitting room has colour TV and an assortment of books and games, with open fires early and late season. Sheila and Trevor place great emphasis on providing good food and personal attention in a relaxed and informal atmosphere. They extend a warm welcome to old friends and look forward to meeting new ones in this their fourteenth season. Children are welcome. Pets by arrangement. There is ample private parking; a car is not however essential as guests are met on arrival at bus or rail point. Windermere is an excellent centre for touring by car or coach. Weekly terms, Bed and Breakfast £49 low season, £7.75 daily. Dinner £5.50. Reductions for pensioners on weekly terms low season and for children sharing with adults. Please ask for colour brochure.

Resident Proprietors Sheila and Trevor Holmes, The Terrace, Windermere, Cumbria LA23 1AJ. Tel. (09662) 3654.

WINDERMERE. Mr D. J. Limbrey, Glenburn, New Road, Windermere LA23 2EE (Windermere [09662] 2649). Elegant family run guest house — tastefully decorated and furnished. Double, single and family bedrooms all with washbasins and most with colour TV. Lounge with open fireplace. Licensed, and delicious home cooking. Open all year with central heating. Car not essential, but there is parking. It is a 15 minute walk to the lake, ideal for exploring Lakeland. Riding, fishing, golf within easy distance. Collection from railway station (free). Children welcome and pets allowed. Mini-breaks from mid-October to mid-May. Evening Meal, Bed and Breakfast from £16.50; Bed and Breakfast from £9.00. Rates reduced for children and senior citizens.

✱ **WINDERMERE. Mr and Mrs A. and S. L. Tasker, Oakthorpe Hotel, High Street, Windermere LA23 1AF (Windermere [09662] 3547).** AA and RAC Oakthorpe Hotel, a listed building, is located within the heart of Lakeland, only two minutes' walk from railway station and buses. An ideal centre for visiting the whole of the National Park with excellent facilities locally for walking, boating and fishing. A warm welcome guaranteed to all by resident proprietors. Accommodation includes two lovely lounges; comfortably furnished bedrooms, individually heated. There are four family rooms and eight rooms with private facilities. Twenty bedrooms in all each with tea and coffee making equipment. Cot, high chair and babysitting available. Ample parking. Best of traditional and Continental cooking served in our restaurant. Evening Dinner, Bed and Breakfast from £20 to £25. Bed and Breakfast £12 to £17. Weekly terms available. See also Display Advertisement in Colour Section of this Guide.

CUMBRIA – LAKELAND SPLENDOUR!

The Lake District has for long been a popular tourist destination; however, the Fells and Pennine areas are also worth exploring. The many attractions of Cumbria include the Ennerdale Forest, St. Bees Head, Langdale Pikes, Bowness-on-Solway, the market town of Alston, Lanercost Priory, Scafell Pike – England's highest mountain – and the Wordsworth country around Ambleside, Grasmere and Cockermouth.

WINDERMERE (Lake District). Mrs Ann Palmer, Yorkshire House, 1 Upper Oak Street, Windermere LA23 2LB (Windermere [09662] 4689). Yorkshire House, built around 1880 of local stone, offers guests bright, warm rooms, good food, with generous portions, at a reasonable price. Situated just off the main bus route, within five minutes' walk of Windermere rail station, short walk Windermere village, so car not essential, but parking provided. Our aim is to help you enjoy your stay in the Lakes, whether short or long. Bowness Bay, one and a half miles south, Ambleside four and a half miles north, cater for water sports, while in Windermere you are nearby the homes of Wordsworth, Ruskin and Beatrix Potter. Three double, one single (bunks), three family rooms with washbasins (one en-suite). Bathroom, two toilets; lounge; diningroom. Licensed. Central heating. Children and pets welcome; cot, high chair, babysitting, reduced rates. Open March to November. Evening Meal, Bed and Breakfast from £12.50; Bed and Breakfast from £8.50. Mid-week Break from £7.50 via The Mountain Goat Bus Company.

WINDERMERE. Mrs B. Bradley, Orrest Close, 3 The Terrace, Windermere LA23 1AJ (Windermere [096-62] 3325). Orrest Close is a Listed Building built about 1847 and believed to be the work of Augustus Pugin, well-known for his work on the Houses of Parliament. Hot and cold in all rooms, heaters, shaving points and electric blankets. Only 100 yards from trains and buses, and close to many restaurants. Tea and biscuits are served at 9.45 pm in the colour TV lounge by the owners. Betty and Brian Bradley have many years' experience of the Lake District and are happy to give advice and suggestions to help you enjoy your holiday. Three double bedrooms, two singles, one twin and three family rooms; sittingroom; diningroom; three bathrooms/toilets. Children welcome, cot, high chair and babysitting. Pets allowed. Car not essential, but private parking. Packed lunches. Bed and Breakfast from £7.25. Reduced rates for children.

WINDERMERE. Geoff and Jean Hilton, "The Archway" Guest House, 13 College Road, Windermere LA23 1BY (Windermere [096-62] 5613). "The Archway" is a small select Guest House with a friendly atmosphere, providing magnificent open mountain views yet close to railway station, bus terminus and shops. Windermere is an ideal centre from which to enjoy the Lake District National Park with its glorious natural scenery and endless outdoor pursuits. Three family, two double, one single bedrooms, all with washbasins; diningroom with separate tables, colour TV lounge. Reductions for children. Pets by prior arrangement. Open all year. Central heating throughout. Ample parking. AA listed. Bed and Breakfast. Optional Evening Dinner (excellent home cooking). Please send stamp for terms and brochure.

WINDERMERE. Miss Betty Holmes, Acton House, 41 Craig Walk, Windermere LA23 2HB (Windermere [096-62] 5340). Acton House is situated in a quiet street off the main road from Windermere to Bowness Bay. Ideal for access to the rest of the Lake District. Traditionally built house of stone and slate with modern plumbing. Three double rooms (one has twin beds) all with washbasins; tea making facilities. No restrictions on access to house or use of sittingroom (colour TV, coal fire); all other rooms heated. Emphasis on comfort and good food. Packed lunches on request. Children over eight welcome. Open March to middle of November for Evening Dinner, Bed and Breakfast from £72 per week. Reductions out of season; extra reductions for Senior Citizens out of season. No pets please.

WINDERMERE near. Mr and Mrs R. H. Leaver, Borwick Fold Farmhouse, Crook, Near Windermere LA8 9HS (Windermere [096-62] 4104). Working farm. Borwick Fold Farmhouse is a traditional 17th century Lakeland stone farmhouse, with a wealth of oak beams and panelling, nestling in a very peaceful spot high up on the fells. It enjoys beautiful all-round views, including the Langdale Pikes, and is well away from holiday crowds and traffic. Situated in the Lake District National Park, it provides a convenient base for fell-walking or touring, and many recreational and sporting amenities are within easy reach. Comprehensive information provided on places to visit, and local events. One double, one twin/single and one family room, all with H&C. Lounge with colour TV. Highly recommended for peace and comfort. Children over five welcome. No pets. Car essential. Open Easter/October. Terms on application.

DERBYSHIRE

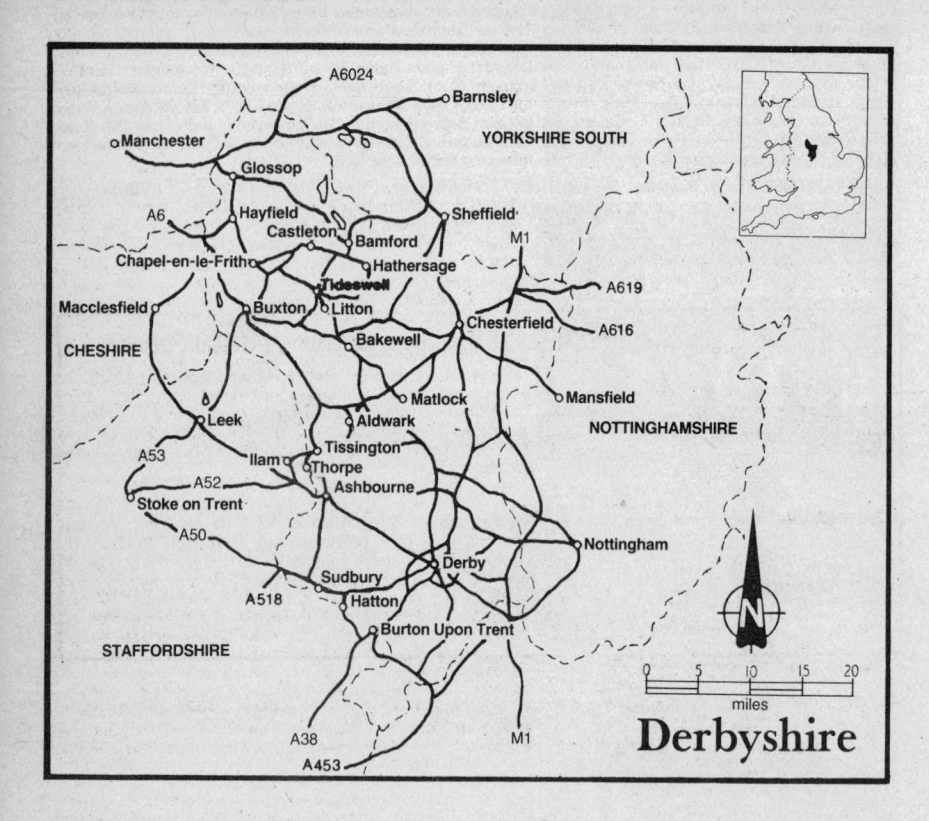

ALDWARK. Mrs D. Forsey, Tithe Farm, Aldwark, Grangemill, Via Derby DE4 4HX (Carsington [062-985] 263). Tithe Farm is peacefully situated in the Peak District National Park, near to the High Peak Trail. Dovedale, Chatsworth, Haddon Hall, Bakewell, Matlock and Ashbourne are all within 10 miles. The three twin-bedded rooms have washbasins, shaver points and tea/coffee making equipment. There is full central heating with log fires in sitting and dining rooms. Traditional farmhouse food is served, with home-baking and garden vegetables in season. Packed lunches available. Ample car parking. Open April to October. Bed and Breakfast from £9. Bed, Breakfast and Evening Dinner from £14.75. Reduced terms for children under 14. SAE, please, for brochure.

ASHBOURNE. Mrs M. J. Davies, Clifton Hall, Clifton, Ashbourne DE6 2GL (Ashbourne [0335] 42265). Clifton Hall is a splendid country house reputed to date back to 1740. Set in nearly three acres of gardens on the edge of Peak National Park. The lovely village of Clifton is south west of Ashbourne, between the A52 and A515 roads, within easy reach of Alton Towers, Chatsworth and many other attractions. Very comfortable accommodation is offered with hot and cold in all bedrooms. Guests' sitting-room with colour TV and tea-making facilities. Early morning tea and light refreshments are available on request and breakfast is served at a time to suit you. Bed and Breakfast only, but there are many fine restaurants in the area for other meals. Free parking within grounds. Open all year. For overnight or weekly terms please send SAE or telephone.

ASHBOURNE (Peak Park). Mrs M. Borg, "Green Croft", Green Farm, Thorpe, Peak Park, Ashbourne DE6 2AW (Thorpe Cloud [033-529] 411). "Green Croft" is located 15 minutes' walk from Dovedale, Thorpe Cloud and walks to other Dales. The centrally heated farmhouse overlooks the village green in the typical Peak District village. Close by is Ashbourne, with its country market. Available to guests is a separate barn, comfortably furnished as a lounge, with colour TV at all times. Two double bedrooms with bathroom en suite (£9-£11). Two family rooms (children charged depending on age), and two further double bedrooms (£8). A good three-course meal is served (£5), with tea/coffee making facilities available to guests. Fire Certificate held. A map will be supplied with confirmation. Open March onwards. A car is essential and there is ample parking. A warm welcome to all our guests.

Mrs C. Brandrick, SIDESMILL FARM, Snelston, Ashbourne, Derbyshire DE6 2GQ. Telephone: Ashbourne (0335) 42710

Rippling mill stream flows past this 17th century farmhouse on peaceful 60-acre dairy farm on the banks of the River Dove. Ideal area for walking and touring Derbyshire and Staffordshire Dales. Ashbourne two miles, Dovedale four miles and Alton Towers seven miles. Good home cooking and a warm welcome guaranteed. Large garden. Open log fire and TV in guests' sittingroom; diningroom. One twin-bedded and one family bedrooms with cot. Bathroom, toilet. Children welcome; reduced rates for those under 12. No pets. Car essential – parking. Open May to October.
Bed and Breakfast from £8. Evening Meal, Bed and Breakfast from £12.50.

ASHBOURNE. Mrs G. Prince, Home Farm, Norbury, Ashbourne DE6 2ED (033524-284 or 286). Working farm. Guests receive a warm welcome to this delightful farmhouse situated in a small hamlet on the borders of Derbyshire and Staffordshire. The house and garden are elevated on a bank separated from the 130 acre dairy farm by a footbridge, which spans the B5033, Darley Moor to Ellastone road. Well situated for Alton Towers, Dovedale, Matlock and other beauty spots, also easy access to many stately homes. Accommodation comprises twin bedded room, with adjacent cloakroom on ground floor; family room (with cot if required) on first floor, bathroom and toilet; own diningroom and lounge with colour TV. Double bed settee in lounge if required. Solid fuel central heating, log fires. Home grown produce (when available). Bed and Breakfast from £7.50. Evening Meal by arrangement. Snacks available until 10 pm. Afternoon tea served in garden. Ample car space. Special rates for children under nine. Sorry no pets.

ASHBOURNE. Mrs A. Wooddisse, Mayfield Cottage, Middle Mayfield, Ashbourne DE6 2JU (Ashbourne [0335] 42538). Two miles from Ashbourne, accommodation is offered in this comfortable Georgian House with large garden and converted Coach House from March to October. Situated in the Dove Valley on the edge of the Peak District within easy reach of Alton Towers, Chatsworth, Haddon Hall, Sudbury and many places of scenic and historic interest. There is one family bedroom with washbasin in the main house and two double bedrooms in the coach house. Two bathrooms, three toilets; sittingroom and diningroom, TV. Children welcome. Pets accepted by arrangement. Car necessary, parking space. Evening Meal, Bed and Breakfast from £10; Bed and Breakfast from £6.50. Reductions for children.

DERBYSHIRE – PEAK DISTRICT AND DALES!

The undulating dales set against the gritstone edges of the Pennine moors give Derbyshire its scenic wealth. In the tourists' itinerary should be the prehistoric monument at Arbor Low, the canal port of Shardlow, the country parks at Elvaston and Shipley, the limestone caves at Creswell Crags and Castleton and the market towns of Ashbourne and Bakewell. For walkers this area provides many excellent opportunities.

Derbyshire BOARD

ASHBOURNE. Mr and Mrs Spencer, Tan Mill Farm, Mappleton Road, Ashbourne DE6 2AA (Ashbourne [0335] 42387). Working farm. Tan Mill Farm is set in beautiful rural surroundings yet only 10 minutes' walk from the old market town of Ashbourne, where the open market is held on Thursday and Saturday. There is a swimming pool, squash courts and park for your enjoyment and it has many good shops offering friendly service. The farm is only yards from the Tissington Nature Trail and here cycles can be hired. There are many places of beauty and historic interest within a radius of 20 miles. A warm welcome, clean bed and good food are assured. Children welcome, cot, reduced rates. Open all year except Christmas. Car preferable, parking. Public transport 10 minutes' walk. Bed and Breakfast from £9.50. Also select site for five touring vans, water point, Elsan emptying point. Local swimming pool with showers.

ASHBOURNE. Mrs E. J. Harrison, Little Park Farm, Okeover, Ashbourne DE6 2BR (Thorpe Cloud [033-529] 341). Working farm. The 125-acres family run dairy farm looks on to Dovedale and is ideally situated for the Derbyshire Dales and Alton Towers. Plenty of wildlife and beautiful walks. Ideal for a get away from it all holiday. Good wholesome farmhouse cooking. An oak beamed farmhouse over 200 years old. Colour TV lounge. One double and two family size bedrooms, all with washbasins; bathroom, toilet; diningroom. Children welcomed at reduced rates. Sorry, no pets. Car essential, parking. Open Easter to end September. SAE, please, for terms for Evening Meal, Bed and Breakfast. AA listed. Pony trekking and cycle hire nearby.

ASHBOURNE. Mrs E. K. Prince, Roston Hall Farm, Roston, Ashbourne DE6 2EH (Ellastone [033-524] 287). Working farm. Spacious traditional farmhouse, situated in quiet village, offers home-produced fresh farmhouse meals. Guest diningroom with inglenook fireplace; comfortable lounge with wood-burning stove and TV. Well situated for Alton Towers, Derbyshire Dales and many stately homes. Ashbourne six miles. Accommodation comprises one double and one family bedroom (one with washbasin); bathroom, toilet. Children over 13 years welcome. Sorry, no pets. Car essential — parking. Roston Hall Farm, a 100 acre beef/arable farm, is open from May to September. Evening Meal, Bed and Breakfast from £12; Bed and Breakfast from £8. Mid-week bookings accepted. SAE, please.

ASHBOURNE. Mrs M. A. Griffin, Coldwall Farm, Okeover, Ashbourne DE6 2BS (Thorpe Cloud [033-529] 249). Working farm. The farmhouse is set in a secluded spot overlooking Dovedale. The comfortable stone-built house is 200 years old and ideally situated for touring the Peak District and visiting Alton Towers. It has an attractive garden. Guests are welcome to watch farm activities; milking cows, calves, sheep and lambs and a Shire horse are kept. Most of the food is home produced. Lovely walks through the woods and by the river on the farm. Two family bedrooms, with washbasins; bathroom, toilet; sittingroom; diningroom. Children welcome, cot, high chair and babysitting available. Sorry, no pets. Car essential, ample parking. Open from March to October for Evening Dinner, Bed and Breakfast or Bed and Breakfast. Terms on request with SAE, please.

ASHBOURNE near. Mr and Mrs P. J. Watson, Weaver Farm, Waterhouses, Nr Ashbourne ST10 3HE (Oakamoor [0538] 702271). Working farm. Situated off A52 on the Weaver Hills close to Ashbourne, Dovedale and Alton Towers. Stone farmhouse with central heating and open fires offering family, twin and double bedrooms with washbasins. Cot. Bathroom with shower and WC. Guest diningroom and lounge with TV. Children welcome. Home produced fresh farmhouse cooking is served. The 320-acre farm with dairy cows, calves, sheep and lambs provides many activities which guests are welcome to watch and they can also enjoy extensive walks and views. Car essential; ample parking. No pets. SAE or ring for terms. A warm welcome awaits you.

ASHBOURNE (Peak District). Mr D. J. Coxon, Dog & Partridge, Swinscoe, Ashbourne DE6 2HS (Ashbourne [0335] 43183). Adjacent to 17th century Inn with restaurant, bars and pool room, the motel offers ideal holiday accommodation. Children's play area in four acres of lawn and among the activities available locally are pony trekking, golf, fishing, cycling trails and many beautiful walks in Dovedale and the Peak District. Alton Towers Leisure Park five miles distant. Double, twin, single and family rooms, all en suite and tea making facilities. All with carports. Cots available. Open all year. Also available self catering chalets accommodating up to five persons. Linen provided. Location for touring vans; shower and toilet block; Elsan point. For full details contact **Mr and Mrs Coxon (Dept. FH)** at above address.

PLEASE SEND A STAMPED ADDRESSED ENVELOPE WITH ENQUIRIES

BOARD Derbyshire 117

ASHBOURNE near. Mrs H. Leason, Overdale, Lode Lane, Alstonefield, Near Ashbourne DE6 2FZ (Alstonefield [033-527] 206 or 275). Overdale, a beautiful, spacious house, situated in one-and-a-half acres of landscaped gardens including shaded walks, orchard, lily pond and tennis court. Alstonefield is a quiet, extremely pretty village adjacent to Dovedale, the spa towns of Buxton and Matlock, Chatsworth House and Haddon Hall. The guest house has full central heating, two family and five double bedrooms, all equipped with washbasins; three toilets, bathroom. A charming sittingroom and pleasant diningroom complete this perfect holiday home in its exclusive setting. Bed and Breakfast including Evening Drink £8. Evening Meal can be supplied if required. Open all year.

BAKEWELL. Mrs J. Walker, The Candle House, Greaves Lane, Ashford-in-the-Water, Bakewell DE4 1QL (Bakewell [062-981] 3726). A listed building of historical interest, this lovely old Georgian terraced house (beautifully modernised) derives its name from the fact that candles for the lead mines were once made in its outbuildings. Ashford is one of Derbyshire's most beautiful villages, famous for its sheep wash bridge and an ideal centre for exploring. Wells are dressed each year, and blessed on Trinity Sunday. Three double bedrooms with washbasins; electric kettles in all bedrooms; bathroom, two toilets; sittingroom; diningroom. Not really suitable for children. Sorry, no pets. Private parking. Bed and Breakfast only from £7-£8. SAE for terms.

BAKEWELL. Mrs Birkhead and Mrs Philps, Castle Cliffe Private Hotel, Monsal Head, Bakewell DE4 1NL (Great Longstone [062-987] 258). Castle Cliffe Hotel overlooks Monsal Dale where visitors can stroll by the grassy banks of the River Wye. Beauty spots of North Derbyshire are within easy reach — Haddon Hall, Chatsworth House, Blue John Caverns at Castleton, Cathedral of the Peak at Tideswell. Comfortable accommodation in three double bedrooms with washbasins, spring interior mattresses, razor points, reading lights, tea/coffee-making facilities and showers in all rooms. Lounge with colour TV, diningroom with separate tables. Choice of Menu. Table licence for residents only. Central heating. Free parking. No objection to pets. Open all year except Christmas. Evening Meal, Bed and Breakfast or Bed and Breakfast. Excellent food and personal attention. Also small furnished flat to let. Terms on application.

BUXTON. Mrs P. A. Green, Thorn Heyes Private Hotel, 137 London Road, Buxton (Buxton [0298] 3539). Victorian elegance in small owner-managed hotel. Tastefully furnished throughout with your comfort in mind. We have full central heating. Electric blankets and teasmades in every room. Some shower/toilet and colour TV en suite. Ample parking; beautiful gardens. Mrs Green makes her own pate, soup and bread rolls whenever possible. Book your holiday in confidence with the people who care. Terms and further details on request. Children and pets welcome.

BUXTON. Mrs M. A. MacKenzie, Staden Grange Farm, Staden, Buxton SK17 9RZ (Buxton [0298] 4965). At Staden Grange we strive to offer a high standard of accommodation, food and service, with a warm welcome and friendly hospitality, made possible by our small size and personal service. Licensed. Four double and one family rooms; a shower room; two bathrooms, two toilets; En Suite arrangements for some of the rooms; small informal diningroom where meals consist of home produce whenever possible, both meat and vegetables; lounge. Children welcome, cot, high chair and babysitting. Pets welcome. Open all year with central heating. Car essential, parking. Staden Grange is a splendid place for touring, walking and riding holidays in a lovely scenic area. There is much of interest in the area. (High Peak, Buxton Opera House, Pooles Cavern and Country Park). Evening Dinner, Bed and Breakfast from £12.00; Bed and Breakfast from £7.50. Reduced rates for children. Also caravan site for five vans with water, shower, sanitation available all year.

Derbyshire BOARD

BUXTON. Mrs S. Pritchard, "Devonshire Lodge", 2 Manchester Road, Buxton SK17 6SB (Buxton [0298] 71487). Have a wonderful holiday in our fine fully-appointed guest house situated in the High Peak of Derbyshire within three minutes' walk of Buxton Opera House and Pavilion Gardens. We offer modern and tastefully-decorated accommodation with good home cooking in a friendly atmosphere. Accommodation comprises one family room, two double rooms and one single room all with hot and cold water, shaver points. Full central heating. Dining room with individual tables and colour TV lounge. Children and small pets are welcome and a babysitting service is available. Bed and Breakfast £7 per night (all inclusive); Bed, Breakfast and Evening Meal £11 per night (all inclusive). 10% reduction for full weekly bookings. Also available a self-contained holiday flat to sleep three to five people. Please write for details.

BUXTON. Mr and Mrs J. Power, The Old Manse Guest House, 6 Clifton Road, Silverlands, Buxton SK17 6QL (Buxton [0298] 5638). For a happy holiday stay at the Old Manse, where you arrive as guests and leave as friends of Jim and Joan. The house, centrally situated in a quiet residential area, has open views, including Grin Low Tower and woods. Close to all amenities — Pavilion Gardens and Opera House. Good and varied home cooking; table licence; colour TV; fitted carpets throughout. Four double, two single and two family bedrooms (all with radiators, comfortable beds and washbasins); two bathrooms, two toilets; sittingroom and diningroom. Children welcome, cot, highchair and babysitting available. Pets permitted (10p nightly). Parking. Fire Certificate held. Open from January to November for Bed and Breakfast only, from £8.50 nightly. Evening Dinner £4. Ideal for touring the Peak District and for mini winter holidays. AA listed. SAE, please, for brochure.

BUXTON. Mrs N. Edge, "Nithen Corner Guest House," 45 Manchester Road, Buxton SK17 6SR (Buxton [0298] 2008). Beautifully appointed guest house with all modern amenities including private car park. Hot and cold washbasins in all bedrooms (four double and two family) also tea-making facilities. TV lounge; separate dining-room. Central heating throughout. Bathroom with shower. Fire Certificate. Pets and children welcome. Cot, babysitting, reduced rates. Situated half a mile from the town centre, within easy reach of local facilities, but on the edge of beautiful open countryside. In the unlikely event of guests being dissatisfied with the abundance of superb home cooking, comfort and service provided, no charge will be made. Open all year. Evening Dinner, Bed and Breakfast from £12.50 daily (inclusive) — £85 weekly (inclusive); Bed and Breakfast from £8 daily (inclusive) — £55 weekly (inclusive). SAE, please.

BUXTON. Mr and Mrs Alan Peet, Kingscroft Guest House, 10 Green Lane, Buxton SK17 9DP (0298-2757). Kingscroft offers a warm welcome to all guests and provides every comfort. Set in an interesting garden, with pleasant diningroom and lounge with colour TV, it is open all year. Four double and two family bedrooms, all with washbasins; two bathrooms, four toilets; central heating. Children welcome (reduced rates). Car not essential but parking provided for nine cars. Kingscroft is licensed and within easy reach of shops and park. Ideal base for touring Peak District, Matlock, Dovedale, Castleton, etc., or relaxing in Buxton which has many attractions during summer season. Evening Meal, Bed and Breakfast (seven nights) £65 per week (fully inclusive); or Bed and Breakfast only £10.80 per night. AA listed. Pets permitted.

FARM HOLIDAY GUIDES LIMITED publish a large range of well-known accommodation guides. We will be happy to send you details or you can use the order form at the back of this book.

BOARD   Derbyshire   119

BUXTON. Mrs A. J. G. Fosker, Brunswick Guest House, 31 St. John's Road, Buxton SK17 6XG (Buxton [0298] 71727). Brunswick House, a quietly situated home from home family guest house. Ideally located, only two minutes' walk from Buxton's Pavilion Gardens, Shopping centre and overlooking the beautiful Serpentine walks. All bedrooms have H&C and television. Tea-making facilities in all rooms. Centrally heated throughout. Relaxing television lounge. Private car parking facilities. Good home cooking and a warm welcome from your hosts. Bed and Breakfast £8 per person sharing double or twin room; Evening Meal, Bed and Breakfast £12.50 per person sharing double or twin room. Further details on request.

BUXTON near. Mrs Moira Wheeldon, Dale Grange Farm, Chelmorton, Buxton SK17 9SG (Taddington [0298] 85206). Working farm. This 220-acre dairy, beef and sheep farm is in Derbyshire Dales, heart of the Peak District. Ideally situated for all local beauty spots. Four miles from Buxton; superb Opera House for entertainment. Bakewell seven miles, and Chatsworth stately home. Local dales and Blue John caverns of Castleton all within easy reach. Comfortable accommodation and good food. Two double or two family bedrooms with hot and cold and central heating. Tea making facilities, electric blankets. Bathroom with shower, lounge with TV. Children welcome at reduced rates. Reasonable terms. Bed and Breakfast, Evening Meal optional. SAE or telephone for terms.

BUXTON. Mrs Muriel Legg, Heawood Guest House, 74 Corbar Road, Buxton SK17 6RJ (Buxton [0298] 4700). Quiet situation within easy reach of the town centre and the surrounding countryside. Ideally placed for touring the Peak District with its beautiful scenery and many places of interest. Accommodation consists of four double, one family rooms with washbasins, (two doubles with bathroom en suite); bathroom, separate shower, two toilets; sittingroom; diningroom. Good variety of menus — all home cooking. No extra charge for early morning tea or light supper. Cot, high chair, babysitting available. Reduced rates if sharing room with two adults. Sorry, no pets. Parking. Open April to October for Evening Dinner, Bed and Breakfast from £11.75 per night; Bed and Breakfast from £7.75 per night. Reduced terms for weekly bookings. April/May and October period 10% discount excluding Bank Holiday weeks.

BUXTON. Mrs J. Nadin, Fernydale Farm, Earl Sterndale, Buxton SK17 0BS (Longnor [029-883] 236). Working farm. Fernydale is a 220-acre dairy farm situated on the B5053 by the village of Earl Sterndale, in the heart of the Derbyshire Peak District. Within easy reach of all the dales, Chatsworth House, Bakewell and Buxton Spa etc. Earl Sterndale is five miles from Buxton and nine miles from the market town of Bakewell. Extremely comfortable accommodation and excellent food. Two double bedrooms (one with extra single bed) both with H&C, tea/coffee making facilities and bedside lamps. Double glazing, central heating and fitted carpets throughout. Bathroom, lounge with colour TV and diningroom. Terms on application for Bed and Breakfast with four course Evening Meal optional. SAE, please, or telephone for brochure. Open from Easter to September.

BUXTON by. Mrs M. Stubbs, Cotterill Farm, Biggin, Hartington, By Buxton SK17 0DJ (Hartington [029-884] 447). Working farm. Cotterill Farm is a mainly dairy farm, well situated overlooking Derbyshire hills with Biggin and Hartington close by. It is an ideal centre for Buxton, Ashbourne, Leek and Bakewell, Haddon Hall and Chatsworth, and for those wishing to walk on the Biggin, Dove, Wolfscote and Beresford Dales. Comfortable accommodation, carpeted throughout. One double and one family bedrooms with washbasins; tea and coffee-making facilities; bathroom, toilet; sittingroom with colour TV; diningroom. Central heating. Children welcome, reduced rates for those under 12 years. Car essential — parking. Open all year for Full Board; Evening Meal, Bed and Breakfast or Bed and Breakfast only. Dinner Monday to Saturday; High Tea on Sunday. SAE for terms.

BUXTON via. Mrs E. Vernon, Whitelee Farm, Sparrowpit, via Buxton SK17 8ES (Chapel-en-le-Frith [0298] 812928). Working farm. Whitelee is a 42-acre beef farm, four miles from Castleton, famous for its caves, four miles from Edale, six miles from Spa town of Buxton and within easy reach of Chatsworth House, Haddon Hall and Derbyshire Dales. Ideal walking/touring centre. The Farmhouse, part dating back to 1600, is fully modernised. AA listed. Three double bedrooms, all with fitted carpets, central heating, washbasins, razor points, bedside lights, spring interior mattresses, electric blankets, tea/coffee-making facilities with supplies. Guests' bathroom/shower room. Soap and towels supplied. Diningroom; sittingroom with TV; many leaflets on Derbyshire which guests may borrow. Excellent standard home-cooked farmhouse food. Open April/October. Pets very welcome, no charge, may sleep in bedroom. Ample parking. Evening Dinner, Bed and Breakfast or Bed and Breakfast. SAE, please, for brochure.

BUXTON near. Mrs S. J. Morgan, Rowan House, Great Hucklow, Near Buxton SK17 8RS (Tideswell [0298] 871715). Situated in the very heart of the Peak District, the peaceful village of Great Hucklow is an ideal centre for a walking and sight seeing holiday. Places of outstanding natural beauty and interest such as Monsal Dale, the Blue John Caverns and Chatsworth House are all close at hand. Rowan House itself has two guest bedrooms, one with washbasin, and a bathroom solely for guests' use. It is centrally heated and has a large comfortable lounge and pleasant diningroom where guests can enjoy the home cooked meals provided. Ample parking space and accommodation throughout the year. Reasonable terms for Bed, Breakfast and Evening Meal. Reductions for children and for stays of seven days or more.

BUXTON. Mrs C. Holland, Brierlow Grange, Ashbourne Road, Buxton SK17 9PZ (Buxton [0298] 3578). Working farm, join in. BRIERLOW GRANGE is a 300-acre family farm with dairy and mixed enterprises, situated in the heart of the Peak District on the A515 Buxton to Ashbourne Road. Enjoy the hospitality and comfort of our spacious home which is within easy reach of Buxton, Bakewell, Matlock Bath, Chatsworth stately home and many other attractions. Double, family and single rooms available, colour TV lounge with open fire, diningroom, full four-course farmhouse Breakfast and Evening Meal available. Children welcome at reduced rates. Open throughout the year. For further details phone **Christine Holland** at above number.

BUXTON near. Mrs Mary Preston-Cox, Glebe House Farm, Heathcote, Hartington, Near Buxton SK17 0AY (Hartington [029-884] 313). This cosy old house is in a quiet position on the edge of a small country village in the heart of the Peak District. Ideal touring centre for the Dales and caverns of Derbyshire, stately homes of Chatsworth, Haddon Hall, Hardwick Hall, etc. The Spa of Buxton, with its many attractions, 10 miles. The house commands excellent views of the surrounding countryside. Accommodation comprises two double, one single and one family rooms (washbasin in family room); bathroom and toilet; sittingroom, diningroom. Children welcome, cot, high chair. Babysitting by request. Pets accepted at small charge. Car essential — parking. Open March to October. Evening Dinner/Meal, Bed and Breakfast from £12; Bed and Breakfast from £7 per night. Reductions for children. Also two caravans available for hire.

BUXTON near. Mrs A. Barnsley, Dale House Farm, Litton, Near Buxton SK17 8QL (Tideswell [0298] 871309). Working farm. Bed and Breakfast and good farmhouse food is provided on this friendly farm in clean, comfortable, spacious accommodation with fine open views, on the outskirts of a pleasant picturesque village with its unique village greens. Within easy walking distance of many well-known beauty spots, centrally situated in the heart of the Peak District National Park. Two double and one family bedrooms; bathroom, toilet; sittingroom; diningroom. Sorry, no pets. Plenty of parking space. Open all year. Bed and Breakfast from £6. Guests assured of a friendly welcome. AA listed.

CASTLETON. Mrs B. Johnson, Myrtle Cottage, Market Place, Castleton, Near Sheffield S30 2WQ (Hope Valley [0433] 20787). Pleasantly situated in the centre of Castleton, famous for its castle and caverns. Ideal base for walking, pot-holing, hang gliding or for touring the beautiful Peak District and Derbyshire Dales. Within 20 minutes' motoring you can reach Buxton, Bakewell, Chatsworth House or the plague village of Eyam. Registered with the English Tourist Board, the guest accommodation comprises two family, one double and one twin bedrooms, all with washbasins; bathroom, two toilets; diningroom. Central heating. Fire Certificate. Children welcome at reduced rates. Babysitting. Regret, no pets. Ample car parking. Open all year except Christmas for Bed and Breakfast only.

The information in the entries in this guide is presented by the publishers in good faith and after the signed acceptance by advertisers that they will uphold the high standards associated with FARM HOLIDAY GUIDES LIMITED. The publishers do not accept responsibility for any inaccuracies or omissions or any results thereof. Before making final holiday arrangements readers should confirm the prices and facilities directly with advertisers.

BOARD   **Derbyshire**   **121**

DERBY. Mr and Mrs A. & D. Harris, Dairy House Farm, Alkmonton, Longford, Derby DE6 3DG (Great Cubley [033523] 359). This is a working dairy farm with accommodation for guests in two double, two single and two family rooms, all with washbasins and tea/coffee making facilities. Two bathrooms, two toilets; lounge and diningroom and colour TV. Open all year with central heating and log fires in inglenook fireplace. It is a comfortable, homely atmosphere with good food and residential licence. Children are welcome and there is cot, high chair and babysitting. Car essential, parking. Pets allowed but not in house. Full Board from £100 per week; Evening Dinner, Bed and Breakfast from £15 per night; Bed and Breakfast from £9. Warm welcome and hospitality guaranteed.

DERBYSHIRE. Dovedale Farm and Country Holidays. Visit the Dove, Churnet and Manifold Valleys. Choice farmhouse accommodation in this scenic and interesting area of Derbyshire. See also Display Advertisement in the Board section of this Guide.

DOVEDALE. Mrs Barbara Challinor, The Old Orchard, Stoney Lane, Thorpe, Ashbourne DE6 2AW (Thorpe Cloud [033-529] 410). The Old Orchard is a modern, split-level dwelling bordering the village green and quietly situated in the heart of the Derbyshire Dales in its own colourful, lawned and terraced garden with running stream. The accommodation comprises two double rooms (two with washbasins) and two single rooms. Visitors' bathroom with shower and toilet. Ample car parking on the premises. We have open fires in the lounge on chilly evenings. Sports available within four mile radius, including swimming, squash, horse riding, hang gliding, fishing and cycling (own cycles). Ideal centre for visiting stately homes: Alton Towers, Matlock Bath Cable Chair etc. Enjoy the pleasures of Dovedale, Thorpe Cloud and Stepping Stones only ten minutes from premises. Open March-November for Bed and Breakfast, and Evening Meal if required. Prices from £7.50.

DOVEDALE. Mrs Julia Brookfield, Green Gables, Thorpe, Near Ashbourne DE6 2AW (Thorpe Cloud [033-529] 386). This is no longer a working farm and the three storey farmhouse has been renovated to offer comfortable accommodation to guests. Two large bedrooms on the second floor have beautiful views of the village green and surrounding hills; both have washbasins and share a bathroom. On the third floor the twin bedded room has retained the old beams and shares a bathroom. The ground floor has hall cum diningroom, lounge with colour TV, full central heating. Children are welcome at reduced rates. Ample parking space. Open from April to October. Evening Meal £4; Bed and Breakfast from £7.50.

DOVEDALE (Near Ashbourne). Mrs F. M. Gould, St. Leonard's Cottage, Thorpe, Ashbourne DE6 2AW (Thorpe Cloud [033-529] 224). One of the oldest cottages in the village, St Leonard's stands in its own grounds of one third of an acre overlooking the village green, near to the entrance to Dovedale. Thorpe Cloud rises in the background. Many historic houses easily reached, walking in Manifold Valley and Tissington Trail. Fully modernised but retaining the original oak beams, the house has four bedrooms with wash hand basins, two bathrooms, three toilets. Bed and Breakfast from £7.50. Evening Dinner, Bed and Breakfast from £11.50. One bedroom en suite — Bed and Breakfast £9; Evening Dinner, Bed and Breakfast £13 (weekly terms). Diningroom and sittingroom, colour TV. A new extension has provided space and comfort for the guests. Open to visitors all day. Open all year except Christmas. Sorry, no pets in the house. Ample parking. Fire Certificate held.

DOVEDALE. Mrs B. Herridge, Bent Farm, Tissington, Ashbourne DE6 1RD (Parwich [033-525] 214). Working farm. This 17th century stone-built farmhouse, on the outskirts of the picturesque village of Tissington, offers friendly, comfortable accommodation on a dairy farm, where home cooking with home produced vegetables, and cosy log fires, enhance your stay. The farm is within the Peak District National Park and adjacent to Dovedale and Tissington Trail, an ideal centre for walking and touring. Visitors' lounge with colour TV; separate diningroom; two family rooms and two double rooms with central heating, washbasins, tea/coffee-making facilities in all rooms; bathroom, showers and toilets. Children welcome, cot and babysitting provided. Sorry, no pets. Ample parking space. Evening Dinner, Bed and Breakfast from £11; Bed and Breakfast from £7. Reductions for children. AA recommended. Open all year.

PLEASE SEND A STAMPED ADDRESSED ENVELOPE WITH ENQUIRIES

DOVEDALE FARM & COUNTRY HOLIDAYS

New Park Farm, Bradley, Ashbourne. (Mrs C. Akers Tel. [0335] 43425)
Peaceful comfortable farmhouse, recently modernised. Good home cooking, special diets catered for. Children welcome, central for walking, Chatsworth, Alton Towers, Matlock.

Manor Farm, Prestwood, Denstone. (Mrs Ball Tel. [0889] 590415)
Jacobean house in scenic Churnet Valley. 16th century 4 Poster bed, plus family room. Antiques throughout, oak panelled dining room, grass tennis court.

Sidesmill Farm, Snelston, Ashbourne. (Mrs C. Brandrick Tel. [0335] 42710)
Pleasantly situated dairy farm on the banks of the River Dove. Ideal touring base for the Dales and Alton Towers.

Henmore Grange, Hopton, Nr Wirksworth. (John & Elizabeth Brassington Tel. [062985] 420)
Converted farm buildings overlooking Henmore Valley and woodland. Centrally situated for Matlock, Chatsworth, Haddon Hall, Ashbourne, Alton Towers and Dove Dale. On edge of two small villages.

Sycamore Farm, Hopton, Nr Wirksworth. (Mrs B. M. Corbett Tel. [062982] 2466)
Elizabethan farmhouse on a mixed farm situated close to the Peak District and Derbyshire Dales.

Spend Lane Farm, Thorpe, Ashbourne. (Mrs V. M. Dean Tel. [033529] 435)
Beautiful Georgian farmhouse with magnificent views towards Thorpe Cloud and the River Dove. Good home cooking. Tea/coffee making facilities.

Shirley Hall Farm, Shirley, Brailsford. (Mrs Sylvia Foster Tel. [0335] 60346)
17th century timbered house, lovely garden close to Shirley Village, excellent woodland walks. Central for Kedleston and Sudbury Halls and Alton Towers. 4 miles from Ashbourne.

Coldwell Farm, Okeover, Ashbourne. (Mrs K. W. Griffin Tel. [033529] 249)
Dairy and sheep farm set in a secluded spot overlooking Dovedale. Guests are welcome to watch farm activities. Centrally situated for visits to Alton Towers, Chatsworth and Peak District.

Little Park Farm, Mappleton, Ashbourne. (Mrs E. J. Harrison Tel. [033529] 341)
Situated in the beautiful and peaceful Dove Valley. The 300 year old farmhouse with oak beams is ideally situated for walking, pony trekking, bike hire and Alton Towers. Visitors' own lounge with TV.

Packhorse Farm, Matlock Moor, Matlock. (Mrs Margaret Haynes Tel. [0629] 2781)
Modernised farmhouse quietly situated in extensive ground. Central for visiting stately homes and the Peak District. Full English Breakfast. Fire certificate. SAE for replies.

Chevin Green Farm, Chevin Lane, Belper. (Carl & Joan Postles Tel. [077382] 2328)
Farm buildings luxuriously converted into B & B accommodation. Overlooking Derwent Valley. Ideal touring centre for Matlock, Ashbourne, Dovedale and the Peak District. Children welcome.

Roston Hall Farm, Roston, Ashbourne. (Mrs E. K. Prince Tel. [033524] 287)
Spacious traditional farmhouse in quiet village 6 miles from Ashbourne. Good home cooking. Comfortable visitors' lounge with TV. Well situated for Derbyshire Dales, Peak District and Alton Towers.

Home Farm, Norbury, Ashbourne. (Mrs Gillyan Prince Tel. [033524] 284/6)
Traditional farmhouse, in peaceful woodland surroundings. Own dining room, and lounge with TV. Central heating. Close to Alton Towers and Derbyshire Dales.

Dannah Farm, Shottle, Nr Belper. (Mrs Joan Slack Tel. [077389] 273)
Large, traditional, old Derbyshire farmhouse on 128-acre working farm, in beautiful countryside on Chatsworth estate at Shottle. Recently modernised. Good home cooking. Children welcome. Centrally situated.

Weaver Farm. Waterhouses, Stoke-on-Trent. (Mrs Watson Tel. [0538] 702271)
Stone built farmhouse situated on Weaver Hills, magnificent views (5 counties). Ideal for Alton Towers, Dovedale and Peak District. Separate lounge. Tea/coffee facilities. Open all year round. Fire certificate.

VISIT THE BEAUTIFUL DOVE, CHURNET AND MANIFOLD VALLEYS.

DOVEDALE. Mrs Joan Wain, Air Cottage Farm, Ilam, Ashbourne DE6 2BD (Thorpe Cloud [033-529] 475). Holidaymakers to the Peak District will enjoy staying at Air Cottage Farm situated at the edge of Dovedale with picturesque views of Thorpe Cloud and Dovedale Valley. The famous Stepping Stones just 10 minutes away and it is an ideal base for touring the Peak District National Park, stately homes and many other places of local historical interest. Unlimited walks in the Manifold Valley and the Tissington Nature Trail and scenic routes for motorists. Within easy reach of Alton Towers and Matlock "Gulliver's Kingdom". Sports available include swimming, squash and horse riding within easy reach. There is a pony on the farm for children to ride. Two double bedrooms and one single (sleeping two); bathroom, two toilets; sittingroom; diningroom. Cot and high chair provided for children. Open March to November, a car is essential — parking. Terms and further details on request.

PACKHORSE FARM
Matlock Moor, Matlock, Derbyshire
Mrs Margaret Haynes : Matlock (0629) 2781

Modern farmhouse with elevated southern view, two miles from Matlock, seven from Chesterfield and 18 from Derby. The 52-acre mixed farm is central for touring Dales and Peak National Park, also for visiting stately homes and country houses. Ideal for walking and outdoor pursuits. Car essential, parking. Open all year. Two double and two family bedrooms, with washbasins; bathroom, two toilets; sittingroom; diningroom. Colour TV. Children welcome. Pets allowed, but outside only. Putting green for guests and small nature reserve on property.

SAE please, for prompt reply and terms for Full English Breakfast. Reductions for children. Fire certificate held.

MATLOCK. Mrs S. Emmott, Home Farm, Stanton in Peak, Matlock (Youlgrave [062-986] 547). Traditional farmhouse with extensive views, in the Peak District National Park, set in the peaceful pretty village of Stanton in Peak, four miles from Bakewell and within easy reach of the Derbyshire Dales, three miles from Chatsworth and Haddon Hall. Spacious bedrooms with washbasins; lounge with colour TV; central heating. Large parking area. Children and ramblers welcome. Ideally situated for all outdoor pursuits.

HELP IMPROVE
BRITISH TOURIST STANDARDS

You are choosing holiday accommodation from our very popular FARM HOLIDAY GUIDES. Whether it be a hotel, guest house, farmhouse or self-catering accommodation, we think you will find it hospitable, comfortable and clean, and your host and hostess friendly and helpful.

Why not write and tell us about it?

As a recognition of the generally well-run and excellent holiday accommodation reviewed in our publications, we at FARM HOLIDAY GUIDES LIMITED present a diploma to proprietors who receive the highest recommendation from their guests who are also readers of our Guides. If you care to write to us praising the holiday you have booked through FARM HOLIDAY GUIDES – whether this be board, self-catering accommodation, a sporting or a caravan holiday, the content of your letter will be evaluated and the proprietors who reach our final list will be contacted.

The winning proprietor will receive an attractive framed diploma to display on his premises as recognition of a high standard of comfort, amenity and hospitality. FARM HOLIDAY GUIDES LIMITED offer this diploma as a contribution towards the improvement of standards in tourist accommodation in Britain. Help your excellent host or hostess to win it!

DIPLOMA
AWARDED BY
READERS
of
FARM HOLIDAY GUIDE
PUBLICATIONS LIMITED

TO..
FOR HOLIDAY ACCOMMODATION
of the HIGHEST STANDARD

AT..

MATLOCK. Mrs Denise Abrehart, Masson Farm, St. John's Road, Matlock DE4 3PQ (Matlock [0629] 2720). Working farm. Situated between Matlock and Matlock Bath this small farm is an ideal base for touring many places of interest. Set alone on hillside, with panoramic views of local countryside, the house is stone built, over 200 years old, with beams and bedrooms with sloping ceilings. Guests are welcome to help feed hand-reared animals which are often tame enough to be petted. Two double and one twin bedrooms; sitting/diningroom; bathroom and shower room. Home cooking with predominant use of own produce. Food is cooked on a wood-burning range. Car essential. Open all year with central heating for colder months. Evening Meal, Bed and Breakfast from £10.50 and Bed and Breakfast from £7.50. Also camping site for tents (no outside facilities except water). Further details on request.

MATLOCK. Mrs S. Pickering, The Cobbler's Cottage, 7 Sycamore Road, Matlock DE4 3HZ (Matlock [0629] 3148). The cottage, built in the mid 1700's, has been lovingly restored by the present owners and a new wing blends with the old. The interior is designed to incorporate mementos from bygone days. Genuine friendly welcome. Perfect centre for touring and walking holidays. Our own personal interest is discovering and walking old medieval packhorse routes, saltways and drovers ways. We will be delighted to help you plan a walk and loan our maps and books. Breathtaking countryside close to Peak National Park. Cable car — Matlock Bath. Stately homes Chatsworth, Haddon Hall, Hardwick House. Double and single rooms with washbasins; bathroom, two toilets; diningroom; lounge. Open all year with central heating. Evening Dinner, Bed and Breakfast from £11.50; Bed and Breakfast from £7.50.

MATLOCK near. Mrs R. B. Clayton, Town Head Farmhouse, 70 High Street, Bonsall, Near Matlock DE4 2AR (Wirksworth [062-982] 3762). Townhead Farmhouse is a stone-built, 18th century farmhouse and barns, tastefully and sympathetically converted to form comfortable accommodation, but still retaining much of its former character. No longer a working farm. The quiet, unspoilt village of Bonsall is within easy touring distance of the Dales, Haddon Hall, Chatsworth, Bakewell, Ashbourne, Crich Tramway Museum. Castleton, Ladybower and Derwent Reservoirs are approximately three-quarters of an hour's drive away. Accommodation is in two twin, one single and three double rooms with washbasins (three with private showers), also razor points in all rooms. Guests lounge and diningroom. Ample parking. Evening Drink at no extra charge. Open from April to October for Bed and Breakfast from £9. Pets by arrangement.

MATLOCK near. Mr C. R. Truman, Sycamore Guest House, 76 High Street, Town Head, Bonsall, Near Matlock DE4 2AA (Wirksworth [062-982] 3903). A.A. listed. A small 18th century family guest house in the village of Bonsall, nestling high on Masson Hill on the edge of the Peak District National Park. Easy access to Matlock Bath (for cable cars), Chatsworth, Haddon Hall, Dovedale, Alton Towers, etc. All bedrooms with hot and cold, plus tea/coffee making facilities. Two bathrooms, two showers, three toilets. Lounge with TV. Diningroom with open fire. Full central heating. Residential licence. Ample car park. Bed and Breakfast from £8.50; Bed, Breakfast and Evening Meal from £13.00.

TIDESWELL. Mrs A. B. Whatley, The Hall, Great Hucklow, Tideswell, Buxton SK17 8RG (Tideswell [0298] 871175). Guests are invited to share our 17th century stone farmhouse which is in a peaceful south facing situation on the edge of the village. In the centre of the Peak District, the house is an excellent base from which to tour the area whether by car, bicycle or on foot. There is plenty to interest everyone from the caves, and dales of the limestone areas, crags and moors of the gritstone, to the large houses such as Chatsworth and Haddon Hall. Only a small number of guests can be accommodated in our family home and, whether for a week's holiday or a one night stay, guests are provided with excellent home cooking, comfortable rooms and a very warm welcome. Sorry, pets not accepted.

WHEN MAKING ENQUIRIES PLEASE MENTION
FARM HOLIDAY GUIDE

BOARD   Devon   125

DEVON

ASHBURTON. Mrs Linda K. H. Wilkinson, Babeny Farm, Poundsgate, Newton Abbot TQ13 7PS (Poundsgate [036-43] 296). Working farm. Farm on Dartmoor with walking, fishing, rough shooting and horses. Seven miles from Ashburton and one and a half miles from C178 Ashburton to Tavistock road. There are two double and one family bedrooms; bathroom, two toilets; sittingroom and diningroom. Children over five years welcome; babysitting and reduced rates. Pets allowed but must be kept in the car at nights. Open all year round; mid week bookings accepted. Car essential — parking. Evening Meal, Bed and Breakfast or Bed and Breakfast only.

ASHBURTON. Mrs D. M. Dent, Adams Hele Farm, Ashburton TQ13 7NW (Ashburton [0364] 52525). Working farm. This 16th century farmhouse nestles on the south facing hill overlooking the Dart Valley and the Moors. The farm consists of 90 acres stocked with cattle, sheep and ponies on pleasant grassland. It is an excellent base for exploring the beauty and unspoilt scenery of Dartmoor. The accommodation for guests consists of two double bedrooms and two family rooms, all with washbasins; two bathrooms, three toilets; sittingroom; two diningrooms. Children are welcome; cot, high chair, babysitting, special mealtimes and reduced rates. Pets by arrangement. Open March to October. Car essential, parking. The South Devon beaches are only 15 miles; Torbay, Plymouth and Exeter within an hour's drive. Excellent fishing, beautiful walks, moorland pony rides and many golf courses within easy reach. A warm welcome to all guests.

ASHBURTON. Mrs B. M. Tuckett, Headborough Farm, Ashburton TQ13 7QR (Ashburton [0364] 52360). Working farm. This farmhouse on a mixed farm offers homely accommodation with plenty of good food. Guests are welcomed with a cup of tea and there are three double bedrooms, with washbasins; bathroom, two toilets; combined sitting/diningroom with TV. Children are welcome and there is a cot and high chair. Sorry no pets. Open March to end of November, with electric heating. A car is not essential but there is parking. Half a mile to public transport. Roast home pork, lamb, beef and poultry; nice sweets and cream. Evening Dinner, Bed and Breakfast from £8 per day with reduced rates for children.

126 Devon BOARD

The Dartmoor Motel

Peartree Cross,
Ashburton,
Devon TQ13 7JW
Tel: (0364) 52232

AA ** MM RAC** ** FULLY LICENSED**

You'll find the Dartmoor Motel 300 yards off the main A38 Dual Carriageway ¼ mile west from the old market town of Ashburton. Ashburton — gateway to the Dartmoor National Park — is the ideal centre for sampling the wide variety of scenery and activities only South Devon can offer in such profusion. Just half-an-hour's drive could take you to the ancient and beautiful Cathedral City of Exeter, or Plymouth with its amalgam of living history and 20th century technology, or Torquay, Paignton and Brixham with their glorious Torbay sea-scapes, bathing and unrivalled holiday facilities.

The 21 bedrooms all overlook pleasant open countryside and have en suite bathrooms. Character four poster honeymoon suite available. Lounge bar (snacks served); coffee shop serving snacks throughout the day; licensed Restaurant; free car parking and filling/service station. Dogs welcome by arrangement (but not in public rooms please). Full fire certificate, central heating throughout and Les Routiers and Ashley Courtenay recommended.

Stay with us once and you'll want to come back.

**The Dartmoor Motel, Ashburton TQ13 7JW, South Devon
Telephone (0364) 52232**

WELLPRITTON FARM

Registered with
English Tourist Board

Member of Dartmoor
Tourist Association

AA Listed

A warm welcome awaits you at Wellpritton, a working farm with a beautiful Devon farmhouse. Set in panoramic countryside on the edge of Dartmoor, one mile from the picturesque village of Holne and five minutes from River Dart Country Park, which offers a host of activities for adults and children alike. Riding, fishing, walking, sailing, and golf are near, and also many places of historical interest. Torbay, Exeter, Plymouth, and beaches within a half hour's drive. Completely modernised accommodation of a very high standard. Central heating, fitted carpets throughout. Washbasins (H&C) in bedrooms, also automatic tea-makers for guests' comfort. Showers in most rooms. Bathroom, toilets, diningroom, lounge with colour TV. Filtered swimming pool, games room. *Really caring personal attention guaranteed with plenty of mouthwatering, farm produced food.* Devonshire cream every day. Children over five welcome. Sorry, no pets in house, but warm kennel provided at no extra charge. Car essential – parking.

Open all year except Christmas. Out of season breaks are offered. Stamp please, for brochure. Fire Certificate held.

**Mrs Sue Townsend, Wellpritton Farm, Holne, Ashburton, Devon.
Tel. Poundsgate (03643) 273.**

ASHBURTON. Gray and Liz Ross, East Burne Farm, Bickington, Newton Abbot TQ12 6PA (Bickington [062-682] 496). Charming 17th century farmhouse in peaceful valley — superb centre for touring, walking, riding, fishing, etc. Guests have use of swimming pool, and the 11½ acres of land are managed primarily to conserve the outstanding variety of bird and plant life. Two double, one single bedrooms (one en suite with shower and WC); two bathrooms, four toilets. Lounge with colour TV; diningroom where an excellent variety of home cooking is served including local meat and vegetables, home-made jams, bread, clotted cream. No micro-wave cookery! The hosts' aim is to maintain a relaxed, friendly atmosphere and to ensure their guests have a truly enjoyable holiday. Children welcome, cot, high chair, reduced rates available. Pets accepted outside only. Car essential, parking. Open all year. Evening Dinner, Bed and Breakfast from £15 per day, £100 per week. Bed and Breakfast from £9 per day, £60 per week. Highly recommended. Also self-catering accommodation.

AA, RAC LISTED   LICENSED
REGISTERED WITH THE ENGLISH TOURIST BOARD

Lovely 16th century former Wool Mill, carefully converted and modernised. Attractive bedrooms all overlooking open countryside, with shower, washbasin and tea-making facilities. Some have WC en suite. One ground floor bedroom. Large comfortable beamed lounge with corner bar and granite archways leading to the dining room and to a cosy sittingroom with colour television. One acre garden. Ample car parking. Beautiful area on edge of Dartmoor National Park, surrounded by farmland. Ideal base for touring South Devon, or visiting Exeter and Plymouth. Children over five welcome. Reduced rates for those under 12. No pets. Evening Meal, Bed and Breakfast or Bed and Breakfast. SAE please for terms.

Mr & Mrs B. J. Cox, Gages Mill, Buckfastleigh Road, Ashburton, Devon TQ13 7JW. Ashburton (0364) 52391.

ASHBURTON. Mrs Mary Lloyd-Williams, Hooks Cottage, Bickington, South Devon TQ12 6JS (Bickington [062-682] 312). Children of all ages especially welcomed here. With large swimming pool and 12 acres of woods, rivers and fields to explore, it is a perfect centre for family holidays, within easy reach of coastal resorts, the moor and countless attractions for all ages. The cottage offers guests a family suite of double with connecting bathroom to twin and family room with double and bunks, lounge with wood-burning stove and colour TV, cot, babysitting, pony to ride. Super, large, home-cooked meals with fresh garden produce, home-made bread, cream, etc. Happy, relaxed atmosphere. Huge reductions for children. Open all year. Particularly glorious for Spring/Autumn breaks. Brochure on request.

ASHBURTON near. Mrs Margaret Petherick, Chase Gate Farm, Holne, Near Ashburton TQ13 7RZ (Poundsgate [036-43] 261). "Chase Gate Farm" is ideal for a happy, homely holiday in beautiful National Park surroundings. A good centre for walking and touring with many places of interest to visit, including Buckfast Abbey, Widecombe-in-the-Moor and Princetown. Plenty of good country cooking, home grown vegetables and home-made pies. One double, one twin-bedded and one family bedrooms, with washbasins and tea-making facilities. Bathroom, two toilets. Sittingroom. Diningroom with separate tables. Children welcome. Car essential — parking. Sorry, no pets. Evening Meal, Bed and Breakfast or Bed and Breakfast. SAE, please, for terms.

ASHBURTON. Mrs B. Hicks, Higher Venton Farm, Widecombe-in-the-Moor, Newton Abbot TQ13 7TF (Widecombe-in-the-Moor [036-42] 235). Working farm. Higher Venton Farm, with its beautiful 17th century thatched farmhouse is set in the Dartmoor National Park on 45 acres of mixed farmland. An excellent centre for touring the beauty spots of Dartmoor and the Torbay area, and there are riding stables nearby. Three double bedrooms; bathroom, toilet; diningroom; TV. Open from January to December for Bed and Breakfast or Bed and Breakfast and Evening Meal. Good home cooking and fresh farm produce. Homely atmosphere. Car essential — parking. Sorry, no pets. SAE, please, for terms and further details.

PLEASE ENCLOSE A STAMPED ADDRESSED ENVELOPE WITH ENQUIRIES

Devon   BOARD

AXMINSTER. Mrs A. E. Spanton, Maudlin Farm, Winsham, Chard, Somerset (Winsham [046-030] 277). Working farm. Situated 10 miles from Lyme Regis, overlooking the picturesque Axe Valley on the borders of the three counties — Somerset, Devon and Dorset. The attractive farmhouse has all modern conveniences and home from home comforts. Ideal location to get away from the noise and bustle of everyday life and enjoy the lovely countryside. Within easy reach of places of interest including Forde Abbey, Cricket St. Thomas Wildlife Park, Charmouth (great for fossil collectors). Accommodation comprises one family, two double bedrooms, with washbasins; bathroom, shower and toilet. Sittingroom and diningroom. Open most of the year, guests will enjoy the friendly atmosphere. Car essential. One mile of own fishing rights available. (Small Caravan Club site). SAE, please.

AXMINSTER. Mrs M. Bond, Birchwood Farm, Kilmington, Axminster EX13 7ST (Axminster [0297] 33867). Working farm. This is a new farm bungalow in a beautiful situation amongst fields and woods on 120-acre dairy farm. Lovely walks, and guests are free to wander where they please or help in farm activities such as fetching the cows or feeding calves etc. Six miles from the sea and six different beaches within 10 miles; three golf courses nearby; tennis courts in the picturesque village. Dartmoor, Exmoor, Torquay all within reach for day trips. A relaxed, homely atmosphere is provided and good quality home cooking a speciality. Two double and one family bedrooms, two with washbasins; bathroom, two toilets; sittingroom; diningroom. Cot, high chair, babysitting and reduced rates for children. Log fires when necessary. Car essential; ample parking. Open May to September. Evening Meal, Bed and Breakfast or Bed and Breakfast only. SAE for terms.

AXMINSTER. Mrs Susan Bowditch, Stonebarrow Farm, Hawkchurch, Axminster EX13 5XL (Hawkchurch [029-77] 338). Working farm. Stonebarrow Farm is a modern bungalow set in unspoilt countryside and has beautiful views of surrounding fields and woodland. The farm is mainly a dairy farm of 140 acres, six miles from the sea. There are also pigs and poultry. Although situated in Devon, it is only half a mile from the Dorset and Somerset Borders. The bungalow is carpeted throughout, has colour TV and fitted bedroom furniture. Most of the meat is produced on the farm and all vegetables in season. There are three double rooms and one family room, two bedrooms with washbasins; bathroom, toilet; sittingroom and diningroom. Children welcome and babysitting offered. Sorry, no pets. Dinner, Bed and Breakfast or Bed and Breakfast only. Reduced rates for children. SAE, please, for terms.

AXMINSTER. Mrs S. Clist, Annings Farm, Wyke Green, Axminster EX13 5TW (Axminster [0297] 33294). Working farm, join in. Annings is situated on a hill with lovely views of the Axe Valley, a quiet spot but not isolated. Fishing available in the large carp pond. A friendly warm welcome and service is assured with scrumptious food and plenty of Devonshire cream. One double, one single, two family bedrooms, three with washbasins; bathroom, shower room, two toilets; sittingroom; diningroom. Car essential; ample car parking. Cot, high chair, babysitting for children and reduced rates for those under 10 years old. Sorry, no pets. Evening Dinner, Bed and Breakfast from £11; Bed and Breakfast from £7. A relaxing holiday guaranteed.

AXMINSTER. Mr and Mrs Cobley, Elford Farm, Dalwood, Axminster EX13 7HB (Axminster [0297] 32415). Working farm. Elford is a 27-acre dairy farm carrying a herd of SR cows. Built circa 1585, the house combines the interesting features and charm of the old, with modern comfort. AA and RAC listed. Fire Certificate granted. Two double, one single and two family rooms with private bath suite (four bedrooms have washbasins). Bathroom, four toilets; lounge, diningroom. Children over three years welcome, babysitting by arrangement. Sorry, no pets. Car essential, parking. Good farm fare with fresh vegetables in season. English Breakfast, four-course Dinner. Guest House now has licensed premises. Near coast, historic houses, wildlife parks, golf, tennis and riding. Open all year. Electric heating. Reduced rates for children if sharing parents' room. SAE, please, for details.

BARNSTAPLE. Mrs Jane Stanbury, Halmpstone Farm, Bishop's Tawton, Barnstaple EX32 0EA (Swimbridge [0271] 830321). Working farm. This is a lovely old manor house dating back to medieval times. A large garden and patio with magnificent views. It is a 235 acre dairy farm. Three double bedrooms, one twin bedroom all with electric heaters; residents' lounge with colour TV; panelled diningroom with log fires on cooler evenings. Morning tea, Continental or full English traditional Breakfast; cream teas; residential licence. Tea and coffee available at all times. Five miles from Barnstaple, six miles from South Molton; easy access to the moors, beaches and coastline. Brochure available on request. Comfort, elegance and personal attention with value for money are our priorities.

BARNSTAPLE. Mr G. Copley, The Gables, Licensed Guest House, Umberleigh EX37 9AB (0769-60461). Situated eight miles south on B3227, a Guest House having an excellent reputation for a friendly relaxed atmosphere, with generous portions of varied and well-cooked food. Ideally situated beside the River Taw on Devon's Holiday Route, and convenient for Exmoor, Dartmoor and both North and South Coasts. One double and two twin bedrooms, with hot and cold, shaver points, electric radiators and tea-making facilities. All with river views. Residents' lounge with colour TV. Diningroom and Bar. Children welcome at reduced rates, cot and high chair available. Pets accepted. Car essential, parking. Open January to 1st November. Bed and Breakfast £7.50 (£49 per week). Bed, Breakfast and Evening Meal £12 (£77 per week). "A Yorkshire Haven in Devon" says our Guest Book — come and see why.

BARNSTAPLE. Mrs L. P. A. Joslin, Stone Farm, Brayford, Barnstaple EX32 7PJ (Swimbridge [0271] 830473). Working farm. Lovely old character farmhouse on 180 acre mixed farm, well situated in peaceful countryside six miles between the market town of Barnstaple and Exmoor. Ideal touring centre for moors and glorious coastline. Retaining original charm with exposed beams and open fireplaces, the thoughtfully modernised accommodation is spacious and comfortable. Four double rooms, two bathrooms, diningroom, drawing room, lounge, colour TV. Plentiful fresh food of the highest quality provided for full Breakfast and excellent four-course Dinner. A friendly, relaxed holiday. No restrictions. Guests welcome to roam. Moderate terms for Bed and Breakfast or Bed and Breakfast and Dinner. Reductions for children. No pets.

BARNSTAPLE
Lower Hearson Country Holidays,
Swimbridge, Barnstaple, N. Devon EX32 0QH

**VALERIE AND TONY WELLS
0271 830702**

16th century country guest house in 12 acres. Three double bedrooms, all en suite, shower/bath. Central heating. Food of high quality with personal and friendly service from owners. **Large heated swimming pool, Snooker room.** Table tennis and darts. Beautiful scenery, within easy reach of Exmoor, Dartmoor and lovely N. Devon beaches. Village shops and pub, one and a half miles Bishops Tawton. Barnstaple five miles. Also available two self catering cottages of high standard with Evening Meals in house if desired.

BARNSTAPLE. North Devon Holiday Centre, 48 Boutport Street, Barnstaple EX31 1SE (0271) 76322 (24-hour brochure service) — (0271) 44915 (Tourist Information). Choose unspoilt North Devon and enjoy a change that offers so much more than the rest. New colour guide and booking service to over 100 recommended Hotels and Guest Houses from peaceful country inns to first class hotels with every amenity you could wish for. Bargain break weekends from £20 per person. Beautiful unspoilt region around Exmoor and the wide sandy beaches and coves of Devon's Golden Coast. First class value assured. See also Full Page Colour Advertisement in this Guide. *

BARNSTAPLE. Mr K. J. Le Voir, Muddlebridge House, Fremington, Barnstaple EX31 2NQ (Barnstaple [0271] 76073). A large period country house, close to beaches, offers food of the highest quality. Two double bedrooms, plus family room with shower/bathroom, central heating, hot and cold in each room. Children welcome, cot and high chair. Car not essential, but ample parking. For self-catering holidays, six superb cottages converted from stone farm buildings sleeping two-eight persons, set in two acres of formal gardens, heated swimming pool, children's play area, snooker room, table tennis etc. Evening Meals available. Residents' bar. Open mid-March to mid-January. See also Colour Display Advertisement. *

BARNSTAPLE. Mrs Hazel Kingdon, Waytown Farm, Shirwell, Barnstaple EX31 4JN (Shirwell [027-182] 396). Working farm. Waytown is a beef and sheep farm on the A39 three miles from Barnstaple which has a Leisure Centre. Our attractive 17th century farmhouse is set in pleasant countryside. Dartmoor can be seen in the distance; within easy reach of Exmoor National Park and sandy beaches. Fishing nearby. Guests made welcome with home cooking (own vegetables, cream, eggs). Accommodation consists of two double and one family bedrooms (all with washbasins); bathroom, two toilets; lounge with TV. All children welcome. Babysitting. Cot, high chair. Ample parking. Sorry, no pets. Open all year. SAE for terms for Bed, Breakfast and Evening Meal (optional). Reductions for children under 12.

BARNSTAPLE. Mrs M. Lethaby, Home Farm, Lower Blakewell, Muddiford, Barnstaple EX31 4ET (Barnstaple [0271] 42955). Working farm. AA/RAC listed, ideal for children as there are swings, pony, Wendy house, slide and numerous beaches nearby. Situated in peaceful countryside half mile off the B3230 road about three miles from Barnstaple and seven miles from Ilfracombe. Guests have a choice of accommodation. Either Bed, Breakfast and Evening Meal in the farmhouse or self-catering accommodation, with or without meals, in adjacent cottage or six-berth caravan. Every effort is made to ensure that guests have a comfortable and happy stay. Excellent catering using fresh produce where possible. Farmhouse bedrooms have tea tray and washbasin and there is a sittingroom with colour TV. Access to house at all times. Evening Dinner/Meal, Bed and Breakfast from £10; Bed and Breakfast from £7. Open Easter to October. SAE, please, for brochure.

Please note that entries marked with an asterisk also have a colour display advert in the colour section in this guide

130 Devon BOARD

BARNSTAPLE. Mr and Mrs D. Woodman, The Old Rectory, Challacombe, Barnstaple EX31 4TS (Parracombe [059-83] 342). Within the Exmoor National Park, easily accessible on a good road, The Old Rectory is tucked away peacefully on the edge of Challacombe. A glance at a map of North Devon will show how excellently the house is placed, either for touring the spectacular coastline or for walking on Exmoor. Superbly furnished bedrooms, with tea/coffee making facilities, washbasins and heating. Bathroom and toilets. Lounge, diningroom. Home cooking. Bed and Breakfast from £55 per week; £8.50 per night. Evening Dinner, Bed and Breakfast from £84 per week; £12.50 per night. No VAT charge. Further particulars on request.

BARNSTAPLE. Mrs Sheelagh Darling, Lee House, Marwood, Barnstaple EX31 4DZ (Barnstaple [0271] 74345). A beautiful old manor house dating back to the 13th century. Offering complete seclusion at the end of a long private drive. Three double and two single bedrooms are comfortable and all have their own washbasins. There are two bathrooms and four lavatories. The sittingroom has colour television. Full English breakfast and three-course dinner is served in a spacious diningroom, where the speciality is home cooking and bread, home-baked daily. Easy driving along quiet roads to coast and moors. Not suitable for children under 12 and there is no reduction for children. Bed and Breakfast £10, Bed, Breakfast and Dinner £13. There are no extra charges. Open April to September.

BARNSTAPLE. Mrs G. Hannington, Fair Oak Farmhouse, Fair Oak Farm, Ashford, Barnstaple EX31 4AU (Barnstaple [0271] 73698). Working farm. Modern farmhouse specially catering for families with children. The house is in a rural position overlooking the Taw estuary. Safe, sandy beaches five miles away. Central for touring North Devon and Cornwall. Extra large bedrooms with washbasins. Lounge with colour TV and separate diningroom. Homely atmosphere, babyminding. AA listed. Fire Certificate. Ample parking. Reductions for children. Regret, no dogs. SAE, please, for details and terms.

BARNSTAPLE. Mrs E. Steele, Holywell, Bratton Fleming, Barnstaple EX31 4SD (Brayford [059-88] 213). Working farm. Large country house in 40 acres — mainly oak woodland — designated as an area of great landscape value. Peaceful haven for a comfortable holiday in beautiful surroundings. We keep Exmoor Horn sheep and Jersey cows. Exmoor National Park is within walking distance and North Devon's spectacular coast scenery is only a few miles away. All bedrooms have their own washbasins, and two have en suite bathrooms. Full English Breakfast including home made marmalade and bread, own honey and free range eggs served in panelled diningroom. Bed and Breakfast £9 per day or £56 per week (Evening Meal available). Regret, no dogs.

DEVON – ENDLESS CHOICES!

People never tire of visiting Devon. There's so much to do, like visiting Alscott Farm Museum, Berry Head Country Park, Bickleigh Mill Farm, Farway Countryside Park, Haytor Granite Railway, Kent's Cavern, Dartmoor National Park and of course Plymouth and its Hoe.

BARNSTAPLE. Mrs Jane Jeyes, North Whitefield, Brayford, Barnstaple EX32 7QW (Brayford [059-88] 388). Working farm. This very attractive and comfortable farmhouse is open from March to October offering holidaymakers seclusion and quiet, yet only one and a quarter miles from village of Brayford and HR B3226. North Whitefield is a small 25-acre stock farm with lovely views. Picturesque walks through woods and rolling countryside and an ideal situation for families with children. Sea approximately 12 miles, and many beauty spots and places of interest in Exmoor within easy reach. Barnstaple, South Molton approximately 10 miles. Two guest bedrooms (one with double, one with two single beds), washbasins, also small twin-bedded room available. Guests' lounge/diningroom featuring large stone and oak beam open fireplace. Cot, high chair (on request), babysitting, reduced rates for children. Sorry, no pets. Car essential — parking. Evening Dinner, Bed and Breakfast from £10; Bed and Breakfast from £7.

BARNSTAPLE. Mrs Andrea Cook, Higher Churchill Farm, East Down, Barnstaple EX31 4LT (Shirwell [027-182] 543). Working farm. This 300-year-old farmhouse is set in beautiful countryside on a 350-acre working sheep and cattle farm — part of the National Trust "Arlington Court" Estate. We are centrally situated between beaches and Exmoor. Traditional farmhouse cooking with as much home produce as possible (milk, cream, eggs, meat and vegetables). Accommodation consists of four bedrooms and two bathrooms, catering for two families. Diningroom with separate tables. Sittingroom with colour TV. Facilities for making tea, coffee and packed lunches. Reductions for children. Cot, high chair and babysitting available. Car essential — parking. SAE, please, for terms for Bed, Breakfast and Evening Meal.

BARNSTAPLE. Mrs S. Sampson, Ashford Holt, Ashford, Barnstaple EX31 4BT (Barnstaple [0271] 45225). Charming Georgian guest house in stock-raising farmlands and private garden facing south with views of the Taw Estuary. Centrally placed for Exmoor, Dartmoor and the beautiful North Devon Coast. Ashford is a small attractive village with church and post office, three miles from market town of Barnstaple. One family and two double bedrooms, all with hot and cold; bathroom, three toilets; lounge with colour TV; separate diningroom. Children welcome, cot, and babysitting by arrangement. Open June to end of August. Sorry, no dogs. Excellent cuisine. Car essential, ample parking. Bathing, riding, tennis, surfing, golf, etc. in area. Evening Dinner, Bed and Breakfast or Bed and Breakfast only. Reduced rates for children sharing parents' room. SAE, please.

BARNSTAPLE near. Mrs J. Turner, Whitstone Farm, Chittlehampton, Umberleigh EX37 9RB (Chittlehamholt [07694] 410). Whitstone Farm is situated in lovely countryside some five miles from South Molton and eight miles from Barnstaple. The North Devon coast with its sandy beaches, Exmoor and Dartmoor are all easily accessible. Guests are sure of a warm welcome to this friendly family run 250 acre working dairy and corn farm with original farm pond stocked with coarse fish, ducks and wild life. The spacious farmhouse provides comfortable carpeted accommodation with double and family rooms with washbasins. Guests' own diningroom where plenty of farmhouse food is served; lounge with colour television . Also snooker and table tennis. Children welcome at reduced rates. Regret, no pets. Bed and Breakfast and Evening Dinner (four course plus coffee) or Bed and Breakfast only. Stamp please or telephone for brochure and terms.

BARNSTAPLE near. Mrs E. M. Petherick, Higher Heale, Parracombe, Near Barnstaple EX31 4QE (Parracombe [059-83] 333). Working farm. A peaceful holiday with all the comfort of log fires, home cooking and farm fresh produce is offered at Higher Heale. The farm lies on the edge of Exmoor, overlooking the lovely Heddon Valley, eight miles from the sea. A car is needed in this rural spot and parking is available. One double and one family bedrooms; bathroom; sittingroom. Children welcome at reduced rates. Open from May to October for Evening Dinner, Bed and Breakfast or Bed and Breakfast. SAE, please, for further details and terms.

BARNSTAPLE near. Mrs Joyce Ley, West Barton, Alverdiscott, Near Barnstaple EX31 3PT (Newton Tracey [027 185] 230). Working farm. West Barton is a family farm of 180 acres with cows, sheep and calves. Reductions for children under 10. Sorry, no dogs. Six miles from sandy beach. Bed, Breakfast and optional Evening Meal. West Barton is pleasantly situated beside the B3232 Barnstaple to Torrington road with Bideford only five miles away. Also within easy reach of Exmoor and Dartmoor and many beaches. Guests will be served with the best of farm produce. One family room, one double with twin beds and one double-bedded room. Cot and highchair available. Garage for car. Dining/sittingroom with TV.

Terms quoted in this publication may be subject to increase if rises in costs necessitate

BARNSTAPLE near. Mrs Margaret Pover, The Old Rectory, Marwood, Near Barnstaple EX31 4EB (Barnstaple [0271] 44433). Detached Georgian former rectory, circa 1800. Listed house. Secluded walled gardens, lawns and orchard. In conservation area and opposite Marwood Hill Gardens. Double bedrooms, all with washbasins, one en suite. Central heating/log fires. Excellent home cooking with wine served with five-course dinner. Happy family home. Open April to October. Children over 10 welcome; sorry, no pets. Private game fishing available. Easy reach Moors, coast, National Trust properties, gardens, golf courses, riding, surfing etc. Early morning tea with biscuits and full English Breakfast. Car essential. Ample parking. Evening Dinner, Bed and Breakfast from £16 per day; Bed and Breakfast from £10.50 per day. Weekly terms. A warm welcome is assured at The Old Rectory.

BARNSTAPLE near. Mrs Dolores Foote, Lower Upcott Farm, Stowford, Chittlehampton, Umberleigh, Near Barnstaple EX37 9RX (Chittlehamholt [076-94] 289). Working farm. In a peaceful setting above the hamlet of Stowford, this 16th century Devon longhouse enjoys lovely views across the valley. The house has recently been modernised without losing the character or features of the old property. Comfortable and homely, with a large garden, accommodation comprises two double and one family bedrooms with washbasins; guest bathroom and shower, two guests' toilets; sittingroom with colour TV; diningroom where good, wholesome food, prepared largely from own produce, is served in a friendly atmosphere. Full English Breakfast and three-course Dinner. Central heating and open fires. Children welcome, cot and babysitting available. Sorry, no pets. Car essential — ample parking. Evening Dinner, Bed and Breakfast. Open all year. Also one four-berth caravan for self-catering holiday. Brochure available. Visitors travelling from A361 (South Molton/Barnstaple) take B3227 to Umberleigh.

BARNSTAPLE near. Mrs K. Andrew, "Linscott Farm," Tawstock, Near Barnstaple EX31 3JY (Newton Tracey [027-185] 213). Working farm, join in. Have a quiet carefree holiday at Linscott Farm; personal attention and best of home cooking assured. Children welcome and they will love the two lovely Shetland ponies, dogs, cats and other small farm animals. The farmhouse is pleasantly situated with picturesque views and modern comforts. Three family rooms, one double and one single bedrooms (three with washbasins); sitting and diningrooms. When guests can tear themselves away from the farm activities, the sea is six miles away and there is a riding stable one mile off. Cot, high chair and babysitting offered. Sorry, no dogs. SAE, please, for terms for Evening Dinner, Bed and Breakfast.

BARNSTAPLE. Mrs F. E. Barnett, West Hill, Parracombe, Barnstaple EX31 4PF (Parracombe [059-83] 384). Working farm. West Hill is a 200-year-old farmhouse in beautiful countryside inside Exmoor National Park, within easy driving distance of several beaches. This smallholding has Jersey cows, calves, sheep, ducks and chickens. The farmhouse, carpeted throughout, has two double, one single, two family rooms, bathroom and shower room. The beamed diningroom and lounge have open log fires. Colour TV. Children very welcome at reduced rates whatever the season. Car essential, ample parking. Guests may use the house at any time. The accent is on happy and carefree holidays for all. Pets welcome. Home and local produce — good food and plenty. Bed, Breakfast and Evening Meal. Fire Certificate. SAE, please, for terms.

BEAWORTHY. Mrs J. Bass, Forda Farm, Ashwater, Beaworthy EX21 5DL (Beaworthy [040-922] 477). Working farm. Situated in a quiet valley away from main roads and four-and-a-half miles south of the busy market town of Holsworthy, 200-acre cattle and sheep farm, centrally placed for exploring the Devon and Cornish coasts and moors with many National Trust and sporting facilities nearby. A warm welcome is assured to all guests visiting the comfortable farmhouse, set in spacious grounds, offering two double and one single rooms. Large diningroom has separate tables; lounge and study with colour TV. Full central heating and log fires. Good home cooking a speciality. Sorry, no pets. SAE, please, or 'phone for rates which include Evening Meal, Bed and Breakfast. Also available, self-contained cottage sleeping eight persons.

BIDEFORD. Mrs C. M. Tremeer, Garnacott Farm, Alverdiscott, Torrington EX38 7HG (Newton Tracey [027-185] 282). Working farm. Situated amidst quiet and peaceful countryside with delightful scenery, mixed working farm of 85 acres carrying cows, sheep, calves and poultry, where visitors are welcome to participate in farm activities. Homely, comfortable accommodation with plenty of good farmhouse cooking using own produce — milk, eggs, cream and vegetables. Within easy reach of North Devon and Cornish beaches and moors. Bideford, Torrington four miles, Barnstaple seven miles and lovely sandy beaches only five miles. Two family bedrooms, one single (two with washbasins); bathroom, toilet. Sitting/diningroom with wood-burning stove and colour TV. Children welcome; babysitting arranged. Sorry, no pets. Car essential — parking. Evening Dinner, Bed and Breakfast £60 weekly (£9 daily); Bed and Breakfast £47 weekly (£7 daily). Reductions for children under 10. Open March to November. AA listed.

Mrs Gillian M. Bowden, Higher Odham, Highampton, Beaworthy, Devon EX21 5LX
Tel. Black Torrington (040-923) 324

This red and white bricked house, surrounded by lawns and flower beds is on a 104-acre dairy, beef and sheep farm, one mile from the village with its public houses, shop and riding stable. Between two market towns, the house is central for moor and sea. Lovely country walks nearby. A happy atmosphere prevails – the Bowdens have two girls and a boy – and most of the food served is grown on the farm. Three double or family bedrooms, one single bedroom (three with washbasins); bathroom, two toilets; two sittingrooms; diningroom. Cot, high chair and babysitting available. Log fires. Available March to October. Car essential; parking. Swing, see-saw, slide and sand pit on lawns. Evening Dinner, Bed and Breakfast £10 daily (£63 weekly) or Bed and Breakfast £6.50 daily (£43 weekly). SAE, please. Reduced rates for children.

BIDEFORD near. Mrs B. A. Ford, Webbery Barton, Near Bideford EX39 4PU (Newton Tracey [027-185] 395). Working farm, join in. Webbery Barton is a 400-acre mixed farm with a large 18th-century farmhouse. Situated three miles from Bideford, five miles from nearest beach, eight miles from Barnstaple with its Leisure Centre. Ideal for touring all North Devon's many beaches and beauty spots. Visitors are encouraged to take part in any farm activities. There is a pony for children to ride. We take only one family at a time so you are assured of personal attention. Reduced rates for children; cot, high chair and babysitting offered. Open Easter to October. Sorry, no pets. Car essential — parking. Bed, Breakfast and Evening Meal or Bed and Breakfast only. SAE, please, for terms or telephone.

BIDEFORD. Mrs Betty Willes, Raddy Farm, Instow, Bideford EX39 4LW (Instow [0271] 860433). Set in quiet countryside typical of North Devon, Raddy Farmhouse, a south facing farmhouse old, but modernised, with lawn at front. Sandy beach at Instow only three-quarters of a mile away; market towns of Bideford and Barnstaple three and six miles away, respectively. Very central for touring the beautiful beaches of North Devon and the much-loved Exmoor and Dartmoor are nearby. Cooking is traditional with most of the food home produced. Colour TV for visitors; babysitting. Two double, one single, two family bedrooms, all with washbasins; bathroom, two toilets; two sittingrooms and diningroom. Sorry, no pets. Car essential, parking. Children welcome at reduced rates. Open May to September for Evening Dinner, Bed and Breakfast or Bed and Breakfast only. Terms on request.

BIDEFORD. Mrs A. Hancock, Midway Farm, Parkham, Bideford EX39 5PT (Clovelly [02373] 330). The Bungalow is pleasantly situated on a smallholding of 19 acres in open countryside, two miles from the A39 and five miles from the coast. Ideal for touring or seaside holidays with bathing, surfing, golf, tennis and riding all within easy reach. Plenty of good food and home-grown produce. Accommodation in two double bedrooms with washbasins; bathroom, toilet; diningroom; sittingroom. Children welcome, cot available; babysitting; TV. Sorry no pets. Car essential. Parking space. Open May to September for Bed, Breakfast and Evening Meal or Bed and Breakfast only. SAE, please, or phone for terms. Reductions for children.

BIDEFORD. Mrs Brenda Slee, Southdown Farm, Higher Clovelly, Bideford EX39 5SA (Clovelly [023-73] 452). Working farm. "Southdown" is a 150-acre dairy farm where guests are warmly greeted into a family atmosphere from Easter to September and welcome to explore the farm. The south facing farmhouse is set in an unspoilt valley with sandy beaches of North Devon only three to four miles away. Golf, riding and surfing at Bideford (10 miles), Bude (15) and historical places of interest nearby. The fully carpeted house offers one family, one double, two single bedrooms, two bathrooms, two toilets; a comfortable sittingroom with colour TV, diningroom. Good home cooking is a speciality using fresh farm produce. Children welcome at reduced rates, cot, high chair, babysitting offered. No pets. Evening Dinner, Bed and Breakfast or Bed and Breakfast. SAE, please. Car essential — ample parking.

BIDEFORD. Mrs M. Ogle, Lower Winsford Farmhouse, Abbotsham, Bideford EX39 3QP ((Bideford [02372] 75083). Lower Winsford Farmhouse is in a rural setting on the edge of Abbotsham village. A very pretty part of North Devon with some beautiful coastal walks and three miles away the smooth sands with safe bathing at Westward Ho! The old port and market town of Bideford is two miles away. Dartmoor and Exmoor are easily accessible. Lower Winsford Farmhouse is situated in large gardens and has a pretty courtyard. The atmosphere is welcoming and relaxing with the house being comfortably furnished. The accommodation comprises of a private sittingroom with TV. Diningroom where good farmhouse cooking is attractively served. There are four double bedrooms all with washbasins and there are two bathrooms. Children over the age of five years are welcome at reduced rates. Babysitting is available. A car is essential and there is plenty of parking space. Regret, no pets. Terms for Bed and Breakfast or Bed, Breakfast and Evening Meal on request. Open from April to September.

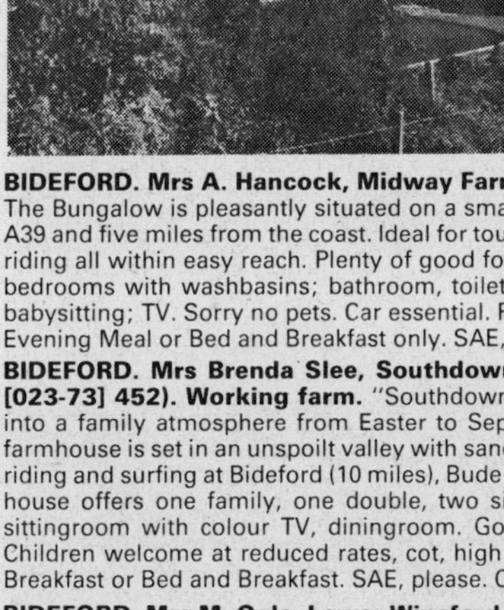

134 Devon BOARD

BIDEFORD. Mr and Mrs L. Spitzer, Sonnenheim Hotel, Heywood Road, Bideford EX39 2QA (Bideford [023-72] 74989). Attractive Georgian residence set in its own grounds of approximately one acre, halfway between Bideford and Northam, close to golf course and Westward Ho! beach, a short walk down to riverside. Large rooms and friendly family atmosphere. Full central heating. AA and RAC listed. Traditional English Breakfast. Some rooms with private bathrooms; comfortable lounge, colour TV. Residential Licence. Children very welcome, cot and high chair, lots of room for them to play in garden. Babysitting offered free of charge. Terms for Bed and Breakfast from £56 per person per week inclusive. Half price for children sharing parents' room. SAE, please, for colour brochure.

BIDEFORD. Mrs S. Clark, Great Ashmansworthy Farm, Woolsery, Bideford EX39 5RE (Bradworthy [040-924] 288). Working farm. A friendly welcome awaits guests at this olde worlde farmhouse in quiet countryside. Visitors are free to look around this 95-acre dairy farm, where fishing is also available. Holsworthy with its cattle market is 10 miles away, as are Bideford and Bude; Clovelly four miles. Children are welcome at reduced rates — cot and babysitting provided. Two double and one single bedrooms are available, or two family rooms with washbasins; bathroom; sittingroom; diningroom; colour TV. Open Easter to end of September. Car essential — parking. Plenty of good food. Terms from about £49 each adult for early morning tea, Bed, Breakfast, Evening Meal. Fire Certificate held.

BIDEFORD. Mrs G. P. Dunn, Southcott Farm, Parkham Ash, Bideford EX39 5PS (Horns Cross [023-75] 287). Working farm, join in. Farmhouse accommodation in beautiful unspoilt countryside, within easy reach of sea. Excellent for touring north Devon and Cornwall. Riding stables nearby, also fishing lakes. Fire Certificate held. Two double and two family bedrooms, all with washbasins; bathroom, toilet; sittingroom and diningroom. Cot, babysitting and reduced rates for children. Sorry, no pets. Log fires. Open all year round. Guests can participate in the activities of this 184-acre mixed farm. Car essential — ample parking. Take A39 to Bucks Cross, turn left, second left, second right. Home cooking and produce. Bed and Breakfast, Evening Meal optional. Reasonable terms.

BIDEFORD. Mrs C. Colwill, Welsford Farm, Hartland EX39 6EQ (Hartland [023-74] 296). Working farm, join in. Relax, enjoy the peaceful countryside, yet be within easy reach of towns, interesting places and picturesque beaches with miles of scenic cliff walks. This 360-acre farm is situated two miles from unspoilt Hartland village; four miles from cobble-stoned Clovelly and the rugged coastline of Hartland Quay. Feel free to wander around the farm and "Pets Corner" at leisure. The farmhouse is comfortably furnished — diningroom, lounge with colour TV; hot and cold in bedrooms. Children welcome at reduced rates — cot, high chair, babysitting always available. Regret, no pets. Plenty of good country food is served using fresh home grown produce. Car essential — parking. Bed and Breakfast, four-course evening meal from £55 weekly. Warm welcome and friendly atmosphere. Open April to October.

BIDEFORD. Mrs Mary Phillips, Hillside, Weare Giffard, Bideford EX39 4QR (Bideford [02372] 72956). A delightful character Georgian farmhouse with oak beams and stonework, situated in the beautiful Torridge valley made famous as the backdrop for 'Tarka the Otter'. All bedrooms have washbasins, shaving points and spring interior mattresses. Golf, fishing, sailing, surfing and exploring the natural beauty of the countryside are all available. Ilfracombe, Lynmouth, Westward Ho! and Clovelly are within easy reach and the golden beaches of Croyde and Woolacombe are a notable feature of the area, with Exmoor and Dartmoor a comfortable drive away. Regret no pets. Car essential. Open from Easter to October for Bed and Breakfast (Dinner optional). There are paintings of the area always on display. Brochure available.

BIDEFORD near. Mrs Yvonne Heard, West Titchberry Farm, Hartland, Near Bideford EX39 6AU (Hartland [023-74] 287). Working farm, join in. Spacious, completely renovated 17th century farmhouse, carpeted and well appointed throughout. One family room with washbasin, one double room and one twin room, bathroom and toilet. Downstairs a lounge with colour TV, diningroom with separate tables where excellent home cooking is served using fresh farm produce. A games room and sheltered walled garden is available for guests' use. The coastal footpath winds its way around this 150-acre mixed farm situated between Hartland Lighthouse and the National Trust beauty spot of Shipload Bay (sand at low tide). Hartland three miles, Clovelly six miles, Bideford and Westward Ho! 15 miles, Bude 18. Children welcome at reduced rates; cot, high chair, babysitting available. Terms on application for Evening Dinner/Meal, Bed and Breakfast or Bed and Breakfast. Open all year except Christmas. Also self catering cottage available.

If you've have found
FARM HOLIDAY GUIDE
of service please tell your friends

BIGBURY. Mrs Julie Widger, Lower Cumery, Bigbury, Kingsbridge TQ7 4NN (Kingsbridge [0548] 830160). Farmhouse set in a very secluded position with fine country views. Two double and one twin-bedded rooms, each with hot and cold vanity unit; one single room. Bathroom, two toilets. Large diningroom; spacious lounge with colour TV. Excellent food with a good variety of home-grown fruit and vegetables and free range eggs. Children welcome at reduced rates; cot, high chair, babysitting available. Sorry, no pets. Large gardens and play area. Wood-burning stoves lit for chilly days as required. Open all year. Bed, Breakfast and Evening Meal £80 per week. Bed and Breakfast £7.50 per night. Lovely sandy beaches nearby. Ideal walking country. Fishing, riding, golf and many places of interest within easy reach. Car essential — parking.

BRADWORTHY. Mr and Mrs P. Lynch, Moorlands Farm, Bradworthy, Holsworthy EX22 7SH (Bradworthy [040-924] 402). "Moorlands," set in a delightfully rural area of North Devon, is a six-and-a-half acre smallholding three quarters of a mile from village overlooking attractive Bradworthy Common. Ideally located for those seeking peace and quiet, touring, walking, surfing. Several unspoiled beaches, or more popular Bude within 20-30 minutes' drive. Dartmoor/Exmoor approximately 20/30 miles. Good fishing abounds including Tamar Lakes, three miles. Eileen and Peter Lynch aim to provide plenty of good traditional food, home or locally produced. Comfortable accommodation, friendly relaxed atmosphere. All rooms have hot and cold with free tea-making facilities. Lounge; Colour TV; outdoor games room with table tennis, darts, etc. Bed and Breakfast £8 to £10; Bed, Breakfast and Evening Dinner £13 to £15. Reductions for children, and weekly rates. Open all year.

Edgemoor Hotel

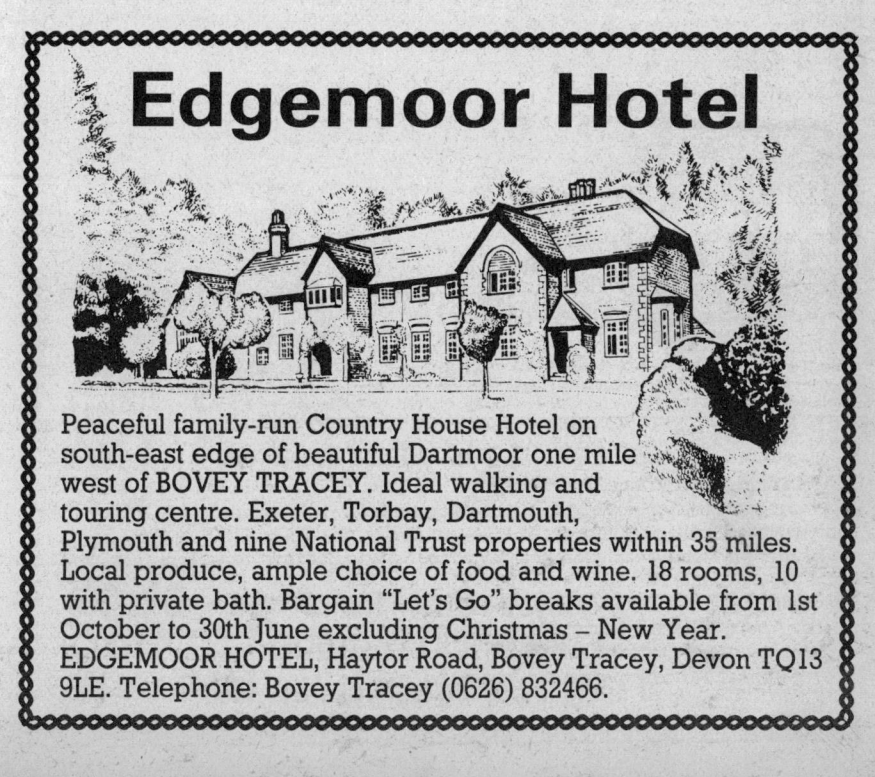

Peaceful family-run Country House Hotel on south-east edge of beautiful Dartmoor one mile west of BOVEY TRACEY. Ideal walking and touring centre. Exeter, Torbay, Dartmouth, Plymouth and nine National Trust properties within 35 miles. Local produce, ample choice of food and wine. 18 rooms, 10 with private bath. Bargain "Let's Go" breaks available from 1st October to 30th June excluding Christmas – New Year.
EDGEMOOR HOTEL, Haytor Road, Bovey Tracey, Devon TQ13 9LE. Telephone: Bovey Tracey (0626) 832466.

BRAUNTON. Mrs Marjorie Cork, Castle Street Farm, North Buckland, Braunton EX33 1HY (Croyde [0271] 890325). Working farm. Situated about one mile from the village of Georgeham, this dairy and mixed farm is within easy reach of beaches. Open Easter to September, Castle Street, a 15th century Longhouse, has two double bedrooms, one could be used as a family room, and also one single/twin bedroom; bathroom/shower and separate toilet for guests. Large sitting/diningroom with colour TV and electric fire. Car essential, ample parking. Bed, Breakfast and Evening Meal. SAE, for details. Reductions for children under 10. Cot available.

BRAUNTON. Mrs Jean M. Barnes, Denham Farm, North Buckland, Braunton EX33 1HY (Croyde [0271] 890297). Working farm. This is a 160-acre beef farm situated in the centre of a small hamlet. A genuine working family farm where guests are allowed to roam around and see the animals (particularly the young calves being fed). All the food is personally prepared by Mrs Barnes to ensure a very high standard, it is good in quality and quantity, and desserts are a speciality. There is a relaxed and happy atmosphere — a home from home — with plenty of room for children to play. Eight bedrooms with washbasins, two bathrooms, toilets plus extra toilet; sittingroom; diningroom, lounge bar. Cots, high chair, babysitting. No pets. Open all year. Car essential — parking. Bed and Breakfast or Evening Dinner, Bed and Breakfast. SAE for terms.

✱ **BRIXHAM. Mr G. Glass, Raddicombe Lodge, 102 Kingswear Road, Brixham TQ5 0EX (Brixham [080-45] 2125).** AA, RAC Listed. Raddicombe Lodge stands in its own grounds, reached by a private drive away from the rush and the noise, overlooking the sea and country with views across Lyme and Start Bay. Situated between Brixham and Dartmouth, the house has a charm and character of its own with open pitched ceilings and lattice windows in many of the bedrooms which all have hot and cold water, mirror lights, shaver lights, over bed or bedside lights and fitted carpets. Separate tables in diningroom. Delicious foods include Brixham crab and fish from the quay. Devon cream, local baked crusty bread and fresh produce from the garden when available, with a fine selection of wines. Central heating. Comfortable lounge, colour TV. Large car park. Room, Breakfast and Evening Dinner from £14.10 to £17.45 including early morning tea, supper time coffee and VAT. Reductions for children sharing room with two adults, according to age. See also Colour Display Advertisement in this Guide.

BUCKFASTLEIGH. Mrs Carole Barnet, Kilbury Manor, Colston Road, Buckfastleigh TQ11 0LN (Buckfastleigh [0364] 43291). Kilbury Manor is a 16th century farmhouse in a quiet country lane in the beautiful Dart Valley, just a few minutes' walk from the town and on the edge of the Dartmoor National Park. The house is set in two acres of garden and orchard. Within walking distance is Buckfast Abbey and the Dart Valley Steam Railway with trains running to the fascinating and historic town of Totnes. Good home-cooked food is served using produce from our own garden. We are happy to provide picnics. Children welcome, cot, high chair, babysitting available. Pets at owners' discretion. Comfortable lounge with colour TV for guests' use; diningroom. Central heating and open fire. Car essential — parking for 12 cars. Open all year. Evening Dinner, Bed and Breakfast from £10; Bed and Breakfast from £5.50. Reductions for children.

BUCKFASTLEIGH. Mr and Mrs E. F. Botell and Mr and Mrs M. Wright, Bossell House Hotel, Plymouth Road, Buckfastleigh TQ11 0DG (Buckfastleigh [0364] 43294). RAC and AA one star licensed Country House Hotel, delightfully situated in three acres of private grounds within Dartmoor National Park, close to Buckfast Abbey and within easy reach of the South Devon beaches. Excellent cuisine, comfortable rooms, ample parking, attractive cellar bar and billiards room. Tennis court, children's play area. Babysitting available and laundry facilities. Local horse riding and swimming. Full Fire Certificate granted, and a friendly welcome is assured from the resident proprietors Mr and Mrs Botell and Mr and Mrs Wright. Open all year the hotel is centrally heated and has seven double, four single and six family rooms, some with private bath or shower. There is a small charge for your pet. SAE, please, for full particulars.

FUN FOR ALL THE FAMILY IN DEVON

Babbacombe Model Village, Torquay; *Beer Modelrama,* Beer, near Seaton; *Dart Valley Steam Railway,* Buckfastleigh; *Torbay & Dartmouth Steam Railway,* Paignton; *Bicton Gardens,* East Budleigh, near Budleigh Salterton; *Grand Western Horseboat Trips,* Tiverton; *The Shire Horse Centre,* Dunstone, Yealmpton, near Plymouth; *Farway Countryside Park,* near Honiton; *Dartmoor Wildlife Park,* Sparkwell, near Plymouth; *Paignton Zoo,* Totnes Road, Paignton; *Plymouth Aquarium,* Plymouth Hoe, Plymouth; *Exeter Maritime Museum,* The Quay, Exeter; *Torbay Aircraft Museum,* Higher Blagdon, near Paignton; *Exmoor Brass Rubbing Centre,* The Smuggler's Den, Queen Street, Lynton; *Dartington Glass,* Linden Close, off School Lane, Torrington; *Yelverton Paperweight Centre,* Leg O'Mutton Corner, Yelverton; *Kents Cavern,* Ilsham Road, Wellswood, Torquay.

ROCKFIELD HOUSE

F.H.G. Diploma and Award Winner

We all need a rest from time to time and ROCKFIELD HOUSE is the perfect place. We are not an hotel, neither do we consider ourselves an ordinary guest house. We offer: An attractive country house in peaceful surroundings on edge of Dartmoor town. Superb touring centre. High quality meals (choice of Breakfast and a four course Evening Dinner with table licence). Spacious bedrooms with good divan beds and tea/coffee making facilities. Tasteful residents' lounge and antique furnished diningroom. Ample parking. Log fires in early and late season and, above all, a warm and friendly welcome.
All you need supply is the time to ring or write for our brochure. Regret no children under 12.

**Lyn and John Allan, Rockfield House, Buckfastleigh, S. Devon TQ11 0BU.
Tel: 0364 43602**

BUCKFASTLEIGH. John and Aileen Hodsall, Furzeleigh Mill Country House Hotel, Dart Bridge, Buckfastleigh TQ11 0JP (Buckfastleigh [0364] 43476). Furzeleigh is a 16th century mill house which has been converted into a modern guest house, while still retaining its old world character. Overlooking Dart Bridge, it is midway between Exeter and Plymouth and ideal for the South Devon coastline. Two single, three family, 11 double bedrooms, all with washbasins (six en-suite); bathrooms, toilets. All bedrooms have comfortable beds and lovely views. The diningroom with its fine oak beams, presents a cosy atmosphere in keeping with good food. Two cheerful lounges and a delightful cocktail bar. Children welcome, cot, high chair. Dog allowed. Open January to November. Only 12 miles from the sea. Car preferable — parking. Terms on request for Evening Meal, Bed and Breakfast or Bed and Breakfast only. SAE, please.

CHAGFORD. Mr G. B. Thompson, Bly House, Chagford TQ13 8BW (Chagford [06473] 2404). Chagford is an unspoilt village set in lovely woodland and river scenery and is also a centre for the wilder beauty of Dartmoor. About 20 miles from the sea, it is equidistant from Exeter, Torquay and Plymouth. Bly House, formerly Chagford Rectory, is idyllically set in five acres of sweeping lawn, garden and woodland, with views to the moor. The centrally heated house is comfortably furnished with antiques, some bedrooms having four poster beds and private bathrooms. Tea-making facilities in all bedrooms. Separate TV lounge. Small children not catered for, our aim being to provide guests with a peaceful holiday in tranquil surroundings, combined with home-cooked food using fresh produce from the garden when possible. Mid-week bookings accepted. Open January to November. Ample parking. Evening Dinner, Bed and Breakfast.

CHAGFORD. Mr and Mrs B. R. Cosford, Claremont Guest House, Mill Street, Chagford TQ13 8AW (Chagford [06473] 3304). Attractive Georgian house situated on the outskirts of a lovely village, close to an excellent range of shops and inns. In the Dartmoor National Park, a superb centre for touring and walking, and within easy reach of all moorland beauty spots. Fishing, riding and golf nearby. Guests welcomed all year and accommodated in one family, one single and three double rooms, all with hot and cold water; shower room, two toilets; residents' lounge with TV open all day; diningroom. Children welcome. Fitted carpets; full central heating. Residential licence. Home cooking and diets catered for. RAC listed and Member of Dartmoor Tourist Association. Evening Dinner, Bed and Breakfast; Bed and Breakfast only. Reductions for children. Terms and brochure on request.

CLOVELLY. Mr and Mrs R. C. Beck, Stroxworthy Farm, Woolfardisworthy, Near Clovelly EX39 5QB (Clovelly [02373] 333). Working farm. Stroxworthy Farm is family run, with a herd of pedigree Guernsey cattle. Guests are made to feel welcome and are free to watch the farm activities, milking and feeding, etc. The picturesque village of Clovelly, with its cobbled street leading to the sea, is nearby. Westward Ho!, with safe bathing, and Bude with its surfing, are within easy reach, as are Dartmoor and Exmoor. Your pleasure and comfort are assured when you relax in either of our two lounges, one with colour TV, and the other with a cosy bar, also a Games Room with a pool table, etc. Diningroom with separate tables where good country food is served, and a popular selection of table wines. Five double, three family and two single bedrooms, all with washbasins. Open from Easter to end October for Evening Dinner, Bed and Breakfast. Terms from £80 inclusive weekly. Reductions for children and Senior Citizens. SAE for Colour Brochure.

CLOVELLY. Mrs Grace Kelly, Jonquil, Burscott Road, Higher Clovelly, Near Bideford EX39 5RW (Clovelly [023-73] 346). Jonquil is set just off the main road into Clovelly, a picturesque cobbled village on the beautiful coast of North Devon. The countryside offers ample opportunity for those who enjoy walking and there are panoramic views over the adjoining farmland. Guests are warmly welcomed all year round and accommodated in centrally heated bedrooms, all with washbasins; bathroom/shower room; lounge/diner with colour television. Bed and Breakfast from £6 per person. Further details on request.

COLYTON. Mrs Ruth Gould, Bonehayne Farm, Colyton EX13 6SG (Farway [040-487] 396). Working farm. Bonehayne Farm, situated in beautiful Coly Valley, set amidst 250 acres dairy farm on banks of River Coly, where daffodils are a feature in Springtime, and Mallard duck and Kingfishers are a common sight. Trout fishing freely available. Woodlands to explore. Visitors welcome to participate in farm activities and make friends with the animals. One family, one double bedroom, with washbasins; bathroom, toilet. Spacious, homely lounge with inglenook fireplace, TV. Varied menu includes roast beef, Yorkshire Pudding, sherry trifle, Devonshire cream etc. Reduced rates, cot, high chair, babysitting for children. Small pets accepted. Parking. Farway Country Park, two riding schools, Honiton Golf Course, weekly cattle market, sea at Seaton, all within four-and-a-half miles. Open April to October. Evening Meal, Bed and Breakfast. Terms on request.

COLYTON. Mrs S. A. Rabjohns, Wiscombe, Linhay Farm, Southleigh, Colyton EX13 6JF (Farway [040-487] 342). Working farm. Ideally situated for touring and exploring all the East Devon coastal resorts and many places of historic and scenic interest, this is a small farm only five miles from Sidmouth and Seaton, both popular seaside resorts. Good sporting and leisure activities within a short radius include fishing, golf, riding school, sailing and swimming. Accommodation comprises one family room and one twin-bedded room. Mrs Rabjohns provides good farmhouse cooking using home produce whenever possible. Children most welcome, with swing and playground for their enjoyment. Ample parking. Write or phone for terms and further details.

COLYTON. Mrs N. A. Rich, Sunnyacre, Rockerhayne Cross, Northleigh, Colyton EX13 6DA (Farway [040487] 422). Working farm. This accommodation is in a farm bungalow on 150-acre dairy/beef farm set in a very scenic, rural position five miles from the coast which has nice beaches. Honiton only three miles away with a golf course and other amenities. Riding stables locally. Places of interest to visit include animal parks and craft centres etc. Farm animals include goats, calves, sheep, chickens, ducks and a dog. Watch the cows being milked. Three bedrooms — one family, one double and one single; bathroom, toilet; diningroom; sittingroom. Open May to September with open fires. Car essential, parking. Children welcome, cot, high chair, babysitting. Regret, no pets. Good home cooking. Evening Dinner, Bed and Breakfast maximum £60. Bed and Breakfast £45. Reduced rates for children.

Terms quoted in this publication may be subject to increase if rises in costs necessitate

COLYTON. Mrs Sheila Lee, Churchstyle Farm, Farway, Colyton EX13 6EQ (Farway [040-487] 383). Working farm. Churchstyle is a very old farmhouse situated beside village church and school with 140 acres of farmland and a dairy herd of 50 and most farm animals including a pony for the children, swing in garden, etc. House has been modernised for guests' convenience but retaining its old world character. Situated 600 feet above sea level at the source of the Coly with panoramic views over the Coly Valley. Food of high quality and a widely varied menu using garden vegetables. A 30-minute drive to beaches (four within seven miles). Countryside Park one-and-a-half miles, many pleasant walks. Two family, one double bedrooms with washbasins; children welcome, cot, high chair, babysitting available. Sorry, no pets. Car essential, parking. Open April/Easter to Autumn. Fire Certificate. SAE for terms for Evening Dinner/Meal, Bed and Breakfast or Bed and Breakfast.

COLYTON. Mrs Judy Bagwell, Perry Hill Farm, Farway, Colyton EX13 6DH (Farway [040-487] 266). Working farm, join in. Attractive Devonshire farmhouse set on a working farm of 134 acres in the heart of the picturesque Coly Valley, four miles from Honiton. Ideally situated for touring and exploring all the East Devon coastal resorts and many places of historic and scenic interest. Guests are invited to participate in the farm activities or simply enjoy the local surroundings with many beautiful walks. Spacious, comfortable accommodation in one double bedroom (with washbasin) and two single rooms; bathroom, toilet; sittingrooms, diningroom. Children welcome, cot, high chair and babysitting is available at any time. Pets accepted with charge for large dogs. Open from April to October, log fires burn on chilly evenings. Car essential — parking. Excellent farmhouse fare and home produce is used in abundance. Evening Dinner/Meal, Bed and Breakfast or Bed and Breakfast. Reductions for children and senior citizens. Further details on request.

COLYTON. Mrs Betty Pearce, Umborne View, Shute, Axminster, Colyton EX13 7QN (Colyton [0297] 52443). Set in quiet and peaceful surroundings, a comfortable bungalow with lovely views, welcomes holidaymakers from January to end November. Warm and friendly atmosphere, "Jerseys" and other animals with which to make friends. Enjoy good farmhouse cooking with Devonshire cream, fresh milk, free range eggs. Accommodation consists of two family rooms, one double, with washbasins; bathroom and shower; one family unit (two rooms with own bathroom). Diningroom. Comfortable lounge. Tea/coffee making facilities. Full central heating. Guests have own keys. Bed, Breakfast and Evening Dinner or Bed and Breakfast. Phone or SAE, please. Terms from £60 weekly. Car essential — parking. Coastal resorts, golf, tennis, horse riding and fishing within easy reach. Fire Certificate held.

COLYTON near. Mrs Brenda Selway, Morganhayes Farm, Southleigh, Near Colyton EX13 6RY (Colyton [0297] 52373). Working farm. Morganhayes is a 130-acre mainly dairy farm where guests are welcome to watch the milking during the evenings. It has a small trout stream running through the grounds. Within easy reach of numerous places of interest including Wildlife Park, Bicton Gardens, Honiton Pottery, Axminster Carpet Factory, Peco Model Railway. Only three-and-a-half miles from sea. A variety of home made dishes including fresh vegetables and fruit from the garden in season. Horse riding available nearby. Two double, one single and one family bedrooms; bathrooms, toilets; sitting/diningroom. Children welcome at reduced rates. Cot, high chair and babysitting available. Log fires. Sorry, no pets. Car essential — parking. Open Easter to October for Evening Meal, Bed and Breakfast or Bed and Breakfast. SAE, please.

COMBE MARTIN. Mrs V. Plesner, The Old Coach House, Leigh Road, Combe Martin EX34 0NE (Combe Martin [027188] 2242). Small, quiet yet friendly guest house open all year, situated on the outskirts of the village, one and a half miles from the sea. Comfortably furnished with accommodation in three spacious double bedrooms and one family room, all with washbasins and shaver points. Diningroom with separate tables; lounge with colour TV. Homely atmosphere and a selection of delicious food with generous portions to satisfy those holiday appetites. Children welcome, cot and babysitting. Pets allowed (small). Car essential, parking. Visitors can be assured of comfortable accommodation combined with a superb location and a friendly atmosphere. Terms and further details on application.

COMBE MARTIN. Mrs Mary Peacock, Longlands Farm, Combe Martin, Ilfracombe EX34 0PD (Combe Martin [027-188] 3522). "Longlands" is situated on the edge of the Exmoor National Park, in a beautiful and peaceful valley. The House stands on a plateau, above its own Lake, enjoying panoramic views. Within easy reach of all well-known North Devon beauty spots, the resorts of Ilfracombe and Lynton and the sandy beaches of Woolacombe. The market town of Barnstaple is about 10 miles. The house has four double and two family rooms, all with washbasins and shaver points; two showers, one bathroom and three WCs. Lounge, TV lounge and sun lounge. Diningroom with separate tables. Home grown food when available. Residential licence. Children welcome — cot, high chair and babysitting provided. Reduced rates for children. Dogs by arrangement. Devon Fire Certificate held. AA listed. Car essential — plenty of parking. SAE, please for Brochure and terms for Bed, Breakfast and Evening meal, or Bed and Breakfast.

140 Devon BOARD

COMBE MARTIN. Mrs I. G. Heywood, South Patchole Farm, Kentisbury, Barnstaple EX31 4NB (Combe Martin [027-188] 3213). Working farm. Guests are welcomed to South Patchole Farm from Easter to October. A mixed farm offering excellent farmhouse fare in homely surroundings with personal attendance. Arlington Court (National Trust) nearby; golf at Ilfracombe and Saunton; Woolacombe, Lynton, Lynmouth and many fine sandy beaches within easy distance, also the market town of Barnstaple. Horse riding, delightful country walks and many places of interest are found locally. Two double bedrooms, two family rooms with H&C; bathroom, two toilets; sittingroom, diningroom with separate tables. Colour TV. Children welcome, cot, high chair and babysitting available and reduced rates for those under 11 years. Car essential — parking. Regret, no dogs. Terms sent on request with SAE. Fire Certificate held.

COMBE MARTIN. Mr and Mrs M. F. Heath, Heathmoor, Holdstone Down, Combe Martin EX34 0PE (Combe Martin [027-188] 3666). This recently modernised country home stands in four acres in Exmoor National Park, 950 feet above sea level, with magnificent all round views. Ideal base for exploring Exmoor and North Devon Coast. Mass of wildlife on doorstep. National Trust Coastal Path adjacent. Personal attention by owners at all times with excellent home cooking and home produce whenever possible. Furnished to a high standard and open all year round. Car essential here and ample parking. Children welcome, reduced rates if sharing parents' room, cot available and owners offer babyminding. Central heating throughout. Fitted carpets. Two miles from village of Combe Martin. Accommodation in two double rooms and one family/double bedroom with shower unit en-suite. Bathroom with shower; two toilets; sittingroom and diningroom. Sorry, no pets. Evening Dinner, Bed and Breakfast; Bed and Breakfast only. SAE, please, for terms.

COMBE MARTIN. Mrs K. H. Roche, Highfield Farm, Long Lane, Kentisbury EX31 4NV (Combe Martin [027-188] 3701). Bed, Breakfast and Evening Dinner. Highfield is a country guest house with a personal touch, described by many guests as 'Home from Home'. Situated in seven acres of grounds and scenery unsurpassed in beauty, it is 800 feet above sea level overlooking Combe Martin and the sea. Glorious Devon aptly describes the surrounding countryside. Central heating, hot and cold water in all bedrooms, adequate bathroom and toilet facilities. Separate tables in diningroom. Comfortable lounge with TV. Residential licence. Children under 10 years of age half price. Good food and comfort in every respect is the aim of the proprietors.

COMBE MARTIN. Mrs M. E. Richards, West Seven Ash Farm, Combe Martin (Combe Martin [027-188] 2494). Working farm. West Seven Ash is a mixed farm of 90 acres, centrally situated for Lynton, Ilfracombe, Woolacombe, Combe Martin, etc. Beautiful beaches, stately homes such as Arlington Court within easy reach. Riding and rambling on Exmoor. Open Easter till October, the farmhouse now has a residential licensed bar and Fire Certificate. Good food served in spacious diningroom, mostly own farm produce — most guests return and bring their friends. Accommodation in four family and two double bedrooms, all with washbasins; bathroom, toilet; sittingroom and diningroom. Children welcome, cot, high chair and babysitting. Pets permitted. Four miles to the sea; car essential — parking. Terms for Evening Dinner, Bed and Breakfast on request. SAE, please, for prompt reply.

CREDITON. Mrs S. M. Bowden, "Woodview", Stoneshill, Sandford, Crediton EX17 4EF (Crediton [036-32] 2001). Working farm. Mrs Bowden, having catered for the public for some years and renowned for good food and friendly atmosphere, now welcomes guests to this new modern bungalow home on the 112-acre mixed farm. One mile from the village of Sandford on the outer edge of the old market town of Crediton. Cathedral City of Exeter nine miles. Beautiful country walks, tennis and golf nearby. Overlooking scenic valley and wood. Only small numbers catered for. One family (or twin bedded room) and one double bedroom, both with washbasins, shaver points and tea-making facilities. Luxuriously furnished lounge/diner with colour TV. Full central heating. Evening Dinner, Bed and Breakfast or Bed and Breakfast only. Open all year except Christmas. Sorry, no pets.

CREDITON. Mr and Mrs R. Barrie-Smith, Great Leigh Farm, Crediton Hamlets, Crediton EX17 3QQ (Cheriton Bishop [064-724] 297). Working farm, join in. Great Leigh Farm is delightfully set in the mid-Devon hills in a quiet position between Cheriton Bishop and Crediton, two miles off the new A30 dual carriageway. Ideally situated for a quiet holiday or for touring Devon and Cornwall. Guests are free to wander over the 80-acre sheep farm and may participate in farm activities. Outstandingly comfortable accommodation with full central heating. Two rooms with bathroom en suite. Children welcome. One family room, one double and one single room. Good home cooking. Open all year. Car essential. No pets, please. Babysitting available. Bed, Breakfast and Evening Dinner from £10. Reduced rates for children.

CREDITON. Derek and Pansy Hill, East Hillerton House Farm, Spreyton, Crediton EX17 5AD (Bow [036-33] 393). Working farm. East Hillerton is set in beautiful unspoilt countryside, some miles from nearest town and a car is essential to make the most of your holiday. Typical Devonshire stock rearing and arable cropping farm of 180 acres with milking cows and beef cattle. The house is surrounded by garden and lawns, plenty of room for children to play and for adults to sit and relax. Comfortable lounge with colour TV; diningroom. Three double, one family bedrooms, all with washbasins; fitted carpets. Plenty of substantial farmhouse fare using home produce and vegetables whenever possible. Children welcome, cot and babysitting. Sorry, no pets. Open all year, except Christmas. Central heating, log fire. Evening Meal, Bed and Breakfast from £10; Bed and Breakfast from £7. Reductions for children.

BOARD Devon 141

CROYDE. Mrs G. M. Adams, Combas Farm, Croyde EX33 1PH (Croyde [0271] 890398). Working * farm. Combas Farm (140-acres) is three-quarters of a mile from the sea. 17th century farmhouse with attractive garden and orchard where children can play. Set in unspoiled valley close to excellent beaches — sand, surf, rock pools. National Trust coastline. Own dairy produce, vegetables, fruit and herbs. Care is taken over presentation and variety of menu. Guests are taken on beer and skittles outing. Tennis one mile, golf three. Access at all times. Tea and coffee available on request. Sorry, no pets. Children welcome, cot, high chair and babysitting. Open May to October. There are two double bedrooms and four family rooms (five with washbasins); bathroom, three toilets; sittingroom; diningroom. Evening Dinner, Bed and Breakfast. Rates reduced for children under 12 years, and for senior citizens early and late season. See full colour advertisement for details.

CULLOMPTON. Mrs B. Hill, Sunnyside Farm, Butterleigh, Cullompton EX15 1PP (Bickleigh [088-45] 322). Working farm. Here at Sunnyside Farm everything is done to give guests a happy holiday. Conveniently situated three-and-a-half miles from M5 it makes an excellent overnight stop and is three miles from the lovely village of Bickleigh, a great tourist attraction, with a craft centre etc. Guests are free to wander round the 150-acre farm and there is a spacious garden for children to play on the lawn and a pony for them to ride. Trout fishing nearby and many places of interest. Comfortable accommodation in two double, one single and two family rooms with washbasins; bathroom, shower, two toilets. Sittingroom has log fire and colour TV; diningroom with separate tables and a sun lounge with panoramic views. Cot, high chair, babysitting and reduced rates for children. Pets allowed. Car essential — parking. Open all year except Christmas. Evening Meal, Bed and Breakfast from £10; Bed and Breakfast from £6.50. AA listed. Fire Certificate held.

CULLOMPTON. Mrs Stella Hurford, Craddock Farm, Craddock, Cullompton EX15 3LH (Craddock [0884] 40306). Working farm, join in. A warm welcome is always assured at Craddock Farm which is situated in the beautiful Culm Valley in the pretty hamlet of Craddock on the B3391 road. The house is spacious and fully modernised. Lounge has colour TV. One double, one twin-bedded and one family bedrooms, all with washbasins. Large lawns, gardens and many amusements and pets for children — cot, high chair and babysitting offered too. Visitors are encouraged to join in farm activities. An abundance of food is served in pleasant diningroom with cream and fresh vegetables daily. Pets permitted free of charge. Open all year. Car essential, parking. Bed and Breakfast from £7 daily for adults; Evening Meal, Bed and Breakfast from £10 daily for adults. Reduced rates for children.

CULLOMPTON near. Mrs Diana F. Gibbins, Wrights Farm, Clyst Hydon, Near Cullompton EX15 2NB (Plymtree [08847] 403). Working farm. We offer you our farming way of life with animals and pets in rural surroundings. Close to Dartmoor, Exmoor and North and South coasts. Outdoor swimming pool and 16th century inn within walking distance. Plenty of healthy home grown produce and a warm and friendly atmosphere. Two double, two family and one single rooms; bathroom, toilet; sittingroom; diningroom. Car essential, ample parking. Children welcome, cot, high chair and reduced rates. Pets welcome. Open April to October. Bed and Breakfast from £6.50; Bed, Breakfast and Evening Meal from £11.00.

DARTMOOR. Miss P. Neal, Middle Stoke Farm, Holne, Near Ashburton, Newton Abbot TQ13 7SS (Poundsgate [036-43] 444). Middle Stoke Farm stands in 60 acres of beautiful, soft, peaceful countryside on the edge of Dartmoor National Park. It is also a Racing Stable, mainly in the winter, in summer months there are several horses around, also sheep — visitors are welcome to take an interest and your own horses are welcome. Every room enjoys extensive views over farmland or the valley of the River Dart. Ideal centre for walking, riding, touring, birdwatching etc. Car not absolutely essential as walks can start from the farm, but preferable. Ample parking. Dartmoor National Park has an extensive programme of Guided Walks. Buckfast Abbey, Dart Valley Railway, Shire Horse Centre are examples of places to visit. Beaches at Torbay within easy reach, approximately 15 miles. Warm welcome in a relaxed atmosphere with plenty of good food will, we hope, want you to return again and again. Two double, two single, two family rooms, with washbasins; bathroom, two toilets; sittingroom, diningroom. Children welcome at reduced rates, cot. Pets £7 per week. Open May to September for Evening Dinner, Bed and Breakfast from £73 weekly (£12 daily); Bed and Breakfast from £55 weekly (£9 daily). All prices plus VAT. SAE, please, or telephone to Miss Neal.

DARTMOOR. Mrs Margaret Phipps, New Cott Farm, Poundsgate, Newton Abbot TQ13 7PD (036 43) 421. Working farm. This working farm in the Dartmoor National Park overlooks miles of Devon countryside. The large garden slopes down to trout ponds where visitors may fish. Ideal area for walking, riding and sightseeing. Homely well-appointed accommodation offering one double, one twin and one family room, all with handbasin, tea and coffee making facilities, electric heating, shaver plugs, towels, etc. Comfortable lounge/diningroom, colour TV, separate tables. Friendly and relaxed atmosphere. Plenty of good fresh food. Children welcome. Ample parking. Bed, Breakfast, Evening Meal. Brochure or phone above for further details.

Dartmoor & South Devon Farm and Country Holidays

Dartmoor and South Devon Farm and Country Holiday Group. A friendly atmosphere has been created by a group of Devonshire families who offer high quality self catering and bed and breakfast, evening meal accommodation. You are assured of a friendly welcome on working farms or delightful country properties. Excellent value. All accommodation inspected by W.C.T.B. Ideal touring centre for Moor to Shore. Please send stamp for brochure to:
Mrs. Linda Harvey, Frost Farm, Bovey Tracey, S. Devon TQ13 9PP.

DARTMOUTH near. Mrs Joan I. Blampey, Hillfield Farm, Hillfield, Near Dartmouth TQ6 0LU (Blacklawton [080-421] 279). Gothic windows are a feature of this old farmhouse, modernised to present day standards of comfort. Four miles from Dartmouth and sea, with several sandy beaches not far away, and Torquay accessible for evening entertainment. One double, one single, four family bedrooms (four with washbasins); bathroom, two toilets; sittingroom, diningroom. Children welcome — cot, high chair, babysitting offered. Pets accepted at small charge. One bedroom to suit disabled guest. Open all year except Christmas. Car necessary, parking. All farmhouse food home produced when in season. Reduced rates for children sharing parents' room; also for senior citizens early/late season. SAE, please, for terms for Evening Meal, Bed and Breakfast or Bed and Breakfast.

DARTMOUTH. Mrs D. E. Keep, "Highcliff", Strete, Dartmouth TQ6 0RU (Stoke Fleming [0803] 770307). "Highcliff", built as the Vicarage, is a Georgian Residence, standing in its own grounds and overlooking the unspoilt scenery of Start Bay with beaches less than a mile in either direction; this is an ideal resting place or touring base for this lovely part of Devon. Here you will be delighted with excellent food and spacious comfort, with all amenities. At the end of each day you will enjoy returning to Highcliff, sure of a warm welcome. AA and RAC recommended. There are six double, two single and two family bedrooms, all with washbasins; three bathrooms, five toilets; lounges and diningroom. Children welcome, cot, high chair and babysitting. Pets allowed free. The house is open from Easter to October for Evening Dinner, Bed and Breakfast or Bed and Breakfast only. SAE, please, for terms. Rates reduced for children.

DAWLISH. Mr and Mrs B. R. Saich, Mimosa Guest House, 11 Barton Terrace, Dawlish EX7 9QH (Dawlish [0626] 863283). This family guest house is AA and RAC listed and lies in a quiet part of town opposite the Manor Gardens, only a few minutes' walk from the sea and shops. Dawlish has a good train, bus and coach service for touring this lovely part of Devon. The town nestles at the foot of Haldon Moor between Exeter and Torquay. Miles of safe, sandy beaches, good sports facilities, golf, tennis, bowling, fishing etc., cinema (free). Lovely walks. Three double, four family, two single bedrooms, with washbasins; shaver points; bedlights (two bedrooms en suite); cotton sheets; five toilets; bathroom and shower; lounge; diningroom with separate tables. Central heating. Children over five welcome. Car not essential. Open Easter to October.

BOARD Devon 143

DAWLISH. Mrs J. A. Smith, Woodhouse Farm, Ashcombe, Dawlish EX7 0QD (Dawlish [0626] 866227). Working farm. Woodhouse is a 270-acre farm, with Friesians and sheep. The comfortable, modernised house has three family and one double bedrooms (three with washbasin); bathroom, two toilets; diningroom and lounge with TV. Only three and a half miles from the lovely beaches of Dawlish and Teignmouth, also Torquay night life only eight miles away; horse riding on Dartmoor. Sailing, fishing and golf nearby. Children's facilities include cot, high chair and babysitting, also reduced rates. Regret, no pets. Car essential with parking provided. Open all year for Evening Dinner/Meal, Bed and Breakfast only. Please send SAE for terms.

DAWLISH. Mr and Mrs T. Crump, MHCI, Radfords Country Hotel, Dawlish EX7 0QN (Dawlish *
[0626] 863322). Come and relax at Radfords in one of our lounges, comfortable bar or lovely garden or alternatively enjoy an action-packed holiday — many activities and sports available here and in the locality. We have family bedrooms or two family suites available, all with a private bathroom; accommodation for at least 24 families. The children will love their special heated indoor pool, the outdoor playground, the freedom of our large gardens and the assorted ponies and dogs there are to talk to. In the evening they can look forward to a swimming gala, live entertainment, a party and their own cartoon show, etc. The adults can look forward to superb food lovingly cooked and served and the various entertainments we arrange for them — from skittle tournaments to a feature film by a cinema company showing a currently popular family film. We also have a fully equipped launderette and an evening babysitter to help make your holiday as relaxing as possible. Mothers can bring babies and small children here with every confidence. AA listed. Member West Country Tourist Board. Please telephone or send for illustrated brochure. See also full page colour display advertisement for further details.

DAWLISH. Mrs E. M. Cracknell, "Brock House," 3 Barton Terrace, Dawlish EX7 9QH (Dawlish [0626] 863311). This is an ideal holiday spot for all ages, well served by bus, coach and train. Safe, sandy beaches within eight minutes' walking distance, also shops and picturesque gardens. The guest house has a homely atmosphere offering accommodation for single person, plus double rooms and family rooms with washbasins. Gas and electric fires; all modern conveniences. Children welcome. Bed and Breakfast only, on daily or weekly basis. There are plenty of restaurants, cafes and takeaway meal shops, usually open on Sundays. Many people enjoy having a real Devon Cream Tea occasionally as a change from an evening meal. Reduced rates OAPs and children under 10 sharing parents' room. Open from March to end of October. SAE for terms. Dawlish is a good centre for touring, being within easy reach of many beauty spots, such as Dartmoor, Torquay, Exeter. SAE for terms. Access to rooms at any time.

EXETER. Mr & Mrs G. Stevens, Venn Farm, Bridford, Exeter EX6 7LF (Christow [0647] 52328). Working farm. Gilbert and Mabel Stevens invite you for a holiday on their small 50-acre stock farm with homely and friendly accommodation in beautiful surroundings of the Teign Valley. Situated between Exeter (eight miles) and the Moors, it is an ideal position for touring, within easy reach of Torbay, the South as well as the many beauty spots and walks on Dartmoor. Bed and Breakfast, with optional Evening Meal, at reasonable prices. Open all year round with a varied menu of good home cooking. Children welcome with babysitting, cot and high chair available. Pets accepted. The house is suitable for disabled guests. Car essential — parking. For further information please write or phone the above.

EXETER. Mrs Mary Brown, Cottles Farm, Woodbury, Exeter EX5 1ED (Woodbury [0395] 32547). Working farm. A charming thatched farmhouse with comfortable accommodation and good home cooking. Our dairy farm is situated in 200-acres of peaceful countryside with wonderful views as far as Dartmoor. Only four miles to Exmouth and the nearest sandy beach, and seven from Exeter where there are many interesting places to visit. Dartmoor and Exmoor are in easy driving distance. Two double bedrooms and one family room with washbasins; bathroom, toilet; lounge/diner. Children welcome; cot and high chair provided; babysitting offered. Bed and Breakfast. Open July, August, September. Reductions for children aged 11 and under.

EXETER near. Mrs J. Williams, Home Farm, Mamhead, Kenton, Near Exeter EX6 8HP (Dawlish [0626] 866259). Working farm. Lovely spot for a quiet holiday, within easy reach of the moors and coast. Beach four miles. This is a 130-acre working farm, with plenty of animals for children to see — donkeys, horses, ducks, peacocks, cows, a red deer. Guests are made very welcome and plenty of good, home-made food is served. Three double, two family rooms, three with washbasins; bathroom, two toilets; sittingroom; diningroom. Central Heating. Pets allowed. Open April-November. Car essential — ample parking. Bed and Breakfast. SAE, please, for prompt reply. Reductions for children according to age. One self-catering flat available, also four caravans.

EXETER near. Mr and Mrs R. H. Cornall, Taylors Farm, Brampford Speke, Near Exeter EX5 5HN (Stoke Canon [039-284] 255). Working farm. Taylors Farm is situated in one of Devon's most peaceful villages in the Exe Valley, only two minutes' walk from river and five miles from Exeter. The house is 16th century, thatched and of historical interest. Although modernised, it still retains open beams and fireplace in lounge. Peaceful, restful and homely holidays, with wholesome food personally prepared. Highly recommended. Two double, two single, one family bedrooms; bathroom, three toilets; sittingroom; diningroom. Children reduced rates. No pets, please. Open March to October. Plenty of parking. Evening Meal, Bed and Breakfast or Bed and Breakfast terms on application. SAE, please, for early reply.

Please note that entries marked with an asterisk also have a colour display advert in the colour section in this guide

EXMOOR. Knowestone Court Hotel, Knowestone, Near South Molton EX36 4RW (Anstey Mills [03984] 457). This former rectory is situated in the delightful thatched village of Knowestone. The private hotel stands in its own secluded grounds with views over miles of unspoilt countryside. Whether you come to walk, fish, shoot, ride or tour in this beautiful area we can offer luxury en suite accommodation at the best place in the locality. Bed and Breakfast £10.50 to £13.50. Dinner (choice of starters, main course and sweets) £6.50. Quality wines less than £4 per bottle. Bar snacks available. Babies free. Children (five to 14) half price. Ask about all year bargain breaks.

Beach and Bracken Exmoor Holidays

From the office beside our Village Inn between Exmoor and the sea we can recommend –

- Farmhouse accommodation with excellent food
- Full range of Inns and Hotels
- Comfortable Self Catering Cottages
- Introductions to all Country Pursuits
- Spring and Autumn Bargains

For advice and free brochure write, ring or call at any time
BEACH and BRACKEN HOLIDAYS (F.H.G.)
White Hart, Bratton Fleming, Barnstaple, Devon EX31 4SA
Tel: Brayford (05988) 702

EXMOUTH. Mrs P. M. Bailey, Lower Coombe Farm, Lympstone, Exmouth EX8 5NA (Exmouth [0395] 264192). Working farm. This fully modernised oak-beamed farmhouse is situated in peaceful surroundings on a 200-acre mixed farm near the picturesque fishing village of Lympstone which was selected to represent Britain in the 1984 European Bloom Competition "Entente Florale" — the beautiful cottage gardens are a delight to see. Three miles to sandy beach at Exmouth, eight to Cathedral city of Exeter. Fishing, sailing, windsurfing, golf and riding locally. Meals are personally prepared using farm produce. Comfort assured in this homely accommodation. Escorted farm walks by arrangement. One double and one family bedrooms; bathroom and toilet; combined sitting/diningroom. Children welcome, babysitting by arrangement. Car not essential, but parking space available. Regret, no pets. Open Easter to October. SAE, please, for terms for Bed and Breakfast with Evening Meal optional. Reductions for children. Mid-week bookings accepted.

EXMOUTH near. Mrs J. L. Hallett, Gulliford Farm, Lympstone, Near Exmouth EX8 5AQ (Topsham [039-287] 3067). Working farm. Three miles from the sea and beautiful sandy beaches of Exmouth, and half-a-mile from the lovely fishing village of Lympstone, on 236 acres of dairy and arable farming, this spacious farmhouse has a beautiful garden with sun terrace, swimming pool, tennis court. Built circa 1594, in an excellent position for touring Devon, with fishing, sailing, golf and riding locally, meals are personally prepared by Mrs Hallett who provides Bed and Breakfast only at the farmhouse. Two lovely cottages, both three-bedroomed, for those who prefer to cater for themselves. The farmhouse has three double and one family bedrooms; two toilets. Lounge with inglenook fireplace, TV, diningroom with separate tables. Cot, high chair, babysitting arranged. Car essential, ample parking. Open all year except Christmas. Tea-making facilities in all bedrooms. SAE for terms and further details for Bed and Breakfast and self-catering cottages.

EXMOUTH near. Mrs C. E. Harding, Wotton Farm, Lympstone, Near Exmouth EX8 5AY (Exmouth [0395] 264401). Working farm, join in. This comfortable farmhouse is on a 100-acre dairy farm, where guests may participate if they wish. Accommodation is in two family bedrooms; bathroom/shower, toilet; dining/sittingroom. Children are welcome and there is a cot, high chair and babysitting available. Sorry, no pets are allowed. Open from April to October with central heating. Car is not essential but there is parking (quarter mile to public transport). Wotton Farm is only two miles from Exmouth's lovely beach. Evening Dinner/Meal, Bed and Breakfast or Bed and Breakfast only. Reduced rates for children.

HOLSWORTHY. Mrs M. I. Hayes, Little Knowle Farm, Pyworthy, Holsworthy EX22 6JY (Holsworthy [0409] 253544). Working farm. Little Knowle Farm dates from the 16th century and has been completely renovated. The lounge with its original oak beams and cloam ovens, is comfortably furnished and has colour TV. The bedrooms have hot and cold, and we also have our own games room. Children are welcome but we regret, no pets. We keep a dairy herd of 90 cows, plus ponies and other cattle. Guests are welcome to watch at milking time and help feed the baby calves. Little Knowle Farm is an ideal centre for touring the West Country. Within a few miles are beautiful moorlands and sandy beaches, with the best surfing in England. A car is essential. Within easy reach of golf, tennis, fishing, riding, bowls, canoeing, rock climbing, walking, squash, archery, wind surfing, heated indoor swimming-pool, discos. Day trips to — Historic Houses, Music museum, Slate Caverns, Pixieland, Farm museum, Clovelly, Lydford Gorge, Ancient castles, Glass factory, Monkey Sanctuary and many more. Bed, Breakfast and Evening Meal: children from £50, adults from £70 per week. No VAT. A warm welcome assured.

HOLSWORTHY. Mrs Hester Gill, Heslden Farm, Bradford, Holsworthy EX22 7AH (Shebbear [040-928] 341). Working farm. Heslden is an 80-acre livestock farm situated amidst lovely Devon countryside, about 15 miles from the coastal resort of Bude, six miles from the market town of Holsworthy. Well-positioned for touring moors, beaches and local attractions. Children particularly welcome and babysitting undertaken free. For the sporting — clay pigeon shooting lay outs. Local facilities include golf, fishing, surfing, horse-riding. Farm participation welcomed. Accommodation consists of one double room, one children's room and one family room. Bathroom. Lounge with TV; diningroom. Car essential. Good home cooking includes fresh milk and cream. Limited number of guests ensures personal attention. For terms for Bed, Breakfast and Evening Meal please enclose SAE. Also self-catering caravan available.

HOLSWORTHY. Mrs Barbara Morris, Chasty House, Chasty, Holsworthy EX22 6NA (Holsworthy [0409] 253511). Set in a peaceful location with lovely views extending to Dartmoor and Bodmin Moor, yet only three-quarters of a mile from the market town of Holsworthy. Swimming, surfing and sandy beaches at Bude, 10 miles away. Dartmoor, Bodmin Moor and Exmoor easily accessible by car. Fishing and sailing at nearby Tamar lakes, and Holsworthy has its own golf course. We offer a happy family atmosphere and welcome children (reduced rates). Lots of toys to play with, calves, hens, cats and pony to enjoy. Plenty of space to run. Babysitting available. Guests have the use of lounge with colour TV. Diningroom; playroom and large garden. Bed, Breakfast and Evening Meal. Sorry, no pets.

HOLSWORTHY. Mrs M. R. Jones, Holladon Farm, Bridgerule, Holsworthy EX22 6LN (Bridgerule [028-881] 268). Working farm. Holladon Farm is a 200-acre mixed farm pleasantly situated on the Devon/Cornwall border, seven miles from coast with Bude being the nearest resort. Within very easy reach of Clovelly and many Devon and Cornish beaches. Golf one mile. Horse riding locally. Excellent home cooking with roast beef, lamb, duck, pork, turkey, etc., on the menu. Two double and three family bedrooms (four with washbasins); bathroom and toilet, lounge, diningroom, colour TV. Children welcome. Cot, high chair and babysitting on request. Sorry, no pets. Car essential, ample parking. The house is open from April to October for Evening Dinner/Meal, Bed and Breakfast or Bed and Breakfast. Fire Certificate held. Reduced rates for children. SAE, please, for terms and brochure.

HOLSWORTHY. Mr and Mrs F. K. Lax, Court Barn Hotel, Clawton, Holsworthy EX22 6PS (North *Tamerton [040-927] 219). AA** RAC**, 2AA Merit Awards, Ashley Courtenay and ExecHotel recommended, BTA Commendation. Keith and Josephine Lax invite you to enjoy the comfort and luxury of their Country House. A warm friendly atmosphere with good cooking is assured, a five-course dinner is served every evening using home and local produce whenever possible. Set in approximately five acres including croquet lawn, putting green with magnificent views of the local countryside, the house is spacious with two lounges, diningroom, intimate bar and sun lounge with pool table. Convenient for fishing, golf, horse riding, tennis, surfing and swimming and also for touring the unspoilt Devon and Cornish countryside and coasts. Children welcome; family rooms available, most with bathrooms en suite. Radio alarms in all bedrooms. Please telephone or write for colour brochure tariff. See also Colour Display Advertisement in this Guide.

HOLSWORTHY. Mr and Mrs Eric and Marion Cornish, Leworthy Farm, Holsworthy (Holsworthy *[0409] 253488). Working farm. Surrounded by beautiful countryside, Leworthy Farm is an excellent centre for touring Devon and Cornwall. It extends to 240 acres and guests will enjoy the farming activities, walks and picnics on the farm. Access is easy to the glorious coastline where there is surfing, swimming and fishing. The standard of food and comfort is very high — AA Award UK Farmhouse of the Year, Farm Holiday Guide Diploma Award, Relais Routiers nominated. Double, single and family bedrooms, en suite available. Sittingrooms; diningroom with separate tables. Residential Licence. Provision is made for children, but regret, no pets. Indoor recreation including badminton, skittles, table tennis, snooker available. Party evenings with live music, hay rides, fishing, pony riding, tennis. Car essential. Winter breaks, complete with inglenook log fires, at out of season rates. Brochure and tariff on request. See also Colour Display Advertisement in this Guide.

Please note that entries marked with an asterisk also have a colour display advert in the colour section in this guide

HOLSWORTHY. Mrs Irene Reader, Headon Farm, Hollacombe, Holsworthy EX22 6NN (Holsworthy [0409] 253721). Working farm. Headon, which is a working family farm, is situated in beautiful unspoiled countryside, some 600 feet above sea level. A dairy herd of Friesians and Devon closewool sheep are kept. Two-and-a-half miles from the ancient market town of Holsworthy; within easy reach of the glorious coastline where swimming, surfing can be enjoyed. Lovely sandy beaches. Fishing at two local lakes, also golf and horse riding available in the district. Two double, one single, three family bedrooms, all with washbasins; bathroom, two toilets; sittingroom with colour TV; diningroom (separate family tables); individual attention, together with good food and comfort — what better proof than the Farm Holiday Guide Diploma won by Headon Farm in 1978. Fire Certificate held. Please send stamp for brochure and tariff. Evening Dinner, Bed and Breakfast, and Bed and Breakfast. Reductions for children. Open April to September.

HOLSWORTHY. Mrs Beryl Holdcroft, Ley Farm, Milton Damerel, Holsworthy EX22 7NY (Milton Damerel [040-926] 259). Working farm. Situated in a secluded position 250 yards from the A388 Bideford to Holsworthy road. Within easy reach of Dartmoor and numerous sandy beaches. The house is spacious and dates from the 15th century and possesses a wealth of character and old world charm. Guests are welcome to wander around the 100-acre farm where they will find cows, calves and poultry. Comfortable family atmosphere and home cooking. Colour TV. Early morning tea and late night snack included. Two family and one single/twin bedrooms; one bathroom, two toilets; sittingroom, diningroom, playroom, kitchenette. Children welcome. Cot, high chair, babysitting available. Sorry, no pets. Open from June to September. Car essential, parking. Evening Meal, Bed and Breakfast or Bed and Breakfast. Reduced rates for children.

HOLSWORTHY. Mrs S. J. Fowler, Hockwill Farm, Newton-St-Petrock, Holsworthy EX22 7LS (Shebbear [040-928] 261). Working farm. Hockwill Farm is a 70-acre farm in the peaceful village of Newton-St-Petrock situated midway between Bideford and Holsworthy. Within easy reach of Exmoor, Dartmoor, 10 miles from the coast and many sandy beaches. Surfing at Bude and safe bathing at Westward Ho! Horses and sheep are kept here. Excellent farmhouse food. Egg and bacon breakfast. Four-course Evening Meal. Early morning tea and late night snack at no extra charge. A welcome cup of tea on arrival. Two double rooms both with washbasins and a single room. Colour TV. Babysitting. Reduced rates for children under 10 years. Guests may be well assured of every comfort in a homely atmosphere. SAE, please, for prompt reply.

HONITON. Mrs Elizabeth Tucker, Lower Luxton Farm, Upottery, Honiton EX14 9PB (Churchstanton [082-360] 269). Working farm. Get away from the toil of everyday life and come to Lower Luxton Farm where a warm welcome awaits you. Set overlooking peaceful Otter Valley facing south, this olde worlde farmhouse, fully modernised, but retaining its charm, is on 120 acres of farmland keeping usual animals and pets to make it a real farm. Guests are welcome to watch the activities. Peaceful walks. Trout fishing on farm. Ideal base for touring south-east Devon. Several places of interest in area. Coast 14 miles; village inn one mile. Good home cooking assured using fresh farm produce (four-course breakfasts and dinners) — including sweets topped with Devon cream — Evening Tea and biscuits included in terms. Family, double, twin or single rooms available with H&C and razor points. Children welcome at reduced rates, also OAP's. Snooker table available for guests. Mid-week bookings and reductions early and late in season. Pets welcome. Terms from £58 per week — Dinner, Bed and Breakfast. SAE for brochure and terms. Open all year.

HONITON. Mrs Sally Cooke, Courtmoor Farm, Upottery, Honiton EX14 9QA (Upottery [040486] 316). Working farm. Enjoy a quiet peaceful holiday on our 170 acres farm comprising mainly dairy and sheep. Guests are free to watch farm activities. The farm is two miles from the village of Upottery with a lane leading off the main A30. No through traffic. There are excellent views of Otter Valley. Good food, mostly home produced meat and vegetables, also home baked bread. Ideally situated for touring the coast and many other places of local interest. Accommodation comprises two double and one twin-bedded rooms (one double can be family room if needed); bathroom; dining room and a sitting room with television and a few children's games. Children welcome; cot and high chair available. Bed, Breakfast and Evening Meal. Car essential. A warm welcome extended to all. Please send for brochure.

HONITON. Mrs P. M. Millett, "Splatt Hayes Farm," Buckerell, Honiton EX14 0ER (Honiton [0404] 850464). "Splatt Hayes" is a lovely old, thatched farmhouse in three acres of land with a cow, goats, pigs, ducks, and poultry etc. Set in the rural village of Buckerell in lovely countryside about eight miles from Devon coast, the house has two family bedrooms, one double, one twin-bedded and one single rooms, all with washbasins. Two bathrooms with toilets and two separate toilets. Comfortable lounge with colour TV and attractive diningroom. Good home cooking with varied menu. Open all year round. Children welcome and babysitting offered. Ample parking — car essential. Regret, no pets. Reduced rates for children. Evening Dinner, Bed and Breakfast. SAE, please.

HONITON. Mrs Shirley Evans, Yarrow Park Farm, Payhembury, Honiton EX14 0HD (Broadhembury [040-484] 245). Working farm. Yarrow Park Farm offers guests every modern convenience and comfort. Situated midway between the M5 at Cullompton and A30 at Honiton, this farm carrying mainly sheep and poultry is in the heart of the beautiful East Devon countryside. Relax in the peaceful garden, enjoy the views. One family, one double bedrooms, bathroom adjacent; lounge-diningroom with TV. Within easy distance from the coast and an hour's drive from the moors. A car is essential to tour this area with its many places of interest. Ample parking. Children welcome at reduced rates. Regret, no dogs. All home grown produce served. Bed, Breakfast and Evening Meal (optional). Open Easter to October. SAE, please, for terms.

HONITON near. Mrs Sylvia J. Retter, Higher Northcote Farm, Monkton, Near Honiton EX14 9QQ (Honiton [0404] 2986). Working farm. Guests are made welcome from May to October on this very old modernised farmhouse lying in pleasant surroundings of 246 acres of grassland for the 180 milking cows; guests have all the benefits of the country and we are only eight miles from the sea. Accommodation in one double, one single, two family rooms, all with washbasins; bathroom, two toilets; sittingroom, diningroom. Children welcome, cot, high chair and babysitting provided. Pets are allowed. Car essential and there is parking. Evening Dinner, Bed and Breakfast or Bed and Breakfast only. Rates are reduced for children. Terms on request.

ILFRACOMBE. Jack and Ethel Park, Sunnymeade Country House Hotel, Dean Cross, West Down, Ilfracombe EX34 8NT (Ilfracombe [0271] 63668). Delightful country house set amidst rolling Devon countryside, yet within easy reach of Devon's famous Golden Coast, 200 yards from bus stop. Choice menu prepared on the premises by chef proprietor. The 10 bedrooms have central heating and tea-makers, some en-suite and two are located on the ground floor. Two bathrooms, plus shower, five toilets. Sittingrooms, diningroom. Residential and Restaurant licence. Children welcome, cots, high chairs and babysitting provided. Large gardens and car park although a car is not essential. AA listed and Member of West Country Tourist Board. Evening Dinner, Bed and Breakfast from £14 daily (£77 weekly); Bed and Breakfast from £8.50 daily. Reduced rates for children. Open all year. Special rates early and late season. A warm welcome from Jack and Ethel Park. Regret, no pets.

ILFRACOMBE near. Mrs M. K. Cowell, Lower Campscott Farm, Lee, Near Ilfracombe (Ilfracombe [0271] 63479). Working farm, join in. Lower Campscott, on a 91-acre farm, offers guests a warm welcome and a happy holiday atmosphere from April to November. Accommodation comprises two double bedrooms; bathroom, toilet; sittingroom and diningroom. Children welcome, but regret no pets. Ideal base for touring the various beauty spots in the area and the unspoilt village of Lee, children will love the many rock pools at Lee Bay. Ilfracombe three miles. Evening Meal, Bed and Breakfast from £77 per week; Bed and Breakfast £49 per week. Also two self-catering cottages fully equipped for four persons in each; electric cooking/heating. Everything supplied except linen. Parking. One caravan also available with gas cooking and heating; shower and flush toilet. Delightful walking country. Weekly terms for caravan £50 to £95.

ILFRACOMBE near. Dawn and Sandy Gilson, Sandy Cove Hotel, Combe Martin Bay, Berrynarbor, Near Ilfracombe (Ilfracombe [027-188] 2243). How would you like to arrive for a week's holiday at a hotel overlooking a beautiful bay, the sea and Exmoor. It has a heated swimming pool and acres of gardens and woods running down to the cliff and edge. The restaurant has extensive à la carte menu and on Saturdays you can enjoy the hot carvery and Swedish Smorgasbord, barbecues, Country and Western cabaret (in the height of the season) and dancing. Guests can use the putting green and games room, fitness room, sauna and sun bed. CHILDREN WELCOME, and FREE AT CERTAIN TIMES OF THE YEAR IF SHARING WITH PARENTS — YOU JUST PAY FOR THEIR MEALS. Babysitting facilities. Pets welcome. Invalids catered for. Open all year. SEE ALSO COLOUR DISPLAY ADVERTISEMENT FOR FULL DETAILS. *

Terms quoted in this publication may be subject to increase if rises in costs necessitate

148　Devon　BOARD

ILFRACOMBE. Mrs B. A. Scothern, "Marlyn" Guest House, 7 Regent Place, Ilfracombe EX34 9AB (Ilfracombe [0271] 63785). This guest house provides comfortable accommodation in a really pleasant part of Ilfracombe, just one minute from the shops and two minutes from the seashore. All the resort's amenities are close at hand. This is a beautiful area in which to spend a holiday. Good walking countryside, an ideal centre for touring North Devon. A warm welcome awaits guests from Easter to October. Seven double, three single and two family bedrooms (all with washbasins); two bathrooms, three toilets; sittingroom, diningroom with separate tables. Residents' licensed bar. Cot, high chair and babysitting available. Gas heating. All rooms nicely decorated and fitted carpets throughout. AA listed. A car is not essential but "lock-up parking" is available. Colour TV. Evening Dinner, Bed and Breakfast and Bed and Breakfast only. Reductions for children and senior citizens. SAE, please, for brochure.

ILFRACOMBE. Mrs M. Johnson, Church Pool Cottage, West Down, Ilfracombe EX34 8NH (Ilfracombe [0271] 66470). West Down is a pretty hamlet in a rural area yet it offers the opportunity to walk, sail, fish, swim, surf board or wind surfing, or take a trip on a steamer to Wales and other coastal areas. Within easy reach of golden sands or charming harbour. An ideal spot for your touring base. Real friendly service and comfortable accommodation. Double, single and family bedrooms with washbasins; bathroom, toilet; sittingroom; diningroom. Children welcome, cot available. Car essential, parking on premises. Handicapped visitors welcome. Pets are welcome. Open April to October. Within easy reach of Exmoor. Evening Dinner/Meal, Bed and Breakfast or Bed and Breakfast only.

ILFRACOMBE. Mr Robert Hill, Chalfont Private Hotel, Church Road, Ilfracombe EX34 8BZ (Ilfracombe [0271] 62224). Choose Chalfont for a relaxing holiday at a reasonable price. Margaret and Rob Hill assure you of a warm welcome, plenty of good food and friendly personal service in a relaxed family atmosphere. Chalfont is situated on a quiet corner within a few minutes' level walk of the town centre and sea-front — 13 comfortable, centrally heated bedrooms (single, double, twin and family) all beautifully appointed with tea-making facilities and some with private facilities. Licensed bar and large colour TV lounge. Snacks and packed lunches are available. Children welcome. Pets by arrangement. Open March to October. Please phone or send SAE for colour brochure and tariff.

ILFRACOMBE near. Mrs Olga M. Basten, Daymer Cottage, Lee, Near Ilfracombe EX34 8LR (Ilfracombe [0271] 63769). Situated on the cliffs overlooking the sea on the outskirts of the unspoilt village of Lee. Only ships pass the front of the house — the road is at the back. Ilfracombe three miles. Plenty of Rock Pools at Lee Bay to keep children happy. Car essential to tour the many beauty spots in the area. Ample parking. This is a very happy household where children and pets are welcome. Three-course Breakfast, four-course Evening Meal. Early morning tea for Mums and Dads and tea and biscuits around 10 pm included in the very reasonable terms. Cot, high chair and babysitting provided. Reductions for children. Open March to October. Terms on request.

ILFRACOMBE. Mr and Mrs John & Diane Parry, Abbeydale Hotel, Torrs Park, Ilfracombe EX34 8AY (Ilfracombe [0271] 63878). Situated in a quiet protected area of Victorian Mansions at the foot of the National Trust Torrs Walks only a short walk away from the busy High Street Shopping Centre, Seafront, Pier, Promenade, picturesque Harbour and Quay. Facilities include a cosy well-stocked Residents' Lounge Bar/TV Video Lounge, Sun Lounge/Games Room and parking within Hotel grounds and in Torrs Park. All bedrooms have colour TVs. Video films are available every day. Weekly terms from June to September include a free mystery coach trip. Dogs are most welcome — free of charge. Special Christmas and New Year programmes. Phone John or Diane Parry for free colour brochure. Some en-suite rooms. Bed, Breakfast and Evening Meal with choice of menu from £78 to £98 per week including VAT.

WHEN MAKING ENQUIRIES PLEASE MENTION FARM HOLIDAY GUIDE

BOARD   Devon   149

IVYBRIDGE. Mr and Mrs D. Johns, Hillhead Farm, Ugborough, Ivybridge PL21 0HQ (Ivybridge [075-54] 2674 or Plymouth [0752] 892674). Working farm. Comfortable accommodation and good, home-produced food. Busy farm with plenty to see. Set in rolling Devonshire countryside within walking distance of Dartmoor. Choice of beaches within 10 miles. Near towns of interest including Plymouth, with its new Theatre Royal, Totnes, Kingsbridge and Salcombe. Pony trekking, golf available nearby. Bed and Breakfast — Adults £7 per night; Bed, Breakfast and Evening Meal £10 per night. Reduced rates for children — cot, baby equipment available. Double and twin bedrooms, family room with double and single bed. Open all year. From A38 at Wrangaton Cross, turn left to Ermington B3210, turn right at first crossroads (signpost Ugborough), across next crossroads, continue three quarters of a mile to Hillhead Cross, turn left — farm 75 yards on left.

IVYBRIDGE. Mrs R. A. Cole, West Peek Farm, Bittaford, Ivybridge PL21 0EU (Plymouth [0752] 892329). Working farm. This 16th century Devon longhouse, situated on a 130-acre mixed farm, nestles into the Dartmoor hills and overlooks the village of Bittaford. It is an ideal centre for walking and touring many places of interest. Local sandy beaches approximately 10 miles; riding stables and golf course within two miles; Ivybridge two and Plymouth 15 miles. Good home cooking is served in a happy relaxed atmosphere. Two family bedrooms; bathroom, toilet; sitting/diningroom with colour TV. Children welcome — reductions, cot, high chair and babysitting available. Open Easter to October for Evening Meal, Bed and Breakfast or Bed and Breakfast only. SAE, please, or telephone for terms. Car essential — parking.

IVYBRIDGE near. Mrs Pat Stephens, Venn Farm, Ugborough, Near Ivybridge PL21 0PE (South Brent [036-47] 3240). Working farm. Venn Farm is situated one mile from A38 dual carriageway and is ideally placed amidst lovely countryside of the South Hams. Near the Moors and within easy reach of the seaside resorts. Children enjoy taking an interest in farm life and there are always young animals around to delight them. The large grounds enable youngsters to explore. Two family bedrooms with washbasins; one double room; bathroom; two toilets; two sittingrooms; diningroom. Guests enjoy the 'carve-your-own' roasts which are a popular feature. Cot, babysitting and reduced rates for children under 10 years. Pets allowed. Car essential — parking. Open from May to September. Evening Meal, Bed and Breakfast. SAE, please, for terms to Mrs P. Stephens.

KINGSBRIDGE. David and Avril Adkins, Hope Cove Hotel, Inner Hope, Kingsbridge TQ7 3HP ✱ (Kingsbridge [0548] 561215). Hope Cove Hotel is a small licensed Hotel, 50 yards to sandy beach with slipway and adjoining National Trust area with magnificent coastal walks. Well appointed bedrooms, some with private bathrooms. Radios in all rooms. Bar, bar lounge and separate television room. Reputation for good food. Reduced rates for spring, early and late summer, special terms for children. Own car park. Ashley Courtenay recommended. Also see Full Colour Supplement of this Guide for full details.

KINGSBRIDGE near. Mr and Mrs C. M. Davies, Maelcombe House, East Prawle, Near Kingsbridge ✱ (Chivelstone [054-851] 300). A small coastal farm nestling beneath wooded cliffs overlooking Lannacombe Bay. The beach is one minute from the comfortable farmhouse which is nearly the most southerly in Devon. Guests have choice of family, double or single rooms. Food is excellent, much being produced on the farm and freshly caught seafood is a speciality. There is much to do, fishing, bathing, spectacular walking, exploring, climbing or just relaxing in the gardens. Prices from £59.50 per week with special reductions for children. There is also a self-catering flat to sleep six, and camping facilities are provided. Telephone or write for colour brochure. See also Colour Display Advertisement in this Guide.

KINGSBRIDGE. Mrs F. Newsham, Marsh Mills, Aveton Gifford, Near Kingsbridge TQ7 4JW (Kingsbridge [0548] 550549). Marsh Mills, a former 14th-century Mill House, is set in four and a half acres of gardens and pastures and overlooks the River Avon. Kingsbridge is four miles away, Plymouth with excellent shopping centre, cinemas and theatres is less than 18, Salcombe popular coastal resort, seven miles away. Salcombe Estuary provides opportunities for small boat and dinghy sailing. Fishing, inshore or deep sea, arranged. Walking, riding, wild life. Sea at Bigbury Bay, also golf, and Thurlestone offers tennis, squash and badminton. A warm welcome is extended to all guests to Marsh Mills. All bedrooms have tea/coffee making facilities and guests have own lounge/diningroom with colour TV. Evening meals by arrangement. Packed lunches if required. Cot and babysitting available. Open all year except Christmas. Car essential, parking. Brochure and prices on request.

KINGSBRIDGE near. Mrs L. M. Smith, Yeo Farm, Topsham Bridge, Woodleigh, Near Kingsbridge TQ7 4DR (Kingsbridge [0548] 550586). Working farm. Beautiful farmhouse tastefully renovated to high standard of comfort, nestling in Avon Valley, bounded by river with one mile of salmon and sea trout single bank fishing lying within property boundary. Behind and to the north of the house are woods rich in bird and animal life. Ideal situation for bird watching and walking; beaches and Dartmoor within 15 minutes. Accommodation comprises two double, one family bedrooms; two bathrooms, three toilets. Sittingroom; diningroom. Central heating and log fires. Children welcome at reduced rates, babysitting available. Pets accepted at small charge. Car essential — parking. Open all year for Bed, Breakfast and Evening Dinner from £12.50; Bed and Breakfast from £8. Good home cooking. Also available two acres for five touring caravans and campers.

150 Devon BOARD

KINGSBRIDGE. Ms Denise Lyndale, Holmfield, West Charleton, Kingsbridge (Frogmore [054853] 721). Holmfield is a spacious, character-filled 17th century farmhouse, three miles from the beach and superb coastal walks. It is right in the heart of the South Hams — walking, fishing, sailing, horse riding, lovely pubs, all close by. Swimming pool for guests' use in the lovely peaceful and sunny garden. Double, single and family bedrooms, all with washbasins, two with four poster beds and one with brass bed. All bedrooms are large and have south facing garden views. Two bathrooms, three toilets; sittingroom; TV lounge; diningroom. Open April 1st to October with central heating. Children are welcome and there is cot, high chair and reduced rates. A full English Breakfast is given in the beamed diningroom with inglenook fireplace. Car essential, ample parking. Bed and Breakfast from £10.

KINGSBRIDGE. Mr N. Oldham, Well Cottage, Galmpton Cross, Near Hope Cove, Kingsbridge TQ7 3EW (0548-561933). Large family run country cottage, situated in the beautiful South Hams area. One mile from Hope Cove with sandy beaches, also one mile from Thurlestone Sands. Fantastic cliff walks from Bolt Tail to Salcombe — seven miles of cliff walk, or three and a half miles by road. The town of Kingsbridge is only five miles away with its many shops. Fishing and boating trips can be arranged, also windsurfing, water skiing and diving for the more energetic. Comfortable accommodation in double and twin bedded rooms each with H/C; large sittingroom with TV; ample car parking. Washing and drying facilities. Children and pets welcome. Babysitting service available. Bed and Breakfast from £8.00, Evening Meal from £4.50 for three courses. Please telephone.

KINGSBRIDGE. Mr and Mrs Peter and Elaine Jones, Little Orchard, Thurlestone Sands, Kingsbridge TQ7 3JY (Kingsbridge [0548] 561279). Little Orchard is an oak-panelled country house set in lovely countryside and we are situated just 400 yards from the beach, which can easily be seen from the house. All rooms are fitted with en suite facilities and we really pride ourselves on the degree of comfort and service provided. Our aim for the evenings is to provide an atmosphere similar to a dinner party with enormous emphasis laid on the standard of cuisine provided. Golfers, fishermen and walkers are all within easy reach of their chosen sport, whilst we ourselves provide windsurfing facilities both for the beginner and expert together with a rescue boat for your safety. R.Y.A. instructors. Open from March to November. Enquiries really welcomed.

KINGSBRIDGE. Mrs G. M. Balkwill, Court Barton, Aveton Gifford, Kingsbridge TQ7 4LE (Kingsbridge [0548] 550312). Working farm. Jill Balkwill welcomes you to her attractive 16th century farmhouse on this 350-acre working farm, for a relaxing, well fed country holiday. The house, standing below the church, is 100 yards from the village of Aveton Gifford, with beautiful country walks over the farm and down to the tidal River Avon. Large swimming pool in a sheltered, private position at rear of house. Games room, with pool, darts and table tennis. Wide range of eating houses in area from snack bars to fine restaurants. Three miles from sandy beaches, and the nearby moors make ideal picnic areas. Three double, one single and two family rooms, all with washbasins; bathrooms, toilets; sittingroom with colour TV; breakfast room. Children welcome at reduced rates, cot, high chair, babysitting available. AA recommended. Fire Certificate held. Sorry, no pets. Car essential — parking. Open all year round for Bed and Breakfast. Terms and brochure on request.

The information in the entries in this guide is presented by the publishers in good faith and after the signed acceptance by advertisers that they will uphold the high standards associated with FARM HOLIDAY GUIDES LIMITED. The publishers do not accept responsibility for any inaccuracies or omissions or any results thereof.
Before making final holiday arrangements readers should confirm the prices and facilities directly with advertisers.

BOARD Devon 151

FAIR TIDES HOTEL

HOPE COVE, NEAR KINGSBRIDGE SOUTH DEVON TQ7 3HF

Licensed family hotel set in unspoilt fishing village surrounded by National Trust Land and close to safe, sandy beaches, golf courses and spectacular cliff walks. A paradise for nature lovers and those seeking peace and tranquillity.

Personal attention and good home cooking assured at all times in a relaxing, friendly atmosphere. Pets and children welcome. Private car park. Open all year. Brochure on request.

Tel: KINGSBRIDGE (0548) 561271
Proprietors: MIKE & BETTY STEVENS

SUN BAY HOTEL
HOPE COVE

This AA and RAC listed two-star hotel overlooks a safe sandy beach and adjoining National Trust headland. The old world fishing village has facilities for swimming, boating, and fishing, also magnificent coastal walks. All the well-appointed bedrooms have private bathrooms. Bar, lounge and separate TV lounge. Good food is served with varied menus. Children and pets are welcome; cot, highchair and babysitting can be provided.

ASHLEY COURTENAY RECOMMENDED

Proprietors: PETER and BETTY PEDRICK

Hope Cove, Nr. Kingsbridge, South Devon TQ7 3HH   Telephone 0548 561371

KINGSBRIDGE. Mrs B. J. Baker, South Allington House, Chivelstone, Kingsbridge TQ7 2NB (Chivelstone [054-851] 272). Enjoy a weekend or longer in the country, either in the house or our luxury flats (sleep four/six), standing in four acres of park land, between Start Point and Prawle Point. Good country hospitality. English Breakfast; cider and home grown vegetables are served with the Evening Meal. TV lounge. We offer single, double and family rooms, hot and cold in all rooms. Play croquet or boules on our lawns. Children's play area. Sailing, fishing, golf, Dartmoor, all close to hand. Cot, high chair and babysitting available. Car essential, parking. Evening Meal, Bed and Breakfast or Bed and Breakfast. Open all year. Terms and further details from proprietors Edward and Barbara Baker. SAE, please.

KINGSBRIDGE. Mrs B. Kelly, Blackwell Park, Loddiswell, Kingsbridge TQ7 4EA (Gara Bridge [054-882] 230). Blackwell Park is a 17th century farmhouse situated five miles from Kingsbridge and two miles from Loddiswell. Many beaches within easy reach, also Dartmoor, Plymouth, Torbay and Dartmouth. Seven bedrooms for guests, all with H&C. Separate tables in diningroom; lounge with colour TV. Large games room with darts, snooker etc. Garden with plenty of grass area for games, and large car parking area. Ample food with choice of menu; home grown produce. Help yourself to tea and coffee at any time. Fire Certificate. Children and pets especially welcome. Babysitting. Open all year round. Reduced rates out of season.

KINGSBRIDGE near (South Devon). Mr I. Garland, Courtlands Manor, Near Kingsbridge TQ7 4BN (Loddiswell [0548] 550282). A small cosy Manor House in four acres of private grounds amongst beautiful Devon countryside. Two miles from Kingsbridge and within a short drive from local beaches and Dartmoor. Courtlands has its own Adventure Centre in the grounds where you can water ski, canoe, sail and ride, etc. Facilities include assault course, games field, gym, sauna. Coach House Bar. Two double, one family and one twin room, all with washbasins. Bathroom, toilet. Diningroom. Accommodation available in Centre also. Children welcome. Cot and high chair. Pets, if under control and left in car. Bed and Breakfast from £8. Evening Meal available. Phone for brochure.

KINGSBRIDGE. Mr and Mrs S. G. Sharley, Nuckwell Farm Guest House, Aveton Gifford, Kingsbridge TQ7 4NZ (Kingsbridge [0548] 550368). Working farm. Our farm is delightfully situated in the centre of our fields with magnificent views over the countryside to parts of Southern Dartmoor some 15 miles away. We are a half-mile from main road so it is peaceful and quiet, yet we are only three miles from Kingsbridge and three and a half miles from the sea at Bantham, which has a lovely sandy beach. The food is all home cooked with varied menus including sweet trolley. Mostly home produced beef, pork and poultry. Five double, one single, three family bedrooms, all with washbasins. One bathroom, two showers and four toilets. Two lounges, one with TV. Cot and babysitting available. Dogs welcome. Open March to mid-November. Ample parking. Terms sent on request with SAE, please. Rates reduced for children.

KINGSBRIDGE. Mr G. H. Lonsdale, Fern Lodge, Hope Cove, Kingsbridge TQ7 3HF (Kingsbridge [0548] 561326). "Fern Lodge" situated in small fishing village of Hope Cove, surrounded by National Trust Land. Facing south, commanding both sea and landscape views. The lovely garden is flanked by palm trees, giving tropical effect. Four double, two single and three family rooms, all with washbasins; three bathrooms, four toilets; lounge, diningroom. Cot, high chair, babysitting, reductions for children. Exceptionally well-furnished. Pets by special permission. Car essential. SAE for terms for Evening Dinner, Bed and Breakfast or Bed and Breakfast only. Open March 1st to November 1st. Central Heating. AA Listed. Fire regulations. SAE for brochure.

FARM HOLIDAY GUIDES LIMITED publish a large range of well-known accommodation guides. We will be happy to send you details or you can use the order form at the back of this book.

THE VENTURE

Good Sea Bathing
Water Ski-ing
Country Walks
Nature Reserve

Fresh Water and Sea Fishing

Licensed Bar

The Venture Guest House and Restaurant is situated directly fronting the beach in the centre of Torcross village at the Southern end of Slapton Sands. Although the house retains its old world charm with thick walls and thatched roof, the interior is fully modernised, with hot and cold water, electric heating, and colour T.V. in all bedrooms. The Bar and Dining Room overlook the sea, and The Venture is noted for the excellence of its home cooked meals. Free car parking is adjacent to the house. Children sharing parents' accommodation are at reduced rates, and the Guest House is open from the 1st March until the last day of October. Boats may be left on the beach outside. Fishing trips can be arranged in Dartmouth, and walking from the house over the unspoiled countryside is enjoyed by many. Dinner, Bed and Breakfast, and Bed and Breakfast. Please send S.A.E. for Brochure and Tariff. Fire Certificate held.

**Proprietors: MR & MRS ROGER JEFFERIS,
TORCROSS, near KINGSBRIDGE, DEVON TQ7 2TQ.
Telephone: KINGSBRIDGE 580 314 (STD 0548)**

"La Mer" Thurlestone Sands

Iris and George Rhodes invite you to share with them this most beautiful unspoilt corner of South Devon. "La Mer" is a marine/country Hotel situated in the South Hams district. The magnificent and uninterrupted views over Bigbury Bay, Burgh Island and Thurlestone Sands, together with a view over miles of countryside at the rear, makes this location popular with the locals as well as the holidaymaker. Plymouth, Torquay, Dartmouth and Dartmoor are within easy motoring distance, Kingsbridge, the main shopping centre, and Salcombe, world famous as a sailing centre are the local towns. The well-known golf and tennis club at Thurlestone is only a short walk across the sands. In the opposite direction is the quaint village of Inner Hope, reached in a few minutes by the cliff path. Safe bathing from the beach alongside the house, while fishing can be enjoyed from the rocks below the house. "La Mer" has all the usual modern conveniences including four flush toilets, four bathrooms, hot and cold in all bedrooms, with shaver points, colour TV, etc. Ten bedrooms (six with private showers), lounge, bar lounge, TV lounge, diningroom, games room. Own car park. Catering standards are well above average. Iris and George Rhodes make all guests feel at home in their comfortable home, and children of four years and over are accommodated. Putting now available at "La Mer". Riding and trekking nearby. Swimming pool facilities next door by arrangement. Kingsbridge and Salcombe four miles. Evening Dinner, Bed and Breakfast terms on application, reduced for children. Residential Licence. Open Easter to September. Brochure and Tariff sent on request, SAE, please.

**Proprietors: Iris and George Rhodes, "La Mer", Thurlestone Sands,
near Kingsbridge, South Devon TQ7 3JY. Kingsbridge (STD 0548) 561207.**

Devon BOARD

KINGSBRIDGE near. Mr H. W. Garner, Greyhomes Hotel, Torcross, Near Kingsbridge TQ7 2TH (Kingsbridge [0548] 580220). AA One Star. Situated in six acres of grounds above Slapton Sands, Greyhomes, a small friendly licensed hotel offers you a peaceful and relaxed holiday. The unique position commands a magnificent view of Slapton Ley and Start Bay. The hotel has a high reputation for good food. There are four self-contained holiday bungalows each situated separately in the grounds with their own paved terrace overlooking the sea. Surrounded by rock gardens and lawns they have the perfect setting for a quiet healthy holiday. The bungalows are fully equipped, modern and convenient and will accommodate four to five people. Be completely self-contained or take the advantage of the hotel facilities. SAE for brochure.

THE PORT LIGHT

**BOLBERRY DOWN
NR. KINGSBRIDGE
S. DEVON**

National Trust coastal area between Salcombe and Hope Cove. Small licensed Hotel with sea and country views.

IDEAL DOG WALKING BASE

For Brochure write or ring : **Kingsbridge (0548) 561384**

Ashley Courtenay Recommended ★ Michelin Guide

KINGSBRIDGE. Mrs C. Lloyd, Lower Norton, East Allington TQ9 7RL (East Allington [054-852] 246). Lower Norton is a stone built farmhouse now run as a guest house within a one acre smallholding, providing vegetables, eggs and milk. The house is surrounded by farmland situated approximately five miles from Kingsbridge and eight miles from Dartmouth; the nearest beach is Slapton. Torbay, Plymouth and Dartmoor are all within 25 miles. One double and three family bedrooms; two bathrooms with toilets; separate lounge and diningroom; utility room and tea making facilities. Children welcome. Cot, high chair and babysitting available. Fire Certificate held. Car essential, parking. Open April to October for Evening Meal, Bed and Breakfast from £59 weekly. Reductions for children. Stamp only please for brochure.

KINGSBRIDGE near. The Crest Hotel, Hope Cove, Near Kingsbridge TQ7 3HF (Kingsbridge [0548] 561304). THE CREST HOTEL has long been noted for its friendly atmosphere, good food and relaxing bar and lounge, all this backed with the Smith family's lifetime in the hotel trade combine to ensure your stay is as trouble free and relaxing as possible. The nine bedrooms are very well appointed giving a choice of double, twin, single and family rooms, some en suite. Teasmade, baby listening etc. available. The elevated sun patio, hotel and lawns face south overlooking the two lovely villages of Hope providing safe sandy beaches, sailing, fishing, diving, swimming plus magnificent National Trust cliff walks, all within 250 yards of the hotel. Pets and children most welcome. Open all year. Dinner, Bed and Breakfast from £15. Off season and winter break discounts. AA listed. Telephone for details.

KINGSBRIDGE. Mrs Jill M. Berrill, Holbeche House, Inner Hope Road, Hope Cove, Kingsbridge TQ7 3HH (Kingsbridge [0548] 561809). This is a modern guest house in a beautiful, unspoilt village, with many delightful walks, two good sandy beaches three minutes' walk away. We offer you a peaceful holiday in a comfortable friendly atmosphere, together with the very best of home cooking prepared from fresh local produce. Two family rooms (one bathroom en suite), two doubles, one single. Central heating. Ample shower/bathroom facilities. Large car park. Children welcome at reduced rates (under fives low season). Free babysitting. Two good pubs within walking distance. Bed and Breakfast £7, with Evening Meal £11; Bed and Breakfast and Evening Meal £75 weekly per adult. Open all year (except Christmas).

KINGSBRIDGE. E. M. Balkwill, Littlecourt, Aveton Gifford, Kingsbridge TQ7 4LE (Loddiswell [054-855] 362). Working farm. Littlecourt is a small friendly guest house with five bedrooms, TV lounge, large garden with parking spaces. Enjoy a farm-style holiday with all modern conveniences on family's 400-acre mixed farm with the River Avon on the south boundary. Aveton Gifford is a village in an area of outstanding natural beauty with the old coaching inns and two shops about five minutes' walk from the house. Many famous beauty spots are within easy driving distance and the nearest sandy beach is three and a half miles and is unspoiled and uncommercialised. Comfortable rooms and a good Breakfast. Children and dogs really welcome.

KINGSBRIDGE

Mr P. Trute
Woodland View Guest House, Kiln Lane, Stokenham, Kingsbridge, South Devon. Tel: Kingsbridge (0548) 580542

Woodland View is situated in the picturesque village of Stokenham within walking distance of two country inns. Only a mile from the sea, many beaches within easy reach. Personal attention is offered in a homely atmosphere with good Devonshire cooking. Seven comfortable bedrooms, some ground floor with a choice of single, double, twin and family, all with hot and cold water and tea/coffee facilities. Bathroom, shower room, three toilets; sun lounge; TV lounge, diningroom. Bed & full English Breakfast and four-course Evening Dinner or Bed & Breakfast only. Ideal base for touring many places of interest. Superb coastal walks. Reduced rates for children; babysitting available. Pets by arrangement. Open Easter to end September. Licensed. Fire certificate held. Ample parking.
TELEPHONE FOR TERMS OR SAE FOR BROCHURE

KINGSBRIDGE near. Mrs P. Venables, Hopedene Guest House, Grand View Road, Hope Cove, Kingsbridge TQ7 3HF (Kingsbridge [0548] 561602). This comfortable guest house enjoys lovely views overlooking the picturesque fishing village of Hope Cove, with its sandy beaches and fine cliff walks. Relaxed, friendly atmosphere, good home cooking. Table licence and Fire Certificate held. All bedrooms have washbasins, razor points and electric heaters. Residents' lounge with colour TV, sun verandah. Large garden and car park. Safe footpath to village, beaches and cliff walks. Reduced rates for children over 4 sharing parents' room. Dogs welcome. Open March to end of October. Special reduced rates Spring and Autumn. No VAT. Registered with English Tourist Board. Evening Meal, Bed and Breakfast or Bed and Breakfast only. SAE for details please.

KINGSBRIDGE near. Mr Kenneth Small, The Cove Guest House, Torcross, Near Kingsbridge TQ7 * 2TH (Kingsbridge [0548] 580448). Torcross, a small seaside village, and The Cove House are a combination which can serve to be one of the most relaxing holidays you have ever had. The Cove House is situated in three and a half acres of its own coastline and is an ideal place from which to enjoy fishing, swimming or just strolling along the beach. Dartmouth, Torquay, Paignton, Plymouth or Dartmoor within one hour's drive. Excellent food is served in the diningroom which immediately overlooks the sea. Attractive licensed bar, and all bedrooms have TV and basins with hot and cold water. Some have private showers. Car desirable but not essential. Ample parking. Children under eight years and pets not catered for. Open from March 1st to November 30th for Dinner, Bed and Breakfast. See full colour advertisement for details.

KINGSBRIDGE near. Mr and Mrs R. Hill, "Eliotts," Galmpton, Hope Cove, Near Kingsbridge TQ7 3EY (Kingsbridge [0548] 561955). Six hundred-year-old thatched cob cottage standing in two acres of orchard/pasture land. Farm animals — popular with children. Close to National Trust walks, beaches and many places of interest. Golf, windsurfing, diving, fishing, sailing, riding, picnics all arranged. Bed, Breakfast and optional Dinner. Open all year. Pets and children of all ages welcome (substantial reduction for children). Well located between Hope Cove, Kingsbridge and Salcombe. Please send SAE or telephone for details. Special rates off season and weekly bookings. No VAT. This is a true character property serving first-class food with comfortable, homely rooms.

KINGSBRIDGE near. Mrs Hutchings, Alston Farm, Slapton, Near Kingsbridge TQ7 2QE (Kingsbridge [0548] 580337). Working farm. Equidistant for Dartmouth and Kingsbridge, "Alston", a family run stock farm, is offering family accommodation for Bed and Breakfast and optional Evening Meal. Adjoining unspoilt country lanes, ideal for lovely walks, near large nature reserve and fish farm, it is approached by a Tarmac road, being two miles from Slapton Sands and sea, with large lawns — several animals. Guests have private bathroom facilities adjoining large family bedroom, also double room or single rooms available, all ages welcome, TV and kettle in bedrooms. Prices: adult — Bed and Breakfast £6; children under 10 — Bed and Breakfast half price. Evening Meal £3, children £2. Contact **Mrs Hutchings** at above for further details. Open all year.

KINGSBRIDGE near. Mrs M. Paice, Trebles Cottage Hotel, Kingston, Near Kingsbridge TQ7 4PT (Bigbury-on-Sea [0548] 810268). A warm welcome and personal attention await you at our small, friendly hotel set in large grounds in an unspoilt village in beautiful South Hams countryside, noted for its mild climate. This is an ideal touring centre and much of interest is easily reached by car, including two golf courses. Six comfortable bedrooms have washbasins or en suite facilities. There is a colour TV lounge, a licensed bar lounge and a diningroom with separate tables where excellent, attractively presented food is served. You will also enjoy our homely atmosphere, finding peace and relaxation. Open March to October. Full central heating. Low season bargain breaks. Ample free parking. No small children or pets. SAE, please, for brochure and tariff showing our excellent value-for-money terms.

KINGSBRIDGE near. Mrs S. Sweeney, Pointridge, Well Street, Loddiswell, Near Kingsbridge TQ7 4RP (Kingsbridge [0548] 550450). Set in the beautiful Avon Valley, Loddiswell is an attractive village only three miles from the market town of Kingsbridge. "Pointridge" is an old farmhouse, recently converted and modernised, now run as a family Guest House. There are five comfortable bedrooms; bathroom and toilet plus shower room and toilet. Colour TV lounge; diningroom. Guests may use the garden. Car essential — parking (some garages available). Being only five miles from the sea and eight miles from Dartmoor, Loddiswell is an ideal touring centre. Children welcome at reduced rates; cot, high chair, babysitting available. Sorry, no pets. A full Breakfast is served and a four-course Dinner with choice of menu. Bed, Breakfast, Evening Dinner from £80 per week; Bed and Breakfast from £9 per person. Open all year.

KINGSBRIDGE near (Hope Cove). Mr and Mrs D. W. Rossiter, Burton Farm, Galmpton, Near Kingsbridge TQ7 3EY (Kingsbridge [0548] 561210). Working farm. Burton Farm, a working dairy and sheep farm, is situated in the unspoilt rural valley of Galmpton, one mile from the picturesque old fishing village of Hope Cove, three miles from the renowned sailing village of Salcombe and five miles from Kingsbridge. Ideal for a relaxing family holiday with easy access to beach for swimming, diving and water sports of all kinds. Many beautiful walks (NT included). A holiday at Burton Farm welcomes you to a friendly relaxed atmosphere with plenty of good farmhouse cooking, with much local produce. Car essential. Well behaved pets welcome, but not in house! Open all year. Reduced rates for children. Bed and Breakfast, optional dinner, cream teas. Telephone or write for details.

KINGSBRIDGE (South Hams). Mrs C. M. Lancaster, Helliers Farm, Ashford, Aveton Gifford, Kingsbridge TQ7 4ND (Kingsbridge [0548] 550689). Working farm. A warm welcome awaits you at Helliers Farm, a comfortable farmhouse, recently modernised, situated off the main 379 Plymouth – Kingsbridge road. Central for moors, and half an hour's drive from the local beaches — Bignury-on-Sea, Bantham, Thurlestone and the city of Plymouth. There are family, double and twin bedrooms, all with washbasins; two bathrooms; diningroom and lounge with TV. Cot and babysitting available. Bed, and excellent cooked Breakfast. Evening Meals by arrangement, but many pubs locally for evening meals. Bedtime drinks served if desired. Open all year. SAE or telephone for details.

✱ LAPFORD. Mrs B. Cullimore, Nymet Bridge House, Lapford, Crediton EX17 6QX (Lapford [036-35] 334). Situated in glorious countryside, charming 14th century cottage-style guest house. Ideal touring centre; golf, fishing, riding and tennis locally. Residential licence. Home cooking. Log fires. Five bedrooms (three en suite). Open all year for Bed, Breakfast and four-course Dinner. Write or phone for colour brochure and tariff. See also Colour Display Advertisement in this Guide.

LYDFORD (near Okehampton). Mrs E. Glass, "Styria" Bungalow, Lydford, Near Okehampton EX20 4AU (Lydford [082-282] 335). You would like to go to Austria this year but won't make it? Come instead to "Styria" for a friendly atmosphere, Weiner Schnitzel and Apfelstrudel (English food served, too). Mrs Glass is the former proprietor of the Malt House, Coryton. The bungalow with a large sun terrace and garden is well situated in the most favoured areas of the National Park being on the outskirts of the ancient village of Lydford renowned for the beautiful National Property of Lydford Gorge and the ancient castle. Just off the A386. Open all year round. Two double and one large single rooms (two with washbasins). Bathroom, two toilets. Diningroom, sittingroom with TV. Table tennis. Riding schools locally. Bed and Breakfast from £6.50 (£42 weekly); Bed, Breakfast and Evening Dinner from £9.50 (£62 weekly). SAE, please, or IRC.

LYNMOUTH. Jan and Peter Patis, Countisbury Lodge Hotel, Tors Park, Lynmouth EX35 6NB (Lynton [059-85] 2388). Attractive old vicarage built into rocky hillside. Sheltered and sunny with lovely views of river, waterfalls and wooded hillside. The garden has picturesque views of Lynmouth village and harbour. Situated on a private drive giving seclusion yet only a few minutes' walk to village and cliff railway to Lynton. Ideal for walking, fishing, riding and enjoying grandeur of Exmoor and North Devon coast. Central heating; colour TV. Eight charming bedrooms (five with private bathroom). Unique bar. Ample parking. Four-course dinner with choice of home cooked menus. Bed, Breakfast and Dinner from £108.70 weekly; from £17.05 daily including VAT. AA/RAC listed. Dogs £4 per week. Open March to December.

LYNTON. Mrs H. E. Blight, Hazeldene, Lee Road, Lynton EX35 6BP (Lynton [0598] 52364). This is a family-run guest house and provides comfortable, well-appointed accommodation. Full central heating makes it an ideal place for an early or late holiday. Mouthwatering home cooking with an ample and well varied menu. Lovely country walks, horse-riding, boating, fishing, tennis, etc., all easily available. Within three minutes' walk of the unique Cliff Railway to Lynmouth. Centrally situated, facing south. Pleasant garden. Spacious and comfortable lounge with colour TV. Dine by candlelight. Good selection of wines. Tea/coffee making facilities, colour TV in all bedrooms. Private car park though car not essential. Mid-week bookings accepted. Children and pets welcome. AA/RAC Listed. Member of West Country Tourist Board. Open January to November. Access/Visa cards accepted. Colour brochure on request. See also Colour Display Advertisement in this Guide.

LYNTON. Dennis and Jean Gay, The Denes, Longmead, Lynton EX35 6DQ (Lynton [0598] 53573). Our guest house has a friendly atmosphere and is situated at the entrance to the Valley of Rocks. It is ideal for walking and exploring Exmoor with its magnificent views over sea, woodland and moor. Convenient for shops, tennis courts, putting and bowling greens, bus station and cliff railway to Lynmouth. Lynton is within easy reach of Combe Martin, Ilfracombe, Doone Valley and many more places of interest. One mile from the sea, the house has eight bedrooms, three toilets, two bathrooms, diningroom and lounge with colour TV. Own car park. Open all year for Bed and Breakfast. Evening Meal optional. Lunches and packed lunches on request. Send for free brochure.

LYNTON. Mrs M. A. Thorne, Pine Lodge, Lynton EX35 6AX (Lynton [0598] 53230). Pine Lodge (AA/RAC listed; Ashley Courtenay recommended) is set in a sunny, sheltered position away from the main road. It has its own private car park and an acre of hilly garden. All rooms are on the ground or first floor and ground floor bedrooms are available for those who find stairs difficult. Each bedroom has its own tea/coffee making facilities and meals are freshly cooked, with strawberries and other garden produce in season. Pine Lodge is the owners' home and the quiet, friendly, relaxed atmosphere brings back many guests year after year. The house overlooks the thickly wooded West Lyn Valley and is an ideal starting place for the beautiful walk over the Cleaves to Watersmeet. For those who enjoy walking or exploring the varied scenery of Exmoor National Park, Pine Lodge is the perfect base. Dinner, Bed and Breakfast from about £98 per person per week.

LYNTON. Mrs R. Pile, Coombe Farm, Countisbury, Lynton EX35 6NF (Brendon [059-87] 236). Working farm. Coombe Farm, set amid 370 acres beautiful hill farming country dates back to 17th century. Ideal holiday base from which to visit lovely Doone Valley and Exmoor countryside. Two double and two family bedrooms, with washbasins and hot drink facilities; bathroom, shower, two toilets; lounge, diningroom. Excellent country fare served. Central heating. Children welcome, cot, high chair and occasional babysitting. Regret, no pets. Car essential, parking space. Guests enjoy watching farm animals, including Devon cattle, Exmoor Horn sheep and horses. Pony trekking, tennis, fishing, golf, nearby. Open mid-April to October. Fire Certificate held. Evening Dinner, Bed and Breakfast from £96 per week; Bed and Breakfast from £8.50 per night. Reductions for children 11 years and under sharing family room. Stamp, please, for brochure.

LYNTON near. Mrs L. E. French, Brendon Barton, Near Lynton EX35 6LQ (Brendon [05987] 201). Working farm. This is a large stockrearing farm where animals are often seen in the farmyard. There are numerous lovely walks in the area such as Doone Valley and Watersmeet. The farm is also near the open moorland, two miles out of the village of Brendon. Horse riding nearby. Open from May to October, guests are accommodated in two family rooms; bathroom, toilet; sittingroom, diningroom. Children are welcome at reduced rates and there is a cot available. A car is essential — ample parking. Pets are allowed if kept under control. Evening Meal, Bed and Breakfast or Bed and Breakfast only. SAE, please, for terms.

Please note that entries marked with an asterisk also have a colour display advert in the colour section in this guide

LYNTON. Mr and Mrs B. Peacock, Seawood Hotel, North Walk, Lynton EX35 6HJ (Lynton [059-85] 2272). Seawood Hotel is set in its own grounds overlooking the sea with breathtaking views of Lynmouth Bay and Exmoor. The Peacock family makes guests very welcome in their charming old-world house, which is now an AA/RAC one star hotel. Five course dinners with imaginative home cooking, for which great praise is received. Both lounges, diningroom and all bedrooms enjoy sea views. The latter all have private bath and/or shower and WC. Four-posters are also available. Full central heating. Residential licence. Pets welcome. Colour brochure on request. Open March to November.

MALBOROUGH. Mrs Joan Luckham, The Lodge Hotel and Restaurant, Malborough TQ7 3RN (Kingsbridge [0548] 561405). The Lodge Hotel and Restaurant is situated in the picturesque village of Malborough, close to Salcombe and halfway between Torquay and Plymouth. We are ideally situated for walking and boating enthusiasts and centrally located for many Devonshire attractions. The lodge is a small licensed hotel, tastefully furnished, with most of the bedrooms en suite. We feature king size beds and all rooms have tea and coffee making facilities and central heating. There is a private car park. We have a well appointed restaurant and guests have access to TV lounge and library or can relax on the patio overlooking our sunny garden. No accommodation suitable for children.

MORETONHAMPSTEAD. Mrs T. M. Merchant, Great Sloncombe Farm, Moretonhampstead TQ13 8QF (Moretonhampstead [0647] 40595). Working farm. Great Sloncombe dates from the 13th century and is a dairy/mixed farm of 145 acres. Guests are able to watch many farming activities, and to wander over the farm. Many interesting walks in the area, and lots of wildlife (including badgers). Situated in Dartmoor National Park and ideal for touring Devon and Cornwall; riding, fishing, golf, swimming available locally, also many interesting places to explore. One mile from Moretonhampstead on the Chagford/Okehampton road, the house has many interesting features, including open fireplaces, panelled hallway and cobbled courtyard. Two double and one twin-bedded rooms; bathroom, toilet; sitting/diningroom. Facilities for children, also reduced rates. Open all year round for Bed and Breakfast, Evening Meal optional. Car essential — parking. Pets accepted. SAE for brochure.

NEWTON ABBOT. Mrs M. R. Chitty, Bittons Guest House, Ipplepen, Newton Abbot TQ12 5TW (Ipplepen [0803] 812489). Delightfully situated Guest House offering every comfort, good food and personal attention. Ideal touring centre within easy reach of both sea and moorland. We offer all that you would expect to ensure a pleasant and happy holiday base. Guest accommodation in three double, one family bedrooms, all with washbasins. Bathroom, two toilets. Guests' lounge and separate diningroom. Central heating in all rooms. Children welcome, cot, high chair available, also reduced rates. Car essential — parking. Open all year for Evening Meal, Bed and Breakfast from £13; Bed and Breakfast from £8. Please write or telephone for further details.

NEWTON ABBOT. Mrs Valerie Brailey, Swallowfield, Conniford Lane, Ipplepen, Newton Abbot TQ1 2SU (Ipplepen [0803] 812114). Swallowfield is a family guest house which enjoys a quiet position on the edge of Ippleden village and offers every comfort, good food and personal attention. Ideal touring centre within easy reach of both sea and moorland. Two double bedrooms and one family room, all with H/C. Central heating throughout. Chidlren welcome, cot and high chair available (reduced rates on request). Car essential. Open all year for Evening Meal, Bed and Breakfast from £12 or Bed and Breakfast from £7.50. Please write or phone for further details.

Terms quoted in this publication may be subject to increase if rises in costs necessitate

NEWTON ABBOT. Mrs Brenda Heath, West Downe Farm, Bickington, Newton Abbot TQ12 6PF (Bickington [062-682] 258). Working farm. West Downe is a mixed farm of 64 acres with the usual farm animals and guests are welcome to wander around the farm at will. Situated one and a half miles off the A38; seven miles Torbay, five miles from Dartmoor and many other places of interest are within 30 to 40 minutes' drive. Horse riding and trekking nearby. The farm house has all the usual comforts. One double, one family size bedroom with washbasins and teasmades. Bathroom, two toilets; sittingroom and diningroom. Colour TV. Children welcome. Cot, high chair and babysitting. Car esential — parking space. Open from March to October for Evening Dinner, Bed and Breakfast. Reduced terms for children. AA listed. Farmhouse food, mainly home produced.

NEWTON ABBOT. Marina and Roger Briggs, "Coombe Hatch," Combeinteignhead, Newton Abbot (Shaldon [062-687] 3433). Guests always enjoy their stay at "Coombe Hatch" a comfortable Guest House, centred in one of Devon's lovely unspoiled villages bordering the banks of the tidal Teign Estuary, where sailing, water ski-ing, fishing and bird watching are enjoyed. A 13th century Parish Church, Post Office, garage, two attractive Olde Pubs. Newton Abbot (with its well known market) two miles. Exotic Torquay four, Paignton seven, Brixham 12. By the river is Shaldon two miles, Teignmouth two and half. Dawlish eight and Dartmoor 10 miles. Good home cooking, Devon beef, poultry and cream etc. Double, family and single bedrooms attractively furnished. Three toilets; bathroom. Attractive lounge and diningroom. Fire Certificate. Open all year round for Bed/Breakfast and Evening Dinner or Bed and Breakfast only. Children welcome, also pets. Reasonable terms. Parking. WE REALLY WOULD LOVE TO SEE YOU.

NEWTON ABBOT. Mrs G. A. Stone, Milton Farm, East Ogwell, Newton Abbot TQ12 6AT (Newton Abbot [0626] 4988). Working farm. Farm Bungalow in pleasant village with good view of Dartmoor, two miles west of Newton Abbot. Village lies equal distance from Torbay, Teignmouth and Dartmoor National Park, all about eight miles. Golf, riding, sailing and fishing all within easy reach. Dairy farm with cows, calves and poultry. Five minutes' walk from bus; railway two miles. Parking. One double room with washbasin; one twin bedded room. Bath with shower. WC separate. Sitting/diningroom. Sorry, no pets. Mostly fresh produce served. Bed and Breakfast from £5. Evening Meal optional. Reduced rates for children. Closed November to mid-April. Details with SAE. Mid-week bookings if required.

NEWTON ABBOT. Mrs M. Gregson, Penpark, Bickington, Newton Abbot TQ12 6LH (Bickington [062-682] 314). Surrounded by farmland and magnificent views, Penpark has five acres of gardens and woodland, also a tennis court. Within easy reach of sea and moor, with riding, fishing and golf nearby, and midway between Exeter and Plymouth in the Dartmoor National Park. Half-mile from A38. Ideal situation for touring the West Country, or for a peaceful secluded holiday. One double and one single bedrooms, with washbasins; bathroom, toilet; sittingroom; diningroom. Children welcome at reduced rates. Car esential; parking for four cars. Bed and Breakfast from £8 per night. Open all year round.

NEWTON ABBOT. Mrs J. Birkenhead, Gale Farm, Bickington, Newton Abbot TQ12 6PG (Bickington [062-682] 273). This imposing Georgian farmhouse is tucked away in total seclusion yet only half mile (three minutes) from A38. Ideal centre for visiting south Devon's many beaches and beauty spots, or for touring Dartmoor National Park. The extremely high standard of accommodation will satisfy the most fastidious and the hearty Breakfast features traditional cooking using home produce. Three double bedrooms; bathroom, toilet; sittingroom and diningroom. Children are welcome. Sorry, no dogs. Car esential; parking. Open all year for Evening Dinner, Bed and Breakfast from £13 per day (weekly terms on request) or Bed and Breakfast from £8 per day.

**If you've found
FARM HOLIDAY GUIDE
of service please tell your friends**

NEWTON ABBOT. Mr and Mrs T. R. Burman, "Three Gables", Ideford, Chudleigh, Newton Abbot TQ13 0BQ (Chudleigh [0626] 853226). This is a modern country residence in a picturesque village off the main Exeter-Torbay-Torquay A380 road. Enjoy a good night's rest in the country and awake to the beautiful views of the moors and a nice English breakfast. Teignmouth is the nearest beach; Dawlish, Torquay, Paignton and Exeter are all within easy reach. Four double, one single and one family bedrooms; two bathrooms and three toilets; sitting and dining-rooms. Cot, high chair and babysitting offered. Car essential, parking. Bed and Breakfast from £4.50 to £6 per night; terms reduced for children under 10; senior citizens' rates. SAE, please, for further details.

NEWTON ABBOT near. Mrs Heather Young, Bremridge Farm, Woodland, Ashburton, Near Newton Abbot TQ13 7JX (Ashburton [0364] 52426). Working farm. In the heart of South Devon, 10 miles from sea and close to Dartmoor, this small working farm stands in eight acres amidst peaceful Devon countryside. Part of the house dates back to the 16th century yet it has been fully modernised, offering every comfort with fitted carpets and wood-burning central heating. The accommodation includes two family rooms and two adjoining rooms with washbasins; lounge with TV; diningroom; bathroom and toilets. Children welcome, cot, high chair and babysitting available. Plenty of farm produce and vegetables. Large garden — ample parking. Car essential. Open all year for Bed, Breakfast and Dinner from £60 weekly. Reduced rates for children. AA listed. SAE or phone for illustrated brochure.

NORTH TAWTON. Mrs M. A. Partridge, Cadditon Farm, Bondleigh, North Tawton EX20 2AW (North Tawton [083-782] 450). Working farm. "Cadditon" is at least 300 years old and although the inglenook fireplaces and oak beams can still be seen, all modern comforts have been added for the benefit of guests. The accommodation comprises one family, one double, one twin-bedded rooms (electric blankets on beds) and all bedrooms fully carpeted with hot and cold water, and tea-making facilities. Bathrooms, toilets. Sittingroom with colour TV and diningroom. This is an ideal base from which to tour Devon; only eight miles from Dartmoor National Park where pony trekking can be enjoyed and Okehampton where there are facilities for golf and swimming. Children are welcome on this 147-acre dairy farm and a cot, high chair and babysitting are available. Sorry, no pets. Car essential — parking. Evening Meal, Bed and Breakfast or Bed and Breakfast (reductions for children and Senior Citizens). AA listed. SAE, please.

OAKFORD. Mrs Lindy Head, Harton Farm, Oakford, Tiverton EX16 9HH (Oakford [039-85] 209). Working farm. Lovely 17th century farmhouse with original fireplaces and witches' window on 32-acre mixed farm that is virtually self-supporting with own cows, pigs, chickens, sheep, home spun wool, etc. Secluded, yet only half-a-mile north of A361 at the end of a private lane, it is an ideal touring centre for Exmoor, the Exe Valley and Devon. Comfortable accommodation in three double bedrooms; bathroom; diningroom serving real country cooking with farm-produced vegetables, meat, eggs, butter; home baking a speciality; guests' lounge with colour TV. Children over four welcome. Pets accepted. Car essential — parking. Open January to December for Evening Meal, Bed and Breakfast from £9; Bed and Breakfast from £6. Horses at livery by arrangement. Vegetarian meals available on request.

OKEHAMPTON. Mrs J. Vanstone, Musehill, Lewdown, Okehampton EX20 4QY (Lewdown [056-683] 391). Working farm. A warm welcome awaits everyone at Musehill, a mixed 80-acre farm, amid peaceful countryside, one mile from the A30, near the Cornish border and central for Moors and sandy beaches. Many beauty spots within easy reach. The old stonebuilt farmhouse is completely modernised and offers accommodation in two family and one double bedrooms (two with washbasins); cot, high chair and babysitting provided for children, also reduced rates. Good farmhouse cooking, (fresh strawberries and raspberries, Devonshire cream, fresh home grown fruit and vegetables). Swing for children. Personal attention assured. Visitors welcome to wander around the farm and join in family activities or just relax on the lawns. Bed and Breakfast (optional Evening Meal). Car essential, parking. SAE, please.

PLEASE SEND A STAMPED ADDRESSED ENVELOPE WITH ENQUIRIES

BOARD Devon 161

OKEHAMPTON. Mrs J. A. King, Higher Cadham Farm, Jacobstowe, Okehampton EX20 3RB (Exbourne [083-785] 647). Working farm. Higher Cadham is a 139-acre beef and sheep farm just off the A3072 Holiday Route, five miles from Dartmoor. It is a 16th century modernised farmhouse with accommodation for guests in two double, one single and one family bedrooms all with washbasins and shaver points; bathroom, toilet; sittingroom with colour TV and Games Room with plenty to amuse the children. There are free tea-making facilities; free fishing and shooting. Plenty of home produced food. Residential licence. Children over three are welcome. Open from April to November. Car is essential and there is ample parking. Sorry no pets. Excellent holiday for all the family. Fire Certificate held and AA listed. Tourist Board recommended. There are no extra charges. Evening Dinner, Bed and Breakfast from £11 per night, £70 weekly; Bed and Breakfast only from £6.50 nightly, £42 weekly. Rates reduced for children under 13 years. Brochure on request.

OKEHAMPTON. Mr and Mrs M. Harbridge, Poltimore, South Zeal, Okehampton EX20 2PD * (Okehampton [0837] 840209). Poltimore is a charming thatched Guest House delightfully situated in the Dartmoor National Park and has been awarded the British Tourist Authority's Commendation for Outstanding Hospitality. It is the perfect place for relaxation and good food and is an ideal centre for walking, riding and touring holidays throughout the year. Home grown produce. Licensed Bar. Colour TV. Log fires. Dogs permitted. Seven bedrooms, three with private bathrooms. Terms from £112 per week for Bed, Breakfast and Four Course Dinner. For the discerning visitor to this beautiful part of Devonshire, there can be no finer combination of situation and hospitality. Self-catering accommodation also available. AA listed. For a Colour Brochure and Terms telephone or write to the Resident Proprietors; Maurice and May Harbridge. See also colour advertisement.

OKEHAMPTON (Dartmoor). Mrs Jean S. Robinson, South Nethercott Farm, Whiddon Down, Okehampton EX20 2QZ (Whiddon Down [064-723] 276). Working farm. South Nethercott Farm is a 170-acre dairy and corn farm 25 miles from the North and South coasts. The modernised farmhouse (originally two cottages) has an open log fireplace in the drawingroom and Scandinavian wood-burning stove in the diningroom. The ceilings are oak beamed. Double bedroom with bathroom en suite. Double room with basin, will sleep three. One single bedroom. Second bathroom. Shaving points. Children over 12 years welcome. Sorry, no pets. Car essential. Situated on A30 holiday route, easy access Plymouth (Roscoff Ferry) and Heathrow (about three-and-a-half hours on motorway) and dual carriageway to within two miles of farm. Open March — November. Good centre for riding, walking, fishing and touring. Very superior farmhouse cooking. Evening Dinner, Bed and Breakfast or Bed and Breakfast only. Commended by British Tourist Authority 1980.

OKEHAMPTON near. Mrs Jean Borthcott, "Town Farm", Bridestowe, Near Okehampton (Bridestowe [083-786] 226). Working farm. Comfortable farmhouse accommodation, on a 150-acre farm in a typical Devon village on the edge of Dartmoor, with two "olde worlde" pubs to relax in after an interesting day touring. East and West coasts approximately 30 miles; the beautiful Lydford Gorge four miles; Morwellham Quay, a museum copper mine eight miles. Ideal location for bird watching and walking. Many National Trust properties within easy reach. Facilities for golf, tennis, horse riding and swimming nearby. Guests are accommodated from May to September — two double, one family bedrooms, with washbasins. Tea-making facilities in bedrooms if required. Bathroom, toilet. Sittingroom, diningroom. Ample home produced fare. The house is always available to guests in inclement weather. Children welcome at reduced rates. Pets accepted. Car essential — ample parking. Evening Dinner, Bed and Breakfast or Bed and Breakfast. Terms on request.

FARM HOLIDAY GUIDES LIMITED publish a large range of well-known accommodation guides. We will be happy to send you details or you can use the order form at the back of this book.

OKEHAMPTON. Mrs A. G. V. Darch, Lovaton Farm, Whiddon Down, Okehampton EX20 2RA (Whiddon Down [064-723] 225). Working farm. Lovaton Farm is a 300-acre cattle and sheep farm in the centre of Devon. It is a large stone-built south facing house, well furnished with a feature fireplace and colour TV. Situated in a very secluded and sheltered setting on edge of Dartmoor National Park. An ideal spot for touring Dartmoor and north and south coasts of Devon and Cornwall. Excellent food, own produce used. Golf, swimming, pony trekking available locally. Rough shooting available on farm. Directions — off A30 at Post Inn to North Tawton Road. Left at South Tawton Road. The farm is two miles from A30 Post Inn, Whiddon Down. One double and two family rooms (two with washbasins); two bathrooms, two toilets; sittingroom, diningroom. Children welcome, cot and babysitting available. Sorry, no pets. Open February to November, with electric and log fires. Car essential, parking. Evening Dinner, Bed and Breakfast or Bed and Breakfast. Terms on application. Reductions for children.

OKEHAMPTON near. Miss Una Cornthwaite, Hayne Mill, Lewdown, Near Okehampton EX20 4DD (Lewdown [056-683] 342). Hayne Mill is the home of the Braddabrook Bearded Collies, an attractive old Mill House lying beside the River Thrushel and sheltered by woodland. The house is situated midway between the North and South coasts between Dartmoor and Bodmin Moor and is very central for hiking, touring and pony trekking. Several good beaches within one hour's drive. Miss Cornthwaite owns the fishing rights (brown trout, sea trout and salmon) and guests may avail themselves of this facility. Delicious home cooking is served including organically grown fruit and vegetables from the garden. Vegetarian and special diets catered for. Two double, one single bedrooms, with washbasins; two bathrooms, three toilets; sittingroom, diningroom. Central heating and log fire. Children welcome, cot, high chair, babysitting and reduced rates under 10 years. Pets by prior arrangement at £1.50 (including food). Car essential — ample parking. Full Board £16; Evening Dinner, Bed and Breakfast £13.50; Bed and Breakfast £8. Open all year — special winter breaks.

OTTERY ST. MARY. Mrs Susan Hansford, Pitt Farm, Ottery St. Mary EX11 1NL (Ottery St. Mary [0404 81] 2439). Working farm. This most attractive 16th-century thatched farmhouse, which is family-run, consists of 190 acres of Arable and Beef. It is situated in the picturesque Otter Valley, half a mile off the A30 on the B3176, in the village of Fairmile, and one mile from Ottery St. Mary. All East Devon resorts, moors and Torbay are within easy reach. Golf, squash, tennis, pony trekking, heated swimming pool and many other facilities nearby. Farmhouse food is served, some of which is home produced. Two double rooms and two family rooms, one with H&C. Two bathrooms and three toilets. Lounge, colour TV, diningroom. Children welcome. Cot, high chair and babaysitting available. Regret, no pets. Open all year. A warm welcome awaits all our guests. SAE for brochure. Prompt reply, or phone for terms.

Venn Ottery Barton COUNTRY HOTEL

Venn Ottery, Nr. Ottery St. Mary, Devon EX11 1RZ

(AA and RAC Listed)

Residential Licence

Telephone:
Ottery St. Mary 2733
(040-481)

Three miles from Ottery St. Mary and only five from the seafront at Sidmouth, this delightful 16th Century Licensed Country Hotel offers the charm of old oak beams and log fires combined with all modern comforts. Tucked away amid farmlands, only six miles from M5, Exit 30, 'Venn Ottery Barton' is family run to high standards and is close to many well-known beaches and picturesque seaside towns including Beer, Branscombe, Exmouth and Charmouth. Exeter 11 miles. Diningroom, lounge with colour TV, separate well-stocked bar (residential licence). Large games room.

There are ten double or twin-bedded rooms, two single and three family, nine with en-suite bath or shower and toilet, all with washbasins and full central heating. All bedrooms are on ground or first floor and all have tea/coffee making facilities (no charge). Terms daily or weekly; reductions for children six to eleven sharing parents' room. Small dogs by arrangement. Open all year. AA and RAC Listed. Bargain breaks. Brochure on request.

OTTERY ST. MARY. Mrs E. A. Forth, Fluxton Farm Hotel, Ottery St. Mary EX11 1RJ (040 481) 2818. Lovely 16th century farmhouse in beautiful Otter Valley with two-acre gardens including stream and trout pond. Licensed. Beamed candlelit diningroom, all local fresh produce. Log fires, central heating. 'Teasmade' in all rooms. Two lounges, one non-smoking. Good home cooking our speciality, and a relaxing friendly holiday guaranteed. Parking. Only five miles from beach at Sidmouth. Children and pets welcome. Reductions early and late season.

OTTERY ST. MARY. Mrs Doreen Turl, Home Farm, Escot, Ottery St. Mary EX11 1LO (Honiton [0404] 850241). Working farm. Situated in beautiful Parkland near the historic town of Ottery St. Mary and Sidmouth, with its lovely sandy beaches, 16th-century Home Farm is a 300-acre mixed farm approximately half-a-mile from A30, eight miles M5. Ideal setting for touring South Devon beaches and moors with many places of architectural interest and pleasure facilities nearby. Guests are welcomed to this family home with its oak beams and comfortable accommodation from April to October. Double, single and family bedrooms (some with washbasins); bathroom, toilet. Lounge with colour TV; diningroom where good, mainly home-produced food is served. Electric and log fires. Children welcome at reduced rates, cot, high chair and babysitting can be arranged. Sorry, no pets. Car essential — parking. Bed and Breakfast. Evening Meal optional. SAE, please, for terms.

PAIGNTON. Mr R. F. Varty, South Mount Hotel, 7 Southfield Road, Paignton TQ3 2SW (Torbay [0803] 557643). Situated at the centre of Torbay, South Mount is an elegant Georgian house in a pleasant garden containing some of the rarer trees and shrubs. Some ten minutes' walk from the beach and close to town, between Kirkham House and Oldway Mansion (buildings of special interest), it is convenient for all the English Riviera has to offer, but is suitably private and ideal for a quiet holiday in peaceful surroundings. South Mount has its own car park, bar, TV lounge. English Breakfast, four-course Evening Dinner with good wines available.

PAIGNTON. Mr and Mrs White, Newbarn Farm, Totnes Road, Paignton TQ4 7PT (Paignton [0803] 553602). New Barn Farm is set in 64 acres of beautiful countryside and has panoramic views which include Dartmoor. Half-mile off A385 Paignton – Totnes road. Two miles from Paignton and sea, four from Totnes and 12 from Dartmoor. Trout fishing and coarse fishing available at our Angling Centre. House has three double bedrooms, two of which can be used as family rooms and the third, twin-bedded, can be used as a single. Two bathrooms, three toilets, two sittingrooms, diningroom. Home produce and clotted cream served. Dogs, and children over four years welcome. Car essential; ample parking. Dinner, Bed and Breakfast £10 per night (£62 weekly); Bed and Breakfast £6 per night (£37 weekly). Dinner by arrangement. Reduction off peak periods (March and October). Open Christmas. Caravan and flat to let. Terms on application. Caravan Club Site. Members only.

PAIGNTON (Torbay). Mrs B. J. Tooze, Elberry Farm, Broadsands, Paignton TQ4 6HJ (Churston [0803] 842939). Working farm. Elberry Farm is situated in the middle of a popular holiday area. Guests have access to the house at all times, facilities for making light refreshments, washing etc. available. Dartmoor and Plymouth within one hour's journey. Pitch and putt outside farm; Broadsands safe beach for children and Elberry Cove is very popular for water ski-ing, both are about 400 yards away. All cooking is done by Mrs Tooze, and vegetables are home grown. Three family and one double bedrooms (three with washbasins). Lounge, diningroom and all modern conveniences. Children welcome. Two cots, two high chairs and babysitting available. The 60-acre farm is open from Easter to October. No pets please. Reductions for children up to 12 years old. Evening Dinner, Bed and Breakfast or Bed and Breakfast only. Terms on request with SAE, please.

FUN FOR ALL THE FAMILY IN DEVON

Babbacombe Model Village, Torquay; *Beer Modelrama*, Beer, near Seaton; *Dart Valley Steam Railway*, Buckfastleigh; *Torbay & Dartmouth Steam Railway*, Paignton; *Bicton Gardens*, East Budleigh, near Budleigh Salterton; *Grand Western Horseboat Trips*, Tiverton; *The Shire Horse Centre*, Dunstone, Yealmpton, near Plymouth; *Farway Countryside Park*, near Honiton; *Dartmoor Wildlife Park*, Sparkwell, near Plymouth; *Paignton Zoo*, Totnes Road, Paignton; *Plymouth Aquarium*, Plymouth Hoe, Plymouth; *Exeter Maritime Museum*, The Quay, Exeter; *Torbay Aircraft Museum*, Higher Blagdon, near Paignton; *Exmoor Brass Rubbing Centre*, The Smuggler's Den, Queen Street, Lynton; *Dartington Glass*, Linden Close, off School Lane, Torrington; *Yelverton Paperweight Centre*, Leg O'Mutton Corner, Yelverton; *Kents Cavern*, Ilsham Road, Wellswood, Torquay.

164 Devon BOARD

PAIGNTON near. Mrs Margaret Godwin, Millmans Farm, Marldon, Near Paignton TQ3 1ST (Paignton [0803] 558213). Millmans Farm is a beautiful old world farmhouse once owned by family of Sir Walter Raleigh, situated in peaceful village of Marldon with its old church and fine inn, within easy reach of all holiday amenities and seaside at Paignton, Torquay and Brixham. Millmans offers first-class traditional food, large comfortable bedrooms with washbasins, a beautiful large lounge with colour TV and diningroom. Millmans has all the ingredients to give a family a happy holiday. Play park nearby. Children welcome, cots. Babysitting and pets by arrangement. Open from June to September. Rates reduced for children. Evening Dinner, Bed and Breakfast. Terms on request.

Millman's Farm House and Cottages. Nr. Marldon Paignton.

PARRACOMBE. Mr and Mrs H. Bearryman, Lower Dean Farm, Trentishoe, Parracombe EX31 4PJ (Parracombe [059 83] 215). Working farm. Charming 17th century licensed farmhouse within the Exmoor National Park offers all the peace of the countryside plus the glorious beaches of north Devon, a short drive away. All 11 bedrooms (doubles, singles, family) have bathroom or shower en suite. Spacious lounge, colour TV, dining room and cocktail bar. Horses for hire. Games room, billiards, pool, table tennis, darts. Golf course five miles. Home cooked food using home and local produce. Ideal for family holidays. Cot, high chair, babysitting facilities. No pets. Open all year. Sea 2½ miles. Car essential. Dinner, Bed and Breakfast or Bed and Breakfast. Reductions for children sharing parents' room. SAE, please.

* PARRACOMBE. Tony and Elizabeth Pring, The Old Rectory, Martinhoe, Parracombe (059-83) 368. Small, secluded country house hotel; superior cuisine; all bedrooms en-suite. Winners AA coveted HBL merit award for fourth successive year. See also Colour Display Advertisement under Devon.

PLYMOUTH. Mrs M. Rogers, New Farm, Battisborough Cross, Holbeton, Plymouth PL8 1JQ (Holbeton [075-530] 289). Working farm. This modern farmhouse, nine miles from the A38, 10 miles from Plymouth and four miles from Newton Ferrers (for sailing), has lovely views of Dartmoor and the sea. Golf at Bigbury, nine miles. Ideal centre for touring South Hams beaches, Dartmoor, or South East Cornwall; National Trust walks. Two double and/or family bedrooms, with washbasins; bathroom, two toilets; sitting-diningroom, TV. Cot, babysitting and reduced rates for children. Guests warmly welcomed from Easter to October. Car essential — parking. Dinner, Bed and Breakfast or Bed and Breakfast. Home produced pork, poultry, cream, butter, milk, eggs, fruit and vegetables. Dogs allowed. SAE, please, for terms.

PLYMOUTH. Mrs Margaret MacBean, Gabber Farm, Down Thomas, Plymouth PL9 0AW (Plymouth [0752] 862269). Working farm. This 120-acre dairy farm is situated one mile from the Wembury and Bovisand beaches. Ideally located for touring — the lovely historic town of Plymouth, Dartmoor and the beaches of Bigbury, Bantham, etc. within easy reach. Many beautiful coastal walks in the area; golf course and riding nearby. Open Easter to November. A variety of bedrooms are available, two with hot and cold water; bathroom, toilet; sitting and diningrooms. Good home cooking using own farm produce with a varied menu so that visitors will not be served the same meal over a two-week period. Children welcome at reduced rates — cot, high chair, babysitting available. Sorry, no pets. Car essential, parking. Colour TV. Evening Meal, Bed and Breakfast. SAE, please, or telephone for terms and further details.

PLYMOUTH. Mrs S. J. MacBean, Coombe Farm, Wembury Road, Plymstock, Plymouth PL9 0DE (Plymouth [0752] 41730). Working farm. Coombe Farm is a Dairy Farm and is situated in a quiet valley on the outskirts of Plymouth. It is within easy reach of Plymouth City Centre, good safe beaches and Dartmoor National Park. It is an ideal touring centre with many places of interest within half an hour's drive. The farmhouse offers peaceful homely accommodation with plenty of good farm produce and home cooking. Lounge, colour TV. Riding, sea fishing, country walks. Children welcome, cot and babysitting. Sorry, no pets. Car is essential and there is parking space. Open Easter to end of September. Evening Meal, Bed and Breakfast or Bed and Breakfast only. Reduced rates for children. SAE, please, or telephone for further details or terms.

PLYMOUTH near. Mrs Dorothy Baskerville, West Pitton Farm, Plympton, Near Plymouth PL7 5BB (Plymouth [0752] 880387). Working farm. Peacefully situated 150 acre farm, in picturesque countryside, one mile from A38 road, approximately six miles historic Plymouth, Dartmoor National Park, lovely beaches. Ideally located for touring; many beautiful coastal walks; golf, sea fishing, riding within easy reach. Bed and Breakfast (evening meal optional) is offered from May to October. Comfortable accommodation provided in one double and one family bedrooms, with washbasins; diningroom etc. Children welcome, but regret no pets. Car essential — ample parking. Further details on request.

The information in the entries in this guide is presented by the publishers in good faith and after the signed acceptance by advertisers that they will uphold the high standards associated with **FARM HOLIDAY GUIDES LIMITED**. The publishers do not accept responsibility for any inaccuracies or omissions or any results thereof. Before making final holiday arrangements readers should confirm the prices and facilities directly with advertisers.

PLYMOUTH near. Mrs B. J. L. George, Barnwell House, Brixton, Near Plymouth PL8 2AD (Plymouth [0752] 880626). Pleasantly situated in a quiet position off the A379 and approximately five miles from Plymouth. Barnwell House (luxuriously converted farm buildings) caters for Bed and Breakfast only. The family atmosphere, every comfort, comfortable lounge, TV, with additional meals nearby, make this the ideal touring centre. There are three double and two family bedrooms, most with washbasins; guests' bathroom, two toilets; sittingroom and one diningroom. Children welcome, cot, high chair and babysitting available. No objection to pets. With gas central heating the house is open all year round. Safe beaches for the children, near the River Yealm for sailing and fishing. Reduced rates for children. SAE or phone for further details and terms.

SALCOMBE. Mrs Manya Norris, Beadon Farm House, Beadon Road, Salcombe TQ8 8LX (Salcombe [054-884] 3454). This Victorian farmhouse faces south with beautiful views over the North Sands valley. A public footpath leads to nearby sandy beaches and coastal walks. Salcombe is a 10 minute walk from the farmhouse so that you can enjoy both the quiet of the countryside and the amenities of this unspoilt fishing town. Car not essential, but parking space for car and boat. Three double rooms with washbasins; one children's room. Guest bathroom. Central heating. Lounge with TV. In addition to a substantial cooked breakfast Mrs Norris offers a two course Evening Dinner with home grown vegetables three times a week. Open all year. Evening Dinner, Bed and Breakfast from £13.50; Bed and Breakfast from £9. Reductions for children and out of season holidays.

SALCOMBE. Mr and Mrs L. Thackstone, Melbury Hotel, Devon Road, Salcombe TQ8 8HJ (Salcombe [054884] 2883). Situated overlooking this beautiful unspoilt estuary, our 14 bedroomed family run hotel offers a warm welcome, comfort, excellent food with choice of menu and attractive wine list. Bar lounge. TV lounge. Spacious diningroom. All rooms have tea/coffee making facilities and many have WC and shower or bath en suite. Car parking in grounds of hotel. Lovely views in all directions. Reasonable terms with reductions for children five to 15 according to accommodation. Regret, no pets. Self-catering cottages and flats sleeping two to eight, plus cot available. Details of holidays at Melbury from proprietors **Lawrie and Anthea Thackstone.**

SALCOMBE. Mrs Madge Bullock, Pine Cottage, Froude Road, South Sands, Salcombe TQ8 8LH (Salcombe [054-884] 2170). A comfortable detached cottage in wooded surroundings with beautiful sea views from all bedrooms; lounge, diningroom and sun terrace. Car preferable, but not essential — parking space provided. Log fires out of season — bedrooms with heaters. Safe, sandy beach within 100 yards for swimming, sailing, windsurfing, diving and fishing. Ideal countryside for walkers and visitors appreciative of wild life, with magnificent views of the estuary and English Channel. Other beaches and coves nearby. Children over three years welcome at reduced rates if sharing parents' room. Substantial cooked breakfast, pot of tea with biscuits early morning and afternoon from £8 inclusive — no extra charge. Bed and Breakfast only. Open from January to December. Reductions for senior citizens. November to March. SAE, please.

SEATON. Mrs W. J. Lee, The Check House, Beer Road, Seaton EX12 2PR (Seaton [0297] 21858). Spend your holiday in an interesting house built by a Victorian baronet. Listed Building. Many unique features and fabulous views. Set in two acres of woodland garden with private path and gate to beach in an area of outstanding natural beauty. Quiet, comfortable accommodation with nine bedrooms, five private bathrooms, one ground-floor. Fire Certificate. Central heating. Log fire for chilly evenings. Licensed. Recommended traditional cooking using local produce. Ideal centre for touring Devon, Dorset, Somerset. Ample car parking. Terms from £9.50 nightly. SAE, please, for brochure. We regret no dogs or small children.

Devon BOARD

SEATON. Mrs R. B. Hallet, Borolands Farm, Axmouth, Seaton EX12 4BP (Colyton [0297] 52680).
The farm is situated approximately quarter-of-a-mile off the main A358 Axminster to Seaton road, up a good private tarmac drive north of the village of Axmouth. The residence is a bungalow suitable for disabled guests. Double and one family bedrooms; bathroom and toilet; sittingroom; diningroom. Central heating. Children welcome and babysitting available. Dog or small pets allowed by arrangement. Car would be an advantage and there is parking. Ideal situation for touring. Sea and river fishing, golf, tennis, horse riding are among the sporting facilities. Historic houses, country and wild life parks nearby. Bed and Breakfast. Evening Meal optional. Open all year round. Reduced rates for children. SAE, please.

SEATON. Mrs M. Gallagher, Thornfield Hotel, 87 Scalwell Lane, Seaton EX12 2ST (Seaton [0297] 20039). Thornfield offers an informal and relaxing atmosphere with plentiful home cooking a speciality. Heated outdoor pool, secluded gardens of over one acre. Comfortable lounge with colour TV. The accommodation is licensed and consists of five double/twin, one single and four family bedrooms, mostly en-suite, some on ground floor; all centrally heated. Tea making facilities. Colour TV's. Solarium. Children welcome, with reductions. Ample parking. Self catering caravan sleeps six, also available. Various sports activities locally including golf, and many places of interest to suit all ages. Generous reductions for off season, spring and autumn breaks. Open all year. AA and RAC. English Tourist Board, four star. Write or telephone for colour brochure.

SEATON. Mr and Mrs P. Millard, Beach End, 8 Trevelyan Road, Seaton (Seaton [0297] 23388). This attractive 60 year old house situated on the Esplanade at Seaton is the nearest guest house to the beach. There is a good range of shops also golf club and harbour close by. Ideal centre for exploring the beauty spots of Devon, Dorset and Somerset. Four double, two single and one family bedrooms, all with washbasins and sea views; two bathrooms; three toilets; sittingroom; diningroom. Cot, high chair, babysitting and reduced rates for children. Sorry, no pets. Open all year, mid-week bookings accepted. Parking. Traditional British cooking our speciality and terms include early morning tea and late evening beverage. SAE for brochure and tariff.

SIDMOUTH. Mr B. D. Nunn, Sidmount Hotel, Station Road, Sidmouth EX10 8XJ (Sidmouth [03955] 3432). A perfect, peaceful setting for a true West Country holiday. Relax in the friendly atmosphere of the Sidmount, a fine Georgian hotel of character set in quiet secluded position in two acres of beautiful gardens which contain over 300 different varieties of trees and shrubs. Superb sea and country views. The 14 bedrooms, reached by a splendid oak staircase, are well appointed, many with private bathrooms. Three lounges; diningroom. Excellent food. Licensed. High standards of comfort and hygiene. Full central heating. Children welcome, cot, high chair. Sorry, no pets. Garaging for three cars, ample parking although car not essential. Full Fire Certificate. Weekly terms for Dinner, Bed and Breakfast from £85 to £129 according to room and season. Reduced rates for children sharing parents' room. Sidmouth is one of the few unspoilt seaside resorts in England nestling in picturesque Lyme Bay with two fine beaches. Colour brochure on request. Open all year.

SIDMOUTH. Mrs Betty Sage, Pinn Barton, Peak Hill, Sidmouth EX10 0NN (Sidmouth [039-55] 4004). Working farm. Pinn Barton is a farm of 330 acres situated on the coast, one and a half miles from Sidmouth, where there is good choice of eating places. There are many safe bathing beaches nearby and lovely walks along the cliffs around the farm. It is very peaceful, being just off the coast road, between Sidmouth and the village of Otterton. Pinn Barton has been highly recommended and you will be given a friendly welcome in comfortable surroundings, and a good farmhouse breakfast. All bedrooms have colour TV; heating, washbasins, razor plugs, tea/coffee-making facilities and electric blankets for chilly nights. There is a diningroom and separate sittingroom for guests (with colour TV and a fire). There is also a bathroom/shower and separate toilet; also the family room has en-suite bathroom. Children are very welcome and there is a cot, high chair, swings, etc. Babysitting by arrangement. Bed and Breakfast including bedtime drink from £7. Reductions for children sharing parents' room. Own keys provided. Stamp, please.

Hotel Elizabeth

(Licensed)

**Resident Proprietors:
Ken and Marion Ridgeway**

Friendly delightful Regency hotel in an unrivalled position on Sidmouth's sea front which spreads itself in the sun between two tree-covered heights Peak Hill (west) and Salcombe Hill (east) – all that's best of both sea and country. There are beautiful gardens, sea and cliff walks, safe bathing from the hotel, golf, sailing, tennis, putting and bowls. Hotel Elizabeth provides all the comfort and service to make your holiday relaxing and enjoyable. Most of the 37 bedrooms have sea view and some have private bathrooms and balconies. All have intercom, radios and coloured televisions and are centrally heated. There is a lift to all floors. The hotel, carefully supervised by the resident proprietors is licensed and offers delicious food including home made soup and sweets prepared by our qualified chef and patissier. Our kitchens are open to inspection.
TERMS: Dinner, bed and breakfast from £115 inc. VAT. Brochure upon request with SAE or stamp please.

**HOTEL ELIZABETH, Esplanade, Sidmouth, Devon EX10 8AT.
Telephone (03955) 3503 (Management).**

SIDMOUTH. Mrs B. I. Tucker, Goosemoor Farm, Newton Poppleford, Sidmouth EX10 0BL (Colaton Raleigh [0395] 68279). Working farm. Goosemoor Farmhouse is an old Devon Long House with bread oven in diningroom. The 25-acre mixed farm is on the Exeter/Lyme Regis bus route about four miles from the sea and has streams running through its meadows. There are many delightful walks in country lanes or over Woodberry and Alsbeare Commons. Guests may wander freely on the farmland. Private fishing. There are four double and one family rooms all with washbasins; two bathrooms, three toilets; sittingroom; diningroom. Children welcome, cot, high chair and babysitting. Sorry, no pets. Open all year with log fires. Central heating throughout. Car not essential but there is parking. Evening Meal, Bed and Breakfast from £60; Bed and Breakfast from £6. Rates reduced for children under 10 years.

SIDMOUTH. Mr and Mrs Lang Williams, Voggis Hill Farmhouse, Harcombe, Sidmouth EX10 0PR (Sidbury [039-57] 271). In a hamlet in a valley of outstanding natural beauty where walks abound as do foxes, badgers and pheasants, Lang and Joan Williams extend a welcome to you from this 16th century Devon farmhouse. Here 20th century comforts blend with additions made over the years enhancing the inglenook atmosphere. Own garden produce. Devonshire cream. Traditional farmhouse fare. Early morning tea, late night cuppa inclusive. Three double rooms with H&C. Bed, Breakfast and Evening Dinner. LICENSED. No children. No pets. Ample parking. Sidmouth three miles. Easter to November. Christmas. Brochure on request.

SOUTH MOLTON. The Manager, Marsh Hall Country House Hotel, South Molton (07695) 2666. *
Ashley Courtenay Recommended — AA**RAC — secluded Victorian Country House set in its own ground with panoramic views. Luxuriously appointed bedrooms, all en suite. Activity weekend breaks in bird-watching and clay pigeon shooting. Stabling available. Bed, Breakfast and six-course Dinner from £28 per person. Christmas breaks also available. See also Colour Display Advertisement in this Guide.

Please note that entries marked with an asterisk also have a colour display advert in the colour section in this guide

SOUTH MOLTON. Mrs R. M. Hayes, Sheepwash Farm, Molland, South Molton EX36 3NN (Bishop's Nympton [076-97] 276). Working farm. A warm welcome is extended to everyone staying at Sheepwash. An old farmhouse of character situated on the outskirts of Exmoor National Park, one-and-a-half miles from A361, within easy driving distance of the glorious North Devon coasts. South Molton, nearby, has swimming pool, bowling green, tennis courts; Barnstaple (regional centre) 18 miles, with leisure centre. Visitors welcome to explore the 300-acre farm; many lovely walks in the area. Swimming pool open to the public close by. One double/twin and one family bedrooms, with washbasins. Two bathrooms, two toilets, lounge; diningroom with TV and log fire. Children welcome. Reductions for under 12s. Cot and babysitting available. Car essential — parking. Small pets allowed if left in cars. Good farmhouse fare with a different menu every day. Facilities provided for hot drinks in bedrooms. Open May to September for Evening Meal, Bed and Breakfast or Bed and Breakfast. SAE, please.

SOUTH MOLTON. Mrs Gillian Carr, Greenhills Farm, Yeomill, West Anstey, South Molton EX36 3NU (Anstey Mills [03984] 300). Working farm. Visitors are always welcome at Greenhills. We are a farm with milking cows, sheep and pigs in the middle of the Exmoor countryside. Ideally situated one mile off A361 in a quiet lcoation wonderful for exploring Devon and West Somerset. Lovely walks, shallow river, picturesque and safe for children. Visitors can watch the milking in a relaxed and friendly atmosphere. The farmhouse has one family and one double bedrooms. Diningroom. Lounge with colour TV, comfortable with olde worlde decor. Early morning and supper drinks included. Good home cooking. Own dairy produce. vegetables from our own garden. Child's small pony available for riding or just playing around with. Evening Dinner, Bed and Breakfast or Bed and Breakfast only. Reduced rates for children.

SOUTH MOLTON. Miss C. F. Bubb, East Crosside, Knowstone, South Molton EX36 4RT (Anstey Mills [03984] 206). East Crosside is set amidst beautiful countryside near Exmoor, six miles from South Molton and one and a half miles from the picturesque village of Knowstone with thatched inn. Farmhouse accommodation on 10 acre smallholding with sheep, goats, poultry, horses and ponies. Riding available also weekly riding holidays and riding weekends. One double and one family bedrooms, two toilets, separate bathroom, sittingroom with colour TV, diningroom. Plenty of good home cooking. Families especially welcome (children over five). Babysitting. Reductions children under 12. Car essential, parking. Open Easter to October. Bed and Breakfast from £6.50 per night; Bed, Breakfast and Evening Meal from £9.50 per night. Weekly reductions.

SOUTH MOLTON. Mrs M. Radford, Woodhouse Farm, South Molton EX36 4JH (South Molton [076-95] 2321). Working farm. Woodhouse Farm is situated two miles south of the market town of South Molton, in unspoilt countryside and within easy reach of Exmoor, the North Coast and Leisure Centre. Beef and sheep are reared on the 150 acres, with several young animals to see. There are three comfortably furnished bedrooms, with hot and cold water. Tea/coffee making facilities available. Bathroom, separate toilet. Large sittingdiningroom with log fires and colour TV. Plenty of good farmhouse food, mostly home produced. Personal attention at all times. Car essential, ample parking. Open May to October. Bed, Breakfast, Evening Meal (optional). SAE, please, for terms.

SOUTH MOLTON. Mrs P. G. Brown, The White House, Bottreaux Mill, South Molton EX36 3PT (Anstey Mills [039-84] 331). This modern house set on A361, offers panoramic views and is ideally situated for touring north and south Devon coasts, Exmoor and Dartmoor. A homely atmosphere and a friendly welcome are guaranteed. Food is good, menus varied with home-grown vegetables and fruit. Riding and pony trekking from nearby stables, for those wishing to view the scenery from the saddle. Two double bedrooms, one with twin beds and a family room, all with washbasins; lounge, colour TV; separate diningroom. Cot, high chair, babysitting. Car essential — parking space. Pets welcome free. Open Easter to October. Evening Dinner/Meal, Bed and Breakfast from £63; or Bed and Breakfast from £53. Reductions for children according to age.

SOUTH MOLTON near. Mrs P. England, Yeo Farm, Molland, Near South Molton EX36 3NW (Bishops Nympton [076 97] 312). Working farm. South Molton five miles — mixed farm with cows, sheep and poultry. Twenty miles from Saunton Sands, three miles from Molland and Exmoor. Bed and Breakfast or Bed, Breakfast and Evening Meal. Terms on application. AA listed. Everybody is sure of a warm welcome at Yeo Farm which lies one-and-a-half miles off the A361 in a secluded valley with the river Yeo running through the farm. It is ideally situated for touring Exmoor, North Devon and Cornwall. The house is over 300 years old, but is fully modernised with hot and cold, and sprung interior mattresses; both the diningroom and the lounge have the original oak beams and open fireplace. Good food is a speciality with cream, eggs and fresh killed meat and poultry on the menu.

SOUTH MOLTON near. Mrs J. M. Bray, East Bowden Farm, Knowstone, Near South Molton EX36 4RP (Rackenford [088-488] 382). Working farm. East Bowden is an 85-acre farm, mainly beef and sheep. It is situated on the edge of the moor with lovely views over open countryside and Exmoor. Rough shooting on the farm, riding and fishing locally. About a mile from 'The Masons Arms', an ancient thatched inn. Guests receive hospitality in the real Devon tradition, with splendid food and value for money — roast beef, pork, chicken, lamb, fresh vegetables, fruit pies and Devonshire cream. One double, one single and two family bedrooms, three with washbasins; bathroom, two toilets; sittingroom with TV; diningroom. Cot, high chair, babysitting. Pets permitted. Open all year round. Car essential — parking. Evening Dinner, Bed and Breakfast or Bed and Breakfast. Terms on request.

SOUTH MOLTON near. **Mrs Hazel J. Milton, Partridge Arms Farm, West Anstey, Near South Molton EX36 3NU (Anstey Mills [039-84] 217). Working farm.** "Partridge Arms" Farm was, until 1909, a country inn, half-a-mile from A361, four miles west of Dulverton on the Devon/Somerset border. Ideal for touring Exmoor National Park or the North Devon and West Somerset coastal resorts. Riding, trekking and fishing available. Guests enjoy the atmosphere of a one-time country inn now a guest house and family farm of over 200 acres. Two ponies on the farm for children's amusement. Open all year, guests can enjoy excellent and varied menu — no dish repeated in any one week. Three double, two single, one family bedrooms (three with washbasins); bathroom, two toilets; two sittingrooms and three diningrooms. Children welcome with reduced rates according to age; cot. Full Fire Certificate. Residential licence. Pets by arrangement. Car essential, ample parking. Evening Dinner, Bed and Breakfast from £69 weekly; Bed and Breakfast from £49 weekly.

STOKENHAM. Michelle and Tony Jeffs-Bonstow, "Old Cotmore Farm", Stokenham, Near Kingsbridge TQ7 2HU (Kingsbridge [0548] 580240). Sympathetically modernised 400-year-old farmhouse situated in delightful open countryside one-and-a-half miles from lovely beaches and National Trust walks. The historic riverside town of Dartmouth is 10 miles distant, and market town of Kingsbridge, seven miles. We offer four charming bedrooms — two double (en-suite), one single, one family, all with washbasins, full central heating, tea-making facilities and colour TV. Open February to November, with log fires in winter. Ample parking and secluded garden to relax. Pets can be accommodated in outbuildings. Bed and Breakfast only from £9. Numerous good pubs of character serving food, and restaurants, within two miles of farm. Please ring or send SAE for brochure.

TAVISTOCK. Mrs B. Anning, Wringworthy Farm, Mary Tavy, Tavistock PL19 9LT (Mary Tavy [082-281] 434). Working farm. This farm is set in a valley with the entrance on the A386. It is mentioned in the Domesday Book and the main part is Elizabethan. It has been modernised for comfort yet retains its old charms such as beams and flagstones. Log fires and a friendly greeting ensure guests of a warm welcome at Wringworthy. The guests have a lounge to themselves with TV; two double bedrooms and one family size; two bathrooms; diningroom. Children over two are welcome and there is a cot and reduced rates. Sorry, no pets. Open from April to September. Car is essential and there is parking. Evening Dinner, Bed and Breakfast or Bed and Breakfast only. It is near sea and there is fishing in Tamar and Tavy. Also near the moors; riding, walking and golfing. Dinner served on five nights a week, with local produce being used. SAE, please, for terms.

TEIGNMOUTH. Mrs C. A. Walker, Cornubia, Thornley Drive, Teignmouth TQ14 9JH (Teignmouth [06267] 4256). The Cornubia is a spacious and cheerful family run hotel, standing in its own grounds overlooking the sea, Shaldon and beautiful Teign Estuary. Ideal for touring Devon and Dartmoor, yet only 10 minutes' walk from the beach, harbour and town of Teignmouth. We have a licensed bar, full size snooker table, heated swimming pool, table tennis and colour television. Bedrooms are light and spacious with tea making facilities. The atmosphere is relaxed and carefree, the rates reasonable. Children are welcome, cot, high chair and babysitting. Pets allowed. Open April to October. Please telephone or write for colour brochure.

TEIGNMOUTH. Mr and Mrs W. G. Halford, The Cottage, West Town, Forder Lane, Bishopsteignton TQ14 9QY (Teignmouth [062-67] 2382). A Georgian Guest House in spacious secluded grounds. In heart of picturesque village overlooking River Teign. Close to the sea and moors with everything for the sporting enthusiast within close vicinity. A comfortable family atmosphere, where children are welcome. Home-grown produce when available. Buses to Teignmouth and Newton Abbot pass the gate hence car is not essential but ample parking available. Two double, three family and one twin bedded rooms, all with washbasins. All family and one double bedrooms have views of garden or river. Fitted carpets in all bedrooms, reading lamps and shaver points. Two bathrooms and two toilets; one shower room; sitting and diningrooms. Cot, high chair, babysitting available. Open all year for Evening Dinner, Bed and Breakfast or Bed and Breakfast only. Rates reduced for children if sharing bedroom. SAE for terms and brochure.

PLEASE SEND A STAMPED ADDRESSED ENVELOPE WITH ENQUIRIES

TEIGNMOUTH. Mrs Joan Webber, Higher Radway Farm, Bishopsteignton, Teignmouth TQ14 9TB (Teignmouth [062-67] 5348). Working farm. The farmhouse, on 250 acres given over to mixed farming, offers every modern comfort, with fitted carpets throughout and TV in lounge. This is glorious country, and from the diningroom there are particularly fine views of the River Teign and the sea. Golf courses less than one mile away; rough shooting. Centrally heated. Open March to October. Three double and one family bedrooms (two with washbasins); bathroom and toilet; sittingroom, diningroom. Pets allowed free of charge. A car is essential — parking available. SAE, please, for terms for Evening Dinner/Meal, Bed and Breakfast or Bed and Breakfast only.

TIVERTON. Mrs C. S. Drake, Upcott Farm, Nomansland, Tiverton EX16 8NT (Tiverton [0884] 860892). Working farm. Bed and full English Breakfast offered all year round in this 300-year-old Devon Longhouse on 120-acre mixed farm in peaceful surroundings, away from main roads, midway between Dartmoor and Exmoor. Ideal centre for touring and walking — Exeter 20 miles, Tiverton and South Molton (market towns), 10 miles. A variety of animals are kept including dogs, cats, geese, chicken, ducks, sheep and cattle, so there is always something interesting for children. Babysitting available. Two double bedrooms, one twin-bedded room; comfortable TV lounge. Car essential. Guests will enjoy the welcoming and friendly atmosphere. Bed and Breakfast from £6.50. Weekly rates on request. SAE, please, or phone evenings.

* **TIVERTON. Mrs Jill Bent, West Pitt Farm, Uplowman, Tiverton EX16 7DU (Tiverton [0884] 820296). Working farm.** Two-and-a-half miles from the M5 (Sampford Peverell interchange), West Pitt is ideally situated within easy reach of both North and South coasts, Exmoor and Dartmoor. Guests are free to explore the 190 acres mixed farm. Delicious cooking and every comfort is our speciality. Three double, one single, one family bedrooms, all with washbasins; bathrooms, toilets; lounge with oak beams; diningroom. Heated swimming pool, grass tennis court, well-stocked coarse fishing pool, games room. Children and pets welcome. Also self-catering farm cottage — sleeps six. See also Colour Display Advertisement in this Guide.

TIVERTON. Mr and Mrs R. C. Pratt, Moor Barton, Nomansland, Tiverton EX16 8NN (Tiverton [0884] 860325). Working farm. Full Fire Certificate. Set in glorious countryside where guests are free to roam the 200-acre mixed dairy farm. Economically situated for touring all Devon. Visit Tiverton market, heated swimming pool, horse riding, canal trips. Equidistant North and South coasts, Exmoor, Dartmoor. Guests return annually to enjoy the free family atmosphere given by Colin, Rita and family and the excellent fresh home cooking including full English breakfast of bacon and eggs. Dinners of home produced beef, lamb, pork, chicken, pies, cream etc., served. All bedrooms have washbasins (one on ground floor). Bathrooms and ample toilet facilities. Central heating. Lounge with colour TV and open log fire. Children welcome at reduced rates, high chair. Evening Dinner, Bed and Breakfast from £78 weekly (£13 daily); Bed and Breakfast from £8.50 per night. House suitable for disabled guests. Open all year.

TIVERTON near. Mrs F. A. Luxton, Thorne Farm, Stoodleigh, near Tiverton EX16 9QG (Rackenford [088-488] 232). Working farm. Thorne Farm is quietly situated in Devon's rolling hills, overlooking wooded valleys with marvellous views. There are pedigree Devon cattle and sheep and visitors are welcome to take an interest in the various jobs on the farm and walk on the 120 acres of farmland. Within easy reach of the Exmoor National Park and many local beauty spots. Food is a speciality, with fresh vegetables, milk, cream, meat and home-made bread. Two double, one family bedrooms; bathroom, two toilets; sittingroom. Reduced rates, cot and occasional babysitting. Sorry, no pets. Open April to October. Car essential; ample parking. Evening Meal, Bed and Breakfast from £64; Bed and Breakfast from £9.50. Reduced rates for children under fourteen years. SAE, please.

TIVERTON. Mrs S. M. Kerslake, Landrake Farm, Chevithorne, Tiverton EX16 7QN (Bampton [0398] 31221). Landrake is situated at the 900 ft. level with extensive views of the pleasant quiet countryside, plenty of lovely walks on the farm. North and South Devon coasts within easy reach, also Dartmoor and Exmoor. Tiverton, with its golf course, tennis, heated swimming pool, canal with horse-drawn barge, country pubs, fishing, riding stables, all within four miles. Freshly grown vegetables and home produced beef, lamb, pork and chicken served with personal supervision. One double, one twin and one family rooms; bathroom, toilet; sittingroom, diningroom. Children welcome, cot, high chair and babysitting. Pets allowed. Open April to October. Car essential, ample parking. Evening Dinner, Bed and Breakfast with reduced rates for children. Terms on application with SAE, please.

TIVERTON near. Mrs Margaret Reed, Trewmans Farm, Cadeleigh, Near Tiverton EX16 8HP (Bickleigh [088 45] 232). Working farm. Mixed dairy farm with cows, calves, ponies, a horse and pets. Children welcome, baby minding. Regret, no dogs. Twenty-two miles from sandy beach. Bed and Breakfast or Bed, Breakfast and Evening Meal. Terms on request. Reductions for children under 12 years. Our farm is situated in the small village of Cadeleigh with post office and inn. Tiverton six miles, Exeter 13 miles. Within easy reach of South and North coast, Exmoor and Dartmoor. Lounge, TV. All modern conveniences. Good farm fare. Open March to November.

The information in the entries in this guide is presented by the publishers in good faith and after the signed acceptance by advertisers that they will uphold the high standards associated with FARM HOLIDAY GUIDES LIMITED. The publishers do not accept responsibility for any inaccuracies or omissions or any results thereof. Before making final holiday arrangements readers should confirm the prices and facilities directly with advertisers.

TORBAY. Mrs J. Ireland, Holt, 7 Greenhill Road, Kingskerswell, Near Newton Abbot TQ12 5HT (Kingskerswell [080-47] 2336). Torquay three miles; Newton Abbot three miles. Welcome to our family guest house in charming village with old church, stream, thatched restaurant, pub and shops. We have our own fields, horses, dogs, puppies, cats, free range hens, baby chicks and a goldfish. Explore the gaiety of seaside resorts, historic towns or beautiful Dartmoor with its Stone-Age antiquities. We only have room for 12 guests in family, double and single bedrooms all with hot and cold basins and tea-making facilities. Bathroom and two WC's. Lounge with colour TV. Separate diningroom. Bed and Breakfast from £7. Evening Meal optional by arrangement. Open April to October.

CLEVELANDS COUNTRY HOUSE HOTEL
Steep Hill, Maidencombe, Torquay, Devon TQ1 4TS
R.A.C. LISTED   REG'D E.T.B.

"Clevelands" is a small, licensed, family hotel situated in a secluded garden setting in the picturesque hamlet of Maidencombe, midway between Torquay and Teignmouth. The hotel is only 150 yards from the beach path leading to a small sheltered cove with safe bathing. The bedrooms, all with sea or country views, have hot and cold water, and central heating. There is a comfortable lounge with colour television, an attractive bar lounge, large sun lounge and a pleasant dining room over-looking the sea. Facilities for riding, sailing, fishing and golf are all within easy reach. Traditional English cooking with home or locally grown produce used whenever possible. Children over three years welcome. Small dogs by prior arrangement. Open early spring until late Autumn. S.A.E. for brochure please.

Mr and Mrs A. Grops   Torquay (0803) 38577

COURTHOUSE
MAIDENCOMBE, TORQUAY, S. DEVON TQ1 4SU
Telephone: [0803] 38335

Originally a 12th Century Manor Court House, mentioned in Domesday, now a family-run Country House Hotel. Steeped in history yet offering guests the best of English fare and present day comforts, including en suite facilities, licensed bar, own car park. Set in rural surroundings in the unspoilt hamlet of Maidencombe 300 yards from the beach, yet only four miles from Torquay. An ideal centre for touring glorious South Devon.

★ Open April to October
★ Midweek or Saturday-Sunday bookings accepted
★ Children very welcome at reduced rates
★ Reduced terms for Spring and Late Summer

RAC Listed

Member of
West Country Tourist Board

To find out more about us, please write, enclosing stamp, for colour brochure to the Resident Proprietors Sheila and Godfrey Walker.

Bowden Close Hotel

AA★★ RAC★★
Member of Torquay Hotels Association & Registered with English Tourist Board. Member of West Country Tourist Board.

Teignmouth Road,
Maidencombe Cross,
Torquay,
South Devon,
TQ1 4TJ
Torquay 38029

"Bowden Close" is a delightful Victorian country house hotel, situated halfway between Torquay and Teignmouth with panoramic views of sea, coast and country, set in lovely grounds. Maidencombe is an unspoilt coastal hamlet with safe bathing from a sheltered beach. It is an ideal area for boating enthusiasts. Two 18-hole golf courses nearby. Riding stables are within walking distance. Charming Devon villages abound with their thatched roofed old pubs. The hotel is very comfortable – central heating, plus open log fire. The accommodation comprises 20 bedrooms, most with shower or bath en suite (all with radios and colour TV); two lounges; spacious lounge/bar; well-appointed beamed ceiling diningroom; sun lounge; excellent sea views. Ample parking. Children welcome. Sea approximately 600 yards. Fire Certificate.

Charming Hotel in beautiful setting. Licensed. Choice wine list.

The Hotel is carefully supervised by the Clarke family providing a good four-course Dinner, Traditional English Breakfast, Lunches and Bar Snacks when required.
TERMS: Evening Dinner, Bed and Breakfast from £90 inc. VAT per week. Spring, Autumn and Christmas breaks. Brochure upon request with SAE or stamp please.

BOWDEN CLOSE HOTEL,
Teignmouth Road, Maidencombe Cross, Torquay,
South Devon TQ1 4TJ. (0803 38029).

TORCROFT HOTEL

CROFT ROAD, TORQUAY TQ2 5UF

(TAS)

Telephone
TORQUAY
(0803) 28292

AA & RAC Listed

Licensed

This comfortable and friendly 21-bedroom Hotel is situated on a quiet tree-lined road, only 400 yards from Abbey Sands. We offer good food, a restful atmosphere, combined with easy access to the town centre, Abbey Gardens and Holiday entertainment. Stamp only for Colour Brochure with pleasure from Resident Proprietors:

HELEN & GRAHAM DAVIES

For your happy Holiday we offer: ○ Ample free parking in grounds for all cars ○ Four-course Dinner with choice of menu ○ Full English breakfast ○ Ornate dining room with separate tables ○ Spacious lounge bar ○ Colour TV lounge ○ All rooms H&C water, shaver sockets, bedside lights ○ Some rooms with shower/w.c. en suite ○ Balcony bedrooms with sea view ○ Ground floor and family bedrooms ○ Fire certificate ○ Evening refreshment service ○ One child under 5 years free early and late season ○ Reductions for OAP's early and late season ○ Parties catered for ○ Regret we do not accept pets.

TORQUAY. Mr and Mrs C. K. Fallowfield, Craig Court Hotel, 10 Ash Hill Road, Torquay TQ1 3HZ (Torquay [0803] 24500). BTA, AA and RAC listed. Licensed. Now under the supervision of Resident Proprietors Chris and Ken Fallowfield, Craig Court Hotel is beautifully situated, facing south in one of the most convenient positions in Torquay, within easy walking distance of beaches, amusements and shops, and open from Easter to October inclusive. Centrally heated. Pleasant sun lounge and lounge with colour TV overlooks a secluded garden; diningroom has separate tables and food is excellent. The hotel has seven double bedrooms (four en suite) and three family bedrooms — all with wash hand basins; three bathrooms and toilets. Children welcome, cot, high chair and babysitting available. Car not essential, parking available. Fire Certificate held. Evening Dinner, Bed and Breakfast or Bed and Breakfast. Bar lunches also available. Reduced rates for children sharing parents' room. SAE, please.

TORQUAY. Mrs R. F. Hitchcock, Kingsway Lodge, 95 Avenue Road, Torquay TQ2 5LH (0803-25288). This clean, comfortable guest house comes well recommended for good home cooked meals as well as for its situation — just 15 minutes' level walk from beach, shops, Abbey Gardens. Central for touring beauty spots in the area. Personal attention at all times. There are four double, one single and one family bedrooms with central heating, spring interior divans and washbasins. Carpeted throughout. Colour TV lounge; diningroom; bathroom, two toilets. Children are welcome at reduced rates. Sorry, no pets. Free parking though car not essential. Open all year for Evening Meal, Bed and Breakfast from £55 weekly or Bed and Breakfast only from £38 weekly.

FARM HOLIDAY GUIDES LIMITED publish a large range of well-known accommodation guides. We will be happy to send you details or you can use the order form at the back of this book.

174 Devon BOARD

TORQUAY. Mr and Mrs A. and F. Lang, Victoria Lodge Hotel, 16 Newton Road, Torquay TQ2 5BZ (Torquay [0803] 211580). Victoria Lodge is a licensed, comfortable hotel and restaurant consisting of six double, one twin and three family bedrooms (some en-suite). The diningroom is spacious and offers a wine list to complement our traditional four-course meals. The bar carries a wide range of soft and alcoholic drinks. Our guests enjoy the benefit of a large comfortable lounge with colour TV. The hotel complies to safety standards and holds a fire certificate, and is RAC listed. Ample parking but a car is not essential, it being a leisurely fifteen minutes' stroll to the sea front, beach and town. Many beauty spots and places of historic interest are within easy reach. Regret, no pets. Write, SAE, please, or phone for brochure.

TORRINGTON. Mrs Jessie Barnes, "River View", 132 Mill Street, Torrington EX38 8AW (Torrington [0805] 23195). Set in an extensive garden, in a lovely valley, overlooking the old toll bridge, "River View" offers rest and relaxation with personal attention and friendly service. The best of food, morning and evening tea served free, electric blankets and washbasins in all bedrooms, central heating — you can afford to spoil yourself at these prices: Bed and Breakfast from £7, Optional Dinner £5, Fisherman's Lunch £2. Excellent facilities for walking, golfing and fishing; beaches of the "Golden Coast" within 10 miles; moorland and larger resorts within 30 miles. Children welcome, reduced rates — cot and high chair provided, babysitting can be arranged. Car essential — free parking. Open February to December. Pay a visit soon — you won't be disappointed.

TORRINGTON. Mrs Y. S. Wassell, Woodland Farm, Little Torrington, Torrington EX38 8QS (Torrington [0805] 22473). Working farm. Woodland Farm is a 141-acre farm with sheep and cattle. The land runs down to the bank of the River Torridge. The historic old farmhouse nestles in a sheltered position in this lovely wooded valley. Two double rooms, both with washbasins and shaver points. One single room. Guest shower room. Bathroom available. Sittingroom with colour TV. Wood fires. Home cooking. Garden. Car essential. Ample parking. Midway Dartmoor/Exmoor. Touring distance Cornish moors. Easy reach coast, Bideford, Westward Ho!, Clovelly. Golfing and fishing locally. Evening Dinner, Bed and Breakfast or Bed and Breakfast only. Open March-November.

TOTNES near. Mrs E. Cavell, "Pippins", Broadhempston, Totnes TQ9 6BJ (Ipplepen [0803] 812056). "Pippins" is a comfortable, old cottage just off the Village Square, three miles off the Newton Abbot/Totnes road (A381), with easy access Dartmoor, Torquay, Buckfast Abbey etc. Broadhempston is a peaceful farming village, ideal for anyone seeking lovely countryside, rest and quiet. The hedgerows are massed with wild flowers for much of the year. The ancient town of Totnes, Steam Railway and the Arts and Crafts of Dartington are 10 minutes away by car. "Pippins" has one family bedroom (washbasin and TV), one double bedroom. Modern bathroom opposite. Remarks in the Visitors' Book show how much the hospitality and creative cooking are appreciated. Being centrally heated, "Pippins" is warm and cosy in winter. Bed and Breakfast from £6. Delicious Evening Dinner £4.25. Special terms for children.

TOTNES near. Mrs S. A. Edwards, Ford Farm, Harberton, Near Totnes TQ9 7SJ (Totnes [0803] 863539). Ford Farm is a 17th-century house in a typical rural village, ideally situated for touring Dartmoor and the coast, within easy reach of Exeter, Dartmouth, Plymouth and Torquay. The owners, Mike and Sheila Edwards, previously owned and ran a restaurant for 11 years, and can assure you of personal, skilled attention, really good cooking and a warm welcome. Guests bringing their own wines will find that these are served at no extra charge. The house is comfortably furnished with many period pieces of furniture. We offer two double bedded rooms with shower, handbasin, WC en-suite, a twin-bedded room and two single rooms, both with washbasins. Bathroom, toilet. Sittingroom, diningroom. Central heating. Children 12 years and over welcome. Pets by prior arrangement. Car essential — parking. Open all year. Special winter breaks. Brochure available on request.

TOTNES. Mrs Anne Barons, Charford Farm, Avonwick, Totnes TQ9 7LT (South Brent [03647] 3263). Working farm. A warm and friendly welcome awaits you at this lovely old farmhouse on a 350 acre dairy, sheep and arable farm. Central for coast, Dartmoor, Plymouth and Torbay; within easy reach of many tourist attractions. Family, double and twin-bedded rooms, all with washbasins and tea-making facilities. Bathroom and separate toilet. Diningroom and lounge with colour TV. Home from home comfort in a relaxed, informal atmosphere. Central heating early/late holidays. Children are very welcome at reduced rates. Cot, high chair and babysitting available, also children's pony. Open Easter to October for Evening Meal, Bed and Breakfast or Bed and Breakfast only. Please telephone or write for terms and brochure.

TOTNES. Mr R. Miller, Buckyette Farm, Littlehampton, Totnes (Staverton [080-426] 638). Much of the appeal of Buckyette lies in its sense of history and tradition. The present house includes part of an earlier farmhouse which was mentioned in the Domesday Book, and the farm itself was developed around a fresh water spring still in use today. Set between Torbay and Dartmoor, it is an ideal holiday centre. Safe beaches, summer shows, discos, night clubs and sporting facilities are easily reached. Car essential. Accommodation consists of double, single and family bedrooms, most with washbasins; bathroom, shower room, three toilets; sittingroom with TV and separate diningroom serving home cooked fresh food. Children are very welcome. Sorry, no pets. Open from May to September. Ample parking. Terms on request. Also self-catering properties.

TOTNES. Mrs Susan Freeth, Wonton Farm, Diptford, Totnes TQ9 7LS (South Brent [036-47] 2210). Working farm. Wonton Farm is situated two miles from the A38 dual carriageway. It is a dairy farm and pony stud. We are central for the Dart Valley Railway (Steam Trains), The Shire Horse Centre, Paignton Zoo, River Dart, Boat Trips and many National Trust Properties, and within easy reach of the coast. There are a number of good Public Houses in the immediate vicinity. The house dates back to the 16th century. There is a large sittingroom with colour TV for guests' use whenever required. Large secluded garden. Three double, one family bedrooms; two bathrooms, three toilets. Children welcome at reduced prices. Pets permitted. Free babysitting. Bed and Breakfast. Evening Meal by Arrangement. Open February to November.

UMBERLEIGH. Mrs K. Baker, Langley Barton, Umberleigh EX37 9EF (Newton Tracey [027185] 464). Working farm. Langley Barton is a 150 acre dairy farm, with a large 17th century farmhouse and was mentioned in the Domesday Book. It is situated about seven miles from the market towns of Torrington, South Molton, Bideford and Barnstaple. The golden sands of Woolacombe and Saunton are about 12 miles as is Exmoor. The accommodation consists of one double room (with H&C), one twin room and a family room. There is also a bathroom and colour TV lounge for guests' use. The tariff is £6.50 per person per night for Bed and Breakfast and £10 per night if Evening Meal is required. Also reductions for the under fives. Please ring for details.

UMBERLEIGH. Mrs S. Walker, Nethercleave Farm, Umberleigh EX37 9AD (Chittlehamholt [076-94] 252). Working farm. A warm welcome awaits you on this 100-acre dairy farm adjoining the River Taw. Situated seven miles from Barnstaple, South Molton and Torrington, it is within half an hour's drive of a variety of surfing and sandy beaches and Exmoor. There are quiet local walks and guests are welcome to explore the farm. Horse riding, tennis and fishing available locally. Fresh home cooking. Guests' lounge with TV. All bedrooms have hot and cold water. Children welcome. Terms from £70 per week.

UMBERLEIGH. Mrs Eileen Chapple, Bouchland Farm, Burrington, Umberleigh EX37 9NF (High Bickington [0769] 60394). Working farm. A warm and friendly welcome awaits guests at this 145 acre mixed farm, which is set in the heart of the countryside (just one mile off the A377 Exeter/Barnstaple road) overlooking the Taw Valley. This is an ideal touring centre for visiting Exmoor, Dartmoor, the sandy beaches and many other places of interest. The mainly stone-built farmhouse is spacious and offers two family rooms with washbasins and tea/coffee facilities, and two double or twin bedded rooms, two toilets. Bathroom with shower. Diningroom with separate tables. Snooker, darts and table tennis. Speciality: good food guaranteed. A four-course Dinner of soup, egg mayonnaise, melon etc; traditional farmhouse roast, steak and kidney, chicken in mushroom sauce; followed by a variety of sweets; cheese, biscuits and coffee. Full English Breakfast. Children welcome, reduced rates under 12. Regret, no pets. Car essential. Open from March to November for Dinner, Bed and Breakfast or Bed and Breakfast. Stamp please for brochure and further details.

The information in the entries in this guide is presented by the publishers in good faith and after the signed acceptance by advertisers that they will uphold the high standards associated with FARM HOLIDAY GUIDES LIMITED. The publishers do not accept responsibility for any inaccuracies or omissions or any results thereof. Before making final holiday arrangements readers should confirm the prices and facilities directly with advertisers.

WELLINGTON (Somerset). Mrs Ann Heard, Lower Westcott Farm, Ashbrittle, Near Wellington, Somerset TA21 0HZ (Clayhanger [039-86] 296). Working farm. Situated on the Devon/Somerset border, Lower Westcott enjoys extensive views of both these lovely counties. The delightful old house is warm, carpeted and offers guests every comfort including freedom of a large garden with lawns and amusements for children. The 210-acre farm has cattle, sheep, pigs, poultry and is convenient to A38, A361 and M5, nine miles from Tiverton with Sports Centre, canal, castle, craft centre, golf, riding and Knightshayes Court. Central for touring Dartmoor, Exmoor, north and south coasts or overnight stop for Cornwall. Two family, one double bedrooms, with washbasins; bathroom; diningroom; TV lounge. Cot, high chair, babysitting and reductions for children. Car essential — ample parking. Evening Meal, Bed and Breakfast from £70 weekly; Bed and Breakfast from £7 per night. Enjoy good home cooking with fresh farm produce. For prompt reply phone or SAE, please.

WINKLEIGH. Mrs E. Cowle, Week House Farm, Winkleigh (Winkleigh [083-783] 282). A warm and friendly welcome awaits you at this 230-acre farm which lies a mile and a half from the pretty old village of Winkleigh and is central for touring the north and south coasts, Dartmoor and Exmoor. Many sporting pursuits can be followed here — rough shooting on the farm, fly fishing on a pond two miles away. The large stonebuilt house has spacious rooms; two bedrooms with washbasins; lounge; diningroom with separate tables. TV. Cot and high chair available; babysitting arranged. Pets allowed. Home cooking and an excellent menu with roast poultry, fresh cream, eggs, vegetables — everything good served. Open all year with the exception of Christmas. Evening Dinner, Bed and Breakfast. SAE for terms.

WOOLACOMBE. Tony and Carole Rogers, Crossways Hotel, The Seafront, Woolacombe EX34 7DJ (Woolacombe [0271] 870395). Homely, family-run, licensed hotel, beautifully situated, overlooking Combesgate beach and the pretty Combesgate valley, and surrounded by National Trust land. Bathing and surfing from the hotel. Well situated for golf courses, horse riding, and many beautiful walks. All bedrooms recently completely refurbished to a very high standard, many en-suite, or with showers. Menu choice for evening dinner and breakfast, and a varied choice of bar snacks available at lunchtime. We have just received two awards from the AA for the high standard of our bedrooms, and for our hospitality; this must be why so many of our guests return year after year — why not join them? Children half-price or FREE. Pets welcome by arrangement.

WOOLACOMBE. Mr and Mrs A. S. Gay, Gull Rock, Mortehoe, Woolacombe EX34 7EA (Woolacombe [0271] 870534). Gull Rock is a family run Guest House with a sun terrace having one of the most breathtaking views in the whole of North Devon. Below are Combesgate, Barracane and Woolacombe beaches, which are backed by glorious National Trust property. Beyond the beaches are Baggy Point and on to the Lighthouse of Hartland Point. One double and six family bedrooms, all large with vanitory units and razor points, and all have sea views. There are ample toilet and bathroom facilities. Diningroom. Wonderful summer lounge has the same lovely sea view and colour TV also. Children are welcome and there is cot, high chair and babysitting by arrangement. Pets by arrangement. Open March to October with central heating. Car essential, parking. Fire Certificate. Write to Pam and Alan Gay with SAE for details of Bed and Breakfast and Bed, Breakfast and Evening Meals.

WOOLACOMBE. Tom and Win Cooper, Seawards, Beach Road, Woolacombe EX34 7AD (Woolacombe [0271] 870249). Well-appointed guest house, hillside situation, facing South and West. Magnificent views across fields and valley to the beach, three quarters of a mile away. Here you will find friendly informality, combined with high standard of totally home-cooked food, well presented. Full English Breakfast and four-course Evening Dinner. Residential Licence. Moderate charges (£70 to £85 per person per week) reflect the fact that Seawards is family-run and attracts no VAT. Children five to ten are welcome, at half-price; 11 to 15 years 75%. Three miles sand and Atlantic breakers for surf-riding. Lovely villages and beautiful countryside, including Exmoor within reach. Plenty of walking for the energetic.

WOOLACOMBE. Mrs A. M. Carroll, Ferndale, Mortehoe, Woolacombe EX34 7ED (Woolacombe [0271] 870546). This house is two minutes from centre of village and one mile from sea. Accommodation for guests in one double and two family bedrooms, all with washbasins. Children welcome and there is cot, high chair, babysitting and reduced rates. Much of the moorland belongs to the National Trust and there are lovely moorland views and walks. Woolacombe with three miles of golden sands only a mile away and Rockham beach with its rock pools, shrimping and rock climbing is 15 minutes' walk. Bull Point Lighthouse is one-and-a-half miles. Open March to October. Good food served and plenty of Devonshire Cream is used. Car essential, parking. Evening Dinner, Bed and Breakfast or Bed and Breakfast only. SAE, please, for terms.

PLEASE SEND A STAMPED ADDRESSED ENVELOPE WITH ENQUIRIES

WOOLACOMBE. Mr and Mrs E. W. and R. G. Adey, "Caertref," Beach Road, Woolacombe EX34 7BT (Woolacombe [0271] 870361). "Caertref" is a small family guest house, two minutes from Woolacombe's glorious beach, one of the most beautiful in North Devon, surrounded by unspoilt National Trust protected landscape. The main aim of the proprietors is to give each guest an enjoyable holiday, in relaxed friendly atmosphere. Accommodation comprises large, comfortable lounge, colour TV; cosy bar, residential licence; hot and cold and shaver points in all bedrooms, two double (one twin-bedded, one with private shower), two single and four family bedrooms; bathroom with toilet plus two toilets; one shower room; sitting and diningrooms. Full central heating. Cot, high chair and reduced rates for children. Pets taken except in high season. Parking. Fire Certificate held. Evening Meal, Bed and Breakfast or Bed and Breakfast from April to end of September. SAE, please, for terms.

WOOLACOMBE. Mr and Mrs V. W. Bassett, Sunnycliffe Hotel, Mortehoe, Woolacombe EX34 7EB (Woolacombe [0271] 870597). This is a friendly hotel where you are really looked after and where someone cares about the success of your holiday; situated amongst beautiful National Trust countryside, with rolling green downs sloping to golden beaches, Sunnycliffe is one of the finest small hotels in North Devon. All bedrooms have sea views, colour TV and tea-making facilities, most with private bathroom, or shower and toilet. The hotel has a reputation for good English food cooked by the highly-qualified proprietor (chef). Only children over 10 years accepted. If you would like a quiet holiday with really good food, Sunnycliffe will welcome you. SAE, please.

WOOLACOMBE. Mrs C. Robbins, Springside, Mullacott Road, Woolacombe EX34 7HF (Woolacombe [0271] 870452). Springside is a seven-bedroomed detached country guest house standing in two-and-a-half acres of land just off the B3343 road on the outskirts of Woolacombe with views over open countryside to the sea. Three miles from Ilfracombe and within easy reach of all the beaches and beauty spots in the area. All bedrooms have washbasins, razor points, bedside lamps, and are fully carpeted. Two bedrooms have private bathroom and toilet. Own keys to bedrooms. Separate tables in large diningroom. Two lounges with colour TV. Residential Licence. Fire Certificate. Central heating. Car essential — ample free parking. Plenty of excellent food is served and is always highly recommended. Children welcome at reduced rates; cot and high chair provided. Sorry, no pets. Open March to November for Evening Dinner, Bed and Breakfast. AA and RAC Listed.

For the Mutual Guidance of Guest and Host

Farm Holiday Guides Ltd. do not inspect or recommend accommodation but advertisers agree to accept our Farm Holiday Guide standards of comfortable and clean accommodation and wholesome and well-cooked food. Advertisers are also bound by the Trades Description Act.

When accommodation has been booked, deposits sent, and letters of acceptance exchanged, both parties – host and guest – have entered into a binding contract.

Friends and families can easily be upset and much bitterness caused if holiday arrangements are not carefully made. The following points can be of real importance:

Guest When enquiring about accommodation, be as precise as possible. Give exact dates, numbers in your party and the ages of any children. State the number and type of rooms wanted and also what catering you require – bed and breakfast, full board etc. Make sure that the position about evening meals is clear – and about pets, reductions for children or any other special points.

Read our reviews carefully to ensure that the proprietors you are going to contact can supply what you want. Ask for a letter confirming all arrangements, if possible.

Host Give details about your facilities and about any special conditions. Explain your deposit system clearly and arrangements for cancellations, charges etc, and whether or not your terms include VAT.

We regret that Farm Holiday Guides cannot accept responsibility for any errors or omissions in descriptions. Prices in particular should be checked before booking because of the early compilation of the Guides, far ahead of the next holiday season.

DORSET

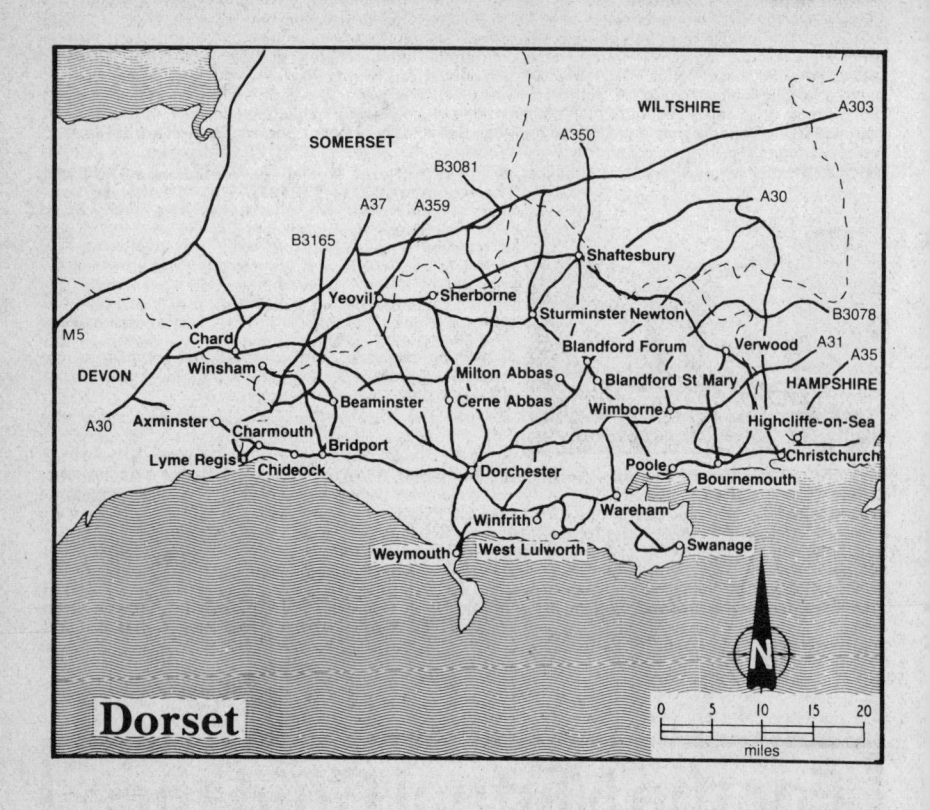

BEAMINSTER. Mrs J. E. Wyatt, Brimley Farm, Stoke Abbott, Beaminster DT8 3JU (Broadwindsor [0308] 68205). Working farm. There is a warm welcome to greet you at Brimley Farm, which is a lovely thatched 16th-century farmhouse. It has been well-modernised inside with family and twin-bedded rooms — private bathrooms and toilet. Ideally situated for visiting places of interest, and various beaches are all within easy reach. Good farmhouse cooking guaranteed, using own garden produce when possible. Children welcome at reduced rates — cot, high chair and babysitting by arrangement. Car essential — ample parking. Sorry, no pets. Open April to October. Colour TV, lounge, diningroom. Evening Dinner, Bed and Breakfast or Bed and Breakfast only. SAE for terms, please.

BEAMINSTER. Mrs C. Poulton, Hursey Farm, Hursey, Broadwindsor, Beaminster DT8 3LN (Broadwindsor [0308] 68323). Hursey Farm is a lovely old farmhouse situated in the tiny hamlet of Hursey on the edge of Broadwindsor in quiet and beautiful Dorset countryside seven miles from coast. Ideal centre for walking, golfing, fishing and touring, with riding available at village stables. Many places of interest, historic houses and gardens, wildlife park, ancient earth works and fossil-rich cliffs of Lyme Regis, plus many lovely towns and villages. Guest accommodation two delightful double bedrooms, one with twin beds, with washbasins; toilet and shower room; separate lounge with TV, and diningroom. Full central heating. Good home cooking using fresh home produce. Sorry, no pets. Car essential — ample parking. Open all year, except Christmas and New Year. Evening Meal, Bed and Breakfast from £80 per week; Bed and Breakfast only from £8.50 per night.

BOARD   Dorset   179

BLANDFORD. Mrs A. M. Martin, Glebe Farm, Winterbourne Houghton, Near Blandford DT11 0PD (Milton Abbas [0258] 880420). Working farm. Glebe Farm is a dairy and arable farm. It is situated in a quiet village in a valley under Bulbarrow Hill in the centre of Dorset. This is an ideal base for touring, with the village of Milton Abbas four miles away, and the towns of Blandford, Dorchester, Sherbourne and Wimborne all within easy reach, and Dorset's beautiful coastline only 20 miles to the south. Open from March to September, the accommodation consists of one double room and one twin-bedded room (both with tea-making facilities); bathroom with toilet. Sitting/diningroom with TV. Car essential. Sorry, no dogs. Bed and Breakfast only. (Good food available at reasonable prices at nearby inns.) SAE, please, for terms.

BLANDFORD. Patricia and John Benjafield, Farnham Farm House, Farnham, Blandford DT11 8DG (Tollard Royal [07256] 254). Working farm. Set in three-quarter acre garden, with heated swimming pool, 19th century farmhouse, part of a 350-acre cereal and beef farm situated in the heart of Cranborne Chase. Ideal touring centre, being within easy reach of the coast and many other places of interest. Bed and Breakfast only is provided all year round, but numerous inns in the surrounding area all serve excellent food. Guests are accommodated in two double, and two family bedrooms (all with washbasins); bathroom, two toilets; sittingroom-cum-diningroom. Cosy log fires provided in winter months. Children welcome, cot, high chair and babysitting available. Pets accepted free of charge. Car essential — unlimited parking. Bed and Breakfast from £9 with reductions for under twelve year olds.

BLANDFORD near. Mrs E. Howlett, Tadpoles, Frog Lane, Shroton, Near Blandford DT11 8QL (Child Okeford [0258] 860033 or 860650). West wing of attractive 17th century house, comfortably furnished and tastefully decorated, standing in own garden in the small village of Shroton at the foot of prehistoric Hambledon Hill. Within easy reach of Salisbury, Bath, Longleat, Dorchester, Poole and many other places of historical interest. On the edge of Hardy country and not far from riding, sailing, golfing, fishing, nature reserves, etc. and many beautiful walks. Coast varies from golden sands to rocky coves. Accommodation in four double bedrooms; cot; two bathrooms, three toilets; sittingroom with black and white TV. Large open fire for winter months. Children welcome. Pets by arrangement. Access to house throughout the day. Open all year for Bed and Breakfast also Evening Meal. Picnic lunches provided if booked in advance. SAE, please, for terms and further details.

BOURNEMOUTH. Mrs Annie Habgood, Northover Hotel, 10 Earle Road, Alum Chine, Bournemouth BH4 8JQ (Bournemouth [0202] 767349). OLD-FASHIONED COURTESY AWAITS YOU AT THE NORTHOVER HOTEL, situated overlooking Alum Chine, 400 yards from sea and sandy beaches and only 20 minutes' walk from Bournemouth Pier. Near bus routes for town centre where there is superb shopping and all types of entertainment. The New Forest, Purbeck Hills and lovely Dorset and Hampshire countryside within easy reach. Choice of double, single or family rooms with double or twin beds, fitted carpets, hot and cold water, shaver points and free tea/coffee making facilities; some with en-suite facilities. Attractive lounge, colour TV; spacious diningroom serving varied and excellent food. Residential licence. Central heating. Under personal supervision of proprietors, the hotel is open all year for Bed and Breakfast from £7.95 or Dinner, Bed and Breakfast from £11.95. Mid-week bookings accepted. Special rates for Senior Citizens early and late season. Children and pets welcome. Ample parking.

BOURNEMOUTH. Mr and Mrs A. E. Rabone, Wenmaur House Licensed Hotel, 14 Carysfort Road, Boscombe, Bournemouth (0202-35081). Spend a carefree holiday at Wenmaur House, a friendly, family hotel. Maureen and Albert Rabone give personal service until midnight in the medium sized hotel, and guests are provided with keys and have access at all times. Large garden at rear of hotel. Short distance to sea. Colour TV lounge. Friendly bar lounge with piano. Children are welcome and are well catered for. Sorry no pets. Open all year, including Christmas. Evening Dinner, Bed and Breakfast from £10.50 daily, £70 weekly; Bed and Breakfast from £7 daily (no VAT). Reductions for children and senior citizens at certain times. Please apply to **Mr and Mrs A. E. Rabone.**

BOURNEMOUTH. Josie & Ian Green, Seaway Hotel, 45 Parkwood Road, Boscombe, Bournemouth BH5 2BS (Bournemouth [0202] 424600). A warm welcome awaits all guests at Seaway Hotel which is situated just off main Christchurch Road, within walking distance of Boscombe shopping area and beach. This small, comfortable family hotel, tastefully decorated, provides home cooked food and good selection of wines. Guests given a key on arrival; access to house at all times. Open throughout year, all 10 bedrooms have hot/cold water, shaver points, gas fires. Colour TV in lounge, also a bar lounge. Children welcome; reduced rates can be arranged. Bournemouth Centre, a few minutes' drive, gives easy access to cinemas, theatres, ice and aqua shows, golf, bowling and the quiet retreat of the New Forest nearby. Evening Meal, Bed and Breakfast from £10 per night; Bed and Breakfast from £7.50 per night. Pets are only permitted out of high season. Stamp only for speedy reply.

DOWNSIDE PRIVATE HOTEL

A small hotel near Alum and Branksome Chines which makes a good base for touring Hardy country and the New Forest etc. Convenient for buses, shops and entertainment. Full English breakfast and four course dinner. Bed and Breakfast from £6 and Dinner, Bed and Breakfast from £8.50 per day. Choice of menu. Weekly rates and special terms for children and OAP's. Residential licence. Open all year. Full tariff and colour brochure on application from the resident proprietors **J. and K. Barge.**

**52 Westbourne Park Road, Bournemouth
Tel. Bournemouth (0202) 763109**

BRIDPORT near. Mr and Mrs D. M. Scott, Betchworth House Hotel, Chideock, Near Bridport DT6 6JW (Chideock [0297] 89478). Betchworth House is a 17th century small licensed Hotel. AA and RAC listed, situated in the charming village of Chideock on A35 between Bridport and Charmouth. We offer a high standard of comfort and excellent home cooking. Only three quarters mile from secluded bathing beach surrounded by glorious hill scenery. There is a choice of two golf courses within four miles. Chideock is an ideal touring centre. Six bedrooms, four with washbasins and two with private facilities en-suite, two separate bathrooms, central heating, guests' lounge and separate diningroom. Pretty cottage garden. Car not essential, but large car park. Children over seven years welcome. Open all year for Bed/Breakfast and Evening Dinner. SAE, please, for terms and brochure.

BRIDPORT. Mrs Denise Wyatt, Blackney Farm, Bridport (Broadwindsor [0308] 68249). Working farm. "Blackney" is an attractive 17th-century farmhouse situated in beautiful quiet countryside on the edge of the Marshwood Vale, one mile off the Bridport/Chard road. Places of interest include Cricket St. Thomas Wild Life Park, Swannery at Abbotsbury, Sherborne Abbey and Castle, Forde Abbey, Chesil Beach. Colour TV lounge, diningroom with oak beams where food of a very high standard is served with fresh garden produce and eggs, cream, milk fresh from farm. Good walking area. Only one mile away from National Trust properties, Pilsden Pen and Lewesdon Hill, the highest hills in Dorset. Within easy reach of all resorts on Dorset coast including Charmouth and West Bay. Swimming, sailing, golfing, fishing six miles; horse riding nearby. One double, two family bedrooms with washbasins, each with adjoining bathrooms; two toilets. Children welcome at reduced rates; cot, high chair, babysitting by arrangement. Large garden with swing and slide. Car essential, parking. Open March to October. Evening Dinner, Bed and Breakfast or Bed and Breakfast. SAE for terms, please.

* **BRIDPORT. Dudley and Shirley Edwards, Marshwood Manor, Bridport DT6 5NS (Broadwindsor [0308] 68442 and 68825).** Farm/guest house, built in Victorian times, set in 50 acres of pasture and woods, bordered by streams, lies in beautiful surroundings only five miles from Charmouth's unspoilt beach. Comfortable, relaxed, informal atmosphere; good food a speciality. Car essential — ample parking. Four double, six family rooms with washbasins. Five bathrooms, two en-suite. Lounges, colour TV. Cots, high chairs, babysitting provided. Large indoor games room. Central heating, log fires. Part of house suitable for disabled guests. Pets welcome. Open all year. Special "off season" rates. See also Colour Display Advertisement in this Guide.

BRIDPORT. Mrs Alison Green, "Bomerhayes", Shave Cross, Marshwood Vale, Bridport DT6 6HW (Broadwindsor [0308] 68472). Four miles from the market town of Bridport, "Bomerhayes" is set in the middle of the glorious Marshwood Vale, surrounded by open farmland. Bed and Breakfast accommodation is offered from Easter to October (tea/coffee available any time at no extra charge). Two double bedded rooms, one twin bedded room (two with washbasins); bathroom, two toilets. Guests' dining/sittingroom; TV; full central heating. Children welcome; reductions under 12 years old; cot, high chair, babysitting available. Pets permitted if kept outside. The hamlet of Shave Cross has 14th century inn where Lunches/Evening Meals are available. Within easy reach of all resorts on Dorset coast including Charmouth and West Bay; Pilsden Pen (Dorset's highest point) and the coast from Golden Cap to Lyme Regis, four miles. Swimming, sailing, golf, fishing, horse riding, all easily accessible. Car essential — parking ample. SAE, please, for terms.

FARM GUEST HOUSE

This farm/guest house, built in Victorian times, set in fifty acres of pastures and woods, bordered by streams, lies in beautiful peaceful suroundings, only five miles from Charmouth's unspoilt beach with its store of fossils. The house has a comfortable, relaxed and informal atmosphere and really good food is a speciality, including home made bread, jams, farm butter etc. The gardens provide fresh fruit and vegetables. Swimming pool in walled garden. Car essential. Ample parking space provided. Four double and six family rooms, with wash basins. Five bathrooms, two en suite. Two lounges, colour TV. Cots, high chairs and babysitting provided. Children can play safely in fields and large indoor games room. French and German spoken. Part of house suitable for disabled guests. Central heating, log fires. Evening Dinner, Bed and Breakfast. Tea/coffee making facilities in all rooms. Reductions for children. Pets welcomed. Riding nearby. Open all year. Special "off season" rates.

DUDLEY & SHIRLEY EDWARDS, MARSHWOOD MANOR
Bridport, Dorset DT6 5NS
Tel: Broadwindsor (0308) 68442 and 68825

BRIDPORT. Mrs S. D. Cove, Revelshay Farm, Bettiscombe, Bridport DT6 5NT (Broadwindsor [0308] 68361). Working farm. An attractive farmhouse, including inglenook fireplace, situated on 91-acre south facing farm. Set in the delightful Marshwood Vale area of West Dorset below Pilsden Pen which is the highest point in Dorset. The popular beaches of Charmouth, Lyme Regis and West Bay only eight miles away. A family farm with cows, calves, beef and sheep, horses and other animals kept. All freshly prepared food using, when possible, produce from the garden. Four family bedrooms, all with washbasins; bathroom, two toilets; sittingroom and diningroom. Children welcome. Sorry, no pets. Car essential — parking space. Open April to October for Bed and Breakfast. SAE, please.

BRIDPORT. Mr and Mrs J. B. Francis, Durbeyfield Guest House, West Bay, Bridport DT6 4EL (Bridport [0308] 23307). "Durbeyfield," a Georgian guest house situated near the small harbour of West Bay and the famous Chesil Beach, is surrounded by beautiful scenery, coastal and old world villages. At West Bay there are fishing trips, bathing, fishing from piers and an 18-hole golf course situated on the cliff top. Mr and Mrs Francis pride themselves on hospitality and good home cooking. Four double, two single and two family bedrooms, all with washbasins; bathroom, shower, two toilets, sitting and diningrooms; colour TV. Fire Certificate held. Pets allowed. Children welcome, cot, high chair and babysitting; reduced rates. Open all year for Evening Meal, Bed and Breakfast or Bed and Breakfast only. Reductions for senior citizens — low season.

BRIDPORT. Mrs L. M. Hutchings, Oakdene, Dunster Farm, Broadoak, Bridport DT6 5NR (Bridport [0308] 24626). Working farm. 120-acre farm comprising cows, sheep and pigs, farmed by husband and father-in-law. Well placed for exploring Dorset, Somerset and Devon. Pilsdon Pen (the highest point in Dorset) can be seen from the bedrooms. Seaside resorts five miles away. Bridport four miles. One double, two family rooms; bathroom, toilet; sittingroom, TV; diningroom. Wood fire. Plenty of good food, mainly home produced. Children welcome, cot, high chair, babysitting arranged. Car essential, parking. Sorry, no pets. Open all year round, except Christmas. Bed, Breakfast and Evening Meal (optional). SAE, please, for terms. Prompt reply. Reductions for children.

BRIDPORT. Mrs S. N. Lancashire, The Sycamores, Verriotts Lane, Morcombelake, Bridport DT6 6DU (Chideock [0297-89] 277). "The Sycamores" is a small detached private house situated high on a hill-side overlooking Charmouth (two-and-a-half miles) and Lyme Regis (five-and-a-half) enjoying wonderful views over National Trust property to the south and south west. Many places of scenic and historic interest are nearby. Golden Cap, the highest hill, on the south coast and the beach at St. Gabriels for fossil hunters one mile. Ideal centre for touring Dorset and East Devon. Safe bathing at Charmouth; golf, fishing, tennis at Lyme Regis. Off shore fishing West Bay and Seatown. Two double, one family bedrooms; bathroom, toilet; sitting/diningroom. Children welcome at reduced rates. Sorry, no pets. Open April to September. Traditional English food served and every assistance given to make guests' holiday a pleasant one. Bed and Breakfast and Evening Meal. Terms on application. Car essential — parking.

Dorset BOARD

CERNE ABBAS. Mr R. Paul, Giant's Head Farm, Old Sherborne Road, Cerne Abbas, Near Dorchester (Cerne Abbas [030-03] 242). Giant's Head Farm is nicely situated in an area rich in historical and Roman association, and two miles from the interesting village of Cerne Abbas. Ideal for motoring holiday. Visit Thomas Hardy's birthplace, the Cheddar Caves, Longleat House and lion reserve, Maiden Castle and Cerne Giant and various wildlife parks. Fishing and bathing at Weymouth 16 miles; eight miles to Dorchester. There are five double bedrooms (with washbasins); lounge and diningroom. Children over seven welcome. Sorry no dogs. Car needed, garage and parking. Good farmhouse cooking guaranteed with free-range eggs. Open most of the year with residential licence. SAE please for terms for Bed and Breakfast plus Light Meals. Touring caravans and tents also welcome. Also Self-Catering accommodation available.

CHARMOUTH. Mrs K. M. Baker, Dodpen Farm, Wootton Fitzpaine, Charmouth DT6 6NW (Hawkchurch [029-77] 372). Working farm. This is a 70-acre farm situated on the southern slope of Dodpen Hill with tree plantations on all boundaries. The 16th century house is approached by a quarter of a mile farm road. Within easy distance of all resorts on the Dorset Coast including Charmouth (three miles) and Lyme Regis (six miles). Good farmhouse food is assured and log fires are blazing when needed. Radiators in all rooms, also electric kettles for drinks, filling flasks, etc. The 40 acres of farmland is mainly dairy. Three double bedrooms, one with washbasin; bathroom and toilet; dining/sittingroom. Colour TV. Also available six berth self-catering caravan. Children are welcome and cot, high chair and babysitting available. Car essential, parking. Open April to October for Evening Dinner, Bed and Breakfast. SAE for terms.

CHARMOUTH. Mrs D. Batten, Northay Farm, Wootton Fitzpaine, Bridport DT6 6NL (Charmouth [0297] 60481). Working farm. Northay Farm is situated in lovely peaceful countryside, away from it all but within easy motoring distance of the seaside, Charmouth three and a half miles, Lyme Regis six miles. A family farm, with cows and sheep and guests are able to wander around and see the animals. There is a homely atmosphere, farmhouse fare is served, own milk, cream, eggs and vegetables in season. There are two family rooms both with washbasins, bathroom, toilet, sitting/diningroom. Evening Meal, Bed and Breakfast with reduced rates for children according to age (cot, high chair and babysitting also). Open May to September. Also six-berth self-catering caravan, fully equipped. Please send SAE for terms.

CHIDEOCK. Mrs P. M. Barker, Spindleberry Guest House, North Road, Chideock DT6 6LE (Chideock [029-789] 617). Spindleberry Guest House is located in the lovely olde worlde village of Chideock three-quarters of a mile from the sea. Spindleberry is situated just off the main road between Bridport and Charmouth surrounded by lovely scenic views. Guests are assured of a warm welcome and good home cooked food. Chideock makes an ideal touring centre for the glorious Dorset countryside as well as parts of Devon. Guest accommodation in two double and one family bedrooms with washbasins; two bathrooms, two toilets; lounge; TV. Children are welcome at reduced rates. Sorry, no pets. The house is suitable for disabled guests. Open all year. A car is not essential here, but parking provided. Evening Dinner, Bed and Breakfast. SAE, please, for terms.

CHIDEOCK near. Mr F. M. Preston, "Conifers," 5 Winniford Close, Chideock, Near Bridport DT6 6SA (Chideock [029-789] 411). A retired hotelier offers a double room with breakfast in his luxury bungalow in this lovely old world village. Guests have sole use of sitting room at all times and also shower room with WC etc. There are pleasant rural views of the surrounding hills and adjacent farmland; country and coastal walks abound. The beach at Seatown is 10 minutes' walk and Charmouth and Lyme Regis close by. Winniford Close is quiet and peaceful and yet only two minutes to restaurants and local shops in village centre. Open all year with central heating. Sorry, no pets or children. Come and you will come again to enjoy the comfort here. Terms £8 full traditional Breakfast.

CHRISTCHURCH. Alan and Beryl Norris, "Sundial House," 8 Bure Road, Friars Cliff, Christchurch BH23 4ED (Highcliffe [04252] 4911). Sundial House is situated in a quiet residential area five minutes' walking distance from a lovely sandy beach. Three miles from Christchurch; Bournemouth seven; Southampton 23. The New Forest easily accessible four miles. Buses between Bournemouth and Lymington 300 yards. The bedrooms, three double (one ground floor), two family, one single, are comfortably furnished having hot and cold and shaver points, electric kettles for morning tea and flasks. There is a large lounge and diningroom with separate tables. Good home cooking with fresh vegetables. Central heating throughout. Access to house at all times. Open all year round for Bed and Breakfast with Dinner optional. Terms on application. Reduction for children in family rooms.

DORCHESTER. Mrs M. M. Stephens and Mrs P. Lazenby, The Court, Frampton, Dorchester DT2 9NH (Maiden Newton [0300] 20242). Working farm. Large country house offers high standard of accommodation to those who appreciate Cordon Bleu cooking. Home grown vegetables and own dairy produce. Relaxing homely atmosphere, 60 acres of lovely gardens, large pond with lovely collection of waterfowl, woodlands, fields and river. Magnificent surrounding countryside. Five double and two single bedrooms (all have washbasins); two bathrooms, three toilets and shower room; diningroom and lounge with log fires. Central heating. Sorry, no children. Pets by arrangement. Car essential — parking. Open from Easter to October for Evening Dinner, Bed and Breakfast. Terms on application.

DORCHESTER. Mrs Marian Tomblin, Lower Lewell Farmhouse, West Stafford, Dorchester DT2 8AP (Dorchester [0305] 67169). This old, historic house, originally a farmhouse, is situated in the Frome valley, four miles east of Dorchester in the heart of the Hardy country. It is two miles from his birthplace and is reputed to be the Talbothays Dairy in his famous novel, "Tess of the D'Urbervilles." Situated as it is in quiet countryside yet so near the county town, it makes an ideal base from which to explore Dorset. There is one family bedroom and two double bedrooms, all with washbasins. Much appreciated by guests are the tea and coffee making facilities. Car essential, ample parking. Regret no dogs. For details of Bed and Breakfast terms, SAE please. Open January-December.

DORCHESTER. Mrs Helen Cox, Wynards Farm Country Guest House, Winfrith Newburgh, Dorchester DT2 8DQ (Warmwell [0305] 852817). Working farm. Wynards farm is a small, residential farming property of approximately 11 acres on the outskirts of the village of Winfrith Newburgh enjoying extensive views — most of central and southern Dorset can be seen. Three miles from Lulworth Cove and Durdle Door — Dorchester, Wareham, Weymouth, Poole and Bournemouth within easy reach, also the beautiful Purbeck Hills. Comfortable accommodation in four double and one family bedrooms (three with washbasins); two bathrooms, three toilets. Access to rooms at all times. Good food using own farm produce when available is served in the attractive diningroom with separate tables. Lounge with TV. Central heating. Children welcome at reduced rates; cot; babysitting by arrangement. Pets accepted. Car essential, parking. Open April to October for Evening Dinner, Bed and Breakfast from £15; Bed and Breakfast from £10 inclusive. Brochure on request.

DORCHESTER. Mrs C. Walford, Rectory House, Fore Street, Evershot, Dorchester DT2 0JW (Evershot [093-583] 273). Lovely 18th-century Rectory situated in the picturesque village of Evershot in the heart of Thomas Hardy countryside. Evershot has its own bakery, shops and village pub and is an ideal centre for visiting many places of interest and seaside resorts. Many beautiful walks can be taken and wonderful scenic views abound. Fishing, riding and sailing facilities are nearby. Guests are accommodated in lovely bedrooms to suit families or couples; own bathroom and washing facilities; separate lounge and diningroom. Large garden. The emphasis is on superb home cooking to add to the enjoyment of your holiday. Open all year (except Christmas and New Year). Central heating. Children welcome, cot, high chair and babysitting available. Sorry, no pets. Car not essential, but there is parking. Evening Dinner, Bed and Breakfast from £85 (weekly); Evening Meal, Bed and Breakfast from £13; Bed and Breakfast from £8.50. Reductions for children.

DORCHESTER. Mrs P. and Mrs C. Mapstone, Chalmington Farm, Cattistock, Dorchester DT2 0HB (Maiden Newton [0300] 20531 or 20303). Working farm. Chalmington Farm is a family run farm of 220 acres, all dairy. It is ideally situated in quiet picturesque countryside for visiting the coast, and the towns of Dorchester, Sherborne and Wells which have many historical features. A warm welcome is given to all guests. Good home cooking using fresh vegetables from the garden; eggs, milk, etc. Comfortable accommodation, with central heating, consisting of one double and two family bedrooms with washbasins; bathroom, toilet; diningroom, sittingroom with colour TV. Children welcome, cot, high chair, babysitting provided. Pets permitted. Car essential — parking. Open from Easter to October for Evening Dinner, Bed and Breakfast or Bed and Breakfast. Reductions for children. SAE, please.

DORSET – RURAL SPLENDOUR!

Absorbing old towns like Dorchester and Shaftesbury, surrounded by panoramic vales, undulating chalklands and peaceful villages contribute to Dorset's great appeal. Included in any tourist's itinery should be, Abbotsbury Village and swannery, Ackling Dyke Roman road, Brownsea Island, Lulworth Cove and, of course, the many locations that constitute Hardy's Dorset.

DORCHESTER. Mr and Mrs Richard and Jayne Childs, The Manor Hotel, West Bexington, Dorchester (Burton Bradstock [0308] 897785/897616). Set in beautiful Hardy country, in the small village of West Bexington, some 500 yards from the Chesil Bank, 16th century Manor House offering peace and quiet, good food, fine wines and Real Ale. Magnificent views along the Dorset coastline — Dorchester 12 miles; Abbotsbury with its Swannery and sub-tropical gardens a few miles away. Golf, boating and fishing trips available at West Bay. Comfortable lounge, cosy Cellar Bar and Buttery, stone-flagged candle-lit diningroom, log fires, colour TV. Radio/Intercom, Tea/Coffee making facilities, washbasins, in all 11 bedrooms (two with bathrooms en suite) which have panoramic sea and country views. Central heating. Children welcome, cot and high chair provided. Sorry, no pets. Short break or longer holidays. AA two-star. Egon Ronay, Ashley Courtenay and Relais Routiers Recommended. Mentioned in leading food and accommodation guides. Open all year. SAE for brochure.

DORCHESTER. Mrs D. M. Fry, Foxholes Farm, Little Bredy, Dorchester DT2 9HJ (Long Bredy [030-83] 395). Working farm. Completely surrounded by hills and trees, this farm with cows, calves, pigs, hens, sheep is just right for a leisurely family holiday with pony rides for the children (extra). Central for many sandy and shingle beaches. Sea five miles; Dorchester nine; Weymouth 15; Bridport 12. Open all year (except one week in December). There are six family bedrooms, tea/coffee making facilities in all adult bedrooms; five with washbasins; two bathrooms, three toilets; sittingroom, diningroom. Full central heating. Car essential, parking space. Children are welcome at reduced rates, with cot, high chair, babysitting available. Dogs accepted at small charge. Come here for a free and easy holiday with no tiresome restrictions. Good English cooking accompanied by a selection of wines. Evening Dinner, Bed and Breakfast. Terms on application with SAE please.

DORCHESTER near. Mrs Margaret Tewson, Conygar House, Broadmayne, Near Dorchester DT2 8LX (Warmwell [0305] 852727). A warm welcome awaits all guests to Conygar House. This delightful house with oak-panelled reception hall, staircase and dining room is quietly situated in five acres of wooded grounds and paddocks with lovely views over the surrounding countryside. Open all year with heating in all rooms and woodburning stoves for cold days. First class accommodation in three double or family rooms all with private bathroom, colour television, and personal keys giving access at all times. Cot and high chair available for younger guests with reduced terms for children sharing room. Superb English breakfast with free range eggs. English Tourist Board registered. Ample parking, car essential. Bed and Breakfast only, Evening Dinner available in local inn, highly recommended. SAE please for terms.

DORCHESTER near. Mrs Marion Colwill, "The Old Cottage", 29 Fore Street, Evershot, Near Dorchester DT2 0JR (Evershot [093-583] 406). Attractive 17th-century house in the quiet, picturesque village of Evershot, in the centre of beautiful Hardy countryside. This is an excellent centre for touring many of Dorset's beauty spots; nearby are beaches and opportunities for fishing and walking. The village has an old inn, church, general stores, bakery and many fine houses. Very comfortable and elegant accommodation comprises one double and one family bedroom, with washbasins and fitted wardrobes; bathroom, toilet; diningroom/lounge. Central heating. Excellent home cooking, morning tea and full English Breakfast (Evening Meal optional). Children welcome, cot and babysitting available. Sorry, no pets. Ample parking space. Open all year except Christmas. Terms on request. Bed and Breakfast £8.50. Children at reduced rates.

Terms quoted in this publication may be subject to increase if rises in costs necessitate

FERNDOWN. Mr W. Hobbs, Broadlands Hotel, West Moors Road, Ferndown BH22 9SA (Ferndown [0202] 877884). A "country house" hotel standing in secluded grounds and an ideal centre from which to explore the New Forest and coastal areas. Within easy reach of Bournemouth with its fine beaches and excellent entertainment. Open all year. Residential licence. Especially suited to those requiring a quiet holiday, comfort and good plain cooking. Evening Dinner, Bed and Breakfast from £17; Bed and Breakfast from £12. Reductions for children. Cot, high chair and babysitting. Two lounges, TV, diningroom. Five double, five single and two family rooms, all with washbasins, fitted carpets and razor points. Pets accepted. Ample parking facilities. AA, RAC listed and registered with the Southern Tourist Board.

HIGHCLIFFE-ON-SEA. Mrs Jean L. Partridge, "Windermere", 6 Saulfland Drive, Highcliffe-on-Sea, Christchurch BH23 4QN (Highcliffe [042-52] 3145). A detached, comfortable house situated within one mile of the sea. The lovely New Forest to the east with its picturesque market towns and country inns; west is Christchurch with its famous Priory and the Rivers Avon and Stour, excellent for salmon fishing. Golf and tennis nearby. Bournemouth eight miles away for its sandy beaches, shopping centre and family summer shows. Sittingroom, diningroom; colour TV; two double, two single and one family rooms (four with washbasins); bathroom, two toilets; central heating. Car not essential, but parking available. Children welcome at reduced rates with cot and babysitting provided. Pets allowed. Open April to end October. Full English Breakfast and four-course Evening Dinner from £55 weekly; Bed and Breakfast from £38 weekly.

LYME REGIS near. Mrs D. G. Billson, Curlew Farm, Trinity Hill, Combepyne, Axminster, Devon EX13 6SZ (Lyme Regis [029-74] 2546). Working farm. Curlew Farmhouse on a 96-acre dairy farm, is a modern bungalow with beautiful views of country and sea (three miles safe bathing). Lyme Regis, Charmouth ideal for fossil hunting. One double, two family bedrooms, all with washbasins; bathroom, two toilets; diningroom; lounge (colour TV). Guests welcome on farm; children may help to feed animals, collect eggs. Cot, high chairs; Mrs Billson is happy to babysit. Open all year, comfortably heated and ideal for mini winter holidays — special low season reductions. Fire Certificate. Ample parking. Good farmhouse fare. Evening Dinner, Bed and Breakfast or Bed and Breakfast only. SAE, for terms. Reductions for children. Pets by arrangement.

LYME REGIS. Mrs C. Perry, Harbour Close, Coombepyne, Axminster, Devon (Lyme Regis [02974] 2657). This is a small holding on the Devon/Dorest border. Coombepyne is a pretty farming village situated in a valley three miles from Lyme Regis and four miles from Seaton. Modern, comfortable house with full central heating; two bathrooms and toilets; one double room, two family rooms; lounge with colour TV. Guests may stay in, if wet. Babysitting. Guests are assured of a warm welcome with plenty of good food and home-produced fare. We have various animals, including a pony, calves, goats and many domestic animals. Open from Easter to November for Bed and Breakfast or Bed and Breakfast and Evening Meal. Ample car parking. Reduced rates for children. SAE, please, for terms.

LYME REGIS. Mrs L. J. Currall, Bullmoor Farm, Musbury, Axminster, Devon EX13 6TE (Axminster [0297] 33368). Working farm, join in. Guests return year after year to Bullmoor Farm, a 140-acre mixed farm with cows, calves, sheep, pigs, chickens etc. Situated approximately three miles from Lyme Regis and five miles Seaton, with many other seaside resorts and some lovely beauty spots and places of interest in the area. Guests are welcome to stay in if the weather is wet, or wander around the farm and participate in farm activities. Three family bedrooms with washbasins; bathroom, toilet. Lounge/diningroom with colour TV and log fire lit when necessary. Excellent variety of good home-cooked food including free range eggs, clotted cream and home grown produce. Children welcome, cot, high chair, babysitting available. Pets accepted. Car essential — parking. Fire Certificate held. Terms on application for Evening Dinner, Bed and Breakfast or Bed and Breakfast. Reduced rates for children. Open all year. Also self-catering bungalow. Details on request.

LYME REGIS. Mrs M. J. Powell, Green Lane Farm, Rousdon, Lyme Regis DT7 3XW (Lyme Regis [029-74] 3262). Working farm. Green Lane is a dairy farm of 70 acres, situated on the border of Devon and Dorset a half mile off the A3052 at Rousdon, three miles from Lyme Regis, four from Seaton. Many places of interest nearby, including Ford Abbey, Bicton Gardens, wildlife parks. Lovely beaches and sporting facilities. One double, two family rooms, with washbasins and radiators. Bathroom/shower, two toilets, sitting/diningroom; TV. Guests assured of warm welcome. Open March to November for Bed and Breakfast from £6.50 per night. Children welcome; cot, high chair and babysitting. Reductions for children 11 years old and under, sharing parents' room. Ample parking. Fire certificate held. Horse riding nearby. No VAT. SAE, please, for terms.

186   Dorset   BOARD

LYME REGIS. Mrs E. E. Dicks, Penlong Close Farm, Rousdon, Lyme Regis DT7 3XW (Lyme Regis [029-74] 2955). Working farm. This dairy farm, set in unspoiled countryside, offers guests a happy and relaxed holiday. Ideal for touring the West Country, or a family holiday with the sea and sand just three miles away. Plenty of home produce served at meals including chicken, eggs, cream, vegetables and fruit. Children love "helping" with the chickens, etc. and often there are calves and lambs to see. There is also a safe garden for them to play in with a swing for their enjoyment. As this is a bungalow it is suitable for disabled people. One family room, one double. Children over three years welcome. Terms on application with SAE, please. Sorry, no pets.

LYME REGIS. Mrs Betty Hodder, 1 Cuckoo Hill, Uplyme, Lyme Regis DT7 3SS (Lyme Regis [029-74] 2292). Cuckoo Hill is a small country house, in a quiet country lane, built on a hillside, with magnificent views over Uplyme and the Devon/Dorset borders. Pleasant walks nearby. One and a half miles to the sea at Lyme Regis, a popular resort. Guests welcome from Easter to September. Cot and babysitting available for children, with reduced rates also. Mrs Hodder caters for one party at a time, and offers Bed and Breakfast, with Evening Meal optional. One family room with washbasin (plus double if required). Sorry, no pets. Ample toilet accommodation. Car essential — parking. SAE, please, for terms. The area is well known for fossil hunting.

OSMINGTON. Mrs Joyce Norman, Dingle Dell, Osmington, Near Weymouth DT3 6EW (Preston (Dorset) [0305] 832378). Not a farm, but situated down a lane on the fringe of the picturesque village of Osmington, in the centre of farming country, with safe bridle-ways and footpaths right by the gate — a beautiful rural setting with the coast only one-and-a-half miles away. This family home of mellow local stone is set in a large garden full of roses and apple trees. The two spacious, attractively furnished bedrooms, with washbasins, have beautiful views over garden and fields, and the famous "White Horse" on the nearby hill. Children welcome. Regret, no pets. This is a quiet corner of Hardy's Wessex, a peaceful and friendly base ideal for exploring the beautiful Dorset countryside whether by car, on foot, or on horseback. Open March to October. Bed and Breakfast from £7.50. Reductions for children sharing parents' room. Car essential — parking.

SHAFTESBURY. Mr and Mrs D. G. Marchington, Estyard House, Fontmell Magna, Shaftesbury SP7 0PB (Fontmell Magna [0747] 811460). The hotel is situated in the village which lies close to the beautiful Cranborne Chase and Blackmore Vale. Many places of interest including cathedral cities, historic houses and attractive countryside are within easy reach of the hotel. AA listed. Home cooking using produce from the garden. Open all year except November and Christmas. Four double, two single bedrooms, all with washbasins; sittingroom and diningroom. Full central heating, car park and garden. Children over 10 years of age welcome. Dogs permitted by arrangement. Dinner, Bed and Breakfast or Bed and Breakfast. Terms on request.

SHAFTESBURY. John and Sheila Harris, Grove House Hotel, Ludwell, Shaftesbury SP7 9ND (Donhead [074-788] 365). Situated in a picturesque village, next to old thatched cottages on the Dorset/Wiltshire border, Grove House is a small one-star AA and RAC private hotel (9th season). Ideally placed for walking and touring holidays. All rooms have country views and tea making facilities and most double and twin bedrooms have en-suite bathrooms. Personally supervised by the resident proprietors, you are assured of good food and wine at reasonable prices. English Tourist Board bedroom category 4. Two to seven day breaks available for most of the year. Car essential but ample parking available within hotel grounds. Diningroom and one lounge for non-smokers.

SHERBORNE near. Mrs Helen Vickery, Butterwick Farm, Holnest, Near Sherborne DT9 5PN (Holnest [096-321] 269). Working farm. Visitors are welcome to wander around this 100-acre family run dairy farm with 70 milking cows and various other animals. Although situated in an isolated spot, car is essential, it is within easy reach of coast, historic towns of Sherborne and Dorchester, Wildlife Park, Butterfly Farm, Tank and Fleet Air Arm Museums. Fishing on the farm (mainly carp and tench) available to visitors free. Ideal walking country. One double, one family bedrooms; bathroom, two toilets. Diningroom; sittingroom with colour TV. Log fires. Access to rooms at all times; tea-making facilities. Excellent home cooking and a friendly welcome extended from Easter to October. Children welcome, cot, babysitting. Some small pets accepted. Ample parking. Evening Meal, Bed and Breakfast £62 weekly; Bed and Breakfast from £6. Reductions for children sharing. Also large caravan for self-catering holidays.

SHERBORNE near. Mrs Ann Osmond, Sunnyside Farm, Holnest, Hermitage, Near Sherborne DT9 6HA (Holnest [096-321] 276). Working farm. A 50-acre dairy farm with various farm pets to interest children. The cosy farmhouse welcomes guests all year round. Good farmhouse cooking served in the diningroom with separate tables. Good riding school and fresh water fishing nearby. The historical town of Sherborne with its Abbey and Castle, and the pretty village of Cerne Abbas within easy reach. All guests are assured of a warm welcome in this homely atmosphere. Log fires on chilly evenings. Outdoor amusements for the children in the large garden with spacious lawns. Accommodation consists of one double (twin-bedded), one single, one family bedrooms with washbasins and shaving points in all rooms; bathroom, toilet; sittingroom with TV. Children welcome at reduced rates. Babysitting arranged. Sorry, no pets. Car essential, parking. Evening Meal, Bed and Breakfast or Bed and Breakfast. Terms on request. SAE, please.

SHERBORNE. Mrs J. Mayo, Almshouse Farm, Hermitage, Sherborne DT9 6HA (Holnest [096-321] 296). Working farm. This is a friendly family farm of 140 acres, with cows and poultry to supply fresh milk, cream and eggs. Other farm animals will attract the children and they can play on the lawns. The attractive stone-built house, overlooking the unspoilt countryside of the Blackmore Vale, was restored from a monastery in 1849. Six miles from Sherborne, with its interesting castle and abbey, one mile off the A352. Good English food and personal attention offered. Open from Easter to September; accommodation comprises three double bedrooms, all with washbasins; diningroom with separate tables and large inglenook fireplace; comfortable lounge with TV and log fires. Some central heating also. Car advisable, parking. Sorry, no dogs. Evening Dinner, Bed and Breakfast or Bed and Breakfast only. SAE, please, for terms. AA Listed.

SHERBORNE. Mrs S. M. Friar, Eldersfield House, Ryall's Lane, Bishop's Caundle, Sherborne DT9 5NG (Bishop's Caundle [096-323] 273). Eldersfield House is a former Victorian gentleman's residence standing in its own secluded grounds and commanding magnificent views of the Dorset hills and Cranborne Chase across the beautiful Vale of Blackmore — Hardy's "engirdled and secluded region". One double, one twin and one single bedrooms, each with hand washbasins; comfortable guests' drawing room with colour television and log fires in chilly weather; central heating in all rooms. Fresh fruit and vegetables in season and special diets by arrangement. Ideal centre for touring Hardy's Wessex and within easy reach of the coast. Open throughout the year except Christmas. Regret, no children or pets.

SHERBORNE. Watkins Farm, Peaceful Lane, Holwell, Sherborne. Working farm. Friendly family farm, overlooking Blackmore Vale countryside. There are plenty of animals for the children and large garden to play in with swing and pony to ride. Ideal touring centre with Pub of the Year in Dorset half a mile. Seven miles historic castle and abbey town of Sherborne, 25 miles to beaches. Lovely walks and small carp fishing pond. One double, one family rooms; bathroom, toilet; sitting/diningroom with log fire and colour TV. Good food and personal attention. Open all year. Children welcome, cot, high chair and babysitting. Car essential, parking. Bed and Breakfast or Evening Meal, Bed and Breakfast. Reduced rates for children. Three quarters mile off A3030 Sherborne to Blandford road. SAE, please, for terms.

SHERBORNE. Mrs P. J. Luxmoore, Caphays House, Caundle Marsh, Sherborne DT9 5LX (Bishop's Caundle [096-323] 325). "Caphays" is a comfortable 400-year-old stone cottage, formerly the old dairy house, and is the ideal place for those wishing peace and quiet. Four miles from the historic abbey town of Sherborne, with its castles, and situated in the Blackmore Vale with its many places of interest made famous by the novels of Thomas Hardy. The house is located half a mile up a "no-through" lane of our own. Two bedrooms — one with twin beds and washbasins; one with three single divan beds; bathroom/toilet; shower room/toilet. Sitting/diningroom with inglenook fireplace and oak beams. Pleasant family atmosphere and home cooking. Children welcome; cot, babysitting, reduced rates. Open January to November for Evening Meal, Bed and Breakfast or Bed and Breakfast only.

SHERBORNE near. Mrs F. Lee, Lower Farm, Adber, Trent, Near Sherborne (Marston Magna [0935] 850367). This picturesque farmhouse is set in a small hamlet on the Dorset/Somerset border near the historic town of Sherborne. It is situated within easy reach of the South Coast, Longleat House, Wells, Cheddar and Exmoor. Guests are welcomed all year round and the accommodation comprises two double, one single and two family bedrooms; bathroom and toilet; sittingroom and diningroom. Children are welcome and a cot, high chair and babysitting are provided. Pets are welcome. A car is essential for touring the beautiful countryside, the farmhouse making an ideal centre for visiting many places of interest. Parking available. Evening Dinner, Bed and Breakfast. Reduced rates for children. Terms on request.

FUN FOR ALL THE FAMILY IN DORSET

Brownsea Island, Poole Harbour; *Abbotsbury Swannery & Gardens*, near Dorchester; *Merley Tropical Bird Gardens*, near Poole; *Worldwide Butterflies*, Compton House, near Sherborne; *Poole Park*, Poole; *Tuckton Leisure Park*, Stour Road, Christchurch; *Wimborne Model Town*, West Row, Wimborne Minster; *The Model Village*, Corfe Castle; *The Tank Museum*, Bovington Camp, near Wareham; *Barney's Fossil & Country Life Exhibition*, Charmouth, near Bridport.

188   Dorset   BOARD

SHERBORNE. Mrs Susan Eavis, Higher Knighton Farm, Beer Hackett, Sherborne DT9 6QT (Yetminster [0935] 872360). Working farm. The house, on this mixed farm of 200 acres, is situated in a high and very pleasant part of Dorset, with good views all round, and many places of interest within easy reach. A car is required here as the rail connection is four miles distant, and there is ample parking space. The three family rooms are spacious; one double; all bedrooms have washhand basins; bathroom, separate shower unit; two toilets (upstairs and downstairs). The rest of the house comprises sittingroom with TV, diningroom. Children welcome, cot available. Babysitting can be arranged. Pets permitted only by arrangement. Centrally heated, the house is open from April to October. Unfortunately, the premises are not suitable for the disabled. Evening Meal, Bed and Breakfast or Bed and Breakfast only. Reduced rates for children. Terms on request, with SAE please.

STURMINSTER NEWTON. Thea Redpath, Old Post Office, Hinton St Mary, Sturminster Newton DT10 1NG (Sturminster Newton [0258] 72366). The Old Post Office is a cosy and comfortable Guest House near the interesting market town of Sturminster Newton. Situated in the beautiful Blackmore Vale, it is an ideal centre for exploring the many picturesque villages and seaside towns that Dorset has to offer. We appreciate the importance of holidays and make every effort to ensure you have a really enjoyable stay. Facilities for hot drinks in all bedrooms, access at all times, good home cooking. One family, two double rooms, both with wash handbasins, guest lounge with coloured television. Bed and Breakfast £7.50. Evening Meals (optional) £4. Reductions for weekly and group bookings.

STURMINSTER NEWTON. Mrs A. P. Dick, MHCIMA, Romaynes Guest House, Lydlinch, Sturminster Newton DT10 2HU (Sturminster Newton [0258] 72508). For an enjoyable holiday in Dorset this Guest House, situated adjacent to the A357, warmly welcome you all year round. Romaynes is spacious and comfortable with over an acre of garden and offers the discerning guest a very high standard of cuisine and personal service. Five bedrooms, three double and two single, all with washbasins, two bathrooms, two toilets. Large comfortable sittingroom, pleasant diningroom overlooking the garden. Children over 12 welcome, but regret no pets. Car essential; ample parking space. Registered with the English Tourist Board. Fire Certificate issued. Please write or phone for brochure and terms.

STURMINSTER NEWTON. Mrs Sally Wingate-Saul, Holbrook Farm, Lydlinch, Sturminster Newton DT10 2JB (Hazelbury Bryan [025-86] 348). Working farm. Situated in the heart of the Blackmore Vale, Lydlinch is three miles from Sturminster Newton, nine miles from Sherborne, and about three-quarter hour from the coast. This is a family farm and the stone-built Georgian farmhouse has many original features. It makes an ideal central base for exploring Dorset, but guests are also welcome to use the swimming pool and take walks over the farm. Clay pigeon shooting on farm; fishing, golf, tennis, etc. locally. Accommodation comprises delightful converted stables sleeping four with their own sitting rooms, shower units, etc. and mini-kitchens, and two comfortable twin-bedded rooms in the farmhouse and a sittingroom. Sorry, no pets. Car essential. Pleasant family atmosphere and good home cooking. Evening Meal by arrangement. Open all year.

FARM HOLIDAY GUIDES LIMITED publish a large range of well-known accommodation guides. We will be happy to send you details or you can use the order form at the back of this book.

STURMINSTER NEWTON. Mrs Sheila Martin, Moorcourt Farm, Moorside, Marnhull, Sturminster Newton DT10 1HH (Marnhull [0258] 820271). Working farm. Marnhull is situated four miles from Sturminster Newton, five from Shaftesbury. New Forest and coast within 28 miles. This is a modern dairy farm of 100 acres lying in the Blackmore Vale in Hardy country. Visitors are welcome to watch the farm activities and laze in the large garden. There is a friendly atmosphere created "down on the farm". Accommodation comprises one large room with double bed; two double bedrooms (one with twin beds, one with double bed), all bedrooms have wash-handbasins. (Shower room with sink and toilet also.) Bathroom, toilet. Sittingroom with colour TV; diningroom. Children over 10 only. Sorry, no pets. Car essential, ample parking. Evening Meals provided from £3 to £4, except Sundays. Bed and Breakfast from £7.50. Weekly lets only in peak season. Open April to October. Further details on request.

STURMINSTER NEWTON. Mrs Carol Williamson-Jones, Boywood Farm, Mappowder, Sturminster Newton DT10 2EQ (Hazelbury Bryan [02586] 416). Working farm, join in. Interesting, modernised farmhouse, on 17-acres mixed farm, situated in open farmland, well off a quiet road in the heart of Dorset. The house, enjoying lovely views, provides a heated indoor swimming pool (Apr/May-Oct), hard tennis court, table tennis on site. Excellent walking country. The three double bedrooms are comfortably furnished; bathroom, toilet; guests' sittingroom has a wood-burner and colour TV. All rooms centrally heated. Children welcome, babysitting available. Pets accepted. Car essential — ample parking. The coast, Bournemouth, New Forest, Salisbury and Bath all within easy reach. Open all year. Guests are welcome to participate in farm activities. Evening Meal, Bed and Breakfast from £13; Bed and Breakfast from £8. Reductions for senior citizens. AA listed.

STURMINSTER NEWTON. Mrs P. Luton-Lozach'Meur, Rowden Mill House, Stourton Caundle, Sturminster Newton DT10 2JT (Bishop's Caundle [096-323] 212). This farmhouse is very quiet with magnificent views and a stream running through the garden. It lies three quarters of a mile from the village at the end of a "No Through Lane". It is an ideal centre for walking in the Blackmore Vale. There are also many places of interest within a 20-mile radius. Accommodation comprises one double/family room with hot and cold, two single rooms. Lounge with colour TV. Open all year. Bed and Breakfast from £7. Weekly rates on request. Evening Meal provided in the village £2-£3. Car essential — ample parking. Children welcome, babysitting. SAE, please, or phone.

STURMINSTER NEWTON. Mrs Gillian Espley, Yew House Farm, Marnhull, Sturminster Newton DT10 1NP (Marnhull [0258] 820412). Yew House Farm is situated six miles south of Shaftesbury, an excellent centre for visiting such places as Stourhead, Longleat, Yeovilton and World Wide Butterflies. Bed and Breakfast accommodation is available in two double bedrooms, one with en suite bathroom; bathroom, toilet; sittingroom. Open January to December with wood burning stove and electric heaters. Car essential, parking. Children are welcome and there is cot and high chair and babysitting is possible. Sorry no pets. Bed and Breakfast from £8.50 to £10.50. Rates reduced for children. A warm welcome is guaranteed to all our visitors.

STURMINSTER NEWTON. Mrs R. Candy, Manor Farm, Todber, Sturminster Newton DT10 1JB (Marnhull [0258] 820384). Working farm. Manor Farm is situated in the Blackmore Vale amid Hardy countryside. A 225-acre farm with 100 dairy cows and various children's pets. Visitors are welcome to wander around the fields and relax in the very quiet countryside. The historic towns of Shaftesbury and Sturminster four miles away. One double, two single and two family rooms (three with washbasins); bathroom, two toilets; sittingroom and diningroom. Children welcome at reduced rates; cot, high chair and babysitting available. Sorry, no pets. Car needed with ample parking provided. Open Easter to October for Evening Dinner, Bed and Breakfast or Bed and Breakfast. Good home cooking a speciality. SAE, please, for reply.

SWANAGE. Mrs Stephanie Lucas, 1 Hillview, Quarr Farm, Valley Road, Swanage BH19 3DY (Corfe Castle [0929] 480865). Working farm. A choice to stay in 1600's farmhouse or a recently built bungalow. Central heating with open fire in sittingroom and colour TV. Stock rearing farm of 150 acres surrounded by lovely walking countryside through woods to Purbeck Hills. Clean sandy beaches at Swanage three miles and Studland four miles. Nature reserve for bird watching six miles. Three double, three family and one single rooms (four with washbasins); two bathrooms, two toilets; diningroom. Children welcome at reduced rates, cot, high chair, babysitting available, also a play area in the grounds. Car essential — ample parking. No objection to pets. Open May till end September. Evening Meal, Bed and Breakfast. Reductions for senior citizens. Terms on request.

WAREHAM. Mrs M. Hoblyn, Graybank Guest House, West Lulworth, Wareham BH20 5RL (West Lulworth [092941] 256). Period Guest House situated in beautiful country surroundings, five minutes from the sea at Lulworth Cove. Comfortably furnished bedrooms with hot and cold water and heating. Lulworth is an ideal base for exploring the magnificent cliff scenery and delightful coves and bays. There are many famous beauty spots within easy reach. The coastal path is close by giving many walks over unspoilt countryside. Graybank Guest House offers every comfort with excellent food. There is a lounge and car park. Tea-making facilities available. Bed and Full English Breakfast from £8.50. Evening Meal (optional) £4.

WAREHAM. Mrs Elizabeth Rudd, Bishop's Cottage Hotel, West Lulworth, Wareham BH20 5RS (West Lulworth [092 941] 261). A well-established licensed Hotel, personally supervised by the owner, large garden now with heated swimming pool overlooking the Cove. Ideal for walking along Dorset's famous coastline or, inland, the Thomas Hardy countryside. The Hotel is open from Easter to October. Friendly atmosphere, good service, all modern amenities; colour TV, sun lounge. Children welcome, cot and baby listening available. No objection to pets. Highly recommended for good food and home cooking. Parking, Bed and Breakfast with Dinner optional with other meals available in own restaurant which specialises in local fish, crabs and lobsters. Special terms for family rooms and also bargain breaks (off season). Colour brochure on request.

WAREHAM. Mr and Mrs D. H. Gegg, "Glen Ness," No. 1 The Merrows, Off St. Helens Road, Sandford, Wareham BH20 7AX (Wareham [09295] 2313). Doug and Iris Gegg welcome guests with a cup of tea at their small friendly guest house, a cedar/stone bungalow in secluded surroundings. Those returning yearly recommend highly the freshly cooked food and varied menu. All bedrooms have fitted washbasins, razor points and interior spring mattresses; bathroom with separate shower, two toilets. Morning tea, evening drinks, packed lunches, flasks filled. Safe off-road parking. Hourly bus service to Poole, Rockley Sands, Corfe Castle, Studland Bay, Swanage. Colour TV in diningroom. Access at all times. Bed, Breakfast and Evening Meal or Bed and Breakfast only. Gas central heating. Tourist Board Registered. Brochure on request. Small dogs allowed.

WEST LULWORTH. Mr and Mrs J. Else, The Old Barn, West Lulworth, Wareham BH20 5RL (West Lulworth [092-941] 305). The Old Barn is situated in a superb position with a glorious view of the rolling Dorset hills, yet only a few hundred yards from the famous beauty spot of Lulworth Cove. Accommodation for one to four persons in self-catering units equipped with Baby Belling cooker, fridge, kettle and all necessities. Continental quilt, linen, electricity and room service is included in the charge. Also available single, double and treble bedrooms with Continental Breakfast. Car essential. Large garden and parking space. To give guests a break from cooking, two nearby hotels will provide Breakfast and Dinner, if required, an ideal arrangement for overnight visitors or those on short stays. Central heating. Fire Certificate. Shops and sea nearby. Entertainment at Bournemouth (22 miles) and Weymouth (15 miles). Daily/weekly terms and details on request with SAE, please.

WEST LULWORTH. Mr and Mrs T. H. Williams, Shirley Hotel, West Lulworth, Wareham BH20 5RL (West Lulworth [092-941] 358). Comfortable, small, friendly hotel of 17 bedrooms, all en suite, with colour TV, radio, bedside lights, tea-making facilities. Situated in a Conservation Area, in the village of West Lulworth, half a mile from the famous Lulworth Cove, with spectacular scenery and cliff walks, pleasure and fishing trips, proximity to Bournemouth (shopping, entertainment); sandy beaches (16 miles); local shingle beaches; many places of interest. Light, airy diningroom with bar; excellent cuisine, varied menu prepared by hosts and served by friendly staff. Lounge with card tables and reading area. Coin-op laundry. Car park. Lovely swimming pool and patio; lunchtime snacks on large lawn adjacent. Children welcome, cot, high chair, baby listening by arrangement, reduced rates. Pets allowed. Brochure available on request giving full details of this licensed, family-run hotel. Activity weekends early and late season. Open March to November.

WEYMOUTH near. Mrs E. M. Perrott, Little Orchard, Rodden, Near Weymouth DT3 4JE (Abbotsbury [0305] 871263). Situated in Rodden, small hamlet in hollow of some of Dorset's most beautiful countryside, this modern house is open from March to November. Sea two miles away, riding at Chickerell (four miles) and golf, tennis, fishing at Weymouth (seven miles). Five double and one single bedrooms, all with washbasins, spring interior mattresses, bedside lights, shaving points and electric blankets during winter; two bathrooms, two toilets; lounge with colour TV and diningroom. Children over seven years welcome, charged according to age and large play area provided for them. Oven fresh cooking, succulent roasts, local produce. Pets allowed. No restrictions — guests given keys. Fire Certificate held. Evening Dinner, Bed and Breakfast from £10, Bed and Breakfast from £7. SAE, please, for further details.

WEYMOUTH. Mrs S. Foot, West Shilvinghampton Farm, Portesham, Weymouth DT3 4HL (Abbotsbury [0305] 871493). Working farm. An old manor house set in the picturesque and unspoiled Waddon Vale, on a 170-acre working arable farm with beef cattle. The scenic coastline from Portland Bill to Lyme Regis is dominated by the famous Chesil Beach. The area is interesting archaeologically. Mr and Mrs Foot aim to provide a comfortable, homely atmosphere with the emphasis on home cooking. Two double and two family bedrooms, all with washbasins; bathroom and toilet. TV lounge; diningroom. Cot, high chair and babysitting offered. Open Easter to end of September. Evening Dinner/Meal, Bed and Breakfast or Bed and Breakfast only. Regret, no pets. SAE, please, for terms and further details.

WINFRITH. Mr and Mrs R. J. Hansford, West Burton Farm, Winfrith, Dorchester DT2 8DD (Warmwell [0305] 852956). Working farm. This family dairy farm with lovely character house, tastefully furnished and carpeted throughout, is situated in open countryside on A352 three miles from Lulworth Cove. Ideal centre for touring. Golf, fishing, pony trekking and beaches locally. Car essential, ample parking. One double bedroom, with washbasin; family suite comprising double bedded room, twin bedded room with washbasin. Tea making facilities in bedrooms. Bathroom, toilet; large sitting/diningroom. Children over five years welcome and babysitting offered, also reduced rates. Sorry, no pets. Open all year, except Christmas. SAE or telephone please, for details of Bed and Breakfast only.

WINTERBOURNE STICKLAND (near Blandford). Mrs E. Chaffey, Stickland Hill Farm, Normandy Road, Winterbourne Stickland, Near Blandford DT11 0LY (Milton Abbas [0258] 880341). A warm welcome awaits you when you come to this beautifully situated new bungalow standing in 12 acres in the heart of the Dorset hills. Open all year, the accommodation comprises one luxury double bedroom with bathroom en suite, electric blanket and colour television, and two double bedrooms with shared bathroom. Both bathrooms with showers. Excellent breakfast includes our own free range eggs. Car essential to tour the fine local beaches and many places of interest. Guests welcome to use family swimming pool. Bed and Breakfast. Further details on request.

DURHAM

JERSEY FARM RESTAURANT & HOTEL
West Town Pasture Farm
Darlington Road, Barnard Castle, Durham

Jersey Farm Hotel lies in Teesdale, one mile east of the market town of Barnard Castle, easily accessible from the M1. The Hotel is an integral part of the working farm, whose pedigree Jersey Herd supplies all the dairy produce on the menu. Single, double, twin and family rooms are available, all with bathroom or shower room en suite. Tastefully decorated they have colour TV and tea/coffee making facilities as standard equipment. The licensed restaurant offers supreme traditional English country fare made from fresh farm ingredients. Occasional 'Eat as Much as You Like' Carvery. Residential and Cocktail Lounges. Guests are welcomed into a friendly family atmosphere, and are free to explore the farm. Many country attractions in area and opportunities for golf, tennis, riding, pony-trekking, water-skiing and bowls are available. Open all year for Dinner, Bed and Breakfast or Bed and Breakfast only. Packed lunches available. Special terms for Winter and Bargain Breaks.

Resident proprietors John and Jean Watson
Teesdale [0833] 38223

PLEASE ENCLOSE A STAMPED ADDRESSED ENVELOPE WITH ENQUIRIES

BARNARD CASTLE. Mrs R. Lowson, West Roods Farm, Boldron, Barnard Castle DL12 9SW (Teesdale [0833] 37676). Working farm. Bed and Breakfast £6.50, which includes tea, biscuits on arrival and at 9 pm. Evening Meal from £5. Children under 10 years half price; 10-13 years £1 less than adults. Tea-making facilities in bedrooms. Bathroom/toilet plus outside loo with washbasin. Heated shower plus washbasin. Partial central heating; diningroom/lounge; TV. Excellent for kite flying. Dairy farm (no bull), blending tourism with farm life. Farmhouse guests' books; puzzles and Lego. Elementary water dowsing. Caravan Licensed Halt for six tourers £2 per night. Also for tents. The farm is situated in the Pennines overlooking Barnard Castle. Entrance to site off A66, 2½ miles east of Bowes, half-mile west of road to Boldron Village, do not enter village.

DURHAM. Mr and Mrs F. J. and B. M. Cornish, Country View Guest House, 40 Claypath, Durham DH1 1QS (Durham [0385] 61436). This 200-year-old terraced, registered Guest House is ideal for the person wishing to explore Durham and surrounding area. Two minutes from the city centre and five to seven minutes from the Cathedral and Castle. Durham is an interesting town on the River Wear, with three fine old bridges; the Cathedral, on a splendid site overlooking the river, has very notable Norman work. Nearest coastal town 30 minutes. Accommodation comprises two double, two single and three family bedrooms, all with washbasins and colour TV. Bathroom, two toilets; sittingroom, diningroom. Full central heating. Children are welcome. Pets permitted. Open all year; mid-week bookings taken. Car not essential. Bed and Breakfast from £8 per person per night. Member of the Northumbria and English Tourist Boards.

MIDDLETON-IN-TEESDALE. Mrs B. J. Killen, West Park, Lunedale, Middleton-in-Teesdale, Barnard Castle DL12 0PS (Teesdale [0833] 40380). Working farm. West Park is a stockrearing farm at one time part of the Strathmore Estates. Now extensively altered and modernised, superior accommodation is offered in four double, one single and one family bedrooms, most with washbasins; two bathrooms, three toilets. Original beamed licensed diningroom and attractive Cellar Bar. Two sittingrooms (one with TV). Children welcome at reduced rates. The farmhouse, half a mile from the approach road, faces south and overlooks Grassholme Reservoir. It has extensive views towards Teesdale and the surrounding fells. The famous Pennine Way runs close to the farm to the West and North. A walker's paradise; also available locally, fishing, golf, riding, sailing, water ski-ing. Open all year. Stamp only for brochure.

MIDDLETON-IN-TEESDALE. Mrs June Dent, Wythes Hill, Lunedale, Middleton-in-Teesdale, Barnard Castle DL12 0NX (Teesdale [0833] 40349). Working farm. Friendliness and comfort are assured at Wythes Hill, a 500 acre hill farm with sheep and suckler herd of beef cattle. Situated right on the Pennine Way route it has commanding views of the surrounding hills and valley of reservoirs. Trout fishing and sailing available. Pony trekking at nearby farm. An area abounding in history with Hadrian's Wall, many castles and the Bowes Museum to visit and only an hour's drive to the Lake District. Guests will enjoy good plain cooking including free range eggs and home produced meat. Accommodation in one double and one family bedrooms; bathroom, shower room, two toilets; diningroom; sittingroom with colour TV. Children welcome, cot, high chair, babysitting provided. Car essential — parking. Evening Meal, Bed and Breakfast from £9; Bed and Breakfast from £6.50 with reductions for children. Open May to September.

TEESDALE. Mrs Ann Flynn, Wood End House, Etherley Bank, High Etherley, Bishop Auckland DL14 0LG (Bishop Auckland [0388] 832279). Wood End House is a stone-built country house conveniently situated on the A68 one mile north of West Auckland in this attractive part of south-west Durham. An ideal touring centre and a convenient stopping place when travelling to or from Scotland. Places of interest to visit include Weardale, the Yorkshire Dales, North York Moors, Durham City, Hadrian's Wall and Beamish open air museum, all within easy reach. Accommodation comprises one family/single room, one double bedroom. Diningroom/sittingroom. Home baked bread and free range eggs are among the good food served by Mrs Flynn. Reductions for children, cot and babysitting provided. Car essential — parking. Open Easter to December for Bed and Breakfast £6.50; Evening Dinner £3.50. Pets accepted.

DURHAM – MOORS, VALLEYS AND INDUSTRY!

At its western extent Durham embraces the moors and valleys of the Pennines but otherwise this is an industrial county, with a strong coal mining tradition. Places worth a visit include Barnard Castle, the Upper Teesdale Valley, the gothic church at Brancepeth and the farm and industrial museum at Beamish.

The information in the entries in this guide is presented by the publishers in good faith and after the signed acceptance by advertisers that they will uphold the high standards associated with
FARM HOLIDAY GUIDES LIMITED. The publishers do not accept responsibility for any inaccuracies or omissions or any results thereof. Before making final holiday arrangements readers should confirm the prices and facilities directly with advertisers.

ESSEX

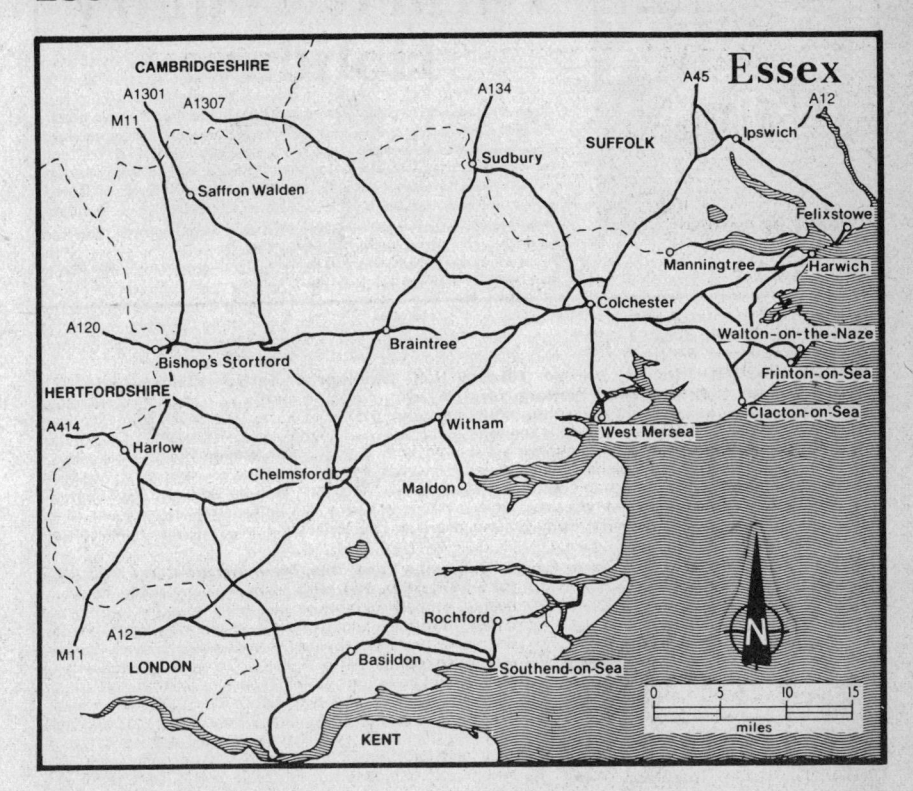

COLCHESTER. Mrs Audrey Daniels, Morants, Colchester Road, Great Bromley, Colchester CO7 7TN (0206) 230240. Within easy reach of England's first recorded town of Colchester, steeped in history (four miles), Constable Country and famous village of Dedham (four miles), the popular and famous seaside resorts of Walton, Clacton and Frinton (12 miles) and the Port of Harwich (12 miles). Morants is a former farmhouse and part of it is 15th-century, set back from the road in 11 acres of parkland. There is a hard tennis court. Golf, sailing and riding facilities all close by. Central heating. Open all year.

HALSTEAD near. Mr and Mrs John West, The Pottery, St. James Street, Castle Hedingham, Near Halstead (Hedingham [0787] 60036). Very comfortable late Georgian house set in medieval village with Norman Castle. (Working pottery behind house with day courses available for people with little or no experience). Situated on Suffolk/Essex borders with lovely rural scenery and villages close by. Local market town, Sudbury. Cambridge, Bury St. Edmunds, Colchester and Aldeburgh are within one hour's drive. Accommodation: Bed and Breakfast — twin and double room, both have electric blankets, central heating, tea-making facilities. Washbasins and shower points. Traditional English breakfast served. Children over 12 years welcome. Sorry, no dogs. Open all year round and will take mid-week bookings. Single £9; double £17. Registered English Tourist Board.

Farm & Country Holidays

The beautiful and peaceful county of Essex offers the ideal location for a weekend break or a quiet country holiday, yet the close proximity of London also makes it the ideal stopping point for those wishing to combine business with pleasure.

The Farm and Country Holiday Group offer a variety of accommodation ranging through Bed and Breakfast, Half Board and Self-catering, and visitors can be sure of the highest standards. Each member is registered with the English Tourist Board. A comprehensive brochure is available and this describes not only the facilities offered, but also the varied tourist attractions to be found locally.

Further information available from **Mrs B. Martin, Newhouse Farm, Mutton Row, Stamford Rivers, Essex. Tel: Ongar (0277) 362132.**

SAFFRON WALDEN. Mrs Lily Vernon, Thistley Hall, Widdington, Saffron Walden CB11 3ST (Saffron Walden [0799] 40388). Working farm. A warm welcome awaits you at this 17th century farmhouse which is uniquely situated in the north west corner of rural Essex, five miles from Stansted Airport, two miles off B1383 (formerly A11) London-Cambridge road (with easy access to M11). On borders of Hertfordshire, Suffolk and Cambridge making it central for touring and sightseeing. The house stands in 30 acres pastures (adjacent to Molehall Wildlife Park) and views of the gardens and countryside can be seen from every window. Accommodation comprises two double rooms (one twin-bedded) with washbasins, family room. Central heating when necessary. Shaver points in bedrooms. Bathroom, shower room, three toilets. Sitting/diningroom. Colour TV. Homely atmosphere and personal attention. Bed and Breakfast from £8.50 per person.

WIX. Mrs H. P. Mitchell, New Farm House, Spinnell's Lane, Wix, Manningtree CO11 2UJ (Wix [025-587] 365). Working farm. A comfortable, centrally heated, modern farmhouse ideally situated for touring the famous Constable countryside, local seaside resorts, historic Colchester and other towns. Convenient for Harwich (Parkeston Quay) Car Ferry to Holland, Denmark, Germany and Sweden. All bedrooms have washbasins and optional colour TV. Also guests' lounge with colour TV. Small kitchen available for making hot drinks at any time, beverages and milk provided free. Children welcome at reduced price, cot, high chair and babysitting provided. Very large play area with swings, etc. Games room with Table Tennis, Darts, Pool, etc. Good farmhouse cooking. Bed and Breakfast. Evening Meal. Open all year. AA and RAC listed. SAE for colour brochure.

ESSEX – CHOICES!

Essex offers the choice between rural farmland, a marshy coastline, and industrial towns. Worth a visit are Abberton Reservoir, Blackwater Estuary, the country park at Danbury, Hatfield Forest and the Naze.

When you have read one you *haven't* read them all – we have *eleven* other publications

---

If you've found
FARM HOLIDAY GUIDE
of service please tell your friends

BOARD   Gloucestershire   195

GLOUCESTERSHIRE

Gloucestershire

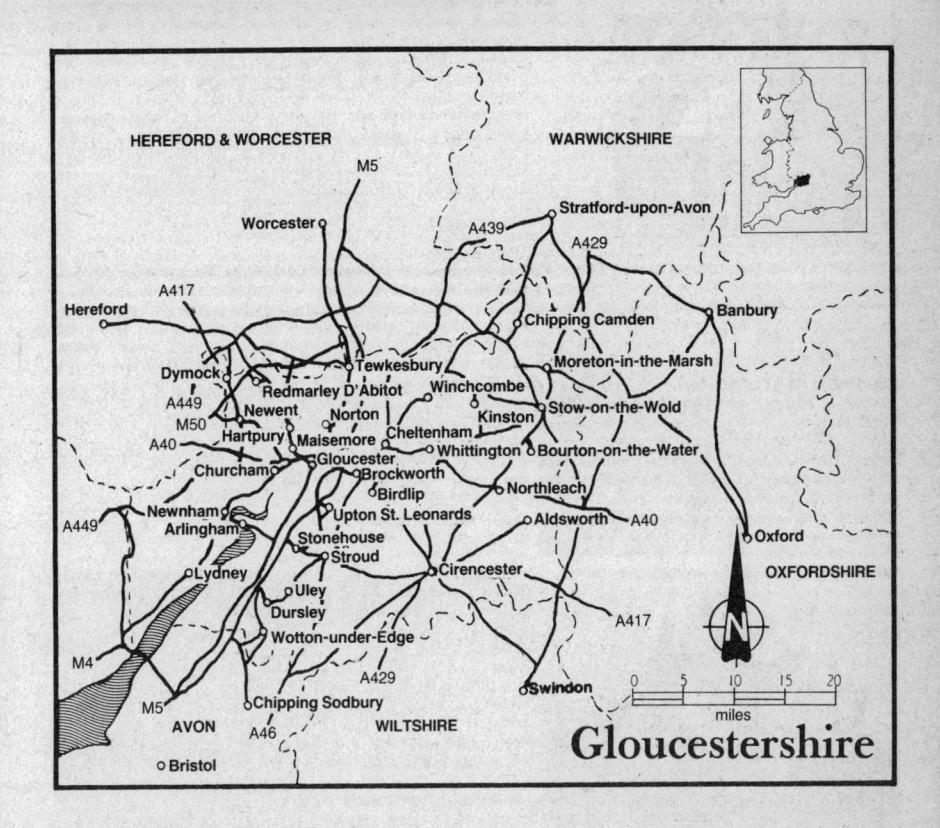

ARLINGHAM. Mrs D. Turrell, Horshoe View, Overton Lane, Arlingham GL2 7JJ (Gloucester [0452] 740293). Guests are given a friendly welcome, all year round, in this comfortable private house enjoying beautiful views of River Severn and Forest of Dean. Within easy reach of A38 and M5, and excellent base for touring the Cotswolds, Bath, Slimbridge Wildfowl Trust, Berkeley Castle and many other places of interest. Dry ski slope, Gloucester Leisure Centre and Three Choirs Festival attract many visitors. Accommodation in two double bedrooms (one en suite), one twin-bedded and one single room, with usual amenities. Children over eight years welcome. Sorry, no pets. Car essential — ample parking. Bed and Breakfast (Evening Meal by arrangement). Reductions for children and Senior Citizens. SAE, please, for terms.

BERKELEY. Mrs Barbara A. Evans, Green Acres Farm, Breadstone, Berkeley GL13 9HF (Dursley [0453] 810348). Working farm. Oak beams, inglenook fireplaces are just some of the interesting features at Green Acres, an attractive, comfortable, friendly guest house on a 47-acre dairy farm. Excellent touring centre for the picturesque villages of the Cotswolds, Malvern Hills, Bath, Royal Forest of Dean, and Wales. Delightful local beauty spots include Uley Tump, Coaley Peak picnic area and nature reserve. Excellent walking locally. Horse riding and golf nearby. Berkeley Castle and Severn Wildfowl Trust among many interesting places to visit. Open February to November, there are two double, one family bedrooms, with washbasins (two rooms en-suite). Bathroom, toilet. Sittingroom, diningroom. Personal attention and an excellent variety of home produced food served. Central heating. Children welcome, cot, high chair, babysitting, reduced rates. Sorry, no pets. Car essential — parking. Evening Dinner, Bed and Breakfast from £12.50; Bed and Breakfast from £8.50. Reductions for senior citizens out of season.

PLEASE SEND A STAMPED ADDRESSED ENVELOPE WITH ENQUIRIES

Gloucestershire BOARD

BIRDLIP. Mrs P. M. Carter, Beechmount, Birdlip GL4 8JH (Gloucester [0452] 862262). Good central base for touring Cotswolds, conveniently situated for many interesting places and picturesque views with lovely walks. "Beechmount" is in centre of Birdlip on A417, B4070 junction. Village and garage, post office/village stores and public house. Prices include morning tea and choice of menu for breakfast. Front door key is provided so that guests may come and go freely. One double, one single, two family bedrooms, all with washbasins; bathroom, separate shower, shaver point; toilet. Children welcome at reduced rates, cot, high chair provided. Pets allowed by arrangement. Parking space. Open January/December for Bed and Breakfast. Evening Meal by prior arrangement. Small family run guest house.

BISHOP'S NORTON. Mrs Denise Carr, Hill Farm, Bishop's Norton GL2 9LX (Gloucester [0452] 730351). Working farm. A warm welcome awaits you at this picturesque 14th century thatched, oak-timbered farmhouse, offering comfortable, homely atmosphere, and good home cooking. Situated in a quiet village in the Severn Valley within easy reach of the M4 and M5/6, it is ideal for touring the Cotswolds, Malverns, Forest of Dean and the Wye Valley, Berkeley and Sudeley Castles, Prinknash Abbey and Wild Fowl Trust. Riding, golfing, boating nearby — fishing within walking distance. Two double, one single, two family rooms, all with washbasins and panoramic views. Two bathrooms, three toilets; sitting and diningrooms. Children welcome, cot, high chair and babysitting available. Pets allowed. Open all year, except Christmas. Log fires. Terms for Evening Meal, Bed and Breakfast on request. Reductions for children. Fire Certificate. Stamp only for brochure.

BISHOP'S NORTON, near Gloucester. Mrs Patsy Spiers, The Green Farm, Wainlodes Lane, Bishop's Norton, Near Gloucester GL2 9LN (Gloucester [0452] 730252). Working farm. This is a delightful half-timbered farmhouse on a 200-acre mixed farm. Pleasantly situated in the Severn Valley within walking distance of the River Severn. Golf, fishing, horse-riding and many other sporting facilities are nearby. A very good centre for exploring the many well-known beauty spots in Gloucestershire and surrounding area. One twin-bedded and one family room, both with hot and cold. Bathroom, toilet; lounge/diningroom. Sorry, no pets. Car is essential and plenty of parking space. Open March to November. Reductions for children. SAE, please, for terms.

BOURTON-ON-THE-WATER. Mrs Helen Adams, Upper Farm, Clapton-on-the-Hill, Bourton-on-the-Water, Cheltenham GL54 2LG (Cotswold [0451] 20453). Working farm. Upper Farm is a mixed farm of 130 acres situated two miles from Bourton-on-the-Water in a peaceful Cotswold village with magnificent views. Centrally located for many places of interest (Stratford, Oxford, Slimbridge, Cirencester), it is ideal for touring, walking or merely relaxing. The 17th century stone farmhouse of historic interest has been restored to give warmth and comfort. There are two double, one family and one single bedrooms, all with washbasins; separate lounge and diningroom. Car essential, ample parking. Children are welcome, cot and high chair. Open April to October. Bed and Breakfast from £8. Reduced rates for children.

BOURTON-ON-THE-WATER. Mr and Mrs J. Weir, Lansdowne Villa, Bourton-on-the-Water GL54 2AR (Bourton-on-the-Water [0451] 20673). In the heart of the Cotswolds, Lansdowne Villa is a large, modernised Georgian House near the village centre of Bourton-on-the-Water. This charming village is surrounded by many beautiful and historic places of interest and straddles the River Windrush. Model Village, Model Railway, Butterfly Exhibition and Birdland in Bourton-on-the-Water are certainly worth a visit. Five double and five family bedrooms with washbasins; three bathrooms, four toilets; sittingroom, TV; diningroom. Central heating. Children welcome at reduced rates if sharing parents' room; cot, babysitting provided. Open all year. SAE, please, for terms for Bed and Breakfast only.

GLOUCESTERSHIRE – THE IDYLLIC COTSWOLDS COUNTY!

A combination of the Cotswolds and The Vale of Severn, Gloucestershire is a popular tourist destination. Visit Chipping Campden, Cirencester, The Cotswolds Farm Park, The Forest of Dean, Keynes Park and Tewkesbury and you will not be disappointed. If you are around at the right time, the Severn Bore can also be quite a spectacle.

BOARD   Gloucestershire   197

CHELTENHAM. Mrs Patricia Linsdell, Blind Lane Cottage, Kineton, Guiting Power, Cheltenham GL54 5UG (Guiting Power [04515] 616). Blind Lane Cottage is 18th century and set in an old world cottage garden overlooking open countryside. Kineton is a farming area in North Cotswolds. Nearby public houses serve evening meals. The following places are within easy reach; Stratford-on-Avon, Oxford, Stow-on-the-Wold, Burford, Tewkesbury, Bourton-on-the-Water, Winchcombe, Chipping Campden and Moreton-in-Marsh. Many well-known historic places of interest to be found in any published guide. Leisure activities include riding, swimming, golf and walking. The immediate area has many public footpaths giving access to some of the most beautiful countryside in England. The Cotswold Way passes the outskirts of Winchcombe. Nearest motorway access Cheltenham, junction 10, M5. Double and single rooms, with washbasins; children welcome; pets allowed. Open all year with central heating. Car essential, parking. Full Board; Evening Dinner, Bed and Breakfast or Bed and Breakfast only. Reduced rates for under 12's. Further details on application.

CHELTENHAM near. Mrs E. A. Daniels, Bouchers Farmhouse, Bentham, Near Cheltenham GL51 5TZ (Gloucester [0452] 862373). This charming Cotswold stone house, until 1962 and for nearly 300 years a farmhouse, is set in one acre of garden and surrounded by unspoilt countryside. Situated at the foot of the Cotswolds; ideal for touring Forest of Dean, Wye Valley and Prinknash Abbey, famous for its pottery. The Cathedral City of Gloucester is six miles away and Cheltenham Spa four miles. Enhanced by all modern comforts, olde worlde charm is maintained throughout the house, a special feature being the beamed ceilings. Two double bedrooms with washbasins and shaver points; one bathroom, one toilet; lounge, diningroom. Children of school age welcome, reduced terms. Car essential, ample parking. Sorry, no pets. Open all year (except Christmas). Bed and Breakfast. SAE, please, for terms or telephone.

CHELTENHAM near (Cotswolds). Mrs D. Trott, "Cosy Cottage", The Avenue, Bourton-on-the-Water, Near Cheltenham GL54 2DT (Cotswold [0451] 21748). Quietly situated in the heart of the Cotswolds, four minutes' walk from the village centre of Bourton-on-the-Water, surrounded by many beautiful and historic places of interest, "Cosy Cottage", a family home, offers clean, comfortable accommodation in a friendly atmosphere. Twin and double bedrooms, with washbasins, tea/coffee making facilities. Bathroom, two toilets. TV lounge, diningroom. Central heating. Good home cooking using organically grown vegetables in season. Car preferable to enjoy the delightful Cotswolds countryside. Parking. Full English Breakfast. SAE or phone for terms and further details.

CHIPPING CAMPDEN. Mrs C. H. North, Meon House, Stratford Road, Mickleton, Chipping Campden GL55 6SU (Mickleton [038-677] 579). Situated twixt Stratford-Upon-Avon and Broadway on the A46. Ideal for touring Cotswold villages and Shakespeare country. All rooms with washbasins and facilities for your morning tea or coffee. Set in 10 acres of plum orchards and pasture. Bed and English Breakfast £9 to £10 per person per night. Open all year. Enquiries to owner, Mrs C. H. North or telephone.

CHIPPING CAMPDEN. Mr and Mrs David Lord, Charingworth Manor, Near Ebrington, Chipping Campden GL55 6NS (Paxford [038-678] 219). Charingworth Manor welcomes you to stay in this beautiful, family-owned part-Tudor, part-Jacobean house on the northern point of the Cotswolds. Within 30 miles of much of England's history and most varied countryside. Excellent cooking, but bring your own wine. Tourist Board recommended. Please write for brochure.

FARM HOLIDAY GUIDES LIMITED publish a large range of well-known accommodation guides. We will be happy to send you details or you can use the order form at the back of this book.

Gloucestershire BOARD

CHIPPING SODBURY near. Mrs J. Pye, Elmlea, King Lane, Horton, Near Chipping Sodbury BS17 6PF (Chipping Sodbury [0454] 312295). Secluded detached bungalow in one acre garden with scenic views over unspoilt countryside. Beautiful spot for walking and birdwatching. Ideal for touring Cotswolds. Easy reach Bristol and Bath. Three miles from Chipping Sodbury where there is a choice of pubs. Elmlea offers one double room and one twin bedroom with tea/coffee making equipment (tea/coffee/biscuits supplied). Comfortable lounge/diner with log stove for chilly evenings. Bathroom, toilet. All tastefully furnished. A warm welcome and personal service April — mid October. Car essential. Ample parking. Sorry, no children or pets. Evening Meal, Bed and Breakfast from £12.50. Bed and Breakfast from £9, including bed-time drink. Weekly bookings welcome.

CIRENCESTER. Mrs E. T. Thring, Rapsgate Park, North Cerney, Cirencester GL7 7EW (North Cerney [0285-83] 270). Rapsgate Park is a charming old Cotswold Manor House in lovely peaceful countryside situated halfway between Cirencester and Cheltenham. Ideally placed for touring — Cotswold villages, Bath, Oxford and Stratford-upon-Avon are within easy reach. Rapsgate makes an excellent holiday base for families, with its large garden and lawn with croquet. Comfortable accommodation comprises two double and two single bedrooms; two bathrooms, three toilets. Sittingroom and diningroom. Children welcome at reduced rates, babysitting available. No objection to dogs. Car essential — ample parking. Open May to end October for Bed and Breakfast. Evening Meal if required. Mid-week bookings accepted. Please write for brochure (with map) or 'phone.

CIRENCESTER (Cotswolds). Mrs R. J. Barton, The Coach House, Manor Farm, Middle Duntisbourne, Cirencester GL7 7AR (Cirencester [0285] 3058). The Coach House is separate from the farmhouse and is personally supervised by Mrs Barton and her daughter Mrs Whitaker. Surrounded by 400 acres of farmland and situated in the small hamlet of Middle Duntisbourne, a peaceful and picturesque valley, this area is ideal for walking and touring. Bath, Stratford-upon-Avon and Oxford are within easy reach, Cirencester being in the centre of the Cotswolds. There is a large lawn and meadow with little river at the back of the house. The TV lounge is open at all times and there are washbasins in all four bedrooms (three double and one family), as well as electric blankets, interior spring mattresses and electric wall heaters. Plenty of parking space. Bed and Breakfast with choice of breakfast. Children under nine years reduced rates. Tea/coffee facilities in all rooms.

COTSWOLDS. Mrs V. Keyte, The Limes, Tewkesbury Road, Stow-on-the-Wold GL54 1EN (Cotswold [0451] 30034). Over the last 10 years this RAC and AA Listed Guest House has established a reputation for its homely and friendly atmosphere. It is just four minutes' walk from town centre; central for visiting Stratford-upon-Avon, Burford, Bourton-on-the-Water, Cirencester, Cheltenham, etc. The Limes overlooks field and has an attractive large garden with ornamental pool and waterfall. Single, twin, double or family rooms, with washbasins; one four-poster bedroom with shower; central heating, TV lounge, diningroom. Children welcome; cot. Open all year. Log fires in winter. Car park. Fire Certificate held. Bed and Breakfast from £8.50 per person.

COTSWOLDS. Mrs Christine A. Long, The Gorse House, Bourton-on-the-Water GL54 2EJ (Cotswold [0451] 20819). Thatched house of particular charm and character situated in secluded, peaceful setting, yet within easy walking distance of the beautiful Cotswold village. Golf, tennis, fishing, bathing within easy reach; pony trekking locally. Wildlife parks, Slimbridge, Stratford-upon-Avon and many interesting houses to visit. Ideal for touring the Cotswolds with its many picturesque towns and villages. Easy access to Motorway (M5). Comfortable accommodation in two double bedrooms (with washbasins), one single and one family bedrooms, all with tea/coffee making facilities. Bathroom, two toilets; sittingroom, diningroom. Television available if required. Restaurants and inns are plentiful to suit all tastes and pockets! Children welcome, cot, babysitting provided. Pets accepted at small charge. Parking, but car not essential. Open all year for Bed and Breakfast from £9.50. Reductions for children and senior citizens.

Terms quoted in this publication may be subject to increase if rises in costs necessitate

Tudor Farm, Clearwell, Coleford, Glos. GL16 8JS
Mrs Sheila Reid. Tel. (0594) 33046

Why not visit our beautiful 13th century house in the village of Clearwell at the edge of the Royal Forest of Dean. This is a lovely unspoiled corner of England, with superb walking, delightful villages and friendly country pubs. We are within a short drive of the Wye Valley and spectacular Symonds Yat in an area of outstanding natural beauty yet only 20 minutes from the Severn Bridge, and the M4 and M5 motorways. Enjoy a large farmhouse breakfast (served at a civilised hour) and dinner freshly prepared from local produce. Afterwards you can relax in our comfortable oak beamed lounge with a drink in front of the inglenook fireplace. Licensed.

DURSLEY. Mrs E. Williams, Claremont House, 66 Kingshill Road, Dursley GL11 4EG (Dursley [0453] 2018). Claremont, a large pleasant house overlooking the Cam Valley and with fine views of the Cotswold Escarpment, offers most comfortable accommodation and a warm welcome to all visitors. It is ideally situated for touring the Severn Vale and many Cotswold beauty spots; convenient for visits to Berkeley Castle, Slimbridge Wildfowl Trust, Cirencester, Bath, Cheltenham and Severn Bridge. Fresh farm produce always available. Double and family bedrooms with hot and cold; bathroom, two toilets; sittingroom and diningroom. Cot, high chair, babysitting and reduced rates for children. Central heating. Car preferable; ample parking. Open all year for Evening Meal, Bed and Breakfast or Bed and Breakfast only.

DURSLEY. Mrs D. Clutterbuck, Standle Farm, Stinchcombe, Dursley GL11 6BH (Dursley [0453] 2736). Working farm. Standle is most peacefully situated yet is an ideal centre for touring the Cotswolds. The house is attractive with beamed ceilings and is tastefully decorated and furnished. Good food attractively served. Milk, eggs, vegetables fresh from the farm. Slimbridge Wildfowl Trust and Berkeley Castle are of local interest. The farm is 140-acre working dairy farm with accommodation for guests in one double and one family rooms, with washbasins; one twin bedded room also. Bathroom, toilet; sittingroom; diningroom. Children are welcome and cot, high chair and babysitting provided. Pets are allowed. Open March to October: Car essential — parking. Evening Dinner, Bed and Breakfast or Bed and Breakfast only. Reduced rates for children sharing parents' room.

DURSLEY. Peter and Lesley Rackley, Burrows Court, Nibley Green, North Nibley, Dursley GL11 6AZ (Dursley [0453] 46230). Converted 18th century mill in one-acre garden with beautiful views of the Cotswolds Escarpment. Ideal touring centre for the Cotswolds, Bath, Bristol and Cheltenham. Cotswold Way walk, Berkeley Castle, Westonbirt Arboretum, Slimbridge Wildfowl Trust, Badminton and several good golf courses nearby. Easy access M4, M5. We have seven double/twin bedrooms with washbasins and tea/coffee making facilities; four bathrooms; guest sitting room, with colour TV; large dining room. Full central heating, log fires. Ample parking. Weekly rates; Bed and Breakfast £49; Dinner, Bed and Breakfast £84. Short breaks: Dinner, Bed and Breakfast for two nights £28; three nights £39. Open all year. Licensed. SAE for brochure.

DURSLEY near. Gerald and Norma Kent, Hill House, Crawley Hill, Uley, Near Dursley GL11 5BH (Dursley [0453] 860267). Cotswold stone house situated on top of a hill with beautiful views of the surrounding countryside, near the very pretty village of Uley. Ideal spot for exploring the various walks in the area including the Cotswold Way, and there are many places of interest within a reasonable driving distance of Uley. Bed and Breakfast offered, although Evening Meals are normally available on request. Choice of bedrooms, with hot and cold water, central heating, shaver points, tea and coffee making facilities. Guest lounge with colour television. Your hosts' aim is to make your stay in the Cotswolds an enjoyable and memorable one, with comfort and hospitality of prime importance. Please 'phone or write for brochure.

Hill House

DURSLEY. Mrs N. M. Hill, Newbrook Farm, Uley, Dursley GL11 5AL (Dursley [0453] 860251). Working farm. Newbrook, a mixed farm of 130 acres, lies under Downham Hill about a mile from Uley Village in a lovely part of the country on the edge of the Cotswolds, with magnificent views all round. Excellent walking area. Newbrook Farm is open January to November and the farmhouse has been modernised, with full central heating; two double rooms, each with an extra bed, and one family room (two with washbasins); bathroom, two toilets. Lounge with colour TV, diningroom. Nearby are Slimbridge Wildfowl Trust, Berkeley Castle, Chedworth Roman Villa, Severn Bridge and the Wye Valley. SAE, please, for terms for Evening Dinner, Bed and Breakfast or Bed and Breakfast only. Car essential — parking.

DURSLEY. Sam and Kay Trump, Hodgecombe Farm, Uley, Dursley GL11 5AN (Dursley [0453] 860365). The farmhouse stands in 13 acres of pasture beneath Uley Bury with uninterrupted views of the distant Severn, the Forest of Dean and the Malverns. Modernised, full central heating. Two double rooms each with extra single bed. One room with twin beds. Guests' own bathroom with shower, also second shower/toilet. Character lounge. Separate diningroom. Open April to October inclusive. Nearby is Slimbridge Wildfowl Trust, Berkeley Castle, two golf courses, all within 15 minutes' motoring. In an area of outstanding natural beauty. Situated on the Cotswold Way. Easy access to the M5 and village pubs. Ample parking. Generous home cooking. Bed and Breakfast from £8. Evening Meal if required £5. Advance booking preferred. Camping £1.50 per tent. AA listed. British Tourist Board registered. Welcome to non-smokers.

DURSLEY. Mrs Catherine C. Cobham, 61A The Street, Uley, Dursley GL11 5SL (Dursley [0453] 860313). Large bungalow, with lovely gardens, situated on B4066, within easy reach of the Cotswold Way, Berkeley Castle, Slimbridge Wild Fowl Trust, Tetbury, Cheltenham and many other places of interest. This is very suitable accommodation for the disabled. Two double bedrooms, with hot and cold; guests' bathroom with toilet. Spacious sittingroom/diningroom with colour TV. Children over 12 welcome. Pets accepted, if kept under strict control, at a small charge. Central heating. Wholefood catering. Ample parking. Bed and Breakfast £8.50 per night. Open March 1st to end December. Mid-week bookings accepted.

DURSLEY near. Mrs D. Steel, Ham Farm, Coaley, Near Dursley GL11 5AS (Dursley [0453] 860112). Working farm. This is a 250-acre mixed farm on the picturesque escarpment of the Cotswolds with swimming pool and playroom. Excellent hill climbing and walking country. Horse riding, gliding club, golf courses within three mile radius. Two double rooms and a single, two with washbasins; two bathrooms, one toilet; sittingroom; diningroom. Car essential, parking. Children are welcome, cot and high chair. Regret no pets. Open all year. Bed and Breakfast from £6.

GLOUCESTER near. Mrs S. J. Barnfield, "Kilmorie", Gloucester Road, Corse, Staunton, Near Gloucester GL19 3RQ (Staunton Court [045-284] 224). Built in 1848 by the Chartists, "Kilmorie" is "Grade 2 Listed" in a conservation area, and is a smallholding keeping farm livestock and fruit, in a lovely part of Gloucestershire countryside. Good home cooking with own produce, meat, eggs when available. Large garden. Central heating. Children are welcome to participate with the animals if they wish, a child's pony is also kept. There are many places of both natural and historic interest to visit, "Kilmorie" is situated close to the borders of Herefordshire, Worcestershire, the Forest of Dean, also the Cotswolds, Malvern Hills, Wye Valley and four Castles within easy reach. River trips can be enjoyed from Tewkesbury and Upton-on-Severn. Three double bedrooms; bathroom, shower, toilet; lounge with colour TV, diningroom. Cot, high chair, babysitting, reduced rates for children. Pets accepted. Ample parking; good bus service. Evening Dinner, Bed and Breakfast from £8.50; Bed and Breakfast £6. Open all year.

GLOUCESTER near. Mrs M. Beale, Benges Farm, Prior's Norton, Near Gloucester GL2 9LT (Gloucester [0452] 730349). Working farm. Guests are welcome from March to October in this pleasant farmhouse with a family atmosphere situated in a small hamlet in the Severn Vale. The farm is 300 acres, mainly arable, with some beef. Nearby the River Severn; golf, fishing and many sporting facilities including a dry ski slope within easy reach. The farm is ideally placed for touring the many beauty spots and places of interest. Two twin-bedded rooms, one single (two with washbasins); bathroom, two toilets. Combined lounge/diningroom. Interesting varied home cooking and traditional English Breakfast served. Evening Meal optional. Bed and Breakfast from £8. Regret, no young children or pets. Car essential. SAE for further details.

HARTPURY. Mrs G. Pugh, Brick House Farm, Hartpury GL19 3DD (Hartpury [045-270] 279). Working farm. This early Georgian farmhouse, surrounded by 200 acres of dairy farming land lies on the Gloucester/Worcester border. Hartpury, with its medieval church, is well situated for touring the Cotswolds, Wye Valley and the Forest of Dean. Visits to Bristol Zoo and Slimbridge Wild Fowl Trust will delight children, who are welcome. Cot available, babysitting facilities to allow parents some freedom in the evenings. Three double rooms, two family, one single (with washbasins); sittingroom with colour TV, diningroom. Bathroom, two toilets. Electric heating. Regret no dogs. Mrs Pugh welcomes guests from April to September. Terms gladly sent on request for Evening Dinner, Bed and Breakfast, or Bed and Breakfast only. SAE, please. Reduced rates for children.

NAILSWORTH. Mrs J. Granger, Barley Hill, Watledge, Nailsworth GL6 0AS (Nailsworth [045-383] 2619). An early Victorian family house, situated in an elevated position overlooking the Cotswold town of Nailsworth and the countryside beyond. The grounds extend to over an acre and back onto National Trust woods and then Minchinhampton Common. Nearby are the villages of Painswick and Badminton, with Bath, Cirencester, Cheltenham and Tetbury being within easy reach. The tastefully furnished accommodation comprises one large double room, and one twin bedded room, both with washbasins and television or radio; bathroom; sitting/diningroom. Central heating. Children welcome, and pets by prior arrangement. Ample car parking. Bed and Breakfast from £9.50. Weekly rates on application. Evening meals by arrangement. Self-catering accommodation also available.

The White House Licensed Guest House, Mrs Turner, Popes Hill, Newnham, Glos.

Telephone: 0452 76463

The farm is set in the lovely Forest of Dean on top of Popes Hill, with panoramic views of the rolling countryside and River Severn. Well laid out garden for guests to relax in. Many interesting places to visit include Wye Valley, The Cotswolds and Malvern Hills, Bath, Cheltenham, Hereford. Ideal. for walking, touring. Friendly welcome. Good home cooking assured. Fire certificate. Diningroom with bar. Kettles in bedrooms. Special diets catered for. Visit ancient open Iron Mines, Castles, Abbeys and many historical buildings, bird sanctuaries and museums, including Westbury Dutch Water Gardens.

FOREST OF DEAN

The Old Vicarage, Awre;

Country House Hospitality

in a lovely Georgian house set in the midst of four acres of interesting and unusual gardens, on the edge of the Forest of Dean.

Guests return for the peace, thoughtful service and cuisine. We are renowned for our home grown foods used to create delicious and imaginative dishes, complemented by either our own wine from the vineyard, or cider from the orchard. Menus are prepared each day according to the seasons and guests interests.

The house has superb panoramic views of the Severn Estuary, Cotswolds and Forest of Dean. All rooms are large, comfortable, elegantly decorated and furnished with antiques. Guests are welcome to be 'at home' at any time. All bedrooms are provided with heaters, electric blankets, tea and coffee facilities and have either H&C or are 'en suite'; in addition there are ample W.C. and bath facilities. Guests have their own dining room, and separate lounge with log fire. There is no T.V. in the lounge, but many books, maps and games, A T.V. is available for private use if required.

The area is fascinating, rich in history, and glorious in all seasons. Excellent for walks and touring with many interesting towns and villages, antique shops, markets, castles and museums. Literature is available to assist exploring.

An ideal holiday for the discerning, searching for a peaceful retreat. Not suitable for children under 12 or pets. **If you would like to book, please telephone 0594-510282 or write for a brochure to Nick and May Bull. The Old Vicarage, Awre, Newnham, Glos. GL14 1EL.**

Gloucestershire BOARD

NEWNHAM-ON-SEVERN. Mrs Margaret MacFarlane, Poulton Court Farm, Awre, Newnham-on-Severn GL14 1ES (Dean [0594] 510249). Working farm. Poulton Court is a 16th century period farmhouse quietly situated near the River Severn to which walks are possible, and on the edge of the Royal Forest of Dean. It is perfect for a peaceful country holiday, as a centre for a touring holiday, or as a midway stop from north to south. Accommodation consists of one twin-bedded room, two double rooms, guests' own bathroom/toilet and sitting/diningroom. Bed and English Breakfast terms also include a bedtime drink. If you wish, a home-baked farmhouse evening meal is also available. Tea-making facilities in all bedrooms. Open all year. Ample parking. Children at reduced rates. Sorry, no pets.

NORTHLEACH. Mrs Patricia Powell, Cotteswold House, Market Place, Northleach GL54 3EG (Northleach [04516] 493 till January 1986, then Cotswold [0451] 60493). This is a listed building of considerable charm and renovated to a high standard, showing a fine blend of old stone and oak beams. It is situated in the heart of the Cotswolds, ideal for touring this beautiful area. Cheltenham, Oxford, Sudeley Castle, Stratford-upon-Avon and many more places of interest. Visitors are welcome all year round for Bed and Breakfast from £8.75 per person per night. Individual room controlled central heating. One double, one twin bedded and one family rooms offered. Two well fitted and well appointed bathrooms. Diningroom. Car parking space in square. SAE, please, for further details.

REDMARLEY. Mrs Anne Arnall, Scar Farm, Redmarley GL19 3JQ (Staunton Court [045-284] 244). Lovely 16th century black and white farmhouse beautifully renovated and full of character, offering a high standard of accommodation. Spacious, comfortable lounge with colour TV, separate diningroom with Inglenook Fireplace; two double-bedded rooms with washbasins plus one with shower and toilet en suite; one twin-bedded room with washbasin and toilet en suite; one single bedroom. All rooms furnished and decorated to a high standard. Relaxed friendly atmosphere, good home cooking using mostly home-grown produce. Pleasant informal gardens with panoramic views to the Malverns and Cotswolds. Quiet, open countryside away from all traffic noise. On the borders of Gloucestershire/Herefordshire/Worcestershire so excellent for touring the many places of interest. Evening Dinner/Meal, Bed and Breakfast or Bed and Breakfast only. SAE, for terms.

STONEHOUSE. Mrs D. A. Hodge, Welches Farm, Standish, Stonehouse GL10 3BX (Stonehouse [045382] 2018). Working farm. Welches Farm is about three miles from Stroudwater Interchange on the M5. Standing near Standish Hospital on the outskirts of Stonehouse. It is a very old Cotswold farmhouse with exposed beams, also an old wood-panelled staircase. It is reputed that Oliver Cromwell stayed at the Welches before the siege of Gloucester in the 17th century. Fairly close to Wildfowl Trail, Berkeley Castle and the Forest of Dean; also National Trust park and woods and many beautiful Cotswold villages. A short distance from the Cotswold Way. Only cotton and linen sheets are used. Large sittingroom — spacious bedrooms. Good food, guaranteed satisfaction. Children welcome, cot, high chair and babysitting. Pets welcome. Car essential — parking. Bed and Breakfast from £8. Reduced rates for children.

STONEHOUSE. Mrs G. P. M. Cozens, Green Farm, Eastington, Stonehouse GL10 3AQ (Stonehouse [045-382] 2452). Working farm. This dairy farm, situated at the foot of the Cotswolds makes an ideal holiday centre and extends a warm welcome. Dating back over 300 years, it offers every comfort. Panoramic views and scenic walks from nearby hills, picturesque Cotswold villages to explore; Bath, Wye Valley and Wales within one hour's drive; Slimbridge, Tetbury, Badminton, Cirencester, Cheltenham, 30 minutes Oxford, Cheddar, Stratford-on-Avon easily reached. One twin and two double rooms with washbasins. Beamed lounge and diningroom. Traditional Farmhouse Breakfast. Open Easter to October. Bed and Breakfast from £7 (morning tea — bedtime drink inclusive). Reductions for children. Excellent value. Evening Meals available at local inns and restaurants. No pets. SAE, please. Tourist Board approved.

PLEASE SEND A STAMPED ADDRESSED ENVELOPE WITH ENQUIRIES

STOW-ON-THE-WOLD. Mr and Mrs G. A. Simms, Mount Pleasant, Oddington Road, Stow-on-the-Wold GL54 1AL (0451) 30732. Mount Pleasant is an old Cotswold stone-built house of character, with gardens, lawns and ample parking space. It is five minutes' walk from the town centre; ideally situated in the midst of many Cotswold villages of beauty and character. Less than an hour's drive to Blenheim Palace, Sudeley Castle, Stratford-upon-Avon, Warwick, Evesham, Cirencester, Cheltenham and many other places of interest. Three double, one family bedrooms with washbasins, some with Cotswold views. Two bathrooms, two toilets. Lounge with TV; diningroom. Central heating. Children welcome at reduced rates if sharing parents' room. Sorry, no pets. Car an advantage. Satisfaction is our aim and a good English breakfast is always served. Bed and Breakfast only from £8 (drinks always available). Open all year. SAE, please.

STOW-ON-THE-WOLD. Mrs F. J. Adams, Banks Farm, Upper Oddington, Moreton-in-Marsh GL56 0XG (Cotswold [0451] 30475). Working farm. Banks Farm is a mixed farm, and the Cotswold stone farmhouse is situated in an elevated position in the centre of the village of Oddington, about three miles from Stow-on-the-Wold. All bedrooms enjoy lovely views over fields to XIth century church. It is centrally situated for all the Cotswold villages, while Blenheim Palace, Oxford, Stratford-upon-Avon, Sudeley Castle, Cheltenham, Cirencester are all within easy reach. Guests and children over 11 years are welcomed to our home from April to October. One double room, one twin bedded room both with washbasins. Car essential, ample parking. Sorry, no pets. Bed and good English Breakfast, morning tea and Bedtime drink from £8 to £8.75. Packed lunches available. SAE with enquiries please.

STRATFORD-ON-AVON. Mrs J. M. Everett, Newbold Nurseries, Newbold-on-Stour, Stratford-upon-Avon CV37 8DP (Alderminster [078-987] 285). Working farm. You can be sure of personal attention and a friendly welcome here. The modern farmhouse has country views on all sides, but is easy to find, standing just off the A34. There are 20 acres of arable crops and half an acre of hydroponically-grown tomatoes. Stratford is seven miles, Warwick Castle, the Cotswold area and Blenheim Palace within very easy reach. Accommodation comprises family and double rooms, with two bathrooms, both having a shower. Dogs are accepted and children sharing a room are half-price. Bed and Breakfast from £8. Local pub serves excellent meals at budget prices.

STROUD near. Mrs B. J. Clarke, Furners Farm, Elcombe, Slad, Near Stroud GL6 7LA (Painswick [0452] 813674). Working farm. Furners Farm with its 17th century farmhouse is a small mixed farm of 10 acres set in the Slad Valley, an area of unspoilt beauty three miles north of Stroud. Cheltenham and Gloucester are 10 miles. There is a nature reserve and riding stables nearby. Ideal centre for walking and touring. The farmhouse is comfortable with a homely atmosphere. Sunny rooms with washbasins and good views. Lounge with colour TV, oak beams and stone fireplace (log fire). Central heating. Home grown produce and home baking. Tea making facilities in rooms. Reductions for children; cot, high chair, babysitting. SAE, please, for terms for Evening Dinner, Bed and Breakfast or Bed and Breakfast only. Weekly rates available.

STROUD near. Miss E. M. MacSwiney, New Inn House, The Camp, Near Stroud GL6 7HL (Miserden [028-582] 336). New Inn House, built in 1694 as a posting-inn, is a Listed Building of Architectural interest. It stands in half-an-acre of grounds in a small Cotswold hamlet 820 feet above sea level amidst unspoilt countryside. Excellent touring centre for Cotswolds and Wye Valley, Bath, Stratford-upon-Avon. Gloucester 10 miles, Cheltenham nine and Cirencester 10 miles. Nearby are the Cotswold Way and Prinknash Abbey; three golf courses within easy reach and riding stables in the village. The Severn Wild Fowl Trust approximately 15 miles. Both bedrooms (one twin-bedded and one single with extra folding bed) have washbasins, tea-making facilities. Three-course Dinner, English Breakfast. Children over 10 welcome. TV. Own garden produce served whenever possible. Dogs welcome if well controlled. Car essential. Leisure Centres at Gloucester and Stroud. SAE, please, for terms. Mid-week bookings accepted. Registered with E.T.B.

FARM HOLIDAY GUIDES LIMITED publish a large range of well-known accommodation guides. We will be happy to send you details or you can use the order form at the back of this book.

Gloucestershire BOARD

TEWKESBURY. Mrs Lynn Bird, Green Gables, Ripple, Tewkesbury GL20 6EX (Upton-on-Severn [068-46] 2740). Large modern house set in the beautiful quiet village of Ripple which is only three miles from Tewkesbury and Upton-on-Severn in the heart of the Severn/Avon Valley, with views of the Malvern and Bredon Hills. Luxurious accommodation with tea-makers and colour TV in bedrooms, and friendly and comfortable lounge for evening relaxation. Open all year, with central heating. Three double, one single bedrooms (two with washbasins). Bathroom, toilets. Children welcome, cot, high chair, babysitting available. Car essential — parking. Bed and Breakfast from £9. Reduced rates for children and senior citizens. Mid-week bookings accepted. Sorry, no pets.

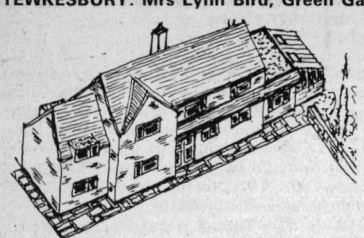

TEWKESBURY. Mrs Bernadette Williams, Abbots Court, Church End, Twyning, Tewkesbury GL20 6DA (Tewkesbury [0684] 292515). Working farm. A large, quiet farmhouse set in 350 acres, built on the site of monastery between the Malverns and Cotswolds, half a mile M5-M50 Junction. Large bedrooms, fully carpeted, with washbasins and tea-making facilities. Centrally heated. Open all year. Large lounge with open fire and colour TV. Spacious diningroom. Good home-cooked food in large quantities. Home produced where possible. Children's own TV room, games room and playroom. Tennis lawn. Play area and lawn, pony to ride. Cot, high chair and babysitting available. Laundry facilities. Ideally situated for touring with numerous places to visit. Swimming, tennis, sauna, golf within three miles. Trout and coarse fishing available on farm. Bed and Breakfast from £7.50. Reduced rates children and senior citizens.

WOTTON-UNDER-EDGE. Mrs K. P. Forster, Under-the-Hill-House, Adey's Lane, Wotton-under-Edge GL12 7LY (Dursley [0453] 842557). Open from April to October, accommodation is provided in this wing of a fine Queen Anne listed house on the edge of ancient wool town of Wotton-under-Edge. Bounded on the east by National Trust Land which is let to the owners who run a breeding herd of cattle. The house is only a few minutes' walk from the town centre where there is much to please the historian; it shelters under the Cotswold escarpment, along which there are beautiful walks with magnificent views of the Severn Vale and river. Ideally situated for Bath, Berkeley Castle, Peter Scott's Wild Fowl Trust and the Cotswolds. The guest wing has four bedrooms with washbasins and tea/coffee making facilities, fine open views. Generous diningroom and comfortable lounge. An evening meal is provided from Monday to Friday with the fruit and vegetables from the garden when available. Sorry, no pets. Bed and Breakfast from £8.20 per night; Bed, Breakfast and Evening Meal (Monday to Friday only) from £12.80. Two-thirds for children 12 years and under.

WOTTON-UNDER-EDGE. Mrs Sylvia Scolding, Varley Farm, Talbots End, Cromhall, Near Wotton-under-Edge GL12 8AJ (Wickwar [045-424] 292). Working farm. This dairy farm of 75 acres is situated near the edge of the Cotswolds. An ideal centre for visiting Wales, Cheddar, Bristol, Bath and Wildfowl Trust. The grey stone farmhouse, recently modernised, has washbasins in all bedrooms — four double or four family rooms. Two bathrooms, three toilets. Lounge with colour TV; diningroom with separate tables. Central heating. Fire Certificate granted. Children welcome, high chair and babysitting available. Sorry, no pets. Car essential — parking. Good English Breakfast. Open Easter to September. Visitors are welcome to walk around the farm and watch the farm activities. Bed and Breakfast or Bed, Breakfast and Evening Meal. Reductions for children. AA and RAC Listed. SAE, please, for early reply.

WHEN MAKING ENQUIRIES PLEASE MENTION
FARM HOLIDAY GUIDE

HAMPSHIRE

ASHURST. Mrs C. Woods, Kingswood Cottage, 10 Woodlands Road, Ashurst SO4 2AD (Ashurst [042129] 2582). Picturesque character cottage set in park-like gardens of one acre with own stream. Direct access to New Forest. The cottage is tranquil and very comfortable, ideal for those wishing to explore the New Forest and the many historic and interesting places close by. Restaurants within five minutes' walk. Children welcome, cot and babysitting. Pets by prior arrangement. Children's meals are available and the gardens are a wonderful playground. Heating available all year round in bedrooms. A wonderful quiet location to explore the beauty of the New Forest and the many places of historic interest in the area. Car preferable, parking. Bed and Breakfast from £8. Reduced rates for children. Open all year.

BROCKENHURST (New Forest). Mr and Mrs T. W. Owton, The Cloud Hotel, Meerut Road, Brockenhurst SO4 7TD (Lymington (0590-22165/22254). A delightful venue for all seasons in a family run hotel. A really magical setting overlooking lovely forest views from public rooms and most bedrooms. Ponies often graze just outside the hotel. Full central heating throughout the hotel with log fires in the lounges in winter. Four cosy lounges include a TV lounge, Bar lounge, Reception lounge and Quiet lounge. The hotel offers a high standard of real home cuisine. Bar Snacks and Cream Teas are also served. All 19 bedrooms have central heating, H&C and radios. Dinner, Bed and Breakfast from £120 to £135 per week. The hotel is open to non-residents. Many special Weekend Activities are organised, viz: Rambling Weekends, Deerstalking Walks, Gourmet Dinners and a 4-day Xmas Programme. A Colour Brochure and leaflet on Special Weekend Activities are available from resident proprietors. Ashley Courtenay recommended. Two night breaks at £45 to £53. See also Colour Display Advertisement.

FORDINGBRIDGE (New Forest). Mr P. Williamson, The Waverley, Salisbury Road, Fordingbridge SP6 1EX (Fordingbridge [0425] 52751). The Waverley is a detached RAC listed guest house situated at Fordingbridge on the edge of the New Forest. Its central position makes it an ideal centre for visitors to this area — within easy reach of the sea and many tourist attractions, such as Beaulieu, Stonehenge, Salisbury, etc. Perfect for walking or riding enthusiasts and people who just want to enjoy the beautiful countryside of the Forest. Comfortably furnished, the accommodation offers a choice of twin, double, family or single bedrooms, all with washbasins. Ample toilet/shower/bath provision. Own car park. Bed and Breakfast for around £8 nightly, £48 weekly. Evening Meal available on weekly terms. SAE, please.

LYMINGTON near. Mrs Nellie Mole, Silver Farm Hotel, Silver Street, Hordle, Near Lymington SO4 0DF (Lymington [0590] 682329). Comfortable small hotel with large garden. High standard of food and personal attention. Relaxing country-house atmosphere. Four double, two family bedrooms, all with washbasins; two bathrooms, two toilets; two sittingrooms, diningroom. Cot, high chair, babysitting and reduced rates for children. Pets permitted free of charge. Central heating. Free Early Morning Tea. Open all year round for Evening Dinner, Bed and Breakfast or Bed and Breakfast only. The hotel stands in pleasant country and forest two miles from the sea. Ideal for touring holiday — Bournemouth and Southampton reached in 30 minutes. Terms on request with SAE, please. Fire Certificate.

LYMINGTON (New Forest). Mrs B. P. Chase, Belford Farm, Silver Street, Hordle, Lymington SO4 0DF (Lymington [0590] 682196). Modern, comfortable farmhouse, near the lovely New Forest, overlooks fields to the front and rear. An ideal touring centre being within easy reach of Bournemouth and Southampton, the Isle of Wight Ferry, Lymington and Beaulieu. Guests are accommodated in two double and one family bedrooms, with washbasins. Bathroom, two toilets. Lounge/diningroom has colour TV and there are fitted carpets throughout. Central heating. Children welcome at reduced rates when sharing parents' room, babysitting arranged. Car essential — parking. Bed and Breakfast from £7.50 per person per night is offered from Easter to October, and guests are welcome to come in and freshen up during the evening. Sorry, no pets.

MILFORD-ON-SEA. Don and Pat Emberson, Compton Hotel, 59/61 Keyhaven Road, Milford-on-Sea SO4 0QX (Lymington [0590] 43117). Compton is a friendly, family hotel. The bedrooms — five doubles (some with showers), four family, four singles (some ground floor) have radio, baby listening, tea-making facilities. Heated swimming pools set in a natural sun trap. The friendly bar, with dance floor and lounge seating, provides nice social evenings. Games room with table tennis, pool and darts. TV room with video. The cooking, English style, and sweet trolley are the product solely of the proprietors. Half Board or Bed and Breakfast. Reduced rates for children. One child sharing under five free May/June/September. OAPs rates May/June/September. Central heating. Parking. Pets welcome. No service charge. Open all year. SAE for details.

Hampshire BOARD

MILFORD-ON-SEA. Mrs Sue Forward, Tregoyd, 16 Whitby Road, Milford-on-Sea SO4 0ND (Lymington [0590] 45548). Enjoy warm and friendly atmosphere of large family house with added feature of games room with table tennis. Large garden overlooking attractive woodland, pleasant walks through woods and along cliff top. Beautiful views of Isle of Wight. Enjoy Milford village with attractive village green. Ideal centre for New Forest, Rufus Stone, Christchurch Priory and Beaulieu. Excellent food including various roasts and fresh vegetables when available. Open all year round. Two double, three family rooms, with washbasins; bathroom, three toilets; sittingroom; diningroom. Reduced rates for children. Cot, high chair, babysitting. Car not essential; parking available. Pets permitted. Evening Dinner, Bed and Breakfast or Bed and Breakfast. SAE, please, for terms.

MILFORD-ON-SEA (New Forest). Mr Nigel P. Jestico, Seaspray, 8 Hurst Road, Milford-on-Sea, Lymington SO4 0PY (Lymington [0590] 42627). Guests staying at this attractive seafront guest house will enjoy uninterrupted sea views to the Isle of Wight and Needles along the coastline to Swanage. Ideal centre for touring the New Forest; within easy reach of Bournemouth and Southampton with their excellent shopping centres. Sporting facilities and entertainment; the ferry to Isle of Wight only four miles distant. The Licensed Bar provides real ale; three sitting rooms; six double bedrooms (two on ground floor) all have washbasins, television and two have shower/toilet en-suite. Diningroom; excellent food, varied menus, and comprehensive wine list. Children at reduced rates if sharing. No pets. Car not essential. Parking. Open from March/October (incl). Evening Dinner, Bed and Breakfast from £110 weekly. Bed and Breakfast from £11 per day. AA Listed. BTA Commended.

PETERSFIELD. Mrs H. S. Wroe, Foxcombe House, South Harting, Petersfield GU31 5PL (Harting [073085] 357). Georgian Country House in peaceful setting on South Downs 250 yards South Downs Way, one mile S. Harting (with three inns serving good food). Ideal for walking, touring and antiques. Uppark, Chichester, Cowdray and Goodwood nearby. One twin bedroom, with bathroom en suite; one double bedroom and one single with washbasins and second bathroom for guests. Sittingroom with colour TV. Large, attractively furnished rooms. Full English Breakfast in beautiful antique-furnished diningroom. Spacious gardens with tennis court. Rates £10 to £12 per person per night. Brochure available on request.

PETERSFIELD. Mrs Mary Bray, Nursted Farm, Buriton, Petersfield GU31 5RW (Petersfield [0730] 64278). Working farm. This late 17th century farmhouse, with its large garden, is open to guests throughout most of the year. Located quarter mile west of the B2146 Petersfield to Chichester road, one and a half miles south of Petersfield, the house makes an ideal base for touring the scenic Hampshire and West Sussex countryside. Queen Elizabeth Country Park two miles adjoining the picturesque village of Buriton at the western end of South Downs Way. Accommodation consists of three double bedrooms; bathroom, two toilets; sittingroom/breakfast room. Children welcome, cot provided. Sorry, no pets. Car essential — ample parking adjoining the house. Terms on application with SAE, please, for Bed and Breakfast only. Reductions for children under 12.

RINGWOOD (New Forest). Mr and Mrs N. E. Thomas, "Carmel," Christchurch Road, Kingston, Ringwood BH24 3AX (Ringwood [042-54] 77703). Norman and Teresa Thomas, having catered for the public for some years and renowned for good food and friendly atmosphere, now welcome guests to their modern bungalow home. It is on the outer edge of the market town of Ringwood, within walking distance of the New Forest. The River Avon, with its walks and fishing, lies just down the lane beside the bungalow. Riding and golf nearby. Central places of interest such as Salisbury, Portsmouth, Corfe, eight miles from Christchurch/Bournemouth. Two large bedrooms (one double and one twin) with washbasins and shaver points. Comfortable guests' TV lounge/diner. Full central heating. Bed and Breakfast, with optional Evening Meal. Open all year. SAE for terms.

ROMSEY. Mrs J. Hayter, "Woodlands", Bunny Lane, Sherfield English, Romsey SO5 0FT (Whiteparish [07948] 223). Small family guest house situated close to New Forest. Places of interest nearby include Romsey Abbey — Broadlands — Beaulieu — Salisbury Cathedral and Isle of Wight Ferry. Ideal relaxing holiday, large garden with country views, lovely walks. Friendly family accommodation with family/double/twin bedrooms, with washbasins (one bedroom with toilet); also coffee/tea making facilities in all rooms. Lounge with colour TV. Bathroom/shower. Diningroom with separate tables. All good home cooking. Bed and Breakfast from £6.50; Bed, Breakfast and Evening Meal £8.50. Weekly terms: Bed and Breakfast, Evening Meal from £60. Reduced rates for children and Senior Citizens. Open January to November.

PLEASE SEND A STAMPED ADDRESSED ENVELOPE WITH ENQUIRIES

SOUTHAMPTON. Mr Brian Tillman (Mopley Farm Ltd.), Mopley Farm Countryside Activity Centre, Mopley Road, Blackfield, Southampton SO4 1YH (Fawley [0703] 891616). This is a small family-run Residential Centre situated in the middle of Cadland Estate on the coast bounded by Southampton Water and the Solent. On the edge of the New Forest, with its beautiful scenery, 15 miles from Southampton, within easy reach of London, the coast with its estuary and beaches, the Centre provides an ideal location for riding (DIY boxes available), walking, bird watching and windsurfing. Trout fishing, clay pigeon and game shooting by arrangement at extra cost. Many interesting places to visit within 10 miles of the Centre. Accommodation comprises four bedrooms; ample shower and toilet facilities; large lounge/diningroom with colour TV and Video. Central heating. Open all year. Children welcome. Sorry, no pets. Terms for Board — Overnight Bed and Breakfast from £8.05 to £9.20 (including VAT); weekly Full-Board from £64.40 to £96.60 (including VAT). Equipment available on hire.

STOCKBRIDGE. Mrs K. R. Harper, Gardener's Cottage, Nether Wallop, Stockbridge SO20 8HE (Andover [0264] 781217). Set at the top of a country lane, through a ford on edge of a very beautiful village. Two acres of garden and paddock, with sheep, bantams, cats, dogs and peacocks. Ten miles Salisbury, 14 Winchester, eight from Andover, Danebury Ring, Longstack Water, Meadows and Gardens, Stonehenge 20 minutes, Avebury Ring etc., Beaulieu, Broadlands, Romsey Abbey and King John's Hunting Lodge all within 20 minutes. The private house offers one twin and one twin family bedrooms, with washbasins; bathroom, two toilets; sittingroom and diningroom. Central heating. Children welcome. High chair and babysitting available. Pets permitted. Open all year. Car essential — parking. Bed and Breakfast from £9.75 per person. Half for children two to ten years.

WINCHESTER. Mrs Carol Brett, Stratton House, Stratton Road, St. Giles Hill, Winchester SO23 8JQ (Winchester [0962] 63919 or 64529). Stratton House is a lovely old Victorian house (circa 1890) set in an acre of grounds in an elevated position on St. Giles Hill which overlooks the city of Winchester and is only five-ten minutes' walk to the city centre. Single, double, twin-bedded and family rooms, many with private bathrooms or showers are available throughout the year. All rooms are centrally heated and have TV. We have a large courtyard for private parking and offer a free collection service from Winchester on arrival. A traditional English country home atmosphere prevails here and guests enjoy home cooking and personal service. Sittingroom; diningroom; three bathrooms, three toilets. Cot, babysitting by arrangement and reduced rates for children. Pets permitted. Evening Meal, Bed and Breakfast from £16 per night. Bed and Breakfast from £12 per night. (Reductions for children).

HELP IMPROVE
BRITISH TOURIST STANDARDS

You are choosing holiday accommodation from our very popular FARM HOLIDAY GUIDES. Whether it be a hotel, guest house, farmhouse or self-catering accommodation, we think you will find it hospitable, comfortable and clean, and your host and hostess friendly and helpful.

Why not write and tell us about it?

As a recognition of the generally well-run and excellent holiday accommodation reviewed in our publications, we at FARM HOLIDAY GUIDES LIMITED present a diploma to proprietors who receive the highest recommendation from their guests who are also readers of our Guides. If you care to write to us praising the holiday you have booked through FARM HOLIDAY GUIDES – whether this be board, self-catering accommodation, a sporting or a caravan holiday, the content of your letter will be evaluated and the proprietors who reach our final list will be contacted.

The winning proprietor will receive an attractive framed diploma to display on his premises as recognition of a high standard of comfort, amenity and hospitality. FARM HOLIDAY GUIDES LIMITED offer this diploma as a contribution towards the improvement of standards in tourist accommodation in Britain. Help your excellent host or hostess to win it!

DIPLOMA
AWARDED BY
READERS
of
FARM HOLIDAY GUIDE
PUBLICATIONS LIMITED

TO..
FOR HOLIDAY ACCOMMODATION
of the HIGHEST STANDARD

AT..

HEREFORD & WORCESTER

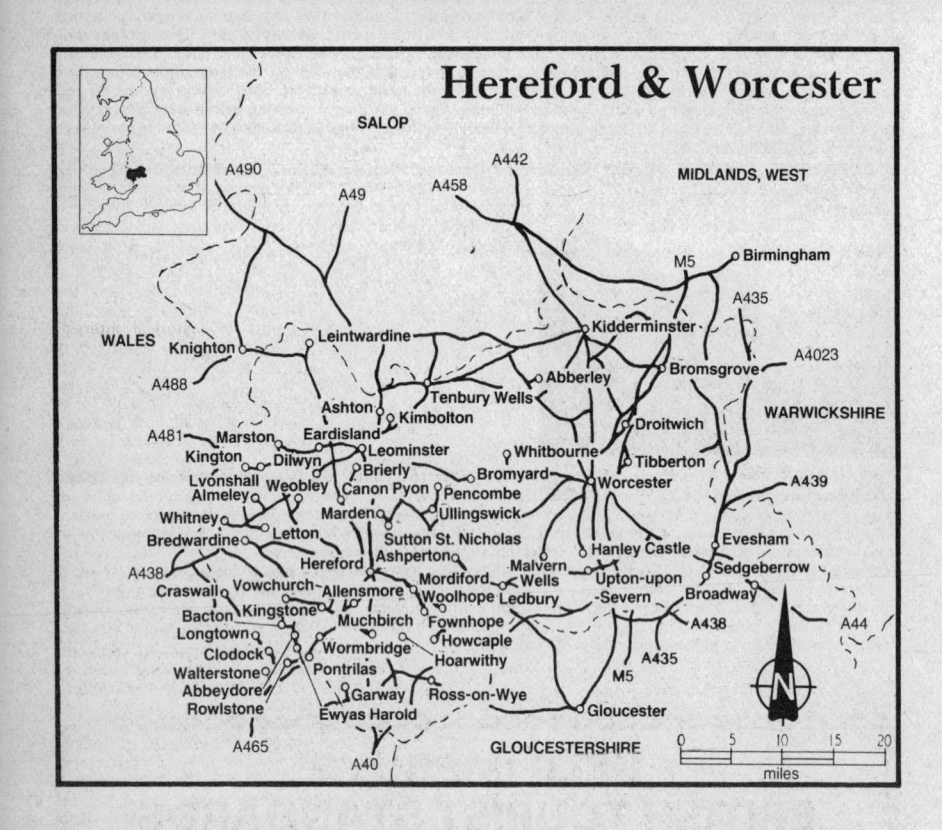

BROADWAY. Mrs Sylvia Riley, "Olive Branch" Guest House, 78 High Street, Broadway WR12 7AJ (Broadway [0386] 853440). This attractive village of Broadway is one of the loveliest places in the Cotswolds and has remained completely unspoiled. This guest house, dating back to the 16th century, is conveniently situated, close to the centre of the village which is well provided with places to eat out, ranging from tea rooms to a four star hotel. Combining modern amenities with old world charm, the house has four double (two en-suite rooms), two family and two single bedrooms, all with hot and cold water; diningroom, separate lounge; TV; shower, toilets. Parking for 8 cars. Cot available. Fire Certificate held. Six miles to Evesham, 10 to Bourton-on-the-Water, 15 to Stratford-on-Avon, 16 to Cheltenham. Open all year except Christmas. Owners' adjacent antique shop is available to browse around in or out of shop hours. SAE, please, for terms for Bed and Breakfast. AA/RAC listed.

BROMYARD near. Mrs J. Keenan, Paunceford Court, Much Cowarne, Near Bromyard HR7 4JQ (Hereford [0432] 820208). Working farm. Paunceford Court is a large country house situated in nice gardens. The house dates back to the 11th century and was the home of De Pauncefort, one of William the Conqueror's knights. Situated beside the lovely 13th century church, St. Mary's with its listed Norman Bell Tower, Paunceford Court makes an ideal centre for travelling to Ledbury, Bromyard, Hereford, Worcester and the Malvern Hills, while Gloucester, Ludlow, Hay etc. are all within an easy hour's drive. Children are welcome, cot, high chair, babysitting and reduced rates. Regret no pets. Open all year. Two double rooms, one with washbasin; bathroom, two toilets; sittingroom; diningroom. Car essential, parking ample. Evening Meal, Bed and Breakfast daily from £11, weekly from £73.50; Bed and Breakfast from £7 daily, £45.50 weekly.

DROITWICH near. Mrs Joyce Ulyet, Valley Farm, Hanbury, Near Bromsgrove (Hanbury [052-784] 678). A lovely old farmhouse dating from the 16th century, sympathetically restored and modernised with a wealth of old beams and a superb inglenook fireplace in the diningroom. Well situated, only ten minutes from M5, and an ideal centre for Stratford, Warwick, Warwick and the Cotswolds and Malverns. Traditional English cooking and fresh home produced farm produce. Two double-bedded rooms and one twin-bedded room, with additional single bed or cot available; excellent toilet facilities; comfortable lounge. Children welcome at reduced rates. Open all year. Bed and Breakfast; optional Evening Meal. SAE for terms.

PLEASE SEND A STAMPED ADDRESSED ENVELOPE WITH ENQUIRIES

DROITWICH. Mr M. F. Howard, Upper Goosehill Farm, Hanbury, Droitwich, Worcester (Himbleton [090-569] 270). Working farm. Luxuriously appointed 15th century farmhouse on 300-acre mixed farm with large area of woodland; good walks. One acre fishing lake. Hunting and shooting in season, by arrangement. Own horses welcome; good stabling. Worcester six miles, with theatre, porcelain works, county cricket, riverside race course and many places of historic interest. Stratford-on-Avon 14 miles. Warwick Castle and Welsh border within easy reach. One double and one single bedrooms, also two family rooms with washbasins. Two bathrooms, two toilets; sittingroom and diningroom. Cot, high chair, babysitting and reduced rates for children. Pets allowed. Open all year. Car essential; ample parking. Near B4090, just off A38. Bed and Breakfast from £9; Evening Meals by arrangement.

EVESHAM. Mrs Jane Green, Beechgrove House, Haselor Lane, Evesham (Evesham [0386] 860220). Situated half-a-mile off the A44 Evesham to Pershore Road with views of both Bredon Hills and the Cotswolds, this house is surrounded by farmland. Evesham and Pershore have many points of historical interest; Broadway and the Cotswolds five miles away. Stratford 14 miles. Children are welcome and there are facilities for table tennis, croquet and darts, etc. Large garden. Dogs by arrangement only. Cooking a speciality, local produce, eggs and home-baked bread. One double room with twin beds and washbasin, shaver point; family room with twin beds for two, folding bed if required, with private bathroom, shaver point; single room with washbasin and shaver point; two bathrooms, four toilets. Colour TV; sittingroom, diningroom. Solid fuel central heating and open fires. Open all year round. Car essential — good parking. Evening Meal, Bed and Breakfast from £11; Bed and Breakfast from £7. Reduced rates for children under 12.

EVESHAM. Mrs M. Alloway, Sedgeberrow House, Winchcombe Road, Sedgeberrow, Near Evesham WR11 6UD (Evesham [0386] 881310). Four miles south of Evesham, a fine old residence set in the Vale of Evesham, only minutes from the North Cotswolds, recently converted as a guest house, carefully retaining its character and restful atmosphere. Large airy rooms. Fine views of farmland stretching to Bredon Hill. Easy drive to Stratford, Cheltenham. Comfortable divan beds, close carpeting, easy chairs. Two guest bathrooms, toilets and showers. Delightful large garden. Central heating, colour television in guests' lounge, pay-telephone, ample private parking. From £9.50 (high season) for Bed and Full English Breakfast. Good, reasonably priced Evening Meals by arrangement, with local fresh vegetables and fruit. Lower weekly terms. Children (five to 12) sharing parents' room half price. Substantial reductions out of season. 'Phone or write for terms and vacancies.

FOWNHOPE. Mrs Mary Blake, Scotland Cottage, Common Hill, Fownhope HR1 4QA (Fownhope [043-277] 453). Working farm. A three-acre small farm, one mile from Fownhope, seven from Hereford, 11 from Ross-on-Wye, overlooking scenic National Trust woods. Ideal walking countryside. This three double-bedded, centrally heated house has two bathrooms; lounge (TV); diningroom; sun lounge. Play area on large lawn for children. Sorry, no pets. Babysitting available. Pedigree Jersey cow provides milk, butter and cream. Hand-milking and butter making can be observed. Bees produce pure Herefordshire honey. Food is home-produced country fare, home-baked desserts (some Canadian) a speciality. Coarse fishing, rough shooting, horse riding, golf, tennis or squash can be arranged locally. Open all year for Dinner, Bed and Breakfast. Special Christmas menu and programme. Rates on application. Reduced rates for children and Senior Citizens.

HEREFORD & WORCESTERSHIRE – THE HEART OF ENGLAND!

A beautiful county which includes The Vale of Evesham and the rugged – if petite – Malvern Hills. It has been designated an "Area of Outstanding Beauty". Places of interest include The Avoncroft Museum of Buildings, Brockhampton, Ross-on-Wye, The Teme Valley and The Hereford & Worcester County Museum.

**HEREFORD. Mrs L. M. Powell, Parsonage Farm, Walterstone, Hereford (Crucorney [087-382] 341).
Working farm.** Parsonage Farm is situated in the heart of the country with some of the most glorious views one could ever wish to see and many rambles down country lanes for you to enjoy. Many of the activities on the farm should both educate and amuse adults and children alike. Pony trekking and mountain climbing close at hand. Excellent country food (four-course Evening Meal). One family and three double bedrooms (two with washbasins); bathroom, toilets; sitting/diningroom with separate tables. Cot, high chair and babysitting available, plus ponies for children to ride. Pets allowed. Open all year except Christmas and New Year. Suitable for the disabled. Car essential. Evening Dinner, Bed and Breakfast or Bed and Breakfast only. Reductions for children and Senior Citizens. SAE, please.

THE FALCON, HOW CAPLE, HEREFORD HR1 4TF

Stonebuilt farmhouse standing in four acres of ground on the B4224 road, six miles from Ross-on-Wye, nine miles Hereford and eight from Ledbury. Central for touring Wye Valley and Malvern Hills. Local golf course and fishing available. Two double and one family bedroom all with washbasins. Bathroom, shower room, two toilets; sittingroom and diningroom. Playroom for children. Pets welcome. Car essential, plenty of parking.

Write or telephone for details. Mrs M. Kennedy – (098-986) 223.

HEREFORD. Mrs Mary Moore, Poole Guest House, Much Dewchurch, Hereford HR2 8DL (Golden Valley [0981] 540291). A warm welcome awaits you at this centrally heated, comfortably furnished Georgian House, standing in own pleasant grounds — nine hole Putting Course on lawn. Ample parking for the essential cars. Situated on the edge of the village. Two miles from the Norman Church at Kilpeck. Central for touring the Wye Valley and mid-Wales. Scenic views from all six bedrooms, five with hot and cold. Stairlift. Three ground floor double bedrooms, one with shower. Comfortable lounge with colour TV. Diningroom where appetising home cooking is served, with home produced vegetables. Mid-week bookings accepted. Open all year round for Evening Dinner and Bed and Breakfast — refreshment tray in bedroom if required. Fire precautions installed. Stamp for brochure, or telephone — evenings.

HEREFORD. Mrs G. C. Andrews, Webton Court, Kingstone, Hereford HR2 9NF (Golden Valley [0981] 250220). Working farm. Webton Court is a Georgian Black and White Farmhouse situated in open country in the heart of beautiful Wye Valley amidst green fields. This is ideal touring country at any time of the year. It would be difficult to find lovelier scenery than round Symonds Yat, Forest of Dean, Chepstow and the Severn Bridge or to the west to the rugged Welsh Mountains. Malvern and Stratford-on-Avon also offer peace and tranquillity. There is accommodation in three double, one single and two family bedrooms all with washbasins; two bathrooms, five toilets; sittingroom; diningroom. Children are welcome, cot, high chair and babysitting. Pets welcome. Open all year with electric heating. Home plain cooking made with fresh garden and farm produce. Roasts of all meats are enjoyed. Early morning tea. Children under ten and Senior Citizens are welcome at reduced rates. Horse riding available in local woods and countryside. Riding lessons, etc. Full Board, Evening Dinner, Bed and Breakfast or Bed and Breakfast only. Fire Certificate granted. Terms on application.

HEREFORD. Mrs Catherine B. Smith, Tremorithic, Bacton, Hereford HR2 0AU (Golden Valley [0981] 240291). Working farm. Have a peaceful away from it all holiday in a 17th century farmhouse offering good home cooking and comfortable accommodation. The house enjoys panoramic views of the Black Mountains and is easily accessible to the Brecon Beacons, Wales and the many beauty spots of the Wye Valley. Open from April to October there are two double and one single bedrooms; bathroom, toilet; sitting/diningroom. Children welcome, cot, high chair and babysitting provided. Pets by arrangement. Car essential — parking. Evening Meal, Bed and Breakfast from £65 per week; Bed and Breakfast from £6 to £8 per night per person including bedtime drinks. Evening Meal from £2.50. Reduced rates for children by arrangement.

THE BOWENS FARMHOUSE
COUNTRY GUEST HOUSE
Fownhope, Nr. Hereford

Tourist Board Recommended   *Recommended by Arthur Eperon*   *AA Listed*
Resident owner: Carol Hart   *Residential Licence*

Peacefully situated in glorious unspoilt countryside, part of the "Wye Valley area of outstanding natural beauty", this charming renovated farmhouse is the perfect place for a relaxing country holiday. Set in an acre of delightful grounds. "THE BOWENS" offers the discerning visitor all the comforts and modern amenities required while retaining the country house atmosphere. All rooms are tastefully decorated and furnished with many period pieces. The oak beamed sittingroom has a large inglenook fireplace — log fires in season — colour TV and views over the garden. The attractive diningroom, where guests can enjoy good, home cooked meals using fresh local meat and own produce when available, also overlooks the garden. There are 10 bedrooms, 5 with private baths or showers, others with showers and vanitory units. All have shaver points, central heating, divan beds with duvets and tea/coffee making facilities. 2 public bathrooms with toilets. Scenic views from all rooms. High standard of comfort and personal service. Featured on BBC "Holiday" programme 1982. Marvellous walking/touring area, with numerous Norman border castles and churches, Roman remains, historic houses, picturesque black and white villages and towns. Cathedral cities of Hereford, Gloucester and Worcester. Golf and fishing by arrangement. Also for the not so energetic we have a putting green and other lawn games for Summer evenings. Ample sporting facilities in surrounding area. Regret not suitable for children under 10 or pets. Ample parking. Fire certificate. Open February-December inclusive. High Season Dinner, Bed and Breakfast from £125 per person per week including VAT. Bed and Breakfast from £82 per person per week. Daily terms available. Bargain Breaks from 17th September 85 — 1st April 86, £35 for any two days. Stamp for brochure and tariff.

Tel. Fownhope 430 (STD 043277)

Cordon bleu dinners by candlelight in 17th century Country House.

"The Steppes"

B.T.A. Commendation Award, Good Hotel Guide, Ashley Courtenay, Farm Holiday Guide Readers Diploma, A.A., Recommended by leading travel writers, Member of English Tourist Board and Heart of England Tourist Board.
Featured on Central Television, January 1983.

"The Steppes" is a delightful old country house set in 1½ acres of grounds and situated in the glorious Wye Valley.

This characterful house retains its historic features, including exposed beams throughout and a grand inglenook fireplace in the dining room, yet it has been sympathetically modernised to provide for all year round comfort, including full central heating. Log fires are lit during the colder months. All bedrooms are furnished to a high standard, including en suite facilities, clock/radio, colour television and tea & coffee making facilities.

Unsolicited praise from previous guests has established "The Steppes" as a gourmet's paradise, with the emphasis on originality of menu and interesting English and Continental dishes. "The Steppes" is licensed and a full range of aperitifs and fine wines is always available. Older children are welcome. Prices including Breakfast, Dinner and en-suite room from £24.00 per person per night.

"The Steppes" is open all year round and we are pleased to offer "Winter Bargain Break" terms.

The area offers the quiet timelessness of the English countryside at its finest and is ideal for the walker being within easy reach of the Malvern Hills and Black Mountains. Here too are grand old houses and castles, picturesque Tudor villages, markets and antique shops.

For colour brochure SAE or telephone: **Mrs Tricia Howland, "The Steppes," Ullingswick, Herefordshire.**
Tel. Burley Gate (0432 78) 424 or Hereford (0432) 820424

212   Hereford & Worcester   BOARD

HEREFORD. Mrs Jean Phillips, Wilton Oaks, Tarrington, Hereford HR1 4ET (Tarrington [043279] 212). Working farm. Wilton Oaks is set in beautiful gardens surrounded by 30 acres of grounds. It has magnificent views over the majestic Malvern Hills and is a short drive away from the historical City of Hereford and the picturesque town of Ledbury. The house is comfortably furnished with full central heating. There are two double rooms available and one twin-bedded room with tea and coffee making facilities provided in the bedrooms, which also have their own vanity units. There is a guest bathroom and toilet available. Additionally, there is also a dining room and separate lounge with colour TV. Bed and Breakfast is provided with Evening Meal by arrangement. Ample car parking space available. Sorry, no pets.

RELAX AT ORCHARD FARM

AA LISTED

A dairy farm with attractive 18th-century house peacefully situated with lovely views. Explore the picturesque local villages or visit Hereford, 4½ miles away. Ideal for touring Wye Valley and central Wales. Three double rooms, one single with washbasins, heaters and tea-making facilities. Two sitting rooms, colour TV, dining room. Excellent food using local produce. Tourist Board Approved. Licensed. Fishing. Children welcome, pets permitted. Bed and Breakfast from £8. Evening Meal from £4.50. Bargain Breaks November to April — Two Days £24. Stamp for brochure to:

Mrs Marjorie Barrell, Orchard Farm, Mordiford, Hereford. Phone Holme Lacy (0432 73) 253.

HEREFORD near. Mrs M. A. Barker, Apple Tree Cottage, Mansel Lacy, Near Hereford HR4 7HH (Bridge Sollars [098-122] 688). This delightful 16th century cottage is situated in a charming little hamlet amidst some of the loveliest countryside in England. Very quiet and peaceful making it ideal for country lovers, birdwatchers and walkers, yet within easy touring distance of the Black Mountains and the Cotswolds. Golf and historical sites nearby. Guests enjoy comfortable accommodation, and a friendly atmosphere prevails. One double and two twin-bedded rooms with tea making facilities. Guests' bathroom. Use of lounge and TV in evenings. Excellent home cooking served using fresh garden produce. English country Breakfast and optional Evening Meal. Children and pets welcome. Car essential; parking. Bed and Breakfast from £8.50. Terms on application for Evening Dinner/Meal. Seven miles NW of Hereford City off the A480.

HEREFORD near. Mrs Mabel C. James, New House, Llanveynoe, Longtown, Near Hereford HR2 0LQ (Longtown Castle [087-387] 210). This accommodation is on a smallholding of ten acres and is surrounded by quiet countryside near the Black Mountains and Offa's Dyke Path. Many rare birds and wild flowers to be seen; pony trekking nearby; many places of interest to visit including Brecon Beacons National Park. A warm welcome and excellent farmhouse fare awaits you all year round. There are two double and two single bedrooms; bathroom, toilet; sittingroom, diningroom. Children are welcome, cot and babysitting (by arrangement) provided. Rates are reduced for children under 10 years old. Dogs permitted. SAE for terms for Evening Dinner, Bed and Breakfast or Bed and Breakfast only.

HEREFORD near. Misses N. L. and M. S. Stoakes, Blacklands Farm, Canon Frome, Ledbury, Near Hereford HR8 2TB (Trumpet [053-183] 493). Working farm. Blacklands is a small, rural farm with a delightful cottage style farmhouse six miles from the picturesque town of Ledbury. A perfect situation for touring the Wye Valley, Malvern Hills, Worcester, Hereford, Ross-on-Wye and the Welsh borders. Car essential, ample free parking. Comfort and plenty of good food, and accommodation in two double rooms with washbasins, one family and one single rooms; bathroom, toilet; sittingroom with colour TV; diningroom. Children welcome at reduced rates — cot, high chair and babysitting. Dogs welcome if they sleep in car. Open January to December for Evening Meal/Dinner, Bed and Breakfast from £55 to £58 per week; £10 to £12 nightly; Bed and Breakfast from £45 to £48 per week; £7 to £8 nightly. SAE, please, for prompt reply.

WORCESTERSHIRE FARM AND COUNTRY HOLIDAYS

THE ENGLISH VALES

Lower Doddenhill Farm, Newnham Bridge, Tenbury Wells. (Mrs Joan Adams, Tel No: [058479] 223)
Comfortable 17th Century red brick and timbered farmhouse, sympathetically restored and set in 220 acres of undulating farmland, having uninterrupted views across the Teme Valley. AA listed. B & B from £7.50.

Caldewell, Pershore Road, Stoulton, Worcester. (Mrs Sheila Booth and Mrs Adrienne Leslie Tel No: [0905] 840894)
Spacious Georgian listed building, 6 miles Worcester, 3 miles M5. Easy reach Stratford, Cotswolds, Malvern. Private lake, railway, friendly farm animals. Excellent facilities for children.

Old House Farm, Tibberton, Droitwich. (Mrs Pat Chilman Tel No: [090565] 247)
Family run dairy farm 1 mile from M5 junction 6, in the peaceful village of Tibberton, large garden with lovely views of Malvern Hills. Ideal touring centre.

Little Lodge Farm, Broughton Green, Hanbury, Droitwich. (Mrs Jackie Chugg, Tel No: [052784] 305)
17th Century black and white farmhouse in superb secluded position. Prettily decorated bedrooms. Warm hospitality. Home cooking. Ideal overnight stop on route north/west country.

Phepson Farm, Himbleton, Droitwich. (Mrs Tricia Havard Tel No: [090569] 205)
Break your journey or have a real farm holiday in comfortable, peaceful surroundings. Handy for M5. B & B from £8. EM by arrangement. Brochure on request.

Trench Farm, Dunhampstead, Droitwich. (Mrs Gwen Jackson, Tel No: [090569] 234)
A comfortable farmhouse in beautiful surroundings. 4 miles M5 motorway. Double room and family room. Children welcome. Excellent food also available locally. Brochure on request. B & B from £7.50.

"Harlington", Pershore Lane, Martin Hussingtree. (Mrs Josie Lane Tel No: [0905] 52354)
Modern bungalow with smallholding on A4538. One mile from M5 motorway, ½ mile from A38. Full English breakfast. Ideal centre for touring Worcester, Malvern, Evesham, Pershore, Cotswolds, Stratford-on-Avon.

Leigh Court, Nr Worcester. (Mrs Sally Stewart Tel No: [0886] 32275)
Friendly comfortable modernised 16th century manor house beside River Teme on sheep/arable farm. Personal service. Excellent food. Fishing. Touring centre. French spoken. Worcester/Malvern 5 miles.

The Hill, Leigh. (Mrs Shirley Lewis Tel No: [0886] 32211)
A picturesque 16th century black and white farmhouse on a working farm with hops, soft fruits and poultry. Worcester 4 miles. Malvern 5 miles. Home produce whenever possible.

The Church House, Shelsley Beauchamp, Worcester. (Mrs Gill Moore Tel No: [08865] 393)
A family run farm with 18th Century farmhouse situated on River Teme. We have sheep, cattle and poultry. Farmhouse food served. Easy reach of Cotswolds and Welsh border.

Middle Woodston, Lindridge, Tenbury Wells. (Mrs Jean May Tel No: [058470] 244)
Comfortable farmhouse on a 10-acre small holding, ½ mile from the road. Meat and vegetables home grown, also home baked bread. Log fires, wash basins in bedrooms. AA listed.

Fir Tree Farm, Fairfield, Bromsgrove. (Mrs Joan McKay Tel No: [0527] 72329)
Tastefully modernised farmhouse on 5-acre small holding in peaceful village, 3 miles from Bromsgrove town. Easy access M5. Excellent bedroom accommodation, separate dining/sitting room.

Manor Farm, Broughton Hackett, Nr Crowle. (Mrs Hilary Morgan Tel No: [090560] 252)
3 miles from M5. Friendly comfortable red brick, timbered farmhouse, with attractive garden. Within peaceful village of Broughton Hackett. Convenient for Worcester, Stratford, The Malverns.

Church Farm, Abberley, Nr Worcester. (Mr & Mrs S. Neath Tel No: [029921] 316)
Victorian farmhouse on arable and beef farm in beautiful countryside. Warm welcome ensured. Good touring base. Children welcome. Wash hand basins. Visitors bathroom. Morning and bedtime drinks.

Eastfield Farm, Kempsey, Nr Worcester. (Mrs Rosemary Prosser Tel No: [0905] 820584)
Comfortable accommodation on dairy farm 4 miles south of Worcester. Easy access M5. Family and twin rooms with H & C. B & B £7.50. Reductions children. Dogs accepted.

Church Farm Holding, Castle Morton, Malvern. (Mrs Sue Rimell Tel No: [068 481] 352)
88-acre dairy farm lying under Malvern Hills, lovely views. Newly decorated farmhouse, visitors lounge/TV. Large farmhouse breakfast. Dogs accommodated.

Moorend Court, Mathon, Nr Malvern. (Mrs S. Williams MHCIA Tel No: [088684] 205)
Magnificent 16th Century country house. Beautiful grounds, trees, wildlife, panoramic views to Elgar's Malvern Hills. Accent high on old English traditions. AA Ashley Courtenay. Cordon Bleu cuisine.

FOR SELF CATERING ACCOMMODATION PLEASE SEE
'WORCESTERSHIRE FARM AND COUNTRY HOLIDAY'
ADVERT IN SELF CATERING SECTION.

FOR GROUP BROCHURE WITH FULL DETAILS SEND 9" × 4"
SAE TO MRS P. HAVARD, PHEPSON FARM, HIMBLETON,
DROITWICH, WORCESTERSHIRE. TEL. (090569) 205.

Hereford Farm and Country Holidays

FARMHOUSE ACCOMMODATION

WEBTON COURT FARMHOUSE, KINGSTONE (Mrs Andrews [0981] 250220)
Attractive Georgian house in quiet and peaceful surroundings. H/C in all rooms, home produce, baking, local food B/B. EM AA listed.

ORCHARD FARM, MORDIFORD (Mrs M. J. Barrell [0432 73] 253)
Dairy farm with attractive stone built farmhouse, lovely views, peaceful surroundings, BB. EM licensed. AA listed B & B from £8.

GREAT HOUSE FARM, STOKE PRIOR (Mrs S. Bemand [056882] 663)
17th century farmhouse on 750 acre family farm. Friendly service and good cooking. Lounge, dining room, TV and tennis court.

HAYNALL VILLA, LITTLE HEREFORD, LUDLOW (Mrs Rachel Edwards [058472] 589)
Comfortable old farmhouse on family run mixed farm. Ideal for touring Shropshire, Herefordshire, Worcester and Welsh Borders. Farmhouse food. Home grown vegetables.

NEW HOUSE FARM, DILWYN (Mrs Farndon [0544] 318289)
In a quiet unspoiled Tudor village. Surrounded by lawns and flower beds. Excellent base for touring Black Mountains, Elan and Wye Valleys.

THE ELMS, EARDISLAND, LEOMINSTER (Mrs Mary Johnson [05447] 405)
Small working farm, high standard. 100 yds back from A44. In one of England's most beautiful villages. AA listed. A NO SMOKING house.

THE FALCON, HOW CAPLE (Mrs Kennedy [098986] 223)
Farmhouse on B4224 road. Central to Malvern and a Wye Valley walk. TV lounge. Wash basins. Tea makers. Games room and fishing available.

RATEFIELD FARM, KIMBOLTON, LEOMINSTER (Mrs E. M. Mears [0568] 2507)
Sheep and beef farm in parkland setting. Lots of animals. Nature trail. Home produce, home made bread, local food. B & B and E.M.

STRETFORDBURY, STEENS BRIDGE, LEOMINSTER (Mrs Moore [056882] 239)
Traditional farmhouse amid beautiful scenery offering excellent accommodation and superb food, suitable as a base for discovering Herefordshire and its surroundings.

WILTON OAKS, TARRINGTON (Mrs J. Phillips [043 279] 212)
Comfortably furnished vanity units in bedrooms, good food, lovely views, very peaceful gardens. Between Hereford and Ledbury, ½ mile off A438 road.

GRANGE FARM, NEWCASTLE, MONMOUTH (Solveig Preece [0600] 2636)
Small stock rearing farm, peacefully situated near the border town of Monmouth within easy reach of South Wales.

DINEDOR COURT, Near HOLME LACY (Rosemary Price [0432 73] 481)
Enjoy the relaxing atmosphere of this 16th Century farmhouse only 3 miles from Hereford beside the river Wye. Children and pets welcome. B & B from £8.00. EM £5.

Ring farm of your choice or for group brochure giving full details send 9" × 4" SAE to:

**Mrs Avril Farndon, Newhouse Farm, Dilwyn, Hereford.
Tel. No. Weobley (0544) 318289.**

HEREFORD. Mrs M. Watkins, Hunt House Farm, Clodock, Hereford (Longtown Castle [087-387] 249). Working farm. Hunt House is on the border of Wales and the Black Mountains area, which includes Brecon Beacons National Park; within easy reach of the Wye Valley and the Forest of Dean. The house, on 150 acres, makes an ideal centre for touring; riding; trekking; fishing and plenty of hill climbing in the area. Beautiful walks around the countryside. Excellent farmhouse. Two double and two single bedrooms; two bathrooms, two toilets; sitting/diningroom. Children over three welcome, babysitting provided. Pets allowed. Car essential — unlimited parking. Open March to November for Evening Dinner, Bed and Breakfast or Bed and Breakfast. Reductions for children. SAE for terms.

HEREFORD. Mrs C. L. McKay, Todd's Hole Cottage, How Caple, Hereford HR1 4TF (How Caple [098-986] 662). Todd's Hole is a lovely 17th century cottage with a charming three-quarters of an acre of garden. Surrounded by beautiful countryside, it is six miles from Ross-on-Wye and nine from Hereford on the B4224. An excellent touring centre it is only a mile from the Wye and has many lovely views and good walking in the pleasant hill country around. Open all year, the house has one double and one single bedrooms (single downstairs); bathroom, toilet; sittingroom, diningroom. A car is needed here and parking is available. No pets. Children welcome at reduced rates and babysitting offered. Bed and Breakfast — Evening Meal by arrangement.

HEREFORDSHIRE. Hereford Farm and Country Holidays. Ring the farm of your choice or send for brochure giving full details of farmhouse accommodation. See also Display Advertisement in the Board Section of this Guide.

KINGTON. Mrs Pat Griffiths, The Beacon, Bradnor Hill, Kington HR5 3RE (Kington [0544] 230182). The Beacon, set in the picturesque countryside of the Herefordshire/Welsh border, is situated high above the little market town of Kington with wonderful views of surrounding hills — Malverns to the east, Black Mountains to the south. Excellent walks; ideal for naturalists; surrounded by National Trust land; 50 yards from the clubhouse of Kington's 18-hole golf course, highest in England and Wales. Spacious, comfortable lounge with colour TV. Bedrooms (double, twin-bedded, family, single) all with washbasins; own toilet and showers. Bed and Breakfast £9 per night; Dinner, Bed and Breakfast £14. Stay for seven nights, we charge for six giving one night and dinner free per person. A wide and varied menu provided, home cooking prepared to highest standard. Car park. Send or 'phone for brochure. Open all year.

KINGTON. Mrs E. E. Protheroe, Bucks Head House, School Farm, Hergest, Kington HR5 3EW (Kington [0544] 231063). Working farm. Newly modernised farmhouse on 290-acre mixed farm which has been worked by the Protheroe Family since 1940 and carries cattle, sheep and crops. Wye Valley, Black Mountains, Elan Valley, Ludlow, Hereford Cathedral, Black and White villages, all within easy reach. Two double, two single, two family bedrooms, with washbasins; two bathrooms, two showers, four toilets; two sittingrooms; diningroom. Cot, high chair and reduced rates for children; babysitting by arrangement. Guests return year after year. Pets free of charge, by arrangement only. Car essential; parking. Central heating. Peaceful walks around the farm and its sheep walk "Hergest Ridge". Evening Dinner/Meal, Bed and Breakfast or Bed and Breakfast only. Eight-berth mobile home also available. AA listed.

LEDBURY. Ms Jane West, Church Farm, Coddington, Ledbury HR8 1JJ (Bosbury [053-186] 271). Working farm. This is a dairy farm with a Black and White 16th century listed farmhouse, close to the Malvern Hills. It is ideal for touring. Warm hospitality assured. There is accommodation in two double and one single bedrooms; bathroom, toilet; sittingroom; diningroom. Children are welcome (reduced rates under 10 years), cot and babysitting provided. Plenty of good English fare, everything home-made wherever possible. Log fires, television, pets allowed. Open all year. Bedtime drink included. Car essential, parking. Situated midway between Ross-on-Wye, Hereford, Gloucester and Worcester. SAE, please, for full details.

LEDBURY. D. J. and J. M. Peirce, Wall Hills Farm, Ledbury HR8 2PR (0531-2681). Working farm. Wall Hills Farm is situated on the A438 Ledbury to Hereford Road. One mile from the market town of Ledbury, with easy access to M50. The farmhouse is approached by a long private drive. The house is a modernised Georgian house with four guest bedrooms: one single, two doubles, with washbasins, one twin room; two bathrooms. Residents' lounge with TV, and diningroom. Car essential. The farm specialises in cattle and sheep. The surrounding area is not only famous for its unspoilt scenery but also for the many places of interest and beauty. Open April to October for Bed and Breakfast (full English Breakfast), Bed, Breakfast and Evening Meal by arrangement.

When you have read one you *haven't* read them all — we have *eleven* other publications

LEDBURY. Mrs Janet Griffiths, Gazerdine House, Munsley, Ledbury HR8 2PZ (Trumpet [053183] 298). Gazerdine House is an outstanding Georgian residence set in spacious grounds with hard tennis court and paddocks grazing sheep and horses. Bedrooms have tea/coffee making facilities, washbasins and lovely views to the Malvern Hills. Guests have use of their own sittingroom with log fire in season. Ledbury is three miles away and Gazerdine is the ideal touring base for Forest of Dean, Wye Valley, Stratford and Welsh Borders. Golf and fishing arranged. Excellent local facilities. Personal family service and elegant comfortable surroundings ensure many guests return again to Gazerdine. Children welcome, cot and babysitting. Bed and Breakfast from £9, weekly terms from £60. Evening Meal optional with good choice of local pubs providing food. Reduced rates for children.

LEOMINSTER. Mrs Ramona Thomas, 100 Bargates, Leominster HR6 8QT (Leominster [0568] 2226). Reached by car, train, bus, bike. Newly-established Bed and Breakfast with comfortable accommodation/friendly atmosphere in Edwardian town-house. Central heating and colour TV. Plentiful breakfast/choice of menu; pretty garden to relax in afterwards. Ideally situated for exploring English/Welsh borderlands or beyond. Castles and ancient churches of the Marches; Cathedral cities; historic towns; Shakespeare country; Welsh hills and Black Mountains; all within easy reach. Open all year round. £6.50 to £8.50 per person (depending on menu); reduction for over three nights. WE AIM TO HAVE YOU ENJOY YOUR STAY. Visitors' Book is our recommendation.

LEOMINSTER. Mrs Pauline Edwards, Stocklow Manor Farm, Staunton-on-Arrow, Pembridge, Leominster HR6 9HT (Pembridge [054-47] 436). Working farm. Delightful countryside surrounds this 350-acre mixed farm which is worked by the Edwards family. Situated near the Welsh borders it is an ideal base for touring the many places of interest. Pembridge with its historic inns three miles, Leominster 11 and Hereford 17 miles. The house is mentioned in the Royal Commission of Historical Monuments Records which note that part of it is late 17th or early 18th century. Overlooking a pretty garden with lawns, shrubs, rose borders and beyond to a large pool with wild fowl, the accommodation consists of two double, one family bedrooms (two with washbasins); bathroom, separate shower, toilet; sittingroom, diningroom; TV; fitted carpets throughout; interior spring mattresses; shaver points. Sorry, no pets. Children welcome at reduced rates. Cot available. Jacko, the donkey, will amuse the young guests. Coarse fishing on the farm. Car essential, ample parking. Evening Dinner, Bed and Breakfast or Bed and Breakfast only. SAE, please, for brochure and terms. Registered with the English Tourist Board.

LEOMINSTER near. Mr and Mrs M. G. B. Warren, Humber Grange Country Guest House, Humber, Stoke Prior, Near Leominster HR6 0NE (Steens Bridge [056-882] 224). "Humber Grange", a beautiful stone built country house, in five acres of private grounds, ideal for all who love and appreciate country life. Individual attention to all guests. Trains and buses meet at Hereford and Leominster stations. Ample free parking. Grass tennis court and trout stream in grounds, free of charge to guests. Three of the five double bedrooms are family size, and there are two singles (four rooms with washbasins). Full central heating. Ponies, dogs and assorted farm animals usually kept. Fire Certificate held. Children minded in the evenings. Colour TV (22 inch) in drawingroom, separate diningroom. Own milk, eggs and kitchen garden produce in season. Terms; Room, Breakfast and Evening Dinner from £70 each weekly (£10 per day); Room and Breakfast from £7 each per night. Reductions for children. No VAT or Service Charge. Brochure on request. SAE.

LEOMINSTER. Mrs Evelyn Mears, Ratefield Farm, Kimbolton, Leominster HR6 0JB (Leominster [0568] 2507). Working farm. Ratefield Farm, once a deer park, laid out by Capability Brown, stands secluded three miles north of Leominster. Ideal for touring Malverns, Welsh Borders, Black Mountains and historical towns of Hereford, Worcester, Ross, Shrewsbury, Ludlow and Ironbridge. Walking, fishing, riding and golf. The farm (beef and sheep) is 40 acres run on traditional lines and has lots of animals. Two double bedrooms, one single and one family rooms, most with H&C and all with tea-making facilities; two bathrooms, sittingroom, diningroom. Children welcome at reduced rates. Cot, high chair, babysitting offered. Dogs by arrangement. Car essential. Ample parking. Open all year for Evening Meal, Bed and Breakfast or Bed and Breakfast. Terms on request.

PLEASE SEND A STAMPED ADDRESSED ENVELOPE WITH ENQUIRIES

LEOMINSTER near. Mrs M. E. Pryce, Brick House Farm, Brierley, Near Leominster HR6 0NT (Leominster [0568] 2719). Guests are assured of a good night's rest at Brick House Farm in the comfortable two double and two family bedrooms. Two of the rooms have washbasins. There is a sittingroom and diningroom where Mrs Pryce serves a good breakfast. Children are welcome and a cot and babysitting are provided. No pets. A car is essential, parking space. The farm is half-a-mile off the A49 and is situated in a secluded hollow where you can enjoy the refreshment of natural surroundings. A short climb gives a view of several counties and Welsh mountains. Open from Easter to October for Bed and Breakfast. Leominster two miles away. Reduced rates for children if sharing parents' room. Terms on request.

LONGTOWN. Mrs I. Pritchard, Olchon Cottage Farm, Longtown, Hereford HR2 0NS (Longtown Castle [087-387] 233). Working farm. An ideal location for a peaceful holiday in lovely walking country close to Offa's Dyke path and Welsh border. A smallholding of 28 acres mostly sheep and cattle. The farmhouse is noted for its good, wholesome home-produced food and many guests return to enjoy the homely, relaxing atmosphere. Magnificent views and many places of interest to visit. Accommodation comprises two family bedrooms with washbasins; bathroom, toilet; sittingroom and diningroom with separate tables. Towels and soap provided. Reductions for children with cot, high chair and babysitting provided. Pets accommodated. Open Easter to September for Evening Meal, Bed and Breakfast or Bed and Breakfast. Car essential — parking provided. Terms on application with stamp for brochure, please.

MALVERN. Douro Cottage, 76 Worcester Road, Malvern WR14 1NU (Malvern [068-45] 4157). Douro Cottage is a charming Regency house of character, with extensive views, only a few minutes' walk from the town centre and conveniently situated for access to the hills and commons, and for public transport. Malvern, itself, in addition to being an unspoilt attractive inland resort, is ideal for touring the Cotswolds, Wye Valley, Welsh Borders, Shakespeare country, etc., and many other places of beauty and historic interest. The house is very comfortable with central heating throughout. The bedrooms all have washbasins, tea/coffee making facilities. Bed and Breakfast from £7 to £8. Reductions for children. Parking nearby. SAE, please.

MALVERN near. Mrs S. Williams, Moorend Court, Mathon, Near Malvern (Ridgway Cross [088-684] 205). Moorend Court is a beautiful country house with oak-panelling, set in lovely grounds in a quiet position with Lakes, wild life and panoramic views to the Malvern Hills. The comfort of the guests is of prime importance, and the bedrooms have kettle with tea and milk provided, TV, armchairs. There is also a lounge where coffee and cream is served after dinner. Meals are a speciality as Mrs Williams is Cordon Bleu trained and the food is of the highest standard. Special diets catered for. Many guests return again and again. Fishing available. Grass tennis court. Four double, one single, two family bedrooms, with washbasins (one bedroom with en-suite facilities); two bathrooms, toilets. Panelled lounge, diningroom. Central heating. Cot, high chair, babysitting, reduced rates for children. Pets permitted. Car essential — parking. Fire Certificate held. Evening Dinner, Bed and Breakfast. Open all year — "Special Winter Breaks". Ashley Courtenay recommended. AA recommended.

MALVERN WELLS. Mrs J. L. Morris, Brickbarns Farm, Hanley Road, Malvern Wells WR14 4HY (Malvern [068-45] 61775). Working farm. Brickbarns a 200-acre mixed farm is situated two miles from Great Malvern, at the foot of the Malvern Hills, 300 yards from the bus service and one-and-a-half miles from the train. The house which is 300 years old, commands excellent views of the Malvern Hills and guests are accommodated in one double, one single and one family bedrooms with washbasins; two bathrooms, shower room, two toilets; sittingroom and diningroom. Children welcome and cot and babysitting offered. Central heating. Car essential, parking. Open Easter to October for Bed and Breakfast from £7 per person. Reductions for children and Senior Citizens. Birmingham 40 miles, Hereford 20. Gloucester 17, Stratford 35 and the Wye Valley is just 30 miles.

MALVERN WELLS. Mrs B. Winfield, Canbury, 37 King Edwards Road, Malvern Wells WR14 4AJ (Malvern [068-45] 2203). Open from April to October, this pleasant family house is situated in a quiet road close to the Malvern Hills and offers comfortable accommodation and a friendly welcome. Ideal walking and touring country, within easy reach of Worcester, the Cotswolds and the Wye Valley. Children over seven years welcome. Accommodation comprises one double/family room, one twin-bedded room, both with washbasin, razor point and tea/coffee making facilities. Bathroom/shower, two toilets; diningroom and sittingroom. Car not essential, but parking available. Sorry, no pets. SAE, please, for terms for Bed and Breakfast.

Terms quoted in this publication may be subject to increase if rises in costs necessitate

PIRTON. Mrs Margaret Thurnham, Pirton Court, Pirton WR8 9EE (Worcester [0905] 820691). You are invited to spend a relaxing holiday at the 'Court', a manor house set in lovely grounds commanding panoramic views of the Malverns and Bredon Hill. Pirton is an excellent centre from which to visit the lovely Vale of Evesham, the Cotswolds, Stratford-on-Avon, etc. The M5 (junction 7) is four miles away. All bedrooms have showers, washbasins, electric heaters, teasmades, radios and shaving sockets. Reduction for children sharing. Excellent home cooking. Full Board or Bed and Breakfast (breakfast is à la carte). Colour TV. Large panelled sittingroom. Cot/babysitting can be arranged. Car essential. Ample parking. Open all year. No pets indoors, kennels available. SAE, please, for terms.

Woodlea Guest House

ROSS-ON-WYE. Mr & Mrs B. D. Adcock, WOODLEA GUEST HOUSE, Symonds Yat West, Ross-on-Wye HR9 6BL. (Symonds Yat [0600] 890206)

A delightful family-owned Victorian Guest House set amidst glorious scenery, with the best valley views in the village, overlooking the famous Wye Rapids, yet only a mile from the A40. Monmouth 4 miles, Ross-on-Wye 6 miles. Licensed and AA/RAC listed. Double, twin, single and family rooms available, all with washbasins, central heating, fitted carpets, shaver sockets, and radio/intercom; some have en-suite shower/toilet. Colour TV lounge, reading lounge, lounge bar, spacious dining room, modern bathrooms. Imaginative and distinctive home cooking, and well stocked bar and cellar. Discounts for children. Dogs by arrangement. Swimming pool. Full fire certificate. Party bookings welcome. B&B from £10.95. Regional winner AA "Best Family Holiday 1984".

ROSS-ON-WYE. Mrs P. A. Ruck, Lower House, Yatton, Ross-on-Wye HR9 7RB (Much Marcle [053-184] 280). Farmhouse accommodation in peace and quiet of the lovely countryside of Herefordshire, not far off the main A449 road, but far enough for peace and quiet. The location is ideal for visiting the Wye Valley, Malvern Hills, Forest of Dean and many more interesting places. The accommodation is two double rooms and one family or single, all with washbasins and razor points. Sittingroom upstairs with TV. Sorry, no pets. Tea or coffee served in the evening. Sorry, no smoking in the house. Also self-catering in converted hop kiln. SAE, please, for details and terms for Bed and Breakfast and Self-Catering.

ROSS-ON-WYE. Mrs Mary Adshead, 'Tamarisk', The Grove, Brampton Abbotts, Ross-on-Wye HR9 7JH (0989-62997). 'Tamarisk' is a semi-detached cottage type residence situated in a quiet village just two miles from the olde worlde market town of Ross-on-Wye and one mile from M50. Emphasis is on home cooking and friendliness. Leafy lanes to explore, scenic drives by car, we are well situated for touring Wye Valley and Forest of Dean. Two double and one twin bedroom with washbasins and shaver points. Towels, soap, morning tea and bedtime drinks included in price. Colour TV lounge, separate diningroom. Ample parking. Bed and Breakfast £7 daily; four course Evening Dinner £4. Reductions for weekly bookings and senior citizens.

ROSS-ON-WYE. Mrs Susan Dick, Merrivale Place, The Avenue, Ross-on-Wye HR9 5AW (Ross-on-Wye [0989] 64929). Merrivale Place is a lovely big Victorian House in the best residential area of Ross. Overlooking hills and trees offering a peaceful setting near the River Wye yet near the centre of town. Guest accommodation in three spacious and comfortable bedrooms all with washbasins; two bathrooms, three toilets; guest sittingroom and a pleasant garden in which to sit for afternoon tea. Separate diningroom. Children welcome. Reduced rates, cot and babysitting available. Sorry, no pets. Car not essential, but parking provided. Open March to October for Bed and Breakfast from £8 per person. Evening Dinner by arrangement — £5. Weekly terms available. Ross is within reach of the Forest of Dean for walking or the Wye Valley, South Wales and Stratford-on-Avon. Come and see the lovely Wye Valley. Further details on request.

ROSS-ON-WYE. Miss A. K. Pugh, Kirkby Guest House, Symonds Yat West, Ross-on-Wye (Symonds Yat [0600] 890253). Welcome to this lovely 15th-century house and gardens overlooking the River Wye. All modern conveniences. Hot and cold water in bedrooms. Colour TV lounge. Excellent cuisine. All home farm produce. Parking.

ROSS-ON-WYE. Deirdre and Gordon Keay, Ryefield House, Gloucester Road, Ross-on-Wye HR9 5NA (Ross-on-Wye [0989] 63030). Set in a pleasant residential area, half-a-mile from the town centre, with easy access to local beauty spots, Ryefield House is a first-class small, private hotel. AA, RAC and ETB approved. Single, twin, double and family bedrooms all with fitted carpets, central heating, washbasins, razor points and tea-making facilities. Two bedrooms have private bathrooms. Lounge with colour TV and residents' bar. Tasty home cooked food. Evening Meal optional. Large attractive garden with ample free parking. Reduced rates for children. Most pets welcome. Personal, friendly service. Open all year (excluding Christmas). Bed and Breakfast from £8.50. Weekly reductions. Full details on request.

ROSS-ON-WYE. Beris and Raymond Vivian, "The Skakes" Guest House, Glewstone, Ross-on-Wye HR9 6AZ (Llangarron [098-984] 456). The Skakes Farmhouse dates from the early 18th century. In 1974 the barn, stable and coachhouse were incorporated with the house and converted into a guest house, retaining much of the original old character. Guests are welcomed and become one of the family, many returning for successive visits, enjoying the relaxed atmosphere and excellent home cooking which includes home-made bread, preserves etc.; fresh food used whenever possible. Double, single and family bedrooms, with facilities for children. Ample toilet facilities. Situated in open country on the A4137 Monmouth to Hereford road, it offers magnificent views and places of interest and beauty within reach: Kilpeck, Black Mountains, Forest of Dean, Cathedral Cities and old castles and buildings. Bed and Breakfast and Evening Meal from £13 or Bed and Breakfast from £9. Reductions for children. Babysitting services available. Open all year round. Restaurant Licence held. Members of ETB.

ROSS-ON-WYE. Mrs F. Davies, Aberhall Farm, St. Owens Cross, Ross-on-Wye HR2 8LL (Harewood End [098-987] 256). Working farm. Aberhall is in the heart of the Wye Valley, four-and-a-half miles from Ross-on-Wye. The farm is 132 acres, mainly stock with some arable in quiet secluded spot, enjoying panoramic views of the beautiful countryside. Aberhall is a 200-year-old house of character, fully modernised with central heating and washbasins in all rooms. Shower and bathroom; two toilets. Games room in cellar. Children welcome. Sorry, no pets. There is plenty to do and see in the area and an all-weather tennis court is provided for guests' use. Interesting places to visit include Symonds Yat, Forest of Dean, Malverns, Brecon Beacons and Black Mountains. Good wholesome cooking. Open March to December. Evening Meal, Bed and Breakfast. Reductions for children. AA recommended. SAE, please, for terms.

ROSS-ON-WYE. Jean and James Jones, The Arches Country House, Walford Road, Ross-on-Wye HR9 5PT (Ross-on-Wye [0989] 63348). The Arches is set in one-third acre of lawns, situated in the beautiful Wye Valley, only 15 minutes' walk from town centre. All rooms are tastefully furnished, centrally heated, with hot and cold water. There is a comfortable residents' lounge with colour TV. Renowned for good home cooking, menus are varied. Evening Meal optional or light snacks available on request. Licensed. Personal service by resident owners. Reduced rates for children. Pets by arrangement. Open all year, except Christmas. Ample parking. One bedroom with private bathroom and WC; family rooms; double rooms; twin-bedded rooms and single, all with tea-making facilities. Bed and Breakfast from £8.50. Weekly reductions. SAE, please. AA and RAC listed. ETB recommended.

ROSS-ON-WYE. Mrs E. Player, Lower Butts, Llangarron, Ross-on-Wye HR9 6PA (Llangarron [098-984] 396). Fully modernised country house offering comfortable, friendly accommodation. All bedrooms have vanity units with hot and cold water, shaver points, etc. Comfortable lounge with large colour TV. Large well-kept garden supplying fresh home grown vegetables and flowers for the house, which is set in quiet village, with church and village stores only two minutes away. Extensive views of Garron and Wye Valleys can be seen within a short distance. Central for Wye Valley, Symonds Yat, Forest of Dean, Black Mountains, etc. Ross-on-Wye and Monmouth only five miles distance, where local markets are held. Trout fishing can be arranged on the Garron Brook, also fly fishing on a local stocked lake. Pets by arrangement. Car essential, parking. Open from April to October. Evening Meal, Bed and Breakfast or Bed and Breakfast only. SAE for terms. Reasonable rates.

ROSS-ON-WYE. Mr and Mrs L. M. Baker, Walnut Tree Cottage, Symonds Yat West, Ross-on-Wye HR9 6BN (Symonds Yat [0600] 890828). This is a charming 19th century cottage with a friendly atmosphere. All rooms have central heating and there is a log fire and colour TV in the lounge. Full English Breakfast served with good homely cooking and personal attention. It is situated in the Wye Valley and is an ideal touring base for the Black Mountains, Golden Valley, Upper and Lower Wye Valley areas, Forest of Dean. Children over 11 years welcome. Small dogs by arrangement. Car essential, parking. Open February to November. Mid-week or Half Board Bookings taken. Bed and Breakfast from £9.50. Evening meals optional (£5.50), no VAT. Licensed. Write or phone for details.

SYMONDS YAT EAST. Mr Alan Pearson, Saracens Head Hotel, Symonds Yat East HR9 6JL (Symonds Yat [0600] 890435). A warm welcome awaits you at this small hotel standing on the east bank of the River Wye as it flows through this quite spectacular and famous gorge. Within the Royal Forest of Dean, with its peaceful woodlands the situation of the hotel makes it an ideal base for exploration. Rooms are tastefully furnished, those overlooking the river have private shower and toilet. Television and private residents' lounge overlook the centuries-old ferry crossing which the hotel is proud to maintain. The restaurant and its chef de cuisine are famous for the excellence of the food and wine. A particular feature is the Lounge Bar with its central open fireplace. A hotel for all seasons but particularly appealing in the early spring or very colourful autumn.

TENBURY WELLS. Mrs J. M. May, Middle Woodston, Lindridge, Tenbury Wells, Worcs. WR15 8JG (Eardiston [058470] 244). Working farm. This comfortable farmhouse is situated half a mile from the A443 in the beautiful Terne Valley, with extensive views over its orchards and hopfields. We are five and a half miles east of Tenbury, ideally placed for exploring The Heart of England. Our 10-acre smallholding provides us with fruit, vegetables, free-range eggs and meat, our speciality being delicious home-baked bread. There is a lounge with log fire, separate diningroom, twin, double and family bedrooms with wash-basins and a large pleasant garden. Open Easter to October. Children welcome. Sorry no pets. Bed and Breakfast from £8.50, Evening Meal optional. AA recommended.

* **UPTON-UPON-SEVERN. Mr and Mrs G. B. Webb, Pool House, Hanley Road, Upton-Upon-Severn WR8 0PA (Upton-Upon-Severn [068-46] 2151).** To anyone wishing to spend a quiet, restful holiday, Pool House, a fine country house, built in 1700's, with its shady lawns and attractive garden, will be found very pleasing. Standing on the banks of the River Severn with its own fishing and mooring rights, it enjoys extensive views of the Malvern Hills. Six double, three family bedrooms — four with washbasins, five en suite. Two bathrooms, six toilets. Sittingroom, diningroom. Excellent cuisine. Licensed. Colour TV. Children welcome, cot, high chair, babysitting can be arranged with Mrs Webb. Sorry, no pets. Car not essential, parking available. Pool House is within walking distance of the old market town of Upton-Upon-Severn. Ideal centre for touring Wye Valley, Cotswolds, Stratford-on-Avon, M5-M50 motorways four miles. Open all year. SAE, please, for terms for Evening Dinner, Bed and Breakfast. See also Colour Display Advertisement in this Guide.

Please note that entries marked with an asterisk also have a colour display advert in the colour section in this guide

BOARD   Hereford & Worcester   221

VOWCHURCH. Mrs Joan Powell, Little Green Farm, Newton, Vowchurch HR2 0QJ (Michaelchurch [098-123] 205). Working farm. Little Green is a farm of 50 acres with modernised farmhouse facing south. Many interesting features still remain in the house which dates back to 1620's. Peacefully situated between the Golden Valley and Black Mountains. Many places of historical interest and natural beauty within easy distance. Literature provided to help guests. Two family, one double bedrooms (all with washbasins and electric heating); electric blankets on all beds. One bathroom, two toilets. Separate tables in diningroom. Colour TV in lounge. Guests are assured of a warm welcome. Good farmhouse fare. Open all year except Christmas. Car essential. Parking. Reduced terms for children and senior citizens. SAE, please. Pony trekking (four miles), fishing, golf (12 miles) and other sporting facilities in the surrounding area.

Mrs Amy Williams, The Croft, Vowchurch, Hereford HR2 0QE. Peterchurch (098-16) 226. Elegant Country House set in delightful gardens and grounds with many mature specimen trees, tennis lawn, orchard and paddocks. Glorious views over beautiful countryside to Black Mountains. Hereford City 10 miles, Hay-on-Wye (World Bookshop) 11 miles. Ideal centre for exploring the Welsh borders, Brecon Beacons National Park, Wye Valley, Forest of Dean, Offa's Dyke etc. The area is rich in historic interest and is also considered to be of outstanding natural beauty. A warm welcome and excellent home cooking await you at The Croft, together with superbly appointed rooms, private bathrooms, tea/coffee facilities, colour TV, comfortable beds. Charming sitting & diningrooms. Licensed. AA listed. Les Routiers. **Daily or weekly terms. Bargain Breaks October - May.** SAE for brochure/tariff. **Dinner, Bed & Breakfast from £18 per day.**

WEOBLEY. Tony and Una Williams, "The Gables Guest House," Broad Street, Weobley, Hereford HR4 8SA (Weobley [0544] 318228). Beautiful old 14th-century Tudor House situated in the centre of one of England's prettiest villages. Open from January to November, "The Gables" is renowned for its hearty English Breakfast. Dinners are optional and can be ordered daily. Several small cafes, restaurants and hotels in the village. An area of great natural beauty with the Malvern Hills and the Welsh Mountains easily accessible, it is also an antique and artist lovers' paradise. "The Gables", set in one acre of lovely gardens, offers choice of double, single and family bedrooms, all with hot and cold water, shaver points, tea/coffee-making facilities. All rooms are beautifully and comfortably furnished; guest lounge with colour TV, two diningrooms. Children over three welcome. Pets accepted at small charge. Car not essential, but there is ample parking. Two golf courses nearby. SAE, please, for terms and further details.

WHITBOURNE. Mrs M. E. Simpson, Upper Elmores End Farm, Linley Green Road, Whitbourne WR6 5RE (Knightwick [0886] 21245). Working farm. A warm, friendly welcome awaits you at Upper Elmores End. A beautifully renovated 16th century black and white farmhouse set in orchards and wooded countryside. The farm is 54 acres of mixed farming. Good farmhouse food, highly recommended and comfortable accommodation. Two double and one family bedrooms, all with washbasins (cot available). Modern bathroom and shower. Large diningroom and large sittingroom with colour TV. Ideally situated for touring Malvern Hills, Wye and Severn Valleys. Lovely country walks. Children welcome, sorry, no pets. Open Easter to October.

WORCESTERSHIRE. Worcestershire Farm and Country Holidays. Selection of farmhouse accommodation in the lovely English Vales. See also Display Advertisement in Board Section of this Guide. For self-catering accommodation see Worcestershire Farm and Country Holidays advert in self-catering section.

WORCESTER near. Mrs A. M. Thacker, Cockshutts Poswick Farm, Upper Sapey, Near Worcester WR6 6XU (Upper Sapey [088-67] 231). Working farm. Cockshutts is a modernised cottage on a 350-acre dairy/mixed family-run farm offering comfortable and friendly accommodation from April to October. It is very quietly situated with extensive views within a short walking distance. Ideal location for touring with many places of interest including the Wye Valley, Malvern Hills, Stratford-on-Avon, Ironbridge, Ludlow and the Welsh Borders all within one hour's drive. Mrs Thacker specialises in good farmhouse cooking, freshly prepared and special diets catered for by arrangement. One double and one family rooms; bathroom, toilet. Sittingroom, diningroom. Children welcome, cot, high chair and babysitting available. Regret, no pets. Car essential, parking. SAE, please, for terms and further details.

WORCESTER near. Mrs Sally Neath, Church Farm, Abberley, Near Worcester WR6 6BP (Great Witley [029-921] 316). Working farm. A warm welcome is ensured at our family run arable and beef farm situated in glorious countryside. Use as a base to tour the Heart of England, taking days out to visit the Steam Railway, Safari Park, Ironbridge Gorge, historic towns, or simply take one of the many unspoilt footpaths over the farm. Accommodation consists of comfortably appointed bedrooms with washbasins; separate shower and toilet facilities. A log fire burns in the diningroom/lounge when necessary, and early morning and late evening tea is freely available. Choose either a local restaurant or Real Ale pub for an excellent Evening Meal. Bed and Breakfast. Reduced rates for children. Open April to October.

WORCESTER near. Mrs Sally Stewart, Leigh Court, Leigh, Near Worcester WR6 5LB (Leigh Sinton [0886] 32275). Working farm. We offer you a friendly informal welcome in this modernised Teme Valley farmhouse, five miles west of Worcester and north of the Malvern Hills. Double or twin bedded rooms available, each with H&C, shaving point, tea-making and supplementary heat. Guests have separate toilet, shower, bathroom, lounge with colour TV and diningroom. Guests may explore the 270-acre farm, including the great 14th century tithe barn. River fishing available. Bed and Breakfast from £8.50. Evening Meals by arrangement. Open Easter/November. English Tourist Board registered. Brochure available.

KENT

ASHFORD. Mrs G. Smith, Brickwall Farm, Woodchurch, Ashford TN26 3RG (Woodchurch [023-386] 314). Guests can be sure of a warm welcome at this lovely Queen Anne Kentish farmhouse, standing in five acres of ground with a large attractive garden, surrounded by farmland. Good centre for visiting the historic towns of Rye, Canterbury and the Cinque Ports. Sports centres at Ashford and Folkestone. Two double bedrooms, with washbasins; bathroom and two toilets; sittingroom and diningroom. Children welcome, cot, high chair and babysitting available. Excellent home cooking, home-grown fruit and vegetables in season. Pets permitted. Open all year. Car essential — parking. Evening Dinner, Bed and Breakfast or Bed and Breakfast only. Reduced rates for children. SAE for terms.

CANTERBURY. Mrs Julie Sole, Broxhall Farm, Lower Hardres, Canterbury (Petham [022770] 205). Working farm. This is a 17th century farmhouse in a quiet, pretty, rural setting with dairy herd, chickens, doves, cats, dog, pony, rabbit. Country walks. Ideal for family holidays with children's play area, cot, high chair and babysitting. Afternoon teas. Riding stables one mile, golf course and park close by. City centre four miles. Channel ports 12 miles. Beaches 10 miles. Local country pub with beer garden and food 10 minutes' walk across the field. One twin/single, one double, one family rooms all with tea making facilities. Open all year. Pets welcome. Bed and full English Breakfast from £8.00 (October-April £7); children under three free, up to 12 half price. Write or phone for details.

CANTERBURY. Mr and Mrs C. W. Fagg, Reeds Mill, Kingston, Canterbury CT4 6JL (Canterbury [0227] 830122). Working farm, join in. Family run, comfortable, modern farmhouse offering "with family" accommodation in double, single and family bedrooms. A very quiet spot, six miles from Canterbury, its central position means that a short drive takes you to any of the East Kent towns, countryside, coasts, or ferries. In well wooded, unspoilt countryside within the "North Downs Area of Outstanding Natural Beauty", an area noted for its flowers, birds and scenery, with a maze of quiet lanes leading to many interesting and historical places. Excellent walking. Bed and Breakfast from £7.50 per night; Bed, Breakfast and Evening Meal from £80 per week.

Complete Seclusion at ELVEY FARM

Completely secluded in the beautiful countryside of the Garden of England, a working farm where we have converted traditional oak-beamed farm buildings into luxury holiday accommodation retaining the timeless charm of the original timbered construction lovingly preserved and restored.

The five ground floor stables, one or two bedroomed with private bath/shower and kitchen/diner, adjoin the old Kent Barn where there are two large family rooms with private bathrooms over the spacious dining and sitting rooms.

The Oast House, built originally for drying hops, has family bedroom, and two twin-bedded rooms in the stone roundel, all with private bath/shower rooms. All bedrooms have colour TV's and central heating.

Pluckley is ideally situated for visiting Leeds and Sissinghurst Castles, Canterbury, Rye, the Coast and Channel Ports with all outdoor activities including gliding and parachuting available locally.

Excellent farmhouse meals featuring home produce, fresh fruit and home made cider will help to make your stay with us a holiday to remember.

MRS. F. HARRIS
ELVEY FARM, PLUCKLEY, NR. ASHFORD, KENT
TEL. PLUCKLEY (023 384) 442

CANTERBURY near. Waltham Court Hotel, Waltham, Near Canterbury CT4 5RY (Petham [022-770] 413). High on the North Downs, five miles south of Canterbury. Quietly situated yet not isolated, Waltham Court stands in grounds of about two acres including a wooded area, the whole in a locality designated as "of outstanding natural beauty". This listed, elegant 19th-century conversion of an 18th-century poorhouse, offers luxury accommodation in twin-bedded and family rooms, each with en-suite shower, washbasin and two adjoining toilets. Television, tea and coffee making facilities are provided in all rooms, with full central heating. Breakfast is served in the Restaurant Diningroom, which is also available for dinner if required. A period bar/lounge completes the many interesting features the house has to offer. SAE or telephone for brochure. Bed and Breakfast from £12.

CANTERBURY near. Mrs Sheila Wilton, Walnut Tree Farm, Lynsore Bottom, Upper Hardres, Near Canterbury CT4 6EG (Stelling Minnis [022-787] 375). Walnut Tree Farm, a 14th century thatched cottage situated in a peaceful valley, completely unspoilt with no new development, in one of the most attractive corners of Kent, is an ideal place for those "wishing to get away from it all" or "en route" to the Continent. Canterbury six miles, Folkestone and Dover 12 miles. The farm is a small-holding of six acres offering good Farmhouse Breakfast, home-made bread, marmalade, preserves and fresh eggs. Accommodation in a period annexe adjacent to the cottage offers excellent family accommodation, one double room, one twin-bedded room, all spring interior mattresses and tastefully furnished with pine furniture. Guest bathroom and toilet. Reductions for children under 13. Regret no pets. Open March to November. Car essential, parking. Bed and Breakfast. Evening Meal by arrangement. Terms from £8.50. SAE for brochure. Excellent pub food five minute's drive away.

PLEASE SEND A STAMPED ADDRESSED ENVELOPE WITH ENQUIRIES

The ideal hotel for visiting south east Kent

- ★ Charming Victorian hotel
- ★ 6 miles Canterbury, 9 miles coast
- ★ 2½ acres including lawns, flower beds and vegetable garden
- ★ Children's play area including sandpit & swing
- ★ Happy atmosphere and good service
- ★ Horse riding, fishing, golf & tennis nearby
- ★ A wealth of historical places to visit just a short car ride away
- ★ Farm Holiday Guide Diploma winner for accommodation & food 1979-80-81

The Woodpeckers Country Hotel Ltd.

Womenswold, Nr. Canterbury, Kent Canterbury 831319 (STD 0227)

RAC   E.T.B. Bedroom Category –

- ★ Heated swimming pool, water slide & diving board
- ★ Television lounge and quiet lounge
- ★ 16 comfortable rooms all with H/C water and tea & coffee-making facilities
- ★ Four-poster, Georgian, brass bedstead, bridal bedrooms all en suite
- ★ Warm air central heating
- ★ Highly recommended for traditional country home baking as reported in *The Daily Express*, *The Guardian*, *The Dover Express* and *The Telegraph*
- ★ Packed lunches
- ★ Licensed. New luxury bar.

'A TASTE OF ENGLAND'

DEAL. Mr and Mrs P. Jailler, Blencathra, Kingsdown Hill, Kingsdown, Deal CT14 8EA (Deal [0304] 373725). "Blencathra", friendly, modern and well-appointed is a licensed guest house with a high reputation for first class food. A holiday here gives you the opportunity for quiet relaxation in the delightful Kentish coastal villages, or of dipping into the history of Canterbury and the Cinque Ports. Situated in an unspoilt peaceful village with panoramic views across the golf course to the sea. Ideal for touring. Open all year. One double, one single and three family bedrooms, all with washbasins and tea/coffee making facilities. Guests have use of two bathrooms and two toilets. Sittingroom with colour TV; diningroom. Children over three years welcome. Central heating. A car is advisable and there is ample parking. Sea seven minutes' walk. Hoverports and ferry terminals easily accessible. Evening Dinner/meal, Bed and Breakfast or Bed and Breakfast only. AA/RAC listed. SAE, please, for brochure and terms.

DOVER near. Mrs B. E. Ritchie, Church Farm, Barfreston, Near Dover CT15 7JQ (Shepherdswell [0304] 830366). Working farm. Church Farm is situated two-and-a-half miles from the A2 road, in the picturesque hamlet of Barfreston with its famous Norman Church. It is 10 miles from the City of Canterbury, eight from Dover and within easy reach of other seaside resorts and Kentish scenery. Guest accommodation comprises one double room with a connecting twin-bedded room and a double room, also one single room. Bathroom; sittingroom and diningroom. Children welcome. Car essential, parking space provided. Open Easter to October. Evening Dinner, Bed and Breakfast. Rates reduced for children. SAE, please for moderate terms.

GILLINGHAM. Mrs B. L. Penn, 178 Bredhurst Road, Wigmore, Gillingham ME8 0QX (Medway [0634] 33267). Wigmore is four minutes from M2 motorway via the A278. Midway between London and Channel Ports, close to the Weald of Kent, Castles and countryside. Hempstead Valley Shopping Centre is also nearby. Bed and Breakfast registered with S.E.E.T.B. 'En Suite' accommodation. Children welcome. Bed and Breakfast from £8. Children under 14, £5. Open all year.

HASTINGLEIGH. Mrs Gorell Barnes, Hazel Tree Farm, Hassell Street, Hastingleigh, Ashford (Elmsted [023-375] 324). Charming old farmhouse dating from medieval times, surrounded by lovely garden. Inglenook fireplaces, mellow oak beams, delightfully and comfortably furnished. New wing built in traditional Kentish style, blends in with the old part of the house. Beautiful views. Ideal centre for exploring an unspoiled part of the Kent countryside on the North Downs. Perfect for naturalists and walkers. Nine miles Canterbury. Within easy reach of the coast and the Continent. Open May to November. Bed and Breakfast from £9 per night. Evening Meal, Bed and Breakfast from £14.50 per night. Weekly terms and reduced rates for children.

MAIDSTONE. Miss R. Berridge, Bydews Place, Farleigh Hill, Maidstone ME15 0JB (Maidstone [0622] 58860). Working farm. Bed and Breakfast in the relaxed, friendly rural Elizabethan farmhouse, one mile from Maidstone town centre, a county town on the River Medway. Four-poster beds and Evening Meals available. This is a seven-acre stock rearing farm, with a wildfowl garden. Kent is famous for fruit and hops with characteristic 'oast houses'; delightful touring countryside; the well-known white cliffs of Dover within easy reach. Historic sites, hill and coast land, Chillington Manor, Sissinghurst, with its famous garden, Chartwell, Cobham Hall, Quebec House, Scotney Castle gardens are only a few of the many places well worth a visit by the holidaymaker. Choice of three double, one single, one family bedrooms (three with washbasins, one en-suite); two bathrooms, two toilets. Two sittingrooms, diningroom. Car not essential, but there is ample parking. Children and pets welcome. Evening Dinner, Bed and Breakfast from £13; Bed and Breakfast £8.50. Non-smokers, please.

MARGATE. Mrs Doris Hendry, Ivydene Guest House, 54 Grosvenor Place, Margate CT9 1UW (Thanet [0843] 23152). Ivydene is a homely and comfortable four storey guest house in a high position overlooking the well-known Dreamland Amusement Park; five minutes' walk to town centre; sandy beaches and all amentities. Many places of interest including Ramsgate and Canterbury within easy reach. Two ground floor chalets suitable for persons confined to a wheelchair. Coin 'phone nearby. The rooms all have washbasins and electric points, four double, four family; bathroom, two toilets; sittingroom, diningroom. Children welcome at reduced rates. Cot, high chair. Pets permitted. Open all year for Evening Dinner, Bed and Breakfast, Evening Meal, Bed and Breakfast or Bed and Breakfast. Senior Citizens May and September, reduced rates.

KENT – THE GARDEN OF ENGLAND!

The pleasant landscape of Kent, including The North Downs and The Weald, is the host of many engaging places to visit. These include Chiddingstone – the half-timbered village, the sophisticated spa town of Tunbridge Wells and Swanton Mill. There are also day trips to the continent and for railway enthusiasts, The Sittingbourne & Kensley Light Railway, The Kent & East-Sussex Railway and the 'World's Smallest Public Railway' from Hythe to Dungeness.

MARGATE. **Northenden Private Hotel, 11 Dalby Square, Cliftonville, Margate CT9 2ER (Thanet [0843] 223889).** It is true to say that the Northenden Private Hotel is your home during your stay and only yards from the sea front. The proprietors pride themselves in being friendly without imposing tiresome restrictions and rely only on the good taste of their guests. There is dancing and entertainment to be enjoyed at the Winter Garden locally, with star-studded variety shows, and the Lido's Old Time Music Night, while on hand is the special weekly party night in the Northenden. With its friendly atmosphere and comfortable bar for a relaxing drink, friendliness is the motto and service the aim. Free baby listening service. Colour TV for hire in bedrooms. For details of Bed and Breakfast or Half Board or Full Board please send SAE or telephone **Marion or Peter Bradbury.**

SEVENOAKS. **Mrs Amanda Webb, Pond Cottage, Eggpie Lane, Weald, Sevenoaks TN14 6NP (Weald [073277] 773).** Beautiful Grade II listed 16th century farmhouse with inglenook fireplace and oak beams. Set in three and a half acres of ground with tennis court, large, safely fenced, pond with fish, kingfishers, wild duck. This is beautiful countryside and yet only 30 minutes by train to London; one hour to the coast at Dover, Eastbourne and Brighton. Sir Winston Churchill's Chartwell, Penshurst Knole and some excellent and historic pubs nearby. Accommodation in one family room/double room (own bathroom, toilet and shower); one single room. Mrs Webb cooks lovely full Breakfasts plus fruit juice, cereal and home made bread. Colour TV in sittingroom. Children welcome at reduced rates; babysitting. Open all year. SAE, please.

TENTERDEN. **Mrs M. R. O'Connor, The Old Post House, Stone-in-Oxney, Tenterden TN30 7JN (Appledore [023-383] 258).** Experience peace and tranquillity of rural England at its best. This guest house overlooks the historic expanse of Romney Marsh and nestles against the hill of the Isle-in-Oxney in the heart of Kentish farmland. Only about 10 minutes' drive to the delightful market towns of Rye and Tenterden where excellent meals can be enjoyed. A warm welcome is offered and traditional English Breakfast. All rooms are equipped with central heating, washbasins, razor points, tea and coffee making facilities. Open all year round. Children over eight years welcome. Pets must be left in car. Bed and Breakfast from £8.50 per person and delicious food can also be had in the village. Car essential; ample parking.

TENTERDEN. **Mrs E. I. Hodson, Tighe, Stone-in-Oxney, Tenterden TN30 7JU (Appledore [023-383] 251).** Tighe, a carefully modernised and very comfortable 17th century farmhouse with oak beams, inglenook fireplaces, antique furniture and surrounded by its own large gardens and farmlands, stands on a height overlooking Romney Marsh with the North Downs in the distance. Five miles from Rye and 35 miles from Dover and Canterbury; eight miles sandy beaches. Being on the borders of Kent and Sussex, this is excellent touring country for both counties which offer a wealth of historic houses, castles and gardens. Local potteries, sea fishing, golf courses, cross channel ferries and steam railways. Three double bedrooms, all with washbasins; bathroom, two toilets; one shower room; sittingroom with colour TV, diningroom. Children over eight welcome — reduced rates, babysitting. No pets. Car essential — parking. Open May to October for Bed and Full English Breakfast from £9.50, weekly tariff £58. SAE, please.

FUN FOR ALL THE FAMILY IN KENT

Dover Castle, Dover; *Rochester Castle*, Rochester; *The Romney, Hythe & Dymchurch Railway*, Hythe, near Folkestone; *Kent & East Sussex Railway*, Tenterden Town Station, Tenterden; *Sittingbourne & Kemsley Light Railway*, Sittingbourne Station; *The Tyrwhitt-Drake Museum of Carriages*, The Archbishop's Stables, Mill Street, Maidstone; *The C.M. Booth Collection of Historic Vehicles*, Rolvenden, near Cranbrook; *Port Lympne Zoo Park & Gardens*, Lympne, Hythe; *Howletts Zoo Park*, Bekesbourne; *Butterfly Farm*, Bilsington, near Ashford; *Bedgebury National Pinetum*, near Flimwell; *Fleur de lis Heritage Centre*, Preston Street, Faversham; *Shell Grotto*, Grotto Hill, Margate.

TONBRIDGE. Mr and Mrs E. H. Thatcher, Dene Court, Shipbourne, Tonbridge TN11 9NS (Tonbridge [0732] 352545). Beautiful views across the Kent countryside with virtually no other house in sight, yet only two miles from Tonbridge with excellent train service to London. Historic homes like Penshurst Place, Leeds Castle, Chartwell, Knole House, Hever Castle and Ightham Mote are within easy reach. The coach-house was converted in 1965 within a 68-foot livingroom and was featured in "House and Garden Book of Holiday and Weekend Houses." Part of the stables have been turned into a family unit with two double bedrooms and bathroom en suite. Traditional English breakfast. Tea and coffee making facilities available. Bed and Breakfast £9. Sorry, no dogs.

WHITSTABLE. Mrs N. Fitchie, "Windyridge," Wraik Hill, Whitstable CT5 3BY (Whitstable [0227] 263506). "Windyridge" is situated in a quiet country lane, 10 minutes away from the M2 motorway, mainline stations and the historic city of Canterbury with its magnificent cathedral and interesting buildings. This charming house has splendid views over the Thames Estuary. Its ceilings are oak beamed; large comfortable lounge with colour TV; spacious garden and verandah for relaxation. Two double, one family bedrooms (all with washbasins); two single bedrooms; two bathrooms, two toilets. Two sittingrooms, diningroom. Car essential, ample parking. Sorry, no pets. Children over nine welcome. Whitstable, two miles away, is noted for its sailing, water ski-ing and golfing opportunities. Approximately 20 miles away lie Ramsgate, Pegwell Bay and Dover. Evening Meal, Bed and Breakfast or Bed and Breakfast only. Morning tea and evening drink by request. Terms on request.

LANCASHIRE

BLACKBURN near. Mr and Mrs F. Hargreaves, Mytton Fold Farm Hotel, Langho, Blackburn BB6 8AB (Blackburn [0254] 48255). Working farm. Third generation to farm this 100-acre mixed farm. In 1985 an extension was built on to the recently converted coaching house, giving 12 luxurious en suite bedrooms, each with telephone, colour TV, trouser press, hairdryer and tea/coffee making facilities. There are two comfortable lounges, one with open fire, the other with a licensed bar, built from local stone. The beautifully furnished restaurant, open to non-residents, specialises in home cooked fresh food, using local produce whenever possible. The building retains the original oak beams and mullioned windows. Full central heating throughout. Convenient for visiting Blackpool, Yorkshire Dales and Lake District. 10 miles from M6 (exit 31). Open all year. AA listed.

BLACKPOOL near. Mrs C. A. Smith, Singleton Lodge, Lodge Lane, Singleton, Near Blackpool FY6 8LT (Poulton-le-Fylde [0253] 883854). Working farm. A warm welcome awaits you at Singleton Lodge, a Georgian country house situated in delightful Lancashire countryside, five miles from the bustle and excitement of Blackpool and the quieter resort of Lytham St. Annes, and it is an ideal base for exploring the beautiful Forest of Bowland, the Lake District and the Yorkshire Dales. There are double and single bedrooms available, all with washbasins, and two bedrooms have bathroom en-suite. All bedrooms have tea/coffee making facilities. Diningroom and comfortable lounge with colour TV. Children welcome — cot and high chair provided. Farmhouse Breakfast fayre served; Dinner by arrangement. Terms on request with SAE, please.

CLITHEROE. Mrs Frances Oliver, Wytha Farm, Rimington, Clitheroe BB7 4EQ (Gisburn [020-05] 295). Working farm. Farmhouse accommodation on dairy farm in Ribble Valley with extensive views. Within walking distance of Pendle Hill. Ideal touring centre for Lake District, Yorkshire Dales, Bronte Country, interesting and historic Clitheroe. Children welcome. Babysitting service. Beautiful picnic area. Packed lunches available. Farm produce when possible, and home cooking. Accommodation comprises family and double rooms; TV lounge; central heating. Ample car parking. Pets by prior arrangement (£1 per day). Bed and Breakfast from £8; Evening Meal £5. Reduced rates for children under 11 years. Open all year.

NORTH WEST LANCASHIRE
Farm Holidays
VALE of LUNE
Close to the coast, Lakes and Dales

Several Farmers' wives in the Lune and Wyre area offer you and your family farm holiday accommodation in some of the most attractive and unspoilt countryside in Britain between the Pennine foothills and Morecambe Bay.

BED AND BREAKFAST

LANE HOUSE FARM, **BENTHAM**, NEAR LANCASTER LA2 7DJ (Mrs Betty Clapham Tel. No. [0468] 61479) A 100-acre dairy farm with extensive views of Yorkshire Dales. 1 mile from Bentham which offers golf, tennis and fishing. Half hour from Junction 34 of M6. Enjoy walking, touring or just relaxing in the countryside B&B from £7.50. E.M. from £5.

GREENHALGH CASTLE FARM, CASTLE LANE, **GARSTANG**, PRESTON PR3 1RB (Mrs Jean Fowler Tel. No. [09952] 2140) 150-acre dairy farm with lovely 17th century beamed farmhouse. Peaceful and secluded yet only 1½ mile from small market town. Good walking, birdwatching or canal fishing on farm. Blackpool or Morecambe 14 miles. Lake District 40. AA Listed. B&B from £8.00.

COLLINGHOLME FARM, **COWAN BRIDGE**, CARNFORTH LA6 2JL (Peter and Anne Burrow Tel. No. [0468] 71775) A 250 year old farmhouse in an area of tranquil beauty a mile from the A65 road between the market town of Kirkby Lonsdale and Ingleton on the edge of the Yorkshire Dales. A warm welcome awaits you. B&B from £7.50.

LUNDHOLME, **INGLETON**, CARNFORTH LA6 3HN (Mrs Nancy Lund Tel. No. [0468] 41207) A 300 acre dairy and sheep farm nestling under Ingleborough. Ingleton 1 mile. Famous for its waterfall, caves, potholing and walking. Ideal centre for the Dales, Lakes and West Coast. Warm welcome plus good home cooking. B&B from £7.00. E.M. from £5.

GALLABER, **BURTON-IN-LONSDALE**, CARNFORTH LA6 3LU (Mrs Mary Dodgson Tel. No. [0468] 61361) A 125-acre sheep and stock rearing farm, situated in a quiet rural position. Ideal for touring the Lakes, Dales and Morecambe Bay. A warm friendly atmosphere awaits you. B&B from £7.50.

GARGHYLL DYKE, **COWAN BRIDGE**, CARNFORTH LA6 2HT (Mrs Gillian Burrow Tel. No. [0468] 71446) You will find a homely welcome on our 260 acre dairy, beef and sheep farm close to the old market town of Kirkby Lonsdale with picturesque Devil's Bridge. Ideally situated for Lakes, Dales and Coast. B&B from £7.50. 1 double, 1 twin.

COTESTONES FARM, SAND LANE, **WARTON**, CARNFORTH LA5 9NH (Mrs Gill Close Tel. No. [0524] 732418) Situated on the North Lancs coast near to M6 Junction 35. This is a family run dairy farm adjacent to Leighton Moss R.S.P.B. reserve, also near to Steamtown Railway Museum. Midway between Lancaster/Morecambe and the Lake District. B&B from £7.00. Reductions for children. E.M. from £4.00.

STIRZAKERS FARM, BARNACRE, **GARSTANG**, PRESTON (Mrs R. Wrathall Tel. No. [09952] 3335) A 130 acre dairy farm. Ideal centre for exploring the Lancashire coast, Lake District and Forest of Bowland or helping on the farm. B&B from £7.00. Reductions for children. Double, family and single room.

TARNACRE HALL FARM, **ST. MICHAEL'S ON WYRE**, PRESTON (Mr and Mrs J. Whewell Tel. No. [09958] 217) Family dairy farm by the River Wyre (fishing available). Central for Blackpool, Lancaster and many places of interest. Golf and boating, 20 minutes. Plenty of good eating places locally. Children welcomed. B&B (Adults) from £8. EM £5.00. Caravan Club CL (motor vans) £1.25 nightly.

For group brochure with full details please send 9" × 4" SAE to Mrs Jean Fowler, Greenhalgh Castle Farm, Castle Lane, Garstang, Preston, Lancs. PR3 1RB Tel. (09952) 2140.

The group is a member of the Farm Holiday Bureau and an associate member of the North West Tourist Board.

CLITHEROE. Mrs M. A. Berry, Lower Standen Farm, Whalley Road, Clitheroe BB7 1PP (Clitheroe [0200] 24176). **Working farm.** Comfortable farmhouse accommodation with Bed and Breakfast, offered all year round (except Christmas) for holidaymakers planning to tour the Lake District and the scenic West Coast — Blackpool an hour's drive away. Convenient centre also for touring the Yorkshire Dales. Visitors are given a warm welcome and can participate in the activities of this 140-acre farm by arrangement with the owners. Golf club and swimming pool nearby. Two double bedrooms, plus single bed in each, one twin-bedded room, all with washbasins (one double room also has a shower); bathroom, toilet; sittingroom; diningroom. Children welcome — cot, high chair, babysitting and reduced rates for the under 12's. Sorry, no pets. Car essential — parking. Public transport half-a-mile. Terms and further details on request.

GARSTANG. Mrs Jean Fowler, Greenhalgh Castle Farm, Castle Lane, Garstang, Preston PR3 1RB (Garstang [09952] 2140). **Working farm.** Greenhalgh is 160 acre dairy/sheep farm. The 300-year-old farmhouse is overlooked by the ruins of Greenhalgh Castle (circa 1490) and is in a beautiful secluded setting yet only half mile from the small market town of Garstang. It is an ideal spot for touring the North West Coast, Lake District or the beautiful Forest of Bowland area. Good walking/birdwatching and canal fishing on farm. Accommodation is very comfortable with pretty beamed bedrooms (two double, one twin) all with washbasins, shaver points and tea/coffee making facilities. Separate guests' bathroom and lounge with colour TV. AA listed. ETB registered. Open Easter to mid-October. Leaflet on request. Bed and Breakfast from £8.

Terms quoted in this publication may be subject to increase if rises in costs necessitate

GARSTANG near. Mrs D. J. Hodge, Lower House Farm, Bilsborrow Lane, Bilsborrow, Near Garstang PR3 0RQ (Brock [0995] 40581). Working farm. Relax deep in the heart of the Lancashire countryside on a working dairy farm. Peaceful surroundings yet only 10 miles from Preston and 15 miles from Lancaster. Ideal situation for the seaside, the Lakes and the Ribble Valley. Excellent walks in the area but car essential. Stay in the recently renovated luxurious farmhouse. One double bedded room and one twin bedded room with adjoining shower room. Table tennis for children and snooker for adults. Own dining/sittingroom, early morning tea and late night drink. Bed, Breakfast and Evening Meal, with reduced rates for children. Sorry, no pets. SAE for details.

GARSTANG (near Preston). Mrs M. Chapman, Nuncroft House, Churchtown, Garstang, Near Preston PR3 0HT (Garstang [099-52] 3233). Nuncroft House is a 200-year-old country house in lovely conservation village. It is off the A586, four/five miles from the M6 from the North Exit 33, Hampson Green; from the south Exit 32, Broughton. The Pennine Hills, the Lake District and the lovely Trough of Bowland within easy reach; Blackpool 11 miles. The village has two inns with excellent catering. Also river and 12th century church. Car essential, parking. Double and family rooms with washbasins; bathroom, two toilets; sittingroom; diningroom. Children are welcome. Sorry no pets. Open all year with central heating. Bed and Breakfast. Terms on request. Rates reduced for children.

PRESTON near. Mrs K. Johnson, Falicon Farm, Fleet Street Lane, Hothersall, Longridge, Near Preston PR3 3XE (Ribchester [025-484] 583). Working farm, join in. Come and enjoy the Ribble Valley and the peace and tranquillity of Falicon Farm, a 13-acre sheep and beef farm, set in quiet country surroundings midway between Preston and Blackburn, within 15 minutes' drive of M6 (Junctions 31 and 32). The centrally heated farmhouse has been recently modernised to ensure guests a comfortable retreat and a happy, memorable holiday. Comfortable accommodation is provided in one double/family room with private bathroom, one twin-bedded room with bathroom en-suite, plus double room with shared facilities. Three bathrooms, three toilets. Sittingroom, diningroom. Children over 10 years welcome, and pets allowed if kept in car. Imaginative cuisine at farmhouse prices! — freshly grown own and local produce used; diabetic and vegetarian diets catered for. Car essential — ample parking. Evening Meal, Bed and Breakfast from £20; Bed and Breakfast from £11. AA listed. Open all year.

PRESTON near. Mrs B. Huggon, Wolfen Lodge, Chipping, Near Preston PR3 2GR (Chipping [099-56] 482). Magnificently situated country house near picturesque prize-winning village in "Area of outstanding Natural Beauty" offers peace and tranquillity in idyllic surroundings. Heart of rural Lancashire on edge of Fells. Ideal walking and touring centre, within one hour's drive of the Lake District, Blackpool and Fylde Coast, Yorkshire Dales and Trough of Bowland. Plentiful home cooking. Bed and Breakfast from £8. Reduced rates for children and Senior Citizens. Car essential. Ring for brochure and full details.

LEICESTERSHIRE

BARKESTONE-LE-VALE. Mrs Sylvia Smart, The Paddocks, Barkestone-Le-Vale, Nottinghamshire NG13 0HH (Bottesford [0949] 42208). Situated in the beautiful Vale of Belvoir, close to Belvoir Castle, within half an hour's drive — Melton Mowbray, Newark, the Dukeries and Sherwood Forest at Nottingham, Oakham (Rutland Water). Large garden with heated swimming pool; Games Room with Pool and table tennis etc. Children love the peacocks, Matilda the Goose, Jemima the Donkey, horses, dogs, etc. Bed and Breakfast from £8; Evening Meal by arrangement. Cot, high chair provided. Three double, two single, one family rooms, with washbasins, shaver points. Full central heating, open fires. Two bathrooms, three toilets; two sittingrooms, diningroom. Horse riding provided; coarse fishing nearby. Visit our speciality craft centre — a converted stable offering many beautiful arts and crafts from local cottage industries with many original items. Car essential — parking. A1 (Grantham) — 15 minutes. BTA Approved.

PLEASE SEND A STAMPED ADDRESSED ENVELOPE WITH ENQUIRIES

**DESFORD. Mrs G. J. Allen, Old Manor Farm, Desford, Leicester LE9 9JF (Desford [045-57] 2410).
Working farm.** Early 17th-century farmhouse on a 70-acre mixed farm, with a dovecote, situated in village of Desford, seven miles from Leicester, with easy access of M1 (Junction 21). Nearby are the Battlefield of Bosworth, Bradgate Park and Twycross Zoo. The accommodation is spacious with a wealth of oak beams and an inglenook fireplace in the diningroom. One double and one family bedrooms (one with washbasin); bathroom, toilet. Children welcome, cot, high chair and babysitting available. Sorry, no pets. Car not essential, but there is parking. Public transport 50 yards. Open March to December for Evening Meal, Bed and Breakfast from £11; Bed and Breakfast from £7.50. Reduced rates for children.

LEICESTER. Mrs Janet S. Clarke, Three Ways Farm, Melton Road, Queniborough LE7 8FN (Leicester [0533] 600472). Three Ways Farm is in the picturesque village of Queniborough. Adjoining the A607, it is within easy reach of the M1, A1 and A47. The spacious modern bungalow is surrounded by fields with views to Charnwood Forest. There is a large flock of breeding sheep. Melton markets Tuesday and Saturday, Leicester, Charnwood Forest, Oakham (Rutland Water). Nottingham half an hour's drive, Belvoir Castle, Burleigh and Belton Houses and Horse Trials within an hour. Large family room, also twin/family room. Visitors' bath/shower. Visitors' toilet. Tea/coffee making facilities. Central heating and electric blankets. Bed and Breakfast. Evening Meal by arrangement. Coarse fishing, riding, tennis and bowls — one mile. Good village pubs serve food.

LUTTERWORTH. Mrs A. M. Knight, Knaptoft House Farm, Bruntingthorpe Road, Near Shearsby, Lutterworth LE17 6PR (Peatling Magna [053-758] 388 or 509). Working farm. Convenient M1 (Exit 20) M6 (Exit 1) A50; nine miles south Leicester, Bruntingthorpe-Saddington X roads. Open all year. Short breaks a speciality. Bed and Breakfast from £8.50. Evening Meal by arrangement. Warmth, comfort, good home cooking. Wholefoods, home produced free range eggs, milk and meat. Own delicious spring water. Diets prepared. Sunny dining and sittingrooms, wood-burners and colour TV. Your wine served. Bedrooms include family room, two rooms with en-suite showers, two ground floor bedrooms adjoining, suitable for the disabled, all with heating, double glazing, tea/coffee making facilities, washbasins. Three toilets and two bathrooms. Pets accepted by prior arrangement. Quietly situated in rolling countryside, 145-acre mixed farm. Coarse fishing. Enjoy local tourist attractions, then relax in our lovely sun lounge. AA. ETB. Access cards accepted. 'Phone for leaflet.

LUTTERWORTH. Mrs Sue Timms, Wheathill Farm, Church Lane, Shearsby, Lutterworth LE17 6PG (Peatling Magna [053-758] 663). Working farm. This 130-acre dairy farm with attractive old house, beamed ceilings and inglenook fireplaces, is situated in a tiny village that dates back to the Saxons. The area is steeped in history and offers many stately houses and castles within easy reach. Sporting needs catered for locally with fishing, golf and gliding. Within nine miles, Leicester contains much of interest including Roman ruins and modern theatres. A warm welcome and good home produced food is assured to all, including children. Five miles M1 exit 20. M6 exit 1. Easy distance N.E.C., N.A.C. One twin room with shower, one double room, H&C; one single. Tea/coffee making facilities in rooms. Bed and Breakfast, Evening Meal. Babysitting by arrangement. For full details and prices an SAE would be appreciated.

MELTON MOWBRAY. Mrs J. S. Goodwin, Hillside House, Burton Road, Burton Lazars, Melton Mowbray LE14 2UR (Melton Mowbray [0664] 66312). Set in the heart of Leicestershire, on the edge of Rutland, this fully modernised cottage overlooks rolling countryside in a small village, two miles from Melton Mowbray, famous for its pork pies and Stilton cheese. Belvoir Castle and Rutland Water are two of the many local beauty spots and places of interest. Accommodation consists of one double and two twin-bedded rooms with washbasins, all centrally heated. Also luxury bathroom and shower room. There is a sitting-room and colour television, and a dining room. Ample space for car parking; pleasant garden. Bed and Breakfast from £8.00. Open all year.

BOARD Leicestershire 231

MELTON MOWBRAY. Mrs M. A. Morris, Manor House, Saxelbye, Melton Mowbray LE14 3PA (Melton Mowbray [0664] 812269). Working farm. Manor House is situated within easy reach of M1 and A1, and five miles from the busy market town of Melton Mowbray in the quiet hamlet of Saxelbye. The Manor House is a fine stone-built farmhouse — a special feature being its 500-year-old staircase where the original stone walls are exposed. The farm of 125 acres is mainly dairy and visitors are welcome to wander around. There is a large garden of lawns and rose beds. Food served is fresh local produce. AA award given in 1978 for excellent cuisine. Two family bedrooms with washbasins; bathroom, two toilets; sitting and diningroom. Children welcome with cot, high chair and babysitting available. Pets by arrangement. Open Easter to October for Evening Dinner, Bed and Breakfast or Bed and Breakfast. Reductions for children. Terms on application. Car essential. Parking.

**Mrs S. Booth
Sysonby Knoll Hotel
Asfordby Road, Melton Mowbray,
Leicestershire LE13 0HP
Tel. (0664) 63563**

Ashley Courtenay   AA   RAC

A small family owned and run Hotel in its own large garden. All bedrooms have TV and tea/coffee making facilities. 11 bedrooms also have bathroom-en-suite. Some ground floor bedrooms, also four poster room. Pleasant dining room overlooking swimming pool and gardens. Cosy bar and two lounges. Traditional English cooking with variety of choice. Reduced rates for weekends and Bargain Breaks available.

MELTON MOWBRAY. Mrs Valerie Anderson, Home Farm, Church Lane, Old Dalby, Melton Mowbray LE14 3LB (Melton Mowbray [0664] 822622). 18th/19th Century Farmhouse; quiet lane on edge of village in lovely Vale of Belvoir. Home Farm and garden are ideal for overnight stop, or base for more leisurely explorers; Belvoir Castle, Stapleford Park, Burleigh and Belton Houses, etc. Lincoln and Coventry Cathedrals, Chatsworth and Peaks are comfortable day trips. Stables in heart of world-famous Quorn Hunt country offer liveries in winter. Long distance riders stop over in summer. Easy access from motorways (M1, M69) and main routes (A1, A6, A46, A47). Seven miles northwest Melton (A606). Open January-November. Twin and family rooms (all H&C). Full central heating. Guests' own sittingroom and diningroom. Children welcome, babysitting. Quiet dogs kennelled (not in house). Car, horse or bicycle essential.

MELTON MOWBRAY. Mr and Mrs B. Brotherhood, Beechcroft, Church Lane, Asfordby, Melton Mowbray LE14 3RU (0664-812314). A spacious Georgian residence (circa 1800) and 200-year-old modernised holiday cottage situated in two acres of lawns and gardens with river frontage. First floor comfortable bedrooms (H&C). Diningroom and residents' colour TV/music lounge. A friendly, informal atmosphere prevails which is extremely restful in a quiet free and easy fashion. Children welcome. Fishing from river bank. Ample parking. Enjoy shopping in the busy market town of Melton Mowbray, well known for its delicacies of Stilton cheese and pork pies, with its bustling street markets on Tuesday and Saturday. Within half an hour's motoring of Belvoir Castle, Stapleford Park and Rutland Water. Bed and Breakfast accommodation from £7. Evening Meals on request. The cottage, fully furnished, is available as a self-catering holiday unit. BTA approved. Brochure and full details on request.

LEICESTERSHIRE – THE EPITOMY OF MIDDLE ENGLAND!
A county of undulating farmland containing such delights as Rutland Water, the canal "staircase" at Foxton, the market town of Oakham, Charnwood forest and the estate church at Staunton Harold.

TILTON-ON-THE-HILL near. Miss J. Layton, Knebworth House, Loddington Lane, Launde, Near Tilton-on-the-Hill LE7 9DB (Tilton [053-754] 257). Knebworth House is two-and-a-half miles off A47 (Tugby), one-and-a-half miles off Oakham/Tilton Road, built in 1868, recently modernised throughout. Accommodation available; two double rooms (one with washhand basin); one twin bedded room with washhand basin; one single room; upstairs bath/shower/toilet; downstairs shower/toilet. Situated on the Leicester/Rutland border in the heart of beautiful Leicestershire; seven miles from Oakham, 15 miles from Leicester, ten miles from Rutland Water (Empingham), 15 miles from Stamford, eight miles from Uppingham and 20 miles from Belvoir Castle; it is a rambler's paradise. Best home cooking served, fresh garden produce, farm eggs; comfortable furnished surroundings, secluded rural countryside. Car essential, excellent parking facilities, cars and caravans. Children catered for at reduced rates — terms on request.

UPPINGHAM near. Mrs D. Renner, The Old Rectory, Belton-in-Rutland, Near Uppingham CA5 9LE (Belton [057-286] 279). This Country Craft Centre welcomes parties of visitors by appointment and the many facilities offered include an interesting exhibit of quality traditional country crafts on sale or to order; traditional country bygones on display; miniature farm; farm walks; picnic facilities; children's play area; cream teas and other light refreshments. Bed and Breakfast accommodation from £8.50 per person. Double and family rooms with washbasins; bathroom, two toilets; sittingroom; diningroom. Car essential — parking. Open all year round and pets are permitted. Also five-acre site for caravans/campers.

LINCOLNSHIRE

BOSTON. Mr and Mrs D. H. Devine, Qu-Appelle Farm, Swineshead Road, Frampton Fen, Boston PE20 1SF (Hubberts Bridge [020-579] 227). This old farmhouse, although not on a working farm, is open from Easter to September and is surrounded by farmland. Three miles from Boston on the A52, there is good fishing nearby, and the location is central for touring Lincolnshire. A local bus passes every two hours. Guests assured of good home cooking and comfortable accommodation. Boston and district has many buildings of interest to the tourist. Three double and one single bedrooms; bathroom, two toilets; sitting and diningrooms. Ample parking space for cars. Evening Meal, Bed and Breakfast or Bed and Breakfast. SAE, please, for terms. A high standard of cooking guaranteed. Regret no pets or children under 11.

GEDNEY HILL (Spalding). Mrs Christine Cave, Sycamore Farmhouse, GEDNEY HILL, Spalding PE12 0NP (Holbeach [0406] 330445). Working farm. Sycamore Farm is a 75-acre mixed farm, pleasantly situated on B1166 on the Lincolnshire, Norfolk, Cambridgeshire borders, and is an ideal touring centre for many places of interest. Our accommodation for guests is in our modernised 100-year-old farmhouse — one double, one twin and one family bedrooms; bathroom; lounge with colour TV; diningroom with traditional sized table and good country food. Open all year except Christmas. Children welcome, cot and babysitting. Pets allowed. Many National Trust, Wild Fowl Trusts and RSPB reserves in abundance; famous windmills, "Royal Houses," Cathedrals and Abbeys, Lincolnshire Wolds, The Fens, The Wash and seaside of the Norfolk and Lincolnshire coast. A warm farmhouse welcome awaits you at Sycamore Farm. Bed and Breakfast from £10 (Evening Meal optional). AA Listed. Les Routiers.

HORNCASTLE near. Mrs P. B. Wattam, The Vicarage, Great Sturton, Near Horncastle LN9 5NX (Baumber [065-86] 258). Working farm. Comfortable 18th century farmhouse on a 600-acre farm situated on the edge of the Lincolnshire Wolds midway between Lincoln and Boston. Only three-quarters of an hour's drive from the coast and within easy reach of the market towns of Louth, Horncastle and Market Rasen. Near Tennyson country. Bed and Breakfast from £9 is offered all year round. Guests are accommodated in one double, one family and one single bedrooms. Bathroom/toilet. Sittingroom and diningroom. Children welcome and cot, high chair and babysitting available. Car essential — ample parking. Mid-week bookings accepted. For further details please write or phone.

WHEN MAKING ENQUIRIES PLEASE MENTION
FARM HOLIDAY GUIDE

LANGTON-BY-WRAGBY. Miss Jessie Skellern, Lea Holme, Langton-by-Wragby LN3 5PZ (Wragby [0673] 858339). Comfortable, chalet-type house set in own half-acre peaceful garden surroundings. All amenities. Central for touring wold, coast, fen, historic Lincoln etc. So much to discover — the county with wonderful skies and room to breathe. Attractive market towns — Louth, Horncastle, Boston, Spilsby, Alford, also Woodhall Spa. Two double bedrooms (can be let as single), with washbasins; bathroom, toilet; sittingroom; diningroom. Children welcome; reduced rates. Some babysitting may be available. Car almost essential; parking. Basically Room and Breakfast, but Evening Meals can be had by arrangement. Bed and Breakfast from £8 per person; Evening Meal £2.75. Open all year.

LINCOLNSHIRE FARM HOLIDAY GROUP
"STAY ON OUR FARM"

Welcome: Our big Lincolnshire farming welcome seems to be renowned far and wide. And whether you're looking for an overnight stay or a fortnight's settled holiday, whether you want bed and breakfast, half-board or prefer to opt for self-catering, whether you're alone or with a family – we believe we have just the place for you where we can give the holidaymaker and business traveller a wide choice of good value places to stay throughout this wide country of fens and flowers, hills and livestock and safe, empty beaches. So see for yourself and send for a free brochure from: 
Anne Thompson, Guy Wells Farm, Whaplode, Spalding, Lincolnshire PE12 6TZ; or telephone Holbeach (0406) 22239.

SPALDING. Mr & Mrs Richard and Anne Thompson, Guy Wells Farm, Whaplode, Spalding PE12 6TZ (Holbeach [0406] 22239). Working farm. AA listed. 'Guy Wells' is a 75 acre family farm growing arable crops and spring flowers, situated ideally for touring National Trust, Wild Fowl Trusts, RSPB reserves, etc., as well as the famous Fenland Churches, "Royal Houses", Cathedrals, Abbeys, the Fens, the Wash and Norfolk and Lincolnshire coasts. Friendly, relaxing atmosphere in delightful spacious 18th century farmhouse, which is centrally heated with guests' oak-beamed diningroom and pleasant lounge with colour TV and wood-burning stove. Bed, Breakfast and Evening Meals available. Excellent accommodation with delicious home cooking. 'Guy Wells' offers you a warm welcome. Bed and Breakfast from £9.

MRS FITTON, ABBEY HOUSE, WEST END ROAD, MAXEY PE6 9EJ
Tel: Market Deeping (0778) 344642

STAMFORD near. Comfortably furnished guest house in one acre of mature gardens. Dating in part from 1190, it belonged to Thorney Abbey and Peterborough Minster before serving as a vicarage and possesses several features of historical interest. Full central heating. All bedrooms are well appointed, offering refreshment facilities and colour TV. The locality abounds in attractive stone built villages, stately homes and castles. Stamford (five miles), Crowland Abbey, Rutland Water, Peakirk Wildfowl Trust and Peterborough Cathedral are close at hand, whilst Ely and Cambridge are reached within the hour. Private Carp Lake. SAE, please, or telephone for details.

LINCOLNSHIRE – OUTSTANDING NATURAL BEAUTY!
The Lincolnshire Wolds are indeed worthy of their designation as an "Area of Outstanding Natural Beauty". Anybody visiting this county should explore The Wolds and visit such places as Bourne, Grantham, Honington, the woodland at Kesteven and the Museum of Lincolnshire life in Lincoln itself.

STAMFORD near. Mrs Liebich, Spa House, Braceborough, Near Stamford PE9 4NS (Greatford [077-86] 310). Nearest roads A1, A15 and A16. A very pleasant house offering comfortable and quiet accommodation and a friendly welcome to visitors. Spa House is about a mile from Braceborough Village and seven miles from Stamford which is an interesting town with some very old buildings. The countryside is unspoilt and has many historic houses. Superbly situated in a secluded setting amidst undulating and wooded countryside, the house and garden are surrounded by a spa, once famous for its healing waters, where King George III bathed, around 1788. Accommodation comprises three double and one single bedrooms; shower, two toilets; large oak-panelled drawing room with open fireplace where good food is served. Open all year with central heating. The terms are; Evening Dinner, Bed and Breakfast from £10 or Bed and Breakfast from £8. 25% reduction for children — cot and babysitting available. Pets permitted.

MERSEYSIDE

WIRRAL. Mrs B. J. Hughes, The Croft, 38 Digg Lane, Moreton, Wirral L46 6AQ (Liverpool [051] 6774175). "The Croft" is a detached bungalow situated in the lovely Wirral Peninsula a half mile from the M53 whose junctions are only minutes from the coast and links directly with the M56, M6, M62 and M1. An ideal base for touring Wales, the Lake District and Cheshire. Chester is only 18 miles. A five mile journey through one of the Mersey Tunnels brings you into Liverpool, home of the Beatles, the ferry to Ireland and many places of interest. Good home cooking; gas central heating — not spared on chilly nights; one double and one single room; bathroom and toilet; lounge with CTV; diningroom. Bed and Breakfast or Dinner, Bed and Breakfast. Parking. Sorry, no pets. Dinner, Bed and Breakfast from £9.75 nightly.

For the Mutual Guidance of Guest and Host

Farm Holiday Guides Ltd. do not inspect or recommend accommodation but advertisers agree to accept our Farm Holiday Guide standards of comfortable and clean accommodation and wholesome and well-cooked food. Advertisers are also bound by the Trades Description Act.

When accommodation has been booked, deposits sent, and letters of acceptance exchanged, both parties – host and guest – have entered into a binding contract.

Friends and families can easily be upset and much bitterness caused if holiday arrangements are not carefully made. The following points can be of real importance:

Guest When enquiring about accommodation, be as precise as possible. Give exact dates, numbers in your party and the ages of any children. State the number and type of rooms wanted and also what catering you require – bed and breakfast, full board etc. Make sure that the position about evening meals is clear – and about pets, reductions for children or any other special points.

Read our reviews carefully to ensure that the proprietors you are going to contact can supply what you want. Ask for a letter confirming all arrangements, if possible.

Host Give details about your facilities and about any special conditions. Explain your deposit system clearly and arrangements for cancellations, charges etc, and whether or not your terms include VAT.

We regret that Farm Holiday Guides cannot accept responsibility for any errors or omissions in descriptions. Prices in particular should be checked before booking because of the early compilation of the Guides, far ahead of the next holiday season.

NORFOLK

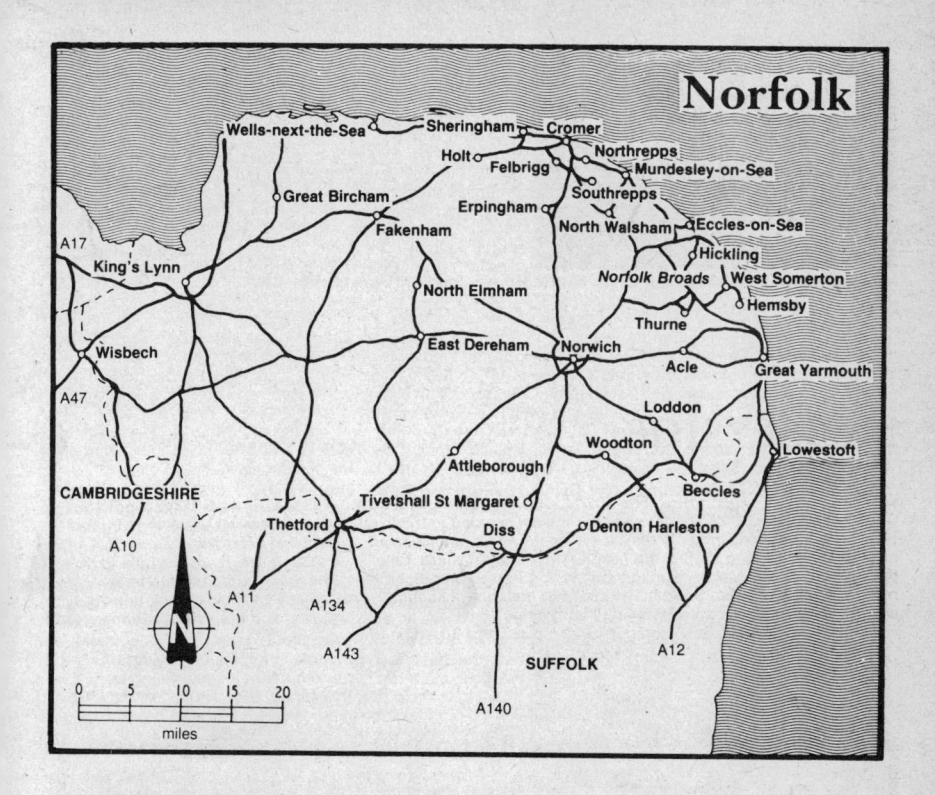

ATTLEBOROUGH. Mr and Mrs P. A. Morfoot, Church Cottage, Breckles, Attleborough NR17 1EW (Great Hockham [095-382] 286). A warm welcome awaits you at this charming and comfortable 200-year-old country home. All home cooking, home made bread. Own eggs. Church Cottage is situated in beautiful Breckland overlooking typical Norfolk farmland. Convenient for touring East Anglia. Approximately 40 miles to Ipswich, Cambridge and all points on the coast from King's Lynn to Southwold. Norwich 22 miles. Broads 30 miles. Ideal for touring historic buildings, churches. Car essential, ample parking. Heated outdoor swimming pool. Two double bedrooms, with washbasins; one single. Bathroom, two toilets; visitors' dining/sitting-room with TV. Children over 10 welcome. Sorry, no pets in house. Central heating. Closed Christmas and New Year. Bed and Breakfast.

AYLSHAM. Mr and Mrs Pauline and Dick Newby, Abbots House, White Hart Street, Aylsham, Norwich NR11 6HG (Aylsham [0263] 734182). This spacious Georgian house is only 12 miles from the fine city of Norwich which is an excellent shopping centre. There are three large centrally heated bedrooms, one double, one twin and one family rooms, all with washbasins and shaver points; guest bathroom and separate shower room. Sitting-room with colour TV overlooks gardens and paddocks. Log fire when necessary. Well behaved children and pets welcomed. Cot, high chair and babysitting. Bicycles on loan. Surrounding countryside offers a wide variety of interests and activities; boating, fishing, wild life parks and unspoilt coastline. National Trust Blickling and Felbrigg Halls three and ten miles respectively. Squash and badminton courts in town and riding facilities nearby. Bed and Breakfast from £10 per person per night plus £6 for Evening Meal.

Norfolk BOARD

BECCLES near. Mrs R. M. Clarke, Shrublands Farm, Burgh St. Peter, Near Beccles, Suffolk NR34 0BB (Aldeby [050-277] 241). Working farm. This attractive homely farmhouse which is pleasantly situated in the Waveney Valley on the Suffolk border, is surrounded by one acre of garden and lawns. The River Waveney flows through the 350 acres of mixed working farmland providing fishing and bird-watching. Ideal base for touring Norfolk and Suffolk; Beccles, Lowestoft, Great Yarmouth and Norwich, all within easy reach. The house has two double rooms and one family room, with washbasins; two toilets, bathroom; sittingroom, diningroom, separate lounge with colour TV. Games room for table tennis, snooker and darts. Tennis court available. Children welcome. Car essential, parking. Open March to October. Good home cooking, which includes farm produce. Evening Meal, Bed and Breakfast, or Bed and Breakfast. No pets. Reductions for children. SAE, please.

CROMER. Mrs Barbara Barrett, The White House, Suffield Park, Cromer NR27 0EJ (Cromer [0263] 512194). The White House is a well-established, friendly Guest House situated in its own spacious gardens, approximately one mile from Cromer town centre, and close to main bus route. The beach, lighthouse, pleasant woodland walks and an excellent 18-hole golf course are all within easy walking distance. Your hosts' aim is to please and make your stay a happy and enjoyable one. Barbecues are a special feature at the White House and enjoyed by young and old alike. Children are especially welcome, also the family dog. Choice of three double, one single, two family bedrooms with all the usual facilities, razor points, washbasins in each one. (Two ground floor bedrooms available.) Bathroom, two toilets. Colour TV in the lounge and separate tables in the diningroom. Cot, high chair, babysitting and reduced rates for children. Central heating. Car not essential, but ample parking space. Evening Dinner, Bed and Breakfast £10.50; Bed and Breakfast £7. Open all year — special low season breaks. Nearby Holiday Chalet available.

CROMER. Mr J. R. Graveling, The Grove, Overstrand Road, Cromer NR27 0DJ (Cromer [0263] 512412). The Grove is an 18th-century holiday home magnificently set in its own three-acre grounds of fields, gardens and trees. There are walks through the fields and woods to cliffs, golf courses and beach. The small fishing town of Cromer is within walking distance, with its pier, lifeboat, fine church, museum, shops and eating places. We have a lounge, games room, venture-type playground for children, and we grow our own vegetables. Ideal holiday for young or old. Six double, two single, three family bedrooms with washbasins; three bathrooms, four toilets; diningroom. Cot, high chair, reduced rates for children. Sorry, no pets. Open April to October for Evening Meal, Bed and Breakfast from £80 per week; Bed and Breakfast from £59 per week.

DEREHAM. Mrs J. Overall, Oak Ring, The Dyes, Hindolveston, Dereham NR20 5DQ (Melton Constable [0263] 861222). 17th century traditional red brick Norfolk House, half-mile off public road, deep in the heart of lovely countryside. Seclusion for resting, bird watching, walking etc. The sea only 20 minutes' drive. Norwich, Blickling, Holkham and many other places of interest all within 20 miles. Our stock includes ponies, sheep and chickens. Children are very welcome; babysitting available. Washbasins in bedrooms. Guests' sittingroom, colour TV. Personal caring attention at all times. Car essential. Bed, Breakfast and Evening Meal.

EAST DEREHAM. Mrs Jane Faircloth, Moat Farm, Mattishall, East Dereham NR2 3NL (Dereham [0362] 850288). Situated in the centre of the village, 11 miles from Norwich, a fine city with cathedral, many interesting buildings and museums, theatre and cinemas. Within easy reach of Sandringham and the Coast. Offering Bed and Breakfast and Evening Meal with traditional farmhouse meals using home grown fare. Family room and twin-bedded room with washbasins; separate bathroom and WC. Lounge with log fire and TV. Sorry, no pets. Cot not provided. Open May to October. AA recommended. Please send SAE for terms.

FAKENHAM. Mrs Maureen Walpole, "Hardlands", East Raynham, Fakenham NR21 7EQ (Fakenham [0328] 2657). "Hardlands" is situated in delightful countryside — four miles from Fakenham on the A1065. An ideal centre for touring almost all of Norfolk including Royal Sandringham Estate, North Norfolk Coast, King's Lynn, Norwich and The Broads. This modern house is set in its own gardens and has five bedrooms with tea/coffee-making facilities; guests have own TV lounge/diner. Central heating. Children are welcome and there is cot, babysitting and reduced rates. A car is essential and there are ample parking facilities. Full English Breakfast with traditional home cooking. Pleasant garden of nearly one acre. Evening Dinner, Bed and Breakfast from £13; Bed and Breakfast from £9. Weekly rates available.

PLEASE SEND A STAMPED ADDRESSED ENVELOPE WITH ENQUIRIES

FAKENHAM near. Mr and Mrs P. T. Sinclair, Toad Hall, East Barsham, Near Fakenham NR21 0LH (Walsingham [0328-72] 317). A rambling old rectory, 17th to 19th century, delightfully situated in the valley of the River Stiffkey. "Toad Hall" has two acres of woodland and garden and lies twixt 12th century church and pub. As a touring centre for old Norfolk, "Toad Hall" is ideal. Sandringham, Blickling Hall and bird sanctuaries within easy reach. Bed and Breakfast mid-April to 31st October. Dinner optional. Two treble bedrooms, four double and one single, all with washbasins. "Toad Hall" occupies a sequestered position — a place to unwind with like-minded people. SAE, please, for brochure. Sorry, no dogs.

FAKENHAM near. Mrs Ann Green, Old Coach House, Thursford, Near Fakenham NR21 0BD (Thursford [032-877] 273). This peaceful Norfolk farmhouse, converted from 17th century coach house, affords modern comforts but retains its charm. Entered from the main King's Lynn to Cromer road (A148), straight drive curving into sheltered sunny courtyard. Norfolk offers miles of sandy beaches, golf, sailing, fishing and riding, also stately homes, museum, bird sanctuary and wildlife park to visit. Main bedroom has four-poster bed, washbasin, shaver point and kettle; second bedroom with twin beds and room for extra bed or cot if required; guests' bathroom/WC; dining/sittingroom with sun lounge and access to garden. Maximum of five guests and only one party at a time. Good country cooking and personal attention. Children welcome and pets by arrangement. Bed and Breakfast from £8.50 per night (£60 weekly); Bed, Breakfast and Evening Meal from £12 per night (£80 weekly). Reduced rates for children. Open all year. See also self-catering entry under Norfolk.

GREAT YARMOUTH. Mrs Margaret Bowles, Gables Farmhouse, Scratby Road, Scratby, Great Yarmouth NR29 3NL (Great Yarmouth [0493] 732107). A pleasantly situated farmhouse, tastefully restored to preserve all its natural charm, including exposed beams and inglenook fireplace. Situated conveniently for Great Yarmouth, Broads, Beach and North Norfolk coast. This farmhouse stands in two-and-a-quarter acres with pleasant gardens and pond-side walk. An ideal holiday area embracing facilities for golf, sailing, birdwatching, mediaeval churches, fishing (sea and fresh water), riding and swimming. Guesthouse accommodation in two double bedrooms (one with own shower/WC), one single room and one family room, each with washbasin; bathroom, two toilets. Tea and coffee making facilities in each bedroom. Sittingroom with TV and diningroom. Good country cooking, produce from kitchen garden. Ample parking. Sorry, no pets. Open April to September.

GREAT YARMOUTH. Mrs Margaret Lake, Old Station House, North Road, Hemsby, Great Yarmouth NR29 4EZ (Great Yarmouth [0493] 732022). A warm welcome and a soothing family atmosphere is assured at this country house 10 minutes from beaches and also in the Broads area; Great Yarmouth six miles. Accommodation is in one double and two family rooms, with washbasins; bathroom, toilet; separate diningroom; tea-making facilities; lounge with colour TV. Children welcome. Sorry no pets. Open from Easter to October, with partial central heating. Good home cooked food is served. Car is not essential, but plenty of parking here. Guests are given own keys and may come and go as they wish. Evening Dinner, Bed and Breakfast from £10.50 per night or from £58 weekly. Bed and Breakfast only from £7.50 per night. Children half price.

NORFOLK – NOT JUST THE BROADS!

There's more to do in Norfolk than messing about in boats – pleasurable though that may be. Other places of interest include the gardens and steam museum at Bressingham, the Broadland Conservation Centre, the flint mines at Grimes Graves, The Norfolk Rural Life Museum, Sandringham – which is often open to the public, and of course Norwich itself.

GREAT YARMOUTH near. Mrs Margaret Adnitt, The Cannons, West Caister, Near Great Yarmouth NR30 5SS (Great Yarmouth [0493] 728557). This is a Georgian country house in two acres of lovely grounds with ample parking. Two miles from beaches, Norfolk Broads and Great Yarmouth, yet in peaceful, rural surroundings. Close to golf course, race course and riding stables. Caister Castle Motor Museum half-a-mile. Offering guesthouse accommodation — also self-catering flats. Home grown produce, choice food. Three double and one family rooms with washbasins and one private bathroom; two bathrooms, two toilets; diningroom/lounge. Children welcome at reduced rates. Sorry, no pets. Open all year. Electric blankets. Evening Dinner, Bed and Breakfast £12 per day; Bed and Breakfast £8.50 per day. Car essential.

GREAT YARMOUTH near. Mrs Winifred Youngs, Street Farm, Horsey, Near Great Yarmouth NR29 4AD (Winterton-on-Sea [049-376] 212). Working farm. Horsey is a National Trust property, a small village situated on the B1159 Great Yarmouth to Cromer road, eleven miles north of Great Yarmouth. It is not commercialised in any way and there are no caravans and no tents. Street Farm is a farm of 280 acres producing cereals and stocked with a suckling herd of cows and calves. Just 20 minutes' walk away from a clean sandy beach stretching for miles and all the main centres of Broadland are within a radius of 15 miles. Double, single and family bedrooms, some with washbasins. Dinner, Bed and Breakfast or Bed and Breakfast, with home cooking a speciality of the hostess. SAE for terms, please.

HARLESTON. Mrs K. Pointer, Paynes Hill Farm, Denton, Harleston IP20 0AW (Homersfield [098686] 628). This is an old beamed farmhouse in peaceful countryside. Central for Norwich, Lowestoft or Yarmouth. Near Waveney for fishing. Otter Trust at Earsham, wildlife park Kessingland. Steam trains and gardens at Bressingham. One single, one family room, with washbasins; bathroom, two toilets; sitting/diningroom. Children welcome; cot, high chair. Sorry no pets. Electric or open fires. Good home grown food and well cooked meals. Personal attention from Mrs Pointer. Parking — car essential. Open May to September. Also two caravans, each sleeps four. SAE for terms, please.

HARLESTON. Mrs J. E. Holden, Weston House, Farm, Mendham, Harleston IP20 0PB (St. Cross [098-682] 206). Seventeenth century Grade II Listed farmhouse set in one acre garden overlooking pastureland. Double, twin, family and single rooms, all with H&C and radiator. One bedroom on ground floor. Comfortable lounge with colour TV. Separate tables in diningroom. Tea making facilities. Hot drink served at night. Reduced rates for children under 12 years. Dogs by arrangement. Parking. AA listed. Tourist Board Registered. Dairy/mixed farm of 330 acres. Good touring area within easy reach of coast, Broads, Norwich, wild life parks and historic monuments. Nearby pubs and restaurants. SAE for terms please.

HICKLING. Mrs J. C. Schreiber, Jenter House, Town Street, Hickling NR12 0AY (069-261-372). Jenter House is situated in the delightful Broadland village of Hickling and near super unspoiled, sandy beaches. Just 15 minutes' walk from the largest and most picturesque broads in Norfolk. A paradise for the ornithologist, fisherman, sailor or holidaymaker. Norwich and Great Yarmouth are within easy reach. Guests will find a warm welcome, excellent accommodation and good country cooking. Bed and Breakfast and Evening Meal. Children welcome at reduced rates. Open all year. AA, RAC, BTA registered. Pets permitted.

HOLT. Mrs M. A. Middleton, Home Farm, Holt Road, Weybourne, Holt NR25 7ST (Weybourne [026-370] 334). Working farm. Built in 1974, traditional style bungalow with farmland views. Two double, one single plus one bunk bedded rooms; bathroom and shower room, both with toilets; combined lounge-diningroom with colour TV. Children welcome at reduced rates, cot and high chair. Regret no pets. Central heating. The house is suitable for disabled guests. Car essential, ample parking. New games room and children's play area. Weybourne has unique steam train link with Sheringham (three miles away), also riding school in the village. Good, plentiful home cooked food. Safe beaches nearby. Heated outdoor swimming pool on farm — 133 acres of mainly arable land with small beef herd and a few pigs. Open May to end September for Evening Dinner, Bed and Breakfast or Bed and Breakfast. SAE for brochure and terms. Also self-catering cottages available.

PLEASE ENCLOSE A STAMPED ADDRESSED ENVELOPE WITH ENQUIRIES

MUNDESLEY-ON-SEA. Mrs Bridget Plummer, The Grange, High Street, Mundesley-on-Sea NR11 8JL (Mundesley [0263] 721556). An outstandingly beautiful, well furnished house in an attractive half-acre garden. Home cooking a speciality. The Grange is open all year and centrally heated. Children are welcome. Scale of reductions for under 12's, under two's free of charge. Three double rooms, one family room; all with washbasins; two bathrooms; three toilets; sittingroom; diningroom. Car is not essential but there are good parking facilities. No pets. Nine hole golf course in village. Ideal for Broads, Norwich, bird-watching, fresh water/sea fishing; convenient beach. Evening Dinner, Bed and Breakfast. SAE, please.

NEATISHEAD (Norfolk Broads). Alan and Sue Wrigley, Regency Guest House, Neatishead Post Office Stores, Neatishead, Near Norwich NRG 8AD (Horning [0692] 630233). An 18th-century guest house in picturesque, unspoilt village in heart of Broadlands. Personal service top priority. Long established name for very substantial English breakfasts. Only 20 minutes from interesting old city of Norwich and six miles from coast. Ideal location for touring East Anglia, all boating activities, sailing, hiring, cruising, sightseeing. Haven for fishermen. Easy access to wildlife and bird watching grounds. Two public houses and one licensed restaurant, all excellent eating facilities, within minutes' walk. Guest house has tastefully furnished rooms (four double and one family, all with washbasins), individually and charmingly decorated, and offers colour TV, tea-making facilities, and two main bathrooms. Dining/breakfast room. Cot, babysitting, reduced rates for children. Pets welcome. Parking. Mid-week reduced rates. Open all year. Bed and Breakfast from £8.50. Reductions for Senior Citizens.

NORTH WALSHAM. Mr Christopher A. Bayne, Paston Hall Hotel, Paston, Near Mundesley, North Walsham NR28 9TA (Mundesley [0263] 720379). Paston Hall Hotel, with its own heated swimming pool and squash court and set in 15 acres of garden and woodland, is an ideal centre for a Norfolk holiday. The Norfolk Broads are half-an-hour's drive away and the beautiful City of Norwich three-quarters-of-an-hour's drive. The Norfolk coast with its fine beaches and interesting little villages is perfect for a relaxed holiday and the Hotel grounds provide a safe play space for all the children. Accommodation for guests in five double, one single and two family bedrooms, seven with washbasins; three bathrooms, three toilets; two sitting-rooms and a diningroom. Children welcome and cot, high chair and babysitting provided. Open April to October, central heating. Car is essential, ample parking. Pets permitted at 50p per night. Full Board; Evening Dinner/Meal, Bed and Breakfast; Bed and Breakfast only. Rates reduced for children. Terms on application with SAE, please.

The information in the entries in this guide is presented by the publishers in good faith and after the signed acceptance by advertisers that they will uphold the high standards associated with FARM HOLIDAY GUIDES LIMITED. The publishers do not accept responsibility for any inaccuracies or omissions or any results thereof. Before making final holiday arrangements readers should confirm the prices and facilities directly with advertisers.

NORTH WALSHAM. Mrs P. Garnham, The Hermitage, Beach Road, Bacton, North Walsham NR12 0EP (Walcott [0692] 650012). The Hermitage is a delightful house adjacent to the beach, 20 yards off the coast road at Bacton. There is a half-acre garden, mainly set to lawns, ideal for children's play. Conveniently situated for visiting stately homes, zoo, Norwich with castle, museum, wildlife park, etc. Good sandy beach adjacent. The house includes lounge with colour TV; separate diningroom; one ground floor bedroom and three first floor bedrooms, all with washbasins and facilities for tea making. Bathroom on first floor. Ground floor shower room and one toilet. Children welcome, cot available. Babysitting by arrangement. Reduced rates for children sharing parents' room. No dogs permitted in the house. Car advisable; ample parking. Evening Meal, Bed and Breakfast from £9.50. Bed and Breakfast from £7.

NORTH WALSHAM. Ernest and Jenny Townsend, Beechwood Hotel, 20 Cromer Road, North Walsham NR28 0HD (North Walsham [0692] 403231). Within three minutes' walk of interesting market town shopping centre and yet secluded in lovely grounds. Beechwood is ideally located for sandy beaches, the Broads, Norwich, and many other interesting places. Open all year, except Christmas. There are seven family rooms, three double and one single all with washbasins; fitted carpets, shaver points and comfortable beds; some have a private bathroom/WC. Two lounges, diningroom (separate tables) and games room. Licensed. Central heating. Ample parking space. AA listed. Ashley Courtenay recommended. Friendly personal service. Write or telephone for brochure. See outside back cover.

NORWICH. Mrs Carolyn Holl, Hillside Farm, Brooke, Norwich NR15 1AU (Brooke [0508] 50260). Working farm. Brooke is seven miles south of Norwich (B145 Bungay to Norwich road), ¾ hour drive to excellent beaches. Hillside Farm, built 1600's, is timber-framed and thatched and has been recently restored. Full central heating. Two family/double rooms with tea-making facilities; has one en-suite loo, bidet, washbasin and TV; also one single room; two bathrooms; large diningroom with inglenook fireplace sitting area. Car essential, ample parking. Children welcome, cot, high chair and babysitting. Fishing in two secluded private lakes; games barn; large garden. Laundry room. Sorry, no pets. Reduced rates for children. Bed and Breakfast, some light suppers. Terms on request.

NORWICH. Mrs Joanna Douglas, Greenacres Farm, Woodgreen, Long Stratton, Norwich NR15 2RR (Long Stratton [0508] 30261). A 17th century period farmhouse with a warm friendly atmosphere — wealth of character, exposed beams and inglenook fireplace. Farm is situated in an idyllic, rural situation — yet only one and a half miles from Long Stratton (A140) with a variety of shops, public houses, sports centre — golfing, fishing, riding, swimming facilities nearby. The beautiful historic city of Norwich is 12 miles away as are other character market towns. Central location provides easy access to Norfolk Broads, coast and the Suffolk Constable country. Car essential. Accommodation comprises one double, one twin, one single rooms; bathroom; sittingroom and TV. Children welcome, cot, high chair, babysitting available. Open all the year round. Bed and Breakfast £8.50. Light Evening Meal £4.

NORWICH. Mrs J. Halsey, Old French Church Farm, Caister St. Edmund, Norwich (Framingham Earl [05086] 2403). Old French Church Farm is a completely modernised Victorian farmhouse situated in an elevated position in open countryside three miles south of the historic city of Norwich. It stands in a large garden with fine country views. Two large bedrooms are let to visitors: both are tastefully decorated, centrally heated and with their own electric kettles. A private guests' bathroom is shared by a maximum of two families. Good walks are available from the house and Caistor St. Edmund is an ideal touring base for Norfolk and Suffolk. Car essential — ample parking. No public transport. Children welcome, cot, high chair and babysitting. Open all year. Evening Meal, Bed and Breakfast from £13.50; Bed and Breakfast from £8.50. Reduced rates for children.

BOARD Norfolk 241

NORWICH. Mrs Margaret Smith, "Flitcham Cottage," Fir Covert Road, Felthorpe, Norwich NR10 4DT (Norwich [0603] 867493). "Flitcham Cottage" is pleasantly situated in typically Norfolk countryside, overlooking farmland bordered by woods. Within easy reach of city and Broads and coast. Old established, guests can relax in large lounge, conservatory or garden, and enjoy a peaceful holiday all year except Christmas and New Year. Full central heating with log fire in lounge. Two double bedrooms and one family room, all with washbasins; bathroom, two toilets; sittingroom, diningroom. Cot provided and babysitting by arrangement. Pets also by arrangement. English and Continental dishes. Bus stop one mile away. Ample parking. Great Witchingham Wild Life Park four miles away. Bed and Breakfast from £7; Bed, Breakfast and Evening Meal from £10.50. Reduced rates for children.

NORWICH. Mrs S. Clarke, The Poplars, Ipswich Road, Long Stratton, Norwich NR15 2TJ (Long Stratton [0508] 30502). Delightful early 18th century timber-framed farmhouse standing well back on A140 in one and a half acres of lawns and orchard. Guests can enjoy year round hospitality in a friendly atmosphere where log fires glow on chilly evenings. Excellent home cooking and varied menu. Accommodation comprises twin-bedded room with own separate bathroom; double bedroom with bathroom en suite; sittingroom, diningroom. Children welcome, cot, high chair and babysitting offered. Sorry, no pets. Car is not essential, public transport 400 yards, but there is parking. New South Norfolk Sports Centre in village and fishing, horse riding and golf available locally. The scenic Norfolk Broads for cruising and sailing 20 miles; the coast 28 miles. Bed and Breakfast from £8; Evening Meal from £6.50. Reductions for children under 10. Mid-week bookings accepted. Closed Christmas.

NORWICH. Mrs A. E. Parker, Elm Farm Chalet Hotel, Horsham St. Faith, Norwich NR10 3HH (Norwich [0603] 898366). Situated just four miles from Norwich in the pretty, quiet village of Horsham St. Faith, Elm Farm Chalet Hotel was started in 1978 when a conversion was made of farm buildings into luxury chalets. Each unit has two self-contained rooms, hot and cold water, tea/coffee making facilities, colour TV; some have own shower/toilet. The 17th century farmhouse, recently modernised, also accommodates guests and has attractive diningroom, coffee lounge, TV lounge. Restaurant licence. Packed lunches supplied. The Hotel stands in one-and-a-half acres of ground with spacious lawns, duck pond and ample parking. Within easy reach of Norfolk Broads, two miles Norwich Airport; ideal base for touring Norfolk and Suffolk coasts. Children welcome, cot, high chair, reduced rates available. Sorry, no pets. Open all year for Evening Dinner, Bed and Breakfast or Bed and Breakfast. Send for brochure and tariff to above.

NORWICH. Mr and Mrs R. M. and B. M. Harrold, Salamanca Farm, Stoke Holy Cross, Norwich NR14 8QJ (Framingham Earl [050-86] 2322). Working farm. At Stoke Holy Cross, Colmans first produced their famous mustard — the original Mill still stands, on the River Tas, and the Harrolds' cows graze nearby. Salamanca Farm, a short walk from the river, was named by a former owner who fought with Wellington in the battle of Salamanca. Norwich, a Cathedral city, with excellent shops and museums, is only four miles away. Large garden. Central heating. Four guest bedrooms, three bathrooms; spacious diningroom, sittingroom with colour TV. Full English Breakfast. Dinner includes home-made soup, traditional farmhouse meat course, exotic sweets, a choice of cheese and coffee. Bed and Breakfast from £8.50. Dinner £4.50. Regret, no dogs. SAE, please, for brochure.

NORWICH near. Mr B. M. D. Wootton, The Old Mill Hotel, Buxton Mill, Buxton with Lamas, Near Norwich NR10 5JF (Buxton (Norfolk) [060-546] 774). The Old Mill Hotel is part of one of Norfolk's famous Water Mills at Buxton with Lamas. An ideal base for a complete holiday, Norwich and the Broads are natural attractions, and the best part of Norfolk's coastline runs, with an almost unbroken stretch of beach, between Sheringham and Great Yarmouth. Barry and Phyllis Wootton give you a warm welcome to this small, historically interesting, licensed hotel. Five bedrooms, each with its own individual character, are most comfortable, beamed, centrally heated, colour TV, and all enjoy picturesque river views. Two rooms en-suite. Pretty diningroom serving first-class food; good selection of wines available. Sittingroom, overlooking the river, leads on to sun terrace. Log fire in cold weather. Patio and garden beside the river for guests' use; coarse fishing in river by arrangement. Car park. Visitors can view craft activities adjacent to the Old Mill. Highly recommended.

PLEASE SEND A STAMPED ADDRESSED ENVELOPE WITH ENQUIRIES

NORWICH near. Mrs R. Snaith, Grey Gables, Norwich Road, Cawston, Near Norwich NR10 4EY (Norwich [0603] 871259). Former rectory in wooded grounds offering excellent food and wine. Lounge with log fire. Elegant candle-lit diningroom where traditionally prepared food is served using fresh fruit and vegetables from our own kitchen garden. Lawn tennis court and bicycles available. All bedrooms have en suite bathrooms, tea/coffee making facilities and colour TV. Children under 10 sharing parents' room accommodated free of charge. Accommodation £14 per person inclusive of English Breakfast. Dinner from £7.

NORWICH near. Mrs G. Vivian-Neal, Welbeck House, Brooke, Near Norwich NR15 1AT (Brooke [0508] 50292). Situated one mile east of Brooke off the B1332, Norwich/Bungay road, Welbeck House is ideal for exploring the Broads, the Norfolk and Suffolk coast, local churches and Norwich which is only seven miles away. You will find a friendly and homely atmosphere in this pink Georgian farmhouse which, with its delightful large garden and superb trees, stands well back from the road. There is plenty of parking space and the bus service is frequent. Open from January till November. Babies and children 12 and over are welcome. Babysitting can be arranged. Pets are welcome free if they sleep in car. There are two double and three single rooms; two bathrooms; three toilets; diningroom. Bed and Breakfast from £8, children and Senior Citizens £7.

NORWICH near. Mr and Mrs A. E. Rackham, Stubbs House, Stubbs Green, Loddon, Near Norwich (Loddon [0508] 20231). Modern comfort in a period setting, with superb food and a warm welcome from Jenny and Andrew Rackham, will ensure a delightful stay at Stubbs House. Centrally heated throughout; two lounges, one with colour TV and log fire for chilly evenings. Washbasins in all bedrooms, some with private shower or bathroom. Residential licence. Special rates offered for two or three days' stay in October, February, March and April, excluding Bank Holiday periods. Summer rates from £90 per week for Dinner, Bed and Breakfast including VAT. Surrounded by lovely countryside and interesting places to visit, a car is essential to make the most of your holiday. Parking space. Further particulars on application. SAE, please. See also Inside Front Cover.

SOUTHREPPS. Mrs C. Codling, Church Farm Guest House, 20 Church Street, Southrepps NR11 8NP (Southrepps [026379] 248). Church Farm Guest House is set on a small-holding in lovely Norfolk countryside, three miles from the coast at Mundesley and Cromer with safe sandy beaches. There are two double bedrooms and one family room, all with washbasins; bathroom, three toilets; sitting room and dining room. Tea and coffee making facilities in rooms. There is a play area for children; pets allowed. A car is not essential, but there is parking. Ten miles from the Norfolk Broads with fishing nearby. Home cooking with fresh garden produce a speciality. Railway station one mile; collection by arrangement. Open January to November. Full central heating. Evening Dinner, Bed and Breakfast or Bed and Breakfast only. High tea for children under five. Bike hire available in village. Caravan and camping site also available, also Rose Cottage, a luxury holiday cottage, sleeps six/seven, central heating and open fire, fitted kitchen including washing machine and colour television.

THETFORD. Mrs Garnier, College Farm, Thompson, Thetford IP24 1QG (Caston [095-383] 318). Recently modernised 600-year-old farmhouse, formerly a priests' college. The two twin-bedded rooms, one double and one single are quite large and all have armchairs, electric blankets and black and white TV (the double room has a washbasin); bathroom, shower room, two toilets. Diningroom. Children over 10 welcome and babysitting offered. Regret no pets. Car essential (or bike), ample parking. Thompson is a small village, off the beaten track, but only three miles from the market town of Watton where there are several restaurants. There is a very old thatched pub in the village which provides bar meals and Evening Dinner. Ideal centre for touring East Anglia on pleasant country roads with very little traffic. Open all year (except Christmas). Bed and Breakfast. Terms on application with SAE, please.

The information in the entries in this guide is presented by the publishers in good faith and after the signed acceptance by advertisers that they will uphold the high standards associated with FARM HOLIDAY GUIDES LIMITED. The publishers do not accept responsibility for any inaccuracies or omissions or any results thereof. Before making final holiday arrangements readers should confirm the prices and facilities directly with advertisers.

WELLS-NEXT-THE-SEA. Mrs E. R. Leather, "Partners", Northfield Lane, Wells-next-the-Sea NR23 1LQ (Fakenham [0328] 711096). Spacious bungalow offering homely accommodation with complete freedom in peaceful half-acre. Tree shaded surroundings. Close to quay and shops. Popular with Senior Citizens, very quiet. Bedrooms light and airy with Continental quilts. Lounge with colour TV. Morning and evening drink. Parking in grounds. Double and family rooms. "Partners" is a short drive from Blakeney-Chey, Sherringham and Cromer. Popular with bird watchers, also the pinewoods at Wells, not forgetting Holkingham Hall, Hunstanton and Sandringham. Open January to November. Home cooked and fresh produce. Bed and Breakfast from £7 per night, Evening Meal £4.50. Children welcome, sorry no pets. A warm welcome is guaranteed.

WELLS-NEXT-THE-SEA. Mrs Anne Taylor, The Cobblers, Standard Road, Wells-Next-The-Sea NR23 1JU (Fakenham [0328] 710155). The Cobblers is a small friendly guest house close to the quay and town centre. Tea and coffee-making facilities and H&C in all rooms, fully centrally heated and double glazed. Members of Les Routiers and English Tourist Board. Open all year except December. Special winter breaks. Come and discover the glorious north Norfolk coast, enjoy miles of unspoilt sands, surrounding countryside and many bird reserves and places of historical interest. One double, one twin, one family and one single bedrooms. Ample parking and access to the house at all times. Bed and Breakfast from £7. Weekly rates by arrangement. We endeavour to make your stay with us a pleasant and memorable one.

WELLS-NEXT-THE-SEA. Mrs J. M. Court, Eastdene, Northfield Lane, Wells-next-the-Sea NR23 1LH (Fakenham [0328] 710381). A homely guest house offering a wam welcome. Bed, Breakfast and optional Evening Meal. Traditional cooking with own garden produce. Close to marshes, lovely coast walks. Central for Cley and Titchwell bird reserve and historical places such as Holkham Hall Estate and Walsingham Shrine. Hot and cold washbasins in bedrooms; central heating; TV lounge with coffee and tea making facilities. Three double bedrooms and one single; one double with own shower. Own front door key. Private car park. Pets welcome. Terms on application. Holder of Farm Holiday Guide Diploma.

WOODTON. Mrs J. Read, George's House, Woodton, Near Bungay NR35 2LZ (Woodton [050-844] 214). This is a charming late 17th century cottage with four-acre market garden. It is situated in the centre of the village, just off the main Norwich to Bungay road. Wonderful holiday area, ideal for touring Norfolk and Suffolk. Historic Norwich, with its castle, cathedral, theatre and good shops is only nine and a half miles and everyone should find something there to suit them. Sea 18 miles. Guest accommodation comprises three double bedrooms, with washbasins. There is a bathroom and toilet. Diningroom and TV lounge. A car is essential to make the most of your holiday and there is ample parking. The house is open to guests from April to September for Evening Meal, Bed and Breakfast. SAE, please, for terms.

FUN FOR ALL THE FAMILY IN NORFOLK

Banham Zoo & Monkey Sanctuary, The Grove, Banham; *Kilverstone Wildlife Park*, Thetford; *Thrigby Hall Wildlife Gardens*, near Filby; *The Otter Trust*, Earsham, near Bungay; *Wildfowl Trust*, Welney; *Kelling Park Hotel & Aviaries*, near Holt; *Cromer Zoo*, Cromer; *Caister Castle Motor Museum*, near Great Yarmouth; *Banham International Motor Museum*, The Grove, Banham; *Bressingham Gardens & Live Steam Museum*, near Diss; *North Norfolk Railway*, Sheringham Station, Sheringham; *Maritime Museum for East Anglia*, Marine Parade, Great Yarmouth; *Iceni Village*, (reconstructed), Cockley Cley, near Swaffham; *Colman's Mustard Museum*, The Mustard Shop, 3 Bridewell Akkey, Norwich.

NORTHAMPTONSHIRE

DAVENTRY (Northants). Mrs Margaret Lainchbury, Weston Hill Farm, Moreton Pinkney, Daventry NN11 6SN (Sulgrave [029-576] 382). Working farm. This attractive farmhouse is situated half-a-mile outside the conservation village of Moreton Pinkney, with beautiful views looking out over unspoiled countryside. It is on the B4525 between Banbury and Northampton, and is an ideal touring centre for the Cotswolds, Stratford-upon-Avon, Oxford, Silverstone, Towcester and Sulgrave Manor, and is convenient for the Royal Show and the M1. It is one mile from the National Trust property of Canons Ashby House. Guests' comfort is catered for with full central heating, fitted carpets and hot and cold in bedrooms. They have the use of their own diningroom, drawing room with open fire and colour TV, and their own bathroom. Bed and Breakfast. Evening Meal optional.

MARKET HARBOROUGH. Mrs Kathleen Randle, Valley View, 3 Camsdale Walk, Middleton, Market Harborough, Leicestershire LE16 8YR (Rockingham [0536] 770874). Stone-built house in an elevated position in a quiet cul-de-sac on the outskirts of the village, with outstanding panoramic views of the Welland Valley, within easy distance of Market Harborough, Corby, Uppingham and Kettering. Bathroom for exclusive use of guests, separate diningroom, large lounge, parking space. Local amenities include East Carlton Countryside Park with Industrial Heritage Centre, Craft Workshops and Nature Trails, Rockingham Castle, used to film 'By the Sword Divided'. Trout fishing locally, and many other historic houses and beauty spots. On A427 Market Harborough/Corby Road. Turn onto the B670 Middleton Road, take third left, School Hill, Camsdale Walk first right.

NORTHAMPTONSHIRE – WHAT TO DO AND SEE!

Rolling farmland and woods contrasted against industrial towns such as Corby and Kettering, this is what makes up Northamptonshire. The canal centre at Stoke Bruerne, the coloured stone church at Stanford-on-Avon and the country parks at Barnwell and Irchester all make for interesting visits.

HELP IMPROVE BRITISH TOURIST STANDARDS

You are choosing holiday accommodation from our very popular FARM HOLIDAY GUIDES. Whether it be a hotel, guest house, farmhouse or self-catering accommodation, we think you will find it hospitable, comfortable and clean, and your host and hostess friendly and helpful.

Why not write and tell us about it?

As a recognition of the generally well-run and excellent holiday accommodation reviewed in our publications, we at FARM HOLIDAY GUIDES LIMITED present a diploma to proprietors who receive the highest recommendation from their guests who are also readers of our Guides. If you care to write to us praising the holiday you have booked through FARM HOLIDAY GUIDES – whether this be board, self-catering accommodation, a sporting or a caravan holiday, the content of your letter will be evaluated and the proprietors who reach our final list will be contacted.

The winning proprietor will receive an attractive framed diploma to display on his premises as recognition of a high standard of comfort, amenity and hospitality. FARM HOLIDAY GUIDES LIMITED offer this diploma as a contribution towards the improvement of standards in tourist accommodation in Britain. Help your excellent host or hostess to win it!

DIPLOMA
AWARDED BY
READERS
of
FARM HOLIDAY GUIDE
PUBLICATIONS LIMITED

TO ....
FOR HOLIDAY ACCOMMODATION
of the HIGHEST STANDARD

AT ....

NORTHUMBERLAND

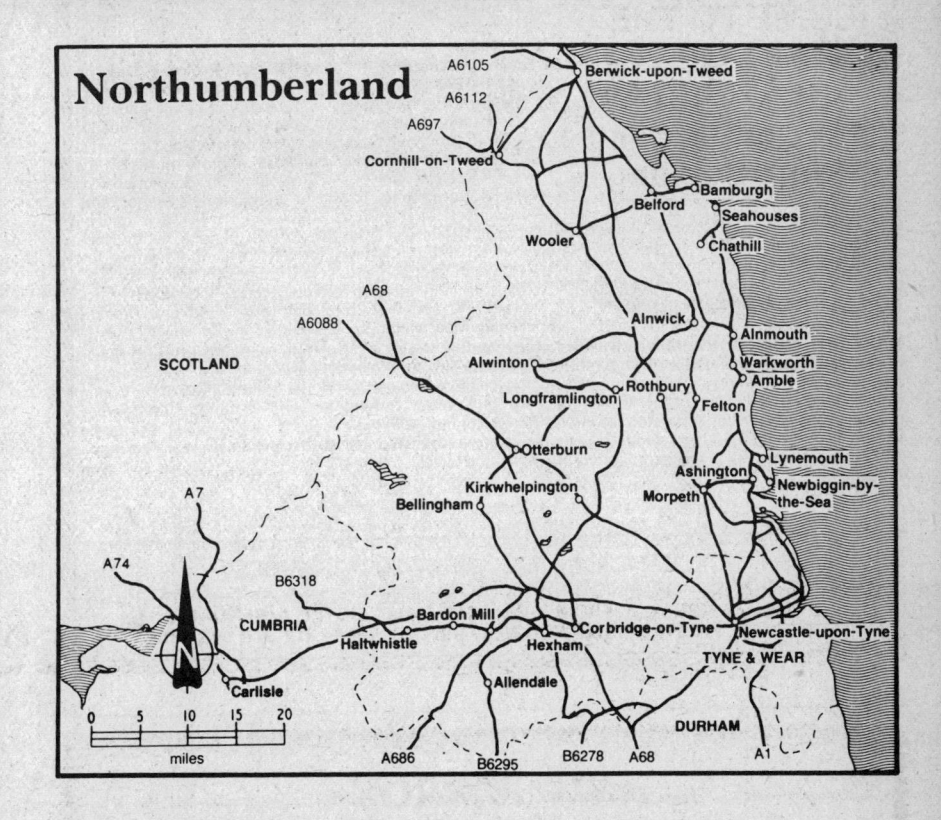

ALLENDALE. Mrs Carol Davison, Oakey Dene, Allendale, Hexham NE47 9EL (Allendale [043-483] 572). Situated approximately one mile from the picturesque town of Allendale and half-a-mile from the golf courses and riding school in an area for touring: 20 minutes' drive from Roman Wall and many buildings of historical interest within easy reach. This small farmhouse, with adjoining byres and hayloft, has now been converted into an attractive home. Comfortably furnished double and family bedrooms (two with washbasins); bathroom, toilet; sittingroom, diningroom. Children welcome at reduced rates, cot, high chair. Parents can enjoy an evening out without worrying about the children, as someone will be on hand to babysit. Open April to October, the house is centrally heated. No pets. An ideal position for overnight stops or for spending a peaceful holiday. Bed and Breakfast from £8; Evening Meal £6.

ALNMOUTH. Sheila and Gordon Inkster, Marine House Private Hotel, 1 Marine Road, Alnmouth NE66 2RW (Alnwick [0665] 830349). "Marine House" is a 200-year-old stone house, once a granary, of considerable charm, recently modernised but retaining original features. Situated on the edge of the village's nine-hole golf links, with fine views of the sea. Personal supervision, home cooking, residential licence, spacious lounge with colour TV. Full central heating. Double, twin and family rooms, H&C, some with own shower and toilet. Children reduced rates. Cellar games room. Parking. Pets welcome. Open all year. Special terms early, late season. Golf courses, sandy beaches, bathing, pony trekking. Excellent centre to explore the magnificent Northumbrian coastline with its castles and wildlife sanctuaries. Ramble on the Cheviot Hills or along the Roman Wall. Evening Dinner, Bed and Breakfast from £18.50; Bed and Breakfast from £12.

Terms quoted in this publication may be subject to increase if rises in costs necessitate

COME TO THE HEART OF GREAT BRITAIN for Comfort and Home Cooking

"THE DALE" HOTEL, established in 1870 and supervised by the present owners for 60 years, offers considerable comfort and is an ideal touring base for visitors seeking a country holiday. It is excellently situated with a southern aspect in the Market Place of Allendale with views from the garden of the beautiful Allen Valley. The main building dates back to the reign of Queen Elizabeth I and improvements during the past few years, while not altering the character of the structure, now provide amenities of a high standard.

The hotel, open from the Spring Holiday to the end of September, as well as over the Christmas festive season is centrally heated and, in addition, all bedrooms of varying size have electric blankets and fires, and washbasins. There are five bathrooms and a sauna, ample toilet accommodation, two lounges and two diningrooms. There is a swing in the garden, table tennis, putting green. A riding school is nearby. A reliable recommendation is the fact that guests return year after year to enjoy the excellent food — home-cooked beef and tongues, home-made cakes, appetising sweets and fresh cream.

Inclusive terms from £89 Full Board; £79 Dinner, Bed and Breakfast; £52.50 Bed and Breakfast, per week.

Allendale itself, the geographical centre of Great Britain, is an unspoiled country village founded before AD 1200 and its unrestricted position 800 feet above sea level gives the visitor a sense of freedom and space enhanced by rolling heather-clad hills. It has a nine-hole course, tennis and bowling, while fishing and fell walking can be enjoyed in the vicinity. Wildlife abounds in the surrounding countryside and Allendale makes an ideal centre from which to tour Hadrian's Wall and visit some of the most interesting Roman camps. Parking.

Please send for brochure with full details of "The Dale" to:

MR and MRS W. A. THOMPSON, "THE DALE" HOTEL, ALLENDALE, HEXHAM, NORTHUMBERLAND NE47 9BD (Allendale 212 STD 043 483).

Bishopfield Farm, Allendale, Hexham, Northumberland, NE47 9EJ

Standing in 200-acres of beautiful countryside, the farmhouse dates to 1740. The furnishings and accommodation are to a high standard with nine letting bedrooms, all with bath or shower rooms en suite and full central heating. Six of the bedrooms are situated in the cobbled courtyard which acts as an annexe to the house and holds a full fire certificate. There are two lounges and a diningroom which has a table to accommodate 18 people. It is the policy of the proprietors to serve good, freshly cooked and locally produced food and they take pride in the cleanliness of the establishment. Centrally situated for many places of interest such as Hadrian's Wall, stately homes and castles, Lake District and Kielder Dam, and many more. Your hosts, **KATHY & KEITH FAIRLESS** are confident that you will return home feeling relaxed, with many pleasant memories and hope that you will want to return to **BISHOPFIELD** again and again.

* Personally owned and run by the Fairless family who are the third generation at Bishopfield.   * All rooms with bath and shower room en suite.   * Fresh locally produced food; home cooking.   * 16th century six-bedroom annexe in cobbled courtyard.   * Full central heating.   * Open log fires in two lounges.   * 1½ miles private trout fishing for guests.   * Dining table seats 18 people with Minton china and silver cutlery.   * Cleanliness and home cooking our speciality.   * Colour TV in all bedrooms.   * Access to rooms at all times.   * Table Licence.

Tel.: Allendale (0434 83) 248.

ALNMOUTH. Mrs M. I. Cleghorn, "St. Julian's", 21 Argyle Street, Alnmouth NE66 2SB (Alnmouth [0665] 830486). This guest house is situated four miles east of Alnwick, off the A1. It is 70 yards from the beach in a small seaside village. Nearby there are numerous beautiful beaches, golf courses, National Trust areas and properties plus places of historic interest. Good walking country. Fishing and riding available in the area. Accommodation in family, twin and single rooms, some with washbasins. Two bathrooms; two toilets. Sittingroom and diningroom. Children are welcome and provided for. Pets welcome. A car is not essential, but preferable. Ample parking. Visitors' lounge with TV. Open May to October. Mid-week bookings accepted. Evening Dinner, Bed and Breakfast from £13. Bed and Breakfast from £8.

ALNWICK. Mrs A. I. Easton, Farm House, West Ditchburn, Eglingham, Alnwick NE66 2UE (Powburn [066-578] 337). Working farm. This 17th-century stone-built house has large garden with pheasants, peafowl, etc., and is situated in unspoilt countryside with beaches all around. Many interesting sights — Chillingham wild cattle, Grace Darling's Museum, hills, castles, etc. Pony trekking, country walks in lovely valleys and all within easy reach of the house. Accommodation is available from March to October. Four bedrooms, double or family (three with washbasins). "Teasmade"; bathroom and toilets; sittingroom and diningroom. Full central heating. Pets by arrangement. A car is essential and there is plenty of parking space. Evening Meal, Bed and Breakfast or Bed and Breakfast. Reductions for children. A warm welcome and good food awaits all guests. Fire Certificate held. AA and RAC listed. SAE for colour brochure please.

ALNWICK. Mrs Jean Robinson, "Ravensmount," Alnmouth Road, Alnwick NE66 2QG (Alnwick [0665] 603773). A spacious detached country house of character in its own grounds, welcomes guests from April to end September. Commanding excellent views of the countryside it is only three-quarters-of-a-mile from the historic town of Alnwick with castles and history dating back to the 13th century. Ideal base for touring central Northumberland. Accommodation in twin-bedded rooms with private bathroom suite, one family and one double bedrooms; three bathrooms, four toilets; diningroom, sittingroom with colour TV. Children welcome — cot, high chair and reduced rates for under-12's. Sorry, no pets. Ample parking provided. Bed, Breakfast and Evening Meal or Bed and Breakfast only. Terms on request.

ALNWICK. Mrs Anne Davison, Alndyke Farm, Alnwick NE66 3PB (Alnwick [0665] 602193). Working farm. This spacious 18th-century farmhouse stands in its own grounds, with excellent views, offering accommodation in one double, one twin-bedded and one family bedrooms (two with washbasins), all have hot drink facilities. Bathroom and toilet. Breakfast and Evening Dinner are served in the diningroom. The lounge has colour TV and wood-burning fire. Guests are assured of comfort and good cooking at Alndyke which is situated near the A1068, one mile from the historical town of Alnwick and three miles to sandy beaches. The farmland runs to the River Aln, with a disused railway line and right of way, giving pleasant walks and uninterrupted views. Alndyke is an excellent centre for touring Northumberland, from the coast to the Cheviot Hills, with castles, country houses, fishing, golf, riding, swimming nearby. Accommodation is available from May to October. Children are welcome from five years old. Car essential. Ample parking. Fire Certificate held. AA listed and registered with Tourist Board Grade Three. SAE for brochure with terms.

NORTHUMBERLAND – BORDER COUNTRY!

You cannot go any further north and remain in England! There is much outstanding scenery, both inland and on the coast, and a host of interesting places to visit. Border Forest Park has everything you would expect, plus many interesting Roman remains. There are also remains at Housesteads and other places of interest include Lindisfarne, the "conserved" village of Blanchland, Hexham, Heatherslaw Mill and Craster.

Northumberland BOARD

ALNWICK. Mrs Marion Oates, Lumbylaw Farm, Edlingham, Alnwick NE66 2BW (Whittingham [066-574] 277). The Oates family offer delightful hospitality in their recently modernised Northumbrian Farmhouse, providing one family and two double bedrooms, fully fitted with washbasins, central heating, hot drink facilities and spectacular views to the surrounding hills. Although the farm is ideally situated for exploring the delights of Northumberland, its 900 acres provide walks rich in history and abundant in wildlife, encompassing a river, a railway line (disused), ruined medieval castle and Norman church. Healthy appetites follow healthy activities and the day begins with a real farmhouse breakfast — and ends in the comfortable lounge after an imaginatively prepared evening meal. Children are welcome, reductions available. Pets by arrangement. Cot, high chair, babysitting, extensive reading selection provided, but above all a relaxed friendly atmosphere and enjoyable food. Please send SAE, or telephone for details.

ALNWICK. Mrs Dorothy Hankin, New Moor House, Edlingham, Alnwick NE66 2BT (Whittingham [066-574] 638). This charming stone-built house, originally a coaching house built approximately 1800, is set in the midst of spectacular countryside. Situated on the junction of the A697 and the B6341, seven miles from Alnwick and four from Rothbury with lovely views over moorland and Cheviot Hills. Sea 10 miles. Excellent centre for walking and sporting activities. Good farmhouse style cooking, much of the fare home produced — fruit, vegetables, eggs and milk. A small Egon Ronay recommended tearoom is run on the premises and pedigree show goats are bred on the smallholding. Three double or family rooms and one single, all with washbasins. Children welcome, cot, high chair and babysitting. Pets allowed. Open March to November. Evening Meal, Bed and Breakfast or Bed and Breakfast. Reductions for children. The aim of the proprietors is to provide a happy informal holiday and they think Northumbria has everything to offer the holidaymaker. SAE, for terms, please.

ALNWICK. Mrs L. Edridge, Norfolk, 41 Blakelaw Road, Alnwick NE66 1BA (0665-602892). A private house where cleanliness and comfort are guaranteed. Good home cooking with garden produce. Refreshments at 9 pm. One double room with H&C, razor points. One twin room with H&C, razor points. Central heating. Double glazing. Bathroom/shower. Separate toilet. TV lounge. Situated in a peaceful area of this market town. Ideal for open countryside and quiet roads. Forestry walks six miles. Northumbrian coastline four miles. Historic houses and castles are plentiful. Bed, Breakfast and Evening Meal. SAE please, or telephone for terms.

BELFORD. Mrs B. J. Bryden, Seafields, 7 Cragside Avenue, Belford NE70 7NA (Belford [06683] 502). A private family house in its own grounds with extensive views offering accommodation all year round. One double, one twin bedded room, with extra single available; bathroom, toilet; lounge; diningroom. Central heating throughout. Children welcome, cot, babysitting and reduced rates. Pets allowed. Car not essential but there is parking. Bus 100 yards. An ideal centre for touring castles, National Trust properties, Farne Islands, Holy Island, the Borders country and enjoying the beautiful beaches. A warm welcome is assured to all our visitors. Bed and Breakfast from £6.50; Evening Meal, Bed and Breakfast from £9.50.

BERWICK-ON-TWEED. Mrs J. Gray, Middle Ord Farm, Berwick-on-Tweed TD15 2XQ (0289) 306323. Working farm. An attractive Georgian residence, built 1783, with a Victorian extension (1907), on mixed cattle, sheep, arable farm, set in unspoilt position surrounded by woodland and walled gardens. Period lounge and diningroom overlook the garden. Colour TV. Tea/coffee making facilities. Three double, one single, one family rooms (one with washbasin). Central heating. Car essential — parking. Open May to October for Bed and Breakfast from £8.50. Many places of interest to visit, and sporting activities are within easy reach. Also available, Middle Orm Farmhouse, for self-catering holidays, from April to October — an 18th century farmhouse, completely detached, to accommodate up to nine people, plus cot for small baby if required. Three double, one twin-bedded room; bathroom; sittingroom; diningroom; kitchen. Fully equipped except linen. Pets accepted. Weekly terms £50 to £140.

CORBRIDGE. Mrs E. Sanderson, 'Low Riding', Aydon Road, Corbridge, Tyne (Corbridge [043-471] 2340). Tourist accommodation in the beautiful Tyne Valley. The house is situated in a residential district of Corbridge (6321). Ideal for visiting The Roman Wall, Housesteads, Kielder, Wallington. One double bedroom, one twin-bedded room, both with wash hand basins. One single room. Shower in bathroom. The house is open all year and is centrally heated throughout. Diningroom with separate tables. Car essential. Parking available. Children welcome. Regret, no dogs. Mid-week bookings taken. BTA commended. Evening Meal available at Corbridge. Terms on request. SAE, please, for quick reply.

CORBRIDGE. Mrs Sue Jones, Low Barns, Thornbrough, Corbridge NE45 5LX (Corbridge [043-471] 2408). Ideal base for country lovers, Low Barns is situated in open countryside, one mile east of Corbridge, within easy reach of the Roman Wall, Hexham, Lake District, Scottish Borders and the breathtaking north east coastline. Recently converted from two farm cottages and a barn, accommodation comprises two double rooms with washbasins, colour TV, tea/coffee making facilities etc., plus one family room. Bathroom, toilet. Sitting/diningroom. Central heating. Local sporting facilities include riding, golf, fishing, swimming, wind surfing, canoeing and rambling. Children over 12 years welcome, pets accepted if kept in car. To reach "Low Barns" take B6350 from roundabout on A69 east of Corbridge, after one mile take private road on right — grey slate sign "Low Barns" on roadside. Open all year. Bed and Breakfast from £8.50. Parking.

CORBRIDGE. Mrs D. F. Sives, Bowland, Aydon Road, Corbridge NE45 5EG (Corbridge [043-471] 2043). This bungalow stands in a quiet, residential area and makes a good stopping-off place en route north or south. Good centre for visiting Hadrian's Wall. Visitors are assured of every comfort and satisfaction. One double and one twin bedrooms; bathroom, toilet; sittingroom; diningroom. Children and pets welcome. Parking available. Breakfast of the highest quality, beautifully cooked and attractively served. Open all year round. SAE, please, or telephone for further details.

CORNHILL-ON-TWEED. Mrs A. T. Robertson, Encampment Farm, Cornhill-on-Tweed TD12 4TF (Crookham [089-082] 254). Working farm. As the name suggests, this farmhouse stands on what was once an army encampment at the Battle of Flodden in 1513. Now used for more peaceful purposes, the farm is delightfully situated with a good view of the surrounding district of Ford Castle, with the Border Abbeys at Kelso, Jedburgh, Dryburgh and Melrose within easy reach. The Cheviot Hills provide scope for walking and climbing, and Berwick-upon-Tweed, with its Elizabethan Walls, is within easy reach. The farmhouse stands on 250-acre crop farm and has three double, one single and one family bedrooms, one with washbasin; bathroom, two toilets; sitting/diningroom. Cot, high chair, babysitting, reduced rates for children. No pets. Open April to October. Car essential, parking. SAE for terms for Evening Meal, Bed and Breakfast; Bed and Breakfast.

GREENHEAD. Mrs Pauline Staff, Holmhead Guest House, Hadrian's Wall, Greenhead CA6 7HY (Gilsland [069-72] 402). If you are visiting Hadrian's Wall, or en route to the Lakes or Scotland, come and stay with us! Our modernised and converted farmhouse stands on the line of the Wall and is only 15 minutes' walk from the highest remaining parts and the Roman Army Museum. Pauline is a qualified tour guide and can organise tours or show slides of the Wall. Holmhead nestles in the Tipalt Valley surrounded by farmland. Approach by driving over ford and half a mile private drive from Greenhead Village which is on the A69, three miles west of Haltwhistle. The bus stops at Greenhead near the golf course. All bedrooms have hot and cold washbasins, shaver points, lovely views. Our upstairs residents' lounge has colour TV, coffee/tea making facilities. Children welcome. All facilities and special rates for them. Babysitting. Full central heating. Open all year. Farmhouse breakfast. Dinner, if required. Excellent food, attractively served. AA listed. Residential and restaurant licence.

HALTWHISTLE. Mrs Mary Dawson, Park Burnfoot Farm, Featherstone Park, Haltwhistle NE49 0JP (Haltwhistle [0498] 20378). Working farm. When visiting the Roman Wall area for an overnight stop or a longer visit, you can be sure of a friendly welcome at this 18th-century farmhouse on a 200-acre working farm, the Park Burn with the waterfalls to the front of the house, and the River South Tyne at the back make an ideal setting. Woodland walk 100 yards away. Two miles from Haltwhistle, one mile from Featherstone castle and about four miles from the best parts of the Roman Wall, the farm is an ideal touring centre; Ullswater and the Scottish Borders within easy motoring distance. One double and one family bedrooms, with washbasins; soap and towels; bathroom with shower, separate toilet; large, warm visitors' lounge. Terms for accommodation and good English breakfast from £7.50, late drink included. Self-catering cottage also available from £45 per week. Recommended by "Home and Garden" '81. Registered with English Tourist Board. AA listed. AA Wayfarer Vouchers welcome.

HALTWHISTLE. Mrs M. S. Murray, Oaky Knowe Farm, Haltwhistle NE49 0NB (Haltwhistle [0498] 20648). Working farm. "Oaky Knowe" is a most attractive 300-acre stock-rearing farm which was featured in the 1977 TV programme "Wish You Were Here." Situated one mile from the Roman Wall and walking distance from Haltwhistle, it is within easy reach of the Lake District, Lowther Wild Life Park, pony trekking and many places of historical interest. Two family and one twin-bedded rooms; bathroom, toilet; sitting and diningrooms. Children welcome (reductions under 10), cot and high chair available — babysitting by arrangement. Pets allowed, but not indoors. Ample parking. Sporting facilities in the area. Evening Meal, Bed and Breakfast or Bed and Breakfast. Prices on request.

HEXHAM. Mrs M. I. Lee, Manor House Farm, Ninebanks, Hexham NE47 8DA (Whitfield [04985] 236). Working farm. Manor House Farm is a stock rearing hill farm situated just off the A686, eight miles from Alston, 15 from Hexham. It is a convenient centre for the Lake District, Roman Wall, Beamish Museum and an excellent stopover for visitors to Scotland. There is pony trekking and golf course nearby. The farmhouse nestles in the beautiful unspoilt West Allen Valley offering visitors a peaceful holiday, with a substantial farmhouse Breakfast to start their day. Single and family rooms; bathroom, toilet; sittingroom; diningroom. Open fires. Children and pets welcome. Open fires. Car essential. Parking. Bed and Breakfast from £8 daily. Reduced rates for children.

If you've found
FARM HOLIDAY GUIDE
of service please tell your friends

HEXHAM. Mrs J. Roberts, Lilac Mount, Catton, Allendale, Hexham NE47 9QR (Allendale [043-483] 553). An attractive, luxurious bungalow offering excellent accommodation and a warm welcome. Set in a delightful North Pennines village surrounded by beautiful countryside, this is a good base for walking and touring. Close to Hadrian's Wall, Kielder Reservoir, Durham, Border country and the magnificent Northumbrian coastline. Golf course and riding stables within one mile. Good cooking a speciality. Rooms (one double, one twin and one family room with washbasins) furnished mainly with fine antiques. Central heating and log fires. House suitable for disabled guests. Ideal overnight stop between York and Scotland. Car essential — parking. Terms from £17 for Evening Dinner, Bed and Breakfast. Bed and Breakfast only from £10. Les Routiers recommended. Open all year.

HEXHAM. Mrs J. Knowles, Hunter Oak Farm, Keenley, Allendale, Hexham NE47 9NT (Whitfield [049-85] 291). A delightful early 18th-century farmhouse in a peaceful rural situation three miles from picturesque Allendale and 12 miles from historic Hexham. Magnificent views across the valley to nearby Hadrian's Wall. The house is centrally heated throughout and comfortably furnished, largely with antiques. One double, one twin and two single rooms all with washbasins. Guests' bathroom (hot showers) two toilets. Sittingroom with colour TV and log fire, separate dining room. Walled garden for sunning. Good food a speciality. Ideal overnight stop between York and Scotland. Bed and Breakfast from £7.50. Four course Evening Dinner from £5.50. Excellent centre for walking or touring in Northumbria. SAE please for brochure.

HEXHAM. Mrs M. G. Carter, East Wood House, Fallowfield Road, Acomb, Hexham NE46 4RN (Hexham [0434] 603188). A small, comfortable, well-appointed country house in a peaceful rural setting with gardens and three and a half acres of land, south-facing with extensive views over the Tyne Valley. Ideal centre for visiting the Roman Wall, the magnificent Northumberland countryside and many places of historic interest. The attractive old market town of Hexham is three miles away. The house is centrally heated. One double, one twin, one single bedroom, all with washbasins. Adjacent guests' bathroom (including shower). Separate guests' diningroom and sittingroom (colour TV). Good food. Bed and Breakfast £7.50. Bed, Breakfast and Dinner from £11.50. Weekly half-board from £77. Dogs welcome by prior arrangement. Open April to October. SAE for brochure.

HEXHAM. Mrs M. E. Grimwood, Heatherlea, 5 Percy Terrace, Bellingham, Hexham NE48 2BY (Bellingham [0660] 20248). Situated on the fringe of Bellingham in the beautiful countryside of the North Tyne near Kielder Reservoir, with a splendid view over the valley, this spacious guest house is set in a village abounding in interesting historical associations. Hadrian's Wall and Roman Camps are within a few miles, en route to Pennine Way, with the Border Forest Park nearby. One double, one single, one family bedrooms, one with washbasin; bathroom, toilet; diningroom; large lounge. Cot, high chair, babysitting. Sorry, no pets. Car essential — parking. Home cooking and packed lunches. Open April to October. SAE for terms for Evening Dinner, Bed and Breakfast or Bed and Breakfast. Reductions for children under 12 years.

HEXHAM near. Mrs Jean Cousin, The Laws, Whitfield, Near Hexham NE47 8JG (Whitfield [049-85] 227). Working farm. A warm welcome and comfortable accommodation awaits guests all year round on this 550-acre mixed farm in a peaceful village 11 miles from the historic town of Hexham. Family room with double bed and bunks, plus single room. Bathroom, two toilets. Sittingroom and diningroom. Children welcome, babysitting available. Pets accepted free of charge. Car essential here and there is ample parking. Ideal base for touring the Lake District, Roman Wall, Kielder Reservoir, Border country and the splendid Northumbrian coastline. Golf course and riding centre within easy reach. Excellent walking country. Village has a post office and general store. Good cooking a speciality. Evening Meal, Bed and Breakfast from £8; Bed and Breakfast from £6. Reduced rates for children.

HEXHAM-ON-TYNE. Mrs E. Stappard, Mount Pleasant Farm, Sandhoe, Hexham-on-Tyne NE46 4LX (Hexham [0434] 603070). Working farm. Traditional farmhouse in lovely countryside on 140-acre mixed farm with cattle and sheep. Good centre for exploring Hadrian's Wall, Roman Camps, Kielder Water, beautiful Northumbrian countryside, Border country or North-East coast. Ideal overnight stop to or from Scotland. Mount Pleasant is one and a half miles north of Corbridge and one mile from A68; three miles from Hexham. One double and one family room (both with washbasins and shaver points); bathroom and toilet; sun lounge (with extensive view of Tyne Valley); lounge with TV; diningroom. Central heating. Open from April to end October. Bed and Breakfast only (Evening meal can be obtained at Corbridge, or local country inns). Parking space (car essential). SAE, please.

HOUSESTEADS. Mrs Brenda Huddleston, Beggar Bog Guest House, Housesteads, Haydon Bridge, Hexham NE47 6NN (Bardon Mill [049-84] 320). A small comfortable Guest House where good food and cleanliness are guaranteed. Situated on B6318, 13 miles from market town of Hexham. The house is ideally situated for use as a base whilst exploring the many historic sites in the area. Particularly, the many Roman forts, museums, Hadrian's Wall and Kielder Dam. Four bedrooms, hot and cold water and tea-making facilities. Lounge where guests can relax at any time. Dinner and packed lunch on request. Children welcome. Registered English Tourist Board. Write or telephone for terms.

KIRKWHELPINGTON. Mrs A. H. Wells, The Old Vicarage, Kirkwhelpington NE19 2RT (Otterburn [0830] 40319). Relax in the tranquil beauty of Northumberland and enjoy the old world charm of this historic Georgian house, originally a 13th-century Pele Tower with the house built around it in 1760. The present owners have sympathetically restored the old house to its former elegance without losing modern comfort and convenience. There is an acre of walled garden, with sweeping lawns. Pet hens lay fresh eggs for breakfast and there is a friendly atmosphere. Children and pets welcome. French spoken. TV lounge. Sunny diningroom. Packed lunches and Evening Meals on request. Bed and Breakfast from £7.50. Kirkwhelpington is just off the A696 between Belsay and Otterburn and is one and a half miles from Wallington Hall.

MORPETH. Mrs Norma Sadler, Rimside House, Longframlington, Morpeth NE65 8DR (Longframlington [066-570] 259). Conveniently situated in the centre of a charming Northumbrian village. Ideal touring centre for coast, castles and National Parks. River fishing, pony riding and golf nearby. Rimside is a stone-built period house with ample car parking facilities, set in three acres. Excellent accommodation, all bedrooms with washbasins, tea-making facilities. Comfortable residents' lounge with colour TV and diningroom serving good home-cooked meals using our own produce where possible. Older children welcome. Sorry, no pets. Open all year. Bed and Breakfast from £8.50. Dinner optional. Bargain break week-ends during low season. Self-catering cottage also available. Registered with English Tourist Board. Phone for full details and brochure.

NEWCASTLETON. Mrs Margaret Jones, Forest Lodge, Kershopefoot, Newcastleton, Roxburghshire TD9 0TJ (Liddesdale [054-121] 392). Superior accommodation and the personal attention of the proprietress will ensure that your overnight stay, weekend break or annual holiday is a memorable one. An acre of garden affords breathtaking views of the surrounding hills. Ideal base for walking, touring, bird-watching and fishing. Nearby are Hadrian's Wall, Scottish Border country, Northern Lake District, Solway Coast and Kielder Dam. Good stopover for travellers from England to Edinburgh and the Highlands. One twin room and one family room with tea-making facilities and good choice of breakfast. Bath, toilet and shower facilities. Central heating. Car essential, parking. Babysitting, cot and highchair. Reduced rates for children sharing with parents. Terms from £7 Bed and Breakfast. Phone for details.

NEWCASTLE-UPON-TYNE. Mrs Alice Southern, Beukley Farm, Great Whittington, Newcastle-upon-Tyne NE19 2LD (Great Whittington [043472] 225). Buckley Farm is a 400-acre mixed farm standing high up in the Northumbrian countryside. The breathtaking views have to be seen to be believed and it is little wonder that Hadrian used this place as a lookout to thwart the oncoming Scots! This is Roman Wall country and all the intrigue and history of that unique era is here for you to explore as well as some of the most beautiful unspoilt countryside in England. Tom and Alice Southern look forward to welcoming you to their splendid farmhouse where comfort and good food are in abundance. This is a holiday you are unlikely to forget — give it a try.

NEWCASTLE-UPON-TYNE. Mrs Janet B. White, Horncastle, Kirkwhelpington, Newcastle-upon-Tyne NE19 2RA (Otterburn [0830] 40247). Working farm. Situated off the beaten track, Horncastle offers a truly rural setting for a peaceful farm holiday. Beautifully furnished rooms, bedrooms with wash handbasins, hot drinks facilities, central heating, two bathrooms make this a particularly lovely farmhouse in which to stay. Super English Breakfasts, and delicious three-course dinners are served six nights of the week. The weekly farm walk with Ian, plus farm trail and fishing pool make Horncastle an interesting farm to stay. Many places to visit — Kielder Water, Hadrian's Wall, Coast and Castle, but most of all a place where hospitality is shown to all our guests. Please send stamp for details or telephone.

PLEASE SEND A STAMPED ADDRESSED ENVELOPE WITH ENQUIRIES

Northumberland BOARD

ROTHBURY. Jeff and Sheila Jefferson, Orchard Guest House, High Street, Rothbury, Morpeth NE65 7TL (Rothbury [0669] 20684). A warm welcome awaits guests in this charming Country Guest House in Rothbury. Set in the Coquet Valley in the heart of the Northumbrian countryside. Ideal touring centre for visiting National Trust properties, historic Castles, Roman Wall and National Park. The area is renowned for walking, fishing and its scenic beauty. In Orchard House we have six bedrooms, double, family or twin-bedded as required, all with washbasins and shaver points. Three bathrooms, shower room and four toilets. Guests' lounge and separate diningroom. Central heating throughout. Open all year. Excellent home cooking and personal attention. Bed and Breakfast or Bed, Breakfast and Evening Meal. Sorry, no pets. Brochure on request, SAE appreciated. AA listed.

WARKWORTH. Mrs J. C. Clarke, Elmwood, 6 Watershaugh Road, Warkworth NE65 0TT (Alnwick [0665] 711357). Pleasant family house surrounded by attractive garden, in peaceful situation on edge of Warkworth with lovely views of sea and castle, about one and a half miles from long sandy beach. Accommodation for up to six guests all year round in single, double or family/twin rooms. Friendly family atmosphere and Mr and Mrs Clarke and their daughters speak French and German. Sittingroom with colour TV and garden for guests' use any time. Children welcome, cot, high chair and babysitting. Pets accepted free of charge. Warkworth is a picturesque village with an old church, famous castle and beautiful riverside walk to Ancient Hermitage. Within easy drive of Scottish Border, Roman Wall, numerous castles and nature reserves. Parking space. Bed and Breakfast from £7.50. Evening Meal by prior arrangement — £5. Reductions for children, and for senior citizens off season only.

WARKWORTH. Mrs S. C. Lillico, 9 Watershaugh Road, Warkworth, Morpeth NE65 0TT (Alnwick [0665] 711583). Friendly, family home on the edge of this historic village, within easy reach of long, unspoilt, sandy beaches. We provide accommodation in double/twin rooms, one with washbasin. Children welcome at reduced rate, babysitting provided. Parking. Bed and full English Breakfast, including evening drink from £7.50 nightly, £52 weekly. Bed, Breakfast and three-course Evening Meal from £11.50 nightly, £80 weekly. Within easy reach of Cheviot Hills, Forest Walks, Farne Islands, historic castles and Roman Wall by car. Tourist Board registered.

SHIELDHALL

WALLINGTON, CAMBO,
MORPETH, NORTHUMBERLAND NE61 4AQ
Stephen and Celia Robinson-Gay
Tel. Otterburn (0830) 40387

This attractive 18th century farmhouse overlooks the National Trust's Wallington Hall and its beautiful surroundings. It is a quarter of a mile off the A696 Newcastle/Edinburgh road and is easily accessible from the A1 and the A68. Central for exploring Northumbria's many castles, churches, Roman wall remains, Lindisfarn and Kielder. Within Shieldhall's east and west wings are two double bedrooms plus a single and a family room — all with private facilities and electric blankets. One oak four poster. French windows in the lounge lead to a well kept garden. Home produce served in charming inglenook dining room. SAE please for brochure and terms.

WOOLER. Mrs M. D. Wilkinson, "Chateauguay," High Humbleton, Wooler NE71 6SU (Wooler [0668] 81561). Modern bungalow with beautiful views situated at the foothills of the Cheviots, and excellent touring centre. Lovely countryside for walking. Pony trekking one mile. Numerous historical houses within easy reach, coast 15 miles. Comfortable accommodation with good home-cooking. Bed and Breakfast from £7.50; Evening Meal provided from £4. Bedtime drink included. Two double, one single room; bathroom, toilet; visitors' lounge with TV, diningroom. Children welcome at reduced rates; babysitting available. Sorry, no pets. Car essential — parking. Open May to September.

WOOLER. Mrs B. Nevins, Turvelaws Farmhouse, Wooler NE71 6AJ (Wooler [0668] 81479). Working farm. A warm welcome awaits you at Turvelaws Farmhouse, half a mile from Wooler at the foothills of the Cheviots. A unique base from which to explore the magnificent county of Northumberland; 14 miles from Scottish Borders, 13 miles from sandy beach, 10 miles from historic Flodden Field. Farm Museum in Wooler. Comfortable accommodation in two double, one family, one single bedrooms; bathroom; sittingroom with colour TV; diningroom. Children over five welcome and babysitting can be arranged. Sorry, no pets. Car essential, ample parking. Open May to October (also Easter) for Evening Dinner/Meal, Bed and Breakfast or Bed and Breakfast. Tea and biscuits at bed-time included in terms. Reductions for children. SAE brings prompt reply.

NOTTINGHAMSHIRE

MANSFIELD. Mrs L. Palmer, Boon Hills Farm, Nether Langwith, Mansfield NG20 9JQ (Mansfield [0623] 743862). Working farm. Farmhouse accommodation in stone-built farmhouse standing in 155 acres of mixed farmland, 300 yards back from A632 on edge of the village. Comfortably furnished with fitted carpets throughout, the house has electric heating, open fire. Large sitting/diningroom with colour TV. One family room, one double room and another room with twin beds. Children welcome and there are many pets for them on the farm. Babysitting arranged. Pets accepted. Situated on edge of Sherwood Forest, six miles from Visitors' Centre; eight miles M1; 10 miles A1. Places of interest include Hardwick Hall, Thoresby Hall, Chatsworth House, Newstead Abbey. Pleasant half-mile walk to picturesque village inn. Car essential, ample parking. Bed and Breakfast only from £7 per night. Non-smokers only. Reductions for children. Open March to October inclusive.

MANSFIELD. Mrs June M. Ibbotson, Blue Barn Farm, Langwith, Mansfield NG20 9JD (Mansfield [0623] 742248). Blue Barn is a family run mixed arable farm on Welbeck Estate, set in quiet countryside between Cuckney and Nether Langwith on the edge of Sherwood Forest. Clumber Park, Creswell Crags, Hardwick Hall, Rifford Country Park and many other places of interest are just a short distance away by car. Visitors are welcome to walk around the farm. Blue Barn is up the second lane on left out of Cuckney on A616. On arrival please bring cars on to lawn through Blue Gate. Double, single and family bedrooms; bathroom, two toilets; sittingroom; diningroom. Open all year. Children are welcome, cot, babysitting and reduced rates. Well controlled pets allowed. Car essential, plenty parking. Tea/coffee facilities in each room. High Tea by arrangement. Bed and Breakfast from £8. Self-catering accommodation for eight also available. AA listed.

WHEN MAKING ENQUIRIES PLEASE MENTION FARM HOLIDAY GUIDE

FARMHOUSE ACCOMMODATION

Sherwood Forest FARM & COUNTRY HOLIDAYS

Bed and Breakfast

BLUE BARN FARM (Mrs J. Ibbotson Tel. No. [062 385] 2248) 250 acre, family run mixed arable farm on Welbeck Estate, Sherwood Forest, Clumber Park, Thoresby Hall, Hardwick Hall and Peak District a short car journey. Bed and Breakfast from £6.50 per person. Weekly terms on application. 1 double, 1 twin bedded room. **Blue Barn Farm, Nether Langwith, Notts.**

NORTON GRANGE (Mrs Palmer Tel. No. [0623] 842666) Georgian stone farmhouse on edge of Sherwood Forest and Dukeries. Mixed arable farm with beef cattle and poultry. Open Easter to mid-September. Bed and Breakfast from £7. **Norton Grange, Norton Cuckney, Mansfield NG20 9IP.**

MOORGATE FARM (Mrs J. Rose Tel. No. [0777] 870274) A family run farm situated in the medieval village of Laxton. Panoramic views of the surrounding district including Sherwood Forest and the Lincolnshire Wolds. Bed and breakfast – Double room from £14 for 2 persons. Twin bedded room from £7.50 per person. (Cot available). High tea £3 on request. **Moorgate Farm, Laxton, Newark, Notts.**

For group brochure giving full details, send 9" × 4" s.a.e. to
**Mrs Shaw-Browne, Sherwood Forest Caravan Park,
Clipstone Park Estate, Old Clipstone, Mansfield, Notts NG21 9BS.**

NEWARK near. Mrs Christine Green, The Mill House, Kneesall, Near Newark NG22 0AZ (Mansfield [0623] 862525). Situated on a hilltop in open countryside this lovely house has a wonderful view from all windows. A warm friendly welcome awaits you in a quiet relaxed atmosphere. Nearby is the Sherwood Forest Visitors' Centre and there are many stately homes, country parks and places of interest to visit. Parking. The A1 is eight miles away. Open April to September. Children over five welcome. Double and family rooms; sittingroom; diningroom. Bed and Breakfast from £8.50 (£6.50 for children, babysitting available). We hope you will be able to visit us in 1986.

Robin Hood Country

OXFORDSHIRE

ABINGDON. Mrs Maureen Lay, Manor Farm, Fyfield, Abingdon OX13 5LR (Frilford Heath [0865] 390485). Working farm. This large Queen Anne style farmhouse is situated in the heart of a historic and attractive village on a working farm (750 acres) with sheep, beef cattle and corn. The proprietors have a young family between the ages of six and sixteen, so facilities for children and reduced rates are available. Ideally situated for Oxford, Abingdon and the Cotswolds. One double and two family bedrooms (one with washbasin); bathroom, two toilets; sittingroom and diningroom. Pets permitted. Parking. Open from January to December for Bed and Breakfast from £8 single.

MORAR FARMHOUSE
Elizabeth Gundrey, Relais Routiers & AA Accommodation

A good day out in the country followed by comfort and friendly hospitality in a very clean farmhouse is the basis for a super holiday. I serve a full English Breakfast and offer a range of home made preserves; the price includes bed time drink, morning tea in bed and a thermos for the day. Farm has beef and dairy cows, wheat and barley. Our pets include dogs, cats, goats, guinea pigs and a ram whose fleece I spin and knit. Our hobbies include barndancing, Morris dancing, bell ringing, gardening — and laughing! Lots to see without travelling far. Bed and Breakfast from £9.10 — 15% reduction for children six to 11, and for senior citizens October to March. Full central heating; log fire in winter; colour TV, piano, water softener. Dogs must sleep in car.

Mrs Janet Rouse, Morar, Weald Street, Bampton, Oxfordshire OX8 2HL. (Bampton Castle [0993] 850162).

BAMPTON near. Mrs Mary J. Rouse, University Farm, Lew, Near Bampton, Oxford OX8 2AU (Bampton Castle [0993] 850297). A warm and friendly welcome awaits you at this 17th century farmhouse. It has been fully modernised for comfort but retains the charm of its traditional character. There are four double and two family bedrooms at University Farm, all with colour TV; six bathrooms, six toilets; lounge with inglenook fireplace and diningroom with oak beamed ceiling. Children over eight welcome. Guests are welcome all year round and there is central heating throughout. Colour TV; large garden. Car is essential and parking space is provided. Ideal base for touring the Cotswolds and visiting Blenheim Palace and Oxford. University Farm is Tourist Board Member and AA listed. National runner-up and winner South-East England in the AA Farmhouse of the Year Awards 1980. Also recommended by Ideal Home Magazine, Daily Telegraph and British Tourist Authority commended. Rates on request with stamp, please.

AA LISTED

Terms quoted in this publication may be subject to increase if rises in costs necessitate

BANBURY near. Mrs Rebecca Trace, Rectory Farm, Sulgrave, Near Banbury OX17 2SG (Sulgrave [029 576] 261). Working farm. Delightful 350-year-old thatched farmhouse set in five acres overlooking Sulgrave Manor, ancestral home of George Washington. This is a working farm keeping sheep, ducks, chickens and ponies. Convenient for Oxford, Stratford, Cotswolds, and canals. House retains many original features — flagstone floors, exposed beams, open fireplaces, bread oven. Excellent home-produced food served in friendly, homely atmosphere. Two double, two family, one twin rooms, all with washbasins; two bathrooms, two toilets; sittingroom, diningroom. Children welcome, cot, high chair and babysitting available. Central heating. Car essential, ample parking. Open all year except Christmas, for Evening Dinner, Bed and Breakfast from £13.50; Bed and Breakfast only from £9. Rates reduced for children and weekly bookings. Licensed.

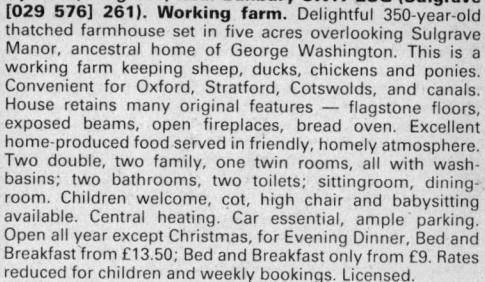

BANBURY near. Mr and Mrs R. H. Nelson, Paddocks Farm Guest House, Culworth, Near Banbury OX17 2BE (Sulgrave [029-576] 491). Paddocks Farm is a 17th-century converted farmhouse, retaining all the charm of its period. Standing in large cultivated grounds, it overlooks fields and farmland. The Guest House, which is licensed, provides substantial home cooked breakfasts and optional evening meals and affords six double guest rooms (four twin, two double-cum-family) and one single, all with washhandbasins, central heating and fitted carpets. Culworth, situated in the heart of undulating countryside, is an attractive unspoilt farming community, with a forge, general store, post office, and pub which serves bar meals. The village is ideally placed for the Cotswolds, Stratford-on-Avon, Warwick, Blenheim, Oxford etc. A cot, high chair and occasional babysitting service is provided. Sorry, no pets. Open January to December. Car preferable — parking for 10-15 cars. Bed and Breakfast from £10. Evening Meal optional extra.

DEDDINGTON. Mrs Audrey Fuller, Earls Farm, Deddington, Oxford OX5 4TH (Deddington [0869] 38243). Working farm. Delightfully situated on edge of village 200 yards from main Banbury to Oxford road, this farm covers 230 acres and carries dairy cattle and cropping fields. Open all year, has two double, one family bedrooms, two with washbasins; two bathrooms, two toilets; sittingroom, diningroom. Children very welcome and facilities for them include cot, high chair, babysitting and reduced rates; also swing and slide. Fishing available on River Swere. Golf five miles away, tennis two. Banbury six miles. This is an ideal touring base. Pets accepted. Car essential, parking. Bed and Breakfast from £8.50 per night. SAE, please, for further details.

DEDDINGTON. Mr and Mrs D. V. Ward, Maunds Farm Guest House, High Street, Deddington, Oxford OX5 4SL (Deddington [0869] 38569). This village farmhouse, no longer a working farm, is a listed ancient building and has a large Inglenook fireplace and other interesting features. It has five double, two single and one family bedrooms, all with washbasins; central heating and continental quilts; two bathrooms, three toilets; lounge, TV room and diningroom. Children over five welcome, and under 10's taken at half price. 10% off peak, OAP reductions. Open all year except Christmas. No pets in house, please. Car essential, plenty of parking, mostly under cover, good sized garden. Deddington lies on the edge of the Cotswolds between Stratford-upon-Avon and Oxford. There are antique shops, a picture shop, silversmiths, fine old church, and the site of a Norman Castle. Evening Dinner, Bed and Breakfast from £13 daily — £82 weekly; Bed and Breakfast from £8.50 daily — £54 weekly. Prices inclusive.

FARINGDON. Mrs Pat Hoddinott, Ashen Copse Farm, Coleshill, Faringdon SN6 7PU (Faringdon [0367] 20175). Working farm. Perfect spot to tour or get away from it all. A 580 acre beef and arable farm set in peaceful National Trust countryside on borders of Oxfordshire, Wiltshire and Gloucestershire. The large comfortable stone and brick farmhouse has lovely views over the garden, swimming pool and lawns, as well as the surrounding farm and woodland, and the Iron Age White Horse Hill. Many historical houses/gardens, wildlife parks, museums, antique and craft shops in nearby Cotswolds, Oxford, Blenheim Palace, Burford, Cirencester, Bath and Avebury. Boating on River Thames (five miles), riding (two miles). Open all year. Great for children (special reductions). Bed and Breakfast from £9 daily, £50 weekly.

PLEASE SEND A STAMPED ADDRESSED ENVELOPE WITH ENQUIRIES

Oxfordshire BOARD

FREELAND. Mrs B. B. Taphouse, "Wrestler's Mead", 35 Wroslyn Road, Freeland OX7 2HJ (Freeland [0993] 882003). A warm welcome awaits you at the home of the Taphouses. We are conveniently located for Blenheim Palace (10 minutes), Oxford (20 minutes) and the Cotswolds (25 minutes). Accommodation comprises of one double and one single room, both with washbasins and at ground level. Our first floor family room has its own "En Suite" shower room with washbasin and toilet. The double and the family room each have a colour television, a black and white portable is available for the single room, if required. No charge for a child under four, cot, high chair and babysitting service available. Pets by arrangement. No hidden extras. Bed and Breakfast from £8.50.

HOOK NORTON (Cotswolds). Mrs Eve Galilee, Bell Bottom House, Bell Hill, Hook Norton OX15 5NG (Hook Norton [0608] 737034). A family home (17th-century), offering warm comfortable accommodation. Hook Norton is a secluded village built of stone and thatch. Most suitable for walking and exploring the Cotswolds. Near Stow-on-the-Wold, Stratford-upon-Avon, Oxford. The house is situated in the centre of village, opposite village bakery. We have our own famous brewery, six inns and village stores. Nearest stations are Charlbury and Banbury. Visitors can be collected, but car very useful! Food good and generous. Children welcome at reduced rates. Pets accepted. Bed, Breakfast and Evening Meal £80 per week (£12 per day); Bed and Breakfast £55 weekly (£8.50 per day). Open 1 March – 30 October. Please telephone.

OXFORD. Mrs E. Neville, Ascot Guest House, 283 Iffley Road, Oxford OX4 4AQ (Oxford [0865] 240259). This pleasant Victorian guest house situated one mile from the city centre offers six most pleasant and comfortable rooms with modern facilities and TV. Tea and coffee always available in the lounge at no extra charge. Cots also available upon request. One four-poster bed. Mrs Neville makes all her guests very welcome and will help plan tours. A good base for visiting the city of "Dreaming Spires". A short drive takes you to Blenheim Palace, the Cotswolds, Stratford-upon-Avon and within a day's drive is Windsor Castle. A vegetarian Breakfast is provided if required.

UFFINGTON. Mrs Carol Wadsworth, The Craven, Uffington SN7 7RD (Uffington [036-782] 449). The Craven, an attractive 17th-century thatched and beamed farmhouse, mentioned in 'Tom Brown's Schooldays', is situated on the outskirts of Uffington. The unspoilt countryside, in the picturesque Vale of the White Horse, provides a lovely walking area, including the famous Ridgeway Path. Ideally situated for visiting Oxford, the Avebury Circle, the City of Bath and the Cotswolds. Three golf courses in area. Children welcome and babysitting offered. Sorry, no pets. Guests welcome all year round to enjoy the friendly atmosphere and good country home cooking. There is central heating and log fires in winter. Bed and Breakfast from £9. SAE for further details and terms.

WITNEY. Mrs Stella R. Pickering, Hawthorn Farm, Standlake, Witney OX8 2QU (Standlake [086-731] 211). Working farm. Hawthorn Farm is a 25-acre smallholding, situated on a bridleway which dates back to Roman times. Originally Victorian, the farmhouse has been extensively modernised to provide comfortable ground floor accommodation. The farm supports a beef and mixed animal herd. Guests who arise early are invited to bottle feed the orphan lambs. Hawthorn Farm is within easy reach of the Cotswolds and makes an ideal centre for visiting Oxford, Abingdon, Woodstock and the Berkshire Downs. The A40 (M40), about four miles from the farm, provides a fast route to London. For the fishing enthusiast there is a trout lake in Standlake Village and day tickets are available. Dogs and well behaved children welcome. Bed and Breakfast. Terms on request.

WOODSTOCK. Mrs P. Jerrams, Cedar Gable, 46 Green Lane, Woodstock, Oxford OX7 1JZ (Woodstock [0993] 812231). A friendly welcome awaits you at Cedar Gable in a detached bungalow which is situated in a quiet secluded position in the Glyme Valley at Woodstock; 300 yards centre of town. A short walk Blenheim Palace and Park; 20 minutes' drive to Oxford; 30 minutes to Cotswolds. English Tourist Board registered with Three Rose Category. Lounge, TV, central heating, double glazed, shaver points; bathroom, shower; parking; front door and bedroom keys. Ideal for handicapped persons. Garden. Sorry, no children under five years. No pets. One double, one twin, one family bedrooms. Bed and Breakfast from £9. Evening Meals by prior arrangement.

WOODSTOCK. Mrs Jean Bolovich, 8 Crecy Walk, Woodstock OX7 1US (Woodstock [0993] 812573). A comfortable family house in a lovely setting five minutes' walk from the centre of Woodstock and Blenheim Palace. Situated eight miles from Oxford, 33 miles from Stratford and a short drive into the Cotswolds, Woodstock offers many shops, pubs and excellent eating places. Diningroom, bathroom, two double rooms (one with shower), one single room, all rooms with TV. Children welcome. Sorry, no pets. Large picturesque garden with swimming pool and sauna. Three garages and forecourt parking but car not essential. Mrs Bolovich extends a friendly welcome to all her guests, please write or telephone to book. Bed and Breakfast from £9.50. Evening Meal available.

SHROPSHIRE

BISHOP'S CASTLE. Mrs P. Allbuary, Green Farm, Wentnor, Bishop's Castle SY9 5EF (Linley [058-861] 394). Modern farmhouse for a quiet and relaxing holiday, situated in superb area of outstanding natural beauty; ideal for touring. Between Long Mynd and Stiperstones. Family room (sleeps up to five), completely separate from main house, own entrance, cloakroom adjacent. Single room in house. Family room supplied with kettle for making drinks. Bathroom; sittingroom, diningroom. Cot, babysitting, reduced rates for children. Car essential — parking. TV, table tennis, darts, for evening entertainment. Village shop nearby, also two pubs with eating facilities. Animals include cats, dogs, tame sheep and ponies and guests may wander freely and make friends with all of them. Licensed riding/trekking centre. Bed and Breakfast from £7.50. Evening Meal bookable daily from £5.

BISHOP'S CASTLE. Mrs R. E. Jones, Cwnd House Farm, Wentnor, Bishop's Castle SY9 5EQ (Linley [058-861] 237). Working farm. Cwnd House is 120-acre mixed farm in the Onny Valley between Stiperstones, setting of Mary Webb's books and film "Gone to Earth" and the Longmynd Hills. Centrally situated for touring mid-Wales, border towns, Montgomery, Powys, Ludlow, Shrewsbury and Stokesay Castles. Also the famous Ironbridge Gorge. Perfect walking country, where buzzard, kestrel and heron are everyday sights, fishing in East Onny. One double and one family bedrooms (family room with washbasin); bathroom, toilet; sittingroom. Children welcome, cot, high chair, babysitting by arrangement. Pets are allowed by arrangement. Open April to October. Car essential, parking. Evening Meal, Bed and Breakfast from £10 per night; Bed and Breakfast from £6 per night. Rates reduced for children and senior citizens. Also four-berth fully fitted caravan to let, with mains electricity, from £35 per week.

BUCKNELL. Mrs Marion Brick, Upper Pedwardine Farm, Brampton Bryan, Bucknell, Shropshire SY7 0DW (Wigmore [056-886] 288). Working farm. Black and white farmhouse of character, and historical interest, dating back to stage-coach days, situated on a 230-acre farm half a mile from 4113 Ludlow to Knighton road, and a mile from the nearest railway station. Commanding panoramic views over the lovely Shropshire countryside, the house is within easy reach of Offa's Dyke, Llandrindod Wells, the Elan Valley, the picturesque villages of Herefordshire and many more places of interest. Interesting walking and birdwatching country. Children of all ages welcome, cot, high chair, babysitting available. Double, single and family bedrooms; bathroom, toilet; diningroom. Central heating. Car essential — ample parking. Bed and Breakfast £5.50; Evening Meal, Bed and Breakfast from £9. Pets accepted. Open all year.

BUCKNELL. Mrs B. Davies, Bucknell House, Bucknell SY7 0AD (Bucknell [054-74] 248). A listed mellow comfortably furnished Georgian Residence in secluded grounds on the fringe of this south Shropshire village. Situated in the picturesque Teme Valley, ideal walking terrain amidst undulating wooded hillsides and the delightful countryside of the Welsh Borderland. Within easy reach on the Welsh side are Knighton, Offa's Dyke, Llandrindod Wells and the Elan Valley. On the English side the olde worlde villages of Herefordshire, The Clun Valley, Housman Country and medieval Ludlow. On rail route for scenic "Heart of Wales", Shrewsbury—Swansea line. One double bedroom with wash unit; one twin bedded room; guests' private bathroom; sitting and diningrooms; central heating. Fishing and tennis available. Car essential. Bed and Breakfast. Terms on application. AA and ETB listed. Open March to November.

BUCKNELL. Mrs N. E. Dark, Brick Cottage, Brampton Bryan, Bucknell SY7 0DQ (Bucknell [054-74] 429). Brampton Bryan is a small village on the A4113 between Ludlow and Knighton in marvellous walking and bird-watching country. "Brick Cottage" is a detached house 200 yards west of the village. An excellent varied and interesting menu is served by Mrs Dark who specialises in homebaked bread. Guest accommodation in two double and one single bedrooms, all with washbasins; bathroom, two toilets. An attractive lounge with TV, diningroom. Central heating. Reduced rates for children under 12, babysitting available. Car essential, parking. Open April to October for Evening Meal, Bed and Breakfast or Bed and Breakfast only. Terms on request.

CHURCH STRETTON. Mrs J. A. Davies, Rectory Farm, Woolstaston, Leebotwood, Church Stretton (Leebotwood [069-45] 306). Working farm. Half-timbered farmhouse built in the early 1600's situated on the edge of the National Trust Long Mynd Hills. Guest accommodation comprises two twin-bedded rooms and one double bedroom, all with private bathrooms and extensive views of Shropshire. No small children. Oil central heating. The house which is open from March to October provides Bed and Breakfast only from £8 to £10 per person. A car is essential and there is ample parking space. There are many attractive places for evening meals locally.

Shropshire   BOARD

CHURCH STRETTON. Mrs H. C. Bovill, Batchcott Hall, Church Stretton SY6 6NP (Lee Botwood [06945] 234). Working farm. This is a stock farm and the farmhouse is situated on the north end of the National Trust Lowsmynd Hill, with magnificent views of the Shropshire Plain. It is five miles from Church Stretton and eleven miles from Shrewsbury. The latter is the market town to the west of the A49 between Picklescott and Woolstaston. This is excellent walking country. There are two double rooms and one twin-bedded room. Also bathroom etc., sitting room with television, dining room and sun room. There is a lawn at front of the house; parking space at back. Terms from £7 per night per person.

CHURCH STRETTON. Mrs C. J. Hotchkiss, Olde Hall Farm, Wall-Under-Heywood, Church Stretton SY6 7DU (Longville [06943] 253). Working farm. William and Chris Hotchkiss and family welcome you to Olde Hall Farm, a modern 190-acre dairy farm. Delightful Elizabethan farmhouse offers accommodation in two twin-bedded rooms, one with extra single bed for child; both have washbasins, teasmades etc. and clean towels daily; a third single bedroom is available. Well appointed bathroom. Residents' lounge with colour TV and books; separate diningroom. Tastefully and comfortably furnished throughout with much of antique quality. Personal service and farmhouse hospitality provided — good wholesome English Breakfast with as much home produced fare as possible. Lovely walking and historic country round about with much of interest to visitors. Children over five welcome. Sorry, we cannot have pets. Open March to November. Car essential, parking. Bed and Breakfast from £7.50, including bedtime drink.

CLEOBURY MORTIMER. Mr and Mrs R. C. Dunaway, The Old Rectory, Hopton Wafers, Cleobury Mortimer DY14 0ND (Ludlow [0584] 890218). The Old Rectory, Hopton Wafers is set amidst lovely countryside with views across to the Malvern Hills, and 10 minutes' drive from Ludlow. This large Georgian house has three acres of grounds and accommodation comprises two double and one single bedroom, each with own bathroom or shower room. Tea making facilities in each room and full English Breakfasts are served at times to suit early or late risers! Evening Meal optional and picnic meals provided on request. Special diets catered for and home produce includes fruit, veg, eggs, honey and milk. Open all year. Please telephone.

CRAVEN ARMS. Mrs Mary A. Lewis, Vron House, Newcastle, Clun, Craven Arms SY7 8QL (Clun [058-84] 257 or 578). Vron House is situated in the unspoilt village of Newcastle in the Clun Valley, 300 yards from the famous Offa's Dyke path, 13 miles from Craven Arms, four from Clun. Many places of historical interest within easy reach. First-class meals and accommodation assured. Three double, one single, one family bedrooms (one with washbasins); two bathrooms, two toilets; sittingroom, diningroom. Sorry, no pets. Open January 1st to December 1st. Car essential — parking. Reduced rates for children under nine. Snacks for non-residents. Camping available. Terms on application for Evening Dinner/Meal, Bed and Breakfast or Bed and Breakfast. SAE, please.

CRAVEN ARMS. Mrs S. J. Williams, Hurst Mill, Clunton, Craven Arms (Clun [058-84] 224). Working farm. "Hurst Mill" is situated in the prettiest part of the Clun Valley, renowned as a completely unspoilt part of England. One mile from the small town of Clun, which has a Saxon Church and a Norman Castle. Within easy reach are Ludlow, Newton, the Elan Valley and Church Stretton. Nearby is the River Clun where you can bathe. Wooded hills provide wonderful walks. Pony trekking locally. The farm has cattle and sheep, crops and ponies. Three double, one single bedrooms; sittingroom; diningroom; parking. Children welcome, cot and babysitting available. Dogs allowed. Evening Dinner, Bed and Breakfast from £11. Open all year.

CRAVEN ARMS. Mrs Veronica M. Oates, Hillside, Twitchen, Clunbury, Craven Arms SY7 0HN (Little Brampton [058-87] 485). South-west facing 200-year-old stone cottage standing in own three acre grounds in quiet hamlet in area of outstanding natural beauty. Offa's Dyke nine miles and many places rich in historical interest within easy reach. Drive leads to ample car park. Large private sittingroom for guests with inglenook log fire. Separate diningroom with individual tables. Accommodation for adults only in one double and two twin-bedded rooms, all with washbasins and tea/coffee making facilities. Two toilets. No objections to pets if kept under control. House open all day. Packed lunches available. Guests assured of a high standard of food and comfort. Fishing, golf etc. are available within reasonable distance. Open April to November. Terms on request for Evening Dinner, Bed and Breakfast or Bed and Breakfast. Transport available.

SHROPSHIRE – HISTORIC BORDER COUNTY!

The lonely Shropshire Hills – an "Area of Outstanding Natural Beauty" – are much favoured by walkers. Those seeking more traditional tourist activities would do well to visit the Acton Scott Working Museum, Ironbridge, Offa's Dyke or the market town of Bridgnorth.

CRAVEN ARMS. Mrs Mary Bason, Beckjay Farm, Clungunford, Craven Arms SY7 0PY (Leintwardine [054-73] 281). Working farm. Beckjay Farm is a mixed working farm of 160 acres with beef cattle, sheep and corn. Situated in a beautiful unspoilt part of the country on the Welsh Border. Ideal for walking, bird watching and peace and quiet. Within easy reach of many places of historic interest. Shrewsbury, Ludlow, Stokesay Castle, Offa's Dyke, Welsh lakes. Good, wholesome, home-produced food served. Vegetarians catered for if required. One double, one single and one family bedrooms; bathroom, toilet; sittingroom and diningroom with log fires, if necessary. Sorry, no pets. Children welcome with reduced rates for under 12's. Cot, high chair and babysitting by arrangement. Car essential, parking provided. Open Easter to November for Evening Meal, Bed and Breakfast or Bed and Breakfast only. SAE, please.

ELLESMERE. Mrs C. Ashley, Cockshutt House Farm, Cockshutt, Ellesmere SY12 0JH (Cockshutt [093-922] 224). Working farm. This beautiful old farmhouse stands on 150 acres on the edge of the North Shropshire Meres. It provides an ideal centre for exploring Snowdonia, South Shropshire, the Welsh resorts and the Midlands. Local activities include fishing, pony trekking, and boating on the local canal, and many beautiful walks. Guests are assured of a friendly family atmosphere and children are welcome at reduced rates — cot, high chair and babysitting services are offered. Excellent meals are provided. One double and two family bedrooms are available from March to October and the house is comfortably centrally heated. Two bathrooms, three toilets. A games room is available for snooker, billiards, darts etc. There is a colour TV in the lounge and a large safe garden for the children to play in. Pets at small charge. Parking for essential car. Evening Dinner, Bed and Breakfast from £49 per week; Bed and Breakfast only from £7 per night. Self catering caravans also available. SAE would be appreciated.

SHROPSHIRE & CHESHIRE FARM AND COUNTRY HOLIDAYS
FARMHOUSE ACCOMMODATION

Burland Farm, Burland, Nantwich. (Mrs Sandra Allwood Tel No: [027074] 210)
Beautiful Victorian farmhouse on working dairy farm. Large comfortable bedrooms, guest sitting and dining rooms – period furnishings throughout. Good country cooking – home made bread. Ideally situated for holidays.

Little Heath Farm, Audlem, Crewe. (Mrs Hilary Bennion Tel No: [0270] 811324)
Beamed farmhouse in canalside village. Spacious bedroom, lounge and diningroom. Convenient for Chester, Shropshire and Potteries. From £8.

Grange Farm, Bomere Heath, Shrewsbury. (Mrs Margaret Cooke Tel No: [0939] 290234)
5 miles north west Shrewsbury. Spacious Georgian farmhouse in beautiful surroundings. Each room equipped with shower, washbasin and radio. Ideal holiday centre. AA approved.

Bank Farm, Wrenbury, Nantwich. (Mrs Caroline Hockenhull Tel No: [0270] 780253)
A modern comfortable farmhouse in quiet countryside. A working dairy farm situated near the historic town of Nantwich. Convenient for Chester and North Wales. Guests have own lounge with TV.

Bradeley Green Farm, Tarporley Road, Whitchurch. (Mrs Ruth Mulliner Tel No: [0948] 3442)
Beautiful Georgian farmhouse, centrally heated, bathrooms en suite, self catering cottage sleeps 4. "Prize winning wildlife wonderland", water gardens, farm nature trail. Trout and carp fishing. Golf close by.

Henhull Hall, Welshmans Lane, Nantwich. (Philip and Joyce Percival Tel No: [0270] 624158)
Large farmhouse on dairy farm. 1 mile from centre of historic Nantwich. Spacious bedrooms, guests lounge and dining room. Children welcome. B & B from £8.50.

Elson House Farm, Ellesmere. (Mrs P. M. Sadler Tel No: [069195] 276)
Be sure of a warm welcome when you visit our home. Elson House Farm, situated 1½ miles from Ellesmere, the home of the Shropshire Lake District.

Lower Huntington Farm, Little Wenlock. (Mrs Pauline Williamson Tel No: [0952] 505804)
Dairy farm with interesting listed black and white farmhouse. Self catering 6 berth static caravan. Ideally situated for Ironbridge. Shrewsbury, Bridgnorth (Steam Railway), Stourbridge, Ludlow, Shropshire hills.

Sproston Hill, Wrenbury. (Mrs J. Wilkinson Tel No: [0270] 780241)
A village in South Cheshire ideally situated for Chester and North Wales. Accommodation comprises twin-bedded and double rooms, both with h & c, own lounge and dining room.

A STRETCH OF PEACEFUL COUNTRYSIDE BETWEEN THE ANCIENT CITY OF CHESTER AND THE BIRTHPLACE OF INDUSTRY AT IRONBRIDGE.

Shropshire BOARD

KNIGHTON. Mrs R. J. Williams, Monaughty Poeth, Llanfair-Waterdine, Knighton, Powys LD7 1TT (Knighton (Powys) [0547] 528348). Working farm. Offa's Dyke runs the perimeter of this 600-acre farm, Monaughty Poeth (site of old monastery), situated in a valley dominated by the ancient castle hill at Knucklas (full of legends of King Arthur) lying between the villages of Llanfair-Waterdine and Knucklas, five minutes' walk from the railway station (Heart of Wales line), with its rampant viaduct which arches the village. Knighton three miles, Clun six, Presteign eight and Llandrindod Wells 20 miles. Beautiful Elan Valley dams 30 miles. Many picturesque walks; good fishing (by appointment) in river Teme which runs through the farm. Two double bedrooms; bathroom, shower room, two toilets. Sittingroom, diningroom. Central heating/open fire. Children welcome. Car an advantage, ample parking. Open all year. Bed and Breakfast from £7.50. Also ample accommodation for touring caravans/campers. Riverside meadow site. No toilets.

LUDLOW. Mr and Mrs Clare & David Currant, Corndene, Coreley, Ludlow SY8 3AW (Ludlow [0584] 890324). Peaceful 18th-century country home standing in two acres of attractive grounds four miles north of Tenbury Wells, in beautiful farming area, in the South Shropshire hills. Well situated for exploring Shropshire, Herefordshire, the Welsh Border, historic towns, stately homes, gardens, museums, nature reserves and lovely walks. Local fishing, riding and swimming. Three ground floor bedrooms (each with private modern bathroom); diningroom; sittingroom with TV and open fire. Central heating throughout. Disabled visitors welcome, house and grounds ideally suited to wheelchair users. Good home cooking, packed lunches, special diets by arrangement. Children welcome, cot, high chair, baby minding. Regret, no dogs (guide dogs excepted). Car essential — parking. Bed, Breakfast, Evening Meal £14.50 per day (£95 per week); Bed and Breakfast £10.50 per day (£70 per week). Reductions for under 12s. Open all year except Christmas.

LUDLOW. Mrs J. S. Bowen, Arran House, 42 Gravel Hill, Ludlow SY8 1QR (Ludlow [0584] 3764). Arran House is ideally situated for exploring Shropshire's beautiful countryside and the medieval town of Ludlow with its fine castle in the heart of the Welsh Marches. This small friendly Guest House is only five minutes from Ludlow town centre and station. Guests are welcome all year round and are comfortably accommodated in two double, two single bedrooms with washbasins and shaver points. Bathroom, shower, toilet. TV lounge; diningroom. Plenty of good home cooking is provided. Children welcome, cot, babysitting available. Pets accepted free of charge. Car not essential, but there is private parking. Evening Meal, £3. Bed, Breakfast, Evening Meal £58 weekly. Bed and Breakfast £6.50. Reduced rates for children.

LUDLOW. Mrs R. M. Edwards, Haynall Villa, Little Hereford, Ludlow SY8 4BD (Brimfield [058472] 589). Working farm. Victorian House set away from farm buildings. Large garden with play area for children and use by residents. Farm is a family business, a mixed farm including a dairy herd. A good centre for touring holidays on Shropshire, Hereford and Worcester borders with many picturesque and historical places to visit. Also good fishing and venues for bird watching locally. Home grown produce is used as much as possible, also home cooking. Full English Breakfast. Overseas visitors welcome. Children made welcome, cot and high chair (reduced rates). Open all year with central heating. Pets by arrangement. Car essential, ample parking. Approximately seven miles Ludlow, four miles Tenbury Wells, seven miles Leominster. Directions: turn off A406 by River Teme at Little Hereford turning for Leysters. House is approximately three quarter mile up lane on right hand side. Evening Meal, Bed and Breakfast from £12; Bed and Breakfast from £8.

LUDLOW. Mrs Helen Williams, Lower Upton Farm, Little Hereford, Ludlow SY8 4BB (Brimfield [058-472] 322). Working farm. AA listed. A friendly welcome assured at this impressive Victorian farmhouse, set in pleasant garden, on peaceful, picturesque Shropshire/Herefordshire border. Mixed working farm of 160 acres set in pretty Teme Valley. Farmhouse has three spacious bedrooms, all with comfortable beds and washbasins — one double, one family and one twin-bedded room. Fitted carpets throughout. Large comfortable television lounge with log burner; separate diningroom. Choice of Breakfasts and menu for Evening Meals offered; packed lunches available. Home cooking. Ideal for touring historic Ludlow; Ironbridge; Severn Valley Railway; Offa's Dyke and Welsh Borders. Bed and Breakfast £7.50; Evening Meal £4 approximately. English Tourist Board and Heart of England Tourist Board member. Information desk. Brochure available.

LUDLOW near. Mrs Margery Wells, 'Redthorpe', Knowbury, Near Ludlow SY8 3JL (Ludlow [0584] 890638). Delightful old world country cottage, high on the Clee Hills, with breathtaking panoramic views. 'Redthorpe' provides an excellent centre for exploring Shropshire, Ironbridge Gorge Museum, the Severn Valley railways. The historic town of Ludlow, with its ruined castle and unspoilt medieval and Georgian buildings within a short distance. Good home cooking, with crusty bread from village bakery. Two double rooms, with four-poster beds, one double room with twin beds, with washbasins and shaver points in all rooms. Lounge with log fire and colour TV. Bed and Breakfast from £7.50; Bed, Breakfast and Evening Meal from £10.50 (weekly £57) — all inclusive. Regret, no pets.

Terms quoted in this publication may be subject to increase if rises in costs necessitate

SOUTH SHROPSHIRE FARM AND COUNTRY HOLIDAYS

FARMHOUSE ACCOMMODATION

MALTHOUSE FARM, LOWER WOOD, CHURCH STRETTON. (Mrs Lyn Bloor [06945] 379)
Comfortable accommodation in 18th Century farmhouse situated amidst the beautiful Long Mynd Hills. Ideal base for hiking or touring Shropshire's lovely countryside and many places of interest.

NEW HOUSE FARM, CLUN. (Mrs Miriam Ellison [0588] 638314)
New House Farm is a traditionally furnished 18th Century farmhouse amid South Shropshire Hills. Near Offa's Dyke, ideally suited for country walks with home cooking and a relaxed friendly atmosphere.

COURT FARM, GRETTON, CHURCH STRETTON. (Mrs B. Norris [06943] 219)
Stone Tudor farmhouse in peaceful area of outstanding rural beauty. Ideally situated for walking, touring or relaxing. Riding or trout fishing can be arranged. Large comfortable rooms. High quality cuisine.

SELF CATERING ACCOMMODATION

SHELDERTON HOUSE, CLUNGUNFORD, CRAVEN ARMS. (Mrs Olwen Evans [05473] 214)
Comfortable farm cottage, fully equipped, sleeps 6 – in the hamlet of Shelderton, nestled amongst woods and hills of natural beauty, within easy reach of many interesting and picturesque places.

STREFFORD HALL FARM, CRAVEN ARMS. (Mrs Caroline Morgan [058 82] 2383)
Part Tudor Cottage, set in the quiet hamlet of Strefford between Ludlow and Church Stretton. Ideally situated to explore the beautiful countryside of South Shropshire. Fully equipped, sleeps 6/8.

QUARRY FARM, NORDAN, LEOMINSTER. (Mrs Elizabeth Fox [0568] 2041)
Comfortable house for five on the outskirts of the friendly Shropshire/Welsh border village of Bucknell. Convenient base for walking and visits in unspoilt countryside. Colour TV, garden, cot, central heating for winter comfort.

CAMLAD HOUSE, LYDHAM, BISHOPS CASTLE. (Mrs Joan Sargent [0588] 638546)
Two farm cottages situated near the market town of Bishops Castle, ideal for Offa's Dyke the Long Mynd and picturesque Ludlow. Comfortable and well equipped with colour TV and table-tennis.

SOUTH SHROPSHIRE IS AN AREA OF OUTSTANDING NATURAL BEAUTY

LYDBURY NORTH. Mr and Mrs R. Evans, Brunslow, Lydbury North SY7 8AD (Lydbury North [05888] 244). Working farm. "Brunslow" is a beautiful Georgian-style farmhouse, centrally heated throughout, ideal for walking and for those who enjoy the peace and quiet of unspoiled countryside. The house is set in large gardens with lovely views in all directions and the farm mainly produces milk; pigs, poultry and calves are reared here and "feeding time" is very popular with younger guests. The cellar has been converted into a games room with billiards, darts and other games. One double, one single and two family rooms, all having washbasins; bathroom, toilets; separate sitting and diningrooms; colour TV. Cot, high chair and babysitting available. Open all year except Christmas for Bed and Breakfast. Evening Dinner if required. SAE, please, for terms. Packed lunches available. Car essential, parking.

NEWCASTLE. Mrs M. A. Stephens, The Plough, Newcastle, Craven Arms SY7 8QL (Clun [058-84] 607). The Plough, once a 16th-century coaching inn, is set in its own grounds in Newcastle Village. It still retains many of its original features intact — the residents' lounge has an inglenook fireplace of original character and the diningroom has a wealth of exposed beam work on ceiling and walls. All rooms are tastefully furnished; each bedroom complete with washbasin (hot and cold water), tea/coffee making facilities. Excellent cuisine and cheerful service. Warm welcome is extended to all our guests. Open March to October.

OSWESTRY. Mrs Ann Lea, Rhydleos, Llansilin, Oswestry (Llansilin [069-170] 227). Working farm. This 80-acre mixed farm and large farmhouse are approached by a good road, two and a half miles from the village of Llansilin, near the Welsh Border. A warm welcome awaits visitors from home and abroad — guests are invited to share a cup of tea with the family at night. Good hill walking, and trout fishing streams; riding two miles away. Several good inns for refreshment. Two double, one single, two family bedrooms; bathroom, toilet; lounge, diningroom. Log fires. Children welcome — cot, high chair, babysitting available. Pets allowed. Open all year for Evening Dinner/Meal, Bed and Breakfast or Bed and Breakfast only. SAE, please, for terms. Reductions for children.

PLEASE SEND A STAMPED ADDRESSED ENVELOPE WITH ENQUIRIES

Shropshire   BOARD

SHAWBURY. Mrs S. J. Clarkson, Longley Farm, Stanton Heath, Shawbury SY4 4HE (Shawbury [0939] 250289). Working farm. Longley Farm is a small farm comprising of sheep and arable. It is the ideal venue for a family holiday, guests being welcome to participate in farming activities. The farmhouse is situated in picturesque countryside with many good local walks. One of our guests' favourite evening strolls is to our popular local pub "The Tiddly," only 200 yards away. We are situated within easy access of the Iron Gorge Museum and the historic town of Shrewsbury. Also within easy reach of the City of Chester. Double and family bedrooms; bathroom/toilet; sittingroom; diningroom. Children welcome, cot, high chair, babysitting available. Central heating. The house, open all year, is suitable for disabled persons. Bed, Breakfast and Evening Meal £70 weekly — £11 daily; Bed and Breakfast £50 weekly — £7.50 daily. Reductions for children under 12.

SHREWSBURY. Mrs Brenda Grundey, Village Farm, Stanton Upon Hine Heath, Shrewsbury SY4 4LR (Shawbury [0939] 250391). Working farm. A warm welcome awaits all wishing to explore the delights of Shropshire, Cheshire, Mid and North Wales. The Ironbridge Gorge Museum, Hodnet Hall, Weston Park, Medieval Shrewsbury and Chester, all within easy reach. A spacious Victorian farmhouse offering good home cooking, open fires, central heating. Two double, one twin and one family bedrooms (all with handbasins). Shower, two toilets. Sittingroom with colour TV; separate diningroom. Cot, high chair, babysitting. Tea-making facilities. Pets under control. Car essential. This 130-acre working farm of beef and arable, offers the opportunity to participate in farm activities. Open all year for Full Board from £75 weekly; Bed and Breakfast with Evening Meal from £12.50 nightly; Bed and Breakfast from £8. Reductions for children.

SHREWSBURY (Telford). Mrs G. C. Evans, New Farm, Muckleton (Shawbury), Telford TF6 6RJ (Shawbury [0939] 250358). Working farm. New Farm is a modernised farmhouse on a 70 acre farm set amidst the beautiful, peaceful surroundings of the Shropshire/Welsh border country, one mile off A53. The attractive and historic towns of Shrewsbury, Chester, Ludlow, Bridgnorth, Ironbridge and also the Potteries are within easy reach. Guests are assured of every comfort with good farmhouse food. All bedrooms have washbasins and one has shower en-suite. Beds are made up with continental quilts, but can be altered to traditional bedding by prior arrangement. Comfortable guest lounge with colour TV; spacious diningroom. Central heating and electric fires. Children welcome, babysitting available. Sorry, no pets. Car essential — parking. Open all year. Evening Meal by arrangement. Reduced rates for children. Please send for tariff and further details.

SHREWSBURY. Mrs Eileen Pickup, Frankbrook, Baschurch, Shrewsbury SY4 2HZ (Baschurch [0939] 260778). Quiet holidays in a comfortable family home one mile from the village of Baschurch. Situated in pleasant farming country in a region of historic interest and natural beauty, the house is a good centre for north and mid-Wales and the border counties. Shrewsbury nine miles, Llangollen 20, Ludlow 38, Chester 40. Local walks, garden for relaxation, plenty of space for children to play. TV. Central heating, with open fire for colder evenings. Sorry, no pets. Car essential — parking provided. Bed and Breakfast £6; Bed, Breakfast and Evening Meal £9. Packed lunches by arrangement. Reduced rates for children under 12 years and senior citizens. Open all year. Mrs Pickup will send sketch of directions to Frankbrook to persons making reservations.

SHREWSBURY. Mrs E. Morgan, The Willows, Halfway House, Shrewsbury (Halfway House [074-378] 233). Working farm. The Willows is a 35-acre beef farm right on the A458 halfway between Shrewsbury and Welshpool, overlooking the Long Mountain and Middletown Hills. Many places of scenic beauty and historic interest to visit. Shrewsbury, Welshpool and Oswestry all within 15 miles. Lake at rear of house with plenty of wildlife. Pretty garden and delightful walks. One family and two double rooms, one with washbasin; bathroom and toilet; lounge and diningroom. Children welcome. Parking space. Open March to October. Solid fuel central heating. SAE, please, for terms for Evening Dinner, Bed and Breakfast or Bed and Breakfast. Reductions for children.

When you have read one you *haven't* read them all — we have *eleven* other publications

---

If you've found FARM HOLIDAY GUIDE of service please tell your friends

SHREWSBURY. Mr E. Griffiths, Sowbath Farm, Shawbury, Shrewsbury SY4 4ES (Shawbury [0939] 250417). Working farm. Our 200-acre dairy farm with its 100-year-old farmhouse is situated two miles from a small village on the A53 in uncommercialised area convenient for exploring Wales, Shrewsbury, Ironbridge or The Potteries. The large house is centrally heated and filled with antique furniture. There are two large family bedrooms, both with hot and cold; one bathroom; diningroom and beautiful lounge with TV. Open all year. Not suitable for disabled guests. Children welcome; free babysitting. Car desirable; plenty of parking space. Large garden. Bed and Breakfast £8, reductions for children sharing. Edward Griffiths welcomes all guests including those from abroad.

WEM. Mrs Elizabeth A. Jones, Lowe Hall Farm, Wem, Near Shrewsbury SY4 5UE (Wem [0939] 32236). Working farm. Lowe Hall Farm, historically famous as the country residence of the ill-famed Judge Jeffries (1648-1689), former Lord Chief Justice of England. Inside is a splendid Jacobean staircase and Charles II fireplace. Several rooms have fine plasterwork with beamed ceilings. An ideal touring centre with Shropshire's Lake District, Chester Zoo, Llangollen, Shrewsbury and Ironbridge all convenient. Two golf courses within seven miles and only a few miles to the Welsh border. Open all year. Ample parking space. Well recommended for outstanding family holiday. Very comfortable accommodation comprising family room with colour TV and washbasin; twin room; bathroom, bath and shower. Excellent full farmhouse Breakfast. Early morning tea and late night drink if required. Bed and Breakfast from £8.50. Reductions for under 12's. For further information SAE, please, or telephone.

WEM near. Mrs P. A. M. Powell, The Woodlands, Wolverley, Near Wem, Shrewsbury SY4 5NQ (Wem [0939] 33268). A Georgian style country house with pleasant views of surrounding district; large airy rooms; fitted carpets; washbasins in all eight bedrooms (three double rooms have private bath or shower). Free-range hens provide eggs, two gardens supply fruit and vegetables. Guests are assured of a warm welcome, log fires and central heating in cold weather. Swings and croquet on lawn, games room, table tennis. 9 hole Pitch and Putt course. Convenient for Chester, Alton Towers, Ironbridge, Gorge Museum, golf, fishing and outdoor swimming pool. Excellent for touring North Wales. Children welcome, cot, high chair, babysitting. Sorry, no pets. Car needed, parking. Shropshire County Council Fire Certificate held. Open from January to December. Residential licence. SAE, please, for terms for Evening Dinner, Bed and Breakfast or Bed and Breakfast only. Reductions for children.

WHITCHURCH. Miss J. Gregory, Ash Hall, Ash Magnor, Whitchurch SY13 4OL (Whitchurch [0948] 3151). Working farm. An early 18th century house, set in large garden, with ample room for children to play, on a medium-sized farm with pedigree Friesians. Situated in the small North Shropshire village of Ash, approximately one and a half miles from A41. Within easy reach of Chester and Shrewsbury (about 20 miles); Crewe 15 miles. An interesting feature of this house are two oak panelled reception rooms and an oak staircase; one of the two guest bedrooms is also panelled. One bedroom has en-suite facilities. Bathroom, toilet; sittingroom, diningroom. Table tennis room, pony riding, and a double lawn tennis court. Children welcome, cot, high chair and reduced rates available. Pets by prior arrangement. Open April to October. Evening Meal, Bed and Breakfast from £9.50; Bed and Breakfast from £7. Weekly terms by request. Sporting facilities in the area include swimming, golf, fishing, squash, etc. Car is desirable, but not essential. Mid-week bookings accepted.

The information in the entries in this guide is presented by the publishers in good faith and after the signed acceptance by advertisers that they will uphold the high standards associated with FARM HOLIDAY GUIDES LIMITED. The publishers do not accept responsibility for any inaccuracies or omissions or any results thereof. Before making final holiday arrangements readers should confirm the prices and facilities directly with advertisers.

SOMERSET

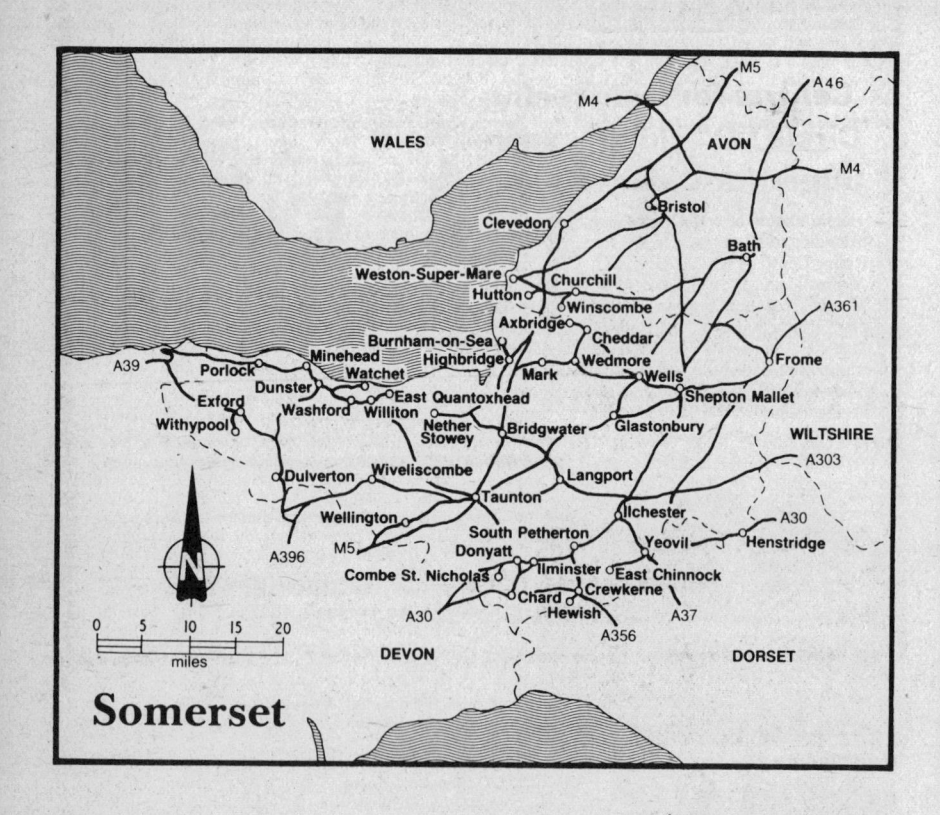

AXBRIDGE. Mrs Benda Bennett, The Laurels, Old Coach Road, Lower Weare, Axbridge BS26 2JB (Axbridge [0934] 732435). "The Laurels" is an old farmhouse just off the A38 with superb views of the Mendip Hills. Within easy reach of Cheddar Gorge and Caves, the coast at Weston-Super-Mare, Wells, Glastonbury, Longleat Safari Park and the shopping centres of Bath and Bristol. Accommodation in two family rooms; cot and high chair available, babysitting provided. TV lounge and diningroom. Central heating and log fires. A chance to ride ponies and help with the animals. Car essential and ample parking space. Pets welcome but not in the house. Bed and Breakfast and Evening Drink from £8. Children under 10 half price. Open all year.

BATH near. Mrs A. J. Warren, The Old Vicarage, Ston Easton, Near Bath BA3 4DN (Chewton Mendip [076-121] 488). Superb country house atmosphere in this delightful attractive house with comfortable accommodation and excellent Breakfast. Peacefully situated within easy distance from Bath, Wells, Glastonbury, Stourhead, Longleat etc. Two double bedrooms, one single and two family rooms; two bathrooms, two toilets; sittingroom; diningroom. Central heating and log fires. Car essential, plenty of parking. Children welcome; cot and babysitting available. Open March to October. Bed and Breakfast including tea/coffee making facilities from £9.

PLEASE ENCLOSE A STAMPED ADDRESSED ENVELOPE WITH ENQUIRIES

AA Listed

Central for sightseeing
Circle "D" riding centre
Super for Cider drinkers

The farmhouse lies on a mixed working farm extending to 250 acres including the Circle "D" Riding Centre, Ponies of Britain Approved and BHS recognised. It is an excellent position for touring and sightseeing in the Mendips and there is a wide variety of sporting facilities in this area. For guests interested in the past this is a house with an atmosphere, that of a by-gone age when it was a coaching inn no less than 400 years ago. It has five double bedrooms and four family rooms, two of which have washbasins; bathroom; shower and two toilets; colour TV lounge and diningroom. Children are made welcome and, besides supplying cot and highchair, Manor Farm is willing to make arrangements for babysitting. Pets are accepted. A car is not considered necessary for your holiday enjoyment but there is ample parking space for those who need it. The beach is nine miles away.

A feature of the hospitality offered at Manor Farm is the Somerset cider served free of charge with evening meals.

Open all year for Evening Meal, Bed and Breakfast or for Bed and Breakfast only. Rates are reduced for children. Terms on request with SAE, please.

MANOR FARM, CROSS, Nr. AXBRIDGE.
(AXBRIDGE [0934] 732577)

BLAGDON. Mrs Jeanne Gilraine, Ubley Hill Farmhouse, Ubley Drove, Blagdon, Near Bristol, Avon BS18 6XN (Blagdon [0761] 62663). Friendly hospitality in peaceful surroundings. Our 250-year-old farmhouse is situated on top of the Mendip Hills enjoying breathtaking views over Blagdon Lake towards the Severn estuary. An ideal centre for West Country touring with easy access to the historic cities of Bristol, Bath and Wells, the caves of Cheddar and Wookey Hole and the beaches of Weston-Super-Mare. Ample scope for rambling, fishing and other rural pursuits. Accommodation comprises two double/family rooms; two bathrooms, two toilets; sittingroom; diningroom. Cot, high chair, babysitting and reduced rates for children. Pets permitted. Car essential — parking. Open all year for Bed and Breakfast. Evening Meal optional. Home produce. SAE, please, for terms.

BRENT KNOLL. Mr and Mrs Gibson, Woodlands Hotel, Hill Lane, Brent Knoll TA9 4DF (Brent Knoll [0278] 760232). Woodlands Hotel nestles into its own wooded grounds and looks towards the Quantock Hills. An idyllic setting, suitable for a restful, relaxing holiday. Family, double and single rooms, most with private shower and toilet. Two sittingrooms; diningroom; cocktail bar. Children welcome. Woodlands pride themselves in their real home cooking and varied menus. Special diets catered for by prior arrangement. Meals served at separate tables in diningroom. Separate television room. Heated swimming pool. Perfectly situated for visiting places of historic interest and scenic beauty, the Woodlands is within easy reach of Bath, Glastonbury Abbey, Wells Cathedral, Longleat House and many stately homes. Horse riding arranged. Golfing, sea fishing, sailing, bowls and tennis nearby at Weston-super-Mare and Burnham-on-Sea. Free holidays offered to those organising parties. Also bargain breaks and special hunting weekends. Livery arranged. Terms on application. See also colour supplement. *

Please note that entries marked with an asterisk also have a colour display advert in the colour section in this guide

Somerset   BOARD

BRENT KNOLL. Mr R. S. C. Robinson, Shrub Farm Guest House, Burton Row, Brent Knoll, Near Highbridge TA9 4BX (Brent Knoll [0278] 760479). This 500 year old farmhouse offers you, your family and your dog a warm welcome. Easy to reach, being within five minutes of M5, and yet situated on a quiet country road at the foot of Brent Knoll, Shrub Farm makes an excellent centre for touring the many beautiful and historic places this area has to offer with Bath, Wells, Exmoor and Cheddar to name but a few. Comfortable accommodation is offered in one single, three double and five family rooms all with hot and cold. There are two residents' lounges, one with licensed bar, TV and electric organ. Garden, sea within five minutes' drive. Bed and Breakfast and Evening Meal. Brochure on request. SAE, please.

BRIDGWATER. Mrs O. M. Duckett, Elm Tree Farm, Stawell, Bridgwater TA7 9AD (Chilton Polden [0278] 722612). **Working farm.** Within easy reach of both coasts, Elm Tree is a farm in the quiet village of Stawell, on the slopes of the Polden Hills, one mile off the King's Sedgemoor Drain. Elm Tree caters for short term guests, offering Bed and Breakfast and optional Evening Meal. Comfortable accommodation with modern conveniences, comprising lounge with colour TV; diningroom; bedrooms with washbasins. Garage and parking space. Children welcome, cot, high chair and babysitting. Meals are of ample proportions and Mrs Duckett's good cooking will appeal to the discriminating guest. Good beaches; most outdoor sports within easy reach. SAE, please, for terms. No weekly or fortnightly bookings taken.

BRIDGWATER. Mrs D. A. Pitman, Barncroft, 20A Taunton Road, Pedwell, Near Bridgwater TA7 9BG (Ashcott [0458] 210294). Enjoy the happy atmosphere at Barncroft which is quietly situated off the main road, in two and a half acres of orchard and gardens. The house is a converted stone barn and accommodation is in two double, one twin and one family bedrooms (one with washbasin); bathroom, two toilets; sittingroom, colour TV; diningroom. Imaginative cooking using home grown vegetables and fruit. Facilities for children. Pets welcome too. Full central heating. Lovely country surroundings yet convenient for Bristol Channel resorts, Longleat, Cricket St. Thomas, Cheddar and Wells; also for coarse fishing. Car rallies in area most Sundays. Two vintage Austins owned. Open from March 5th to January 30th. Evening Dinner, Bed and Breakfast from £11.50 (£77 weekly); Bed and Breakfast from £7.50 (£49 weekly).

BRIDGWATER near. Mrs J. M. Jones, The Counting House, Dodington, Nether Stowey, Near Bridgwater TA5 1LE (Nether Stowey [0278] 732326). Situated at the foot of the Quantock Hills, overlooking the Bristol Channel, the Counting House is completely secluded and is an ideal location for touring both countryside and coastline. It offers homely accommodation with good sized bedrooms, three double, one single, all en suite. Sittingroom (shared); diningroom. Children welcome. Pets permitted. Car essential — ample parking. Open all year. Bed and Breakfast from £8.50, with Evening Meal £13.50. Nether Stowey, one mile away, offers all the usual facilities. Caravan also available.

BRIDGWATER near. David and Sheila Horsell, "Pear Tree Guest House," 16 Manor Road, Catcott, Near Bridgwater TA7 9HF (Chilton Polden [0278] 722390). "Pear Tree Guest House" is a converted farmhouse, situated in a village three-quarters of a mile off the A39, within easy reach of many tourist and beauty spots. Good food is guaranteed with home-grown vegetables whenever possible. Three double, one single, three family bedrooms, all with washbasins; two bathrooms, two toilets; lounge with colour TV, diningroom. Children welcome, cot, high chair and babysitting available. The house is partially suitable for the disabled. Open all year, a car is essential and parking space available. Evening Dinner, Bed and Breakfast; Bed and Breakfast. Reductions for children sharing room. An ideal holiday spot for people of all ages. SAE, please, for further details.

BRISTOL near. Mrs Mary Keel, Rickford Farm, Burrington, Blagdon, Near Bristol BS18 7AJ (Blagdon [0761] 62104). Rickford Farm is part of a 350-acre dairy farm (main farm is quarter mile away) set in the picturesque village of Burrington, famous for the Rock of Ages. This comfortable farmhouse nestles on the edge of the Mendip Hills and is within 300 yards of acres of beautiful common land and numerous walks. Well situated for Bath, Wells, Cheddar (five miles). Fly fishing is available at Blagdon (two miles) and Chew Valley Lakes. Accommodation comprises one double, one single and one family room; guests have their own bathroom. Nearby pubs and restaurants provide good evenings meals. Cot, high chair and babysitting. Reduced rates for children. Ample car parking.

BRUTON. Mrs D. Dabinett, Holland Farm, South Brewham, Bruton BA10 0JZ (Upton Noble [074-985] 263). **Working farm.** Holland Farm is set amidst beautiful countryside, in very peaceful surroundings, making for a very relaxing holiday. A warm welcome awaits, and guests usually have dinner with the family as visitors often like hearing about the farming day. Bedrooms are comfortable with bedside lamps, washbasins and early morning tea-making facilities. Food is excellent and plentiful (dinner is four-course). Longleat House and Safari Park, Yeovilton Air Museum, Cheddar and Wookey Hole Caves, Butterfly Farm, Tropical Bird Gardens, and other interesting places to visit. Opportunities for bird-watching. Open Easter to September. AA listed. Children over four years and pets are welcome. Dinner, Bed and Breakfast from £12.50. Bed and Breakfast from £8.

BURNHAM-ON-SEA. Mrs A. Puddy, Cote Farm, East Huntspill, Near Highbridge, Burnham-on-Sea (Burnham-on-Sea [0278] 784158). **Working farm.** Homely and friendly accommodation is provided in this family farmhouse. Hot and cold in bedrooms; central heating when required, car essential — ample parking. Cote Farm is situated in the heart of Somerset, close to Cheddar, Wells, Wookey Hole, Minehead and Dunster, five miles Burnham-on-Sea; within three miles of five well-known rivers for anglers. Sorry, no pets. Terms on application (SAE, please).

Terms quoted in this publication may be subject to increase if rises in costs necessitate

HOME REARED ROAST BEEF – FARM BAKED BREAD

Churchill Green Farm
CHURCHILL GREEN, CHURCHILL, SOMERSET (AVON)
Phone Churchill 852438

David and Janet Sacof

AA Listed   Licensed

This is a charming old 17th century farmhouse, with modern comforts and yet the character has not been spoiled. It commands splendid views of open countryside at the foot of the Mendip Hills, and is an excellent centre for trips to Wells, Bath, Weston-Super-Mare, Cheddar and the varied and beautiful countryside of North Somerset. Golf, fishing, riding, swimming, tennis and many more sporting facilities are available nearby, clay pigeon shooting arranged, or you can spend your day relaxing in the quiet of two acres of garden by the full-sized swimming pool surrounded by over 20 acres of our own farmland, with no nearby main roads to disturb the peace. Pony for small children.

The bedrooms have hot and cold water, reading lamps and comfortable beds — two of which are antique and unique Canopy "Tester" beds! Although the house is centrally heated, log fires are lit whenever necessary. The house is open all year round and the atmosphere is relaxed and friendly.

Please write direct or telephone for further details and brochure and tariff, which may vary according to the time of year, with reductions for children, who are most welcome.

See also self-catering section of this guide for details of cottage.

FAIRLANDS, CHEDDAR

FAIRLANDS HOUSE is an ancient and beautiful farmhouse dating back to the 17th century. **Farmhouse accommodation** is available at very reasonable prices and we take great pleasure in inviting you to share our home with us. The rambling house and grounds offer a leafy romantic setting for a really relaxed holiday or over-night stay.

We welcome children of all ages, as this is a family home. The extensive stone-walled gardens filled with mature trees provide a delightful and safe area in which children can play, while mum and dad can relax in garden chairs. We have several vintage motor cars and you can play croquet and see our pony and cats.

In the mornings you can come down to a full, cooked, English breakfast, with as much as you can eat, served on a magnificent Oak Refectory table. In the evenings you can watch television in the homely and comfortable sitting room or let us look after the children while you go out and enjoy yourselves.

We also have **TWO STONE-BUILT SELF-CATERING COTTAGES**, described in the second half of this guide. Enjoy the peace of another century and within a few minutes walk onto the Mendip Hills – an Area of Outstanding Natural Beauty – to see some of the finest views in Somerset. It is possible to walk for miles in unspoilt countryside, ride at one of the local stables, enjoy golf, sailing, fishing, shooting, caving, bird watching and climbing. You can visit the glorious Cathedral city of Wells, the ruins at Glastonbury, Bath – famous for its Georgian beauty – is 45 minutes away and many theatres and concerts are 35 minutes away in Bristol. There are a host of stately homes and Museums and the seaside is only 20 minutes away at Weston-super-Mare and Burnham-on-Sea. Les Routiers, AA, RAC, BTA registered. Please send for a brochure and prices to:

SUE BLAKENEY-EDWARDS, FAIRLANDS HOUSE, CHURCH STREET, CHEDDAR, SOMERSET Tel. [0934] 742629

CHARD. Mr and Mrs John Jeffery, Bere Farm, Winsham, Chard TA20 4JQ (Winsham [046030] 207). Working farm. Bere Farm, situated half a mile from Winsham in West Dorset on the border with Somerset, with easy access from the B3162 from Chard to Bridport, makes a good centre for visiting Cricket St. Thomas Wild Life Park, Forde Abbey, Cheddar Caves, Wookey Hole and the wonderful coastline of Lyme Bay. A 200-acre sheep and corn farm with quiet and picturesque walks along the fields and stream. The late Georgian farmhouse is spacious with elegant rooms and lovely views surrounded by a large garden. Comfortable beds with washbasins in all bedrooms; separate bathroom, shower and toilets. Drawingroom with colour TV, diningroom, large playroom. Also tea/coffee making facilities. Children are welcome and there is cot, high chair, babysitting and reduced rates under seven. Car essential — ample parking. Open all year round for Bed and Breakfast at daily or weekly rates.

CHEDDAR. Mr & Mrs J. P. Barker, Gordon's Hotel, Cliff Street, Cheddar (Cheddar [0934] 742497). Gordon's Hotel, once a farmhouse, is set at the foot of the beautiful Cheddar Gorge in glorious Somerset and is within walking distance of the Caves, Marineland, Cheese Factory, Butterfly Land and shops, only 10 miles from the sea. The Hotel is privately run to ensure a homely holiday. Gordon's is a One Star Hotel with a TV lounge, licensed bar and superb Old World Restaurant. Outside there is parking and a heated swimming pool. All 14 bedrooms have TV and teasmades, some have private showers and some private bathrooms en suite. Children welcome, cots and high chair; horse riding arranged. Open February to December, Bed and Breakfast from £8.75, reduced rates for children. SAE for brochure.

DULVERTON. Mrs A. M. Spencer, Dassels, Dulverton TA22 9RZ (Anstey Mills [039-84] 203). Dassels is a superb Georgian style Country Guest House, magnificently situated on the edge of Exmoor, three miles west of Dulverton on the outskirts of East Anstey, set in nine-and-a-half acres of tranquil grounds with panoramic views. A spacious house, large diningroom, separate lounge, TV and log fires. Ten bedrooms, most with washbasins, six en suite. A high standard of comfort is maintained and Dassels is noted for its excellent home cooked food, farm produce, delicious sweets served with clotted cream, fresh bread and rolls baked locally. A beautiful area near the Exmoor National Park where horse riding, walking, fishing and nature study are available. Many beauty spots within easy reach, also places of archaeological and historic interest, easy access to North Devon and West Somerset coastal resorts. Residential Licence, ample parking, fire certificate, stabling. Open all year. Children welcome. Dinner, Bed and Breakfast from £13.50.

DULVERTON. Mrs Heywood, South Greenslade Farm, Brompton Regis, Dulverton TA22 9WU (Brompton Regis [039-87] 207). Working farm, join in. This is a traditional West Country farmhouse in a sheltered position on the farm at the end of a one mile No Through Road, 400 yards from shores of Wimbleball Lake, a large reservoir with fishing (trout), sailing, nature reserve, walks. It is warm, clean and comfortable and open from beginning May to end September. There are two family rooms, each with double and single bed with washbasins; bathroom, toilet; sittingroom; diningroom with large table. A car is essential and there is ample parking. Three quarters of a mile from Haddon Hall, high moorland and woods with deer and Exmoor ponies, in Exmoor National Park. Cattle and sheep kept on farm, interested visitors made most welcome — hand milking, donkeys, sheepdogs etc. Superb spot for country lovers liking peaceful surroundings, walking. Bristol Channel coast 16 miles, Atlantic coast 40 miles. Bed and Breakfast from £7.50. Children from £5. A warm welcome is assured.

DULVERTON. Mrs P. J. Vellacott, Springfield, Dulverton TA22 9QD (Dulverton [0398] 23722). Working farm. Springfield is a farm of 270 acres rearing cattle and sheep, overlooking the River Barle. It is in the Exmoor National Park and within easy reach of North Devon and Somerset coastal resorts. Tarr Steps, a famous beauty spot, is one mile away; Dulverton four miles. Hunting in season; riding and fishing available nearby. All bedrooms (one double, one twin-bedded, one/two singles if children); diningroom and sittingroom with TV, face south, with magnificent views. Guests' bathroom and separate toilet upstairs. Cot, high chair, babysitting for children. Sorry, no pets. Car essential — parking space. Open May to October. Evening Dinner, Bed and Breakfast or Bed and Breakfast only. Reductions for children. SAE, please, for terms.

DULVERTON. Mr and Mrs A. H. B. Matthews, Hiccombe House, Brompton Regis, Dulverton (Brompton Regis [03987] 228). This comfortably furnished 16th century country house lies in a secluded wooded valley close to Wimbleball Lake in Exmoor National Park. Perfect walking/fishing centre (deep freezing facilities). Within touring distance of South/North coasts, Dartmoor, etc. Central heating. Three double bedrooms, with washbasins, electric blankets and kettles, Bathroom, showerroom; sittingroom with log fire and colour TV; diningroom with separate tables. Excellent home cooking with fourcourse evening meal and coffee. Fresh cream always used and home produced vegetables whenever possible. Sorry, no children or pets. Car essential — parking. Open April/October. Dinner, Bed and Breakfast £15.50–£17 or Bed and Breakfast only £9.50–£10.50. Also self-contained cottage flat. SAE, please, for brochure.

DULVERTON. Mrs W. M. Wescott, Higher Foxhanger Farm, Brompton Regis, Dulverton TA22 9PA (Brompton Regis [039-87] 242). Working farm. "Higher Foxhanger", a farm in the beautiful Exmoor National Park, is open from April to November. This is a quiet farmhouse with two family rooms — with washbasins; interior sprung mattresses; bathroom, toilet; sittingroom, diningroom with separate tables; fresh farm produce served. Evening Dinner, Bed and Breakfast or Bed and Breakfast. Children welcome. Cot and high chair available. Good tarmac road to farmhouse. Within easy reach of several beauty spots and lovely walks all round. Car essential. Dulverton five miles; Minehead 13 and the sea 12. Reductions for children. SAE brings prompt reply to enquiries.

DUNSTER. Mr and Mrs A. J. Hill, The Old Manor, Lower Marsh, Dunster TA24 6PJ (Dunster [0643] *
821216). The Old Manor is a delightful 15th-century guest house standing in spacious grounds about a mile from Dunster village, well situated for touring Exmoor, the Quantocks and Brendon Hills. Ten minutes' walk to quiet beach with riding stables and Minehead Golf Course. Number of National Trust properties worth visiting in the area. Four double, two single, five family bedrooms, with washbasins; three bathrooms, four WCs. Lounge with TV; diningroom. Restaurant and Residential licence. Children welcome, cot and high chair. Car preferable. Parking space. Open Easter to end September. Evening Dinner, Bed and Breakfast from £16; Bed and Breakfast from £10. Morning coffee, cream teas and snack lunches are available for visitors wishing to relax in the house or garden. High reputation for comfortable holidays under personal supervision. SAE, please, for terms and brochure. Also self-catering accommodation, for details see Self-Catering Section (Dunster, Somerset).

EAST BRENT. Mrs Lorna M. Walker, Manor Farm, East Brent, Highbridge (Brent Knoll [0278] 760887). Fully modernised Georgian country farmhouse. Ideally situated for family holidays, in quiet rural position. Two miles from M5 (J22). Six miles Weston-Super-Mare. Close to sandy beaches, at Burnham on Sea, Berrow and Brean all within four miles. Cloe to Mendip and Quantock Hills, Bristol, Bath, Cheddar and Glastonbury. Excellent accommodation, one double and three family rooms. High quality farmhouse fare. Open May to September. Bed and Breakfast £7.50 or Evening Meal, Bed and Breakfast £12. Reduction for children and weekly stays. Write or phone for brochure and bookings. Also cottage for six/nine available.

EAST QUANTOXHEAD (Bridgwater). Mrs F. D. Miller, Court Farm, East Quantoxhead, Bridgwater TA5 1EJ (Holford [027-874] 320). Working farm. Court Farm is a lovely old farmhouse, set in an unspoilt village at the foot of the Quantocks. The farm is 300 acres of mixed farmland and the fields border the Bristol Channel. The district abounds in historical interest and holiday facilities; riding, sailing, fishing are within easy reach. Excellent base for touring Exmoor. Spacious comfortable bedrooms, one family, one double and one twin bedded rooms. Beautiful views. Farmhouse breakfast with home-made bread, fresh eggs and milk. Bed and Breakfast guests are welcome from April to October. Children at reduced rates; cot, high chair; babysitting. Pets are permitted. A car is essential and there is ample parking. SAE, please, for terms.

EXMOOR. Ann and Philip Durbin, Cutthorne, Luckwell Bridge, Wheddon Cross TA24 7EW (Exford [064-383] 255). Working farm. Cutthorne is a traditional 18th century farmhouse totally secluded in 25 acres of glorious Exmoor countryside, 1000 ft. above sea level — on the southern slopes of Dunkery. An ideal haven for a quiet holiday, with excellent walking, fishing, pony trekking, birdwatching and hunting. The spacious and comfortable accommodation includes diningroom and lounge with log fires and central heating in season. Our three bedrooms boast magnificent views, and our master bedroom has a four-poster bed. Two luxury bathrooms. We offer you a full English Breakfast, high tea for the children, and candlelit Dinner. Fresh produce and home-baked bread. Stabling for horses. Pets by arrangement. Reductions for children. Bed and Breakfast from £7.50. Dinner £5.50. Open Easter-November. Brochure available.

PLEASE SEND A STAMPED ADDRESSED ENVELOPE WITH ENQUIRIES

FROME. Mrs Mandy Hulme, Highcroft Farmhouse, West Woodlands, Frome BA11 5EQ (Frome [0373] 61941). Comfortable old stone farmhouse, formerly part of Longleat estate, in scenic country setting, two miles south of Frome, one mile from Longleat House. Easy access to Stourhead, Bath, Wells, Glastonbury, with many other local attractions. Large, pleasant rooms, with rural views, centrally heated throughout. Double, twin-bedded and family rooms available with or without shower/washbasin. Children welcome. Pets by arrangement. Guests' lounge with television. Full English breakfast with home-made bread. Evening meals available using home grown produce. Lovely mature gardens available to guests with barbecue facilities. Ample secure car parking. Daily rates from £8 Bed and Breakfast, £12.50 with Evening Meal. Weekly rates available. Open all year.

FROME near. Mrs J. Down, Gloucester Farm, Lullington, Near Frome BA11 2PQ (Frome [0373] 830293). Working farm. Approximately 10 miles from Bath and three miles from Frome, Gloucester Farm is a dairy farm of 230 acres situated in a very quiet, unspoilt village of "old world charm" attached to a beautiful park. Ideal base for touring being within easy reach of Longleat, Stourhead, Cheddar, the cathedral cities of Wells, Exeter and Salisbury, the New Forest and seaside resorts of the Bristol Channel. Sports in Frome. Riding, fishing, golf available in the area. Lounge with colour TV; family rooms available with hot and cold water. Sorry, no pets. Bed and Breakfast £7.50, children under 10 years £6.50. Evening Meal by arrangement using home grown produce — £5.50. Many interesting country pubs in the locality.

Berewall Farm Glastonbury

This friendly family run farmhouse situated on a dairy farm 1¼ miles from Glastonbury offers first class accommodation. Home cooked food with a choice of menu all meals. Licensed bar. There are nine bedrooms, 4 family, 5 twin/doubles, all rooms en suite, central heating. Tennis, horse riding (fun ponies) for the children, swimming pool, clay pigeon shoots available on the farm. Central for touring many local attractions. Special winter terms, open all year including Christmas.

Mrs J. I. Nurse, Berewall Farm, Cinnamon Lane, Glastonbury BA6 8LL or phone Glastonbury (0458) 31451.

GLASTONBURY. Mrs J. M. Gillam, The Dower House Farm, Butleigh, Glastonbury BA6 8TG (Baltonsborough [0458] 50354). Quiet farmhouse, over 200 years old, not isolated, where every attention is given to guests. Within easy reach of all local beauty spots, beautiful Vale of Avalon and historic houses; the nearest coast only 20 miles. Good food served with fresh vegetables from secluded garden used, and local butter, cheese and free-range eggs. Open from February to November, there are five double and one family bedrooms, with washbasins (one bedroom is ground-floor with en-suite facilities); bathroom, two shower rooms, four toilets. Attractive sittingroom and diningroom. Cot and babysitting offered for children, who are welcome, also reduced rates. Many attractions locally for children including butterfly farm, aeroplane museum, rural museum, cheese-making and steam engines (Cranmore). No objection to pets but *not* in bedrooms. Car essential, parking. Evening Dinner/Meal, Bed and Breakfast or Bed and Breakfast only. An ideal touring centre. Also self-catering accommodation for four persons. SAE for prompt reply.

HIGHBRIDGE near. Mrs G. W. Hunt, Northwick Farm, Mark, Near Highbridge TA9 4PG (Mark Moor [027-864] 228). Working farm. Large Georgian farmhouse on 70-acre farm, set in pleasant country only two miles from M5 junction 22 and five miles Burnham-on-Sea. Panoramic views of Mendip and Quantock Hills across open farmland and an ideal base to tour the West Country, many well-known resorts and places of historical interest — Cheddar, Wells, Glastonbury, Taunton, Exmoor within easy reach. Every comfort is offered to guests with beamed diningroom (separate tables), colour TV lounge, traditional farmhouse cooking from fresh farm fare, home and local produce — ample portions. Three double and one family bedrooms, with washbasins; bathroom, two toilets. Car essential — ample parking. Fishing, riding, golf nearby. Warm and friendly to guests seeking quiet and a peaceful holiday. Open all year except Christmas. Moderate terms, reduced for children under 12. SAE for prompt reply, please.

HIGHBRIDGE. Mrs V. M. Loud, Alstone Court Farm, Alstone Lane, Highbridge TA9 3DS (Burnham-on-Sea [0278] 789417). Working farm. Seventeenth century farmhouse, situated on outskirts of town, two miles from M5 Edithmead inter-change, on a mixed farm of 200 acres. The land adjoins Bridgwater Bay, ideal as touring centre for Somerset. Within easy reach of Burnham-on-Sea, Weston-Super-Mare, Wells, Cheddar Gorge, Wookey Hole and the Mendips. Ideal for sea and coarse fishing. Horse-riding on the farm — qualified instructor. Spacious comfortable bedrooms — two family, two double, two twin-bedded rooms. Lounge with colour TV, large diningroom. Central heating. Home produce when available. Children welcome. Ample parking space. Evening Meal, Bed and Breakfast. Terms on request with SAE, please.

HIGHBRIDGE near. Mrs B. M. Puddy, Laurel Farm, Markcauseway, Near Highbridge TA9 4PZ (Mark Moor [027-864] 216). Working farm. Laurel Farm is over 300 years old with 120 acres, 76 milking cows, and chickens. The farmhouse is about one-and-a-half miles from Mark village and church, and on the Wells to Burnham-on-Sea B3139 road; it makes an ideal touring centre or halfway house as the M5 motorway is two miles away, junction 22. There is a large sittingroom with colour TV; log and coal fires September to May. Electric blankets and hot/cold in all bedrooms. Central heating. Nicely decorated and fitted carpets throughout. Diningroom has separate tables. Three double, one single and two family bedrooms; bathroom, three toilets. Sorry, no pets. Car essential, three undercover garages. Open all year for Bed and Breakfast. Evening Dinner by arrangement.

ILMINSTER near. Mrs J. Durman, Whitehouse Farm, Rapps, Near Ilminster TA19 9LG (Ilminster [046-05] 4417). Working farm. A square Georgian House set in large garden at the end of private drive, in quiet countryside. Two miles from Ilminster, nine miles from Taunton. Situated off the A358 road. Working farm, mainly beef and sheep, a bit of arable; many animals on farm — goats, ponies, dogs, etc. Cider is made at the farm, and may be sampled. Home produced vegetables and meat served in diningroom; separate tables. Ideal for touring or a quiet, relaxed holiday. Two double and one family bedrooms, with washbasins; bathroom, toilet; sittingroom. Children welcome, cot, high chair, babysitting. Pets allowed. Open from March to October. Car essential — parking. Evening Dinner, Bed and Breakfast from £65 per week; Bed and Breakfast from £7 per night. Reduced rates for children under 12 years.

LYMPSHAM. Alan and Nanci Bailey, Lower Wick Farm, Wick Lane, Lympsham BS24 0HG (Brean Down [027-875] 333). Pleasantly situated in the Somerset countryside a little under 10 minutes' drive from Junction 22 of the M5, being six miles from Weston-super-Mare and five miles from Burnham-on-Sea. We offer quality accommodation which includes, Bed, Breakfast and Evening Dinner, with Full Board on Sundays, in a farmhouse updated for your comfort. No facilities for young children. Double rooms have toilet and shower en-suite. Quiet lounge and TV lounge. Spacious lawn for sunbathing. Home grown produce whenever possible. No VAT or service charge. Pets permitted by arrangement. Car essential — parking. Open all year. For terms and brochure SAE, please, or phone.

MINEHEAD. Mrs R. Dyer, Burnells Farm, Knowle Lane, Dunster, Minehead (Dunster [0643] 821841). Comfortable farmhouse situated in the lovely Avile Valley with beautiful view of Exmoor and two miles from sea. One mile from Dunster. Three double bedrooms, three family rooms, with washbasins; bathroom, shower, two toilets; sittingroom; diningroom. Open all year. Car essential, parking. Children welcome, cot, high chair, babysitting and reduced rates. Pets accepted. Dinner, Bed and Breakfast and packed lunch if required. Bed and Breakfast from £6.50 per night. Evening Meal, Bed and Breakfast from £9.50 per night, £65 weekly. Special terms for senior citizens.

If you've found FARM HOLIDAY GUIDE
of service please tell your friends

Somerset BOARD

MINEHEAD. Mrs Sheila Bailey, Stoates Farm, Allerford, Minehead TA24 8HN (Porlock [0643] 862061). Stoates Farm is surrounded by National Trust lands within the Exmoor National Park with beautiful views across the Vale of Porlock to Dunkery Beacon, the highest point on Exmoor. All bedrooms are tastefully decorated and kept to a high standard. Meals are served in a cosy dining-room with fresh farm eggs being used and fresh vegetables whenever possible. Our aim is to provide good home cooking for you whilst you holiday in this beautiful walking country with breathtaking scenery. Riding, fishing and golf are just minutes away or just enjoy the peace and quiet of the countryside. Open all year except Christmas. Evening Meal, Bed and Breakfast.

EMMETT'S GRANGE

Large Moorland Farm standing in quiet position, surrounded by beautiful country. Many sporting facilities nearby including fishing, riding and hunting. Stabling. Large comfortable farmhouse, open Easter to September. Three double rooms with washbasins and one single room; one bathroom and one shower room; three toilets; dining-room; sittingroom with bay window and lovely view. Colour TV. Central heating and open fire. Excellent home cooked food. Children and dogs welcome. Car essential. SAE, please for details to **Mrs F. H. Brown, Emmett's Grange, Simonsbath, Minehead TA24 7LD (Exford [064-383] 282).**

MINEHEAD. Mr and Mrs J. A. Soar, Bilbrook Lawns Hotel, Bilbrook, Near Minehead TA24 6HE (Washford [0984] 40331). A delightful Georgian Hotel standing in its own grounds of lawns, pine trees and shrubs, offering superb accommodation and service in a friendly and relaxing atmosphere. It is much recommended for its excellent cuisine and reasonably priced table wines. All bedrooms have tea-making facilities and TV. Some with WC and bath or shower en-suite. Ground floor and single bedrooms are also available. Weekly — Bed, Breakfast and Dinner from £105. Bargain Breaks — two nights Bed, Breakfast and Dinner from £32. Ample car parking. Brochure gladly sent by Resident Proprietors **Tony and June Soar.**

MINEHEAD. Mrs S. J. Baker, Styles Farm, Rodhuish, Minehead TA24 6QN (Washford [0984] 40255). **Working farm.** An interesting cattle, arable and horse farm with picturesque farmhouse and garden. Situated in 325 acres of beautiful Exmoor National Park, close to beaches at Blue Anchor, Dunster and Minehead. Excellent walking country with pony trekking and other activities available locally. Bedrooms are double or family, as required, all with attractive view. Spacious dining/sittingroom with log fire and oil central heating, colour TV. Bathroom and toilet. Children welcome at reduced rates. Babysitting available. Guests welcome from April to November. Good home cooking with farm produce, and clotted cream served. Sorry, no pets. Car essential — parking. Evening Dinner, Bed and Breakfast or Bed and Breakfast only. Please send SAE for terms and further details.

Terms quoted in this publication may be subject to increase if rises in costs necessitate

BOARD Somerset 273

MINEHEAD. Mrs Carole Turner, "Green Close", Wootton Courtenay, Minehead TA24 8RA (Timberscombe [064-384] 482). Green Close is a small bungalow guest house situated in a peaceful and quiet rural area and set in three acres with panoramic views of the beautiful EXMOOR NATIONAL PARK. Guests are assured of friendly comfortable accommodation and good country cooking. Ideally situated for touring and walking. The Doone Valley. Dunkery Beacon, Dunster Castle, Riding, Fishing, Golf, all within easy reach. Sea five miles. Accommodating one family or one double and one single. Dinner, Bed and Breakfast or Bed and Breakfast. Open Easter to October.

MINEHEAD. Mr A. C. Cole, The Langbury Hotel, Blue Anchor, Minehead TA24 6LB (Dunster [0643] 821375). The Langbury is a small, friendly, family hotel, occupying an elevated position on the West Somerset coast and enjoying wonderful views of sea and nearby Exmoor. Guests are assured of every comfort and plenty of good food. There is a licensed bar, own private swimming pool and pleasant gardens. The area has ample opportunities for riding, walking, fishing, etc., together with the amenities provided by the nearby resort of Minehead. All bedrooms have colour TV and tea-making facilities; there are five double, two single and two family rooms, all rooms have washbasins and some with private shower/WC; one bathroom, two toilets; two sittingrooms and one diningroom. Children welcome — cot, high chair, babysitting and reduced rates. Pets allowed free. Open March to October with central heating and log fires. Car is essential, ample parking. Evening Dinner, Bed and Breakfast from £15 per day.

MINEHEAD. Mr and Mrs G. Collop, Alcombe Cote Guest House, 19 Manor Road, Alcombe, Minehead TA24 6EH (Minehead [0643] 3309). Alcombe Cote is a charming 19th century residence situated at the entrance to Alcombe Coombe and within a short distance of Exmoor. Ideal base for exploring the coast and countryside by foot, car or coach. Castles, manor houses, churches, ancient monuments and historic villages abound, also many famous beauty spots and the West Somerset Steam Railway in Minehead. Two double, one single, one family, two twin bedrooms with washbasins; two bathrooms, two toilets, diningroom. Lounge has large log fire as well as central heating. Babysitting and reduced rates for children. Sorry, no pets. Open March to November. Parking. Evening Meal, Bed and Breakfast from £9.50 daily (£60 weekly); Bed and Breakfast from £6.50 daily.

MINEHEAD near. Ian and Jean Hamilton, Fern Cottage, Allerford, Near Minehead TA24 8HN (Porlock [0643] 862215). Fern Cottage dates from circa 1600. Run as a friendly little country guest house, it is attractively furnished and equipped to give guests every comfort whilst enjoying this wonderful Exmoor valley. Log fires and central heating for those who prefer early and late season holidays. Home cooked meals served in traditional style in the diningroom. Lounge. TV room. Bed and Breakfast £9. Bed and Breakfast and Dinner £14. Weekly £90 including VAT. No service charge.

MINEHEAD. Mr and Mrs R. A. Ferrier, Marston Lodge Hotel, St. Michael's Road, North Hill, Minehead TA24 5JP (Minehead [0643] 2510). Marston Lodge stands in half an acre of grounds and is situated on the picturesque North Hill overlooking the Bay and Exmoor. All rooms at the hotel have views of the sea or garden and every comfort is given to ensure a worry-free holiday. Personal service at all times and home cooking. Accommodation in seven double, one single and three family rooms, all with washbasins; two bathrooms, four toilets; TV lounge and lounge bar; diningroom. Children welcome and pets allowed. Open all year. A car is not essential here, but there is ample parking space. The town and sea are only half-a-mile away. Sea fishing, golf and horse riding nearby. Dinner, Bed and Breakfast, Bed and Breakfast or Full Board. Reductions for children sharing parents' room. SAE, please, for further details.

274 Somerset BOARD

✱ MINEHEAD. Mr and Mrs J. M. Showell, Harley House Hotel, Irnham Road, Minehead TA24 5DL (Minehead [0643] 2850). Minehead is the perfect centre for touring the outstanding beauty of Exmoor and for a delightful seaside holiday. The hotel occupies a remarkably open, sunny position in a quiet side road, just by the town centre and lies in a large walled garden with a croquet lawn and putting green. Ample car parking in forecourt. Six double bedrooms (some en suite), one single, three family, all with washbasins and gas or electric fires. They overlook the surrounding hills while the lounge, a particularly peaceful, charming room, looks on to the garden. Bathroom, shower room, three toilets: Diningroom. TV. Cot. Pets allowed. Breakfast a la carte. The four-course dinner is the best of traditional English cooking, with delicious and unusual sweets a speciality. Evening Dinner, Bed and Breakfast or Bed and Breakfast only. Reductions for children and for Senior Citizens out of season. RAC listed. Colour brochure. See also Full Colour Advertisement for details.

PORLOCK. Mr S. Fitzgerald, "Seapoint", Upway, Porlock TA24 8GE (Porlock [0643] 862289). Charming Edwardian house situated on the edge of Porlock, an unspoilt Exmoor village. We enjoy extensive views across Porlock Bay and are surrounded by the beautiful Exmoor Hills. We have earned a reputation for the quality of our service and food and provide delicious traditional, wholefood and vegetarian menus. Pleasantly furnished guest accommodation comprises two family and one double bedrooms, all with washbasins and central heating. The sittingroom, overlooking the bay, has colour TV and log fires are an added comfort during chilly weather. Warm and friendly atmosphere with children and pets welcome. Moderate terms. Ample parking.

SHEPTON MALLET near. Miss P. J. Cary, The Laurels, East Pennard, Near Shepton Mallet BA4 6TW (Ditcheat [074-986] 293). The Laurels is an old fashioned stone-built house now modernised, situated 200 yards off the A37 five miles from Shepton Mallet. Ideal for touring or a quiet holiday, yet within easy reach of well-known beauty spots such as Cheddar Caves, Wells Cathedral, Bath Abbey, Longleat House and lion reserve, Glastonbury Tor, etc. Kennel/cattery half mile. Two double bedrooms, bathroom, two toilets; sittingroom. Car essential — ample parking space. Open Easter to October. Sea 30 miles. Evening Meal, Bed and Breakfast or Bed and Breakfast only. Moderate terms.

SHEPTON MALLET. Mrs J. V. White, 2 Haydon House, Prestleigh Road, Evercreech, Shepton Mallet BA4 6JY (Evercreech [0749] 830031). Period stone-built house with a lovely garden situated in the friendly village of Evercreech. Comfortably furnished family house with a warm, friendly atmosphere and first-class home cooking with a varied and imaginative menu. Lovely walks in the area. Within easy distance Royal Bath and West Showground, one mile, Cheddar Caves, Wookey Hole, Tropical Bird Gardens near Bath, Longleat. Weston-super-Mare, Cathedral City of Wells, Shepton Mallet, Castle Carey and many other places of interest within an easy driving distance. Accommodation for guests in two double and one family bedrooms (two with washbasins); bathroom, two toilets; two sittingrooms (one with TV), diningroom. Children welcome, cot and babysitting provided. Pets accepted by prior arrangement. Parking. Open all year with central heating. Bed and Breakfast from £8 (including tea/coffee in the evening). Dinner provided on request. SAE, please.

SHEPTON MALLET. Mrs M. White, Barrow Farm, North Wootton, Shepton Mallet (Pilton [074-989] 245). Working farm. This farm accommodation is AA listed and registered with the English Tourist Board. Barrow is a dairy farm of 146 acres. The house is 15th century and of much character, situated quietly between Wells, Glastonbury and Shepton Mallet. It makes an excellent touring centre for visiting Somerset's beauty spots and historical places, for example, Cheddar, Bath, Wookey Hole and Longleat. Two double rooms, one family room, one twin bedded room are available each having hot and cold and tea/coffee making facilities. There is a bathroom, two toilets, two lounges, one with colour television, and dining room with separate tables. Guests can enjoy farmhouse fare in generous variety, home baking a speciality. Bed and Breakfast with optional four-course Dinner available. Car essential; ample parking. Children welcome; cot and babysitting facilities. Open March to November; sorry no pets.

SOUTH PETHERTON. Mrs G. N. Vaux, Rydon Farm, Compton Durville, South Petherton TA13 5ER (South Petherton [0460] 40468). Working farm. Standing in an elevated position, only one mile A303 trunk road and approached by a private road. Set in truly rural surroundings, the house is built of local hamstone and has mullioned windows. It faces west with views of the Quantock Hills and there are many local beauty spots, historical properties, private and National Trust. North and south coasts within easy reach; local forest trails; fishing, riding, walking and wild life park less than 10 miles. Bristol, Bath, Glastonbury, Wells and Cheddar Caves within one-and-a-half hour's drive. Excellent sports and recreational field in the village with bowls, tennis and children's play area. Good farmhouse fare with local meat, cheese, cream and fresh eggs; own fruit and vegetables a speciality. Large garden. Warm welcome. Double, single, family bedrooms. Usual facilities. No pets. Terms on enquiry. Evening Meal, Bed and Breakfast or Bed and Breakfast. Open April to October.

Please note that entries marked with an asterisk also have a colour display advert in the colour section in this guide

THE LONG HOUSE HOTEL

Pylle Road, Pilton, Shepton Mallet, Somerset BA4 4BP

The LONG HOUSE HOTEL in an idyllic village location, offers super meals that have got us written about in the best guidebooks and newspapers, really comfortable rooms with your own bathroom en suite, and all this for £124.95 per week, half board including VAT, (though two and five night breaks are also available). Naturally there's a car park, and you are welcome to bring your well-behaved pet.

For a colour brochure and full details please write or telephone
PAUL FOSS on Pilton (074-989) 701.

STOKE-SUB-HAMDON. Mrs E. Holloway, Manor Farm, Chiselborough, Stoke-Sub-Hamdon TA14 6TQ (Chiselborough [093-588] 203). **Working farm.** Mr and Mrs Holloway will give you a warm welcome at Manor Farm for a country holiday in the heart of rural Somerset. The farm has about 500 acres of land devoted to mixed farming. The house is an attractive stone building dated about 1861, but looks of an earlier period. The rooms are large and airy and offer every comfort including hot and cold in all bedrooms. Guests at Manor Farm enjoy the owners' high class Cordon Bleu cooking and fresh produce — personal attention is guaranteed. There are many places of interest to visit in the surrounding area — Chiselborough is in excellent walking country — Ham Hill has wonderful views of the Quantocks and the Mendips. The sea is only 18 miles away by car. Riding, golf, tennis, fishing available nearby. Children are welcome; cot, high chair and babysitting. Sorry, no pets. Open from April to October. Car essential, parking. Evening Dinner, Bed and Breakfast from £14; Bed and Breakfast from £9 nightly. Reductions for children if sharing parents' room.

TAUNTON. Mrs Diana Taylor, Nerrols Farm, Priorswood Road, Cheddon Fitzpaine, Taunton TA2 8QL (Taunton [0823] 89502). **Working farm.** A warm welcome to guests, whether your stay is one or more nights, in this large 16th-century farmhouse surrounded by peaceful gardens, lakes and countryside. There are many animals and family ponies on the 210-acre dairy farm. Ideal for touring north and south coasts, Quantocks, Exmoor National Park and many local places of interest. Accommodation comprises one double, two single and one family bedrooms (two with washbasins); two bathrooms, two toilets. Inglenook fireplace in oak-beamed diningroom and large guests' sittingroom. Log fires. Good home cooking using own produce whenever possible. Central heating. Children welcome, cot, high chair, babysitting. Sorry, no pets. Open all year round for Bed and Farmhouse Breakfast. Evening Meal optional. Reductions for children. Please write or telephone for terms.

TAUNTON. Mrs Marisa Heard, Water Farm, Stogumber, Taunton TA4 3TT (Stogumber [09846] 494). Water Farm is situated in a small valley between Exmoor and the Quantocks. Open all year except Christmas, it is ideal for a relaxing summer holiday, short stays or away-from-it-all weekends. Log fires and four poster bed. This 250-year-old farmhouse based on a working farm provides guests with all day access and can arrange mealtimes to suit visitors' needs. Special diets catered for. Two double bedrooms, one family and one single room, one with washbasin, all with tea/coffee making facilities. Central heating. Comfortable sitting/diningroom. TV. Children welcome. Sorry, no pets. Perfect location for touring. Terms and further details on application. Reduced rates for children.

Somerset BOARD

TAUNTON. Mrs Claire Mitchem, Whittles Farm, Beercrocombe, Taunton TA3 6AH (Hatch Beauchamp [0823] 480301). Whittles Farm is a 200 acre dairy farm, situated at the end of a "No Through Road", one mile from the village of Beercrocombe and seven miles from the historic county town of Taunton. Nearby are forest walks, beautiful and historic gardens. Golf, fishing, riding available locally. Car essential. The superior 16th century farmhouse is luxuriously appointed, carpeted, spacious, comfortably and tastefully decorated, with inglenook and log burners. Accommodation consists of one double, one twin and one family room with en suite bathrooms. Tea/coffee making facilities. Drawing room, diningroom, sittingroom with colour TV. Excellent farmhouse food is carefully prepared (Evening Meal optional). Personal service. Children welcome over 11 years. Brochure. Open March to October inclusive. AA listed.

TAUNTON. F. R. and C. H. Jarvis, St. Quintin Hotel, Caravan and Camping Park, Bridgwater Road, Bathpool, Taunton TA2 8BG (Taunton [0823] 73016). St. Quintin Hotel, Caravan and Camping Park is an AA and RAC two-star hotel. Family run for over 45 years and renowned for good food and ready service. Open all the year round. One mile from M5, exit No. 25, on the A38. Excellent centre for much of Somerset, Dorset, Devon, Avon and Wiltshire. Plenty of seaside and countryside to see and explore. Cycle hire, row-boat hire, coarse fishing available. Also Caravan and Camping Park for tourists (AA three pennant and RAC appointed) and Holiday Homes (caravans) to let. Hotel week-end bargain breaks available end of September to June. Choice of double, single and family rooms (all with washbasins, tea/coffee making facilities and colour TV); bathrooms, toilets; sittingroom, diningroom. Children welcome, cot, high chair and reduced rates available. Sorry, no pets. Evening Dinner, Bed and Breakfast from £19.75 per day. Bed and Breakfast from £16.75 per day (reductions for weekends and four days' stay and over). Car not essential, ample parking.

TAUNTON. Mrs Pauline Sellick, Escott Farm, Williton, Taunton TA4 4JQ (Stogumber [0984] 56253). Working farm. This is a mixed farm with cattle, sheep and arable, situated overlooking Quantock Hills. Nearby places of interest are Exmoor National Park, Dunster Castle and the Doone Valley. Five miles from the sea, 10 miles to Minehead. Riding, golf, fishing nearby. Trout fishing available on the farm. Good farmhouse Breakfast. Car essential, ample parking. Children welcome. Sorry, no pets. Also six-berth caravan available. Outside flush toilet and mains electricity. A warm friendly welcome assured. Telephone or SAE for further details.

TAUNTON. Mrs M. M. Garner-Richards, Watercombe House, Huish Champflower, Taunton TA4 2EE (Wiveliscombe [0984] 23725). West Somerset. Charming well appointed Country House on a smallholding with river frontage, welcomes House Guests. Peace and tranquillity in a fold of the Brendon Hills. Enchanting gardens and grounds. Fishing in the river or at Clatworthy, half-mile away. Sailing at Wimbleball Lake, two miles. Sea is within easy reach. Easy access to the wonderful expanse of Exmoor. We offer excellent home cooking using a high proportion of home grown produce. Enjoy a full English Breakfast; Evening Meals optional. There are washbasins and tea-making facilities in the bedrooms. Weekly terms from £85 per person including Evening Meal. Bed and Breakfast (per person per night) from £8.50. Registered with the Tourist Board.

TAUNTON. Mrs Dianne Roberts, Haynes Down Farm, Skilgate, Taunton (Bampton [0398] 31626). Working farm. Devon/Somerset Borders. Come and stay in peaceful, rolling countryside approximately 10 miles north of Tiverton. Close to the beautiful moors of Exmoor and 15 minutes' drive from the lovely reservoirs of Wimbleball and Clatworthy, where fishing and boating facilities are offered. There are many local places of beauty and historical interest including Knightshayes Court with its 40 acres of formal and woodland gardens, Coombe Sydenham Hall and Country Park, Dunster Castle and Cleeve Abbey. The south Devon coast is one hour away, Minehead is half an hour. Bedrooms: one double, one twin. Sittingroom. Open May to October. Bed and Breakfast £8.50; Bed, Breakfast and Evening Meal £14.00. Reduced for weekly bookings.

TAUNTON. Ms Mary Palmer, Hunters Lodge, Churchinford, Taunton TA3 7DW (Churchstanton [082-360] 253). Working farm. A homely old farmhouse on a 30-acre farm with horses, cattle, sheep and an indoor riding school. Delightful garden which guests are free to walk around. Heated swimming pool. Situated on the Somerset/Devon borders in beautiful countryside and forest area of the Blackdown Hills. Trout lake one mile. Guests met at Taunton, if required. One double and three family bedrooms, three with washbasins; bathroom/shower, two toilets. Sitting-room, diningroom. Children welcome — cot available. Pets can be accommodated in kennels at small extra charge. Electric heating. Parking, though car is not really necessary. Open all year round. Bed and Breakfast from £6.50. Evening meal £3.00.

TAUNTON. Mrs S. Hawkins, Preston Farm, Lydeard St. Lawrence, Taunton TA4 3QQ (Stogumber [0984] 5649). Working farm. Preston Farm is a 14th-century farmhouse commanding panoramic views of the Quantock Hills and the coast of Wales. Half-way between Taunton and Minehead, it is a good base for touring Exmoor. Car essential. There are two family rooms and one single; bathroom and toilet for guests' use; log fires in the dining and sittingrooms when it is cold; colour TV; patio for guests' use. Open from Easter to October. Plenty of car space. Guests able to walk around the farm anytime. Regret, no pets. Children welcome and a cot and high chair are available. Babysitting can be arranged. Bed, Breakfast and Evening Meal from £8.50, children under 12, half price. Weekly rates on request. Bed and Breakfast from £6.50.

TAUNTON. Mrs Ann Broom, April Cottage, Stoke St. Gregory, Taunton TA3 6JD (North Curry [0823] 490749). A 17th-century farmhouse with beamed ceilings and inglenooks set in the heart of the picturesque Somerset countryside surrounded by fields and at the end of a private lane. Close by is historic Sedgemoor, many National Trust properties; Taunton, Bath, Wells, Cheddar, the Quantock Hills and Exmoor National Park are all within easy motoring distance as are north and south coastal resorts. Bed and traditional English Breakfast £6.50 per night. Bed, Breakfast and four-course Evening Meal £10 per night. Also available tastefully converted barn, fully furnished with all modern conveniences, sleeping 4/6, meals available if required. For further details send SAE or telephone.

TAUNTON near. Mr and Mrs John Brightwell, Crinkle Birr Cottage, Higher West Hatch, Near Taunton TA3 5RP (Hatch Beauchamp [0823] 480548). Working farm. Old cottage with four acres of orchards and grassland in small village south of Taunton. Jacob sheep kept, hens, ducks, cats and friendly Labrador. Lovely countryside between Quantock and Blackdown Hills. Good touring centre to Exmoor and North Somerset and within easy reach Dorset coast. Good food with home produce. Spinning wheels and small furniture made in workshop in grounds. Open all year. Bed and Breakfast or Bed, Breakfast plus Evening Meal by arrangement. Children welcome at reduced rates. One double bedroom, two singles, all with hot and cold water. Two bathrooms, toilets. Pets by arrangement, free. No buses. Car essential — parking. Warm, friendly welcome assured. SAE for terms or telephone.

TAUNTON near. Mrs D. Matilda Jee, Ruttersleigh Farm, Staple Fitzpaine, Near Taunton TA3 5SH (Buckland St Mary [046-034] 392). Working farm. Peaceful and relaxing, safe for children, quiet for adults, this family farm on Blackdown Hills has a Channel Island herd which can be stroked. Beautiful scenery, surrounded by trees; plenty of wild life can be seen if quietly approached. Neroche Forest Trail quite near. The 16th century farmhouse has two double and one single bedrooms (one double and single adjoining makes an ideal family room); shower room with hand basin and loo; lounge/diningroom; log fire. Cot, babysitting, reduced rates for children. Car essential — parking. Sorry no pets. Open all year. Friendly atmosphere and good plain farmhouse cooking; plenty of cream and fresh milk every day. SAE, please, for terms for Evening Meal, Bed and Breakfast or Bed and Breakfast only.

TEMPLECOMBE. Mr and Mrs N. Barton, Oak Vale, Henstridge, Templecombe BA8 0SP (Stalbridge [0963] 62524). Secluded Queen Anne farmhouse set in one and a half acres of garden and orchard on the edge of the village. Views of the Blackmoor Vale. Open January to November with central heating. One suite of two bedrooms (one double, one single), with own bathroom. Also two double bedrooms, bathroom, toilet. Sittingroom, dining-room. Car essential, parking. Children welcome, cot, high chair, babysitting and reduced rates. Regret, no pets. Use of spacious front garden. Full English or wholefood Breakfast. Bed and Breakfast single £10, double £18 per night. Special weekly rates. Also ground floor converted stables for self-catering accommodation for six available. Apply above.

THEALE. Mrs E. Taylor, Alvion House, Theale, Near Wedmore BS28 4SL (Wedmore [0934] 712026). The farmhouse has beams and inglenooks. With three acres, it is set in a sunny sheltered hollow of the Mendips and enjoys breathtaking views. Easy reach Cheddar, Wells, Glastonbury and Weston. Full country Breakfasts, delicious four course Dinners with succulent roast meats, home made soups and pastries. Fruit and vegetables from the gardens. Animals to interest the children who are specially welcome while parents are pampered. Central heating, log fires. Vegetarians catered for. Two family, two double rooms. Dinner, Bed and Breakfast £65 to £75. Open all year, including Christmas.

WATCHET. Mrs Diana Brewer, "Wood-Advent" Farm, Roadwater, Watchet (Washford [0984] 40920). Working farm, join in. Situated in the Exmoor National Park, a 340-acre farm, mainly sheep, cattle and arable. The large farmhouse has great charm and character, guests may relax in the large gardens or admire them from the diningroom or lounge which has a colour TV. The emphasis on personal care and good home cooking, the food mostly produced on the farm — delicious beef and clotted cream. An ideal centre for touring Exmoor's beauty spots of which there are so many. Family, double or single rooms available. Children of all ages catered for at reduced rates. Car essential — parking. Open February/November. SAE, please, for terms and further details.

WEDMORE. Mrs D. M. Nicholls, Crickham Farm, Crickham, Wedmore BS28 4JT (Wedmore [0934] 712471). Working farm. Crickham Farm, a lovely grey stone farmhouse, standing in 80 acres of farmland, has every modern comfort, yet loses none of its character. It lies one mile from Wedmore, three from Cheddar and is within easy reach of Cheddar, Bristol, Bath, Wells. It is 20 minutes from Weston-Super-Mare, Burnham-on-Sea and Brean. M5 junction 22½ miles from farm. Secluded garden. Home cooking with fresh farm produce and cream. Car essential. Pony riding on farm included in terms. Ample parking. One double, two family rooms, with washbasins; lounge, TV; diningroom. Open Easter to October. Children welcome, cot, high chair, babysitting. Bed and Breakfast — Evening Meal by arrangement. SAE, please, for details.

WEDMORE. Mrs Cynthia Comer, Totney Farm, Blackford, Wedmore BS28 4PB (Mark Moor [027864] 217). Working farm. Totney Farm is a large modernised farmhouse, approached by a private road, five miles from the M5 Junction 22. The farm is a 300-acre Dairy Farm with the house set in a spacious garden with peaceful surroundings and extensive views of the Mendip Hills and local countryside. We are within the popular touring areas of Weston-Super-Mare, Burnham-on-Sea, Glastonbury, Wells, Cheddar, Wookey Hole Caves and the Quantock Hills. Coarse fishing, golf and most sporting facilities locally. Only a small number of guests are accommodated to ensure personal attention. Children are welcome, cot, high chair and babysitting. No pets. Car essential, parking. A traditional English Breakfast and Four-Course Evening Dinner plus a Jug of Somerset Cider is served. Good food is our speciality. Half price rates for children of 14 years and under sharing parents' bedroom (large family bedroom with washbasin). Evening Dinner, Bed and Breakfast £12 per day; Bed and Breakfast £8 per night. (Youngsters 14 to 16 at two-thirds rate in own rooms). A warm welcome assured to all our guests.

WEDMORE. Mrs L. G. Callow, Chards Farm, Blackford, Wedmore BS28 4PA (Wedmore [0934] 712262). Working farm. This 28-acre beef rearing farm is in a quiet, though not remote, locality adjoining the B3139 road, midway between Wells and Burnham-on-Sea, and central for Cheddar, Weston-Super-Mare, Glastonbury, Wookey Hole and many other places of interest. There are two family bedrooms; bathroom, toilet; large lounge/diningroom with colour TV. Children welcome. Cot, high chair and babysitting available (after children are in bed). Well-trained dogs allowed. Car essential, ample parking space. Open April to October. Bed and Breakfast from £6. Good farm fare with generous helpings. Swing on lawn for children. Reductions for children. SAE, please.

WELLINGTON. Mrs Caroline Nicholas, Stallenge Thorne Farm, Hockworthy, Wellington TA21 0NJ (Clayhanger [039-86] 228). Working farm. This farm, situated in peaceful surroundings on the Devon/Somerset border, is a children's country paradise with a large milking herd, horses and ponies. Ideal for touring Exmoor and both coasts, yet only 10 miles from the motorway. The large farmhouse, built in 1675, is full of character. The panelled diningroom has separate tables. Evening Meals are mostly traditional farmhouse 'roasts' with fresh vegetables, whenever possible. Lounge has colour TV. A holiday with all home comforts. One double, two family bedrooms (washbasins). Children under 12 reduced rates. Car essential — parking. Evening Meal, Bed and Breakfast or Bed and Breakfast. Terms on application.

WELLINGTON. Mrs M. A. Heard, Westcott Farm, Ashbrittle, Wellington TA21 0HZ (Clayhanger [039-86] 258). Working farm. Westcott Farmhouse is a 17th century house facing south with delightful views situated one-and-a-half miles from A361 Taunton/Barnstaple main road. The farm is 190 acres mixed, with numerous animals. Ideal for touring the magnificent West Country with Exmoor and Quantock Hills within easy reach. Fox and stag hunting nearby. Sports Centre and pony trekking eight miles away. One single and two family bedrooms, with washbasins; bathroom; lounge/diningroom with TV. Home produced food served whenever possible. Children welcome, cot and babysitting available. No pets. Car essential. Open all year. Evening Meal, Bed and Breakfast from £70. Reductions for children.

WELLS. Mrs N. Cole, Manor Farm, Worth, Near Wookey, Wells BA5 1LW (Wells [0749] 73428). A 17th century farmhouse offering homely, clean accommodation with every comfort assured. All rooms H/C and TV. Visitors' lounge, colour TV. Children welcome, cot, babysitting. Fire Certificate. Drinks Licence. Eight bedrooms, three bathrooms. Open all year. Ample home produced cooking. Sorry, no pets. Manor Farm is a small mixed farm in a beautiful rural setting close to Mendip Hills, with picturesque shallow river running through it with wild ducks and geese. Visitors are invited to relax and enjoy themselves here. Ideal for touring a vast number of beauty spots, natural and historical, wildlife parks, modern entertainments, the beach. London one and a half hours by rail. Walking distance from restaurant, bus and pub. Bed and Breakfast from £7; Bed, Breakfast and Evening Meal from £11. Self-catering cottage also from £100 per week. Write or phone for brochure.

WELLS. Mrs Pat Higgs, Home Farm, Stoppers Lane, Upper Coxley, Near Wells BA5 1QS (Wells [0749] 72434). Working farm. Home Farm is situated in the heart of all the historic beauty spots, just off A39 — Wells (one-and-a-half miles) — Glastonbury (five miles); Bath, Cheddar Gorge, Wookey Hole Caves, Weston-super-Mare. We offer a varied type of holiday for all ages of the family — beaches nearby for children; National Trust properties; Fleet Air Arm Museum; Steam Trains and Vineyards. All rooms (three double, one single, three family) have washbasins, razor points. Each one has a pleasant view, some of the garden, majority of the Mendip Hills. Two bathrooms, plus shower, three toilets. Cot available; babysitting by arrangement; reductions for children sharing parents' room. Pets accepted in low season. Central heating. Lounge with colour TV; diningroom. Large lawns and garden for guests' use. Good farmhouse cooking assured. Open all year (except Christmas). Terms and further details on request.

WELLS. Mrs Janet Gould, Manor Farm, Old Bristol Road, Upper Milton, Wells BA5 3AH (Wells [0749] 73394). Working farm. Manor Farm is a listed Elizabethan Manor House superbly situated on the slopes of the Mendip Hills one mile from the centre of Wells. It is a beef farm of 130 acres. Three large rooms for visitors, all with hot and cold water and electric heating. Full English Breakfast, with choice of menu, is served in the panelled diningroom. This room, with colour TV and games for children is available for visitors to use as a sittingroom. They can also relax in sun chairs in the peaceful garden and enjoy the lovely view towards the sea. Ideal for walking in the Mendip Hills and an excellent centre for exploring local places of historic interest. Children welcome. Open January to December for Bed and Breakfast from £7 per person. Reductions for children and week-long stays. Parking. Fire Certificate held. Brochure on request.

WELLS. Mr and Mrs B. E Lane, "Quodlibet", Reservoir Lane, Wells BA5 2QZ (Wells [0749] 75530). A quiet, attractive setting overlooking Cathedral City of Wells and Mendip Hills. Ideal for walking (West Mendip Way nearby). Within easy reach of Weston-super-Mare, Burnham-on-Sea, Brean Sands, Cheddar Gorge, Glastonbury, Wookey Hole, Bath, Bristol, etc. Two twin rooms, one double. Guests' own bathroom with bath/shower; own lounge/diner and colour TV. Evening Drink, early morning tea inclusive. High tea/packed lunch/flask filled. Laundry by arrangement. Non-smokers preferred. House and garden plants when available. Free parking. Central heating. Open January – October inclusive. From £7.50 per night. SAE for further details.

WELLS, near. Mrs M. E. Brown, Fenny Castle Guest House, Wookey, Near Wells BA5 1NN (Wells [0749] 72265). Guest House part Edwardian/Georgian style, situated in own farm grounds, three miles from City of Wells, five miles Glastonbury, one mile off A39 Wells/Glastonbury road through country lane. Good coarse fishing in River Sheppey nearby. Accommodation on two floors, fitted carpets, electric heating, spring interior mattresses; three double, one single, two family bedrooms, all with washbasins. Electric blankets used in winter; razor points, tea/coffee making facilities in all rooms. Bathroom, two toilets. Sitting, diningrooms. Licensed Residential and Restaurant. Variety of good farmhouse food, all home produced cooking. Snacks provided, plain and fancy. Packed lunches arranged night before. TV lounge. Children welcome at reduced rates. Pets allowed. Open all year except Christmas/Boxing Day. Car essential, parking. Evening Meal, Bed and Breakfast or Bed and Breakfast. SAE for terms and tariff.

WELLS near. Mrs Pamela Keen, Crapnell Farm, Dinder, Near Wells (Shepton Mallet [0749] 2683). **Working farm.** Crapnell Farm is a 300-acre mixed farm of arable and dairy situated on the Mendip Hills in beautiful surroundings. It is a listed 16th-century house with much character. It is within easy reach of Wells, Cheddar, Wookey Hole, Bath, Longleat and many more interesting places. All rooms are large and very comfortably furnished with H/C, tea/coffee facilities. TV lounge; snooker room; large spacious garden with a swimming pool. Packed lunches if required. You will find a warm friendly welcome in a relaxed atmosphere. Children very welcome. March/October. Ample parking. Evening Dinner, Bed and Breakfast or Bed and Breakfast only.

WELLS near. Mrs D. D. Frayne, Rushlands Farm, Knowle Lane, Wookey, Near Wells BA5 1LD (Wells [0749] 73181). Working farm. Rushlands is situated down a lane from the village with open views. Central Somerset for visiting places like Glastonbury with Abbey ruins and Tor; Wells, with its magnificent cathedral, Wookey Hole caves, Longleat and the lions. You will find a friendly atmosphere and enjoy home cooking with fresh vegetables. Three double (one twin-bedded), one single, two family bedrooms, five with hot and cold and razor points. Bathroom, three toilets; sittingroom and diningroom. Central heating. Children welcome. Babysitting at times. Sorry, no pets. Car essential — parking. Fire Certificate. SAE for terms for Evening Meal, Bed and Breakfast or Bed and Breakfast. Reduced rates for children under 12 years.

* **WESTON-SUPER-MARE near. Mr and Mrs D. J. Brown, Batch Farm Country Hotel, Lympsham, Near Weston-Super-Mare BS24 0EX (Edingworth [093-472] 371). Working farm.** Batch Farm Country Hotel is licensed and AA and RAC two star. It is a charming spot in a lovely part of England. Modern accommodation with old world charm. Ideal centre for touring; acres of freedom for the children; fishing, riding, swimming, tennis, golf locally. Guests welcome Easter to October. Double, single and family bedrooms — all with H&C, shaver sockets, and some bedrooms with bathrooms en-suite. All rooms have panoramic views of hills and countryside. Fully licensed lounge bar, also three lounges, one with colour TV; large diningroom with separate tables. Traditional home cooking. Personal attention by Resident Proprietors and their family and staff, whose ambition is to make your holiday a happy one. Sorry, no pets. Please enclose stamp only for colour brochure and terms. See also Colour Display Advertisement in this Guide.

**HOME BAKING
FRESH VEGETABLES
JERSEY CREAM
at . . .**

POOL FARM, near Weston-super-Mare, Somerset. Tel: Yatton (0934) 833138.

Let the children sample the excitement of life on a working farm. There are horses, ponies, calves, chickens and ducks to see, and sometimes help to feed, and delicious food to enjoy. Although modernised and centrally heated, the farmhouse retains much of its old world charm. Inglenook fireplaces, with open fires on chilly days; two spacious lounges, one with colour TV. All bedrooms have washbasins and two are on the ground floor. Five bath/shower rooms, six toilets. Good facilities for children, and someone available for babysitting. Pleasant gardens. The house makes a good base for touring Bath, Wells, Glastonbury, Cheddar, Longleat and Bristol. Weston-super-Mare with its beaches, fine open-air swimming pool, tennis courts, golf course etc., only four miles distant. Open all year except Christmas and New Year. Dog allowed (owners must bring food).

For more details write or telephone Josephine and Graham Murphy.

WESTON-SUPER-MARE near. Mrs E. V. Howson, Lower Farm House, Lympsham, Near Weston-Super-Mare BS24 0DY (Edingworth [093-472] 206). Lower Farm stands in five acres of lawns, gardens and playfields with swings. The farm, which accommodates visitors in double, single and family bedrooms, has horses, domestic animals, and there are peacocks in the grounds. Unrestricted views of the Mendip Hills; Cheddar Gorge, Wookey Hole, and Bristol Zoo all within easy reach. Also miles of sandy beaches, golf, riding and fishing nearby. Children welcome. Ground floor suitable for disabled person. Open from March to November. Reductions for children. Senior Citizens at reduced prices. Pets welcome. SAE, please, for terms.

WEST SOMERSET FARM & COUNTRY HOLIDAYS

Come to the part of Somerset which inspired the poetry of Coleridge and Wordsworth.

The wooded slopes of the Brendon and Quantock hills, offering marvellous opportunities to walkers, riders and lovers of nature generally. There are horse riding centres and golf courses, both fresh and sea water fishing (the North and South coasts are within easy reach), sailing and windsurfing. Winding lanes will lead you to small, hidden villages where you may find painters and potters at work or perhaps a game of cricket in progress. Self-catering accommodation available, also Bed & Breakfast with optional Evening Meal.

For further information, contact: Mary Hunt, The Mount, Ford, Wiveliscombe, Somerset. (Wiveliscombe [0984] 23992/23725).

WILLITON. Mrs S. J. Watts, Rowdon Farm, Williton TA4 4JD (Stogumber 0984-56280). Working farm. Take a break from the stress of your busy world. Come "DOWN ON THE FARM" for rest, peace and tranquillity. Our clean and comfortable farmhouse has an idyllic setting. Four miles from the coast and with panoramic views of the Quantock Hills. Quiet walking, riding, fishing country. Rural industries and noteworthy beauty spots within easy reach. A pleasant room with H&C, fresh farm produce and personal attention to your well being. We also have self catering on the farm with a good choice of bar meals and restaurants locally. AA listed. Open all year.

WIVELISCOMBE. Mary Hunt, The Mount Country House, Ford, Wiveliscombe TA4 2RL (Wiveliscombe [0984] 23992). The Mount is set in six acres in the pretty hamlet of Ford, West Somerset. The rooms are tastefully furnished retaining old worlde charm and many features. It makes an ideal base to explore the beauty of Somerset and Devon, whether for walking, touring or simply relaxing. It is within easy reach of Exmoor and the Quantock and Brendon Hills, with many places of interest to visit; riding and fishing nearby. A warm welcome and personal service await you. Hot and cold in all bedrooms. Log fires. Home cooking. Lounge, TV. Ample parking. Relais Routiers recommended. Open all year. Special winter rates. Long or short stay. Bed and Breakfast nightly from £11 (weekly from £63). Dinner, Bed and Breakfast nightly from £16.25 (weekly from £99.75).

SOMERSET – THE CREAM AND CIDER COUNTY!
Wookey Hole, the great cave near Wells, is the first known home of man in Great Britain. Other places of interest in this green and hilly country include The Mendips, Exmoor National Park, Cheddar Gorge, Meare Lake Village and The Somerset Rural Life Museum. The villages and wildlife of the Quantocks, Poldens and Brendons should not be missed.

Somerset / Staffordshire   **BOARD**

YEOVIL. Mrs M. Tucker, Carents Farm, Yeovil Marsh, Yeovil BA21 3QE (Yeovil [0935] 76622). Working farm. Carents Farm is half-a-mile off A37 Yeovil/ Ilchester road, Dorset Border two miles. It is a 350-acre arable and beef farm with 17th century Hamstone farmhouse and looks out over peaceful fields and lawns. Accommodation for guests in two double bedrooms and one family room, one with washbasin; bathroom, two toilets; lounge with colour TV and diningroom with separate tables. The bedrooms are comfortably furnished with fitted carpets, spring interior mattresses and tea/coffee making facilities in all rooms. This is a suitable tourist centre for Dorset villages, north and south coasts, Cheddar Caves, Bath, Longleat, Wells. The food is good and well cooked. Children are welcome and babysitting provided. Sorry, no pets allowed. Open from January to November with electric heating and log fires in the winter. Car essential, large parking area. Rates reduced for children. SAE, please, terms on application.

YEOVIL near. Mr and Mrs Merchant, Barrows Country House, East Chinnock, Near Yeovil BA22 9EJ (West Coker [093-586] 2390). This Victorian mansion, open all year, is situated just off the A30 midway between Yeovil and Crewkerne. It is in beautiful, rolling countryside, ideally placed for walking or touring. The maximum of 10 guests have available six bedrooms, all with hot and cold water; three bathrooms, four WC's; two sittingrooms, each with TV; separate diningroom; full central heating. The resident proprietors, who give personal service to all guests, hold a residential licence and specialise in good English fare using home-grown produce. The large garden includes a croquet lawn. Children over five years welcome. Sorry, no pets. Car park. Bed and Breakfast, optional Evening Dinner. No service charge. No VAT. Brochure and terms on request.

STAFFORDSHIRE

CODSALL. Mrs Denise E. Moreton, Moors Farm and Country Restaurant, Chillington Lane, Codsall, Near Wolverhampton WV8 1QH (Codsall [090 74] 2330). Working farm. Moors Farm is a livestock farm with its own farmhouse restaurant, situated in a pleasant rural valley one mile from Codsall village which has shops, pubs, churches and its own railway station with links to Shropshire and Wales or the Birmingham National Exhibition Centre. The farm has a variety of animals including cows, pigs, sheep and poultry and there is a pony for hire to experienced riders. Kitchen uses home produced meat, dairy products and garden vegetables. Fishing, riding, tennis, golf and swimming within easy reach. Ideal situation for touring. Accommodation comprises three double, and three family rooms, all with hot and cold, tea/coffee making facilities; two bathrooms. Sittingroom, diningroom, 'Oak-Room' licensed bar, with log fires. Open all year. Fire Certificate held. Bed and Breakfast or Evening Dinner, Bed and Breakfast. AA/RAC listed. British Relais Routiers approved.

LEEK near. Mrs E. Lowe, Fairboroughs Farm, Rudyard, Near Leek ST13 8PR (Rushton Spencer [02606] 341). Working farm. The house dates from early Tudor period with oak beams and open fires. The rooms are large and comfortable with fitted carpets and H&C washbasins. There is a shaver point in each room and linen is provided fresh daily. There is a diningroom and separate lounge with colour TV for use of visitors. There are magnificent views and, being situated in the Staffordshire moorlands, we are within easy reach of the Peak Park, Potteries and Cheshire. Fishing areas nearby at Rudyard and Tittesworth Reservoirs. This is a working beef/sheep farm of 140 acres. We endeavour to make everyone welcome — children in particular! Bed and Breakfast from £8.50 single, £15 double. Evening Meal available on request. Reduced rates for children. AA listed. CC/CL.

PLEASE SEND A STAMPED ADDRESSED ENVELOPE WITH ENQUIRIES

STAFFORDSHIRE MOORLANDS

The countryside of the **Staffordshire Moorlands** is the most dramatic in Staffordshire and includes some of the best scenery in the Peak National Park. It is an area for people with a taste for upland scenery where open moors contrast with rock outcrops and deep wooded valleys and dales carved by fast flowing streams. It is challenging countryside ready made for adventurous pastimes such as climbing, hiking, pony-trekking, cycling and hang-gliding all of which can be sampled in the Staffordshire Moorlands.

There are quiet villages nestling in the hills and lively towns with markets, mill shops and antiques. There are rural crafts, horse-drawn canal trips, scenic train journeys, and many other attractions including Alton Towers — Britains most popular leisure park. The Staffordshire Moorlands is also an ideal base for visits to the Potteries and museums of Stoke-on-Trent and the historic houses and other attractions of the Peak National Park. Get away from the crowds and enjoy the warmth of traditional hospitality in the Staffordshire Moorlands. Brief particulars and telephone numbers included here. Phone accommodation of choice or for more information about the area contact Tourist Information Centre, Stockwell Street, Leek, Staffordshire. Tel. No. (0538) 385181.

BOARD

The Hermitage, Froghall (Frank or Wilma Barlow, Tel. No. (053871) 515). Beautiful period farmhouse with oak beams and old world charm. Overlooks Churnet Valley, easy access to Alton Towers. Bed and breakfast from £8.00.

Travellers Rest, Nr. Leek (Elaine and Jeff Barton, Tel. No. (0538) 382186). Conveniently placed comfortable accommodation. Tea/coffee facilities, private bathroom, own lounge/dining room. Colour T.V. Reasonable rates. Lunches, evening meals available. Licensed.

The Hatcheries, Leek (Mrs. B. Birchall, Tel. No. (0538) 383073/386230). Two minutes town centre, secluded position overlooking the Moorlands. B & B from £9.50. All bedrooms colour T.V., H & C, tea and coffee makers, car park, C.H., S.P.

STAFFORDSHIRE MOORLANDS

Admiral Jervis, Oakamoor (Allan and Marjorie Boulton [0538] 702187). Riverside Inn, picturesque setting. 2 miles from Alton Towers, 10 miles from Stoke-on-Trent. Family owned and run. Excellent food. All rooms – showers, T.V., tea/coffee, C.H., B & B from £12.00 p.p.

White House, Grindon (Philomena Bruce, Tel. No. [05388] 250). 17th Century former inn in quiet village overlooking Manifold Valley. C.H., T.V., H & C., tea and coffee facilities in all rooms. B & B £8–£9.00.

Triphena, Leek (Mrs. Buxton, Tel. No. [0538] 384998). Pleasantly situated double fronted Victorian town house overlooking recreation grounds – few minutes from town centre. Family atmosphere. C.H., T.V. Lounge. B & B from £7.00. Evening meal £2.25.

Hollybush, Hollington (Mrs. Clayton, Tel. No. [088926] 314). Country farmhouse within easy reach of Alton Towers, Peak National Park and beautiful Staffordshire Moorlands. Own suite of rooms inc. T.V., Full Board £52.50 p.w. B & B £6.50 p.p.

Park House, Nr. Longnor (Mrs. Floyd, Tel. No. [029884] 423). B & B in homely atmosphere in picturesque cottage situated in Peak Park. Horse-drawn scenic rides and driving tuition available.

The Old Vicarage, Endon (Mrs. Grey, Tel. No. [0782] 503686). In quiet setting off A53 Leek to Potteries road. B & B (with evening drink) £8.00. Children and non-smokers especially welcome.

Cheddleton Heath House, Nr. Leek (Peter and Mary Hall, Tel. No. [0538] 360364). 2 miles south of Leek. Victorian house with large garden and ample parking space. B & B from £7.00. Evening meal £3.50. Guest Lounge.

Porch Farm, Grindon (Mrs. S. Hulme, Tel. No. [05388] 545). Traditional Peak Park Stone farmhouse overlooking the Manifold Valley. Convenient for Dovedale, Potteries, Alton Towers. Ideal walking and touring. B & B from £7.50.

Peak Weavers Hotel, Leek (Mr. and Mrs. Jones, Tel. No. [0538] 383729). Georgian mansion in own grounds close to town centre. Licensed restaurant. Car Park. All rooms with T.V., tea/coffee facilities. B & B from £11.00.

The Old Malthouse, Alton (Mr. A. R. Lee, Tel. No. [0538] 702 408). Superbly situated in North Staffordshire's Rhineland near Alton Towers, Dovedale and Derbyshire Peaks. Homely, B & B. Please apply for rates.

Keekorok Lodge Farm, Upperhulme (Mrs. J. Lomas, Tel. No. [053834] 218). Olde Worlde farmhouse in secluded position. Excellent views. Ideal for walking, Wedgwood, Chatsworth, Alton Towers. Twin Double/Family rooms, C.H., H.C., Visitors bathroom, T.V. Lounge, choice of breakfasts.

The Old Vicarage, Alstonefield (Mrs. L. Macaskill, Tel. No. [033527] 215). Dovedale, ideal centre for touring and walking. High standard accommodation retaining friendly atmosphere of family home. B & B from £9.00. Also self-catering flat for 4 from £70.00.

Park View, Cheadle (Mrs. Mahoney, Tel. No. [0538] 755412). Easy reach Alton Towers and Potteries, adjacent to Leisure Centre. Parking, colour T.V. family rooms with wash-hand basins. Bed and breakfast £8.50. Evening meal £3.00 (pre booked).

Pethills Bank Cottage, Bottomhouse (Mrs. Yvonne Martin, Tel. No. [05388] 555 or 277). Situated in open countryside on boundary of Peak National Park. 2 D (1 en-suite) 1 TW, T.V., tea/coffee facilities in all rooms. B & B from £7.50.

East View, Hulme End (Mrs. Moorcroft, Tel. No. [0298] 884). Situated by B5054, attractive cottage by Manifold Valley Trail, close to Dovedale. Two twin or double rooms with H & C., T.V. Lounge, large garden, ample parking. B & B from £7.00.

The Old Chapel, Wetton (Mrs. P. Rhoades, Tel. No. [033527] 378). Beautifully modernised spacious accommodation in Peak National Park. Close to Manifold Valley, Dovedale and Milldale. Magnificent views. 3 twin rooms (2 en-suite). B & B from £8.00 evening meal available.

Bank End Farm, Longsdon (Barbara Robinson, Tel. No. [0538] 383638). Adjoining 15th Century farmhouse near Leek. Modern bedrooms, bathroom en-suite. Visitors lounge and dining room. Licensed bar. Heated swimming pool. Fishing. B & B from £10.00.

Sleighbury House, Leek (Mrs. L. A. Savage, Tel. No. [0538] 382200). Victorian family house with large garden. 3 twin rooms with H.C., 1 single. Guest lounge with colour T.V. B & B from £8.00 (inc. evening drink).

Whimbrell, Ipstones (Mrs. Squire, Tel. No. [053871] 749). Comfortable modern stone residence on edge of Peak Park. Close to Alton Towers, Dovedale and Churnet Valley. B & B £7.50, evening meal £4.50.

Choir Cottage, Cheddleton (Elaine Sutcliffe, Tel. No. [0538] 360 561). 17th Century cottage. Four-poster bed, en-suite shower/toilet, colour T.V. Meals served in adjoining house. Only fresh produce – all diets catered for. B & B from £8.50.

New Cottage Farm, Quarnford (Mrs. A. Walker, Tel. No. [02607] 665). Modernised farmhouse in Peak Park overlooking Dane Valley. Close to Roaches, Three Shires Head and Lud's Church. B & B £7.00.

Weaver Farm, Waterhouses (Mrs. Watson, Tel. No. [0538] 702271). Stone farmhouse situated on Weaver Hills with magnificent views. Ideal for Alton Towers, Potteries and Peak District. Separate lounge, tea and coffee facilities. Fire Certificate. Sleeps 12. B & B £8.00 evening meal £4.00.

Leasows Farm, Hilderstone (Mrs. Webb, Tel. No. [088924] 221). Alton Towers, Wedgwood, Shugborough, Dovedale easy reach from Leasows Farm. C.H. throughout. B. & B from £10.00. Evening meal by arrangement. Also large self-catering apartment (sleeps 6). Brochure available.

Micklea Farm, Longsdon (Mrs. White, Tel. No. [0538] 385006). In quiet village off A53 near to Potteries, Peak District, Alton Towers. Own lounge and T.V. B & B £8.50, evening meal £4.50.

Aldwyn Cottage, Alstonefield (Audrey Williams, Tel. No. [033527] 213). Homely accommodation in cosy cottage close to Dovedale and Manifold Valley. Excellent walking and interesting scenery. Full English breakfast. B & B £7.00–£7.50.

The Manor, Cheadle (Mrs. Woolridge, Tel. No. [0538] 753450). Georgian House ideally situated for the Potteries, Peak District and Alton Towers. 3 double rooms in house, 6 chalet bedrooms (2D, 4F). Evening meal on request. From £12.50 (S) – £18.54 (D) inc. VAT.

Glenwood House Farm, Ipstones – See 'Self Catering'.

Glenrock Cottage, Alton – See 'Self Catering'.

STAFFORDSHIRE MOORLANDS

SELF CATERING

Alders Cottages, Alstonefield (Mrs. Allen, Tel. No. (033527) 201). Three modernised cottages in picturesque village near Dovedale. AA listed (TBA) open fires and central heating. Each cottage sleeps 6. Pleasant garden overlooks the hills. Phone for details.

Glenwood House Farm, Ipstones (Joyce Brindley, Tel. No. (053871) 294). A 58 acre working farm, overlooking the Churnet Valley. 4 miles from Alton Towers and Peak National Park. Bed and breakfast and Self Catering. S.A.E. for brochure.

Garden Cottage, Onecote (Mrs. Gladys Burton, Tel. No. (05388) 380). Restored stone cottage in centre of village in Peak Park. Sleeps 4/5. Fully equipped inc. colour T.V., woodburning stove etc. Own garden and parking £45 to £75 p.w.

Lake View, Rushton (Mrs. Cheetham, Tel. No. (02606) 241). Holiday flat with beautiful views over Rudyard Lake. Sleeps 2/4. Elec. blankets. Linen provided, beds made for arrival. Colour T.V., radio. Lawn with garden chairs. Parking. £50 to £70 per week. Brochure.

Heather Farm, Nr. Oakamoor (Mrs. Creswell, Tel. No. (0538) 702362). Restored 18th Century farmhouse situated in 10 acres of glorious countryside. 3 miles from Alton Towers. Sleeps 7. £80 to £120 p.w.

The Limes, Rushton (Mrs. K. Goodfellow, Tel. No. (0625) 872863). Large comfortable house in village. Garden, private drive and parking. Ideal for children and country walks. Excellent local with catering facilities. 5 bedrooms. £65 to £95 p.w.

Jasmine Cottage, Rudyard (Mrs. Johnson, Tel. No. (0538) 385080). 18th Century stone cottage in sunny position. 2 bedrooms (1D, 1T). All amenities including colour T.V., coal and electric fires. Parking for 2 cars. Pets welcome £50 to £80 p.w.

Crowgutter Farm, Ipstones (Mrs. Sheila Leeson, Tel. No. (053871) 428). Large secluded farm house which has been divided to form spacious self-contained holiday home. Overlooks beautiful Churnet Valley. Sleeps 7. From £70 to £110.

Bramhouse Farm, Wetley Rocks (Mr. P. E. Meakin, Tel. No. (0782) 550527). New Lodge House delightfully located in landscaped gardens and lawns. Tastefully furnished with 3 bedrooms, sleeps 8. £70 to £90 p.w.

Bank End Cottage, Brown Edge (Mrs. K. Meredith, Tel. No. (0782) 502160). Self catering cottage in beautiful country village. Sleeps 5. Fully furnished and equipped – colour T.V. Ample parking. Visit Peak District and Potteries. From £50 to £100 p.w.

10-11, The Square, Oakamoor (Dot Merry, Tel. No. (0538) 702744). Artist offers self catering accommodation, sleeps 4, pets welcome. £75 p.w. (Special winter rates). Free week's holiday if you have your pet's portrait painted.

Lower Berkhamsytch Farm, Nr. Leek (Mr. and Mrs. Mycock, Tel. No. (05386) 213). Stone built house on dairy farms with excellent views on edge of Peak National Park. House divided to provide self-contained holiday home. Sleeps 2/4. Linen if requested. £40 to £70 p.w.

Islington Villa, Longnor (Mr. Nadin, Tel. No. (029883) 291). Self-catering cottage, sleeps 5 plus cot. Fully equipped, T.V., garden, parking. Also 4 berth caravan, facilities as above. Open all year. S.A.E. for brochure.

Glenrock Cottage, Alton (Maggie Naish, Tel. No. (0538) 702502). Situated in the Churnet Valley on Staffordshire Way. Fully modernised, central heating, T.V., 1 double room, 1 family room. Self-catering or bed and breakfast.

2 Rose Cottage, Endon (Mrs. Perkin, Tel. No. (0782) 502358). 17th Century Cottage, sleeps 4. One large room with bed-settee and coal fire, 1 large bedroom. Well equipped kitchen, shower cubicle, outside w.c. From £40 to £50 p.w.

Tythe Barn Holiday Homes, Alton (Mrs. J. Ratcliffe, Tel. No. (0538) 702852). Near Alton Towers. Two spacious self-contained holiday homes in attractive 17th Century farmhouse. Pleasant gardens overlooking countryside. Sleeps 6. AA listed. Apply for rates.

Bank Top Farm, Nr. Waterhouses (Jean Salt, Tel. No. (05386) 331). Modernised cottage on dairy and sheep farm. Within easy reach of Alton Towers and Manifold Valley. Fishing close by. Sleeps 5. £65 to £95 p.w.

Lockwood Hall Farm, Chealde (Bill and Frances Sherratt, Tel. No. (0538) 752270). Family house on dairy farm with beautiful views overlooking Churnet Valley. 4 miles Alton Towers. Convenient for Potteries, Dovedale, Chatsworth. Sleeps 10 (cot available). Terms on request.

Limestone View Farm, Nr. Waterhouses (Mrs. Wendy Webster, Tel. No. (05386) 288). Cottage on dairy farm attached to farm house overlooking fields. Sleeps 6. Open fire giving full central heating. Colour T.V. linen provided. Pets. Parking. Telephone for details.

The Old Vicarage, Alstonefield – See 'Board' section.

Leasows Farms, Hilderstone – See 'Board' section.

NATIONAL GARDEN FESTIVAL
STOKE-ON-TRENT STAFFORDSHIRE

▲ **Fun and Festivities for all Ages**
There's so much to see and enjoy at the most exciting family entertainment of the year. Traditional craftsmen, the Butterfly Tower, beautiful lakes; hot-air balloons, nature reserves, 'History of the Potteries' exhibitions, children's play areas and adventure playgrounds, show houses and lots, lots more.

OPEN EVERY DAY 10.00am–DUSK
1st MAY – 26th OCTOBER 1986

Staffordshire's Vale of Trent
Farm and Country Holidays

Sample the warm hospitality of Farm or Country accommodation amidst the peaceful and beautiful countryside of central Staffordshire.
Rich in local traditions and easily accessible, the Vale offers the visitor a feast of things to do and see. Historic houses, castles, picturesque villages still performing ancient ceremonies and working museums recreating Staffordshire's industrial heritage are in abundance here.
Roam at will over the lovely heath and forest of Cannock Chase, enjoy a leisurely trip aboard a traditional narrowboat it's a marvellous way of seeing some of Staffordshire's finest scenery, or simply look for bargains in one of the several interesting market towns in the area.
Brief particulars and telephone numbers below.
Phone accommodation of choice or Secretary Mrs. D. E. Moreton. Tel. (09074) 2330.
For Group leaflet please send stamped addressed envelope (9" × 4").

FARMHOUSE ACCOMMODATION
Fishers Pit Farm (Mrs. Sylvia Aitkenhead, Tel. No. [0283] 840204).
A warm and friendly welcome awaits you on this 85-acre dairy working farm, one mile east of Abbots Bromley. Centrally situated for all of Staffordshire's many attractions.
Oaklands Farm (Mrs. Angela Badham, Tel. No. [0283] 840503).
Comfortable accommodation and home cookinig on peaceful and pleasant 12 acre smallholding, within easy reach of Cannock Chase, Alton Towers and the Potteries. Terms £7 evening meal available.
Ashmore Brook Farm (Mrs. Helen Broome, Tel. No. [05432] 55753).
Partly Georgian and partly oak beams, Ashmore Brook has spacious rooms comfortably furnished. Situated 1½ miles from city centre, ideally placed for all Midlands activities.

VALE OF TRENT

FARMHOUSE ACCOMMODATION – continued

The Home Farm (Mrs. Joan Brown, Tel. No. [078574] 252)
168-acre dairy/arable farm, 6 miles M6 junction 14, 6 miles Newport, 3½ miles Eccleshall. Every home comfort, tastefully furnished accommodation. Warm welcome to all. Lovely secluded gardens, grass tennis court.

Dairy House Farm (Mrs. Harris, Tel. No. [033523] 359)
Working dairy farm. Oak beamed farmhouse. Residential licence. Evening meals. Visitors' diningroom and lounge. Colour TV. Tea/coffee facilities. Washbasins in bedrooms. Near Alton Towers.

Marsh Farm (Mrs. Mary Hollins, Tel. No. [0283] 840323)
Situated 1 mile north of Abbots Bromley. Famous for horn dancing and many interesting historical aspects. Close to the Staffordshire Way, Blithfield Reservoir and within easy reach of Alton Towers and the Potteries.

Offley Grove Farm (Mrs. Margaret James, Tel. No. [078579] 205)
178-acre working farm, offers comfortable renovated accommodation, 5 miles Newport, Salop, 4 miles Eccleshall, 15 minutes M54 and M6. Accessible Shropshire, Staffordshire and Cheshire. Visitors lounge and dining room.

Moors Farm & Country Restaurant (Mrs. D. E. Moreton, Tel. No. [09074] 2330)
Attractive fully licensed farmhouse in beautiful countryside 5 miles northwest of busy Wolverhampton. Bedrooms have H & C, tea/coffee facilities. Children over 4 years; no dogs. AA/RAC listed.

Holly Grange Farm (Mrs. Bridget Noakes, Tel. No. [08893] 2405)
Centrally heated farmhouse tastefully decorated with many antiques. Guests' lounge with colour TV. Tea/coffee facilities in rooms. Convenient for Alton Towers, Potteries etc. Childrens play area.

The Old Vicarage (Mrs. Janet Powis, Tel. No. [0283] 820993)
An early 19th Century Georgian 6 bedroomed house adjacent to open fields on the edge of an attractive village set in around 2 acres of garden.

White Oak Farmhouse (Mrs. Pat Richardson, Tel. No. [095276] 246)
Modernised Victorian Farmhouse situated in attractive open countryside surrounded by the Earl of Bradford's estate. Conveniently situated for Cosford Aerospace Museum, Severn-Valley Railway. Terms from £8.00.

Chantry View Farm (Mrs. Brenda Skipper, Tel. No. [0283] 75200)
Farmhouse set in beautiful countryside with magnificent view. Guests TV lounge and bathroom. Welcome tray in rooms. Convenient for Alton Towers, Lichfield, Cannock Chase, Potteries, Peak District.

Dower House Farm (Mrs. Elizabeth Denham Smith, Tel. No. [0283] 216417)
Dairy farm with 18th Century stone house. Home cooking. French spoken. 5-van caravan site. Self contained cottage for disabled. Fishing. T.V. Tea/Coffee facilities. Basins H & C. Prices on request.

Popinjay Farm (Mrs. K. Stockton, Tel. No. [08893] 66082)
Pleasantly situated west of Uttoxeter but within easy reach of Uttoxeter race course, Alton Towers, pottery museums and the beautiful Churnet and Dove Valleys.

Manor Farm (Mrs. Susan Stubbs, Tel. No. [088921] 391)
This 16th century farmhouse is half timbered in the village of Kingstone 4 miles west of Uttoxeter. We offer homely accommodation and good food in comfortable surroundings.

Stanton Barns Farm (Mrs. J. R. Tavener, Tel. No. [03316] 2346)
A picturesque, old, stone farmhouse in a secluded position, with land bordering the River Trent. Only 20 minutes from the M1, Derby. 3 miles Calke Abbey.

SELF-SERVICED ACCOMMODATION

The Grange (Mrs. Rita Cooper, Tel. No. [082786] 219)
Tastefully furnished cottage situated in Lullington. Pleasant outlook, several times winner of the best kept village. Sleeps 2/3, with linen supplied, 9 miles from Lichfield.

Silver Trees Caravan Park (Mrs. S. A. Cooper, Tel. No. [08894] 2185)
Comfortable chalet, and caravans, on beautiful Cannock Chase. Facilities include swimming pool, tennis court, games and TV room, play area, showers, shop, laundry. Touring and motor caravans also welcome.

Farewell Manor (Mrs. L. H. Hammersley, Tel. No. [05436] 2248)
Gorton Lodge Farm. 17th Century ivy covered farmhouse set along a quiet lane yet with easy access to A51. Working farm. Large garden. 3 miles Lichfield. Ideal touring base.

Birch Cottage (Mrs. Carolyn Heydon, Tel. No. [088926] 271)
Alton Towers country. Modernised sandstone cottage. Sleeps 6 plus baby in 3 bedrooms. Storage radiators and open fire. Garden adjoining woodland. Beds made before arrival.

Curborough Hall Farm (Mrs. G. Hollinshead, Tel. No. [05432] 22595)
Elmhurst Dairy Farm: Tastefully converted farm buildings into 3 cottages each accommodating up to 6 persons. Approximately 1½ miles from the City of Lichfield. Brochure on request. From £62 per week.

Priory Farm (John and Barbara Myatt, Tel. No. [088922] 269)
Secluded and picturesque accommodation on working dairy farm. Converted fishing house provides commodious bed sitting room for 2-4 persons with modern kitchen, shower room, colour television, fridge.

Honeysuckle Cottage (Mrs. Elizabeth Denham Smith, Tel. No. [0283] 216417)
Facilities for disabled visitors. Sleeps 6. Outdoor swimming pool. Lovely surroundings. TV. Peaceful. Electricity on meter. Linen provided. No pets please. 5 van caravan site.

MACCLESFIELD. Mrs Joyce Brown, Barnswood Farm, Rushton, Macclesfield, Cheshire SK11 0RA (Rushton Spencer [026-06] 261). Working farm. Barnswood is a 100-acre dairy farm overlooking the picturesque Rudyard Lake which is owned by British Waterways; sailing and coarse fishing are permitted. It is a two miles long reservoir, 400 yards down the farm fields. The farm is on the A523, 28 miles from Manchester Airport, nine miles from the silk town of Macclesfield; Jodrell Bank, Dovedale and the Peak District, Alton Towers, many stately homes, all within a 15-mile radius. Two double and one family bedrooms (two with washbasins), all with view of Rudyard Lake; bathroom, two toilets; sitting/diningroom. Colour TV. Children welcome at reduced rates. Sorry, no pets. Open Easter to November. Car essential, parking available. Fire Certificate. SAE, please, for terms for Bed and Breakfast. AA listed.

RUGELEY. Mrs R. A. Read, Lower Newlands Farm, Newlands Lane, Rugeley WS15 3JD (Burton-on-Trent [0283] 840370). Working farm. The 16th-century oak-beamed farmhouse is situated in open countryside within reach of the Peak District, Cannock Chase, Alton Towers and various stately homes such as Sudbury Hall and Shugborough Hall. Lichfield Cathedral and the picturesque village of Abbots Bromley are close by. Trout fishing in the River Blythe is available free. Breakfast and the four-course dinner are served in the diningroom with plenty to eat. Lounge with colour TV for use in the evening. Large lawn and garden where children can play and guests can sit outside if they wish. Cot, high chair, babysitting available. Car essential — parking. Evening Dinner, Bed and Breakfast from £70 per week per person plus VAT; Bed and Breakfast from £49 per week per person plus VAT. Reductions for children under 11.

UTTOXETER. Mr P. J. Tunnicliffe, Moor House Farm, Wood Lane, Uttoxeter ST14 8JR (Uttoxeter [08893] 2384). Working farm. Situated beside the Uttoxeter Race Course and about a mile from the town itself, Moor House Farm offers you a friendly atmosphere with excellent cuisine — variety a speciality. There are two double, one single and one family bedrooms; a bathroom and two toilets; sittingroom and diningroom. Children are welcome and a cot and highchair are provided. Babysitting can be arranged. Open all year, the farm is within easy distance of many places of interest such as Shugborough, Chatsworth, Kedleston, Alton Towers and the Blue John Mines. Uttoxeter itself has a Leisure Centre with swimming pool and a Cattle and Market Day on Wednesdays. Car an advantage with public transport one mile away. Evening Dinner, Bed and Breakfast £12 per person, Bed and Breakfast £7.50 with reductions for children and senior citizens. Terms on application.

SUFFOLK

BECCLES. Mrs F. Prime, Mill House, Wangford, Beccles NR34 8AZ (Wangford [050-278] 694). Mill House stands in a large garden, overlooking the village. Lowestoft is 11 miles away. Beccles eight and Southwold three-and-a-half miles. Guests will find they have easy access to heaths, woods, the sea, the Broads, stately homes and a bird sanctuary. Golf, tennis, riding and fishing can be enjoyed in the vicinity as well as bathing. Open all year round except Christmas and New Year. Two double and one single bedrooms (two with washbasins and shaver points); bathroom and two toilets; sittingroom, diningroom. Children welcome. Regret no pets. A car is necessary, parking available. Bed and Breakfast only. SAE, please, for terms.

SUFFOLK – CONSTABLE COUNTRY!
To be precise Dedham Vale is Constable Country and it is only one of Suffolk's attractions. The others include the country parks at Brandon and Clare Castle, Debenham, Lavenham, Newmarket, The Museum of East Anglian Life and the river port of Woodbridge.

BECCLES. St. Peter's House Hotel, Old Market, Beccles NR34 9AF (Beccles [0502] 713203). James of St. Peter's offers a warm welcome to all guests, with comfortable accommodation, varied traditional English food and fine wines. St. Peter's has lawns sweeping down to the River Waveney and moorings are for residents and diners. (Boat hiring facilities nearby). Two double, two twin and one family bedrooms (one twin on ground floor) with washbasins, shaver points and tea/coffee making facilities. The house is early Georgian with Gothic touches and is scheduled as Grade I listed building. Unique feature is the Strawberry Hall Gothic Restaurant. Fully licensed bar, bar meals, traditional ale and Suffolk cider. Beccles is ideal for touring East Anglia and about 20 miles from Norwich; ideal for birdwatching, too. Car not essential, but there is parking space near. Children welcome, cot, high chair. Bed and Breakfast or Bed, Breakfast and Evening Dinner (the Restaurant is licensed). Special two-day breaks available during winter months. St. Peter's is open all year. Weekly and daily terms on application.

BURY ST. EDMUNDS. Mrs Elizabeth Nicholson, The Grange Farmhouse, Beyton, Bury St. Edmunds IP30 9AG (Beyton [0359] 70184). The Grange is a very attractive, traditional Suffolk farmhouse standing in six acres with a large secluded garden. Situated in the picturesque village of Beyton, five miles east of the historical market town of Bury St. Edmunds, just off A45. Within easy reach of Cambridge, Newmarket, Ely Cathedral, medieval wool town of Lavenham, Constable country; an ideal stopover point for travellers to and from the European Ferries at Felixstowe and Harwich. Local amenities include golf, riding, swimming and tennis. Two National Trust properties nearby and Theatre Royal in Bury. Choice of comfortable bedrooms, all with washbasins; bathroom, two toilets. Central heating, plus log fires in winter evenings. Excellent home cooking for Bed and Breakfast (evening meal optional). Colour TV in guests' lounge. Cot, high chair, babysitting available, reduced rates for under 10's. Sorry, no pets. Car essential, ample parking. Open all year. Please send for brochure. We look forward to hearing from you.

BURY ST. EDMUNDS near. Miss R. Thew, High Green House Guest House, Nowton, Near Bury St. Edmunds IP29 5LZ (Sicklesmere [028-486] 293). Very good centre for visiting all of East Anglia, two miles from Ickworth, 10 miles from Lavenham. Fully modernised Tudor house set in one acre pleasure garden with extensive views of surrounding countryside. Attractive accommodation comprises one family room (with four-poster and toilet), two twin rooms (one with shower), plus two bathrooms. Two ground floor single rooms (one with bath adjoining), toilet. One of these rooms suitable for disabled guests. Lounge with colour TV. Ample parking — car essential. Children and pets welcome. Bed, Breakfast and Evening Meal or Bed and Breakfast. Open all year. Winter Bargain Breaks. Further details on request.

BURY ST. EDMUNDS. Mrs M. J. Slater, Buttons Green Farm, Cockfield, Bury St. Edmunds IP30 0JF (Cockfield Green [0284] 828229). Working farm. Buttons Green Farm is a 15th century farmhouse situated in quiet surroundings. It is three and a half miles from Lavenham and historic Bury St. Edmunds is eight miles away. Easily accessible to Constable country, Cambridge and Norfolk's Brecklands and forests; unspoilt Aldeburgh and Southwold just over one hour's drive away. The house is comfortable with modern amenities but retains its old world charm. Two twin-bedded rooms (one with washbasin), one single bedroom; bathroom, toilet; lounge and fully timbered diningroom with inglenook. Children welcome — cot and babysitting available. A warm welcome is assured from April to October and good and varied food is served. This is a Grade II listed building. Car essential — ample parking space. Bed and Breakfast, Evening Dinner or Bed and Breakfast is offered. Reduced rates for children under 12 years. SAE, please, for further details.

Terms quoted in this publication may be subject to increase if rises in costs necessitate

Suffolk BOARD

BURY ST. EDMUNDS. Mrs N. B. Less, Broad Acre, 10 Parklands Green, Fornham St. Genevieve, Bury St. Edmunds IP28 6UH (Bury St. Edmunds [0284] 69340). A large attractive house in a quiet location offering excellent accommodation and cooking, and set in delightful partly wooded grounds of one-and-a-half acres. The village of Fornham St. Genevieve is two miles north of the historic market town of Bury St. Edmunds. Cambridge, Newmarket, Thetford and medieval wool towns such as Lavenham are within easy reach. The house has three double bedrooms, one twin-bedded and a single bedroom, all with hot and cold water. Shower-room, bathroom and diningroom/lounge with TV are for guests' exclusive use. Children are welcome from three years old and there is a reduced rate up to age 10. Sorry, no pets. Open year-round for Bed and Breakfast; Evening Meals available. Write or 'phone for bookings or full details.

COLCHESTER. Mrs C. A. Somerville, Rosebank, Lower Street, Stratford St. Mary, Colchester, Essex CO7 6JS (Colchester [0206] 322259). Attractive 14th-century part Manor House, with river frontage and fishing rights in peaceful village in the Dedham Vale, which is renowned for its period architecture and old inns. Our boathouse is reputed to have featured in Constable's paintings. Guests are accommodated in three double, and one family bedrooms, all with washbasins; two bathrooms and three toilets. Diningroom. Central heating. Rooms are comfortable and attractive with television plus tea and coffee making facilities. Family bedroom has toilet en-suite. Delightful chalet set in the grounds, twin-bedded with bathroom en-suite. English Breakfast of your choice — good cooking. Terms £10.50 to £12 for Bed and Breakfast. Open all year except Christmas week.

EYE. Mrs G. E. Jones, Barley Green, Laxfield Road, Stradbrooke, Eye IP21 5JT (Stradbroke [037-984] 281). Barley Green is a Tudor Farmhouse in eight acres, surrounded by a garden and ponds. A haven for wildlife, haunt of the Kingfisher. It is conveniently situated for visiting historic places, Norwich, Bury St. Edmunds, Ely and Ipswich, also Blooms nursery and steam museum. Within travelling distance of coast, Minsmere Bird Reserve, Aldeburgh Music Festival and small nature reserves. Barley Green offers a tranquil setting for stop-over night breaks or longer stays to enjoy the Suffolk countryside. Available double bedroom, en-suite bathroom, twin-bedded room and single room. Hall, diningroom and sittingroom. Full English Breakfast and Dinner available. Brochure for terms. Non-smokers preferred.

FELIXSTOWE. Mrs N. Matthews, Redhouse, Levington, Ipswich IP10 0LZ (047-388-670). Victorian farmhouse in heart of countryside with views over the Orwell Estuary in AONB. Ideal for walkers, riders, artists, sailors or anyone wanting a quiet place 'away from it all', yet only six minutes from Felixstowe. Many walks and bridleways — riding holidays arranged. Visit 'Constable' country or explore the unspoilt coastline. The Continent is closer than you think. You can have a great day out to Belgium for as little as £7 adult return, half for children. No passport needed if you are British. Bed and Breakfast from £9. Evening Meal £5 by arrangement. Home cooking, fresh produce and eggs. Reductions for children. No pets.

FRAMLINGHAM. Mrs S. M. Webster, Elm Lodge Farm, Fressingfield, Eye IP21 5SL (Fressingfield [037-986] 249). Working farm. Elm Lodge is a spacious Victorian farmhouse with 112 acres, mainly arable, overlooking a large common where animals graze in summer. Within easy reach of coast — Southwold 18 miles, and many places of interest including historic castles, churches, stately homes and towns such as Framlingham. Equidistant Norwich, Bury St. Edmunds and Ipswich — 30 miles approximately. Open Easter to October. One double bedroom (with washbasin), one single and one family bedrooms; bathroom, toilet; diningroom; sittingroom with convector heater or open fire, colour TV. Reductions for children. Cot, high chair, babysitting. Sorry, no pets. Car essential — parking. Telephone or SAE for terms, please, for Evening Meal, Bed and Breakfast or Bed and Breakfast only.

FRAMLINGHAM. Mrs S. T. Stocker, Woodbridge Road, Broadwater, Framlingham (Framlingham [0728] 723645). This is a lovely Georgian house set in beautiful surroundings with gardens, woodland, four-acre vineyard and flower farm. The little town of Framlingham is one mile away with its interesting castle and church and the coast, bird sanctuary at Minsmere and Snape Festival Hall are within easy reach. There is a small flock of Jacob sheep. Accommodation comprises twin-bedded room with en-suite bathroom, two double rooms with wash handbasins, two single rooms. Diningroom and drawing room with TV. Central heating and log fire. Open all year. Dinner (optional) and Breakfast. Fully licensed; Broadwater wine usually for sale. Weekly terms. No VAT. SAE, please, for terms.

FRAMLINGHAM. Brian and Phyllis Collett, Shimmens Pightle, Pennington Road, Framlingham, Woodbridge IP13 9JT (Framlingham [0728] 724036). Shimmens Pightle is situated in an acre of landscaped garden, containing a growing vegetable enterprise, surrounded by farmland, within a mile of the centre of Framlingham with its famous castle and church. Ideally situated for the Heritage Coast, Snape Maltings, Easton Farm Park, local vineyards, etc. Central for Constable country, Norfolk Broads, Ipswich, Norwich and Bury St. Edmunds. Many good local eating places. Double and twin-bedded rooms on ground floor, with bathroom between, and extra WC; use of lounge. Central heating and log fires. Morning tea and evening drinks offered. No pets indoors. Tourist Board registered. Terms from £9 for Bed and traditional Breakfast.

FRAMLINGHAM. Mrs Ann Proctor, Grove Farm, Laxfield, Framlingham, Woodbridge IP13 8EY (Ubbeston [098683] 235). Working farm. This is a Georgian farmhouse standing in a 30-acre mixed farm with pigs and sheep, ponies and pedigree breeding dogs. Beautiful view of village and only 12 miles from the coast. Within easy reach of Norwich, Norfolk Broads, historic houses with quaint unspoilt villages. The accommodation is in two double and two family bedrooms (with washbasins); diningroom; lounge with colour television; bathroom, three toilets; full central heating. Children welcome, cot, high chair and babysitting. Sorry, no pets. Open March to November. The emphasis is on a friendly atmosphere with good home cooking, meat, vegetables, honey, etc., mainly produced on farm. Car essential, ample parking. Bed and Breakfast or Bed, Breakfast and Evening Meal; children under 12 years reduced rates. Please phone or send SAE for terms.

FRAMLINGHAM near. Mrs J. R. Graham, Woodlands Farm, Brundish, Near Woodbridge IP13 8BP (Stradbroke [037-984] 444). Woodlands Farm has a cottage-type farmhouse set in quiet Suffolk countryside. Near historic town of Framlingham, with its castle, and within easy reach of coast, wildlife parks, Otter Trust, Easton Farm Park and Snape Maltings for music lovers. Ideally suited for family holidays. Open all year. Family room with private shower, washbasin and WC. One double bedroom with bathroom en suite. One single bedroom sharing bathroom and WC. Diningroom and sittingroom, with inglenook fireplaces for guests. Good home cooked food assured. Full central heating. Car essential, good parking. Cot and babysitting. Sorry, no pets. SAE, or telephone, for terms for Bed and Breakfast or Evening Meal, Bed and Breakfast. Reduced rates for children under 10.

HALESWORTH. Mrs Elizabeth George, Fen Way, School Lane, Halesworth IP19 8BW (Halesworth [098-67] 3574). A spacious bungalow in its own seven acres of meadow situated in a completely rural position on the outskirts of the busy little country town of Halesworth. All meals are served in a delightful sun lounge overlooking unspoilt farmland. Farming is not carried on commercially, but the George family are the proud owners of pets including sheep and lambs. Convenient for the beach (nine miles); Broadland, churches and castles; steam museums, trust houses and gardens; something to interest everybody in this area. Two double bedrooms, one twin bedded room, all with washbasins; shower room, two toilets; lounge, diningroom. Central heating. Facilities for making hot drinks available. Children over eight years welcome. Regret no pets. Open all year. Parking. Bed, Breakfast and Evening Meal or Bed and Breakfast. Telephone or SAE for terms.

HALESWORTH. Mrs Eileen Webb, "Saskiavill", Chediston, Halesworth IP19 0AR (Halesworth [098-67] 3067). "Saskiavill" is set back from the road and stands in one and a half acres of garden. The spacious bungalow offers holidaymakers an ideal touring base for the fine City of Norwich, the coast and nearby Minsmere Bird Sanctuary. The village has many thatched cottages and an old church and is only two miles from the market town of Halesworth. Convenient for golf courses, nature reserves, museums, trust houses, gardens, etc. Three double, one family bedrooms, with washbasins; two bathrooms, two toilets; sittingroom, diningroom. Children welcome at reduced rates, babysitting available. Sorry, no pets. Car essential — parking. Open all year for Evening Dinner/Meal, Bed and Breakfast or Bed and Breakfast. Varied menus with good home cooking including home made pastries, bread and preserves. Telephone or SAE for terms. Reductions for Senior Citizens out of season.

HARLESTON. Mrs Anne Wilson, Oak Hill Farm, Metfield, Harleston, Norfolk IP20 0JX (Fressingfield [037-986] 321). Working farm. A period farmhouse with exposed beams, very quiet and peaceful, situated about quarter of a mile off the road and reached by private drive. Comfortable accommodation in one double, three family bedrooms with washbasins; bathroom, three toilets; sittingroom, diningroom. Children are welcome at reduced rates, and cot and babysitting offered. Comfortably heated with open fires. Pets permitted, but to sleep in cars. Open all year round except Christmas. Within easy reach of the Broads and many stately homes to visit. Norwich 22 miles, the East Coast 15 miles. The accent is on home produced food and good cooking, farm butter and cream. Riding and canoeing in the area, five minutes' walk from village. Fire Certificate held. Plenty of freshwater fishing nearby. Evening Dinner/Meal, Bed and Breakfast or Bed and Breakfast. SAE, please, for terms.

PLEASE SEND A STAMPED ADDRESSED ENVELOPE WITH ENQUIRIES

HITCHAM. Mrs Mollie Loftus, Little Causeway Farmhouse, Hitcham IP7 7NE (Bildeston [0449] 740521). This 16th century Tudor farmhouse situated in the heart of the beautiful Suffolk countryside, near to Lavenham, Constable country and many other places of interest. Guests are welcome all the year round to enjoy the comforts at this most attractive farmhouse, the accommodation being two double bedrooms (one twin); lounge, diningroom; bathroom. Central heating. Car is essential and there is ample parking. Regret, no pets allowed. This is a lovely part of Suffolk and worth seeing. Bed and Breakfast with Tea and Coffee-making facilities in bedrooms. Reduced rates for weekly bookings.

IPSWICH. Mrs J. Van Slooten, Woolney Hall, Creeting St. Mary, Ipswich IP6 8QB (Stowmarket [0449] 711201). Working farm. Delightful, modernised 17th-century farmhouse in 20 acres, rich in wildlife including foxes and pheasants, and a nightingale an annual visitor. The secluded house, set back from a little-used lane, but only three miles from main trunk routes, is heavily beamed, the inglenook fireplaces having wood stoves for chilly evenings. Guest rooms have washbasins and views of tranquil rolling countryside. The good farmhouse meals offered use home-produced Jersey milk, cream, eggs, meat, vegetables and fruit. Usually only one or two parties are welcomed at a time to ensure the best comfort and hospitality. Centrally positioned for exploring East Anglia. Open Easter to November. Brochure and terms on application.

IPSWICH. Mrs Brenda Elsden, Wetherden Hall, Hitcham, Ipswich IP7 7PZ (Bildeston [0449] 740412). Working farm. Wetherden Hall is a working farm of 250 acres mostly arable, but also pigs, cattle, chickens and geese. In a quiet position on the edge of a picturesque village; close to Lavenham, Bury St. Edmunds, Ipswich, Cambridge and in Constable country. Good touring centre. Car essential. Ample parking. Large attractive bedrooms; one double, one single and one family room. Bathroom; toilet. Large sitting/diningroom. Children over 12 years welcome. Sorry, no pets. Bed and full traditional Breakfast. Choice of several local inns and restaurants for varied evening meals. SAE please for terms. AA listed.

MONK SOHAM. Mrs Sue Bagnall, Abbey House, Monk Soham IP13 7EN (Earl Soham [072-882] 225). Working farm, join in. A Victorian Rectory in 10 acres of quiet Suffolk countryside surrounded by secluded gardens with ponds and a swimming pool. The remainder of the grounds are shared with a couple of Jersey cows, some sheep, friendly pigs and poultry. There are three centrally heated double bedrooms with private bathrooms. Guests have exclusive use of the diningroom and the drawing room with television and a log fire. We provide good home cooking using our own dairy produce, meat, honey and vegetables. Reduced rates for children. Open all year. Ideal base for touring East Anglia.

The information in the entries in this guide is presented by the publishers in good faith and after the signed acceptance by advertisers that they will uphold the high standards associated with FARM HOLIDAY GUIDES LIMITED. The publishers do not accept responsibility for any inaccuracies or omissions or any results thereof. Before making final holiday arrangements readers should confirm the prices and facilities directly with advertisers.

NEEDHAM MARKET. Mrs R. Hackett-Jones, Pipps Ford, Norwich Road, Needham Market IP6 8LJ (Coddenham [044-979] 208). Pipps Ford is a 16th century Tudor farmhouse on most beautiful stretch of Gipping River, a Conservation Zone of outstanding natural beauty. (Reputed to have been manor house of Richard Hakluyt, famous 16th century traveller and writer. Also the home of Sir William Harvey's wife.) Completely secluded, yet handy to key roads and near to a Roman camp site; ideal for touring coast, Constable country, Lavenham, Aldeburgh, etc. Bird-watching, fishing, golf, swimming, tennis, near. Comfortable old house with modern amenities, central heating throughout, log fires in winter. Sittingroom, diningroom, breakfast and meals in the conservatory. Good interesting home cooking, vegetables fresh home grown, home made bread, honey, eggs, milk, bacon, pork — home produced. Full English Breakfasts. Two doubles with private bath and WC each. Super family suite with antique four-poster bed and separate adjacent bedrooms for children. SAE, please, or telephone.

NEWMARKET. Mrs R. J. Cole, The Old Rectory, Ashley, Newmarket CD8 9DU (Newmarket [0638] 730751). This house is situated in a peaceful village well placed for Cambridge, Ely, Bury St. Edmunds and Newmarket. This attractive early Victorian flint built house, set in walled gardens, offers one double room and one twin bedded room, both well furnished to a high standard and one newly fitted bathroom. Children are welcome, cot, high chair and babysitting are available. Dinner is available by arrangement, and there are good facilities locally. Terms on application. Telephone or SAE, please. Open all year, except Christmas.

SAXMUNDHAM. Mrs Margaret Gray, Park Farm, Sibton, Saxmundham IP17 2LZ (Yoxford [072-877] 324). **Working farm.** Accommodation in a friendly farmhouse in gentle Suffolk countryside six miles from our "bird watcher's paradise" coast and 25 miles from Ipswich and Norwich. Mrs Gray enjoys looking after guests who are treated as members of the family. Individual tastes catered for and mostly local and garden produce is used in cooking. One double, one twin bedrooms, both with hot and cold water; bathroom, toilet; diningroom. Cot, high chair, babysitting and reduced rates for children. Sorry, no pets. Open from March to November. Mid-week bookings accepted. Car essential — parking. Evening Dinner/Meal, Bed and Breakfast from £13.50; Bed and Breakfast from £7.50. Mrs Gray aims to give guests an enjoyable holiday so that they go home feeling refreshed and relaxed.

STOWMARKET. Mrs Diana Ridsdale, Cherry Tree Farm, Mendlesham Green, Stowmarket IP14 5RQ (Mendlesham [044 94] 376). Situated in the peaceful mid-Suffolk village of Mendlesham Green, Cheery Tree Farm offers an ideal centre for exploring the Suffolk countryside. Hearty English Breakfasts and Evening Meals are served in our oak-beamed diningroom. We bake our own bread, produce our own preserves and honey and provide home-grown fruit and fresh vegetables. The comfortable bedrooms, one double and one family, have full central heating and each is fitted with a vanity basin and shaver point. There is also a guest bathroom with shower, bath and WC. A spacious oak-beamed lounge with inglenook fireplace is available for the comfort of our guests. Car is essential and there is parking for three cars. Children over three are welcome. Regret, no pets. Open all year, with mid-week bookings available.

STRADBROKE. Mr and Mrs G. Bailey, Meadow Farm, Rookery Lane, Battlesea Green, Stradbroke IP21 5NE (Stradbroke [037 984] 287). Veronica and George Bailey welcome you to VEGETARIAN WHOLEFOOD in their 16th century half-moated farmhouse in five acres, with donkeys, Shetland ponies, hens, geese, ducks and peacocks plus a vintage car. Accommodation comprises three bedrooms, one with double bed, one single and one with two singles. A separate bathroom and shower room both with handbasin and toilets; a sitting room and dining room both with wood/coal-burning stoves. Additional accommodation is in a 70-year-old Living Van providing one double and one single bed with electric light and heat. The Suffolk Heritage Coast is within a half-hour drive as are Bird and Otter Sanctuaries, castles, museums, gardens, Snape Maltings and walks.

PLEASE SEND A STAMPED ADDRESSED ENVELOPE WITH ENQUIRIES

WESTLETON. Mrs Mary E. Macgilp, Argyll House, Westleton, Near Saxmundham IP17 3AE (Westleton [072-873] 210). Argyll House is quietly situated in the village of Westleton, surrounded by beautiful countryside. The sea is two miles away, with good bathing. Darsham Railway two-and-a-half miles, with an abundance of small old villages in the area to interest visitors. Minsmere Bird Reserve, two miles. Open all year round, the guest house has two double and two single rooms with washbasins; two bathrooms and two toilets; sitting and diningrooms. Mrs Macgilp offers good food, personally cooked and served. Evening Meal, Bed and Breakfast. SAE, please for terms.

WOODBRIDGE near. Mr and Mrs W. F. Ardley, Queen's Cottage, Hacheston, Near Woodbridge IP13 0DS (Wickham Market [0728] 746273). All guests receive a warm welcome at this 16th century timbered, thatched house with inglenook fireplace. Situated in a delightful part of Suffolk, adjoining an area of outstanding natural beauty, it is within easy reach by car of the unspoilt coastline and also the interesting and historic towns of Framlingham, Woodbridge, Aldeburgh. Ideal centre for touring, walking, golf, birdwatching, fishing, sailing and visiting famous gardens and stately homes. Two double rooms and one single, all with washbasins, shaver points, tea making facilities. Two bathrooms, two toilets, diningroom, lounge with colour TV, parking, garden. Children over 12 welcome. We regret, no pets. Open May to September. Bed and Breakfast. Evening Dinner by arrangement. Send SAE for brochure and terms.

SURREY

HORLEY near. Mr and Mrs G. H. Tucker, Chithurst Farm, Chithurst Lane, Horne, Smallfield, Near Horley RH6 9JU (Smallfield [034284] 2487). Working farm. Chithurst Farm is situated amidst the Surrey countryside approximately one and a half miles from main road and villages of Horne and Smallfield. Conveniently near Surrey/Kent/Sussex border. Attractive town of East Grinstead with its old High Street, shops and houses is four miles away, as is Crawley with its modern shopping precint and weekly market. London only 35 minutes by train. Less than half hour drive is Reigate, Dorking and the North Downs. Ashdown Forest to the south and Kent to the east. Coast one hour's drive. Chithurst Farmhouse, an attractive 16th century house with beamed rooms and sloping floors, offers Bed and Breakfast accommodation in one single room, one double room, one twin bedded room with additional bed if required. Cot on request and babysitting. Farm is a working dairy farm. Visitors welcome to look around. Numerous good eating places in vicinity. Directions sent on booking. Bed and Breakfast from £9.

LINGFIELD. Mrs Vivienne Bundy, Oaklands, Felcourt, Lingfield RH7 6NF (Lingfield [0342] 834705). Oaklands is a spacious country house of considerable charm dating from the 17th century. It is set in its own grounds of one acre and is about one mile from the small town of Lingfield and three miles from East Grinstead, both with rail connections to London. It is convenient to Gatwick Airport and is ideal as a "stop-over" or as a base to visit many places of interest in south east England. Dover and the Channel Ports are two hours' drive away whilst the major towns of London and Brighton are about one hour distant. One family, two double and one single bedrooms, one with washbasin; three bathrooms, two toilets; sittingroom; diningroom. Cot, high chair, babysitting and reduced rates for children. Gas central heating. Open all year. Parking. Bed and Breakfast from £9. Evening Meal by arrangement.

SOUTH GODSTONE. Mr and Mrs D. I. Nunn, The New Bungalow, Old Hall Farm, Tandridge Lane, Oxted RH8 9NS (South Godstone [0342] 892508). Enjoy a relaxing family holiday and a warm welcome in a spacious modern bungalow set in the heart of a small family farm. One double/family room and one twin bedroom; use of TV lounge and diningroom. Bath/shower can be taken at any time. All rooms are centrally heated and fully carpeted. Good facilities for young children. Ideally located for day trips to London and the south coast. Bed and Breakfast with optional Evening Meal from £60 per week. Open April to October.

SURREY – LOVELY COUNTRYSIDE, CLOSE TO LONDON!
If you are staying in Surrey and only using it as a base for London you will be missing out. Try to find time to visit the Alice Holt Forrest, Leith Hill – the highest point in South-East England, Witley Common and the Downs at Epsom.

SUSSEX

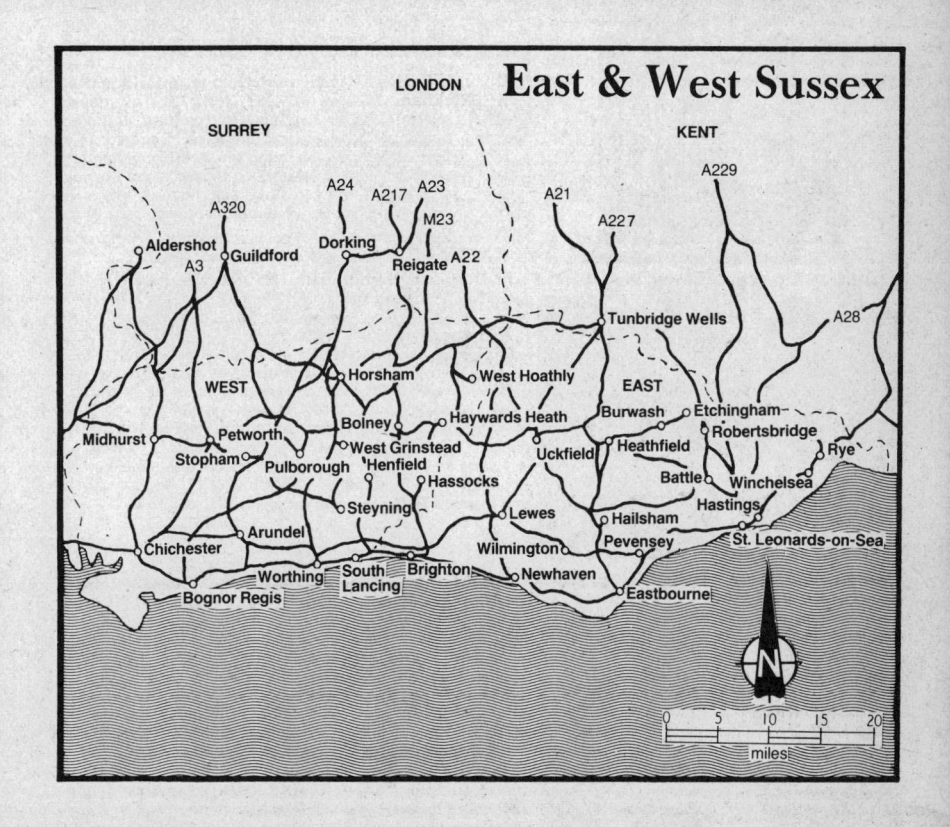

EAST SUSSEX

BATTLE. Mr and Mrs Adam Rolland, Burnt Wood, Powdermill Lane, Battle TN33 0SU (Battle [042-46] 2459). A country house in 18-acres with its own swimming pool, tennis court, small farm, large garden and vegetable garden. Two double rooms have en suite bathrooms. Two double and one single share well-equipped shower-room. One double has own basin and WC. Situated conveniently for walks, fishing, golfing, sightseeing; castles, towns, houses and famous gardens. London is one-and-a-half hours away by rail or road. Car almost essential; ample parking. Colour TV in drawingroom or there is a large sun room. Excellent food, mainly home produced. Bed and Breakfast from £8. Evening Meal available. English lessons for overseas visitors easily arranged. Telephone for terms.

BUXTED. Mrs Mary F. Charman, Heatherwode Farm, Pound Green, Buxted TN22 4JN (Buxted [082-581] 2131). Spacious and comfortable Victorian farm guest house on Kent/Sussex border, within easy reach of the South East coast, plus fast trains to London from Haywards Heath. Beautifully situated for many places of historic interest including National Trust properties, Bentley Wildlife, Glyndebourne, Chartwell, Hever Castle, Penshurst Place, Bluebell and Tenterden steam railway. Surrounded by many villages of character and unspoilt countryside. We offer informal and relaxing holidays, full English Breakfast, coffee and tea making facilities. One double with hot and cold, one family room. Bathroom, shower, toilet. Sittingroom; diningroom. Children welcome. Car essential — parking. Bed and Breakfast £8. Open January to November.

EASTBOURNE. Mr and Mrs K. & G. Smith, Ranworth Private Hotel, 86-88 Pevensey Road, Eastbourne BN22 8AE (Eastbourne [0323] 33520 (Reservations) 23196 (Guests). Ranworth is situated close to lovely "carpet" gardens, beach and pier — three minutes sea front and coach station — central to all amusements. Accommodation for 30 guests in double, twin, single and family bedrooms, all have shaver points, hot and cold, radio, room call service and baby-listening service. No basement rooms. Children welcome, cot and babysitting available. Small dogs accepted free of charge. Own keys and access at all times. Unrestricted street parking although car is not essential. Colour TV. Licensed bar. Fire Certificate. Reduced rates for children, 10% reduction for senior citizens early and late season. Bed and Breakfast, or Bed, Breakfast and four-course Dinner. Open March to October; attractive terms (reduced off season). Special Christmas programme. Mid-week bookings accepted. SAE, please, or phone Resident Proprietors **Ken and Gina Smith.**

ETCHINGHAM. Mrs E. Sirrell, Woodlands Farm, Burwash, Etchingham TN19 7LA (Burwash [0435] 882794). Working farm. Woodlands Farm stands one third of a mile off the road surrounded by fields and woods. This peaceful and beautifully modernised 16th century farmhouse offers comfortable and friendly accommodation in double or twin bedded rooms (one has four poster bed) together with excellent farm fresh food. This is a farm of 55 acres with mixed animals, and is situated within easy reach of 20 or more places of interest to visit and half an hour from the coast. Open all year with central heating. Children are welcome and dogs and cats permitted. Car essential, parking. Evening Meal, Bed and Breakfast from £12; Bed and Breakfast from £9. Rates reduced for children.

HAILSHAM near. Mr and Mrs R. E. Gentry, The Stud Farm, Bodle Street Green, Near Hailsham BN27 4RJ (Herstmonceux [0323] 833201). Working farm. The Stud Farm keeps mainly cattle. It is peacefully situated between A271 and B2096 amidst beautiful undulating countryside. Ideal for walking and touring lovely East Sussex, being within easy reach of Eastbourne (12 miles), Bexhill (10 miles) and Hastings (15 miles). There are many places of historical interest in the vicinity and the coast is only eight miles away at Pevensey. Guests do not have to share bathrooms. Upstairs there is a family unit (only let to one set of guests — either two, three or four persons — at a time), consisting of one twin-bedded room and one double-bedded room with handbasin and shaver point and their own bathroom with toilet. There is also downstairs one twin-bedded room with shower, handbasin and toilet en suite. (No nylon sheets used). Guests have their own sittingroom with TV and diningroom and sunroom. Children over 10 years welcome. Sorry, no pets. Open all year. Central heating in winter. Car essential — parking available. Bed and Breakfast from £8.70. Evening Meal from £5. SAE, please.

HAILSHAM. Mrs Leigh Wadey, Champneys Farm, Wartling on the Hill, Hailsham BN27 1RU (Herstmonceux [0323] 832208). Working farm. Built around 1680, Champneys is a listed building nestling in one of the prettiest parts of East Sussex. It is heavily beamed and has two guest bedrooms, each with twin beds and own bathroom. Large lounge and diningroom with inglenook fireplace. Here the hedgerows are full of wild roses and honeysuckle. Nearby attractions include Herstmonceux Castle and the Royal Greenwich Observatory. We have a mixed farm of 60 acres and produce our own organically grown vegetables. Children over 12 welcome. Open from April to October. Car essential. Evening Meal, Bed and Breakfast. Prices on application.

PLEASE SEND A STAMPED ADDRESSED ENVELOPE WITH ENQUIRIES

BOARD East Sussex 297

HAILSHAM. Mr and Mrs E. V. Penrose, "Rucklands," 225 London Road, Hailsham BN27 3AP (Hailsham [0323] 842328). Standing in an acre of mature garden on the B2104, one mile north of the market town of Hailsham and eight miles from the sea, this guest house is within easy reach of numerous places of historic interest and nearby seaside towns, including Eastbourne, Pevensey, Bexhill, Lewes, etc. Lounge, diningroom with separate tables, where fresh garden produce features on the menu; two double, two single and two family bedrooms, most with washbasins; bathroom and two toilets. Open all year. Evening Meal, Bed and Breakfast from £9 or Bed and Breakfast from £6. Reduced rates for children. Car not essential but there is ample parking. SAE, please, for moderate terms. No VAT or service charge.

HASTINGS. Mrs B. M. Beck, Lower Lidham Hill Farm, Guestling, Near Hastings TN35 4LX (Hastings [0424] 814225). Working farm. Lovely, fully beamed 18th century farmhouse situated on 100-acre farm, just off the A259 Hastings – Rye road, turn off at Harborough Nursery. Ideal for touring with Battle seven miles; Hastings five miles and Rye six miles; sea just five miles away. Two family rooms sleep seven. Bathroom/toilet; sitting/diningroom. Children welcome — cot, high chair and babysitting provided. Well behaved pets accepted. Open all year for Bed and Breakfast. Car essential — parking. SAE for terms please.

HEATHFIELD. Mrs Edna Lines, Mount Pleasant Farm, Chapel Cross, Heathfield TN21 9DB (Rushlake Green [0435] 830472). Working farm. Mount Pleasant Farm is situated well away from the road with ample parking, surrounded by its own working farmland and animals. Superb views across the South Downs and to the sea. Market town of Heathfield two miles; Eastbourne 15 and Brighton approximately 22 miles. Spacious farmhouse, fully carpeted, central heating and comfortable lounge with colour TV. Diningroom with separate tables overlooking secluded garden and lawn. Double and twin-bedded rooms with showers and washbasins, two single-bedded rooms, tea-making facilities in all bedrooms. Cot, high chair available on request. Babysitting. Bathroom with shower, washbasin; two toilets. No objection to pets. Car essential — parking. Many local places of interest and gardens and historical houses to visit. Most sports facilities available locally; sea fishing at Newhaven. Open April to October for Evening Dinner, Bed and Breakfast from £68 per week; Bed and Breakfast from £9 per person, £55 per week. Reductions for children under 12 sharing parents' room. ETB.

HEATHFIELD. Mrs R. Field, Rose Bank Farm, Horam, Heathfield TN21 0JR (Chiddingly [0825] 872683). Working farm. Rose Bank is a family-run, 100 acre dairy farm situated in a quiet country lane about 12 miles from Eastbourne and the sea. The house is well modernised with central heating and log fires in cold weather. Plenty of home cooked food. Two double bedrooms; bathroom, two toilets; sittingroom/diningroom. Children welcome, cot and high chair. Sorry, no pets permitted. Open all year round for Evening Meal, Bed and Breakfast or Bed and Breakfast only. Terms on request. Car essential — parking.

MIDHURST. Mr and Mrs G. A. Hart, Lower Cranmore Farm, Peace Lane, Heyshott, Midhurst GU29 0DF (Midhurst [073-081] 3193). Working farm. Modern farmhouse in 60 acres (grass, livestock) set in beautiful part of the country. Fishbourne, Bognor are famous for Roman remains; polo at Cowdray Park, walks may be enjoyed on the South Downs Way. Chichester, Guildford can be reached in less than an hour; sea 20 miles. Gardeners will be interested in Royal Horticultural Society gardens at Wisley. Open all year, the house has central heating and open log fire, offers one family and one double bedrooms; bathroom, two toilets; sitting and diningrooms. Cot, high chair, babysitting available, reduced rates for children. Sorry, no pets. Car essential — parking. Home produced cooked food is served. Terms for Evening Meal, Bed and Breakfast or Bed and Breakfast will be sent on application. SAE, please.

PULBOROUGH. Mrs D. C. Lerwill, Frithwood Farm, Lee Place, Codmore Hill, Pulborough RH20 1DF (Wisborough Green [0403] 700394). Working farm. This 16th century beamed Sussex Farmhouse situated "away from it all", two miles from A29 with lovely scenery and good walks. The old Arun canal and river nearby. Goodwood Racecourses, Singleton Open Air Museum, Petworth House and Arundel Castle are but a few of the interesting places to visit. Home produce from the 32-acre mixed farm used whenever possible providing excellent fresh food; full English breakfasts. Warm welcome extended to all guests. Two double, two single rooms; bathroom and toilet; dining/sittingroom. Children welcome, babysitting by arrangement. Sorry, no pets. Car essential, parking. Open Easter to October. Bed and Breakfast. Reductions for children. SAE, please, for terms.

ROBERTSBRIDGE. Mrs M. Hoad, Parsonage Farm, Salehurst, Robertsbridge TN32 5PJ (Robertsbridge [0580] 880446). Working farm. A warm welcome awaits anyone visiting this 15th century farmhouse which has oak beams and panelling and lies in a quiet unspoiled hamlet half-a-mile from the main A21. It is within easy reach of many of the popular South Coast resorts and, inland, many places of historical interest and natural beauty. Plenty of country walks and there is fishing. A genuine working farm with sheep, calves and beef cattle. Chickens roam the farmyard. Good plain cooking of mostly home produced food. Colour TV, Electric blankets in winter. Bedtime drinks available if required. There are one single, one double and one family rooms; bathroom, toilet; sittingroom, diningroom. Children over seven welcome at reduced rates. Sorry, no pets. Open from November to August (except Christmas week). A car is an advantage here and there is ample parking. Evening Meal, Bed and Breakfast or Bed and Breakfast only. SAE, please, for terms.

East Sussex / West Sussex   BOARD

RYE. Pat and Jeff Sullivin, Cliff Farm, Iden Lock, Rye (Iden [079-78] 331 (long ring, please). Our farmhouse is peacefully set in a quiet elevated position with extensive views over Romney Marsh. Cliff Farm is a working smallholding with sheep, goats, chickens, ducks and pets. The ancient seaport town of Rye is two miles away with its narrow cobbled streets. We are ideal touring base, although the town and immediate district has much to offer — golden beaches, quaint villages, castles, gardens, etc. Comfortable guest bedrooms with washbasins, tea/coffee making facilities; two toilets; own shower/dining/sittingrooms. Home produce. Open March–October for Bed and Breakfast from £8. Reduced weekly rates. AA/RAC Listed.

WINCHELSEA. Denis and Irene Coxell, Snailham House, Broad Street, Icklesham, Winchelsea TN36 4AT (Hastings [0424] 814556). Snailham House has the best of both worlds, set in the heart of beautiful countryside and yet only about five miles from the ancient historic town of Rye and also the popular resort of Hastings. The area has much to offer — pretty villages, castles, historic houses, gardens, steam railways, caves and quaint pubs. An ideal base for touring or for an "away from it all" weekend. The five double, one single and one family bedrooms all have washbasins, razor points, tea making facilities and supplies as well as magnificent views. The main lounge has colour TV and the "quiet" lounge overlooks the terraced lawns. Children welcome, cot and high chair. Open from April to October inclusive. Regret no pets. Car desirable and there is parking. Residential Drinks Licence. Evening Meal, Bed and Breakfast from £88 to £95 per week (£14 daily); Bed and Breakfast from £9.50. Rates reduced for children. SAE, please, for brochure. "AA Guest House of the Year" (S.E. England 1981).

WINCHELSEA. Mrs Diana R. Longly, Snaylham Farm, Broad Street, Icklesham, Winchelsea TN36 4AT (Hastings [0424] 814296). Working farm. This charming modernised 17th century farmhouse features an inglenook fireplace, oak beams and a bread oven. It is set in approximately 200 acres of beautiful fruit and arable farmland with glorious views and walks. Situated half a mile from the A259 coast road, five miles from the picturesque town of Rye and historic Hastings. Brighton, Tunbridge Wells, Dover and Canterbury are all within easy reach. The accommodation consists of two double bedrooms and one twin bedded room, all with electric blankets, shower room and bathroom, both with shaver points. Bed and full English breakfast with free range eggs, homemade preserves, own honey. Open all year. SAE for terms.

WEST SUSSEX

BOGNOR REGIS. Mr and Mrs G. E. Soothill, Black Mill House Hotel, Princess Avenue, Bognor Regis PO21 2QU (Bognor Regis [0243] 821945). A well-appointed hotel with pleasantly large windows facing south; it is always comfortably warm out of season. The hotel is situated in the quieter west end of Bognor Regis, only 300 yards from the the sea and Marine Gardens. It has all the characteristics of a large private house surrounded by gardens and enclosed lawns. The hotel is centrally heated throughout. Radio, intercom and razor points in all 26 bedrooms; five bathrooms. plus 11 private bathrooms. There is an attractive Cocktail Bar (Restaurant and Residential Licence), large Games Room with darts, small snooker table, model railway 'O' gauge, two Lounges (separate colour TV). Full Board or Dinner, Bed and Breakfast; picnic lunches, afternoon teas available. Children special offers; babies under 2 years FREE, with two children — younger child FREE under 10 years. Washing and ironing facilities, cots, high chairs, supper trays provided. "Baby Listening Service." Open all year. Out of season Mini-Breaks, two days from £41.50 Full Board, also Spring and Summer Short Breaks. Dogs welcome. Colour brochure giving details of the hotel and inclusive terms, will be gladly sent on request. AA*/RAC*. Ashley Courtenay Recommended and Members of S.E. England Tourist Board. Own Car Park.

BOGNOR REGIS. Mrs B. M. Hashfield, Taplow Cottage, 81 Nyewood Lane, Bognor Regis PO21 2UE (Bognor Regis [0243] 821398). The Cottage lies in a residential part, west of the town centre, 600 yards from the sea and shops. Proximity to many beaches and contrasting towns and countryside make for an ideal touring centre. Chichester, Goodwood Racecourse, Arundel Castle, Brighton, Portsmouth and Southsea are but a few places of interest within easy reach. Accommodation comprises one double, one twin-bedded and one family bedroom, all with vanity units. Lounge, diningroom, central heated throughout. The cottage is well appointed and the area is served by public transport. Parking space available. Bed and Breakfast from £8.50. Dogs by prior arrangement. SAE, please.

HAYWARDS HEATH. Mrs R. B. Coghlan, Ludwell Grange, Station Road, Horsted Keynes, Haywards Heath RH17 7EG (Danehill [0825] 790524). Ludwell Grange is a listed ancient building dating from 1540 but modernised and comfortable. The ground floor rooms have the original oak panelling, beams and open fireplaces. There is a large mature garden, an orchard and kitchen garden providing home grown vegetables. Ideal area for country walks, visiting country houses and gardens. Bluebell Railway and the sea at Brighton 18 miles. Horsted Keynes, an old picturesque village, is four miles by bus from Haywards Heath. Excellent train service to London. Village shop is adequate, a post office and several pubs serving excellent meals. Open all year except Christmas fortnight. Three double, one single rooms, with washbasins; two sittingrooms, diningroom. Children over eight welcome, babysitting by arrangement. No pets. Parking for four cars. Bed and Breakfast from £11 per person nightly or from £70 weekly; Evening Meal from £6 per person.

HENFIELD. Mrs M. Wilkin, Great Wapses Farm, Henfield BN5 9BJ (Henfield [0273] 492544). The Tudor/Georgian Farmhouse is set in rural surroundings, ten miles north of Brighton, off the B2116 Albourne/Henfield road. Hickstead is nearby. There are horses, calves, chickens etc. The three comfortable rooms (one with four poster bed) all have their own bathroom, shower, TV and tea/coffee making facilities. The family suite has its own sitting room and refrigerator. Children and well behaved dogs are welcome. Open all year round for Bed and Breakfast. Snacks usually available by arrangement. There is also an attractive self-contained comfortable cottage sleeps two/three. Let on weekly basis £80 including electricity, TV etc.

HORSHAM. Mr J. F. V. Christian, Brookfield Farm Hotel, Winterpit Lane, Plummers Plain, Horsham RH13 6LY (Lower Beeding [040-376] 568). Working farm. Brookfield is a British Tourist Board registered modernised farmhouse with full central heating. It is situated adjoining a golf course in beautiful countryside, with its own lake for boating, fishing and swimming. A large lounge with a log fire and coloured television. Open throughout the year and offering Bed and Breakfast accommodation with Evening Meals available. Licensed bar. Golf driving range. There is ample car parking space. Persons travelling abroad may leave their cars safely with us. A courtesy car service to and from Gatwick Airport is maintained. Hire Cars available by arrangement as we are agents for "Granada" car hire, who operate a fleet of modern cars. Children welcome, cot, high chair, babysitting. Pets accepted. Evening Dinner/Meal, Bed and Breakfast from £16.68, Bed and Breakfast from £11.50 per day. Reductions for children.

HORSHAM near. Mrs S. E. Martin, Saxtons Farm, Nuthurst, Near Horsham RH13 6LG (Lower Beeding [040-376] 231). Working farm. This comfortable, modernised Georgian farmhouse is four miles south of Horsham and ideally situated for touring or exploring the surrounding countryside. Many places of interest to suit all tastes, including stately homes and gardens, show jumping at Hickstead, wildlife parks and the New Forest not too far away. The farm is run as a family unit and guests are assured of a warm welcome and good home cooking. Tea and coffee making facilities in bedrooms. Four double and one single bedrooms, all with washbasins; bathroom and shower, three toilets; sittingroom, two diningrooms. No pets, please. Car essential — parking. Open from January to December for Evening Meal, Bed and Breakfast or Bed and Breakfast. SAE, please.

West Sussex BOARD

HORSHAM. Mrs E. C. Sawyer, Swallows Farm, Dial Post, Horsham RH13 8NN (Partridge Green [0403] 710385). Working farm. Swallows Farm is a 200-acre mixed farm, including Shire horses, and is situated in mid-west Sussex; it has been farmed by the family for over 50 years. The farmhouse is Grade Two listed, and is situated half-a-mile from the busy A24 which goes from London to the coast, Gatwick Airport, and many places of historic interest such as Arundel Castle, Petworth House, the South Downs, and many well-known gardens are all within 20 miles. Open March-October. SAE for brochure, or phone please.

LANCING. Mr and Mrs L. W. Buckle, Beach House, 81 Brighton Road, Lancing BN15 8RB (Lancing [0903] 753368). Only one minute walk to the beach, this comfortable, friendly Guest House makes an ideal centre for touring the south east and visiting many places of interest. Open all year, the house has four rooms with views over beach, green and sea, two with views over Downs; all have washbasins, tea-making facilities. Full central heating. Lounge with colour TV, diningroom. Guests have own key to give access at all times. Situated on the coast road between Worthing and Brighton, five minutes' walk to local shops with fishing and boating available. Safe, sandy beaches. Children welcome at reduced rates. Car not essential, parking for six cars provided. Sorry, no pets. Bed and Breakfast. Mid-week bookings taken. SAE, please, for full details.

LIPHOOK near. Mrs Angela Jenner, Home Farm, Hollycombe, Near Liphook, Hampshire GU30 7LR (Liphook [0428] 722171). Working farm. Family run farm in tranquil surroundings with south-facing Sussex farmhouse set in attractive yards and buildings with garden overlooking beautiful Millard Valley. One and a half miles to Liphook (A3) with fast trains to London (50 miles) for day trips. Many places of interest within 25 miles. Arundel Castle, Goodwood Race Course, Portsmouth, also National Trust houses, footpaths and golf courses. One twin or family room, one double and two single, one bathroom, one shower room; some basins and razor points in bedrooms. Beamed sitting/diningroom. Children welcome, babysitting. Central heating. Car essential. Bed and Breakfast; some Evening Meals. Hot Snacks by arrangement.

MIDHURST. Mrs J. C. Francis, Mizzards Farm, Rogate, Petersfield, Hants GU31 5HS (Rogate [073-080] 656). Beautiful 17th-century farmhouse carefully modernised in peaceful setting by river, quarter mile from main road. Superb Guest Suite with marble bathroom. Breakfast in vaulted diningroom. Use of swimming pool. Lovely gardens and panoramic views. Excellent local pubs provide evening meals. Within easy reach of South Downs and coast, with riding, polo, golf, racing and sailing. Warm family atmosphere. Children welcome. Open all year with central heating. A car is essential and there is parking. Bed and Breakfast from £10 per person per night.

PETWORTH. Mrs Isobel Gray, Old Post House, Duncton, Petworth GU28 0JY (Petworth [0798] 42938). This is a period cottage set on north end of Duncton Village, on the South Downs, three miles from Petworth. Accommodation in two double bedrooms and one single room all with washbasins and tea making facilities (one room twin bedded); bathroom, toilet; diningroom. Central heating. Children over 10 years welcome (no reduction). Sorry, no pets. Places of interest in the area include Roman Baths and numerous country houses. There are lovely walks on the Downs and through the woods, and polo in Cowdray Park. Open March to October for Bed and Breakfast from £9.50. Evening Meal at 6.30 pm if advised before 5 pm. Price for Evening Meal, Bed and Breakfast from £14 to £16 per person.

PETWORTH near. Mrs Diana Caplin, Little Selham, Near Petworth GU28 0PS (Lodsworth [07985] 402). Little Selham is a wing of a large country house situated well away from main roads. It has a large secluded garden with swimming pool and is very close to the south downs in excellent walking country. Ideal centre for touring West Sussex with Chichester, Worthing, Brighton, Arundel, Portsmouth, Petworth and Midhurst within easy driving distance. Many historic places of interest in the area. Approximately 16 miles from the sea. Accommodation in three double bedrooms, two bathrooms, diningroom, drawing room. Central heating. Parking available for six cars. Open February 1st to October 31st. Premises suitable for disabled guests. Children over 10 years welcome. Bed and Breakfast from £9.50.

PETWORTH. Mrs Carol Bamber, East Lavington Farm, Graffham, Petworth (Graffham [07986] 276). This is a beautiful old farmhouse dating back to 17th century with delightful gardens and woodland. The land is not actually farmed but we have all sorts of chickens and ducks. The surrounding countryside is of outstanding beauty, excellent walking, and riding which can be arranged next door at a livery yard and riding school. The South Downs Way is only one mile away. Only three miles from Petworth with beautiful Petworth House and Park, eight miles from Chichester, with its cathedral and yacht basin, four miles from Goodwood, three miles from Midhurst with polo at Cowdray. There is also golf at Cowdray and Pulborough, swimming in Petworth and tennis in Graffham. Sea 10 miles. Arundel with castle six miles. Open all year. Children welcome, cot, high chair and babysitting. Bed and Breakfast. Warm welcome.

PETWORTH. Mr and Mrs N. Moss, River Park Farm, Lodsworth, Petworth GU28 9DS (Lodsworth [079-85] 362). Working farm. Guests are welcome to walk over River Park's 340-acres of farmland and adjoining woodland which has a good network of footpaths. Bullocks are kept for beef, and there is a flock of breeding ewes. The house which is completely secluded by farmland dates from 1600. Three bedrooms and a staircase are extensively beamed. Three double bedrooms have washbasins and shaver points and all beds have electric blankets. There is a breakfast room and lounge which guests are welcome to use. A four-and-a-half acre lake which attracts a great variety of wildlife is available for coarse fishing. Full English Breakfast, including home-baked bread, free range eggs and milk from our Guernsey house cow. Evening Meals available locally or Mrs Moss serves cooked meals most evenings. Open Easter to end of September. Central heating. Children welcome — babysitting. Bed and Breakfast from £7.50.

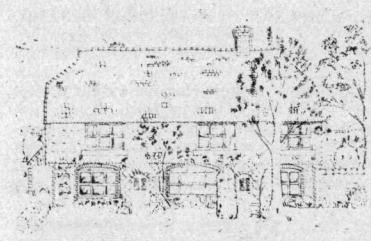

PETWORTH. Mrs E. Jenkins, Pikeshoot Cottage, Coultershaw, Petworth GU28 0JE (Petworth [0798] 42928). This is an old miller's stone cottage on the River Rother with a large garden run as a smallholding with goats, hens, dogs etc. It is one mile south of Petworth on the Chichester road (A285). Home grown produce is used whenever possible and a warm welcome is extended to all guests. Two double bedrooms and one family room, one with washbasin, and one bathroom, one toilet, a sitting room and a dining room. A car is essential and there is some parking space. Children welcome; cot, high chair and babysitting facilities available. Evening Dinner, Bed and Breakfast from £16.00; Bed and Breakfast from £10.00.

PULBOROUGH. Mrs A. M. Steele, New House Farm, West Chiltington, Near Pulborough RH20 2LA (West Chiltington [079 83] 2215). In the centre of West Chiltington village, this 15th century farmhouse, with its oak beams and inglenook fireplace, is within easy reach of many places of historic interest, including Parham House, Roman Villa, Fishbourne, Goodwood Cowdray Park; the West Sussex golf course is of interest to sports enthusiasts. The farmland covers 175 acres. Open January to November. AA listed. Car essential, ample parking. Two family bedrooms, one single room with washbasins, shaver points, tea/coffee making facilities and colour TV. Two bathrooms and toilets. Sitting/diningroom. Children over 10 welcome. Sorry, no pets. Sea 12 miles, Horsham nine, Brighton 20. Within easy reach of Gatwick Airport. Bed and Breakfast from £9.50 to £11. Evening Meals by arrangement. Reductions for children according to age and if sharing parents' room. Off season reduced price packages.

PULBOROUGH. Mrs L. C. Shiner, Coldharbour Farm, Sutton, Pulborough RH20 1PR (Sutton (Sussex) [079-87] 200). Working farm. Coldharbour Farm is a beef/arable farm of 160 acres situated in beautiful, quiet position on the north side of the South Downs. Built in the 16th century, its accommodation comprises three twin-bedded rooms (one with private bathroom), all with washbasins; guests' sittingroom with colour TV. All rooms are fully carpeted and centrally heated. Good English farmhouse cooking is provided. A drive of 20 minutes to Chichester, Arundel, Petworth, Goodwood; 12 miles to sea; two miles to Bignor Roman Villa, many beautiful walks including the South Downs Way. Children over 10 welcome. Pets permitted. Open April to October. Evening Dinner, Bed and Breakfast. Car essential, ample parking space. SAE, please, for terms and details.

WEST SUSSEX – COASTAL RESORTS AND DOWNS!

Although dominated perhaps by Bognor Regis, West Sussex does have much to offer. Places like Marden-Stoughton Forest, Midhurst, and its historic inn, the open-air museum at Singleton and the National Butterfly Museum at Bramber are worth a visit.

West Sussex / Warwickshire   BOARD

PULBOROUGH. Mrs Janice Langley, Rock Mill, Washington, Pulborough RH20 3DA (Ashington [0903] 892941). Genuine Sussex Smock Windmill with magnificent views from all rooms. Quietly situated with large grounds and swimming pool for guests' use, yet ideally placed for access to all parts of West Sussex. Close to South Downs for lovely walks. Mrs Langley is well known for her cooking, and guests are assured of a warm welcome. Children over 10 welcome. Pets by arrangement. Open all year except Christmas. Three double bedrooms with washbasins; bathroom, two toilets; sittingroom; diningroom. Car essential, parking. Evening Dinner, Bed and Breakfast from £20 per night; Bed and Breakfast from £12 per night. Reduced rates for children.

STEYNING. Mrs C. G. de Boer, Wappingthorn Farm, Steyning BN4 3AA (Steyning [0903] 813236). Wappingthorn Farm is two miles from beautiful old market town of Steyning. Footpaths in unspoiled woodland, seaside four miles, coastal towns of Worthing (seven miles); Brighton (12 miles); castles, country parks, historic monuments, all within easy reach. One twin bedded room with washbasin, also one twin bedded room and one family room with washbasin and shower, all rooms have fitted carpets, spring interior mattresses and TV. Showers, toilets. Central heating. Breakfast and Evening Meal served in diningroom which also has TV and several games. Family apartment — two rooms, plus private bathroom. Sittingroom. Tea/coffee can be made in each room. Nice garden and sun patio, large lawns, heated swimming pool, pond. Horse riding, fishing, shooting available. Free parking. Children welcome, cot, high chair and babysitting; also nice playground. Dogs accepted. Open February to November. Evening Dinner from £5.50; Bed and Breakfast from £7 per night; £48 weekly. Afternoon teas served.

STEYNING. Mr A. and Mrs P. J. R. Barnicott, Down House, King's Barn Villas, Steyning BN4 3FA (Steyning [0903] 812319). Tourist Board and AA listed. Well situated Edwardian guest house in large sunny gardens at end of private road. Panoramic views of South Downs. Less than 10 minutes' walk from historic Steyning. Many beautiful villages and stately homes in the area. One family room with bath; two double rooms and three single rooms all with washbasins and shaver points. Two bathrooms, TV lounge; large diningroom; garden furniture. Ample parking. Children over five welcome. Pets permitted. The house has gas central heating and is open all year round for Bed and Breakfast only. There are also two holiday flats for two/three or four people, attached to the guest house. Postage only or phone for full terms.

WARWICKSHIRE

COVENTRY near. Mr and Mrs Derek and Sandra Evans, Camp Farm, Hob Lane, Balsall Common, Near Coventry CV7 7GX (Berkswell [0676] 33804). Camp Farm is a farmhouse 150 to 200 years old. It is modernised but still retains its old world character. Nestling in the heart of England in Shakespeare country, within easy reach of Stratford-upon-Avon, Warwick, Kenilworth, Coventry, with its famous Cathedral, and the New National Exhibition Centre site. Camp Farm offers a warm, homely atmosphere and good English food, service and comfortable beds. The house is carpeted throughout. Diningroom and Sunlounge with colour TV. Bedrooms — five double, three family rooms and five single, all with hot and cold. Part of the house suitable for disabled guests. Children welcome. Cot and high chair. Babysitting on request. Fire Certificate granted 1974. All terms quoted by letter or telephone.

LEAMINGTON SPA. Mrs D. J. Cotterill, The Granary, Fenny Compton, Leamington Spa CV33 0XE (Fenny Compton [029-577] 214). Modern hillside country house converted from old farm buildings in quiet situation and overlooking open farmland. Attractive garden borders Oxford Canal. Ground floor accommodation comprises three double centrally heated rooms, each having shower rooms with full facilities en-suite. Tea trays. Also guests' lounge/diningroom. Bed and Breakfast only. Choice of good evening meals at local inns (nearest three minutes' walk). No facilities for children or pets. The hamlet of Fenny Compton Wharf is on the A423, or may be reached from the A41 via the villages of Northend and Fenny Compton. Ideal for touring Warwickshire, Oxfordshire, Northamptonshire and the Cotswolds.

LEAMINGTON SPA. Miss Deborah Lea, Crandon House, Avon Dassett, Leamington Spa CV33 0AA (Fenny Compton [029577] 652). Working farm. A specially warm welcome at this comfortable, well equipped farmhouse, set in 20 acres of beautiful countryside. Our small farm provides produce used in our excellent farmhouse fare. Three double rooms; sittingroom, diningroom; bathroom, toilet. Central heating with log fires in chilly weather. Car essential, ample parking. Ideal centre for visiting the Heart of England. Children and pets welcome. Evening Dinner, Bed and Breakfast from £14; Evening Meal, Bed and Breakfast from £12; Bed and Breakfast from £9. Bedtime drink. Reduced rates for children. Open all year.

LEAMINGTON SPA. Mrs R. Gibbs, Hill Farm, Lewis Road, Radford Semele, Leamington Spa CV31 1UX (Leamington Spa [0926] 37571). Working farm. Guests are welcome all year to this friendly, comfortable farmhouse on 350 acres mixed farm, ideally situated for Warwick, Stratford-upon-Avon, Leamington, Coventry, Royal Showground, Birmingham and N.E.C., and the Cotswolds. Children welcome; reductions for under 12's. Cot and high chair. Large garden with swing. Babysitting. Excellent farmhouse fare using home produce. Central heating. Log fires in chilly weather. Two double, one family bedrooms (all with washbasins, teasmade); beautiful bathroom, two toilets. Guests' sittingroom, colour TV and diningroom. Car preferable; ample parking. Supper drinks available. Evening Meal optional on request. Tourist Board listed. 1984 AA Recommended.

RUGBY near. Mrs Helen Sharpe, Manor Farm, Willey, Near Rugby CV23 0SH (Butterworth [04555] 3143). Working farm. Manor Farm is a dairy farm on the edge of a peaceful village. It is situated two and a half miles from the Fosseway/A5 Junction and only a short distance from Motorways M1, M6 and M69. It is an ideal touring base for the historical towns of Warwick, Stratford-upon-Avon, Coventry Cathedral and Market Bosworth Battlefield. Comfortable and centrally heated, the accommodation comprises one double room, with guests' lounge and diningroom. Parking space. Sorry, no smokers, no children, no pets. Open all year round for Bed and Breakfast or Bed, Breakfast and Evening Meal. SAE, please, for terms.

SHIPSTON-ON-STOUR near. Mrs Jean Johnson, Winter's Yard, Ascott, Near Shipston-on-Stour CV36 5PP (Long Compton [060-884] 280). A comfortable village house in an utterly peaceful setting. Relax and enjoy yourselves. Rooms equipped to a high standard with colour TV, tea and coffee making facilities, adjoining bathroom. You can expect to eat good wholesome food, home-baked bread and fresh produce. Sorry, no pets. Riding available on our quality horses. Ideally situated for Stratford-upon-Avon, Oxford and the Cotswolds. Car essential — parking. Bed and Breakfast £9 per person per day. Further details on request.

STRATFORD-UPON-AVON. Mrs Marian J. Walters, Church Farm, Dorsington, Stratford-upon-Avon CV37 8AX (Stratford-upon-Avon [0789] 720471). Working farm. A friendly welcome awaits you throughout the year at our Georgian farmhouse, with open fires and central heating. Stratford-upon-Avon, Warwick, N.E.C., Royal Showground, Cotswolds and the Vale of Evesham are all within easy driving distance. Guests are free to explore the beef, arable and horse farm. Gliding, fishing, boating and horse riding are all nearby. One family room and two double bedrooms, all with washbasins. Bed and Breakfast. Evening Meal optional. Good fresh home-produced food. Children welcome at reduced rates. Cot and high chair available. AA Listed. Please write or phone for further details and terms. Open all year.

STRATFORD-UPON-AVON. Mrs J. Wakeham, Whitfield Farm, Ettington, Stratford-upon-Avon CV37 7PN (Stratford-upon-Avon [0789] 740260). Situated down its own private drive, off the A429, this 220-acre mixed farm (wheat, cows, sheep, geese, hens) is ideal for a quiet and relaxing holiday. Convenient for visiting the Cotswolds, Warwick, Coventry, Stratford, Worcester. Fully modernised house with separate lounge and colour TV; two double and one family bedrooms with washbasins; bathroom, two toilets; diningroom. Sorry, no pets. Reduced rates for children, cot, high chair and babysitting by arrangement. Car essential — parking. Open all year (except Christmas) for Bed and Breakfast from £7 per night. Home produced food served. SAE, please.

STRATFORD-UPON-AVON. Mrs G. Hutsby, Thronton Manor, Ettington, Stratford-upon-Avon CV37 7PN (Stratford-upon-Avon [0789] 740210). Working farm. Enjoy the peace of a 16th century stone manor house in beautiful surroundings on a mixed farm off the A429. Gardens, including a grass tennis court, fly fishing and coarse fishing are available. Ideal for visiting Stratford, Warwick, Cotswolds, NEC and the Royal Show. Two family bedrooms and one twin bedded room, all with washbasins; bathroom and shower room. The beamed house is centrally heated throughout and has a large sittingroom with colour TV, diningroom and kitchen for guests' use. Bed and Breakfast with Evening Meal available on request. Open all year.

STRATFORD-UPON-AVON. Mrs J. M. Everett, Newbold Nurseries, Newbold-on-Stour, Stratford-upon-Avon CV37 8DP (Alderminster [078987] 285). Working farm. This smallholding has a modern farmhouse set in 25 acres with lovely views of open country on either side. Tourist attractions in the area include Shakespeare-land seven miles away, Warwick Castle, the Cotswolds and Hidcote Manor Gardens, a National Trust Property. Children are welcome, cot and babysitting provided. Pets permitted free of charge. One family room and two doubles, two bathrooms; sittingroom and diningroom. Open from March to October. Car essential, ample parking. A warm welcome and a full traditional English Breakfast is given to all guests. Bed and Breakfast from £8. Local pub serves excellent Evening Meals.

STRATFORD-UPON-AVON. Mrs M. Turney, Cadle Pool Farm, The Ridgway, Stratford-upon-Avon CV37 9RE (Stratford-upon-Avon [0789] 292494). Working farm. Situated in picturesque grounds, this charming oak-panelled and beamed family house, is part of 450 acre mixed working farm. It is conveniently situated two miles from Stratford-upon-Avon town, between Anne Hathaway's cottage and Mary Arden's House, also only eight minutes from The Royal Shakespeare Theatre. Ideal touring centre for Warwick, Kenilworth, Oxford, the Cotswolds and Malvern Hills. Accommodation comprises two twin-bedded rooms, and one family suite of rooms, all with private bathrooms, and central heating. There is an antique oak diningroom, and lounge with colour TV. The gardens and ornamental pool are particularly attractive, with peacocks and ducks roaming freely. Children welcome at reduced rates; cot, high chair, babysitting. Sorry, no pets. Open all year.

STRATFORD-UPON-AVON. Mrs M. J. Jordan, Pebworth Fields Farm, Pebworth, Stratford-upon-Avon CV37 8XP (Stratford-upon-Avon [0789] 720318). Working farm. This unusual Colonial-style farmhouse lies in the middle of 100-acre stock and arable farm. A large entrance hall with a grand staircase leads to light, spacious rooms (two double, one family, one with washbasin); the sitting/diningroom opens to a balcony partly surrounding the house and overlooking the garden, with lovely views of the countryside. Visitors find this an ideal centre for touring the Cotswolds, Stratford-upon-Avon, Warwick and the Vale of Evesham. Car essential, ample parking. Children welcome at reduced rates. Sorry, no pets. Open May to September for Bed and Breakfast. SAE, please, for terms.

STRATFORD-UPON-AVON. Mrs Robin Hutsby, Nolands Farm, Oxhill CV35 0RJ (Kineton [0926] 640309). Working farm, join in. Conveniently situated midway between Stratford-upon-Avon and Banbury, off the A422, Nolands Farm extends to approximately 300 acres. Guests are welcome to participate and enjoy various aspects of life on the farm. Lovely walks, well stocked lake and garden for relaxation. Guests' drawing room with colour TV, separate annexe overlooking stable yard. Accommodation comprises two double rooms en suite, two double, one family, one single bedrooms, all with washbasins; two bathrooms. Tea/coffee facilities. Central heating plus open log fires. Riding by arrangement. Open all year. Bed and Breakfast from £6.50 per person.

STRATFORD-UPON-AVON near. Mrs Joan James, Whitchurch Farm, Wimpstone, Near Stratford-upon-Avon CV37 8NS (Alderminster [078-987] 275). This large Georgian farmhouse is set in parklike surroundings, four-and-a-half miles from Stratford-upon-Avon, on the edge of the Cotswolds and ideal for a touring holiday. It is open to guests all year with central heating. The accommodation is in three family rooms with washbasins; bathroom, toilet; sittingroom, diningroom. Log fires. Children are welcome; there is a cot and babysitting is offered. Sorry, no pets. A car is essential and there is parking space. Good farmhouse English breakfast served. Reduced rates for children. Bed and Breakfast from £6 – £7.50 nightly. AA and HETB registered.

TYSOE. Mrs Pendleton, Church Farm, Tysoe CV35 0SF (Tysoe [029-588] 385). Working farm. This family run farm is pleasantly situated beneath the Edge Hills, midway between Banbury and Stratford. Built in 1617, the comfortable farmhouse offers accommodation in two double and one family bedrooms with washbasins; bathroom and separate toilet; guest lounge. Children are most welcome and babysitting, cot, high chair are available. Take the opportunity while in Shakespeare country to enjoy the theatre at Stratford, walks in the beautiful Cotswolds or to wander round Chipping Campden and Banbury's large cattle market. Church Farm is open all year and offers Bed and Breakfast or Evening Meal/Dinner, Bed and Breakfast. Good home cooking or excellent pub meals locally.

WARWICK near. Mrs J. Stanton, Redlands Farm, Banbury Road, Lighthorne, Near Warwick CV35 0AH (Leamington Spa [0926] 651241). A beautifully restored 15th century farmhouse built of local stone, the "Old Farm House" is set in two acres of garden with its own swimming pool, well away from the main road yet within easy travelling distance of Stratford and Warwick. Guest accommodation in one double (with bathroom), one single and one family bedrooms; bathroom, beamed lounge with TV; diningroom. Rooms are centrally heated and the farmhouse also has open fires. Evening Meal, Bed and Breakfast from £11.50; Bed and Breakfast from £8.50. Garden produce used whenever possible. No extra charge for evening drinks. Children welcome — facilities available. No pets. A car is recommended to make the most of your stay.

WARWICKSHIRE – SHAKESPEARE'S COUNTY!

Stratford-Upon-Avon is the county's, and indeed one of the country's, biggest attractions. However, other interesting places which should not be overshadowed include the Windmill at Chesterton, the country parks at Coombe Abbey, Hartshill Hayes and the Yew garden at Packwood House.

MOONRAKER HOUSE
40 Alcester Road, Stratford-upon-Avon

Moonraker Guest House (AA recommended) is on the north side of Stratford-upon-Avon, five minutes' walk from the town centre. It is the perfect centre for exploring the Cotswolds, Vale of Evesham, Shakespeare's countryside, Warwick and Kenilworth castles and Blenheim Palace. Moonraker has family, double and twin rooms tastefully furnished, hot and cold water, central heating, tea/coffee making facilities. ALL bedrooms have private showers, toilet en suite, fitted hair dryers and colour TV. There is comfortable lounge/diningroom. We believe in giving our guests a hearty English breakfast. Dinner is available by arrangement. Car Park. Terms on request on receipt of SAE, please.

Telephone: Stratford-upon-Avon (0789) 67115
Proprietors: Mr and Mrs M. V. Spencer

WARWICK. Mrs Carolyn Howard, Willowbrook House, Lighthorne Road, Kineton, Warwick CV35 0JL (Kineton [0926] 640475). Willowbrook is a peaceful house with charming views in four acres of paddocks and garden, 10 minutes' walk from Kineton Village; handy for Stratford-upon-Avon (nine miles), Warwick (10 miles), Banbury (10 miles) and the Cotswolds. Accommodation consists of two twin-bedded rooms with washbasins; bathroom, shower room, two toilets; visitors' sittingroom with colour TV; diningroom. Central heating with log fires for chilly evenings. Chickens, sheep and horse kept, and there is a riding school in the village. Children welcome. Bed and Breakfast, Evening Meal by request with imaginative home cooking. Open March through October.

The information in the entries in this guide is presented by the publishers in good faith and after the signed acceptance by advertisers that they will uphold the high standards associated with FARM HOLIDAY GUIDES LIMITED. The publishers do not accept responsibility for any inaccuracies or omissions or any results thereof. Before making final holiday arrangements readers should confirm the prices and facilities directly with advertisers.

WILTSHIRE

CHIPPENHAM. Mrs J. M. Summers, "Summer Cottage", 20 Chittoe Heath, Bromham, Chippenham SN15 2EH (Bromham [0380] 850338). Chittoe Heath is a small hamlet situated between Devizes and Chippenham just off A342. "Summer Cottage" is set in half an acre of quiet surroundings, facing view to the front overlooking beautiful historic Roundway Hills, and in the distance Salisbury Plain, with woods at the rear. Parking space for three cars. Three double bedrooms, with hot and cold. Lounge with TV. Within easy reach of ancient area of Avebury and Silbury Hill. Five minutes' drive to Lacock; Bath, Stonehenge, Castle Coombe, Longleat and Wells Cathedral are all easily accessible. Evening Meal by arrangement. Children welcome at reduced rates. Open March to October. SAE, please, for terms for Bed and Breakfast.

CHIPPENHAM. Mrs K. M. Addison, The Old Rectory, Lacock, Chippenham SN15 2JZ (Lacock [024-973] 335). Working farm. Situated in the National Trust village of Lacock and standing in its own grounds with tennis and croquet, The Old Rectory offers easy access to a variety of interesting things for the visitor to see and do. Lacock Abbey, the home of Fox Talbot, is one of the few abbeys Henry VIII did not destroy, and a visit to the Fox Talbot Photographic Museum is well worthwhile. The village is centrally placed for touring such places as Bath, Avebury, Stonehenge, Salisbury and many other towns and villages. Pleasant drives and walks through the West Country. Elegant accommodation is offered, with washbasins in all bedrooms. Ample free parking space. Bed and Breakfast from £10 per person per night.

CIRENCESTER near. Mrs Yvonne Edmonds, Old Manor Farmhouse, Ashton Keynes, Near Swindon SN6 6QR (Cirencester [0285] 861770). A XVth century Manor House full of character on the edge of the Cotswolds, close to the Cotswold Water Park (windsurfing, sailing, fishing, etc.). M4 12 miles. All bedrooms are beamed and offer four poster, twin beds, family accommodation. Washbasins in every room and a warm friendly atmosphere is assured. Coffee/tea making facilities in every room, and a large lounge with colour TV is always available for residents; separate beamed diningroom with inglenook fireplace. Evening meals available, by arrangement, using only the best fresh foods. Ample parking space. Children most welcome. SAE, please, for terms.

COTSWOLDS. Mr and Mrs P. B. Hartland, 2 Cove House, Ashton Keynes SN6 6NS (Cirencester [0285] 861221). A 17th century manor house situated in an acre and a half of beautiful gardens in a quiet village on the Wiltshire/Gloucestershire border, five miles south of Cirencester. Accommodation is in large rooms (two with bath/shower room). Babysitting and reduced rates for children. Dogs by arrangement. Open all year. An ideal centre for visits to such historic cities as Gloucester, Bath, Bristol and Oxford, all within one hour by car, and to many beautiful Cotswold villages. The Cotswold Water Park is in the immediate vicinity and fishing, sailing, windsurfing, are available. The Hartlands are members of the Royal Shakespeare Theatre and can arrange bookings, given sufficient warning. Car essential. Bed and Breakfast from £9.50 (Evening Meals available). SAE, please.

DEVIZES. Mr and Mrs C. Fletcher, Lower Foxhangers Farm, Rowde, Devizes SN10 1SS (Seend [038-082] 254). Working farm. Lying in a secluded hollow by the Kennet and Avon Canal, two and a half miles west of Devizes on the A361, Lower Foxhangers is nicely placed for touring Wiltshire, rich in places of historic, scenic and recreational interest. Heated swimming pool and tennis courts within three miles; horse riding and public golf course seven miles. The canal provides boating, fishing in season and excellent walking along the towpath as an alternative to the open Downs or woodland walks nearby. The spacious 18th century farmhouse provides double and twin bedrooms with washbasins; two bathrooms, three toilets. Lounge with colour TV. Separate diningroom. Cot and high chair available. Pets welcome. Open Easter to October. Bed and Breakfast £8 per person. Leaflet by return.

Terms quoted in this publication may be subject to increase if rises in costs necessitate

BOARD Wiltshire 307

DEVIZES. Mrs Michael Maude, Etchilhampton House, Devizes SN10 3JH (Devizes [0380] 2927). Beautiful 200-year-old Georgian house standing in a four-acre garden surrounded by lovely countryside. Very peaceful and relaxing setting with hard tennis court and croquet lawn for guests' enjoyment. Excellent touring centre for many interesting places including Bath, Avebury, Salisbury, Stonehenge and Lacock. Three miles east of old market town of Devizes. Very comfortable accommodation in three twin, one family bedrooms, all with washbasins; one single room; bathrooms, toilets; sittingroom; diningroom. Children and pets welcome. Cot, chair and babysitting available. Central heating. Car is advisable, ample parking. Open all year for Bed and Breakfast from £10; Evening Meal by arrangement. Reductions for children.

MALMESBURY. Mrs Sandra Doel, Hayleaze Farm, Crudwell, Malmesbury SN16 9EY (Crudwell [06667] 368). Working farm. Quietly situated on the Wiltshire/Gloucester border, this family dairy farm makes an ideal base for touring the Cotswolds. Being only 10 miles from J17-M4, this also makes a convenient place to break a journey. The accommodation is available from April to October and has a double room and a family room, both with washbasins; bathroom, toilet; sittingroom; diningroom. Central heating. Car essential, ample parking. Children are welcome, cot, high chair, babysitting and reduced rates. Bed and Breakfast from £8.

MALMESBURY. Mrs D. Freeth, Vancelettes Farm, Sherston, Malmesbury SN16 0LU (Malmesbury [0666] 840253). Working farm. This farmhouse, on a 70-acre mixed farm, is situated at side of quiet country road, one-third-of-a-mile from the Cotswold type village, one-and-a-half miles from Westonbirt Arboretum. Convenient for Tetbury, Cheltenham, Cirencester, Bath, Slimbridge, Castle Combe, ideal touring centre. Varied menu, home-produced vegetables. Two double, one twin bedrooms, with washbasins; bathroom, toilet; sitting/diningroom. Children welcome, reduced rates — cot, high chair. Pets permitted. Car essential — parking. Open April to end October. Mid-week bookings except July and August. Evening Dinner, Bed and Breakfast or Bed and Breakfast. SAE, please, for terms.

MALMESBURY. Mrs C. Parfitt, Angrove Farm, Rodbourne, Malmesbury SN16 0ET (Malmesbury [066-62] 2982). Working farm. Homely farmhouse accommodation in a secluded position. Junction 17 — M4 five miles away. Ideal for a quiet relaxing holiday. Drink making facilities available at all times. Hot and cold in all rooms. Clean towels daily. Separate lounge with TV. Farmhouse is centre of 204 acres currently farmed with beef cattle. Angrove Wood lies behind farmhouse. River Avon bounds the farm; own trout and coarse fishing available. River is trout stocked. Many interesting walks. Central for Slimbridge, Cotswolds, Bath, Bristol, Bradford-on-Avon, Doddington, Longleat. Choice of Breakfast menu including whole foods. Set four-course Dinner, plus coffee. Advance weekly bookings only taken (Saturday to Saturday). Personal attention with an aim to please. Good plentiful food. Open May to September inclusive. Sorry, no dogs. Terms and brochure on request.

MELKSHAM. Mrs J. Podger, Seend Bridge Farm, Seend, Melksham SN12 6RY (Seend [038-082] 534). Bed and Breakfast in 18th century Wiltshire Farmhouse. Secluded, yet only three miles from Bath/Devizes road. First-class centre for visiting places of historic and scenic interest. Bath, Longleat, Stonehenge, Avebury, Stourhead, the Mendip Hills and Caves, Salisbury Plain, the Cotswolds and many places within an hour's travel. Recommended by Egon Ronay; Daily Telegraph and Routiers. Evening meal on request.

Wiltshire BOARD

MELKSHAM. Mrs B. Pullen, Frying Pan Farm, Broughton Gifford Road, Melksham SN12 8LL (Melksham [0225] 702343). Working farm. Frying Pan Farm makes an ideal touring centre; Lacock National Trust village and Bath are not far away. Open for guests from Easter to October with one double bedroom and one family bedroom; bathroom; sitting/diningroom. Children are welcome. Sorry no pets. The house is cosy and comfortable with solid fuel heating. A car is not essential but there is ample parking. Public transport one-third of a mile. Bed and Breakfast. Reduced rates for children.

MERE. Mrs M. E. Frost, Chetcombe House Hotel, Salisbury Road, Mere BA12 6AZ (Mere [0747] 860219). This Country House Hotel, set in one acre of lovely gardens, is situated just off the A303 on the eastern approach road to the picturesque little town of Mere. Ideal as a stopover en route to the West Country, or as a centre to explore the delights of Wiltshire. Close to Stourhead and Longleat, with Stonehenge, Salisbury, Wilton and Shaftesbury all within 20 mile radius. All bedrooms have hot and cold running water and are south-facing with lovely views. The hotel has a residential licence and is open all year. Bed and Breakfast from £10; Evening Meal available £5.50. Special rates for families and low season breaks.

SALISBURY. Mrs P. A. Helyer, Little Langford Farm, Little Langford, Salisbury SP3 4NR (Salisbury [0722] 790205). Working farm, join in. Little Langford Farm is a dairy and arable farm situated in the beautiful rolling Wiltshire Downs just eight miles North West of the lovely Cathedral City of Salisbury. Guests have freedom of the farm. The beautiful Victorian farmhouse stands in its own grounds with large pleasant garden and countryside view. It has spacious tastefully furnished rooms, double/family, twin and single with tea/coffee making facilities. Guests' bathroom. Separate diningroom and lounge with colour TV. Three-quarter size billiard table. Excellent touring area. Near Stonehenge, Wilton House, Stourhead, Longleat, New Forest. Quaint village pubs nearby. Open all year.

SALISBURY. Ms Pamela Allan, Harestock Cottage, Southampton Road, Whiteparish, Salisbury SP5 2QU (Whiteparish [07948] 370). Pam and George invite you to Harestock Cottage where the emphasis is on wholefood cooking. Excellent base for touring; nearby places include Salisbury, New Forest, Stonehenge, Southampton, Wilton House, Romsey Abbey, Broadlands, Beaulieu and Winchester. Accommodation in double and family rooms (some with washbasins). Tea making facilities. Spacious lounge with colour TV, log fire and central heating. Children welcome, cot, high chair, babysitting provided, reductions for them if sharing parents' room. Pets accepted. Car essential, parking. Beehives, chickens and a milking goat are kept (own cheese and yoghurt); one acre garden produces organically grown vegetables using raised beds, polytunnel and we are experimenting with hydroponics (NFT). Bed and Breakfast from £8 daily (£49 weekly); Evening Meal from £5.50. Please send for brochure.

SWINDON. Mrs Patricia Harris, Worsall Farm, Coleshill, Near Highworth, Swindon SN6 7PS (Swindon [0793] 762274). Working farm. Situated in the foothills of the Cotswolds, within four miles of the Thames, 17th-century farmhouse of great charm and character, surrounded by National Trust Villages and Properties. Guests are accommodated all year round — three twin-bedded rooms, one double bedded room (three with washbasins). Two bathrooms, three toilets. Lounge; TV sittingroom; diningroom where Cordon Bleu and traditional home cooking is served with varied menus (open to non-residents for dinner). Log fire and central heating. Car essential — ample parking. Regret, we cannot accommodate children under 10 years. No pets. This is excellent hunting, shooting and fishing country. Lechlade four and a half miles, Burford 12 miles. Blenheim Palace, Woodstock and Oxford within easy driving distance. Evening Dinner, Bed and Breakfast from £18.50; Bed and Breakfast from £10. SAE, please, for brochure.

When you have read one you *haven't* read them all — we have *eleven* other publications

WARMINSTER. Mrs Jean Crossman, Stalls Farm, Longleat, Warminster BA12 7NE (Maiden Bradley [098-53] 323). Working farm. Stalls Farm is a 281-acre dairy farm on Wiltshire/Somerset border, situated at Longleat on road from Longleat House to Safari Park. Pleasant garden with terrace, lawns and pond. Lovely walks. Ideally situated for visiting Longleat, Stourhead, Bath, Cheddar, Wells, Salisbury, Stonehenge, Avebury, Castle Combe, Rode Bird Gardens, Claverton Manor, Westbury White Horse, etc. A car is essential. All bedrooms with comfortable divans, fitted carpets and washbasins. Children welcome, cot and high chair. Access to house at all times. Open all year. SAE or phone for terms. Guests accommodated for winter breaks. Full central heating. AA recommended.

WESTBURY. Mrs M. Hoskins, Spinney Farmhouse, Chapmanslade, Westbury BA13 4AQ (Chapmanslade [037-388] 412). Off A36, three miles west of Warminster; 16 miles from historic city of Bath. Close to Longleat, Cheddar and Stourhead. Reasonable driving distance to Bristol, Stonehenge, Glastonbury and the cathedral cities of Wells and Salisbury. Golf, pony trekking and fishing available locally. Hot and cold and tea/coffee-making facilities in all rooms. Family room available. Guests' lounge with TV. Central heating. Children and pets welcome. Ample parking. Open all year. Bed and Breakfast £9. Reduction after two nights. Evening Meal £6. Farm fresh food in a warm friendly family atmosphere. Registered with ETB and AA.

WILTSHIRE – "WHITE" HORSE COUNTY!

Many "White" horses adorn The Wiltshire chalk downs and the prehistoric theme continues with Stonehenge and Avebury. Also of interest are the landscape gardens at Studley, Chiselbury Camp, The Kennet and Avon canal with lock "staircase", Salisbury Plain, and the abandoned city Old Sarum.

For the Mutual Guidance of Guest and Host

Farm Holiday Guides Ltd. do not inspect or recommend accommodation but advertisers agree to accept our Farm Holiday Guide standards of comfortable and clean accommodation and wholesome and well-cooked food. Advertisers are also bound by the Trades Description Act.

When accommodation has been booked, deposits sent, and letters of acceptance exchanged, both parties – host and guest – have entered into a binding contract.

Friends and families can easily be upset and much bitterness caused if holiday arrangements are not carefully made. The following points can be of real importance:

Guest When enquiring about accommodation, be as precise as possible. Give exact dates, numbers in your party and the ages of any children. State the number and type of rooms wanted and also what catering you require – bed and breakfast, full board etc. Make sure that the position about evening meals is clear – and about pets, reductions for children or any other special points.

Read our reviews carefully to ensure that the proprietors you are going to contact can supply what you want. Ask for a letter confirming all arrangements, if possible.

Host Give details about your facilities and about any special conditions. Explain your deposit system clearly and arrangements for cancellations, charges etc, and whether or not your terms include VAT.

We regret that Farm Holiday Guides cannot accept responsibility for any errors or omissions in descriptions. Prices in particular should be checked before booking because of the early compilation of the Guides, far ahead of the next holiday season.

YORKSHIRE

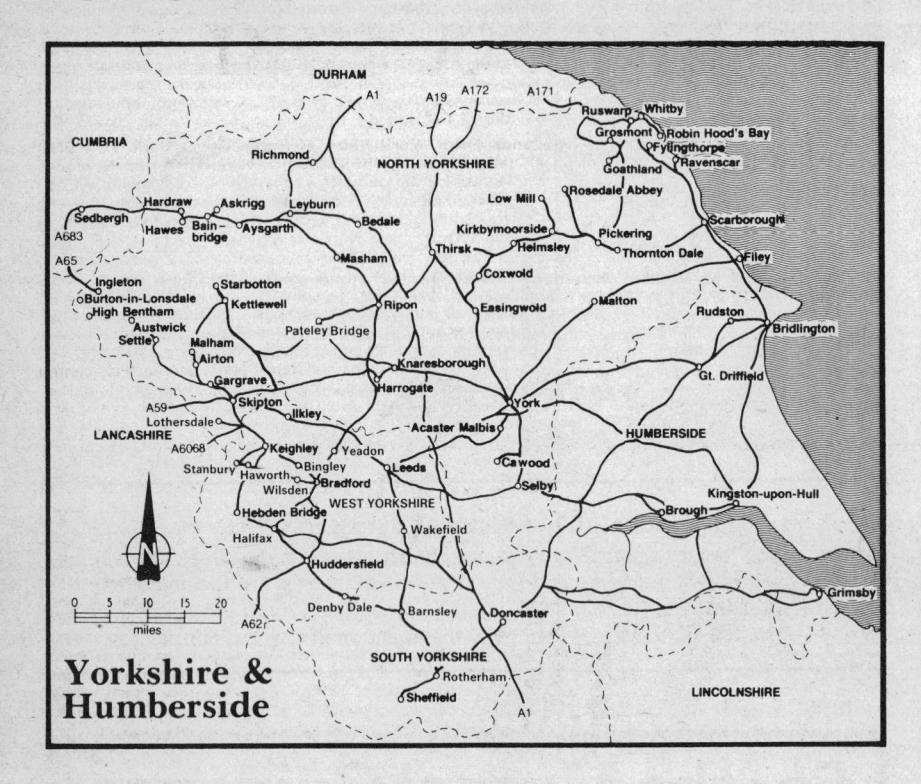

EAST YORKSHIRE (Humberside)

BRIDLINGTON. Mrs J. M. Thompson, The Grange, Bempton Lane, Flamborough, Bridlington YO15 1AS (Bridlington [0262] 850207). Working farm, join in. This attractive 140-year-old house is situated on 475 acres of dairy and arable land, half-a-mile from Flamborough Village on the B1229, 100 yards off the road with tarmac drive and ample parking space. It has a large garden with tennis court, children's play area, swings and slides. Within easy reach of sandy beaches at Bridlington or Filey, also Yorkshire moors and Wolds. Golf at Flamborough, Puffin and Gannet colonies at Bempton. Guests welcome all year except Christmas and New Year, and can look around the farm and even help with the milking. One double, one single and one family bedrooms, all with tea-making facilities; two bathrooms and toilets; sittingroom and diningroom. Children welcome at reduced rates. Cot, high chair, babysitting available (free of charge). Pets permitted. Car essential — ample parking. Terms on request for Bed and Breakfast only. Evening meals in Flamborough or Bridlington four miles away.

BRIDLINGTON near. Miss Brenda M. Jackson, Brentwood, Ruston Parva, Driffield YO25 0DG (Driffield [0377] 44298). Modern bungalow, situated on a farm, ideal location for visiting Bridlington, eight miles; Filey 15 miles; Scarborough 22 miles; historic City of York 30 miles. Among many places of interest for the holidaymaker to visit — Hornsea potteries, Sewerby Hall, Sledmere House, Burton Agnes Hall, all within easy reach. Situated in a quiet village, half-a-mile from main Driffield-Bridlington road (four miles Driffield), accommodation comprises one double, one family bedroom, shaver point. Bathroom/toilet. Lounge/diningroom with colour TV. Children welcome at reduced rates, babysitting. Pets accepted by prior arrangement. Large garden; ample parking space. Good food and warm welcome assured. Bed and Breakfast (Evening Meal optional). Open from April to October, it is suitable for disabled guests. SAE, please, or telephone for further details and terms.

PLEASE SEND A STAMPED ADDRESSED ENVELOPE WITH ENQUIRIES

POCKLINGTON near. Mrs A. Pearson, Meltonby Hall Farm, Meltonby, Near Pocklington YO4 2PW (Pocklington [07592] 3214). Meltonby Hall Farm is in a small village at the foot of the Yorkshire Wolds, offering a relaxed, homely atmosphere, providing a good base for historic York 13 miles, coast 30 miles, as well as the beautiful North Yorkshire Moors with their forest drives, not forgetting Stately Homes. Pocklington is two and a half miles away with its magnificent water lilies. Own and local produce used. Double and twin room, cot and high chair if required. Guests' own bathroom, diningroom/lounge. Open Easter to October with central heating and open fire. Car essential, parking. Children welcome, babysitting and reduced rates. Bed and Breakfast £7; Bed, Breakfast and Evening Dinner £12.50 with slight reductions for weekly bookings. Reduced rates for children under 12. Registered E.T.B.

YORK. Mr and Mrs Peter Scott, Newlands Farm, York Road, Barmby Moor, York YO4 5HU (Wilberfoss [07595] 308). Working farm. Newlands Farm is on the main A1079 between the villages of Wilberfoss and Barmby Moor. Situated on the main route between York and the Humber Bridge, an ideal centre to explore York and district, coast within easy reach. The farm is a highly productive small-holding with a variety of animals, including rare Angora Goats; the house is set well back from the main road and surrounded by conifers. One double, one twin-bedded, one family bedrooms, all with washbasins, tea-making facilities and TVs. One room with private bathroom. Outdoor swimming pool, swings, slide and mini tennis court. Reduced rates, babysitting for children. Pets welcome. Full central heating. Car essential — parking. Guests welcome to participate in farm activities which may be of interest to people who wish to derive an income from a small acreage. Bed and Breakfast £6.50–£7.50. Farmhouse teas and light suppers served.

YORK. Mrs J. M. Liversidge, Cuckoo Nest Farm, Wilberfoss, York YO4 5NL (Wilberfoss [075-95] 365). Working farm. Cuckoo Nest Farm is an 80-acre stock and arable farm quietly situated but convenient for touring the Dales, 200 yards from the main A1079 road. An active working farm, with calves and often pet lambs. Visit York, seven miles, Hornsea pottery, forest drives, abbeys, steam railway, stately homes and other places of interest. Restaurants in the immediate area. No facilities for children under two years, but rates reduced for the under 12's and babysitting is offered. Oak beamed diningroom, lounge with TV. Central heating. One double and one family rooms, both with washbasins, electric blankets, heating and shaver points; bathroom, two toilets. A car is fairly essential although the farm is on a bus route, parking. Sorry, no pets. Bed and Breakfast from January to November. Light supper served if required. SAE, for terms, please.

NORTH YORKSHIRE

ARKENGARTHDALE. James and Doreen Binge, Croft House, Arkengarthdale, Near Richmond DL11 6EN (Richmond [0748] 84321). Arkengarthdale runs northwards out of Swaledale towards Tan Hill and is the most peaceful, unspoiled Dale in the National Park. Croft House is at its heart, ½-mile north of the tiny village of Langthwaite. Unforgettable views in all directions, ideal walking country, good touring base. No public transport, so car is essential. Parking. The house is off the road, has central heating and open fires. The three guest bedrooms have tea/coffee making facilities and guests have the use of two bathrooms, drying room, library and TV. Special diets catered for; dogs are permitted; open all year. Bed and Breakfast £8.00; four-course Dinner by arrangement £5.00.

ASKRIGG. Mr and Mrs J. L. Whitfield, Winville Private Hotel, Askrigg, Leyburn DL8 3HG (Wensleydale [0969] 50515). Winville is a former family mansion which has been tastefully transformed into a small comfortable, friendly hotel. All bedrooms are en suite, with additional facilities for tea or coffee making. Comfortable lounge and diningroom and Licensed Bar for the use of guests. A walled garden and ample parking space are available at the rear of the hotel. Situated in the centre of this most pleasing village which has featured in the TV "Vet" series. Also ideal for visiting Hardraw Scar, Aysgarth Falls, Richmond and Bolton Castles, whilst a little farther away you have Ingleton Falls and caves, and the Lakes are within easy distance. Good walking for walking. Proprietors will assist with information. Traditional Yorkshire dishes served using fresh vegetables, also home baked sweets. All terms on application (write or telephone). Reduced rates for children, weekly bookings and senior citizens.

North Yorkshire BOARD

ASKRIGG. Mrs Patricia Tate, Prospect House, Moor Road, Askrigg, Leyburn DL8 3HH (Wensleydale [0969] 50371). A warm comfortable family house quietly situated on the outskirts of the village with a fine view across Wensleydale. Ideally placed for walking, touring or fishing. Aysgarth Falls, Lake Semmerwater, Mill Gill Force, Bolton Castle, Hardraw Force are all within hiking distance, whilst York, the Lakes, Fountains Abbey, Richmond Castle are all easily accessible by car. One twin room with washbasin and one double room. Excellent home cooking with home grown produce. Parking space. Sorry, no pets. SAE, please for terms for Dinner, Bed and Breakfast or Bed and Breakfast, and Brochure.

Dweldapilton Hall Hotel AA★★RAC

**Appleton-le-Moors
N. Yorks YO6 6TF
(075-15-227)**

Appleton-le-Moors was mentioned in the Domesday Book, only then it was called Dweldapilton. The Hotel is a Victorian Country House set in extensive gardens with the Yorkshire Moors as a backdrop. The Dales, York and the coast are all near by. The hotel with its gracious lounge, diningroom and snug bar has all the modern comforts with private bathrooms, a lift and full central heating (and of course, log fires). Open all the year for those who want to relax in superb surroundings. A full brochure on request.

Proprietor Richard Ambler.

ASKRIGG. Mrs B. Percival, Milton House, Askrigg, Leyburn DL8 3HJ (Wensleydale [0969] 50217). Askrigg is situated in the heart of Wensleydale and is within easy reach of many interesting places — Aysgarth Falls, Hardraw Falls, Bolton Castle. This is an ideal area for walking. Milton House is a spacious house with all modern amenities. There are two double bedrooms and one family room, all have washbasins; bathroom with shower, two toilets; visitors' lounge with TV; diningroom with separate tables. Children are welcome (at reduced rates). Central heating. It is open all year and Askrigg is one of the loveliest villages in the Dales. You are sure of good home cooking, a friendly welcome and a homely atmosphere. Car essential, parking space. Pets are allowed. Evening Meal, Bed and Breakfast or Bed and Breakfast only. Terms on application with SAE, please.

BAINBRIDGE. Mrs A. Harrison, Riverdale House, Bainbridge, Leyburn DL8 3EW (Wensleydale [0969] 50311). Riverdale House overlooks village green and stocks in centre of a lovely village in Upper Wensleydale, which is a National Park area. Good touring centre for the Dales and other places of interest — Aysgarth Falls, Hardraw Scour, Richmond and Bolton Castles, Ingleton Falls and Caves are but a few. Excellent walking over hills and moors. Good food a speciality, all fresh produce, traditional roasts, home made soups, delicious puddings, plus a carefully chosen wine list. All bedrooms well appointed and very comfortable with tea/coffee making facilities. Fire Certificate granted. Leyburn 11 miles. Many rooms with private bathrooms. SAE for brochure or telephone from November to 31st March **(Aysgarth [096-93] 381)** — thereafter as above.

BARNARD CASTLE. Mrs S. M. Jeffrey, Lodge Farm, Scargill, Barnard Castle, Co. Durham DL12 9SY (Teesdale [0833] 21238). Working farm. Small quiet farm in the Yorkshire Dales between Teesdale and Swaledale beef and sheep rearing with several pets including a Jersey cow. Traditional old stone farmhouse, centrally heated, well off the road with extensive views over woodland, fields and moors. Fishing available, attractive walks and abundant wildlife. Ancient market towns and castles nearby. Two double and one single bedrooms; sittingroom available with colour TV. Children welcome, well behaved pets accepted. Ample parking. Bed and Breakfast from £6.50. Occasional Evening Meals available. Reductions for children. Open all year.

BOARD North Yorkshire

BEDALE. Mrs G. E. Spence, Oak Tree Farm, Well, Bedale DL8 2PE (Bedale [0677] 70262). Working farm. This is a quiet farmhouse on a 200-acre dairy farm, and a good base for exploring the Yorkshire Dales and moors. There are many places of interest in the area to visit; York, Durham, Fountains Abbey, Bolton Castle, the famous fishing town of Whitby, are only a few. Accommodation in three double rooms; bathroom and toilet; diningroom. A car is necessary, parking space available. SAE, please, for details and terms for Full Board, Evening Dinner/Meal, Bed and Breakfast or Bed and Breakfast only.

BEDALE. Mrs Elizabeth Y. Pilgrim, The Manor, Exelby, Bedale DL8 2HB (Bedale [0677] 22929). The Manor is a period house of great charm in peaceful surroundings, set in two acres of land, two miles south of Bedale, and ideally situated for Dales and Moors. All rooms are generously proportioned with beamed ceilings, items of antique furniture and tasteful decor. The large lounge has colour TV and there is a separate diningroom. The bedrooms have washbasins, shaver sockets and tea making facilities. Ground floor accommodation available. No evening meal but excellent facilities nearby. Ample car parking. Bed and Breakfast £7.50. Reductions for children. SAE, please, for brochure.

CARLTON-IN-COVERDALE. Mrs Anne Dinsdale, Town Foot Farm, Carlton-in-Coverdale, Leyburn DL8 4BA (Wensleydale [0969] 40651). Working farm. One hundred acres in Yorkshire Dales National Park. The farmhouse has a secluded position in the village. Private parking. Car essential. Good farmhouse cooking. Free range eggs. Guests' kitchen available for sandwich making, filling of flasks, washing clothes etc. Ingredients and facilities for making hot drinks. Two double rooms, one twin room, all with washbasins. Poly/cotton sheets used and towels supplied. Guests' lounge with TV; oak-beamed diningroom. Sorry, no pets. Open from Easter for Evening Meal, Bed and Breakfast or Bed and Breakfast only. Terms on request. SAE, please.

COVERDALE (Leyburn). Mrs Gillian M. Smith, "Abbots Thorn," Carlton-in-Coverdale, Leyburn DL8 4AY (Wensleydale [0969] 40620). Peaceful Coverdale, in the heart of Herriot country and the Yorkshire Dales National Park, offers unspoilt countryside and sweeping hills. Abbots Thorn is an old house of character which has been thoroughly modernised to offer every comfort to our guests with central heating and coal fires in cool weather. Good walking from the house. All rooms face south with views across the Dale. One double, one twin, one family room, all with washbasins, tea-making facilities. Bathroom and toilet for guests' use only. Colour TV in lounge. Separate diningroom. Children welcome. Pets permitted. A car is essential for touring this lovely scenic area and there is parking space opposite the house. Wensleydale, Wharfedale and Swaledale are all nearby, plus several historic buildings. Full English breakfast and four-course Evening Dinner. All home cooking. Open April to end of September.

COVERDALE (Leyburn). Mrs P. Suttill, Coverham Abbey Farm, Middleham, Leyburn DL8 4RN (Wensleydale [0969] 40209). Working farm. Three hundred acres set in a lovely quiet position next to ruins of Coverham Abbey. Central for touring Dales and places of historical interest. Two double rooms or family rooms, with washbasins. One double room. Bathroom, two toilets. Central heating. Log fires. Separate lounge and diningroom. Colour TV. Home cooking. Children welcome. Babysitting available. Pets accepted free of charge. Car essential — parking. SAE, please, for terms for Bed, Breakfast and Evening Meal or Bed and Breakfast. Reductions for children.

DENT. Mrs Marlene Williamson, Ivy Dene, Gawthrop, Dent, Sedbergh LA10 5TA (Dent [058-75] 353). Ivy Dene is situated in the Yorkshire Dales within easy reach of the glorious Lake District and ten miles from the M6. Ideal centre for walking and only half-a-mile from the picturesque village of Dent with its cobbled streets. Accommodation comprises two double and one family bedrooms, with washbasins; bathroom; sittingroom with TV/diningroom. All home cooking and baking is served. Sorry, no pets. Children welcome at reduced rates. Car essential — parking. Open March to November for Evening Dinner/Meal, Bed and Breakfast or Bed and Breakfast. Terms on request.

EASINGWOLD. Mrs Margaret Helm, Hunters Lodge, Husthwaite, Easingwold, York YO6 3SY (Coxwold [034-76] 539). Hunters Lodge is situated 250 feet up on the Hambleton Hills with glorious views westwards towards the Dales. Set in over an acre of garden and paddock, the outstanding modern house has many extra facilities for wet weather — large lounge and snug (colour TV); table tennis room; **indoor swimming pool**, heated from Whitsun to October; sauna and solarium (extra cost). Accommodation available — two double bedrooms, one family room, all with washbasins and full central heating. All rooms furnished and decorated to a high standard. Car essential and ample parking space. Children welcome. Cot, high chair, babysitting provided. Easingwold and A19 two miles; York 15 miles. Ideal touring centre for moors and Dales with many delightful pubs and hotels for meals. You are sure of a warm welcome, comfort and help in planning excursions to local places of interest. Open all year for Bed and Breakfast from £9. Reduced weekly terms and winter rates, also for children under 10. SAE, please, for further details, or telephone.

WHEN MAKING ENQUIRIES PLEASE MENTION FARM HOLIDAY GUIDE

North Yorkshire BOARD

FILEY near. Mrs Joan Greenwood, Cannonfields Guest House, 44 Muston Road, Hunmanby, Near Filey YO14 0JY (Scarborough [0723] 890933). A small guest house in two acres of lovely gardens, an ideal centre for Filey, three miles with its beautiful beach. Scarborough, Bridlington, Wolds and North Yorkshire Moors and Granton Golf Course within easy reach. Ground floor bedroom available for invalids; easy access. All bedrooms have fitted carpets, hot and cold basins, razor points and comfortable beds. Two bathrooms, with showers; four toilets. Excellent food attractively served. Home grown produce. Separate tables; lounge with colour TV. Central heating. Bowling and putting greens. Twelve guests only. Children over eight welcome. SAE, please, for brochure and tariff to resident proprietors. Open Easter to October. Fire Certificate. Five-course dinner and tea-making facilities. Reduced terms for children. Two 28-foot caravans to let in grounds.

GLAISDALE (Whitby). Mrs S. E. Burtt, York House, Glaisdale, Whitby YO21 2PZ (Whitby [0947] 87357). Working farm. Stone built coaching house with oak beams and log fires, dating back to 1780. Situated in North Yorkshire Moors National Park. Now a 185-acre dairy and sheep farm, pleasantly situated in beautiful peaceful Dale of Glaisdale 'twixt moors and sea. Good home cooking with generous helpings of farm produce: free range eggs, cream, milk, meat and vegetables. One double, one twin, and one family bedrooms with washbasins; tea/coffee making facilities. Bathroom and two toilets. Lounge with beams and colour TV. Diningroom with separate tables. Full central heating. Children over 5 years, babysitting offered. Boating, golfing, fishing, riding nearby. Small pony on farm for use of guests. Many local beauty spots and places of interest. Coastal resorts nearby. Car essential. Sorry, no pets in house, kennels in area. SAE or telephone for terms with reductions for children. No VAT.

GOATHLAND. Mrs V. A. MacCaig, Prudom House, Goathland, Whitby YO22 5AN (Whitby [0947] 86368). Situated nine miles from the coast, Goathland offers some of the finest walking countryside and is an ideal touring centre. An added attraction is the North Yorkshire Moors Historical Railway Trust running through the village. Delightful scenery. Prudom House is situated in attractive well-maintained gardens in the centre of the village. Careful restoration of the farmhouse has provided guests with modern amenities whilst retaining its character. Open beams a feature and log fires. All bedrooms provided with razor points and H/C. Comfortable accommodation and good food. Children are welcome, cot, high chair, babysitting and reduced rates. Dogs allowed. Open all year except Christmas and New Year. Please phone or send SAE for brochure.

GOATHLAND. Mr J. A. Lusher, Whitfield House Hotel, Darnholm, Goathland, Whitby YO22 5LA (Whitby [0947] 86215). On the fringe of Goathland in the beautiful North York Moors, this residential licensed, family run hotel has 11 bedrooms (four with en-suite bathrooms), and central heating throughout. It offers a friendly atmosphere with colour TV Lounge, cosy Bar Lounge and excellent food. Ideally situated for walking or touring the National Park, the North York Moors Railway is close by, and Whitby and the coast just nine miles away. Children three years and over welcome (reductions when sharing parents' room). Dinner, Bed and Breakfast or Bed and Breakfast only. Morning Tea, Evening Drinks and packed Lunches on request. Open all year. AA* approved. Write or phone for brochure and tariff.

GOATHLAND. Colin and Christine Chippindale, Barnet House Guest House, Goathland, Whitby YO22 5NG (Whitby [0947] 86201). Barnet House is stone-built, standing in its own grounds just outside the delightful village of Goathland, an ideal centre for walking and touring the North Yorkshire moors, dales and coast. Guests are assured of comfort, friendly atmosphere, excellent menu, including home grown produce, freshly prepared and tastefully served; lounge with colour TV. Three double, three twin-bedded, and one family rooms, all with washbasins and razor points, individually heated, with magnificent views over surrounding moorland. Bathroom, shower room, three toilets. Reductions for children. Sorry no pets. Ample parking. Open from March to November for Evening Dinner, Bed and Breakfast. Brochure on request.

GREWELTHORPE. Mrs T. A. Barker, High Bramley Grange, Ilton Road, Grewelthorpe, Near Ripon HG4 3DH (Kirkby Malzeard [076-583] 410). Working farm. Spacious farmhouse set in half an acre of lawns and garden on a dairy farm situated in a scenic area at the foot of Yorkshire Dales. The charming village of Grewelthorpe is an ideal centre for touring, pony trekking or visiting the interesting country market town of Ripon, eight miles away. Comfortable accommodation in two double and one twin-bedded rooms; two bathrooms, two toilets. Sittingroom with colour TV, diningroom. Central heating. Children welcome, cot available. Sorry, no pets. Open April to end October inclusive, Bed and Breakfast is provided from £7 (drink and snack at bedtime included). Car essential — parking. Reduced rates for children.

GROSMONT. Mrs D. Hodgson, Fairhead Farm, Grosmont, Whitby YO22 5PN (Whitby [0947] 85238). Working farm, join in. Grosmont is a beautiful Eskdale village with steam railway. Whitby is six miles and York 40 miles. The farmhouse, which is on a 172 acre dairy farm, is pleasantly set in quiet area with superb views half a mile out of village. Children are welcome. Sorry, no pets. It makes an ideal touring base for moors and coast. Accommodation is in one double, one single, one family room; bathroom, toilet; sittingroom; diningroom. Rates are reduced for children and there is a cot and babysitting done by arrangement. Open all year for Bed and Breakfast, with Evening Meal if required. Parking space. SAE, please, for terms.

HARROGATE. Mrs V. E. Smith, "Clint Banks", Clint, Harrogate (Harrogate [0423] 770712). Clint Banks is a spacious, detached country house, run by Mrs Smith and her family giving good, friendly service. Situated in a small, quiet village the house has superb views across the Nidd Valley and is an ideal centre for touring the Dales, Herriot country and York. Peaceful, relaxed atmosphere with good traditional cooking. The rooms are large and well furnished — one family room with bathroom en-suite, one family and one double rooms with washbasins, one single room. Bathroom, two toilets. Sittingroom with colour TV, diningroom. Central heating. Children welcome, babysitting available. Sorry, no pets. Car essential — parking. Open all year for Bed and Breakfast from £8; Dinner, Bed and Breakfast £13.50 (bedtime drink included). Weekly rates on request. Reductions for children.

HARROGATE. Mrs M. M. Manning, "Sherwood," 7 Studley Road, Harrogate HG1 5JU (Harrogate [0423] 503033). A warm welcome awaits you at "Sherwood," quietly situated, yet only 300 yards from town centre and 100 yards from New Conference Complex, Valley Gardens and swimming pool. Harrogate is the "Gateway to the Yorkshire Dales," halfway from London to Edinburgh and five miles from the A1. The good, homely accommodation has been highly recommended, and personal attention guaranteed at all times. Full central heating. No restrictions, guests have their own keys. Three double bedrooms, all with washbasins; bathroom, toilet; sittingroom with colour TV; diningroom. Full three-course English Breakfast from £9; evening tea/coffee included in prices. Reductions for children and for senior citizens (low season). SAE, please.

HARROGATE. Mrs N. Iveson, Newton Hall, Ripley, Harrogate HG3 3DZ (Harrogate [0423] 770166). Newton Hall is a 17th century farmhouse where guests receive a warm welcome. A working farm with cattle, sheep and crops, four miles from Harrogate quietly situated away from the noise of traffic, with lovely views across open countryside, and half a mile from the charming village of Ripley with its beautiful castle. Ideal for touring the Yorkshire Dales. Family, twin and double rooms, all with washbasins and electric blankets. Bathroom, shower-room; lounge with colour TV; diningroom. Home produced milk, butter, preserves and free range eggs. Bed and Breakfast only; there are a number of places nearby where Evening Meals may be obtained. ETB registered. SAE, please, for terms and further details.

HARROGATE near. Mrs B. Sowray, Bowes Green Farm, Bishop Thornton, Near Harrogate HG3 3JX (Harrogate [0423] 770114). Working farm. Set in the midst of the Yorkshire Dales on a 300-acre mixed farm, this beautiful 17th century farmhouse offers all modern comforts to guests from Easter to end of October. Many beauty spots and places of historical interest in the vicinity such as Fountains Abbey, Ripley Castle and the market towns of Knaresborough and Ripon. Large sun garden. Two twin-bedded rooms and two double rooms all with washbasins; bathroom, toilet, shower; diningroom with separate tables and lounge with colour TV. Central heating. Best fresh farm produce served. Children from 14 years old welcome. Regret, no dogs. Car essential, parking space. Evening Dinner, Bed and Breakfast or Bed and Breakfast only. Mrs Sowray was awarded the Farm Holiday Guide Diploma for holiday accommodation of the highest standard. Terms on application with SAE, please. Also furnished cottage to let, sleeps five.

HARROGATE near. Mr and Mrs Peatfield, Fewston House, Fewston, Near Harrogate HG3 1SU (Blubberhouses [094-388] 637). Fewston House, standing in one acre of gardens, surrounded by extensive woodlands, welcomes guests all year round, and every effort has been made to ensure an enjoyable holiday. The house is warm and comfortable with a wood-burning fire in the sittingroom, colour TV. Mrs Peatfield speaks fluent French and some German. Diningroom where an excellent cuisine is served with varied menus using own vegetables, home made bread, marmalade, free range eggs. Choice of double, family bedrooms, with washbasins; bathroom, toilets. Central heating. Children welcome, babysitting, reduced rates. Pets by prior arrangement. Car essential — parking. Nearby are Swinsty and Fewston Reservoirs favoured for fly fishing. Idyllic location for restful holiday or touring Dales, moors; easily accessible to Harrogate, Bolton Abbey and numerous other places of interest. Evening Meal, Bed and Breakfast from £12.50; Bed and Breakfast from £8.50.

HARROGATE. Mrs J. Nelson, Bishop Keld Close Farm, Felbeck, Pateley Bridge, Harrogate HG3 5DR (Harrogate [0423] 711677). Working farm. Spacious stone-built bungalow in beautiful Nidderdale. Just off the Ripon/Pateley Bridge road (B6265) close to the Herriot country. Homely comfortable accommodation. Very central for touring Yorkshire Dales. Pateley Bridge two miles; Harrogate 14; Ripon nine. Museums, rocks, caves, fishing, bird watching, beautiful quiet walks. One family room with washbasin; one double with washbasin; one twin. Two bathrooms, shower or bath. Colour TV. Central heating. Choice of breakfast, tea and snack at bedtime. Everyone made most welcome at this working farm. Ample parking space. Details and terms for Bed and Breakfast only sent on request. Evening Meal available one mile away. SAE, please. Open Easter to end of October.

HARROGATE. Mrs Janice Kellett, Moorfield House, Bishop Thornton, Ripley, Near Harrogate HG3 3LE (Sawley [076586] 680). Moorfield House is an old but modernised house of character and charm, standing in its own beautiful garden surrounded by farmland, offering all the peace of the countryside plus the famous Fountains Abbey two miles away. An ideal house from which to tour the beautiful Dales, Pateley Bridge, Ripon, Knaresborough and Harrogate. Accommodation consists of one double, one twin-bedded and one family rooms, all with washbasins; bathroom and toilet; comfortable lounge with colour TV and gleaming brasses and log fires; diningroom with separate tables. Central heating. Children welcome at reduced rates if sharing parents' room. Car essential and parking provided. Open Easter to October. SAE, please, for terms for Evening Dinner, Bed and Breakfast. Highly recommended. Guests return each year.

HARROGATE. Mrs A. Wood, "Field House", Clint, Near Harrogate HG3 3DS (Harrogate [0423] 770638). "Field House" is situated five miles from Harrogate and a mile above the attractive village of Hampsthwaite commanding beautiful views over the Nidd Valley. Ideal for exploring the Dales and Moors with ancient abbeys, castles and country houses. The market towns of Skipton, Ripon and Knaresborough and the historic City of York all within easy reach. Accommodation is in one twin and one double room with private bathroom. Private sittingroom with TV, etc. Open all year. Car essential — private parking. Bed and Breakfast with Evening Meals readily available. A warm welcome guaranteed in a peaceful, friendly atmosphere. Telephone or SAE, please, for terms.

HARROGATE near. Mrs Mary Sowray, Gillmoor Farm, Bishop Thornton, Ripley, Near Harrogate (Sawley [076-586] 233). Working farm. This old oak beamed farmhouse quietly situated on a 150 acre dairy farm seven miles from Pateley Bridge, the heart of lovely Nidderdale, Knaresborough, Harrogate and Ripon. Three miles from Brimham Rocks and the famous Fountains Abbey. Ideal for touring Yorkshire Dales and Moors. Riding and pony trekking from farm. Diningroom; large, comfortable lounge with colour TV; two double, one family rooms (all with washbasins); bathroom, shower, toilets. Children welcome at reduced rates, babysitting offered. Menus of highest standard — guests return year after year. Open from Easter to October. Car essential — parking. Evening Dinner, Bed and Breakfast or Bed and Breakfast only. Small controlled dogs allowed. SAE, please, for terms. Also luxury furnished cottage to let.

HARROGATE near. Mrs Joyce Kellett, Hatton House Farm, Bishop Thornton, Near Harrogate HG3 3JA (Harrogate [0423] 770315). Working farm. A warm welcome and the best of hospitality awaits you at "Hatton House" Farm. Set in peaceful farming atmosphere the house is designed for the comfort and well-being of guests. Four double bedrooms, all with washbasins; electric blankets on all beds, bathroom with toilet, bath and shower. There is an attractive diningroom with separate tables, and a large comfortable lounge to relax in. Colour TV. Central heating and log fires. All home cooking, beautifully served and presented. Situated one mile from Bishop Thornton village on a farm-maintained road. A car is essential, parking space. Children from 12 years of age welcomed. Regret, no dogs. Terms for Evening Dinner, Bed and Breakfast on application with SAE, please. Open March to November. Highly recommended. Mrs Kellett has been awarded the Farm Holiday Guide Diploma for Holiday Accommodation of the Highest Standard.

HARROGATE near. Mrs G. A. King, "High Winsley Cottage", Burnt-Yates, Near Harrogate (Harrogate [0423] 770662). High Winsley Cottage is situated in the peaceful countryside on the edge of Nidderdale, half way between Harrogate, with its elegant shops, gardens and Conference Centre, and Pateley Bridge, pretty market town of Nidderdale. The accommodation is two twin bedrooms and one double room; two bathrooms; dining and sittingrooms; pleasant gardens and sun terrace. Excellent cuisine with plenty of fresh home grown garden produce; free range eggs and home baked bread. Every comfort assured and needs catered for. A car is essential, plenty of parking space. Open Easter until October. SAE, please, for brochure and terms for Bed, Breakfast and Evening Meal.

HARROGATE. Mrs E. Payne, North Pasture Farm, Brimham Rocks, Summerbridge, Harrogate HG3 4DW (Harrogate [0423] 711470). Working farm. North Pasture Farm offers farmhouse Bed, Breakfast and Evening Dinner. Guests receive a warm welcome, and best of hospitality, home cooking, well prepared and served. The farm is a 135-acre dairy farm next to Brimham Rocks, four miles from Fountains Abbey and nine miles Harrogate. The house is of historic interest with datestone 1657 and the front part dates back to the early 1400's. John Wesley preached in the room which is now the lounge. There is colour TV, H&C in all rooms, and central heating. Sorry, no dogs. SAE, please.

BOARD **North Yorkshire** 317

HARROGATE. Anne and Bob Joyner, Roan Guest House, 90 King's Road, Harrogate HG1 5JX (Harrogate [0423] 503087). AA — RAC listed. "Bonza!", "Exceptional value!", "Good food!", "Quiet!", "Never had it so good!" — just a few testimonials visitors have written in our book on leaving. Situated in a tree-lined avenue in a central position close to all amenities. Conference and Exhibition Centre two minutes' walk. Valley Gardens, town and local swimming baths close by. Our house is centrally heated, with tea/coffee making facilities in all rooms, hot and cold throughout. Some rooms en suite, home cooking (no Microwave here). Four-course dinner, plus tea or coffee upon request. Ideal centre for touring Dales/Herriot country.

HARROGATE near. Mrs Jo Austin, Hookstone House Farm, Low Lane, Darley, Near Harrogate HG3 2QN (Harrogate [0423] 780572). A 300-year-old cottage farmhouse, 10 miles west of Harrogate, in picturesque Nidderdale Valley. Ideally situated for touring the many local attractions — Herriot countryside to the north and Bronte country to the south, golf, walking or fishing (on local reservoir). A traditional Yorkshire welcome, comfortable bedrooms (washbasin in double bedrooms); separate guest sittingroom with colour TV — central heating and log fires await all our guests. Fresh farm and local produce used in home-cooked fare. Special diets can be arranged. Bed and Breakfast or Dinner, Bed and Breakfast. Open all year. Please send for further details.

HARROGATE. Mrs H. M. Phillips, Shutt Nook Farm, Chain Bar Lane, Killinghall, Harrogate HG3 2BS (Harrogate [0423] 67562). Working farm. Shutt Nook Farm is a mixed, 150-acre family run farm, ideally situated for touring the Yorkshire Dales. The spa town of Harrogate is just three miles away, and Ripley Castle, Fountains Abbey and the ancient City of York are all within easy reach. There are one double, one twin and two family bedrooms, two with washbasins; bathroom, toilet; sittingroom, diningroom. Children welcome, cot, high chair and babysitting. Sorry, no pets. Open May to September. A car is recommended and there is parking. Evening Dinner, Bed and Breakfast; Bed and Breakfast. Reduced rates for children.

HELMSLEY. Mrs C. S. Robinson, Valley View Farm, Old Byland, Helmsley YO6 5LG (Bilsdale [043-96] 221). Old Byland is a very small quiet village with beautiful views. Valley View Farm is family run and has pigs, sheep, beef cattle, one cow and two acres of arable land. It is our aim to make our guests' holidays very enjoyable with home cooked food and some home produce. Three double bedrooms; sittingroom; diningroom; two bathrooms. Open April to October with central heating. Children are welcome with cot, high chair and babysitting. Car essential, parking. The village is set on the edge of the North Yorkshire Moors close to Sutton Bank, Helmsley, Rievaulx Abbey York 30 miles, Scarborough 35 miles. Good walking country. Full Board from £84; Evening Dinner, Bed and Breakfast from £12 per night; Evening Meal, Bed and Breakfast from £10 per night. Bed and Breakfast from £7.50.

HELMSLEY. Mrs J. Milburn, Barn Close Farm, Rievaulx, Helmsley (Bilsdale [043-96] 321). Working farm. Farming family offer homely accommodation on mixed farm in beautiful surroundings near Rievaulx Abbey. Ideal for touring, pony trekking, walking. Home-made bread, own produced meat, poultry, free range eggs — in fact Mrs Milburn's excellent cooking was praised in "Daily Telegraph". Modern home — two double bedrooms with washbasins, one family room; TV lounge; diningroom. Children welcome, babysitting. Sorry, no pets. Open all year round, open log fires. Car essential — parking. Reduced rates for children under 10 sharing parents' room. Evening Meal, Bed and Breakfast or Bed and Breakfast only. Terms and brochure sent on receipt of SAE.

HELMSLEY near. Mrs Anna Taylor, Carr House, Ampleforth, Near Helmsley YO6 4ED (Coxwold [03476] 526). Working farm. Carr House — 16th century farmhouse in peaceful, beautiful 'Herriot' countryside, half an hour from York. Recommended by *Sunday Observer* "a fresh-air fiend's dream — good food, good walking and a warm welcome". Tour the Moors, Dales, National Parks, York coast, nearby famous Abbeys, Castles and Stately Homes. Carr House provides a comfortable, relaxing homely base. Two double, one twin-bedded rooms. Two bedrooms, en-suite, one with four-poster bed. ETB and YHTB approved. Enjoy a full Yorkshire farmhouse Breakfast with home-made butter and preserves, fresh eggs. Bed and Breakfast £7, with Evening Meal £12 daily — £49 to £75 weekly. Sorry, no pets or children under seven. Open all year; closed Christmas, New Year. SAE, please, for brochure. Farm Holiday Bureau Member.

INGLEBY GREENHOW. Mrs M. H. Bloom, Manor House Farm, Ingleby Greenhow, Near Great Ayton TS9 6RB (Great Ayton [0642] 722384). Working farm. NORTH YORKS MOORS NATIONAL PARK. Outstandingly delightful accommodation of the highest standard in picturesque farmhouse on working farm of 164-acres in idyllic parkland, surrounded by hills and forests. Ideal for relaxing, walking and touring. All modern comforts, excellent food, fine wines, log fires. All rooms have central heating. Separate entrances, lounge and diningroom for guests. There are two twin-bedded rooms, one double room and a family room, with two delightful bathrooms and three toilets. Brochure on request. Half Board from £18.50.

INGLETON. Mrs Mollie Bell, "Langber Country Guest House", Ingleton (Via Carnforth) LA6 3DT (Ingleton [0468] 41587). Working farm. Ingleton, "Beauty Spot of the North", in the National Parks area. Renowned for waterfalls, glens, underground caves, magnificent scenery and Ingleboro' mountain — 2,373 ft. An excellent centre for touring Dales, lakes and coast. Golf, fishing, tennis, swimming and bowls in vicinity. Pony-trekking a few miles distant. Guests are warmly welcomed to "Langber", a detached country house, having beautiful views with seven acres of gardens, terrace and paddock. Sheep, lambs, goats and a pony. There are three family, two double and a single bedroom — all with washbasins and razor points. Bathroom, shower and three toilets. Sunny, comfortable lounge and separate diningroom. Central heating and fitted carpets. Babysitting offered. Open all year except Christmas. Fire certificate granted. AA and RAC listed. SAE for Evening Dinner, Bed and Breakfast or Bed and Breakfast only. Reductions for children under 13 sharing parents' room. Self-catering cottage also available.

INGLETON. Mrs J. Sharp, Ivescar Farm, Chapel-le-Dale, Ingleton, Via Carnforth LA6 3AX (Ingleton [0468] 41424). Working farm. This delightful and peaceful hill farm is situated on the southerly facing slopes of Yorkshire's highest mountain, Whernside, sheltered to the north by a beautifully wooded limestone scar with views of the Ribblehead viaduct on the Settle to Carlisle railway. Ingleborough Caves and White Scar Caverns both within few miles of Ivescar, also Ingleton Glens with magnificent waterfalls. Two typical Dales inns 10 minutes' drive. Within an hour of sea, Lake District, James Herriot country. One double and one family bedrooms; bathroom, toilet; sittingroom, diningroom. Children welcome, cot, high chair, babysitting provided. Pets accepted. Car essential — ample parking. Open March to November for Evening Meal, Bed and Breakfast; Bed and Breakfast. Reductions for children.

KIRKBYMOORSIDE near. Mrs Robinson, Eller House Farm, Farndale, Near Kirkbymoorside YO6 6LA (Kirkbymoorside [0751] 23223). Working farm. Friendly accommodation on a 150 acre stock farm. There are two double and one family bedrooms, a sitting room and a dining room serving good food. Children are welcome and there is a cot and a high chair. Babysitting can be arranged. No pets. Car essential. Kirkbymoorside is nine miles away and there is easy access to the moors, the coast and York. Ideal for walking. Open April to October. Evening Meal, Bed and Breakfast from £11 per day (£75 weekly); Bed and Breakfast from £7. Reduced rates for children. SAE or phone for full details.

KIRKBYMOORSIDE. Mrs M. P. Featherstone, Keysbeck Farm, Farndale, Kirkbymoorside YO6 6UZ (Kirkbymoorside [0751] 23221). Working farm. Friendly accommodation on a 200-acre farm. There are one double, one single or twin bedrooms; a sittingroom; diningroom with open log fire where good food is served. Car essential, parking. Open all year round. Children are welcome and there is babysitting available. Sorry no pets. Evening Meal, Bed and Breakfast £10; Bed and Breakfast from £7. Reduced rates for children and weekly lets.

LEYBURN. Mrs Ann Margaret Tunstall, Robin's Garth, Harmby, Leyburn DL8 5PD (Wensleydale [0969] 23495). "Robin's Garth" is situated in the quiet rural village of Harmby, close to the market town of Leyburn in the heart of Wensleydale. Aysgarth Falls, Middleham and Bolton Castles and many more places of interest within easy reach. There are three double bedrooms, all with washbasins; bathroom, showerroom, two toilets; diningroom and large comfortable lounge in which to relax; tea and scones served in the evening (price inclusive). Cot, high chair and babysitting for children; reduced rates for those under 12 years. Open fires and central heating. Pets permitted. Car not essential, but needed to make the best of holiday; parking. Open from April 1st to November 1st. Bed, Breakfast and Evening Meal provided. SAE for terms and brochure please.

LEYBURN. Mrs H. B. Dinsdale, Lowgill Farm, Aysgarth, Leyburn DL8 3AL (Aysgarth [09693] 275). Working farm. Lowgill Farm is set in the heart of Dales country, the rooms are large and airy with beautiful views over the Wensleydale countryside. A perfect base for touring, one mile from Aysgarth, nine miles from the market town of Hawes; nearby are Aysgarth Falls and passes to Swaledale and Wharfdale. Accommodation on this 100-year-old farm comprises two double and one family bedrooms; two bathrooms, two toilets; sitting and diningroom. Children are welcome. Well behaved dogs are permitted. A car is preferable here and parking provided. Open March to November for Bed and Breakfast only from £6.50. In Spring the lambs are a special attraction and the feeding and milking of cattle is of interest to visitors all year. Some self-catering accommodation also available. Guests enjoy a quiet and peaceful holiday in this delightful countryside.

LEYBURN. Mrs H. M. Richardson, "Sunnyridge," Argill Farm, Harmby, Leyburn DL8 5HQ (Wensleydale [0969] 22478). "Sunnyridge" is a spacious, modern stone-built bungalow, with attractive gardens, situated on a smallholding of 12 acres. In an outstanding position, the bungalow enjoys magnificent views from every room. In the midst of "James Herriot" country, there are many places of interest nearby — the old market towns of Richmond, Hawes and Leyburn, historical Middleham, Jervaulx and Castle Bolton are but a few for the holidaymakers to enjoy. Open from Easter to October, guests are accommodated in one double and one family bedroom; bathroom/toilet; sittingroom, diningroom. Children welcome, cot, high chair and babysitting available. Pets accepted by arrangement. Central heating. Car preferable, parking. Evening Meal, Bed and Breakfast from £10; Bed and Breakfast from £6. Reductions for children.

LEYBURN. Mrs P. M. Keeble, Hammer Farm, East Witton, Leyburn (Bedale [0677] 60306). Working farm. Hammer is a typical Lower Dales farm of 250 acres. Pedigree and commercial cattle. Sheep and rare breeds of poultry. Centrally situated for Dales, Herriot country, York, Ripon. Within walking distance Jervaulx Abbey, Middleham Castle. No more than five adults or one family accommodated. Guests' bathroom. TV. Garage. 'Phone. All guests free to participate on farm. Excellent walking in Dales, moors, woods and rivers. Fishing. Six racecourses within one hour. Pub 10 minutes by car, 30 minutes walking. Top quality food — free range eggs. A really traditional farm life. Bed and Breakfast from £9.50 (Dinner £4.50); six nights full Board £80. Children £65. Open May 1st – October 1st.

LEYBURN near. Mr and Mrs B. & S. Fletcher, Ivydene Guest House, West Witton, Near Leyburn DL8 4LP (Wensleydale [0969] 22785). Situated between Leyburn and Aysgarth on the A684, in the heart of Herriot country, Ivydene Country Guest House, a 17th century listed building, celebrating its 300th anniversary in 1986 (the owners are not quite as old!). Sheila and Barrie Fletcher offer you hospitality second to none with food to match. Ideally situated for touring Dales and Lakes. Six comfortable bedrooms, with scenic views (four-poster bed available), hot and cold, shaver point and tea-making facilities. TV lounge and separate diningroom. Licensed. Ample parking. Bed, Breakfast, Evening Meal. Daily and weekly terms. SAE for brochure or telephone the above.

MALHAMDALE. Mrs E. Bristow, Tudor Guest House, Bell Busk, Skipton BD23 4DT (Airton [07293] 301). Commended in AA 1984, BTA 1985. Built in 1849 this family-run licensed home is beautifully situated in the country, with one acre of gardens and a magnificent view over hills and streams. It is near to the Lakes, Bronte Country, Harrogate and York. Enjoyable walks can be taken around Malham, Bolton Abbey, Grassington etc. There is a lounge with colour television, games room with snooker, table tennis, darts, etc.; central heating and electric blankets. Ample parking. Also morning tea facilities. Bed and Breakfast £7.75. Four-course Evening Meal and coffee £4.75. Open all year. Also available, self-contained flat on first floor of guest house, plus cottages to sleep four or six. Sorry, no pets. SAE for brochure.

MALTON. Mrs J. Sturdy, Eden House Farm, Old Malton, Malton YO17 0RT (Malton [0653] 2093). Working farm. This is a comfortable farmhouse on 280-acre arable farm. There are two double and one family rooms; two bathrooms and two toilets; diningroom and a private sittingroom with TV and radio. Children welcome, cot, high chair and babysitting. Pets are allowed. Open from January to December with solid fuel heating. There is a pleasant garden for the use of guests. A car is essential and there is parking. Ideal centre for York, Coast and North Yorkshire Moors. Bed and Breakfast from £8.00 per night. Reduced rates for children.

MALTON. Bob and Marion Shaw, Abbotts Farm, Ryton, Malton YO17 0SA (Malton [0653] 4970). A comfortable family farmhouse at the end of a lane and surrounded by fields and trees. Ideal for country lovers wishing to relax in natural surroundings. Near old market town of Malton and central for North Yorkshire. Within easy reach of the coast, Moors, Castle Howard and Herriot Country as well as towns and villages such as Pickering (terminus of North Yorkshire Moors Railway), Whitby, Scarborough, Kirkbymoorside, Helmsley and the beautiful and historic city of York, with interest for everyone — Minster, City Walls, Castle Museum, Railway Museum and more. Abbotts Farm has lovely open views and a large sun garden. Accommodation is in two large double bedded rooms, with single and bunk beds for children, and a single bedroom. Central heating, open fires in cool weather in pleasant dining/sittingroom. Hearty Yorkshire Breakfast served. Tea, coffee and biscuits served any time, small charge. Special facilities for families — reduced terms for children (any age) sharing adults' room. Babysitting. Children's teas at reasonable price. Babies under one year free, cot, high chair etc. Lunches and Evening Meals available at many good local inns and hotels. Bed and Breakfast from £8.50 (no VAT). E.T.B. Registered. Sorry, no pets. (Also available, self-catering cottage on farm).

MALTON. Mrs G. M. Cass, Grange Farm, Birdsall, Malton YO17 9NP (North Grimston [094-46] 217). Pleasantly situated farmhouse, central for North Yorkshire Moors, Wolds' coast, York, old market towns, Castle Howard and other stately homes and abbeys. Good food, home cooking and baking. Three double bedrooms, bathroom, toilet, own sittingroom, TV. Children welcome; reduced rates. Sorry, no pets. Solid fuel and electric heating. Car essential — parking. Open from March to October for Evening Meal, Bed and Breakfast or Bed and Breakfast only. SAE, please, or telephone for terms.

MALTON. Mrs S. K. Scott, White House Farm, Barthorpe, Malton YO17 9RW (Bishop Wilton [075-96] 206). Working farm. This farmhouse is situated on dairy farm, quiet and not near main road. Good area for bird watching or walking. Large garden where visitors may walk or sit. Convenient for York or coast and North York Moors. Guests are treated as family and accommodated in one double bedroom with one single available sometimes; two bathrooms, two toilets; sittingroom; diningroom. Log fires when needed. Children welcome; cot and reduced rates. Dogs permitted. Car is essential and there is lots of parking. Open from April to October; mid-week bookings accepted. Bed and Breakfast. Terms on application. Evening Meal optional.

MALTON. Mrs Susan M. Hodsman, Kennels Farm, Eddlethorpe, Malton YO17 9QT (Burythorpe [065-385] 213). Working farm. Relax and sample Yorkshire hospitality in this spacious family farmhouse on a 270-acre mixed farm situated in quiet countryside at the foot of the Yorkshire Wolds. Approximately three miles south west of the market town of Malton, it is an ideal centre for North Yorks Moors, Wolds' coast, old market towns, Castle Howard and other stately homes and abbeys, and the historic walled city of York. Bed and a good Yorkshire breakfast provided from April to October. One double, two family bedrooms; bathroom, toilet; sittingroom, diningroom. Central heating. Children welcome, cot, high chair and babysitting can be provided by arrangement. Sorry, no pets. Car essential — parking. Bed and Breakfast from £7. Evening drinks included. Reductions for children. Mid-week bookings accepted.

MALTON. Mrs S. Jefferson, The Quarry Guest House, Amotherby, Malton YO17 0TG (Malton [0653] 3623). Peacefully situated in its own three acres of grounds with ample parking. Every comfort assured with four double, one single and one family rooms, all with washbasins; central heating; reading lights; shaver points, tea making facilities; two bathrooms and toilets. Lounge with colour TV, diningroom with table licence. Home cooking with garden produce. Children welcome with cot, high chair and babysitting available. Ideal touring centre close to Castle Howard, zoo and abbeys. Within easy reach of East Coast, York and Moors. Pony trekking, fishing, golf nearby. Evening Dinner, Bed and Breakfast from £12.50; Bed and Breakfast from £8. Reduced rates for children sharing parents' room. Brochure sent on receipt of SAE.

MIDDLEHAM. Mrs Susan Constantine, Sundial House, Middleham, Leyburn DL8 4QG (Wensleydale [0969] 22615). Built around 1750, Sundial House is a family home with the emphasis on comfortable accommodation and excellent home-made food, and located just 50 yards from Middleham Castle. There is one family room and one double bedroom; bathroom with shower, three toilets; lounge with TV; diningroom; walled garden; central heating. Central for the Dales, York, Fountains Abbey, Jervaulx and Richmond. Children over 12 welcome (at reduced rates). Sorry, no pets. Car essential, parking space. Open all the year for Dinner, Bed and Breakfast or Bed and Breakfast only. No VAT. 'Phone or send for our entertaining brochure.

PATELEY BRIDGE. Mrs Joan Simmons, Moorhouse Cottage, Pateley Bridge, Harrogate HG3 5JF (Harrogate [0423] 711123). Restored 18th century farmhouse set in quiet picturesque location with open views over Nidderdale. Central for the beautiful Yorkshire Dales, numerous Market Towns, Abbeys, Castles and historic York. For longer excursions North Yorkshire Moors, coast and the Lake District are all within reach. The house is furnished in keeping with its age with many original features, including a range with open fire in the guests' lounge. One family, one double, one single room. Two bathrooms. Good varied wholefood cooking with home grown produce. Vegetarian meals on request. Colour TV. Children welcome, cot available. No pets. Car advisable. Ample parking. Evening Meal, Bed and Breakfast £10.50. Bed and Breakfast £7.50.

PATELEY BRIDGE (near Harrogate). Mrs K. Whiting, Greengarth, Greenwood Road, Pateley Bridge, Near Harrogate HG3 5LR (Harrogate [0423] 711-688). Modern spacious bungalow situated in Pateley Bridge in the beautiful Nidderdale Valley known as "Little Switzerland". Many beauty spots and places of historical interest such as Fountains Abbey, Ripley Castle, Brimham Rocks and caves, spa town of Harrogate, 15 miles, with lovely Vally Gardens. Local trout fishing and riverside walks. One family room, one double room, one with twin beds; washbasins, razor points. Gas central heating; shower — bathroom; three toilets; combined dining/sittingroom. Colour TV. Ample parking space. Bed and Breakfast £7.50; Bed, Breakfast and Evening Meal £12. Reduced rates for children. Sorry, no pets.

PICKERING. Mrs H. D. Dale, Bell End Farm, Rosedale, Pickering YO18 8RE (Lastingham [075-15] 431). Working farm. Home cooking and farmhouse cooking guaranteed at this farmhouse with holiday accommodation available from January to mid-December. Two double and three family bedrooms; bathroom; two toilets; two sittingrooms; two diningrooms. Cot and high chair. Pets permitted. Car essential; ample parking facilities. Close by a main road and central for visiting seaside, York and other historical places. Evening Dinner/Meal, Bed and Breakfast from £10; Bed and Breakfast from £7. Reduced rates for children. SAE, please, for further details.

BOARD **North Yorkshire** **321**

PICKERING. Mrs W. Wood, Brickyard Farm, Marton Lane, Pickering YO18 8LW [0751] 72880). **Working farm.** The farm is one mile from the market town of Pickering, and stands at the side of a quiet country lane. Easy travelling distance for North Yorkshire Moors, Moors Railway, Forest Drives, East Coast, many historical buildings and York. The house has two double bedrooms, one family room, one single room with washbasins and tea-making facilities. Bathroom, separate toilet. Diningroom and sittingroom. Good farmhouse cooking. Ample parking — car essential. Reduced rates for children if sharing parents' room. Open all year round. Evening Meal, Bed and Breakfast from £14.50. Send for brochure. SAE, please.

PICKERING. Mr & Mrs T. D. Cowley, Medd's Farm House, Rosedale West, Pickering YO18 8SQ (Lastingham [07515] 358). Working farm. Don and Eileen Cowley welcome you to this old, now centrally heated farmhouse set within the beautiful North Yorkshire Moors National Park. It is remote and ideal for an away from it all holiday. Superb walking and riding country. One family and four double bedrooms, all with washbasins; bathroom, two showers, toilets; sittingroom; diningroom. Cot, high chair, babysitting and reduced rates for children. Pets under strict supervision only. Residents' bar. Open from March to October for Evening Meal, Bed and Breakfast from £12.50 or £82 per week; Bed and Breakfast from £8.50. Take the road to Thorgill from Rosedale Abbey; house is half-mile beyond Thorgill.

PICKERING. Stan and Hilary Langton, Vivers Mill, Mill Lane, Pickering YO18 8DJ (Pickering [0751] 73640). VIVERS MILL is an ancient watermill situated in peaceful surroundings, quarter mile south of Pickering Market Place on Pickering Beck. The Mill is a listed building, constructed of stone, brick and pantiles, part possibly dates back to the 13th century. The Mill, with its characteristic beamed ceilings is being renovated whilst maintaining most of the machinery, including the waterwheel and millstones. Pickering is an excellent centre from which to explore the North York Moors National Park, Ryedale and the spectacular Heritage Coast. It is the terminal station for the preserved North Yorkshire Moors railway and is only 26 miles from historic York. Visitors are assured of a friendly welcome with nourishing, traditional food. Large lounge and nine comfortable bedrooms, most with WC, shower or bath. Tea/coffee making facilities. Bed and Breakfast from £70 per person per week. Reductions for family room.

PICKERING. Mrs Jenny Bentley, Square Farm, Lockton, Pickering YO18 7QB (Pickering [0751] 60233). Working farm. Square Farm is situated in the North Yorkshire Moors National Park within easy reach of many noted beauty spots. The coast, York, Scarborough and Whitby are a short drive away. There are many stately homes and other places of historic interest within easy reach. A working steam railway operates from Pickering. Guests are assured of a warm welcome with good home cooking using fresh produce. There are two family bedrooms and one double room, with washbasins; two bathrooms and toilets; sitting and diningroom. Car essential, ample parking. Pets are not allowed in the house. Terms on request for Bed and Breakfast. Evening Meal optional.

PICKERING. Mr and Mrs J. and M. B. Bean, The Moorlands Country House Hotel, Levisham, Pickering YO18 7NL (Pickering [0751] 60229). Guests are assured of a warm Yorkshire welcome at Moorlands, a charming detached house, with Residential Licence, set in four acres of secluded gardens with wonderful views. Situated within the National Park there is good access to many beauty spots and places of interest. The coast, York, Scarborough, Whitby are a short drive away. Eight bedrooms, with H/C handbasins, ensure that all requirements can be met; bathrooms with showers and toilets. Guests' diningroom/lounge and separate TV room. Good home cooking using fresh produce, mostly home grown. Car essential — ample parking. Children welcome. Full Board; Evening Dinner/Meal, Bed and Breakfast from £13.50; Bed and Breakfast £9. Reductions for children. Open all year. No smoking or pets in house.

PICKERING. Mrs M. A. Angelow, Moordale House, Dale Head, Rosedale Abbey, Pickering YO18 8RH (Lastingham [075-15] 219). Situated amidst North Yorkshire Moors and open farmland, this family run guest house offers a warm friendly welcome and good home cooking enhanced by home grown vegetables and local produce. This is an excellent area for horse riding, walking or touring. One double, one single and one family bedrooms, all with washbasins; bathroom, shower room, three toilets. Cot, high chair and babysitting for children. Pets by arrangement only. A car is essential to make the most of your holiday and parking is available. Evening Meal, Bed and Breakfast from £10.50 per person per night; Bed and Breakfast from £7.50. Weekly terms available.

North Yorkshire   **BOARD**

PICKERING. Mrs E. Bowes, "Ravenfield," 16 The Mount, Thornton Dale, Pickering YO18 7TF (Pickering [0751] 74616). Thornton Dale, one of the prettiest villages in Yorkshire, with stream flowing through centre. Ravenfield situated in a very quiet part of village, ideal for quiet night's sleep or touring coast, moors, forest, Scarborough, Whitby, Flamingo Park Zoo, Castle Howard, North Yorks Moor Railway, all near. One double, one family rooms with hot and cold water, one single bunk bedded room; bathroom, toilet; sittingroom, diningroom. Central heating. Pets permitted. Own keys provided. Visitors' book reads "Excellent," "Real Yorkshire hospitality," "Wonderful holiday, will come again." Good Yorkshire breakfast served. Four restaurants, three pubs in village for meals; many more good eating places near. Children made very welcome, cot and babysitting offered. Also reduced rates. Open all year for Bed and Breakfast from £7 (including light supper). Parking provided. SAE, please, for early reply.

PICKERING. Miss H. P. Flinton, "Hurrell," Hurrell Lane, High Street, Thornton Dale, Pickering YO18 7QR (Pickering [0751] 74245). "Hurrell" is a large detached stone-built house standing in its own grounds of three-quarters of an acre, with splendid views of the North Yorkshire Wolds. Quietly situated on the eastern side of the village 50 yards from the main road and within easy reach of the North Yorkshire Moors, coast, many pleasant country walks and numerous places of historic interest, riding, golf, and the North Yorkshire Moors Railway. Home cooking, superior accommodation and a warm welcome. Three double bedrooms, two with washbasins; bathroom, toilet; sittingroom; diningroom. Car essential — parking. Evening Meal, Bed and Breakfast or Bed and Breakfast only. SAE for terms.

PICKERING near. Mrs M. Green, "Easthill", Thornton-Dale, Near Pickering YO18 7LP (Pickering [0751] 74561). Large detached family house, set in two-and-a-half acres of ground and private woodland with tennis court, in one of the most picturesque villages in Yorkshire. Situated on edge of North Yorks Moors and National Park, ideal centre for touring moors, coast and forest, Scarborough, Whitby, Flamingo Park Zoo, Castle Howard within easy reach. Pleasant country walks; riding, golf available. Open all year, a friendly atmosphere avails, good home cooking ensured. Five double, one single, two family bedrooms (with washbasins, two en-suite). Ample bathroom/toilet facilities; sittingroom, diningroom. Central heating. Children welcome, cot, high chair, babysitting, reduced rates. Car advisable — parking. Evening Meal, Bed and Breakfast £11.75; Bed and Breakfast £8. Brochure on request.

PICKERING near. Mrs J. Avison, Chester Villa, Thornton Dale, Near Pickering YO18 7RB (Pickering [0751] 74513). Chester Villa is a small farm one mile from the village, fishing is available in the stream flowing behind the house. Riding school half a mile away. Convenient for visits to the Yorkshire Moors, East Coast, historical houses and Flamingo Park Zoo. All bedrooms have washbasins (one twin, two double, one family rooms); bathroom, two toilets; sittingroom, colour TV; diningroom. Cot. Plenty of parking space. Reductions for children sharing bedrooms. Open from Easter to November. Price on application. SAE, please, for reply.

RAVENSCAR. Mrs Joan Greenfield, Smuggler's Rock Country Guest House, Ravenscar YO13 0ER (Scarborough [0723] 870044). Smugglers Rock is a stone built Georgian farmhouse twixt Whitby and Scarborough with panoramic views over the surrounding North Yorkshire National Park and sea. The farmhouse has a homely and relaxed atmosphere. Home cooking is served in our old world diningroom. There is open fire and colour TV in our beautiful open beamed lounge. Private facilities are available and we have our own car park. AA and Tourist Board listed. This is an ideal country holiday area with the many picturesque seaside villages on the heritage coast and beautiful Dales just a few miles inland. Please send for brochure.

RICHMOND. Mrs Dorothy Hodgson, Hackney House, Reeth, Richmond DL11 6TW (Reeth [074-884] 302). Hackney House is a very comfortable guest house, situated in beautiful surroundings in the Yorkshire Dales National Park, and only 10 miles west of the historical market town of Richmond. Three double, two single and two family bedrooms, some with washbasins; two bathrooms and toilets; sittingroom and diningroom. Children welcome at reduced rates. Open all year. A car is essential, ample parking. Reeth itself lies at the confluence of the rivers Arkle Beck and Swale, and is the ideal centre for all local beauty spots and moorland walks. Evening Dinner, Bed and Breakfast from £11. Fire Certificate held. Parties of up to 16 catered for (rambling clubs, etc.). SAE please, for further details.

RICHMOND. Mrs Yvonne Woodward, 1 Orchard Lane, Reeth, Richmond (Richmond [0748] 84627). The village of Reeth is set in the heart of Swaledale and the house is on its outskirts, with open views of the surrounding hills. Nearest market town is Leyburn, seven miles. Buses to Richmond (12 miles). Small, family-run guest house with three double bedrooms, all with washbasins; bathroom, two toilets; sittingroom; diningroom. Children welcome at reduced rates. Sorry, no pets. Oil-fired central heating. Open all year round. Car essential for touring this area; parking. Much of historical interest and lots to see and do. Evening Dinner, Bed and Breakfast from £11 per day; Bed and Breakfast from £7.50 per day.

PLEASE SEND A STAMPED ADDRESSED ENVELOPE WITH ENQUIRIES

RICHMOND. Mrs M. Baylis, Dalton Hall, Newsham, Richmond DC11 7RG (Teesdale [0833] 21420). Dalton Hall was built in the 14th century as a fortified house. It has been extensively modernised but still retains its original character. Part of the house was used by the BBC for the filmimg of James Herriot's series "All Creatures Great and Small". The house is set in its own grounds with delightful views yet only five minutes' drive from A66 and seven miles from Scotch Corner. Charming country inn within walking distance which serves excellent bar snacks. One family bedroom with washbasin; bathroom, toilet; diningroom. Car essential, parking. Bed and Breakfast from £7.50. Reduced rates for children. Babysitting. Pets welcome. Open all year.

RICHMOND. Mrs Margaret F. Turnbull, Washton Springs Farm, Richmond DL11 7JS (Richmond [0748] 2884). Working farm. An attractive Georgian farmhouse on mixed farm set high in the hills three miles from Richmond. Featured on ITV's "Wish You Were Here" holiday programme, the rooms are spacious and furnished to a high standard having received the Guest Accommodation Good Room Award. Unusual bay windows overlook lawns which slope down to a sparkling stream. This is a busy family farm, north west of Richmond, gateway to the Dales and glorious Herriot country. Enjoy good farmhouse cooking with home produced meat, local fruit and vegetables. Guest bedrooms have central heating, colour TV, facilities for tea/coffee making; six bedrooms in the stable courtyard have en-suite bathrooms or showers. Table licence. Many interesting places and picturesque villages to explore. Golf, riding, fishing available. Evening Dinner, Bed and Breakfast from £14; Bed and Breakfast £8.50. Reductions for children if sharing. Sorry, no pets. Brochure on request.

RIPON. Mrs Veronica Priem, Riga, Primrose Drive, Ripon HG4 1EY (Ripon [0765] 2611). Riga is a lovely house in peaceful, garden setting, within few minutes' walk of historic Ripon's ancient Cathedral, Market Square, excellent shops and restaurants. Ideal touring centre for the rich green valleys and dramatic limestone scenery of Yorkshire's beautiful Dales and Herriot country, stately homes, castles, caves and National Trust properties, including nearby magnificent ruins of Fountains Abbey in Studley Royal Deer Park. Two spacious twin-bedded rooms with washbasins and tea-making facilities, sunny single room, all with attractive outlook. Private parking. Excellent traditional or wholefood breakfasts with home-made jams and marmalades. Home-baked wholewheat bread always available. Non smokers. Open March to end of October.

ROSEDALE. Mrs Linda Sugars, "Sevenford House", Thorgill, Rosedale Abbey, Pickering (Lastingham [075-15] 283). "Sevenford House" — a beautiful country house, with four acres of lovely gardens, set in the heart of the North Yorkshire Moors National Park, enjoys fine panoramic views over Rosedale Abbey Village and the surrounding Dale and Moorland. An ideal centre for touring forests and moors, the picturesque coast, ruined abbeys and Roman roads, and visiting market towns, the Lyke Wake Walk, Castle Howard and other stately homes, Flamingo Park Zoo, steam railways. In the locality — two charming pubs, restaurant, 18 and nine-hole golf courses, painting studies on the Moors; riding (BHS approved courses); pony trekking at Cropton and Rosedale. Guests are comfortably accommodated, all year round, in two double, two family bedrooms, with washbasins; bathroom, two toilets; sittingroom, diningroom. Children welcome, cot, high chair, babysitting facilities. Car essential — parking. Bed and Breakfast from £8 per night. Children under 12 years half price.

ROSEDALE. Mrs B. Brayshaw, Low Bell End Farm, Rosedale, Pickering YO18 8RE (Lastingham [075-15] 451). Working farm. The farm is situated in the North Yorkshire Moors National Park about 15 miles from the nearest seaside resort of Whitby. Scarborough and Bridlington are within easy reach, also York, Pickering and Helmsley, all places of historic interest. The farm, a 173 acre dairy and sheep farm, is one mile from the village of Rosedale Abbey and there are many lovely walks to be taken in the area. A car is essential with ample parking space. Sorry, no pets. One double, one bunk-bedded, one family rooms; bathroom and toilet; combined sitting/diningroom with colour TV. Children welcome at reduced rates. Cot, high chair, babysitting available. Central heating and open fires. Open May to September. Evening Dinner, Bed and Breakfast or Bed and Breakfast. Terms on request.

SCARBOROUGH near. Mrs Sheila Anderson, Basin Howe Farm, Sawdon, Near Scarborough YO13 9EB (Scarborough [0723] 85631). Basin Howe Farm is a smallholding rather than a large farm and accommodates only one family at a time. An ideal place for children, away from main roads but only 20 minutes' drive from Scarborough, about an hour from York. Interesting walks, forest two minutes away. The smallholding has a herd of goats of all ages and the owners are breeding English goats in preference to the Swiss breeds. Open from April to October, guests are accommodated in one double-bedded room, smaller room with two single beds; bathroom; large sitting/diningroom. Children welcome, cot, high chair and babysitting available. Pets accepted but must sleep outside. Car essential, parking. Evening Meal, Bed and Breakfast from £7.50; Bed and Breakfast from £5. Special diets catered for. Reductions for children.

SCARBOROUGH near. Mrs Gillian Watson, Grange Farm, Staintondale, Near Scarborough YO13 0EN (Scarborough [0723] 870203). **Working farm.** A recently modernised, comfortable stone-built Georgian house halfway between Whitby and Scarborough. Cleveland Way nearby for walking and pony trekking within reach. Not a roadside farm, so peace and quiet guaranteed. Children welcome. They will enjoy the calves and sheep and a very friendly black Labrador dog who loves going for walks. The food is excellent and home-produced and a light supper snack included in terms. One double and two family bedrooms, all with washbasins; bathroom with shower and separate toilet; sittingroom and separate diningroom. Central heating. Open from Easter to October for Evening Dinner, Bed and Breakfast or Bed and Breakfast. Reduced rates for children. Dogs welcome at small charge. SAE for terms.

PLANE TREE FARM COTTAGE, STAINTONDALE, SCARBOROUGH, YORKSHIRE

Mrs Marjorie Edmondson offers only good food and garden produce (when possible) at this old farm cottage on the 108 acre farm in Stainton Dale. This mixed farm grows corn and potatoes and breeds sheep and pigs. Staintondale is situated between Scarborough and Whitby, very scenic countryside and an area excellent for walking and touring.

The cottage, which has open sea views, has one double and one family room, lounge, dining room, bathroom, separate toilet and central heating. Children welcome, also pets kept on lead (a small charge is made for pets). Also six berth caravan.

Well recommended. SAE please for terms, Bed and Breakfast or Dinner, Bed and Breakfast, to *Mrs M. A. Edmondson. Telephone Scarborough (0723) 870796.*

SCARBOROUGH near. Mrs June Simpson, Hazel Hall Farm, Snainton, Near Scarborough YO13 9PN (Scarborough [0723] 85413). **Working farm.** Stonebuilt in 1700. Hazel Hall is situated on the hillside with panoramic views of the Vale of Pickering. Forest drives north to purple moors, sea to the east and ancient York to the west. Although a working farm with its accompanying tractors and animals, the orchard, garden and swimming pool attract relaxation. Hazel Hall has been discreetly modernised for comfort, without spoiling its old world charm. Fire certificate held. Each family room has its own shower and WC. Mrs Simpson personally prepares the farmhouse cooking and helps her guests to plan their daily itinerary. Evening Meal, Bed and Breakfast from £80 per week.

SCARBOROUGH. Mrs R. Glaves, "Milestone" Bungalow, 15 Racecourse Road, East Ayton, Scarborough YO13 9HP (Scarborough [0723] 862507). A large, comfortable bungalow with all amenities on the outskirts of this lovely village, which has two high-class restaurants, two pubs serving good bar meals, and the entrance to beautiful Forde Valley, the Forest Drive, and only four miles from Scarborough and all its attractions. Two double bedrooms (one double-bedded with vanity unit and one twin-bedded); bathroom, separate toilet; sitting/diningroom. Bed and Breakfast from £7.50 per person per day. Car parking. Open April to October.

SCARBOROUGH. Mr and Mrs S. Maw, Wayside, Snainton, Scarborough YO13 9AF (Scarborough [0723] 85264). A very warm welcome awaits every guest to "Wayside". Plenty of excellent food with fresh vegetables and home produce. Central for lovely drives over North Yorkshire Moors and Wolds. Forest drives and walks nearby. Whitby, Scarborough, Filey and Bridlington all within easy reach. A day in York is a must. Three double bedrooms (two on ground floor), all with washbasins. Bathroom, two toilets (on ground floor); sittingroom; separate tables and personal attention in diningroom. Children over seven welcome. Fire Certificate held. Tea-making facilities in all rooms. Member of English Tourist Board. SAE for terms. Bed and Breakfast. Evening Dinner served until end of June.

SCARBOROUGH. Mrs Elisabeth Blackborrow, Manor Farm, Sawdon, Near Scarborough YO13 9DY (Scarborough [0723] 85391). **Working farm, join in.** Welcome to Manor Farm, a mixed stock farm where comfort, relaxation and plenty of home prepared food (including home-made bread) are assured. Accommodation in the large comfortable stone built farmhouse is in two double rooms, one with washbasin; a pleasant sittingroom for guests to come and go as they please, and diningroom. The East Coast, Yorkshire Moors, North Yorkshire Steam Railway, forestry for drives and walks are just some of the interesting places within easy reach. Bed and Breakfast including Morning Tea and Light Supper from £6. Evening Meal by arrangement. Open February to November.

SCARBOROUGH. Mrs Jane M. Hodgson, Studley House, Ebberston, Scarborough YO13 9NR (Scarborough [0723] 85285). Working farm. Studley House is a 19th-century farmhouse which offers comfortable accommodation in a quiet, restful situation. It is close to the North Yorkshire Moors, the Dales, the Forests and the sea. Ebberston is central for access to market towns. General store opposite the farm. Gardens may be used for relaxation at any time. Guests of all ages welcome. Bunks for children. Shower. TV and tea-making facilities in lounge. Central heating. There is accommodation for six guests in a friendly atmosphere. Local fishing available. Ample parking space. Open April to November. Winter breaks by arrangement.

SCARBOROUGH. Mrs Gwen Owen, Teydale Farm Guest House, Whitby Road, Cloughton, Scarborough YO13 0DZ (Scarborough [0723] 870886 or 870213). Pleasantly situated with an unspoilt rural outlook to a National Park, this farmhouse is midway between Scarborough and Whitby, and within easy reach of both Yorkshire Moors and the sea. Two family bedrooms with washbasins and teasmades; diningroom with separate tables; colour TV lounge; bathroom and all modern conveniences. Car essential and ample parking. Children welcome, cot, high chair and babysitting. Good food, soup, turkey, roast beef and Yorkshire Pudding, lamb, fish, and a good variety of sweets. Scarborough with all its holiday amenities, sea two miles. Open Easter to October. Sorry, no pets. SAE, please, for terms for Bed and Breakfast only. Light supper snacks served along with the evening tea.

SCARBOROUGH. Mrs D. M. Medd, Hilford House, Crossgates, Scarborough YO12 4JU (Scarborough [0723] 862262). Detached country guest house, quietly situated in own grounds adjoining A64. Near Scarborough, but handy for touring all coast and countryside of North Yorkshire. Three double, one single and one family bedrooms all with H&C and central heating. Bathroom, two toilets; diningroom with separate tables and guests' lounge with colour TV. Cot, high chair and babysitting available. Full fire certificate held. Open all year round. Personal supervision ensures complete satisfaction of guests. Own home grown fruit and vegetables served in season, also fresh Scarborough cod and local meats. Private car parking. Bed and Breakfast from £6.50; Evening Dinner, Bed and Breakfast from £10. Reductions for children sharing. Member of English Tourist Board and Yorkshire/Humberside.

SCARBOROUGH. Mrs K. M. Warters, Roundhills Guest House, 80 Limestone Road, Burniston, Scarborough YO13 0DG (Scarborough [0723] 870276). Set in one-and-a-half acres. Excellent centre for touring coast, Dales, moors and forestry. Magnificent scenery. Panoramic views from all rooms of either moors, Dales or sea. Fishing, swimming, golf, tennis and horse riding nearby. Personal attention; Bed and Breakfast only. Accommodation in double, twin, single and family bedrooms, and all are newly furnished in modern style with washbasins, shaver points and heating. Lounge/diningroom. Colour TV, sun lounge, bathroom, four toilets. Large car park. Three miles North Bay. Open all year except Christmas. SAE, please, for terms. No VAT to pay.

SCARBOROUGH. Mrs K. Major, The Melbourne Hotel, 57 Moorland Road, Scarborough YO12 7RD (0723-371172). The Melbourne is a small friendly hotel near Peasholme Park, the beach, swimming pools and the cricket ground. Accommodation comprises three double, one single and two family bedrooms, all with washbasins. Bathroom and toilet. Sittingroom and diningroom. Children are welcome and the hotel has cot, high chair and babysitting is provided. Pets are permitted. Central heating allows the hotel to stay open from January to December and mid-week bookings are accepted. A car is not essential, but would always prove an asset when based in this particularly attractive part of the country. Terms from £8.50 per day Bed, Breakfast and Evening Dinner. Reductions for children sharing.

NORTH YORKSHIRE – RICH IN TOURIST ATTRACTIONS!

Dales, moors, castles, abbeys, cathedrals – you name it and you're almost sure to find it in North Yorkshire. Leading attractions include Castle Howard, the moorlands walks at Goathland, the Waterfalls at Falling Foss, Skipton, Richmond, Wensleydale, Bridestones Moor, Ripon Cathedral, Whitby, Settle and, of course, York itself.

SETTLE. Mrs B. Nolan, Liverpool House Guest House, Chapel Square, Settle BD24 9HR (Settle [072-92] 2247). Liverpool House is an 18th century house in a quiet, but central, part of Settle, and is comfortably furnished to suit a house over 200 years old. The house is personally run by Brenda and Philip Nolan and has a Residential Licence and Fire Certificate. Brenda's menus include traditional Yorkshire dishes, but please book dinner in advance. There's a choice of full English or light Breakfast. All eight bedrooms have hot and cold, central heating, razor points and tea/coffee making facilities. The Gatehouse lounge has colour TV, and the Terrace room is for relaxing with drinks. There is a private car park. Sorry, no pets. Please phone or send SAE for a brochure.

SETTLE. Mrs L. J. Gorst, Hollin Hall Farm, Rathmell, Settle BD24 0AJ (Settle [072-92] 2523). Working farm. Ideal for touring Dales and other Yorkshire beauty spots, Hollin Hall is a sheep and beef cattle farm of 108 acres in a quiet position overlooking the Ribble Valley two and a half miles from Settle. Within easy reach of the Trough of Bowland and the Lake District. Homely and friendly atmosphere and guests are made welcome from Easter to October. Two double-bedded rooms with washbasins, one twin-bedded room. Bathroom, toilet. Sittingroom; diningroom with separate tables where good home cooking is served. Children welcome at reduced rates. Sorry, no pets. Car essential, ample parking. Garden. SAE, please, for terms for Evening Dinner, Bed and Breakfast or Bed and Breakfast.

SETTLE near. Mr & Mrs Robert Jones, The Rowe House, Horton-in-Ribblesdale, Near Settle BD24 0HT (Horton-in-Ribblesdale [072-96] 212). The Rowe House is a lovely 18th-century house in an acre of land in beautiful, peaceful surroundings at the foot of Penyghent and near the historic Settle/Carlisle Railway. The area is renowned for its natural beauty, pot-holes, botany and ornithology. We are licensed and offer our guests very good home cooking with our own produce, whenever available with free range eggs from our own poultry. All bedrooms have washbasins and there is a comfortable lounge with open fire and separate, pleasant diningroom. We are open all year except Christmas and New Year.

SKIPTON. Mr and Mrs R. T. Shelmerdine, Eshton Grange, Gargrave, Skipton BD23 3QE (Gargrave [075-678] 383). Working farm, join in. Modernised 18th century farmhouse offers comfortable accommodation especially suitable for keen young walkers with pot-holing, pony trekking in the vicinity. This Scheduled Building on a 20-acre stock farm and Shetland pony stud is situated in the popular Yorkshire Dales and National Park. Skipton nearby and two miles from the interesting old village of Gargrave. Many holiday amenities in the area. The house comprises five double bedrooms with TV; one with bunk beds, also a bathroom exclusively for guests' use. Sittingroom. Three toilets; diningroom. Bed and Breakfast from £8. Evening Meal extra. Open all year. Children welcome, high chair and babysitting by arrangement. Car — parking. Further details on request. SAE, please.

SKIPTON near. Mrs J. Harrison, Crook House Farm, Bracewell, Near Skipton (02005-205). Situated on A59 between Gisburn and Skipton, we offer guests every home comfort and excellent food. Lounge/diningroom with TV; family or double bedroom; bathroom with constant hot water. We are situated in beautiful countryside near Bronte country, Lakes and Dales. Pennine Way close by. Babysitting available. Reduced rates for children. Ample car parking space. Evening Meal and Bed and Breakfast or Bed and Breakfast only. SAE, please, for further details.

SKIPTON near. Paul and Jean Dolan, Park Bottom Guest House, Litton, Near Skipton (Arncliffe [075-677] 235). Peace and tranquillity prevail in the picturesque hamlet of Litton, and guests are assured of a warm and friendly welcome at Park Bottom, a new centrally heated house. Ideal touring centre and excellent walking countryside. Comfortable accommodation in three double bedrooms with en suite shower, washbasin and WC. One family room with en suite shower, washbasin and WC and two rooms with washbasins. There is a log fire in the main lounge and a separate TV lounge which guests are welcome to use during the day. Diningroom. Residential licence. Dogs not allowed in house but welcome if staying in car. Car essential — ample parking. Bed, Breakfast and Evening Dinner from £14; Bed and Breakfast from £12. Small activity groups welcomed. Further details on request.

THIRSK. Mrs P. M. Stevens, Skipton Hill Farm, Thirlby, Thirsk YO7 2DQ (Thirsk [0845] 597286). Working farm. Skipton Hill Farm is a fully modernised traditional farmhouse, nestling under the cliffs of the glorious Hambleton Hills with panoramic views over the Vale of York to the Yorkshire Dales. We welcome you with comfort, peace and lots of good food. Ideal walking, touring, riding, gliding and hang-gliding (off Sutton Bank). Golf at Thirsk, plus five other courses in the locality, and racing at York, Ripon, Thirsk, Catterick, Wetherby and Sedgefield. We are well away from busy roads, but within easy reach of York, Harrogate and the Coast. Thirsk five miles. Good local pubs serving bar meals. Children and well-behaved pets welcome. Open all year.

THIRSK. Mrs K. M. Hope, High House Farm, Cold Kirby, Thirsk YO7 2HA (Thirsk [0845] 597557). Working farm. High House is a family dairy and stock rearing farm standing on the Hambleton Hills in a most glorious stretch of the North Yorks Moors National Park, with panoramic views of the Vale of York. An ideal quiet holiday location with plenty of freedom for walking and exploring the Herriot country. Coast 35 miles. Visit Kilburn (two miles) to see the White Horse carved into the hillside, also Robert Thompson's "mouse" oak furniture. Other places of interest within easy reach include Coxwold, Shandy Hall (birthplace of Laurence Sterne), and Newbrough Priory with beautiful lake and gardens. Thirsk and Helmsley eight miles, York 27 miles. Riding and Gliding just 15 minutes away. Accommodating one family at a time, personal attention is assured. Room with two double beds, room with double and single bed; bathroom, toilet; comfortable sittingroom, diningroom. Car essential — parking. Open all year. Terms on request.

THIRSK. Mrs Legge, The Old Rectory, Scawton, Thirsk YO7 2HG (Thirsk [0845] 597294). Rectory with character set in lovely grounds with superb view over Rievaulx Terraces and situated in North Yorkshire Moors National Park. Fully modernised facilities: double and single rooms, each with own bathroom; sittingroom; diningroom; full central heating. Sittingroom has open fire and colour TV. Superb old village with 16th-century pub and 12th-century church. Pub has good home-cooked bar meals including evenings. Lovely walks from rectory. Close to historic Rievaulx Abbey, Helmsley and Yorkshire Moors. Children over 10 welcome. Pets allowed in outside kennels. Car essential, parking. Fishing by arrangement. Open all year except Christmas. Bed and Breakfast from £8.

THIRSK. Skipton Hall Private Hotel, Skipton-on-Swale, Thirsk YO7 4SB (Thirsk [0845] 567457). The Hall is a Georgian House in its own grounds, where a warm welcome awaits you. All bedrooms have H&C and Tea/Coffee making facilities; TV lounge. All tastefully furnished with many antiques. It is the ideal touring centre for the Yorkshire Dales and Moors, Historic York, Harrogate and several Stately Homes. Skipton Hall is situated in the small village of Skipton-on-Swale on the A61 between Thirsk and Ripon and only four miles from the A1 and A19. It is peaceful and relaxing with lovely views of the River Swale. There are five double, one single and one family bedrooms, all with washbasins; three bathrooms, four toilets; sittingroom; diningroom. Open all year round with coal and electric fires. Children are welcome and there is cot, high chair and babysitting. Pets are allowed. Car essential, parking. Reduced rates for children. Evening Dinner, Bed and Breakfast from £16; Bed and Breakfast from £11. We will be delighted to send you our brochure. Fire Certificate. Residential Licence. Access/Visa accepted.

THIRSK. Mrs Joan Knowles, Manor Farm, Little Thirkleby, Thirsk YO7 2BA (Thirsk [0845] 401216). Working farm. Manor Farm is a beautifully situated stock and arable farm in a peaceful hamlet in Herriot country. Views of White Horse and Hambleton Hills; one mile A19; 21 miles York; five miles Thirsk. AA and Les Routiers approved. Ideally situated for walking and touring Moors, Coast and Dales. Gliding, golf, fishing, riding, swimming locally. Guests welcome all year in this comfortably furnished farmhouse with central heating and open fires. Two double (additional child's bed) and one single room. Electric blankets. Bathroom, two WCs. Lounge with TV. Tea/coffee making facilities. Bed and Breakfast. Excellent local restaurants for evening meals. Brochure on request. Also self-catering farm cottages.

THIRSK. Mrs Helen G. Proudley, Doxford House, Front Street, Sowerby, Thirsk YO7 1JP (0845) 23238. A warm welcome awaits guests at this handsome Georgian house which overlooks the greens in Sowerby, a delightful village one mile south of Thirsk (James Herriot's TV series). Centrally situated for touring the North York Moors and the Dales National Park; within easy reach of York, Harrogate and the East Coast; places of interest include Coxwold, Shandy Hall, Newbrough Priory with beautiful lake and gardens. Ideal walking and riding countryside. Golf at Thirsk. Accommodation has full central heating, with hot and cold in all bedrooms (one en suite); one ground floor bedroom suitable for the disabled. Bathrooms, toilets. Residents' lounge with colour TV, diningroom, separate games room with snooker, table tennis and darts. Large garden with a paddock and friendly animals. Children and pets welcome. Cot, high chair, babysitting available. Open all year. Evening Dinner, Bed and Breakfast from £12; Bed and Breakfast from £8. Reductions for children.

WHITBY. Mrs Susan Evans, Honey Ridge, 100 Ruswarp Lane, Whitby YO21 1ND (Whitby [0947] 605965). Honey Ridge has panoramic views including Esk Valley and Abbey; one-and-a-half miles from beaches and historic town, surrounded by moors and picturesque villages: walking, riding, fishing, boating, steam railway etc. Close to bus and train, private parking. Family room and double room — duvets, washbasins, shaver points and TV. Guests' bath/shower room, central heating. Terrace, lawns and sun lounge. Lounge/diningroom (illustrated) has colour TV, log fire. Children welcome — babysitting by arrangement. Four-course Evening Dinner and Breakfast. Choice of menu. Early morning tea. Flexible times, diets catered for. Garden produce including free range eggs, honey and dairy goat products. Snacks available. 'Phone for brochure and rates (week half-board £80).

WHITBY. Mr & Mrs Pattinson, Farm Hotel, Boggle Hole Road, Near Robin Hood's Bay, Whitby YO22 4QQ [0947] 880 308). Working farm. Small, family run hotel with small restaurant having a large a la carte menu. Dance on Saturdays; open to the public. Pool and games room. 135-acre farm which is mixed but mainly arable, hence only seasonal participation for holidaymakers. Ideal centre for touring North Yorkshire. Beach approximately two miles down country road. Pony trekking nearby. Hotel has two bars with large light meals menu. Open Easter to Christmas Eve. Children half price if sharing. Bed and Breakfast from £8. Apply to Mr & Mrs Pattinson for further details.

WHITBY. Mrs K. Mortimer, New House Farm, Glaisdale, Whitby YO21 2QA (Whitby [0947] 87208). Working farm. The farm is a family farm, the present owners being the third generation. It consists of 118 acres of hill land. Over the years many new buildings have been erected but most of the original ones remain. The farm is situated in the Dale of Glaisdale and lies midway along the bottom of the Dale itself. Stock kept are mostly beef type cattle and a breeding flock of 365 Swaledale ewes, although there are the usual sheep dogs and farm cats. Hens are kept by my children, so breakfast eggs are always fresh. Summertime finds us still feeding the occasional pet lamb so bottle feeders are welcome. At the front of the house is a large lawn where visitors may sit and admire the magnificent views. For the children the grass may be a source of outdoor entertainments. The accommodation is clean and friendly taking up to six/seven people. Full English Breakfast and substantial supper are the meals available. Lots of walking. Whitby 12 miles. Steam trains at Gromont. Bed and Breakfast from £7.50; Supper, Bed and Breakfast from £9.25. Reduced rates for children.

WHITBY. Mrs Avril Mortimer, Hollins Farm, Glaisdale, Whitby YO21 2PZ (Whitby [0947] 87516). Hollins Farm is a small-holding ten miles from the historical coastal town of Whitby, surrounded by picturesque countryside and moorland with lovely walks. Places of interest include Moors Steam Railway, Pickering Market Town with its medieval castle and the famous City of York. Many scenic villages such as Hutton-le-Hole with its extensive folk museum. The accommodation comprises one large family or double room (sleeps four/five) with washbasin also twin-bedded room. Bathroom, sittingroom, sun lounge. Cot and babysitting. Parking — car essential. Bed and Breakfast with optional Evening Meal. Home produced meat, vegetables and dairy products. Open March–October. Phone or send SAE for terms.

WHITBY. Mrs M. G. Wilkinson, High Whins, Tranmire, Ugthorpe, Whitby YO21 2BW [0947] 840546). A warm, family atmosphere greets guests in this large stone-built farmhouse situated in beautiful little valley. Surrounded by moorland it is only six miles from beach and 10 miles from the historical town of Whitby. Pony trekking, fishing, golf available locally. This is a lovely part of North Yorkshire with delightful old villages, beautiful valleys and moorland with many interesting things for the holidaymaker to see and do. Excellent beaches and good walking country. Visitors can sample Real Ale in a local inn — only two miles. Accommodation in two double, one family rooms, all with hot and cold water; bathroom, two toilets; own sittingroom and diningroom. Open all year with central heating. Car essential — parking. Details and terms sent on request.

WHITBY. Mrs V. M. Lee, Firtree, Beckhole, Goathland, Whitby YO22 5LE (Whitby [0947] 86288). This 17th century stone-built house has mullioned windows and overlooks the Green of the picturesque hamlet of Beckhole in a sheltered valley one mile from Goathland village. The property has been listed as a building of historical and architectural interest. The area is part of the North Yorkshire Moors National Park and is an area of outstanding natural beauty. Two double, one twin-bedded rooms, all with washbasins; bathroom, toilet; combined dining/sittingroom. Children over 10 years welcome. Sorry, no pets. Car essential, parking available. Open April to September for Evening Dinner, Bed and Breakfast or Bed and Breakfast. SAE, for details.

PLEASE SEND A STAMPED ADDRESSED ENVELOPE WITH ENQUIRIES

WHITBY. Mrs B. A. Howard, Cote Bank Farm, Aislaby, Whitby YO21 1UG (Whitby [0947] 85314). **Working farm.** Situated in the National Park and looking south over the Esk Valley, in a peaceful, secluded setting, bordered by 150-acres of woodland, this 100-acre dairy farm offers Yorkshire hospitality and good cooking, using mainly local produce. Varied menu provided. The 18th century house is surrounded by gardens and has mullioned windows and spacious rooms. Large sittingroom, colour TV, books, games; separate diningroom; bathroom, toilets. Two double/family rooms with washbasins, also one single room. Pets not allowed in house (kennels locally). Car essential, parking. Open all year except Christmas. Bed and Breakfast, Evening Meal optional. Bedtime drink included. SAE, please, for terms.

WHITBY. Mrs Marion N. Cockrem, Dale End Farm, Green End, Goathland, Whitby YO22 5LJ (Whitby [0947] 85371). Working farm. Comfortable 17th century stone built farmhouse on a moorland farm of 135-acres with sheep, cows, pigs, ponies, poultry, etc. Situated in the North Yorkshire Moors National Park, making an ideal location for walking, touring and fishing. One double and two family bedrooms, with washbasins, divan beds, bedside lights. The guests' lounge is furnished with antiques, horse brasses, oak beams and open inglenook fireplace; TV; background central heating; diningroom, separate tables, serving generous portions of home-produced food with variety in menus. Pets allowed. Children welcome, cot and babysitting. Children's playground. Mrs Cockrem offers hospitality with every home comfort and is open all year for Bed, Breakfast and Evening Meal or just Bed and Breakfast. SAE, please.

WHITBY near. Mrs P. Beale, Ryedale House, Coach Road, Sleights, Near Whitby YO22 5EQ (Whitby [0947] 810534). Whitby — three miles. Friendly guest house of charm and character at the foot of the moors; magnificent scenery, picturesque villages, harbours, sandy beaches and North York Moors Railway nearby. Double, twin, family and single rooms on first floor with hot and cold, heating (according to season). Lounge with colour TV, selection of guide books; light, airy diningroom (separate tables) with beautiful views over large garden and Esk Valley. Good home cooking with choice and variety; all local produce. Children over two years welcome. Flexible mealtimes; choice of evening and light meals, packed lunches. Regret no pets. Adults: Bed and Breakfast from £7.50. Evening Dinner £3.95. Weekly reductions. Open February to November. Registered English Tourist Board. Established 10 years.

WHITBY near. Mrs Marjorie Pearson, "Seadale," Runswick Bay, Near Whitby TS13 5HR (Whitby [0947] 840440). A small friendly guest house where good food, comfort and cleanliness are assured. Situated in a picturesque seaside village in the country within the National Park area. Surrounded by lovely walks and an excellent centre for touring all places of interest. "Seadale" is open from April to October, and has all modern conveniences including spring interior mattresses in all beds. Colour TV lounge. Separate tables in diningroom and good home cooking. Car parking space. There are two bedrooms — one double and one twin-bedded. Short stays welcome. Sorry, no pets. Reasonable terms (no VAT) for Bed and Breakfast. Evening Meal available, if required. SAE, please.

WHITBY near. Mrs Elaine Macgregor, Rock Head Farm, Glaisdale, Near Whitby YO21 2PZ (Whitby [0947] 87355). Working farm. Highly recommended by all guests, renovated Yorkshire farmhouse dating from 1692, with wash-stands, what-nots and peat stoves. Friendly and comfortable atmosphere. Good home cooking with generous helpings. This working farm makes an ideal centre for touring the North Yorks Moors, picturesque coast and countryside, North Yorkshire Steam Railway. Many lovely walks, and the historical coastal town of Whitby within easy reach. Two double rooms, two twin-bedded rooms (one with handbasin), one single room; two bathrooms/toilets; sittingroom and diningroom. Car essential — parking. Evening Dinner, Bed and Breakfast from £12; Bed and Breakfast from £7. Light supper/bedtime drink included. Farm reared beef! Open all year.

WHITBY. Mrs Jean Lister, Browside Farm, Glaisdale, Whitby YO21 2PZ (Whitby [0947] 87228). Working farm. This 70-acre dairy and mixed farm, 10 miles from the town of Whitby and other coastal villages. Ideal for walking on North Yorkshire Moors; four miles from North Yorkshire Moors Railway. Local beauty spots are Egton Bridge, Rosedale, Hutton-le-Hole. Home grown produce whenever possible. One double, one family bedrooms, one with washbasin; bathroom, toilet; sittingroom, diningroom. TV. Cot, high chair, babysitting. No pets, please. Car essential — parking. Open from Easter to September for Evening Meal, Bed and Breakfast or Bed and Breakfast only. Large garden. Personal service. SAE, please, for terms.

WHITBY. Mrs M. H. Heald, Halfway House Farm, Eskdaleside, Sleights, Whitby YO22 5ES (Whitby [0947] 810189). Set in the beautiful Esk Valley and enjoying panoramic views, this 18th century stone farmhouse combines traditional beamed ceilings and open fires with modern facilities and full central heating. Whitby and the coast are only five miles away and the North Yorkshire Moors Steam Railway one and a half miles. The lay-out of the accommodation lends itself especially to use by one family at a time. The twin-bedded room is let to families with older children who share the bathroom, which is en-suite with the family room. The farm comprises goats, pigs, bees as well as a flock of sheep. Anyone interested can join in and help. A car is advisable, nearest bus one mile; rail link one and a half miles. Cot, high chair and babysitting. Pets by arrangement. Open April to October. Evening Meal, Bed and Breakfast from £11; Bed and Breakfast from £7.50, reduced rates for children.

WHITBY. Mrs Doreen Lister, Yew Grange, Glaisdale, Whitby YO21 2PZ (Whitby [0947] 87352). Working farm. Guests are welcome from Easter to October on this 110 acre mixed farm in an ideal location for walking or touring. Whitby 10 miles, and there are many local beauty spots and places of interest within easy reach including North York Moors Steam Railway, Folk Museum at Hutton-le-Hole and the famous City of York. Home produced vegetables and meat are served when available and visitors receive personal and friendly attention. Morning tea and bedtime drink included. One double, one single and one twin bedrooms; bathroom and toilet; sittingroom with TV, diningroom. Children welcome, cot, high chair and babysitting available. Sorry, no pets. Car essential, ample parking. Phone or SAE, please, for terms. Reductions for children.

North Yorkshire BOARD

YORK. Mrs W. Howe, Belmire Farm, Whitwell-on-the-Hill, York YO6 7JT (Whitwell-on-the-Hill [065-381] 385). Belmire Farm is situated 300 yards from the A64 York to Scarborough road, overlooking the River Derwent. The countryside is beautiful and rich in places of interest, stately homes and castles, including Castle Howard three miles. The ancient city of York is only 12 miles from Belmire; Scarborough, Whitby and Bridlington 28 miles distant. The Yorkshire Dales and Moors are easily accessible. Excellent meals are served using largely home cooking. Guests welcome from April to November. Two double and one single bedrooms; bathroom and two toilets; sittingroom and diningroom. Children over 12 years welcome. Sorry, no pets. A car is essential here and parking space available. Evening Dinner, Bed and Breakfast or Bed and Breakfast only. SAE, please, for terms.

YORK. Mr Keith Jackman, The Dairy Guest House, 3 Scarcroft Road, York YO2 1ND (York [0904] 39367). The Dairy is a tastefully renovated Victorian house, offering comfortable accommodation at a reasonable price. Situated only 200 yards south of the Medieval City Walls, it is within easy walking distance of the city centre. Decorations and furnishings are in the style of "Habitat — Sandersons — Laura Ashley — Dolly Mixtures", with an emphasis on pine and plants. All bedrooms have washbasins, shaver points and continental quilts; one has a private bathroom, and one a private shower room. There is a lounge with colour TV and tea/coffee making facilities; full central heating and a lovely enclosed courtyard. Breakfast choice ranges from Traditional British to Wholefood/Vegetarian. Highly recommended. Bed and Breakfast £9.

YORK. Mrs C. W. Fell, The Hall Country Guest House, Slingsby, York YO6 7AL (Hovingham [065-382] 375). The Hall is a Regency house of character set in five acres of delightful grounds, with croquet lawn and stream, situated in a 'real' English village with a ruined castle. A genuine Yorkshire welcome awaits every guest, many of whom return year after year. Excellent varied cuisine with fresh produce. Ideally situated for visiting York, the North Yorks Moors, coast and also stately homes such as Castle Howard (three miles). Five double rooms, two family and one single. Some with showers. One en suite. A car is essential. Ample parking. Brochure available. Open Easter to October.

YORK. Mrs K. Alexander, Calm Cottage, Warthill, York (York [0904] 488092). Georgian Country House in two acres of grounds in small village with duck pond and village pub, five miles from the city of York. House is situated down a private drive behind the village church, and is open at the back to farmland. One double and one family bedrooms. Beams in sittingroom and bathroom. TV. Good home country cooking served in diningroom. Central heating and open fires. Children welcome — babysitting and reduced rates. No pets, please. Parking, though car not essential. Open from March to October for Evening Dinner, Bed and Breakfast or Bed and Breakfast only. SAE, please, or telephone for terms.

YORK. Mrs M. J. Robinson, The Grange, Flaxton, York YO6 7RL (Flaxton Moor [090-486] 219). Working farm. Open all year for BED AND BREAKFAST. This is a family farm situated in 130 acres of delightful countryside outside the picturesque village of Flaxton, one mile from A64 between York and Malton, midway between LONDON AND EDINBURGH/GLASGOW. A modernised farmhouse set in its own gardens, separate from the farm buildings. Single, double and family rooms all with washbasins; electric blankets, razor points, plus facilities for making tea. Bath/shower can be taken anytime. Colour TV. Ample free parking. Meals available locally. Children half price if sharing parents' room. Overseas visitors welcome. Flemish spoken. SAE, please, or phone between 5 pm and 8 pm.

YORK. Mrs J. Fowler, Holtby Grange, Holtby, York YO3 9XQ (York [0904] 489933). Working farm. Holtby Grange is a 90-acre arable farm set in peaceful countryside and guests are welcome to walk around. York easily reached, being only five miles away. The two main roads (A64 and A166) provide easy access to coast, moors and historical places of interest. A hearty Yorkshire breakfast is served in the separate diningroom. Other facilities are a spacious lounge with open fire and colour TV; one family, one twin and one double bedrooms, all with washbasins, shaver sockets, electric blankets and teasmades. Bathroom with electric shower, two toilets. Large attractive gardens. Pets allowed, but not in house. Cot, high chair and reduced rates for children under 14 sharing parents' room. Babysitting if required. Car essential — parking. Open from April to October. 10% reduction on a full week's booking of Bed and Breakfast and Evening Meal (adults only), or 5% discount on Bed and Breakfast only. Bed, Breakfast and Evening Meal from £12 per person; Bed and Breakfast from £8. Send stamp only or telephone for further details. Registered with English Tourist Board and Yorkshire and Humberside Tourist Board.

YORK & YORKSHIRE
Explore city & country from the centre of it all –
THE MANOR COUNTRY GUEST HOUSE
Acaster Malbis, York YO2 1UL

In delightful country 4½ miles from the city. Six acres of grounds and woodland almost adjoining the River Ouse. A friendly, homely house. All guest bedrooms have central heating, hand-basins with hot and cold water, electric razor points, electric blankets, and bedside or bedhead lights. Some rooms have showers. One ground-floor bedroom (with shower). Lounge has open coal fire and TV. **NO SERVICE CHARGE.** Centrally placed in the county and mid-way between London and Edinburgh/Glasgow.

The Manor from across the lake

Join us if you like it really quiet!

Single bedrooms, twin-bedded rooms, double-bedded rooms, rooms with double bed and single bed, and four-or-five person family rooms. **Stairlifts to both floors.** Also one four-berth caravan in secluded woodland clearing. CHILDREN WELCOMED. Please book as early as you can, particularly for popular school holiday periods. Give details, if possible, of requirements, period, dates, etc. Detailed and illustrated brochure with maps, from:

Miss F. H. PEACOCK,
Tel. York (0904) 706723
(9 am to 9 pm)

Reduced charges November to Easter

Please be sure to send a stamp or a 6" x 9" stamped and addressed envelope with your enquiry. Enquiries from abroad, please send **Four** International Reply Coupons (obtainable from Post Offices).

YORK. Mrs Jackie Cundall, Wellgarth House, Wetherby Road, Rufforth, York YO2 3QB (Rufforth [0904-83] 592). Wellgarth House is a new detached house, set back off the road (B1224) on the very edge of the village, approximately four miles from York. All rooms with washbasins, television and central heating. Comfortable lounge with colour television; separate diningroom. Keys are provided. Reduced rates for children. Bed and Breakfast from £7.50. Ideal touring base and convenient for those travelling from North to South. A car is essential and there is ample parking. Two local inns are within walking distance, both providing food. Personal attention is assured at all times. SAE, please, for brochure. Registered with the English Tourist Board. Also furnished town house at York.

YORK. Miss Wendy Peacock, The Manor Country Guest House, Acaster Malbis, York YO2 1UL (York [0904] 706723 — 9 am to 9 pm). The Manor is situated by the River Ouse in six acres of delightful grounds and woodland, only 12 minutes from York by car. Packed lunches supplied. All meals, both hot and cold are "help yourself," with resultant variety of dishes. Reservations made for room and full buffet breakfast, with optional cold buffet evening meal at 6 pm. Facilities in bedrooms for making tea and coffee. Children welcome at reductions according to age, when sharing parents' room. Large car park. Open all year except Christmas. All bedrooms have washbasins, central heating, electric blankets and razor points. Some rooms with showers. Showers in all bathrooms. Stairlifts to both floors. One ground floor bedroom. Also two double bedrooms at "Oak Tree", 200 yards from the Manor, with similar full amenities. No service charges and no "extras". Send 9½" × 6" SAE, or stamp for illustrated brochure; please state requirements and dates if possible. Enquiries from abroad please send four International Reply Coupons. Reduced charges from beginning of November to Thursday before Easter.

YORK. Mrs Kathleen Jackson, Townend Farm, Great-Ouseburn, York YO5 9RG (Green Hammerton [0901] 30200). Working farm. Comfortable, well furnished farmhouse on a working 380-acre farm in a beautiful, unspoilt village half-way between York and Harrogate; within easy reach of Yorkshire Dales, Moors and Herriot country. Full English Breakfast is prepared with fresh farm produce. Two double bedrooms (with washbasins), one single bedroom. Tea/coffee making facilities in all rooms, plus electric blankets, shaver points. Bathroom, three toilets (bath/shower may be taken anytime). Sittingroom with colour TV; diningroom. Colourful, secluded garden for guests' use at rear of house. Children welcome at reduced rates; cot, babysitting available. Pets accepted. Car essential — ample parking. Open all year. Bed and Breakfast from £8.

YORK. Mrs P. Stockhill, Marina Guest House, Naburn, York YO14 4RW (York [0904] 27365). Off A19, superior accommodation overlooking York Marina and the River Ouse. Guests are offered a pleasant stay in country surroundings, yet only two and a half miles from the city of York. Six double, one single and two family bedrooms, all tastefully furnished. Hot and cold water in each, and some rooms have private shower. Two bathrooms, four toilets; three sittingrooms and a diningroom. Children welcome at reduced rates. No pets permitted. Central heating. Open from January to December. To start the day a Full English Breakfast is served. Dinner is available on request. Private car park. Car essential. Brochure available on request.

YORK near. Mr and Mrs J. and J. Richardson, School House, Coxwold, Near York YO6 4AD (Coxwold [03476] 356). Once an old coaching house, School House is now a private house set in the beautiful village of Coxwold in the heart of "James Herriot's Yorkshire". Surrounded by sweeping moorland, picturesque dales, ancient market towns, Abbeys, Castles and Cathedrals. Coxwold is an excellent centre for visitors of all ages. School House, under personal supervision of Mr and Mrs Richardson, is noted for excellent traditional Yorkshire cooking. Your hosts make every provision for a happy and relaxed holiday. Four double bedrooms, tea-making facilities and TVs. Two bathrooms, four toilets; three diningrooms. Children welcome at reduced rates, cot. Pets accepted. Central heating. Car essential — parking. Open March/October for Evening Meal, Bed and Breakfast, or Bed and Breakfast only. Terms on request.

PLEASE SEND A STAMPED ADDRESSED ENVELOPE WITH ENQUIRIES

YORK. Mrs C. M. Farnell, Beech Tree House Farm, South Holme, Slingsby, York YO6 7BA (Hovingham [065-382] 257). Working farm. A 260-acre mixed farm carrying cattle, sheep, pigs and poultry. Set in a peaceful valley near Castle Howard, York and Flamingo Park Zoo with a wealth of historical monuments to explore. Within easy reach of the North Yorkshire moors, North Yorkshire railway, Wolds, Dales and Yorkshire coastline, York 20 miles. There are two double (one twin bedded), one single bedrooms; bathroom, toilet; sittingroom and diningroom. Children welcome at reduced rates. Cot, high chair, babysitting available. Sorry, no pets. Car essential — parking. Open February to November for Evening Meal, Bed and Breakfast, or Bed and Breakfast. Good home cooking, fresh vegetables, etc. SAE, please, for terms.

YORK. Mrs P. M. Brewer, Home Farm, Whitwell-on-the-Hill, York YO6 7JJ (Whitwell-on-the-Hill [065-381] 428). Smallholding, farmhouse and buildings situated in pleasant country village off main A64, within easy reach of Castle Howard, Kirkham Abbey, York, coast, moors. Local tennis, horse riding. Putting green on lawn, clock golf, tennis, table tennis. Comfortable accommodation offered. Two single rooms both with hot and cold; one double, plus one family room with washbasin; twin bedded room; also TV. Toilet and bathroom (toilet plus shower outside). Lounge, colour TV; diningroom. Open all year. Garage. Home cooking. Evening Meal by arrangement. Bed and Breakfast. Farm Holiday Guide Diploma.

WEST YORKSHIRE

HAWORTH near. Mrs Brenda Taylor, Ponden Hall, Stanbury, Near Haworth BD22 0HR (Haworth [0535] 44154). Working farm. Ponden Hall is a 400-year-old farmhouse with mullioned windows, open fires and oak-beamed interior overlooking Ponden Reservoir, adjacent to the Pennine Moorland. Ponden was visited regularly by the Bronte family and is, reputedly, "Thrushcross Grange" in Emily Bronte's "Wuthering Heights". Haworth is three miles away with its steam railway, Parsonage and cobbled streets. Horse riding, boating, walking are on the doorstep. We farm 12 acres on a small scale. The Georgian extension houses our hand-loom weaving studio. Double and family bedrooms. Bed and Breakfast £7 to £7.50 per person. Children half price. Home-cooked evening meal £4. Pets welcome. Access third-of-a-mile rough, but wide track from main road. Open all year except December 25th and 26th.

HUDDERSFIELD. Mrs Christine Mellor, New Ing Farm, Rochdale Road, Golcar, Huddersfield HD7 4NN (Huddersfield [0484] 651967). Stay in our 18th century Pennine handloom weaver's farmhouse and enjoy the panoramic views from our two acre smallholding with its goats and free-range poultry. Explore "Last of the Summer Wine" country, Bronteland, Yorkshire Dales and Peak District. The comfortable centrally heated accommodation has two double rooms, one twin room; bathroom; diningroom; and lounge with colour TV. Children welcome at reduced rates. Babysitting available. Open all year. Bed and Breakfast from £8, Evening Meal by arrangement. Real Yorkshire hospitality only 10 minutes from M62. Please write or phone for directions.

HUDDERSFIELD near. Mrs Margaret Wood, Perch House Farm, Denby Dale, Near Huddersfield (Huddersfield [0484] 863177). Perch House Farm stands on a hill overlooking green fields and woodlands, within easy reach of the M1, on the A636 road. Near to the village where 'Last of the Summer Wine' was filmed. Near towns and cities and sports centre. This 150-year-old farmhouse has guest accommodation in one double and one family bedrooms; bathroom; toilet; sittingroom; diningroom. Children are welcome and babysitting is offered. Open all year with open fires. Pets at 20p per day. Car is not essential, but there is parking. Full board; Evening Meal, Bed and Breakfast or Bed and Breakfast only. Rates reduced for children sharing parents' room and senior citizens.

ILKLEY. Mrs Enid M. Hunter, Craigend Lodge Vegetarian Guest House, Cowpasture Road, Ilkley LS29 8RS (Ilkley [0943] 609897). This Yorkshire stone house offers first-class catering which is entirely vegetarian, designed on health lines, and highly recommended by both meat eaters and vegetarians. Delightful moorland position with walks and climbing. Ideal country house for those recuperating. Help yourself to meals, make tea or coffee anytime, happy, friendly atmosphere; sunbathing lawn, garden chalet for relaxing. Visit Windermere, museum, tennis, paddling, swimming baths. Six double, three single, three family bedrooms, all with washbasins; twin bedded room on ground floor with shower; two bathrooms, three toilets; lounge; diningroom. Children welcome, reduced rates, cot, high chair, babysitting by arrangement. Disabled guests welcome but regret house not suitable for wheelchairs. Pets, small charge. Parking. Full Board, Evening Dinner/Meal, Bed and Breakfast. Bed and Breakfast only from £5 to £7. Mid-week bookings available for any number of days. Fire Certificate. SAE, please. Easter to November.

KEIGHLEY near. Mrs W. Cocks, High Hob Cote Farm, Colne Road, Oakworth, Near Keighley BD22 0RW (Haworth [0535] 42376). This pleasant 18th-century farmhouse is situated in 30 acres of pasture, facing south and overlooking Haworth and Haworth Moors, the home of the Bronte Family of "Wuthering Heights" fame. The Worth Valley Steam Railway is also in Haworth. The farm is one mile from the Pennine Way and 10 miles from Skipton and the beautiful Dales National Park. Car advisable. Two family bedrooms have washbasins and gas fires; one single bedroom. Electric blankets, tea-making facilities in all bedrooms. Bathroom, two toilets; diningroom; sittingroom with TV. Children welcome. Pets accepted. Open from April to November. Bed and Breakfast from £7. Also furnished cottage to let. SAE for details.

ISLE OF WIGHT

BRADING. Mr G. L. Ruthven, Stoneham, The Mall, Brading PO36 0DB (0983-407315). Stoneham is a mid 17th century village house with Georgian facade set in a half acre of garden. There is a guests' livingroom with colour TV and separate diningroom, both with open fireplaces and beamed ceilings. The house is centrally heated. Accommodation comprises one family and two double rooms, each with washbasin and tea-making facilities. There are two bathrooms. Good public transport facilities within walking distance. Ideal spot for walking and cycling enthusiasts and beach two miles away. Bed and Breakfast only from £7 per night. Children under 12 half price if sharing room. Regret, no pets. Please send SAE for details.

CARISBROOKE. Mrs Jane Cross, "Alvington View," Calbourne Road, Carisbrooke PO30 5SR (Isle of Wight [0983] 527700). Alvington View is a smallholding, set in open country with panoramic views of the Solent and surrounding countryside. Being situated in the centre of the island it makes an ideal base for touring. It is only half-a-mile out of Carisbrooke which has historic castle and church. At Alvington View we keep a few goats, pigs, ducks, chickens and bantams (with plenty of chicks and ducklings hatching out during the summer). There is a swimming pool in the garden for the use of the guests. One double, one single and two family bedrooms; bathroom, toilet; sittingroom with colour TV; diningroom. Children welcome, cot, high chair, babysitting and reduced rates. Open all year with central heating and log fires. Pets allowed. Car not essential, but parking available. Evening Meal, Bed and Breakfast or Bed and Breakfast only. Rates also reduced for Senior Citizens.

CHALE. Mr and Mrs J. Bradshaw, The Clarendon Hotel and Wight Mouse Inn, Newport Road, Chale PO38 2HA (Niton [0983] 730431). Visitors are most welcome to The Clarendon Hotel and Wight Mouse Inn. Every comfort and hospitality assured. Children welcome. Beautiful sandy beaches close by. Guests' bedrooms are beautifully appointed and have central heating, tea and coffee making facilities and lovely views of unspoilt coastline or St. Catherines Downs. Several rooms have colour TV and many have en-suite bathrooms. The hotel diningroom is locally renowned, using local produce whenever possible, and there is an excellent wine cellar. Our pub, attached to the hotel, has great atmosphere — open fires, real ale, children's games room. Local musicians and entertainers featured nightly. Please phone for brochure or send SAE.

CHALE near. Mrs Julie Young, Atherfield Farm House, Atherfield Green, Near Chale, Via Ventnor PO38 2LF (Chale Green [098-379] 270). Working farm. Atherfield Farm House is situated in the peace and quiet of the countryside, although within walking distance of main coastal road and beaches. Home from home comforts, no petty restrictions. Good home cooking. Large garden to sit or play in. Two double, one single and two family bedrooms all, except single, with washbasins. Bathroom, three toilets. Lounge with colour TV. Diningroom with separate tables. Cot, high chair, baby listening and reduced rates for children. Fire Certificate held. Open May to September. Weekly terms for Bed and Breakfast from £48; Half Board £60. SAE, please, or telephone for brochure.

NEWPORT. Mrs D. Harvey, Newbarn Farm, Gatcombe, Newport PO30 3EQ (Chillerton [098-370] 202). Working farm. Newbarn Farm, a 165-acre arable/stock farm, is situated in a secluded downland valley in the centre of the island. Ideal for walking. All attractions and beaches within easy reach by car. Ample parking. Public transport one mile. Two family rooms with washbasins, razor points and tea-making facilities. Central heating. Swimming pool in garden. Open April to October. Children over five years welcome. Sorry, no pets. Car essential — parking. Evening Dinner, Bed and Breakfast from £14; Bed and Breakfast from £10. Also self-catering accommodation in wing of farmhouse, sleeps up to six persons. Fully equipped. Weekly terms £90 to £200 (fuel included).

RYDE. Mrs M. J. Long, The Brambles, Gatehouse Lane, Upton Cross, Ryde PO33 4BS (Isle of Wight [0983] 65556). Private farmhouse accommodation, one mile from Ryde, in a lovely scenic area. Two double rooms and one family room all with hot and cold water. Two bathrooms with showers. Lounge with colour TV. Separate diningroom. Children welcome; babysitting arranged. Very homely atmosphere. Good home cooking and a warm welcome to all our visitors. Terms: Bed and Breakfast from £6.50, with Evening Meal from £8.50. Children under 12 half price if sharing parents' room.

SANDOWN. Nicholas and Daphne Rayner, Montrose, Alverstone, Near Sandown PO36 0EZ (0983) 402885. A small country guest house with home cooking and fresh garden produce. Situated in a quiet village, three miles to the beach. Lovely country and river walks all around. One double, one family room, one twin-bedded; double and family room with washbasins. Bathroom, toilet. Colour TV lounge, diningroom with separate tables. Children welcome, cot, high chair available, also half price for children under 12 years. Open May to September for Evening Dinner, Bed and Breakfast from £56 to £63 including early morning tea. SAE, please.

SANDOWN near. Mrs Geraldine Watling, "The Grange", Alverstone, Near Sandown PO36 0EZ (Isle of Wight [0983] 403729). Enjoy a peaceful holiday at our small family Guest House. Ideally situated for all aspects of the Island. Two miles from sandy beaches, the East Yar nature walk and Nunwell trail pass through the village. A traditional farmhouse Breakfast to start the day, and excellent menu for your Evening Meal. Tastefully decorated throughout. Lounge with colour TV; central heating. Prices from £10 per day for Bed and Breakfast and from £88 per week for Bed, Breakfast and Evening Meal. Reduced rates for children. Write or telephone for further details.

SANDOWN near. Mrs R. A. Mallard, Middle Barn Farm, Bathingbourne, Near Sandown PO36 0LY (0983) 865282. Bathingbourne is situated in a quiet road, half a mile from the Sandown/Newport road and about three and a half miles from Sandown. It is an ideal centre for touring the island, which has plenty to offer visitors. Plenty of space for parking; large lawned garden for children. Lots of good home cooking, with farm and local produce. Large lounge with colour TV. Diningroom with separate tables. Washing line for smalls. Children welcome, cot, high chair, babysitting offered. No need to go out if weather is bad. Everything done here to make guests comfortable. Accommodation in two double and two family bedrooms, all with washbasins; bathroom, three toilets. Open May/October. Evening Dinner, Bed and Breakfast or Bed and Breakfast only. Rates reduced for children. Terms on request.

CLIFTONVILLE HOTEL
Tel. 098-386 2197. 6 Hope Road,
Shanklin, Isle of Wight PO37 6EA.
Proprietors: Mr & Mrs G. Jenkins

Cliftonville Hotel is pleasantly situated midway between station and beach (300 yards from sea) within easy distance of shops and entertainments. Car not essential. Hot and cold washbasins; 13 amp and razor points in all bedrooms. Ideal for family holidays. 14 bedrooms, colour TV lounge, TV in family rooms, tea-making facilities. Garden seating, swings, rotary lines. The hotel assures homeliness, excellent food and no restrictions. The island has safe, sandy beaches and many pleasant walks along cliff tops or to chines and downs. Ideal for Spring and Autumn holidays. Open May to September. From £12 per day, reduced rates for children under 17 sharing. Please send SAE for brochure. Member of the Isle of Wight Tourist Board. Ample parking. Mid week booking daily or weekly.

SEAHORSE AWARD

The Nodes Country Hotel

A well run hotel – with a happy country house atmosphere

TOTLAND BAY. Mr Robert Godden, The Nodes Country Hotel, Alum Bay Old Road, Totland Bay PO39 0HZ (Isle of Wight [0983] 752859). A charming old Country House Hotel standing in two-and-a-half acres of grounds, in the heart of the magnificent West Wight countryside, enjoying lovely rural views to the coast. Riding, fishing and sailing close by; several safe sandy beaches for excellent swimming; Golf Club only five minutes' drive. Many delightful walks to Alum Bay, Totland Bay and Freshwater Bay. The Hotel, open April to October, is fully centrally heated, furnished to a very high standard. Bedrooms have fitted carpets, hot and cold, razor points, bedside lights, radio/baby listening, etc. The new wing has six bedrooms, each with own shower/toilet. Comfortable lounge with colour TV and log fire. Courtyard Bar. Traditional country cooking, local and own produce, varied menu, excellent selection of wines. Parking in grounds, but car not essential. Children welcome. Bed, Breakfast and Evening Dinner from £16 daily (£96 weekly); Bed and Breakfast from £10 daily (£65 weekly). Please send for Colour Brochure. AA/RAC approved.

TOTLAND BAY. Mrs V. M. Swain, Garrow Hotel, Church Hill, Totland Bay PO39 0EU (Isle of Wight [0983] 753174). Licensed: 15 bedrooms, 7 with private bathrooms. Children over 5 welcome: Car Park (16): Newport 13 miles, Yarmouth 3 and Freshwater 2. Standing high above Totland Bay in its own extensive grounds, the views from Garrow Hotel are truly magnificent. Peacefully located yet conveniently close to beach, shops, bus services etc., with walks in National Trust Countryside and an 18-hole Golf Course nearby. Most of the charming guest rooms have sea views and some are available on the ground floor, well suited to the elderly or infirm. Proprietors Larry and Vi Swain have provided two separate lounges for the comfort of their guests, one with colour television, and the accent in the delightful diningroom is firmly on home cooking and baking which, with the friendly and efficient service, make our meal times a joy to all. Open from Easter to October.

VENTNOR. Mr and Mrs J. Chalus, Peartree Farm Guest House, Whiteley Bank, Wroxall, Ventnor PO38 3AF (Isle of Wight [0983] 862538). Situated in country surroundings near the picturesque village of Godshill and within walking distance of main bus route. Sun lounge, TV lounge, diningroom with separate tables; family bedrooms, double and single rooms, all well-furnished and carpeted, with washbasins; bath, two showers, five toilets. Cot, high chair, babysitting on request; reduced rates for children. Ample parking space. Fire Certificate held. Licensed. Ample outdoor space for children to play. No dogs. Ground floor accommodation suitable for disabled guests. Terms on request for Evening Dinner, Bed and Breakfast or Bed and Breakfast only. SAE, please.

Terms quoted in this publication may be subject to increase if rises in costs necessitate

---

HELP IMPROVE BRITISH TOURIST STANDARDS

You are choosing holiday accommodation from our very popular FARM HOLIDAY GUIDES. Whether it be a hotel, guest house, farmhouse or self-catering accommodation, we think you will find it hospitable, comfortable and clean, and your host and hostess friendly and helpful.

Why not write and tell us about it?

As a recognition of the generally well-run and excellent holiday accommodation reviewed in our publications, we at FARM HOLIDAY GUIDES LIMITED present a diploma to proprietors who receive the highest recommendation from their guests who are also readers of our Guides. If you care to write to us praising the holiday you have booked through FARM HOLIDAY GUIDES – whether this be board, self-catering accommodation, a sporting or a caravan holiday, the content of your letter will be evaluated and the proprietors who reach our final list will be contacted.

The winning proprietor will receive an attractive framed diploma to display on his premises as recognition of a high standard of comfort, amenity and hospitality. FARM HOLIDAY GUIDES LIMITED offer this diploma as a contribution towards the improvement of standards in tourist accommodation in Britain. Help your excellent host or hostess to win it!

DIPLOMA
AWARDED BY
READERS
of
FARM HOLIDAY GUIDE
PUBLICATIONS LIMITED

TO...
FOR HOLIDAY ACCOMMODATION
of the HIGHEST STANDARD

AT...

CHANNEL ISLANDS / Guernsey

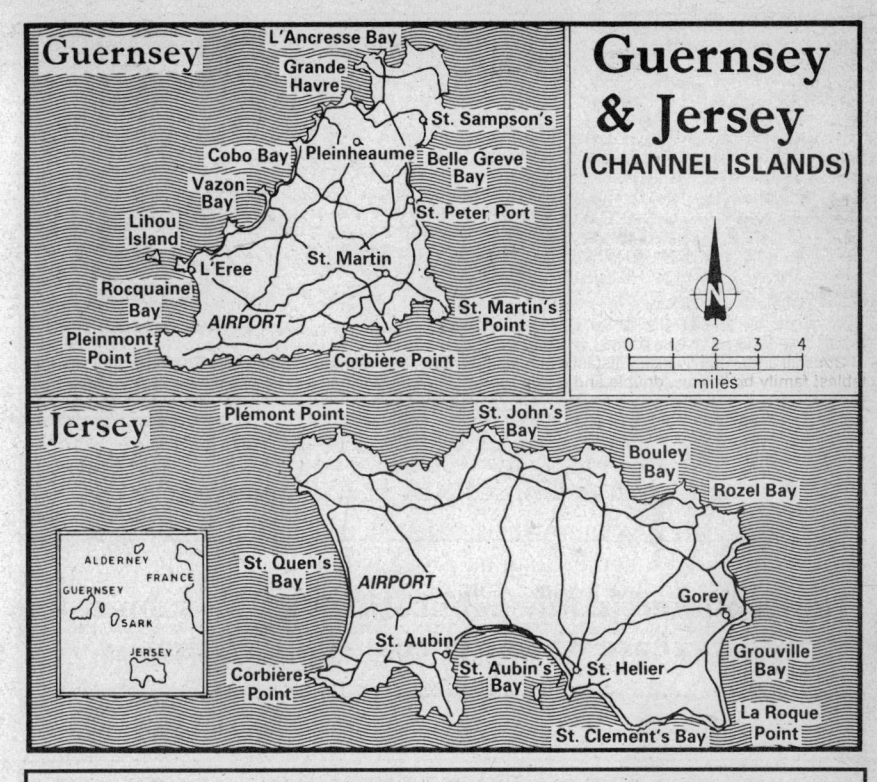

Victoria Arms Inn
VICTORIA ROAD, ST. PETER PORT
Telephone: (0481) 25076

A friendly pub. H&C in all bedrooms. 5 minutes walk from town centre and buses to all parts of the island.

Bed and Full English Breakfast from £8.00

Open all Year

MONICA and JACK VICKERMAN

GUERNSEY

MRS M. ARMENTA, PINEWAY, DE LA TERRE, NORGIOT, ST. SAVIOURS, GUERNSEY   Tel. 0481-64051

Pineway Guest House is a large modern bungalow situated in rural Guernsey near the reservoir with lovely walks through country lanes. We are adjacent to the West Coast which has superb sandy beaches which are within 20 minutes walking distance. We are a family run Guest House with all home comforts and good food and pleasant atmosphere. Facilites for making hot drinks with no extra charge. Showers, baths free. Hot and cold in all rooms and access to bungalow all day. Children welcome with cot, high chair and babysitting on request. Open April to October. Car essential, parking.

BED & BREAKFAST & EVENING MEAL £10 PER DAY; FAMILY/EN SUITE B/B & EM £13 PER DAY
Reduced rates for children.

CHANNEL ISLANDS / Jersey BOARD

HOTEL DES ILES
Gorey Village
Telephone: 0534 54324
Guest House Register A

Comfortable family hotel in the delightful village of Gorey, 300 yards from a safe sandy beach. Gorey harbour, castle and golf course nearby. Centrally heated and comfortably furnished, with hot/cold, razor points, radio and baby listening service. Residents lounge with colour TV. Licensed bar. Excellent home cooking at separate tables. This hotel is continually recommended.

*Terms: Room, Breakfast and Evening Dinner from £11 to £15 according to season. *No service charge. *25% to 50% special reduced rates for children. *One child free early/late season.*

Please write for brochure to resident proprietors Betty and Brian Davies enclosing unaffixed stamp.

Old Court House Inn
ST. AUBIN'S HARBOUR   Tel: 0534 41156

Family run 17th century Inn situated on the harbour at St. Aubin. The oak-beamed Restaurant dating back to A.D. 1643 was its original "Court Room", specialities include "Fruits de Mer", Lobster, Crab, etc. 3 attractive bars. Comfortable bedrooms, some with bath; also a 2-bedroomed "Penthouse" suite. Room with Breakfast terms only. Please write for brochure.

CASTLE HOUSE HOTEL
9 CASTLE STREET, ST. HELIER
Guest House Register 'A'
Tel. Visitors (0534) 33409; Reservations Summer (0534) 25788; Winter (0534) 42668

This elegant Georgian building has been run as a comfortable guest house by the Jordan family for over 25 years. Positioned close to the centre of town the house is within easy reach of the main shopping area, the harbour, the bus station, the Esplanade and the beach. Comfortable, large family rooms with H&C and razor sockets. Central heating and Residential Bar. Multi storey car park opposite. Midweek bookings accepted. Bed, Breakfast and Dinner from £12 according to season. Reductions for children sharing parent's room.

Please write or phone proprietors: Thomas and Mary Jordan.

ALFRISTON HOUSE
ST. PETER, JERSEY
Guest House Register 'A'   Tel: 0534 42704

A small friendly country Guest House with bus stop outside for town and beach. Most rooms have central heating.
* All bedrooms have colour TV's
* Tea/coffee making facilities in all rooms
* Ground and first floor bedrooms
* Excellent food with fresh farm produce
* A sandy garden with aviary
* Own car park
* A warm and friendly welcome awaits you.

**WRITE OR PHONE TO RESIDENT PROPRIETORS:
MR & MRS JENKINS**

Farm Holiday Guide
ENGLAND
1986

Village Inns · Activity Holidays
Caravan and Camping

VILLAGE INNS

DEVON, COMBE MARTIN. Mrs Norah Denham, The London Inn, Leigh Road, Combe Martin EX34 0NA (Combe Martin [027-188] 3409). This charming old world Inn is situated near beautiful country and only one mile from the sea. The proprietors' aim is to please. The rooms are very comfortable with all modern conveniences. The cuisine is excellent. There are two bars; one in period style, with log fire; the other with a small intimate dance area and music. At the rear of the Inn there is a beer garden. "An Inn to please all tastes," accommodation is in seven double, two single and two family bedrooms, all with washbasins; ample bathroom and toilet facilities; lounge and diningroom. Children are welcome and a cot is available. Pets allowed. A car is not essential, but there is ample parking space. You can enjoy the pleasures of a Devon holiday at any time of the year here. SAE, please. Reasonable terms. Reduced rates for children.

KENT, CANTERBURY. Mr J. Cork, Bow Window Inn, High Street, Littlebourne, Canterbury (0227) 721264. This attractive inn lies on the A257 in a picturesque village within four miles of historic Canterbury. Here one may wine and dine well beneath old oak beams and take in the ambience of centuries of hospitality. English and Continental dishes are always available and there is an excellent selection of wines. The accommodation comprises eight bedrooms and adheres to a very high standard of comfort. All bedrooms have private bathroom, colour TV and tea/coffee making facilities. The inn is carpeted throughout and fully centrally heated, comforts complemented by a courteous and willing staff. Two of the guest rooms have their own sun lounge. Many places of historical interest within easy reach, and the inn provides an excellent stopping place for visitors "en route" to the Continent — Folkestone and Dover approximately 12 miles. Ample parking space (25 cars).

YORKSHIRE (North), SELBY near. Mrs C. Sharp, Anchor Inn, Market Place, Cawood, Near Selby YO8 0SR (Cawood [075-786] 363). The Anchor Inn stands in pleasant country surroundings, nine miles from York and 40 miles from the sea. Ideal for walking, fishing and touring. Of historical note, there is an old world church and ancient castle, once the home of Cardinal Wolsey, which is now a farm. Open all year with three twin and one family bedrooms; sittingroom with TV, diningroom and bar. Children are welcome.

PLEASE ENCLOSE A STAMPED ADDRESSED ENVELOPE WITH ENQUIRIES

ACTIVITY HOLIDAYS

GENERAL

FALMOUTH. Antron Barn, Mabe, Near Falmouth. Two miles from Falmouth beaches. Mabe village is centrally placed for the Fal and Helford estuaries, Lizard and north coast beaches. Antron Barn is a secluded architect-designed modern house, partly converted from an old granite barn, with spacious lawns, big trees (with tree swing) and large sun terrace with views of lake and valley and glimpses of the sea. Golf (nine-hole rough 300 yards, clubs provided), croquet and your own games on lawns (about one acre), fly and coarse fishing one mile. Riding in village. Inside is an enormous L-shaped wood panelled living/diningroom, full of light and space. Modern kitchen, telephone and bathroom, separate shower, two toilets; garage; TV, barbecues, table tennis. Sleeps six to eleven; double bed plus single; two rooms with two single beds in each; two bunks; two folding beds in table tennis room (three bedrooms with fitted washbasins and cupboards). Cot. Linen not supplied. Particularly suitable for off-season with extensive under-floor heating and double glazing. £70 to £370 per week. Particulars from **Mr and Mrs Duncan Ogilvie, 19 Canynge Road, Clifton, Bristol BS8 3JZ (0272) 736688.**

AN INVITATION TO **St. Brannocks Hotel**
NEWQUAY, CORNWALL
MODERN SEQUENCE DANCE HOLIDAYS

For the fifth successful year, we offer specific off season dates to BRING YOUR PARTNER. Choose either a full week, or a four day break. Our friendly three star hotel offers all rooms en suite with central heating. Ashley Courtenay recommended restaurant. RESIDENT M.C.'s. Offer practice dances, afternoon tea dances, and dancing each evening to specialist sequence bands. Large ballroom with maple sprung floor. WE WOULD BE PLEASED TO HOST YOUR CLUB HOLIDAYS AND REQUEST M.C.'s TO WRITE FOR AVAILABLE DATES. In the morning or after dancing, enjoy a relaxing swim in our warm indoor heated pool, or take advantage of the Sauna and Solarium facilities. We can also offer your club the facility of coach travel to Newquay and return with morning tours to places of interest in the County if required. 1987 TERMS AVAILABLE.

CONTACT: DORIS STEPHENS, ST. BRANNOCKS HOTEL NEWQUAY. STD. 0637-872038

Activity Holidays

CUMBRIA, KESWICK (LAKE DISTRICT). Coledale Holidays, Coledale Cottage, Braithwaite, Keswick CA12 5TN (Braithwaite [059-682] 475). A guided walking holiday based at this peaceful fellside cottage at the edge of Braithwaite. Enjoy a strenuous week conquering the fell tops or a gentle one discovering the flora and fauna at low level, or a mixture of both — the choice is yours! Local sightseeing trips are offered using our minibus or car with selected guides. We cater for individuals or groups. Activities such as rock climbing, sailing, windsurfing, water ski-ing, riding are also available. At the end of the day come back to home cooking and relax in the garden or by a log fire. Open all year. Phone or write for brochure.

DEVON, KINGSBRIDGE. Mr Keith Chell, Slapton Ley Field Centre, Slapton, Kingsbridge TQ7 2QP (Kingsbridge [0548] 580466). An educational charity offering a wide variety of natural history courses for individuals and family groups, led by expert tutors. Courses cover painting, archaeology, birds, seashore, walking and natural history, and are aimed at all ages and abilities. Setting is the impressive South Devon coast, within a 200 ha nature reserve, plus close proximity to Dartmoor. Courses run from mid-February till October. There are 38 bedrooms, 10 bathrooms and 14 toilets. Oil/electric heating. Car not essential, though parking available. Pets are accepted, though not encouraged. From £118 weekly; family rates. Full details on request.

cotswold rambling

"Walking Holidays for anyone to whom a leisurely break rambling through the beauty of the unspoilt South Cotswolds appeals. With your country accommodation pre-booked; your luggage moved for you, and the comprehensive map and information package we supply, you are free to explore this glorious part of England at your own pace.
4/7 days – £65/£130 including dinner, B&B and transport to and from nearby station. Reductions for children and groups. Dogs welcome. Come anytime: holidays possible at short notice.

BROCHURE: COTSWOLD RAMBLING (A27),
"PETTY CROFT", HILLESLEY, WOTTON-UNDER-EDGE, GLOS GL12 7RB
Telephone Dursley 0453-842920

PONY TREKKING AND RIDING

DEVON, EXETER near. Mr D. L. Salter, Haldon Lodge Farm, Kennford, Near Exeter EX6 7YG (Exeter [0392] 832312). Working farm. Peace and seclusion are assured on this private residential site. The Salters offer a family holiday for all ages, with a special invitation to younger members to join in pony riding and enjoy a free and easy farm holiday with them. Exeter four-and-a-half miles. Dawlish (short car drive away) ideal centre for touring all South Devon resorts and Dartmoor. The three six-berth residential holiday caravans adjoin a large lawn with a background of fields, pine trees, rhododendrons. Six comfortable beds, blankets, pillows. Fully equipped kitchen, carpeted lounge (TV), bathroom (H/C) flush toilet, electricity and mains connected. Horses and ponies nearby are an interest to everyone. Horse lovers and children we invite to explore the beautiful Teign Valley forest on horseback. Day pony treks arranged for small parties. The well-known Nobody Inn is one of the many attractive country inns where you can have a drink and a meal in the midst of a friendly atmosphere. Pets allowed. Terms: Pony Riding from £30 per week. Caravans March to December from £30 per week. Tourers from £2.50 per day; campers from £1.50 per day.

DEVON, EXMOUTH. Mrs Sandra Joy, Goodmores Farm, Marley, Exmouth EX5 5BA (0395) 264-115. Farmhouse accommodation and riding holidays for all the family, unaccompanied children live as family. Informal atmosphere, friendly qualified staff. Attractive gardens, barbecues, fun competitions, badminton, lovely walks and rides over beautiful open common land with magnificent sea views. Quality horses and ponies to suit all abilities. We have own pony trekking centre nearby. Riding school offers all-weather menage, show jumping area and cross-country course for more experienced riders and beginners welcome. We are close to seaside town of Exmouth with miles of sandy beaches and sport facilities. Central for touring Devon and places of interest. Open all year for weekends, weeks, or longer. All activities personally supervised by **Sandra Joy.**

RIDING

DEVON, LYDFORD. Mrs Z. Myers, Classical Riding Academy, Lydford EX20 4BL (Lydford [082-282] 271). The Classical Riding Academy at Manor Farm lies in 13 acres of ground in a sheltered position by the White Lady Falls entrance to the beautiful Lydford Gorge; off main Okehampton – Tavistock road. Licensed as a riding establishment where instruction in Classical Riding is given in indoor and outdoor schools. Choice of terms from Bed and Breakfast to Full Board with or without riding instruction. Open all year the farm is an excellent centre for riding, fishing, golf, tennis and touring. Many safe beaches within an hour's drive. Dartmoor on the doorstep: Exmoor and Bodmin Moor within easy reach: many National Trust properties, interesting Stately Homes. Pubs and eating places abound. The accommodation to a high standard of comfort offers two family rooms, one double and two twin rooms, all with washbasins; TV if required; tea/coffee makers; three with private bathrooms. Lounge with TV and video. Licensed diningroom serving beers, wines and spirits to complement the excellent food. Tea rooms in the grounds. Brochure on Riding Instruction sent gladly on request.

NORTH YORKSHIRE, YORK. Mrs and Miss Kemp-Welch, B.H.S.I.I., Moor House, Wigginton, York YO3 8RB (York [0904] 769029). This is a British Horse Society Approved small family Riding School, with indoor and outdoor schools, cross-country jumps and jumping paddocks. Riding terms are from £19 for three days and £23 for four days. We are five miles from York. Car desirable and parking available. There are hotels and guest houses nearby. Full details on request.

ACTIVITY FARMING

EAST SUSSEX, LEWES. WORKING WEEKENDS ON ORGANIC FARMS is an exchange scheme with a wide variety of host farms and smallholdings throughout the UK ("Organic" simply means building up natural fertility and avoiding the use of persistent poisons). You live with the family and receive practical experience in return for your help; haymaking, sowing, planting, collecting the eggs, mucking out, weeding, composting, harvesting, feeding the animals, seaweed gathering . . . are typical tasks. Midweek and longer stays also available. A wonderful way to get to know the country. For brochure, please send stamped addressed envelope to **WWOOF (FHG), 19 Bradford Road, Lewes, East Sussex BN7 1RB.**

SPECIAL INTEREST

KENT, SEVENOAKS. Galleon Leisure Holidays, 52 High Street, Sevenoaks TN13 1JG 0732-452355 or 01 859 0111. Treat yourself to a different sort of holiday this year! We are specialists in Leisure Painting Holidays and you can choose from one of our many courses, whether a beginner or devoted Leisure Painter. We also run a number of special activity holidays, including ski-ing, rambling and farm holidays. Find out more by sending for the Galleon Leisure Painting and Activity Holidays brochure. Telephone or write to the above.

If you've have found FARM HOLIDAY GUIDE of service please tell your friends

CARAVAN AND CAMPING HOLIDAYS

AVON

BRISTOL near. Mrs C. B. Perry, Cleve Hill Farm, Ubley, Near Bristol BS18 6PG (Blagdon [0761] 62410). Working farm. This is a dairy farm set close under the Mendip Hills and visitors are welcome to explore the land. Trout fishing and bird watching close at hand and many lovely walks in beautiful countryside. Within easy touring distance of Bristol, Bath, Wells (beautiful cathedral), Cheddar and Wookey Hole Caves, Longleat, etc. Horse riding at Churchill, four miles. Several lovely old churches worth a visit. One Stately and one Bluebird caravan available from April to October. Electric light, Calor gas cooker, water. Fully equipped except linen. Stately has bathroom with hot and cold water (10p electric meter). Bluebird has toilet close by. Small shop one mile, larger shop three miles. Weekly terms from £40 to £80. Well controlled pets allowed.

CORNWALL

BODMIN. Kelly Green Farm, St. Kew Highway, Bodmin. Working farm. Two six-berth caravans on this 250-acre mixed farm. All blankets and pillows supplied and kitchens fully equipped. Guests required to bring own linen. Flush toilets, tap water in each van, electric light, heating, fridges, TV, Calor gas cookers and shaving points. Toilet and shower on site. Plenty of activity on the farm. Guests are welcome to browse around and watch the milking of 90 cows, sheep shearing, silage, hay-making and corn harvesting. Situated in the beautiful Allen Valley and within easy reach of both north and south coasts. Available from Easter to October. Slide and swing for children, also parking for a few touring vans. Well behaved dogs allowed. SAE for terms and further details. **Mrs Nancy Harris, Trekelly Meadow, Tremeer Lane, St. Tudy, Bodmin PL30 3DT (Bodmin [0208] 850275).**

BODMIN. Mrs M. J. Matthews, Pengelly Farm, Blisland, Bodmin PL30 4HR (Cardinham [020-882] 261). Working farm. Modern six-berth caravan situated four miles north of Bodmin on a 180-acre mixed farm, quiet and secluded with extensive views of beautiful countryside. It is central for both north and south coasts, with pony trekking nearby. There are two bedrooms, kitchen and lounge, also toilet, shower, electricity, fridge and fire. Parking alongside van. Children welcome and pets allowed. The picturesque village of Blisland has a shop and post office. At Bodmin there is a heated swimming pool, tennis courts, launderette and supermarkets. There is a licence for certified location for five touring caravans on a separate field of the farm. Weekly terms from £45.

BODMIN. Miss Nina D. Puddick, Little Trehudreth, Blisland, Bodmin PL30 4JW (Bodmin [0208] 850132). Little Trehudreth is a 16th-century dwelling with one caravan situated in unspoilt beautiful countryside between both coasts on the edge of Bodmin Moor, one mile from A30. Ideal for exploring the magnificent coasts and moorland. Nearby facilities include top surfing beaches, sailing, riding, bird watching and walks. The picturesque village of Blisland, also one mile away, has a shop/post office, pub and church. Our caravan accommodates six. It is completely self-contained and includes separate double bedroom, flush toilet, shower, electric lighting and heating, fridge, cooker, TV. Linen provided. Ample parking. No additional charges. Evening babysitting by arrangement. Terms from £65–£85 per week. SAE, please.

346   Caravans and Camping

BUDE. Mr and Mrs H. D. Redman, Trenance Farm Guest House, Crackington Haven, Bude EX23 0JQ (St. Genny's [08403] 273). Luxury holiday caravan accommodating six/eight people, enjoying beautiful views, set in National Trust countryside with a wealth of coastal and moorland beauty. The caravan has bathroom/shower, Calor gas cooking and heating; fridge. Everything supplied for your holiday needs, including linen. Children welcome; pets accepted by prior arrangement. Half an acre of land available for touring vans and campers. Hot showers, toilets, plus electric hook-up, and farm shop on site. Car essential — ample parking. Crackington Haven is a beautiful bay with sandy beach, safe for swimming and surfing. Lovely coastal walks. Ideal touring centre. Within easy reach of Widemouth Bay, Bude, Boscastle, Tintagel and many scenic places. Half a mile to shop and pub. Golf, tennis, riding, sea and river fishing easily accessible. Available all year. Self-catering in Guest House accommodating up to twelve; also Bed and Breakfast. Terms and further details on request.

BUDE. Mrs V. B. Vickery, Killock Farm, Bude EX23 9PZ (Kilkhampton [028-882] 504). Working farm. Killock Farm (300 acres) is situated just off the A39, a short distance from sandy beaches noted for surfing and near golf course. All visitors are made welcome and enjoy the freedom of the farm. There are two Wonderland caravans, each in its own paddock. Fully equipped with full size gas cooker, fridge, iron, TV and electric lighting. Shower and toilet block on site also pet donkey, skittle alley and large pond for children to fish in. Open May to October. SAE for details and terms.

LAUNCESTON. Mrs M. Colwill, Trewithen, Laneast, Launceston PL15 8PW (056686) 343. Working farm. A luxury six-berth residential caravan pleasantly sited in a garden on a mixed farm, with lovely views of the surrounding hills and moors. Fully equipped, five separate rooms; double bedroom, bunk bedroom, shower room and toilet, fitted kitchen with Calor gas cooker and fridge, lounge with TV and heater (seats can be made into two single beds). Hot and cold water throughout. Visitors are welcome to look around the farm to see the animals. Shops within three miles. This is a good area for touring, 20 minutes from the coast and its lovely sandy beaches. Pony trekking on moors nearby. Heated swimming pool at Launceston. Personally supervised. Pets allowed. SAE for terms please.

LIZARD PENINSULA. Mrs Yolande Drayson, Transingove Farm, Cury, Helston TR12 7QY (Mullion [0326] 240429). Working farm. If you are seeking a quiet peaceful holiday come to our four-berth caravan situated in its own secluded, sheltered spot on hard ground with a grass area. This 23-acre farm is located down a quiet country lane within easy reach of numerous beaches, one-and-a-half miles to nearest sandy cove; many other places of interest in the area; 18-hole golf course one mile, riding stables on next farm, market town of Helston five miles, Cury Village with stores one-and-a-half miles. Mains water from tank with tap at side of caravan; Calor gas cooking, electric light, power point, modern chemical toilet. Everything provided except linen. Available May to October. Weekly rates from £40 include gas/electricity.

LOOE. Mrs E. M. Lee, Trevollard, Lanreath, Looe PL13 2PD (Lanreath [0503] 20206. Working farm. This luxury six-berth caravan is sited on a secluded sunny spot on the farm with plenty of space for parking and children to play. It has electric lights, hot and cold water, fitted kitchen with full size Calor gas cooker, electric kettle, toaster and fridge. Bathroom with flush toilet; double end bedroom. Lounge has TV, Calor gas fire, convertible settee and two single bunks. Only four miles from the coast across the ferry to Fowey. Looe and Polperro seven miles. Area is renowned for its lovely coastline, coastal walks and sandy beaches. Fishing, pony riding, golf available. Shops nearby. Children and pets welcome. SAE, please, for further details.

NEWQUAY. Mrs Joan Luckraft, Nancolleth Farm Caravan Park, Summercourt, Newquay, Cornwall TR8 4PN (Mitchell [087-251] 236). Working farm. Nancolleth is a 250-acre mixed farm with secluded south facing caravan park, surrounded by trees. There are four modern six-berth caravans in garden setting. Two new 28' fully serviced models (shower, toilet and hand basin). Two 26' 1980 models with own outside flush toilets and shower room. Each caravan has two bedrooms, colour TV, fridge, gas cooker, H&C water, shaving point, electric light, gas fire, fully equipped and cleanliness guaranteed. Open May to October. Children welcome, safe grass area with swing and see-saw for them. Sorry, no pets. This is a small site with privacy and peace — not commercialised — and away from crowds. Cornwall's finest beaches and Newquay six miles. Ideal for touring Cornwall. Milk delivered. Shops three miles. Mrs Luckraft's aim is to provide an enjoyable and relaxing holiday in her clean and comfortable caravans and she welcomes her visitors personally.

Terms quoted in this publication may be subject to increase if rises in costs necessitate

Caravans and Camping 347

NEWQUAY. Mrs F. Whybrow, Treworgans Farm, Cubert, Newquay TR8 5HH (Crantock [0637] 830200). Midway between Crantock and Cubert, one-and-a-half miles from the sea, this one-acre farm site in rural surroundings with capacity for 20 caravans has seven six-berth caravans available from Easter to end of September. All have flush toilets, Calor gas cookers, some have two separate bedrooms, and fridges; four have hot and cold showers and water heaters. Mains drainage, room heaters, electricity. Fully equipped except linen. The site has a toilet block with flush toilets, showers, washbasins, etc. Shopping facilities 5 yards. Children are welcome and pets permitted. The site is not isolated, and approached by a tarmac path from a B-class road. Ample parking space. One acre reserved for campers. No touring caravans. SAE for terms.

ST. AGNES. Mrs Mary Thorley, 'Treleaver', Mithian Downs, Near St. Agnes (St. Agnes [087-255] 2486). Working farm. Single Bluebird caravan 27' × 12' on 20 acre smallholding. 5/6 berths. Set in sheltered valley two miles from the coast. Available May to October. Separate fully equipped kitchen with mains water, mains electricity, Calor gas cooker. Chemical toilet in caravan and outside flush toilet adjacent. Children welcome, and pets if safe with farm animals. Terms £45–£75. Beach hut on St. Agnes beach available.

TINTAGEL. Mr R. L. Wickett, Bossiney Farm Caravan Site, Tintagel PL34 0AY (0840-770481). Working farm. Bossiney Farm is a small family run farm site, situated on the B3263 main road between Tintagel and Boscastle in the hamlet of Bossiney. There are cliffs on the opposite side of the road, through which one can walk to Bossiney Cove, a safe, sandy bay. Selection of four, five and six-berth caravans, terraced with rural views. All vans have mains water, electric lighting, Calor gas cooking and small fridge, TV, some with toilets and showers. Cleanliness guaranteed. Toilet block offers free hot water to hand basins; razor point; showers. Available April to October. Ideal for touring all Cornwall and much of Devon with local walks, sandy beaches and beauty spots within easy reach. Weekly rates from £28 plus VAT for vans; £1.50 plus VAT for tourers and campers. Stamp for brochure.

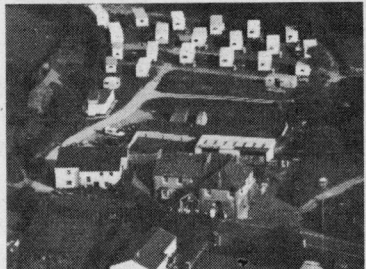

TINTAGEL AREA. SMALL PEACEFUL SITE situated in a pleasant rural setting a few minutes from the delightful little village of St. Teath, an ideal location for sandy beaches. Surfing, sailing, horse riding, fishing, moors, excellent touring centre. Our 2, 4, 6-berth caravans all have flush toilet, colour TV, fridge, fire. Some with showers. For our colour brochure write to: **Trepentor Caravans, 3 Race Hill, Launceston PL15 9BA. Tel: (0566) 4549.**

TRURO near. Mrs Hazel Bowerman, Tre-Knoll Farm, Ladock, Near Truro TR2 4QB (St. Austell [0726] 882451). Very informal, quiet and relaxed atmosphere on this 10-acre smallholding where all the animals are treated as pets. Overlooking the beautiful Ladock Valley, Tre-Knoll is centrally situated and ideal for touring the whole of Cornwall. Truro six miles; Newquay 10 miles; innumerable beaches within easy reach. The four-berth caravan has Calor gas cooking, electric lighting, heating, hot and cold water, fridge and Elsan. Double bedroom. There is a flush toilet at the house and baths can also be arranged. Full details and terms on request.

WADEBRIDGE. Lady Jungius, Trevorrick Farm, St. Issey, Wadebridge PL27 7QH (Rumford [08414] 574). Working farm. Ideal for a peaceful holiday in lovely country surroundings, near beautiful beaches, a caravan is available on a beef and stock rearing farm. Seven-berth, 31' long, with kitchen, dinette, livingroom, built-in bathroom with lavatory; hot and cold water; electric light, cooker, water heater, TV, airing cupboard; fridge. Children welcome; well behaved dogs allowed. The caravan is privately sited in its own fenced garden, not overlooked, facing south. Good approach road. Beautiful walking country, with surfing, water ski-ing, boating, pony trekking in area. Milkman calls; village shops one mile. Weekly terms on application. SAE, please.

WIDEMOUTH BAY near. Mrs Marian Winnard, Honeys Meadow, Jacobstow, Bude EX23 0BX (Canworthy Water [056-681] 493). Two luxury caravans 28' and 23' set in private one and a half acre grounds. A quiet country holiday with extensive views over farmland. Ideally situated for touring all Cornwall and parts of North Devon. Both caravans have a bathroom with shower, flush toilet, Calor gas cooker, mains hot and cold water, gas fire, fridge, television and a double end bedroom. Shops, launderette, garage, public house and Post Office are two minutes away. Beaches within easy reach. Season from April to September. Very reasonable rates. Brochure available with SAE.

FARM HOLIDAY GUIDES LIMITED publish a large range of well-known accommodation guides. We will be happy to send you details or you can use the order form at the back of this book.

CUMBRIA – English Lakeland

AMBLESIDE (English Lakeland) GREENHOWE CARAVAN PARK, GREAT LANGDALE, AMBLESIDE LA22 9JU (096 67 231). An English Tourist Board Rose Award Park. Four, six or eight-berth caravans are offered for hire on this quiet, secluded, wooded site which is easily approached from the B5343, only six-and-a-half miles from Ambleside. Caravans have full gas cooking, electric lighting, WC, Shower, heating and colour TV. This one of the finest centres from which to explore the Lake District. Children are welcome here. Pets allowed if kept under control. No space is available for touring caravans or for campers. Rates for hiring range from £60 to £180 per week. Open from 1st March to 15th November.

AMBLESIDE. Mrs S. E. Jump, The Grove Farm, Ambleside LA22 9LG (Ambleside [0966] 33074). Three modern six-berth caravans available, to families only, on private site at The Grove Farm. Each caravan is installed with shower, toilet, hot and cold water, light, heat, cooker, TV and fridge. The caravans have panoramic views and are situated one-and-a-quarter miles above the village of Ambleside in the beautiful Stock Valley. An ideal spot for walking, touring and boating. Full details and terms on receipt of SAE.

CARLISLE. Mrs Anne E. Ivinson, Green View, Welton, Near Dalston, Carlisle CA5 7ES (Raughton Head [069-96] 230). An orchard in corner of our field is setting for this 28' four-berth caravan, with views over village green and farmland to Caldbeck Fells. Fringe of Lake District, in heart of farming country, caravan is in small rural hamlet of Welton on the Carlisle/Caldbeck road. An ideal touring centre, Caldbeck four miles, Carlisle nine; the Northern Fells and Lakes Ullswater and Bassenthwaite are easily accessible. The van has fully equipped kitchen (four burner cooker with grill and oven), hot and cold water, lounge with gas fire and bed settee; dinette; entrance hall; bathroom with flush toilet; basin and shower; full width end double bedroom; Calor gas cooking and heating. Electric light, fridge, TV, kettle, electricity by 10p meter. Linen hire available. Pets allowed if kept under control. Car essential, parking by van. Laundry/Freezer facilities provided. Shop/post office, craft shop and pub in Welton. Terms from £45. Open March to end October. SAE, please, for terms and further details. Also cottage to let and two pine chalets.

CARLISLE. Mrs P. E. Johnston, Yeast Hall, New House Farm, Newby West, Carlisle CA2 6QZ (Carlisle [0228] 23545). Working farm. Two attractive caravans on private farm site — 28 foot Fairview five-berth, 30 foot Willerby six-berth, each with lounge, kitchen, bedroom, bathroom and each completely private in own enclosure. Situated three-and-a-half miles west of Carlisle, one-quarter mile from road down private lane. It is ideally situated for visiting Lake District, Solway Coast, Scottish Borders, Roman Wall, Eden Valley, etc. Vans are very well equipped, with everything supplied except linen, and thoroughly cleaned between visitors. Electric lighting, heating. One Calor gas, one electric cooker, water heater. TV available. From £38 weekly. Further details with pleasure. Phone or write (SAE, please).

CONISTON. Mrs E. Youdell, Spoon Hall, Coniston LA21 8AW (Coniston [0966] 41391). This 33' six-berth caravan is situated on a 50-acre working hill farm one mile from Coniston, overlooking Coniston Lake. It has flush toilet, shower, gas cooker, electric lighting and fire. Children are welcome and there is a cot. Pets are allowed free. Available all year round. Pony trekking arranged from farm. Weekly terms on request.

CONISTON near. Mrs J. Halton, Scarr Head Bungalow, Torver, Near Coniston LA21 8BP (Coniston [0966] 41328). Working farm. Scarr Head Bungalow is a very small cattle breeding farm, three miles south of Coniston. Just off the Coniston/Ulverston road, the farm is situated close to the bridleway which leads to Coniston Old Man and Walna Scar and has tarmac access. Two 22' four-berth caravans are sited in a sheltered sunny position in a large garden to one side of the property, well spaced, all concrete standing, and fully paved paths, quiet peaceful surroundings and a nice outlook. The caravans are very clean and comfortable having full gas cookers, electricity, running water inside. Shaving point, fridge for necessities, car parking and flush toilet nearby. Linen not supplied. Available March to October. Ample parking and separate space for a touring caravan. Lovely walking terrain, central for touring. Ideal small site. SAE for particulars and prompt reply.

GRANGE-OVER-SANDS. Greaves Farm Caravan Site, Field Broughton, Grange-over-Sands. Available March to October, Greaves Farm Caravan Site is situated in a flat, grassy farm orchard. Quiet but not isolated, there are two six-berth caravans for hire each with colour TV, fridge, gas cooker and room heater and electricity for light and TV, as well as sites for 20 caravans. On site there is a toilet block with showers and hot and cold water. Parking alongside caravans. Personally supervised by owner. Children and pets welcome. An ideal base for touring the Lakes. Caravan hire from £65 to £85 weekly and £2.50 per night for touring vans. Contact **Mrs E. Rigg, Prospect House, Barber Green, Grange-over-Sands LA11 6HU (Cartmel [044 854] 329).**

KENDAL. Mrs E. Bateman, High Underbrow Farm, Burneside, Kendal LA8 9AY (Kendal [0539] 21927). Working farm. The caravan is one six-berth with end bedroom with two single beds in it. It is sited just off our private road before you get to the farmyard on a small piece of ground, fenced and mown. Lovely views and pleasant walks. Ideal spot for touring Lake District and Yorkshire Dales. It has Calor gas cooker and fire, electric lights, fridge, fire, TV and shaving points. Flush toilet in van. Open March 1st to October 31st. Children and pets welcome. Shopping Burneside two miles; Kendal four miles. Weekly rates from £50. Holiday cottage (sleeps four) also to let from £75 a week.

KENDAL near. Mrs B. Pickthall, Borrans Farm, New Hutton, Near Kendal LA8 0AT (Kendal [0539] 21753). Three six-berth well equipped caravans with separate end bedrooms, TV, fridge, Calor gas cookers and a shower and toilet block at the end of the farmhouse. The caravans are situated in a field next to the farmhouse overlooking the farmyard where children can see all the farming activity — cows being milked etc. We are within easy access of the Lakes and Yorkshire Dales. Horse riding and fishing close by with many different country lanes for an evening walk. Children are welcome and there is a cot. Pets allowed. Available March 31st to October 31st. Weekly from £55–£65.

CARAVANS
TO LET

Good range of well-equipped modern caravans available on genuine farm site at Threlkeld, near Keswick. Magnificent views. Convenient for northern Lakes. Site facilities include flush toilets, H/C showers, shaver points, laundry room, shop, pony trekking.
Long SAE for details please.
Rates £40 to £115. Ask for special 10% discount.
We specialise in early/late cheap holidays.
Weekend lets available.

ANNABLE HOLIDAY CARAVANS
2 Spring Gardens, Watford, Herts. WD2 6JJ
Tel: Garston (0923) 673946 or Stourbridge (0384) 395960.

KESWICK. Setmabanning Farm, Threlkeld, Near Keswick. Working farm. At Threlkeld, a genuine farm site, just off the Keswick to Penrith road, with milking cattle and hill sheep, overlooking Saddleback with Helvellyn behind. River Glendermackin runs through the site, marvellous for walkers, within easy reach of Derwentwater, Ullswater, Grasmere and Windermere etc. Sailing, boating, steamer trips can be enjoyed. Wide choice of Kingsize, excellently equipped, modern caravans with mains water, drainage, and gas fires. Flush toilets, hot and cold showers, shaver points, laundry room and pony trekking on site. Farm and village shop. Parking beside caravans. Special rates early and late, weekends a speciality. Rates from £35 to £115. SAE — **C.M.C. Holiday Caravans, 23 Brooks Road, Wylde Green, Sutton Coldfield B72 1HP (021-354-1551).**

KESWICK near. Setmabanning Farm, Threlkeld, Near Keswick. Working farm. This site is a genuine farm site, just off the main Penrith to Keswick road, some four miles from Keswick, strategically placed for all northern lakes. Main road quarter mile. For hire selection four/five berth caravans furnished and equipped to the highest standard; full oven cookers; sink units; lounges; single and double beds; fires etc. Some with private toilet and shower. Toilet block with showers, laundry and shop, also shop in village quarter mile. Children and pets welcome. Water and drainage laid on. Superb walking and climbing in this beautiful and interesting countryside. For hiring these vans, 25' and 30', weekly rates are from £59 to £105. Open Easter to 31st October. SAE, please, for further details **Mrs D. Robson, 68 Station Road, Stanley, Co. Durham DH9 0JP (Stanley [0207] 232329).**

LAMPLUGH. B. Simpson, Inglenook Caravan Park, Lamplugh CA14 4SH (Lamplugh [0946] 861240). Inglenook Caravan Park is an AA listed site pleasantly situated in the picturesque village of Lamplugh and centre of the North Western Lakes, ideal for touring the Lake District. The luxury holiday vans for hire have all services and add pleasure to your holiday. The immediate countryside provides for walking, climbing; fishing and pony trekking only minutes away. Sandy beaches just seven miles. Ample golf courses in the area. The site shop provides most requirements. Mr and Mrs Simpson, the proprietors, make every effort to make your holiday enjoyable. H&C showers, toilets and laundry available on site. Hook-ups. Open to all tourers and tents and a listed site of the Caravan and Camping Club. Sites are available for the sale of new Static Vans. March/November. SAE for details.

MILLOM. Mrs S. R. Capstick, Whicham Hall, Silecroft, Millom LA18 5LT (Millom [0657] 2637). Working farm. Whicham Hall, situated in Whicham Valley, a beautiful unspoilt part of the Lake District, provides a perfect holiday for those who want a change from a busy noisy life. The large six-berth caravan on quarter-acre, very private site, has water, electricity, gas cooking and fridge and heating, also shower and flush toilet. The 300-acre beef and dairy farm is two miles from Silecroft beach and golf course, and 12 miles from Coniston. Silecroft post office and general store is just a mile away. Children are welcome, as are family pets. Open Easter to October. Weekly from £50. SAE, please, for further details.

MUNGRISDALE near. Thanet Well Caravan Park, Hutton Roof, Near Mungrisdale. A small quiet farm site just north of the Penrith/Keswick road, with 40 vans, set in light woodland on a ridge with magnificent views over the valley to the nearby mountain range. Two six-berth caravans to let, all fully equipped except linen. Electric kettle, fridge, TV hire, lighting, mains water, Calor gas cooking and heating; all vans have one double bedroom and one bunk bedroom. Toilet block with hot and cold showers, laundrette. Shop on site. Children welcome. One small dog by arrangement. Open from March to October. Early/late weekends. Beautiful peaceful surroundings, pony trekking nearby. Lakes Ullswater and Derwentwater are within easy reach. Fell walking and many places of interest to visit in this area. SAE, please, for terms, **Mrs Anne E. Ivinson, Green View, Welton, Near Dalston, Carlisle CA5 7ES (Raughton Head [06996] 230).**

SEDBERGH. Mrs R. Udall, Merlin Cragg, Howgill, Sedbergh LA10 5HU (Sedbergh [0587] 20719). Six-berth Pemberton caravan set amidst picturesque and peaceful country surroundings affording easy access to Lakes and Yorkshire Dales; one and a quarter miles from Sedbergh. Ideal walking centre. The van is on private land with good approach road and parking and has flush toilet and hot and cold water. All-electric; TV. Children are welcome and they may bring their pets. Open all year round, mid-week bookings accepted. Terms from £48 weekly.

SEDBERGH. Mrs E. D. Hill, High Branthwaite, Howgill, Sedbergh LA10 5HU (Sedbergh [0587] 20579). Working farm. High Branthwaite is a dairy farm at the foot of the Howgill Fells, one and a half miles from Sedbergh, 11 miles from Kendal. Two Ace Emperor 24' caravans, standing at opposite ends of a half-acre paddock, have electric light and heaters. Cooking by Calor gas. Flush toilet with washbasin and water heater nearby. Caravans fully equipped, including linen. Children welcome and pets permitted. Farm produce available. Ideal location for touring Lakes and Dales, fell walking, fishing, bird watching. Available March to October from £55 and weekends early and late season. Also Bed and Breakfast available in one family room sleeping four.

WINDERMERE. Mrs J. E. Park, Causeway Farm, Windermere LA23 1JT (Windermere [096-62] 3802). Working farm. Causeway Farm is a 200-acre beef farm situated north of Windermere off the A592 behind Orrest Head from which one can see the entire lake and surrounding mountains. Fishing, swimming, pony trekking, golf, boating are all available close by. The four-berth caravan is situated in the orchard behind the farmhouse, enjoying the benefits of a quiet position, yet only one-and-a-half miles from Windermere village. Electric lighting, heating. Calor gas cooker, fridge; toilet and hot and cold water supply 10 yards away. No linen supplied. Open all year. Children and pets welcome. SAE, please, for terms.

DERBYSHIRE

ASHBOURNE. Mr N. Martin, The Alamo, Kniveton, Ashbourne DE6 1JL (Ashbourne [0335] 42276). Two miles from Ashbourne, near Alton Towers, Chatsworth House, Sudbury Hall and Museum this large four-berth caravan is situated on a 15 acre farm with panoramic views of Dovedale and the Derbyshire Peaks. Free electricity. Toilet in the caravan and another toilet plus hot water and handbasin are available on site. Children and pets are welcome and babysitting can be arranged. Cheap eggs and milk are available. Open all year. Car essential. £50 per week. CU-HT-P-PD-R-TV.

BUXTON near. Mr and Mrs J. Melland, The Pomeroy Caravan Park, Street House Farm, Flagg, Near Buxton SK17 9QG (Longnor [029883] 259). Working farm. This newly developed site for 30 caravans is situated five miles from Buxton, in heart of Peak District National Park. Ideal base for touring by car or walking. Site adjoins northern end of now famous Tissington and High Peak Trail. Only nine miles from Haddon Hall and ten from Chatsworth House. Landscaped to the latest model standards for caravan sites; tourers and campers will find high standards here. New toilet block with showers, washing facilities and laundry; mains electric hook-up points. Children welcome; dogs on lead. There is a 22' six-berth Eccles caravan for hire here, with Calor gas heating and mains electricity for lighting and shaver point; it has full size cooker. Elsan toilet inside. Fully equipped except linen. Open Easter to end of October. SAE, please, for weekly and nightly rates. Back-packers welcome.

Caravans and Camping 351

DOVEDALE. Mrs Joan Wain, Air Cottage Farm, Ilam, Ashbourne DE6 2BD (Thorpe Cloud [033-529] 475). Air Cottage Farm is situated at the edge of Dovedale with picturesque views of Thorpe Cloud and Dovedale Valley; 10 minutes from the famous Stepping Stones. Within easy reach of "Alton Towers" and Matlock's Gulliver's Kingdom. There is one four/six berth caravan available, with gas cooking, lighting and fridge. Hot and cold water on site and separate flush toilet. Children are welcome and there is a pony for them to ride. Pets permitted. Eggs and milk can be provided. Open from March to October. Terms on request.

DEVON

ASHBURTON. Mrs Rhona Parker, Higher Mead Farm, Ashburton TQ13 7LJ (Ashburton [0364] 52598). Working farm. Six-berth caravans, inside flush toilets, electric light, gas or electric cooking. Genuine farm site. Caravans set in part of 170-acre farm, 12 miles Torbay and three miles from edge of Dartmoor. Riding half a mile. Golf and fishing within seven miles. Stock car racing and National Hunt racing seven miles. Children and pets very welcome. This is a family-run site and all caravans are cleaned after every let and checked by owner who lives on site. Prices from £38 to £85 per week — 10% reductions if only two occupy caravan. Also three cottages — one two-bedroomed, one three-bedroomed, the other four-bedroomed from £60 to £160. Open March to November.

AXMINSTER. Mrs G. Webber, Higher Manor Farm, Combpyne, Axminster EX13 6SY (Lyme Regis [02974] 3376). Working farm. Six-berth caravan situated in beautiful countryside, in the hamlet of Combpyne, close to the coast. Four miles to the picturesque seaside town of Lyme Regis. Shop one mile. Caravan comprises double bedroom with washbasin and wardrobe, also shaver point; dining area with TV; kitchen equipped with gas cooker, electric fridge, toaster and all essential utensils. Gas fire; inside toilet. Pleasant cliff walks nearby, and the town of Lyme Regis is noted for fossils, also for its connections with authoress Jane Austen. SAE for details please.

CHITTLEHAMHOLT (North Devon). Snapdown Farm Caravans, Chittlehamholt. Six only, six-berth caravans, in lovely unspoilt countryside, down a quiet lane on a 161-acre farm. The caravans, backing onto trees, are well spread out, each with hard standing for a car and each with electricity, fridge, colour TV, gas cooker and fire and inside flush toilet. Outside seats and picnic tables, barbecue and children's adventure and play area in small wood adjoining. Two well appointed showers and small laundry room with spin dryer, iron, etc. Snapdown is within easy reach and central for all North Devon coast and Exmoor. Terms £35 to £90 including VAT and all gas and elctricity in caravans. Discount for two people only, early and late season. Available March-November. Illustrated brochure from **Mrs M. Bowen, The "Star" Agri. Eng. Co., The Square, South Molton EX36 3BU (South Molton [076-95] 2505).**

COLYTON. Mrs S. Gould, Bonehayne Farm, Colyton EX13 6SG (Farway [040-487] 396). Working farm. This is a six-berth Pemberton caravan situated in a secluded spot in the farmhouse garden, overlooking the river, fields and woodlands where foxes, badgers and deer, Mallard duck and Kingfishers too are a common sight. There are farm animals to make friends with on this 250-acre working farm and good trout fishing down on the river. The caravan contains a separate double end bedroom, kitchen with electric cooker and fridge. Large lounge dividing into two further double bedrooms (one twin). Mains water and electricity, flush toilet and shower room just outside. Fully equipped except linen. TV available. Farm produce obtainable from the house. Colyton two miles and the sea four-and-a-half miles. SAE please for full details.

COLYTON. Mrs M. A. Virgin, Shortlands Farm, Southleigh, Colyton EX13 6SA (Farway [040-487] 236). Working farm. This 28' six-berth caravan is on a 32-acre dairy farm. Woodland walks and wildlife park near. Within easy reach of golf courses, Seaton Tramway (four miles) and Beer (the old smugglers' village) which has the Peco Railway. The caravan has an end double bedroom. Flush toilet, electricity, gas cooker, fridge, running water. Meter installed. No linen supplied. The caravan stands in a small orchard through which runs a small brook. Open from Easter to October. Children of all ages welcome and pets permitted. A car is essential and there is parking space. Local post office for sweets and cigarettes. Main shops two-and-a-half miles away. SAE, please, for terms.

CULLOMPTON. Mrs J. Davey, Pound Farm, Butterleigh, Cullompton EX15 1PH (Bickleigh [08845] 208). Working farm. A Pound Farm holiday combines finest English scenery with traditional beauty of village of Butterleigh. Enjoy family break from April to October on this 80-acre sheep and dairy farm. Spacious comfortable caravan accommodation for six, in grass paddock with paths and parking for two cars. Well-equipped except linen. Electric cooker, kettle, toaster, fridge, heater, TV, lights, four power points. All cutlery, utensils, blankets. Adjoining caravan is flush toilet, two washbasins in utility room with shaving point, hot/cold water, electric light and two-bar heater. Four miles from M5, Cullompton, Tiverton, Silverton, Bickleigh — traditional thatched olde worlde village in heart of beautiful Exe Valley. Well-stocked coarse and trout ponds only two miles away plus our own two ponds (coarse and carp) for private fishing only. SAE, please, for terms and details.

352 Caravans and Camping

HOLSWORTHY. Mrs H. Gill, Helsden Farm, Bradford, Holsworthy EX22 7AH (Shebbear [040-928] 341). Working farm, join in. Enjoy a relaxing self-catering caravan holiday on a Devon livestock farm, amidst glorious countryside, about six miles from the market town of Holsworthy. Ideally situated for touring moors, beaches and many local attractions. The caravan is a spacious five-berth, with fridge and TV. Facilities 25 yards from caravan include shower, flush toilet, games room with snooker, table tennis and darts. Also clay pigeon shooting. Local facilities include golf, fishing and horse riding. It is an ideal family holiday where children are particularly welcome. Baby minding if required. Farm participation welcomed. For prices and vacancies SAE, please.

HONITON. Mrs Sue Wigram, Riggles Farm, Upottery, Honiton EX14 0SP (Luppitt [040-489] 229). Working farm. Three beautifully situated caravans on 450-acre dairy/arable farm, nine miles from Honiton, easy access to many lovely beaches and local attractions. Visitors welcome on farm. Farmhouse meals available some evenings. Milk and eggs sold at farm. Children's play area, table tennis; cot and linen hire available; tumble and spin drier. Caravans are in two peaceful acres near farmhouse. Each is fully equipped for two/eight people, with two separate bedrooms and spacious living areas. Own bathroom with shower, flush toilet, washbasin. Gas cooker, heater, colour TV, fridge. From £50 per week inclusive (10% reductions for couples, not school holidays). For brochure please telephone or send SAE.

ILFRACOMBE. Mrs H. Y. Verney, Cheglinch Farm, West Down, Ilfracombe EX34 8NW (Ilfracombe [0271] 62148). Working farm. Although this is a working farm, the caravan is situated in a quiet private paddock of one eighth of an acre. This is a six-berth "Astral Gay Dawn" caravan with Calor gas cooking and electric lighting. A separate flush toilet and washing facilities with mains water (hot and cold) and drying cabinet for use of caravan guests only is available approximately 10 yards from the caravan. A high standard of cleanliness is maintained at all times. All guests warmly welcome including children. Pets permitted. This is an ideal centre for touring beaches and moors. 500 yards from main Barnstaple/Ilfracombe road, three miles from Ilfracombe, 10 miles from the market town of Barnstaple, and five miles from the golden sands of Woolacombe Beach. Terms on application.

ILFRACOMBE. Mrs J. Blackmore, Hillcrest Farm, Bittadon, Barnstaple EX31 4HN (Ilfracombe [0271] 63537). Working farm. On our 500-acre farm we have a fully equipped six-berth caravan, 27', separate end bedroom, inside toilet, cold water on tap, Calor gas cooker; refrigerator, kettle, light, iron and fire on 10p meter. Also separate bathroom with shower, hot and cold basin and flush toilet. Available all year. Ample parking and garden area. 700' above sea level in quiet hamlet of Bittadon. Easy access to beautiful Woolacombe beaches, Ilfracombe, Exmoor and Combe Martin. Visitors are welcome to walk about and enjoy farm activities. One small, well-behaved dog accepted by arrangement at £5 per week.

ILFRACOMBE. Mrs K. A. Richards, East Hagginton Farm, Berrynarbor, Ilfracombe EX34 9SB (Combe Martin [027-188] 2262). Working farm. East Hagginton Farm is a 180-acre farm approached off a B-Road; sea, shops and golf course all within one mile. Peaceful surroundings, with views of Bristol Channel. The caravan, which sleeps six, is sited in quarter-acre paddock at rear of farmhouse and is fully equipped except linen. Flush toilet adjacent. Electric heater and cooker, fridge and TV. Babysitting if required. Regret no pets. Car parking. Available Easter to October. SAE, please, for terms.

NEWTON ABBOT. Mr & Mrs J. Murray, Silver Birches, Teign Valley, Trusham, Newton Abbot TQ13 0NJ (Chudleigh [0626] 852172). Two luxury 23 ft. and 29 ft. four-berth caravans in an attractive two acre garden on the bank of the River Teign. Each has mains water, electricity, shower/bath, flush toilet, washbasin, immersion heater, Calor cooker, fridge, TV available. Ideally situated two miles from A38 on B3193. Dartmoor, Exeter, Torquay easily accessible. Sea 12 miles. Car essential — ample parking. Excellent centre for fishing (river and reservoir), bird watching, forest walks; 70 yards private salmon and trout fishing. Golf courses and horse-riding within easy reach. Shops two-and-a-half miles. Milk delivered. We personally clean caravans and ensure your comfort. Pets by arrangement. E.T.B. registered. Open March – October. Terms from £50 per week. Bed and Breakfast available in bungalow.

SEATON. Mr J. M. Salter, Manor Farm Caravan and Camping Site, Seaton (Seaton [0297] 21524). Working farm. Come and spend a super holiday on a site second to none! This is a working farm approached by tarmac roads on A3052. Both caravan and camp sites have glorious views to the sea and are one mile from the sea and Seaton, within easy walking distance. The luxurious modern facilities include flush toilets, hot and cold showers and washbasins, hair dryers, laundry rooms, chemical disposal points, washing up facilities, mains water taps, shop, play area, public telephone. Dogs allowed. Most sporting facilities are available nearby. We also have caravans for hire. SAE for brochure, or telephone.

SOUTH BRENT. Nick and Sue Coveyduck, Edeswell Farm Caravan and Camping Park, Rattery, South Brent TQ10 9LN (South Brent [036-47] 2177). SOUTH DEVON PICTURESQUE FARM Caravan and Camping Park. Quiet rural setting in 18 acres. Ideally situated for touring Dartmoor, Torbay, South Devon coast, or just relaxing. Midway between Plymouth/Exeter, half a mile from main A38 on the A385. Shop, trout fishing, TV lounge, Bar, Lounge, Bar Meals, launderette, leisure area — table tennis, badminton, pool, video games, woodland playground. Fully serviced de-luxe caravans — £40 to £180 per week. Everything included. NEW LUXURY UNITS — own shower, flush toilet, hot and cold, fridge, fire, gas, electricity, cooker, two and three bedrooms. PETS, TOURERS AND TENTS welcome — showers, hot and cold water, flush toilets.

Please note that entries marked with an asterisk also have a colour display advert in the colour section in this guide

Caravans and Camping 353

SOUTH MOLTON. Mrs P. M. Grimshire, Rugglepitt Farm, West Anstey, South Molton EX36 3PW (Anstey Mills [039-84] 345). Working farm. One six-berth caravan, 26', in excellent condition on a private farm site in peaceful Devon countryside bordering Exmoor. Available from March to October. Double end bedroom, spacious kitchen and lounge. Electric lighting and fridge, black and white TV. Calor gas cooker and heater, mains water and drainage. Elsan toilet in van. Flush toilet nearby. Parking space. Easily approached by a good B road. Fully equipped except for linen. Cot available. Farm carries a dairy herd of cows and sheep, etc. Visitors welcome to wander around the farm observing simple rules. Riding nearby, also some fishing. Children and well behaved pets welcome. Within easy reach of Moors and many beautiful spots. Shop two miles. Farm produce available. Weekly rates £35 to £60. SAE, please.

TORQUAY near. John and Rosemary Baines, Brook Orchard Caravan Park, Brookedor, Kingskerswell, Near Torquay TQ12 5BJ (Kingskerswell [08047] 5165). A small, pretty holiday park in level orchard setting, on edge of old village. Centrally placed for Torbay entertainments, the peace of Dartmoor, the beauty of Devon's beaches and countryside, with a tremendous variety of holiday attractions. Pleasant, clean caravans with flush toilets, mains water, electricity, fridges and gas cookers. Car parking adjacent to caravans. Central building with hot/cold water, basins, showers, laundry. Shop, TV hire. Calor gas sales. Elsan disposable. Children and well behaved dogs welcome. Rates from £42 per week. Tourers from £3 per night (no awnings). Closed February only. Telephone or SAE for brochure.

WESTWARD HO! Star Holidays (FG), Golf Links Road, Westward Ho! EX39 1HF (Bideford [023-72] 72238). EXMOOR, DARTMOOR & CLOVELLY WITHIN EASY REACH. Self-catering at its BEST. Luxury caravans and chalets with hot and cold shower, flush toilet, colour TV, full size cooker and fridge. No dogs! Cleanliness assured, highly recommended, considered the best chalet/caravan park in Westward Ho! Three miles of golden sand, safe bathing, surfing, fishing, horse riding, golf. Write or phone now for colour brochure with details of discounts and special offers for two persons and the small family in chalets and large caravans, some with three bedrooms. See also colour display advertisement. *

WESTWARD HO! Roslyn Caravan Gardens, Merley Road, Westward Ho! Four to seven berth luxury caravans and one chalet in this small garden site near the sea, with perfect sea views. All mains services with electricity, gas, water drainage, colour TV, fridge, fire, toilet, washbasin, shower or bath, hot and cold water. Fully equipped. Laundry room, washing machine etc. Free car parking on site. Children welcome. No pets peak months. Available from Easter to October. Shopping facilities opposite. Three miles of sandy beach for fishing, surfing, horse riding and golf nearby. Licensed club — not on site. Under owners' personal supervision. **Mrs J. Barclay (EG), Merley Road, Westward Ho! EX39 1JS (Bideford [02372] 75281).**

WOOLACOMBE. Twitchen House and Mortehoe Caravan Park. A fleet of luxury and modern caravans are available on this country mansion site, nine different types of caravan giving a wide choice of accommodation at a price to meet the individual holidaymaker's needs. All caravans are on concrete bases, and have mains drainage, water, toilets, heating in lounge, electricity and fridges. Most have TV, hot and cold water to sinks, showers etc. All are fully equipped except for linen. Terms which are fully inclusive, start from £40 per week. Excellent site facilities are available, including licensed club with bar, cafe, pool, family area and entertainment; launderette and supermarket etc. Pets permitted out of season. Member of WCTB. Registered with ETB. SAE, please, for colour brochure and tariff. **Woolacombe Caravan Hirers (Dept FHG), Garden Cottage, 27 East Street, Braunton, Near Devon EX33 2EA (Braunton [0271] 816580).**

WOOLACOMBE. North Morte Farm, Mortehoe, Woolacombe. Working farm. This genuine farm Site is situated at the top of Mortehoe Village, overlooking Rockham Bay. The Beach is 500 yards from the Park and is safe for bathing. The surrounding countryside is made up of Farm and National Trust land. Fishing, Horse Riding, Golf, etc. are all within easy reach. The Village is five minutes' walk and has several shops, cafes and pubs. Woolacombe with its three miles of golden sand and entertainment for all the family, is one mile away. There are two large fields containing Holiday Caravans each with ample parking space alongside. Facilities include flush toilets, showers, hot and cold running water, washing machines, dryers, ironing-hair drying facilities, shop and children's play area. Accommodation for tents also. For details and brochures SAE to **R. C. and M. R. Easterbrook, Dept. FHG, North Morte Farm Caravan and Camping Park, Mortehoe, Woolacombe, N. Devon EX34 7EG (Woolacombe [0271] 870381).**

DORSET

BOURNEMOUTH near. Mudeford, Near Bournemouth. This site is just a few minutes' level walk away from beach, quay and harbour, and just three miles from the border of the New Forest. Excellent river and harbour fishing, also facilities for water ski-ing, golf, sailing, judo, gliding, bowls and horse riding in area. Good sea bathing, lovely sands. Buses pass the site which is just six miles from Bournemouth. Bluebird Consort four/six berth, own toilet, fridge, gas fire, colour TV. Site facilities include showers, flush toilets, laundry room (with iron). Children and pets welcome. Shops nearby. SAE, please, for terms to **Mrs D. M. Davis, 7 Chessel Avenue, Boscombe, Bournemouth BH5 1LQ (Bournemouth [0202] 37587).**

BRIDPORT. Mrs P. M. Huxter, Bidlake Farm, Broadoak, Bridport DT6 5PY (Bridport [0308] 22675). Working farm. One large residential caravan situated 100 yards from the farmhouse on small secluded site on 250-acre dairy farm carrying herd of 60 cows. Sleeps up to five in one double bedroom, one room with bunk beds and z-bed in sittingroom. Fully fitted kitchen with fridge; fully fitted bathroom; sittingroom with TV. All services including full central heating, connected. Children are welcome, also pets. Milk and eggs supplied from farmhouse; shopping and cinema at Bridport, two miles away. West Bay for bathing, fishing, boating etc., three miles. Good country walks over the numerous footpaths across surrounding countryside. Excellent riding establishment within one mile. Weekly terms from £55. SAE, please, with enquiries.

ETB　　　**MANOR FARM HOLIDAY CENTRE**　　　**AA**
Charmouth, Bridport, Dorset

Situated in a quiet rural valley, Manor Farm is the nearest caravan and camping site to Charmouth beach, a level ten minutes' walk away.

Luxury 6-berth Caravans for Hire with toilet/shower, refrigerator, full cooker, TV, gas fire.
30-acre Tourist Park for touring caravans, dormobiles and tents.
Centre facilities include * Toilets; * Hot showers; * Fish and chip takeaway; * Licensed bar with family room; * Amusement room; * Launderette; * Shop and off-licence; * Swimming pool; * Electric hook-up points; * Calor gas and Camping Gaz; * Ice pack service; * Chemical disposal unit.

Send SAE for colour brochure to **Mr R. E. Loosmore or Tel: 0297 60226**
See also Colour Display Advertisement in this Guide.

CHARMOUTH. Mrs D. J. Chapman, Stubbs Farmhouse, Monkton Wyld, Charmouth DT6 6DE (Charmouth [0297] 60464). Working farm. One six-berth caravan in a secluded spot near farmhouse, with far reaching views along valley. This mixed farm is situated two-and-a-half miles from Charmouth – three miles from Lyme Regis. Ideal for touring or walking. Golf and plenty of places of interest within a few miles. The caravan is fully equipped with Calor gas cooker and fire, electric fridge, double and single end bedrooms, colour TV and flush toilet. Open May until October. No linen supplied. Full details and rates available on request. SAE, please.

LYME REGIS. Mrs A. M. Hounsell, Carswell Farm, Uplyme, Lyme Regis DT7 3XQ (Lyme Regis [02974] 2378). Working farm. Carswell Farm is a carries dairy cows and pigs and is situated in a wooded valley, two-and-a-half miles from the sea. Ideal for family holidays with safe sandy beaches at Lyme Regis and Charmouth. Lovely walks, golf, fishing, riding nearby. Interesting places to visit. Four six-berth caravans (with inside flush toilet and shower). All have hot and cold water. Children are welcome and well controlled pets allowed. Shops one mile (village). Fully equipped, except linen (sleeping bags and blankets provided), the caravans have electric lights, fire and fridge; gas cooker. Available 1st May to 1st October. SAE, please, for terms and further details.

LYME REGIS. Mrs J. Tedbury, Little Paddocks, Yawl Hill Lane, Lyme Regis DT7 3RW (Lyme Regis [029-74] 3085). A six-berth caravan on Devon/Dorset border in a well-kept paddock overlooking Lyme Bay and surrounding countryside. Situated on a smallholding with animals, for perfect peace and quiet. Lyme Regis two-and-a-half miles, Charmouth three-and-a-half miles. Both have safe beaches for children. Easy driving distance to resorts of Seaton, Beer and Sidmouth. The caravan is fully equipped except linen. It has shower room with handbasin and toilet inside as well as flush toilet just outside. Electric light, fridge and TV. Calor gas cooker and fire. Car can be parked alongside. Dogs welcome. Terms from £46. SAE, please.

LYME REGIS. Mrs C. Grymonprez, Beechfield Cottage, Yawl Hill, Uplyme, Lyme Regis DT7 3RW (Lyme Regis [02974] 3216). Panoramic seaview and surroundings. Only two static caravans privately sited in peaceful countryside on our one acre well-kept field — hedge screened. One cosy six-berth with end bedroom, one modern eight-berth with two bedrooms and shower. Both caravans are fully equipped (except linen) with fridge, mains electricity, water, inside flush toilet, gas cooker and fire, TV. Cleanliness guaranteed. Parking alongside caravans. Prices according to season but include gas and electricity. Lyme Regis is only two-and-a-half miles, Charmouth three-and-a-half miles. We produce organically grown vegetables and herbs. Free range eggs, milk and home-made bread are available. Also Bed and Breakfast.

PLEASE SEND A STAMPED ADDRESSED ENVELOPE WITH ENQUIRIES

Caravans and Camping 355

POOLE. Rockley Sands, Poole. Please contact us for details of our caravans sited on the fabulous Rockley Sands Holiday/Leisure Centre. All our caravans have own bath/shower, toilet, electricity, heating, fridge, H&C, separate bedrooms and are fully equipped with everything you will require on holiday for up to six persons. Estate amenities include full entertainment programme, shops, go-carts, crazy golf, beach, water ski-ing, fishing, boat trips. Free club membership and free entrance to swimming pool. Superb area for sightseeing. Bournemouth only seven miles. All bookings and caravans personally supervised by owner, Mrs Jennifer Pretty. Dogs welcome. Open April–October. SAE, please, to **Rio Caravans (ENG), 80 Parkway Drive, Bournemouth BH8 9JR (Bournemouth [0202] 34423).**

SHERBORNE near. Mrs Ann Osmond, Sunnyside Farm, Hermitage, Near Sherborne DT9 6HA (Holnest [096-321] 276). Working farm. This is a 50-acre dairy farm with various farm pets. Outside toys for children. Large garden with lawns to sit on. Good riding school nearby, also fresh water fishing. Seven miles from the historical town of Sherborne and five miles from the pretty village of Cerne Abbas. The 32' residential caravan sleeps six persons and has Calor gas cooker, TV, fridge; flush toilet in bathroom; hot and cold water at all taps. Open all year. Well controlled pets allowed. Shops three miles away. SAE, please, for terms.

GLOUCESTERSHIRE

WOTTON-UNDER-EDGE. The Manager, Cotswold Gate Caravan Park, Canonscourt Farm, Bradley Wotton-under-Edge GL12 7PN (Dursley [0453] 843128). Working farm. Cotswold Gate Caravan Park is a haven of peace for travellers who wish to break their journey; within easy access to both M5 and M4 motorways, situated under the Westridge spur of the Cotswolds amidst farming country. Ideally located for touring both the Cotswolds and the Severn Vale. Adjacent to the Site, Streamleaze nine-hole, par 3 Golf Course has been developed, incorporating a half-acre lake for fishing. The "Bull Pen" offers a welcome range of Real Ale, Wines, Farmhouse Cider and Minerals for refreshment after walking, driving, or just soaking up the country air. Open March to end October.

HEREFORD & WORCESTER

LEOMINSTER. Miss P. Moore, Meadow Bank Farm, Hamnish, Leominster HR6 8EF (Steensbridge [056-882] 267 or 254). Working farm. There are three secluded caravans for hire on this farm, four to eight berths. They have mains water, TV, gas cooker, all necessary utensils etc.; fridge and everything except personal linen. Flush toilets in all vans. Shower available. Fishing on farm; golf locally. Horse riding for all ages and experience — Country Hacks or lessons on farm (20 horses/ponies). Children welcome. Pets allowed under proper control. Only site rules are for reasonable peace and quiet with friendly atmosphere. Shops Leominster two miles, swimming pool. Miss Moore enjoys people coming to stay at her caravans and helps in every way she can with information about interesting places to visit. Available March to October. Weekly terms £35 to £50 according to season. Visitors return again and again. Full particulars on request.
LOWER MAESCOED. Mrs J. M. Bambrough, Maerdy Farm, Lower Maescoed HR2 0HP (Longtown Castle [087 387] 237). Modern, comfortable, six-berth caravan, peacefully sited on family mixed farm amidst beautiful countryside on the Herefordshire/Gwent Borders. Ideally located for touring the Black Mountains, Brecon Beacons and Wye Valleys. Local shops three miles. Milk, bread and green-groceries delivered to farm during week. Available 31st March to 31st September, caravan facilities include electricity, water, gas, fridge, heater, WC, gas cooker. End double bedroom, pulldown double bed and two single couch beds. No shower, but visitors welcome to use bathroom in house. Car essential, parking. Rates on application include electricity, gas and linen.

KENT

**BENENDEN. Mrs Anne Cyster, Walkhurst Farm, Benenden TN17 4EN (Cranbrook [0580] 240677).
Working farm.** There are two new luxury holiday caravans on this farm site of two acres, half hour by car from the sea. Benenden village is about half a mile and there are many historic buildings in the surrounding area to visit. Golf Club nearby and also Riding Stables. This is a very beautiful part of Kent, especially in May when the apple blossom is out. The caravans sleep eight; French doors go into lounge with a Calor gas fire for heating and TV; the seating area makes a double bed; kitchen/dining area lets down into double bed; Calor gas cooker, fridge, crockery, cutlery, etc. Toilet with washbasin and shower room. Hot and cold water. Double bedroom; wardrobes; another bedroom with bunk beds and wardrobe. Bed linen is provided. Open all year. Peaceful and ideal for children. Weekly £70–£100. Sorry, no pets. Meals can be provided.

LEICESTERSHIRE

UPPINGHAM near. Mrs D. Renner, The Old Rectory, Belton-in-Rutland, Near Uppingham LE15 9LE (Belton [057-286] 279). Working farm, join in. This Country Craft Centre welcomes parties of visitors by appointment and the many facilities offered include an interesting exhibit of quality traditional country crafts on sale or to order; traditional country bygones on display; miniature farm; farm walks; picnic facilities; children's play area; cream teas and other light refreshments. Car essential — parking. Five-acre site for caravans/campers is in a pastoral setting and facilities include septic tank, disposal point, cold water tap, dustbins, electricity hook-up points, washing machine and iron, shower and WC.

NORFOLK

MUNDESLEY-ON-SEA. Mr A. E. Crawford, The Bellevue Caravan Park, Heath Lane, Mundesley-on-Sea, Norwich NR11 8ER (Mundesley [0263] 720259). This is a beautiful caravan holiday park for people who require a quiet, uncommercialised holiday away from it all. The proprietors do everything to make the holiday a success. The caravans for hire are modern, well appointed, 24' to 32' long, two, three and four-berth, with drainage, running water and electricity. Bellevue is quiet with only 61 caravans and like a large private garden with lawns, rosebeds, rockeries, surrounded by trees, sheltered and secluded in the heart of the country, but within easy walk of the beautiful sandy beach, buses, golf course and shops. The toilet blocks have modern fittings, washbasins, hot water, laundry room, baths, etc. The six caravans owned by the proprietor for hire have flush toilets, colour TV and gas fire; the other 55 are privately owned and not sub-let. Mundesley is a quiet, pretty village with water and windmill. Nearby are the Broads, Cromer, Norwich, Great Yarmouth, Walsingham Shrine, etc. Free picture brochure. SAE, please. Caravans for sale with site, from £850.

NORTHUMBERLAND

ALNWICK. Mrs J. W. Bowden, "Anvil-Kirk," 8 South Charlton Village, Alnwick NE66 2NA (Charlton Mires [066-579] 324). One six-berth caravan on single private site. Hard standing and lovely spacious surroundings. Three-quarters of a mile from the A1; six miles north of Alnwick and six miles also from the lovely clean beaches of Beadnell, Seahouses, Crestor village; nine miles from the Cheviot Hills. Many castles nearby — Bamburgh and Alnwick being the largest; wild cattle and bird sanctuaries; Ingram valley for the hill walker, Berwick and Morpeth markets. Holy Island is a must with its tiny castle and harbour with fishing boats. Many places to eat out within a radius of 10 miles. The caravan has mains water and electricity; full size Calor gas cooker, fridge, TV, end bedroom (bunk beds); flush toilet in bathroom. Open Easter to October. Children and pets welcome. Milk and bread delivered, papers and greengrocery daily. Weekly terms from £65. SAE, please. Also Bed and Breakfast available in house.

SHROPSHIRE

CRAVEN ARMS. Mrs V. M. Davies, Bush Farm, Clunton, Craven Arms SY7 0HU (Little Brampton [058-87] 330). Working farm. Sited in the beautiful secluded and peaceful Clun Valley riverside site, this stock-rearing, 60-acre farm has two six-berth mobile homes with fitted double bed and small bedrooms, double bed-settees. One 42', the other 36', both have fitted kitchens, fridge, bathroom with flush toilets. All-electric (10p meter); shaving points; hot and cold water; immersion heaters; carpets throughout. Children and small pets welcome. Fully equipped except linen. Car essential — ample parking. There is good trout and grayling fishing in the River Clun. Pleasant walking and touring country near the Welsh borders, with castles, Offa's Dyke, museum, market towns of Ludlow, Shrewsbury and Leominster and Roman sites. Inn five minutes' walk from site. Shops two miles. Pre-arrival shopping service by arrangement. Six acres for tourers and campers with flush toilet block and washbasins. Weekly hiring rates, on request with SAE, please.

SOMERSET

BROADWAY HOUSE
Caravan and Camping Park

AA 4 pennant site
RAC appointed
*Heated Swimming Pool

In the quiet surroundings of Somerset and sheltered from the north by the slopes of the Mendips, your family can have complete privacy together with all the amenities of modern caravan living.

This caravan park has 4-8 berth caravans some with shower and toilet, and is situated one mile from Cheddar, renowned for its famous Caves and Gorge, and one mile from the old world village of Axbridge on the A371, very near Bristol and also within easy reach of Wookey Hole, Bath, Wells Cathedral and the magnificent Roman baths.

The amenities include heated swimming pool, two modern toilet blocks, with babies and invalid facilities, laundry room, colour television room, children's play area and table tennis, shop, fully licensed bar with bar billiards and small dance area (bar snacks also served). Also family room with video films and pool table.

The site has well drained, flat fields for touring caravans, tents and Dormobiles and at night the fields are lit by street lights. Numerous drinking water taps and waste water disposal points are provided. Plug-in electricity available.

There is also a flat available sleeping eight people; fully fitted and equipped. Situated in central Cheddar this first floor flat is one minute from the swimming pool and five minutes from Cheddar Gorge. SAE for brochure.

PROPRIETORS: Mr & Mrs C. K. NEVILLE
Mr & Mrs D. R. MOORE
Telephone: CHEDDAR [0934] 742610
CHEDDAR, SOMERSET

Rose award park 1985

WHEN MAKING ENQUIRIES PLEASE MENTION FARM HOLIDAY GUIDE

Caravans and Camping

DULVERTON. Higher Town, Dulverton. Working farm. Six-berth 22' caravan adjoining picturesque Exmoor National Park, near Devon/Somerset border. Situated in a lawn in pleasant rural surroundings, with lovely views, the caravan has plenty space and a play area for children. Fully equipped for six, except for linen. Electricity connected for TV, fridge, lighting and heating. Gas cooking. Cold water connected to sink; flush toilet. Double end bedroom, fold-away double bed, two single beds in separate partitions. Children welcome, pets allowed on request. Visitors are welcome to walk over the 200 acres of the beef and sheep farm. Riding nearby, fishing in the vicinity. Rates from £34. Open from Spring Bank Holiday to October. **Mrs M. M. Jones, Higher Town, Dulverton TA22 9RX (Anstey Mills [039-84] 272).**

WIVELISCOMBE. Mrs J. P. E. Welch, Washers Farm, Raddington, Wiveliscombe (Clayhanger [039-86] 269). Working farm, join in. Washers Farm is a 220-acre beef and sheep farm in this beautiful rural area. Easily accessible but completely peaceful and unspoilt. Steep combes adjoin the secluded single site where deer and other wildlife may be seen and which slopes down to a stream. The very nice caravan is suitable for two to six persons. It is comfortable and spacious with Calor gas, electricity and water connected. Fridge. Flush toilet. Children and very well-controlled pets are very welcome around the farm. Lots of places to go and things to do, including fishing locally or on the farm. Exmoor a few miles. Sea 15 miles. Open May to October from £45 weekly. Please telephone or send SAE.

Call in for a night or longer
any time of the year!

St. Quintin Hotel, Caravan & Camping Park

Bridgwater Road, TAUNTON, Somerset TA2 8BG
Telephone: Taunton 73016 (Code 0823)

AA★★   RAC★★   AA▶▶   RAC appointed   CC

Services available: HOTEL – TOURING CARAVAN AND CAMPING PARK – HOLIDAY HOMES (Caravans let weekly) – LICENSED RESTAURANT

"Renowned for good Facilities and Friendly Service"

1 mile from M5 Junction 25 on the A38 Bridgwater Road.
Bargain breaks.

An outstanding Holiday Touring Centre and Staging Post for much of the West Country – an almost endless variety of places to visit and things to do within easy reach.

OPEN THE YEAR ROUND

SUFFOLK

LOWESTOFT. Mr G. Westgate, Beach Farm Caravan Park, Arbor Lane, Pakefield, Lowestoft (Lowestoft [0502] 2794) or (Norwich [0603] 743919). Beach Farm Caravan Park is situated on A12 Kessingland/Lowestoft road. Five minutes from lovely clean beaches and sea within easy reach of Oulton Broad. Residential and holiday static caravans on the six acre site, with 60 pitches available for touring caravans or tents. Caravans are fully equipped with water, cooking facilities, TV. Showers, toilets, shop, laundry and games room on site. Heated swimming pool available. Children are welcome. Pets permitted on touring park only. Caravan hire from £45 weekly. Tourers/campers (four people) from £3.45 per day, including VAT.

PLEASE SEND A STAMPED ADDRESSED ENVELOPE WITH ENQUIRIES

SUSSEX

EAST SUSSEX

ROBERTSBRIDGE near. Mrs J. A. Higgs, Blackshaw House, Padgham Farm, Ewhurst, Near Robertsbridge TN32 5TH (Northam [07974] 2194). Six-berth caravan, hot/cold water, bath, toilet inside. Calor gas cooking, electricity (meter). One end double bedroom, one bunk bedroom, large lounge; kitchen, fridge, electric fire, colour TV. Stands in its own garden overlooking beautiful views. Bodiam Castle within walking distance along River Rother, Dixter Gardens 2 miles, Battle Abbey 5/6 miles, ancient town of Rye 8 miles, sandy beach (Camber) 10 miles. Shops, 1½ miles. Homemade cakes; milkman calls, very peaceful surroundings. Terms: July/August £80 per week, other months £70 per week. Open March to November.

ROBERTSBRIDGE near. Mrs G. Downey, Catts Green Farm, Staplecross, Near Robertsbridge TN34 5UR (058-083-248). Working farm. A new very luxurious six-eight berth caravan in pleasant, rural, wooded area near Battle, Rye and Hastings. Catts Green Farm has beef, fruit and market garden; home-made bread and cakes are supplied to order. Fully equipped except for linen, the caravan has two end bedrooms, bathroom and flush toilet, electricity. Calor gas, mains water and TV. Available from March to November. Children welcome and pets permitted if kept under control. SAE for terms.

WEST SUSSEX

HENFIELD. Mrs R. Griffiths, Farmhouse, Tottington Drive, Small Dole, Henfield BN5 9XZ (Henfield [0273] 493157). Working farm. In a level field beside the farmhouse, the six-berth caravan is a modern, comfortable 23' Belmont. Fully equipped, all electric, with mains water and flush toilet alongside. Fresh milk and eggs available on our small dairy farm; village shop, post office and pub a few minutes' walk. Car essential — ideal country base for touring Sussex, also for walkers, farm footpaths lead onto South Downs Way. River Adur and Woods Mill Nature Trail are nearby. Nearest beach Shoreham five miles; Brighton and Worthing 10 miles east and west. SAE, please, for terms. Campers also welcome.

For the Mutual Guidance of Guest and Host

Farm Holiday Guides Ltd. do not inspect or recommend accommodation but advertisers agree to accept our Farm Holiday Guide standards of comfortable and clean accommodation and wholesome and well-cooked food. Advertisers are also bound by the Trades Description Act.

When accommodation has been booked, deposits sent, and letters of acceptance exchanged, both parties – host and guest – have entered into a binding contract.

Friends and families can easily be upset and much bitterness caused if holiday arrangements are not carefully made. The following points can be of real importance:

Guest When enquiring about accommodation, be as precise as possible. Give exact dates, numbers in your party and the ages of any children. State the number and type of rooms wanted and also what catering you require – bed and breakfast, full board etc. Make sure that the position about evening meals is clear – and about pets, reductions for children or any other special points.

Read our reviews carefully to ensure that the proprietors you are going to contact can supply what you want. Ask for a letter confirming all arrangements, if possible.

Host Give details about your facilities and about any special conditions. Explain your deposit system clearly and arrangements for cancellations, charges etc, and whether or not your terms include VAT.

We regret that Farm Holiday Guides cannot accept responsibility for any errors or omissions in descriptions. Prices in particular should be checked before booking because of the early compilation of the Guides, far ahead of the next holiday season.

YORKSHIRE

NORTH YORKSHIRE

BARNARD CASTLE. Mrs J. Dixon, East House, Langleydale, Barnard Castle, Durham DL12 8SL (Teesdale [0833] 37225). Working farm. This large modern caravan is located in the beautiful valley of Teesdale, on the fringe of James Herriot and Hannah Hauxwell country. It faces south overlooking thousands of acres of North Yorkshire Moors. This beef and sheep farm is ideal for a relaxing holiday. It has 350 acres of grassland where you are welcome to take walks. Places of historic interest are Bowes Museum, Beamish Open Air Museum, Durham Cathedral, Raby Castle with its herd of deer, Hadrian's Wall, High Force, Cauldron Snout and many country churches. Just over an hour's drive takes you to the Lake District, seaside, Lowther Wild Life Park. Six-berth caravan with gas cooker, fire and immersion heater. Electric lights, fridge, TV and points. Toilet and shower inside. May to October. SAE for terms.

FILEY near. Mrs Joan Greenwood, Cannonfields, 44 Muston Road, Hunmanby, Near Filey YO14 0JY (Scarborough [0723] 890933). Two six-berth Lynton (28') caravans are situated in the two-acre grounds of the guest house on the edge of the very attractive village of Hunmanby, three miles from beach at Filey and between Scarborough and Bridlington. Fully equipped except for linen, the caravans have flush toilets, water, gas cooker, electric lights, television and fridge. Car parking. Putting green, bowling green and table tennis room for recreation. Children are welcome, also pets. Shopping facilities in village, five minutes' walk. Available April to October. Terms from £45 weekly.

HARROGATE. Mrs E. Lister, Hallfield House Farm, Dacre, Harrogate HG3 4AW (Harrogate [0423] 780398). Working farm. A variety of local amenities are easily reached from this four-berth caravan situated on small mixed farm amidst the unspoilt countryside of the Yorkshire Dales. Horse riding, fishing, walking, tennis, bowls, caves etc. Harrogate, Ripon, Knaresborough, Otley, Skipton and Pateley Bridge can be visited. The caravan is well equipped. Everything supplied except linen. There is hot and cold water, gas cooker, fridge, electricity and adjacent flush toilet and shower. Children are welcome; cot and high chair provided. Babysitting by arrangement. Pets allowed. Open from May 1st to 31st October. Terms from £45 weekly.

RUSWARP. Mr A. R. Harland, Brooklyn House, Ruswarp, Whitby YO21 1NG (Whitby [0947] 602859). Situated in the grounds of "Brooklyn" House with open views of the surrounding countryside is the six-berth Ace Emperor Caravan (24' × 9' 4"). Ruswarp village five minutes' walk, Whitby one-and-a-half miles. The spacious interior comprises the lounge, with wide comfortable seating, which can become two single beds. This area can be partitioned off from the dinette, which easily converts into a comfortable double bed. An interior door leads to the double end bedroom, complete with wardrobe and dressing table. The Emperor is self-sufficient with its own water supply, TV and internal chemical toilet compartment. Flush toilet with hot and cold washbasin nearby. Pets are welcome. Terms from £40 per week. SAE, please, for full details. Brochure for Tree House Cabins also available.

The information in the entries in this guide is presented by the publishers in good faith and after the signed acceptance by advertisers that they will uphold the high standards associated with FARM HOLIDAY GUIDES LIMITED. The publishers do not accept responsibility for any inaccuracies or omissions or any results thereof. Before making final holiday arrangements readers should confirm the prices and facilities directly with advertisers.

SCARBOROUGH. Mrs A. Richardson, Backlays Farm, Langdale End, Scarborough YO13 0LP (Scarborough [0723] 82226). Working farm. This is a 192-acre sheep and beef farm situated one-and-a-half miles from Langdale End Village completely surrounded by Forestry Commission woods, and is most suitable for quiet walks and pony trekking five miles away. There is unlimited room for playing in grass fields on farm. Milk, eggs and potatoes may be purchased at the Farm. Ideal for a quiet and restful holiday. One 24' six-berth caravan with two bedrooms. Electric lighting and heating and fridge. Electricity on meter. Calor gas cooker with gas included in charge from £30 per week. Chemical toilet outside van. Fully equipped except sheets and pillow cases. Water on tap in van. Open all year. Children welcome. Pets allowed but not in caravan. Shops are seven miles at Scalby and Ayton.

WHITBY. Mrs A. G. Shardlow, Beckside Farm, Sneatonthorpe, Whitby YO22 5JG (Whitby [0947] 880550). Working farm. One 20' static caravan, accommodating five persons, plus cot, situated on modern dairy farm on edge of North Yorkshire Moors, overlooking small beck and wooded area, five miles from the sea. The beautiful coastline, with sandy beaches and rocky coves, is an ideal location for fishing, riding, boating on river; visiting tea gardens, craft centres, steam railway, zoo and enjoying many lovely walks. The caravan is equipped with cooker, fridge, TV, hot and cold water, mains sanitation, gas heater and all necessary utensils. Shower on site. Everything supplied for your holiday requirements, except linen. Fresh eggs and milk may be obtained on request. Children's play area and parking space. Available April to October, SAE for weekly terms.

THE FLASK CARAVAN PARK

Fylingdales, Robin Hood's Bay, Whitby, N. Yorkshire YO22 4QH

This small park is ideally situated within easy reach of Robin Hood's bay, Scarborough, Whitby and the Moors. There are 15 six-berth caravans all with magnificent views. Each caravan has all mains electric, shower/WC; colour TV; gas cooker, fire, refrigerator and separate bedrooms etc. All caravans are to N.F.S.O. and British Tourist Board standards. Play area and shop. Cafe and Inn adjoin park. Available March to October. The park is personally supervised by the owners. SAE for brochure.

Proprietor: Mr G. Allison   **Tel: Whitby (0947) 880592**

WHITBY. Mrs K. E. Noble, Summerfield Farm, Hawsker, Whitby YO22 4LA (Whitby [0947] 601216). Summerfield Farm (with Georgian Farmhouse) is situated two miles from Whitby and 17 from Scarborough. Surrounded by 70 acres of corn and sheep pasture. Few minutes' walk across fields to "Cleveland Way" Footpath leading to Robin Hood's Bay (an old fishing village). Rugged and beautiful coast, bring hammer and chisel for fossiling. Sandy beach one mile. Riding stables, boating on river, tea gardens, steam railway, zoo, fishing, peaceful valley and moorland villages to visit. Secluded and quiet private farm site offers well-kept luxury six-berth Red Barn caravan in half acre of cut grass; fenced and safe for play area; parking. Double end bedroom, bathroom/shower, mains water, electricity and gas free, hot water, sanitation, colour TV, gas cooking, fridge. Toilet on site. Pets welcome. April to October. Shops one mile; Whitby two miles. No linen. Eggs/milk on request. SAE for terms.

YORK. Miss F. H. Peacock, The Manor Country Guest House, Acaster Malbis, York YO2 1UL (York [0904] 706723 from 9 am to 9 pm). "Lynton", 29' four-berth (but would sleep six) stands alone in a secluded clearing in the six-acre grounds of the Guest House. The caravan is very spacious and well equipped, has mains water supply to sink, and electric lighting. A double bed in separate room at one end, twin beds in partitioned-off lounge, and foldaway bed between. Calor gas cooker with two burners, grill and oven. Refrigerator and food store. Separate dinette. Flush toilet near house. Calor gas fire in lounge. Blankets, crockery and cooking utensils supplied. Meals may be taken at Guest House when desired. York four-and-a-half miles away. River adjoining grounds. Bookings taken from December 28 for following year. Please send stamp or 9½" × 6" SAE for illustrated brochure. Enquiries from abroad, please send four International Reply Coupons.

When you read one you *haven't* read them all — we have *eleven* other publications

ISLE OF WIGHT
CAMPING HOLIDAYS

SANDOWN. Mr and Mrs R. W. G. Flood, Cheverton Farm Camping Site, Apse Heath, Sandown PO36 9PJ (Shanklin [0983] 862869). Working farm. In an ideal centre for touring the island, this camping site offers facilities from 1st April to 31st October. There are flush toilets, hot showers, washbasins and lighting. Children and pets welcome. Lovely country walks all around. Terms from 90p per person per night. Two acres for campers.

CHANNEL ISLANDS

VAUGRAT CAMPING
GUERNSEY
Mr & Mrs J. A. Lainé
Le Hougues, Route de Vaugrat, St. Sampson's, Guernsey.
Telephone 0481 57468   R.A.C. LISTED

The Vaugrat Camping Site is centred around a granite farmhouse, the farm buildings have been converted to contain a ladies and gents toilet block consisting of showers with hairdrying and shaving points and washing and ironing facilities. The reception area contains a shop, take-away food service, a TV room and coffee barn. The site is flat and well drained. It has reception areas and children's adventurous playgrounds. The site is only minutes walk from sandy Port Grat and Grande Haure Bays which are safe for family bathing. Car and Tent Hire can be arranged. Buses H1 and H2 regularly pass nearby. Open May to September.

HELP IMPROVE BRITISH TOURIST STANDARDS

You are choosing holiday accommodation from our very popular FARM HOLIDAY GUIDES. Whether it be a hotel, guest house, farmhouse or self-catering accommodation, we think you will find it hospitable, comfortable and clean, and your host and hostess friendly and helpful.

Why not write and tell us about it?

As a recognition of the generally well-run and excellent holiday accommodation reviewed in our publications, we at FARM HOLIDAY GUIDES LIMITED present a diploma to proprietors who receive the highest recommendation from their guests who are also readers of our Guides. If you care to write to us praising the holiday you have booked through FARM HOLIDAY GUIDES – whether this be board, self-catering accommodation, a sporting or a caravan holiday, the content of your letter will be evaluated and the proprietors who reach our final list will be contacted.

The winning proprietor will receive an attractive framed diploma to display on his premises as recognition of a high standard of comfort, amenity and hospitality. FARM HOLIDAY GUIDES LIMITED offer this diploma as a contribution towards the improvement of standards in tourist accommodation in Britain. Help your excellent host or hostess to win it!

DIPLOMA
AWARDED BY
READERS
of
FARM HOLIDAY GUIDE
PUBLICATIONS LIMITED

TO..
FOR HOLIDAY ACCOMMODATION
of the HIGHEST STANDARD

AT..

Farm Holiday Guide
ENGLAND
1986
SELF-CATERING ACCOMMODATION

SELF-CATERING HOLIDAYS

LONDON

ORSETT VILLAGE (Essex). Working farm. The special attraction of this cottage is its situation, just 22 miles from the heart of London, yet quietly nestled in the centre of a pretty Essex village. The cottage has Tourist Board four star accommodation for five, plus baby, in three bedrooms. Spacious comfortable lounge, modern fully equipped kitchen. Telephone, garden, two minutes' walk shops, village pubs. AA recommended. Golf, horse-riding, sailing, windsurfing, fishing, swimming, tennis available locally. 30 minutes train London and Southend-on-Sea. 10 minutes M25 for Cambridge and Canterbury. £110 to £180 weekly inclusive electricity, CH, all linen, VAT. Also single luxury six-berth caravan at Lorkins Farm from £70 weekly. Fullest details: **Mrs Wordley, Lorkins Farm, Orsett RM16 3EL (0375 891439).**

AVON

BATH near. By post — Mr and Mrs M. Saville, Motcombe Farm, Marshfield, Via Chippenham, Wilts SN14 8AJ (Bath [0225] 891201). Self-contained Cotswold cottage in 40 acres, surrounded by glorious countryside, south facing, in superb setting overlooking a Gothic castle across a green valley. Peace and seclusion; traffic free, yet only six miles from M4 and Bath. Three bedrooms; sleeps five/six people. Well-equipped; beautifully furnished. Near golf, fishing, riding; ideal walking, bird watching, touring area. No pets. Well behaved children welcomed. Linen available. SAE brings details from Mrs E. Saville.

BRISTOL near. Myrtle Cottage, Goose Green, Near Bristol. A 250-year-old country cottage recently modernised and equipped to a high standard of comfort, situated in pleasant rural area overlooking meadows, midway between Bristol and Bath. Ideal centre for visiting the Cotswolds, Slimbridge, Longleat, Cheddar and Wells. Bath with its Georgian architecture and Roman remains is only 20 minutes' drive, as is Bristol, with Brunel's Suspension Bridge and S.S. Great Britain. Leisure Centre nearby for swimming, badminton and squash. Sleeps six, in one double bedroom and two twin-bedded. Fully fitted kitchen/diner. Lounge with colour TV. Bathroom. Garden. Garage. Car essential. Night storage heating provided for out of season lets. Linen an optional extra. Children welcome, but sorry no pets. Complies with British Tourist Board Standards. Terms £70 to £125 per week. Open all year. **SAE to Mrs S. Thompson, Myrtle House, Goose Green, Syston Hill, Warmley, Near Bristol BS15 5LU (Bristol [0272] 564961).**

Signs are you'll find more to do around Britain, around a Hoseasons Holiday-Home.

Cafeteria or take-away food
Children's play area
Colour TV provided
Tennis court
Entertainment
Bar
Pony Trekking within 3 miles
Shop

When you choose a Hoseasons holiday home your freedom of choice really begins. You can come and go as you please in a holiday village that has something to please all the family. Whether it's a chalet, a bungalow, a country lodge, or even a caravan, your accommodation is a real 'home-from-home'. Kitchens are fully-equipped and most homes have TV.

Linen, with blankets or duvets, is provided and your private bathroom includes a bath and/or shower.

Every home is heated.

Only Hoseasons offer 120 holiday villages and locations all around Britain. The brochure shows a variety of activities within easy reach.

While the children are pony trekking, mum and dad can enjoy a round of golf. Keen anglers will note that Hoseasons do a nice line in fishing locations.

Together you can get out and about to enjoy the beaches, sight-seeing and visits to some local beauty spots.

Most villages have a heated swimming pool, shop, club with entertainment and bars. Other useful facilities, varying from place to place, include a restaurant, launderette and a children's play area. Should you not wish to cook there are meals-inclusive holidays too! Hoseasons 1986 brochure gives full details of all our holidays, which start from as little as £10 per person per week.

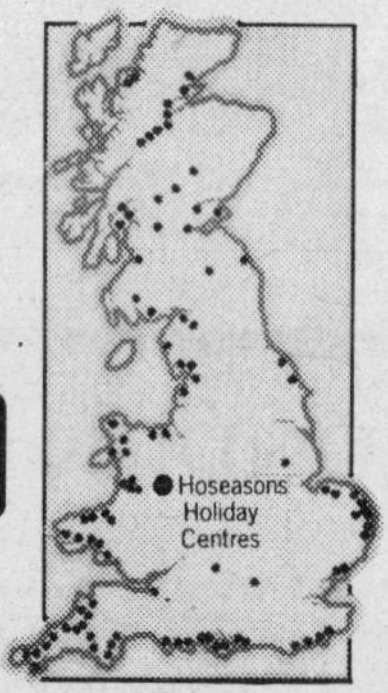

You'll also find details of our special rail fare discount scheme.

Send now for your free 172 page full colour brochure to Hoseasons Holidays Ltd., H14, Lowestoft, NR32 3LT.

● Hoseasons Holiday Centres

Dial-a-Brochure
0502 87373
day or night
Bookings: 0502 62292.

Please rush me my 1986 Hoseasons Holiday-Homes brochure

Mr/Mrs/Miss_____ BLOCK CAPITALS

Address_____

Town_____

Postcode_____

HOSEASONS HOLIDAYS
H14
Britain's No.1 in Holiday-Homes

SELF-CATERING   **Avon**   **367**

BRISTOL near. Mrs C. B. Perry, Cleve Hill Farm, Ubley, Near Bristol BS18 6PG (Blagdon [0761] 62410). Working farm. This is a dairy farm, set close under the Mendip Hills. Visitors are welcome to watch farm activities, if they follow the Country Code. Chew Valley and Blagdon Lakes are close at hand, giving trout fishing and birdwatching. Beautiful countryside with many lovely walks. Within easy touring distance of Bristol, Bath, Wells (beautiful Cathedral), Cheddar and Wookey Hole caves and Longleat, etc. Also within easy reach of Wales. Riding at Churchill, approximately four miles. Guests are made to feel at home and accommodated in part of the farmhouse. One double room, plus landing bed, cot; bathroom, toilet; sittingroom with bed settee. Fully equipped kitchen. No linen supplied. Well controlled pets allowed. Terms from £40 to £80. SAE, please.

BRISTOL near. Colin and Josephine Smart, Leigh Farm, Pensford, Near Bristol BS18 4BA (Compton Dando [07618] 281). Working farm. Personal attention and comfortable accommodation is our aim. Visit our beef and sheep farm which is ideally situated for touring Bath, Bristol, Wells and Glastonbury. Enjoy the rare breeds of cattle and sheep, eat free range eggs and relax on our large lawns. An attractive natural stone conversion offers a choice of family accommodation. Three bedroomed oak-beamed character cottage sleeping maximum eight. Bungalows, either one or two bedroomed sleeping two to five persons. Crockery, cutlery, etc. supplied. Linen hire. Cots. Shower rooms with washbasin and WC. Hot water by immersion heater. TV. Pay phone. Ample parking. Cattery/kennels nearby. Open all year. SAE. AA listed.

WHEN MAKING ENQUIRIES PLEASE MENTION FARM HOLIDAY GUIDE

POOL HOUSE – CHURCHILL GREEN FARM

Situated in the garden of Churchill Green Farm Guest House (licensed with small bar) this single storey L-shaped cottage, built around the swimming pool, has a main entrance and access to the garden. Private, quiet and ideal for families wishing to stay at reasonable cost in North Somerset, this is a superb position, with open views to the Mendip Hills. Open pastureland surrounds the cottage and two horses are kept in the paddock at the end of Pool House. There is room for six in two double bedrooms, and possible sleeping accommodation in the lounge; bathroom, toilet; all-electric kitchen. Linen is supplied. Oil-fired heating throughout. Suitable for disabled visitors. Parking. Weekly cleaning is available.

> The use of the swimming pool is included in weekly terms. Oil and electricity metered. Board accommodation offered at Farmhouse. "The Farmhouse itself" is available for Self-Catering Holidays at certain times of the year.

SAE, please for terms and further details to:
Mrs J. A. Sacof, Churchill Green Farm, Churchill, Avon, Somerset. (Churchill 852438)

Avon / Berkshire / Cheshire   SELF-CATERING

CHEW VALLEY. Mrs Jill Quantrill, Bonhill House, Bishop Sutton, Bristol BS18 4TU (Chew Magna [0272] 332546). Working farm. Bonhill House Cottage, a converted coach house originally built in 1842, offers delightful family holiday accommodation and is set in the beautiful Chew Valley area of the Mendip Hills. Standing adjacent to the main farmhouse and surrounded by picturesque countryside, the cottage comprises of a fully equipped kitchen/diner, lounge, WC, bathroom, two bedrooms, one with double bed and the other with two singles (cot can be supplied). Off the road parking. Colour TV, drying and freezer facilities. This is a working farm with on site stabling and livery facilities. Bath, Wells and Cheddar 12 miles; Bristol 10; Weston-super-Mare 20; Longleat 5.

EDINGWORTH. Mrs J. A. Spanner, Delhorn Farm Stables, Weston Road, Edingworth BS24 0JH (Edingworth [093-472] 596). DELHORN FARM HOLIDAY COTTAGES. SELF CATERING ACCOMMODATION WITH CHARACTER. *Cottage No.1:* Comprising kitchen, lounge diner, two double bedrooms, toilet and shower room, self contained, suitable for up to four persons. Semi-detached to main farmhouse (18th century). *Cottage No.2:* Comprising kitchenette, lounge diner, one double bedroom, toilet and shower room. Purpose built two years ago, suitable two/three persons only. Detached and self contained, with character. Both cottages enjoy rural views to Brent Knoll and the Mendip Hills. Situated A370 Bridgwater to Weston-super-Mare Road. SAE, please.

BERKSHIRE

NEWBURY near. Mr and Mrs A. Carmichael, The Barracks, West Ilsley, Near Newbury RG16 0AU (East Ilsley [063-528] 374). A haven for country lovers — an unpretentious yet very pleasant holiday apartment in small downland red-brick house nestling in a peaceful valley, one mile from a typical Berkshire village. The comfortable accommodation comprises livingroom with TV; two bedrooms (double beds); bathroom and fully equipped kitchen. Linen supplied, except towels. Cot and playpen available. Ideally situated for touring the many places of interest in this delightful part of England; Oxford, Bath and the Cotswolds. Windsor, Newbury and the New Forest all within easy reach! While just over a mile away lies the historic Ridgeway, ancient highway across England. Regret, no pets. SAE for particulars or telephone.

CHESHIRE

CHESHIRE. Cheshire Farm Holidays. For a selection of farmhouses and self-catering farm accommodation, please refer to the Display Advertisement for Cheshire Farm Holidays in the BOARD section under Cheshire. **Mrs Chris Hollins, Green Farm, Balterley, Crewe (0270) 820214.**

MALPAS. "Greystones," High Street, Malpas. Large pre-19th century, two-storey house with oak beams downstairs. Large garden to rear, garage and parking space. Situated in charming Cheshire village of Malpas with bus and shops close by. Nearest sandy beaches of North Wales coastline, about 40 miles. Within easy driving distance of Chester (12 miles). Well placed for touring all North Wales. Several golf courses in area. Well furnished and equipped for a comfortable holiday. Fitted carpets throughout. Ground floor, entrance hall. Large kitchen, livingroom and diningroom, bathroom, two toilets. Sleeps seven. Cot if required. Brushed nylon linen — £1.50 per week. SAE to **Mrs D. M. Fitton, Malt Kiln, lghtfield, Whitchurch, Shropshire SY13 4NX (Calverhall [094-876] 251).**

MALPAS. Mrs Angela Smith, Mill House, Higher Wych, Malpas SY14 7JR (Redbrook Maelor [094-873] 362). "The Granary" is situated in a peaceful rural position, near the Welsh Border and ideal for touring North Wales or visiting historic Chester. Three miles from shops and two miles from public transport so a car is essential and parking available. Accommodation is for four/five people. Two double bedrooms, cot if required. Bathroom, toilet; sittingroom and kitchen with electric cooker etc. Centrally heated, making it suitable for out of season holidays. Linen supplied. Terms are from £50 to £100 weekly. Metered electricity.

MALPAS. Mrs Doris Bevin, Pitt's Farm, Malpas SY14 7AJ (Threapwood [094881] 224). Working farm. Set in the middle of Pitt's Farm, a farm where guests are welcome to participate freely, is Oak Cottage with accommodation for six in one double room, one with bunk beds and a third with two single beds. Recently completely renovated, it is carpeted throughout, except the kitchen/diner which is fully equipped including fridge-freezer, electric cooker, washing machine and toaster. There is also a bathroom, shower room and sittingroom. Linen supplied. Board accommodation is also available in three double, two single and three family rooms with two sittingrooms and one diningroom. Children are welcome and a cot and highchair are available. Babysitting can also be arranged. Sorry, no pets. A car is essential with the shops and public transport two miles away but there are many places of interest within easy driving distance such as Chester (17 miles) and North Wales (30 miles). SAE, please for terms and further details.

CHESHIRE – FLAT AND INTERESTING!
Although Chester is well known as a tourist destination the rest of this low-lying green county also hosts a variety of attractions. These include Alderley Edge, Arley Hall Gardens, Delamere Forest, Eccleston, Stylal, Lyme Park, Mow Cop and the country park at Tegg's nose.

SELF-CATERING   Cheshire / Cornwall   369

NANTWICH near. Sproston Hill Cottage, Wrenbury, Near Nantwich. Sproston Hill Cottage is a luxurious self-catering holiday home set in the peaceful tranquillity of Wrenbury, a small typically English country village in South West Cheshire. Accommodation comprises lounge with colour TV; diningroom; family bedroom; twin bedroom; bathroom, downstairs shower room; fully fitted kitchen; full central heating throughout. Ideal base for exploring the surrounding countryside — Chester 16 miles away, Derbyshire and the Peak District 30 miles, Snowdonia National Park one and a half hour's drive. Alton Towers 35 miles and Wedgwood Pottery 25 miles. Local places of interest include Stapeley Water Gardens and Bridgemere Nurseries, both the largest of their kind in Europe. Available all year. Car essential, parking. Terms on request. **Mrs J. E. Wilkinson, Sproston Hill Farm, Wrenbury, Near Nantwich CW5 8HH (Crewe [0270] 780241).**

CORNWALL

ALTARNUN. Little Penpont and Penpont Mill, Altarnun. Altarnun is about eight miles from Launceston, a quarter mile from the A30 on the way to Bodmin Moor. It is a charming village and has won many awards, such as Britain in Bloom, Cornwall's Tidiest Village, etc. The approach from either side is between steep banks starred with flowers and overhanging trees, and at the end of a journey is as welcoming as a cool drink on a hot day. Penpont Mill is the oldest cottage in the village, with immensely thick walls and windows set in deep embrasures, which upstairs are floor level. Both cottages have been most carefully adapted to very comfortable holiday homes, and make a perfect touring centre, within easy reach of coasts, moors and woodlands. Full details including rents and all vacancies will be most gladly sent on receipt of SAE. See also under Port Isaac. **Mrs M. M. Cook, The Beach House, Port Gaverne, Port Isaac PL29 3SQ (Port Isaac [020-888] 296).**

BODMIN. Mrs Marjorie West, Penwine Farm, St. Mabyn, Bodmin (St. Mabyn [020-884] 286). Working farm. This cottage has been converted from a barn with all modern conveniences. It has open fireplace in the sittingroom and a pine staircase. Separate kitchen fully equipped with all cooking utensils and facilities. Electric fires. Bathroom with shower, basin and toilet. One double bedded room with cot; one twin bedded room; single bed in wide corridor; sittingroom with colour TV and dining area. Linen not supplied. Garage and shop half a mile. The sea is only eight miles away. Cottage is 200 yards from the road, a car is essential here and there is ample parking. All concrete surround and drive. Milk, butter and cream when available. It is half a mile from Camelford/Bodmin main road. Easy motoring distance to North Cornwall beaches. Available April to October. Weekly terms from £70 – £100, excluding electricity.

BODMIN. Pennytinney, St. Kew, Bodmin. Working farm. Farmhouse on 200 acre dairy and beef farm, situated two miles from the small fishing village of Port Isaac and 10 minutes' drive from the North Cornwall beaches. Here you can enjoy bathing, boating, surfing, horse riding and pony trekking. The house accommodates seven in three double bedrooms and one single bedroom; bathroom, toilet; lounge and kitchen with electric cooker, fridge, TV and sink. Linen not supplied. Children and pets welcome. Car essential, parking space. SAE, please, for details of terms. **Mr T. Wellington, Hayle Farm, St. Kew, Bodmin PL30 3HE (Port Isaac [020-888] 395).**

BODMIN. Mrs Ann Warne, Trevisquire Manor, St. Mabyn, Bodmin PL30 3DF (St. Mabyn [020-884] 297). Working farm. This attractive stone-built chalet, on a mixed farm of 230 acres, is situated amid beautiful scenery overlooking a lovely wooded valley. Ideal for a "get-away-from-it-all" holiday. Comfortably furnished for two in double bedroom; bathroom (shower, flush toilet); well equipped kitchen with full-size electric cooker; fridge, toaster, kettle, stainless steel sink unit. Everything supplied including linen at extra charge. Colour TV. Electricity by 10p slot meter. Good centre for touring; Wadebridge five miles; Bodmin seven miles; Polzeath nine miles; Tintagel 12 miles. Sorry, no pets. Shops one mile; sea nine miles. Car essential — parking. SAE, please, for prompt reply. Early booking advised.

Coombe Mill offers 17th century cottages and riverside cabins

"COOMBE MILL" offers 17th CENTURY COTTAGES and RIVERSIDE CABINS.

Tasteful conversions of 17th century Farm Buildings with their immense granite walls are the heart of "COOMBE MILL". Located in the Camel Valley "COOMBE MILL" also offers twelve 'Riverside Cabins' placed by this picturesque river. Private fishing allows you to pit your wits against the trout and salmon. This 27 acre farm setting, complete with livestock thrills adults and children alike. A car is advisable due to location, but we have easy access to beautiful sandy beaches only six miles away. The rugged moors of Bodmin for walking and riding which can be arranged for both novice and experienced riders.

COTTAGES: All with four-poster bed sleep 2, 4, 6, 8. Prices £60–£320 including bedding. Open all year.

RIVERSIDE CABINS: Complete with colour T.V. fitted bedrooms, carpeted throughout and 'Pined' lounge/dining room. Ideal 4 sleep 6. Prices £63–£195 including electricity allowance (Three bedroomed Cabin available).

Special price for couples during June, July and September. 'Farm Shop' Launderette, Children's Play Area, Home-Made 'Take-Away' Cooking. Fishing Rod Hire.

New for 1986: TENNIS COURTS.

Apply for brochure from resident proprietors **Jennifer and Jimmy Conchie "COOMBE MILL" St. Breward, Bodmin Moor, Cornwall PL30 4LZ. Tel. (0208) 850344.**

BODMIN. Mrs Gill Hugo, Bokiddick Farm, Lanivet, Bodmin PL30 3HP (Bodmin [0208] 831481). Working farm. This delightful bungalow enjoys uninterrupted views of the picturesque Helman Tors. Set in its own large grass garden it makes for a delightful holiday. The bungalow is on a 120-acre dairy farm which the guests are welcome to explore, also to watch the milking. Donkey for the children. The bungalow has two bedrooms (one double and one with double and bunk beds). Bathroom, separate toilet; lounge/diningroom with colour TV, large cedar wood conservatory overlooking garden. Kitchen is fully fitted with electric cooker, fridge/freezer, kettle and immersion heater. Electricity by 50p meter. Everything supplied except linen. Plenty of parking space. Central for safe, sandy beaches of North Coast, Daymer Bay, Polzeath and Rock, also south coast harbours of Looe, Polperro and Fowey. Sea and river fishing, golf courses, horse riding, tennis and squash courts, also beautiful National Trust Houses of Lanhydrock and Pencarrow, close by. Lanivet village with general stores, pub, garage, cafe, post office, two miles. Bodmin five miles. Registered with English and Cornish Tourist Board. Farmhouse accommodation in farmhouse close by. Please phone or send for brochure with SAE.

BODMIN. Mrs E. Tidy, Penbugle Farm, Bodmin PL31 2NT (Bodmin [0208] 2844). Working farm. This modernised old world cottage on a 130-acre beef and sheep farm is ideally situated in the centre of Cornwall, 12 miles from north and south coasts with good surfing beaches. Bodmin town one mile; Bodmin Moor three miles. Rough shooting and Clay Pigeon shooting available. Excellent trout fishing nearby. Places of historic interest — Lanhydrock House, Pencarrow House, Restormel Castle. Children are welcome to look at the animals. Five people accommodated in two double bedrooms, cot; bathroom, toilet; lounge (wood supplied for stove); kitchen with electric cooker, fridge and dining area. Linen supplied by arrangement at extra charge. No pets allowed. Car essential — parking. Available all year. Weekly terms on request. SAE, please, for prompt reply. AA Listed.

SELF-CATERING **Cornwall** **371**

BOSCASTLE. Mrs D. J. Wickett, Tregaina Farm, Trevalga, Boscastle PL35 0ED (Boscastle [084-05] 282). Working farm. "Tregaina" on the North Cornish coast is a dairy farm of 60 acres. Children have a wonderful time here as there is a Friesian herd and domestic animals. Parents are not forgotten and there is safe bathing and surfing locally, and any part of Cornwall can be visited in a day. Car essential — parking space. Open March to November. The accommodation is in a modernised wing of the farmhouse with three bedrooms sleeping eight; cot; sitting/diningroom; kitchen with units, electric cooker and fridge; linen supplied; bathroom, inside toilet. Pets allowed. Large sun lounge. Shops and sea two miles. Terms, including electricity, on request with SAE, please.

BOSCASTLE near. Alan and Beryl Tomkinson, Courtyard Farm, Lesnewth, Near Boscastle ✱ (Otterham Station [084-06] 256). Picturesque group of 17th century luxury stone cottages overlooking beautiful National Trust Valley with fabulous views of the sea. All the cottages are individually designed and furnished and equipped to the very highest standard with colour TV etc. They are warm and comfortable and are open all year round. Virtually all the coastline around Boscastle is National Trust owned and provides fabulous walks and beaches. Our cottages are not the cheapest, but do offer you quality and comfort at reasonable rates. Accommodation for eight — two double rooms, two single rooms; sittingroom; diningroom; kitchen; bathroom/toilet. Children welcome, cot, high chair. Sorry no pets. Fishing, shooting, half mile; bathing, hill climbing, two miles. Please write or phone at any time for our free colour brochure. Also see Colour Advertisement in the Full Colour Section of this Guide.

BOSCASTLE. Tresquare, Boscastle. Working farm. This delightful dormer bungalow quietly situated in its own grounds with beautiful valley views overlooks Boscastle. Superior accommodation, comfortably furnished, carpeted and fully equipped except linen. Sleeps nine in three bedrooms (one double, two family rooms). Cot. Large lounge with colour TV. Sun lounge; diningroom; kitchen with electric cooker, fridge, kettle, larder; bathroom; two toilets; immersion heater. Electric and coal fires. Storage heaters. Metered electricity. Large garden and sun terrace. Car essential — private parking. Picturesque harbour, cliffs, shops, valley within walking distance. Tintagel Castle, several sandy surfing beaches nearby. Walking, fishing, riding, golf amidst beautiful scenery. Ideal touring centre. Also spacious, quiet, four-bedroomed country bungalow sleeping seven; sea views. Both from £50 weekly. SAE, please, stating number in party, dates etc. to **Mrs G. Congdon, Tremorle, Boscastle PL35 0BU (Boscastle [084-05] 233).**

SHAW'S COTTAGE HOLIDAYS
(South West England)

Choice of **SEASIDE & COUNTRY** cottages,
houses, flats, farms & bungalows
in South West England
(Cornwall, Devon, Dorset, Gloucestershire & Somerset)

FREE BROCHURE

Shaw's Cottage Holidays,
Celtic House, Maes Square, Pwllheli, Gwynedd,
N. Wales LL53 5HA

Telephone (0758) 614800 (24 Hours)

Cornwall SELF-CATERING

BUDE. Mr and Mrs M. Cummins, Mineshop, Crackington Haven, Bude EX23 0NR (St. Gennys [08403] 338). Several traditional Cornish cottages, and six Canadian cedar lodges (AA listed), in an unspoilt and uncommercialised area of outstanding natural beauty, sleeping from four to nine people. Most are available throughout the year. Nightstore heating free early and late. Peaceful wooded valley setting leading to sandy beach at Crackington Haven, with rock pools and surfing. National Trust cliff land, coastal footpath and valley walks. Electric cookers, fridges, immersion heaters, bathrooms, modern fitted kitchens, electric heaters in all rooms, colour TVs. Pets welcome. Linen optional extra. Bude nine miles (cinema, golf, fishing, tennis, dry-ice and roller skating, etc.). Widemouth Bay six miles, Boscastle and Tintagel 9-12 miles. Car essential — parking. SAE, please, for illustrated brochure and terms.

BUDE. Mr E. D. Congdon, Kitsham, Poundstock, Bude EX23 0DZ (Week St. Mary [028-884] 336). Working farm. Detached country cottage, personally supervised on owner's beef and sheep farm. Pleasantly situated with garden in refreshing, peaceful countryside. Two and a half miles off A39. Surf, sea and sandy beaches and unspoilt North Cornish coast three miles. Many sporting facilities at Bude including boating on canal, golf, tennis and swimming in tide-swept pool. Ideal for visiting places of historic interest. Exmoor, Dartmoor and Bodmin Moor. Fishing in stream. Log fire. Accommodating six people plus baby in one double, one single and one room with double, single and cot; bathroom, toilet; sittingroom with colour TV; diningroom with Rayburn cooker. Electric cooker, fridge/freezer and larder. No linen supplied. Pets by arrangement only. Car essential, ample parking. Terms from £40-£170. Also farmhouse flat, sleeps four. Views over countryside. Colour TV. All electric. 50p meter. Safe sandy beaches three miles. Terms on application.

BUDE. Millook House and Little Millook, Poundstock, Near Bude. Two AA listed cottages sleeping six and eight people respectively, situated at the end of the wooded valley at Millook, 100 yards from the rock-bound, pebbled shore abounding with prawning pools and lobster hides, available for holiday letting all year. This part of the coastline is scheduled as being of Outstanding Natural Beauty. Coastal footpath with magnificent views. Walks through the wooded valley. Electric cooker, fridge, immersion heater, nightstore heating free early and late, colour TV, all rooms with electric heaters. Linen optional extra. Open fires. Pets welcome. Sands at Widemouth Bay one and a half miles. Bude five miles (cinema, 18-hole golf course, outdoor swimming pool, tennis, etc.). Car essential — parking. SAE, please for illustrated brochure and terms to **Mr and Mrs T. Cummins, Mineshop, Crackington Haven, Bude EX23 0NR (St. Gennys [08403] 338).**

BUDE near. The Doll's House, Week St. Mary, Near Bude. This delightful, cosy old cottage, full of character, is situated four and a half miles from Quinceborough Farm on the outskirts of the village of Week St. Mary. Tastefully decorated and fully equipped to a high standard, the cottage accommodates four persons in one double and one twin bedded room, one with sea view. Bed linen supplied at no extra cost. Lounge with open beams and open fire, colour TV. Fitted kitchen with electric cooker, fridge, iron and vacuum cleaner etc. Bathroom. Large garage. Grassed garden to rear. The village itself has many historic buildings, village green and lovely old church, also post office, general store and country pub. Weekly market on Saturdays. Sea within easy reach. Nearest beach is Widemouth Bay. Excellent holiday base. Open all year. Car essential. Terms on request. **Mrs Patricia M. Rowland, Quinceborough Farm, Widemouth Bay, Bude EX23 0NA (Widemouth Bay [028-885] 236).**

FUN FOR ALL THE FAMILY IN CORNWALL

Woolly Monkey Sanctuary, Murrayton, Looe; *Padstow Bird & Butterfly Gardens,* Fentonluna, Padstow; *Bird Paradise,* Hayle; *Bodmin Farm Park,* Fletchers Bridge, Bodmin; *Newquay Zoo,* Trenance Park, Newquay; *Cornish Seal Sanctuary,* Gweek, Helston; *Mevagissey Model Railway,* Mevagissey; *The Forest Railroad Park,* Dobwalls, near Liskeard; *Age of Steam,* Crowlas, near Penzance; *Lappa Valley Railway,* Benny Halt, Newlyn East; *Poldark Mining & Wendron Forge,* Wendron, near Helston; *Cornwall Aero Park,* Royal Naval Air Station, Culdrose; *Museum of Nautical Art,* Chapel Street, Penzance; *St. Agnes Leisure Park,* St. Agnes.

SELF-CATERING   Cornwall   373

BUDE. LANGFIELD MANOR SET IN THREE ACRE PRIVATE WOODED GROUNDS complete with heated swimming pool. Carefully converted into six self catering apartments, including one at ground floor level. Situated overlooking Bude golf course, yet only a few minutes' walk to the town centre, shops and central beaches. The swimming pool (complete with diving board and water chute) and sunbathing terraces are floodlit at night. Licensed bar for residents opens onto poolside terrace. Billiard room, games room, table tennis, laundry, daily maid service; car park. Apartments have private hall; lounge/diner; separate fully fitted kitchen with fridge/freezer. Choice of one, two or three bedrooms with bath or shower. For a holiday that is totally different from ordinary self catering and hotel holidays, please send stamp for brochure to resident proprietors: **R. J. & B. Dinshaw, Langfield Manor, Bude EX23 8DP (Bude [0288] 2415).**

BUDE. Mrs Patricia M. Rowland, Quinceborough Farm, Widemouth Bay, Bude EX23 0NA (Widemouth Bay [028-885] 236). Working farm. A variety of self-catering accommodation is available at Quinceborough Farm, including a hay barn, which has recently been converted into three cottages, each sleeping six to eight persons. These cottages won the CoSira and Country Landowners Cornwall Award for 1982. Also available is a large, modern bungalow sleeping up to 10. The sea and country views from all of the properties are magnificent. Each dwelling is equipped and furnished to a very high standard and all have colour TV, fridges, electric cookers, etc. Bed linen is provided and cots and high chairs are available on request, free of charge. Guests are invited to use our heated outdoor swimming pool, games room and tennis court and to ramble over the fields, etc. Pets and children are welcome but, as this is a working farm of 120 acres, they must be under control. Our best recommendation is that people return regularly for what they consider to be the ideal family holiday. SAE, please, for further details.

BUDE. "Lower Quinceborough," Marine Drive, Widemouth Bay, Bude. "Lower Quinceborough" is an extremely attractive character bungalow with many luxury features — double glazing etc. Situated just two minutes' walk from the sandy, surfing beach of Widemouth Bay with spectacular, uninterrupted views of the sea. Comfortable accommodation for six/eight in two large family bedrooms; all rooms have fitted carpets, are well-decorated and furnished. Fitted kitchen has electric cooker, fridge, vacuum, etc. Colour TV. Bed linen. Electric and open fires. Garage. Garden and use of heated outdoor pool, games room, and tennis court at Quinceborough Farm (half a mile away) add to your holiday enjoyment. Bude, three miles distant, offers golf, riding, putting, tennis, fishing and boating on canal etc. Good base for touring Cornwall and Devon. Port Isaac, Boscastle, Tintagel, Clovelly, Bideford etc., all within easy reach. Open all year. Children and pets welcome. SAE, please. **Mrs Patricia M. Rowland, Quinceborough Farm, Widemouth Bay, Bude EX23 0NA (Widemouth Bay [028-885] 236.**

BUDE. Mrs P. Gilhespy, 2 Church Cottages, Marhamchurch, Bude EX23 0EN (Widemouth Bay [028-885] 570). A choice of two very old and charming cottages occupying a unique position in the centre of this lovely village. The larger cottage has three bedrooms and accommodates up to six people. The smaller has two bedrooms and can also take up to six people. Both cottages have been carefully restored and have all modern amenities including colour TV. Mrs Gilhespy is a practising artist and her husband works in wood; many examples of their work are to be seen in and around the cottages. Pets and children are welcome here; each cottage has its own garden and share a children's play garden. Many of Mrs Gilhespy's guests return every year, surely the best recommendation of all. SAE, please, for further details.

BUDE. Mrs C. J. Greenaway, Rattenbury Farm, Marhamchurch, Bude EX23 0HF (Widemouth Bay [028885] 327). There is accommodation for 10 at Rattenbury Farm. This is in a wing of a fine 16th century farmhouse tucked away in the heart of the countryside which is only a few miles from the lovely Cornish beaches. It is a typical beef and sheep farm. The spacious and well furnished accommodation provides a lounge with colour TV, diningroom and a large kitchen with electric fridge, cooker and washing machine. Upstairs there are three bedrooms, a family room with a double and bunk beds, and the other two each with a double and a single bed. Cot and linen hire available. 50p meter. We are one mile from the village of Marhamchurch and three miles from Bude and Widemouth Bay. A car is essential and there is parking.

Cornwall   SELF-CATERING

BUDE. Mrs J. M. Grigg, Park Farm, Marhamchurch, Bude EX23 0ES (Widemouth Bay [028-885] 502). Park Farm is part of a large farmhouse situated amongst other cottages and approximately 500 yards from the village of Marhamchurch; Bude and Widemouth Bay, both well known for surfing, are approximately two miles away. The accommodation provides for nine people. All five bedrooms are carpeted throughout. Bathroom and separate toilet. Kitchen/diningroom with sink unit, electric cooker, fridge, mains water, also large scrub top farmhouse table. The slated hallway leads into the cosy sittingroom, black/white TV also included. Linen not supplied. No pets. Electricity included. SAE, please, or phone.

CAMELFORD. Mr Clive Ahrens, Mayrose Farm, Helstone, Camelford PL32 9RN (Camelford [0840] 213507). Working farm. Mayrose Farm is set in a beautiful rural area where your family can enjoy the experience of living on a typical Cornish farm. In an area of outstanding natural beauty, with lovely panoramic views over the wooded Allen Valley noted for its wild flowers. The farmhouse (owners' home) and the four cottages are all constructed of local stone and Delabole slate roofs, with their own private gardens equipped with garden furniture. The 18-acre farm is full of interest with animals used to the attention of children. St. Teath, one and a half miles, has village store, post office and off-licence, with the White Hart Inn providing excellent cuisine and a welcome for children. One of the cottages sleeps four and the other three sleep six each. All fully equipped including colour TV, electric cooker, fridge, etc. Nice bathrooms. Ample parking. Pets allowed. Open March to December. Terms from £55. Full details on request. AA listed.

CAMELFORD. Elm Cottages, Helstone, Cornwall. Elm Cottages, originally Elm Farm, sleep seven with three double bedrooms in each, all carefully equipped and having fitted carpets throughout. Night storage heaters for Spring or Autumn. There is a modern kitchen with electric cooker and fridge; colour television. Children and pets welcome. Car essential. Ideal for a comfortable, quiet and relaxed holiday with many short distance excursions to wonderful beaches and the magnificent North Cornish coastline. There is plenty to suit everyone in this part of the county. Places of interest and beauty include Camelford town, Tintagel with its castle ruins, Port Isaac and the lovely harbour of Boscastle. **Mrs Hircock, The Elms, Helstone, Camelford PL32 9RL (0840-213729) and [0840] 770571).**

CORNWALL. The Helpful Holiday Agency, Coombe 1, Chagford, Devon TQ13 8DF Tel: (06973) 3593/2478, will help you choose from over 400 cottages, houses, flats and bungalows all over the West Country.

COVERACK. Mrs O. Yeats, Polcoverack Farm, Coverack TR12 6FP (St. Keverne [0326] 280497). Working farm. Seven stone-built two and three bedroomed cottages cared for and equipped to a very high standard in sylvan surroundings on 170-acre farm; half mile from safe, sandy beach and unspoilt fishing village of Coverack. Enjoy the best of both worlds — seaside plus farm. A child's paradise; helping with the animals or exploring fields, woods and streams whilst grown-ups play tennis or soak up the peace and tranquillity of the sunny gardens. Week-day changeovers. Regret, no pets. Please send SAE for full details and illustrated brochure. Registered with English and Cornish Tourist Boards.

CRACKINGTON HAVEN. Mrs P. Henshall, Rosecare Farm, St. Gennys, Bude EX23 0BE (St. Gennys [084-03] 375). Working farm: Traditional stone farm buildings situated on small active mixed farm recently converted into character cottages; tastefully and comfortably furnished; fully equipped and with all modern conveniences, including colour TV. Full sized electric cooker and refrigerator and storage heating. Accommodation for two to eight persons and well behaved dogs. Suitable for the disabled. Situated in tranquil farmland hamlet, but within easy reach are many amenities including riding, surfing, fishing, water ski-ing etc. and bathing beaches — nearest being one-and-a-half miles. Linen hire and laundry services available on premises, also licensed restaurant in 16th century farmhouse. Please send SAE for brochure.

FALMOUTH. Trebarvah Woon Cottage, Constantine, Falmouth. Trebarvah Woon is a modernised cottage ideally situated for touring the many beauty spots of South Cornwall, being two miles from Gweek, the little creek of the Helford River. Set by the roadside with its own garden, the cottage offers privacy without isolation. Formerly a smallholding there are meadows for children's play or a breath of fresh air before retiring. Two double bedrooms upstairs; one twin-bedded downstairs. Modern kitchen and livingroom with a modern toilet/bathroom. TV. Electric cooker, refrigerator, fires. "Off Peak" electric central heating available as an extra. Nicely furnished. Beds have spring interior mattresses. Cot available. Fully equipped with linen etc., except for towels and iron. Kiddies welcome and also the family dog. Premises thoroughly cleaned and checked by owners between each let. Sea about four-and-a-half miles away. SAE, please. **Mr T. P. Tremayne, "The Home," Penjerrick, Falmouth TR11 5EE (Falmouth [0326] 250427 and 250143).**

SELF-CATERING **Cornwall** **375**

FALMOUTH. Nantrissack, Constantine, Falmouth. NANTRISSACK is an impressive farmhouse standing in a delightful garden. It is ideally situated for touring this lovely southern coast of Cornwall. Being two miles from Gweek — the little creek of the Helford River — it is also ideal for visiting Falmouth and the Lizard Peninsula. The farm and small woodland with a freshwater stream is available for those who wish to walk. The furnishing is nice. Beds have interior sprung mattresses. Bathroom with hot and cold water in all bedrooms. Partial central heating. New 30' Sun Lounge. Colour TV. Terms from £65 per week. **Mr T. P. Tremayne, The Home, Penjerrick, Falmouth TR11 5EE (Falmouth [0326] 250427 and 250143).**

FALMOUTH. Navas Hill House Cottage, Trenarth Bridge, Mawnan Smith, Falmouth. This cottage is a peaceful haven in a glorious area of Cornwall, far from the holiday traffic but ideal for exploring the beautiful countryside and beaches; fishing trips and golf available within easy distance. There is accommodation for six, in two double bedrooms; cot; bathroom, toilet; sittingroom, diningroom; kitchen with electric cooker, sink unit, ample cupboards. Everything supplied except linen. Shops one mile. Two miles from the sea. Sorry, no pets allowed. A car is essential and there is ample parking. Open from Easter to October. Weekly terms from £60 plus. **Mr G. T. Trethowan, Navas Hill House, Trenarth Bridge, Mawnan Smith, Falmouth (Mawnan Smith [0326] 250656).**

FALMOUTH. Dolvean Holiday Flats, 48 Melvill Road, Falmouth. Six completely self-contained, well-equipped all-electric flats situated 250 yards from safe, sandy bathing beach and sea front, and within a short distance of the Dell railway station and buses to town centre. Each flat has a full-size cooker and fridge, colour television, lounge or lounge/diner with a double bed-settee, one or two double or twin bedrooms, and a bath or shower room and toilet. Bed linen supplied. Pets permitted. Cot available. Electric coin meter. Four flats each sleep up to six and two take two to four. Open all year. Mid-week bookings accepted. Weekly terms £50 to £200, plus VAT. Stamp, please, to **Mr John Myers, 48-50 Melvill Road, Falmouth TR11 4DQ (Falmouth [0326] 313658).**

HAYLE. The Towans, Hayle. Chalet situated among sand dunes adjoining three miles of golden sands in St. Ives Bay. Ideal spot for touring, or a haven for the family on the sand or grass. Accommodation for six in three double bedrooms; bathroom; toilet; sittingroom; diningroom/kitchen with built-in units and all-electric appliances. Fully equipped except for linen. Sorry, no pets. Shops and sea 200 yards. Car parking. Riding, golfing, fishing all near. Unnecessary to leave the area to enjoy the holiday as shops, post office, hotel and entertainment all within 500 yards. Weekly terms excluding fuel from £40 to £100. SAE, please, to **Mrs Enid L. Johns, "Kerana Tiga," 12 Penview Crescent, Grange Road, Helston TR13 8RX (Helston [032-65] 2489 — evenings only).**

HAYLE. Mrs J. C. Hodge, Trenerth Farm, Leedstown, Hayle (Leedstown [0736] 850583). Working farm. This self-contained cottage, with accommodation for six people, is situated in the centre of a 100-acre dairy farm. It comprises two bedrooms, each with a double and single beds, bathroom with constant hot and cold water, spacious airing cupboard. Modern kitchen fitted with electric cooker, fridge, vacuum cleaner, iron, etc. TV is also available in the sittingroom. Separate diningroom. No linen supplied. Many beaches are available on both sides of the coastlines, the nearest ones being Gwithian, Praa Sands and Marazion with St. Michael's Mount all being within eight miles of the farm. The main shopping towns are Camborne and Hayle, four miles. Open May to September inclusive. No pets, please. SAE for weekly terms.

HELFORD RIVER near. Mrs Anne Matthews, Boskensoe Farm, Mawnan Smith, Falmouth TR11 5JP (Falmouth [0326] 250257). Working farm. Picturesque farmhouse set in three acres of garden and orchard on 400-acre farm, accommodation for eight persons. Five minutes' walk to village of Mawnan Smith, with good selection of shops. The lovely river is approximately one mile away and is famous for its beautiful coastal walks and scenery. Several quiet beaches close by for picnicking, bathing; also excellent sailing and fishing facilities. Other properties also available. Apply for brochure.

HELSTON. Barn Cottage and Parc-an-Fox, Manaccan, Helston. Traditional Cornish stone-built cottage over 250 years old, with beamed ceiling in sittingroom. Also a converted barn comfortably furnished and modernised. One cottage sleeps six and the other sleeps eight. Each has cot; three bedrooms, modern bathroom/shower. Spacious sittingroom and dining/kitchen with electric cooker, fridge, immersion heater (10p meter), twin tub washing machine, colour TV. No linen supplied. A car is essential; ample parking; large secluded garden with stream, surrounded by trees. Situated in sheltered valley amid unspoilt countryside, one mile from the sea. Three miles from Helford River, Frenchman's Creek. Boat for hire for sailing and fishing two miles away. Safe bathing from numerous beaches and excellent walking. Very safe for children and pets. Babysitter available. Helston 12 miles, the home of the Floral Dance. Open all year. SAE, please, stating number of persons and dates required. **Mrs J. Jane, Parc-an-Fox, Manaccan, Helston TR12 6EP (St. Keverne [0326] 280624).**

376 Cornwall SELF-CATERING

HELSTON. Mrs A. Nicholas, Old Mill House, Gweek, Helston TR12 6UA (032622-217). Old Mill Cottage (stream diverted) sleeping six plus cot. Basic rent when only two people staying. It is in a sheltered quiet position at the edge of the village; shop/post office, inn, restaurants, seal sanctuary. Helston, the quaint old Cornish town of the Floral Dance, is four miles. All bedding provided, Polycotton top sheets, nylon under. Comfortable lounge/diner (hatch to kitchen), colour TV with r.c., electric fire, log fire. Kitchen with electric cooker and Rayburn for cooler days. Two south facing bedrooms, double and twins, back bedroom — bunks; bathroom, heater, toilet; second toilet downstairs. Garden meadow behind. Parking on forecourt. Excellent for many coves. Four deck chairs. Pets by arrangement. Children welcome, cot, high chair and babysitting. Available all year. Please apply to above for terms.

FAMILY CHALETS & CARAVANS IN CORNWALL

Park adjoins 3 miles of sandy beach, Ideal for camping, Licensed clubs, Entertainment. Indoor heated swimming pool. Pets Welcome

FREE Colour Brochure

Mr. F. JAMES
St. Ives Bay Chalet & Caravan Park
Upton Towans, Hayle, Cornwall TR27 5BH
Tel: Hayle **0736 752274** 24 Hour Service

name _____
address _____
BLOCK CAPITALS PLEASE

HELSTON. Fuchsia Cottage, Tregarne, Manaccan, Helston. Secluded, spacious country bungalow (owners' home) in large mature garden, one mile from quiet fishing cove of Porthallow. The well carpeted, fully equipped accommodation includes three double bedrooms, two with double beds, one with bunks/twin beds, all with Continental quilts; large dining/kitchen with electric cooker, twin-tub washing machine, fridge/freezer, electric water heater and toaster. Large lounge, inglenook with stone fireplace, TV, radio; bathroom with WC. High chair and cots available on request. Electricity by meter. Car essential. Access is down a private lane. Ample car parking. Lovely area for walking, touring, boating, fishing, coastal path. Shop, pub, beach one mile. Ideal for a peaceful holiday. Great for children. Pets by arrangement. Available April to October. Special rates for Senior Citizens, except during June, July and August. Telephone after 4 pm and at weekends for further details, **Mrs P. M. Jones, 4 Pinewood Drive, Little Haywood, Stafford ST18 0NX (Little Haywood [0889] 882184).**

HELSTON. The Loft, Tregarne Farm, Manaccan, Helston. Working farm, join in. Tregarne is a small hamlet set in a wooded valley close to the lovely coves and beaches of The Lizard Peninsula and the picturesque Helford River. Part of a stone-built barn 'The Loft' comprises sitting-room (colour TV); all-electric diner/kitchen; one double, one bunk-bedded room (cot); shower room, separate WC and is fully equipped (excluding linen) for four/five persons. Situated on a working farm where visitors are welcome to 'muck in', The Loft is ideal for a relaxing family holiday amidst traditional country and close to unspoilt coves. Nearby leisure activities include fishing, sailing, swimming, riding, etc. Available Easter to October. Weekly terms from £50. **Mrs P. A. Lugg, Tregarne Farm, Manaccan, Helston TR12 6EW (St. Keverne [0326] 280304).**

PLEASE SEND A STAMPED ADDRESSED ENVELOPE WITH ENQUIRIES

SELF-CATERING   Cornwall   377

"HALWYN"
MANACCAN, HELSTON, S. CORNWALL

Situated in an area of outstanding natural beauty, **HALWYN** is an ancient Cornish farmstead with the original old farmhouse and the former farm buildings architecturally converted to a choice of holiday homes. Superbly set in parklike surroundings in an idyllic sunny valley one mile from the sea at Porthallow and two miles from the Helford River.

There is **HALWYN FARMHOUSE**, a spacious five bedroom character house with beams and inglenook, for up to twelve people. **HALVILLA COTTAGE**, a large four bedroom cottage for up to ten. **COURTYARD COTTAGE**, two small single storey cottages for four/six. **THE GRANARY** and **THE HAYLOFT** both two bedroom apartments. All are equipped with colour TV, heating and electricity inclusive. No meters. Everything included except linen.

Two acres of grounds. Indoor heated swimming pool with adjoining paddling pool (open May to mid-September). Small lake with boat, badminton court, children's play area and putting green. Unspoilt coast ideal for those who enjoy a quiet holiday. Many sandy beaches. Safe bathing and boat hire. Open all year round with special low rates and log fires out of season when Cornwall can be at its best. Well behaved dogs welcome. **Stamp for colour brochure to MR & MRS H. DONALD or Telephone ST. KEVERNE (0326) 280359.**

HELSTON Mrs S. Harris, Tregarne Farm Cottage, Tregarne, Manaccan, Helston TR12 6EW (St. Keverne [0326] 280362 or Truro [0872] 560509). **Working farm.** Set in small private gardens adjoining grassy orchard and yard of a small mixed farm in the hamlet of Tregarne one mile from the sea and close to Helford River with opportunities for sailing, fishing, bathing, diving, walking and riding. The cottage contains one double and two twin-bedded rooms and cot, sittingroom with inglenook fireplace and wood-burning stove; kitchen/diner with electric cooker, fridge, washing machine, combined WC and shower room, additional outside WC, and is fully equipped for six excluding linen. All-electric with slot meter. Small B/W TV available on request. Children and well behaved pets welcome. Weekly terms from £60 to £160. Open all year. Special rates for Senior Citizens off season.

HELSTON. "Mor Gwel" and "Volnay," Porthoustock, St. Keverne, Helston. On the beach in the quiet fishing village of Porthoustock, two cottages, well equipped and comfortable for six people in three double bedrooms. Colour TV, Teasmade, electric blankets and washing machine are just some of the equipment supplied. Bed linen and towels are not provided and electricity is on 50p meter. Children welcome with cot and highchair available. Shops, pubs and garage are available in St. Keverne. The scenery, beautiful walks, extremely good fishing and the large shingle beach suitable for launching boats, make the underwater paradise of the Manacle Rocks accessible to divers. Bed and Breakfast, boat hire and fresh crab and lobster available. Phone for brochure. **Mr and Mrs B. G. Viccars, "Hernan Dowr," Porthoustock, St. Keverne, Helston TR12 6QW (St. Keverne [0326] 280788).**

HELSTON. Mr D. C. S. Farquhar, Porthpradnack, Mullion, Helston TR12 7EX (Mullion [0326] 240226). At Mullion Cove on the Lizard Peninsula is Porthpradnack, a well built house with two flats, each with two bedrooms, bathroom and toilet. One has livingroom/kitchen, the other a separate sittingroom and kitchen. Kitchens are fully equipped and have fridges, electric cooker etc., TV. Cots, high chair (no extra charge) but linen is not supplied. Each flat has separate front door. A telephone is available to tenants. They are available all year. Pets permitted by arrangement. Car essential — parking bay. Weekly terms from £50 to £135 in high season. Enquiries to: **Mr D. C. S. Farquhar, as above.**

Cornwall SELF-CATERING

HELSTON. Willow Cottage, Porthallow, St. Keverne, Helston. This is a comfortable, homely cottage set in the little fishing village of Porthallow. Accommodation is for six people in three bedrooms (one double, one double plus single, one single); bathroom, toilet; sittingroom with colour TV; diningroom; kitchen with electric cooker, fridge, sink unit. Bed linen provided. Shops 100 yards, sea 50 yards. Car essential, ample parking. Pets permitted if well behaved and controlled. Electric fire (50p meter). Local fishing trips, boats for hire, pony riding, golf all within the vicinity. Delightful countryside and scenery — beautiful walks. There is a limited bus service in the village. This charming cottage would be ideal for a family holiday, with plenty to do or just relax in comfort and enjoy the peace and quiet of Cornwall. Terms weekly from £50 to £150. Please apply to **Mrs E. M. M. Lugg, Polpidnick Farm, St. Martin, Helston TR12 6DU (Manaccan [032623] 268).**

HELSTON. Carpenters and Appletree Cottages, St. Martins Green, Helston. Two adjoining stone-built cottages, tastefully modernised and furnished with a high standard of cleanliness; garden with parking space and lawn at rear. Situated in small village of St. Martins Green, just over a mile from the glorious Helford River which offers boating and fishing of most kinds. Village has general stores/post office, church and pub (half-a-mile away, an easy stroll). Ideal for touring Lizard Peninsula with its many lovely coves, beaches and character fishing villages. For the walker many lovely coastal and country walks; golf six miles. Both cottages have open beamed lounge/diners; fitted carpets; large fully fitted kitchen with table and chairs; all-electric (10p meter). Carpenters sleeps six; Appletree sleeps four. Cots available. Usual toilet facilities. SAE, please, to **Mrs C. A. Lawrence, Trevithian Cottage, Lanarth, St. Keverne, Helston TR12 6RG (0326-280658).**

HELSTON near. Troon Cottage, Breage, Near Helston. Take a break in this charming old cottage, attractively furnished to a high standard, situated in a quiet country lane near the sea. Modern kitchen, colour TV, all equipment provided, beds made up ready — sleeps two to five. Large storage heaters ensure warmth during cooler months, cost included in rent. Secluded garden, patio, garage. Children welcome, cot provided. Breage is ideal centre for exploring the numerous beaches and National Trust coastal walks in the area, within easy motoring distance of Land's End, The Lizard, Falmouth, St. Ives and many other well known beauty spots. Excellent for spring or autumn holidays. Ring or write to **Mrs Graham, Beech Close, Whitehill Avenue, Bexhill, Sussex TN39 3RX (Cooden [04243] 3182).**

HELSTON, RUAN MINOR (near The Lizard). Little Treveddon, Ruan Minor. Working farm. Little Treveddon consists of a character farmhouse and Cornish-stone, converted barn facing south, set in secluded garden and lawn. Situated approximately three miles from The Lizard and Kynance Cove; one and a half miles from Cadgwith fishing cove and beach of Kennack Sands. Ten miles from Helston, where the famous "Floral Dance" is held on May 8th, and within easy reach of many beaches, fishing, cliff walks, golf and horse riding. Little Treveddon contains three bedrooms (sleeps six); lounge, diningroom; bathroom; kitchen (electric cooker, fridge); colour TV; nightstore heating and fitted carpets. Treveddon Barn sleeps seven; lounge with French doors; kitchen/diner; bathroom and all furnishings as above. Cot available. Pets with permission. Available all year for holiday letting. SAE for colour brochure and terms. **Mr and Mrs P. J. Hodge, Trezebel Farm, Manaccan, Helston TR12 6JB (Manaccan [032-623] 392).**

LAUNCESTON. Higher Bamham Farm Holiday Cottages, Launceston. Set in beautiful countryside, with magnificent rural views, and only half mile from the market town of Launceston. These five cottages situated around a courtyard are luxuriously converted from old farm buildings. Three are adjoining and two are detached, with plenty of parking space available. One of the many outstanding features is the large (36' × 15') indoor heated swimming pool with adjoining paddling pool set in a large garden; we have also a stretch of private trout and salmon fishing. Amenities of the area include golf, riding stables, squash and tennis courts all within one mile. For your brochure please contact: **Jackie Chapman, Higher Bamham Farm, Launceston PL15 9LD (Launceston [0566] 2141).**

LAUNCESTON. Mrs H. H. Rowe, Godcott, North Petherwin, Launceston PL15 8NX (North Petherwin [056-685] 223). Working farm. Solid stone farm cottage situated on parish road. The dairy farm is set in beautiful Cornish countryside and fishing, surfing, golf, squash, tennis and other sporting facilities can be enjoyed in Bude, Launceston (new heated indoor swimming pool), Holsworthy and surrounding districts. Near Devon Border so guests can enjoy the facilities of both Devon and Cornwall. Six people accommodated in one double, one twin and one room with bunk beds and cot. Bathroom and toilet; sittingroom; kitchen/diner with electric cooker, fridge, etc. Linen supplied. Colour TV; open fire if needed, also Rayburn. Immersion heater; mains water and electricity (meter 10p). Car essential — parking. Pets welcome. Open January to December; terms from £40 weekly. SAE, please.

LAUNCESTON near. Hillside, Badharlick, Egloskerry, Near Launceston. This large cottage, set in rural farming community, stands in its own grounds with half an acre of lawn; on the border of Devon and Cornwall it is an ideal touring centre. Golf course four miles, pony trekking nearby. Within easy reach of Dartmoor and the Cornish Hills. A real family retreat. Accommodation for six/eight in two double, one family bedrooms, cot available. Bathroom and toilet upstairs, toilet downstairs; large sittingroom with TV; diningroom; kitchen with electric cooker and all necessary utensils. Storage heaters. Linen supplied. Well controlled pets allowed. Car essential, parking in cottage grounds. Three-quarters of a mile from shops. Open all year. SAE, please, for terms to **Mrs O. M. Francis, Badharlick Farm, Egloskerry, Near Launceston PL15 8SU (Pipers Pool [056-686] 275).**

SELF-CATERING Cornwall

LAUNCESTON. Mr and Mrs E. J. Broad, Lower Dutson Farm, Launceston PL15 9SP (Launceston [0566] 2607). Working farm. Whether fishing family or not, everyone is made equally welcome on this 200 acre family farm where they may feel free to stroll across the fields to the river and/or lake. It is centrally situated for touring the coasts and the counties of Cornwall and Devon. Both houses available are comfortably furnished, with colour TV and all equipment, the larger also having a separate room with table tennis, darts, snooker, etc. There is no close season for fishing the well stocked lake for carp, tench, rudd etc. or, if preferred, the River Tamar provides good pools and sport for trout and salmon. Space does not allow a detailed description but full particulars will be sent immediately on receipt of SAE.

LAUNCESTON. Mrs M. Coumbe, West Penrest, Lezant, Launceston PL15 9NP (Stoke Climsland [0579] 70362). Working farm. This cottage for six people is set on a mixed farm, one mile from the village — with its shop, church and public house. It is ideally situated for touring north and south coasts, Dartmoor and Cornish Moors. The historic town of Launceston is five miles away, with its Leisure Centre (heated swimming pool etc.). Plymouth 20 miles. There are two bedrooms, one with double bed and the other with double bed and bunks; lounge with colour TV; bathroom and two toilets; dining/kitchen with electric cooker, fridge, toaster, kettle. All fully equipped except linen which may be hired at extra charge. Immersion heater. Pets allowed. Car essential here and there is a garage and parking space. Large garden. Children welcome, cot. It is in an area of great natural beauty and has wonderful views of the Cornish Hills. A warm welcome assured from March to November. SAE, please, for terms.

LAUNCESTON. Mrs O. M. Leask, Badharlick, Egloskerry, Launceston PL15 8SU (Pipers Pool [056-686] 308). Situated in peaceful, secluded country surroundings (no through traffic), 15 miles from North Cornish coast. Small cottage provides good family accommodation without frills but with all modern conveniences at a reasonable price — £69 per week; May, June and September £55 per week. Fully furnished and well-equipped for five. One double bedroom, one larger room with three single beds. Cooking by gas (included in rent). Electric fires, hot water and fridge (10p meter). TV and own carport. DOGS WELCOME. Full details on request. Also available in nearby cottage, Bed and Breakfast (double room, twin beds) and use of delightful 26 foot sun lounge. £6 per person per day.

LAUNCESTON. Dozmary Pool Cottage, Bolventor, Launceston. Enjoy a quiet holiday in a quaint country cottage in this delightful part of Cornwall in the heart of Bodmin Moors overlooking Dozmary Pool. Approximately one mile Jamaica Inn, 10 miles Launceston, Bodmin and Liskeard. Ideal centre for touring north and south coast and the legendary King Arthur country. The cottage comprises two small double bedrooms, sitting/diningroom; B/W TV; electric coal effect fire. Bathroom, toilet. Kitchen, fully equipped, has electric cooker, fridge, etc. Linen supplied on request. Ideal location for children and pets. Car essential — ample parking. Open all year; weekly terms — £70. SAE, please, **Mrs Mary Rich, "Nathanla," Altarnun, Launceston PL15 7SL (Pipers Pool [056-686] 426).**

LAUNCESTON. Mrs P. Sobey, Higher Dutson Farm, Launceston, Cornwall PL15 9SP (Launceston [0566] 2930). Working farm. Two bungalows converted from an old barn are available on this dairy and sheep farm 1½ miles from Launceston with beautiful views of the surrounding countryside. Each can sleep 5 and 6 respectively. Each have bathroom, electric cooker, fridge, etc. Livingroom with colour TV, electric fire, mainly carpeted and tastefully decorated. Cots available. Linen supplied at extra cost. Pets by arrangement. Trout fishing on River Tamar and River Ottery which flow through the farm. Ample parking. Terms from £40 p.w. Also olde worlde beamed cottage with 3 bedrooms to sleep 7 (off farm). Very spacious with inglenook fireplaces, all mod. cons. Lovely country setting. Numbers and dates with SAE please. Available all year.

LAUNCESTON near. Mrs A. E. Moore, Hollyvag, Lewannick, Near Launceston PL15 7QH (Coads Green [056-682] 309). Working farm. Part of 17th century farmhouse, self-contained and full of old world charm with own lawns, front and back. Set in secluded position in wooded countryside with views of the moors. Central for North and South coasts. Family farm with ducks on the pond, horses, sheep and poultry. Sleeps four/six, fully furnished with all modern conveniences, folding bed and cot available. Colour TV, fridge, electric cooker, solid fuel heating if needed. Babysitting available free. Linen not provided. Within five miles of market town; golf, fishing and riding nearby. Terms from £50. Brochure on request.

LAUNCESTON. Mrs D. J. M. Courtenay, Trethinna, Launceston (Pipers Pool [056-686] 207). Working farm. There are no restrictions in this self-contained furnished flat, which is part of a large farmhouse with its own entrance. Guests who want peace and relaxation will enjoy a holiday here. All Cornwall and a good part of Devon are within easy reach by car for day trips. Two double bedrooms; bathroom with flush toilet. Lounge/diningroom, with night storage and a put-u-up as an extra bed if required. Large kitchen with electric cooker, fridge and immersion heater for hot water. Cot for child. Parking space. Shops two and a half miles. Pets are allowed. Open all year. Terms sent on request. SAE, please, for prompt reply.

Cornwall SELF-CATERING

LISKEARD. Mrs L. Kidd, Lower Trengale Farm, Liskeard PL14 6HF (0579) 21019. Three delightful cottages carefully converted from a traditional stone barn near to the farmhouse. Comfortably furnished and fully equipped, storage heating, colour TV and all linen supplied with beds made up for guests' arrival. Delicious home-cooked Evening Meals available to give busy mothers a proper holiday. See also Board Section in this Guide.

LISKEARD. Mrs E. Coles, "Cutkive Wood Chalets", St. Ive, Liskeard PL14 3ND (Liskeard [0579] 62216). Six self-catering Cedar Chalets set in 41 acres of private woodland and pasture, totally secluded. Personally supervised, our spacious chalet bungalows have open plan living room with colour TV, two double bedrooms, bathroom and separate WC. Fully equipped electric kitchen. Picturesque resort of Looe is but 15 minutes' drive. Trout and sea fishing easily accessible. Walking and riding on Bodmin Moor, two miles. Nature Trails and bird watching in our own grounds. Championship Golf Course of St. Mellion, five miles. On site shop, home made bread, fresh milk, eggs and own garden produce. Pets corner, goats, ducks, hens, rabbits, quails etc. Adventure Playground. Pets allowed. Car essential. Write for brochure.

* **LOOE. Mr and Mrs A. Wright, Treworgey Cottages, Duloe, Liskeard PL14 2PP (Looe [05036] 2730).** Dream old-world country cottages, sleep two to six, three miles from Looe. Individual private gardens and breathtaking views. Heated pool. Furnished and equipped to an extremely high standard including colour TV's, log fires, washer driers, linen. Delicious home-cooked meal service. Golf, riding, sea, nearby. Open all year. Well behaved pets welcome. Please send for free colour brochure. See also Colour Display Advertisement in this Guide.

LOOE. Mrs A. E. Barrett, Tredinnick Farm, Duloe, Liskeard PL14 4PJ (Looe [05036] 2997). Working farm. This accommodation is part of a large farmhouse on a mixed farm of dairy, beef, sheep and corn. Situated with beautiful views of the Cornish countryside just four miles from Looe and Polperro. Beaches, swimming, fishing, bowls, golf and horse riding all within easy reach. The house has part central heating and comprises three bedrooms, one with washbasin, sleeping eight, plus cot. Bathroom. Large lounge with woodburner and colour TV. Fully equipped kitchen. Electricity by 50p coin meter. Utility room with washing machine and tumble dryer; extra toilet. Children welcome. Sorry, no pets. Large lawns and ample parking space. Send 1st class stamp for further details.

LOOE. Mr and Mrs A. T. Hunt, "The Millpond", Polliscourt, St. Martins, Looe (Looe [050-36] 2736). On the fringe of Looe, a cluster of beautifully furnished cottages, **of rare and exceptional quality,** only 350 yards from the beach and coastal footpath. Country lanes, riding, fishing and golf. Colour TV and linen included, with beds made up for your arrival. Electric blankets and comprehensive heating for out of season breaks. Regret, no pets. For colour brochure, please telephone as above. See also Full Page Colour Display Advertisement.

* **LOOE. Mrs G. B. Dolley, Plaidy Beach Holiday Apartments, Plaidy Park Road, Looe PL13 1LG (Looe [050-36] 2044).** Situated in a commanding position on the Cornish Riviera overlooking a sheltered beach — eight completely self-contained flats varying in size accommodating from two to nine occupants. About 15 minutes' walk into Looe where shark fishing, boating, tennis are available, while riding stables, golf about 10 minutes by car. Shops 400 yards. All flats have coastal views and are tastefully decorated. Fitted carpets, colour TV; shower/bathroom, toilet. Kitchens have electric cooker, fridge, kettle, generous quantity of equipment. Electricity by coin meters. Blankets, pillow provided, linen by hire. Extra children's beds, cots, high chairs. Launderette/ironing facilities. Free car parking. Pets welcome. Many places of interest to visit. Monkey Sanctuary, Organ Museum, hill climbing on Bodmin Moor. Terms from £45-£140 (low season); £85-£220 (high season). These rates refer to minimum size up to maximum size of flats. West Country Tourist Board and Cornwall County registered. SAE or telephone for brochure as above. See also colour display advertisement.

LOOE. 1 Longcross, Lansallos, Looe. This semi-detached cottage is situated between the towns of Polperro, one a half miles and Fowey, three and a half miles, Looe four miles. The cottage has a level approach and on a fine day commands magnificent views. It is available from May to November and there is accommodation for seven in two double, one twin and one single bedrooms; cot; all spring interior mattresses. Bathroom, inside toilet. Lounge-cum-diningroom with TV. Kitchen with fridge, sink-unit, hot and cold, electric cooker. Electric fires. Linen is not provided. Large garden. Car essential, parking space. Coastal walks within easy reach. SAE, please, with enquiries to **Mrs M. M. Julian, Penglaze, Brent, Polperro, Looe (Polperro [0503] 72251).**

Please note that entries marked with an asterisk also have a colour display advert in the colour section in this guide

SELF-CATERING Cornwall 381

LOOE (East). Lugano, 4 Pendrim Road, East Looe. Cottage situated on the hillside in East Looe with outstanding views of the harbour and the river estuary. Extensively modernised and completely redecorated throughout, the cottage is fully equipped to accommodate a maximum of eight people and is available from May 1st to October 31st. The lounge is fitted with a patio door leading onto a sun-deck — excellent for sun-bathing. Diningroom, modern kitchen with electric cooker, etc. Two double, one family bedrooms; cot and high chair available. Electric heating. Everything provided except linen. Car not essential, but there is a garage about 150 yards away and parking. Sea 700 yards, shopping and public transport 400 yards. Weekly terms from £60 to £195 (including electricity). Reductions in off season. The cottage has been inspected by the Cornwall Tourist Board and is on their approved register. **Mr D. B. Rees, 15 Sweethay Close, Staplehay, Taunton, Somerset TA3 7HG (Taunton [0823] 87083).**

LOOE. Mrs R. M. Rowe, Treweers Farm, Lansallos, Looe PL13 2QJ (Polperro [0503] 72252). Treweers Cottages are situated on a B class road, one and a half miles from the fishing village of Polperro. It is four miles to Fowey and Looe and one mile from the hamlet of Lansallos with its National Trust Coastline, walks and coves. There is riding, golf and fishing nearby. The cottages have beamed ceilings and open plan stairs; fitted carpets; all-electric and TV; ample parking space. Linen is not supplied. Accommodation for five in two double bedrooms and one single; bathroom, toilet; sittingroom; kitchen/diner with electric cooker. Electric fires. Children are welcome. Sorry no pets. Available May to end of October. Please send SAE for brochure.

MARAZION near. "Sunnyside," Perranuthnoe, Near Marazion. This fully modernised furnished cottage has superb views and is situated in the small, unspoilt village of Perranuthnoe, two miles from Marazion. The village has a shop, pub and ancient church. Sunnyside is only five minutes' walk from the sandy family beach. There are good coastal walks and fishing from the rocks. Nearby are St. Michael's Mount and many tourist attractions, within easy reach of St. Ives, Penzance, the Land's End Area, Helston and the Lizard Peninsula. The cottage has fine coastal views from livingroom and bedrooms. The livingroom has sliding glass doors on to a sheltered patio and small secluded garden. Upstairs, the bedroom verandah has a panoramic view of Mount's Bay. It sleeps four but a fifth folding z-bed can be supplied. Bed linen is provided but please bring your own towels, otherwise the cottage is fully equipped including TV and a modern all-electric kitchen. Also Night Storage heaters for winter use. Apply to **Mrs F. S. Roynon, "Treetops", Perran Downs, Goldsithney, Near Penzance TR20 9HJ (Penzance [0736] 710482).**

MARAZION near. "An Gwythow", Perranuthnoe, Near Penzance. Spacious, modern self-contained cottage situated in beautiful, quiet, unspoilt village of Perranuthnoe, 250 yards from sandy beach. Central for St. Ives, Marazion, Falmouth, Land's End, etc. Perran Sands faces due south and is sheltered by low cliffs, has rocky pools, sandy beach and superb cliff walks. Four/six people can be accommodated all year round in the two double bedrooms plus cot; bathroom and toilet; sittingroom; diningroom; modern kitchen with everything supplied including linen if required. Suitable for disabled holidaymakers. Local farm providing milk, cream and eggs. Weekly terms from £40. Details from **Mrs C. G. Coles, "Palm Trees", Wheal Whidden, Carbis Bay, St. Ives TR26 2QX (Penzance [0736] 798055).**

MEVAGISSEY. Mrs J. L. Owens, Mevagissey House, Vicarage Hill, Mevagissey PL26 6SZ (Mevagissey [0726] 842427). Mevagissey House offers family Bed and Breakfast accommodation and self-catering cottages, all situated within three and a half acres of lovely woodland, surrounded by farm land. Ideal location on the St. Austell side of Mevagissey, nestling on the hillside, with superb views across the valley to the harbour and open sea beyond. Comfortable accommodation is provided in the house, with colour TV, tea and coffee making facilities in each room and use of lounge. There are also three cottages: "Dormer" sleeping two/three; "Coach House" with accommodation for five/six and "Goose" for seven/nine persons. Each cottage is fully equipped, including bed linen (except towels) and colour TV. Car not essential, parking. Five minutes to shops and public transport. Available March to end of October. Weekly terms from £70 to £240 including electricity. Further information on request.

CORNWALL – SOMETHING FOR EVERYONE!

Sea, sand, cliffs and quite often the sun, but that's not all you will find in this interesting county. Cornwall has many fascinating places to visit, such as the Charlestown Shipwreck Centre, the Tropical Bird Gardens at Padstow, Cornwall Aeronautical Park near Helston, Botallack Tin Mine, The Cornish Seal Sanctuary, Perranporth and of course, St. Michael's Mount.

Cornwall   SELF-CATERING

MEVAGISSEY. Mr and Mrs A. H. Robins, Invermore, School Hill, Mevagissey PL26 6QT (Mevagissey [0726] 842348). Four flats to let in the square of Mevagissey, a quaint old Cornish fishing village. Recommended by Cornwall Tourist Board. Each flat will sleep up to six people and all are self-contained and fully equipped. Two double bedrooms and cot; bathroom, toilet; sittingroom with bed settee; diningroom; kitchen. No linen supplied. Near shops and just two minutes from the sea. Car not essential, but parking available. Pets are permitted. Open all year with weekly terms from £40 – £120, VAT exempt. SAE, please.

MOUSEHOLE (Penzance). Mr and Mrs D. Pike, Polvellan Holiday Flats, The Parade, Mousehole, Penzance TR19 6PT (Penzance [0736] 731602) — 24 hours. Five self-contained flats, open all year. Overlooking sea, some with part or full sea view. All-electric with colour TV. Two ground floor and three first floor flats in large stone-built house with gardens and patio. Sleep from two/six persons. Near bus stop, village shops and harbour — 80 yards to beach. Children welcome, cots and high chairs available. Pets welcome. Mousehole is an unspoilt Cornish fishing village. The Harbour forms a sun trap enclosing a small sandy beach well recommended for safe bathing. A sea water pool is nearby. Fishing and boat trips are available from the Harbour. Terms from £45 per week. Free brochure — from **Mr and Mrs D. Pike.**

MULLION. "Kittiwake," Polurrian Cliff Road, Mullion. Owners' large detached bungalow in one-third of an acre overlooking the sea. Uninterrupted view across Mount's Bay to Penzance. Attractively and comfortably furnished. Colour TV. Storage heaters. Sleeps seven in three bedrooms (two have basins). Fully fitted modern bathroom including shower and bidet. Modern and extensively equipped kitchen — double oven, fridge/freezer, dishwasher, washing machine, food mixer/blender, etc. 10 minutes' walk to the village – nine to the sandy beach. Many other beaches, coastal walks, golf, local fishing harbours, the Helford River, boat trips from Falmouth and much else. SAE please, giving dates required to **Weyman, The Vicarage, Westcott, Dorking, Surrey RH4 3QB (Dorking [0306] 885309).**

TALL TREES, TREBUDANNON NEWQUAY

Lovely old farm cottage situated in the tiny hamlet of Trebudannon, secluded, yet close enough to town and beach holiday entertainments. A trout stream meanders through the land and down the lovely Colan Valley to the sea. Three bedrooms, plus cot; bathroom; toilet; lounge; diningroom. Colour TV; cooker; fridge and immerser; continental quilts; washing machine; 50p meter. Log fires. Everything supplied except linen. Car necessary; parking. Pets allowed. SAE, please, stating number of people and dates required, for terms and brochure to:

MRS JOY WELDHEN,
TREBUDANNON FARM,
TREBUDANNON, NEWQUAY TR8 4LP
(St Columb [0637] 880346)

TALL TREES

NEWQUAY. Mrs C. L. Pascoe, 30 Veor Road, Newquay TR7 3BX (Newquay [06373] 77740). This three-bedroomed bungalow, situated at the end of a very quiet road with views of Porth Island and beach, offers accommodation for seven people in two double bedrooms and one with beds for three, plus cot. There are gardens to front and rear. Three minutes' walk to the beach, a few minutes' drive along the main road to the town centre or by a very pleasant walk across the barrowfields, all on level. There is a lounge/diner with TV; separate kitchen with electric cooker, fridge, etc; bathroom, and separate toilet. Linen supplied. Children welcome. Pets by previous arrangement. Open from May to October. For further information SAE, please or telephone.

NEWQUAY. Mrs R. Pascoe, "Bella's Villa", 35 Linden Avenue, Newquay (Newquay 063-73-3670). Holiday accommodation in new property. Self-contained Flat, sleeps five persons in two bedrooms; lounge/diningroom and kitchen recess. Shower room/toilet. Own entrance. Drying space on sun patio. All electric — cooker, fridge, kettle, iron, fires. Colour TV. Linen supplied but no towels. Car not necessary, although there is private parking, overlooking a large and well kept garden. Shops at the end of the Avenue. Park, Zoo and sporting complex three minutes' walk. Sea 10 minutes' walk. Occupies a quiet and sheltered position, and guests are assured of every comfort. Pets by arrangement. Available Easter to October. SAE, please or telephone.

NEWQUAY. 59 Carneton Close, Crantock, Newquay. This spacious modern first-floor flat with lock-up garage is situated in a peaceful residential cul-de-sac. The village of Crantock is four miles from Newquay and has one of the finest beaches in Cornwall. Tradesmen call, and shops, two inns and a church are within easy walking distance. The accommodation (for six people) comprises two double bedrooms, one with an extra single bed; bed-settee in dining area of lounge; colour TV; electric heating; bathroom; toilet; kitchen with fridge and electric cooker, etc. No linen supplied. Pets are allowed. Open from Easter to October. There is 50p electric meter. SAE, please, for terms to **Mrs Wendy Carne, "Kalsia," Broadshard, Crewkerne, Somerset TA18 7NF (Crewkerne [0460] 73068).**

SELF-CATERING　　Cornwall

NEWQUAY near. Mrs F. Wearne, Rosewastis Farm, St. Columb Major, Near Newquay TR8 4LT (St. Columb [0637] 880270). Working farm. A semi-detached farm cottage surrounded by farmland and accommodating seven people is available from April to end of October for self-catering holidays. Modernised, it has three bedrooms, diningroom, lounge, kitchen and shower room with WC. Tastefully furnished; TV, cooker, fridge. Large garden and parking space (car essential). Situated on the A39 road, one mile from ancient market town of St. Columb, within easy reach of lovely Cornish beaches. Central for touring. This is a 214-acre mixed farm where guests can really "get away from it all." No linen supplied. Well controlled pets allowed. SAE, please, for terms.

PADSTOW near. Mrs S. May, Trewithen Farm, St Merryn, Near Padstow PL28 8JZ (Padstow [0841] 520420). Working farm. Trewithen is a 124-acre family run farm with cattle, sheep, cereals etc., quiet and secluded but near many lovely beaches, all good for swimming, surfing, sailing etc. Near Trevose Golf Club and good riding stables. The flats are fully equipped except linen. Very comfortable and guaranteed to be clean and fresh. Sorry, no pets. Accommodation for seven in two double and one family bedrooms; cot; bathroom, toilet; sittingroom/kitchen with electric cooker, fridge, fire, iron, colour TV. Car essential — ample parking. Available Easter to October. Also another flat available, sleeping five with one family bedroom and studio couch in lounge. SAE, please, for weekly terms.

PENZANCE. Penwith Cottages, Penzance. From Penzance to Land's End, we have carefully selected a wide variety of Cottages and Farmhouses which we regard as ideal for your holiday requirements. Either set in picturesque countryside with lawned gardens, or on the coast with spectacular sea views. All properties are registered with the English and Cornish Tourist Boards and are comfortably furnished together with colour TV. Sleeping four to nine, plus cot. Pets are most welcome. Do write with SAE to the following address for a brochure, or telephone for friendly help and advice to choose your perfect Cornish holiday — **Penwith Cottages, Chyandour Office, Penzance, Cornwall TR18 3LW (Penzance [0736] 65306).**

PENZANCE. Rockhaven is an olde worlde farmhouse set in four acres of peaceful countryside, midway between Penzance, Helston and St. Ives. The sea and nearest sandy beach being Praa Sands just moments away by car. Views extend to St. Ives and there is absolute tranquillity, yet many popular resorts are within easy reach. The location is ideal for walking, touring, horse riding and there is a Golf Club nearby. The house is luxuriously furnished, sleeping four in comfort. The open beamed lounge has a colour TV. Well equipped kitchen includes dishwasher and washing machine. The heating is electric and is included in the rate. Please telephone **01-661 7845** on Sundays or after 9.30 pm weekdays.

ROCKHAVEN,
Penzance, Cornwall.

PENZANCE. "The Cottage", Brane, Sancreed, Penzance. Working farm. Attractive rural farm cottage, sleeps seven in four bedrooms (two double, one twin-bedded, one single room). Bathroom with shower; lounge (TV); kitchen/diner with electric cooker, fridge, immersion heater; electric fires. Garden. Ample parking. Situated between Penzance and Land's End, car is essential as cottage is quietly located in countryside on a dairy farm. Short drive to many sandy beaches, beauty spots, places of historic and archaeological interest. Beautiful walks in the vicinity including National Trust land. Terms from £50 to £110. SAE, please, to **Mrs E. Wherry, Brane Farm, Sancreed, Penzance TR20 8RD [St. Buryan [073-672] 368).**

PENZANCE. Mr and Mrs G. B. Hocking, Rospannel, Crows-An-Wra, Penzance TR19 6HS (St. Buryan [0736] 72262). Granite farm cottage, situated in centre of quiet 85-acre farm, next to farmhouse, overlooking a peaceful, unspoilt valley. Tarmac drive to garage adjoining cottage, one mile from A30. Ideally situated for touring West Cornwall; many coves and beaches within five miles. Nearest beach, shop, etc. three miles. Sleeps five. Two bedrooms, electric radiators, washbasin and upstairs toilet. Linen supplied for overseas clients only. Dining/sittingroom has a large granite inglenook fireplace and colour TV. Fully equipped electric kitchen, including fridge and spin dryer. Only one cottage, so personal service guaranteed. SAE, please, for details, stating dates required.

PENZANCE. Mrs T. Thomas, Trevear Farm, Sennen, Penzance TR19 7BH (Sennen [073-687] 205). Trevorrian farmhouse and Trevear cottages are easily accessible, set in quiet countryside, on adjoining farms, approximately one-and-a-half miles from Sennen Cove beach. The surrounding area is of outstanding natural beauty with a variety of sports available within a 10-mile radius. The farmhouse is extremely spacious, sleeping 12 in five bedrooms. The cottages sleep six each. All bedrooms are fully carpeted, bed linen is not supplied. All are fully equipped with electric cooker, fridge, china, etc., heaters, television, storage heaters. Separate laundry facilities at Trevorrian farm for all guests. Personal supervision with emphasis on cleanliness and comfort. Pets by arrangement. SAE, please.

Cornwall SELF-CATERING

PENZANCE. Boswednan Farm Cottage, Tremethick Cross, Penzance. Working farm. Granite cottage in a tiny hamlet of four farms, quarter mile down a lane, two miles from Penzance on the St. Just road. Sheltered and secluded, yet within easy reach of numerous beaches and the impressive scenery of both north and south coasts. Information provided of local entertainments, restaurants, beaches and other holiday facilities. Accommodation of good standard, comfortably furnished and equipped for six people. Large lounge with TV and open fire, kitchen with dining area, electric cooker and fridge; one double and one single bedrooms, plus one room with 4' double bed, plus single bed. Linen not provided. Car essential — parking. Available May to October. Babysitting can be arranged. Terms from £50 to £120 weekly; electricity extra. Well behaved dogs allowed, by arrangement only. **Mr & Mrs G. N. F. Broughton, Orchard House, Wall, Gwinear, Hayle TR27 5HA (0736-850201).**

PENZANCE. Mrs R. P. Preston, Boscobba, Polking Horne, Gulval, Penzance TR20 8YS (Penzance [0736] 63811). High quality self-catering in splendid farmlands, overlooking bay, only two miles from town centre. Boscobba, self-catering, ground floor and garden in converted granite farmhouse. Three bedrooms sleep six/seven. Unique functioning Cornish fireplace. Open all year. £65 to £250, according to season and party. Boscobba Vean. Delightful detached smaller single storey, stone cottage nearby. Sleeps two/four. Winter let. £40 to £190. Private garden. Resident owner provides linen. TV. Laundry. Ample parking. Total peace. This is a magical area, abundant in wildlife and interesting walks. Nearest beach one and a half miles. End of lane situation, safe for children. Pets welcome. Further details on request.

PENZANCE. Mr and Mrs S. M. Adey, St. Michael's Farm, Nanceddan, Ludgvan, Penzance TR20 8AW (0736-740-738). The Croft, adjoining farmhouse, converted from old smoke house, provides cosy accommodation yet retains typical croft character. Loft, double bedroom and ground-floor, open-plan, with bunkroom, kitchen/lounge and modern bathroom. Ideal two adults, two children; carpeted throughout, all-electric. Situated in beautiful country position overlooking Mount's Bay and St. Michael's Mount — superb sea views. Five minutes by car from beach. Penzance three miles; St. Ives three miles. Numerous country walks including access to wild valley. Favourites are the donkey, pony and Jersey house cow giving fresh milk and clotted cream. Home-made cheese available. Fully equipped except for linen. Shops half-a-mile. Car essential. Sorry, no pets.

PENZANCE. Mrs F. J. Osborne, Bosworlas Farm, St. Just, Penzance TR19 7RQ [0736] 788-709). Working farm. Bosworlas House is centrally situated for touring St. Just, St. Ives, Sennen Cove, Porthcurno, Newlyn and Penzance on the West Coast. Fishing, pony riding, surfing, short scenic flights, coastal walks and many places of historical interest nearby. St. Just (one-and-three-quarter miles away) has take-away meals, licensed restaurants, post office, banks, self-service shops, newsagents, etc. Accommodation for 10 people in two double bedrooms and two family rooms which include cots; bathroom, two toilets; sitting-room with TV; separate diningroom and kitchen, fully fitted with electric cooker, fridge, Hygena sink unit and cupboards. Pets permitted only by arrangement. Open all year round. Car essential — parking. All comforts and good beds. Fully equipped except linen. SAE, please, for terms and further details.

PENZANCE near. Nos. 1 and 2 Praze Cottages, Cape Cornwall, St. Just, Near Penzance. Situated on the only cape in England, two modernised detached cottages standing in own ground. One sleeps three people in one double and one single room; the other sleeps four in two double rooms. Bathroom and shower; hot and cold water, toilet. All-electric kitchen, cutlery, crockery, etc. supplied. Panoramic sea views from the lounge. TV. Parking space. Pets welcome. Cot and high chair available. Open all year. Ideal for out of season breaks. There are sandy beaches, fishing coves, cliff walks, all within easy reach. Penzance seven miles; St. Ives 15; Land's End five. SAE, please, for prompt reply to **Mrs A. N. Rawlinson, 16 Carn, Bosavern, St. Just, Penzance TR19 7QX (Penzance [0736] 788671.**

SELF-CATERING Cornwall 385

PENZANCE. Mrs James Curnow, Barlowenath, St. Hilary, Goldsithney, Penzance TR20 9DQ (Penzance [0736] 710409). Working farm. These two cottages are on a dairy farm, in a little hamlet right beside St. Hilary Church, with quiet surroundings and a good road approach. A good position for touring Cornish coast and most well-known places. Beaches are two miles away; Marazion two-and-a-half miles; Penzance six miles; St. Ives eight; Lands End 16. Both cottages have fitted carpets, lounge/diner with TV; modern kitchen (fridge, electric cooker, toaster, iron); bathroom with flush toilet, shaver point. Electricity is on 50p meter. One cottage sleeps five in three bedrooms (one double, twin divans and one single). The second cottage sleeps four in two bedrooms (twin divans in each). Linen not supplied. Cot by arrangement. Available all year from £55 to £150 weekly.

PENZANCE/ST. IVES. Nanceddan Farm Holidays, Penzance/St Ives. Working farm. AA listed. Midway between St. Ives and Penzance, each approximately five miles. Luxury self-catering holiday homes of one, two and three bedrooms, converted from barns and cattle sheds. Completely self-contained with bathroom and/or shower, WC, shaver point, airing cupboard. Automatic timing electric cooker, fridge, colour TV, heater. Carpeted throughout. Laundry facilities. Ample parking space. Beautiful views of countryside, St Michael's Mount, Mount's Bay. Still a working farm with cattle and fruit. Regret, no pets. Friday to Friday bookings available. Send medium SAE for illustrated colour brochure to; **N. and D. V. Richards, Nanceddan Farm, Ludgvan, Penzance TR20 8AW (or phone Penzance [0736] 740238 or [0736] 740293).**

POLPERRO. Crumplehorn Cottages, Polperro. Dating from early 1700 these traditional Cornish cottages face due south and enjoy the maximum of sunshine. Catering for two/seven persons having open-beamed ceilings, local stone fireplaces, sun patios, gardens and car parking, they offer the discriminating holidaymaker the unique opportunity of enjoying the comfort of "today" with the charm and character of "by-gone-days." Completely on the level and close to the harbour they blend with the local community and are not part of a "holiday complex." OPEN ALL YEAR with nightstore heating available for out-of-season holiday comfort. CCC and AA inspected/approved and under the personal supervision of resident owners to guarantee a high standard of comfort/cleanliness. Also cottages/flats at nearby holiday resort of Looe with similar accommodation/facilities. SAE, please, for illustrated brochure to **Mr and Mrs Murray Collings, Brook Cottage, Longcoombe Lane, Polperro PL13 2PL (Polperro [0503] 72274).**

POLZEATH. 2 The Martins, Polzeath, Wadebridge. This modern, centrally heated bungalow is in a lovely position for a holiday at any time of the year, with a magnificent view over the beach and Pentire Point. About two minutes' walk from the beach and shops. Walks can be enjoyed along surrounding National Trust lands, also golf, riding, sailing, surfing, water ski-ing, fishing etc. Accommodates up to nine people, plus cot. ETB registered Category 4. Amenities include colour TV, pay phone, garden, fitted carpets except in kitchen, bathroom and separate toilet. All linen is supplied and the duvets, furnishings, etc., are non-allergy. Apply to **Mrs J. Wheadon, Hardicott Farm, Milton Abbot, Tavistock, Devon PL19 8PY (Milton Abbot [082-287] 206).**

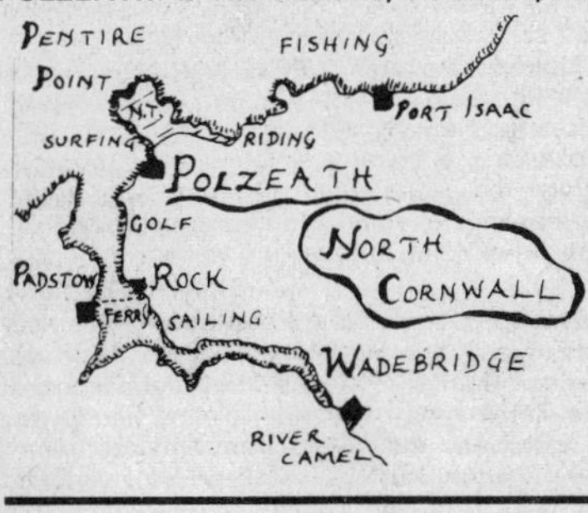

POLZEATH. Curlew, High Cliff, Polzeath, Near Wadebridge. Curlew is in a unique position overlooking the sea and very close to a large sandy beach, ideal for surfing and very good for children of all ages. Pony trekking, sailing and golf at St. Enodoc are within easy reach. Very well situated for cliff walking. Curlew sleeps eight in five bedrooms (all single beds), equipped with Hot and Cold. Good kitchen facilities all electric. Sittingroom with TV. Parking for cars. Garden. Very safe for children. Cot available. Close to shops. Ideal as touring centre. Apply **Mr and Mrs Woodcock, 38 Alleyn Park, Dulwich, London SE21 8SA (01-670 7837).**

POLZEATH. Gullsway and September Tide, Highcliffe, Polzeath. Gullsway and September Tide. Gullsway is a large house divided into three self-contained apartments. The bungalow September Tide shares the garden. They are adjacent to the cliff walk near Old Polzeath and overlook the beautiful surfing beach. Local activities include most watersports, golf, riding, walking N.T. coastline. Accommodation for seven, five, and five in the apartments of the house and for six in the bungalow. Well equipped, colour TV, cots, shared washing machine and dryer. Linen not supplied. Children and pets welcome. Access to the beach is across the car park. Shops at Polzeath are at the top of the beach. Wadebridge, nearest market town, is six miles. SAE, please, or telephone **Mrs A. Hambly, Rosewarne Wollas, Camborne, Cornwall TR14 8LL (0209-712632).**

POLZEATH. Pendeen, Rock, Polzeath. Delightful, detached modern house overlooking golf course, one-and-a-half miles from sandy beaches — Rock, Daymer Bay, Polzeath, offering facilities for sailing, ski-ing, surfing, fishing. Pendeen has three double, and one single bedrooms; cot available. Accommodation for eight persons; bathroom, separate toilet; diningroom; lounge, TV. Kitchen and kitchenette. All-electric and fully equipped except linen. Metered electricity. Garage and parking space. Shops quarter of a mile. One house-trained pet allowed. Also well equipped 30 feet, all-electric, five-berth caravan. SAE for terms to **Mrs W. Francis Mably, Trewint Farm, St. Minver, Wadebridge PL27 6PU (Trebetherick [020-886] 3363).**

POLZEATH. Mrs Christine Hawkey, Treglines Farm, St. Minver, Wadebridge PL27 6QT Trebetherick [020-886] 2534). Working farm. Treglines is situated just one and a half miles from the safe, sandy beach and shops of Polzeath and three miles from the sailing, water ski-ing, golfing area of Rock. One has the advantage of being within easy reach of all facilities whilst enjoying life on the farm. The front half of the farmhouse is completely self-contained with its own two entrances and overlooks pleasant countryside and garden, which is for visitors' use. The house is comfortably furnished and equipped to accommodate up to eight people in four bedrooms. It has a good sized diningroom, lounge (colour TV), kitchen and bathroom. Heating and cooking — electricity. Sorry, no pets. Linen not provided. SAE, please.

PORT GAVERNE. Mr D. G. Bolton, "Gullrock," Port Gaverne, Port Isaac PL29 3SQ (Port Isaac [020-888] 218). Working farm. "Gullrock" is one of the gems of North Cornwall. Situated in Port Gaverne, a small cove of great charm and natural beauty, "Gullrock" is no distance from the beach and yet far enough away to retain the peace and quiet which so many people seek. The cottage/flats, of which there are eight, are spacious, comfortable and well-equipped, each has its own entrance from either the courtyard or a quiet lane. Dating from 17th century, the atmosphere of the building is retained within the central grass courtyard around which nestle the cottage/flats. Brochure on application to the resident proprietor.

PORT ISAAC. Mrs M. E. Warne, Tresungers Farm, Port Isaac PL29 3SY (Port Isaac [0208] 880307). Working farm. Ideal spot for anyone desiring quiet holiday, this farmhouse, on 160-acres of mixed farmland offers furnished self-contained wing for self catering holidays from March to November. Approximately 400 yards from B3314 coast road, just over two miles from sea at Port Isaac. Accommodation for five/six people in two double bedrooms, one with extra single bed; also cot available; bathroom, toilet; sitting/diningroom; well equipped kitchen with electric cooker, fridge, etc. and including bed linen. Regret, no pets. Shops just over two miles. Car essential — parking. Electricity on meter. Golf, pony trekking, bathing and surfing within easy reach. St. Endellion Church about one and a half miles away. Terms on receipt of SAE, please.

PORT ISAAC. Mr and Mrs P. Bower, "Halcyon Flats," The Terrace, Port Isaac PL29 3SG (Port Isaac [020-888] 378). Port Isaac nestles in a coastal valley, unspoilt and little affected by its 600 years history. Narrow alleys and streets lead down to the harbour where you can watch the local catch being landed and buy fresh crab, lobster and mackerel. Port Isaac and neighbouring Port Gaverne offer safe bathing and both are a short walk from the flats, as are a number of pubs and eating places. Halcyon Flats stand high on the cliff top and all lounges enjoy magnificent views of sea and surrounding coast, each flat has its own front door key and is equipped to a high standard with full sized electric cooker, fridge, TV; parking. Sleep two to eight. Children and pets welcome. Linen optional extra. Cornwall Tourist Board approved. Colour brochure available.

PORT ISAAC. Carn Awn, Port Gaverne, Port Isaac. Carn Awn stands on its own in the hamlet of Port Gaverne, and overlooks the harbour and sea. Fishing, swimming, boating and delightful rock pools for the children. Magnificent coastline where you can walk for miles along coastal paths. Many other beaches within reach. Plenty of shopping facilities. Car essential, parking. Accommodation for six people in three double bedrooms; cot available; bathroom, separate toilet; large sitting/kitchen/diningroom. All electric. Linen may be hired. Well behaved dogs welcome. Open all year. Also available flat, sleeps four, in Port Isaac. SAE, please, for terms to **Mrs S. A. May, 24 Silvershell Road, Port Isaac PL29 3SN (Bodmin [0208] 880716).**

SELF-CATERING   Cornwall   387

PORT ISAAC. The Dolphin, Port Isaac. This delightful house, originally an inn, is one of the most attractive in Port Isaac. Fifty yards from the sea, shops and pub. Five bedrooms, three with washbasins. Two bathrooms and WCs. Large diningroom. Cosy sittingroom. Spacious and well-equipped kitchen with electric cooker, dish washer, washing machine. Sun terrace. Port Isaac is a picturesque fishing village with magnificent coastal scenery all round. Nearby attractions include surfing, sailing, fishing, golf, tennis, pony trekking. The Dolphin sleeps nine but reduced rates offered for smaller families and off-peak season. Weekly terms: £120 to £265 inclusive. SAE for details to **Mrs Thomas, 2 Stephenson Terrace, Worcester, Hereford and Worcester WR1 3EA (Worcester [0905] 20518).**

PORT ISAAC. "Edwarma Cottage," 14 Church Hill, Port Isaac. A charming olde worlde white walled period cottage has been extensively renovated and brought up to luxurious living standards. Its elevated position offers extensive views of the village, harbour and sea from bedrooms. Only 50 yards from the harbour, beach and shops — an ideal holiday spot. Port Isaac, one of the most attractive quaint old Cornish villages, has much to delight the holiday-maker and artist. Sailing, surfing, golf, pony trekking, all within easy reach. An ideal centre for touring or just relaxing. Many lovely walks on National Trust land. Six people accommodated in three double bedrooms; bathroom, toilet; sittingroom, diningroom; kitchen with cooker, fridge, etc. No linen supplied. No pets. Car essential — parking. Open from February to November. Radiators and electric fires. TV. Electricity by 50p meter. SAE for terms. **Mrs J. Orchard, "Arabia Cottage," 34 Church Hill, Port Isaac PL29 3RQ (Port Isaac [020-888] 450).**

PORT ISAAC. Salters Cottage and Penny Cottage, Port Gaverne, Port Isaac. Port Gaverne is a hamlet adjoining Port Isaac on an inlet in the magnificent rugged North Coast, and its shingle beach is one of the safest bathing beaches in Cornwall. Salters and Penny Cottages are about 100 yards from the sea, made from the old fishermen's netting lofts and fish "cellars," dating from the days when Port Gaverne had a flourishing herring and pilchard trade. The cottages are fully equipped and most comfortably furnished and Penny Cottage, being all on the ground floor, is most suitable for the elderly or disabled. Salters Cottage has a piano. I will be most happy to send you full details of rents and all vacant dates on receipt of SAE. (See also under Altarnun). **Mrs M. M. Cook, The Beach House, Port Gaverne, Port Isaac PL29 3SQ (Port Isaac [020-888] 296).**

PORT ISAAC. The Lodge, Treharrock, Port Isaac. Pleasant, south facing and convenient bungalow, set in its own small, natural garden and surrounded by fields and woodland with streams — no other houses visible from it. About two miles inland from Port Isaac, a sheltered, secluded spot at the end of driveway to Treharrock Manor. Rugged North Cornish cliffs with National Trust footpaths and lovely sandy coves in the vicinity. Excellent sandy beach at Polzeath (five miles), also pony trekking, golf etc. in the area. South facing sun room on to terrace; black and white TV. Accommodation for six plus baby. Bathroom, toilet; sittingroom; kitchen/diner. Open all year. Linen extra. Pets allowed. Car essential — parking. Terms from £100 to £200 per week (heating included). SAE to **Mrs E. A. Hambly, Home Farm House, Little Gaddesden, Berkhamsted, Hertfordshire HP4 1PN (Little Gaddesden [044-284] 3412).**

PORT ISSAC. Mrs Kathy Alford, Penhill, Pendoggett, Bodmin PL30 3HJ (Port Issac [020-888] 278 or Bodmin [0208] 880278). Pendoggett is a small village two miles from the north Cornwall coast and is an excellent centre for touring, walking, surfing and sea-fishing. The accommodation, situated at Penhill, commands spectacular views down the valley to Port Gaverne and over Port Isaac Bay. Village stores and Egon Ronay recommended restaurant situated nearby. Available are a bungalow and three flats set in large grounds with ample parking space and safe play area for children. The bungalow sleeps six, two flats sleep four and the third flat sleeps two/three. All are furnished to a high standard with electric cookers, fridges, TVs etc. Available April to October. Children and pets welcome. Weekly terms from £30 to £150. Electricity by 50p meters.

PORTHLEVEN. Mr and Mrs M. James, Bethany, Sunset Drive, Porthleven TR13 9JD (Helston [032-65] 62374). Two self contained flats overlooking the sea, harbour and beaches. Balcony flat sleeps nine, ground floor flat sleeps four/six. Fully equipped except linen. Colour TV and storage heaters. Open all year. This lovely village is noted for its picturesque beauty, fishing, sailing, swimming and rock climbing. Mr James has his own motor boat so fishing trips can be arranged. Central for all parts of the Peninsula. SAE, please, for illustrated brochure.

PORTHLEVEN (Helston). Lynwood Holiday Bungalows, Porthleven. Properties fully-equipped, except linen, in well sheltered sunny position in private road in wooded valley of unspoilt south west Cornish fishing village from which The Lizard Peninsula, St. Michael's Mount, Land's End, Falmouth, Truro and Penzance are readily accessible. Ten minutes' walk from harbour and shops; bus stop 100 yards; three miles stretch of beach one side of harbour, rocky shore on other. Long sandy beach at Praa Sands (four miles) and many other nearby beaches and coves. Ample parking. Dogs by arrangement. SAE, please, to **Mr and Mrs C. Bromfield, 4 Lynwood Bungalows, Tolponds, Porthleven, Helston (Helston [03275] 61649].**

Terms quoted in this publication may be subject to increase if rises in costs necessitate

PRAA SANDS near. Lower Kenneggy Farm, Rosudgeon, Near Praa Sands. Working farm. A comfortable, modernised cottage near the farm, with its own garden and ample parking space. The cottage accommodates six persons, with three bedrooms, fully fitted kitchen, diningroom and lounge with TV; bathroom and toilet; airing cupboard with immersion heater. Metered electricity; linen not supplied. Children are welcome, cot provided. Sorry, no pets. Lower Kenneggy is a country area with sea views, but close to Marazion (three miles) and Praa Sands (one mile) beaches; seven miles from Penzance and Helston. SAE, please, for terms to **Mrs P. Laity, Lower Kenneggy Farm, Rosudgeon, Penzance TR20 9AR (Penzance [0736] 762403).**

ROCK near. Tregenna Bungalow, St. Minver, Wadebridge. Working farm. This furnished bungalow to let without attendance all year is situated in a sheltered valley looking out over The Saltings to the River Camel. It stands on a 100-acre dairy farm. Three bedrooms, two double beds, two single beds, bunk beds, and a cot; bathroom; lounge with TV; diningroom; kitchen with electric cooker, fridge, kettle, iron, immersion heater, solid fuel Rayburn, night storage heaters for use if required. Three miles shops and sea. Rock, Daymer Bay and Polzeath ideal for golfing, sailing, swimming, surfing, water ski-ing and pony trekking. Car essential, parking. Sorry, no pets. Electricity extra. SAE, please, for terms. **Mrs M. J. Polkinghorne, Tregenna Farm, St. Minver, Wadebridge PL27 6RH (Wadebridge [020-881] 2879).**

SALTASH. Mr Roger Adlam, Trenance Farm, Tideford, Saltash PL12 5JB (Landrake [075-538] 319). Working farm. A small friendly dairy farm of 87 acres. The house is half of the lovely old Cornish farmhouse, the family living in one half and the visitors in the other. The farmhouse has large comfortably furnished rooms, a large spacious livingroom with a lovely old Cornish fireplace. The rooms are well-equipped and attractive. Two double bedrooms and one family room; cot; bathroom, toilet. All electric kitchen with cooker and fridge. Linen supplied. Ideal for a family holiday with gardens around and room for children to play and explore and watch farm activities. Ideally situated for touring Devon and Cornwall. Plymouth nine miles. Dartmoor and North Cornish Coast within easy distance. Available Easter to October. Car essential, ample parking. AA listed. Sorry, no pets. Weekly terms from £65 to £165, including fuel.

SEATON BEACH. This apartment for five to seven people is situated at Seaton Beach, just a few yards from the beach. One double and one family bedroom; bathroom, toilet; sittingroom; diningroom. Electricity for cooking and heating (slot meter). Children welcome. Pets permitted. Blankets and pillows supplied, but no linen. An ideal area for holidays with plenty to see and do. Available from March to October, with terms from £49 to £159 weekly. Parking available. Apply **Mr John Fowler, John Fowler Holidays, Dept. 23, Marlborough Road, Ilfracombe, Devon (Ilfracombe [0271] 66666).**

SOUTH WEST CORNWALL including HELFORD RIVER AND THE LIZARD PENINSULA. For peace, tranquillity, beautiful scenery and secluded bathing beaches, this part of Cornwall is hard to beat. The Helford River itself is one of the most beautiful stretches of water in the West Country and is a mecca for sailing enthusiasts, while the Lizard Peninsula, with its famous beauty spots, is ideal for bathing or walking along lovely coastal paths. Alein and Jane are agents for many comfortably furnished, well equipped cottages, houses, etc., in the area and although they vary in price according to position, quality of furnishings, etc., they are all, in their opinion, ideal for a really pleasant holiday. Send for the very comprehensive colour brochure to **Alein and Jane Hinton, Collingdale, Vicarage Lane, Manaccan, Helston TR12 6JH (Manaccan [032-623] 415).**

ST. COLUMB MAJOR. The Bungalow, Lower Trenowth, St. Columb Major. Working farm. This fully furnished bungalow situated in the beautiful Vale of Lanthearn, four miles from the well-known surf beaches of the North Cornish coast and two miles from the market town of St. Columb, sleeps seven people. Two double bedrooms, one with bunk beds, and one single bedroom; bathroom; sitting/diningroom with TV; kitchen, all-electric, well equipped. No linen provided. Ample parking space. Pets allowed if under strict control. Open all year. SAE, please, for terms and full details from **Miss H. J. Thomas, Lower Trenowth Farm, St. Columb Major TR9 6EW (St. Columb [0637] 880308).**

ST. IVES BAY. Mr & Mrs A. Kay, Cove Bungalow, 33 Riviere Towans, Phillack, Hayle (Hayle [0736] 753673). Cove holiday bungalow could not be much closer to the sea, the garden extends down to the Cornish Coastal Footpath and just below is a fine beach of golden sand. Access to the beach is by a short footpath; there are no roads to cross. The bungalow is very well furnished with fitted carpets, colour television and it is double glazed. From the lounge window you will enjoy superb sea views to St. Ives harbour and Godrevey Lighthouse. Will sleep 5/6 maximum. Private car park. SAE or phone for letting rates and available dates. Also Bed and Breakfast accommodation available in luxury bungalow next door.

SELF-CATERING   Cornwall   389

Trenoweth, St. Keverne Cornwall, TR12 6QQ

Trenoweth is situated on the Lizard Peninsula, three miles from Helford River and three-quarters of a mile from village of St. Keverne and fishing cove of Porthallow. Unspoilt area, ideal for a quiet, relaxing holiday. Safe bathing, coastal paths, fishing and boating locally, riding schools in the vicinity; 18-hole golf course at Mullion. Trenoweth overlooks four acres of woodlands which lead down to the sea, just over half-mile away. Cottages are converted farm buildings round a grass courtyard; completely modernised and self-contained. Sleeping four/five. Also Garden Wing sleeping eight. Fully equipped except linen and towels; each has TV and electric fires. Cots, high chairs available. The woodland contains interesting bird life and flowers and there is a children's play area away from the buildings for badminton etc. Babysitting available. Well behaved dogs by arrangement. September to June. Full details on request.

John and Heather Tanswell. Tel. 0326 280500.

ST. KEVERNE. Badger Cottage, St. Keverne. Working farm. This cottage faces south overlooking its own private garden which is formed out of an old marl pit and has a lawn running through the length of it. Shrubs on the bank opposite hide the badger holes and there are attractive semi-circular steps leading up to the cottage. Downstairs is one very long (32 feet) room divided, sitting-room from kitchen/dining area, by curtain. The accommodation is for six people in three bedrooms, cot available; bathroom and two toilets. Well-equipped with everything except linen. Colour TV. Electricity on meter. Trellegast Barton is a lovely old Tudor farmstead, a quarter-of-a-mile from St. Keverne, about one-and-a-half miles from the sea. Cows, donkeys, hens, dogs, cats, etc. Milk is made into cream. Super washing machine on farm and drying space, also use of freezer. Visitors are welcome to watch milking etc. Bring boots! Exclusive information on local walks and drives, etc available. Telephone kiosk. Long SAE, please, or stamps. **Mrs Rachel Roskilly, Tregellast Barton, St. Keverne, Helston TR12 6NX (St. Keverne [0326] 280479).**

TINTAGEL. Mrs G. E. Sanders, Fentafriddle Farm, Trewarmett, Tintagel PL34 0EX (Camelford [0840] 770580). Fentafriddle Farm overlooks the North Cornish coastline; the nearest beach, Trebarwith, less than a mile. Tintagel, Delabole, Camelford are also within easy reach. The farmhouse flat is spacious and comfortable, self-contained with own entrance. Fitted carpets throughout. It sleeps five/six in three double bedrooms and one single; bathroom; lounge/diner with colour TV. The kitchen is well equipped with breakfast table, fridge, electric cooker and 50p meter; fitted sink unit, worktop and cupboards. Garden for guests' use and ample parking space (car essential). Bed linen supplied. Sorry, no pets. Available March to November. Terms on request.

TINTAGEL. Ocean View, Halgabron, Tintagel. Working farm. Ocean View is a spacious bungalow with panoramic views of the North Cornwall coast and overlooks beautiful Rocky Valley. Situated on a dairy farm in a quiet hamlet the bungalow is one-and-a-half miles from Tintagel and three miles from Boscastle. Accommodation for seven persons in two comfortably furnished double bedrooms and one family room; bathroom, toilet; lounge with colour TV and diningroom. Fitted carpets except in kitchen. Sheets supplied. Large, well-fitted kitchen with electric cooker and refrigerator. The accommodation is suitable for disabled visitors. Children welcome, pets by arrangement. Car essential — parking. Open all year. Weekly terms on application. **Mrs M. A. Nute, Clifden Farm, Halgabron, Tintagel PL34 0BD (Camelford [0840] 770437).**

TRURO. Mrs P. M. Mead, Pengreep, Ponsanooth, Truro TR3 7JH (Stithians [0209] 860347). Three comfortable furnished cottages scattered around 200-acre agricultural estate in tranquil surroundings with fields, woods, wild flowers and birds. They are all-electric and will sleep 4, 5 or 6 people. They are six miles inland from Falmouth, a busy port with good restaurants, sailing, sandy beaches and walks nearby. The North Coast is eight miles away with surfing beaches and spectacular cliffs. Wind-surfing centre at Stithians Reservoir, nearby. Cornish cream, pasties, saffron cakes are good things to eat. Available April to October with electric heating. Electric kitchens. All fully equipped except linen. Children are welcome, cot. Pets at small charge. Own car essential, parking. Shopping facilities one mile. Weekly terms from £40 to £120.

PLEASE SEND A STAMPED ADDRESSED ENVELOPE WITH ENQUIRIES

HALGABRON HOLIDAY COTTAGES
in Rural Setting with Sea Views

All five cottages are clean, comfortable and furnished to a very high standard including colour TV. The one-bedroomed & three-bedroomed cottages have superb views of Rocky Valley & the cliffs, and the two-bedroomed cottages overlook farmland. Brochure with full information on request.

or

HALGABRON HOUSE

We also have just two letting bedrooms in Halgabron House where we offer Bed and Breakfast at £56 per week per person, with an optional Evening Meal at £6 per night.
If you want to know more we will be happy to help:
Pauline & Ivan Upright, Halgabron House, Halgabron, Tintagel, Cornwall
Camelford (0840) 770667

TRURO near. Mr C. P. Warner, "The Old Barn," Lower Tresithick Farm, Carnon Downs, Near Truro (Truro [0872] 863687). Working farm. Four persons can be accommodated in "The Old Barn" now converted to a self-contained cottage, simple but comfortable; full of character with exposed beams in the upstairs lounge. The cottage has one double bedroom, one bedroom with two 3' 6" beds, cot; bathroom; sittingroom; diningroom-cum-kitchen which is large and homely with plenty of storage space, electric stove, fridge. Linen, except sheets, supplied; colour TV. Pets permitted. Car not essential but parking available. Lower Tresithick is a small working farm tucked away in a little valley above the creeks of the Fal Estuary. A long, bumpy lane leads only to the farm so peace and privacy are assured, although local shops and the main Truro/Falmouth Road are reached by a five minutes' walk. The local creek and boatyard are a 10-minute walk away. Mr and Mrs Warner can offer sailing lessons at their own local beach. Riding available on the farm. Lots of space for children to play in surrounding woods and fields. April/October. SAE for terms.

TRURO. Greenbank Cottage, Feock, Truro. This 300-year-old single storey cottage sleeps six in spacious accommodation. Large L-shaped living/diningroom with fire; colour TV; night-storage heating; double bed; sun lounge with French window to garden and covered patio; one bedroom with bunks, one with single divans. Large kitchen, all-electric. Fridge/freezer; shower/bathroom, separate WC. Parking. Feock is a select village in lovely wooded setting on the River Fal, offering best sailing in Cornwall. Lovely walks and scenery close to King Harry Ferry and very central to Cornish resorts. Village shop and beach only minutes' walk. The cottage is comfortable, clean and well-equipped. Available April to October. SAE, please, for terms. **Mrs J. Westmancoat, Greenbank House, Feock, Truro TR5 6RG (Truro [0872] 862221).**

TRURO. Mrs R. K. Court, Polglaze Farm, Philleigh, Truro TR2 5NB (Portscatho [087-258] 403). Working farm. The farmhouse is situated in the hamlet of Philleigh in peaceful country surroundings. It adjoins the church and the Roseland Inn. There is also a Post Office (two mornings a week); numerous beaches within easy reach. The River Fal and King Harry Ferry two miles away. St. Mawes is five miles with its boating facilities and ferry to Falmouth. The farm is a 100-acre dairy farm and there is accommodation in three double bedrooms for six people; cot; bathroom, toilet; sittingroom; kitchen/diner with electric cooker, fridge, storage heater. Two miles from shops. Everything provided except linen. Car essential, parking. Open Easter to October. Weekly terms on enquiry with SAE, please.

SELF-CATERING Cornwall 391

TRURO near. Mrs Hazel Bowerman, Tre-Knoll Farm, Ladock, Near Truro TR2 4QB (St. Austell [0726] 882451). "Tre-Knoll" was built almost 200 years ago, situated on a hill overlooking the beautiful Ladock Valley, it offers a first-floor flat overlooking green fields with accommodation for four persons. One double bedroom with hot and cold water; studio couch converting to two singles in sitting/diningroom; own bathroom with toilet; fully equipped kitchen, electric cooker, fridge, all cutlery, crockery etc. Linen included. Children welcome. Pets allowed but not female dogs in season. Electric heating throughout. In the centre of Cornwall, ideally placed for touring whole county. Truro six miles; Newquay 10 miles; innumerable beaches within easy reach. Very informal, quiet and relaxed atmosphere. All animals on this 10-acre smallholding are treated as pets. Terms (including electricity for heating, hot water), on request with SAE. (10p meter for 13 amp sockets). Also four-berth caravan.

TRURO. Mrs Penwarden, Garvinack Farm, Truro TR4 9EP (Truro [0872] 560385). Choice of two farm bungalows accommodating four to six people available at any time of year. Situated in the middle of Garvinack Farm with superb views, half a mile from the A30 and five miles from either Truro or the north coast at Perranporth. Both with lounge and TV. Separate diningroom, kitchen with electric cooker and fridge, oil fired Aga/Rayburn if required. One bungalow with double bed, the rest twins. Well equipped to modern standards with continental quilts a feature in one. Please supply own linen. Two miles from shops. Car essential and parking provided. Leaflet available.

TRURO. Higher Hewas, Ladock, Truro. Working farm. This former farmhouse is set amid agricultural land with pleasant country views. Visitors will enjoy perfect peace here, yet sea only eight miles away and all the well-known Cornish resorts are within easy reach. Lovely walks all round; interesting castles and manor houses to visit. The house has four bedrooms accommodating seven people; cot for child; bathroom, toilet, sittingroom; diningroom; kitchen with electric cooker, fridge, etc. Linen not supplied. TV. Shops two miles. Car essential, parking. Open May to October. Pets welcome. Weekly terms from £80. Full details on application: **Mrs P. Blake, Lower Hewas, Ladock, Truro TR2 4QH (St Austell [0726] 882318).**

WADEBRIDGE. Mrs M. J. Drayson, Trevine, Chapel Amble, Wadebridge PL27 6ES (0208 880 220). Working farm. Delightful self-catering accommodation retaining the original charm and character, and set in the heart of the beautiful Cornish countryside. TREVINETTE is a large stone cottage between the farmhouse and an old watermill. Sleeps six. THE COTTAGE is a separate wing of the 18th-century farmhouse. Sleeps 2/4. BRIDGE COTTAGE, originally an old herdsman's dwelling, enjoys a secluded situation in a wooded valley on the edge of the farm. Sleeps six. All premises include colour TV, washing machines, cots and high chairs, swings. Something for everyone in the surrounding area with entertainment, discos, Folk Clubs, restaurants, beaches and sports all within reach, as well as National Trust properties and walks. Open March to October.

WADEBRIDGE. Walts Farmhouse, Trewethern, Amble, Wadebridge. This is a farmhouse of great character, well furnished and situated in the quiet hamlet of Trewethern, across road from farm. Four miles from safe beaches — Rock, Polzeath, Port Isaac, Port Gaverne. Lovely walks along lanes, surfing, sailing and fishing at beach. Golf available. Village shop and beautiful church one mile away. Accommodation for nine in four double bedrooms, with two cots available; one single room; bathroom, toilet; sittingroom; diningroom; TV; kitchen with electric cooker, Rayburn, iron, fridge. Fully equipped except linen. Sorry, no pets. Car essential — parking. All communications with SAE, please, to **Mrs V. M. Davey, Carns Farm, Trewethern, Amble, Wadebridge PL27 6ER (Port Isaac (020-888) 393).**

WADEBRIDGE. Nos. 1 & 2 Villa Cottages, Cannalidgey, St. Issey, Wadebridge. Working farm. Two modernised semi-detached cottages, situated in a small hamlet, with large gardens, on a 170-acre cattle, sheep and cereal farm. Each cottage accommodates five, plus baby. It is ideal location for touring Cornwall, within easy reach of excellent sandy beaches, surfing, fishing, pony trekking and golf. Both cottages furnished and equipped to a high standard comprise one double and one family room; bathroom/WC; lounge/diner (one with separate lounge, diningroom); colour TV. Kitchen with electric cooker, fridge and all necessary equipment. Linen on request. Electricity by 50p meter. Car essential — parking. Shops within three miles. Available all year. Weekly terms £50 to £430. AA listed and registered with Cornish Tourist Board. SAE, please, for details to **Mrs E. D. Old, Roscullion, Little Petherick, Wadebridge PL27 7RX (Rumford [0841] 540212).**

WADEBRIDGE. Gamekeeper's Cottage, Burlawn, Wadebridge. Gamekeeper's Cottage is an 18th century charming Cornish cottage, quietly situated in its own idyllic wooded surroundings, two miles from Wadebridge. Terraced garden with stream and small pond. Tastefully modernised yet retaining original character. Stone fireplaces, exposed beams, slate floor in diningroom; kitchen; bathroom. Mains water. Attractive diningroom; sittingroom with TV; two bedrooms (one with double and single beds, the other with three singles). Parking. Sandy beaches, surfing, sailing, fishing, pony trekking, golf at famous St. Enodoc course, all within easy reach. Beautiful walks in Forestry Commission lands bordering cottage. For terms apply **Mr and Mrs P. U. G. Sharp, Tregawne Farm, Withiel, Bodmin PL30 5NR (Lanivet [0208] 831303).**

CUMBRIA – English Lakeland

AMBLESIDE. Esthwaite Farm Holidays, near Sawrey, Ambleside. Selection of seven delightful holiday flats located in a traditional farmstead (two flats ideally equipped for handicapped visitors). Close to Esthwaite Water and Hill Top (the famous home of Beatrix Potter). Two miles from beautiful Lake Windermere, near Grizedale Forest with its Nature Trails and "Theatre in the Forest". Each flat has comfortable accommodation for four adults, is furnished and equipped to a first class standard with cooking and heating and has livingroom with TV, kitchen, two bedrooms with single beds, shower room with WC and washbasin. Use of washing machine and drying room. Linen not provided. Six flats have wood burning stoves. Coarse fishing on private lakeshore inclusive. Rowing boats at extra charge. Open all year. Weekly terms from £45. Apply to **Esthwaite Estates Ltd., Graythwaite Estate Office, near Ulverston LA12 8BA (Newby Bridge [0448] 31248).**

AMBLESIDE. Mrs E. M. Smith, Gale Crescent Holiday Apartments, Ambleside LA22 0BD (Ambleside [0966] 32284). Newly converted from a guest house, this large Victorian house with outstanding views over the village and fells, lends itself beautifully to four well-equipped comfortable holiday apartments complying with grade three Tourist Board standard. Two flats for two people (double bedrooms), and two flats for four (family and single bedrooms). Also available is a spare double bedroom with its own shower, toilet etc., which can be let with any of the flats to accommodate larger parties. In the garden is a delightful detached cottage for two comprising lounge, kitchen area, double bedroom, shower room etc. All units have colour TV and high standards of furnishings. Brochure on request.

AMBLESIDE. Mr and Mrs N. C. Murphy, High Bank Cottage, Old Lake Road, Ambleside LA22 0AE (Ambleside [0966] 32384). Accommodation for up to six people in this cottage (part house) which is central for walking; swimming pool easily accessible by car or public transport. Steamer. Motor boat cruises and rowing boats for hire on nearby Lake Windermere. Two family bedrooms; bathroom and toilet upstairs, also toilet downstairs; sittingroom with TV; dining/kitchen with gas cooker, electric fridge, stainless steel sink. Linen supplied. Shops and car park 100 yards. Pets permitted at a small charge. Car not essential. Open all year. SAE for terms. Gas and electricity 50p meters.

AMBLESIDE. Mr and Mrs G. R. Pickup, The Dower House, Wray Castle, Low Wray, Ambleside LA22 0JA (Ambleside [0966] 33211). The Dower House Cottage has beautiful views over the superb Lakeland and Windermere countryside with many major peaks and woodlands in Wray Castle Park, and direct access to the Lake shore. The cottage accommodates five people having one twin bedded room and one single room; studio couch in the lounge converts to a double bed; bathroom, toilet; large well equipped kitchen with electric cooker and fridge; metered electricity. No linen supplied. Available all year, the Dower Cottage is three miles from the shops and a car is essential, with parking at owners' risk. Pets not permitted. Children over 11 years. Weekly terms, excluding fuel, on request with SAE, please.

AMBLESIDE. Mr and Mrs A. J. Marsden, Betty Fold, Hawkshead Hill, Ambleside LA22 0PS (Hawkshead [096-66] 611). Betty Fold is a large country house in its own spacious grounds with magnificent views and set in the heart of the Lake District National Park. The quaint village of Hawkshead is nearby and Coniston and Ambleside are within four miles; the beauty spot of Tarn Hows is 15 minutes' walk away. As well as being a Guest House, Betty Fold offers self catering accommodation with units for two, four or six persons. These consist of "Garden Cottage", in our grounds, a flat which is part of the main house and a fine Lakeland cottage, five minutes' walk away. All accommodation is centrally heated and facilities such as linen, colour TV, cots provided, also heating, power and lighting. Pets welcome. Dinner available in Guest House. See also advertisement in BOARD SECTION of this guide.

AMBLESIDE. Mrs N. T. Hall, Croftlands, Hawkshead, Ambleside LA22 0JT (Hawkshead [096-66] 300). This small self-contained flat is available as self-catering holiday accommodation from March to end of October. There is accommodation for four people in one family bedroom (two single and two bunk beds); cot; studio couch in livingroom; bathroom, toilet; fully equipped electric kitchen. Linen not supplied. Dogs permitted if under strict control. Car desirable, parking space is available. The flat is part of a Lakeland stone country house, set in its own grounds in an elevated position commanding lovely views of historic village of Hawkshead and Esthwaite Water. Ambleside five miles; Windermere ten miles; Hawkshead three-quarters mile. Many beautiful walks. SAE, please, for terms.

AMBLESIDE near. Bank Cottage, Hawkshead, Near Ambleside. This Lake District Cottage is situated in the centre of the village next to shops, and within easy reach of local places of interest such as Tarn Hows, Lake Windermere, Coniston Water. Ideal for walking, fishing, climbing, horse riding. Five people can be accommodated in three bedrooms (one double bed, three single beds); combined sitting/diningroom; bathroom. Fitted carpets throughout. Everything people require is provided, including TV, continental quilts and towels. Pets accepted by permission only. Parking nearby. Available all year. Night storage heaters are provided during winter months, otherwise coal or electric fires at charge. Electric cooker, fridge, kettle, etc. SAE, please, for terms, etc. to **Mrs E. Brown, Holly How Cottage, Coniston LA21 8DD (0966 41642).**

WHEN MAKING ENQUIRIES PLEASE MENTION
FARM HOLIDAY GUIDE

SAWREY KNOTTS

FAR SAWREY
NR. AMBLESIDE
CUMBRIA
LA22 0LG
Tel. Windermere (09662) 2105

Sawrey Knotts commands incredible views of Windermere Lake and the surrounding area from its peaceful setting on a hillside near the West bank of the Lake.

Eight acres of daffodil and bluebell woodland and gardens with azaleas and rhododendrons make a safe recreation area for both children and adults. Riding is one of the attractions and, whether experienced or not, we will take you across some of the most beautiful countryside in the Lakes.

All flats and cottages are self contained and have colour TV. Open all year. Children welcome; cot available. A dog is accepted by arrangement. There is a small licensed restaurant.

Details and brochure on request. SAE, please.

APPLEBY (Eden Valley). Mrs Joyce Hunter, Low Abbey, Kirkby Thore CA10 1XR (Kirkby Thore [0930] 61207). Working farm. Low Abbey in the Eden Valley, is mixed farm with two self-catering homes, available from Easter to September inclusive. Two miles from Kirkby Thore village, five from Appleby. The village has two shops, post office, newsagents, church, chapel and garden centre. Excellent walking country (Pennine Way five miles away); at Appleby there is swimming pool, golf course, horse fair and pony trekking. Handy for day trips to Lakes (Ullswater 13 miles), Pennines and Yorkshire Dales. The cottages are on the farm down a private lane. Comfortable and carpeted throughout accommodation comprises livingroom with open fire (fuel provided), colour TV; kitchen with electric cooker, fridge; bathroom, immersion heater; three bedrooms — one double bedded with cot, one double bedded and one with double bed and bunks. No linen. Lawn, garden and ample parking. Electricity extra. Milk delivered daily. Weekly terms from £60 to £110. SAE for details.

BEWCASTLE. Bank End Farm, Bewcastle, Roadhead, Carlisle CA6 6NU (Roadhead [06978] 644). Two warm, well-equipped Cottages (thoroughly modernised) welcome you to a peaceful and relaxing holiday on our hill sheep smallholding beside the river below Bewcastle Fells. Both Cottages are centrally heated (one has open fire), have fully fitted kitchens, electric cooker, fridge, ample cutlery, china, cooking equipment; good bathrooms, bedrooms, ample beddding, dining areas, sittingrooms, colour TV, fitted carpets, etc. Utility room has washer, drier, freezer. Home baking and meals from Farm kitchen. Children welcome, cot, etc. (pet lambs/hens to feed). Pets welcome. Good walking, fishing, touring — Borders, Lakeland, Kielder Water, Hadrian's Wall. Rental includes fuel. Please phone for brochure and tariff. Bed and Breakfast (optional Evening Meal) available.

PLEASE SEND A STAMPED ADDRESSED ENVELOPE WITH ENQUIRIES

Cumbria SELF-CATERING

BOWNESS-ON-WINDERMERE. Oakbeck, 53 Craig Walk, Bowness-on-Windermere. Bowness is a major centre for touring the Lake District, with excellent shops, cinema, pier and all the amenities of Lake Windermere (fishing, sailing, water ski-ing, boating). Golf, tennis, putting, badminton, squash, bowls, swimming, riding are all nearby. Oakbeck enjoys an elevated position in a quiet residential area, yet within a short walk of Bowness. Built of Lakeland stone, it is furnished in traditional style and shares an attractive garden through which a stream runs. Entrance hall; lounge with fireplace; colour TV; diningroom; kitchen; tiled bathroom with shower, shaver point; two twin, one single bedrooms. Drying facilities. Electric heating by 50p meter. Private parking. £90 to £160 per week. Send SAE for brochure or telephone **Mr I. R. Fraser, 37 Lucy's Mill, Mill Lane, Stratford-upon-Avon, Warwickshire CV37 6DE (0789-297309/293198).**

BROUGHTON-IN-FURNESS. Mr & Mrs J. M. Hart, Ring House Farm, Woodland, Broughton-in-Furness LA20 6DG (Broughton-in-Furness [065-76] 578). Ring House Farm is a secluded 18th-century Lakeland farm house in three acres of land catering for non-smokers only. The cottages have olde worlde charm with modern amenities including washbasins in bedrooms, central heating, electric under-blankets, colour TV, washing machine/drier. Woodland is a peaceful hamlet within easy reach of Lake Coniston, the Coniston Hills and the Duddon Valley. Ring House is an ideal base for hill walkers and country lovers. Various recreational activities can often be arranged, including pony trekking, sailing, windsurfing, rock climbing and fell walking. The cottages accommodate four and six respectively. Resident proprietors. Rates £80 – £180. Open all year. Brochure available.

BROUGHTON-IN-FURNESS. Broughton Mill, Broughton Mills, Broughton-in-Furness. Broughton Mill is an old Corn Mill which has been converted into two self-contained flats. The "Corn Mill" accommodation has a large livingroom with kitchen and sitting area, separate bathroom and WC, all on one level. Above are three bedrooms to sleep nine, one with two single beds, one with a double, and one with two doubles and one single bed. "The Malt Kiln" has large livingroom with kitchen area, separate bathroom and WC, two bedrooms (one with three singles, one with one double bed). Studio couch in livingroom. Both flats have mains electricity for cooking, heating, lighting; comfortable beds and fitted wardrobes. Ample parking. No pets. Open all year. Very peaceful, picturesque area, sea at Foxfield three miles. Also the "Threshing House," fully equipped, suitable for two persons. SAE, please, for terms **Mr and Mrs W. D. Hannah, Greenbank Farm, Broughton-in-Furness LA20 6AY (Broughton-in-Furness [06576] 357).**

BROUGHTON-IN-FURNESS near. Mr A. Allis-Smith, Dry Hall, Broughton Mills, Near Broughton-in-Furness (Broughton-in-Furness [06576] 523). Dunnerdale-Broughton Mills. Available all year and for off-season weekends, this attractive cruck-beamed, open plan cottage, attached to 17th century, traditional, stone-built farmhouse having small stock (geese, rabbits, hens, sheep and organic vegetable garden) is situated in an elevated position and lies in 30-acres of quiet hills and woods in unspoilt Dunnerdale amidst ideal walking countryside, and yet close to centre of lakes (Ambleside 30 minutes, Coniston 10 minutes), sandy, quiet beaches of Cumbria coast (15 minutes); sea and river fishing, pony trekking, sailing. Charming old world character, together with luxury fittings, TV, fridge, electric cooker, make this a very comfortable base for a splendid holiday at any time of the year. Sleeps four, plus cot. Car essential, parking available. SAE, please, or telephone for further details.

CARLISLE by. Millstone Cottage, Blackhall Wood, By Carlisle. Working farm. Millstone Cottage has been converted from an old barn into a well designed and spacious unit accommodating six to eight people comfortably. Situated on the farm of 365 acres of dairy and arable land it is within easy access of the Lake District (half hour), Carlisle (10 minutes), Gretna Green, Hadrian's Wall, the Cumbria Coast (half hour) and other places of interest and beauty. Some trout and salmon fishing, also some rough shooting can be arranged (guests must bring their licence and tackle). Cot available; bathroom, toilet; sittingroom with colour TV. Dining/kitchen (modern, all electric); washing machine. Linen extra. Sorry, no pets. Car essential — parking. Shops two miles. Pay telephone. Open all year round. Heating and electricity extra. Terms according to season from **Mr John Cox, Blackhall Wood, By Carlisle CA5 7LH (Dalston [0228] 710342).**

✱ **CARLISLE near. Mrs M. M. Sisson, Bessiestown Farm, Penton, Near Carlisle CA6 5QP (Nicholforest [022-877] 219). Working farm.** Ideal for family holiday or touring the Lake District and South Scotland, three self-catering cottages on small beef/sheep rearing farm situated in a quiet, rural area approximately 17 miles north of Carlisle, only three miles from Scottish Border. Convenient for Roman Wall, Galloway and Solway Coast or pleasant country walks, shooting, fishing and golf within a 15 mile radius. Evening Meals available in the farmhouse if desired. Residential licence. AA/RAC listed. See also Colour Display Advertisement in this Guide.

Please note that entries marked with an asterisk also have a colour display advert in the colour section in this guide

SELF-CATERING Cumbria 395

CARLISLE. Mrs A. E. Ivinson, Green View, Welton, Near Dalston, Carlisle CA5 7ES (Raughton Head [069-96] 230). Two SCANDINAVIAN PINE CHALETS, NEW 1984, set in one and three-quarter acres with views over fields to Caldbeck Fells. Sleep six in three bedrooms, heating in all rooms. Bathroom with heated towel rails included, shower, two WC's. Open plan south-facing sittingrooms with colour TV. All-electric fitted kitchen including fridge/freezer, toaster. Equipped to Tourist Board Standards Category 4. Situated on the B5299 in the small, picturesque hamlet of Welton on the northern fringes of the Lake District, 11 miles M6, exit 41, it is ideal for touring the Caldbeck Fells, nearby Lakes and Scottish Borders. Weekly terms from £74. Car essential. Suitable for the disabled. Open all year. AA listed. Member of Cumbria and Lakeland Self-Catering Association. SAE, please.

CARLISLE. Well Cottage, Welton, Near Dalston, Carlisle. This AA listed, semi-detached cottage has been completely modernised throughout, yet still retains its character. Situated on the B5299 in the small, picturesque hamlet of Welton, on the northern fringes of the Lake District, 11 miles from M6 exit 41, it is ideal for touring the Caldbeck Fells, nearby Lakes and Scottish Borders. Accommodation is for six people in three bedrooms (one single and one with three single beds, original oak beams in the latter). All-electric fitted kitchen/dinette, fridge/freezer, immersion heater; hall with second WC; large new lounge with colour TV, electric fire, picture window with view over lawn and fields to Caldbeck Fells. Small sun lounge leading to garden at rear; new bathroom with vanity unit, pampas green suite, shaver point, shower; fully equipped, linen may be hired; 50p meter for electricity. Centrally heated, double glazed. Car essential, parking space. Open all year. Also residential caravans to let; terms from £145. Local village shop/post office and Inn; golf, pony trekking and fishing available in the area. Member of Cumbria and Lakeland Self-Catering Association. Also new in 1984 two pine chalets. Terms from £74. SAE to **Mrs A. E. Ivinson, Green View, Welton, Near Dalston, Carlisle CA5 7ES (Raughton Head [069-96] 230).**

CARLISLE near. Holly View, Penton, Longtown, Near Carlisle. Working farm. "Holly View" is situated on a 250-acre working farm, with cattle, sheep, pigs, ponies, dogs and cats. Set in a quiet locality near the Border Forest, 17 miles north of Carlisle, three miles England/Scotland Border, it is an ideal base for touring Lake District, Solway and Galloway Coasts, Scottish Borders, Kielder Forest and Dam, the Roman Wall. There is a play area, tennis, pony rides and shooting by arrangement at the farm. Fishing three miles. Beautiful country walks. The bungalow, accommodating six people, is nicely decorated, furnished and carpeted. One double, one family bedroom; cot. Bathroom with shower; sitting/diningroom; fully equipped kitchen has cooker, fridge, kettle and immersion heater. Electric fires. TV. Continental quilts are supplied, but no linen. Electricity by 50p slot meter. Children welcome, high chair. Pets accepted free of charge. Car essential — parking. Weekly terms from £50 to £100. **Mrs Jane Lawson, Craigburn Farm, Penton, Carlisle CA6 5QP (Nicholforest [022-877] 214).**

CARTMEL. Bluebell Wood Cottage, Woodbroughton, Cartmel. In the lovely Cartmel Valley, one mile from Cartmel, three miles from the sea, the cottage is off the main road in private woodland, and has a secluded garden. Fully equipped to sleep four in two twin-bedded rooms. Bed linen supplied. Lounge with electric fire, TV, Radio. All electric kitchen with dining area, fridge, deep freeze, cooker, immerser, wall heater. Modern bathroom with toilet. No service. Available all year, but no reduced rates. Shopping one and a half miles. Car essential — parking. Not suitable for disabled. Children welcome, pets allowed. Electricity included. Golf, tennis, hill climbing, fishing, pony trekking within easy reach. **Mrs I. J. McCabe, High Beckside Farm, Cartmel, Grange-over-Sands LA11 7SW. (Cartmel [044-854] 528).**

COCKERMOUTH. Mrs Roberta Clark, Mosser Gate Farm, High Mosser, Cockermouth CA13 0SR (Cockermouth [0900] 822387). Working farm. Mosser Gate is a hill farm with sheep and cattle and is completely modernised, but has kept its oak beams, warmth of character and open fires. It is situated on the peaceful fell road to Loweswater Lake with direct access to fells from which wonderful views of the district, coastline and Scottish Hills can be seen. Loweswater, Crummock and Buttermere Lakes are all within easy reach. Children always delighted with the miniature railway from Ravenglass to Eskdale. Riding, fishing, golf. Keswick 12 miles; Cockermouth four-and-a-half miles. April/end October. Two double, two single, two family bedrooms; three bathrooms with toilets; sittingroom, diningroom. Cot, babysitting. Sorry, no pets. Evening Dinner, Bed and Breakfast £11 – £11.50 per day; Bed and Breakfast from £7. Rates reduced for children. Evening tea and home-made cakes included in terms. (Flasks and packed lunches also available).

COCKERMOUTH. Mrs C. Harrington, Low Rogerscale Farm, Lorton, Cockermouth CA13 0RG (Cockermouth [0900] 85247). Well equipped holiday accommodation providing comfort for up to seven people. Linen supplied. Ideal centre for visiting the Lakes and beautiful surrounding area. Pony riding, golf and fishing all within easy reach and perfect for the keen sportsman. Enjoy a relaxing family break amidst comfort, splendid scenery and the opportunity to get out and about. Further details on request. SAE, please.

COCKERMOUTH. Mrs B. M. Chester, Bouch House Farm, Embleton, Cockermouth CA13 9XH (Cockermouth [0900] 823367). Working farm. The cottage is situated near the farmhouse and has picturesque views of the Bassenthwaite Valley and surrounding countryside. Own gardens, with deck chairs available. Only one and a half miles from Cockermouth, a pleasant historical market town with good bus service and recreation facilities, including fishing, golf and swimming pool. Well situated for touring Lakes and coastline — nearest Lakes are Bassenthwaite, Buttermere, Crummock and Lowes Water. Accommodates six people, with cot available; bathroom, shower unit, toilet; sittingroom. Colour TV. Fully equipped kitchen. Linen supplied. Pets permitted. Car advisable — parking. Open all year. Terms from £60 weekly. SAE, please.

COCKERMOUTH. Mrs J. Hope, Cornhow Farm, Loweswater, Cockermouth CA13 9UX (Lorton [090-085] 200). Working farm. Ideal for a family holiday, spacious, fully modernised house adjoining an 18th-century farmhouse on a 250-acre dairy and stock-rearing farm. Situated in the beautiful Loweswater Valley it is well-placed for all country activities and central for the coast and lakes (Crummock half a mile). Fully equipped for eight people, the house is quiet and comfortable and accommodation comprises four double bedrooms; two bathrooms, two toilets; sittingroom. Electric cooking facilities and solid fuel heating. Everything supplied for the ease and enjoyment of your holiday. Private fishing. Children welcome and they may bring their pets. Open all year, a car is essential and there is parking. Three miles from shops. Weekly terms £80 to £170 (inclusive of electricity). No linen supplied. Further details on request with SAE, please.

Eden Valley & Alston Moor Country Holidays in Lakeland

That Other Eden

Eden Valley and Alston Moor Country Holidays offer a warm welcome in a variety of self-catering accommodation – farmhouses, cottages, flats, caravans.

We can offer country pursuits in the peace and tranquillity of the vast and sometimes wild landscapes that are all around. There is something for everyone. For a wide choice of self-catering accommodation send a stamped addressed envelope to: Anne Ivinson (FHG), Green View, Welton, Dalston, Carlisle, CUMBRIA. Tel: Raughton Head (06996) 230.

No agents fee.

REGISTERED WITH THE ENGLISH TOURIST BOARD

COCKERMOUTH. Mrs J. A. Christopherson, Hill Farm, Brandlingill, Cockermouth CA13 0RD (Cockermouth [0900] 822346). Working farm. Hill Farm Cottage is quiet and secluded but within easy reach of many outdoor activities. Lovely scenery, Whinfell and the Lorton Valley can be seen from the garden. Car essential; parking. Shops and public transport three and a half miles. Accommodation for six people in two double and one single bedrooms (one of the double rooms has extra single bed); bathroom, toilet; sittingroom; diningroom; kitchen. Electricity for cooking and heating. Linen supplied. Children welcome; sorry, no pets. Available April to October. Slot meter for electricity. Terms on request.

CONISTON. "The Kibble", 9 Green Cottages, Torver, Coniston. "The Kibble" is a charming 19th century Quarry Cottage with attractive old pitch pine doors and staircase. It is situated one and a half miles from Coniston Water, in the quiet, picturesque hamlet of Torver, on the outskirts of Coniston Village, approximately 10 miles from Ambleside and eight miles from Great Langdale. Equally suitable location for touring by car, or for the more strenuous, fell walking on the popular Coniston Mountains, i.e. Dow Cragg, Walna Scar and the Coniston Old Man. Excellent wildlife, birdwatching and fishing. Informative literature on where to go and what to see to get the most out of your holiday. Annually inspected. Colour TV. Garden. Accommodation for two/six persons. SAE, please, for brochure — **Mrs J. Toms, Middlefell Farm, Great Langdale, Ambleside LA22 9JU (09667-684).**

CONISTON. Yew Tree Bungalow, Coniston. Working farm. Attractive, comfortable bungalow attached to farmhouse, situated in its own grounds and enjoying breathtaking views of the Yewdale Valley and Wetherlam. This beef and sheep farm provides lovely walks and the opportunity to have a truly relaxing, get-away-from-it-all holiday for the whole family. The bungalow can accommodate five in one double and one single/bunk bedroom. Children welcome — cot. House suitable for disabled guests. Fully equipped except for linen. Pets allowed. Fishing, hill walking etc. 15 minutes' walk from Tarn Hows on the main road between Ambleside and Coniston. Weekly terms from £65. Reduced rates for winter weekends. Apply **Mrs Jean Birkett, Yew Tree Farm, Coniston LA21 8DP (Coniston [0966] 41433).**

CONISTON. Hanson Ground, Coniston. Hanson Ground is situated at the northern end of the road running along the eastern shore of Coniston Lake, approximately one and a half miles from Coniston and Hawkshead. It was originally the first floor of a barn belonging to the adjacent 16th century farmhouse and, though secluded, is ideally placed for exploring southern Lakeland. Facilities for sailing and riding are within easy reach. Grizedale Forest borders the east of the property which has a secluded garden and balcony overlooking the lake. Four people accommodated in two double bedrooms, cot; bathroom, toilet; sitting/diningroom; modern all-electric kitchen. No linen supplied. Sorry, not suitable for disabled guests. One and a half miles from shops. Pets allowed, but not encouraged. Small charge of £5 per pet. Car essential — parking. Available all year round. Weekly terms from £60 low season and £70 during school holidays. Extra beds and/or Bed and Breakfast now available. SAE to **Mrs M. C. Dutton, Knipe Ground, Coniston (Coniston [0966] 41221).** Please phone after 6 pm.

SELF-CATERING   Cumbria   397

CONISTON. Mrs B. Thompson, How Head Cottage, Coniston LA21 8AA (Coniston [0966] 41594 and 41303). Centrally heated, self catering accommodation overlooking Coniston Water, with outstanding views of the Coniston Fells and surrounding countryside. Just over a mile from Coniston Village, ideally situated for walking or touring, with Tarn Howes, Hawkshead and Windermere quite near. Accommodation for four, carpeted throughout and nicely furnished; lounge with drop-down double bed, bedroom with twin beds. Shower room with toilet. Modern kitchen with electric cooker and fridge. Guests must supply own linen. Sorry, no pets. Shops one mile. Parking. Open all year. Weekly terms from £80 – £150. SAE, please.

CONISTON near (Lake District). Mrs J. Halton, Scarr Head Bungalow, Torver, Near Coniston LA21 8BP (Coniston [0966] 41328). Working farm. This delightful self-contained holiday bungalow in quiet picturesque surroundings, has a lovely outlook and extensive views of the Coniston Mountains. It is completely detached, and stands in its own half acre of level garden and grounds. Tarmac drive and ample parking. Ideal for walking, touring lakes, etc. Bathroom and toilet, kitchen with electric cooker, fridge, hot and cold water, two double and one single bedrooms, large sitting/diningroom. Village Inn very handy. Coniston three miles. Fully equipped except linen. Available all year. SAE, for terms, etc., stating number of persons and dates required.

CONISTON. Clifton Villa, Yewdale Road, Coniston. Clifton Villa is situated in the centre of Coniston village, approximately half a mile from Coniston Water. It has all modern amenities including electric cooker, fridge, TV. All beds supplied with linen and continental quilts. There is accommodation for six, in three double bedrooms (one double bedded and two twin bedded); cot available; bathroom, toilet; sittingroom; diningroom; kitchen. Electricity by 50p meter. Children are welcome. Pets by arrangement only. Car is not essential but there is parking nearby. Open all year. Nearby there is fell walking, fishing, boating and pony trekking. Weekly terms from £65. SAE, please, or telephone **Mrs A. M. Raven, Mountain View, Yewdale Road, Coniston LA21 8DU (Coniston [0966] 41412).**

CONISTON. Mrs D. A. Hall, Dow Crag House, Coniston LA21 8AT (Coniston [0966] 41558). Two bungalows to be let as holiday chalets, on bus route, one mile from Coniston village on A593. Resident owner. Larger bungalow has sittingroom, kitchen/diningroom, three bedrooms sleeping seven; bathroom, separate toilet. All electric including cooker, refrigerator, immersion heater, fires. Small bungalow comprises livingroom, two small bedrooms, bathroom and toilet combined. Small chalet furnished to sleep two. Electric cooker, immersion heater, Courtier stove, refrigerator, fires. Both chalets fully equipped except linen. Parking space. These holiday chalets are set in private garden with direct access to the Fells and Hills. Superb views overlooking lake. Freedom, yet safe for children. Sport available includes mountaineering, boating, fishing, tennis and bowls. Available March till early November. Terms on application with SAE, please.

CONISTON. Mr and Mrs T. Holliday, High Arnside, Coniston LA21 8DW (Ambleside [096-63] 2261). High Arnside is a well preserved and comfortable old Lakeland farmhouse, reputedly 16th century, but well-equipped for holiday letting. Nine people can be accommodated in four double bedrooms, one room with single bed and cot. Bathroom, toilet; sittingroom, diningroom; all electric kitchen, fully provided except linen. The house is open all year. Sorry, no pets allowed. Car is essential and there is parking for three or four cars. Shops three-and-a-half miles. Terms include fuel. Also available is cottage to sleep six and chalet to sleep four. SAE, please, for terms.

CONISTON (Lake District). Mrs M. Wilkinson, Station House and Cottage, Torver, Coniston LA21 8AZ (0966-41392). Semi-detached cottage for two, traditional style bungalow built 1860. Village, Torver, Coniston Old Man and South Lakeland Fells on the doorstep. Coniston Lake one mile. Half an acre of low level gardens and walks. Double bedded room with washbasin, hot and cold water. Sittingroom. Bathroom. All-electric kitchen. Electric storage heaters and fires. Ample parking space. Dining facilities in village. Travelling shop and village shop. Colour TV. Open all year round. Sorry, no pets. SAE for brochure.

GRANGE-OVER-SANDS. Mr and Mrs E. Smith, Aynsome Manor Park, Cartmel, Grange-over-Sands ✱ LA11 6HH (Cartmel [044-854] 433). Established 16 years. Luxury self-contained flats for two to four adults. Open all year round. AA listed and Member of Cumbria Tourist Board. Extensive peaceful lake, gardens and woodland. All-electric, TV, fridge, bathroom etc. Ideal centre lakes and coast. Out of season breaks from £15 for 3 nights. Low season £25 weekly; high season £75 to £100 weekly; brochure on request. SAE, please. See also colour display advertisement.

HARTSOP. Mr G. F. C. Mellstrom, The Manor House, Grove Farm, Hartsop, Patterdale. A most attractive and homely Lake District residence, comfortably furnished and well equipped — ideal for two-family holiday. sleeping 12 including children. Situated between Ullswater and Brotherswater and within the triangle of Penrith, Keswick and Windermere. Property consists of six bedrooms, fully equipped kitchen with Aga cooker. Sitting/diningroom. Music/study room. Separate utility area. Full oil fired central heating, electricity and heating services included in rent. Dogs welcome — two good sized dog kennels. Fishing available. SAE for terms and details, please to **Downlands Farm, Bramshott, Liphook, Hants GD30 7QZ (Liphook [0428] 724600).**

FISHERGROUND FARM

A traditional fell farm on the quieter side of the Lake District. Accommodation comprises two new cottages and three holiday caravans (4 to 8 berth). New in 1983, the caravans are fully serviced with up to 3 bedrooms, kitchen, bathroom with shower and WC. Units share an acre of orchard with stream and shallow pool. All with colour TV. Ideal for family holidays. Coast, horse riding, narrow gauge railway, lakes, boating, historic buildings and forts; walking, climbing, fishing. Bar meals nearby. Pets welcome. Brochure on request.

**Apply to Mrs J. F. Hall
Fisherground Farm, Eskdale
Cumbria CA19 1TF
Telephone (09403) 319**

HARTSOP (Southern Lakes). Mr G. F. C. Mellstrom, The Weaving Cottage, Grove Farm, Hartsop, Patterdale. Working farm. Sleeps four. A traditional Lakeland cottage, modernised to high standard with outstanding views of the fells. Situated in unspoilt peaceful village between Ullswater and Brotherswater, within easy reach of Penrith and Windermere. Fully furnished and well equipped, providing ideal base for self-catering holiday; climbing and walking. Accommodation consists of sitting/diningroom with TV; electric fire, double settee; double bedroom; second bedroom with two single beds. Kitchen. Bathroom. Night storage heating. Large SAE for details to **Downlands, Bramshott, Liphook, Hants GU30 7QZ (Liphook [0428] 724600).**

HAWKSHEAD near. Well Cottage, Satterthwaite, Near Hawkshead. This charming 18th century cottage enjoys a village situation in the peaceful Grizedale valley, three miles south of Hawkshead. It stands detached in a walled garden with parking space. The accommodation offers the opportunity for six people to enjoy a holiday in an old world atmosphere with modern amenities. There are three bedrooms and a cot if required. The lounge/diningroom has an open fire, beamed ceilings, oak settee, old spice cupboard, comfy furniture and a coloured TV. The bathroom has a modern suite and the kitchen is well equipped and houses an electric cooker, fridge, Formica work tops, units, etc. A quiet corner of Lakeland with something to interest everyone. Private fishing. **Mrs J. M. Stoker, 2 Home Farm Cottages, Grizedale, Hawkshead, Ambleside LA22 0QN (Satterthwaite [022 984] 292).**

HAWKSHEAD near. Kentra, Satterthwaite. Charming cottage with old oak beams, but completely modernised in the peaceful unspoilt farming and forestry village of Satterthwaite. Comfortably furnished and carpeted; TV; bathroom; fitted kitchen, automatic cooker and fridge; sunny patio. One bedroom with double bed and one with two singles. Night store units for heating, with lounge wall fire for extra warmth. Lovely views across the valley from the south-facing picture windows. Wildlife museum, nature trails and Theatre in the Forest; fishing, walking. Picturesque Hawkshead is nearby for shopping; rest of Lake District easily accessible. Regret, no pets. SAE for brochure to **R. Brammall, Wain Garth, Satterthwaite, Cumbria LA12 8LP (Satterthwaite [022-984] 343).**

HESKET NEWMARKET. A. F. S. Chance, Howbeck Farmhouse, Hesket Newmarket, Wigton CA7 8JN (Caldbeck [069-98] 306). Howbeck Farm Cottage is an 18th century cottage, recently modernised, on the fringe of a peaceful village with shop, garage and pub adjacent to B5305 Penrith/Wigton road. Overlooks Caldbeck Fells. Centre of Lake District within a few minutes' drive. Pony trekking, fishing, golf, swimming, sailing, wildlife park, restaurants and craftshops nearby. Carlisle, Penrith, Wigton within 12 miles. Easy day expeditions to Northumberland (Hadrian's Wall), Galloway, Scottish Borders. Seaside 18 miles. Two double bedrooms (4 matching beds). Cot/high chair. Bathroom/toilet. Sittingroom — TV, open fire. Two storage heaters. All-electric kitchen/diningroom, fridge. Car essential; ample parking. Pets by negotiation. Open all year. From £50 weekly. SAE for brochure.

HOLMROOK. G. & H. W. Cook, Hall Flatt, Santon, Holmrook CA19 1UU (Wasdale [09406] 270). Working farm. This comfortably furnished house is set in own grounds with beautiful views. The approach road is a short but good lane off Gosforth/Santon Bridge Road. Ideal centre for climbers and walkers. Within easy reach of Muncaster Castle and Narrow Gauge Railway from Ravenglass to Eskdale, about three miles from the sea and Wastwater. Accommodation comprises two double bedrooms, two single and child's bed; cot; bathroom, two toilets; sittingroom; diningroom; all electric kitchen with cooker, fridge, kettle, immersion heater, stainless-steel sink unit. Fully equipped except linen. Open Easter to Christmas. Pets by arrangement. Shopping about two miles and car essential; house sleeps seven. Electricity by 50p meter. SAE, please, for weekly terms.

KENDAL. Scardale, Gatebeck, Kendal. Working farm. Modern bungalow accommodating six people, available for self-catering holidays from Easter to October. Situated on a dairy and mixed farm with lovely views from the sittingroom over farm buildings to Lakeland Fells, Kendal, Kirkby Lonsdale, Milnthorpe six miles and Holmescales Riding Centre one mile away. Three double bedrooms (cots by arrangement), sittingroom, dining area in kitchen; bathroom, toilet. Electric cooker, fully equipped except linen. Fitted carpets throughout (except kitchen), colour TV, storage heaters. Children welcome and pets accepted by prior arrangement. Car essential — garage, parking space. Shops/public transport one and a half miles away. Weekly terms £90–£110 including coal, but not electricity. Large lawn and garden, the house is suitable for disabled visitors. **Mrs Kathleen Robinson, Broadlea, Burton Road, Oxenholme, Kendal LA9 7ER (Kendal [0539] 20452) or (Crooklands [04487] 219).**

KENDAL. Mrs J. Clark, Grisedale Farm, Whinfell, Kendal LA8 9EN (Selside [053-983] 208). Working farm. Surrounded by lovely hills and fells and beside a delightful stream, where visitors can fish for trout and children can paddle, is this part of the farmhouse which is let furnished without attendance. One can enjoy a quiet relaxing holiday here. Grisedale is a 156-acre beef farm; hill climbing nearby; golf and tennis seven miles. Three double bedrooms; cot; bathroom; dining/sittingroom; kitchen with electric cooker, fridge. Pets permitted. Fully equipped except for linen. The house is available from Easter to October. Terms include electricity. SAE, please.

KENDAL. The Barn, Field End, Patton, Kendal. Recently converted, architect-designed barn on 120 acres farmland, four miles north of Kendal. A quiet country area with River Mint passing through farmland and lovely views of Cumbria hills. The barn consists of two spacious houses, one with four double bedrooms, one with three double bedrooms. Each house has full central heating for early/late holidays, lounge with open fire, diningroom, kitchen with cooker, fridge and washer. Bathroom. Downstairs shower room and toilet. Garage. Many interesting features include oak beams, pine floors, patio doors. Central to Lakes and Yorkshire Dales National Parks. Electricity at cost. Pets by arrangement. For brochure of this property apply to **Mr and Mrs E. D. Robinson, 1 Field End, Patton, Kendal (Kendal [053984] 220 or [0539] 21636).**

KENDAL near. Low Fold, Kentmere, Near Kendal. This farm cottage can accommodate six people in three double bedrooms; cot available if requested. There is a sittingroom; dining/kitchen (electric cooker and fridge); bathroom and toilet. No bed linen supplied. Sorry, no pets. The shops are four miles and the sea three-quarters of an hour by car. A car is essential and there is parking available. Electricity by 50p slot meter. Open all year. This traditional farm cottage has panoramic views of the beautiful Kentmere Valley. It is ideal for walking and for touring the Lake District. Kendal is eight miles away, Windermere seven. Weekly terms on request. Also small camp site adjoining farm. **Mr Frank E. Salkeld, c/o High Fold Farm, Kentmere, Near Kendal LA8 0JP (Staveley [0539] 821531).**

KENDAL. Mrs D. M. Dobson, Broad Oak, Crosthwaite, Kendal LA8 8JL (044-88-334). Working farm. This homely bungalow situated on farm (dairy, sheep and free range hens) in beautiful Winster Valley. Sleeps six in two bedrooms. Cot, high chair, baby bath and screen available. Please bring own linen. Bathroom, plus second toilet. Large lounge/kitchen with open fireplace (some logs and coal provided). Convector heater. Electric cooker, fridge, spin dryer and immersion heater. Colour TV. Electricity on meter. Garage and parking space. Adjacent field for recreation. Dogs allowed if kept under control. Village shop/post office two miles; Kendal six miles; Windermere eight miles; Morecambe 16 miles. Available April to October. Weekly rates £70 to £90.

KENDAL. Mrs E. Barnes, Brackenfold, Whinfell, Kendal LA8 9EF (Grayrigg [053-984] 238). Working farm. Brackenfold is a 147-acre dairy/sheep farm set in a quiet country area. There are beautiful scenic views from the farm and also a river running through the middle of the farm which is suitable for paddling and picnicking. Brackenfold is situated centrally for touring the Lake District and the Yorkshire Dales. All children are welcome and babysitting is available. Milk can be obtained from the farm. The accommodation is part of the farmhouse and sleeps six in two double bedrooms, cot; bathroom, toilet; sitting/diningroom; fully equipped kitchen with electric cooker, fridge, etc. Shops four miles, sea 20. Sorry, no pets. Open March to November. SAE, please, for terms.

CUMBRIA – LAKELAND SPLENDOUR!

The Lake District has for long been a popular tourist destination however the Fells and Pennine areas are also worth exploring. The many attractions of Cumbria include the Ennerdale Forest, St. Bees Head, Langdale Pikes, Bowness-on-Solway, the market town of Alston, Lanercost Priory, Scafell Pike – England's highest mountain – and the Wordsworth country around Ambleside, Grasmere and Cockermouth.

KENDAL (Lake District). "Garth Cottage," Castle Garth, Kendal. Available all year. This stone-built house is just across the field from Kendal Castle ruins, where Henry VIII's sixth wife, Katherine Parr, lived. "Garth Cottage" is warm and comfortable with modern conveniences (electric cooker, fridge, fitted carpets, colour TV, shaver point in bathroom) and is fully equipped for two to five people. Please bring your own linen. One double and three single beds. Sorry, no pets. Free parking. Only five minutes' walk to shops, bus and railway station. Kendal is well situated for easy access and good roads to all Lake District beauty spots and only about nine miles from the Yorkshire Dales. Terms from £40 weekly. SAE, please, for brochure to **Mrs E. Steele, 53 Burton Road, Kendal LA9 7JA (Kendal [0539] 23400).**

KENDAL. The Bungalow, Dawson Fold, Lyth Valley, Kendal LA8 8DE. This bungalow accommodates six and is situated in the Lyth Valley, six miles from Bowness-on-Windermere within easy reach of South Lakeland, Kendal, Grange-over-Sands and Morecambe. The village of Levens four miles away with post office, butchers/bakers and two general stores. The places of historical interest in the area being Sizergh Castle, Levens Hall, Windermere Steam Museum and Haverthwaite to Lakeside Railway. There are two double bedrooms and one twin bedded; bathroom; lounge with dining area; kitchen with electric cooker. Open March to October with electric heating. Car essential. Children welcome. Regret no pets. SAE, please, or phone for terms: **Ms C. Walling, Dawson Fold, Lyth Valley, Kendal LA8 8DE (Crosthwaite [04488] 248).**

KENDAL. Mrs E. Bateman, High Underbrow Farm, Burneside, Kendal LA8 9AY (Kendal [0539] 21927). This newly converted cottage adjoins the 17th century farmhouse in a sunny position with beautiful views. Ideal spot for touring the Lake District and Yorkshire Dales and with many pleasant walks around. There are two bedrooms (one with double bed, the other with two singles). Children are welcome and a cot is available. Bathroom with shower, toilet. Large livingroom/kitchen with fitted units, fridge and cooker. TV. Electricity by 50p meter. Understairs store. Fitted carpets throughout. Own entrance porch. Sorry, no pets. Shops at Burneside two miles away, Kendal four miles, Windermere eight miles. Linen optional. Car essential — parking. Terms from £75 weekly. There is also a 6-berth holiday caravan to let from £50 per week. Open all year.

KENDAL near. 17 Low Cottages, Endmoor, Near Kendal. This stone-built, white painted cottage is situated in a quiet village with lovely views over the countryside and river. Comfortably furnished and equipped for four. One double and one twin bedrooms; bathroom; sunny lounge overlooking small garden; TV; large dining/kitchen with electric cooker, fridge. Electric heating and immersion heater. Everything provided except linen. Cot available. The cottage is only seven miles from Lake District National Park, with hill walking, sailing, pony trekking, etc., and five miles from the historic market town of Kendal. Easy access to Yorkshire Dales; the Market Town of Kirkby Lonsdale and seaside are eight miles away. Two miles M6, exit 36. SAE, please, to **Mrs I. H. Gorman, 146 Manchester Road, Rochdale, Lancashire OL11 4JQ (Rochdale [0706] 53333).**

KENDAL near. 'Windy Ridge', Low Cottages, Endmoor, Near Kendal. Traditional stone-built cottage in quiet village, sleeps four. South Lakes area with easy access to National Park, Yorkshire Dales and Fylde coast. Open views over woods and trout river. Accommodation includes sittingroom with TV; rear hall; modern kitchen with fridge, electric cooker and pine furnishings; front bedroom with double bed; rear bedroom with two single bunks; tiled bathroom with WC. Cooking, heating and hot water are by slot meter. To the front is a small sunny garden with a local stone patio. The cottage is tastefully decorated and furnished and has fitted carpets. Everything provided except bed linen and towels. Children and pets most welcome. SAE, please. **Mrs L. M. Newman, 4 Birchfield, Endmoor, Kendal LA8 0JA (Crooklands [044-87] 542).**

KENDAL near. Mrs K. M. Parsons, Low Levens Farm, Levens, Near Kendal LA8 8EH (Sedgwick [0448] 60435). Working farm, join in. The farmhouse dates back to 1190. The flat is contained in part of the farmhouse with separate entrance. Panelled, spacious lounge with TV, gas heater. Large kitchen/diner, all modern conveniences and equipment. One twin bedroom, one room with one double and two bunks, bed-settee in lounge; bathroom and toilet. Situated on banks of River Kent with free fishing permit. Lovely view of Whitbarrow, within easy reach of lakes and sea. Village nearby with post office, hairdresser, two self-service shops and butchers. Farm supplies milk and eggs. Children welcome, swings, climbing frame and orchard to play in. Small dogs allowed if kept on lead. Easily reached from A6 and M6. Weekly terms on application.

PLEASE ENCLOSE A STAMPED ADDRESSED ENVELOPE WITH ENQUIRIES

SELF-CATERING Cumbria 401

KENDAL near CROOK. Plumgarths Holiday Flats, Plumgarths. Plumgarths is an early 17th century * house standing in extensive, peacefully secluded grounds surrounded by open farming country between Windermere and Kendal, just nine miles from M6 exit 36. This picturesque house has been sympathetically converted into six spacious, self contained flats sleeping up to seven. Also Chalet in the grounds. Choose the one that suits you best — one, two or three bedrooms, first floor or ground floor (no steps). All have colour TV and open fire in the livingroom, fully equipped electric kitchen, bathroom and toilet. Everything is supplied except linen (available for hire). Background central heating October/May. Cot and high chair on request. Dogs by arrangement. We are open all year to welcome you and to care for your comfort. Three night Breaks November/March. Write or phone **Jonathan and Fidelia Somervell, Plumgarths Holiday Flats, Crook, Kendal LA8 8LE (0539-821325).** See also Colour Display Advertisement.

KESWICK. Mrs M. R. Tatters, Birkett Bank, St. Johns-in-the-Vale, Keswick (Threlkeld [059-683] 692). The accommodation here is a furnished farm cottage situated in Vale of St. John four-and-a-half miles from Keswick. Two bedrooms (one is large with two double beds, other has one double bed); bathroom; sittingroom with TV; dining/kitchenette — electric cooker, lighting, fridge, immersion heater. Cottage is an old stone one, built in 1787, comfortably furnished. Parking space for cars. Children welcome. Dogs allowed. Penrith 14 miles, Carlisle 28 miles. Terms and further particulars on request with SAE, please, for speedy reply.

KESWICK. Mrs A. D. Teasdale, Doddick Farm, Threlkeld, Keswick CA12 4SY (Threlkeld [059-683] 687). Working farm, join in. The stone built modern bungalow, all electric, lies 12 miles from M6 and six miles from Keswick, just off A66. It overlooks valley, river and magnificent mountain scenery; all the lakes and fells, with their opportunities for walking and climbing, lie within a 20-mile radius. Visitors are free to go around the 156-acre mixed farm. The house accommodates five people in two bedrooms, one with double bed, one with double bed and a single; cot if required. Lounge with TV; spacious kitchen with electric cooker, fridge, sink unit and modern equipment; everything except linen. Suitable for disabled. One mile from village and 30 miles from the sea. Ample parking. Open all year. SAE, please, for terms which depend on season and do not include fuel.

KESWICK. Miss M. Thoburn, Seldom Seen, Thornthwaite, Keswick CA12 5SA (Braithwaite [059-682] 452). Set in its own grounds with a stream running nearby, the cottage is situated in a peaceful village, three and a half miles from Keswick, with uninterrupted views of Skiddaw and Derwent Valley. It is ideal for walking or rambling on the wooded fells which surround it. Sleeping four/five in double and twin bedded rooms, cot and folding bed. Blankets supplied. Linen hire available. Bathroom and toilet. Fully equipped kitchen, cooker, fridge, iron etc. Colour TV. Coal or Calor gas fire in comfortable livingroom. Children and pets welcome. Open all year, fuel included in price. For brochure and terms SAE, please.

KESWICK. Lowthwaite Farm Cottage and Bothy, St. John's-in-the-Vale, Keswick. Working farm. Two attractive cottages, situated either side of a traditional stock rearing and dairy farm, provide ideal holiday accommodation all year round. St. John's-in-the-Vale is a beautiful valley in the Lake District and Lowthwaite Farm makes an excellent centre for touring — South via Thirlmere and Ambleside to the Lakes, or North to the Pennines and Hadrian's Wall. Day excursions to the sea at St. Bees or Maryport delight all ages. Boating on the Lakes, pony trekking available nearby. Excellent walking country. Fully equipped to a high standard, cottage sleeps four and Bothy four/six. Each has sittingroom; bathroom/toilet; kitchen with electric cooker and ample equipment. Electricity by coin meter. No linen supplied. Children welcome, sorry no pets. Solid fuel central heating. Car essential — parking. Shops/public transport two miles. Free range eggs, milk available. SAE, please, for terms to Watson Lewis and Co., St Andrew's Churchyard, Penrith CA11 7YE (Penrith [0768] 64541).

KESWICK. Mr and Mrs M. J. Pye, Fieldside Grange, Keswick CA12 4RN (Keswick [0596] 74444). These fully self-contained and centrally heated apartments, sleeping from two to seven persons, have been converted from an old Lakeland farm. Individual units are comprehensively equipped including electric cooker, fridge and bed linen. There is a colour television lounge and a games room for wet days. The grounds of one-and-a-half acres offer magnificent views over Keswick and the surrounding fells, giving peace and quiet for those who enjoy tranquillity yet plenty of space for children to play away from traffic hazards. Full fire precautions. Open all year. Pets welcome. Cots available. Weekly terms from £65 to £140. Send stamp only please for full details.

Please note that entries marked with an asterisk also have a colour display advert in the colour section in this guide

KESWICK. Horse Shoe Crag, Fieldside Close, Keswick. The property is situated near the Lake District National Park, one mile to the east of Keswick Town Centre. It commands a wonderful and extensive view over the Lakeland Fells. Horse Shoe Crag stands in its own grounds and access is by a private drive with ample parking facilities. The flats are newly built and equipped to make delightful and carefree holidays involving the minimum of housework. Each flat is electrically heated and can accommodate up to six. Electricity by 50p slot meter. Open all year. Lower flat two twin and one double bedrooms; upper flat one double, one twin and two single rooms. All with fitted units. Each flat has fitted kitchen with cooker, fridge, etc. Lounge with local stone fireplace, electric fire and colour TV, and bathroom with airing cupboard. SAE for terms and brochure to **Mrs J. Swainson, Lime Grove, Fieldside Close, Keswick CA12 4LN (Keswick [0596] 72150).**

KESWICK. Mire House, St. Johns-in-the-Vale, Keswick. Mire House is a farmhouse situated in the Vale of St. John four miles from Keswick. The house still retains the oak beams in the sittingroom and offers a quiet relaxing holiday in peaceful surroundings. There is accommodation for six people in three double rooms, one single; cot; bathroom; sittingroom with open fire; kitchen with fitted sink and cupboards with utensils; electric cooker, fridge, iron, immersion heater. Linen not supplied. Children welcome and one pet allowed. Ample parking. Available Easter to January. SAE, please, for terms. **Mrs I. Birkett, Birkett Mire, Threlkeld, Keswick CA12 4TT (Threlkeld [059-683] 608).**

Mire House

KESWICK. Mr J. N. Baxter, "Heathfield," Crosthwaite Road, Keswick CA12 5PG (Keswick [0596] 72407). Two modern, self-contained flats (sleeping six), comprising livingroom, three double bedrooms; kitchen; bathroom with WC. All-electric fully-equipped kitchen with cooker, fridge, airing cupboard and immersion heater. Fully equipped except linen. Situated in beautiful Lake District National Park in the hamlet of Guardhouse, near the Glendermakin River commanding wonderful views of the Saddleback Range of Fells. Ideal starting point for Fell walkers. Pony trekking three miles; golf course nearby. Car essential; ample parking in grounds. Drying green behind property. Colour TV; electricity 50p coin meter. Open all year. Telephone after 5 pm.

KIRKBY LONSDALE. Mr and Mrs M. Dixon, Harrison Farm, Whittington, Kirkby Lonsdale, Carnforth, Lancs. LA6 2NX (Kirkby Lonsdale [0468] 71415). Working farm. This farmhouse in the village of Hutton Roof, three miles from the shops at Kirkby Lonsdale and 15 miles from the sea, has fine views of surrounding Dales and opens on to the Crag. Good walking area and central for touring the Lake District, Yorkshire Dales and Morecambe. The house sleeps seven in three bedrooms — one room with two single beds, one with double bed and the other a double bed and cot, if required. Sittingroom, diningroom/kitchen with electric cooker, kettle, fridge, etc., TV. Everything supplied except linen. Garage parking. Pets permitted. Other cottages available for five, six, seven and eight people. SAE brings quick reply.

KIRKBY STEPHEN. Low Ploughlands, Little Musgrave, Kirkby Stephen. Low Ploughlands is situated in a lush green area, about 200 yards from the River Eden. Nearby are small woods and pleasant walks may be enjoyed. Small stretch of trout fishing available. Appleby, 10 miles, has swimming baths, castle, golf, pony trekking. The Lakes and Dales are within easy reach; shop and post office two miles at Great Musgrave. A concrete road leads to the house which accommodates nine in four bedrooms; cot, bathroom, toilet; sittingroom, diningroom; TV; kitchen with fridge. For the children there are pony rides on "Sunny." Car essential — garage. Pets allowed. SAE, please, for terms to **Mrs E. Bainbridge, Ploughlands, Little Musgrave, Kirkby Stephen (Brough [093-04] 256).**

PENRITH. Skirwith Hall Cottage, Skirwith, Penrith CA10 1RH. Situated on a large dairy farm in the picturesque Eden Valley, this cottage is half of a Georgian farmhouse. Every home comfort. Open fireplace, night storage heaters, electric heaters, colour TV. Accommodates seven to nine adults and there is a cot available. Children welcome. Pets allowed. Electric cooker, plus Rayburn. Car essential, parking. Two miles to shops. It is set in a landscaped garden with Briggle Beck at the bottom. On the outskirts of unspoiled Skirwith village in the shadow of Crossfell, the cottage is within easy reach of the Pennines, Yorkshire Dales and Lake District. Ideal centre for walking, touring or just relaxing in idyllic surroundings. Weekly terms including fuel £69 to £115. **Mrs Laura Wilson, Skirwith Hall, Skirwith, Penrith CA10 1RH (Culgaith [076-888] 241).**

The information in the entries in this guide is presented by the publishers in good faith and after the signed acceptance by advertisers that they will uphold the high standards associated with FARM HOLIDAY GUIDES LIMITED. The publishers do not accept responsibility for any inaccuracies or omissions or any results thereof. Before making final holiday arrangements readers should confirm the prices and facilities directly with advertisers.

PENRITH. "Privet House," Rosgill, Bampton, Penrith. Working farm. This small, cosy farmhouse is ideally situated in open countryside in the peaceful hamlet of Rosgill, near the Haweswater and Ullswater. Guests may laze by the River Lowther which flows through the 350-acre beef and sheep farm. The market town of Penrith is 10 miles and the M6 (junction 39) only four miles. Interesting places to visit include Lowther Park, Pottery, Flourmill and many historic buildings — leaflets and brochures readily available. Many outdoor activities and plenty of opportunities for walking in countryside and fells. Five people accommodated in one double and one family bedrooms; cot. Bathroom/toilet; sittingroom/diningroom with TV; well-equipped kitchen. No linen. Pets allowed. Car essential — parking. SAE, please, for terms to **Mrs M. W. Weightman, Rosgill Hall, Rosgill, Penrith CA10 2QX (Shap [093-16] 248).**

PENRITH. Thwaite Hall, Hutton Roof, Greystoke, Penrith. This farmhouse is a 16th-century listed building which has been modernised but still retains its oak beams and mullioned windows with open fires, overlooking Carrick Fells. Nearby is Keswick, and Ullswater Lake for sailing; walking, climbing, golfing, pony trekking and hunting within easy reach in quiet, peaceful, open countryside. Both houses have double bedrooms and one single and both sleep six. There are cots, bathroom, toilet, sittingroom and diningroom in each. Kitchens have cooker, refrigerator, sink unit, fully equipped with plugs. No linen supplied. Pets are allowed. Open all year. Car is essential, parking. SAE, please, for terms. **Mrs E. Taylor, Hill Top Farm, Penruddock, Penrith CA11 0RX (Greystoke [085-33] 340).**

PENRITH. Rampshowe, Orton, Penrith. Working farm. Rampshowe is 150-acres fell farm with sheep, lambs, beef cattle and calves. Delightfully positioned in the peace and quiet of Birbeck Fells, with a river flowing through the fields, lovely waterfall and pool for bathing. Ideal area for birdwatchers. Local angling club. Shops, post office, pub serving snacks and restaurant at Orton (three miles) Unspoilt, rural countryside, yet only five miles from M6 motorway. Accommodates eight people in three double bedrooms, cot; bathroom, toilet; sittingroom, TV, diningroom with electric storage heaters and coal fire with back-boiler. Large kitchen with fridge, cooker, electric kettle, vacuum cleaner, spin drier etc., only linen required. Pets must be well-controlled. Car essential — parking. Open all year. Terms include most of fuel. The house stands on its own, with garden and large farmyard. Logs provided for fire. SAE to **Mrs M. E. Mawson, Sproat-Ghyll Farm, Orton, Penrith CA10 3SA (Orton [058-74] 244).**

SATTERTHWAITE. Mrs S. H. Brown, High Dale Park Farm, High Dale Park, Satterthwaite LA12 8LJ (Satterthwaite [022-984] 226). Our cottage is situated down a private lane in the heart of Grasmere village. Private but very convenient. The cottage is particularly attractive to those without their own transport as it is only one minute's walk from both bus stops and shops. The garden, which borders the River Rothay on one side, provides a spectacular view of the Helvellyn Foothills. Being built of traditional lakeland stone, our fully equipped cottage stays cool in summer but is very cosy during winter months. Grasmere is "as full of walks as an egg is of meat" said the poet. Come to Grasmere "The Jewel of the Lakes" and enjoy a truly wonderful holiday.

SEASCALE. Mr H. M. Tyson, Little Ground, Wasdale, Seascale CA20 1EU (Wasdale [094-06] 253). Little Ground Cottage is nicely situated in the unspoilt valley of Wasdale, approximately one mile from Wastwater, and enjoys magnificent views of the Wasdale Screes. Recently modernised, the cottage can accommodate six or seven, plus baby, in three double bedrooms; cot; bathroom; inside and outside toilets; diningroom; all-electric, well equipped kitchen. Everything supplied except linen. Shops four miles, sea seven. Car essential to gain the most from your holiday and parking space is available. Pets permitted. This is a good touring centre, within comfortable driving distance of many places of historic and scenic interest. SAE, please, for terms and further details.

SEDBERGH. Edmondsons, Main Street, Dent, Sedbergh. Situated in Dent village in Yorkshire Dale, 10 miles from M6 and 23 miles from Lake District. The newly converted cottage retains old oak beams and mullion windows and is comfortably furnished for four people. Cot available. Two double bedrooms, one of which has twin beds and vanitory unit. Bathroom, toilet; sitting/diningroom. Carpeted throughout. Basement garage with interior stairs to cottage. Night storage heater, also electric fire in lounge. Children welcome. Pets permitted. Car essential. Open all year round. Terms on request from **Mrs R. Hodgson, Main Street, Dent, Sedbergh LA10 5QL (058-75 206).**

SILECROFT. Mrs S. Mansergh, Kellet Farm, Silecroft LA18 4NU (Millom [0657] 2727) Farm Cottage. A cosy 17th century period cottage retaining traditional features, carefully and sympathetically modernised with good quality furnishings and close carpeted throughout. Own walled lawn garden. All modern facilities. Two bedrooms sleeping up to four plus cot. **Hartrees House** has five bedrooms sleeping up to 10. South-facing, standing in open countryside. Fully modernised with all facilities. **Hartrees Cottage** has two bedrooms, with views over open fields to Lake District Fells, sleeping four/five. Completely modernised and fully equipped. The properties are close to a sandy beach and golf course (both quarter-mile), village shop and inn, and railway station. A quiet base for exploring Lake District. Ample parking. Pets allowed in some of the properties.

FUN FOR ALL THE FAMILY IN CUMBRIA

Appleby Castle Conservation Centre, Appleby; Brockhole National Park Visitor Centre, near Ambleside; Grizedale Forest Wildlife Centre, Hawkshead; Lowther Wildlife Adventure Park, near Penrith; Muncaster Castle, Ravenglass; Levens Hall, near Kendal; Ravenglass & Eskdale Railway, Ravenglass; Lakeside & Haverthwaite Railway, Haverthwaite, near Newby Bridge; Windermere Steamboat Museum, Rayrigg Road, near Bowness-on-Windermere; Fell Foot Park, Newby Bridge, Lake Windermere.

SILLOTH. 32 Skinburness Drive, Silloth. End house of a block of four, with gardens front and back. Full gas central heating with gas fire in lounge, fitted carpets throughout; colour TV. Golf and pony trekking one mile. Central lakeland one hour's drive; Gretna Green and Scottish Borders 33 miles. Carlisle 23 miles east. Six people accommodated in two double and one bunk bedded rooms; cot; bathroom, inside/outside toilets; sittingroom; diningroom. Kitchen with electric cooker, fridge, kettle and iron. Linen supplied. Half a mile from shops and less than five minutes from the sea. Pets allowed. Car essential — parking and garage. Open from February to December. Weekly terms from £50 – £95. Further details on receipt of SAE to **Mrs E. Shuttleworth, Hawkshead Hill, Ambleside LA22 0PW (Hawkshead [096-66] 432).**

STAVELEY. Fairfield, Station Road, and Nos. 2 and 6 Church View, Staveley. Two furnished cottages and one furnished house available all year. Situated in picturesque village of Staveley. All within easy reach of shops, playground, bowling green. House accommodates nine in three doubles and one treble room; cottages five each in two double rooms and one single. Children and pets welcome. Cot. Electric heating (coin meter) or coal fires. Kitchen has gas or electric cooker, fridge, stainless steel sink, all utensils etc. Linen supplied. Car not essential, but parking. Staveley on A591 between Kendal and Windermere at foot of beautiful Kentmere Valley. All sporting facilities (Lakeland Outdoor Pursuits) within five mile radius. Weekly terms from £45. SAE, please. **Mrs D. E. Canon, Eagle and Child Hotel, Staveley, Kendal LA8 9LP (Staveley [0539] 821320).**

TROUTBECK (Windermere). Mrs M. Tyson, Troutbeck Park, Troutbeck, Windermere LA23 1PS (Ambleside [0966] 33398). Working farm. Troutbeck Park Holiday Cottage adjoins the farmhouse on this 2,574-acre hill farm, one mile off the main road. Situated at the head of Troutbeck Valley, it was once owned by Beatrix Potter, who left it to the National Trust. A beautiful place with an abundance of wild life, from flowers and plants to a large selection of animals. Peaceful and relaxing, yet handy for shopping areas. Up to five people accommodated. One family bedroom (one double and one single beds); cot on request. Flush toilet; sittingroom with double bed; kitchen-diningroom with electric cooker, water heater, fridge, etc. No linen supplied. Shops one-and-a-half miles. No pets. Car essential — parking. Easter-November. Terms on request (including electricity).

ULLSWATER. South View, Dacre, Penrith. Working farm. South View farmhouse is situated in the small village of Dacre, two miles from Lake Ullswater and four miles from Penrith and M6. There is a large walled garden and plenty of parking space. Car essential. Fully equipped for six people, except linen. Children welcome and cot available on request. Pets allowed if well controlled. The house consists of one double bedded room, two twin bedded rooms; bathroom with toilet; diningroom; sittingroom with electric fire and colour TV. Kitchen with electric cooker and fridge. Water heated by immersion heater. Terms from £70 including electricity. SAE, please, to **Mrs N. Bennett, Hollins Farm, Dockray, Penrith CA11 0JY (Glenridding [085-32] 374).**

ULPHA. Church House Cottage, Ulpha. Church House is situated in the beautiful Duddon Valley so loved by Wordsworth, in the Lake District National Park. Ideal for walking and climbing. The cottage, which sleeps eight people and a baby, has been completely modernised and is fully furnished apart from linen and towels, including colour TV and Teasmade. Four double bedrooms, dining/sittingroom; bathroom, separate WC; modern kitchen, electric automatic cooker, refrigerator, spinner-rinse; adjoining barn can be used as a playroom where darts, table tennis and blackboard are provided. Covered parking for two cars; car essential. Well-behaved pets welcome. Let without attendance from £80 to £150 weekly; fortnightly lets only in school summer holidays. All enquiries enclosing SAE to **Church House (Ulpha) Estates Ltd., Church House, Ulpha, Broughton-in-Furness LA20 6DX (Broughton-in-Furness [06576] 425).**

WASDALE. Church How Cottage, Netherwasdale, Wasdale. Church How Cottage is a detached, traditional lakeland stone building situated within the grounds of The Old Vicarage in unspoilt Wasdale. Although built about 150 years ago, the Cottage has been very extensively modernised and refurbished throughout to an exceptionally high standard way beyond that usually found in holiday accommodation. The Cottage consists of three bedrooms, fitted and fully tiled kitchen, fully tiled bathroom and large living/diningroom. The ground floor and one bedroom have exposed beam ceilings which help to retain the olde worlde character. The Cottage adjoins an attractive oak woodland which guests are free to use. Two pubs are nearby where meals can be obtained. Available all year. **Mr M. Friend, 5 Hill brow Court, Portsmouth Road, Esher, Surrey KT10 9UA (Esher [0372] 68098).**

WIGTON. The Stables, Rosley, Wigton. The Stables, converted 1975, is approached by its own drive from the B5305 Penrith/Wigton road in the hamlet of Rosley on the northern fringes of the Lake District, overlooking Caldbeck Fells. Easily accessible to the Northern Fells, Lake Ullswater and Bassenthwaite; Caldbeck, Wigton and Carlisle within 10 miles. Golf, riding, pony trekking, fishing nearby, birdwatching on the Solway, and Lowther Wildlife Park. Two double bedrooms, one single, sleeps five to six and cot available; bathroom with shaving point; sittingroom with picture window; all-electric kitchen, fridge. Bed linen provided. Pets permitted. Car essential — parking. Five miles from shops and 15 miles from sea. Open March to October. Terms from £60 to £150 per week. SAE, please, to **Dr Michael Elderkin, Rosley House, Rosley, Wigton CA7 8BZ (Wigton [Cumbria] [0965] 42665).**

THE STABLES

PLEASE SEND A STAMPED ADDRESSED ENVELOPE WITH ENQUIRIES

Lakeland Balcony Flats in Windermere

and other *Canterbury Flats* in the same development. Five minutes walk from Bowness promenade with its steamer pier, rowing boats and glorious views over Lake Windermere to the mountains beyond. Close to a variety of interesting shops and restaurants. 1, 2 and 3 bedrooms, sleeping 2-4, 4-6 or 6-8. An ideal base for exploring the Lake District.

The flats are available all year for weekly lettings and for short breaks of 2 nights or longer between November and March. Special terms at Christmas/New Year (4 nights min.). All flats have lounge, kitchen, twin or double beds, bathroom/W.C., colour TV and video, garage or parking. Heating is by storage heaters. Bed linen is provided, cots can be hired.

Colour brochure of CANTERBURY FLATS from Bowness Holidays (WJB), 22 Quarry Rigg, Windermere or by telephoning (09662) 5216 or (0227) 69803 (24 hours).

For the Mutual Guidance of Guest and Host

Farm Holiday Guides Ltd. do not inspect or recommend accommodation but advertisers agree to accept our Farm Holiday Guide standards of comfortable and clean accommodation and wholesome and well-cooked food. Advertisers are also bound by the Trades Description Act.

When accommodation has been booked, deposits sent, and letters of acceptance exchanged, both parties – host and guest – have entered into a binding contract.

Friends and families can easily be upset and much bitterness caused if holiday arrangements are not carefully made. The following points can be of real importance:

Guest When enquiring about accommodation, be as precise as possible. Give exact dates, numbers in your party and the ages of any children. State the number and type of rooms wanted and also what catering you require – bed and breakfast, full board etc. Make sure that the position about evening meals is clear – and about pets, reductions for children or any other special points.

Read our reviews carefully to ensure that the proprietors you are going to contact can supply what you want. Ask for a letter confirming all arrangements, if possible.

Host Give details about your facilities and about any special conditions. Explain your deposit system clearly and arrangements for cancellations, charges etc, and whether or not your terms include VAT.

We regret that Farm Holiday Guides cannot accept responsibility for any errors or omissions in descriptions. Prices in particular should be checked before booking because of the early compilation of the Guides, far ahead of the next holiday season.

Cumbria / Derbyshire — SELF-CATERING

WINDERMERE. High House Cottage, Windermere. Working farm. High House is a 300-year-old, 300-acre farm with beef and sheep, situated about two and a half miles from Windermere and around one and a half miles from the main A591 Kendal to Keswick Road. Places of interest include Brockhole, Lowther Wild Life Park, Beatrix Potter's cottage and Wordsworth's Dove Cottage. The cottage is equipped with immersion heater, fridge and electric cooker, electric overblankets and continental quilts on all beds. Accommodates five people. One double and one family rooms; bathroom, toilet; combined sitting/diningroom. No linen supplied. Car essential — parking. Weekly terms from £60 – £80. Apply to **Mrs D. Whitwell, 6 Kent Drive, Staveley, Near Kendal LA8 9NZ (Staveley [0539] 821476).**

WINDERMERE. 5, 22 and 24 Bannerigg, Windermere. Spacious modern maisonettes in a quiet location, but only 200 yards from village centre, making for convenient shopping and easy access to other parts of Lake District (300 yards from station). Nos. 22 and 24 have three bedrooms (six-nine people), whilst No. 5 is a smaller ground floor unit for two-four people. All have large livingrooms, well appointed kitchens and bathrooms, gas central heating, colour TV, electric cooker, fridge, etc., and fitted wardrobes in many bedrooms. Extremely warm and cosy throughout, maintained to a high standard. Pets allowed. Parking at rear. Cot, high chair available. Weekend/short lets out of season. Open all year. Send large SAE to **Mrs H. Cameron, 23 Brook Meadow, Higher Bartle, Preston, Lancs PR4 0AA or phone Preston (0772) 721764.**

WINDERMERE near. 1 and 2 "Sunny Brow Cottages," Brow Lane, Staveley. Both have great character, comfort and all modern amenities. No. 1 is large with three double bedrooms, spacious lounge and diningroom. No. 2 is smaller with double bedroom and small room with bunk beds suitable for children, lounge/diningroom. Both are carpeted throughout, have fitted kitchens, excellent bathrooms, open fires (coal provided), electric radiators, immersion heaters, TV. Electricity by 50p meter. Ideal touring base for Lakes and Kentmere Valley. Splendid location at foot of fells on sheep farm, but shops nearby. Reasonable terms. Apply quoting "Sunny Brow" to: **Holidays in Lakeland, Stock Park Mansion, Newby Bridge, Ulverston, Cumbria LA12 8AY (0448-31549).**

DERBYSHIRE

ASHBOURNE near. ROSE COTTAGE, Riverside, Milldale, plus GREEN COTTAGE and COLDWALL COTTAGE, Dovedale. Very picturesque stone cottage with superb views in delightful settings by river and close to Dovedale. Ideally situated for quiet peaceful holidays walking/touring in the Peak District with stately homes, cycling, trekking, fishing, and Alton Towers close for those seeking a more active holiday. These 'AA' listed properties have recently been sympathetically modernised to a high standard retaining their old beams and character. They sleep up to six and have fitted carpets, electric cooking/heating, all modern conveniences, cots. Terms £55 – £135 per week. Leaflet giving full detailed information about all properties from: **Mrs Y. Bailey, 4 Woodland Close, Thorpe, Ashbourne, Derbyshire (Thorpe Cloud [033529] 447).**

ASHBOURNE near. Mount Pleasant Farm Cottage, Snelston, Near Ashbourne. Modern self-catering farm cottage at Snelston (off the A515 Sudbury to Ashbourne road), in beautiful setting — ideal for walking and touring in the Peak District. Market town of Ashbourne — two miles; Alton Towers — eight miles; golf course half a mile. Available all year, the cottage is fully equipped to accommodate six holidaymakers and linen is supplied. Three double bedrooms, plus cot. Bathroom, toilet. Large lounge with black and white TV. The diningroom/kitchen includes refrigerator, electric cooker. Electric heating. Pets welcome. Large garden for the children, also babysitting provided if required. Car essential, parking. Further enquiries and terms (including fuel) to **Mrs A. M. Hollingsworth, Mount Pleasant Farm, Snelston, Near Ashbourne DE6 2OJ (Ashbourne [0335] 42330).**

ASHBOURNE near. Alder's Cottages, Alstonefield, Near Ashbourne. Near Dovedale, the Alder's Cottages (AA listed) are in the centre of Alstonefield, an attractive limestone village, three times winner of the best-kept village award, and now a conservation area dating back to Saxon times. Each cottage accommodates six people. They have been recently modernised and furnished in the country style; three bedrooms, bathroom with coloured suite, cot available. Comfortable lounge with large storage heater and open fire. There is a large well equipped living kitchen with electric cooker, fridge, twin tub washing machine. Colour TV. A pleasant garden overlooking the hills of Dovedale. Linen provided for overseas visitors only. Electric 50p meter. Pets by arrangement. Toilet rolls, soap etc. provided. This quiet and peaceful area is ideal for anyone wishing to enjoy the unspoilt countryside of the Peak National Park. Fly fishing arranged. **Mrs E. R. Allen, The Post Office Stores, Alstonefield, Near Ashbourne DE6 2FX (Alstonefield [033-527] 201).**

SELF-CATERING Derbyshire

DOVEDALE FARM & COUNTRY HOLIDAY GROUP

Shirley Hall Farm, Shirley (Mr J. Foster Tel: [0335] 60346) The Saddlery Flat: 1 bedroom, private bathroom. Sleeps 3/4 on working farm. 3 bedroom bungalow: adjoining pleasant village. Superb views. Woodland walks. Central for Chatsworth, Alton Towers, and Kedleston. Fishing. Ashbourne 4 miles.

Hayes Farm, Hulland Ward (Mrs Audrey Gray Tel: [0335] 70204) Unwind in our peaceful valley, superb 3 bedroom bungalow on small friendly dairy farm. Close to Ashbourne, Dovedale, Matlock and the Peak District.

Yew Tree Farm, Alstonefield (Mrs K. W. Griffin Tel: [033529] 249) 17th Century farm house, with adjoining field and shed suitable for ponies. Large garden. Centrally situated for visiting the Peak District and Alton Towers. Pets and children welcome.

Merryfield Farm, Kniveton (Mrs E. J. Harrison Tel: [033529] 341) The farmhouse looks on to the beautiful Derbyshire hills. Can accommodate six people. Ideally situated for walking, bike hiring, Alton Towers, other places of interest. Garden to sit out. 3 miles Ashbourne.

Rose Cottage, Snelston (Mrs Moore Tel: [033524] 230) Beautifully situated, secluded, fully equipped 2 bedroom bungalow. Pine kitchen/living area. Glorious views, lovely quiet countryside. Hard tennis court. Easy access Peak District, Alton Towers.

Culland Mount Farm, Brailsford (Mrs C. Phillips Tel: [0335] 60313) Farm cottage, self-contained adjoining farmhouse, with superb view. On modern dairy farm. Spacious accommodation for 5, TV, carpeted, central heating, car essential. Terms from £55.

Chevin Green Farm, Belper (Carl and Joan Postles Tel: [077382] 2328) Attractively converted farm buildings overlooking the Derwent Valley. Convenient to many attractions – Matlock, Ashbourne, Dove Dale and the Peak District. Children welcome.

Biggin Mill Farm, Nr Kirk Ireton (Mrs Lynn Richards Tel: [0335] 70459) Delightful stone cottage which has just been tastefully renovated to accommodate 4 people very comfortably, overlooking large lawn that is bordered by a bubbling stream.

"VISIT THE BEAUTIFUL DOVE, CHURNET AND MANIFOLD VALLEYS".

ASHBOURNE near. Throwley Moor Farm and Throwley Cottage, Ilam, Near Ashbourne. Working farm. Self catering accommodation in farmhouse and cottage on this beef and sheep farm near Dovedale and Manifold Valley. Within easy reach of Stately Homes and places of historic interest. An ideal touring centre. The cottage accommodates seven people and the farmhouse 12. Ample toilet facilities; sittingrooms and diningroom (kitchen/diner in cottage). Electric cookers and fridges. Pets permitted. Car essential — parking. Available all year; terms according to season. Guests must supply own linen. Nearest shops three miles away. SAE, please, for further details to **Mrs M. A. Richardson, Throwley Hall Farm, Ilam, Near Ashbourne DE6 2BB (Waterhouses [053-86] 202/243).**

ASHBOURNE near. Yew Tree Farm, Alstonefield, Near Ashbourne. Yew Tree Farmhouse is an attractive 17th century farmhouse with original fireplaces and beams etc. It is ideally situated for touring the Peak District and visiting Alton Towers, as it stands on the edge of the unspoilt village of Alstonefield. There is a large garden with ample parking space and an adjoining field and stable suitable for guests to bring ponies. Accommodation for five in two family bedrooms; cot; bathroom, toilet; sittingroom and diningroom; electric kitchen. Children and pets welcome. Car essential. Shops 200 yards. Open all year. Terms on request. **Mr and Mrs K. W. Griffin, Coldwall Farm, Okeover, Ashbourne DE6 2BS (Thorpe Cloud [033-529] 249).**

ASHBOURNE. Mrs J. A. Gray, Hayes Farm, Biggin, Hullandward, Derby DE6 3FJ (Ashbourne [0335] 70204). Working farm, join in. Relax in our peaceful valley. Superb bungalow on small dairy farm. Panoramic views of unspoilt countryside. Join in farm activities. The bungalow has its own garage, lawns and garden. It is 70 yards from farmhouse and buildings. There is a utility room with washing machine, separate toilet, pantry, modern fitted kitchen, split level electric cooker, Rayburn (free coal), diningroom, lounge, colour TV; bathroom with toilet; two double bedrooms and one twin bedded room. Close to Peak District, Matlock Bath, Dovedale, Chatsworth House and other stately homes. Terms from £65 to £98 per week, all year.

If you've found FARM HOLIDAY GUIDE of service please tell your friends

Derbyshire SELF-CATERING

BAKEWELL. Mrs Birkhead and Mrs Philps, Castle Cliffe Private Hotel, Monsal Head, Bakewell DE4 1NL (Great Longstone [062-987] 258). Furnished accommodation available at this private hotel. The flat consists of one double bedroom, bathroom, toilet, all-electric kitchen, sittingroom. Guests are asked to provide own linen. Shopping one mile away. Car essential — parking. Available all year. The flat overlooks Monsal Dale where you can stroll by the grassy banks of the River Wye. Within easy reach of beauty spots such as Haddon Hall (Duke of Rutland), Chatsworth House (Duke of Devonshire), Blue John Caverns at Castleton, Cathedral of the Peak at Tideswell. Sheffield 16 miles, Chesterfield 12 and Buxton nine. Terms on application.

BUXTON. 17 Silverlands, Buxton. Silverlands is just three minutes' walk from the Market Place in Buxton and is a large converted house (three flats) in a cul-de-sac. An ideal base for exploring the caves and caverns of Derbyshire, the Dove and Manifold Valleys, Haddon Hall, Chatsworth House and Buxton's own Pavilion Gardens, with swimming, dancing, children's playground, miniature railway and 20 acres of beautiful gardens. The flats sleep four to seven people and are fully equipped except linen (can be hired). Toilet facilities. Sitting/diningrooms and kitchen with electric cooker, fridge, TV. Small dogs allowed. Parking. Terms from £60 weekly. Electricity metered. SAE, please, to **Mrs D. Goodwin, "Winley Way," Heathcote, Hartington, Near Buxton SK17 0AY (Hartington [029-884] 478).**

CASTLETON (Peak National Park). Harry Eyre Cottage, Spring House Farm, Castleton. 17th century farm cottage, recently restored to a high standard. Central heating. Fully equipped, including linen, for up to six people. One double and one twin-bedded room; two bathrooms; kitchen/diner; lounge. Pets permitted by arrangement only. Children welcome. Ample parking. Private terrace with view to Mam Torr — 'The Shivering Mountain'. Open all year. Terms £65 to £135 (excluding electricity and heating). Also luxury 30 ft. caravan in private position on farm, with superb views. Mains water (flush WC) and electricity. Equipped to high standard (including linen) for up to six people. April to October £60 to £90, inclusive of heating, lighting, cooking, etc. Off season by arrangement. The farm lies half mile from A625, in the beautiful Hope Valley. **Mrs C. Bell, Spring House Farm, Castleton S30 2WB (Hope Valley [0433] 20962).**

DERBY. Dovedale Farm and Country Holidays. Visit the beautiful Dove, Churnet and Manifold Valleys. Excellent farmhouse accommodation and self-catering holidays. See also Display Advertisement in the Board and Self-Catering sections of this Guide.

MATLOCK. Meadow Cottage, Low Moor, Pikehall, Matlock. Working farm. This semi-detached cottage is situated on owners' 300-acre farm between four market towns in the centre of the Derbyshire Dales. Good walking area. Nature Trails half-a-mile. Many historical houses in the area including Chatsworth and Haddon Hall. The cottage has fitted carpets throughout and lawned garden with parking space. Milk and eggs may be purchased from the farm daily. Accommodation for five in two double and one single rooms, cot; bathroom, toilet; sitting/diningroom. Kitchen has sink unit, fridge, electric cooker, kettle and water heater (10p meter). Pets permitted. Car essential — parking. Available all year. SAE, please, for terms to **Mrs M. Bunting, Low Moor, Pikehall, Matlock DE4 2PP (Parwich [033-525] 234).**

SHEFFIELD near. Mrs A. H. Kellie, Shatton Hall Farm, Bamford, Near Sheffield S30 2BG (Hope Valley [0433] 20635). Working farm. Paddock Cottage is attached to Shatton Hall Farm and has an east-facing terrace and its own car park. In the heart of the Peak District it faces away from the farm, and has lovely views. The modern conversion combines character and convenience; a bar kitchen is part of the living area with a wood burning stove — fuel provided. There are two double bedrooms, a double put-u-up and a cot available. Night storage heaters included in rent but electricity metered for cooker and immersion heater. Sleeps six. Children welcome, also well controlled pets. Duvets supplied. Car essential and there is parking for two cars. Open all year round. Terms range from £50 weekly in low season to £140 in high season.

PLEASE SEND A STAMPED ADDRESSED ENVELOPE WITH ENQUIRIES

DERBYSHIRE – PEAK DISTRICT AND DALES!

The undulating dales set against the gritstone edges of the Pennine moors give Derbyshire its scenic wealth. In the tourists' itinery should be the prehistoric monument at Arbor Low, the canal port of Shardlow, the country parks at Elvaston and Shipley, the limestone caves at Creswell Crags and Castleton and the market towns of Ashbourne and Bakewell. For walkers this area provides many excellent opportunities.

SELF-CATERING Devon 409

DEVON

APPLEDORE. Mariner's Cottage, Irsha Street, Appledore. Elizabethan fisherman's cottage right at the sea edge — the high tide laps against the garden wall. Extensive open sea and estuary views of ships, lighthouses, fishing and sailing boats. The quayside, rocky beach, shops, restaurants and fishing trips are all close by. Riding, sailing, tennis, golf, sandy beaches, historic houses and beautiful coastal walks, and the Country Park, are all near. Mariner's Cottage (an historic listed building), sleeps six, plus baby, in three bedrooms and has a modern bathroom, fitted kitchen, diningroom and large lounge with colour TV. A modern gas fire makes Mariner's good for winter holidays. From £30 per week. Picture shows view from garden. SAE, please, for brochure of this and other cottages to **F. A. Baxter, Boat Hyde, Northam, Bideford, N. Devon or 'phone (Bideford [023-72] 73801) for prices and vacancies.**

ASHBURTON. Mr and Mrs G. E. D. Ross, East Burne Farm, Bickington, Newton Abbot TQ12 6PA (Bickington [062-682] 496). This 17th century farmhouse, in a peaceful, sunny valley, is an ideal centre for touring, walking, riding, fishing, golf, etc. or just relaxing. It has a heated 16' × 32' swimming pool and a wealth of bird and plant life as well as friendly farm animals — calves, sheep, hens and dogs. The three self-catering units, sleeping two-seven, have been converted from old farm buildings. All are clean, comfortable and equipped to a very high standard, with colour TV, fridges, electric cookers etc. Kester has two double and two single bedrooms. The Pound has two double bedrooms (and no stairs) and the Old Barn is available with one or two bedrooms, both with en suite facilities. Linen service available. Dogs only by arrangement. Shops three miles. Sea nine miles. Car essential.

ASHBURTON. Mr and Mrs C. A. Coulter, 30 East Street, Ashburton, Newton Abbot TQ13 7AZ (Ashburton [0364] 52589). Ashburton is a small charming town, full of historic interest, situated on edge of Dartmoor, within the bounds of Dartmoor National Park. The Parish of Ashburton is surrounded on three sides by moorland, woods and rolling hills and, to the west, some of the most beautiful reaches of the River Dart. It is near Widecombe-in-the-Moor, Haytor Rock, Becky Falls and many other beauty spots, and within easy reach of Torbay, Teignmouth and other seaside resorts. Flat is fully furnished and carpeted; lounge with colour TV; kitchen/diner; all essentials; two bedrooms (one double and one twin-bedded). Constant hot water to kitchen and bathroom. Completely self-contained. No linen supplied. Pets allowed. Car desirable — parking. Open all year. Shops nearby. SAE, please, for terms.

AXMINSTER. Mrs C. Willoughby, Coaxdon Hall, Axminster (Axminster [0297] 32155). Charming, comfortable and self-contained annexe to country manor house, near Axminster. Set in seven acres of Devonshire countryside with coast six miles. Numerous sporting and recreational facilities nearby. Historically connected with King Charles II. Completely self-contained and fully-equipped, the annexe accommodates four to six in two large double bedrooms; all-electric heating, cooking etc; bathroom, toilet; sitting/diningroom; fully-equipped kitchen. Everything supplied except linen. Tennis court available every day. Ample parking. Shops one-and-a-half miles. Small pets permitted. Open April to end of September. Terms depending on season. Electricity on meters. SAE, please.

AXMINSTER. Laurel Cottage, Smallridge, Axminster. This rebuilt and modernised cottage is adjacent to Devonshire House and has a pretty, secluded garden, bordered by a brook. Situated in the attractive village of Smallridge, two miles from Axminster, within easy reach of the beaches at Seaton, Lyme Regis and Charmouth, it is ideal for exploring Devon, Dorset and Somerset. Accommodation for four in one family bedroom containing two single and two bunk beds; cot and Z-bed downstairs if required; bathroom, two toilets; combined livingroom/diningroom; utility room, kitchen with all-electric appliances, cooker, fridge, iron etc. Fully equipped except for linen. Space and water heated by electricity through 50p meter. Pets accepted. Car essential — garage. Shop and post office nearby; sea 15 minutes' drive. Weekly terms from £20 to £85. All details given on receipt of SAE, please, to **Mrs B. R. Simpson, Devonshire House, Smallridge, Axminster EX13 7LY (Axminster [0297] 32458).**

AXMINSTER. Mrs M. A. Johnson, Trebblehays Farm, Membury, Axminster EX13 7UA (Stockland [040-488] 362). Working farm. Comfortably furnished modern bungalow situated on dairy farm near Devon/Somerset border. Set in beautiful countryside, overlooking River Yarty. Panoramic views. Large fenced garden. One-and-a-half miles from A30. Axminster, Chard, Seaton, Lyme Regis and wildlife park all within easy reach. Good country pub within a few minutes. Five people accommodated in two double bedrooms, plus cot and folding bed. Bathroom, toilet; spacious lounge/diningroom with picture window, open fire, TV. Kitchen/breakfast room with oil-fired Rayburn early/late season, fridge, electric cooker, etc.. electric fire. Fully equipped except for linen. Sorry, no pets. Car essential, parking. SAE, please, for terms.

AXMINSTER. Cider Room Cottage, Hasland Farmhouse, Membury, Axminster. This delightfully converted, thatched cider barn, with exposed beams, adjoins main farmhouse and overlooks the outstanding beauty of the orchards, pools and pastureland, and is ideally situated for touring Devon, Dorset and Somerset. Bathing, golf and tennis at Lyme Regis and many places of interest locally, including Wildlife Park, donkey sanctuary and Ford Abbey. Membury Village, with its post office and stores, trout farm, church and swimming pool is one mile away. The accommodation is of the highest standard with the emphasis on comfort. Two double rooms (sleep five), cot if required; shower room and toilet; sitting/diningroom with colour TV; kitchen with electric cooker, fridge, kettle and iron. Linen supplied if required. Pets by arrangement. Car essential — covered parking. Open all year. Terms on application with SAE, please. Babysitting can be arranged and fresh eggs and vegetables purchased from owners. Apply to **Mr D. A. Steele, Hasland Farm, Membury, Axminster EX13 7JF (Stockland [040-488] 558).**

BARNSTAPLE. Mrs M. Bartlett, Sandick Farm, Swimbridge, Barnstaple EX32 0QZ (Swimbridge [0271] 830243). Working farm. Spacious old type country cottage in secluded situation 200 yards from Sandick Farm, well modernised with own lawn and yard. The 250-acre dairy farm has 70 acres of woodland which is open to visitors. The situation is particularly suitable for country lovers yet five miles from Barnstaple, which has indoor leisure centre, cinema and many other facilities. The local village in Swimbridge has a pub, butcher's shop and general stores and is two miles away. Open all year and accommodates six in two double bedrooms; cot; bathroom, two toilets; sittingroom; diningroom. Car essential, parking. Reductions for out of season holidays. SAE, please, for terms.

BARNSTAPLE. Mrs R. Gard, Brinscombe Farm, Arlington, Barnstaple EX31 4SW (Shirwell [027-182] 529). Working farm. Brinscombe is a 180-acre hill farm peacefully situated and approached by a concrete drive. It is ideally situated for touring the Exmoor National Park and North Devon beaches. Reservoir is two miles away for fishing; riding stables at the next farm. Arlington Court is about one-and-a-half miles — a National Trust property, open to the public. Barnstaple nine miles with Leisure Centre; nearest beach is at Combe Martin — six miles. The house is L-shaped and has been modernised and furnished to a high standard. It is fully carpeted with colour TV; fitted kitchen; coloured bathroom suite. Sleeps six in two family bedrooms; cot; sittingroom and diningroom. Everything supplied except linen. Shop three miles. Open all year. Car essential, ample parking. Personally cleaned between each booking. No pets, please. A comfortable stay and a warm welcome is guaranteed. SAE, please for weekly terms.

BARNSTAPLE. Mrs R. Baxter, Hillcrest, Bowden Twistead, Muddiford, Barnstaple EX31 4HR (Shirwell [027 182] 370). Hillcrest, as the name suggests, is located on a hilltop with magnificent panoramic views across the rolling countryside, sea and distant moorland. The area is perfect for walking, riding (stables nearby), golf (courses at hand) and sea and coarse fishing. For the sun worshipper, seaside resorts and surfing beaches within a 10 mile radius. Barnstaple, about nine miles away has superb shops, with market days, Tuesday and Friday. Shirwell village shop, four miles, has petrol, post office, newspapers, telephone and general stores. Accommodation (self-contained) comprises two twin-bedded rooms, bathroom, separate toilet, large lounge/diner with double bed settee and colour TV. Lounge patio doors lead to patio and guests' private garden. Kitchen with electric cooker, fridge. Cot, high chair if required. Well behaved pets allowed. Car essential — ample parking space. Linen not provided. Details on request.

BARNSTAPLE. Mrs C. M. Wright, Friendship Farm, Bratton Fleming, Barnstaple EX31 4SQ (Parracombe [059 83] 291). Friendship bungalow is quietly situated down a short drive from the farmhouse, in its own garden, and surrounded by fields. There is ample parking space. The farm is situated 12 miles from Barnstaple and Ilfracombe, at the junction of roads B3226 and B3358, within easy reach of the beaches of Woolacombe and Combe Martin. Exmoor is literally on the doorstep. The accommodation comprises three bedrooms (sleeps seven plus cot). Linen not supplied. Lounge with colour TV. Well equipped kitchen/diningroom. Bathroom, laundry room, washing machine. Metered electricity. Weekly terms, low season from £60, high season £105.

BARNSTAPLE. Mrs Andrea Cook, Higher Churchill Farm, East Down, Near Barnstaple EX31 4LT (Shirwell [027-182] 543). Working farm. Holiday accommodation in wing of farmhouse, on 350-acre beef cattle and sheep farm. Guests welcome to walk around the farm and enjoy lovely views over Arlington Court National Trust farmland. Central for beaches and Exmoor. All-electric kitchen, bathroom, large beamed lounge with dining area, colour TV. One double bedroom, one with bunks and single bed. Fully carpeted. Cot, high chair and babysitting available. Milk and clotted cream from our Jersey cow. Free range eggs. Two ponies. Terms inclusive of linen and electricity. Children welcome. No pets. Car essential. SAE, please, for terms and further details.

BARNSTAPLE. Mrs Margaret R. Friend, Brightlycott Farm, Barnstaple (Shirwell [0271-82] 330). Working farm. Wing of delightful 17th century farmhouse accommodating seven/eight persons. Well-equipped and entirely self-contained. Three bedrooms, one with double bed, single bed and cot, one double-bedded room and one with twin beds. Bathroom with flush toilet, immersion heater, airing cupboard. Spacious all-electric kitchen with 50p meter. Lounge with ¾-size Billiard Table, TV. No linen supplied. High standard of cleanliness maintained and personally supervised by Mrs Friend. Ample parking space and large lawns, garage and outside flush toilet. Brightlycott is a large dairy farm with milking parlour, etc., consisting of 250 acres, and only two miles from Barnstaple. National Trust property nearby — Arlington Court, also big Leisure Centre at Barnstaple. Cattle Market and Pannier Market on Tuesdays and Fridays, early closing on Wednesdays. Woolacombe, Ilfracombe, Saunton, Croyde beaches all within easy reach. Exmoor and Dartmoor. Ideal holiday spot. Pony trekking and riding nearby. Dogs allowed if kept under control. SAE for brochure, with details, dates and terms.

BARNSTAPLE. Malt Cottage, Churchill, East Down, Barnstaple. This delightful modernised cottage is set amongst the most glorious countryside overlooking the National Trust Property of Arlington Court, with Exmoor in the distance. The fine and varied beaches of North Devon are within easy reach. The cottage is attached to a small farm where children are welcome to help with sheep, ducks, chickens and Emily. It comprises kitchen/diner with larder off, beamed sittingroom, two double bedrooms, one single, two with washbasins; bathroom with shower and separate toilet. Outside the kitchen door is a walled courtyard for the exclusive use of the cottage. No linen. Details **Mrs A. Mant, Churchill House, Churchill, East Down, Barnstaple EX31 4LT (Shirwell [027-182] 380).**

BARNSTAPLE. Huish Farm, Marwood, Barnstaple. Working farm. This 17th century farmhouse, in a quiet, yet not secluded position is three-and-a-half miles from market town of Barnstaple and five miles from Saunton. A ten-minute walk takes you to Dr Smart's famous gardens with lakes (open to public from March to October). Three spacious double bedrooms (one room contains four beds). Bathroom, separate toilet; sittingroom; large kitchen with all essentials. Carpeted throughout; TV, cot and high chair provided. Plenty of room for children to play. Nine people accommodated. Electricity and VAT included in price. No linen supplied, pets permitted. Car essential, parking. Open March to December. Terms from £75 to £150 weekly. Out of season daily terms £12 per day including electricity and VAT. Fresh milk supplied daily. Apply to **Mrs V. M. Chugg, Valley View, Marwood, Barnstaple (Barnstaple [0271] 43458).**

BARNSTAPLE. Mr and Mrs C. L. Hartnoll, Little Bray House, Brayford, Barnstaple EX32 7QG (Brayford [059-88] 295). Little Bray House is an old farmhouse set in peaceful Exmoor country, only 10 miles from the beautiful North Devon coast. It offers large comfortable self-catering accommodation, sleeping from two to seven people, and each cottage/apartment is fully equipped with TV and private bathroom. Washroom and drying facilities are available. Large gardens, tennis court and one mile trout fishing; also an indoor badminton court, ping pong room and playroom for under fives. Pets welcome. We keep a few animals and can advise about local riding and places to go. Reasonable, fully inclusive prices. No VAT. Duck pond. Amusements for children. SAE, please, for brochure.

BARNSTAPLE. North Devon Holiday Centre, 48 Boutport Street, Barnstaple EX31 1SE (0271) * 76322 (24-hour brochure service) — (0271) 44915 (Tourist Information). With our Free Colour Guides and unbiased recommendation and booking service, we can spoil you for choice in the beautiful unspoilt region around Exmoor and the wide sandy beaches and coves of Devon's Golden Coast. Over 400 selected properties including thatched cottages, working farms, beachside bungalows with swimming pools, luxury manor houses etc. from only £40 per week in Spring and Autumn. First class value assured. See also Full Page Colour Advertisement in this Guide.

Please note that entries marked with an asterisk also have a colour display advert in the colour section in this guide

Devon SELF-CATERING

BARNSTAPLE. Mrs J. Lawson, Smemington Farm, Tawstock, Barnstaple EX31 3JD (Barnstaple [0271] 42485). Self-contained part of this farmhouse to let for self-catering holidays. Own entrance and driveway. In pleasant rural surroundings, one mile from River Taw (fishing available through local angling club). Acommodation for up to six — two double, one single bedrooms; bathroom and toilet; sittingroom; kitchen/diningroom with electric cooker. Night storage heater and immerser. Airing cupboard; spin dryer; fridge; iron; TV. Guests supply own bed linen. Pets allowed. Car essential, parking. Shops three miles. Open April/September with special reductions April, May and September. SAE, please, for terms and details.

BARNSTAPLE near. Mrs J. Tythcott, Churchcombe, Yarnscombe, Near Barnstaple EX31 3NE (Torrington [0805] 23239). Working farm. Churchcombe is a 200-acre farm, the highest point between Exmoor and Dartmoor. Torrington three-and-a-half miles, Instow and many other beaches seven miles. Pony available free. Accommodation in farm cottage for six in two double rooms (with two extra single beds); modern bathroom, shaver point, upstairs toilet; kitchen, electric cooker, fridge, electric water heater; sittingroom with TV; diningroom; electric fire. Completely modernised and fully carpeted. Blankets provided and bed linen for double beds. Metered (10p) electricity. Car essential, ample parking. SAE, please, or telephone for further information.

BARNSTAPLE near. Mrs Veronica M. Ley, Stock Farm, Brayford, Near Barnstaple EX32 7QQ (Brayford [059-88] 498). Working farm, join in. This completely self-contained part of farmhouse is beautifully situated on 170-acre beef and sheep farm in beautiful countryside with lovely views over the moors and along the Bray Valley. Ideal for touring and walking; two miles from Exmoor and seven miles from the sea. Visitors are welcome to join in the working life of the farm. The house has three bedrooms, sleeping seven, all fully carpeted. Fitted electric kitchen/diner. The oak beamed lounge is full of character. Colour TV. Own garden, lawn and drying area. Personally cleaned; bedding available by arrangement. Cot and babysitting. Separate play area for children. Excellent sporting facilities. Terms from £40 to £120. Also seven-berth caravan, all-electric with TV and own shower room. SAE, please. Seaside accommodation also available at Croyde Bay.

BEAWORTHY. Bidlake Barn Cottage, Germansweek, Beaworthy. This is an attractive stone cottage in 70 acres (all of which may be walked over) with sensational views on each side. It is fully modernised and comfortably furnished. Two bedrooms with two single beds in each; spacious sitting/diningroom with TV; immersion heater, night storage heating. Fully fitted electric kitchen. Everything except linen. Dartmoor and the sea both 35 minutes; fishing, trekking available locally. Shops three miles. Sorry, no pets. Open all year. Weekly terms according to season from £35 – £60. Electricity extra. Apply **Mrs Russell, Bidlake Farm, Germansweek, Beaworthy, Devon.**

BEER. 1 and 4 Belmont Terrace, The Causeway, Beer. Situated in a quiet part of the pretty unspoilt fishing village of Beer, the two cottages, built at the turn of the century, sleep seven and nine persons, plus cots. Both have car parking, three and four double bedrooms and colour TV. The sheltered, pebble beach is five minutes' walk down the winding main street. Beach hut and four chairs available as an extra. Nearby there is golf, tennis, riding, sailing and fishing, and a good supply of fresh fish. Boats can be hired and deep sea fishing trips are very popular. Beer is a good centre for visiting Dorset, Somerset, Exmoor and Dartmoor. The cottages are serviced by the owners and are always in good order. Sorry, no pets. Available all year round. Further details from **Mrs P. E. Adams, Two Longwood Lane, Failand, Bristol, Avon BS8 3TQ (Bristol [0272] 393642).**

BIDEFORD. Mrs Veronica Stansfield, Cross House, Fore Street, Northam Near Bideford EX39 1AN (Bideford [02372] 72042). Westward Ho! Northam. Short walk beach, country park, golf course. Cross House is an historic 18th century listed building that provides ideal accommodation for family holidays. The wing has exposed beams, inglenook fireplace and original slate floor in the livingroom. Accommodates seven in three bedrooms. The Cottage accommodates two adults and one child. Ample parking, secluded garden with barbecue. Colour TV. Pets welcome. Cot and high chair available. Use of washing machine. Rental of wing includes central heating which is run at owners' discretion. Weekly terms: Cottage £35 to £75; wing £80 to £180. Contact for further details.

FUN FOR ALL THE FAMILY IN DEVON

Babbacombe Model Village, Torquay; *Beer Modelrama*, Beer, near Seaton; *Dart Valley Steam Railway*, Buckfastleigh; *Torbay & Dartmouth Steam Railway*, Paignton; *Bicton Gardens*, East Budleigh, near Budleigh Salterton; *Grand Western Horseboat Trips*, Tiverton; *The Shire Horse Centre*, Dunstone, Yealmpton, near Plymouth; *Farway Countryside Park*, near Honiton; *Dartmoor Wildlife Park*, Sparkwell, near Plymouth; *Paignton Zoo*, Totnes Road, Paignton; *Plymouth Aquarium*, Plymouth Hoe, Plymouth; *Exeter Maritime Museum*, The Quay, Exeter; *Torbay Aircraft Museum*, Higher Blagdon, near Paignton; *Exmoor Brass Rubbing Centre*, The Smuggler's Den, Queen Street, Lynton; *Dartington Glass*, Linden Close, off School Lane, Torrington; *Yelverton Paperweight Centre*, Leg O'Mutton Corner, Yelverton; *Kents Cavern*, Ilsham Road, Wellswood, Torquay.

BIDEFORD. Webbery Cottages, Webbery, Alverdiscott, Bideford. Once the home farm and stables of the old Manor of Webbery, our architect-designed conversions of farm buildings offer a high degree of modern comfort and luxury. In a courtyard setting at centre of private five-acre grounds with views extending to Exmoor, Bideford Bay and Lundy Island, two all-electric two-bedroom cottages, plus one oil centrally heated three-bedroom cottage. All tastefully furnished. Colour TV. Fitted carpets. Fridges. Cot available. Separate laundry room. Ample parking. Fresh farm produce in season. Quietly situated between market towns of Bideford and Barnstaple. Beaches, birdwatching, fishing, golf, riding, sailing, surfing, walks nearby. No VAT. Also Mini-Breaks/Weekends. Brochure with pleasure. **Mrs Pamela Andrews, The Garden Cottage, Webbery, Alverdiscott, Bideford EX39 4PU (Newton Tracey [027-185] 430).**

BIDEFORD. Mr and Mrs A. Hooper and Mr J. F. Hooper, Riversdale, Weare Giffard, Bideford EX39 4QR (Bideford [023-72] 72479). "Riversdale" is situated at the southern end of the picturesque village of Weare Giffard, four miles from Bideford. The original farmhouse and barns have been carefully converted to provide self-catering accommodation; each of the four fully-furnished dwellings are completely self-contained having electricity, gas cooking, fridges, linen and colour TV; some being close carpeted throughout. The village is ideally situated for visiting the North Devon beauty spots and coastal resorts. We offer private game fishing on a mile of the River Torridge, one of Devon's loveliest rivers. Golf is available within a mile. Post Office and gift shop on site. Adequate parking on the premises in this beautiful wooded valley. SAE, please, for brochure and details.

BIDEFORD. Rendles Down, Monkleigh, Bideford. Working farm. Rendles Down is on its own, full of character, spacious yet cosy, and with all modern conveniences. It has a garden and ample parking space and is well equipped for nine. Surrounded by fields and woods, the farm overlooks the picturesque village of Weare Giffard in the Torridge Valley. Within easy reach of sandy beaches, Exmoor, Dartmoor and all the facilities available to tourists in North Devon. Situated quarter of a mile from Bideford to Torrington main road and one mile north east of Monkleigh. Double and twin-bedded rooms; bathroom, toilet; sittingroom; diningroom. Electricity for cooking. Electric heating, also coal/log fire. Telephone. Linen supplied if required. Children welcome. Pets by arrangement only. Car essential. Open all year; mid-week bookings accepted September to April. Terms from £60 to £160 weekly. Logs supplied free. Apply **Mrs G. Beer, Ley, Monkleigh, Bideford EX39 5JZ (Bideford [02372] 73336).**

BIGBURY BAY. Waves Edge, Challaborough, Bigbury Bay. Waves Edge is a detached four-bedroom bungalow in a magnificent position overlooking the sea. It is situated in nearly half an acre of lawned garden leading on to a low cliff with direct access to the sandy beach. It is well-equipped, centrally heated, attractively furnished, sleeping eight guests. Ample parking. No pets. Advantageous terms May and September. Challaborough is part of a beautiful coastline including superb sandy beaches such as Bigbury, Bantham, Thurlestone, Hope Cove and Wonwell. Walkers can explore for miles along scenic cliffs and nearby is Thurlestone Golf Course. Surf, sail, swim and fish to your heart's content. SAE **Mrs. C. Cooper, 1 St Ronans, Middle Warberry Road, Torquay TQ1 1RP (Torquay [0803] 23493).**

BIGBURY near. Buckleys Harraton, Modbury. Buckleys Harraton is a large country cottage situated on Plymouth-Kingsbridge main road, near Modbury, five miles from sandy beaches of Bigbury Bay. Within easy reach Cornwall (15 miles), Dartmoor (10 miles). Four bedrooms. Sleeps eight/10 (studio couch). Darts, snooker, piano. Open fire. Also small bungalow nearby, with garden. Three bedrooms. Sleeps six. Saturday bookings. Also main part of Bennicke Farmhouse (self-contained) in peaceful situation reached by a lane, quarter mile from road. Garden. Three bedrooms, sleeps eight. Sunday bookings. All have mains water, electricity and TV. Well-behaved dogs allowed. Linen is not provided. SAE for details. Terms £75 to £128 weekly. No VAT. **Miss C. M. Hodder, Bennicke Farm, Modbury, Near Ivybridge PL21 0SU (Modbury [0548] 830265).**

DEVON – ENDLESS CHOICES!

People never tire of visiting Devon. There's so much to do, like visiting Alscott Farm Museum, Berry Head Country Park, Bickleigh Mill Farm, Farway Countryside Park, Haytor Granite Railway, Kent's Cavern, Dartmoor National Park and of course Plymouth and its Hoe.

Devon SELF-CATERING

BRAUNTON. Mrs E. A. L. Fowler, Boode Farm, Braunton EX33 2NN (Barnstaple [0271] 812227). Boode Cottages are a pair of adjoining, semi-detached cottages situated on the farm, one mile from Braunton, with good shopping facilities, and three miles from the famous beach and golf club at Saunton. Well situated for exploring north Devon's many beaches, seaside and market towns and the Exmoor countryside. There are also attractive walks on the farm itself. The cottages are self contained but very suitable for two families wanting to holiday together. One cottage: three twin rooms to sleep six people; other cottage: one double, one twin, one child's room to sleep five people; bathroom; well equipped kitchen/diningroom and comfortable sittingroom with French windows opening onto a small, sunny garden. Some central heating, power points in all rooms. Fully equipped except towels and bed linen. Car essential — parking. Pets permitted. Open March to December. Terms from £40 to £120 weekly.

BRAUNTON. Mrs Jean M. Barnes, Denham Farm, North Buckland, Braunton EX33 1HY (Croyde [0271] 890297). Working farm, join in. A newly converted, self-contained cottage adjoining main farmhouse, situated in the heart of a small hamlet. Very high standard of accommodation, very spacious. Sleeps six plus. Three bedrooms, one bathroom, kitchen, diningroom, sittingroom with extra double bed settee if required. Colour TV. Electricity on meter. Two garages available. Evening Meals provided at farmhouse if required. Visitors are allowed to take part in farming activities and there is ample room for children to play. Linen supplied at extra charge.

BRAUNTON near. Mr and Mrs H. C. Hammond, Upcott Farm, Nethercott, Near Braunton EX33 1HT (Braunton [0271] 814195). Working farm. Who could resist a holiday in this delightful Elizabethan style cottage where interesting features of "yesterday" have been preserved? With its old world frontage, small walled lawn and forecourt and walled yard on the east side, it is set in 120 acres of farmland carrying sheep and cattle. Central for touring with Georgian village approximately one mile away. Braunton two-and-a-half miles, the sea three miles. Fully furnished accommodation for six in two double rooms, with double and single beds in each, and one single room. Cot, high chair; sittingroom; diningroom; bathroom, toilet; fully equipped kitchen. Electric meter. Sorry, no pets. Parking — car essential. Linen not supplied. Shops one-and-a-half miles. SAE, please, for terms.

BRAUNTON near. Mrs L. M. Bowden, Pickwell Manor Farm, Georgeham, Near Braunton EX33 1LA (0271-870205). Working farm. Situated on a cattle and sheep farm in the quiet hamlet of Pickwell, Holmelea cottages are large, roomy and well appointed with ample parking and garden. Lundy Cottage, chalet and flats are recent modern conversions of well-built stone stables and coach houses with parking and field for play area, also table tennis room. All face South with views over farmland extending out to sea as far as Lundy Island and Hartland Point. Woolacombe Bay with three miles of safe, golden sands is one half mile, 20 minutes' walk across the fields. Shop, Post Office, pubs, etc., one mile away in village of Georgeham. Accommodation for four/eight people, two/three double bedrooms, cots. Bathroom, toilet. All electric kitchen. No linen. Open April—November. Terms on application.

BUCKFASTLEIGH. Mrs L. A. Astley, Summersbridge Cottage, Higher Coombe, Buckfastleigh (Buckfastleigh [0364] 42388). Dartmoor National Park — olde worlde country cottage, fully modernised, picturesque. Electric. TV. Fridge. Sleeps five. Parking. Pets permitted. Buckfastleigh is a small town on fringe of Dartmoor. Nearby is Buckfast Abbey and Dart Bridge. The Dart Valley Steam Railway is of interest to all ages. Within easy reach Torbay.

CHITTLEHAMPTON. Mrs N. M. Bendle, South Bray, Chittlehampton, Umberleigh EX37 9QT (Chittlehamholt [076 94] 239). Working farm. South Bray is a 150-acre dairy and sheep farm, situated in peaceful, scenic countryside within easy reach of Exmoor National Park and North Devon's beaches. Accommodation is in half of our spacious, traditional stone farmhouse, completely self-contained with guests' own lawn, garages and entrances. It comprises four double bedrooms (plus cots and extra beds as required), bathroom, large lounge/diner with TV and fully-equipped kitchen, with fridge, freezer, washing machine and walk-in larder. Facilities for children include a large lawn, swing, picnic table and table-tennis room. All amenities, plus fresh farm milk, are included in the price; reductions are offered for low-season holidays. Linen not provided. Available April to October.

PLEASE ENCLOSE A STAMPED ADDRESSED ENVELOPE WITH ENQUIRIES

THE HELPFUL HOLIDAY AGENCY

will help you choose and book from over 400 cottages, houses, flats and bungalows all over Devon, Cornwall and Somerset. Many are on farms – very close to the sea and in the beautiful wooded valleys around the high Moors. At some you can help on the farm; to some you can bring your own horse/pony. Some are lovely inside, some fairly basic (but cheap). In our free colour brochure we tell you what all of them, and their surroundings, are REALLY like, snags and all; and we advise further on the telephone.

Su and Euan Bowater, Helpful Holidays Ref. 1., Coombe, Chagford, Devon TQ13 8DF.
Tel: (06473) 3593/2478 (24 hrs) Telex: 42513

COLYTON near. Mrs M. Chichester, Wiscombe Park, Southleigh, Near Colyton (Farway [040-487] 252/344). Self-contained flats to let in a country mansion; also Whitmoor Cottage. The Mansion stands in its own grounds of 600 acres, in an area of outstanding natural beauty. The land and trout farm are farmed by the family and there are many animals around including working Shire Horses. Ideal for children and those who like country life, but not for those who prefer to be near urban amenities. Easily accessible, being only two miles from A3052 and not far from A30. Car essential for exploring the many places of interest within easy reach, such as Dartmoor and Exmoor, sea at Beer and Branscombe four miles; Sidmouth six. Lovely walks, but golf, riding, fishing and tennis are easy to come by. Well-behaved pets welcome. Flats sleep two-nine people and are completely self-contained, well equipped and comfortably furnished. The self-contained part of Whitmoor Cottage sleeps eight to 10. All rooms face south. Further details on request. See also Colour Display Advertisement. *

COLYTON. Mrs S. Gould, Bonehayne Farm, Colyton EX13 6SG (Farway [040-487] 396). Working farm. Bonehayne Farm, situated in the beautiful Coly Valley amidst 250-acres working farmland on the banks of the River Coly. Daffodils are quite a feature in Springtime. Mallard Duck and Kingfishers too are a common sight. Trout fishing freely available and woodlands to explore. This is an annexe of the farmhouse, completely modernised and tastefully furnished with fitted carpets to accommodate up to six persons. Two double bedrooms and one with bunk beds. Lounge with colour TV and inglenook fireplace containing large wood burner which also runs the central heating system, making it really ideal for out of season holidays at no extra cost. Kitchen/diningroom with electric cooker, fridge, electricity by meter; bathroom, and toilet; cot and babysitting available. Fully equipped except linen. Parking space. The sea four miles. Weekly terms on application.

COLYTON. Mrs C. E. Pady, Horriford Farm, Colyford, Colyton EX13 6HW (Colyton [0297] 52316). Working farm. Horriford Farmhouse lies at the end of a winding Devon Lane, near a ford. The wing of the farmhouse is let, fully furnished — four bedrooms, sleeping seven. Easter to end of October. Many original features remain in this ancient house. An oak screen passage, mullion windows, inglenook fireplace with bread oven, newel staircase, oak beams. Close to the sea, yet in secluded valley deep in the peaceful countryside. Walks with fine views close to the farm which is an all-grass dairy farm in an area of outstanding natural beauty. A herd of 80 Friesian and Guernsey cows is kept. Visitors are welcome to watch farming activities. Seaton one-and-a-half miles; Beer two miles; Lyme Regis and Sidmouth six miles; Exeter 22 miles. A good base to explore unspoilt East Devon. Two-bedroom cottage also available 20 yards from farmhouse. SAE for details and terms.

Please note that entries marked with an asterisk also have a colour display advert in the colour section in this guide

Devon   SELF-CATERING

COMBE MARTIN. Self contained holiday flats with mains services, flush toilets, bathrooms and full size cookers. Adequate blankets and pillows; electric or gas fires, electric irons, fridges and TVs. Half-a-minute from beaches and shops at Combe Martin. Free parking. Children are welcome; cots available. Well-behaved dogs accepted. Everything provided except linen. Accommodation for two to eight persons. Available all year. Moderate terms. Reductions for Spring and Autumn holidays. Central for touring. Putting, tennis, golf, within easy distance. Combe Martin has the appeal of a small coastal village and is the gateway to Exmoor National Park; while Ilfracombe (five miles away) is North Devon's premier resort. AA recommended and English Tourist Board Standards. SAE, please, to **Mr D. Ainsworth, Sun Ray, Moory Meadow, Combe Martin EX34 0DG (Combe Martin [027-188] 2180).**

COMBE MARTIN. "Lynton Cottage," Victoria Street, Combe Martin. This picturesque country cottage stands in its own ground in the main village street, an ideal area for touring. Woolacombe 10 miles; Ilfracombe five miles. The sea is five minutes by car or a 20 minutes' walk. Shops in the village. The cottage can accommodate eight to nine people in four double rooms, one with extra single bed; three bedrooms with hot and cold water; cot available; bathroom and toilet (one inside, one outside); two sitting-rooms with TV; diningroom; fully equipped kitchen with double sink unit, gas cooker (50p meter), and fridge. Everything supplied except linen. Fully furnished, with fitted carpets and very easy stairs. Electricity, immersion heater, electric fires — 10p meter. Parking space nearby. Open all year. SAE, please, for brochure to **Mrs D. Smallridge, Thorns Cottage, Victoria Street, Combe Martin (Combe Martin [0271-88] 2270).**

CREDITON. Mrs Joyce M. Venner, Thornton, Washford Pyne, Crediton EX17 4QZ (Tiverton [0884] 860253). Charming thatched country cottage situated in its own grounds in a small, quiet hamlet midway between the north and south Devon coasts, near Exmoor and Dartmoor. The Cottage, personally supervised, is fully equipped for six people. Double, single and family bedrooms (carpeted), plus cot. Comfortable sittingroom has hearth fire and TV. Kitchen/diner with electric cooker, iron; kettle, fridge, water heater, larder, also a Rayburn. Linen not supplied. Bathroom, toilet. Large lawn and plenty of parking space near quiet road — car essential. Shops and public transport two and a half miles. Children welcome and are invited to walk over the farm. Dogs by prior arrangement. Available April to October. Reasonable terms. Further details on request with SAE, please.

CROYDE BAY. "Palma Villa" and "Lucerne," Leadengate Close, Croyde Bay. Superior detached holiday bungalows, nearest possible to the sand dunes, and golden sandy beach, yet only a few minutes from the olde world village. Highly recommended, each has a private lawned garden, patio and ample parking space. The sitting-rooms are most pretty and individually designed. Furnished to a high standard. Bathroom, some with separate toilet; bedrooms with washbasins; heating in all rooms. Free television. Open March to December. Small dogs allowed. Fully illustrated photographed brochure sent. Terms from £30 weekly, no VAT. Apply to **Mrs J. Lawson Steer, "Lime Grove," 47 Saunton Road, Braunton EX33 1HD (Braunton [0271] 812074).**

CULLOMPTON. Mrs D. Tucker, Woodbeare House Farm, Plymtree, Cullompton EX15 2DD (Plymtree [088-47] 256). Working farm. This accommodation is homely and part of the owner's own home. Self-contained and private, it is set in lovely unspoilt countryside with the Blackdown Hills in the background. Enjoy the freedom of the farm. It is an excellent touring centre for Exmoor, Dartmoor. Golf, fishing, riding nearby. The M5 and Cullompton three miles; Honiton, Exeter nine; Sidmouth and Exmouth 12. Registered with English Tourist Board. Accommodation for 10 in three bedrooms; bathroom with toilet; diningroom. All-electric kitchen. Linen not supplied. Children welcome. Car essential — parking. SAE, please, for terms.

CULLOMPTON. Beechgrove, Symonsburrow, Hemyock, Cullompton. This bungalow, set in the beauty of the Blackdown Hills on the Devon/Somerset border close to the Wellington monument, is comfortably furnished for six people. Accommodation comprises two double and one single bedrooms; bathroom/toilet; sitting/diningroom; kitchen equipped with electric cooker. Linen for hire. Electricity by 10p meter. Colour TV. Car essential with ample parking with easy access to private drive. Ideally situated for touring, being central to north and south Devon coastlines (approximately 25 miles to beach), On the farm itself there are family pets for the children to see and spacious garden with patio suite. Lots of beautiful country walks in the surrounding area and riding stables nearby. Cot and high chair available free. Open from April to October. Controlled pets welcome. **Mrs R. M. Parsons, Great Symonsborough Farm, Hemyock, Cullompton EX15 3XA (Hemyock [0823] 680494).**

PLEASE SEND A STAMPED ADDRESSED ENVELOPE WITH ENQUIRIES

DEVON'S GOLDEN COAST
Cottages – Bungalows – Houses

We offer the widest selection of superior self-catering accommodation of the highest standard for 2-13 persons in Combe Martin, Ilfracombe, Woolacombe, Croyde, Instow, Westward Ho!, and throughout North Devon. All properties personally inspected/supervised; virtually all with colour TV; most within walking distance of sandy beaches; several with washing machines and telephones.

Free colour brochure from:
**MARSDEN'S HOLIDAYS, Dept. FHG, Croyde, North Devon EX33 1NF.
Tel. (0271) 890479.** *Member of the West Country Tourist Board*

CULLOMPTON. Mrs P. J. Gibbins, Hethen Hill Farm, Clyst Hydon, Cullompton EX15 2NF (Plymtree [088-47] 432). Self-contained wing of a large, impressive farmhouse is tastefully furnished and can accommodate up to eight visitors in three spacious bedrooms. The modern kitchen is equipped with fridge, electric cooker and automatic washing machine. Ample toilet facilities; sittingroom/diner. Cutlery, crockery, cooking utensils provided. Guests welcome to use heated swimming pool set in natural sun trap, with paddling area for small children. Also attractive garden in which to relax. Hethen Hill Farm is a dairy farm located in the peaceful village of Clyst Hydon. Visitors can savour the olde worlde feeling and atmosphere of this traditional village with its beautiful church and 16th century thatched inn. SAE for terms and details.

DARTMOOR. Mr G. B. Thompson, Bly House, Chagford TQ13 8BW (Chagford [064-73] 2404). Stable Cottage is an attractive cottage of character recently converted from the stables and coach house of Bly House Hotel (see Hotels section). Although less than five minutes' walk from the village, it is in a quiet, rural position on the slopes of Nattadon Hill with views of Dartmoor. Access to the moor from Hotel grounds. Large kitchen/diner with new fitted units, electric cooker, refrigerator, automatic washing machine. Spacious lounge with wood-burning stove, colour TV, French windows. Two bedrooms — one with double and single bed, one with twin beds. Washbasin, shaver points in both rooms. New bathroom. Fitted carpets. Electric radiators. Towels/linen not supplied. Electricity by meter reading. Dogs welcome, but no cats, please. Ample parking.

DARTMOOR (Edge of). Bungalow sleeping six/seven persons available from March to October in this area of great natural beauty — woods, rivers, rocky Tors. Prehistoric remains and ancient crosses are frequently found, while stone circles near the source of the river Teign (Grey Wethers) near Gidleigh and the enclosure of Grimspound near Postbridge are particularly notable. Bungalow has three double bedrooms; bathroom, toilet; sittingroom. Electricity for cooking and heating (slot meter). Children are welcome, but regret, no pets. Car essential — parking. Shops three miles. Terms from £39 to £139 weekly. Apply **Mr John Fowler, John Fowler Holidays, Dept. 23, Marlborough Road, Ilfracombe [Ilfracombe [0271] 66667].**

Terms quoted in this publication may be subject to increase if rises in costs necessitate

418 Devon SELF-CATERING

DARTMOOR. Mrs Angela Bell, Wooder Farm, Widecombe-in-the-Moor, Near Ashburton TQ13 7TR (Widecombe-in-the-Moor [036-42] 391). Working farm. Modernised granite cottages and converted coach house on 108-acre working family farm nestled in the picturesque valley of Widecombe, surrounded by unspoilt woodland, moors and granite Tors. Three-quarters of a mile from village with post office, general stores, inn, church and National Trust Information Centre. Excellent centre for touring Devon with a variety of places to visit as well as exploring Dartmoor by foot or on horseback. Accommodation is for two to seven. Facilities include electric cooker, fridge, electric kettle and fires, colour TV; laundry room, airing cupboards, fitted carpets, cot, high chair, ironing board, iron, ample crockery and utensils; blankets. Everything except linen provided. Large gardens and courtyard. Easy parking. Children welcome. Electricity metered. Open all year, so take advantage of off-season reduced lets. Weekend lets also available. SAE, please, for brochure.

DARTMOOR NATIONAL PARK. Mrs Sue Booty, Rogues Roost Farm, Poundsgate, Ashburton TQ13 7PS (Poundsgate [036-43] 223). Working farm, join in. Two self-catering units available at Rogues Roost, a working farm of 100 acres. Situated in the Dartmoor National Park; ideal for riding, walking and fishing and within easy reach of many places of interest. Torbay is 22 miles away; Exeter and Plymouth 25. Visitors may join in the farm activities. The first unit, part of a large farmhouse, sleeps eight. Accommodation comprises four bedrooms, bathroom, two toilets, large sittingroom with log fire, diningroom/kitchen. Open Easter to October. The second unit is a bungalow to sleep four; two double bedrooms; sittingroom; diningroom; bathroom, separate toilet; kitchen with electric cooker, fridge. Cot or child's bed available. Dogs by prior arrangement. Car essential. Farm produce. Terms include bed linen and hot water. SAE, please.

DARTMOUTH. Mrs M. E. Turner, Higher North Mill, Hansel, Dartmouth TQ6 0LN (Stoke Fleming [0803] 770219). Working farm. Set on the bank of the River Gara, one of the most beautiful parts of England, Higher North Mill is surrounded by lovely country; river runs through the grounds with small brown trout for the fisherman. From March to November, two interesting self-contained properties are available — MILL COTTAGE, in a sunny position by the river has two double bedrooms and one with bunk beds; cot; bathroom; open-plan living/dining/kitchen area. BUNTINGS, bottom floor of the Mill, consists of one double bedroom, one with two single beds; cot; living/diningroom with views down to the river. Both properties have well-equipped kitchens, cooker, fridge, etc (50p meter for electricity). Bed linen, but not towels provided. Within easy distance — Slapton Sands, the sea, many sandy coves, cliff walks, fabulous walking, riding; miles of country and pretty villages to explore; attractive pubs. Go sailing, fishing, golfing, river boat trips. Steam railway, castles, houses, gardens, caves, craft centres to visit. Also two double bedrooms in Mill House for Bed and Breakfast, or extension to the cottages. Brochure and terms on request.

DARTMOUTH near. Mrs B. S. Wall, Lower Fuge Farm, Strete, Near Dartmouth TQ6 0LL (Stoke Fleming [0803] 770541). A holiday here at Fuge can be peaceful, with picturesque farm walks. We have a 240-acre dairy farm; sheep, calves, goats. We are one mile from Strete village, two miles from two pretty beaches, Blackpool and Slapton. This completely self-contained part of a farmhouse has two family and one double, fully carpeted bedrooms, sleeping 10 (cots available). Linen provided and beds ready made. Nice bathroom. Fitted electric kitchen/diner with fridge/freezer, tumble dryer, Kenwood Chef, high chairs. Lounge is large, fully carpeted with three piece suite, easy chairs, colour TV. Garden with spacious lawn for playing/sunbathing. Electricity metered. Car essential. Ample parking. Pets allowed by prior arrangement. Further details on request.

DARTMOUTH near. Mrs M. J. Britton, Little Coombe Farm, Dittisham, Near Dartmouth TQ6 0JB (Dittisham [080-422] 240). Working farm. Little Coombe Farm Cottage nestles alongside the farmhouse which is one of the oldest in the district. Lovely views across ponds, down towards the ancient village of Dittisham and from high grounds views of Dartmoor, Torbay and Dartmouth. The farm has an interesting cross section of animals and poultry, the ponds and adjoining woods abound with wild life. Horse riding, tuition if needed. Slapton and Blackpool bathing beaches close by. Dartmouth, Salcombe and Plymouth a short drive away. The cottage accommodates six people. Two double bedrooms plus put-u-up. Bathroom, toilet; fully fitted kitchen with electric cooker, fridge. Beamed lounge, log fire, colour TV. Cot available. Weekly terms from £85 to £175. Golf, tennis, fishing, bathing all within six miles.

DAWLISH. Brookdale House, 5 Brookdale Terrace, Dawlish. Self-contained flats and flatlets to sleep two-six people. Prime sea front position with shops, buses and trains all within 100 yards. NO HILLS TO CLIMB. Well maintained in decor and furnishings. Each unit has full size cooker, refrigerator, colour television, shower or bath, WC. Carpeted throughout. Full fire alarm system. Special spring and autumn bonanza: all flats £48 for two and £60 for four. Dogs accepted by prior arrangement. Stamp please for brochure. **Mr & Mrs A. Papworth, "Summerlands", 2 Longlands, Dawlish EX7 9NE (Dawlish [0626] 865111).**

When you have read one you *haven't* read them all — we have *eleven* other publications

Edencliffe
Exclusive Apartments
AA APPROVED

Superior accommodation at a peaceful sea-front location with large gardens and private footpath to uncrowded beach-front. Midway between Dawlish and Teignmouth.

The Main Hall

Self-contained flats with private bathrooms. Free colour TV in each flat and free hot water. Free night storage heating for Early and Late Holidays at reduced terms. Lodge and Coach house available all year. Electric cookers and refrigerators. Free car parking. Launderette on site. Bus stop close by. Regret no pets.

Please send large SAE for details to:

Mr and Mrs Patrick-Mitchinson
Edencliffe (Dept. F),
Holcombe, Dawlish EX7 0JW.
(0626 863171)

DAWLISH. Mr and Mrs P. J. Jameson, Shell Cove House, The Old Teignmouth Road, Dawlish EX7 0LA (Dawlish [0626] 862523). Beautiful Georgian country house in unique position, fully furnished and modernised to highest standards, personally maintained by resident proprietors (since 1968) who take pride in a happy family atmosphere. Beautiful views of gardens and sea, three-quarters of a mile from Dawlish, between the coastal road from Exeter to Torquay and the sea. Own timbered grounds of over six acres with private cliff path to Shell Cove which has a lovely secluded beach only otherwise accessible by boat. Large heated swimming and paddling pools; croquet and badminton lawns, tennis court, parking. Good facilities and games for children. Dinghies welcome. Spacious flats; own key, private bathroom, full central heating, colour TV, bed linen, gas cookers, electric fridges. Also TV lounge, games room, laundry room and occasional barbecues. ETB Category 4 (Top Grade) 4 star. See also colour display advertisement. *

DEVON. Large selection of holiday properties in south-east, south, south-west and up to West Midlands and East Anglia. Some suitable for the disabled. Available all year and out of season short breaks. See also quarter page display advertisement under the Kent section of the guide. **Fairhaven Holiday Cottages (Dept. 6), Fairhaven House, 37 Stuart Road, Gillingham, Kent ME7 4AD (Medway [0634] 570157).**

EXETER. Mrs B. Berman, Newhouse Farm, Tedburn St. Mary, Exeter EX6 6AL (Tedburn St. Mary [064-76] 254). **Working farm.** ETB Category four. Self-contained part of 18th-century farmhouse on a 56-acre sheep and soft-fruit farm, on a hillside with beautiful views. Exeter six miles. Ideal for touring Devon and exploring many places of interest. Dartmoor and coast within easy distance. Car essential. Shops, pubs, restaurants one and a half miles. Children very welcome (we have two boys). Visitors may walk anywhere. Sorry, NO PETS. Equipped and comfortably furnished for six. Only personal belongings need be brought. Sitting/diningroom with oak beams, inglenook with wood-burning stove and colour TV. Telephone in units (metered). Three bedrooms with either double or single beds. Continental quilts on all beds. Modern electric kitchen with automatic washing machine. Shower/WC on ground floor. Cot and high-chair available. The rent INCLUDES ELECTRICITY, CENTRAL HEATING, HOT WATER, WOOD, LINEN and TOWELS. Write or phone for leaflet.

Please note that entries marked with an asterisk also have a colour display advert in the colour section in this guide

EXETER. Lower Westcott, Talaton, Exeter. This is a 130-acre mixed farm situated in peaceful countryside half-mile from Talaton Village on the B3176, 12 miles from Exeter City, an excellent shopping centre, five miles Cullompton and Ottery St. Mary, five miles M5 exit 28. Easily accessible East Devon coastal resorts, Dartmoor and Exmoor. Freedom of farm offered to visitors. Fresh eggs available if required. Detached holiday farmhouse offers all year round accommodation for five, three bedrooms, one double, one twin-bedded, one single. Large lounge, TV. Fully equipped electric kitchen. Fitted units, etc. Bathroom with heated towel rail. Fitted carpets. Central heating. Car essential, parking. Play area. Sorry, no pets. SAE for particulars and terms to **Mrs C. H. Down, Westcott Court, Talaton, Exeter EX5 2RN (Whimple [0404] 822394).**

FURSDON HOUSE, CADBURY, NR EXETER, DEVON. (Tel. 0392 860860)

Deep in the Devon countryside – a high standard of self-catering accommodation set in 600 acres of superb scenery. Peaceful and quiet. Working home farm (produce available), fishing, tennis, children's play area, log fires etc. Write or phone for brochure to the Estate Office (Farm Holidays).

Beach and Bracken Exmoor Holidays

From the office beside our Village Inn between Exmoor and the sea we can recommend –

- Farmhouse accommodation with excellent food
- Full range of Inns and Hotels
- Comfortable Self Catering Cottages
- Introductions to all Country Pursuits
- Spring and Autumn Bargains

For advice and free brochure write, ring or call at any time
BEACH and BRACKEN HOLIDAYS (F.H.G.)
White Hart, Bratton Fleming, Barnstaple, Devon EX31 4SA
Tel: Brayford (05988) 702

EXMOOR. Mrs Philippa McCarter, Fernham Farm, Brayford, Near Barnstaple EX32 7QQ (Brayford [059-88] 330). Traditional Devon farmhouse in beautiful secluded position on very attractive 150-acre sheep farm on edge of National Park with River Bray forming one of the boundaries. Lovely views. Fishing in river and on local Reservoir. Excellent riding facilities locally. The small farmhouse flat is well decorated, equipped and furnished, with central and other heating. Electric blankets. Accommodation for four people in one double bedroom; cot; bathroom; toilet; sittingroom with two beds; TV; kitchen with fridge, Calor gas cooker. Linen extra. Pets permitted. Car essential — parking. Small shop one-and-a-half miles away; three miles from other shops. Sea 12/15 miles away. Available March to October. Terms from £50 to £75. Meter for electricity. Numerous good pubs and restaurants within easy reach.

EXMOOR. Farmhouse to accommodate nine to fourteen people. Four double, one single bedrooms; bathroom, two toilets; sittingroom and diningroom. Kitchen has electric cooker, etc. Blankets and pillows provided, but no linen. Children welcome. Pets permitted. Two miles from shops. Car essential for touring this lovely area, now a National Park, and there are many picturesque combes near the Bristol Channel where the "Lorna Doone" country is situated. Wild ponies and red deer are found on Exmoor and an annual pony fair is held at Bampton. Densely wooded Watersmeet Valley (NT) is worth seeing. Farmhouse available from March to October with terms from £59 to £169 weekly. Slot meter for electricity. Apply **Mr John Fowler, John Fowler Holidays, Marlborough Road, Dept. 23, Ilfracombe (Ilfracombe [0271] 66666).**

GEORGEHAM. "Devonair," 27 David's Hill, Georgeham. "Devonair" is a comfortable, modern two-bedroomed bungalow situated in the attractive village of Georgeham which has its own stores, dairy, small post office and village inns. Ideally placed for golf at Saunton and Ilfracombe, the leisure centre in Barnstaple and beautiful sandy beaches at Putsborough, Croyde, Saunton and Woolacombe. The bungalow sleeps six plus cot, has fitted carpets, oil-fired central heating, well equipped kitchen and bathroom, colour television, own drive, lawned garden overlooking surrounding farmland. Available throughout the year. Very sorry, no pets. For further details please contact **Mrs R. P. Kirby, "Alderman's Place," Heath Lane, Woburn Sands, Milton Keynes MK17 8TN (Milton Keynes [0908] 583414).**

HARTLAND. Mrs M. J. Goaman, Hescott Farm, Hartland, Near Bideford EX39 6AN (Hartland [02374] 318). Working farm. Hescott is one of the oldest working farms in the unspoilt parish of Hartland. It comprises of some 300 acres, with mixed cattle, sheep and arable farming. Hartland parish is bounded by the Atlantic on two sides with a number of pretty, secluded beaches along its fine coastline. Breathtaking scenery of Hartland Quay and Clovelly. Guests are welcome around the farm. Pets accepted. Self-contained part of the farmhouse sleeps six, the old barn accommodates six and the old stable the same. Storage heating plus coal fires, electric cookers and fires. Registered with English Tourist Board, ideal for Summer, Autumn, Spring and Winter holidays. Walkers can take the coastal footpath, other activities include angling visits to Tamar Lake. Brochure on request.

HOLSWORTHY. Mr Charles Clarke, Thorne Farm, Holsworthy EX22 7JD (Holsworthy [0409] 253342). Thorne Farm is situated deep in the north Devon countryside and mentioned in the Domesday Book. Some of the old stone farm buildings have been converted into 10 holiday flats and a special effort has been made to combine their character with the comfort and convenience needed in a holiday home. Each of the flats has two bedrooms and contains interior sprung double, single and bunk beds (sleep up to six people). Fully furnished and equipped (except bed linen and towels). Electric cookers, fridges, colour TVs and central heating are provided. Amenities include children's play area, heated 40' × 20' swimming pool, two squash courts, ample car parking (car essential); shop; laundry room and clothes lines. Garden produce available. Newspapers to order. Licensed bar. Games room. Mains water; electricity by 10p and 50p meter. Open from mid-March to mid-November with terms from £57.50 to £200 per week. Pets by prior arrangement. Part of the farm has been set aside as a Nature Reserve and Nature Trails help one find many species of wildlife. Seaside resorts within eight miles, and many smaller beaches within easy reach. SAE, please, for further details.

HONITON. Mrs A. Russell, Godfordland Farm, Awliscombe, Honiton EX14 0PP (Honiton [0404] 2959). This accommodation is situated quarter mile from road with private entrance. Sleeps six in two large bedrooms; large kitchen/diner, sittingroom. Overlooking glorious views of East Devon. Small garden, ample parking. Pets by arrangement. All mod cons. All-electric, meter read. Shopping facilities two and a half miles, Sidmouth 10 miles provides safe bathing. Village with church, pub with good food. Beautiful walks. Good centre for touring — Dartmoor within easy reach and other places of interest. Good train service from Honiton. Car essential. TV hired and babysitting by arrangement. No linen. Open all year round with electric heating. Send SAE for details or telephone **Mrs Russell.**

HONITON. Mrs L. M. Summers, Wessington House, Awliscombe, Honiton EX14 0NU (Honiton [0404] 2280). This holiday cottage at Wessington House is nicely situated in a peaceful part of East Devon, and has its own lawn and excellent rural views. Within easy reach of all East Devon resorts and places of interest, including Dartmoor and Exmoor. Honiton (one mile) with its shops, church and golf course. The cottage is comfortably furnished with carpets and fully equipped kitchen; diningroom; colour TV in lounge; bathroom, toilet; one double and two single bedrooms (five people accommodated). Cot available. There are two open fireplaces and three storage heaters. No linen supplied. Pets permitted. Car essential — parking. Open all year round. SAE, please, for terms.

ILFRACOMBE near. Mrs E. J. Richards, Hole Farm, Berrynarbor, Near Ilfracombe EX34 9SB (Ilfracombe [0271] 65328). Working farm, join in. Spacious traditional farmhouse, with oak beams, on 70-acre working farm, secluded yet easy access to village facilities. Car essential, ample parking. Wonderful play areas for families, a relative sun trap. One and three-quarter miles Ilfracombe town centre, three quarters mile from picturesque village of Berrynarbor, adjacent Ilfracombe Golf Course and overlooking Watermouth Castle and Bristol Channel. Varied local facilities; many places of interest within easy reach. Farmhouse sleeps 12 in four bedrooms; bathroom with bath, toilet, washbasin. Extremely large kitchen; diningroom, lounge. Comfortably furnished and fully equipped. Electric cooker, fridge, airing cupboard, iron, electric fires, colour TV, hot water, electricity included in charge. Cots, babysitting available. Pets welcome. Also caravan, sleeps seven, fully equipped, B/W TV. Separate shower room with toilet, washbasin adjacent to van. No linen either properties. Open May — mid September.

422　Devon　SELF-CATERING

ILFRACOMBE. Golden Coast Holiday Village, Dept. 18, Worth Road, Ilfracombe EX34 8TG (Ilfracombe [0271] 63543). The name of these 20 holiday bungalows conjures up the pleasures to be found in this area. They are delightfully situated in the secluded grounds of a country house overlooking the sea, and the views are magnificent. The bungalows accommodate from two to six persons, and have one double bedroom, one twin bedded room, with cots available, bathroom, inside toilet; combined sitting/diningroom, colour TV in all units. The kitchen facilities include sink units, full sized cookers and refrigerators. Linen not supplied, but there is a laundry room, all electric. Both shops and sea are under a mile away. Dogs allowed. Car not essential, but advantageous. Parking available. Weekly terms from £29 to £189. Free use of heated swimming pool; licensed club; entertainment; restaurant. In the main house there is accommodation in self-contained apartments for two to four persons. These apartments have private bathrooms. SAE, please, for further details.

ILFRACOMBE. Mrs K. A. Richards, East Hagginton Farm, Berrynarbor, Ilfracombe EX34 9SB (Combe Martin [027-188] 2262). Working farm. This is part of a farmhouse on 180-acre farm with milking cows, horses, sheep and other farm animals. The house is situated on a good road, one mile from the sea, shops and golf course. Well placed for touring Devon's many beauty spots. Guests are quite welcome to roam the farm with no restrictions. Children welcome and we will babysit if required. Large lounge with electric fire and colour TV. Milk may be purchased from the farm. Everything provided, all that guests require to bring are sheets, pillow cases and towels. Bedrooms; one with double bed and two singles; the other with double bed and bunks. Both have washbasins with hot and cold water. Available Easter/end of October. SAE for brochure and weekly terms.

ILFRACOMBE. Mrs M. Thomas, Twitchen Farm, West Down, Ilfracombe EX34 8NP (Ilfracombe [0271] 62720). Working farm. Twitchen Bungalow is part of the farm and guests have all the advantages of a farm holiday. About three miles from Woolacombe and Ilfracombe, convenient for beaches and day trips to Exmoor, Clovelly, etc, this 280-acre farm has hundreds of lambs in the spring and plenty of space to roam free from traffic worries. There is one family room and two double rooms, sittingroom with colour TV, log fire in winter. Dining/kitchen and scullery; separate bathroom and WC. Drying and airing facilities – fully equipped except for bed and table linen (overseas visitors may hire this). Personal supervision ensures well-aired beds and high standard of cleanliness. Open all year, reduced rates for out of season bookings; suitable for disabled. Electricity on meter. SAE, please, for reply by return.

ILFRACOMBE near. Mrs Pam Parke, Middle Lee Farm, Berrynarbor, Ilfracombe EX34 9SD (Combe Martin [0271 88] 2256). In the Sterridge Valley, Berrynarbor has a good village store, butcher, post-office and pub. Excellent for walking, touring or relaxing in or out of season. Sea one mile. To accommodate up to 6 — two self-contained 'Farmhouse Flats', and two 'Barn Cottages', south facing and tastefully furnished; one double and one twin bedrooms, bed-settee in lounge. Bathroom, colour TV, electric fires. All have patios, sun-terraces. To accommodate up to 3 — two 'Shippen Studios'. Luxurious. Double bedroom, shower-room and open-plan living area (bed-settee), colour TV. Own patio. Linen included. Cot and high chair available. Pets accepted. Ample parking. Open all year. Also Farmhouse accommodation. Good food with garden produce. SAE please for brochure.

ILFRACOMBE. The Old Castle Coach House, Watermouth, Ilfracombe. The Old Castle Coach House is 200 yards from the sea in a gloriously wooded valley on the Devon coast between Ilfracombe and Combe Martin. Watermouth is an unspoilt, natural and very beautiful private estate. Sailing, golf, tennis, swimming within easy reach. Architect-designed conversions produced eight delightful cottages surrounding a sunny courtyard. They are tastefully furnished and very well equipped with modern, fitted kitchens and bathrooms, automatic cookers, immersion heaters, fridges, electric kettles, colour TV and night storage heaters. All are completely self contained and have from two to three double bedrooms. There is a large private garden and dogs are allowed. Special low season rates. Details from **Mrs Patricia Gale, Moorings, Watermouth, Ilfracombe (Telephone: 0271-62553 or 0271-62834).**

SELF-CATERING   Devon   423

ILFRACOMBE. Mrs F. M. Irwin, Smythen Farm Luxury Holiday Cottages, Sterridge Valley, ✻ Berrynarbor, Ilfracombe EX34 9TB (Combe Martin [0271 88] 3515). Working farm. Situated on the edge of Exmoor National Park superior holiday cottages to let on family farm of 165 acres. Two miles to village with village stores, butcher's shop and Inn. Fishing, golf, pony trekking in the area and miles of golden sands. One, two and three bedroomed cottages to sleep from two to 11 persons. Magnificent sea and coastal views. Fully equipped except linen. SAE, please, for terms and brochure. See also Colour Display Advertisement in this Guide.

ILFRACOMBE near. Mrs A. M. Richards, Moules Farm, Berrynabor, Near Ilfracombe EX34 9SX (Combe Martin [027-188] 2594). Working farm. Moules Farm is a dairy farm well situated in this attractive Devonshire village, two minutes' walking distance of shops, post office, restaurant, inn, church and bus. Within easy reach of Woolacombe Sands and Exmoor. Accommodation consists of a cottage attached to farmhouse, and flat in farmhouse. Both are tastefully furnished, completely modernised, carpeted throughout. Fully equipped including bed linen. Available all year, the cottage has two family bedrooms with one double and bunk beds per room, shower/WC. Living/diningroom/kitchen with electric cooker, immersion heater, fridge, fires, TV. Flat has family bedroom, small double bedroom, bathroom, separate WC. Living/diningroom/kitchen with facilities as above. Pets by arrangement. Stamp for tariff and brochure please.

INSTOW. Beach Haven, Sandihills, Instow. Beach Haven is a detached holiday bungalow quietly situated right in the dunes next to the sandy beach at Instow. A long, brambled sandbank gives bungalow, small lawned garden and patio with picnic table a feeling of seclusion. Many beautiful walks along the coast and in nearby open countryside, and safe bathing from the beach. Beach Haven sleeps five plus baby in two bedrooms (one double and one twin), and studio couch in lounge. Lounge/diner with colour TV, kitchen, shower room, WC. Own parking space. SAE, please, for brochure of this and other properties to **S. B. Baxter, Boat Hyde, Northam, Bideford or phone (Bideford [023-72] 73801) for prices and vacancies.**

INSTOW. Tide's Reach Cottage, 17 Whitehouse Close, Instow. Tide's Reach Cottage is a modern cottage right on the edge of a long sandy beach with safe bathing and with only a quiet road between the cottage garden and the sands and dunes. There are beautiful views across the beach and dunes and out to sea from the cottage which sleeps six, plus cot, in three bedrooms. It has a modern, fitted kitchen; gas fired central heating. Garage with table tennis; colour television, garden and private parking area. Instow is the main sailing centre for North Devon and there are superb coastal walks, fishing and a ferry operates to Appledore. Four miles from the market town of Bideford. Other beaches within easy reach. Photograph shows view from cottage window. SAE, please, for brochure of this and other cottages to **F. I. Baxter, Boat Hyde, Northam, Bideford, N. Devon or 'phone (Bideford [023-72] 73801) for prices and vacancies.**

KINGSBRIDGE near. Mrs J. Tucker, Mount Folly Farm, Bigbury-on-Sea, Near Kingsbridge TQ7 4AR (Bigbury-on-Sea [0548] 810267). Working farm. A delightful family farm, situated on the coast, overlooking the sea and sandy beaches of Bigbury Bay. Farm adjoins golf course and River Avon. Lovely coastal walks. Ideal centre for South Hams and Dartmoor. The spacious wing comprises half of a farmhouse, self-contained with separate entrance. Large, comfortable lounge with sea views; colour TV. Well equipped kitchen/diner — all electric; metered. Sleeps six persons in three bedrooms; one family, one double and one single; two with basins and sea views. Cot available. Bathroom and toilet. All rooms attractively furnished. Visitors made welcome. Nice garden; ideal for children. Babysitting can be arranged. Car essential — parking. Available all year. SAE, for terms, please.

KINGSBRIDGE. Manor Farm Cottage, South Allington, Chivelstone, Kingsbridge. Well-equipped semi-detached country cottage pleasantly situated with a large garden and a stream running through the grounds. An area of outstanding natural beauty seven miles from Kingsbridge. Many excellent beaches within easy reach. Sailing, fishing, golf at Thurlestone and Bigbury. Accommodation for eight plus baby in two double and one family bedrooms; cot. Bathroom, toilet; sittingroom and kitchen/diner. Constant hot water from oil-fired Rayburn; electric cooker, fridge, iron, vacuum cleaner, kettle, cutlery, spin dryer, etc. Blankets supplied, but no linen. Car essential — parking space. Shop one mile. Available January to December. Friday bookings commencing 3 pm ending 10 am. Weekly terms from £40 to £100 (including fuel). **Mr F. W. Baker, Manor Farm, South Allington, Near Kingsbridge TQ7 2NB (Chivelstone [054-851] 231).**

PLEASE SEND A STAMPED ADDRESSED ENVELOPE WITH ENQUIRIES

Devon — SELF-CATERING

IN SOUTHERNMOST DEVON
A TOUCH OF LUXURY

THE ROCKHOUSE MARINE APARTHOTEL

A Delightful Choice ON THE WATERSIDE
IN A BEAUTIFUL - *Secluded Bay*

- Luxurious Holiday Apartments.
- Waterside Bar in idyllic beach setting.
- Heated pool ● Games Rooms.
- Watersports abound.
- Secluded sandy coves.
- Evening Entertainment.
- Pets welcome by arrangement.
- Laundry room.
- Baby Listening.

ROCKHOUSE MARINE MUST OCCUPY ONE OF THE MOST UNIQUE AND DELIGHTFUL POSITIONS IN SOUTH DEVON.
A Holiday Venue one rarely finds – but often dreams of.
Write or phone now for our brochure to Trevor Illingworth, R.H.M.H., Thurlestone Sands, Near Kingsbridge, South Devon TQ7 3JY. Tel 0548 561285.

KINGSBRIDGE near. Mrs F. R. Munday, Wakeham Farm, South Milton, Near Kingsbridge TQ7 3JQ (Kingsbridge [0548] 560252). Situated in the attractive village of South Milton, in the notable South Hams, the farmhouse stands back from the road; within easy reach of the beach, golf and tennis at Thurlestone, about a mile-and-a-half away. Handy for the village shop; three miles from Kingsbridge; five miles from Salcombe — a must for those interested in boats. Lovely walks in National Trust property at Bolt Head and Bolt Tail. Three double bedrooms sleep six; cot; combined sitting/diningroom; bathroom and toilet; kitchen with electric cooker and fridge, water heater, fully equipped except linen. TV available. Sorry, no pets. Electricity extra. Car essential — parking. This accommodation is part of the farmhouse. SAE, please, for terms.

KINGSBRIDGE. Mrs Beryl M. Honeywill, Beeson Farm, Beeson, Kingsbridge TQ7 2HW (Kingsbridge [0548] 580531). Working farm. A delightful family farm situated in the lovely South Hams hamlet of Beeson. Front of farmhouse flat — one mile from nearest beach; seven miles from Kingsbridge. Ideal centre for beaches and Dartmoor. Flat comprises separate entrance, front garden. Large comfortable lounge, adjoining well-equipped kitchen/diner, all electric (metered). Two bedrooms with sea views — one double room, opposite a large family room (flat sleeps five). Separate toilet, bathroom shared. All rooms attractively furnished. Proved to be popular holiday for young families. Babysitting provided. Sorry, no pets. Available May to October. SAE for terms etc., please.

KINGSBRIDGE near. Mrs B. Goodman, Mattiscombe Farm, Stokenham, Near Kingsbridge TQ7 2SR (Kingsbridge [0548] 580442). Working farm. Only a mile from the three-mile stretch of beach at Slapton Sands the self-contained flat at Mattiscombe Farm is ideal accommodation for up to eight. There are four double bedrooms, a lounge/dining room, a bathroom and a toilet. Electric cooking and heating, 50p meter. Linen supplied if required. Mattiscombe Farm is a 150 acre mixed farm six miles from Kingsbridge, ten from Dartmouth and close to many beaches. A car is essential, the nearest shops are a mile away, as is public transport. Good fishing and many places of interest nearby. Children welcome, cot supplied. No pets. Open April to October. SAE, please, for terms.

KINGSBRIDGE. Mrs Ruth Bate, Woolcombe Farm, East Allington, Near Totnes (East Allington [054-852] 275). Working farm. Woolcombe Farm is situated 200 yards off the A381, four miles Kingsbridge. Totnes, Plymouth, Torbay and Dartmoor National Park all within easy reach. Visitors welcome around the farmyard and can watch the dairy herd being milked. There are also plenty of baby pigs to see. A self-contained part of the farmhouse, sleeping six, plus cot, is available to let. The kitchen/diner has an automatic electric cooker, fridge and is fully equipped. The sittingroom has TV and electric fire. On the first floor there are three double bedrooms, one with two single beds and washbasin etc.; one with double bed, cot and airing cupboard and the other has two single beds. Toilet and washbasin. (Bath not included in accommodation, small charge for use). Sheets and blankets provided, but not for the cot. Babysitting by arrangement. Regret, cannot accept pets. Open from May to September. Terms include electricity.

KINGSBRIDGE. Keynedon Mill, Frogmore, Kingsbridge. Keynedon Mill is a detached farmhouse in the attractive South Hams area, in a little hamlet a quarter-mile from the village. Moors, coves, beaches, Plymouth, Torbay within easy reach. This is a roomy house with three double bedrooms; cot; bathroom/toilet; sittingroom; diningroom with double bed settee; kitchen with Rayburn for slow cooking and hot water, also electric cooker, fridge etc. No linen available. Pets permitted. Car essential — parking. April/May to October. Meter 10p. SAE, please, for terms to **Mr R. Heath, 4 Winslade Close, Frogmore, Kingsbridge TQ7 2NX (Frogmore [054-853] 233).**

KINGSBRIDGE. Mrs E. Marshall, Sea View, Hope Cove, Kingsbridge (Kingsbridge [0548] 561 272). Flat sleeps six; large sittingroom with colour TV; two large bedrooms and one small one with two bunk beds; kitchen with electric cooker, fridge; bathroom; also Calor gas. All hot water is supplied in this well-furnished accommodation, carpeted throughout. Car park for three cars. Two minutes from sea. Only linen not supplied. Shops two minutes. Hope Cove is a pretty fishing village, with many cliff walks and safe bathing. Golf course and other sporting activities in six mile radius.

KINGSBRIDGE. Mrs D. M. Tolchard, Bickerton Farm, Hallsands, Kingsbridge TQ7 2EU (Chivelstone [054-851] 220). Working farm. This is a detached cottage five minutes' walk from the sea at Hallsands, a small, unspoilt village on the coastline between Dartmouth and Salcombe. Four miles from Torcross and the freshwater lake and nature reserve at Slapton Lea. Sleeping six, there is one large bedroom with single beds, one double room, cot, and divan in the sittingroom. The kitchen is all-electric with immerser, cooker, fridge, kettle, etc., everything supplied but linen. TV and night storage heater in the sittingroom, for early and late holidays. Pets are permitted and the cottage is open all year round with weekly terms on request. SAE, please. Car essential — parking. Also three-bedroomed cottage nearby.

KINGSBRIDGE. E. Javin, Ocean View, c/o Atlantic Lodge, Hope Cove, Kingsbridge (Kingsbridge [0548] 561873). This is a a new luxury bungalow, situated in the small fishing village of Hope Cove. It is in the finest position in Hope Cove and all the front rooms overlook the sea. It is just two minutes to the beach along a private path. There are four double bedrooms, two bathrooms, plus cloakroom, also lounge with patio doors onto the terrace. A superb kitchen with electric cooker, hob, fan extractor, fridge, freezer, automatic washing machine; economy seven heating for off season. Parking for two cars. Open all year. Hope Cove is one of the few places where commercialism has been restricted. Special rates for early and late holidays. SAE for brochure and details.

KINGSBRIDGE. Mrs R. E. Lethbridge, Pittaford Farm, Slapton, Kingsbridge TQ7 2QG (Kingsbridge [0548] 580357). Working farm. Fully equipped self-contained wing of 17th century farmhouse on 105-acre mixed farm two miles from Slapton beach, and the well-known Slapton Ley nature reserve where guided walks and bird watching expeditions are arranged. Riding and fishing nearby. Own large lawned garden. Very peaceful. The accommodation, which has beamed ceiling and stone fireplace, is very well equipped including electric fire, electric cooker, iron, vacuum cleaner, refrigerator and colour TV. Sleeps six plus baby. Three double bedrooms, cot; bathroom, toilet; sitting/diningroom. No linen supplied. Children welcome. Pets by arrangement only. Open all year from £70 to £95 per week. Car essential; parking. Two miles from shops and public transport.

KINGSBRIDGE. Keynedon Cottage, Frogmore, Kingsbridge. Keynedon Cottage is situated on the road between two villages where there are shops and pubs, backing on to farmland about quarter-mile from farmstead — visitors are welcome to walk around. The cottage is within two miles of beaches and coves, within easy reach of Dartmoor, Torbay and Plymouth. Accommodation, one family, two double and one single bedrooms, loan of cot, bathroom with toilet. Sittingroom has bed-settee, electric fire and black/white television. Kitchen supplied with electric cooker, heater, fridge, kettle, iron, cleaner and spin dryer. Electricity on 50p meter — linen supplied extra — pets allowed — parking. SAE, please, for terms and brochure: **Mrs M. J. Heath, Keynedon Barton, Frogmore, Kingsbridge TQ7 2AS (Frogmore [054-853] 247).**

KINGSBRIDGE. Mrs Jill Balkwill, Court Barton, Aveton Gifford, Kingsbridge TQ7 4LE (Kingsbridge [0548] 550312). Working farm. Stone Barton is a modern, four-bedroomed house, with large garden, patio and barbecue and is attached to the main farmhouse. Comfortably furnished, it is ideal for a relaxing country holiday with central heating in colder weather and colour TV provided. Just 100 yards from the village. Games rooms, garden and a large swimming pool are available for guests, and with beaches, moors, golf courses, fishing etc. close by, the choice is open for a busy or lazy holiday. Accommodates eight/ten people in four double bedrooms; cot; bathroom, two toilets; sittingroom; diningroom; excellent fully fitted modern kitchen. Linen supplied. No pets, please. Car essential — parking. Available all year round. Terms on application, pamphlet available.

KINGSBRIDGE. Mr and Mrs A. R. Wotton, "Andryl", Lower Farm, Beeson, Kingsbridge TQ7 2HW (Kingsbridge [0548] 580527). Working farm. "Andryl" is situated in a sheltered sunny position on Lower Farm, Beeson. The flat is part of "Andryl" and sleeps six, with bathroom, separate toilet, airing cupboard and well equipped kitchen/diner with TV. Linen is optional. The garden has a swing, and there are other attractions for the children including baby pigs, chicks, ducks, goslings and a pony. The cows are milked on the adjoining farm, where the sheep and cart horses can also be seen. Beesands is half-a-mile away, and other beaches are very near. Kingsbridge is the nearest town, while Dartmouth and Salcombe are within easy reach. Babysitting can be arranged. Available Easter to October. Pets are not allowed. Car essential, parking. SAE, please, for terms and brochure.

KINGSBRIDGE. "Savernake," Thurlestone Sands, Kingsbridge. This substantial house, with a beautiful and unobstructed view of the sea and Thurlestone Rock, stands in its own grounds, adjoining the dunes and beach. The area is of outstanding beauty with wonderful cliff walks. Golf, tennis, quarter mile. Sailing and riding in area. Accommodation for 10 in three twin-bedded double rooms with washbasins; three single rooms (one with washbasin); cot; bathroom, three toilets; lounge and diningroom. Kitchen fully equipped with electric cooker, fridge, kettle and toaster. Linen not supplied. Village shop one mile. SAE to **Mrs M. D. Horsfall, Century Cottage, Foxdon Hill, Wadeford, Chard, Somerset TA20 3AN (Chard [046-06] 2475).**

PLEASE SEND A STAMPED ADDRESSED ENVELOPE WITH ENQUIRIES

Devon   SELF-CATERING

KINGSBRIDGE. Mrs F. M. Rogers, Croft Farm, West Charleton, Kingsbridge TQ7 2AL (Frogmore [054-853] 213). Croft is a pleasant south-facing farmhouse, two miles from Kingsbridge, making an excellent centre for touring the South Hams, and visiting many unspoilt beaches. Much of the farmland adjoins the Kingsbridge/Salcombe Estuary. The accommodation, quite self-contained, sleeps 10-12 comfortably having four bedrooms, all with washbasins. Two cots and a high chair. Diningroom 24' × 15' with well-equipped kitchen corner and a huge oval dining table. Comfortable sittingroom with TV; playroom with table tennis and quarter-sized billiards table top, children's books, etc. Bathroom with WC; larder; full-sized electric cooker, fridge/freezer, electric clothes airer, and usual equipment. Constant hot water. Well-furnished but no linen. Ample parking. Lawn. Please state dates and number in party. SAE for prompt reply. Also available cottage for six at Bigbury. Two miles sandy beaches.

KINGSBRIDGE. Mrs Kemsley, Luke's Barn, Addlehole, Kingsbridge TQ7 2DX (Kingsbridge [0548] 3401). Situated one-and-a-half miles from the market town of Kingsbridge, ground level flat is offered for self-catering holidays from April to October (inclusive). Accommodation for five people in bedroom with double and single beds, and bedroom with full length bunk beds. Cot on request. Lounge/diningroom. Fully equipped electric kitchen including crockery, cutlery, etc. Electric heating. Linen supplied by arrangement. Electric meter (50p). The flat is annexed to the main house in rural and peaceful surroundings. A separate building with its own entrance, modern and clean. Children welcome, pets permitted if well-behaved. Car essential, parking. Shops, public transport one-and-a-half miles. Weekly terms from £50 to £105 (excluding fuel).

KINGSBRIDGE. Mr D. Murphy, Hendham House, Woodleigh, Kingsbridge TQ7 4DP (Kingsbridge [0548] 550335). Here is the perfect answer for two families spending holidays together and looking for somewhere really spacious. The house was built in 1779 and stands in its own grounds surrounded by farming country and with lovely views. Dartmoor is near and there are plenty of beaches less than 10 miles away. An evening stroll takes you down the lane to a picturesque bridge over the River Avon. We let part of the house, with six bedrooms to sleep 10 or more; two bathrooms, kitchen with dishwasher, electric cooker, fridge, sittingroom with TV; large garden and parking space. Electricity, hot water and central heating are included. Registered with the English Tourist Board. From £25 per person per week.

KINGSBRIDGE. Mrs M. Darke, Coleridge Farm, Chillington, Kingsbridge TQ7 2JG (Kingsbridge [0548] 580274). Working farm. No. 2 Coleridge Cottage is situated on Coleridge Farm which is half a mile from Chillington village where there is a post office, grocery store, butcher, doctor and garage. Many beaches are within easy reach of the cottage, the nearest being Slapton Sands and Torcross, two miles. The cottage is modernised and semi-detached comprising kitchen/diningroom, lounge, three double bedrooms and one single with bunk beds, upstairs bathroom and WC. Cot. Fully equipped. Electric cooker, fridge, spin dryer, TV, cutlery, crockery, kitchen utensils, blankets and pillows. There is a small garden and parking. Electricity is by 50p meter. SAE, please, for terms and brochure. Available May to October.

KINGSBRIDGE. Mrs A. M. Ling, Hope Barton, Hope Cove, Kingsbridge TQ7 3HT (Kingsbridge [0548] 561393). Working farm. 1983 saw the expansion of our holiday enterprise with the conversion of three cottages from the 100-year-old stone buildings to join the existing "Granary" — a converted loft with magnificent views and every comfort in which many people have enjoyed holidays for the last 12 years on the 140-acre mixed livestock farm part owned by the National Trust. In 1985 we completed a bungalow-style conversion suitable for physically disabled people. All are equipped to a very high standard, having heating for out of season holidays; colour TV; electric showers; laundry room. Being a mere half-mile from the beach, we can offer a unique blend of farm and seaside in peaceful and beautiful surroundings. Available April to January. SAE, please.

KINGSBRIDGE. Mr and Mrs M. B. Turner, Cross Farm, East Allington, Totnes TQ9 7RW (East Allington [054-852] 327). For a peaceful holiday in the heart of the South Hams, come to Cross Farm, a mixed farm situated in beautiful countryside at the head of a valley only four miles from Kingsbridge and within four to six miles radius of many lovely beaches and coves. East Allington village is just a mile away with shops and character Inn. Good centre for visiting Plymouth, Torbay and Dartmoor. Riding facilities nearby. Accommodation in 17th century self-contained farmhouse wing to sleep 12 persons, plus two cots, in four bedrooms. Also, two superior semi-detached cottages in lovely valley to sleep nine persons, plus two cots, in four bedrooms each. All accommodation is very comfortably furnished and equipped to a high standard with all mod cons including colour TV, showers and automatic washing-machines. Heated for early/late holidays. Recreation barn with billiards, table-tennis etc. and play area for children. Baby-sitting by arrangement. SAE for brochure and terms, please.

KINGSBRIDGE (Hope Cove). 14 Weymouth Park, Hope Cove, Kingsbridge. Modern two bedroom bungalow lies in a beautiful and unspoilt area of the South Hams, in a picturesque fishing village which has two safe bathing beaches. There is a village store and two inns. The main shopping centre of Kingsbridge is five miles away, and Salcombe with its beautiful estuary stretching up to Kingsbridge is only six miles. Sailing and motor boats can be hired there. Accommodation comprises two bedrooms, sleeps four. Fully equipped kitchen, lounge with TV. WC and bathroom. Large garden. Pets allowed. SAE, please, for brochure to **Mr M. J. Watts, Huish Cottage, South Huish, Near Kingsbridge TQ7 3EJ (Kingsbridge [0548] 561703).**

KINGSBRIDGE near. Mrs J. Lucas, Stockadon Farm, Loddiswell, Near Kingsbridge TQ7 4EQ (Kingsbridge [0548] 550255). Working farm. Chestnut Cottage lies in secluded countryside, about 70 yards from the main farmhouse and two miles from the nearest village of Aveton Gifford. The farm is 214 acres, growing corn and potatoes and fattening beef cattle. The sandy beaches are five miles distant, Kingsbridge six miles and Salcombe ten miles. Plymouth, Torbay and Dartmoor are within easy driving distance. There are four bedrooms (one downstairs), large kitchen/diningroom; and separate sitting room. There is an electric cooker, fridge, colour TV, and storage heating — all inclusive. Open all year round. Send SAE for details and terms, or telephone.

KINGSBRIDGE near. Maycombe, Beeson, Near Kingsbridge. Situated in the delightful hamlet of Beeson, this stone-built house combines the charm of 200 years ago with modern comforts. Sunny, sheltered garden. All rooms carpeted and well furnished; nightstore heaters make the house cosy early/late season. All-electric and well equipped kitchen. Charming lounge with original stone fireplace. Accommodation for six people. No linen supplied. Pets permitted. Car essential — parking. Open all year. Beeson is situated among the beautiful coastal scenery and the unspoilt rural countryside of the South Hams — lovely for walking, good bathing, fishing, boating; pleasant for a winter holiday too. Terms from £75 to £180 weekly. Please send SAE for leaflet to **Mrs J. V. Garner, Greyhomes Hotel, Torcross, Near Kingsbridge TQ7 2TH (Kingsbridge [0548] 580220).**

KINGSBRIDGE near. Cotmore House, Stokenham, Near Kingsbridge. Cotmore House is set high with lovely views of sea and country. It is a very good tourist centre and handy for many sandy beaches and places of interest. It is only one and a half miles to coast, six miles to Kingsbridge, 11 miles Dartmouth. It is a spacious detached house in one acre of grounds. There is a 36' lounge/diningroom with sun room off. Kitchen and downstairs cloakroom. Three bedrooms; one double, one twin-bedded, one with bunk beds plus cot. Small bedroom with studio couch. Bathroom with shower and bidet. Separate toilet. Children welcome, cot. Pets are allowed. Kitchen with fridge, auto washing machine, iron, toaster; also TV. It is available March to October with electric heating. Shops two miles. Car essential, double garage. Weekly terms on request. **Mrs D. N. Hutchings, No. 1 Blue Waters, Lower Widdicombe, Near Kingsbridge TQ7 2EG (Kingsbridge [0548] 580491).**

KINGSBRIDGE (South Hams). Mrs Jill Darke, South Huish Farm, Kingsbridge TQ7 3EH (Kingsbridge [0548] 561237). Working farm. Orchard View Cottage is situated on 200-acre mixed farm, just 10 minutes' walk from Thurlestone Sands beach, safe for children, and three miles from Hope Cove fishing village. Five miles from sailing at Salcombe and main shops in Kingsbridge. Within easy reach of golf courses and wind surfing. One double, one single and one family bedrooms, cot; bathroom, two toilets; sittingroom and fully equipped dining/kitchen; colour TV. Garden and parking. Sorry, no pets. Car essential; parking. Three miles from shops. Open all year. Terms are from £90 to £150 weekly.

LYNTON. Mr and Mrs K. J. Moore, Dean Steep Holiday Bungalows, Lynton EX35 6JS (Lynton [0598] 53272). Purpose-built bungalows, available April to October, within Exmoor National Park close to sea, moors, National Trust walks. Dean Steep has a beautiful lawned setting and each bungalow has a panoramic view of Exmoor. Accommodation — two double bedrooms, plus cot. Lounge/diner, bedsettee, electric heaters, colour TV. Bathroom, toilet. Fully equipped kitchenette. Six bungalows have night storage heaters in the lounge. Parking in grounds. The area is a wealth of lovely scenery and Dean Steep is within easy reach of Lynmouth, Valley of Rocks, Doone Valley, etc. If you enjoy a peaceful holiday in beautiful countryside, this is the place for you. Children and pets welcome. SAE for brochure and tariff.

EXMOOR VALLEY

Two delightful genuine Devon Cottages and a Modern Bungalow

The two modernised cottages are XVI century and situated in their own sheltered valley yet only half a mile from a main road, facing South, with a trout stream running through the garden. The bungalow sits on a hill behind with superb views of Exmoor. All are located on an 86-acre farm containing riding stables, sheep, cows and plenty of interest for the children, plus all the other attractions and sporting activities of the area.

RIVERSIDE COTTAGE sleeps nine in three bedrooms, two with hot and cold; bathroom, separate toilet; kitchen; diningroom and lounge with large open log fire. Terms from £110 weekly off season.
NEW MILL COTTAGE sleeps six in two bedrooms, one with hot and cold; large bathroom; separate toilet; kitchen and lounge with open log fire. Terms from £95 weekly off season.
NEW MILL BUNGALOW sleeps six in three bedrooms; bathroom, toilet; kitchen; diningroom and lounge with open fire. Night storage heaters available if required. Terms from £95 weekly off season.

All have mains electricity, flush toilet, colour TV, fridge, full cooking facilities, s/s sinks, spin rinsers and fitted carpets. Furniture is comfortable, interior sprung mattresses, and linen provided, if required. All thoroughly inspected before arrival. Pets are welcome at £10 each weekly. Safe for children and pets to play. Horse riding over Exmoor from farm. Stables are "Ponies of Britain Approved."

SAE to R. S. Bingham, New Mill Farm, Barbrook, Lynton, North Devon (Lynton [059 85] 3341).

LYNTON. Mr H. D. King-Fretts, West Lyn Farm, Barbrook, Lynton EX35 6LD (Lynton [0598] 53618). West Lyn Farm sleeps 12 plus cot. Set in 134 acres of farmland within the Exmoor National Park; owned by Devon's own Atlantic oarsman Hugh King-Fretts. The house enjoys panoramic views across Channel to Wales and is double glazed throughout. Miles of recognised coastal walks to Lynton, Lynmouth and Watersmeet from the farm. Spacious accommodation — large kitchen/diner with electric cooker, oil fired Rayburn at extra cost if required, washing machine, fridge, freezer. Lounge with colour TV, three piece suite, bed/settee. Four bedrooms, one double, one twin, one bunk and one family. Bathroom, toilet. Cot available. Ample gardens, patio. Well behaved dogs welcome. Short walk to Channel View Park with shop, bar, restaurant, launderette, telephone, etc. Terms from £80 – £120 per week. SAE, please, for brochure.

NEWTON ABBOT. Mrs Julia Birkenhead, Gale Farm, Bickington, Newton Abbot TQ12 6PG (Bickington [062682] 273). Gale Farm is a Georgian farmhouse in the quiet, secluded Kester Valley, and only half-a-mile from the A38. The self-contained flat is south-facing, with its own gardens and car-parking. Accommodation consists of a large livingroom with stone fireplace and colour TV, large kitchen/diner and modern bathroom. The kitchen is well equipped with fridge and automatic washing machine; linen is supplied. The flat sleeps four/six in 2/3 double bedrooms. Heating and cooking is by electricity (50p meter) also open fires. Cot and high chair available, and babysitting. Three miles to shops, quarter-mile to public transport — car essential. Available all year. Terms on application.

Terms quoted in this publication may be subject to increase if rises in costs necessitate

SELF-CATERING   Devon   **429**

NEWTON ABBOT. Mrs G. A. Newton, Five Wyches Farm, Bovey Tracey, Newton Abbot TQ13 9LE (Bovey Tracey [0626] 832310). Working farm, join in. Situated on 40-acre working farm on the edge of Dartmoor National Park surrounded by magnificent scenery, this wing of a beautiful, listed 15th century thatched farmhouse offers accommodation for eight to ten people in two double, one twin-bedded and one bunk-bedded rooms. Cot available. Attractive beamed lounge with inglenook fireplace; colour TV; kitchen/diner with electric cooker, fridge, water heater, radiator. Bath and WC. Rooms carpeted throughout, tastefully furnished and very clean. Torbay is 14 miles away. There are excellent opportunities for riding, fishing, golf, swimming. Good shops in Bovey Tracey (one mile). Linen not provided. Outside facilities for pets. Car not essential, but ample parking. Open all year. Metered electricity. SAE, please, for terms.

NEWTON ABBOT. Mr & Mrs R. A. Manuell, Higher Burne Farm, Bickington, Near Newton Abbot TQ12 6PA (Ipplepen [0803] 812844). This is a dairy farm situated in the peaceful Devon countryside, yet only five miles from Newton Abbot, one mile from the A38 and close to Dartmoor. The self-contained, spacious accommodation is well equipped, with its own entrance and ample parking. Swings for children and visitors very welcome to participate in farm activities. Available early July to mid September, accommodation comprises kitchen, lounge/diner, two bathrooms (one with shower), two double and two single bedrooms (cot supplied). Sleeps four/five persons, sixth person by arrangement. Hot water, linen, towels provided. Pets by arrangement. Weekly terms from £80. Further details on request.

NORTH DEVON. Middle Haxton, Bratton Fleming, Barnstaple. Working farm. Well built stone and brick house situated in beautiful countryside, with good views, half-a-mile from village of Bratton Fleming, shops, etc., and eight miles from market town of Barnstaple, 11 miles from South Molton. Within easy reach of Exmoor and surrounding district, beaches, Woolacombe, Ilfracombe, Combe Martin, Lynton, etc. House surrounded by livestock rearing farm of 179 acres (72½ hectares) in own grounds; very peaceful. Ideal for children. (Cot). Accommodation for eight in four double bedrooms; bathroom, toilets; sittingroom; diningroom; fully equipped electric kitchen. Everything except linen. One dog allowed. Open May-October. Car essential, parking. Please enclose SAE when applying to **Mr and Mrs F. J. Huxtable, Higher Haxton Farm, Bratton Fleming, Barnstaple EX31 4RZ (Brayford [05988] 306).**

NORTHAM. The Moorings, Northam, Bideford. The Moorings is a riverside bungalow near the sea in the beautiful Torridge Estuary. Down a private drive, with fields around, and away from all the traffic, it partly overlooks the estuary which is half-a-mile wide at this point and is a haven for bird life. A short path leads to a private beach (public have access). Across the river lies Instow's sandy beach and yachting centre. Fishing village, superb beach, championship golf course and country park with lakes all within two miles. Bideford is two miles away (shops, market and port). The bungalow is fully equipped for six, plus baby, with a modern fitted kitchen/diner, bathroom, games room with table tennis; three bedrooms; large lounge with colour TV, woodburning stove and French windows to terrace and garden; heating. Very suitable for winter letting. From £30 weekly. Photo shows beach below bungalow. SAE, please, for brochure of this and other cottages to **F. N. Baxter, Boat Hyde, Northam, Bideford, N. Devon or 'phone (Bideford [023-72] 73801) for prices and vacancies.**

OKEHAMPTON. Giffords Hele Farm Cottage, Giffords Hele, Meeth, Okehampton. Working farm. Giffords Hele Farm dates from the Domesday era. The recently restored cottage wing stands in its own part-walled garden and, built of stone cob, has been carefully modernised to retain its exposed beams, deep windowsills and period character. Natural pine, co-ordinated spreads and drapes and full carpeting give romantic bedrooms and a log-burning stove in the comfortable lounge fuels central heating. Colour TV. A relaxing holiday is assured on our mixed 175-acre working farm where hedges, wild flowers and woodland still have their place. Whether its our fishing on the River Torridge which borders the farm, or visits to Dartmoor or the coast, there is plenty to see and do. Good livestock/produce market and shops in Hatherleigh (two miles) and excellent local pubs. Linen/babysitting and occasional dogs by prior arrangement. Accommodates five/six, plus cot in two/three bedrooms. £65–£165 weekly. Send SAE for full colour details: **Claire Pratt, Chapel Cottage, Meeth, Okehampton EX20 3QN (Okehampton [0837] 810625).**

WHEN MAKING ENQUIRIES PLEASE MENTION
FARM HOLIDAY GUIDE

Devon SELF-CATERING

* OKEHAMPTON. Mr M. W. Harbridge, Poltimore, South Zeal, Okehampton (Okehampton [0837] 840209). Delightful self-catering accommodation situated in the side of a hill in the grounds of a BTA Commended Country Guest House, comprising a 17th century granite barn converted into two apartments, each sleeping up to six persons, and an attractive holiday chalet for two persons. The Barn apartments have charming beamed sittingroom with dining area; modern kitchen with electric cooker, fridge, etc. Colour TV, electric fires, night store heating. Fully equipped including electric blankets and duvets. Weekly terms £35 to £150. The Chalet has twin-bedded room, sitting/diningroom with further sleeping accommodation for two, if required. Fully equipped kitchenette; furnished to a high standard. Weekly terms £15 to £85 according to season. All West Country attractions within easy reach. See also Colour Display Advertisement.

OTTERY ST. MARY. Mr Malcolm Joyce, Foxholes, West Hill, Ottery St. Mary EX11 1XE (040-481 3151) (24 hour answering or (0392) 860422). A lovely modern ground floor apartment in an exclusive area of East Devon in a peaceful wooded setting, two miles from all the facilities of Ottery St. Mary, within half-a-mile of local supermarket. Heated swimming pool and squash courts only two miles away. Large garden with patio. Perfect for honeymoons, but suitable for disabled. Hall and spacious lounge/diner with bed settee; patio doors to garden. Modern very well equipped kitchen with breakfast bar. Large fully-tiled shower room with shower, basin and WC. Double bedroom with duvet. Services: Colour TV — Private parking — Electric fan heater — Automatic washing machine — Electricity included.

OTTERY ST. MARY. 1 Coombelake Cottage, Fairmile, Ottery St. Mary. This bright, end-of-terrace cottage is one and a quarter miles from Ottery St. Mary, situated amidst pretty countryside with many East Devon towns and villages within easy reach. Accommodation is for five people in two double and one single bedrooms. Cot available. Bathroom/toilet; sittingroom with colour TV; well-equipped kitchen/diningroom with electric cooker, fridge, Rayburn solid fuel, etc. All crockery provided and almost everything likely to be needed is supplied, except linen. Pets permitted. Car essential — parking. Small garden. Available all year — short breaks out of season. Electricity by 50p meter. SAE, please, for terms. **Mrs Susan Hansford, Pitt Farm, Ottery St. Mary EX11 1NL (Ottery St. Mary [040841] 2439].**

PAIGNTON. Mrs Margaret Godwin, Millmans Farm, Marldon, Paignton TQ3 1SJ (Paignton [0803] 558213). Pretty beamed cottages situated in the garden of Millmans Farm in the peaceful village of Marldon, with its old church and Inn. Within easy reach of Torbay and its amenities, seaside at Paignton, Brixham, Torquay and near Dartmoor. The two-bedroomed cottages are fully equipped and sleep four/five. The beautiful lounge/diners have colour TV and every comfort. Shower room and toilet upstairs; suitable for disabled visitors. Linen and cots, high chair available. Pets accepted by prior arrangement. Car not essential, but there is parking. Shops 200 yards, public transport 100 yards. There is a swimming pool in the garden. Horse riding — golf — sailing — windsurfing nearby. Terms on request with SAE, please.

Millman's Farm House and Cottages. Nr. Marldon Paignton.

PAIGNTON (Torbay). Mrs Edith McGuire, Wulfruna Holiday Flatlets, 9 Esplanade Road, Paignton TQ4 6EB (Paignton [0803] 557819). For a happy family holiday in Torbay, we have eight one-room and one two-room flatlets available for self-catering all year round. Situated on sea front overlooking lovely Torbay, with level walks to town centre, within minutes of beach, harbour, theatres, amusement parks, squash, tennis courts, bowling greens. Excellent touring centre. Each flatlet is fully equipped, full-size cookers, fridges, etc. Own key, some with private toilet/bath or shower. Guests may bring own linen or hire. Regret, no pets. Unsuitable for children under five. Ample parking, but car not essential as public transport is within five to 10 minutes. Moderate terms from £55 per flatlet to £120 per week according to season. Accommodation includes hot water and colour TV in all rooms. Special terms available September to May. Send stamp for brochure stating EXACT requirements.

SELF-CATERING   Devon   431

PAIGNTON. Mrs C. Moore, Treetops, Moles Cross, Marldon, Paignton TQ3 1SY (Kingskerswell) [080-47] 3222). Working farm. The flat is self-contained and maintained to a high standard. Built only ten years ago, and situated with a rural outlook, with many interesting walks around. The flat is our own winter residence, comprising three bedrooms, one with balcony. Lounge/diningroom with colour TV and video. Beautifully fitted kitchen with breakfast bar, fridge/freezer, automatic washing machine. Bathroom with toilet and shower. Fitted carpets throughout. Parking space for two cars. There is a farm shop on the premises for fruit and vegetables, fresh farm eggs and potatoes etc. Situated two miles from Torquay, three miles Paignton, Dartmoor 12 miles, Totnes six miles. Ideally situated for all types of holiday activities.

PLYMOUTH. Mrs M. F. Hosford, Briar Hill Farm, Newton Ferrers, Plymouth PL8 1AR (Plymouth [0752] 872252). Working farm. Newton Ferrers is on the estuary of the River Yealm and is an ideal centre for sailing and fishing, or just relaxing on the sandy beaches and enjoying the lovely cliff walks. Good touring base for Dartmoor, approximately ten miles from Plymouth and within easy driving distance of many other places of scenic and historic interest. The house accommodates five people in two double bedrooms plus bed settee; bathroom, toilet; sittingroom, diningroom, well equipped kitchen. Linen supplied on request. Approximately 100 yards to shops. Small dog permitted. A car is preferable with off-the-road-parking. Available Whitsun to September. Weekly terms from £70, includes Calor gas, but not electricity.

PLYMOUTH near. Pool Mill Farm, Newton Ferrers. Working farm. An 18th century farm in 14-acres of pasture with a stream running through the property, and cottages of stone and slate built around livery yard, are available from Easter to December for self-catering holidays. National Trust land surrounds Newton Ferrers, with many lovely walks, some using one man ferry across river. Good local pubs serving reasonably priced food. Beautiful sandy beaches at Mothecombe and Stoke about two miles away. Plymouth and Dartmoor 12 miles' drive. Riding can usually be arranged and a dinghy can be hired. Fresh food may be ordered to await your arrival. Information and maps on local events and sightseeing provided. Cottages sleep two to ten in one to four bedrooms, larger ones having two bathrooms and wood burning stoves. All are fully equipped except linen. Slot metered laundry facilities. Access to telephone. Pets accepted. Car essential, parking. Shopping one-and-a-half miles. Weekly terms from £50 to £300 (excluding fuel). Stamp appreciated. Further details on request to **Mr Len Smith, 81 Veasy Park, Wembury, S. Devon PL9 0EP (Plymouth [0752] 862964).**

Compton Pool Farm – South Devon
E.T.B.

West Country Tourist Board

STANDARD
Top E.T.B. Category

1986 REGISTERED WITH THE ENGLISH TOURIST BOARD

We warmly invite you to enjoy a country holiday in our
LUXURY PERIOD FARMYARD COTTAGES WITH MANY RECREATIONAL FACILITIES

Close to Dartmoor and all South Devon's many attractions yet only 3 miles from the sea at Torquay, these pretty cottages have been converted to a very high standard from the old stone barns of an elegant Georgian farmhouse. They are tastefully furnished in farmhouse pine and are fully equipped with modern appliances including heaters in every room. Set in 12½ acres of lovely countryside all cottages have superb views.

Our facilities include a heated indoor swimming pool, tennis court, games barn, playground, colour TV, cots and high chairs, laundry room, public telephone, and partial central heating which is free in the low season. To make your holiday complete babysitting, in-cottage catering, riding and sailing, all at very reasonable rates, can easily be arranged.

For further details send a large SAE to:

MRS DONNA BROWN (FHG), COMPTON POOL FARM, COMPTON, NR. PAIGNTON, S. DEVON TQ3 1TA
TELEPHONE: 08047 2241.
We look forward to welcoming you to COMPTON POOL FARM

PLYMOUTH. The Sheiling, Court Road, Newton Ferrers, Plymouth. The Sheiling is a charming country house standing in its own secluded grounds and arranged in four comfortable self-contained flats and a tiny cottage. It faces south and is let for holiday periods. Situated above and overlooking The Pool, River Yealm and amidst lovely country and coastal scenery. Excellent yacht anchorage. Nine miles of cliff land (some National Trust land) with tiny coves and beaches. The sailing and fishing village of Newton Ferrers is half-a-mile downstream, and across the water the twin village of Noss Mayo, both providing churches, shops, sailing school, country clubs, yacht club, etc. Golf within easy reach. Plymouth nine miles and many other places of interest within reach. Excellent touring centre. Car essential — parking. Small dogs allowed. Accommodation for two/eight people. No linen supplied. Open all year. SAE to **Mrs Frances Goodwin, Dean House, Holbeton, Plymouth PL8 1LH (Holbeton [075-530] 216 or Plymouth [0752] 872224).**

PORLOCK. Mrs M. C. Richards, Broomstreet Farm, Porlock, Somerset (Brendon [059-87] 268). On coast edge of Exmoor, self contained part of farmhouse. Accommodation for seven people, also a cot, three bedrooms, one larger with extra bed, also bathroom and toilet upstairs, downstairs livingroom and kitchenette. Terms £80 per week. The National Park stretches for miles over the hills. Trout fishing is available in local rivers; licence available on application. Boating at Lynmouth and Porlock Weir. Pony riding near. Hunting with Devon and Somerset Stag Hounds, also with Exmoor Fox Hounds.

SALCOMBE. Flat 1, Glenthorne House, Salcombe. Centrally situated for all amenities, holiday flat with small garden and estuary views, near town centre and quay. Fully equipped accommodation for six persons in one double bedroom and one room with two sets of bunk beds (one full size). Sittingroom, kitchen/diner. Electric cooker, fridge and all utensils supplied. Central heating. Blankets provided but visitors must bring own linen. Children welcome — playground nearby. Pets by prior arrangement only. Car not essential, but there is parking. Weekly terms £85 to £240 (£10 service charge for gas/electricity). Further details from **Mrs A. Newman, Druids Mead, Shirehampton Road, Stoke Bishop, Bristol, Avon BS9 1BL (Bristol [0272] 681894).**

SALCOMBE. Mrs Janet Rogers, Ilton Farm, Malborough, Kingsbridge TQ7 3BZ (Salcombe [054-884] 3635). Working farm. Ilton Farm is situated just off the main Kingsbridge to Salcombe road (A381) two miles from Salcombe and within easy reach of several beaches. Part of the farmhouse is available for self-catering holidays and accommodates up to six people. Two double and one single bedrooms, cot; bathroom; sittingroom with TV; kitchen with electric cooker, kettle, fridge and seating for six people. No linen supplied. Shops one mile. Car essential, parking. Open from April to October. Electricity by 10p meter. Also available two-bedroomed bungalow in Malborough. Terms on request. SAE brings prompt reply.

SEATON. Nos. 1-4 Mulberry Cottages, Fore Street, Seaton. Four semi-detached cottages in charming Mews-type setting 200 yards from beach in centre of town off main shopping street in private cul-de-sac. Quiet, secluded and old world yet fully modernised. Open all year round, long winter lets. Cottages sleep from four to six; two cottages with three bedrooms, two with two bedrooms all upstairs; cot available. All cottages have sittingrooms with TV, etc. bathrooms with toilets, fully fitted kitchens with either electric or gas cookers, fridges, etc. Linen hire available. Either full or part central heating. Pets by prior arrangement. Garaging provided. Rates on application, electricity extra. SAE for details to **Mr H. J. Pountney, 11 Fore Street, Seaton EX12 2LE (Seaton [0297] 21297/22566).**

✱ **SEATON. Mr and Mrs E. P. Fox, West Ridge, Harepath Hill, Seaton EX12 2TA (Seaton [0297] 22398).** West Ridge bungalow stands on elevated ground above the small coastal town of Seaton. It has one and a half acres of lawns and gardens and enjoys wide panoramic views of the beautiful Axe Estuary and the sea. Close by are Axmouth, Beer and Branscombe. The Lyme Bay area is an excellent centre for touring, walking, sailing, fishing, golf etc. This comfortably furnished accommodation is ideally suited for up to five people. Cot can be provided. Available March to October. £85 to £195 weekly (fuel charges included). Full gas central heating; colour TV. AA listed and approved. SAE for brochure. See also Colour Display advertisement for full details.

SEATON near. Mrs E. Pady, Higher Cownhayne Farm, Cownhayne Lane, Colyton EX13 6HD (Colyton [0297] 52267). Working farm. Higher Cownhayne is a family farm with milking cows, beef cattle, breeding horses, children's ponies and farm dogs and cats. Private trout fishing. Private aircraft landing strip, 400 yards long, suitable for Cessna Piper, Rally Club or Helicopter. Also model aircraft flying. North Hill Glider School 12 miles from farm. Farm has own registered riding stables with lessons and trekking at an hourly rate. Within easy reach of seaside resorts. Two flats and a caravan available, sleeping from four to 10 persons. All fully equipped including TV. Linen may be hired (overseas visitors only). Cot available. Sorry, no pets. Parking space. Shops half-mile. SAE, please, for all replies.

SELF-CATERING   Devon   **433**

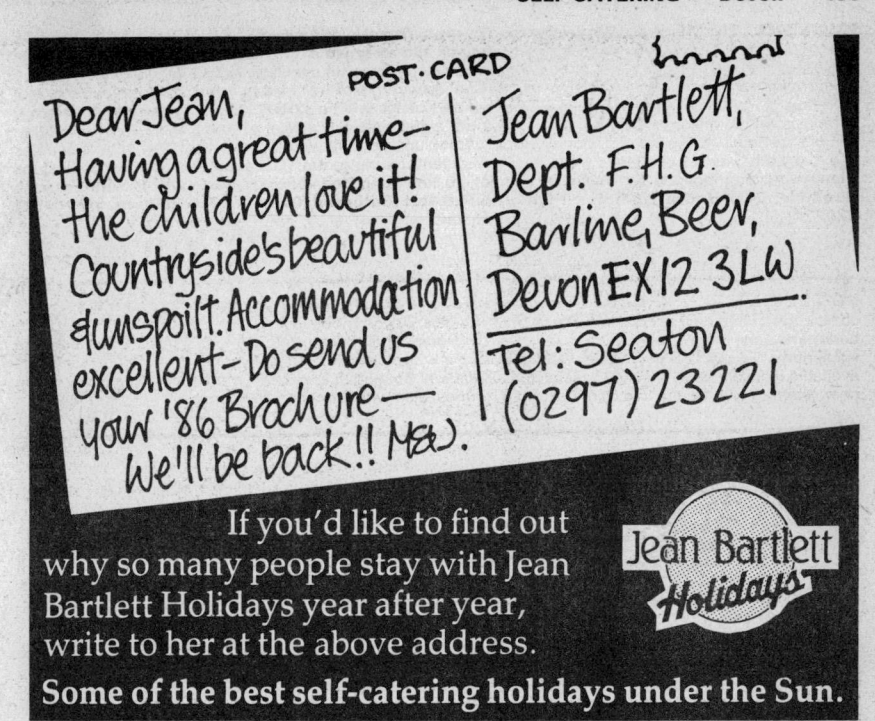

POST·CARD

Dear Jean,
Having a great time — the children love it! Countryside's beautiful & unspoilt. Accommodation excellent — Do send us your '86 Brochure — We'll be back!! M&J.

Jean Bartlett,
Dept. F.H.G.
Barline, Beer,
Devon EX12 3LW.

Tel: Seaton
(0297) 23221

If you'd like to find out why so many people stay with Jean Bartlett Holidays year after year, write to her at the above address.

Jean Bartlett Holidays

Some of the best self-catering holidays under the Sun.

SIDMOUTH. 1 Barton Paddocks, Tipton St. John, Sidmouth. Working farm. Comfortable three bedroom house in centre of small friendly Devon village. Sleeps six, cot, colour TV, storage heaters, all-electric — 50p meter. Garage and parking. Small garden. Within easy walking distance of Post Office/Stores, Pub with catering facilities and playing fields. This area abounds with footpaths running alongside the River Otter, through woods and uphill to spectacular views over East Devon to Dartmoor. Sidmouth, four miles away, provides safe bathing and adequate shopping facilities. The coastal walks are of particular beauty. Springtime visits are strongly recommended. Pets by arrangement. SAE for terms. **Mrs P. Hamilton-Cox, Cotley Farm, Fluxton, Ottery St. Mary EX11 1RJ (Ottery St. Mary [040-481] 2778).**

SOUTH DEVON. Inner Hope Cove and Bantham. Two thatched cottages in Inner Hope Cove stand in a picturesque square, 100 yards from beach, slipway and National Trust Footpath. Each has kitchen, living/diningroom, three double bedrooms, bathroom/WC. Outside is a lawn, garage and ample parking. The Bantham house, close to beach, has glorious views over sea and river, with footpath to river. Kitchen, bootroom, WC, sitting/diningroom; three bedrooms to sleep eight, bathroom/WC. All are furnished comfortably, carpeted, fully equipped, heated by electricity. Each has TV, cot, high chair. Golf, tennis, and boating nearby. SAE to **Hope Holidays, Kerse Farm, South Milton, Kingsbridge TQ7 3LA (Kingsbridge [0548] 560234).**

SOUTH MOLTON. Mrs M. Robins, Dunsley Farm, West Anstey, South Molton EX36 3PF (Anstey Mills [03984] 246). Working farm. Dunsley Farm is a 120-acre farm carrying beef and sheep in delightful countryside approximately six miles from Dulverton, with easy access to the local beauty spots of Exmoor. Situated approximately three miles off A361, adjoining a quiet country road, it is an ideal area for walking or touring. A modernised farm cottage, to accommodate up to six persons, has two bedrooms; bathroom; kitchen with electric cooker, fridge. Large lounge with an open fire, electric heaters and TV. Linen supplied. Electricity by 10p slot meter. Children welcome, cot, high chair and babysitting available. Pets accepted by prior arrangement. Coarse fishing on the farm; riding and pony trekking available nearby. Open all year. For further information SAE, please, or phone **Mrs Robins.**

SOUTH MOLTON. Mrs A. E. Hill, Great Rapscott Farm, South Molton EX36 3EL (Filleigh [059-86] 247). Working farm. Simply furnished farm cottages, warm and comfortable. Attractively set in buildings beside the stonebuilt farmhouse of busy 250-acre family farm. Lovely surroundings with panoramic views over deep-wooded valleys, and peaceful stream, ideal for fishing and family picnics. Not far from Exmoor and safe beaches. Price £69 to £115, electricity included. Dogs £5. Total units 2. Persons one to five. Open all year.

434 Devon SELF-CATERING

SOUTH MOLTON. Mrs R. E. Ley, Drewstone Farm, South Molton EX36 3EF (South Molton [076-95] 2337). Working farm. Completely self-contained part of a large farmhouse with own entrance situated on the 180 acres of sheep/cattle farm within easy reach of South Molton town which has swimming pool, tennis, squash etc. Barnstaple town and sandy beaches. Exmoor, Lorna Doone country, Lynton, Lynmouth, all within easy reach by car. The accommodation comprises of three double bedrooms, one with two single beds and one single bedroom; cot; bathroom, toilet; sittingroom; kitchen/diningroom fully equipped with fridge, cooker, iron etc. Electric fires, TV, fitted carpets throughout. All-electric, which is supplied from 50p meter. Pets allowed. Linen not supplied. Sleeps six/eight. Open all year. Reasonable terms on request.

SOUTH MOLTON. Mrs G. E. Bray, West Millbrook, Twitchen, South Molton EX36 3LP (North Molton [059-84] 382). Working farm. Very fully equipped bungalow and farmhouse flat on West Millbrook Farm, some of whose 150 acres are in Exmoor National Park. Cattle and sheep reared. Ideally situated for touring North Devon and West Somerset and within easy reach of the Lorna Doone Valley. Swimming and pony trekking nearby. The bungalow sleeps 14 to 16 in four double-bedded rooms, one with additional bunk beds, another two single beds. Convertible couches for use in sittingrooms, diningroom or utility room. Can sleep six to eight in fewer rooms at reduced price. Fully carpeted, games room, electric cooker, fridge, sink units, airer, tumble dryer and iron, TV; bathroom, shower-room; cot, high chair, playpen. Linen extra charge. The farmhouse flat sleeps two to eight. Car essential, parking. Central heating if required. Weekly terms from £25 to £170 plus VAT. SAE for coloured brochure. Electricity metered.

SOUTH MOLTON. Mrs Sheila M. Coe, Higher Ley Farm, North Molton, South Molton (North Molton [059-84] 281). Working farm. Higher Ley Farm is a 75-acre mixed farm on the edge of Exmoor. The holiday flat is part of the farmhouse and is comfortably furnished. It has diningroom, lounge with TV, kitchen, bathroom and three bedrooms. Sleeping seven. Cot and high chair also provided. Babysitting is available. Fully equipped except sheets. Milk and eggs available on the farm and there is a chance for children to meet the farm animals. The area offers beautiful countryside for walking and riding and the opportunity to explore an unspoilt coastline from rocky cliffs to long sandy beaches. Well behaved pets welcome. Open April to October. From £80 per week.

SOUTH MOLTON near. "Robert House", Molland, Near South Molton. This house stands in its own grounds with garden and fine views facing south. It is situated in the Exmoor National Park conservation area. Excellent riding, walking. In small agricultural village within walking distance of the moor. Beautiful Cathedral at Exeter 26 miles. Attractive village pub. South Molton eight miles. Accommodation for six/eight people in two double and two single bedrooms; cot available; bathroom, two toilets; sittingroom; kitchen/diner. Fully equipped with oil-fired Rayburn, electric cooker, fridge, etc. No linen. Shops eight miles. Sea 20 miles. Pets are permitted. Car is essential here and there is ample parking. It is open all year and weekly terms are from £60 to £100. Apply to **Mrs R. Fanthorpe, Thatch Cottage, Molland, Near South Molton EX36 3NG (Bishop's Nympton [076-97] 479).**

STARCROSS. Country Services, Exstowe, Starcross EX6 8PD. Please telephone Mrs Smith (any time) — (Starcross [0626] 890333/890321). We are a small agency specialising in letting selected cottages in the lovely South Hams area of South Devon. Dartmouth/Salcombe. All our cottages are extremely well-furnished and immaculately clean. Super cottages in various lovely locations. Superb coastal walks and beaches. A paradise for ornithologists. Sailing or fishing on the beautiful Kingsbridge Estuary. Dittisham-on-the-Dart (illustrated): Delightful quayside cottages on the enchanting River Dart. Sailing or motor boats (life-jackets supplied) available for hire. Sailing instruction by experts. We offer a very personal service — we want you to have a really super holiday!

WHEN MAKING ENQUIRIES PLEASE MENTION FARM HOLIDAY GUIDE

SELF-CATERING Devon 435

**TAVISTOCK. Mrs J. E. Yeo, Kilimanjaro, Brentor, Tavistock PL19 0NF (Mary Tavy [082-281] 469).
Working farm, join in.** Kilimanjaro has a roadside position four-and-a-half miles from Tavistock and half-a-mile from the village of Brentor. Beef and sheep are reared on its 96 acres. The land runs up to the Tor on which the Church of St. Michael is built. Fishing, riding and walking facilities within easy reach and the well-known Lydford Gorge is only four miles away. Children welcome; cot and high chair available. There are two double and one single bedrooms, sleeping five; bathroom, toilet; sitting/diningroom; kitchen with electric cooker, fridge, spin dryer, etc. Linen supplied. Shops four-and-a-half miles away. Parking space. From May to October weekly terms are from £55 to £75. Electricity metered. Pets permitted.

TAVISTOCK near. Mrs E. M. Abel, Higher Godsworthy, Peter Tavy, Near Tavistock PL19 9NY (Mary Tavy [082-281] 211). Working farm. Situated in the Dartmoor National Park on a hill farm where the main enterprise is sheep and beef, the cottage has three bedrooms (one has double bed and the others each have two singles). Cot available. Bedrooms fully carpeted. Linen supplied. Bathroom/toilet with shaving point. Lounge; colour TV; large beamed kitchen/diningroom with cooker, fridge, larder. Utility room with spin dryer. Pets permitted. Hot water supplied. 50p meter for cooking and heating. Car essential — parking. Open all year round. Terms on request. Local market town (Tavistock) four miles. Facilities for golf, tennis, horse riding and swimming nearby. Ideal centre for guided walks on the moor — National Trust properties within easy reach, also Morwellham Quay, a Museum Copper Mine.

TIVERTON. Mrs M. Kelland, Ayshford Court, Sampford Peverell, Tiverton (Tiverton [0884] 820271). Stone built, semi-detached cottage by the side of the Grand Western Canal, situated in lovely open countryside in local beauty spot. Only one mile from M5 Intersection 27. Cottage contains three double bedrooms with two double and two single beds; cot also; large kitchen/diner with electric cooker, fridge; large lounge with colour TV; bathroom, toilet. Ample electric fires. Shops one mile, sea 15 miles, so car is essential and there is parking at the back. Lawn at the front. Sorry, no pets allowed. Open all year. (Everything supplied except linen). Electric meter. Weekly terms from £30 to £80.

TIVERTON. Mr and Mrs W. G. Davey, Middleway, Pennymoor, Tiverton EX16 8LX (Cheriton Fitzpaine [036-36] 335). Nicely situated midway between Dartmoor and Exmoor, within one hour's driving distance of most north and south Devon holiday resorts, self-catering accommodation is available for four people all year round. One double bedroom (additional double bedroom available with toilet and washbasin should there be four/five in the party); cot; bathroom, toilet; and fully equipped kitchen. Everything supplied including linen. Colour TV. Shops three miles. Car essential. Pets permitted. An ideal holiday spot for sporting enthusiasts, with hunting available in season (ten packs); plenty of inns within easy reach. Fresh farm produce available daily. Babysitting facilities. SAE or phone for terms.

TORBAY. Mrs D. J. Naish, "Orchard Lea", North Whilborough, Newton Abbot TQ12 5LP (Kingskerswell [080-47] 3370). Orchard Lea Maisonette is part of a large early Georgian cottage. Self-contained, with separate entrance. On the edge of a small village, it is completely surrounded by gardens and orchards and is not overlooked. There are two bedrooms with double and single beds in each; livingroom with colour TV; bathroom and toilet; immersion water heater and all-electric kitchen with fridge. Electricity is metered. Mains water, drainage, etc. All necessary blankets, cutlery and crockery. Village shops one mile. Newton Abbot and Torquay both three-and-a-half miles; River Dart nearby, also Dartmoor and other South Devon beauty spots. Tradesmen call at the house. Heaters and cot available. Enclosed parking space. Tennis, golf, riding, fishing and bathing all within easy reach in Torbay area. SAE, please, for terms.

TORBAY. Mr and Mrs R. Hawkes, Whilborough Farmhouse, North Whilborough, Newton Abbot TQ12 5LP (Kingskerswell [080-47] 2011). Self-catering conversions of 17th century farm buildings in peaceful hamlet. Thatched stone cottage, bungalow and main house wing. All sleep up to six persons. Mains service. Furnished and fully equipped with cutlery, crockery, electric cookers, refrigerators, immersion heaters, colour TV's and many comforts. Cots, high chairs, linen etc., on request. Guests' private car park and three-quarter acre paddock. Convenient base for seaside, rivers, moors. Torbay resort amenities and Newton Abbot market town. Many attractive country walks. Please send SAE or telephone for full details.

When you read one you *haven't* read them all —

we have *eleven* other publications

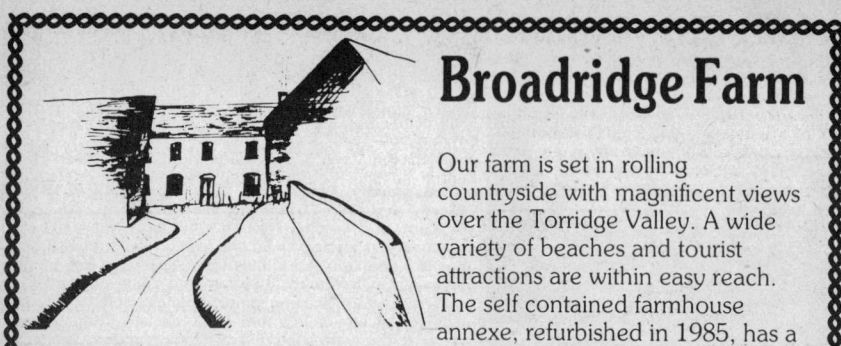

436　Devon　SELF-CATERING

Broadridge Farm

Our farm is set in rolling countryside with magnificent views over the Torridge Valley. A wide variety of beaches and tourist attractions are within easy reach. The self contained farmhouse annexe, refurbished in 1985, has a kitchen/dining room, sitting room with colour TV, bathroom and three bedrooms. We provide all linen; laundry and cleaning services can be arranged. The farm, at the end of its own lane, and with 6 acres of woodland, is ideal for children. There is a large garden with swing, climbing frame and paddling pool. A cot, high chair and push chair are available and baby sitting can be arranged. We keep a house cow, pigs, sheep and chickens and the family will be welcome to explore the farm and help at feeding and milking times. We offer a relaxed and friendly farm holiday with fresh farm produce for your self-catering needs. We can also provide a 'welcome' pack including a hot meal. Sorry no dogs.

For further details please contact Sue Plinston, Broadridge Farm, Little Torrington, Devon EX38 8QR. (Torrington [0805] 22252).

TORQUAY. Rogana Holiday Flats, Higher Warberry Road, Torquay TQ1 1SQ. Seven spacious self-contained flats in a detached Edwardian type house standing in its own grounds of lawns, shrubs and flower beds. Car parking at rear. Each flat is completely independent with its own entrance, ensuring absolute privacy. All flats have private bathroom and most have two separate bedrooms, plus lounge with TV; kitchen etc. Laundrette. Good decor and furnishing. Within walking distance of shops and beaches. We like children and do not object to dogs if previously arranged. SAE, for brochure, to resident proprietors who will endeavour to ensure your comfort and a high standard of cleanliness at all times. **Mr and Mrs F. H. Hughes, Rogana Flats, Higher Warberry Road, Torquay TQ1 1SQ (Torquay [0803] 23584).**

TORRINGTON. Mrs M. Bealey, Week Farm, Torrington (Torrington [0805] 23354). Good quality accommodation in our farmhouse flat, enjoying scenic views in beautiful surroundings. The accommodation comprises spacious, well equipped kitchen/diner; lounge with colour TV; room with double bed, one with twin beds, convertible bed and cot if required; bathroom with WC. Electric cooker, heaters and spin dryer. The farm has a beef, sheep and arable unit and is situated about one mile from Great Torrington which has a heated swimming pool, tennis, golf and Dartington glass factory. Within easy reach of many beaches and the beauty of Exmoor and Dartmoor. Linen for hire. Electric meter. Advance orders. No pets. Children welcome. SAE, please, for details, or phone. Terms from £50.

Terms quoted in this publication may be subject to increase if rises in costs necessitate

SELF-CATERING   **Devon**   **437**

**TORRINGTON. Mrs Beryl Heard, Furze Farm, Torrington EX38 7HA (Torrington [0805] 23360). 
Working farm.** This is a 17th century farmhouse set in 185 acres of peaceful countryside. Family dairy farm approximately one mile from Torrington which has heated swimming pool, golf course, Dartington Glass Factory and many picturesque walks. It is 10 miles to Westward Ho! beach. Lounge/diner with colour TV; games room with ¾ size snooker table, table tennis, darts etc. Log fire when chilly. Central heating. Bedroom accommodation — one double with washbasin, one family room; large bathroom with separate toilet. Cot and high chair available. Children under 12 sleeping in parents' room half price. Evening Meal optional by arrangement. Bed and Breakfast from £6 nightly; Bed, Breakfast and Evening Meal £10 nightly. Full English Breakfast. Home produced food wherever possible. Open March to September. Pets welcome. Warm welcome assured to all our guests.

TOTNES. Mr R. Miller, Buckyette Farm, Littlehempston, Totnes (Staverton [080-426] 638). Buckyette Farm offers a variety of holiday accommodation converted from the old farm buildings and retaining much of the original character and charm. "The Little Stable", "The Linhay", "The Big Stable" and "The Coach House" are all open-plan and sleep up to six people. "Lower Lodge", "Higher Lodge", "The Harness Room" and "The Shippon" are of more conventional design and accommodate from two to eight people. All contain either showers or bathrooms, toilet, TV, fridge, electric cooker and usual equipment. No linen or towels supplied. Metered electricity. Children welcome. Sorry, no pets. Car essential. All the attractions of Torbay and Dartmoor are within five/six miles. Terms from £45 to £138 weekly. Bed and Breakfast accommodation also available.

TOTNES. Mrs D. A. McCoy, The Old Rectory, East Allington, Totnes TQ9 7PX (East Allington [054-852] 288). Spacious flat sleeping six-eight in a large country house on the outskirts of rural South Hams village centrally placed but secluded. Well furnished and appointed the flat provides a comfortable base for holiday pursuits. Guests have use of three-acre gardens. Accommodation includes kitchen/diner with fridge, electric cooker and appliances. Sittingroom (colour TV and bed settee), two bedrooms (one double plus divan; three singles); bathroom. heating by electric fires on coin meter, bed linen provided. Ample car and boat parking. Children welcome, but not pets. Cot and babysitting available by arrangement. Beaches within five miles, Totnes nine, Torbay 15. Brochure.

TOTNES. Mrs S. C. Hodges, Higher Poulston, Halwell, Totnes TQ9 7LE (Harbertonford [080-423] * 345). Eight lovely holiday cottages tastefully converted in 1981 from three old stone farm buildings set in peaceful countryside with superb views, four miles from Totnes, eight miles from beaches. Spacious rooms, modern comforts and conveniences whilst retaining the building's original character. One, two and three-bedroomed cottages sleeping two to seven people. Fitted kitchen/diner, electric cooker and fridge; sittingroom, TV; modern bathroom, vanitory units in some bedrooms, cot, high chairs available. Night store heating. Children's play area. Car essential — parking. Sorry, no pets. No linen. Open all year. Owners live in adjoining farmhouse and look forward to welcoming you. AA listed. SAE, please. Weekly terms from £50. See also Colour Display advertisement for details.

TOTNES. Mrs M. Burgess, The Mill House, Gara Bridge, Totnes TQ9 7JT (Gara Bridge [054-882] 261). Working farm. Cider Press Cottage (the wing of Mill House) is in an idyllic setting beside the River Avon, set amidst woodland and meadows, near Dartmoor and the coast and within easy reach of historic Totnes, Dartmouth and Kingsbridge. The cottage comprises a large light sittingroom and well equipped kitchen/diner with French windows into the garden. Two double bedrooms upstairs and bathroom; central heating throughout, TV etc. Guests are invited to mingle with the ducks, geese, goats and ponies and explore both grounds and river — we have canoes! Fly fishing is available nearby and horses may be hired from us. Holidays offering Western riding/tuition available at special rates. SAE, please, for brochure.

TOTNES. Mrs D. Reddaway, Lower Yetson Farm, Ashprington, Totnes TQ9 7EG (Harbertonford [080-423] 386). Working farm. Self-contained accommodation consisting of the front half of the farmhouse on 164-acre mixed farm. About three miles from the Elizabethan town of Totnes and one mile from Ashprington and Tuckenhay, eight miles from the sea. A small fishing river runs through the farm. Three large bedrooms sleeping six people; large kitchen/diner with electric cooker, fridge, fire, colour TV and piano. Fully equipped except bed linen. Farm and garden produce available. Car essential. Children welcome. Babysitting offered. Sorry, no pets. Weekly terms on application with SAE, please.

438   Devon   SELF-CATERING

* UMBERLEIGH. Mrs S. D. Francis, Collacott Farm, King's Nympton, Umberleigh EX37 9TP (South Molton [07695] 2491). Four character cottages, tastefully converted from stone barn, set in lovely countryside with farmhouse and cottages grouped round cobbled yard. Sleep two-eight, beautifully furnished, well equipped, heating, colour TV, bed linen, cots, high chairs, swimming pool, games and laundry room. Dogs permitted. See also colour display advertisement.

UMBERLEIGH. Mrs H. C. Johnson, Great Deptford, Umberleigh EX37 9AH (Chittlehamholt [076-94] 256). Working farm. The Annexe, completely self-contained, with own entrance through small garden, is part of the 17th century farmhouse, situated right on this 130-acre dairy farm. The accommodation is for five/six in one double and one treble rooms; cot available also high chair and babysitting; bathroom with toilet; open plan sitting/diningroom; kitchen is all electric with automatic cooker, kettle, fridge and clothes drier. Linen is supplied if requested at extra charge. The house is suitable for disabled guests. Dogs by arrangement. Shops three-quarters of a mile — fresh milk and eggs from farm; butcher calls weekly. Open May to October. Car essential, parking. The setting of the farmhouse ensures peace, quiet and safety from traffic; TV and plenty of space for playing on wet days. Shallow stream safe for children. Exmoor and Dartmoor nearby and lovely sandy surfing beaches of North Devon within easy driving distance. Weekly terms on request. SAE, please.

UMBERLEIGH (Exmoor). Sletchcott, King's Nympton, Umberleigh. Sletchcott is a beautifully modernised, detached, historic newly re-thatched Devon Longhouse (grade 2 listed) with two huge inglenook fireplaces, original bread oven and impressive oak beams. It has nightstore heaters and colour TV; furniture and equipment are to a very high standard. The house stands on a south-facing hill, down a short drive in its own three acres of garden, orchard and paddock. The view from all windows is glorious — across the valley to King's Nympton, with Dartmoor in the distance. The whole area of Taw Valley is very beautiful and famous for riding, fishing, walking, etc. Sletchcott is marked on Ordnance Survey Map 180. Inspected and listed by the AA. Registered West Country Tourist Board. Please send SAE for particulars to **Mrs D. H. Young, Little Orchard, 26 Clive Road, Esher, Surrey KT10 8PS (Esher [0372] 64514).**

WELLINGTON. Mr and Mrs L. J. Tristram, West End, Holcombe Rogus, Wellington, Somerset TA21 0QD (Greenham [0823] 672384). Working farm, join in. The 16th century olde worlde farm cottage has an inglenook fireplace and bread oven. It is approached by a private tarmac road and surrounded by a large garden. Situated on 120-acre farm, over which guests are free to wander. Half-a-mile from the small village of Holcombe Rogus which has general store with post office, butcher, public house, church. Within easy reach of Exmoor, Taunton, Exeter and the coast. Excellent walks in unspoilt countryside; extensive views. Six people accommodated in three double rooms, cot; bathroom, toilet; sitting/diningroom. Kitchen with electric cooker, fridge, kettle, iron, etc. No linen. Pets allowed. Car an advantage, ample parking. Open all year. TV provided. SAE, please, for terms.

* WESTWARD HO! John and Gill Violet, West Pusehill Farm, Westward Ho! EX39 5AH (Bideford [02372] 75638 or 74622). Situated in picturesque and peaceful country surroundings one mile from Westward Ho! beach and two and a half miles from the market town of Bideford. Each of the 11 cottages has been carefully converted, being equipped and furnished to an extremely high standard. Varying in size, they accommodate two to eight people. Prices from £65 to £370. Facilities include: heated swimming pool, residents' bar, sauna, solarium, children's play area, pets' corner, games room and laundry. Write or phone anytime for full colour brochure. See also colour display advertisement in this guide.

WOOLACOMBE. John and Rita Sandifer, Burnside, Mortehoe, Woolacombe EX34 7EA (0271-870312). Burnside is an attractive modern house, very pleasantly situated being only one/two minutes' walk from seafront and bus terminus. The flats are all self-contained and each has its own private bathroom and toilet. All electric, fully furnished and equipped for two/four or four/seven people. Bed linen is supplied if required. This is a popular resort, suitable for all ages — three miles of golden sands and lovely little bays. Next to coastal path and National Trust property which provides lovely walks. Outdoor activities include surfing, riding, fishing. Good touring centre. SAE for brochure.

WOOLACOMBE. Mr B. A. Watts, Resthaven, Esplanade, Woolacombe EX34 7DH (Woolacombe [0271] 870298 or 870248). Resthaven is a modern house on the seafront, with magnificent views of the Devon coast, immediately opposite Combesgate beach and 200 yards from Woolacombe sands, the most perfect in the West country. Bathing and surfing from the house. Garage for hire, also parking space. Flat one (first floor) has lounge, kitchenette with electric cooker, fridge; bathroom, toilet; two family bedrooms and one double, one single room, all with washbasins; flat two (ground floor) has one family bedroom, one double room with washbasin; lounge, kitchenette with electric cooker, fridge; bathroom/toilet. Interior sprung mattresses. Fully equipped except for linen. TV. Open March to November. Weekly terms according to season. Full or part livery available. Scenic riding country. SAE, please, for details.

Please note that entries marked with an asterisk also have a colour display advert in the colour section in this guide

SELF-CATERING   Devon / Dorset   **439**

WOOLACOMBE. Mrs P. Bradley, Westering, Springfield Road, Woolacombe EX34 7BX (Woolacombe [0271] 870207). Two completely self-contained flats in detached house in quiet part of village. Easy three minutes' walk to Devon's finest beach with three miles of perfect golden sands. Village offers shops, pubs, restaurants, putting, riding, etc. The flats are comfortably furnished to a high standard, carpeted throughout, with full-size gas cooker, refrigerator, TV. Both enjoy marvellous views of beach, bay and countryside. The flats are two-bedroomed, with separate lounge, bathroom or shower, sleeping four and six. Each has private entrance. There are no meters. Children welcome (cot available). Pets are accepted. Free parking. Available April-November.

WOOLACOMBE. Mrs Diana R. Dennis, Spreacombe Manor, Braunton EX33 1JA (Woolacombe [0271] 870536). Working farm. Riddells and Styles are two houses in the wing of a large scheduled Georgian Manor House set in an area of outstanding natural beauty four miles from the sea, together with the coachman's cottage immediately adjoining. The houses are completely self-contained and surrounded by 200-acres of woodland and 250-acres of farmland. The houses each accommodate six persons in two/three bedrooms and are fully furnished with all-electric kitchens and night storage heaters. Pets welcome. Cots, high chair, laundry room. Initial shopping service. Prices (on application) include VAT, electricity, colour TV etc. Extensive literature and photographs available on request.

WOOLACOMBE. Mrs Diana R. Dennis, Spreacombe Manor, Braunton EX33 1JA (Woolacombe [0271] 870536). Working farm. Spreacombe Gardens comprises six holiday bungalows set in former vegetable garden of large Georgian Manor House. Two bungalows have four bedrooms accommodating eight people and four bungalows have three bedrooms accommodating six people — fully furnished with all-electric kitchens. Large grassed play area with swing, slide, sandpit and three ton roller (!) all surrounded by 250-acres of farmland and 200 acres of woodland, scheduled as being an area of outstanding natural beauty and within four miles of the beach. Pets welcome. Cots, high chairs, laundry room. Initial shopping service. Prices (on application) include VAT, electricity, colour TV, etc. Extensive literature and photographs available on request.

DORSET

ABBOTSBURY. Withybank, Gorwell Farm, Abbotsbury, Weymouth. Working farm. Situated in a secluded valley, 11 miles west of Weymouth, this furnished chalet bungalow on Gorwell Farm is three miles by road from the coast. General stores, post office, butcher in village. Accommodation for five adults. One double, one twin bedrooms, and one single bed in sun lounge; bathroom and toilet; sitting/diningroom, kitchen with electric cooker, fridge and immersion heater. No linen supplied. Cot available. Pets accepted by arrangement. Car essential — parking. Electricity extra. Open from March to November. Brochure on application, with SAE, please, to **Mrs E. J. Pengelly, Gorwell Farm, Abbotsbury, Weymouth DT3 4JX (Abbotsbury [0305] 871284).**

BEAMINSTER. Edward and Bridget Pardey, "Sandiford Farm," Mosterton, Beaminster DT8 3HN (Broadwindsor [0308] 68338). Four detached natural stone farm buildings, tastefully converted into three cottages and a shop with self-contained flat, situated in the centre of the village. The cottages and flat are comfortably furnished to a high standard, each with a small garden, lounge, coloured television, dining area. Fully equipped kitchen (electric cooker, refrigerator, washing machine). Bedrooms, bathroom and toilet. Sleeping four/ten people. There is a large car park and play area for children. Mosterton is on the A3066 within easy motoring distance of the unspoilt Dorset coastline and Thomas Hardy country. Mrs Pardey also runs West Dorset Holiday Cottages, letting other cottages in the villages locally.

440 Dorset SELF-CATERING

BEAMINSTER. Ron and Carol Poulton, Hursey Farm, Hursey, Broadwindsor, Beaminster DT8 3LN (Broadwindsor [0308] 68323). Set in the grounds of a lovely old farmhouse, Hursey Farm cottages have been skilfully converted from traditional stone farm buildings into three pretty self-contained holiday cottages. Tastefully renovated with natural pine, they retain many character features. Each dwelling has an attractive sittingroom with TV; well-appointed kitchen and bathroom and two bedrooms to sleep four plus. Cooking, lighting and heating are all-electric. Pets by arrangement only. Linen supplied, if required, at extra charge. Car essential — parking. Hursey is a tiny hamlet on the edge of Broadwindsor situated in the quiet and beautiful Dorset countryside, seven miles coast. Ideal centre for riding, walking, golfing, fishing and touring. Many places of interest, historic houses and gardens, wildlife park, ancient earth works and fossil rich cliffs of Lyme Regis, plus many lovely towns and villages to visit. Terms from £50 to £138 weekly. SAE, please.

BEAMINSTER. "South Lodge", Seaborough, Beaminster. Delightful, secluded, south-facing cottage overlooking open farmland about 10 miles from sea, within few miles of many places of interest — ancient earthworks, historic houses and gardens, wildlife park, beaches, fossil-rich cliffs at Charmouth and Lyme Regis. Seaborough is a small hamlet about four miles north of Beaminster, four south of Crewkerne. Up to six people accommodated, plus cot, if required, in two family bedrooms (one with washbasin); two bathrooms, two toilets. Lounge with colour TV; diningroom. Fully fitted kitchen, electric cooker, fridge, washing machine. Two storage heaters for winter use. Bed linen supplied.— no extra charge. Large garden — ample parking space — car essential. Shops/public transport two miles. Children welcome. Pets by prior arrangement. Sporting facilities within easy driving distance — golf, sailing, fishing, riding. Available all year. Brochure and terms on application. **Mr and Mrs D. A. Bishop, "Oldcotes", Hursey, Broadwindsor, Beaminster DT8 3LN (Broadwindsor [0308] 68461).**

BEAMINSTER near. Mrs M. Frost, Childhay Manor, Blackdown, Near Beaminster DT8 3LQ (Broadwindsor [0308] 68228). Working farm. Situated on a tributary of the River Axe, a portion of this lovely 14th century manor farmhouse has been modernised and decorated for holiday lets. The 300-acre farm has milking cows and pigs, horses are bred for National Hunt Chasing. Fresh cream and yoghourt made; dairy produce, eggs and honey can be purchased. Within easy reach of Bristol, Bath, Wells Cathedral, Cheddar Gorge and Wookey Hole Caves; 20 minutes from Lyme Regis and Charmouth. Golf and riding nearby. Trout fishing available. Accommodation for six people; cot; bathroom, toilet; large lounge/diningroom; kitchen with electric cooker and fridge. Shops half-a-mile; sea 10 miles. Parking; car essential. No pets. Open all year. Tennis court. Colour TV. Free milk. Weekly terms from £60 including electricity.

BLANDFORD. Littlemarsh, Leigh Cross, Ibberton, Blandford. Working farm. Spacious self-catering bungalow set in secluded, unspoiled countryside, especially pretty in springtime. On an old world stock farm, sheep, cattle and horses graze the surrounding grassland. A short walk takes you to the farmyard with its variety of poultry and livestock (milk, eggs, butter available) or into the tiny village nestling under Bulbarrow Hill, famous for its views of Blackmoor Vale. Within easy reach of Dorset's beautiful coast and many historical sites. Three bedrooms, sleeps six plus cot; bathroom, toilet; lounge (colour TV, open fire); kitchen/diningroom (all-electric, fridge, oil-fired Rayburn if required); utility (automatic washing machine); garage. Children, pets welcome. Brochure on request. Available April – October inclusive. **Mrs P. C. M. Harris, Marsh Farm, Ibberton, Blandford DT11 0EN (Hazelbury Bryan [025-86] 423).**

BLANDFORD. Mrs Patricia C. M. Harris, Marsh Farm, Ibberton, Blandford DT11 0EN (Hazelbury Bryan [025-86] 423). Working farm. Self-catering ground floor flat in attractive farmhouse. This old world stock farm is situated in the heart of Dorset in secluded, unspoilt countryside close beneath Bulbarrow Hill, with its incomparable views of the Blackmoor Vale. It is ideal for walking, riding or just getting away from it all. Within easy reach of Dorset's beautiful coast. You may pass through "Hardy" country on the way, or visit Dorchester, our historic county town. Two double bedrooms, one with bunk beds; shower room, toilet; kitchen, all-electric; sitting/diningroom. Children and pets welcome. Ponies by arrangement. Milk and eggs from farm. Parking. Brochure and terms on request. Available all year round.

BLANDFORD near. School Cottage, Courtney Cottage, Shroton, Near Blandford. This small cottage, recently converted, attached to attractive 17th century house. Ideal for couple, or young couple with two children. Can sleep four, or six if put-u-up in sittingroom used as bedroom. Situated in delightful rural village at foot of prehistoric Hambledon Hill. Within easy motoring distance of Salisbury, Bath, Longleat, Dorchester, Poole and many other places of historic interest. Also within motoring reach of riding, sailing, golfing, fishing. Nature Reserves. It is in the famous Hardy country with its delightful walks and varied coastline. Two double bedrooms with cot; bathroom, toilet; sittingroom; kitchen/diner — fully equipped, electric. Everything except linen. Pets by arrangement. Shops three minutes. Open all year round with special winter terms. SAE, please, for details and terms to **Mrs E. Howlett, Tadpoles, Frog Lane, Shroton, Nr. Blandford DT11 8QL (Child Okeford [0258] 860033).**

Camellia Court
BOURNEMOUTH
Ideal Location

"Camellia Court" is a detached property situated on West Cliff adjacent to Alum Chine and only minutes (300 yards) from the beach. It consists of five spacious self-contained flats sleeping two to seven people, all having separate kitchens with gas cookers and electric fridges, bath, WC. Colour TV supplied. Linen can be supplied if required, and two of the flats are on ground level. Laundry and exterior drying space available. Although a car is not essential, there is a parking space, plus lock-up garages. Ideal for a quiet holiday, there is a large beautiful garden and the property lies in a peaceful cul-de-sac road between two Pinetree Chines. Buses run nearby. Cots and high chairs are available. Open Easter to September, weekly terms are from £50 with gas/electricity slot metered, and central heating provided. Member English Tourist Board and Holiday Flats Association. Colour Brochure on request.

Mr H. J. Balestra, "Camellia Court", 5 Milner Road, Westbourne, Bournemouth BH4 8AD (Bournemouth [0202] 761212).

BLANDFORD near. East Wing, Courtney Cottage, Shroton, Near Blandford. This is the East wing of attractive 17th century house which has been divided into two. Exceptionally well furnished to accommodate four in two double bedrooms and connected bathroom. Ground floor has sittingroom and diningroom with TV. Fully equipped electric kitchen. Linen not supplied. Shops three minutes' walk. Pets by arrangement. Available all year. (Special winter terms). Easy motoring distance of Salisbury, Bath, Longleat, Dorchester, Poole. Riding, sailing, golfing, fishing, beautiful walks. Nature Reserves and many historically interesting places to visit. SAE, please, for terms and details to **Mrs E. Howlett, Tadpoles, Frog Lane, Shroton, Nr. Blandford DT11 8QL (Child Okeford [0258] 860033).**

BOURNEMOUTH. Bournemouth Holiday Homes, Dept. 24, 858 Christchurch Road, Bournemouth BH7 6DQ (Bournemouth [0202] 426677). For more than a quarter of a century Bournemouth's oldest private holiday accommodation agency has been providing a free and reliable **advance** booking service for self-catering holidays at bargain prices in individually-owned, fully furnished HOUSES, BUNGALOWS, COTTAGES, FLATS AND MAISONETTES in BOURNEMOUTH, POOLE, CHRISTCHURCH, HIGHCLIFFE-ON-SEA, RINGWOOD AND ENVIRONS (plus one or two CHALETS/CARAVANS close to NEW FOREST). All premises are personally inspected and accurately described and there is accommodation for up to eight persons to suit most pockets. Children of all ages are welcome at several properties and a few accept well-trained pets at extra charge. Most bookings run from "Saturday to Saturday" only. Please be sure to send three "second class" postage stamps (or equivalent) when applying for detailed literature.

BRIDPORT near. Pound Cottage, Netherbury, Near Bridport. Double-fronted, 17th-century cottage with beamed ceilings, situated in the centre of a delightful picturesque West Country village, away from traffic, six miles from sea at West Bay. Lyme Regis, Exeter and Dartmoor to the west, Bournemouth, New Forest to the east. Small town of Beaminster one-and-a-half miles. Good touring and walking area. Accommodation comprises small entrance hall, large sittingroom with colour TV, diningroom; kitchen, bathroom, separate toilet all on ground floor. Upstairs two bedrooms — one with double bed, the other two single beds. Cot provided. All rooms are well carpeted, decorated and furnished with electric fires. Electric cooker, immersion heater, fridge and washing machine; well supplied with cutlery, china, cooking utensils, blankets, pillows, but no linen. Sunny, secluded garden. No pets accepted. Electricty by 50p meter. Car essential, parking. AA inspected and listed. Available March–October. SAE **Mrs V. M. Barnes, Anvil Cottage, Sea Lane, Chideock, Bridport DT6 6LD (Chideock [0297] 89544).**

442 Dorset SELF-CATERING

BRIDPORT. Moorbath Cottage, 1 Atrim Common Cottages, Broad Oak, Bridport. Dorset Coast: light and airy three bedroom cottage, set in rolling open countryside within two-and-a-half miles of the market town of Bridport, itself only one mile from the sea at West Bay. One double, two single and a pair of bunk beds, plus an 'Adeptus' sofa that will form two singles if required. Blankets, crockery and pans provided. Electricity for cooker, immersion heater and lighting included. Logs for fire extra. Modern kitchen and bathroom. Location is rural, peaceful and designated of 'Outstanding Natural Beauty' by the local planning authority. Further details from **Mr Peter Dixon, 20 Simpson Street, London SW1 (01-228 6005).**

BRIDPORT. Mrs N. Smith, Crooch Farm, Whitchurch Canonicorum, Bridport DT6 6RF (Charmouth [0297] 60818). Working farm. Well converted self-contained part of farmhouse on a dairy farm, situated in the Char Valley on the edge of Marshwood Vale, within half-a-mile of pretty village with local shop and Post Office. Only two miles from sandy beach at Charmouth. The accommodation is pleasantly furnished. Livingroom with TV, open-plan to dining area and well equipped kitchen. Staircase to three double bedrooms, with double, two single and bunk beds, to accommodate up to six people. Cot available. Bathroom and toilet. Metered electricity. No pets, please. Parking. Available April to October. SAE, please, for more details and terms.

BRIDPORT. Stokemill Farm, Broadoak, Bridport. In the heart of Marshwood Vale, quiet, secluded, within easy driving distance of Bournemouth/Exmoor coast, West Bay, Eype, Seatown; Charmouth within five miles. Pilsdon Pen, Lambert's Castle and Lewesdon Hill within easy reach. Orchard and two fields adjoining, pretty gardens, lawns. Children and pets welcome, ample space to play safely. Tastefully furnished, fully carpeted, storage heaters, firewood supplied for open fires in diningroom (inglenook) and sittingroom. Accommodation for six in three double bedrooms; bathroom, two toilets; sittingroom with colour TV; diningroom; kitchen with electric cooker, fridge, all equipment. Car essential — covered parking. SAE, please, for terms. **Mrs M. Hazell, Culverhayes, Clanville, Castle Cary, Somerset BA7 7PQ (Castle Cary [0963] 50492).**

BRIDPORT. Mrs M. E. Fry, Wanehouse Farm, Morcombelake, Bridport DT6 6DJ (Chideock [0297] 89405). Working farm. Ground floor flat for four persons, part of farmhouse. Situated on A35, convenient for the South Dorset coastline. From the livingroom there is a beautiful view of sea and National Trust Land. Livingroom has convertible double bed and dining area; kitchenette with fridge, electric cooker. Shower, washbasin, toilet. One bedroom with double bed, or two single beds if preferred; cot available. TV included. Private parking for essential car. Electricity by 50p slot meter. No pets. Open from Easter until end of September, central heating extra. Charmouth with its sandy beach is three miles, and Lyme Regis seven. SAE, please, or telephone for terms.

BRIDPORT. Nos. 1 and 2 Marshwood Cottages, Marshwood, Bridport. A pair of fully modernised country cottages of character with their own lawns, situated in the village and within easy reach of the sea. Each provides accommodation for five plus cot. Bathroom, toilet. Sitting/diningroom with colour TV; de-luxe fitted kitchens with electric cookers, fridges, irons etc. Regret no pets. Car necessary, parking. Also available immaculate bungalow with small field adjoining. Well-maintained and under personal supervision. Marshwood lies on the Dorset/Devon/Somerset border, approximately seven miles to beaches at Lyme Regis and Charmouth. Beautiful surrounding countryside to explore and historic landmarks. Registered with the English Tourist Board. SAE, please, for details to **Mrs P. B. Bowditch, Colmer Farm, Marshwood, Bridport DT6 5QA (Hawkchurch [029-77] 278).**

BRIDPORT. Blackmore Farm, Whitchurch Canonicorum, Bridport. Blackmore Farm is situated in unspoilt countryside. Lawns almost surround the house and excellent views include National Trust properties. There are also many buildings of historical interest within easy reach. The house has been modernised and includes all modern conveniences. Private drive to farmhouse. There is accommodation for four/five persons. Two double, one single bedrooms. Bathroom and toilet. Kitchen with electric cooker, fridge and other utensils. Children welcome. Regret no pets. Metered electricity. Garage and parking space. Car essential. Available March to November. Please apply for terms to **Mrs D. H. Brooks, Higher Monkwood Farm, Pilsdon, Bridport DT6 5PF (Broadwindsor [0308] 68329).**

BRIDPORT near. Mrs D. M. Austin, Woolcombe Farm, Toller Porcorum, Dorchester DT2 0DP (Maiden Newton [0300] 20264). Working farm. This stone and slate cottage is near the farmhouse in a secluded valley away from the main roads. There is a small grass garden in front and parking and garage nearby. The accommodation is for five adults in two double and one single rooms (a camp bed can be provided, and a cot, if necessary). Sittingroom with open fire and TV; all electric kitchen with cooker, fridge, etc.; bathroom. Water heated by electricity. There are two storage heaters and electric fires. No linen supplied. Shops three-and-a-half miles away; sea six/eight miles. Pets permitted. Car essential. Children welcome at this farm which is two-and-a-half miles from Toller Porcorum village, three-and-a-half miles from Maiden Newton, six miles from Bridport. For terms, SAE, please, to **Mrs D. M. Austin.**

The information in the entries in this guide is presented by the publishers in good faith and after the signed acceptance by advertisers that they will uphold the high standards associated with FARM HOLIDAY GUIDES LIMITED. The publishers do not accept responsibility for any inaccuracies or omissions or any results thereof. Before making final holiday arrangements readers should confirm the prices and facilities directly with advertisers.

SELF-CATERING Dorset

BRIDPORT near. The Coach House, Candida House, Whitchurch Canonicorum, Near Bridport. Standing away from the large main house, this attractive conversion of a former coach house is built in the local Dorset Hamstone. Attractive grounds with bridge and stream. Situated in a picturesque village, two miles from the sea and the Chesil Beach, making an ideal base for exploring south west Dorset and neighbouring Somerset with its quaint thatched cottages, Abbotsbury Swannery, Lyme Regis and Cricket St. Thomas Wildlife Park. Large open-plan lounge with dining and kitchen area; bathroom with toilet; one double and one bunk bedded room; colour TV. Ample parking for two cars. Village shop and pub 200 yards. Sorry, no pets. **Mrs K. J. Bain, The Hut, Mount Park Road, Harrow-on-the-Hill, Middlesex HA1 3JZ (01-422-3390).**

BRIDPORT near. The White House, Candida House, Whitchurch Canonicorum, Near Bridport. Skilfully converted to form one completely self contained half of a Georgian Rectory, The White House stands in two acres of wooded and lawned gardens. A quiet and peaceful setting in a small village, yet only five miles from bustling Bridport and two miles from the sea at Charmouth. Excellent sporting facilities at Lyme Regis; golf nearby and wonderful coastal walks along 11 miles Chesil Beach. Lounge with dining area, breakfast kitchen, separate toilet and washbasin, bathroom with toilet, large upstairs sitting area, one double and one twin bedroom also one room with four single beds. Fuel on request for open fire in lounge, also two storage heaters and electric fire. Sorry, no pets. Ample parking. Colour TV. Terms on request from: **Mrs K. J. Bain, The Hut, Mount Park Road, Harrow-on-the-Hill, Middlesex HA1 3JZ (01-422-3390).**

CHARD. Old Forge Cottage, Holditch, Chard. Ideal for peace and seclusion in glorious unspoilt countryside within easy reach of the sea. This delightful old world cottage with oak beams stands just outside Holditch on the Devon/Dorset/Somerset borders, affording splendid views over beautiful countryside. Charmouth and its sandy beaches seven miles distant. Lyme Regis, with safe bathing and recreational facilities eight miles. The cottage is completely modernised and tastefully furnished with fitted carpets throughout, for up to four people. One twin-bedded room and two bunk rooms; sittingroom with colour TV; kitchen with dining area; modern bathroom; second toilet; electric cooker, fridge, vacuum cleaner, modern sink unit, immersion heater, night storage heaters throughout (included in terms). Everything supplied except linen. Electricity by 10p meter. Phone; walled garden; garage. Chard four-and-a-half miles. Terms £50 to £90 weekly. Open all year. Regret no children under 12 years. No pets. All enquiries to **Mrs P. A. Spice, Orchard Cottage, Duke Street, Micheldever, Near Winchester, Hants SO21 3DF (Micheldever [096-289] 563).**

CHARD near. Mrs M. A. Barrow, Chaffeigh Farm, Thorncombe, Near Chard TA20 4NX (046030-313). Working farm. Comfortably furnished modern bungalow set in beautiful West Dorset countryside on family farm. Own large walled garden. Lovely views and walks. Fully equipped for six plus baby. Large sitting/diningroom with open fire and colour TV; bathroom and toilet; three bedrooms with 4' 6" double and two single and two bunk beds; cot; spring interior mattresses and fitted carpets; pleasant kitchen with electric cooker, fridge etc. Immersion heater, radiators, electric fire. Beautiful lake and streams on farm; super children's swimming pool in village; excellent Wild Life Park and Abbey with gardens nearby. It is 20 minutes' drive to beaches. Discount for two weeks. Pets by arrangement only.

CHARMOUTH. Nag's Head Cottage, Fishpond, Charmouth, Near Bridport. This modernised detached cottage is situated in a quiet but not isolated area, with magnificent views over the Marshwood Vale and within easy reach of National Trust properties. As there is no public transport in the area, a car is essential — ample parking. Accommodation — diningroom/sittingroom with open coal fire; well equipped kitchen with oil-fired Rayburn cooker and small electric cooker; bathroom, toilet with washbasin; double bedroom with twin beds. Upstairs, large bedroom with four beds and single bedroom. Linen not supplied. Electric convectors in all bedrooms. Regret no pets. Open 1st April to 31st October. Deposit on booking. SAE, please, to **Mrs S. Redmond, Peters Gore, Fishpond, Charmouth, Near Bridport DT6 6NW (Hawkchurch [029-77] 364).**

CHARMOUTH. Mrs P. F. Morgan-Smith, Stonebarrow House, Charmouth DT6 6RA (Charmouth [0297] 60839). Spacious flat on first and second floors of farmhouse overlooking the pretty village of Charmouth with its sandy beach. Extensive views over Lyme Bay and inland up Char Valley. Accommodation for six people in three double bedrooms, one with double bed and dressingroom, the others with twin beds. Cot and high chair supplied. Large sittingroom with colour TV; sun room, fitted all-electric kitchen/diningroom; bathroom with airing cupboard. Ample parking. Everything but linen supplied. Electricity by 50p coin meter, including night storage heaters in all rooms. Conveniently situated for expeditions into a beautiful part of the country. Children welcome and babysitting undertaken. Large garden including orchard and climbing frame. No dogs, please. SAE, please, with enquiries.

Dorset SELF-CATERING

CHARMOUTH. Mrs J. R. White, Little Catherston Farm, Charmouth, Bridport DT6 6LZ (Charmouth [0297] 60368). Working farm. West Dorset is a good area for a holiday. Many delightful walks on National Trust Land — "Golden Cap" the highest point on the South Coast. Charmouth is well known for fossils. Golf at Lyme Regis and West Bay, also fishing. Exeter and Weymouth some 30 miles. Wildlife Park near Chard. The beach, about three-quarters of a mile, is sandy and safe for children. Many car parks. The self-contained flatlet, part of the farmhouse, sleeps four. Large bed/sittingroom with double bed. Small room with full size bunk beds. Kitchen meter for electricity. Bathroom, separate toilet. No linen. Car parking. Dogs allowed if kept under control. Open from Easter to end of October. SAE, please, for terms.

ETB **MANOR FARM HOLIDAY CENTRE** AA
Charmouth, Bridport, Dorset

Situated in a quiet rural valley, ten minutes' level walk from the beach.
1983 Built Luxury Two-Bedroomed Houses
*Sleep 4-6 *Lounge with colour T.V. *Fully fitted kitchen/diner *Fitted carpets *Double glazing *Central heating *Parking space.
Three-Bedroomed House and Bungalow
*Sleep 6 each *Lounge with colour T.V. *Central heating available *Parking within grounds *Enclosed garden.
Luxury six-berth Caravans
*One or two bedrooms *Toilet *Shower *Refrigerator *Full cooker *Television *Gas fire.

FULL CENTRE FACILITIES AVAILABLE INCLUDING SWIMMING POOL, SHOP, FISH AND CHIP TAKEAWAY, BAR, LAUNDERETTE, ETC.

Send SAE for colour brochure to **Mr R. B. Loosmore or Tel. 0297 60226**
See also Colour Display Advertisement in this Guide.

DORCHESTER. Mr M. W. Evans, Medway Farm, Askerswell, Dorchester DT2 9EW (Powerstock [030-885] 225). Working farm. Designed as a granny-flat, and built on two floors, into one end of a handsome 19th century slate barn, this accommodation is ideal for two people. Medway Farm is a 150-acre cereal and stock farm situated in outstandingly beautiful country, four miles from the sea. Connemara ponies are bred on the farm so there are often foals to entertain visitors. Wildlife abounds — deer, badgers, foxes and game birds are regularly seen while part of the chalk down is designated as a site of special scientific interest — especially interesting to the botanist and biologist. Available from April to October, the flat is fully equipped; electric cooking and heating; no linen supplied. Children welcome. Sorry, no pets. Car essential, parking. Shops four miles — public transport half-a-mile. Weekly terms £55 to £75. Further details on request.

DORCHESTER. Mrs J. M. Morris, Huish Farm, Sydling St Nicholas, Dorchester (Cerne Abbas [03003] 265). The perfect place for a peaceful holiday for two people only, this self-contained flat in thatched farmhouse, is set amidst beautiful countryside, within easy reach of the coast, and near Cerne Abbas village abounding with historical interest dating back to the 14th century, including remains of the Abbey. The Cerne Giant, 180 feet high, is a curious figure cut in the chalk hillside to the north-east of the village. Upstairs, one very large sunny room with twin beds, private bathroom, toilet; downstairs, large kitchen equipped with large electric cooker, fridge and all utensils. Linen not supplied. Car essential, ample parking. Own entrance, own sunny corner in garden. Pets are permitted. Weekly terms from £45 including fuel. SAE, please, for further details.

DORCHESTER near. Pitt Cottage, Ringstead Bay, Near Dorchester. An attractive part thatched stone-built cottage, surrounded by farmland and situated on the edge of a small wood about quarter-of-a-mile from the sea, commanding outstanding views of Ringstead Bay on the Dorset Heritage Coast. The cottage has recently been renovated and is equipped to sleep six; three bedrooms (two beds in each), two bathrooms, sitting room with open fire and large kitchen/dining area. Cot/high chair by arrangement; washing machine; TV; electric radiators in all rooms. Car essential. Available 22nd March to 31st October from £65 per week. For details, please contact **Mrs Hoare, 3A Redcliffe Place, London SW10 (01-352 4862 — weekday evenings): from 1.1.86 contact Mrs Russell (01-672 2022).**

PITT COTTAGE

LYME REGIS. Mrs V. A. Denning, Lower Holcombe Farm, Uplyme, Lyme Regis DT7 3TQ (Lyme Regis [029-74] 3679). Working farm. Lower Holcombe Farm is a dairy farm of about 100 acres. Children are welcome on the farm to see the milking, etc. Babysitting in the evening can be arranged. Six persons can be accommodated in the flat which is attached to the farmhouse. Carpeted throughout. There is a garden and a washing line. Situated a mile from the village of Uplyme which has a church and village school. Two minutes from village shop and post office. Lyme Regis is a seaside town with a safe, sandy beach and golf course two miles away. The market town of Axminster is four miles. Two double bedrooms, cot and high chair. Bathroom with washbasin, toilet and bath. Small kitchen with electric cooker, fridge and sink unit. Living/diningroom with TV. Suitable for the disabled. Sorry, no pets. Car advisable, parking. Terms do not include fuel (metered). SAE, please.

SELF-CATERING Dorset

LYME REGIS near. Mrs J. M. Masters, Coombehayes Farm, Uplyme, Near Lyme Regis DT7 3SU (Lyme Regis [029-74] 2439). Working farm. Attractive stone cottage built within thick walls of an old barn adjoining 18th century farmhouse. Quiet, south-facing, beautiful views. Shops half-a-mile, sea one and a half miles at Lyme Regis with safe, sandy beaches and interesting harbour. Golf, tennis, riding nearby. Comfortably furnished to high standard. Fully equipped except linen. Maximum seven persons. Carpeted throughout. Entrance hall, spacious lounge with colour TV and electric fire. Large, modern kitchen. Three double bedrooms (one double bed, five singles), upstairs bathroom with WC. Electric radiators all rooms. Cot, high chair, playpen. Metered electricity (50p). Regret, no pets. Ample parking. Available all year. Early booking essential. SAE, please, for brochure, terms and vacancies.

LYME REGIS. Mr and Mrs I. L. Collier, Amherst Farm, Uplyme, Lyme Regis DT7 3XH (Lyme Regis [02974] 2773). This cottage is part of the farmhouse and is set in a secluded West Country Valley. The cottage is totally separate with its own front door. This is a trout farm and fishery. Fly fishing is available by the hour or by the day to our guests and other visitors. The cottage is only two miles from the beach at Lyme Regis, but is ideally situated for all parts of the West Country holiday area. Ideal walking and bird-watching centre. Accommodation for four in two double rooms plus cot. Bathroom; sittingroom; diningroom/kitchen with Belling electric cooker. Central heating. Car essential, parking. Shops one and a half miles. Children welcome. Sorry, no pets. Available from March to October. Weekly terms including fuel from £80 to £175.

LYME REGIS. Mrs S. Denning, Higher Holcombe Farm, Uplyme, Lyme Regis DT7 3SN (Lyme Regis [029-74] 3223). Working farm. Completely separate part farmhouse on dairy farm which was a Roman settlement. Surrounded by pleasant country walks, golf, fishing and safe sandy beaches. Accommodation has three bedrooms. Two double and three single beds, lounge with inglenook fireplace, colour TV, kitchen/diningroom with fitted units, all amenities. Bathroom, toilet. Linen not provided. Pets by arrangement. Electric heating; 50p slot meter. Babysitting by arrangement. Plenty of parking. Car not essential; one mile from shops and village of Uplyme; two miles from coast of Lyme Regis. Open all year round. SAE for details.

LYME REGIS. Mr and Mrs J. D. Manfield, Court Hall Farm, Pound Lane, Uplyme, Lyme Regis DT7 3TT (Lyme Regis [029-74] 3179). Working farm. Half of the 16th century manor house, now dairy farm, is let as a self-contained unit and furnished to a high standard. Large entrance hall, drawingroom (panelled on two walls), beamed ceilings, large hearth fireplace, colour TV; well equipped, modern kitchen with electric cooker, heating, fires, washing machine and fridge. Upstairs bathroom, three bedrooms, cot, some babysitting. Maximum persons eight. Sunny lawn, swings for children. Regret no dogs. Marvellous holiday area, beautiful scenery. Early booking essential. Linen on hire. Undercover and outside parking. Open March to mid-December. SAE, please, for brochure, terms and vacant dates.

LYME REGIS. Mrs A. M. Hounsell, Carswell Farm, Uplyme, Lyme Regis DT7 3XQ (Lyme Regis [029-74] 2378). Carswell Farm is situated in a wooded valley, two and a half miles from the sea. Ideal for family holidays with safe, sandy beaches at Lyme Regis and Charmouth. Lovely walks, golf, fishing, riding nearby. Interesting places to visit. Bungalow on farm accommodates six people and has TV. Two double, one single bedrooms; bathroom; toilet; sittingroom; diningroom. Electricity for cooking and heating. No linen supplied. Children over seven welcome. Well controlled pets allowed. One mile from the shops. Car essential — garage. Open from April to October. SAE, please, for details.

MILTON ABBAS. Mrs V. O. Davey, Little Hewish Farm, Milton Abbas, Near Blandford DT11 0LH (Milton Abbas [0258] 880326). Working farm. Three modernised farm cottages at Little Hewish Farm in Hardy country, situated one mile from the unique village of Milton Abbas with its picturesque thatched cottages, lake and abbey. It is within easy driving distance of the coast with sandy beaches at Bournemouth, Studland, Swanage and Weymouth, with many coastline walks between. The cottages contain two and three bedrooms sleeping four and six persons. Cot if required. Sittingroom; dining/kitchen; bathroom and separate toilet. They are comfortably furnished and fully equipped including fridge, spin dryer and hot water. Fully carpeted. TV. Electricity by 50p meter. Linen extra. Nightstore heaters. Sorry, no pets. Car essential, parking. Available all year. Please phone or SAE for details.

POOLE. Chatsworth House, 11 Chatsworth Road, Parkstone, Poole. Poole, with its vast natural harbour and safe sandy beaches, would be ideal for your 1985 holiday. Situated between the New Forest and the beautiful Purbeck Hills, Poole and nearby Bournemouth offer excellent facilities. The two self-contained flats are spacious, clean, well furnished and fully carpeted. Each comprises two double bedrooms, lounge/diner, kitchen, etc. and can accommodate six people. TV. Parking space; garden. Children welcome (cot available), but no pets. Available May onwards. £68 to £148 per week. Brochure available from **Mrs S. M. Jones, 18 Park Avenue, Solihull, West Midlands B91 3EJ or telephone (021-705 1281) evenings.**

POOLE near. 'Green World Cottage' and 'The Stable Cottage', Organford, Near Poole. Working farm. Farm-style country holiday for two families may be enjoyed in two modern conversions of farm buildings on the 180-acre working farm of Old Slepe. Accommodation for six people in each cottage with spacious livingrooms, bedrooms, modern kitchens, oil-fired central heating and hot water; electric cooker, refrigerator. The cottages are simply but comfortably furnished and have coin-slot TVs, pay telephone. Four miles from Poole Harbour on the A35, there is a river and lake on the premises and mobile boats could be parked on farm. Riding and private fishing available. Local amenities include shops, post office, interesting pubs and a variety of country walks and places to visit. Delivery service for local produce easily arranged. Electricity and oil included in rent. Wareham, Swanage and Bournemouth with fine sandy beaches within easy driving distance. Cottages can be rented separately. For full particulars please apply to **Mrs D. Selby-Bennett, Slepe Green, Organford, Near Poole (Lytchett Minster [0202] 622541 and 624774 or 01-821-9290).**

SHAFTESBURY. 25 Bittles Green, Motcombe, Shaftesbury. Pleasant green sandstone cottage, two miles from Shaftesbury, historic Saxon hill-top town. Surrounded by picturesque countryside on edge of Blackmore Vale, pleasant walks, ideal base for touring. This very comfortable cottage is well equipped, sleeps five, plus baby in a large bedroom with a double and single beds; smaller bedroom with two singles; cot and high chair available. Bathroom with toilet. Sittingroom has TV; electric and gas fire for heating. Kitchen includes electric cooker, kettle, fridge, washing machine and immersion heater. Electricity by 50p slot meter. Carpeted throughout. Children welcome; pets allowed. Large peaceful garden. Terms from £50 to £90 weekly. SAE, please, to **Mrs R. Pettifer, Avenue Farm, Motcombe, Shaftesbury SP7 9NY (Shaftesbury [0747] 2076).**

SHAFTESBURY. Meadow Hayes Cottage, Bedchester, Shaftesbury. This cottage is situated on the edge of a small village with a large secluded garden with a swing and slide. It is about half a mile from the farm with a dairy herd and poultry. It ensures a holiday where comfort and cleanliness are a prime consideration. Tastefully converted from two cottages it comprises hall, lounge with open fire, diningroom, kitchen, larder; three bedrooms, sleeping six/seven, cot. Bathroom. It is fully equipped and has fitted carpets, colour TV, electric cooker, fridge, washing machine, electric heaters. Parking. Ideally situated for visiting Longleat, Stonehenge, Stourhead, Bournemouth, Poole, Salisbury. Five miles Shaftesbury and nine from Blandford. SAE, please, to **Mrs T. Kendall, Brach Farm, Twyford, Shaftesbury (Fontmell Magna [0747] 811356).**

SHAFTESBURY. Mampitts Farm Cottage, Shaftesbury. Working farm. This comfortable farm cottage is situated by a peaceful private road adjoining an 82-acre farm overlooking unspoilt countryside. It has been comfortably modernised to accommodate five people, plus cot, in one double, one family rooms (three beds); bathroom, diningroom; large lounge with colour TV; kitchen and dining area. Fully equipped with electric cooker, fridge, washing machine, etc. Utility room, toilet; fitted carpets; central heating. An attractive walled flower garden with lawns and patio. Cot, high chair and linen available. Large parking area. Within easy reach of shops, many sporting facilities, Salisbury, Stonehenge, Sherborne Castle, Cheddar Caves, Bath, Weymouth, Poole Harbour. Open all year. SAE, please, to **Mrs T. Kendall, Brach Farm, Twyford, Shaftesbury (Fontmell Magna [0747] 811356 before 9 pm).**

SHERBORNE. Mrs R. P. Wade, Stockbridge Farm, Sherborne DT9 6EP (Holnest [096-321] 272). This pleasant farm cottage accommodates five people in two double bedrooms and one single. Children are welcome and there is a cot, high chair. Bathroom with WC. Sittingroom, hall/diningroom, sun parlour, TV, cloakroom with hot and cold and WC. Kitchen with electric cooker and fridge. The heating of water and cottage is by electricity. Pets allowed by arrangement. Personal supervision. Farm milk. Own garage and drive. Sherborne three miles; shop one mile; Weymouth and coast 22 miles. Mid-week bookings permitted. Terms from £30 per week. Apply — **Mrs Wade.**

SHERBORNE near. Mr and Mrs T. Claypole, Manor Farm Country House, Holnest Park, Near Sherborne DT9 6HA (Holnest [096-321] 474). The Manor Farm stands in delightful parkland with fine views over the Blackmore Vale, now converted to five comfortable self-catering apartments, plus an attractive three-bedroomed cottage. An ideal spot for exploring the Dorset countryside with its beautiful scenery, unspoilt villages and lovely coastline. Riding nearby. Available April to October. Please send for brochure.

STURMINSTER NEWTON. Mrs R. J. Primrose, Lymburghs Farm, Marnhull, Sturminster Newton DT10 1HN (Marnhull [0258] 820310). Working farm. Lymburghs Bungalow on dairy and stud farm amongst peace and tranquillity of Blackmore Vale with open views across lush pastures. Faces south with large, relaxing garden. Bungalow is light and modern comprising three bedrooms (one double, two twin) suitable for four adults and two children. Kitchen with electric cooker, fridge; lounge with dining area and TV. Fully equipped for all your holiday needs, except linen. Situated between Shaftesbury and Sturminster Newton. Ideal for touring and visiting many places of interest including Stourhead, Longleat, Cricket St. Thomas, Sherborne Castle, Stonehenge etc. Sea 26 miles. Coarse fishing on River Stour. A warm welcome awaits guests. Regret, no pets. Phone/write for further particulars.

DORSET – RURAL SPLENDOUR!

Absorbing old towns like Dorchester and Shaftesbury, surrounded by panoramic vales, undulating chalklands and peaceful villages contribute to Dorset's great appeal. Included in any tourist's itinerary should be, Abbotsbury Village and swannery, Ackling Dyke Roman road, Brownsea Island, Lulworth Cove and, of course, the many locations that constitute Hardy's Dorset.

SELF-CATERING Dorset 447

STURMINSTER NEWTON. Mrs Sally Wingate-Saul, Holbrook Farm, Lydlinch, Sturminster Newton DT10 2JB (Hazelbury Bryan [025-86] 348). Working farm. Situated in the heart of the Blackmore Vale, Lydlinch is 3 miles from Sturminster Newton, 9 miles from Sherborne and about three-quarters-of-an-hour from the coast. This is a family farm in beautiful and peaceful surroundings, one mile from village and pub. It makes an ideal central base for exploring Dorset, but tenants are also welcome to use the swimming pool and take walks over the farm. Clay pigeon shooting on farm; fishing, golf, tennis, riding, etc. locally. Accommodation for 6 people comprises two twin-bedded rooms, one with bunk beds. Bathroom with separate WC. Well-appointed kitchen/diningroom. Fitted carpets throughout. Sittingroom with open fire and colour TV. Also converted stable annexes for 4 people. SAE for particulars, or telephone.

STURMINSTER NEWTON. Mrs Sheila Martin, Moorcroft Farm, Moorside, Marnhull, Sturminster Newton DT10 1HH (Marnhull [0258] 820271). Working farm. This is an upstairs flat with own entrance and Yale key. It is part of the farmhouse. Kept very clean, there is a friendly, welcoming atmosphere. We are a 110-acre Dairy Farm, in the Blackmore Vale in Hardy country. Guests are welcome to wander around, watch the farm activities and laze in the large garden. New Forest, Wildlife Park, Cheddar and the coast all within easy reach. Accommodation for four people in two double bedrooms, one with a double bed, one with two singles. Bathroom, separate toilet. Sitting/diningroom with colour television. Well-equipped kitchen with full-sized electric cooker, fridge, sink unit and wall cabinets. Everything including linen supplied; electric heaters in all rooms. Open Easter-October. Village shop 400 yards. Sea 28 miles. Car essential. Sorry, no pets. Weekly terms from £65-£100. SAE, please.

STURMINSTER NEWTON. Foxes and Willows, Yew House Farm, Marnhull, Sturminster Newton. Foxes and Willows are two purpose-built Swedish cottages, each situated in secluded positions on the farm with magnificent views of the Blackmore Vale. The accommodation in each cottage comprises one double bedded room and one twin bedded; shower room with washbasin and toilet, tiled throughout. Compact kitchen equipped with electric cooker, fridge, washing machine, tumble-dryer. Spacious livingroom, brick fireplace with woodburning stove. Interior mainly pine, furnishings comfortable and colourful fitted carpets throughout. Colour TV. Outdoor swimming pool. May to September. No pets, please. Linen included. Car essential, parking. Quarter mile to shops and public transport. The farm is situated six miles south of Snaftesbury, an excellent centre for touring places such as Stourhead, Longleat, Yeovilton and World Wide Butterflies. Colour brochure from: **Mrs Gillian Espley, Yew House Farm, Marnhull, Sturminster Newton DT10 1NP (Marnhull [0258] 820412).**

STURMINSTER NEWTON. Meadow Cottage, Well Common, Todber, Sturminster Newton. The cottage is situated overlooking lovely green field in very peaceful surroundings. It accommodates five in one double bedroom and two singles; cot; bathroom, toilet; sittingroom; diningroom; kitchen. Electric heating. Linen not supplied. Village shop half a mile, nearest town is Shaftesbury four miles. Car essential, parking. Regret no pets. SAE, please, for terms. **Mrs R. Candy, Manor Farm, Todber, Sturminster Newton DT10 1JB.**

VERWOOD. Mr and Mrs G. Froud, West Farm, Verwood BH21 6LE (Verwood [0202] 822263). Working farm. The Cottage is situated on West Farm, about 200 yards from the B3081 Verwood to Cranborne road. It is six miles from Ringwood and the New Forest, 12 miles from Bournemouth and its beaches and 20 miles from historic Salisbury. There are many lovely walks through local surroundings. There are three bedrooms; one double, one single and one twin-bedded, also bed-settee in lounge; sleeps total of six people. Cot and high chair provided on request. All bedding provided, but no linen, towels or tea towels. Downstairs lounge with TV, diningroom, kitchen, bathroom and toilet. Kitchen has electric cooker, kettle, fridge and all crockery and cutlery for six people. Immersion heater, also sink water heater in kitchen. Electricity by 50p meter. Electric fires and night storage heaters. Lawned garden with trees and views over lake, meadows and woods. Car parking. Sorry, no pets. Shops one mile. Available April to September. Terms range from £65 to £85 per week, plus VAT.

WAREHAM. Colonel and Mrs A. M. Barne, Culeaze, Wareham BH20 7NR (Bere Regis [0929] 471209 or 471344 after 6 pm). Working farm. An upstairs flat attractively decorated and comfortably furnished overlooking a lovely garden. The River Piddle runs through the property and the house is surrounded by farm and "pick your own fruit" farm, well off the road. Lulworth Cove, seven miles, is the nearest point of coast; Studland Bay has fine, sandy beach. Dorset is full of beautiful and historic places and buildings, all worthwhile visiting. Accommodating four people in two double bedrooms; bathroom, toilet; sittingroom, diningroom. Modern electric kitchen, fully equipped including linen. Children welcome. Pets accepted if kept under control. Available April/September. Electricity included in terms during June, July and August. Bere Regis (one-and-a-half miles) has a few shops. Bournemouth 15, Wareham seven miles. SAE, please, for further particulars, or telephone.

WEYMOUTH. Higher Farm Cottage, Shop Lane, Langton Herring, Weymouth. Within a short walk to the Fleet, a natural bird Sanctuary with lovely walks, the cottage is situated between Weymouth and Abbotsbury in the middle of the village of Langton Herring. Open all year, there is accommodation for eight persons in two double and one family bedrooms with one cot. Linen not supplied. Cooking and heating by electric or Rayburn. 50p meter. Car essential, parking. Pets by arrangement only. For further details and terms **Mrs S. M. Simon, Manor Farm, Stourton Caundle, Sturminster Newton DT10 2JW (Stalbridge [0963] 62471).**

WINSHAM. Ammerham Villa, Winsham, Near Chard, Somerset. Ammerham Villa is set in unspoilt countryside on Dorset/Somerset borders near River Axe, Forde Abbey and Cricket St. Thomas Wild Life Park. Dorset coast eleven miles away. The sunny cottage has two reception rooms, modernised kitchen and downstairs WC. Two double bedrooms with single beds, plus small bedroom with bed and cot. Bathroom with WC. Small garden and garage. Extra parking. Prices start at £60 per week. Electricity extra. Available March to October. No pets. Full details (SAE) from **Canon A. T. Johnson, The Rectory, Semley, Shaftesbury, Dorset (East Knoyle [074-783] 362).**

DURHAM

SPENNYMOOR. Brickyard Farmhouse, Byers Green, Spennymoor. Working farm. Modernised farmhouse, central to many places of historic and general interest. The house sleeps six in two twin bedrooms and two single bedrooms, plus cot. Separate toilet, bathroom, lounge and roomy well equipped kitchen. Gas fires and gas cooker, hot and cold water. The local pleasant countryside provides many walks, picnic areas, golf courses. Horse riding by arrangement. Bus service through the village. Post office and shops in village. A car is essential; no parking problems. Available throughout the year. Terms £50 per week. Heating and cooking on meter. Details from **Mr R. Ellis, The Old Hall, Byers Green, Spennymoor DL16 7PS (Bishop Auckland [0388] 602786).**

ESSEX

ESSEX. Farm and Country Holidays. Essex farmhouses have a lot to offer the visitor. Ideal location of properties in beautiful countryside, some seaside, provide varied holidays for people of all ages. Very close to London, visitors may enjoy the Essex coastline, busy ports, forts and castles, yachting centres and Epping Forest to name just a few holiday pursuits. For further details apply to **Mrs Beryl Martin, Newhouse Farm, Mutton Row, Stamford Rivers, Ongar. Tel: (0277) 362132.** See also Group Display Advertisement in the **Board** section of this Guide.

GLOUCESTERSHIRE

BERKELEY. Mrs Barbara A. Evans, Green Acres Farm, Breadstone, Berkeley GL12 9HF (Dursley [0453] 810348). Working farm. Four new cottages, previously farm buildings, recently renovated to a very high standard, available for self-catering holidays on a 45-acre dairy farm. Fully equipped to meet all your holiday requirements including linen; all-electric kitchen. Central heating. Lovely gardens and lawns. Excellent touring centre for the picturesque villages of the Cotswolds, Malvern Hills, Bath, Royal Forest of Dean, and Wales. Delightful local beauty spots include Uley Tump, Coaley Peak picnic area and nature reserve. Excellent walking locally. Golf and horse riding close by. Berkeley Castle and Severn Wildfowl Trust among many interesting places to visit. Evening meals available at farmhouse. Breakfast packs. Garden produce obtainable from the farm. Car essential — parking. Shops three miles; public transport three-quarters of a mile. Further details and terms on request.

Terms quoted in this publication may be subject to increase if rises in costs necessitate

SELF-CATERING **Gloucestershire**

BLAKENEY near. Mr & Mrs G. Hoinville, Oatfield Farm, Gatcombe, Near Blakeney GL14 4AY (Dean [0594] 510372). Early 17th century farmhouse and farm buildings (all listed buildings) converted into attractive, spacious, self-contained units (one, two and three bedrooms), modernised but with the original character retained. The entire complex is set in an isolated, quiet, rural spot and occupies six acres entirely surrounded by farmland and woodland, yet only half a mile from the village and the Forest of Dean. Facilities include a hard tennis court, a games room, utility room, colour TV in each unit. Children welcome (with well behaved parents!). Sorry, no pets. Car essential — ample parking. Prices range from £120 to £250 per week, all inclusive.

BOURTON-ON-THE-WATER/STOW-ON-THE-WOLD. Mr W. P. Harrison, Olive Hill Farm, Wyck Rissington, Bourton-on-the-Water GL54 2PW (Cotswold [0451] 20350). Choice of four comfortably furnished Cotswold cottages with colour TVs and central heating. (1) Peaceful country cottage in the picturesque village of Wyck Rissington near Bourton-on-the-Water surrounded by fields and with panoramic views. Sleeps four/six. (2) Charming 17th-century cottage in Stow-on-the-Wold with beamed ceilings and inglenook. Sleeps three/four. (3) Tiny one-bedroomed cottage in Stow-on-the-Wold. Sleeps two. (4) Quaint little historic cottage near Stow-on-the-Wold with views over open countryside, log fire. Sleeps two/three. Open all year. Winter week-ends welcome. Please 'phone for further details and terms.

BROCKWORTH. Abbotswood Farm, Brockworth. Working farm. This cottage lies at the foot of the Cotswold Hills at the end of a lane surrounded by farmland. The cottage is 16th century with thick stone walls and oak beams. There is accommodation for 10 people in two double bedrooms and two family bedrooms; cot; bathroom; sittingroom with TV; diningroom; well equipped kitchen with electric cooker. Dogs accepted. Open all year with electric heaters in all rooms. Fully equipped except linen. Children are welcome. Car essential, parking. Shops one mile. **Mrs S. House, Colliers Elm Farm, Bulley, Churcham GL2 8BJ (Tibberton [045-279] 240).**

CHELTENHAM (Cotswolds). Mrs J. V. Kinch, Starvall Farm, Farmington, Northleach, Cheltenham GL54 3NF (Cotswold [0451] 60263). Working farm. Two farm cottages — one detached, the other semi-detached (Hillview), with gardens and superb views, situated on a mixed farm (corn and dairy) of 600 acres in the heart of the Cotswolds. Bourton-on-the-Water (three miles) offers many tourist attractions, with many beautiful and historic places of interest, including Model Village, Model Railway, Butterfly Exhibition and Birdland. Cheltenham 14 miles; Cirencester 12; Stratford-on-Avon 26; Cotswold Wildlife Park 13. Both cottages have three bedrooms, sleeping five, plus cot and high chair if required. Well-equipped kitchens with electric cooker, fridge, kettle, laundry facilities. Linen may be hired. Electricity by 50p meter. Sittingrooms have colour TV, electric fires, also solid fuel stoves. Children welcome, but sorry, no dogs. Car essential — ample parking; shops/public transport two miles. Cherry Tree Cottage has garage. SAE, please, for details.

CIRENCESTER. "Riverside Cottage", "Park View Cottage", "Tree Tops Cottage", Cirencester. These modernised, comfortable Cotswold holiday cottages are situated amongst 400 acres of farmland in a beautiful rural area four miles from Cirencester. All standing in own grounds. "Riverside" and "Tree Tops" sleep four; "Park View" sleeps seven. Each cottage has bedrooms; bathroom; kitchen and diningroom, lounge. "Park View" has a double garage and there is ample parking space at "Riverside" and "Tree Tops". Each bed is interior sprung with electric blanket. Electric cooking and heating with open fires in all lounges. Cot. Everything supplied except linen. Refrigerators. Electricity slot meters. Pets welcome. Middle Duntisbourne is quarter mile off Cirencester/Gloucester road (A417). Awarded 1980 Farm Holiday Guide Diploma for cottages of high standard. Bed and Breakfast is also available. SAE, please, for terms. **Mrs R. J. Barton, Manor Farm, Middle Duntisbourne, Cirencester GL7 7AR (Cirencester [0285] 3058).**

GLOUCESTERSHIRE – THE IDYLLIC COTSWOLDS COUNTY!

A combination of the Cotswolds and The Vale of Severn, Gloucestershire is a popular tourist destination. Visit Chipping Campden, Cirencester, The Cotswolds Farm Park, The Forest of Dean, Keynes Park and Tewkesbury and you will not be disappointed. If you are around at the right time, the Severn Bore can also be quite a spectacle.

450　Gloucestershire　SELF-CATERING

CIRENCESTER near. Mrs J. Baxter, Shawswell Farm, Rendcomb, Near Cirencester (North Cerney [028-583] 439). Working farm, join in. Shawswell is a mixed farm of 530 acres situated in its own picturesque valley one-and-a-half miles from the village of Rendcomb at the end of a "No Through Road". Magnificent views; peaceful countryside; relaxed friendly atmosphere. Visitors are welcome to participate in farm activities, especially interesting for children, or enjoy the many pleasant walks across the farm land. Dogs welcome, but must be kept under strict control. Four cottages and part of ancient stone farm house (separate front door). Properties accommodate from four to six people. Cot available. Three cottages and part farm house have gardens. All fully equipped except linen, with electric cookers, fridges, hot/cold water. Electricity by 50p meters. Excellent base for touring the beautiful Cotswolds, towns and villages, wildlife parks, Sudeley and Berkeley Castles. Car essential. Local shop, post office in village (main shops Cirencester four miles). Rates £55 to £150 weekly. Full leaflet on request.

GLOUCESTER. Mrs J. A. Davies, Singleton Farm, Mussell End, Sandhurst, Gloucester GL2 9NT (Gloucester [0452] 730283). Working farm. Singleton cottage offers accommodation for four plus an infant in two bedrooms, one with double the other with two single beds; bathroom, toilet; sittingroom; large breakfast room/kitchen. Heating and cooking by electricity, 50p slot meter. Cot available. Babysitting can be arranged. Set within the pleasant surroundings of a mixed, family farm where the children can feed the poultry while mum and dad relax in the gardens, it is within easy driving distance of many well-known attractions. Three miles from the Cathedral City of Gloucester, about seven miles from M5 north and south junctions and with the Forest of Dean and Cotswolds close by. Village shop and Post Office one mile from the cottage. Linen supplied. Open all year. Terms from £75 per week.

HARTPURY. Mrs G. Pugh, Brick House Farm, Hartpury GL19 3DD (Hartpury [045-270] 279). Working farm. Brick House Farm Cottage is tastefully modernised and set on the farm, surrounded by 220 acres of dairy farming land on the Gloucester/Worcester border. Sleeping facilities for six in three double rooms, two of which have single beds. Separate lounge with colour TV; diningroom; bathroom and two toilets. Kitchen facilities include electric cooker, fridge, etc. Linen is not supplied. Pets allowed. Provisions shop one mile from cottage. Car essential — ample parking. Cottage well suited for touring the Cotswolds, Wye Valley and Forest of Dean. All sports within six miles and coarse fishing on river running through farmland. Visits to Bristol Zoo and Slimbridge Wild Fowl Trust will delight children. March to October. SAE, please, for terms.

MORETON-IN-MARSH. Dorn, Moreton-in-Marsh. This semi-detached cottage stands in own large garden in the quiet hamlet of Dorn. Accommodates six persons, with cot and high chair available. Ideal for exploring the Cotswolds. Oxford 30 miles; Cheltenham 16 miles; Stratford 16 miles. Good shops and laundrette at Moreton (one mile). Cottage has bathroom and toilet; sittingroom; kitchen with electric cooker and fridge. No linen supplied. Colour television. Pets permitted. Car essential — parking. Available Easter to end of October. Electricity by 50p meter. SAE for details: **Mrs C. M. Righton, New Farm, Dorn, Moreton-in-Marsh (Moreton-in-Marsh [0608] 50782).**

REDMARLEY. Shepherds Hill, Redmarley. Working farm. Large luxury holiday cottage situated in an elevated position in quiet open countryside with panoramic views of Severn Valley, Cotswolds and Malverns. Belonging to a mixed farm. Furnished and equipped to the highest standard with solid fuel central heating. There are two double bedrooms with hot and cold washbasins; one twin-bedded room and one single room. Bathroom with shower; hall; cloakroom with toilet and washbasin; lounge, TV. Diningroom. Kitchen with modern electric equipment. Immersion heater. Secluded lawn for sunbathing. Ample parking space. The lovely country towns of Ledbury, Tewkesbury, Ross-on-Wye, Upton-on-Severn and Malvern within easy reach by car. Also half-timbered fully furnished farm flat available. SAE, please, for details to **Mr R. E. Arnall, Scar Farm, Redmarley GL19 3JQ (Staunton Court [045-284] 244).**

TEWKESBURY. Mrs Sheila Warner, Southwick Farm, Gloucester Road, Tewkesbury GL20 7DG (Tewkesbury [0684] 292106). Working farm. A holiday on this 200-acre arable farm, half-a-mile off the main road, will be memorable for opportunities it affords to tour the Cotswolds, Malverns, Severn and Wye Valleys or visit Bristol Zoo, West Midland Safari Park, Cotswolds Wildlife Park, Peter Scott's Wildfowl Trust, Warwick Castle and Stratford. Pursuits include riding, golf, fishing, tennis and cruising down river at Tewkesbury. Attractive feature of cottage is outdoor heated swimming pool which visitors may use. Six adults and baby accommodated in two double bedded rooms and one twin bedded room, with cot provided. Sittingroom, diningroom, bathroom, toilet; kitchen with electric stove, kettle, iron, fridge. Pay phone in porch. Fully equipped, except linen. Pets allowed. Car essential — ample parking. Little shop, half-a-mile; town shops two miles. Weekly terms from £80, including fuel, April to October. Registered with the English Tourist Board. SAE, please.

PLEASE SEND A STAMPED ADDRESSED ENVELOPE WITH ENQUIRIES

SELF-CATERING   Gloucestershire / Hampshire   451

ULEY near. Mr and Mrs C. N. Mander, Owlpen Manor Cottages, Owlpen, Near Uley GL11 5BZ (Dursley [0453] 860261). Working farm. The tiny hamlet of Owlpen nestles against woods and hills in its own remote and picturesque valley and is one of the treasures of Cotswold scenery. The famous Tudor manor house is the spectacular focus to the group of luxury cottages now restored to very high standards. Guests may enjoy a heritage of peace and beauty in homely comfort and at leisure throughout the year whether it is a party of two or 10 people. Choose from the enchanting Court House, the elegant Grist Mill, three roomy farmhouses, a smaller weaver's cottage or three cosy retreats for two. Everything — central heating, linen, cleaning after departure, colour TV etc — included in rentals ranging from £125 to £425 including VAT weekly; or try a two-day break from £56. At Owlpen there are sheep and cattle, plus 245 acres of beechwoods providing logs, walks and shooting. Lake for fishing. Take-away food and wines. Golf, gliding and five miles private footpaths. Four-poster beds. Centrally located for touring Cotswolds and Bath. SAE, please.

WESTBURY-ON-SEVERN. Mrs Bridget Hyslop, Chaxhill House, Westbury-on-Severn GL14 1QP (Westbury-on-Severn [0452-76] 555). Working farm. Visitors are welcome to take walks, picnics and enjoy this dairy farm which is six miles from the Forest of Dean, and seven and a half miles from Gloucester. This fine Georgian farmhouse pictured here has a flat accommodating four people on the entire top floor. Fitted kitchen, lounge, bathroom and three bedrooms. Magnificent views. Terms from £65 to £90 per week. Also modern Farm Manager's house accommodating six. Fitted kitchen, lounge, bathroom, three bedrooms; utility room with washing machine, dryer and second WC. Lawned garden. Terms from £95 to £110 per week. Both properties are within a stone's throw of the farmyard, and furnished to a high standard with colour TV's; cots and highchairs available. No linen supplied. Please ring or write for brochure.

WINCHCOMBE. Orchard Cottage, Stanley Pontlarge, Near Winchcombe — TEWKESBURY, Magpie Cottage, 4 Chance Street, Tewkesbury. ORCHARD COTTAGE, set amid pear trees of orchard on Cotswold escarpment, three miles from Winchcombe. Rural privacy, own access and garden. Four people accommodated in two bedrooms; bathroom; sitting-diningroom (log-coal burning stove); night storage heaters; fully equipped except linen; kitchen with electric cooker, etc. Car essential — parking. Shops one mile. £65—£120 weekly (including heating). Secluded town cottage at 4 CHANCE STREET offers holiday accommodation for four people. Sitting-diningroom (log-coal burning fire); two bedrooms; bathroom; small kitchen (electric cooker); everything provided except linen. Car not essential; shops nearby. £60—£100 weekly (including electricity). Children welcome at both properties — pets by arrangement. Open all year. Ideal centres for exploring, walking, sightseeing, all sports. Stratford-Upon-Avon, Cheltenham, other interesting towns, villages within easy reach. **Mrs S. M. Rolt, Stanley Pontlarge, Near Gretton, Winchcombe GL54 5HD (Winchcombe [0242] 602594).**

HAMPSHIRE

RINGWOOD (New Forest). Mrs H. Montgomery, Brookfield, Hightown, Ringwood BH24 3DY (Ringwood [0425] 478362). Attractive self-contained flat on top floor of bungalow accommodating maximum two guests, available for self-catering holidays all year round. Twin bedroom, shower room, lounge and kitchen/diner, overlooking rear garden and fields. Colour TV. Everything supplied, including linen. Electric cooker, convector heaters (50p electric meter). Central heating included. Situated on the edge of the New Forest, one and a half miles from the small market town of Ringwood, an ideal centre for walking, riding, fishing, golf and visiting the many National Trust properties, historic houses and gardens, wildlife parks and all the scenic beauty of the New Forest. Sandy beaches at Bournemouth and Mudeford Bay. Car essential. Parking. £60 to £110 weekly.

HEREFORD & WORCESTER

ABBEYDORE. Kerrys Gate, Abbeydore. Working farm. Farmhouse and cottage situated on quiet country roadside in Golden Valley. Both detached with private gardens, offering pleasant views of surrounding woods and farmland. Ten miles from Hereford and seven from the Welsh border. Ideal for walking or touring. Within easy reach of Wye Valley, Black Mountains, Forest of Dean, market towns and ancient castles. Farmhouse sleeps eight in four bedrooms. Cottage sleeps six in three bedrooms, plus cots. Linen may be hired. Modern bathrooms and kitchens with electric cookers and fridges. Comfortable sittingrooms with TV. Electric heating and carpets throughout. Children welcome. Pets by prior arrangement. Shops four miles. Electricity by 50p meter. Open all year. Farmhouse £60-£110. Cottage £50-£100 per week. **Mrs M. Jenkins, Black Bush Farm, Abbeydore, Hereford HR2 0AJ (Golden Valley [0981] 240281).**

ALMELEY. 1 Church Terrace, Almeley. Pleasantly situated house near centre of peaceful village with Wye Valley and Radnor Hills beauty spots nearby. Many excellent eating houses in district. Nine hole golf course at Kington; pony trekking; hang gliding; canoeing on Wye, sailing, picnic areas, walks in Black Mountains and Brecon Beacons; world famous secondhand bookshop at Hay-on-Wye. Accommodation for eight in three double bedrooms, two singles, plus cot; bathroom, toilet; sittingroom; diningroom; kitchen with electric cooker, fridge, etc. No linen supplied. Shops in village, quarter mile. Car essential, parking. Sorry no pets. Open Easter/November. SAE, please, for terms **Mrs Patricia M. Jones, Pontywal Farm, Bronllys, Brecon, Powys (Talgarth [0874] 711281).**

COTHERIDGE. Mrs V. A. Rogers, Little Lightwood Farm, Cotheridge WR6 5LT (Cotheridge [090-566] 236). Working farm. Little Lightwood Farm offers excellent holiday accommodation in the Teme Valley three and a half miles west of Worcester, just off A44 road to Leominster. It has beautiful views of the Malvern Hills and is ideally situated for visiting many places in this area. The farm carries a herd of 55 cows and their calves. The accommodation offered is a self-catering chalet for six people (£35 to £80); two small converted cottages each for two people (£25 to £65). Bed and Breakfast is also available in the farmhouse from £7.50 per person. Children are most welcome.

DROITWICH. Mr M. F. Howard, Upper Goosehill Farm, Hanbury, Droitwich, Worcestershire (Himbleton [090-569] 610). Working farm. Holiday flat accommodating up to six adults available from April to November inclusive situated on 300-acre mixed farm. Single and family rooms. Bathroom, toilet. Sittingroom, diningroom. Electric cooking/heating. Children welcome. Pets permitted. Car essential, ample parking. One mile shops/public transport. Fishing/shooting/hunting/horse riding by arrangement in season. Own horses welcome — good stabling. Many places of historic interest at Worcester, six miles — theatre, porcelain works, cricket, race course. Droitwich brine baths. Stratford-on-Avon 14 miles. Warwick Castle and Welsh border within easy reach. Terms from £75 per week, including fuel.

FOR YOUR PERFECT HOLIDAY IN THE HEART OF ENGLAND

AA Approved; Member of English and Heart of England Tourist Boards

The old world charm of Forge Cottage (illus.), Manor House and Hall Farm (a large Georgian Farmhouse skilfully converted into five self-contained apartments). Properties combine comfort and character and have been carefully modernised to provide the amenities of a modern home with a welcoming atmosphere. Accommodation for two to six people depending on which property you choose. Furnished and equipped to a high standard with fully fitted kitchen, modern bathroom, colour TV, electric fires. 50p slot meter. Laundering facilities. Ample parking space.

Personally supervised to ensure your satisfaction and comfort. Cot and high chair provided. Regret no pets. There are lawned gardens with chairs for sunbathing. Tennis court for the energetic. The beautiful Cotswolds are only a short distance away, together with the Vale of Evesham renowned for its fruit (particularly pick-your-own strawberries, plums etc.). Historic Stratford, Cheltenham and Worcester are within half-an-hour's drive and there are stately homes and farm parks in the vicinity. Golf, fishing, swimming, squash, riding, nearby.

Mrs D. Stow (FHG), Lower Portway Farm, Sedgeberrow, Evesham WR11 6UN
Tel. (0386) 881298

SELF-CATERING — Hereford & Worcester

HAY-ON-WYE. Wooden House, Cwm-Yr-Afor, Whitney-on-Wye & Rose Cottage, Bronydd, Clyro. Cabalva Farms — holiday cottages in the Wye Valley. Three superb country cottages on a large estate just inside the Welsh border and four miles from the old market town of Hay-on-Wye. Wooden House is a cedar wood, riverside cottage sleeping seven/eight, Rose Cottage is a black and white stone built cottage in a small hamlet, recently modernised and sleeps four/five and Cwm-Yr-Afor, beautifully secluded by a small stream and completely renovated, sleeps four/five and is full of old world charm. All of our cottages have spectacular views across the Wye Valley to the Black Mountains and beyond and have been furnished and equipped to a high standard complete with colour TV and linen. Salmon, trout and coarse fishing to hand on our own stretch of the Wye, and golf, trekking, canoeing and sailing close by. Brochure from **Mrs Helen Williams, Cabalva Farmhouse, Whitney-on-Wye HR3 6EX (Clifford [04973] 324).**

HEREFORD. Hereford Farm and Country Holidays. Selection of farmhouse accommodation. Ring, farm of your choice or for group brochure giving full details send 9" × 4" SAE to **Mrs Avril Farndon, Newhouse Farm, Dilwyn, Hereford (Weobley [0544] 318289).** See also Display Advertisements in the Board and Self-Catering Sections under Hereford & Worcester.

HEREFORD. 2 Church Cottage, Bishopstone, Hereford. Working farm. Pleasant semi-detached cottage, available all year for self-catering holidays. Six miles west of Hereford, the cottage stands in a large garden overlooking orchards, pastureland and the local church. Ideally situated for walking and touring the Wye Valley area. Pub restaurant with facilities for children within easy reach. Accommodation — sleeps six in three bedrooms with bathroom, sittingroom with TV, diningroom, kitchen and all modern conveniences. Fully equipped except for bed linen which may be hired. Cot available. Carpeted throughout with electric heating and Rayburn for winter use. 50p electric meter. Car essential — parking. Children welcome. Pets by prior arrangement: SAE, please, for terms. **Mrs V. Carrington, Bishopstone Court Farm, Bishopstone, Hereford HR4 7JQ (Bridge Sollars [098 122] 254).**

HEREFORD. The Meads, Craswall, Hereford. The Meads is in an ideal situation enjoying the peace and tranquillity of the countryside. This detached bungalow, situated in the Black Mountains, Hay-on-Wye 10 miles, Hereford 16 miles, Abergavenny 14 miles, is renowned for beautiful walks and pony riding. Local stores and services in joining village two miles. The house is equipped for five people and linen is supplied. Open all year with Rayburn fuel, radiators. Double bedroom, single bedroom with bunks, also studio couch in sittingroom; fully equipped diningroom/kitchen includes sink-unit, fridge, electric cooker and Rayburn; separate sittingroom with TV; bathroom. Garden and parking for a car which is essential. Children welcome, cot and high chair available. Pets are allowed. Local fishing. SAE, please, for terms to **Mrs J. Watkins, White House Farm, Vowchurch, Hereford HR2 0RE (Peterchurch [098-16] 212).**

HEREFORD. Kingsfield Farm, Marden, Hereford. Working farm. Lovely old farmhouse, standing in its own farmland, one and a half miles from village. Ideal for walking, birdwatching and touring. Recently renovated, exposing old beams and fireplaces. Well equipped electric kitchens, bathrooms. Log burners in sitting rooms (free wood). Can be rented as one house, sleeping eight, two bathrooms, etc., or two independent houses by locking central door downstairs. One side sleeping three in one double and one single bedrooms and the other sleeping five in one treble and one double bedrooms. Ideal for friends/ families wanting certain amount of independence. Also cottage and bungalow, lovely views, close Hereford. All properties with spin dryers, books, games, colour TV. No pets. Hire service linen. Terms: £50 to £112. Special rates for winter lets. **Mrs D. Pritchett, Hermitage Farm, Canon Pyon, Hereford HR4 8NN (Hereford [0432] 760217).**

HEREFORD. Rose Cottage, Craswall, Hereford. Rose Cottage is a modernised stone built cottage, retaining its original character situated at the foot of Black Mountains, on a quiet country road. Hay-on-Wye, Hereford, Abergavenny, easily accessible and ideal for walking and touring. Many churches and castles of historic interest; close to River Monnow where trout fishing is available. Pony trekking, hang gliding nearby. A car is essential and there is ample parking. Rose Cottage is comfortably furnished with full central heating and wood fire (heating and hot water included). Linen provided free of charge. Electricity by meter reading. Two bedrooms, one with double bed, one with three single beds. Cot can be provided. Bathroom, toilet. Kitchen fully equipped with electric cooker, kettle, fridge etc. Sittingroom; diningroom. TV. Dogs are allowed. Registered with the English Tourist Board. Available all year round. Terms on application. **Mrs M. Howard, The Three Horseshoes, Craswall HR2 0PL (Michaelchurch [098123] 631).**

HEREFORD & WORCESTERSHIRE – THE HEART OF ENGLAND!

A beautiful county which includes The Vale of Evesham and the rugged – if petite – Malvern Hills. It has been designated an "Area of Outstanding Beauty". Places of interest include The Avoncroft Museum of Buildings, Brockhampton, Ross-on-Wye, The Teme Valley and The Hereford & Worcester County Museum.

454 Hereford & Worcester　　SELF-CATERING

HEREFORD. 2 Hermitage Cottages, Canon Pyon, Hereford. One of four properties, a bungalow and three cottages, sleeping from three to five (or eight in two adjoining cottages), situated 3½ to 7 miles north of "The Garden of the West" — City of Hereford, with its beautiful Cathedral and River Wye. Market day Wednesday. All properties well situated, with lovely views over surrounding farm land, hop yards, orchards and wooded hills. Well furnished to a high standard, with modern electric kitchens and bathrooms. Spin dryers, radiators, books, games, colour TV. Log burners in two houses. Linen hire. Car advisable. No pets. Many repeat bookings. Our farm is open for "Pick Your Own" strawberries, gooseberries, blackcurrants and cox, and the Nursery for tomatoes, where there is also a farm shop. Terms: £50 to £112. Special rates for winter lets. **Mrs D. Pritchett, Hermitage Farm, Canon Pyon, Hereford HR4 8NN (Hereford [0432] 760217).**

HEREFORD. Tupsley Court Holiday Cottage, Tupsley, Hereford. The farm cottage is situated on the side of a hill occupying a superb south east position overlooking open farm land on the edge of the city boundary of Hereford. The River Lugg flows along the border of the farm where one can walk to the river across the fields. The cottage is at the end of a private drive and is set in its own garden with lawn and parking space. It was built in 1967 and has been well maintained. Sleeps six; three double bedrooms. Bathroom, toilet; sittingroom; diningroom/kitchen. Electricity for cooking and heating (50p meter). No linen supplied. Parking. Sporting activities available in town. Terms on request from **Mrs R. J. Eaton, Hallaton House, 27 Hafod Road, Hereford HR1 1SG (Hereford [0432] 55754).**

HEREFORD near. J. R. Stedman, Yarkhill Court, Near Hereford (Tarrington [043-279] 233 — weekdays or Stow [0451] 30487 Saturday/Sunday). The front self-contained section of the farmhouse, standing in a large garden and commanding magnificent views of the Frome Valley and the hills beyond, comprising large dining/sittingroom; kitchen, cloakroom and WC downstairs and one double and two single bedrooms upstairs with additional beds; bathroom and WC upstairs. It has colour television, refrigerator, electric cooker, immersion heater and fitted carpets throughout. Children and pets welcome. Car essential; parking. Situated seven miles from Hereford and eight miles from Ledbury, this is an excellent centre for the Wye Valley, the Forest of Dean, the Malvern Hills and the castles of the Welsh Marches together with many picturesque villages such as Pembridge, Eardisland and Weobley. Electricity is included in rent. Available April to October. Terms from £60 to £100 weekly.

HEREFORDSHIRE FARM AND COUNTRY HOLIDAYS

LONGFIELD COTTAGE, KINGSTONE (Mr Robert Andrews [0981] 250220). Attractive Victorian farm cottage, garden, lawn, sleeps 7. Good touring, Wye valley, Welsh mountains and Malvern. £50 to £100.

OLDCOURT FARM, LOWER MAES-COED, LONGTOWN (Mr and Mrs P. B. D. Banks [087 387] 235). 2 well appointed cottages in courtyard of 14th Century house, sleeps 4-6, catering available. Working livestock farm, outstanding views, own fishing.

THE FORGE, BYFORD (The Estate Office [098122] 235 day or 317 weekends, evenings). Superb setting on River Wye. Well equipped secluded cottage sleeps 6. Private and salmon and coarse fishing in season included.

BIRCHER HALL, LEOMINSTER (The Lady Cawley [056 885] 218/476). Modernised west wing sleeps 5. 2 bathrooms. Large panelled lounge, garden. Kitchen-diner. Electric and oil heating. Tourist centre. Modernised converted stable house, sleeps 3. Electric and wood burning heating. Spacious lounge bathroom etc. Small garden.

THE CALLOW, WALFORD-ON-WYE (Mrs N. J. Moore [0989] 64599). Detached farm cottage in beautiful position overlooking Goodrich Castle. Large lawned garden. Sleeps 5. Heating available. From £55 per week.

MARLBROOK HALL, ELTON, LUDLOW (Mrs Valerie Morgan [056 886] 230). Three bedroomed house, situated on the edge of small rural village, near the historic town of Ludlow. Ideal for walking.

THE LEEN, PEMBRIDGE, LEOMINSTER (Mrs B. J. Norman [054 47] 305). Cottage for 5 on 400 acre farm, near black and white village of Pembridge, Leominster. 2 trout pools. Near Offa's Dyke.

WOONTON COURTFARM, LEYSTERS, LEOMINSTER (Mrs Elizabeth Thomas [056887] 232). Beautifully situated bungalow on mixed farm, sleeps 6. Sitting room, log fire, kitchen, fully equipped. Children, pets welcome. Also caravan site.

HIGH HOUSE FARM, LEDBURY (Mrs Gill Thomas [053184] 231). 470 acre family farm. Two self-contained 3 bedroom houses. Fully equipped to a high standard. Ideal for touring Wye Valley, the Malverns and the Cotswolds.

Ring farm of your choice or for group brochure giving full details send 9" × 4" SAE to Mrs Avril Farndon, Newhouse Farm, Dilwyn, Hereford. Tel. Weobley [0544] 318289.

HEREFORDSHIRE. Herefordshire Farm Cottages. A warm welcome awaits you in our farm cottages. *
Many of them are tasteful conversions of old farm buildings, full of character but with every modern convenience. Try a holiday with us and feel the freedom of self-catering in our lovely countryside. Situated throughout Herefordshire near rivers, woods, historical houses and golf courses are our granaries, hop kilns and stables or spacious farmhouses. The choice is yours! SAE to **Ashton Court Farm, Ashton, Leominster HR6 0DN (058 472 245).** See also Colour Display Advertisement in this Guide.

HOW CAPLE. Rugden Granary Flat, How Caple. Working farm. In the beautiful Wye Valley (three miles from M50), this lovely old stone building has recently been converted into a well furnished flat with pine fittings. Situated on a fruit farm, with sheep and ponies, there are delightful views from the flat over gardens and fields. Visitors have use of hard tennis court. An excellent touring centre for Symonds Yat, Forest of Dean, Black Mountains, and the picturesque towns and villages of Herefordshire. Ross-on-Wye and Monmouth, where local markets are held, a short drive away. Comfortable accommodation for six persons, the flat comprises hall, large sitting/diningroom with colour TV, paperbacks, etc.; three double bedrooms; well-equipped all-electric kitchen contains cooker, spin dryer, etc. Electricity by 50p meter. Linen supplied on request. Car essential, parking. Shops/public transport half a mile. Children welcome (cot, high chair). Sorry, no pets. **Mrs John Cross, Rugden House, How Caple, Hereford HR1 4TF (How Caple [098-986] 224).**

KINGTON. Lilwall Green Farmhouse, Near Kington. Working farm. The accommodation, close to the Welsh border, consists of the whole of the farmhouse, standing within its own farmland, which visitors are welcome to explore, comprising of three bedrooms, bathroom, kitchen, lounge and diningroom, with all modern conveniences including TV and fridge. Carpeted throughout. Accommodates six people. Ample parking with garage. Pets permitted. Electric heating. Personally cleaned before each letting. Peaceful, with pleasant views of surrounding countryside. Central for visiting mid-Wales, Wye Valley, Brecon Beacons, Black Mountains, Rhayader Dams etc. Reasonable rates. SAE, please or telephone for further details. **Mrs J. Hughes, Oaklands Farm, Kington Hereford HR5 3HB (Kington [0544] 230500).**

KINGTON. Bradnor Farm Cottage, Kington. Working farm. Bradnor Farm Cottage is situated just off Offa's Dyke Path, on Bradnor Hill, common land owned by the National Trust. Only 100 yards away from the highest golf course in England and Wales. An ideal spot for walking, golfing and enjoying panoramic views of several counties, the Black Mountains and the beautiful Welsh Border, only two miles away. The well-furnished detached farm cottage, sleeps six persons. Sitting/diningroom with TV and electric fire. Fully modernised kitchen with fridge, electric cooker etc. Bathroom and separate WC. Immersion heater. Guests supply own linen. Electricity by 50p meter. Sorry, no pets. Car essential — ample parking. Shops three quarters of a mile. SAE, please. **Mrs J. E. Burgoyne, Nash's Oak, Lyonshall, Kington HR5 3LT (Lyonshall [054 48] 272).**

KINGTON. Crossways Cottage, Huntington, Kington. Working farm. The cottage nestles in the Arrow Valley 200 yards from farmhouse and River Arrow. On border of England and Wales with the small market towns of Hay-on-Wye and Kington on either side. Offa's Dyke Path nearby and Black Mountains seven miles. Abundance of wild life in countryside. Five people accommodated. Two double, one single bedrooms; cot; bathroom, toilet; sittingroom with TV; diningroom. Kitchen with electric cooker, fridge. No linen supplied. Pets permitted. Car essential — parking. Open January to December. Shops one mile and five miles. SAE, please for terms to **Mrs M. A. Hammond, Lower Hengoed, Huntington, Kington, Herefordshire HR5 3QA (Clifford [04973] 277).**

KINGTON. The Harbour, Upper Hergest, Kington. This bungalow is on a good second-class road facing south with beautiful views, from its elevated position, across the Hergest Ridge and Offa's Dyke. The Welsh border is a mile away. Shops are two-and-a-half miles away. Kington Golf Club nearby. Accommodation for five/nine in two double rooms (one with extra single bed) downstairs and two double dormer bedrooms; two cots; bathroom, toilet; sittingroom (TV, radio); diningroom; sun porch for relaxing; kitchen with electric cooker, fridge, food store and usual equipment. No linen. Suitable for disabled. Children and pets welcome. Car essential — parking. Available all year, also mobile home sleeping two/six with bathroom and flush toilet. SAE, please, to **Mr A. J. Welson, New House Farm, Upper Hergest, Kington HR5 3EW (Kington [0544] 230533).**

Hereford & Worcester — SELF-CATERING

KINGTON. Mrs J. Pritchard, Lilwall Farm, Kington HR5 3EZ (Kington [0544] 230545). Working farm. Lilwall Farm is a family farm of about 190 acres and the wing of the attractive black and white farmhouse is available as self-catering holiday accommodation from May to October. There is a large lounge with oak beams and TV, dining area; fully-equipped kitchen; bathroom/toilet; spacious hallway; bedrooms with three single beds; double bedroom, with cot, if required. Fully carpeted throughout. No linen supplied. Shops two miles. Car essential. Pets permitted. Ideally situated for touring mid Wales, Black Mountains, Wye Valley, Offa's Dyke and golf courses; all within easy reach. Weekly terms from £50 (including fuel) SAE, please.

KINNERSLEY. Sunny and Myrtle Cottages, Lower Ailey Farm, Kinnersley. Working farm. Two detached cottages in nice sunny positions away from other houses (except farmhouse). Each is surrounded by lawn and fence and set away from the road amid quiet countryside. Good approach roads. Near Wye Valley and Welsh hills where pony trekking can be enjoyed. Hereford 12 miles; Hay on Wye nine miles and many surrounding Black and White villages to explore. The farm has chickens, sheep, cattle, cider fruit and cereals, and also two pet donkeys. Fully furnished, the cottages sleep four/five people. Bathroom, sittingroom; kitchen with electric cooker etc. Car essential — parking. Children welcome; cot and high chair supplied if needed. Well controlled pets allowed. Open all year round. Terms from £75 to £90 weekly. Details from **Mrs G. M. Thomas, The Elms Farm, Kinnersley, Hereford HR3 6PA (Eardisley [05446] 480 or 373).**

LEDBURY near. Mrs E. M. Ross, Grove House, Bromesberrow Heath, Near Ledbury (Bromesberrow [053-181] 584). Garden wing (sleeps six), Grooms cottage (sleeps two to four) and Cherry Tree cottage (sleeps two to four) are all part of Grove House, a mellow farmhouse set in 10 acres of land devoted to horses. Riding is available to guests and riding tuition available if required. Hard tennis court, boating pond and use of private swimming pool. Good centre for visiting Welsh border, Malverns, Forest of Dean, Cotswolds, Stratford-on-Avon, etc. and many places of interest. Garden wing, suitable for disabled, sleeps six (one double, one family room); folding bed in sittingroom; cot available; bathroom; toilet. Electric kitchen and heating. Grooms cottage sleeps two adults and two children. Very small, but pretty and ideal for honeymooners. Upstairs bedroom with double half-tester bed; downstairs room, sittingroom/kitchen/folding bed and a shower and toilet. Cherry Tree cottage with a four-poster bed in bedroom, bathroom, small galley kitchen, good sittingroom with day bed and folding bed. Children and pets welcome. Weekly from £25 to £107. Meals and Bed and Breakfast available in house.

LEDBURY near. Homend Bank Cottage, Stretton Grandison, Near Ledbury. A detached cottage in the heart of rural Herefordshire in an elevated position offering beautiful views. Recently modernised with three bedrooms, bathroom with shower and WC, kitchen, livingroom and diningroom; also downstairs WC. Large garden. Ample parking. Car essential. Night storage heaters included; all other electricity through meter. No linen supplied. Pets welcome. Cot available. Ideal base for touring Welsh Borders, Cathedral towns of Hereford and Worcester, Malvern Hills, Cotswolds and Stratford, all within easy reach. Terms are from £100 per week. Apply to **Mr P. W. A. Hughes, R. H. & R. W. Clutton, Estate Office, Madresfield, Malvern WR13 5AH (Malvern [06845] 3614).**

LEDBURY near. The High House Farm, Preston Cross, Near Ledbury. Working farm. High House Farmhouse (part 13th century), is divided into two holiday houses, equipped to very good standard. Superb views towards Ross-on-Wye (eight miles) and Gloucestershire. Fully electric kitchen/diner; sittingroom; bathroom and toilet; three bedrooms, all with fitted carpets; TV; telephone. Garage (car essential). All rooms have either night storage or electric heaters. Each house sleeps seven, plus cot. No linen supplied. Electricity extra. Farm buildings are nearby (this is a working stock and arable farm). Dogs allowed, under strict control. Children welcome. Historical market town of Ledbury three miles. Malvern eight miles. Weekly terms from £80 to £140. Reductions off season. **Mrs G. M. Thomas, White House Farm, Preston Cross, Near Ledbury HR8 2LH (Much Marcle [053-184] 231).**

LEOMINSTER. Mrs J. S. Connop, The Broome, Pembridge, Leominster HR6 9JY (Pembridge [054-47] 324). Working farm. Holiday accommodation offered in wing of large 17th century farmhouse situated mid-way between picturesque black and white villages of Eardisland and Pembridge. Recently modernised but retaining old world charm of oak beams and a wood-burning stove. Kitchen has new electric cooker, fridge, iron, mixer, etc. Colour TV in lounge. Accommodates eight. Available all year. Broome is 120-acre working farm in beautiful rural Herefordshire. Ample parking space. Own front door opens on to gardens, lawns and flower beds. Bed linen charged at £1.50 per person per week. Metered (10p) electricity. Terms from £42 to £85.

SELF-CATERING   Hereford & Worcester   457

DOCKLOW MANOR

HOLIDAY COTTAGES IN RURAL HEREFORDSHIRE FOR 2-6 PEOPLE

Quietly secluded in 10 acres of garden/woodland, the delightfully renovated stone cottages are grouped around an attractive stone-walled pond amidst shrubs, roses and honeysuckle. The cottages are homely, cosy and spotlessly clean. Fitted carpets, well equipped kitchens, colour TV, electric blankets. Laundry facilities. Bed linen is provided and beds are made up for your arrival. Wander round our rambling gardens and meet our friendly peacock, ducks, hens and goats. The more energetic can play croquet, lawn tennis, table tennis or take a dip in our outdoor heated swimming pool. Docklow is an ideal base for Ludlow, the Welsh border castles and market towns, Wye Valley, Brecon and Malvern hills. OPEN ALL YEAR. Short breaks low season.

For brochure telephone 056 882 643.
Carol and Malcolm Ormerod, Docklow Manor, Leominster, Herefordshire.

LEOMINSTER. Sytches Farm, Eardisland, Leominster. Working farm. This substantial brick-built farmhouse is peacefully situated in the tranquil Herefordshire countryside. It is a comfortable base for exploring the many attractions of the area with its pretty half-timbered villages. The spacious accommodation provides a diningroom and lounge with TV and open fires; large kitchen/diner; upstairs there is bathroom and four bedrooms (one double, one twin, one with three single beds and a double with a single bed also). Outside there is a covered play area and garden and guests are welcome to walk the surrounding fields. Children welcome, cot, high chair, babysitting. Dogs accepted. Also facilities for laundry. March to October. Details from **Mrs G. M. Price, Grove House, Monkland, Leominster HR6 9DF (Pembridge [05447] 228).**

LEOMINSTER. Mrs O. S. Helme, Ford Farm, Fordbridge, Leominster HR6 0LE (Leominster [0568] 2784). Working farm. Fishing almost on the doorstep. Situated on the banks of the River Lugg, two flats adjoining farmhouse, fully furnished and self-contained, yet retaining oak beams of original granary. Sun lounge and terrace overlook river with steps to riverside with boat, canoes and over one mile of fishing. Ideal for children; table tennis, nine-hole golf course and riding nearby. On mixed farm, 500-acres, with woodlands, and in good touring area. Flats sleep four and six people; bathroom, toilet; sitting/diningroom; kitchen with fridge, electric cooker. Bedroom arrangements are in two double bedrooms and bunk room and one double bedroom and bunk room. Pets by arrangement. Cot, high chair. Shops one mile. Buses run daily to Leominster and Hereford. SAE, please, for terms. April to November.

LEOMINSTER. Park View, Staunton-on-Arrow, Leominster. This is a detached cottage comprising entrance porch, lounge with TV, kitchen with dining area, fridge, cooker; pantry, hall, bathroom with toilet; airing cupboard and immersion heater. One double bedroom with washbasin downstairs; upstairs one double and one twin-bedded rooms. Cot. Ample parking space at rear of house. Ideal for the family holiday, large garden for children to play, with lawn and shrubs. Fully equipped except linen. Electric fires. Park View stands well away from the road by the tarmac drive to the farm and looks out to the west over the Hereford countryside to the hills of the Radnor Forest in Wales. Village, one mile, has post office and general stores. Coarse fishing nearby. Baker calls twice weekly. Good area for walking. Car essential to see the best of this fine area. Open all year. Terms and brochure on request. **Mrs P. Edwards, Stocklow Manor Farm, Pembridge, Leominster HR6 9HT (Pembridge [054-47] 436).**

LEOMINSTER. The Hollies, Hyde Ash, Ivington, Leominster. Leominster three miles, Hereford 10 miles. The Hollies is a fully modernised detached country cottage with fitted carpets, fully equipped for six people. Large modern kitchen with dining area, electric cooker, fridge/freezer, washing machine, spin drier; bathroom and toilet. Diningroom. Sittingroom with open fire and colour television — logs and coal supplied. One double, two twin bedrooms; cot and linen supplied. Immersion heater, airing cupboard; electricity metered. Set in quiet open countryside next to small family farm. Car essential, ample parking. Lawn. Children welcome. Sorry, no pets. Terms with SAE, please. **Mrs M. Wood, Little Dilwyn, Dilwyn, Hereford HR4 8EY (Ivington [056-888] 279).**

458   Hereford & Worcester   SELF-CATERING

LLANGARRON. "Barnfield", Trehumfrey Farm, Llangarron, Ross-on-Wye. Working farm. "Barnfield" is a new bungalow on 170-acre dairy farm, with views towards Black Mountains. It is in a secluded setting off private farm drive amidst attractive surroundings. Central for touring the beautiful Wye Valley and Welsh Borders with mountains, rivers and breathtaking scenery. Ross six miles, Monmouth seven. Fishing private lake; swimming, tennis, golf, riding within six miles. Bungalow comfortably furnished, accommodating six in three double bedrooms, cot; bathroom, toilet; sittingroom; diningroom. Kitchen with electric cooker, fridge, iron, etc. No linen supplied. Shops one-and-a-half miles. Pets permitted. Available all year. Fitted carpets, TV, etc. Weekly terms on application, with SAE, from **Mrs J. E. Ball, Trehumfrey Farm, Llangarron, Ross-on-Wye HR9 6NX (Llangarron [098-984] 234).**

LYONSHALL. Offa's Cottage, Lyonshall. Offa's Cottage (part 17th century) was built on Offa's Dyke, and was modernised in 1970. It is a secluded cottage, full of olde worlde charm, with panoramic views of Radnor Forest and the Shropshire Hills. An ideal location for rambling and touring, with golf course and coarse fishing nearby. The comfortably furnished accommodation is for four adults and four children (plus cot) in two double rooms plus one bunk-bedded room (with two bunk beds). Bathroom, toilet; sittingroom; diningroom; well equipped kitchen with hot and cold water, electric cooker, fridge, separate pantry. Everything supplied except linen. Available all year. Pets welcome. Village half-a-mile. Ample parking. SAE for terms, please, to **Mrs M. A. Eckley, The Holme, Lyonshall, Kington HR5 3JP (Lyonshall [054-48] 216).**

Whitewells Farm Cottages

Seven skilfully converted cottages, full of character and charm and fully equipped for an enjoyable holiday at any time of the year. Sleep two to six. Linen, towels, washing up liquid, etc. supplied, also colour TV, fridge, toaster, kettle and iron. Cot and high chair for children. Pets allowed. Coin operated washing machine and tumble dryer in laundry room. There is also a new cottage with facilities for disabled guests and those in wheelchairs. A good welcome and clean, comfortable accommodation assured. Property has been the subject of a BTA Award. Ideally placed for touring Cotswolds, Wye Valley, Forest of Dean and Shakespeare country. Much to see and do. For brochure and terms please apply to:
Mr & Mrs Patrick Morton, Whitewells Farm, Ridgway Cross, Near Malvern, Worcester WR13 5JS. (Ridgway Cross [088-684] 607).

MALVERN. Mrs E. Templeton, Douro Cottage, 76 Worcester Road, Malvern WR14 1NU (Malvern [068-45] 4157). The accommodation to let is a self-contained flat at Douro Cottage which is a Regency house of character, a few minutes' walk from the town centre and convenient for access to the hills and commons. Malvern is an attractive, unspoilt inland resort and is an ideal centre for touring the Cotswolds, Wye Valley, Welsh Borders, Shakespeare country, etc., and many places of historical interest. The flat consists of two bedrooms, one with double bed, one with two single beds; bathroom, sittingroom; fully equipped kitchen with gas cooker and refrigerator. There is central heating and gas fire. Terms from £55 – £85 per week. Bed linen not included. Parking nearby. Incoming telephone calls acceptable.

ROSS-ON-WYE. Pot Acre Cottage, Llangarron, Ross-on-Wye. This comfortably furnished cottage situated half-a-mile from the village of Llangarron, five miles from Ross-on-Wye and three miles from Symonds Yat is ideally placed for touring the Wye Valley, Forest of Dean and Black Mountains. Riding available two miles away. There are three bedrooms (two double and two single beds); ground floor has a sittingroom; dining/kitchen and pantry, all fully equipped for six people, with the exception of linen. Mains water and electricity, hot and cold water, modern bathroom; electric cooker, fridge. Car essential — parking. Weekly terms on application from **Mrs J. Scudamore, Llangarron Court, Ross-on-Wye HR9 6NP (Llangarron [098-984] 243).**

ROSS-ON-WYE near. Mrs S. Dixon, "Swayns Diggins", Harewood End, Hereford HR2 8JU (Harewood End [098-987] 358). This bright, self-contained first floor flat has private balcony and panoramic south facing views across unspoilt countryside. Fitted carpets throughout and full heating. Fully equipped kitchen has fridge and Baby Belling cooker. Sittingroom, with colour TV, and bed-settee. Twin bedroom with shower and toilet en suite. *Linen provided. Electricity included.* Free use of small outdoor swimming pool. Post office/store one-and-a-half miles. Hereford — Black Mountains — Wye Valley — Forest of Dean and many other places of interest within easy reach. Open all year. Weekly terms £55 to £95. Mid week bookings accepted out of season. Fresh milk, free range eggs etc. available. House-trained dogs welcome. Ample parking.

ROSS-ON-WYE. Holly Cottage, Llangrove, Ross-on-Wye. Holly Cottage is situated near the edge of the small village of Llangrove, facing the Forest of Dean. It is 450 ft. above sea level and two miles north of A40 road at Whitchurch. Sleeps seven/six in three bedrooms (two double, two single beds, plus cot; single bed on landing — curtained). Comfortable sittingroom; kitchen and bathroom. Small grassy garden. Ample parking. Fridge, washing machine, spin drier, electric cooker and fires. Immersion heater. Electricity charged. Linen not supplied. TV. Pets welcome. Phone for terms, **Mrs A. C. Williams, The Nurseries, Llangrove, Ross-on-Wye HR9 6ET (Llangarron [098-984] 252).**

SELF-CATERING Hereford & Worcester

WORCESTERSHIRE FARM & COUNTRY HOLIDAYS

THE ENGLISH VALES

Old House Farm, Tibberton, Droitwich (Mrs Pat Chilman, Tel. No. [090565] 247) Comfortable, self contained annexe, on dairy farm. Large garden with lovely views of Malvern Hills. 1 mile from M5 Junction 6. Ideal touring centre.

Church Farm, Knighton-on-Teme, Worcester (Mrs C. D. Hurst, Tel. No. [0299] 266216 or [058479] 358) Georgian farmhouse on 230 acre mixed farm (now 2 self-contained appartments) situated in Teme Valley. Sleeps 5/6 – £100/£120 per week no extra charges. AA listed.

Abbey Manor Farm, Worcester Road, Evesham (Mrs Pru Jeffrey, Tel. No. [0386] 3802) Converted barn providing for self-catering in "character" cottages. Comfortable accommodation sleeping 4-6, colour TV; fitted kitchen, laundry. Traditional farmyard setting with old orchard.

Hill Top Farm, Knighton on Teme, Tenbury Wells (Mr Philip Porter, Tel. No. [058479] 336) Porters Cottage – a delightful, newly restored 16th Century timber framed cottage. Sleeps 4. Granary Cottage, a quaint old granary. Sleeps 2-6. Both comprehensively equipped. Beautiful peaceful countryside.

Lower Portway Farm, Sedgeberrow, Evesham (Mrs Daphne Stow, Tel. No. [0386] 881298) A welcoming atmosphere in comfortable and well furnished cottages or apartments in quiet village near Evesham. Fully equipped including colour TV. Ample car parking. Lawned gardens.

Oakhurst Cottage, Leigh (Mrs Sally Stewart, Tel. No. [0886] 32275) Comfortable modernised farm cottage on 270 acre Teme Valley Farm. Sleeps 4. Cot available. Fishing. Parking in small garden.

For farmhouse accommodation please see 'Worcester Farm and Country Holidays' advert in board section.

FOR GROUP BROCHURE WITH FULL DETAILS SEND 9" × 4" SAE TO MRS P. HAVARD, PHEPSON FARM, HIMBLETON, DROITWICH, WORCESTERSHIRE. TEL (090569) 205.

ROSS-ON-WYE. Mrs H. Smith, Old Kilns, Howle Hill, Ross-on-Wye HR9 5SP (Ross-on-Wye [0989] 62051). In Wye Valley, formerly the site of lime kilns, Old Kilns is a modernised country house situated 500 ft. above sea-level with beautiful views of the Wye Valley and Black Mountains. Six acres own grounds. Ross-on-Wye and M50 (Birmingham — South Wales Motorway) three miles. Symonds Yat four miles; Hereford 14 and Gloucestershire 16 miles. Central for touring Cotswolds, Malverns, Stratford and the Severn Bridge (20 miles). Travel through beautiful countryside to Chepstow with Abbey and Castle. Forest of Dean, ideal for picnics. Fishing (salmon and coarse), boating, canoeing, tennis, bowls, golf, swimming, riding available in the vicinity. Six people accommodated in one double and one twin-bedded rooms; lounge with double bed-settee; colour TV; dinette and kitchen. Bathroom and toilet downstairs. Linen can be hired. AA recommended. Children welcome — two cots, two high chairs, babysitting service. Also four-berth caravan. Ample parking space. SAE brings terms and details by return.

ROWLSTONE. Mrs E. M. Price, Church Farm, Rowlstone HR2 0DP (Golden Valley [0981] 240708). Church Farm is situated in beautiful countryside close to Black Mountains for walking and pony trekking. The two roomed flat with separate entrance is available from July to September. The family bedroom sleeps four. A cot is available. The bathroom is shared. The kitchen-cum-sittingroom has electricity for cooking and heating. Sorry, no pets. Please supply own linen. Car essential. Two-and-a-half miles from shops and one-and-a-half miles from public transport. Terms and further details on request.

The information in the entries in this guide is presented by the publishers in good faith and after the signed acceptance by advertisers that they will uphold the high standards associated with FARM HOLIDAY GUIDES LIMITED. The publishers do not accept responsibility for any inaccuracies or omissions or any results thereof. Before making final holiday arrangements readers should confirm the prices and facilities directly with advertisers.

Hereford & Worcester / Kent   SELF-CATERING

TENBURY WELLS near. Mrs Hurst, Church Farm, Knighton-on-Teme, Near Tenbury Wells WR15 8LT (Rock [0299] 266216 or Newnham Bridge [058-479] 575). Working farm. Adjacent to 16th century church and approached by gated road, this tranquil Georgian Farmhouse is converted into two self-contained apartments (one ground floor, one first floor). Each consists of one double bedroom and one twin bedded room, large lounge/diningroom with bed-settee, TV; well equipped kitchen; bathroom on first floor, shower on ground floor. Garden facing the beautiful Teme Valley. Central for Ludlow, Malverns, Clee Hills, Bewdley with its Severn Valley Railway and Safari Park. Overseas visitors welcome. Weekly rates from £80. March to November. No dogs. Telephone for further details.

WESTHOPE. Kiln House, Westhope, Hereford. Working farm. Kiln House is an immaculate conversion of an old hop kiln and is set in peaceful, picturesque countryside and situated six miles north of Hereford. There is privacy and ample space for parking. Village shop one mile away. Good pubs and restaurants in locality. The accommodation is spacious and well laid out: fully furnished/equipped, carpeted throughout and with central heating. Sleeps six in two double and one twin bedrooms; modern kitchen, diningroom, sittingroom with TV, bathroom. Cot and high chair. Linen supplied at extra charge. Small dogs allowed. Weekend breaks — off-peak period. Terms £50, £80, £120. Apply to **Mrs J. M. Fowler, Fullbridge Farm, Westhope, Hereford HR4 8BN (Canon Pyon [043-271] 310).**

WORCESTER. Worcestershire Farm and Country Holidays. Farmhouse accommodation and self-catering holidays. See also Display Advertisements in the Board and Self-Catering sections of this Guide under Hereford and Worcester.

WORCESTER near. Oakhurst Cottage, Leigh, Near Worcester. This comfortable semi-detached cottage, located within the Teme Valley in the village of Bransford, sleeps four in one double and one twin-bedded room. A cot and high chair are available by arrangement. There is a through dining/sittingroom with coal/electric fire and TV. Also, a modern kitchen and bathroom and a small garden with ample off-street parking. Petrol station/shop quarter-of-a-mile. The Malvern Hills and Worcester are each five miles away and Shakespeare's Stratford-on-Avon, the Welsh border country, Birmingham as well as the lovely valleys of the Severn and Wye are all within easy reach. River Teme fishing available and lovely walks on the 270-acre sheep and arable farm. **Mrs Stewart, Leigh Court, Near Worcester WR6 5LB (Leigh Sinton [0886] 32275).**

WORMBRIDGE. Mrs M. E. Thomas, Granary Flat, Lower Jury Farm, Wormbridge HR2 9EE (Wormbridge [098-121] 229). Working farm. Granary Flat is attached to the early 16th-century farmhouse on Lower Jury Farm situated in a peaceful valley. Close to the Black Mountains, Golden Valley, market towns and places of historic interest. The flat has a wealth of exposed beams, and the lounge (with colour TV) and bedrooms are fully carpeted. There are lovely views to the distant hills and the Grey Valley. Children are welcome to help with the farm animals and hay-making. Shooting for experienced guns. Registered with the English Tourist Board. Accommodates four/five people. Usual conveniences. Kitchen with electric cooker, fridge and dining area. Linen supplied. Pets permitted. Car essential — parking. Open April to October. Terms from £50 to £90 per week. Slot meter (50p) for electricity.

KENT

BENENDEN. Yew Tree Farm, Benenden, Cranbrook TN17 4HH. This 16th century farm cottage, one of a pair, stands on the edge of an orchard on the outskirts of a small hamlet called Iden Green which has one shop and a pub. The cottage accommodates five in three bedrooms plus a cot; bathroom and toilet; sittingroom; dining/kitchen, all-electric. Children and pets by arrangement. A car is essential; parking space; large lawn. Available from April to October, and has solid fuel or electric heating. Weekly terms from £70 to £120. Fully equipped. **Miss Cyster (0580-240509).**

BENENDEN. 1 Primrose Cottage, Benenden. Working farm. The cottage is opposite the main house and is about 100 years old. Beautiful peaceful countryside and much of historical interest in the area. Accommodation for six in three double bedrooms; bathroom, toilet; sittingroom. Kitchen has electric cooker, fridge, table and chairs, sink unit, etc. Linen supplied. Oil filled electric radiators, and logs provided for fire in sittingroom during cold weather. Colour TV. Cleaner calls at least once a week. Shops half-a-mile. Car essential — parking. No pets. Weekly terms from £75—£120 — Easter to October. November—Easter £50—£60. SAE to **Mrs Anne Cyster, Walkhurst Farm, Benenden TN17 4EN (Cranbrook [0580] 240677).**

PLEASE SEND A STAMPED ADDRESSED ENVELOPE WITH ENQUIRIES

COUNTRY HOLIDAYS IN RURAL KENT

Our charming cottages are set in rolling countryside on a private farm, but only 10 miles from the sea. It is an ideal centre for touring, seaside and sight-seeing. Canterbury, Dover, Tunbridge Wells and Leeds Castle are within an hour's drive, while Rye, Tenterden, Chilham and the famous garden at Sissinghurst Castle are considerably nearer. For railway enthusiasts, the unique Romney, Hythe and Dymchurch Light Railway is at Hythe and the Kent and East Sussex steam railway is at Tenterden. Day trips to France (passport required) are an attractive proposition and, for those who wish to visit London, the train journey takes only one hour from Ashford.

For shopping, Ham Street is one mile away and can provide for all household needs, while Ashford and Tenterden (seven miles) have all the facilities of country towns.

Both coast and countryside offer many attractions for the visitor and added to these are two hundred acres of farmland and woods which we own and which are available to you during your visit.

The Oast Houses were recently converted to unique holiday cottages with modern standards of comfort, but retain their original interesting features. Hillside is a delightful bungalow with a large secluded garden and lovely views. Leacon Oast and Hockley Oast sleep six and Hillside sleeps five.

All the houses are comfortable and very well equipped, including television. Electricity is on 50p meters. The kitchens are all-electric and have a cooker, fridge, iron, electric kettle and spindryer, together with a full range of utensils. Heating is either by electric fires, mobile calor gas heaters or solid fuel Rayburns. Two of the houses have open fireplaces. A cot is available on request. Bed linen and towels are not provided. We personally supervise the cottages and are available to help you enjoy your holiday.

LEACON OAST HOUSE

HILLSIDE COTTAGE

HOCKLEY OAST HOUSE

Enquiries to: **Mrs V. A. Dawes, Leacon Hall, Wareholme, Ashford, Kent. Tel. Ham Street 2331.**

HELP IMPROVE BRITISH TOURIST STANDARDS

You are choosing holiday accommodation from our very popular FARM HOLIDAY GUIDES. Whether it be a hotel, guest house, farmhouse or self-catering accommodation, we think you will find it hospitable, comfortable and clean, and your host and hostess friendly and helpful.

Why not write and tell us about it?

As a recognition of the generally well-run and excellent holiday accommodation reviewed in our publications, we at FARM HOLIDAY GUIDES LIMITED present a diploma to proprietors who receive the highest recommendation from their guests who are also readers of our Guides. If you care to write to us praising the holiday you have booked through FARM HOLIDAY GUIDES – whether this be board, self-catering accommodation, a sporting or a caravan holiday, the content of your letter will be evaluated and the proprietors who reach our final list will be contacted.

The winning proprietor will receive an attractive framed diploma to display on his premises as recognition of a high standard of comfort, amenity and hospitality. FARM HOLIDAY GUIDES LIMITED offer this diploma as a contribution towards the improvement of standards in tourist accommodation in Britain. Help your excellent host or hostess to win it!

DIPLOMA
AWARDED BY
READERS
of
FARM HOLIDAY GUIDE
PUBLICATIONS LIMITED

TO..
FOR HOLIDAY ACCOMMODATION
of the HIGHEST STANDARD

AT..

Kent　SELF-CATERING

DEAL. Miss E. B. Phillips, Clanwilliam House, 1 Marine Road, Walmer, Deal CT14 7DN (Dover [0304] 374059). This is a lovely old bungalow built in 1878 and has been well maintained by successive owners. Standing on Walmer seafront it has a verandah with old stone pots and geraniums. Deal Castle is just next to it and Walmer Castle is one mile away where Her Majesty the Queen Mother was installed as Lord Warden of the Cinque Ports in 1979. The hovercrafts at Dover and Ramsgate are nearby and Canterbury and Sandwich are within easy reach. Five people can be accommodated in two double and one single bedrooms; cots can be hired. Fully equipped kitchen; linen can be hired. Dogs permitted at 15p per day. Children welcome and the house is suitable for the disabled. Please book early as this is a popular house and families return regularly. Open Easter to November. Personal service and babysitting (by arrangement). Weekly terms from £50 to £150 approx. Prefer two weeks minimum. Electricity on slot meter. Deal Music Festival July/August — two weeks. Canterbury Festival September.

DEAL. 1 Griffin Street, Deal. Renovated house in Conservation Area. Near shops, 100 yards from sea front. Four double bedrooms, with washbasins. Lounge; kitchen/diner with electric cooker, fridge and all essentials. Bathroom, separate WC. Colour TV. Gas fires. Fitted carpets. Cot and high chair available. Electricity by 50p slot meter. Also available spacious flat, sleeping five persons, at Alfred Square, Deal, and cosy Cottage, with garden, at Walmer, sleeping three persons. Free parking at all accommodation. Weekly terms from £50 to £250. Sorry, no pets. SAE, please, for brochure to **Mr Dennis Johnson, "Pebbles", Wellington Parade, Walmer CT14 8AB (Deal [0304] 373694 and 368165).**

DEAL. 64 Middle Street, Deal. Deal is a quiet unspoilt town with unrivalled views of the sea. Excellent facilities for sailing and fishing, and lots of golf courses in the area. Tennis, bowls, riding and squash also available. Trips to the Continent can be enjoyed and the historic towns of Canterbury, Sandwich and Dover, as well as seaside resorts are within 20 miles. The period Cottage accommodates five people in one double, one twin and one single bedrooms; cot; bathroom, toilet; sittingroom; fully fitted kitchen/diner with split-level electric cooker, washing machine and fridge. Colour TV. Fitted carpets throughout. Pets permitted (extra charge). Parking. Available all year round. Shops and sea front 50 yards away. Slot meter for electricity and gas. SAE, please, for terms to **Mr Martin L. Horncastle, 743B Finchley Road, London NW11 8DL (01-458-7057).**

Fairhaven Holiday Cottages (Dept 6)
Fairhaven House, 37 Stuart Road, Gillingham, Kent ME7 4AD
Phone: Medway (0634) 570157 (24 hour brochure service)

LARGE SELECTION OF SUPER SELF-CATERING HOLIDAY PROPERTIES OF ALL SIZES IN THE SOUTH-EAST, SOUTH, SOUTH-WEST AND UP TO WEST MIDLANDS AND EAST ANGLIA. SOME SUITABLE FOR THE DISABLED. AVAILABLE ALL YEAR AND OUT OF SEASON SHORT BREAKS. SOME AVAILABLE FOR LONG LETS.

HAWKHURST. Mrs L. C. Johnson, Highwell, Heartenoak Road, Hawkhurst, Cranbrook TN18 5EU (Hawkhurst [058 05] 2152). Enjoy a peaceful holiday in the self-contained annexe to our attractive Edwardian house. Offering a high standard of accommodation with linen, colour TV, modern kitchen and a delightful country view from the large comfortable sittingroom. Set in acre of gardens down a country lane, the house is half a mile from Hawkhurst Village which is a recommended regional touring centre for Kent and Sussex. Famous and picturesque gardens and castles, plus coast, within easy reach. Accommodation for two in double bedroom, plus single or cot. Weekly terms from £45 to £75. Available all year.

If you've found
FARM HOLIDAY GUIDE
of service please tell your friends

LANCASHIRE

LANCASTER near. Mrs D. R. Battersby, Hornby Castle, Hornby, Near Lancaster (Hornby [0468] 21291). This 16th century castle is situated in the Lune Valley on the edge of the Lake District, nine miles from the sea and seven miles from the M6. It stands on its own hill with superb commanding views on all sides, set in beautiful extensive grounds and skirted by a river. There are four cottages and two flats available for holiday letting all year round within the castle and grounds, accommodating two to six people. Cot and camp beds available. Each property has great charm and character, is attractively furnished and fully equipped except for linen. Fishing and shooting are available on the estate. Shops in Hornby village quarter-of-a-mile away. Contact **Mrs Battersby** for terms and further details.

LUNE VALLEY. Working farm. Camp Lodge adjoins Camp House Farm, in very pleasant rural surroundings. Views of Hornby Castle and Ingleborough. Within walking distance of River Lune and River Wenning. It is within easy reach of the Lake District, Yorkshire Dales and Morecambe. The stone-built cottage accommodates seven people in three double bedrooms, with extra single bed if required, or cot. Bathroom; toilet; sittingroom with TV; kitchen/diner with electric cooker, fridge, kettle, toaster, spin dryer and all equipment. Electricity on 50p meter. No linen supplied. Pets permitted. Car essential — parking. Garden and large lawn. Open all year. One mile from shops. SAE, please, for terms: **Mrs Y. Towers, Cartref, Greenbank, Caton, Lancaster LA2 9JD (Caton [0524] 770400).**

PLEASE ENCLOSE A STAMPED ADDRESSED ENVELOPE WITH ENQUIRIES

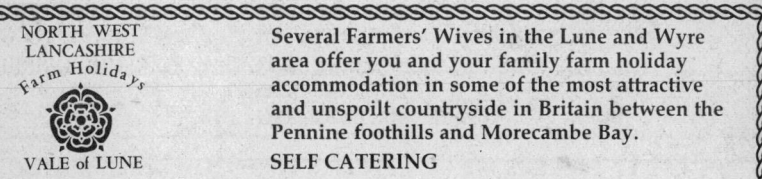

NORTH WEST LANCASHIRE
Farm Holidays

VALE of LUNE

Several Farmers' Wives in the Lune and Wyre area offer you and your family farm holiday accommodation in some of the most attractive and unspoilt countryside in Britain between the Pennine foothills and Morecambe Bay.

SELF CATERING

BRACKENTHWAITE FARM, YEALAND REDMAYNE, CARNFORTH LA5 9TE (Mrs A. S. Clarke Tel. No. [04482] 3276) Modernised cottage, sleeps 4 on 100 acre mixed farm in lovely walking area. Near Leighton Moss Bird Reserve and on fringe of the Lake District. Fishing and riding available nearby. Colour TV, storage heaters, suitable throughout the year.

LANE HOUSE, BENTHAM, NEAR LANCASTER LA2 7DJ (Mrs Betty Clapham Tel. No. [0468] 61479) Six berth caravan in orchard overlooking Yorkshire Dales. Electric light and socket. Gas fire, cooker and fridge. Running water. Parking by caravan.

OXENFORTH GREEN, TATHAM, LANCASTER (Mrs B. Mason Tel. No. [0468] 61784) Recently converted accommodation adjoining farmhouse. Sleeps 4 plus cot. Well equipped fitted kitchen, lounge with gas fire and colour T.V. 2 shower rooms and storage heaters.

TARNACRE HALL FARM, ST. MICHAELS-ON-WYRE, NEAR PRESTON (Mrs F. Whewell Tel. No. [09958] 217) Self contained fully furnished 1st floor three roomed flat in farmhouse with beautiful views. In good touring area, sleeps 4-6 plus cot. Storage heating, shower, toilet etc. From £52 weekly. Short lets out of season.

LUNDHOLME, INGLETON, CARNFORTH LA6 3NH (Mrs Nancy Lund Tel. No. [0468] 41307) Ingleton, beauty spot of the North. Fully furnished cottage sleeps 8 from £50 per week and caravan sleeps 6 on working farm. SAE for brochure.

For group brochure with full details, please send 9" × 4" SAE to Mrs Jean Fowler, Greenhalgh Castle Farm, Castle Lane, Garstang, Preston, Lancs. PR3 1RB. Tel. (09952) 2140.

The group is a member of the Farm Holiday Bureau and an associate member of the North West Tourist Board.

PRESTON. Ash View, Wheel Lane, Pilling, Preston. Working farm. This cottage is situated near the 85-acre dairy farm, within easy reach of Yorkshire Dales and Lake District. The attractive market town of Garstang is six miles away; University town of Lancaster 11 miles; Blackpool 12¼ miles. Lots to see and do in the area. Cottage sleeps four people in one double and one twin bedroom, plus cot if required. Shower, washbasin, toilet. Lounge with colour TV. Diningroom. Well-equipped kitchen with electric cooker, fridge, iron, etc. Guests must supply their own linen. House is on ground level, though not suitable for wheelchairs. Car essential, parking. Available from Easter to November. Shops three-quarters of a mile. Sea one mile. Terms from £56 per week including VAT. SAE, please, or telephone for further details to **D. W. & V. Lawrenson, Bonds Farm, Wheel Lane, Pilling, Preston PR3 6HN (Pilling [039-130] 409).**

LEICESTERSHIRE

MELTON MOWBRAY. Mr and Mrs B. Brotherhood, Stable Cottage, Church Lane, Asfordby, Melton Mowbray LE14 3RU (Melton Mowbray [0664] 812314). This 200-year-old modernised holiday cottage sharing two acres of garden and lawns with river frontage offers free fishing from river bank. Accommodation for six people in three double bedrooms, cot, bathroom, WC and hall. Kitchen/diner with electric cooker, fridge etc; lounge. Fully furnished — cutlery, crockery, linen included. Ample parking. Electricity by coin meter. Good shops and inns in village. Enjoy shopping in busy market town of Melton Mowbray (well known for its delicacies of Stilton Cheese and Pork Pies) with its bustling street markets on Tuesday and Saturday. Within half an hour's drive from Belvoir Castle, Stapleford Park, Charnwood Forest and Rutland Water. Well suited for daily excursions to Stratford-on-Avon, Lincoln and Leicester. Available February to November. Terms from £60 weekly. Please write for full details.

OLD HALL COTTAGES near Rutland Water

Six comfortable stone built cottages in quiet surroundings in and around the beautiful gardens of 17th century Old Hall in Langham. Sleep four-eight, TV, fridge, central heating, parking, etc. Children welcome. Village has pubs serving food, small shops and dairy. Easy reach of Rutland Water, Shakespeare Theatre, picnic spots and many places of interest. Fishing, sailing, riding, golf within a few miles. SAE, please, for details to:
Mrs D. Abel-Smith, Old Hall Cottage, 36 Burley Road, Langham, Oakham, Rutland LE15 7HY. (Oakham [0572] 2964).

LEICESTERSHIRE – THE EPITOMY OF MIDDLE ENGLAND!
A county of undulating farmland containing such delights as Rutland Water, the canal "staircase" at Foxton, the market town of Oakham, Charnwood forest and the estate church at Staunton Harold.

LINCOLNSHIRE

WOODHALL SPA. Clements Farmhouse, Kirkby-on-Bain, Woodhall Spa. Clements Farmhouse is set in secluded position amidst peaceful countryside and offers homely accommodation for seven/eight people throughout the year. Car essential; two garages and ample parking. Grassy garden. Two miles from village and shops. Woodhall Spa, three miles, has attractive woodland walks, championship golf course, cinema, shops, heated swimming pool, tennis courts, etc. Leisure Centre at Tattershall four miles — squash courts, boating and fishing lakes. Ideally situated for touring. The house is spacious and carpeted throughout. Livingroom with TV, diningroom; electric and open fires. Kitchen has electric cooker, fridge and iron. Bathroom and toilet; four/five bedrooms. Electricity is by coin meter. Children welcome and cot and high chair provided. Linen not supplied. Pets by special arrangement only. Apply **Mrs G. B. Laughton, Wellsyke Farm, Kirkby-on-Bain, Woodhall Spa LN10 6YU** (Woodhall Spa [0526] 52151).

NORFOLK

ACLE. Blacksmith's Cottage, 1 The Street, Halvergate, Acle. A newly restored period cottage offering excellent accommodation for six people plus baby. Situated in the centre of this small village close to the church and village green, the cottage offers the following well furnished accommodation. Lounge and diningroom, each with inglenook fireplace and beamed ceiling. Fully fitted kitchen and modern bathroom. Three double bedrooms, one with double bed, one with twin beds, one with bunk beds. Attractive and sheltered gardens are feature of the property and there is ample parking for up to three cars. Ideally situated for touring the Norfolk coast and Broads area. Open all year round. Linen provided; colour TV; electricity by meter. Sorry, no pets. For details SAE to **Mrs J. Parker, 51 Intwood Road, Cringleford, Norwich NR4 6AA** (Norwich [0603] 58768).

ASHILL, near Swaffham. Mrs D. Ralli, Panworth Hall Farm (0760-440-852 & 0953-881206). This accommodation comprises eight two-storey traditional farm cottages, all attractively furnished and decorated on the owners' 650-acre farm where guests are welcome to watch farm activities. Children and well behaved pets are very welcome. This is a rural area and a car is essential. Shops, pub, village green, etc. ½-mile at Ashill. Each cottage sleeps 5 plus baby (cot, pot, high chair all provided) in two double and one single bedroom. Sittingroom, three cottages have dining rooms, bathroom, modern kitchen. Night storage heaters and double glazing. Coal for the open fires, a daily newspaper and colour TV are all provided free of charge. Ample car parking space. Own gardens. Good central touring area for sandy beaches in North Norfolk. Also Norwich, The Broads, Sandringham, Cambridge. Six of the cottages are particularly suitable for families wishing to share a holiday together since they are adjoining. Idyllic 17th century Thatched Cottage at Snetterton also available. Brochure **Mrs Ralli.** Terms: Panworth Hall Cottages — £70 to £156; Thatched Cottage — £70 to £168.

FUN FOR ALL THE FAMILY IN NORFOLK

Banham Zoo & Monkey Sanctuary, The Grove, Banham; *Kilverstone Wildlife Park,* Thetford; *Thrigby Hall Wildlife Gardens,* near Filby; *The Otter Trust,* Earsham, near Bungay; *Wildfowl Trust,* Welney; *Kelling Park Hotel & Aviaries,* near Holt; *Cromer Zoo,* Cromer; *Caister Castle Motor Museum,* near Great Yarmouth; Banham International Motor Museum, The Grove, Banham; *Bressingham Gardens & Live Steam Museum,* near Diss; *North Norfolk Railway,* Sheringham Station, Sheringham; *Maritime Museum for East Anglia,* Marine Parade, Great Yarmouth; *Iceni Village,* Reconstructed, Cockley Cley, near Swaffham; *Colman's Mustard Museum,* The Mustard Shop, 3 Bridewell Akkey, Norwich.

466 Norfolk SELF-CATERING

BECCLES. Hillside, 15 Kells Way, Geldeston, Beccles. This bungalow situated in small country village, very quiet and near River Waveney is within easy reach of Great Yarmouth, Norwich, Lowestoft and seaside. Accommodates four/six people; one double, one twin bedroom; bed settee in lounge, colour TV, small inglenook fire, beams; diningroom; bathroom/shower, toilet; kitchen, electric cooker etc. Carpets throughout. Sorry, no pets. Cot available. Bed linen supplied. Car essential — parking. Shops nearby. Terms on request. **Mrs J. A. Rolt, "Conifer," 17 Kells Way, Geldeston, Beccles, Suffolk NR34 0LU (Kirby Cane [050-845] 689).**

BLAKENEY. 4 Mariners Hill, Blakeney & Starlings, 82 High Street, Blakeney. All year round, beautiful house and attractive cottage available to visitors hoping for a holiday that combines true relaxation, first class accommodation and splendid scenery. Mariners Hill is a flint/brick-built house sleeping eight, with spectacular views over the quay and marsh. Small, secluded, walled garden. Extremely well furnished and equipped. Colour TV, dishwasher, washing machine and fridge/freezer. Starlings is a pink-washed quaint cottage with a part covered courtyard. With ample accommodation for six, it provides TV, Rayburn for extra warmth in winter and the ultimate in comfort. Good dinghy sailing and bird watching at hand, golf courses nearby. Weekly terms: house: from £100; cottage: from £50. Further details on request. **Mrs B. Harris, The Merchants House, 86 High Street, Blakeney, Holt NR25 7AL (Cley [0263] 740863).**

BURNHAM OVERY STAITHE. "Flagstaff House," Burnham Overy Staithe, King's Lynn, and "Clare Cottage," Burnham Market. Flagstaff House is right on the Quay, the old home of Captain Woodgett of the Cutty Sark. Each half of the house sleeps five comfortably in three bedrooms and has wonderful views over the creeks and marshes. Two extra people can be accommodated in summer house. Clare Cottage is an old world cottage in the nearby market town of Burnham Market, only five minutes from the sea and much favoured for its comfort, convenience and quiet seclusion. Sleeps eleven. All houses are well equipped with all modern conveniences, including washing machine, dishwasher, TV, electric storage heaters, etc. Telephone. The area is well known for dinghy sailing, bird watching, windsurfing, golf, fishing and miles of deserted sandy beaches and sand dunes. Apply to **Mr C. W. C. Green, Red House Farm, Badingham, Woodbridge, Suffolk IP13 8LL (Badingham [072-875] 637).**

CROMER. Hobby Cottage, Driftway Farm, Felbrigg, Cromer, Norfolk. Completely modernised, comfortable cottage at the end of a quiet farm lane. Two miles from sandy coast and within easy access of North Norfolk bird sanctuaries, stately homes and Norfolk Broads. The cottage sleeps 4/6, having a sittingroom with bed settee; two double bedrooms (one with double bed, one with twin beds); diningroom, well-equipped kitchen and bathroom. Garden and parking for two cars. Car essential. Available March-October. From £75–£110 per week, including electricity. No linen. Enquiries, with SAE please, to **Mrs E. Raggatt, The Ferns, Berkley Street, Eynesbury, St. Neots, Cambs. PE19 2NE (Huntingdon [0480] 213884).**

CROMER. 2 and 3 Storeys Loke, Northrepps, Cromer. Cottages available for self-catering holidays in the centre of Northrepps village, three miles from Cromer and 22 miles north of Norwich. The nearest beach is approximately two miles away at Overstrand. The cottages sleep four each and have been extensively modernised. Comfortably furnished sitting/diningroom; well equipped, fitted kitchen with fridge and electric cooker; two bedrooms (one double, two single beds); modern bathroom with heater and shaving point. Hot water and heating by electricity. TV. Milk and eggs available in village. Children are welcome, also pets. Parking. Shops nearby. Open all year. This unspoilt area of Norfolk offers much for the holiday-maker. Many beauty spots, country walks, attractive villages and stately homes. Yarmouth 30 miles. Terms on request from **Mrs B. Roper, Shrublands Farm, Northrepps, Cromer NR27 0AA (Overstrand [026-378] 434/660).**

DEREHAM. Mrs V. Hawker, The Old Rectory, Stanfield, Dereham NR20 4HY (Fakenham [0328] 700224). The Barn Cottages are situated in the Old Rectory grounds at Stanfield, a small rural village between Fakenham and Dereham — ideally placed for visiting the coast, historic houses, nature reserves, Broads etc. The ancient barn has been thoughtfully converted into three attractive beamed self-contained cottages sleeping six, four and two (latter ideal for disabled). Own garden and each has delightful views over undulating farmland. All fully equipped excluding linen. Children and pets welcome. Cots available. Car essential. Ample parking. Quarter mile from General Stores, 13 miles from coast and equidistant Norwich and King's Lynn. All terms moderate. SAE for brochure please.

PLEASE SEND A STAMPED ADDRESSED ENVELOPE WITH ENQUIRIES

SELF-CATERING Norfolk 467

CROMER

A Selection of Several Delightful and Picturesque Cottages

Holiday Properties at Northrepps

All cottages are completely modernised, very comfortably furnished and fully equipped to very high standards. They are all in Northrepps, a small hamlet just a mile inland from Overstrand Beach with its endless stretches of golden sands and superb bathing, ideal for all ages. This part of the coast is zoned as an Area of Natural Beauty and it has facilities for golf, sailing, fishing (both sea and fresh water), riding, bird watching, etc. Inland the terrain consists of rolling well-wooded farmland with quiet market towns, superb churches and famous stately homes open to the public most days during the season. The well-known Blakeney Nature Reserve is only a short distance away.

Your Cottage near the sea

All properties are fully electric: cooker, water heater, fridge, TV. All have ample electric fires and many now have night store heaters as well. Cots are available on request. Pets are welcome. Ample parking for cars. Well-equipped village store. Many of these properties stand well back from any road with safe play areas for children and pets. Inclusive charges range from £95 to £195 per week depending on season and size of property.

Detailed brochure and terms on application (SAE, please) to:

**Northrepps Holiday Properties, Cromer, Norfolk NR27 0JW
Telephone Cromer (0263) 512236.**

DISS. Knoll Cottage, Redgrave, Diss. Knoll Cottage overlooks the Village Green of Redgrave, four miles west of Diss. Convenient for visiting historic centres — Norwich, Ipswich, Bury St. Edmunds, near Banham Zoo, Bressingham Steam Museum, potteries, glass factory, sailing, fishing and the Broads. The cottage is spacious, comfortably furnished and equipped. Accommodation for seven people and a baby. Large sittingroom with open fire — logs provided. Colour TV. Small diningroom; kitchen/breakfast room; electric cooker and Rayburn which heats the water (oil provided). Downstairs — twin-bedded room, cloakroom and toilet. Upstairs — two double bedrooms, single bedroom and bathroom/toilet. Small enclosed garden. Shops across Green. Linen provided. Available all year. Weekly terms from £90 to £130. Children and pets welcome. Further details from **Mrs H. G. Bennet, 10 Swan Lane, Harleston IP20 9AN (Harleston [0379] 852068).**

DISS. "Hall Cottage", Heywood, Diss. Small, traditional, oak-beamed farm cottage in peaceful rural surroundings, yet not isolated. Attractive market town of Diss, four miles; mid-way between Norwich and Ipswich (20 miles); Norfolk Broads and coast 30 miles. Several local attractions — riding school at Diss; new covered swimming pool one and a half miles; Bressingham Gardens and Steam Museum; Banham Zoo and Car Museum; Kilverstone Wild Life Park. Stately homes within easy reach. Snetterton car racing circuit eight miles. Convenient for Yarmouth and Newmarket Races. Five people can be accommodated; one double and one twin-bedded rooms, also one single room; cot; bathroom, toilet; sittingroom with TV. Fully equipped kitchen — electric cooker, fridge, etc; 50p electricity meter. No linen supplied. Car essential — parking. Shops one-and-a-half miles. Open May to October. Terms on application. SAE, please. **Mrs I. Burton, Heywood Hall, Diss IP22 3TD (Tivetshall [037-977] 280).**

WHEN MAKING ENQUIRIES PLEASE MENTION FARM HOLIDAY GUIDE

Norfolk SELF-CATERING

ECCLES-ON-SEA. Mrs J. S. Pestell, The Old Rectory, Hempstead with Eccles, Lessingham, Norwich NR12 0SH (Stalham [0692] 80793). The Old Rectory is set in six acres of garden and woodland in rural East Norfolk, about half-a-mile from the quiet, sandy beach at Eccles. The Norfolk Broadland centres of Stalham and Hickling are approximately four miles distant; Yarmouth, Norwich and Cromer about 19 miles. The Old Rectory is considered particularly suitable for adults or parents with baby or toddler, requiring quiet accommodation. One flat accommodating four people. Bathroom, toilet; kitchen/diningroom with electric cooker, fridge, full cooking utensils, TV. The flat is suitable for disabled guests. Half-a-mile from shops. Pets permitted. Car essential — parking. Electricity on 10p meter. Further details and terms on application. Send SAE stating number of adults and children in party.

ERPINGHAM near. The Lady Walpole, O.B.E., Wolterton Hall, Norwich NR11 7LY (Cromer [0263] 761210) or (Matlaske [026-377] 274). Wolterton is situated 17 miles from Norwich in lovely unspoiled North Norfolk countryside, eight miles from the coast, five-and-a-half miles from the market town of Aylsham. Use of tennis court, lake fishing available, pony riding for children. Two Houses, one maisonette, two cottages, three flats as furnished self-catering holiday accommodation. East Lodge 1 sleeps four; one double, one twin-bedded rooms; East Lodge 2 sleeps five; two twin-bedded, one single bedrooms. Stable House sleeps six; three twin-bedded rooms. Garden House sleeps six; one double, one twin-bedded, one bunk-bedded rooms. North Lodge Maisonette sleeps six; three twin-bedded rooms. North Lodge Flat; one double bed sittingroom, one single bedroom. Nelson Flat; two twin-bedded, one single bedroom. North Flat; one twin-bedded room. All have spring interior mattresses, fully equipped except linen. All-electric with fridge, cooker, immersion heater, fires. Regret, no pets. Brochure on request with SAE, please.

FAKENHAM. Mrs Ann Green, Old Coach House, Thursford, Fakenham NR21 0BD (Thursford [032-877] 273). Working farm. 16th century oak-timbered barn converted in 1985 to first and second floor accommodation, completely self-contained, situated on south side of courtyard to the farmhouse, on a 70-acre working farm. Comprising: Lower floor — open plan living area with open fire (also electric heating); kitchen (electric cooker etc.); two double bedrooms. Upper floor — bathroom, separate WC and third bedroom. Duvets/pillow cases supplied, please bring own linen/towels. Very tastefully furnished and well equipped for six people. Cot. Small south facing terrace type garden and parking area. Car essential, public transport 200 yards, shops one mile. From £80 to £180 per week (electricity extra by meter reading). Norfolk offers miles of sandy beaches, golf, sailing, fishing, riding and many other interesting pursuits. See also Board Section under Norfolk.

FAKENHAM. Nelson Cottage, Colkirk, Fakenham. Built in traditional Norfolk flint, the cottage is situated in a quiet position on the outskirts of Colkirk village, facing South, overlooking farmland. It has a garden and garage. Nelson Cottage sleeps six. Two twin bedrooms, one double bedroom; bathroom; lounge; diningroom; kitchen and downstairs toilet. Cot provided. Washing machine; TV. Children welcome. Car essential. Dogs allowed. Terms on application. **Mrs C. Joice, Colkirk Hall, Colkirk, Fakenham NR21 7ND (Fakenham [0328] 2261/3086).**

GREAT YARMOUTH. SCRATBY. Six/eight-berth, two storey brick chalets. HEMSBY — four/six-berth single storey brick chalets. All situated on Norfolk coast. Five minutes' walk from long, sandy beaches. Six miles from Great Yarmouth and within easy reach of historic Norfolk and the picturesque Broads. Well appointed and maintained sites, ample parking, restaurant, shops, club house; free heated swimming pool (Scratby). Colour TV. Heaters in all bedrooms. Full sized cooker, fridge, bathroom. Guests must provide own towels, tea towels and table linen. Bed linen supplied free. Cot available. Bus stops within yards of sites. Arrangements for pets. Open March to October inclusive. Terms from £28 weekly, excluding electricity. Also long weekends from £20. SAE, please, for brochure to **F. G. Downes, Castaway, Back Path, Winterton-on-Sea NR29 4BB (Winterton-on-Sea [049-376] 548 and 373).**

NORFOLK – NOT JUST THE BROADS!

There's more to do in Norfolk than messing about in boats – pleasurable though that may be. Other places of interest include the gardens and steam museum at Bressingham, the Broadland Conservation Centre, the flint mines at Grimes Graves, The Norfolk Rural Life Museum, Sandringham – which is often open to the public, and of course Norwich itself.

SELF-CATERING   Norfolk   469

GREAT YARMOUTH near. Mrs Margaret Adnitt, The Cannons, West Caister, Near Great Yarmouth NR30 5SU (Great Yarmouth [0493] 728557). Three self-catering flats in Georgian country house in two acres of lovely grounds. Ample parking. Within two miles of the beaches, Norfolk Broads and Great Yarmouth, yet peaceful rural surroundings. Close to golf course, racecourse and riding stables. Caister Castle Motor Museum half-a-mile away. Each flat accommodates four people in one double bedroom; bathroom, toilet; sittingroom with bed-settee; extra bedroom/en suite bathroom available. All-electric kitchen with fridge, cooker, cupboards, cutlery, etc. Linen supplied. Shops two miles. Sorry, no pets. A car is essential. Available March to October. Weekly terms from £70. Electricity meters. SAE, please.

HEMSBY. Laburnum, Hall Road, Hemsby, Near Great Yarmouth. A south-facing brick built bungalow in private grounds. Ideal for a quiet and peaceful holiday. Large attractive garden. Near sea and Broads. Two bedrooms, one double and two single beds. Cot available. Pleasant lounge with French doors opening on to lawn. Kitchen/diner, bathroom, fitted carpets throughout. Garage. Colour TV. Oil fired central heating. Open all year round. Pets allowed. Fishing, swimming, riding, golf can be enjoyed locally. SAE for terms to **Mrs W. E. Cooper, The Spinney, Hall Road, Hemsby, Near Great Yarmouth NR29 4LF (Great Yarmouth [0493] 730559).**

HOLT. Mrs M. A. Middleton, Home Farm, Holt Road, Weybourne, Holt NR25 7ST (Weybourne [026-370] 334). Working farm. Three self-catering cottages in enclosed courtyard. Recently converted from flint barns, they overlook the farmyard and accommodate four-six each, with cot on request. Bathrooms, toilets; lounge-diningrooms; well equipped kitchens with electricity on slot meter. One of the cottages is suitable for disabled guests. Sorry, no pets. Car essential — parking. Open from March to November, also Christmas period. New Games Room and children's play area. Weybourne has unique steam-train link with Sheringham (three miles away), also riding school and shops in village. Safe beaches nearby. Heated outdoor swimming pool on farm. Farmhouse accommodation also available. SAE, please, for terms.

CARPENTERS COTTAGES

Carpenters Close is a quiet private L-shaped terrace of the early eighteenth century, built in traditional flint and pantiles. Situated on the edge of Holt, a pleasant market town in a conservation area near the coast, they are ideal for exploring and enjoying the varied attractions of north Norfolk.

The cottages have been sympathetically converted, furnished and equipped to provide the comforts of a modern home.

All the rooms are bright and cheerful with fitted carpets and have – our guests tell us – a very homely atmosphere. Each sittingroom includes colour television, fireside chairs, a sofa (that can easily be converted into a comfortable double bed) and Magicoal fire.

Most cottages have twin-bedded rooms. Blankets, pillows and quilt are provided, with bed linen and towels available on request, in which case the beds will be made up for your arrival. With central heating, the cottages are welcoming the whole year round, and special rates apply for groups and for shorter stays out of season.

Children and pets are welcome. There is parking within our own private courtyard. And cleanliness, comfort and good repair are assured by our personal supervision.

JEREMY SIDDALL, Carpenters Close, Norwich Road, Holt, Norfolk [0572] 56515.

HOLT near. Mill Road, The Green, Briston, Near Holt. A pair of attractive, traditional flint cottages with gardens and parking, in a village four miles from Holt, eight miles from Blakeney. Carefully maintained, cleaned between lets, centrally situated in lovely country. Sandy beaches, nature reserves, stately homes and many holiday attractions. Sailing, fishing, riding, bird watching, walking all within easy reach. Accommodating six/eight. Modernised and well equipped. Shops in village. Pets permitted. AA and National Tourist Board approved. Available all year, weekly or long weekends. Terms and details apply **R. Webb, 33 Blackmores Grove, Teddington, Middlesex TW11 9AE (01-977-4197).**

KING'S LYNN. The Manager, The Ken Hill Estate, Ken Hill, Snettisham, King's Lynn PE31 7PG (Heacham [0485] 70001). Two modernised detached cottages on this estate are offered for holidays. One sleeps six in two double bedrooms, cot; bathroom with inside toilet; sittingroom with studio couch; diningroom; tiled kitchen with electric cooker, fridge, immersion heater; TV. Fully equipped except linen. This cottage is 150 yards from shops. The other, slightly larger, has three double bedrooms and is a mile from shops. Both are a mile-and-a-half from beach, convenient for Norfolk Coast (sailing, riding, golf, bird watching). The larger cottage also has cot and TV. Cars advisable, parking. Nearby King's Lynn, Norwich, Ely and Cambridge. Interesting places in the vicinity include Sandringham House, Holkham Hall, wildlife parks and museums. Pets allowed. Fuller information on request.

KING'S LYNN. Mrs Angela Ringer, The Grange, West Rudham, King's Lynn PE31 8SY (East Rudham [048 522] 229). Working farm. We have a choice of four well equipped cottages, sleeping eight, six, five and four people. The larger cottages are detached in large gardens. All have washing machines, televisions, fridges etc. A car is essential as the village is approximately one and a half miles away. Ideally situated for a quiet country holiday, but within easy reach of Sandringham, King's Lynn, Fakenham and Brancaster. All but the smallest cottage suitable for children. Regret, no pets. TELEPHONE ENQUIRIES PREFERRED.

KING'S LYNN. Hall Farm, Little Massingham, King's Lynn. The farmhouse is situated in pretty farmland setting and there are farming activities all around. Within easy reach of beautiful Sandringham, also north Norfolk coast and market towns of Swaffham and Fakenham. Rooms are spacious, with ample room for eight. Two double, one single, one family room plus cot. Lavatories upstairs and downstairs. Livingroom, television room (colour), playroom with table tennis table. Sunny kitchen with electric cooker, fridge, washing machine, telephone. Children welcome. No linen supplied. Carpeted throughout. Car essential. One mile from shops and public transport. £80 weekly. **Mrs E. Ward, Hall Farm, Gayton, King's Lynn PE32 1PJ (Gayton [055-386] 213).**

MELTON CONSTABLE near. "Greenfields", Gunthorpe, Near Melton Constable. "Greenfields" is a bungalow in a peaceful, rural village, with unspoilt views of green fields and woodland, six and a half miles from Blakeney. The area has many interesting places worth visiting, the city of Norwich (25 miles), National Trust properties, famous Fair Organ Museum, steam trains, nature reserves, pleasant countryside and sandy beaches. Accommodation for five/seven persons comprises two double, one single bedrooms, plus extra bed and cot if required. Lounge with TV; diningroom; kitchen fully equipped with electric cooker and fridge/freezer. Bathroom with shaver point and toilet. Everything supplied except linen. Available throughout the year. Reduced rates off season. For further information please contact **Mrs H. J. Craske, 3A Curtis Lane, Sheringham NR26 8DE (Sheringham [0263] 823586).**

MUNDESLEY-ON-SEA. Seaward Crest, Mundesley-on-Sea. Mundesley-on-Sea is an attractive seaside village situated centrally on the Norfolk coast, within 10 miles of the Norfolk Broads, seven miles from Cromer and 20 miles from Norwich. The clean sandy beaches stretch for miles with safe bathing and natural paddling pools. This attractive brick-built chalet, semi-detached, is in delightful setting with lawns, flower beds, trees and ample parking. Beach 500 yards away and shops 200 yards. There is an excellent golf course close to the site and bowls and riding within easy reach. Large lounge/diningroom, tastefully furnished including double bed-settee and TV. Kitchenette with electric cooker, fridge, sink unit, etc. One double, one twin-bedded rooms. Cot. Bathroom and toilet. Lighting, hot water, heating and cooking by electricity (50p slot meter). Fully equipped except for linen. Weekly terms from £35. Details, SAE, please, **Mrs J. Doar, 41 Stonechurch View, Annesley, Nottinghamshire NG15 0AZ (Mansfield [0623] 757725).**

The information in the entries in this guide is presented by the publishers in good faith and after the signed acceptance by advertisers that they will uphold the high standards associated with FARM HOLIDAY GUIDES LIMITED. The publishers do not accept responsibility for any inaccuracies or omissions or any results thereof.
Before making final holiday arrangements readers should confirm the prices and facilities directly with advertisers.

Norfolk Village Cottages

Cottage farm, Lower Tasburgh, Norwich. A 16th century, pink thatched farmhouse in a quiet village eight miles south of Norwich. In its own pretty gardens, the cottage is close to an ancient watermill and trout stream. There are three bedrooms to sleep six, dressing room bathroom, diningroom, sittingroom and kitchen. Double garage.

Wymondham Lodge, Ketteringham, Norwich. A delightful thatched lodge cottage set in parkland and backed by an avenue of stately oaks. The cottage stands in lawned gardens of one quarter-acre, a mere 15 minutes from the centre of Norwich. There are two beamed bedrooms to sleep four, sittingroom, diningroom, bathroom and kitchen. Garage.

Each is superbly equipped (well above Tourist Board standards), with colour television, all linen for the beds (ready made for guest's arrival) and night store heating for a warm welcome all year round. Guide books and brochures, flower arrangements and a tea tray set to welcome you, assure you of our personal supervision and attention. Sorry no pets.

SAE please for illustrated brochure and terms to Mrs B. C. McFadyen, Swardeston Vicarage, Norwich. Telephone: Mulbarton [0508] 70550.

SNETTISHAM. Woodside Cottage, Park Lane, Snettisham. Sandingham four miles. Ideal touring centre for North Norfolk coast — renowned for its wildlife sanctuaries — safe beaches for children. Woodside Cottage is in a quiet location 200 yards from Village Centre — completely modernised — furnished to a high standard — sleeps four/five. One double and one twin-bedded room, each with hand basin and shaver points. Bathroom incorporating shower unit. Lounge/diner with Put-u-Up, TV. New kitchen containing electric cooker, fridge, washing machine. Towels and linen not supplied (except to overseas visitors). Cot available. Central heating out of season. Small garden. Parking space. Pets by arrangement. Full particulars — **A. F. Crisp, 18 Manor Road, Dersingham, King's Lynn PE31 6LD (0485) 40221.**

STALHAM. 5 Broadside Chalet Park, Stalham. The chalet faces on to a pleasant lawn where children can play in complete safety. It is furnished to a high standard, carpeted throughout. Two double bedrooms; bathroom, toilet; lounge; kitchenette; electric cooker, fridge, TV, iron etc. Sleeps four-six; studio couch in lounge. Linen supplied. This is an attractive site in the small Broadland town of Stalham. Heated swimming pool, paddling pool and playpark for children. Useful general store on site; resident warden. Three miles from sandy beaches of Sea Palling; half-hour's drive to Norwich, Yarmouth. From £48 weekly. SAE, please, to **Leisure Time, 8 The Ridgeway, Southgate, London N14 6NU (01-886 4440).**

PLEASE SEND A STAMPED ADDRESSED ENVELOPE WITH ENQUIRIES

472   Norfolk   SELF-CATERING

STALHAM. Broadside Chalet Park, 63 and 64 Broadside Park, Stalham. This chalet accommodation is available from April 1st to October 31st and for weekends for the rest of the year. It is three miles to the sea; 15 miles from Norwich. Ample parking on site. Each unit accommodates six in two double rooms and a double bed settee; sittingroom; bathroom, toilet; kitchen area with electric cooker, fridge, toaster, electric kettle and all utensils for six persons. Fully equipped except linen. Children are welcome and there is a cot. Pets are allowed under control. Electric heating throughout (50p meter). Fishing on Broads within quarter mile; bathing on site; Historic Buildings; working windmill. Children's playground with pool on site. Day boats for hire within quarter mile. River trips from Wroxham. From £35. **Mrs H. B. Davey, Harbord House, Brumstead Road, Stalham NR12 9DF (Stalham [0692] 80778).**

* **THURNE. Hedera House and Plantation Bungalows, Thurne.** Hedera House is a comfortably furnished Georgian style house able to sleep up to 12 people, comprising spacious lounge and dining area with colour TV, kitchen with split level hob and double oven, breakfast bar, five double (with handbasin) and two single bedrooms, bathroom, shower and two WC's. Heating available for all seasons. Plantation Bungalows is a select group of ten individual holiday homes, roomy and comfortably furnished and carpeted. Colour TV, fully fitted bathroom and kitchen, electric radiator heating in lounge and bedrooms. Cavity wall insulation. Electric meter. Norfolk is rich in places of historic interest, beautiful beaches, Broads, villages and countryside, all within easy motoring distance of Thurne. Fishing, boating, nearby golf course, horse riding. Free mooring and launching facilities for small craft. See also Full Colour Advertisement in this Guide. SAE to **Miss Carol Delf, Thurne Cottage, The Staithe, Thurne NR29 3BU (0692-670242 or 0493-844568).**

WALCOTT-ON-SEA. Eryl-Y-Don, Helena Road, Walcott-on-Sea, Norwich. TWO similar chalet-type bungalows side by side, some 40 paces from the sea-front. Set in their own lawned gardens they are completely private and reached by a private road. Fully furnished, each sleeps FOUR persons. Walcott is a quiet village with a clean, sandy beach, about half-a-mile long. WALCOTT, one mile south of "Bacton in AA books". Cromer is about 10 miles north of Walcott, Great Yarmouth about 18 miles south. The Norfolk Broads and other places of historic interest are all within easy access from Walcott. Enquiries by telephone **(Walcott [0692] 650798)** OR by letter with SAE to **F. A. Webster, Min-Y-Don, St. Helen's Road, Walcott-on-Sea, Norwich NR12 0LU.**

WINTERTON-ON-SEA. Timbers, The Lane, Winterton-on-Sea. Comfortable, well-furnished ground floor flat in timber cottage situated in quiet sea-side village just eight miles north of Great Yarmouth. Broad sandy beach and sand dunes (nature reserve) for pleasant walks. Three miles from Norfolk Broads (boating and fishing). Flat carpeted throughout and is fully equipped for self-catering family holiday. Ideal for children, and pets welcome. One double, one twin-bedded and one small single bedroom. Sleeps five, plus cot. Bed linen provided and maid service every other day for general cleaning. Attractive beamed sittingroom with colour TV. Secluded garden. Car parking. Available June to September. Terms £70 to £175 per week. For full details and photographs write — **Mr M. J. Isherwood, 79 Oakleigh Avenue, London N20 9JG** or telephone **01-445-2192.**

WYMONDHAM. Boundary Farm, Wramplingham, Wymondham. Comfortable, modernised, period farmhouse on a family country estate looking South over cultivated fields and scattered woodlands, 200 yards from the nearest road. Ideal as a central point for touring and exploring East Anglia. Good fly and coarse fishing on the estate. Sleeps six, plus cot. Bed linen provided. Bathroom, toilet. Lounge with colour TV. Diningroom. High chair. Kitchen with electric cooker, fridge, kettle and iron. Immersion heater. Payphone. Full oil-fired central heating. Half an acre of grass garden. Everything supplied except towels and table linen. Car essential, parking. Well trained pets by arrangement when booking. Terms include electricity, kerosene and VAT. For further details contact: **D. V. Gregory, Lombe Estate Office, Hall Farm, Great Melton, Norwich NR9 3BQ (Norwich [0603] 811312).**

Please note that entries marked with an asterisk also have a colour display advert in the colour section in this guide

---

Terms quoted in this publication may be subject to increase if rises in costs necessitate

NORTHUMBERLAND

ALNMOUTH. Mrs Joan Hill, Rosedale Lodge, Foxton Road, Alnmouth NE66 3NQ (Alnwick [0665] 830561). Situated in the grounds of a family house, in the beautiful coastal village of Alnmouth, with its picturesque views and white, sandy beaches. Only five miles from the A1, it is close to Warkworth, Alnmouth, Berwick and Bamburgh castles. The cottage has one double and one twin-bedded room; a large sitting/diningroom includes double bed-settee and TV. Kitchen with cooker and fridge. Bathroom. Electricity payable at metered rate. Linen not supplied. Parking. Pets welcome. A very large garden behind the cottage leads to a path down to the beach 500 yards away. Available all year. Telephone or SAE for further details.

ALNMOUTH. S. and G. Inkster, Marine House Private Hotel, 1 Marine Road, Alnmouth NE66 2RW (Alnwick [0665] 830349). This cottage, expertly converted from a coach house and hay loft, stands next to the main building. It faces a nine-hole golf links and sea, ensuring uninterrupted panoramic views. Alnmouth is an excellent centre for exploring the magnificent Northumbrian coastline with its castles, wildlife sanctuaries and white sandy beaches. The Cheviot Hills and Roman Wall are within easy reach by car. The cottage has one double, one twin-bedded and small room with three ft. bunk beds; (Z-bed or cot available). Shower room, toilet and vanitory basin; Tudor style lounge/diningroom with colour TV; kitchen with electric cooker, fridge, iron. No linen supplied. Metered 50p electricity. Parking. Pets permitted. Shops 200 yards; regular bus service. Guests may use hotel facilities. Evening dinner and packed lunches can be ordered. Weekly terms from £90. Winter lets available.

ALNWICK. Birling Vale, Warkworth, Alnwick. Birling Vale is an attractive stone-built, detached house standing in a very pleasant, secluded garden, approximately one-third mile from picturesque village of Warkworth which is beside the River Coquet and dominated by an ancient Norman Castle. Birling Vale is only half-a-mile from lovely sandy beaches; 15 minutes from trout and salmon rivers, and within a comfortable drive to places of interest, including Hadrian's Wall, Holy Island and Scottish Borders. The house which is tastefully furnished and fully equipped including colour TV, has two bedrooms with double beds and third bedroom with single divans. Oil for full central heating is provided free of charge. Well trained dogs welcome. Weekly terms from £50 off season; £140 mid-season; £180 high season. SAE to **Mrs Janet Brewis, Woodhouse Farm, Shilbottle, Near Alnwick NE66 2HR (Shilbottle [066-575] 222).**

ALNWICK. Mrs Holly Petrie, Summerhill Court, Alnwick NE66 2QF (Alnwick [0665] 602807). Summerhill Court is a small country house with three cottages and lodge within the grounds. Pleasant gardens. Old fashioned and species roses, stables adjacent. Accommodation for two/six persons, traditionally furnished, fully self-contained and equipped including colour TV. Ideally situated approximately one-and-a-half miles from centre of Alnwick, three miles from coast and 35 miles from Scottish borders. Terms £45/£120 per week.

When you have read one you **haven't** *read them all —
we have* **eleven** *other publications*

ALNWICK. Village Farm, Shilbottle, Alnwick. Working farm. Top quality accommodation in 17th century farmhouse, three Scandinavian chalets and two luxury farm cottages, all sleeping four/six. The Farm is on a quiet road beside a lovely old church and near the A1. Unspoilt sandy beaches are within three miles. An ideal centre from which to explore Northumberland with its many Castles, historic buildings and beautiful countryside. Fishing in famous rivers and our own stocked trout pond. Pony riding and fresh eggs free to all guests. Pets welcome. Brochure from **Mrs J. C. M. Stoker, Shilbottle Town Foot Farm, Alnwick NE66 2HG (Shilbottle [066-575] 245).**

BELFORD. Mr John McNish, Outchester Farm, Belford NE70 7EA (Belford [06683] 336). Outchester Farm and Ross Farm are both in superb countryside between Bamburgh and Holy Island, one mile from Budle Bay which is part of the Lindisfarne Nature Reserve, and near magnificent beaches. The attractive stone-built farmhouse has been converted into two self-contained apartments and the various farm cottages recently modernised. They are comfortably furnished, have good beds and are well equipped including TV. Children welcome and cot available. Nightstore heaters. Ample car parking space. Linen and towels not supplied. Electricity by 50p meter. Sorry, no pets. Please write or phone for brochure (**Mr John McNish**).

BERWICK-UPON-TWEED. Mrs R. A. Cadzow, Inland Pasture Farm, Scremerston, Berwick-upon-Tweed TD15 2RJ (Berwick-upon-Tweed [0289] 306072). Working farm. No. 5 Inland Pasture Cottages, faces south with beautiful views over beach towards Holy Island and Farne Islands. Situated in a quiet and peaceful area away from traffic and about quarter-mile from all farm buildings. The cottage is Tourist Board approved and sleeps six. Three double bedrooms; bathroom, kitchen with electric cooker and kettle etc. Cot available on request. One dog only allowed. Electric heating and lighting. Available April to October. Car advisable — parking. Convenient for golfing, fishing (permits required), climbing, bathing, pony trekking/riding. Many interesting houses and historical places to visit. Terms from £50 to £100 weekly.

BERWICK-UPON-TWEED. Felkington Farm Cottages, Berwick-upon-Tweed. Working farm. These stone-built cottages for self-catering holidays are ideal for trips to the coast and countryside. Situated half way between Edinburgh and Newcastle, they are close to the Scottish borders, the Farne and Holy Islands and the Cheviot Hills. Both sleep six people (plus baby), and are fully equipped with colour TV, washing machine, cot, open fire (wood provided) and heaters in all rooms. There are table tennis and pool tables and a children's playground. Children and pets are most welcome. For terms and brochure please contact **Mrs M. Martin, Felkington Farm, Berwick-upon-Tweed TD15 2NR (0289) 87220.**

BERWICK-UPON-TWEED. Mrs Sheila Marshall, The Sheiling, Allerdean Greens Farm, Berwick-upon-Tweed TD15 2TB (Berwick-upon-Tweed [0289] 87257). This semi-detached cottage, four miles south of the historic town of Berwick-upon-Tweed and near the coast, is available for self-catering holidays from April to October. With the Northumbrian National Park, the Cheviot Hills and Holy Island within easy reach, this is an ideal centre for tourists. The comfortable accommodation is for five people in two double, one single bedrooms, cot, bathroom, toilet; sitting/diningroom; well equipped electric kitchen. Everything except linen supplied. Shops four miles, sea three miles. Car essential, parking. Pets welcome if kept under control. Weekly terms from £50 to £60. Electricity metered. SAE, please.

BERWICK-UPON-TWEED. Numbers 7 and 8, Grindon Farm, Berwick-upon-Tweed. Working farm. These are stone-built cottages on one level on a large arable farm three miles from the village of Norham and midway between Berwick-upon-Tweed and Coldstream. Number 7 accommodates six people comfortably and number eight, four people. Situated near the Northumberland Coast and Scottish Borders. There are nine-hole and 18-hole golf courses within an eight mile radius. Permits for fishing on the River Tweed can be purchased in Norham. Car essential. SAE, please, to **Mrs A. T. Barr, Grindon, Berwick-upon-Tweed TD15 2NN (Berwick-upon-Tweed [0289] 82212).**

CORNHILL-ON-TWEED. Mr and Mrs W. Potts, Shidlaw, Cornhill-on-Tweed TD12 4RP (Birgham [089-083] 225). Situated on a large, modern, Tweed-side farm, in a beautiful region, the comfortably furnished cottage has a modern kitchen with electric cooker, fridge, water heater, etc. Livingroom/diningroom with open fire, colour TV. Three bedrooms sleeping six; bathroom and toilet. Cot on request. Accommodation suitable for disabled guests. Car essential — parking. Shops six miles; sea 16 miles. Pets allowed. Open May to October. Fishing on the Tweed; golf and racing at Kelso. Tourists can journey through historic, unspoilt Border countryside with abbeys and castles galore. Riding school nearby. SAE for brochure. Terms from £50 weekly.

Terms quoted in this publication may be subject to increase if rises in costs necessitate

SELF-CATERING Northumberland

HALTWHISTLE. Smithy Cottage & Cobblestone Cottage, Shield Hill, Haltwhistle. Smithy Cottage and Cobblestone Cottage, stone-built cottages on easily accessible working farm on edge of Northumberland National Park, one mile from Hadrian's Wall, three quarters of a mile from the A69. Sleeping four/six and six/eight respectively, both have modern kitchens, log stoves with central heating and are comfortable, clean and tastefully furnished to ETB Category ***, AA listed. Quiet, relaxing surroundings in superb area for walking, bird watching, archaeology and central for touring. Within 35 miles there is the Lake District, Kielder Water, Gretna Green and Southern Scotland. Hexham and Carlisle much nearer and on the doorstep, Hadrian's Wall, forts, sites, Nature Trails, reserves and forest, rivers and moorland. One mile Haltwhistle town, shops, restaurants, pubs, heated open air swimming pool. Bed and Breakfast also available. SAE, please, for brochure. **Mrs W. Laidlow, White Craig Farm, Shield Hill, Haltwhistle NE49 9NW (Haltwhistle [0498] 20565).**

HAYDON BRIDGE (Hexham). Mrs V. R. A. Drydon, West Deanraw, Langley-on-Tyne, Haydon Bridge, Hexham NE47 5LY (Haydon Bridge [043-484] 228). Detached bungalow situated on a farm in rural Northumberland, approximately three miles from the village of Haydon Bridge, and 10 miles from the market town of Hexham. The property enjoys delightful views of the Tyne Valley, and is an ideal touring base for Hadrian's Wall, Kielder Reservoir, Border country, the magnificent Northumbrian coastline, Cumbria and the Lake District. Accommodation comprises one double and one twin bedrooms (extra children's beds available); livingroom with sofa bed; colour TV; diningroom. Fully fitted kitchen, all-electric, includes fridge, washing machine, immersion heater, plus open fireback boiler if required. Terms and further details on request.

LONGFRAMLINGTON. Rimside Cottage, Longframlington. Rimside is a stone-built terraced country cottage in the picturesque village of Longframlington, south of the Cheviots in the beautiful Coquetdale Valley, and with views of rolling farmland and countryside. Bordering the Northumberland National Park and within easy reach of Holy Island, Roman Wall and Castles of Bamburgh, Alnwick, Callaly and Warkworth. Fishing Coble trips to Farne Islands (seals and sea birds). Salmon and trout fishing on River Coquet. Two large bedrooms (sleep five), extra bed if required; lounge; TV; kitchen (electric cooker, fridge); bathroom, toilet; immersion heater. Cot and high chair available. Electric fires, fully equipped except linen. Alnwick and Morpeth, 10 miles. Sandy beaches only 20 minutes' drive. Excellent spot for health-giving holiday. Open all year. Pets welcome. Weekly terms from £50. SAE, please, to **Mrs Bell, 3 Sweetbriar Close, Morpeth NE61 3RP (Morpeth [0670] 512192).**

MORPETH. Mrs Jean Robson, 1 Berkley Terrace, Whalton, Morpeth NE61 3XB (Whalton [067075] 209). Berkley Cottage stands in a pretty country village with easy access to the coast, the Roman Wall, several country houses including Wallington Hall, Cragside and Belsay Hall. Open April to November, there is accommodation for five in two double bedrooms and one single room. Comfortable sittingroom, well equipped kitchen, bathroom and toilet. Linen not provided. Car essential, parking. Children welcome. The ideal choice for visitors who want the opportunity to tour the local area, yet who need the guarantee of clean, comfortable accommodation in pleasant surroundings. Weekly terms from £70. Metered electricity. Details on request.

MORPETH. Mrs Isabel Murray, Cartington House, Thropton, Morpeth NE65 7JW (Rothbury [0669] 20229). Working farm. One good well-furnished cottage on 1,300-acre farm with crops, cattle and sheep, stands 640 feet above sea level with wonderful views of the Coquet Valley and Cheviot Hills. Sleeps six people, having two bedrooms, livingroom and kitchen; Calor gas cooker, electric kettle, fridge and TV. Tenants need only provide linen. Two miles from shops so car is essential, good road passes farm. Easy distances to lovely beaches and Alnmouth, Bamburgh and Lindisfarne. Roman Wall, plenty of forest walks and hill climbing for energetic. Also stately homes and castles to visit. Many superior self-catering house in Spittal, Berwick-on-Tweed (150 yards from sea) and ideal for touring all the above places. Terms on application with SAE, please.

NEWCASTLE-UPON-TYNE (Mid-Northumberland). Nos. 1 and 2 Shop Cottages, Kirkharle, Kirkwhelpington, Newcastle-upon-Tyne. The little hamlet of Kirkharle, birthplace of the famous landscape designer Capability Brown, is situated amidst some of the most beautiful and spectacular scenery in the north of England. Kirkharle is approached on the A696, 18 miles north-west of Newcastle and 82 miles from Edinburgh. The two cottages are situated on the edge of a wood, along a small private track. Built of local stone, with slate roofs, they are newly modernised to a high standard, and Tourist Board approved. Sleep four or six; cot by arrangement. Bathroom, toilet; sittingroom; kitchen with electric cooker. Electric heating. No linen supplied. Pets allowed. Children welcome. Car essential — parking. Shops five miles. Ideal touring situation. Open January to December. Terms from £35 to £100 weekly. Apply to **Mrs K. J. Anderson, Little Harle Tower, Kirkwhelpington, Newcastle-upon-Tyne NE19 2PD (Otterburn [0830] 40229).**

---

*If you've found FARM HOLIDAY GUIDE
of service please tell your friends*

SEAHOUSES. The Dunes, St. Aidans, Seahouses. Spacious one, two and three bedroomed holiday flats situated in the west wing of a large house, formerly hotel, with beautiful views over the surrounding coastline and countryside. 100 yards from the beach, overlooking the sea and white sands, with views of the Farne Islands and Bamburgh Castle, three miles away. This location suits everyone, situated in a quiet, residential area, but only 400 yards from main shops, amusements and harbour. Each flat is comfortably furnished, including electric cooker, fridge and TV. Linen not supplied. Ample parking. Children and pets welcome. SAE, please, for details, or telephone. **Mrs J. Hill, Rosedale Lodge, Alnmouth NE66 3NQ (Alnwick [0665] 830561).**

WOOLER. 25 Peth Head, Wooler. The house is situated in the town of Wooler at the foothills of the Cheviots with many places of historical interest close by. Half hour's drive to many fine beaches and walks and beautiful scenery nearby. Accommodation for four people, one large livingroom, kitchen (electric cooker, fridge, sink unit, cupboards, table and chairs). No linen supplied. Bathroom and toilet. One large bedroom with double bed and two folding single beds and cot. Pets by arrangement. Car essential. Lock-up garage included. Open all year. Terms from £30 to £60 plus VAT (fuel not included). Further details from **Mrs V. Brown, "Flowermead," 33 Glendale Road, Wooler NE71 6DL (Wooler [0668] 81833).**

NOTTINGHAMSHIRE

FARMHOUSE ACCOMMODATION

Sherwood Forest FARM & COUNTRY HOLIDAYS

Self Catering Accommodation

THE WILLOWS (Mrs Lamin Tel. No. [0602] 268330) 'The Willows' A self contained three bedroom unit on 19th century sheep and arable farm. Close to Nottingham, Sherwood Forest and many sporting facilities. Sleeps 4/6. Price from £60. **Top House Farm, Arnold, Nottingham NG5 8PH.**

EASTWOOD FARM (Mrs S. M. Santos Tel. No. [0602] 663018) Self catering cottage and flat, on working farm, ½ mile from village. Warm and well equipped. Home produce available. Open all year. From £45. SAE for brochure please. **Eastwood Farm, Hagg Lane, Epperstone, Nottingham NG14 6AX.**

CLIPSTONE PARK ESTATE (Mrs Shaw-Browne Tel. No. [0623] 823132) Clipstone Park, a farming manor since 1068, family farm of 1000 acres with woodlands, caravan park and riding centre, fishing, boating lake, wooded walks. 2 holiday caravans with double room from £60 per week. April to September. **Clipstone Park Estate, Old Clipstone, Mansfield NG21 9BS.**

NORWOOD COTTAGE (Mrs White Tel. No. [0246] 850271) Stone built cottage near Hardwick Hall. Quiet situation on family farm of 320 acres. Good touring centre from £55–£85 per week. **Hardwick Park Farm, Teversal, Sutton-in-Mansfield, Notts.**

For group brochure giving full details, send 9" × 4" s.a.e. to **Mrs Shaw-Browne, Sherwood Forest Caravan Park, Clipstone Park Estate, Old Clipstone, Mansfield, Notts NG21 9BS**

NOTTINGHAMSHIRE – ROBIN HOOD COUNTRY!
Sherwood Forest is now a country park and is one of Nottinghamshire's leading attractions. This county is rich in terms of its parks. There are others at Burntstump, Clumber, Holme Pierrepont and Rufford. Nottingham itself is a surprisingly attractive city.

SELF-CATERING Nottinghamshire / Oxfordshire / Shropshire 477

NOTTINGHAM. Mrs S. M. Santos, Eastwood Farm, Hagg Lane, Epperstone, Nottingham NG14 6AX (Nottingham [0602] 663018). Working farm. Eastwood Farm (170 acres producing beef and cereals) is situated on a private road, half-a-mile from the village, surrounded by large garden and undulating, lightly-wooded farmland. The Cottage and the Mews Flat, sleeping four/five respectively, form part of the 150-year-old range of brick and pantiled buildings. Each unit has two bedrooms, bed-settee and cot; bathroom with WC; well equipped electric kitchen and sitting/diningroom with TV. For your day's outing: Sherwood Forest, the Dukeries, Derbyshire Peak District or Lincolnshire Bulb Fields; local sports centre, golf and fishing; nine miles from Nottingham with two theatres and good shopping. Eggs and home-made bread available. Pets welcome. AA listed. ETB Registered. £52 to £80 weekly including central heating. Electricity extra. Linen hire. SAE for brochure, please.

OXFORDSHIRE

SHIPTON-UNDER-WYCHWOOD. Mr and Mrs P. Fletcher, Lane House Farm, Shipton-under-Wychwood OX7 6BD (Shipton-under-Wychwood [0993] 830348). Delightful bungalow and two charming cottages on the eastern edge of the Cotswolds — one of England's most attractive holiday areas. Excellent touring centre, within easy reach beautiful country villages, Oxford, Cheltenham, Cirencester, Burford, Stratford-on-Avon and innumerable other attractions. The three properties are carpeted throughout, central heating, bathrooms, sittingrooms, fully equipped kitchens with fitted units, electric cookers, micro-wave ovens, automatic washing machines; each unit has colour TV. Linen included, towels extra. THE BUNGALOW is suitable for Wheel Chairs. Children welcome, cot, high chair. No objection to dogs. Car essential — parking. Shopping facilities within few minutes' walk, children's play park, post office, pubs, churches, etc. Single bank fishing on River Evenlode (quarter-mile away). Available mid-March to mid-January. Brochure, terms on request.

SHROPSHIRE

BISHOP'S CASTLE. Walcott Hall, Lydbury North, Bishop's Castle. Spacious flats at Stately Home. Secluded location in own grounds; splendid scenery and ideal area for peaceful holiday for young and old. All flats fully-furnished and recently decorated and sleep four/nine. Larger parties by arrangement. Village shop half-a-mile; local market towns, castles, villages and hill country of the Border Counties provide opportunities for exploration and walking. Coarse fishing available in pools and Lake. **Mrs M. Smith, Danby Registrars Ltd., 41 Cheval Place, London SW7 1EW (01-581-2782).**

BRIDGNORTH. Mrs S. E. Powell, Harpswood Country Cottages, Bridgnorth WV16 6TZ (074-635-231). These semi-detached Victorian cottages in large lawns and peaceful surroundings provide the sort of holiday that everyone will enjoy. Clee Hill or Long Mynd for walks, trout fishing by arrangement with owner, or coarse fishing on River Severn. Two miles from Bridgnorth on B4364 Bridgnorth/Ludlow road. The small market town has good shopping facilities, Sports and Leisure Centre, tennis, golf, indoor heated pool, cinema, theatre, museums and Severn Valley Railway, also other places of historical interest. Shrewsbury, Ironbridge, Ludlow within 20 miles. Each cottage accommodates six adults. One double and two twin bedded rooms; bathroom and toilet downstairs; lounge; kitchen. Electric cooker/heating. Ample car space. Children and pets welcome. Terms from £65 to £90 weekly.

BUCKNELL. Church Cottage, Bucknell. This is a tastefully modernised Olde Worlde cottage in small village set in delightful Teme Valley with easy access to picturesque mid-Wales. Offa's Dyke, Church Stretton Hills, Wenlock Edge and historic towns of Ludlow, Shrewsbury and Hereford. The cottage sleeps six: one double and two twin bedded rooms, cot by request. Modern kitchen; lounge; diningroom; TV; electric fires. Parking. Small enclosed lawn. Village has butcher, General Store, Post Office, country pub. On rail and bus routes. Open all year round. SAE, please, for terms. Also Farmhouse Bed and Breakfast. Evening Meal by arrangement. **Mrs Christine Price, The Hall, Bucknell SY7 0AA (Bucknell [054-74] 249).**

Shropshire SELF-CATERING

CHURCH STRETTON. Mrs H. C. Bovill, Batchcott Hall, Church Stretton SY6 6NP (Leebotwood [069-45] 234). Working farm. Attached farm holiday cottage with beautiful views situated on the side of the Long Mynd Hill National Trust area, 900 feet above sea level. To the west of the A49, it is 10 miles from Shrewsbury and five from Church Stretton. Three bedrooms (sleeps six), cot; bathroom with toilet; airing cupboard; sittingroom with Baxi fire (logs provided); black and white TV; well-equipped kitchen/diner. Old farmhouse larder with rail for drying clothes. Sheets can be provided (extra laundry charge). Pets permitted. Car essential — parking. Use of en-tout-cas tennis court. Fishing in two acre trout pool. Eggs supplied. Terms from £65 weekly. SAE, please.

CLEOBURY MORTIMER. Mr C. E. Pearce, Cleeton Court Farm, Cleeton St. Mary, Cleobury Mortimer, Worcestershire DY14 0QZ (Stoke St Milborough [058-475] 354). Working farm. Cleeton Court Farm dates back to the 15th century and is a working mixed farm of approximately 120 acres, situated amidst beautiful countryside on the slopes of the Clee Hills in south Shropshire. Unlimited walking and many places of interest within easy reach including Severn Valley Steam Railway, West Midland Safari Park, historic and picturesque Ludlow with its famous castle and fine old buildings. Acton Scott Farm Museum nearby. Church Stretton Hills and Welsh Mountains easily reached by car. One modernised, all-electric, self-contained holiday flat, being the original half timbered wing of the farmhouse available with sleeping accommodation for five persons; large lounge/diningroom; colour TV; fully equipped kitchen. Car essential — parking. Children welcome, cot, high chair provided. Sorry, no pets. Weekly terms from £46 to £75. AA and British Tourist Board approved. SAE, please.

CRAVEN ARMS. Mrs P. E. North, The Old Shop, Clunton, Craven Arms SY7 0HP (Little Brampton [058-87] 327). Self-contained, centrally heated, single storey flat in centre of the small village of Clunton on the River Clun, within six miles of the Welsh Border. Superb walking country with relatively quiet roads and much of historic interest. Sandy beaches within 90 minutes' drive. The flat, a wing of owners' home, is entirely on ground floor and suitable for disabled guests. Entrance hall; comfortable lounge with double bed settee, fitted carpets, double glazing and open fire; dining kitchen with pine units, electric cooker, kettle, fridge and constant hot water. Shower room with WC and washbasin. Bedroom with two single beds, plus camp bed if required. Cot available, babysitting by arrangement. Linen not supplied. TV, games and books provided. Garden. Pets welcome. Car essential, parking. Village shops one-and-three-quarter miles. Fishing and riding locally. Terms on request. Ideal for winter breaks.

CRAVEN ARMS. Horse Shoe Cottage, Upper House, Clunbury, Craven Arms. Craven Arms — the Clun Valley — an area covering Ludlow and Offa's Dyke — Horse Shoe Cottage is a small garden cottage in the grounds of (17th century) Upper House, Clunbury, Craven Arms, in a picturesque National Parkland village. Separate drive to cottage — glorious walks — sleeps four. Fully modernised and equipped — night storage heaters — carpeted. One double, one single bedroom (with bunk beds); cot available. Lounge; kitchen (cooker, fridge, water heater). No linen, but can be provided for overseas visitors. In addition, to let a modern newly-built bungalow in the grounds overlooking hills. Both properties suitable disabled persons. Pets welcome. Excellent base for exploring numerous places of interest in this lovely area. Member of English Tourist Board, and personally supervised by Mr and Mrs Williams. Terms and brochure on request — **Mr C. H. Williams, Upper House, Clunbury, Near Craven Arms SY7 0HG (Little Brampton [058-87] 203).**

CRAVEN ARMS near. The Riddings Cottage, Newcastle-on-Clun, Near Craven Arms. Cottage stands in acre of rough ground, facing south, with glorious views down wide valley to Radnor Forest. Within easy reach of historic Montgomery, Ludlow (castles and fine half-timbered houses), Offa's Dyke, Clun Castle and various ancient British hill forts. Fishing, pony trekking in area. All main windows double glazed (keeps cold out in winter). Accommodation for six in three double bedrooms; cot; bathroom, toilet; sittingroom; diningroom/kitchen (fully equipped). Everything supplied except linen. 50p coin-operated slot meter for electric heating and domestic. Wood-burning stove in kitchen/diner. There is one shop at Newcastle-on-Clun three and a half to four miles away and other shops at Clun and Newtown, eight miles away. Car essential, garage. Pets permitted on request. Available April to November and for winter long lets. Terms from £55 to £65 per week. SAE, please, to **Mrs N. J. Monk, The Vicarage, Ashton Keynes, Near Swindon, Wilts SN6 6PP (Cirencester [0285] 861566).**

* **LUDLOW. Deepwood Cottage, Ludlow.** Superior, two-storey modernised and extended cottage, with garage, in excellent condition available all year for self-catering holidays. In a quiet rural position with good walking and an ideal base for touring, the house accommodates seven people. Large lounge with wood-burning stove (logs provided); diningroom and fitted kitchen. Colour TV. Downstairs cloakroom and toilet. One double room with bathroom en-suite, two twin bedrooms, one single room and second bathroom with shower. Fitted carpets throughout. Electric heaters (central heating optional). Coin box phone. Children welcome, cot and high chair available. One pet allowed. Linen an optional extra. Metered electricity. Golf, tennis, riding at Ludlow three and a half miles. Weekly terms from £90 – £180. Available all year. For details contact **Mrs N. C. Powell, Deepwood Farm, Ludlow SY8 2JQ. Telephone (Bromfield [058-477] 208).** See also Colour Display Advertisement in this Guide.

LUDLOW. Miss H. Morris, Coldoak Cottages, Snitton Lane, Knowsbury, Ludlow SY8 3LB (Ludlow [0584] 890491). 200-year-old solid, stone cottage four and a half miles from Ludlow, facing south, set well back in field ensuring privacy yet only 130 yards from road. Surroundings are quiet and beautiful and visitors will enjoy extensive views of Herefordshire and Wales beyond. Cottage sleeps visitors in one double bedroom, one twin bedded and one single bedroom; comfortable sittingroom with beamed ceiling, colour TV, well stocked book shelves; well equipped kitchen. Linen supplied. Children over five years welcome. Pets permitted. Large attractive garden with sitting out area. Post Office and village shop, pub, milk and paper delivery. Car essential, parking. Open all year. Weekly terms from £85. Metered electricity.

Please note that entries marked with an asterisk also have a colour display advert in the colour section in this guide

LUDLOW. Mrs C. R. Meredith, The Avenue, Ashford Carbonnell, Ludlow SY8 4DA (Richards Castle [058-474] 616]. Spacious completely self-contained flat in lovely Georgian House — set in its own quiet grounds on edge of village — three miles from historic Ludlow. With easy access by wide outside staircase, the flat affords excellent views over surrounding farmland to Clee Hills. Within easy reach of Hereford, Shrewsbury, Worcester, Wenlock Edge, Ironbridge, Brecon. Furnished to a high standard of comfort, sleeping six, two double, one twin; bathroom/WC; fully equipped kitchen/diner, electric cooker, fridge; lounge, colour TV; cot/high chair; electric fires; immersion heater by 50p meter; full night storage central heating by separate meter; ample parking and private garden; linen and garage on request. Open all year. Terms on request.

LUDLOW near. The Granary, Tana Leas Farm, Clee St. Margaret. Situated close to village in a designated area of outstanding natural beauty. Accommodation converted from an old first floor stone granary with extensive views of the Welsh Border Hills. Comprises Entry Hall — Living, Dining, Kitchen area — Bathroom — three Bedrooms, one with twin beds and two single rooms. Heating by electric storage heaters and wood-burning stove. Colour TV and Radio — Washing Machine. Linen and Towels supplied. Regret, no pets. Its situation makes it ideally suited for those wanting a quiet and secluded holiday. Extensive choice of walks available. **Mr & Mrs R. C. H. Mercer, Tana Leas Farm, Clee St. Margaret, Craven Arms SY7 9DZ (Stoke St. Milborough [058-475] 272).**

LYDBURY NORTH. Mrs Mary Wall, 6 Lynch Gate, Lydbury North SY7 8AE (Lydbury North [058-88] 267). Old stone cottage, modernised, with unspoilt views. Owner lives next door. One large bedroom with double bed and cot; one bedroom with single bed and one with two single beds. Bathroom, toilet; sittingroom; diningroom; kitchen with electric cooker, fridge, modern sink unit. Electricity on 50p meter. Linen supplied. Pets permitted. Car essential — parking. Shops three miles. Plenty of walks on National Trust Property. Borrow hill with its ancient Roman Fort, Church Stretton for gliding and hang gliding. Historic Ludlow with its castle, and Stokesay Castle with its Elizabethan gateway only a few miles away. The old stagecoach road from London runs by the cottage and less than an hour's ride away by car is the beautiful Wenlock Edge, Bridgnorth and the first ever iron bridge. Terms from £30 to £70. SAE, please.

NEWCASTLE ON CLUN. Mr and Mrs J. K. Goslin, The Riddings Firs, Crossways, Newcastle-on-Clun, Craven Arms (Kerry [068-688] 467). Ideal holiday location on the Welsh Borders, designated as being of outstanding natural beauty, for those seeking complete peace and relaxation — attractive self-catering family accommodation, for four to five people, in self-contained traditional farmhouse annexe with own private entrance. Fully equipped and attractively furnished including colour TV, central heating. Open plan arrangement comprises one double, two bunk beds and bed settee; electric cooker, fridge, etc.; shower, toilet, washbasin. Children especially welcome. Pleasantly situated in excellent walking country; several interesting market towns, several inns with dining facilities, castle within easy reach. Pony trekking and trout fishing can be arranged. Babysitting available. Self-catering terms £45 to £55 per week. Linen supplied at extra cost if required. Alternatively, Bed, Breakfast and Evening Meal. Also six-berth caravan, with beautiful views, Calor gas cooking and lighting: £45 to £55 per week. Out of season and week-end visitors welcome.

OSWESTRY. Mrs Glenice Jones, Lloran Ganol Farm, Llansilin, Oswestry (Llansilin [069-170] 287). Working farm. A luxury self-catering bungalow on mixed farm in quiet valley. Farm and bungalow are situated over the border in the Welsh hills in Clwyd. Five people accommodated in two double and one single bedrooms; bathroom, toilet; sittingroom, diningroom; colour TV; telephone. Long kitchen with dining area; automatic washing machine and fridge. Linen supplied. Extra charge for pets. Two and a half miles from the shops. Car essential — parking. Shooting, horse riding and trout fishing on farm; fishing, golf and trekking in surrounding area. Open all year round, the bungalow is suitable for disabled guests. Storage heaters, fitted carpets and garden furniture provided. Glass conservatory. Weekly terms from £60. Bed and Breakfast also available with family in house adjoining. From £8 per night.

SHREWSBURY near. Mr T. W. E. Corbett, The Home Farm, Leebotwood, Church Stretton SY6 6LX (Dorrington [074-373] 628). Cottage is a modernised stone cottage in a magnificent position with extensive views at the foot of Lawley Hill, five miles from Church Stretton, nine miles from Shrewsbury and one mile from the village of Longnor. It is set in one-third acre of garden and orchard, and offers excellent facilities for walking, riding, golf, tennis and swimming. There are one double and two single bedrooms, with two folding down beds in addition. Downstairs there is a bathroom, kitchen/diningroom and sittingroom with TV; electric cooker, fridge. Weekly terms include off peak electricity and wood for open fire. Open season from May to October. SAE for terms, please. Registered with English Tourist Board.

SOUTH SHROPSHIRE. For comfortable, well-equipped, self-catering accommodation and also farmhouse accommodation, see the Display Advertisement for South Shropshire Farm and Country Holidays Group under Shropshire Board in this Guide.

PLEASE SEND A STAMPED ADDRESSED ENVELOPE WITH ENQUIRIES

SOMERSET

BATH near. Mrs Audrey Rich, Whitnell Farm, Binegar, Gurney Slade, Near Bath BA3 4UF (Oakhill [0749] 840277). Working farm, join in. A peaceful Manor House with unique character set in beautiful gardens and relaxing countryside with views and sunsets, fading away over the Mendip Hills. Situated just off the B3139 Wells to Bath road. Central for touring the undiscovered parts of Somerset, with Cheddar Caves, Wookey Hole, Glastonbury, the West Coast, Golf, Riding, Fishing, and many holiday attractions within easy reach. We welcome guests to a mixed family farm in two self-contained apartments. FORECOURT — all on one level and suitable for disabled. Fully equipped with three bedrooms for seven people. LAWNSIDE — front entrance. Fully equipped with two bedrooms for four people. Open all year with Bus Service. For booking, telephone or send SAE, please, to **Mrs Rich** for Brochure.

BATH near. Easton Croft, Ston Easton. Working farm. A large detached stone built farm cottage in the Mendip Hills. On a working farm, cows, calves, sheep, horses. Our farm shop sells meat, eggs, etc. A good touring area for Wells, Cheddar, Wookey Hole, Bath, Weston-super-Mare. Car essential. Four double bedrooms, sleeping eight, and cot. Linen not provided. Large kitchen/diner, sittingroom. Electric fires in all rooms. Park-Ray with downstairs radiators available. TV, spin-dryer, electric cooker, fridge, Hoover, electricity by 50p meter. Trout and coarse fishing and two golf courses nearby. Pony riding available. **Mrs Clothier, Home Farm Bungalow, Ston Easton, Near Bath BA3 4DF (Chewton Mendip [076-121] 273).**

BRENT KNOLL. Mrs J. B. Harris, West Croft Farm, Brent Knoll, Highbridge TA9 4BE (0278-760259). Holiday cottage in centre of picturesque village near shop. Sleeps six. Has cot, washing machine, colour TV. Parking space and garden. No linen provided. Three and a half miles from safe, sandy beaches and near many beauty spots including Cheddar Caves, Wells, Bath, Mendip and Quantock Hills. Flat in farmhouse also available; sleeps four/six. Weekly terms from £65 inclusive.

BRIDGWATER. Burton Farm Holiday Accommodation, Stogursey, Bridgwater. Burton Farm is situated one mile from the village of Stogursey and one-and-a-half miles from the beach at Shurton Bars. Riding and pony trekking can be arranged on Quantock Hills. All accommodation — The Bungalow, farmhouse, cottage — is fully equipped apart from bed linen and electricity is on a 10p meter. The Bungalow sleeps four with two bedrooms (one double and two single beds); the farmhouse sleeps six with three bedrooms (one double and four single beds); the cottage sleeps six with three bedrooms (one double and four single beds). All have TV and all-electric kitchens; bathrooms and bath/shower. Pets by arrangement. Parking. Weekly terms from £50–£120. SAE, please, for brochure to **Mrs M. Payne, Pardlestone Farm, Kilve, Bridgwater TA5 1SQ (Holford [0278-74] 237).**

BRIDGWATER. Mr and Mrs C. W. Webber, Currypool Mills, Cannington, Bridgwater TA5 2NH (Spaxton [027-867] 215). A delightful country cottage, pleasant bungalow and comfortable chalet available for self-catering holidays, all situated near the Quantock Hills, 200 yards from the A39 Bridgwater to Minehead road. Horse riding and fishing nearby. Lovely walks in delightful surroundings. Milk is delivered and groceries can be obtained from the village (one-and-a-half miles). The cottage and bungalow sleep eight and the chalet sleeps four. Each has lounge with TV; fully equipped kitchen, bathroom. No linen supplied. Cots for hire. Metered (10p) electricity. SAE, please, for terms and further details. Open all year.

BRIDGWATER. "Moorland Court", Moorland, Bridgwater. Working farm. Set within unspoilt countryside on the edge of the tidal River Parrett, Moorland Court will appeal to visitors seeking a tranquil, relaxing holiday. This fine Somerset farmhouse provides spacious accommodation comprising entrance hall, lounge dining-room, modern kitchen/diner, three double bedrooms, bathroom, shower, separate WC. Well-appointed to cater for six persons, child's cot available. Colour TV. Central heating. Linen not provided. As this farmhouse is part of working dairy farm, no pets please. Large south facing garden at rear with parking area. Country inn (250 yards), post office/general store in village (one mile), shopping centre, launderette in Bridgwater (five miles). Interesting walks, Quantock Hills four miles, Somerset coastline eight miles. Riding, golf, fishing, sandy beaches 10 miles. Available all year. Brochure — **Mrs J. A. Griffin, "Chinook", Moorland, Bridgwater TA7 0AX (Westonzoyland [027-869] 506).**

Terms quoted in this publication may be subject to increase if rises in costs necessitate

SELF-CATERING   Somerset   481

BRIDGWATER. Mrs Jane C. Ellicott, Durleigh Farm, Durleigh, Bridgwater TA5 2AW (Bridgwater [0278] 455724). Working farm. Part of a lovely farmhouse situated in the beautiful Somerset countryside accommodating six people. Two double bedrooms, one single, one family, cot provided; bathroom, diningroom/lounge with TV. Fully equipped kitchen with electric cooker, fridge, kettle and all utensils. Linen supplied. Sorry, no pets. Available from April to October, weekly terms on request. Many sporting activities include golf, pony trekking over Quantocks. Many different beaches to choose from. Indoor sports and nightclubs in town. Excellent fishing facilities from neighbouring reservoir. Among the places of historical interest are Bath with Roman Baths, Cathedral City of Wells 18 miles, Battle of Sedgemoor eight miles and Dunster Castle and village 34 miles, as well as Bridgwater itself. Shopping facilities one mile. Pets welcome.

BRIDGWATER. Mrs S. Honeyball, Manor Farm, Waterpitts, Broomfield, Bridgwater (Kingston St. Mary [082-345] 266). Working farm. Manor Farm Cottage is situated on a 125-acre working dairy farm on the edge of the Quantocks. The cottage is part of a lovely farmhouse enjoying panoramic views overlooking the Quantocks and makes an ideal family home. The surrounding countryside offers superb walks and it is within easy reach of both coasts. Golf course, pony trekking and fishing locally. Accommodation comprises one double, two single rooms, plus cot. Bathroom. Sittingroom with TV; kitchen/diner fully equipped with Rayburn or electric cooker, kettle, fridge, etc. No linen. The cottage is carpeted throughout (except kitchen). Children welcome. Pets by prior arrangement only. Babysitting can be arranged. Car essential — parking. Fresh milk, free range eggs, clotted cream, butter obtainable from the farm. Open April to October. Stabling available. SAE or phone for terms. Bed and Breakfast also available.

BRIDGWATER. Mr and Mrs R. Tucker, Catcott Burtle Farm, Burtle, Bridgwater TA7 8NE (Chilton Polden [0278] 722321). Working farm. This self-catering flat is part of the farmhouse on a dairy farm in a small quiet Somerset village nestled between the Mendip Hills and the Poldens. Within easy reach of Cheddar Gorge, Wells, Glastonbury, Bath. Seven miles from Burnham-on-Sea and a 15 mile drive to Weston-super-Mare. Accommodation for seven in three bedrooms, lounge, diningroom, kitchen, bathroom and toilet. Fridge, TV, electric cooker and heating included in price. No linen supplied. Sorry, no pets. Car essential — parking. Shops quarter of a mile away. Available from May to September. Weekly terms on request. SAE, please.

BRIDGWATER near. Mrs D. C. Coram, Hedging Farm, North Newton, Near Bridgwater TA6 0DF (North Petherton [0278] 662344). Working farm. Comfortable accommodation offered for self-catering holidays from May to September in completely re-modernised part of farmhouse. Situated on a mixed farm in the centre of Somerset, it is within easy reach of historic attractions, ideal touring base. Quantock Hills, sea 12-14 miles, canal fishing five minutes' walk. Sports Centre, riding stables and lovely countryside nearby. Small shop and country pub one mile. Accommodation comprises large lounge with TV, fully equipped kitchen/diningroom; sleeps four-six in one double bedroom, one twin-bedded room; bed-settee available in lounge; bathroom and toilet; cot if required. (All carpeted except kitchen). Electric cooking facilities and heating. Linen supplied as extra if needed. Children welcome. Sorry, no pets. Babysitting arranged. Car essential, parking. Four miles off M5 motorway from Exit 24. SAE, please.

BURNHAM-ON-SEA near. Mrs W. Baker, Withy Grove Farm, East Huntspill, Near Burnham-on-Sea ∗ (Burnham-on-Sea [0278] 784471). Six converted holiday bungalows and one barn flat, well-equipped and comfortable. Sleep five-six persons. Outdoor heated swimming pool, licensed bar, farm shop, games room and skittle alley. Available Easter to November. Also farmhouse accommodation, all bedrooms with washbasins, guests' lounge with colour TV, separate tables in diningroom. Good country fare. See Colour Display Advertisement in this Guide.

BURNHAM-ON-SEA near. Mrs F. V. Lindsay, "Maitland Cottage," Ham Road, Brean, Near Burnham-on-Sea TA8 2RN (Brean Down [027-875] 342). This fully self-contained half of a large country cottage is set in open countryside with panoramic views from the large sun balcony. There is a fenced-in garden with washing line and a river nearby for fishing. Easy touring to Cheddar Gorge and the cities of Bath and Wells; Brean Sands one mile; Brean Down (National Trust) two-and-a-half miles, Burnham-on-Sea four and Weston-Super-Mare seven miles. Berrow Golf Course within easy reach. Five persons accommodated in one double and one single bedrooms, cot available; shower room and toilet; lounge/diner; kitchen with fridge, cooker, double drainer and all utensils. Linen not supplied. Pets permitted. Car essential — parking. Cottage available from May to October from £65 weekly, inclusive of electricity.

Please note that entries marked with an asterisk also have a colour display advert in the colour section in this guide

482　Somerset　SELF-CATERING

CHARD. Rosecot, Dommett, Buckland St. Mary, Chard. This renovated farm cottage retains its olde worlde charm with its inglenook fireplace and exposed beams. Adjoining the farmhouse of a working dairy farm but with its own entrance, it faces one of the best views in Somerset. Ideal for those wishing a self-catering holiday in the peace and quiet of the countryside. Locally you will discover beautiful walks, there is also a forest trail and picnic area one mile away. A car is essential but within easy driving distance you can visit resorts both north and south, wild life parks and many places of historical interest. The cottage is fully equipped with one double bedroom and a modern bed-settee in the lounge. Heating and cooking are by electricity and there is a meter. Shower room and toilet. Open from April to October. Linen not supplied. Children welcome, cot available. SAE for terms please, to **Mrs L. Dicks, Roses Farm, Dommett, Buckland St. Mary, Chard TA20 3JH (Buckland St. Mary [046-034] 558).**

CHARD. Mrs P. P. Maidment, Manor Farm, Knowle St Giles, Chard TA20 3DA (Chard [046-06] 3102). Working farm. Manor Farm is situated half-a-mile from main A358 road, two miles from Chard and three miles from Ilminster. This is a modernised self-contained farmhouse, dating from 15th century. It is a dairy farm of 100 acres, with a Friesian herd of cows. The spacious lounge has TV; sun lounge; bathroom upstairs and cloakroom downstairs; sleeps five, cot; babysitting by arrangement. Modern fully equipped kitchen with electric cooker and fridge. No linen supplied. Pets permitted. Car essential — ample parking. Open all year. Terms on request, with SAE please. It is an ideal centre for touring Somerset, Devon and Dorset. Coast 15 miles. Wildlife Park four miles away; Arts and Crafts Museum half-a-mile.

CHARD. Mrs D. Long, Hornsbury Hill Farm, Chard (Chard [046-06] 2231). Working farm. Hornsbury Hill Farm is about 27 acres, a small calf rearing and beef cattle farm. It is on the main A358 road, one-and-a-quarter miles from Chard. This makes it ideal for touring Somerset, Devon and Dorset and it is within easy reach of several lovely coastal resorts. There is an arts and crafts museum quarter of a mile away. Cricket St Thomas Wildlife Park three miles. General store just down the road. There are lawns at the front of the house and a large yard at the back with plenty of room for children to play. Spend a quiet holiday here or visit several seaside places. Forde Abbey and gardens four miles. Accommodation for six people; two double, one single rooms; cot; kitchen has fridge and electric cooker. Hot and cold water. Colour TV. No linen. Pets permitted. Parking. Open all year round. SAE, please, for terms.

CHARD near. Mrs Susan J. Adams, Manor Farm, Forton, Near Chard TA20 2LZ (Chard [046-06] 3240). Working farm. Part of 16th century farmhouse (self-contained) of historic interest. Interesting wood structure with murals on walls of large bedroom which will sleep up to three persons. Cot supplied if desired. One small bedroom with double bed, fully equipped kitchen; separate shower room, toilet; large sitting/diningroom; Super-ser gas heater. Children can play in safe garden and observe life on this Somerset Dairy Farm set in beautiful countryside. Special attractions of the area include Cricket St Thomas Wildlife Park, Forde Abbey and many different sea-side resorts. Members of the West Country Tourist Board. No dogs allowed. Shops one mile. There is also a badminton court; rackets provided for grown-ups. Car essential. Weekly terms from £80 to £100; all electricity and linen included.

CHARD near. Mrs Pauline Wright, Rull Farm, Otterford, Near Chard TA20 3QJ (Buckland St. Mary [046-034] 398). Working farm. This accommodation is part of the farmhouse and consists of two double bedrooms and one single. Cot, high chair and babysitting available. Bathroom and toilet upstairs. Kitchen with electric cooker, fridge and spin dryer. Fully equipped except linen. Milk, eggs and cream obtainable from the farm. Situated on Somerset/Devon border, not far from the sea — nearby towns are ideal for touring. Lovely country walks. Car essential — parking. Available all year. SAE, please, for terms.

CHARD near. Mrs Elsie Wheaton, Court Farm, Winsham, Near Chard TA20 4JE (Winsham [046-030] 432). Working farm. The two-storey cottage adjoining the farmhouse is quite private and has its own lawn. Two double bedrooms, one of which also has single bed; cot; airing cupboard with hot water tank; steep stairs; bathroom; toilet and washbasin downstairs, next to small utility room. Comfortable sittingroom; TV. Kitchen/diningroom — electric cooker, fridge, electric fires or Rayburn. Everything provided, except linen. Electricity by meter. No pets. Car space; car essential. Shop nearby. Available May to end September. The beef farm is situated on Somerset/Dorset border, standing among attractive countryside and bounded by the River Axe. Nearest beaches 12 miles. SAE, please, for terms.

CHARD near. Mrs F. A. Turner, Lower Synderford Farm, Thorncombe, Near Chard TA20 4QA (Winsham [046-030] 204). Working farm. Completely self-contained flat above the farmhouse, with own entrance and garden available for sun bathing. Accommodates five people. One double and one single bedrooms with bunk beds, cot; bathroom, toilet; sittingroom; dining alcove; kitchen with electric cooker, fridge, iron, etc. No linen supplied. Sorry, no pets. Car essential — parking. This is a working farm of 75 acres on Somerset/Dorset border and many pleasant river and country walks can be enjoyed nearby. Within easy reach of Cricket St. Thomas Wild Life Park and Forde Abbey, with its gardens and fruit farm. Nearest seaside resort is Lyme Regis, 10 miles away. Available from April to September only from £55 weekly. Electricity by 10p meter. SAE, please.

WHEN MAKING ENQUIRIES PLEASE MENTION
FARM HOLIDAY GUIDE

FAIRLANDS, CHEDDAR

FAIRLANDS HOUSE is an ancient and beautiful farmhouse dating back to the 17th century and we take great pleasure in inviting you to share our home with us. The house and grounds have a leafy, romantic atmosphere of a by-gone age. We have several vintage motor cars and you can play croquet and see our pony and cats.

The **TWO SELF-CATERING COTTAGES** are situated in this peaceful and relaxing environment. Delightfully and immaculately converted from old stables, each cottage has a well-equipped kitchen and a dining/living area. There is a double bedroom and a second bedroom fitted with bunk beds and is ideally suited for a family of 4. A further two people can be accommodated on a bed-settee. The cottages are fully and tastefully equipped with every facility and TV. The bathroom includes a separate shower and there is night-storage heating.

Enjoy the peace of another century and within a few minutes walk onto the Mendip Hills, an area of Outstanding Natural Beauty, to see some of the finest views in Somerset. It is possible to walk for miles in unspoilt countryside, ride at one of the local stables, enjoy golf, fishing, caving, shooting, bird watching and climbing.

You can visit the glorious Cathedral city of Wells, the ruins at Glastonbury, Bath – famous for its Georgian beauty is only 45 minutes away and many theatres and concerts are within 35 minutes at Bristol. There are a host of stately homes and museums and the seaside is only 20 minutes away at Weston-super-Mare and Burnham-on-Sea.

We also provide **FARMHOUSE ACCOMMODATION**. Please refer to the **Board** section at the front of this guide.

Les Routiers, A.A., R.A.C., B.T.A. registered. Please send for a brochure and prices to:
Sue Blakeney-Edwards, Fairlands House, Church Street, Cheddar, Somerset. Tel: [0934] 742629.

CHEDDAR. Two cottages. CLOUDS HILL COTTAGE. Sunny, detached house sleeps up to six. Fourth bedroom and second toilet downstairs, comfortable livingroom overlooking secluded garden, kitchen/diningroom (gas cooker), double glazing, gas central heating, garage, general feeling of comfort. THE COACH HOUSE. Pretty stone cottage, sleeps two to four, tastefully converted, exposed beams, double bedroom, bathroom, cosy livingroom (convertible with spring interior mattresses), gas fire, kitchen (gas cooker), large garden, parking. Both cottages are for the discerning holiday-maker, well-equipped, colour TV, quiet, views, beautiful leafy surroundings, lovely walks, conveniently situated near the village's old centre, shops, caves and Gorge. Pets welcome. AA inspected. English Tourist Board. Reasonable terms. **M. Earle, The Old Manse, Barrows Croft, Cheddar (Cheddar [0934] 742496).**

CHURCHILL. Mrs J. A. Sacof, Churchill Green Farm, Churchill, Avon (Churchill [0934] 852438). **Working farm.** Superb position with open views to the Mendip Hills, Pool House is situated in the garden of Churchill Green Farm Guest House (licensed with small bar), a single storey L-shaped cottage built around the swimming pool. Private, quiet and ideal for families wishing to stay at reasonable cost in North Somerset. Open pastureland surrounds the cottage and two horses are kept in the paddock at the end of Pool House. Accommodation for six in two double bedrooms, possible sleeping accommodation in the lounge; bathroom, toilet; all-electric kitchen. Linen supplied. Oil-fired heating throughout. Suitable for disabled visitors. Parking. Use of swimming pool included in weekly terms. "The Farmhouse itself" is available for self-catering holidays at certain times of the year. SAE, please for terms and further details.

FUN FOR ALL THE FAMILY IN SOMERSET

Cheddar Caves, Cheddar Gorge; Madame Tussaud's, Wookey Hole, near Wells; Cricket Wildlife Park, near Chard; Ambleside Water Gardens & Aviaries, near Weston-Super-Mare; Tropical Bird Gardens, Rode; Brean Down Bird Garden, Brean Down, near Weston-Super-Mare; Marineland, Cheddar; Minehead Model Town & Pleasure Gardens, Minehead; East Somerset Railway, Cranmore Station, near Shepton Mallet; West Somerset Railway, Minehead Station, Minehead; Cheddar Motor Museum, near Cheddar Caves; The Fleet Air Arm Museum, Royal Naval Air Station, Yeovilton, near Ilchester.

Somerset SELF-CATERING

CREWKERNE near. Mrs J. Venning, Court Mill, Merriott, Near Crewkerne TA16 5NL (Crewkerne [0460] 72862). Five fully modernised, hamstone cottages sharing private lane off village street. All with gardens of various sizes. Lane leads down to farmyard where guests are welcome to wander; access to stream and fields. Lyme Regis, Charmouth, Dorset and West Bay are all a pleasant half-hour drive, also Cheddar Caves, Wells, Cricket St Thomas Wildlife Park. Accommodation for five to eight people; cots available. Bathrooms, toilets; washbasins in some bedrooms; sitting-rooms; kitchens or kitchen/diners. Fully equipped with fridges, Colour TV, etc. Linen can be hired. Two minutes from shops. Pets permitted. Parking. Open from April to October. Terms on application; electricity on 50p meter.

DONYATT. Edith & Bob Hearn, "Ashdale", Park House, Park Lane, Donyatt TA19 0RN (Ilminster [04605] 2924). Peaceful, secluded yet certainly not isolated, Park House is set in an acre of beautiful garden, surrounded by the most magnificent unspoilt countryside and within easy reach of the sea and numerous places of interest. There is a choice of three separate, self-contained apartments: The Garden Flat with its own private garden, has two bedrooms suitable for two/three persons, whilst The Cloisters and The Little House are both one double bedroomed flats ideal for two persons. All have bath or shower room, toilet, kitchen, lounge, diningroom or lounge/diner. They are well equipped and furnished with colour TV, patio table and chairs, use of swimming pool. Car advisable, ample parking. Pets welcome. Open March to October, weekly terms from £75. Further details on request.

DULVERTON. Keens Cottage, Brompton Regis, Dulverton. Working farm. Stone built detached cottage in sheltered and secluded 50 yards square lawn, 200 yards from farm and 400 yards from Wimbleball Lake, a large reservoir with fishing. The 240-acre hill/livestock farm has horses, donkeys, sheep and cattle and those interested are welcome to join in the farm activities. The accommodation is suitable for six people plus two children. Two double bedrooms, one twin bedded room and one small room with bunk beds. Sittingroom; livingroom; bathroom, toilet; well equipped kitchen — fridge, automatic washing machine, colour TV, electric cooker, immersion heater. Electric fires; four off-peak storage heaters, also oil-fired Rayburn heats house and water (costs extra). Electricity 50p meter. Mains services and telephone. Children welcome; pets permitted. Car essential; parking. Terms from £90 to £120 plus VAT. Apply **Mr and Mrs F. A. Heywood, South Greenslade Farm, Brompton Regis, Dulverton TA22 9NU (Brompton Regis [039-87] 207).**

DULVERTON. L. H. F. Young and Sons, Upcott Farm, Brushford, Dulverton (Dulverton [0398] 23481). Working farm. Completely self-contained and furnished accommodation adjoining the farmhouse at Upcott. Three miles from Dulverton on good road, but quiet. The farm is 650 feet above sea level on an East/West ridge overlooking valleys on both sides. Beautiful countryside, close to Exmoor and 20 to 30 miles to coasts. Suitable for up to six people with one bedroom (double and bunk beds); cot; bathroom, toilet; sitting/diningroom with studio couch; fully equipped kitchen — electric cooker, fridge, etc. No linen supplied. Well controlled pets allowed. Car essential — parking. Available all year round. Terms from £30 – £80. Electricity payment on meter reading.

DUNSTER. Mr and Mrs A. J. Hill, The Old Manor, Lower Marsh, Dunster (Dunster [0643] 821216). Three flats adjoining lovely guest house, available May-September. Ideal touring centre. Riding stables, golf nearby. Flat 1 — accommodates four: large room as kitchen; lounge (TV) with dining alcove; one room (double bed, two singles); bathroom, airing cupboard. Flat 2 — accommodates six; lounge (TV); kitchen/diner; three double bedrooms (one double-bedded and two twin-bedded); bathroom, airing cupboard and WC. Flat 3 — accommodates two in bedsitter; twin beds, TV; kitchen/diner; bathroom; toilet nearby but not for exclusive use of flat. Regret, no dogs or cats. Shops, sea half mile. Children over five. Evening meals available in the Guest House. Residential licence. SAE, please, for brochure. See also under Board Section (Dunster, Somerset).

DUNSTER. "Packhorse Cottage," Dunster. Ideally situated in cul-de-sac leading directly to River Avill, Packhorse Bridge, Deer Park and many delightful walks, all within a few yards. Dunster, renowned for its ancient castle and Old Yarn Market, is adequately served by shops, a post office, garages and licensed hotels. A short drive will take you to the centre of Exmoor National Park or the sea. For those so inclined riding, trekking and fishing are at hand. The cottage comprises a sittingroom with TV, a fully equipped kitchen/diningroom, two double bedrooms (additional bed if required); bathroom and toilet. Available all year round. Pets permitted. Weekly terms from £45. For full details SAE, please to **Lt. Col. and Mrs A. K. Cocks, Venns Cottage, Burrow, Wootton Courtenay, Near Minehead TA24 7UD (Timberscombe [064-384] 375).**

**When you have read one you *haven't* read them all —
we have *eleven* other publications**

SELF-CATERING Somerset 485

EXMOOR. Mrs P. L. Challis, Wychanger, Luccombe, Minehead TA24 8TA (Porlock [0643] 862 526). Two flats in converted coach-house, sleeping four and six, in delightful village amidst glorious countryside between Minehead and Porlock. Extremely comfortable. Electric blankets on all beds. Storage heaters. Colour televisions. Spacious and secluded grounds with immediate access from the paddock into the wood which leads to Moor. Farm, two miles away, offering glorious walks and views. Table tennis, stabling and grazing available. Children and pets most welcome. Luccombe is a very small, delightful, peaceful old world village situated "at the foot of" Dunkery between Minehead and Porlock. There is a also a delightful thatched cottage available nearby. Open all year. Terms and further details on request.

EXMOOR. Miss J. Trow, West Knowle House, Brushford, Dulverton TA22 9RU (Dulverton [0398] 23835 after 9 pm). Comfortable self-catering flat in country cottage, two miles from Dulverton, to sleep four, no pets. Two bedrooms, one with double bed, one with two singles, lounge/diner with studio couch, TV, bathroom, separate toilet, cooking and heating by electricity; plus central heating. Fully equipped but no linen. Dulverton ideal for all activities of this lovely area, close to moor, wooded valleys and within easy reach of North Devon coast. Good centre for guided walks, birdwatching, fishing. There are riding stables easily accessible or stabling can be provided with the flat, horse owners bringing own horses. Details of riding facilities on application.

EXMOOR. Mrs F. Edwards, Westermill Farm, Exford, Near Minehead TA24 7NJ (Exford [064-383] 238). Working farm. Six delightful Scandinavian pine log cottages in small paddocks, plus a holiday cottage attached to farmhouse for self-catering. Campsite for tents by shallow river. All on a beef and sheep farm in the centre of Exmoor National Park. Four waymarked walks over 500 acres. Two-and-a-half miles of shallow river for bathing, fishing or paddling. Cottages are charmingly furnished, sleeping four to eight. Colour TV. All-electric. Pets and children welcome. Small shop, but uncommercialised. SAE, please.

EXMOOR. "Hernlea", 9 Crawter Drive, Doverhay, Porlock. "Hernlea" is situated in Porlock, a large village within the Exmoor National Park, only a few miles from the Devon border. On the first floor there are double, twin and bunk-bedded rooms, a bathroom and separate toilet; on the second, a living/dining room and well equipped kitchen with electric cooker, fridge, kettle, iron, Hoover and an immersion heater. Colour television is available. Own linen to be supplied. Children welcome; small dogs by arrangement. Riding, fishing, bowls, tennis and putting can be enjoyed and swimming is possible off the shingle at Porlock Weir. There are sandy beaches at Minehead and Lee Bay. For further information apply **M. D. Leach, Willowbank, Dumpers Lane, Chew Magna, Bristol, Avon BS18 8SS (Chew Magna [0272] 332465).**

EXMOOR. Springfield, Ash Lane, Winsford. This cottage stands in a breathtaking position in the heart of Exmoor facing South across the moor. It contains three well furnished bedrooms — one double, one twin and one with full-size bunks and a single bed — a large livingroom with an inglenook fireplace, a modern kitchen/breakfast room with gas cooker and fridge, a well-fitted shower room, cloakroom and entrance lobbies. Central Heating and cot available. There is a large garden surrounded by old hedgebanks and parking for two cars. The position is ideal for those wanting to enjoy the peace of this beautiful countryside or to explore Exmoor on foot, on horseback or by car. Full details from **Mrs A. P. Hughes, Manor Cottage, Overleigh, Street BA16 0TR (Street [0458] 43556).**

EXMOOR NATIONAL PARK. Working farm. Two Stable Cottages situated in the centre of the EXMOOR NATIONAL PARK above the unspoilt moorland village of Withypool. Surrounding countryside ideal for walking, riding and other country activities. River, reservoir and sea fishing nearby. Within easy reach of the North Devon sandy and surfing beaches. Both cottages are very well equipped, fully heated, colour TV and are open all year. Home cooked meals available. Dogs/horses welcome. ALSO Bed and Breakfast available in our lovely COUNTRY HOUSE with panoramic moorland views. Family run. One very pretty double room with bathroom en suite. Colour TV in sittingroom. **Mrs J. N. Best, Bigmoor, Withypool, Minehead TA24 7RP (Exford [064-383] 230).**

SOMERSET – THE CREAM AND CIDER COUNTY!
Wookey Hole, the great cave near Wells, is the first known home of man in Great Britain. Other places of interest in this green and hilly country include The Mendips, Exmoor National Park, Cheddar Gorge, Meare Lake Village and The Somerset Rural Life Museum. The villages and wildlife of the Quantocks, Poldens and Brendons should not be missed.

Somerset SELF-CATERING

EXMOOR NATIONAL PARK. Mr and Mrs R. Paul, Whites Farm, Elworthy, Lydeard St. Lawrence, Taunton TA4 3PX (Stogumber [098-46] 283). Working farm, join in. Spacious self-contained accommodation for six in the old Farmhouse, and accommodation for four in the Cider House, with beautiful views over the surrounding hills. Whites Farm lies at the foot of the Brendons within the eastern boundary of the National Park. The north coast is just six miles away, and we are in a good central position for touring the West Country. Riding and fishing can easily be arranged. The farm has an assortment of animals and children are very welcome. Open all year. Car essential — parking. SAE or phone, please, for further details.

HIGHBRIDGE. Mrs M. P. Frost, Ham Farm, Brent Knoll, Highbridge TA9 4BJ (Burnham-on-Sea [0278] 783120). Working farm. Three miles from safe, sandy beaches and two-and-a-half miles from M5, this is a 100 acre dairy farm situated in the charming village of Brent Knoll. Good centre for visiting the many places of interest in Somerset, only three miles from Burnham and Berrow golf course. A flatlet on the farm is to let, with accommodation for five in a double bed/sittingroom; a room with bunk beds (extra bed or cot available); kitchen/diningroom (electric cooker, fridge); bathroom with toilet. All equipment except linen. TV. Shops one mile. Regret, no pets. Visitors welcome all year. Babysitting arranged. Car essential — parking. SAE, please, for terms.

HIGHBRIDGE near. Mrs A. W. Rich, North Grove Farm, Burton Row, Brent Knoll, Near Highbridge TA9 4BY (Brent Knoll [0278] 760421). Working farm. This modern cottage in the farmyard sleeps five in three bedrooms; bathroom; sitting/diningroom with colour TV; kitchen with stainless steel sink unit, electric cooker and fridge; immersion heater. (Electricity on 10p meter). Very comfortable with electric heating and fitted carpets. Children are welcome. Sorry no pets. Car essential, parking. Open from April to October. The farm is 200 acres, with beef cattle, sheep, pigs and hens for the children to see. Burnham and Bream are four miles away and Weston-super-Mare eight miles. Berrow Golf Club three miles. Fishing nearby. Glastonbury, Wells and Cheddar, Mendip and Quantock Hills and Exmoor nice day outings. Visitors can walk through our orchard up the hill to top of Brent Knoll. SAE for terms please. Also flat, sleeps six.

MARK. Mrs E. Harris, Yarrow Farm, Mark, Near Highbridge TA9 4LW (Mark Moor [027-864] 270). Working farm. Self-contained half of farmhouse, situated approximately one mile from the village of Mark and within easy reach of many places of interest, including Weston-Super-Mare, Burnham-on-Sea, Wells, Cheddar, Bath and Bristol. Fishing and riding in locality. This is a 120-acre dairy farm, children welcome, but sorry, no pets. House equipped for seven with cot and high chair on request. Three bedrooms, one with twin beds and one with one double and one single, third has double bed. Bathroom/shower; toilet and shaving point upstairs with another toilet and sink in cloakroom downstairs. Lounge has TV; French windows to garden. Large kitchen with carpeted dining area — electric cooker, toaster, fridge, washing machine. Linen not provided. Milk free. Weekly terms. Metered electricity.

MARK. "London House", Mark, Near Highbridge. Three self-contained, fully furnished flats situated in picturesque village of Mark. Ideal touring centre. Nearby village inn. Easy access to M5 motorway. Within easy reach of Cheddar, Wells, Glastonbury, sandy beaches (Burnham-on-Sea, Weston-super-Mare). Ideal for anglers, horse riding. Rosedene flat: fridge, TV. Two bedrooms, sleeps approximately six. Lounge, kitchen/diner, bathroom, toilet, shower. Willowdene flat: fridge, TV. Three bedrooms, sleeps eight. Lounge, kitchen/diner, bathroom, toilet. Ashdene flat: fridge, TV. Lounge with studio couch, large bedroom, sleeps five, kitchen/diner, bathroom, toilet. Ample parking facilities. Own linen. Other bedding supplied. 50p meters. Pets by arrangement. SAE, please, to **Mrs Sylvia Puddy, "Beavers Lodge Farm", Lympsham, Near Weston-super-Mare BS24 0DE (Edingworth [093472] 246).**

MINEHEAD. Mr D. Stephens & Sons, Luckyard Farm, Wheddon Cross, Near Dunster, Minehead TA24 7HF (064 385) 220. Secluded, comfortable farm cottage commanding superb views of the river Quarme, Exmoor and Winsford. The perfect base for those who love to roam 200 acres of woods and sheep pastures. The farm is run by three brothers, all excellent, attentive hosts and grateful for visitors' help and interest on the farm. The cottage sleeps six in one double bedroom and two single rooms, cot if required; sittingroom, diningroom; bathroom, toilet; good cooking facilities. Blankets supplied. Children welcome, pets allowed. Open all year round, the very best of Exmoor is only five minutes' drive, pub, village shops and riding two miles; sea, golf and Minehead 11 miles. Car essential, parking. Metered electricity. Fish for small brown trout and rough shoot by arrangement. Terms and details on request.

MINEHEAD. Halse Bungalow, Winsford, Minehead. Halse Bungalow is close to open moorland with pony trekking stables about one mile away. There is fishing in local rivers and reservoirs. Six people can be accommodated in two double and one twin-bedded rooms plus cot. Linen is not supplied. Bathroom, toilet; sittingroom; kitchen/diner with electric cooker. This bungalow is suitable for disabled visitors. Children welcome. A car is essential and there is parking. The shops are one mile away; public transport four miles. Open from March to October. Weekly terms on application (electricity extra) for **Mrs E. Baker, Bales Mead, West Porlock, Minehead TA24 8NX (Porlock [0643] 862565).**

MINEHEAD. Butts Green, Wootton Courtenay, Minehead. Charming little house in peaceful setting, 200 yards from village and 10 minutes' walk from moors. Four miles from the sea. Ideal area for walking, touring or just sitting around in the lovely garden. Comfortably furnished, a real home with log fires, etc. Sleeps five/six in three bedrooms; bathroom, toilet; sittingroom; all-electric kitchen. Guests must supply own linen. Pets allowed. Regret no small children. There is a summerhouse and garage. Quarter of a mile from shops. Available all year, with weekly terms from £45 to £500. **Apply to Mrs E. J. Taplin, Huntscott Cottage, Wootton Courtenay, Minehead (Timbercombe [064-384] 258).**

SELF-CATERING   Somerset   487

MINEHEAD. "Hillgarth", 53 Manor Road, Alcombe, Minehead. Hillgarth is an attractive detached period cottage on the outskirts of the village of Alcombe, situated at the entrance to lovely Alcombe Coombe, just 100 yards or so from the Exmoor National Park boundary, and about one and a half miles from Minehead beach. Accommodation comprises: on ground floor; Entrance hall, lounge having colour TV, convertible settee/double bed; diningroom; small kitchen; bathroom with washbasin and WC; refrigerator. Upstairs: Main double bedded room with cot space, and two twin-bedded rooms. Airing cupboard with immersion heater. Heating is by two storage heaters, electric fires, and one open fire in diningroom (fuel not provided). Electricity by 10p slot meter. Well equipped for up to eight persons. Linen is not supplied. Shopping facilities half mile. Ample parking. Open all year. **Mrs M. E. Veale and Mrs M. J. Lowman, Dunster Lodge, Manor Road, Alcombe, Minehead TA24 6EW (Minehead [0643] 3007).**

MINEHEAD. Mr and Mrs T. C. B. Guy, Bougham Farm, Timberscombe, Minehead TA24 7UN (Timberscombe [064-384] 345). Working farm. Two delightful architect-designed bungalows in quiet position overlooking a trout pond. Glorious far reaching views towards the moors. Lovely walks. Also charming country cottage. All sleep up to six people, are fully equipped and furnished to a very high standard. Night storage heating available. All-electric. Well away from traffic and with ample parking space. The bungalows are very convenient for shopping and the small village has excellent stores. The cottage is situated in the most lovely setting about one mile from the village. Being within the Exmoor National Park the area is completely unspoilt. The cottages are three miles from the sea.

MINEHEAD. Mr P. G. Hudson, Landacre Farm, Withypool, Minehead (Exford [064-383] 223). Working farm. Beautiful, modernised period farm cottage located in heart of Exmoor National Park, situated in dry tarmac yard, surrounded mainly by open moorland. Perfect walking and riding country with the River Barle and ancient Landacre Bridge 300 yards. Accommodation for five in two double and one single bedrooms; cot; bathroom and toilet; sittingroom with black and white TV, open log fire; diningroom. Kitchen with Rayburn, electric grill, fridge. No linen supplied. Pets permitted. Car essential — double garage. Open all year round except February. Sea 12 miles; shops three miles. Terms on application. Also modernised bungalow, sleeps two/three, suitable for elderly, partially disabled.

MINEHEAD. Mrs K. Lanyon, The Great House, Timberscombe, Minehead TA24 7TQ (Timberscombe [064-384] 544). A fine Georgian house built in 1720, listed as being of special architectural interest, converted into three spacious flats, each sleeping two to four. The house is on the edge of a small village within the Exmoor National Park with its beautiful countryside and it has an exceptionally peaceful atmosphere. All the bed and living-rooms face south and are comfortably furnished and carpeted throughout. The small kitchens are fully equipped and have electric cookers and fridges. Bathrooms adjoin each main bedroom and constant hot water is supplied. There are electric fires in all rooms and colour TV in each flat. Coin operated telephone. Ample parking. Village stores, post office and 15th century church within two minutes' walk. £45 to £90 weekly.

MINEHEAD. Mrs Diana M. Williams, Little Ash Farm, Withypool, Minehead TA24 7RR (Winsford ✱ [064-385] 344). Working farm. Self-contained and surrounded by fields and open moorland, Little Ash Farm Cottage accommodates up to eight people in two double and two twin-bedded rooms; bathroom, toilet. Furnished and equipped to a high standard the lounge and diningroom have open fires (logs supplied), colour TV, gas heater and electric fire. Kitchen with new pine furniture (all utensils supplied), gas cooker, gas fridge and spin dryer. Most of the rooms have fitted carpets. Lawn for children to play. Ideal for walking, riding, fishing and touring. Many places of local interest. Car essential. Open March to November. Regret, no pets. See also Colour Display Advertisement in this Guide.

MINEHEAD near. Mrs D. M. Salvidge, Thornes Farm, Bicknoller, Near Taunton TA4 4ED (Williton [0984] 32384). Working farm. Thornes Farm is situated at the foot of the Quantocks and has wonderful views of the Exmoor National Park. This is the centre of good hunting country and a stable is available on request. A ground floor flat, part of the farmhouse, overlooking the garden is open all year round; comfortably furnished for five, it has a large kitchen/diner equipped with electric cooker, fridge, immersion heater. Rayburn cooker for winter use. The lounge has TV and electric fire. Three bedrooms — one double, one twin, one single, cot and high chair available. Bathroom and inside toilet. Please supply linen. Parking for essential car. Shops and sea two miles. Sorry, no pets. SAE, please, or telephone. 10p meter.

PORLOCK. Lucott Farm, Porlock, Minehead. Isolated farmhouse on Exmoor, with wood burning fireplaces and all modern conveniences. It lies at the head of Horner Valley and guests will delight in the wonderful scenery. Plenty of pony trekking in the area. Ten people accommodated in four double and two single bedrooms, cot; bathroom, two toilets; sittingroom; diningroom. Kitchen has oil-fired Aga and water heater. No linen supplied. Shops three miles; sea four miles. Car essential — parking. Open all year. Terms (including fuel) on application SAE please to; **Mrs E. A. Tucker, West Luccombe Cottage, Porlock, Minehead TA24 8HT (Porlock [0643] 862810).**

Please note that entries marked with an asterisk also have a colour display advert in the colour section in this guide

Somerset   SELF-CATERING

QUANTOCKS (Bridgwater). Mrs D. Dosson, Crossfields, Spaxton, Bridgwater (Spaxton [027-867] 240). Delightful, freshly decorated farmhouse for six with large lawn. The house consists of lounge with TV and electric fire, diningroom, kitchen with electric cooker, fridge, hot and cold water, bathroom and toilet combined. Two double-bedded rooms, one with washbasin, one twin-bedded, all with cheering open views of farmland and Quantock Hills. If peace is what you require, this is the holiday house for you, approached by stone farm track through fields. A wooded covert for pheasants, a stream close by and orchard, all add to the tranquillity of this area. Exmoor, Cheddar, Wells within easy reach. Riding, fishing, golf four miles; M5 five miles. One pet allowed. No linen. SAE for terms, please.

SHEPTON MALLET. Pennard Hill Farm Cottage, East Pennard, Shepton Mallet. Situated on the top of Stickleball Hill, with panoramic views, the Cottage is an excellent base for visiting the historic town of Glastonbury, City of Wells and within easy reach of Bristol, Bath, Taunton and the coast. Completely rural setting but nearby a host of fine pubs and restaurants. This well-equipped, semi-detached property has all modern conveniences and pleasant garden. Accommodation for four people, plus baby in two double bedrooms; bathroom/toilet; sittingroom, diningroom; kitchen with electric cooking facilities. No linen supplied. Children welcome, cot. Sorry, no pets. Available all year from £30 to £70 (reductions in winter). Car essential — parking. Mid-week bookings available. **Mrs P. Miller, Pennard Hill Farm, East Pennard, Shepton Mallet BA4 6UG (Pilton [074-989] 217).**

SOMERSET. West Somerset Farm and Country Holidays. Choice selection of self-catering holiday homes and farmhouse accommodation in an area rich with opportunity for walkers, riders and lovers of nature with wild animals, flowers and birds. Magnificent scenery of Brendon and Quantock Hills, intriguing folly of Willet Tower looks out over both and acts as a landmark for miles around. Golf courses, fresh water or sea fishing readily available, also sailing and windsurfing both inland and coastal. Local painters, potters, weavers etc. are of a high standard and a visit to the famous Somerset levels enable visitors to watch basket-making. Local pubs offer good beer, locally produced cider, skittles and good company. All properties registered with ETB. Brochure available. **Mary Hunt, The Mount, Ford, Wiveliscombe (Wiveliscombe [0984] 23992).** See also Display Advertisement in the Board Section of this Guide.

SOMERSET. The Helpful Holiday Agency, Coombe 1, Chagford, Devon TQ13 8DF Tel: (06473) 3593/2478, will help you choose from over 400 cottages, houses, flats and bungalows all over the West Country.

TAUNTON. Parswell Bungalow, Clatworthy, Wiveliscombe, Taunton. "Parswell Bungalow" stands high up on the Brendon Hills with breathtaking views of the lovely country surrounding. This is a good spot for touring Exmoor and fishing enthusiasts will find Clatworthy and Wimbleball ideal. The bungalow is kept warm all winter by two large night storage heaters. There are three bedrooms (two double bedded and one twin bedded rooms), cot; lounge; kitchen and bathroom/toilet. Kitchen has electric cooker, fridge, kettle, black and white TV. No linen supplied. Suitable for disabled guests. Shops four-and-a-half miles. Pets permitted. Car essential — parking and garage. Open all year. Domestic electricity by 50p meter. Off-peak electricity for night storage heaters (charge as per Electricity Board). SAE, please, for terms; **Mrs L. Coles, Broadway Head, Clatworthy, Wiveliscombe, Taunton TA4 2SQ (Wiveliscombe [0984] 23485).**

TAUNTON. Mrs S. J. Packer, Lower Tarr Farm, Tarr, Lydeard St. Lawrence, Taunton (Lydeard St. Lawrence [09847] 357). Working farm. A listed period farmhouse of great character, set in beautiful countryside, with easy access to the Quantock Hills and Exmoor. The county town of Taunton is 10 miles away. Accommodation for five persons is in heavily beamed and plaster panelled rooms with inglenook fireplaces. One double and one family rooms with cot; sittingroom; bathroom and two toilets. Gas cooking and central heating, fuel is included. Car essential, parking available. High chair and babysitting service. Regretfully, no pets allowed, but there are pets and plenty of friendly farm animals on site. Guests can participate by arrangement on the 50-acre mixed farm. Open April to September.

WASHFORD. Mrs Ann Fletcher, Bye Farm, Washford, Watchet TA23 OJT (Washford [0984] 40383). Working farm. Bye Farm is a 136 acre mixed farm between Quantock Hills and Exmoor. Visitors are welcome to walk, help feed calves, etc. Bye Cottage and Bye Bungalow stand in sunny positions in their own gardens some distance from farmhouse and each other. River Washford and West Somerset Steam Railway run through the farm. Safe, sandy beach close by, at Blue Anchor. Area has many species of birds and wildlife. Accommodation in each property for six/seven people in three double bedrooms, cots; bathroom, toilets. Well equipped kitchens; sittingrooms; (diningroom in cottage). Linen not supplied. Pets welcome. Car essential — parking. Available March to December. SAE, please, for terms. A39 Williton — Minehead Road; turn second right in Washford.

WEDMORE. Mr & Mrs Squires, Hall Farm, Sand Road, Wedmore BS28 4BZ (Wedmore [0934] 712007). Enjoy your holiday in this converted cider barn with old ceiling beams, which is adjacent to Hall Farm. The farm, not a working farm, is nicely situated in the heart of Somerset Cider Country and is near Cheddar, Wells and Glastonbury, ten miles from the Bristol Channel coast and about six from M5 turn off. Four people can be accommodated in one double bedroom and sittingroom with double put-u-up. Cot available. Bathroom, toilet and fully equipped modern electric kitchen. Everything supplied except linen and towels. Shop five minutes' walk. Pets permitted. Car preferable. AA listed. SAE, please for terms.

Terms quoted in this publication may be subject to increase if rises in costs necessitate

SELF-CATERING   Somerset   489

WEDMORE. Many Stones, Cocklake, Wedmore. Charming country cottage, with its own secluded garden, situated in the hamlet of Cocklake, one mile from the attractive village of Wedmore, three miles from Cheddar. Ideally situated for touring the Mendips and Quantocks. Recently modernised, yet retaining many of its old features and charm, Many Stones is well appointed to accommodate six/eight people. Two double bedrooms, one family, plus cot. High chair (babysitting may be arranged). Bathroom. Large well-equipped kitchen/diningroom; sittingroom with wood-burner stove and colour TV; downstairs cloakroom. Everything supplied except linen. Sorry, no pets. Car essential — ample parking. Weekly terms £90 to £150 (includes fuel for wood-burner and electricity). Night storage heating. Available Easter to end September. Booking forms etc. from **Mrs S. M. Wills, Rose Farm, Cocklake, Wedmore BS28 4HB (Wedmore [0934] 712129).**

WEDMORE. Porch Cottage, Blackford, Wedmore. Pleasantly situated in rural surroundings, adjoining B road 3139, approximately mid-way between Wells and Burnham-on-Sea. Cheddar, Wookey Hole, Weston-super-Mare quite near, also many other places of interest. Comfortably furnished. Large dining/lounge, electric fire, black/white TV. Kitchen has electric cooker, ample china, cutlery and cooking utensils. One double and one family bedrooms, both with washbasins. Sleeps five/six. Bathroom, shower. Cot available. Ample parking space. Open all year. Terms vary from £35 to £75 weekly. Apply **Mrs L. G. Callow, Chards Farm, Blackford, Wedmore BS28 4PA (Wedmore [0934] 712262).**

WEDMORE. Mr and Mrs Hugh and Jane Tucker, Court Farm, Mudgley, Wedmore BS28 4TY (Wedmore [0934] 712367). Working farm. Wedmore is a charming Georgian village with historic connections, pleasant shops, banks, post office etc. Accommodation is situated on dairy farm one and a half miles from village, comprising of two super cottages called "The Hayloft" and "Keepers Cottage" recently tastefully converted from stone-built barn, with superb views over Somerset levels to Polden Hills. Both comprise of lovely open plan kitchen/lounge/diner, delightfully equipped, plus colour TV. Shower room and family bedroom for four with beamed ceilings. Also sofa-bed in "The Hayloft". Cot and high chair available. Special rates for larger parties (up to nine persons) booking both cottages. Linen available. Patio with garden furniture. Laundry room. Garage. Parking. Well behaved dogs accepted by arrangement. Coarse fishing. Electricity included. Open Easter-October. First-class stamp for brochure, please.

WELLS. Mrs N. Cole, Manor Farm, Worth, Near Wookey, Wells BA5 1LW (Wells [0749] 73428). Working farm. Picturesque riverside farm cottage available all year. Sleeps six, offering clean, homely, well-equipped accommodation. (Category 3 with the English Tourist Board). Electric or log fire (logs supplied in winter). Colour TV. Set in 14 acres of beautiful countryside close to the Mendip Hills. Within easy reach of a vast number of places of interest such as natural and historical beauty spots, wildlife parks, modern entertainments, the beach, London one and a half hours by rail. Walking distance from restaurant, bus, pub and shop. Bed and Breakfast £7; Bed, Breakfast and Evening Meal £11. Brochure on request.

B+B
SELF CATERING
Pony Trekking
Trout Fishing
Farm Animals
Children's Play Area
Relax in our Fields
Enjoy the shallow Brooks
Swimming Pool
Friendly, Homely B+B

WELLS. Mrs E. M. Masters, Ebbor Farm, Wookey Hole, Wells BA5 1AY (Wells [0749] 73067). Working farm. Ebbor Farm is a stone-built Victorian house on the outskirts of Wookey Hole, approximately a half mile from the cave entrance and swimming pool. The farm, on 200 acres, has a dairy herd of 130 cattle and adjoins the Ebbor Gorge Nature Reserve. Accommodation for six in a spacious self-contained wing of the farmhouse, with its own entrance and garden. Fully fitted kitchen/diner with electric cooker, fridge. Three bedrooms, sittingroom with colour TV and open fire; bathroom, toilet. Electric fires; electricity metered. No linen supplied. Children welcome; cot. Sorry, no pets. Horse riding nearby. Terms on application. Open May to September.

WELLS near. Mrs E. J. Rider, "Simba", Coxley, Near Wells BA5 1QZ (Wells [0749] 74399). Two-and-a-half miles from Wells, the flat is an extension to the rear of a modern house with lovely views of local farmland and the Mendip Hills. Accommodation comprises livingroom/kitchen with refrigerator and cooker, TV. Bedroom with twin beds. Bathroom with toilet, bath and washbasin. All fitted carpets, gas radiators and double glazing. All rooms are on the ground floor and the flat has a separate entrance. Post Office, stores, local Inn and garage close by. On the Bristol bus route, it is conveniently situated for touring Somerset, Avon and Devon. Close to Glastonbury, Bath, Bristol, Cheddar Gorge, Weston-Super-Mare, Burnham-on-Sea and Longleat Safari Park. Sorry, no pets or children. Adequate parking space. Open all year. Moderate charges.

PLEASE SEND A STAMPED ADDRESSED ENVELOPE WITH ENQUIRIES

Self-contained Farmhouse Cottages
IN AN AREA OF OUTSTANDING NATURAL BEAUTY

In the west wing of an old farmhouse, two self-contained and self-catering cottages have been renovated in traditional style, and have been fully furnished and well equipped for holiday letting.

One cottage accommodates six people and the other four people in double and single bedrooms. Each have bathroom, toilet, sittingroom/diningroom. Kitchens have full modern equipment including fridge, washing machine, electric cooker, etc. Fitted carpets and colour television. Linen is not supplied except for overseas visitors.

The farmhouse is in the middle of a working farm of 120 acres, mainly beef cattle, situated in the Mendip Hills, an area of outstanding natural beauty. Fishing, shooting, riding and golf all within easy reach; Wookey Hole, Cheddar Caves, Wells Cathedral, Glastonbury, historic houses etc., can be visited. Open all year. Winter lets from £50 (C.H. included). Open log fires optional extra.

Full particulars from: ANNE and ARTHUR HILL, PARK FARM, HAYDON, WEST HORRINGTON, WELLS, BA5 3EH (Wells [0749] 73471).

WIVELISCOMBE near. Oddwell Cottage, Brompton Ralph, Near Wiveliscombe. Standing in garden at foot of Brendon Hills is charming 300-year-old cottage with beamed ceilings and inglenook fireplace for cosy coal fires. Equipped for six; two bedrooms — one with three single beds, other with double bed; small bed/sittingroom with put-u-up; modern bathroom, toilet; dining/livingroom; kitchen with oil-fired Rayburn, electric cooker, fridge, immerser, iron, etc., separate larder. Linen supplied if required. Available all year. Indoor games, books provided. Cot, high chair. Trout fishing, riding, walking, pony trekking. Nine miles to sea and half-mile to shops. Car essential, ample parking; garage and small extension garage in keeping with character of cottage. Pets by arrangement. Weekly terms from £45 to £105. SAE, please, to **Graham and Lorna Durling, "Pilgrims," 52 Carbery Avenue, Southbourne, Bournemouth, Dorset BH6 3LG (Bournemouth [0202] 422427).**

YEOVIL. Mrs A. James, Newton Farm, Yeovil (Yeovil [0935] 74305). Working farm. Nicely situated on the Dorset/Somerset border standing in its own garden on a 300-acre farm, this spacious and comfortable bungalow is available for holiday letting as required. Absolutely secluded, yet only half-a-mile from Yeovil and the main train line to London, this is an excellent centre for tourists. Car not essential. Cheddar, Longleat and many other places of interest within comfortable driving distance. Horse riding available close by. Accommodation for six in two double bedrooms; double bed-settee in sittingroom; cot; bathroom, toilet; diningroom; all-electric kitchen, fully equipped. Everything likely to be needed is supplied except for linen. Shops half-a-mile. Babysitting service. Personally supervised. Pets permitted by arrangement. SAE, please.

The information in the entries in this guide is presented by the publishers in good faith and after the signed acceptance by advertisers that they will uphold the high standards associated with FARM HOLIDAY GUIDES LIMITED. The publishers do not accept responsibility for any inaccuracies or omissions or any results thereof. Before making final holiday arrangements readers should confirm the prices and facilities directly with advertisers.

STAFFORDSHIRE

STAFFORDSHIRE. Staffordshire Moorlands — For details of farmhouse and country accommodation see Group Display Advertisement in Board section of this Guide under Staffordshire.
VALE OF TRENT. For details of farmhouse accommodation, please send 9" × 4" SAE to **Mrs Beryl McEwan, The Farmhouse, 34 Shirrall Drive, Drayton Bassett, Tamworth, Staffs.** See also Group Display Advertisement in the **Board** section of this Guide.

SUFFOLK

BECCLES. Mrs S. J. Greene, Little Beck Farm, Becks Green Lane, Ilketshall St. Andrew, Beccles NR34 8NB (Ilketshall [098-681] 226). Accommodation attached to farmhouse comprises pine fitted kitchen with electric fridge and cooker; open-plan lounge and diningroom with TV and electric fire; shower, washbasin and toilet; second lounge. Two double bedrooms; one with two extra single beds makes a good family room; bathroom. Sleeps six plus cot. Electricity 50p meter. Central heating may be used by arrangement. Linen provided. Large gardens, patio with barbecue. Quietly situated with ample parking. We feel privileged to live in this attractive spot and welcome others to share it. Village stores one mile. Three miles within five miles. Coast 10 miles. Bookings throughout year. SAE for terms, please.

BECCLES. Mrs M. D. Patrick, Bulls Green Farm, Toft Monks, Beccles NR34 0HA (Aldeby [050-277] 276). Working farm. Two semi-detached country cottages, adjacent to farm, in a rural area close to Norwich, Yarmouth, Lowestoft and Broads. Car essential. Local grocery shop, fine old public house in village. Beccles three miles away. One double, two single beds, cot provided. Linen not provided. Hot and cold water; shower; colour TV; electric cooker and heaters; fridge (10p coin meter); outside flush toilet (three metres from back door). No pets allowed. Parking next to cottage. Ample space for children to play. SAE for terms. Open Easter to October.

BURY ST. EDMUNDS near. Bridge Cottage, Walsham-Le-Willows, Near Bury St. Edmunds. Bridge Cottage is illustrated in the book "English Cottages", with introduction by John Betjeman. It was built in the 17th century and has been attractively modernised. There are fitted carpets and comfortable beds; it is centrally heated and well furnished. The kitchen is well equipped with electric cooker and fridge. Plenty of hot water. Well behaved pets are welcome. Electricity included in rent. Colour TV. The cottage sleeps four, plus cot. Tennis court and swimming pool available by arrangement. Walsham-le-Willows is in the centre of East Anglia — 11 miles from Bury St. Edmunds and has shops and post office. Weekly terms £80 – £120. Available all year. **Mrs H. M. Russell, The Beeches, Walsham-Le-Willows, Near Bury St. Edmunds IP31 3AD (Walsham-Le-Willows [035 98] 227).**

EYE. Mrs Jenny Grover, Park View, Hall Farm, Yaxley, Eye IP23 8BY (Mellis [037-983] 423). Working farm, join in. The cottage is on a 250 acre stock and arable farm, where cattle, pigs and horses are kept. It stands beside a large meadow and has its own lawns and gardens. There are three bedrooms also bed setting; bathroom and separate WC. Downstairs there is a large lounge/diner with television; kitchen with electric cooker and fridge. All rooms are carpeted and have electric heaters. Electricity is from 50p meter. Baby's cot and babysitting available. Pets welcome. Village shop, Post Office and Cherry Tree Inn half-a-mile; Ipswich, Norwich and Bury St Edmunds, 20 miles; East Coast, 27 miles. Situated off the main A140 at Yaxley. Linen is supplied and pets are allowed. Open April to October. Car not essential but parking available. Weekly terms from £80. SAE, please.

FRESSINGFIELD. Mrs N. V. Upsdale, Lawn Farm, Fressingfield, Eye, Norfolk IP21 5SD (Fressingfield [037-986] 267). Situated at the heart of rural East Anglia, Fressingfield lies in North Suffolk midway between Ipswich and Norwich, one of the driest and sunniest parts of England. Newly renovated wing of Lawn Farm has lovely beamed sittingroom with open fire. Modern fitted kitchen with new electric cooker, fridge and all necessary equipment, ironing facilities. Five people accommodated in two double bedrooms (one twin-bedded), single room. Ample storage space. Oil-filled radiators. Modern bathroom. Children welcome, cot, high chair provided. Pets permitted. Car essential, parking space. Garden. Within easy reach are numerous places of interest — Norfolk Broads, the coast, charming resorts of Southwold and Aldeburgh, Minsmere Nature Reserve; many small market towns, Wildlife Parks, Museums and Craft Centres. Available all year. Weekly terms from £70 to £140 — bed linen, logs, electricity included.

Suffolk / Surrey   SELF-CATERING

HALESWORTH. Elizabeth House, Westhall, Halesworth. This delightful red-brick house with gardens and lawns, set on the hillside of a charming Suffolk village overlooking a valley of quiet countryside is available for holiday letting all year round. Westhall is an interesting village with its 12th century Norman Church, typical village pub and shop and rolling farmlands. Only seven miles from Southwold and Suffolk's Heritage coastline, this is an excellent base from which to tour Norfolk and Suffolk. Many places of interest, both historical and scenic, within easy driving distance. Lovely walking terrain. The accommodation, for six, comprises lounge (TV), diningroom, three double bedrooms; cot for baby; bathroom, toilet, modern kitchen with electric cooker, fridge, kettle, toaster, cutlery, crockery and cooking utensils. Electric heater. Car essential — parking. Children welcome. Pets permitted. Bargain breaks November to April. SAE, please, or telephone (evenings) to **Mrs O. A. D. Johnson, Becks End Farm, Westhall, Halesworth IP19 8OZ (Brampton [050279] 239).**

HALESWORTH. Blue Haw Cottage, The Street, Wissett, Halesworth. Compact self-contained bungalow sleeping two/four. One double bedroom (two single three-foot beds); one sittingroom/bedroom (full sized double bed in cupboard); kitchen/diner with electric cooker, fridge etc. Bathroom with bath, shower, basin and flush toilet. Children welcome and pets allowed. Car essential, parking space. Garden and patio. Within easy reach of Minsmere Bird Sanctuary, Framlingham Castle, windmills, Oulton Broad. Halesworth two miles. Village shop 50 yards. Swimming and riding Southwold and Walberswick nine miles. Norwich 22 miles. Available all year round. Babysitting by arrangement. Terms from £30 weekly. Apply **Mrs J. M. Macfarlane, Saffron Cottage, Wissett, Halesworth IP19 0JG (Halesworth [09867] 3631).**

HALESWORTH near. Mrs Elizabeth Warren, "Elm Farm", St. James Lane, St. James, Near Halesworth IP19 0HR (St. Cross [098-682] 431). Working farm. A spacious self-contained flat, sleeping up to five persons, set amid a family-run small farm. Especially suited for young children with a variety of farm animals to see. Pets considered. Farm produce is available and milk and papers can be delivered. The flat is fully equipped (linen extra), and there are radiators and electric fire. Available from April to October. Own transport essential. Ideally situated for many holiday activities, including horseriding, fishing and golf. Eight miles from the Broads and 12 miles from the sea. Terms from £50 to £80.

KESSINGLAND. Kessingland Cottages, Rider Haggard Lane, Kessingland, Near Lowestoft. An exciting three-bedroom newly built semi-detached cottage situated on the beach, three miles south of sandy beach of Lowestoft. Fully and attractively furnished with colour TV and delightful sea and lawn views from floor to ceiling windows of lounge. Accommodation for up to eight people. Well-equipped kitchen with electric cooker, fridge, hot and cold water; immersion heater. Electricity by 50p meter. Luxurious bathroom with coloured suite. No linen and towels provided. Only 30 yards to beach and sea fishing. One mile to wildlife country park with mini-train. Buses quarter mile and shopping centre half a mile. Parking, but car not essential. Children and disabled persons welcome. Available 1st March to 7th January. Weekly terms from £40 in early March and late December to £150 in peak season. SAE to **Mr S. Mahmood, 156 Bromley Road, Beckenham, Kent BR3 2PG (01-650-0539).**

SAFFRON WALDEN near. Mrs R. H. Alexander, Joslyns Farm, Great Sampford, Saffron Walden CB10 2NY (Great Sampford [079-986] 264). Working farm. On the Suffolk, Essex, Cambridgeshire borders, attractive 17th century detached beamed farm cottage set in its own grounds in a peaceful country lane surrounded by farmland and adjacent to our arable and stock farm. Ideally situated for quiet walks or visiting the many places of interest in historic and picturesque East Anglia. The cottage is fully equipped and comfortably furnished, has three bedrooms (sleeps 5/6), bathroom, toilet, sitting/diningroom (open fire and TV); kitchen with electric cooker, fridge etc. Nightstore heating free. Cot and high chair. Pets by prior arrangement. Village shops one mile.

SAXMUNDHAM. Mrs Mary Kitson, White House Farm, Sibton, Saxmundham IP17 2NE (Peasenhall [072-879] 260). Working farm. The flat is a self-contained part of late Georgian farmhouse standing in 130-acres of quiet farmland. It is a working farm with pigs, chickens, ponies, donkey. Fishing on farm. Accommodation in two double and one single bedrooms (sleeps five/six), cot; livingroom; shower/toilet on first floor. Entrance hall, kitchen/diner on ground floor. Situated one-and-a-half miles from village shops, etc. Ten miles from coast at Dunwich, Minsmere Bird Sanctuary, Snape Maltings. Linen optional. Pets permitted. Car essential — parking. Available all year. SAE, please, for terms.

SURREY

GODSTONE. Mr Oatway, Godstone Farm, Tilburstow Hill Road, Godstone (Godstone [0883] 842546). Cottage and flat on busy children's farm on Surrey/Kent border. A "Holiday with a Difference" for energetic, animal loving children. They can help with calves, pigs, rabbits, chicks, ponies and other farm jobs or play in adventure playground, in the woods or by the stream. Farm is one hour London and one hour coast and within walking distance of shops. Cottage sleeps four/five, and recently converted flat sleeps four. Both with fitted carpets, pine furniture and open fires. Car essential — parking available. Weekly rates from £55 to £120. Open all year.

SUSSEX

EAST SUSSEX

BATTLE. Mrs G. Malins, Old Farm Place, Catsfield, Battle TN33 9BN (Crowhurst [0424-83] 262). ✱
Situated in the hamlet of Henley Down within four miles of the sea at Bexhill amongst unspoilt farmland, a well furnished self-contained wing of attractive old farmhouse. Sleeps five with separate front door, car parking and use of small garden. Kitchen/diningroom and WC downstairs; sittingroom, three bedrooms, bath and WC upstairs. Everything provided except towels and sheets. Colour TV; electric cooker, fridge, deep freezer and night storage heaters with separate meter (not coin). Fortnightly bookings preferred in summer. From £50 per week depending on season. Available all year. SAE, for details. See also Colour Display Advertisement.

BATTLE. The Coach House, Burnt Wood, Battle. This accommodation is a newly converted coach house on a small private estate of 18 acres. It is available all year with wood stove and electric fires. Own transport essential, parking for three cars. Shops one mile. The accommodation sleeps four to six; one family bedroom and one room with bunk beds. Sittingroom with colour TV; bathroom; kitchen. Fully equipped including linen. Children are welcome and there is a cot. Electric meter. Weekly terms from £52.50. Open all year except Christmas. Tennis and bathing on premises; fishing 500 yards. **Mrs Jane Rolland, Burnt Wood, Powdermill Lane, Battle TN33 0SU (Battle [042-46] 2459).**

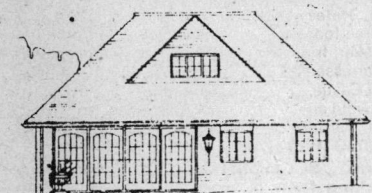

EAST SUSSEX. Large selection of holiday properties in south-west, south, south-east and up to West Midlands and East Anglia. Some suitable for the disabled. Available all year and out of season short breaks. See also quarter page display advertisement in the Kent section of guide. **Fairhaven Holiday Properties (Dept. 6), Fairhaven House, 37 Stuart Road, Gillingham, Kent ME7 4AD (Medway [0634] 570157).**

HAILSHAM near. Mrs B. J. Richards, The Merrie Harriers, Cowbeech, Near Hailsham (Herstmonceux [0323] 833108). This cottage stands in the grounds of the village inn. There is accommodation for up to five persons in two double bedrooms, cot available. Bathroom; kitchen with electric cooker, fridge, immersion heater; lounge/diningroom with inglenook fireplace, beams, colour TV. Large garden. Fully equipped including linen. Pets permitted. Car essential — parking. Village store 100 yards; sea eight miles. Open all year. Ideal spot for touring the many places of interest; including Eastbourne, Hastings, Battle, Herstmonceux Castle, Pevensey and the Downs. Weekly terms from £60. Electricity meter. Large SAE, please, for further details.

HASTINGS. Mrs Norris, Crowham Manor Farm, Westfield, Hastings TN35 4SR (Brede [0424] 882441). Working farm. Crowham Manor is set in the middle of a working farm in beautiful countryside. It lies between the historic towns of Battle and Rye, four miles from the sea at Hastings. Holiday guests can fish in the River Brede and have the use of a hard tennis court 100 yards from the house. The maisonette lies at one end of a large house and has its own entrance porch; a staircase leads to spacious accommodation consisting of kitchen, sittingroom, three large bedrooms and a separate bathroom and lavatory. It is well equipped for six, with washing machine and colour TV. Children and pets welcome. No linen supplied. Open all year. Car essential. Shops half-mile. Weekly terms on request.

UCKFIELD. Mr & Mrs C. P. and A. S. Wright, Brownings Farm, Blackboys, Uckfield TN22 5HG (Framfield [082-582] 338). Working farm. Five comfortable, well equipped cottages, including two Oast houses and a converted stable building, on 400-acre stock and arable farm. Situated in beautiful wooded countryside on edge of the High Weald Area of Outstanding Natural Beauty within easy reach of Ashdown Forest, South Downs and Sussex Coast and resorts of Eastbourne and Brighton. Many local places of interest including historic houses and castles, beautiful gardens and zoos and wildlife parks. Each cottage has well-equipped kitchen/diningroom with electric cooker, fridge, kettle, toaster and iron, a comfortable lounge with colour TV, electric heating and fitted carpets. Some cottages have telephones, automatic washing machines, cots and high chairs, and open fires. Bed linen is provided with beds made ready for visitors' arrival. Guests are welcome to watch farm activities or follow the FARM TRAILS, use the outdoor SWIMMING POOL and visit the CRAFT WORKSHOPS. Village one mile with shops and two public houses with restaurants. Gardens. Parking. Open all year. FREE illustrated brochure on request. Registered with English Tourist Board. Prices from £70 per week.

EAST SUSSEX – A POPULAR DESTINATION!
Apart from its famous resorts East Sussex has many attractions, such as, Ashdown Forest, Ditchling Common Country Park, Lullington Heath Wildlife Refuge, the Medieval town of Rye and Hastings Country Park.

WEST SUSSEX

HASSOCKS. Mrs Gill Pace, New Close Farm, London Road, Hassocks BN6 9ND (Hassocks [07918] 3144). Self-catering annexe flat (ground floor) on 90 acre farm has spacious garden overlooking farmland to South Downs. Accommodation for four persons in one double bedroom and one bedroom with double bunks. Cot and high chair. Interior of flat has been entirely rebuilt, redecorated; fully carpeted. Lounge/diningroom with colour TV. Fully equipped kitchen; 50p coin meter for heating etc. Bathroom. Please bring own linen. Ideally situated for touring Sussex — Brighton approximately nine miles, Hickstead (All-England Show Ground) five miles, South Downs three miles, Bluebell Railway etc. Car essential, hard stand for parking. Local pub with restaurant, Friars Oak, three quarters of a mile. Farm Nature Trail. Open all year. Terms from £85 to £95. Sorry, no pets.

PETWORTH. Mr and Mrs D. V. A. Craddock, The Manor House, Duncton, Petworth GU28 0JY (Petworth [0798] 42380). Manor House Cottage is a recent conversion from an 18th century Sussex hovel, it is adjacent to Duncton Manor and enjoys superb views over the South Downs in its farmland surroundings. The accommodation comprises a large beamed livingroom, double bedroom with en-suite bathroom, twin-bedded gallery bedroom and fully equipped modern kitchen. The location is ideal for Goodwood, Cowdray Park with polo and golf and is 15 miles from excellent south coast beaches. There are also many other places of interest in the neighbourhood. Linen supplied. Electric meter. Weekly terms from £100 to £120 including wood for the stove heater.

PULBOROUGH. Mrs L. C. Shiner, Coldharbour Farm, Sutton, Pulborough RH20 1PR (Sutton (West Sussex) [07987] 200). Working farm. This bungalow attached to the farmhouse on a 160-acre farm is in a beautiful quiet position on the north side of the South Downs. A drive of 20 minutes to Chichester, Arundel, Petworth; 12 miles to sea, five miles to shops. Accommodation comprises two double rooms, one with double and single beds, sleeping five. Cot available. Bathroom, sittingroom/kitchen with electric cooker, fridge, colour TV. Convector heaters. No linen supplied. Pets allowed. Car essential — ample parking. Electricity by 50p meter. Many lovely walks including 'South Downs Way'. Open all year. SAE please for further details.

STEYNING. Mr A. and Mrs P. J. R. Barnicott, Down House Flats, King's Barn Villas, Steyning BN4 3FA (Steyning [0903] 812319). Two fully furnished and equipped holiday flats with panoramic views of the South Downs, attached to well situated Edwardian guest house standing in large, sunny gardens, at the end of private road. Ample parking. Less than ten minutes' walk from the historic town centre of Steyning. Ground floor flat has two double bedrooms, lounge, modern kitchen, bathroom/toilet and small rear garden/courtyard. First floor flat has one double bedroom, large lounge with sleeping alcove, modern kitchen, bathroom/toilet. Both flats have their own gas-fired boiler which provides hot water and full central heating. Electric cookers and fridges. Colour TV free of charge. Linen supplied. Children over five years welcome. Dogs on short visits only. Coin box telephone in communal porch. Postage only or phone for full terms. Tourist Board and AA listed.

WEST GRINSTEAD. Mrs A. Hartnett, Belmoredean Farms, Maplehurst Road, West Grinstead, Horsham RH13 6RN (Cowfold [040-386] 301). Working farm. Belmoredean Farms is 400-acre arable farm, with beef cattle, situated in beautiful countryside, five miles south of Horsham; half-an-hour's drive from Brighton and one hour from London. South Downs, Chanctonbury, Petworth, Singleton Museum easy distance. West Cottages are off the road in half-acre garden surrounded by farmland. Local shops one mile. Modern kitchen and bathroom, sittingroom, diningroom, three bedrooms. All-electric. Sleeps five plus cot. Well furnished; colour TV. Ample parking. Terms from £63 to £98. Also detached Georgian farmhouse surrounded by farmland. Services as above. Solid fuel central heating. £65 to £125.

WEST SUSSEX – COASTAL RESORTS AND DOWNS!
Although dominated perhaps by Bognor Regis, West Sussex does have much to offer. Places like Marden-Stoughton Forest, Midhurst, and its historic inn, the open-air museum at Singleton and the National Butterfly Museum at Bramber are worth a visit.

# WARWICKSHIRE

ALCESTER. Beams, 16 Mill Lane, Oversley Green, Alcester. This 200-year-old terraced cottage has new wing and garage added in period style. Central heating supplies hot water. Rear views of river meadows. Alcester, half-a-mile, dates from Roman times; Stratford-upon-Avon, eight miles. Cottage, comfortably furnished to accommodate four in two double bedrooms, sittingroom; diningroom; bathroom; kitchen with electric cooker, fridge and sink unit. (The dining kitchen and TV lounge are open plan with beamed ceilings and period decor). Available all year. Shops half-a-mile; pets permitted. Everything except linen supplied. Weekly terms include heating and water but cooker is metered. SAE, please, for further particulars and terms: **Mrs B. Ross, 3 Newport Drive, Alcester B49 5BL (Alcester [0789] 764491).**

SHIPSTON-ON-STOUR. Church View Cottage, Shipston-on-Stour. Church View Cottage adjoins a delightful old Cotswold Farmhouse, one of the beautiful original houses in the picturesque little village of Great Wolford. Located on a 90-acre dairy farm, the accommodation comprises a charming 10'6" × 17' lounge with leaded windows and oak beams, comfortably furnished with colour TV and double bed settee, fully fitted kitchen with electric cooker and fridge, ample working surfaces, small bathroom/toilet with handbasin and electric shower, bedroom equipped with bunk beds, a washbasin, Continental quilts and linen. Children welcome and pets accepted. Milk provided free. The ideal choice for a family of four looking for a relaxing, comfortable holiday. Open April to October, cot, high chair if required. Babysitting can be arranged. Weekly terms from £60. **Mrs Shirley Wrench, Hillside Farm, Great Wolford, Shipston-on-Stour CU36 5NQ (Barton Heath [060 874] 389).**

WILTSHIRE

DEVIZES. Mrs M. I. Marks, Mulberry Lodge, Rowde, Devizes SN10 2QQ (Devizes [0380] 3056). Come and relax in Wiltshire. Devizes two miles. Self contained, fully equipped furnished flat sleeping five/six in wing of Georgian farm house. Large bedroom with double and single beds, second bedroom (curtain divided) with two windows, three single beds, cot; annexe with single beds; bathroom, toilet; sitting/diningroom; TV, electric fires. Kitchen with electric cooker and fridge; 10p meter. Linen not included. This small farm is on fringe of village; ideal for children. Badminton on lawns (garden, orchard). Touring centre (Avebury, Longleat, Bath, Salisbury, Stonehenge). Swimming pool, fishing. Shops nearby. Ample parking by door. Weekly terms or weekends. Senior citizens welcome. SAE, please, for brochure.

DEVIZES. Mr C. Fletcher, Lower Foxhangers Farm, Rowde, Devizes SN10 1SS (Seend [038-082] 254). Working farm. Colin and Cynthia Fletcher invite you to enjoy a farm holiday by the Kennet and Avon canal in Wiltshire. Boating (dinghies or canoes); coarse fishing in season. Walk canal towpath, downland or woods. Easy reach of Bath, Longleat, Stonehenge and the villages of Avebury, Lacock. Horse riding, public golf course, tennis, heated swimming pool within 15 minutes' drive. Accommodation in 37' mobile home with two bedrooms, bathroom, kitchen, sittingroom with TV; sleeps four. Situated in farm orchard. Open April to September, from £70 – £110 per week. Farmhouse Bed and Breakfast also available. Leaflet and booking form by return. Children and pets welcome.

MARLBOROUGH. Miss E. L. Kilpatrick, Herridge Farm, Collingbourne Ducis, Marlborough SN8 3EG (Collingbourne Ducis [026-485] 270). This attractive brick and flint cottage is set in peaceful surroundings on a racehorse stud farm. Within easy reach of Cotswolds, Bath, Oxford, Stonehenge, Salisbury and Winchester. Birdwatching, walking, golf, racing, swimming within 20 miles. Shop two miles. Steep stair. Small garden; accommodation for six and baby. Two double bedrooms, one single, bathroom downstairs. Sittingroom with open fire, colour TV. Diningroom with central heating stove. Kitchen with electric cooker, fridge and washing machine, immersion heater, electric fires. Well trained pets allowed. Car essential. Linen and fuel extra. Electricity 50p meter. Open all year round. Saturday bookings. £45-£100 weekly; £20 deposit. SAE, please.

SALISBURY. Mr and Mrs Peter and Heather Coward, Jervoise Farm, Coombe Bissett, Salisbury SP5 4LN (Coombe Bissett [072-277] 230). Two attractive properties available at Jervoise Farm, approximately five miles south of Salisbury, giving magnificent views over open farmland. FARMHOUSE FLAT, tastefully converted, sleeps eight, plus baby — fully fitted kitchen/diner (electric cooker, fridge, washing machine etc.); shower room; upstairs lounge with colour TV, electric fire, single chair bed; two double bedded rooms, plus single beds and cot. Fully carpeted. Electricity by 50p meter. Parking for two/three cars. FARM COTTAGE, sleeps six, plus baby — enclosed by fences, safe for young children — kitchen/diner, fully equipped (electric cooker, fridge, washing machine, etc.); bathroom; lounge with colour TV, electric fire; three bedrooms (double, single beds, cot). Electricity by 50p meter. Ample parking. Outdoor swimming pool, nine-hole putting green available for tenants' use. Golf course. Racecourse, riding stables within short distance. Please phone or write for brochure.

Wiltshire SELF-CATERING

SALISBURY. Mrs E. Pickford, Red House Farm, East Knoyle, Salisbury SP3 6AT (East Knoyle [074-783] 294). Splendid touring area amongst lovely countryside. Four miles from Saxon hilltop town of Shaftesbury. On Wiltshire/Dorset border within easy motoring distance Bath, Bournemouth, Longleat, Salisbury, Stonehenge, Stourhead, Sherborne, Wilton etc. Barn conversion by architect; small beamed cottage, fully equipped, sleeps four. Cot available. Kitchen/diner, electric cooker, fridge, spin dryer. Sittingroom with colour TV, night storage heater. Shower room with washbasin and toilet; two double bedrooms, one with vanitory unit; dimplex radiators. Towels and bed linen supplied. All electricity by meter. Small enclosed garden with patio. Use of heated pool and barbecue in season. Sorry, no pets. Open all year. SAE for details.

WARMINSTER. Olde Cheese House, Upton Lovell, Warminster. Working farm. The Olde Cheese House is warm and cosy, situated on a small farm half-a-mile from the A36. Self-contained and flanked by a drive with iron gates, garage and parking space, in a secluded garden overlooking fields in the heart of Wylye Valley. Three double bedrooms and one single for six; cot; bathroom and two toilets; sittingroom, TV, open fire; diningroom/kitchen, electric cooker, fridge, electric oil-fired radiators in all rooms, gas heater, metered electricity, immersion heater, bed settee, high chair. One dog allowed. Linen may be hired. Shop one mile. Shooting on farm. Riding horses may be hired locally. Open all year. Interesting places to visit; Longleat, Wilton House, Stonehenge, Salisbury, Bath. Weekly terms £46-£80. Weekend breaks available in winter. Large SAE, please, for brochure to **Mrs P. D. Dyke, Beechcroft Farm, Upton Lovell, Warminster BA12 0JW (Warminster [0985] 50383).**

WILTSHIRE – "WHITE" HORSE COUNTY!

Many "White" horses adorn The Wiltshire chalk downs and the prehistoric theme continues with Stonehenge and Avebury. Also of interest are the landscape gardens at Studley, Chiselbury Camp, The Kennet and Avon canal with lock "staircase", Salisbury Plain, and the abandoned city Old Sarum.

For the Mutual Guidance of Guest and Host

Farm Holiday Guides Ltd. do not inspect or recommend accommodation but advertisers agree to accept our Farm Holiday Guide standards of comfortable and clean accommodation and wholesome and well-cooked food. Advertisers are also bound by the Trades Description Act.

When accommodation has been booked, deposits sent, and letters of acceptance exchanged, both parties – host and guest – have entered into a binding contract.

Friends and families can easily be upset and much bitterness caused if holiday arrangements are not carefully made. The following points can be of real importance:

Guest When enquiring about accommodation, be as precise as possible. Give exact dates, numbers in your party and the ages of any children. State the number and type of rooms wanted and also what catering you require – bed and breakfast, full board etc. Make sure that the position about evening meals is clear – and about pets, reductions for children or any other special points.

Read our reviews carefully to ensure that the proprietors you are going to contact can supply what you want. Ask for a letter confirming all arrangements, if possible.

Host Give details about your facilities and about any special conditions. Explain your deposit system clearly and arrangements for cancellations, charges etc, and whether or not your terms include VAT.

We regret that Farm Holiday Guides cannot accept responsibility for any errors or omissions in descriptions. Prices in particular should be checked before booking because of the early compilation of the Guides, far ahead of the next holiday season.

YORKSHIRE

EAST YORKSHIRE

DRIFFIELD near. Manor Farm Cottage, Foxholes, Near Driffield. Manor Farm Cottage is a detached brick cottage with garage and enclosed garden in small wolds village 12 miles from East Coast and within easy drive to Yorkshire Moors and York. Three double bedrooms accommodating six. Bathroom, toilet, sittingroom with colour TV and open fireplace with electric fire. Diningroom. Fully equipped electric kitchen. Immersion heater in bathroom. Open from May to October. Pets are allowed. SAE, please, for terms and further details to **Mrs M. Lamplough, Manor Farm, Foxholes, Near Driffield YO25 0QH (Thwing [026-287] 255).**

DRIFFIELD. The Forge, Front Street, Burton Fleming, Driffield. Spacious accommodation for a self-catering holiday in this fully furnished house situated near the centre of the village of Burton Fleming, close to the shops, Post Office, public house. Ideal for touring country or seaside. Bridlington, seven and a half miles, Filey six miles, and Scarborough 12 miles. Three double bedrooms, with a double and a single bed in each, also two single bedrooms and two cots, one bathroom and toilet; sittingroom, television, kitchen/diner, electric cooker, fridge, washing machine, immersion heater. Please bring own linen. Swimming pools at Bridlington and Scarborough; within easy reach of York, Whitby and Flamingo Park. SAE, please, for terms to **Mrs E. Wilson, Glebe Farm, Rudston, Driffield YO25 0UG (Kilham [026-282] 201).**

RUDSTON. Hind Cottage, Rudston House, Rudston, Near Driffield. Hind Cottage is a clean, well-equipped cottage of character on a farm in the village of Rudston, where authoress Winifred Holtby was born. Five miles from Bridlington, handy for coast and country. It sleeps six/seven people in two double and one single rooms; cot provided. There is a bathroom with toilet; sittingroom with TV; diningroom and kitchen with electric cooker and fridge, etc. Electric fires and open coal fire if required (50p electric meter installed). Sea fishing, pony trekking locally. Cottage available Easter to Christmas. Terms £80 per week in season, £90 in August. Reduced rates out of season. **Mrs Angela Dawson, Rudston House, Rudston, Near Driffield YO25 0UH (Kilham [026-282] 400).**

NORTH YORKSHIRE

AUSTWICK. Blythesgarth Cottage, Eldroth, Austwick. Detached cottage on a farm two miles from Austwick and six from Settle. Panoramic views of Ingleborough and the surrounding countryside. Ideal situation for exploring the Yorkshire Dales and within easy reach of the Lake District and West coast. Sleeps six in three bedrooms, two with double bed, one with two singles. Cot available. Bathroom with WC; lounge; kitchen/diner with electric cooker, fridge, immersion heater, kettle, iron. Electricity extra. Comfortably furnished and fully equipped (except linen). TV. Garage. Car essential. Part central heating, included in rent from October to May. Sorry, no pets. Open all year. Stamp only, please, for brochure and terms to **Mrs M. Booth, Slated House, Eldroth, Austwick, Lancaster LA2 8AG (Clapham [046-85] 365).**

BEDALE. Mr F. E. Hudson, Winterfield House, Hornby, Bedale DL8 1NN (Richmond (N. Yorks) [0748] 811619). Two cottages situated in a beautiful parkland setting between Bedale and Leyburn, both facing south. Approached by a long private drive to the main house, they are away from traffic and ideally suited to children. Seven miles from Leyburn, within easy reach of the Moors, two national parks, Wharfedale, beaches and Lake District etc. Village shop and post office one mile; market town of Bedale four miles. Car essential — parking. Winterfield Cottage, modern, detached with own garden. Kitchen/diningroom, larder, sittingroom, TV; downstairs WC; three bedrooms (one double, one twin, one single). Bathroom. Garden Cottage, older and covered with roses and virginia creeper. Small lawn. Kitchen, diningroom, sittingroom, TV; one double and one twin bedrooms; bathroom, WC; also outside WC. Cots provided. Slot meter (50p) electricity. No linen supplied. Well controlled dogs allowed. Terms on request.

Terms quoted in this publication may be subject to increase if rises in costs necessitate

BURTON-IN-LONSDALE. Poachers Cottage and Badgers Gate Barn, Leeming Lane, Burton-in-Lonsdale. Beautiful 17th century stone cottage and superb 17th century barn in picturesque village near Kirkby Lonsdale. Quiet and unspoilt with lovely wooded scenery, within half an hour's drive of Windermere and 15 minutes from Yorkshire Dales. Many interesting walks and places to visit — all amidst glorious scenery. Both the cottage and barn are superbly equipped and maintained to very high standards. Both have lounge with stone fireplace (log fires and central heating are inclusive); well fitted and equipped kitchens. The cottage has two bedrooms; one double, one with three singles and fully tiled shower/WC/basin. The barn which has a fantastic lounge with magnificent oak beams, sleeps six with one double bedroom, one with two singles and a comfortable sofa bed. Fully tiled luxury bath/shower/WC/basin, and second WC/basin. Please telephone or write for further details: **Mrs Sandra Wood, The Goodies Farmhouse, Firbank, Sedbergh, Cumbria LA10 5BF (0587-21087 or 0468 62184).**

BURTON-IN-LONSDALE. Mrs S. M. Howard, West View, High Street, Burton-in-Lonsdale, Via Carnforth, Lancashire LA6 3JP (Bentham [0468] 61401). West View Cottage is centrally situated in the picturesque village of Burton-in-Lonsdale which lies on a very pretty stretch of the River Greta surrounded by high fells and dales which make delightful walking country. Within half-an-hour's drive of Windermere, Trough of Bowland and Morecambe, and 15 minutes from Yorkshire Dales National Park. The cosy, 18th century end-terrace cottage is comfortably furnished. Entrance/sittingroom has exposed beams, open fire and colour TV. Downstairs shower room with WC and washbasin; well fitted kitchen/diningroom; electric cooker, fridge freezer, storage heater. One twin bedroom with storage heater and washbasin; one double with single bed. All fuel, electricity and linen included in rent. Garden, parking space. SAE for brochure.

FILEY near. "The Poop", Watson's Lane, Reighton, Near Filey. "The Poop" is situated in its own private garden overlooking the horses' four-acre field. Only one mile from the sea, with outstanding views of Filey Bay, the cedar wood bungalow is an ideal base for those seeking peace and quiet or for touring the Moors and coast. There is accommodation for six people plus a baby. The bungalow is equipped with modern conveniences (colour TV) for all year letting, weekend lettings out of season. Holiday facilities are available at nearby Bridlington and Scarborough. Pets by arrangement. Local bus and rail service. Shops five minutes' walk. Suitable for disabled guests — ramp to sun lounge, extra wide doors. Parking. Electricity by 50p meter. Please send SAE and telephone **Mrs R. A. Alderton, "Stubberhill", Watson's Lane, Reighton, Near Filey YO14 9SD (Scarborough [0723] 890394).**

GLAISDALE, near Whitby. No. 10 High Street and High Leas (Flat), Glaisdale. The cottage is a large family house situated on the main village street with an enclosed garden at the rear overlooking fields and Dales; five minutes' walk from the moors. Fully equipped kitchen; three large bedrooms; large bathroom. Lounge with B/W TV. Electricity by 50p meter. Pets welcome. HIGH LEAS FLAT adjoins the owner's country residence, surrounded by gardens and overlooking the Dales and moors. Fully equipped kitchenette/diner; sittingroom with B/W TV. Electricity included in terms. One double bedroom; bathroom, toilet. No linen supplied. Pets are welcome. Open Easter to November, special terms early and late season. Glaisdale is a village 10 miles from Whitby and there are many interesting places to visit including the North Yorkshire Moors Railway, the fishing ports of Staithes and Sandsend, and Robin Hood's Bay. High Leas is half mile from village. Ideal walking country. Weekly terms on request from **Mrs Susan Harland, High Leas, Glaisdale, Near Whitby YO21 2PX (Whitby [0947] 87255).**

GOATHLAND. Darnholme Farm, Darnholme, Goathland, Whitby. This large mobile home on single private site is conveniently situated in the North Yorkshire Moors National Park on the outskirts of this popular moorland village. An ideal base for walking and touring. A short nine mile journey takes you to the sandy beaches at Whitby. A great favourite with railway enthusiasts is the steam train running through Goathland to Pickering. Accommodation sleeps four in two double bedrooms with fitted cupboards, bathroom with flush toilet, lounge with TV, fitted kitchen with full size cooker, fridge, immersion heater. Everything supplied except linen. Electricity on 50p meter. Regret, no pets. SAE, please, or telephone **Mrs H. Graham, Hunt House Farm, Goathland, Whitby YO22 5AP (Whitby [0947] 86250).**

GROSMONT. Mrs D. Hodgson, Fairhead Farm, Grosmont, Whitby YO22 5PN (Whitby [0947] 85238). Working farm. Grosmont is a beautiful Eskdale village with steam railway. The modernised farmhouse which is on a 172 acre dairy/sheep farm is pleasantly situated in quiet area, with superb views, half mile from Grosmont village. Downstairs — good size lounge with open fire, colour TV; diningroom; kitchen, fridge, washer, full size cooker. Upstairs — three bedrooms; bathroom/toilet; three double beds; two single; cot; sleeps six to eight. Heating/cooking by electricity. (50p slot meter). Ample parking space. Children welcome. Sorry no pets. Ideal touring base for moors and coast. Reduced terms early and late season. SAE please or telephone. Open all year.

HAROME. Mrs I. Rickatson, Summerfield Farm, Harome, York YO6 5JJ (Nunnington [043-95] 238). Working farm. Enjoy walking or touring in North Yorkshire Moors National Park. Lovely area 20 miles north of historic city of York. Modernised, comfortable and well equipped farmhouse wing; sleeps four/six plus cot. Kitchen equipped with electric cooker, fridge and washing machine. Sit beside a log fire in the evenings. Linen not supplied. Weekly terms from £60 to £80. Open March to November. Mid-week bookings are possible in April and October. For further information send SAE, or phone.

HARROGATE. Mrs O. Hammond, Harewell Hall Glasshouses, Harrogate HG3 5QQ (Harrogate [0423] 711487). This flat is part of a 17th-century farmhouse. It accommodates five in one double, one single and one twin-bedded room plus cot; bathroom; sitting room; kitchen with electric cooking facilities. Children welcome. Sorry, no pets. Car essential, plenty of parking space. Shops one mile, public transport half-a-mile. Open from June to September. This accommodation is in the centre of the Yorkshire Dales and has many beautiful walks, day fishing, rock climbing, caves, musuem and sports centre all within easy reach. Terms include fuel. Rates on application.

RUDDING PARK HOLIDAY COTTAGES – HARROGATE

Luxury Cottages & Lodges on a private Estate have been converted to make ideal holiday homes for 2/9 persons. Each Cottage has been sympathetically restored retaining its traditional charm. They are equipped to the highest standard including central heating, washing machine and telephone. Situated in an attractive rural setting close to picturesque Follifoot Village yet only 3 miles south of Harrogate. Heated swimming pool, mini golf and children's playground available for our guests. Illustrated brochure:

**Rudding Park Holiday Cottages, Follifoot, Harrogate HG3 1DT
TEL: (0423) 870439.**

HARROGATE. Mrs Betty Ingleby, Dougill Hall, Summerbridge, Harrogate HG3 4JR (Harrogate [0423] 780277). Dougill Hall Flat occupies the top floor of the Hall, which is of Georgian design, built in 1722 by the Dougill family who lived on this farm from 1496 to 1803. It is in Nidderdale, half a mile from the village of Summerbridge, just by the River Nidd, where there is fishing available for visitors. There are good facilities for horse riding, tennis, swimming, squash, etc. Well situated for the walking enthusiast and within easy reach of the Dales, the beautiful and ancient city of York, Fountains Abbey, How Stean Gorge and many other places of interest. The flat sleeps up to seven people. Well equipped, with electric cooker and fridge, iron, vacuum cleaner. No linen supplied. Pets permitted. Car essential, parking. The old Cooling House flat attached to the house is now available and sleeps four. SAE, please, for terms.

HAWES. River View, Dyers Garth, Hawes. A spacious three-bedroomed terraced cottage, River View is situated in a cul-de-sac overlooking "Duerley Beck" an attractive trout stream which runs through Hawes, a market town in the centre of Yorkshire Dales National Park and on the Pennine Way. The cottage has the benefit of storage heaters and also an open coal fire for out of season lets which is an attraction. An ideal situation for walking, fishing and visits to local scenic attractions which include Hardraw Scar, Aysgarth Falls and coach museum, Bolton Castle with the Lake District approximately 30 miles away. The cottage accommodates six plus baby (cot); three double bedrooms, bathroom, sittingroom with TV and fully equipped kitchen/diner. Shops 30 yards. Parking one car. SAE, please, for terms to **Mrs Sheila Alderson, "Inverdene," Hawes DL8 2NJ (Hawes [096-97] 408).**

HELMSLEY. Bank Cottage, Sproxton, Helmsley. A beautiful detached stone character cottage situated on the edge of the small village of Sproxton by the B1257 road. The cottage has several interesting features and lovely views from the rear over surrounding woodland and countryside. Week-end booking in winter. Accommodation:— sleeping seven, plus cot, in four bedrooms — one double bedroom, bunk bedded room, one single bedroom. Downstairs one twin-bedded room with beamed ceiling. Electric heaters all rooms. Sitting/diningroom with beamed ceiling, storage heater, stone open fireplace. Electric fire, radiator, colour TV on meter (50p for five hours). Kitchen with single beam, sink unit, electric cooker, fridge and washer, units. Gas heater. Fully equipped. Bathroom and toilet downstairs with immersion heater. Pets permitted. Large garden, garage and parking space. Ideal for touring and walking on North Yorkshire Moors and visiting historical places including York; coastal resorts 30 miles away. Other cottages available, also new stone bungalow and four-bedroomed house (built 1981 and 1983) and converted chapel near Pickering. Babysitting available. Apply, SAE, **Mrs B. Armstrong, Golden Square Farm, Oswaldkirk, York YO6 5YQ (Ampleforth [04393] 269).**

Lily Hall Farm
Uppermarsh Lane, Oxenhope, Near Keighley, W. Yorkshire

A choice of holiday is available at this farm which is situated about 300 yards from Farmhouse in open country in the 17th century hamlet of Upper Marsh, one mile from Haworth and ideal for exploring Bronte country. A LUXURY, DETACHED COTTAGE with panelled kitchen, split level oven and hob; spacious lounge with dining area and colour TV; one double, one twin and one single bedrooms, bathroom, large porch and entrance hall. Carpeted throughout. Duvets, blankets, pillows supplied but no linen or towels. Heating included in price; no meters. Sorry, no pets. The owners are always on hand to give help and information and they also offer BED AND BREAKFAST ACCOMMODATION at the AA listed farmhouse. Good value, from £8 per person. Optional Evening Meal.

Tel: Haworth (0535) 43999. Mr & Mrs J. S. W. Scholes – Proprietors.

KNARESBOROUGH. 2 Low Hall Cottages, Farnham, Knaresborough. Working farm. This fully modernised nicely furnished farm cottage is situated about 300 yards from Farmhouse in open country with lovely views. Near Yorkshire Dales and only 15 miles from historic city of York and many historic houses such as Harewood House and Newby Hall. Local fishing and golf available; lovely area for country walks. The farm is mainly arable with single suckled herd of Hereford Cattle. Guests have the freedom of the farm. Accommodation for five in two double bedrooms; cot; bathroom, toilet; sittingroom, dining/kitchen with all electric facilities; pay telephone. Everything except linen supplied. Shops one-and-a-half miles. Pets allowed and it is available all year. Car essential, parking. Weekly terms on request with SAE, please, to **Mr T. M. Hall, Low Hall, Farnham, Knaresborough HG5 9JF (Copgrove [090-14] 262).**

LEYBURN. "Karnten," Main Street, Askrigg, Leyburn. Comfortable family cottage, converted from an old coach house, makes an excellent base for both walking and touring the Dales, Lake District and the West Coast. The cottage, situated in the picturesque Wensleydale village of Askrigg, is open all year. Accommodation comprises three bedrooms and a bed/sittingroom, sleeping eight people, plus a cot. The main living/diningroom has a feature stone fireplace and colour TV. The newly-modernised kitchen is fully equipped, electric cooker; fridge; storage/electric/coal heating. Everything supplied except linen. Children and their pets welcome. Car preferable, but not essential — carport. Shops/public transport 100 yards approximately. Storage heaters included in terms; electricity on meter; coal extra. Please send SAE for brochure and terms to **Mrs H. Owen, 57 Vernon Road, Ward Green, Barnsley, South Yorkshire S70 5HQ (Barnsley [0226] 243718 (evenings) 743156 (daytime).**

LEYBURN. Lime Tree Cottage, Spennithorne, Leyburn. Lime Tree Cottage is situated in Spennithorne, a beautiful little unspoilt village in Lower Wensleydale two miles from the market town of Leyburn. Spennithorne is well placed as a centre for touring and walking in Yorkshire's two National Parks, The Yorkshire Dales National Park only four miles distant and the North York Moors National Park, 25 miles to the east. The cottage has accommodation for four persons, one bedroom with twin beds and one bedroom with two single beds. The furnishings are of a high standard and everything is provided with the exception of sheets, pillowcases and towels, which visitors are asked to bring with them. There is car parking available in Spennithorne House Stable Yard behind the cottage. Children are welcome (cot). Pets allowed. Two miles from shops, available from April to November 1st inclusive. Weekly terms from £80 to £115. Enquiries welcome, write or phone please — **Colonel P. T. Van Straubenzee, D.S.O., D.L., Spennithorne House, Leyburn DL8 5PR (Wensleydale [0969] 23200).**

MASHAM. Nelson House and Flats, Sunnyside House, Masham. Very comfortable accommodation in cottages and apartments equipped to a high standard, in old Wensleydale town. Ideal fishing, pony trekking, golf, walking or touring in Yorkshire Dales or Moors. Many places of historical interest. Flats overlook large market square, Sunnyside Cottage, Coach House in grounds of Sunnyside, edge of town. Colour TV, bed linen, Irons, drying facilities, showers, as well as baths in most units. Fitted carpets, electric cookers, fridges, fitted kitchens, immersions heaters. Flats sleep two to six persons; cottages four to eight. SAE, please, for brochure **Mrs J. I. Airton, Sunnyside, Masham HG4 4HH (Ripon [0765] 89327).**

PLEASE SEND A STAMPED ADDRESSED ENVELOPE WITH ENQUIRIES

MASHAM. Lyme Croft, Park Drive, Masham. Detached modern bungalow in market town of Masham. Golf, bowling, fishing, tennis, children's playground and lovely walks. Ideal for touring Yorkshire Dales and Herriot Country, also for visiting York, Harrogate and Richmond. The bungalow is fully equipped, except linen, and sleeps five. One double and one family room; bathroom and separate WC. Entrance hall; large lounge with gas fire and TV; dining/kitchen with coal fire, electric cooker, fridge. Fitted carpets and curtains. Garage and parking. Garden to front and rear. Electricity and heating included in rent. Sorry, no pets or children under seven years. SAE, please, for further details. **Mrs N. E. Dyson, Gebdykes Farm, Masham HG4 4BT (Ripon [0765] 89343).**

YORKSHIRE DALES AND NORTH YORKSHIRE MOORS

Good selection of self catering properties in locations ranging from high moors to peaceful dales and bustling market towns.

For free colour brochure
☎ **0532 668118** 24 HRS
or write
148, HARROGATE ROAD LEEDS LS7 4NZ

Kings Cottages

NORTH YORK MOORS NATIONAL PARK (GLAISDALE). Two stone-built cottages situated on quiet "No Through Road," with splendid views, overlooking the Esk Valley. Spacious and well-maintained garden and grounds. Each cottage (recently renovated and modernised) has two bedrooms with beamed ceilings, lounge, bathroom and large dining/kitchen. All modern electrical appliances are provided. Glaisdale is an ideal centre for touring, walking, or just relaxing. Ten miles from historic seaport of Whitby, four miles from North York Moors Steam Railway, one mile from magnificent moors. Footpaths are profuse, allowing full appreciation of the beautiful countryside. Open all year. SAE to: **Mr and Mrs J. R. Hoggarth, Thorneywaite House, Glaisdale, Whitby YO21 2QU (Whitby [0947] 87338).**

PICKERING. Mrs J. Carter, Grove House, Levisham, Pickering YO18 7NN (Pickering [0751] 72351]. Grove House is a beautiful old country residence set in one acre of garden, bounded by woodland, pine forest and moors; ideal for walkers and nature lovers. A picturesque railway runs through the valley and the car can be left at home for trips to Pickering on market day, and Whitby. Grove Cottage is newly converted from the Groom's cottage in the garden to form a completely self-contained unit and restored to a high standard. The accommodation consists of entrance hall and large kitchen with sink unit, electric cooker, fridge and dining area. Separate bathroom with shower and WC. One bedroom, fully fitted with twin beds. Comfortable lounge with convertible bed-settee. Electricity is charged by meter. Linen is not provided. A warm welcome to all guests.

PICKERING. Mr P. R. Holmes, Townend Farm, Pickering YO18 7HU (Pickering [0751] 72713). A well appointed detached house situated on a country road on the outskirts of Pickering. It has a large garden, garage and sun porch leading on to a patio. Two bedrooms upstairs; third bedroom and bathroom downstairs. Also dining room, sitting room, kitchen with fridge, electric cooker, colour television, electric fires and gas central heating. The property is checked before the arrival of visitors as our aim is to cater for those who wish for the best. House trained pets welcome. Pickering is a good centre for touring the North Yorkshire Moors, Forestry and parks. Riding, golf and own fly fishing in the vicinity. Winter weekends available. SAE for enquiries.

PICKERING. 1 Hallgarth, Pickering. The glorious Yorkshire Moors and Dales appeal to lovers of beauty and countryside and this end-terrace stone house is a grand centre for touring the lovely surroundings. Situated in the centre of an interesting market town, it is available all year. Accommodation for six. One double and one single bedrooms; cot; bathroom; inside and outside toilets; lounge and diningroom; kitchen with electric cooker. Fridge and iron, washer, etc. Solid fuel central heating. Electric blankets, fires, immerser. Fully furnished except for linen. High chair, baby bath, Car essential, parking nearby. Pets allowed. Metered electricity. North Yorkshire Moors, Rievaulx Abbey, Castle Howard and Pickering Castle, all a "must" for tourists. SAE, please, to **Mr R. Dobson, 3 Westgate Avenue, Bolton, Gt. Manchester BL1 4RF (Bolton [0204] 33869).**

PICKERING. Mrs M. Petch, Grindale House, Eastgate, Pickering YO18 7DW (Pickering [0751] 72736). Well appointed furnished cottage, sleeps four. Cottage includes fishing rights, colour TV, Dimplex radiators and fires. Very well equipped and cleaned weekly. Well behaved pets welcome at no extra charge Very convenient for both coastal and moorland areas. Ample parking. SAE, please, stating dates preferred.

PICKERING. Mrs D. Dove, Mount Terrace, Pickering YO18 8JH (Pickering [0751] 72546). This cottage, overlooking the Castle, stands in two acres of trees and lawns, within easy walking distance of Pickering and a short drive from the moors and various historic ruins. Apart from the house of the owner, who personally supervises the cottage, the nearest houses are about 200 yards away. Accommodation for three, in a double bedroom and a single room which also has bath, wash-basin and immerser. Sitting-room with country views, TV and electric fire. Dining kitchen with electric cooker and fire; separate walk-in pantry. Outside flush toilet. Blankets provided, bring your own linen and towels. 10p electric meter. Milk delivered if required. Sorry, no pets. Car essential, parking available. Shops 10 minutes, sea 16 miles. SAE for details.

RICHMOND. Mrs Kathleen Hird, Smarber, Low Row, Richmond DL11 6PX (Richmond [0748] 86243). Working farm. Spacious stone-built farm cottage set along a private road high on the north side of Swaledale overlooking the River Swale, one mile from Low Row. Accommodating seven people in three double bedrooms; cot provided; bathroom, shower; sittingroom. Fully equipped electric kitchen with cooker and fridge. No linen supplied. The house has part central heating. Sorry, no pets. The cottage has a private garden and is ideal for children. Many places of historic interest to visit including Folk Museum at Reeth (five miles), Swaledale Woollens at Muker (six miles), Aysgarth Falls (10 miles), Richmond and Barnard Castles. Interesting and scenic walking country. Car essential — ample parking, plus garage. Available from March to November. Weekly terms from £55 (fuel not included).

RIPON. 45 Allhallowgate, Ripon; "Braeside," Kirkby Malzeard; Rose Cottage, Winksley. All old stone cottages. Rose Cottage recently completely modernised and refurbished throughout. Close to beautiful Dales, 25 miles from York. Lovely walking country. Facilities for riding and pony trekking; golf, tennis, swimming, all nearby. Braeside and Rose Cottage in pretty Dales villages. Ripon excellent touring centre. Many houses of historical interest in area. Fully equipped except linen. Pets allowed. Car essential (except Ripon), parking outside. Open all year round. Cot supplied if requested. Bedrooms — two doubles, one double, one double. All cottages have TV, two with central heating. Winter weekends from £28 including log fire. Weekly terms from £52 to £90. Stamp for brochure, please. **Mrs K. Bailey, Peacock Farm, Winksley, Ripon HG4 3NR (Kirkby Malzeard [076-583] 338).**

RUSWARP (Whitby). Mr A. R. Harland, "Brooklyn", The Avenue, Ruswarp, Whitby YO21 1NG (Whitby [0947] 602859). Enjoy the freedom of an inexpensive camping style holiday in our two and four berth holiday cabins. Situated in the two-acre grounds of Brooklyn House overlooking the tranquil Esk Valley, central for the seaside at Whitby (one-and-a-half miles) or touring the Yorkshire Dales. Each cabin is of wooden construction and occupies its own secluded grounds amidst oak and ash trees. They are self-contained, with own water/electricity supply, TV and exterior chemical toilet. Flush toilet with hot and cold washbasin in the grounds. Weekly rates from £25 to £45. Pets are welcome. Please state number of people and dates required. SAE for brochure. See also advertisement for six-berth caravan in the Caravan and Camping Section of this Guide.

SCARBOROUGH near (North York Moors). Forge Valley Cottage, Castlegate, East Ayton, Near Scarborough. This charming 18th century beamed cottage is set in a picturesque National Park location overlooking Forge Valley, the River Derwent and the 14th century castle of Ayton. The cottage provides a comfortable holiday home of a high standard and sleeps four persons in one double room and one twin-bedded room. Cot available. Bathroom; sitting-room and dining/kitchen with electric cooker, electric heating (50p meter). Linen supplied. There is private car parking and a pretty garden with lovely views over old fashioned meadows. Only three minutes' walk to shops and public transport. Set within an area of outstanding beauty, the cottage is an ideal centre for walking or touring the Moors, countryside and coast. Sorry, no pets. Open February to December. For brochure apply to **Mrs S. Ward, 38 Castlegate, East Ayton, Near Scarborough YO13 9EJ (Scarborough [0723] 862937).** Registered with English Tourist Board; Member of Yorkshire and Humberside Tourist Board.

SCARBOROUGH. Mrs Cyril Brand, Church Road Farm, Ravenscar, Scarborough YO13 0LZ (Scarborough [0723] 870109). Working farm. A fully furnished two-bedroomed stone-built accommodation attached to a small farmhouse in the village of Ravenscar. Solid fuel fire in the lounge which provides hot water and radiators downstairs. Accommodating four in two bedrooms (one with double bed, one two single beds); kitchen, sittingroom; bathroom and toilet. Cot provided, please bring own cot bedding. Kitchen fully equipped including electric cooker, fridge, tumble dryer, percolator, cutlery, crockery, pans, iron, kitchen unit. No linen supplied but can be arranged at an extra charge of £10. Village shop five minutes' walk away. Sorry, no pets. Car essential, parking space. Open April to end of December. Terms, which include solid fuel, from £50 weekly. Electricity — coin operated meter. Very good area for walking and riding. Scarborough and Whitby within easy reach and well situated for touring Yorkshire.

SELF-CATERING **North Yorkshire** **503**

SCARBOROUGH. Mrs Patricia Marshall, Spikers Hill Farm, West Ayton, Scarborough YO13 9LB (Scarborough [0723] 862537). Three delightful three-bedroomed cottages and one two-bedroomed cottage situated on a private 600-acre farm in North Yorkshire's National Park, five miles from Scarborough. All cottages are modernised with every convenience; electric cooker, fridge, stainless steel sink, etc. Luxury fitted carpets; TV's (two are colour). Bed linen is supplied. Also two luxury king-size caravans; hot and cold running water; all-electric kitchens; fridge, cooker, kettle, etc. Flush toilet, end bedroom with washbasin; lounge with fitted carpet and TV. Cottages and caravans are equipped and cleaned to highest standards. AA and English Tourist Board approved. Stamp, please, for brochure and terms.

SCARBOROUGH. Mrs Pamela Thomas, The Manor House, Langdale End, Near Hackness, Scarborough YO13 0LH (Scarborough [0723] 82232). NORTH YORKSHIRE NATIONAL PARK — a small country estate comprising stone-built Manor House converted into three self-contained apartments, plus cottages and large farmhouse set in 11 acres of beautifully landscaped gardens. Only six miles from Scarborough. Ideal centre for touring or walking coastland, moorland or forest. Private trout beck for residents. Pony trekking, golf, sea-fishing and sailing all available locally. Fully equipped (linen hire available), with log fires (fuel included) and fan heaters for all rooms. Cots, high chairs available. Pets welcome. Open all year. Provision store on site, plus range of home grown and home cooked produce. **Serviced** out of season breaks. Telephone or SAE for brochure.

SCARBOROUGH. 59 Esplanade, Scarborough. The flat is situated opposite the Italian Gardens, in one of the most exclusive positions on the South Cliff in Scarborough. Fully equipped to sleep six persons with two single beds in one bedroom, one double bed in second bedroom, each with washbowls and hot and cold water. The third room has a studio couch to sleep two persons. Large well fitted kitchen/breakfast room containing modern dining suite, modern gas cooker, large fridge, stainless steel double drainer sink unit, cooking equipment etc. Bathroom, immersion heater, separate toilet. Spacious lounge, beautifully furnished, TV, modern gas fire. Flat is close carpeted throughout, own separate entrance, completely self-contained. Ample parking space. No linen supplied. Apply **Mrs L. Bramald, 36 North Park Avenue, Roundhay, Leeds 8 (LS8 1EJ) (Leeds [0532] 667477).**

SCARBOROUGH. Surgate Brow Farm, Silpho, Scarborough. Working farm. The farm is situated in the National Park on the edge of Langdale Forest, in ideal country for walking and touring. The house is secluded, but within easy distance of the Scarborough coast and the moors. The self-contained flat sleeps five in two bedrooms — one with a double and small single bed and the other with two single beds. There is a cot available. Bathroom; sittingroom; kitchen with electric cooker, fridge, spin dryer, etc. Linen can be supplied at small charge, but please bring own cot bedding. Pets permitted. Suitable for disabled visitors. Open from April to October from £60 weekly. SAE for further details to **Mrs D. Brydon, Thirley Beck Farm, Harwood Dale Road, Scarborough YO3 0DW (Scarborough [0723] 870346).**

SCARBOROUGH. Dehra-Dun Holiday Flats, 10 Trinity Road, Scarborough. A long-established business situated in a quiet residential area within easy reach of the south bay, Spa, and town centre. Something to suit everyone. We can offer a completely self-contained luxury ground floor flat — maximum six. An attractive first floor flat with private bathroom for two/six. A spacious three-bedroom maisonette with private bathroom — maximum nine. Also flatlets: some ground floor, sleeping two/six persons, excellent bathroom facilities. All our properties are personally supervised and furnished to a high standard. Reduced terms early and late season. Car parking. Open all year. No VAT. Please send SAE for particulars and brochure to **Mr and Mrs G. E. Meller, 10 Trinity Road, Scarborough YO11 2TA (Scarborough [0723] 363528).**

SKIPTON. Mrs Bristow, Tudor Guest House, Bell Busk, Skipton BD23 4DT (Airton [07293] 301). Charming cottages in the Yorkshire Dales to sleep four or six on a quiet cul-de-sac lane. The larger cottage is 17th century with beams and mullioned windows furnished and equipped to a high standard. Guaranteed cleanliness. It has electric cooker, fridge and microwave in breakfast kitchen. Colour TV and Dralon suite in the lounge. Bathroom. Private garden. Linen provided for beds. Heating in all rooms. Small cottage available to sleep four and a ground floor self-contained flat in Tudor Guest House (see under Malemdale for picture of house). A good area for touring or walking near Malham, Grassington, Ingleborough, Harrogate, etc. Sorry no pets. SAE for brochure.

NORTH YORKSHIRE – RICH IN TOURIST ATTRACTIONS!
Dales, moors, castles, abbeys, cathedrals – you name it and you're almost sure to find it in North Yorkshire. Leading attractions include Castle Howard, the moorlands walks at Goathland, the Waterfalls at Falling Foss, Skipton, Richmond, Wensleydale, Bridestones Moor, Ripon Cathedral, Whitby, Settle and, of course, York itself.

SKIPTON. Bolton Abbey, Skipton. Six holiday cottages are available at various locations on the Bolton Abbey Estate, a private family estate in Wharfedale, encompassing moors, woodland, agricultural land and the ruins of the 12th century Bolton Priory on the banks of the River Wharfe. The cottages are all former estate cottages or farmhouses and have been tastefully modernised and equipped whilst retaining the character of a traditional Dales cottage. They provide an excellent base for walking or touring, and fly fishing is available on five miles of private estate water on the River Wharfe at reduced rates for guests. A brochure giving full details of each cottage and weekly terms is available from (SAE, please): **The Estate Office, Bolton Abbey, Skipton BD23 6EX (Bolton Abbey [075-671] 227).**

SKIPTON. Mr M. H. Skidmore, The Grange, Hellifield, Skipton BD23 4LE (Hellifield [072-95] 296). The accommodation is in a compact three bedroomed house, which is part of The Grange situated on the outskirts of the small village of Hellifield which nestles at the foot of the Yorkshire Dales. Commanding views of Pendle Hill, it is close to Settle, Skipton, Malham, Trough of Bowland and only a short drive to Wensleydale, Swaledale, the Lakes and the West Coast. Ample garden and green fields. A very warm welcome awaits you here in this completely unspoiled part of Yorkshire from Mr and Mrs Skidmore. Accommodation for eight in two double bedrooms and one single; cot; bathroom, toilet; sittingroom; diningroom, well equipped kitchen with electric cooker, fridge, etc. Everything except linen. Shops quarter mile. The house is open all year round. Sorry, no pets. A car is essential and there is parking. Weekly terms from £30 to £85. SAE, please.

YORKSHIRE DALES 1986

DALES HOLIDAY COTTAGES

We have a wide range of personally inspected, Self Catering holiday properties. Many in the heart of 'Herriot Country'.

Phone, or write to FAY AMES
Otley Street, Skipton, BD23 1DY
North Yorkshire
Tel: (0756) 69821 or 60919

SKIPTON. Mr and Mrs R. T. Shelmerdine, Eshton Grange, Gargrave, Skipton BD23 3QE (Gargrave [075-678] 383). Working farm, join in. Modernised 18th century farmhouse on stock farm and Shetland pony stud situated in popular Yorkshire Dales and National Park. This top-floor flat is equipped for self catering (linen etc.) and is particularly suitable for the young walker. Accommodation consists of shower and WC, kitchen, large open plan roof room with great character containing dining, sitting and sleeping accommodation for four. TV. Separate twin bedded double room. Cot. There are excellent drying facilities in the farmhouse and an Evening Meal and Bed and Breakfast also available. Open all year. Terms on application. SAE, please.

SKIPTON. Mrs Judith M. Joy, Jerry and Bens, Hebden, Skipton BD23 5DL (Grassington [0756] 752369). Jerry and Ben's stands in two acres of grounds in one of the most attractive parts of the Yorkshire Dales National Park. Seven properties; Ghyll Cottage (sleeps eight); Mamie's Cottage (sleeps eight); Paradise End (sleeps six); Robin Middle (sleeps six); High Close (sleeps nine); Cruck Rise (sleeps six); Raikes Side (sleeps two/three). All have parking, electric cooker, fridge, colour TV, electric heating and immersion heater; lounge, dining area, bathroom or shower; cots if required. Fully equipped, including linen if requested. Washing machine and telephone available. Well behaved pets accepted. Open all year. Fishing and bathing close by. Terms from £46 per week. SAE, please for detailed brochure. Suitable for disabled.

SLEIGHTS, near Whitby. Mrs June Roberts, White Rose Holiday Cottages, 5 Brook Park, Sleights, Near Whitby YO21 1RT (Whitby [0947] 810763). Sleights. A detached stone house set in its own grounds with private parking. Sleeps 5 adults, 2 children, plus cot. An attractive stone cottage sleeps 4 plus cot. The village of Sleights is one of the prettiest in Yorkshire, winding up the hillside from the River Esk to Blue Bank. It is well situated for both coast and country. **Ruswarp.** An attractive cottage, sleeps 4 plus cot. Situated close to the river and opposite Ruswarp Mill. All AA listed. Open all year, reductions out of season. Personally supervised and cleanliness guaranteed.

THIRSK near. Mrs Jean Knowles, Manor Farm, Little Thirkleby, Near Thirsk YO7 2BA (Thirsk [0845] 401216). **Working farm.** These comfortable semi-detached farm cottages, sleeping five to six people, are situated on a farm in the peaceful hamlet of Little Thirkleby (cul-de-sac), one mile A19, four miles Thirsk (James Herriot market town); 21 miles York, 45 miles Whitby. Close to Hambleton Hills and central for exploring beautiful North Yorkshire. Lawns, parking space, spin drier, ironing facilities, open and electric fires. Coal and logs can be purchased, night storage heating, TV, full size cooker and fridge. Linen hire possible. Eggs, milk, bread can be ordered for arrival. Visitors are welcome to walk over farm. Cot and extra bed available. Furnished, and thoroughly cleaned between lets. Well equipped with guide books and maps, and advice is always available to help holiday makers. Riding, gliding, fishing, golf within few miles. Dog one cottage only. Outhouse available for one used to sleeping outside. Bed and Breakfast available at farmhouse. Excellent local inns and restaurants.

THORNTON-LE-DALE AND PICKERING. Three houses situated in the pretty village of Thornton Dale overlooking stream flowing through centre of village. Scarborough 15 minutes' drive. North Yorkshire Moors five minutes. Two of the houses are identical and consist of: three bedrooms (two double, one single); bathroom; large kitchen/diner with TV, fridge and electric cooker. The other house is situated in the small market town of Pickering. Within easy reach of the Yorkshire Moors, the coast, Flamingo Park Zoo. Scenic Steam Railway (Pickering to Whitby). This house consists of two bedrooms (one double, one twin bedded); lounge with gas fire and TV; kitchen/diner with gas cooker and fridge. Open all year. Shops three minutes. Sorry, no pets. Weekly terms on request from **Mrs G. Balderson, Welcome Cafe, Chestnut Avenue, Thornton Dale, Pickering (Pickering [0751] 74272 or [0751] 74218 after 9 pm).**

WHITBY. Rose Cottage, 3 Iburndale Lane, Sleights, Whitby. Rose Cottage is situated in the delightful valley of Sleights, only four miles from the picturesque old fishing town of Whitby. This cosy country cottage is fully modernised. Well equipped with fitted carpets, situated just off the main road. Accommodation for six people, plus baby in two double bedrooms, with extra bunks in one, cot; bathroom, inside and outside toilets; sittingroom with TV, electric fire and a piano. The kitchen/diner has an electric cooker, fridge, immersion heater, slot meter (50p). Everything is supplied except linen. The cottage has part solid fuel central heating and is most comfortable in winter and spring. Pet dogs permitted. Shops nearby, also churches and country inn. Boating and fishing can be arranged at Ruswarp. Car preferable — parking. Available all year. To avoid disappointment book early for this popular holiday home. SAE, please, to **Mrs Miriam Dunn, The Coach House, 145 Coach Road, Sleights Hall, Sleights, Whitby YO22 5EH (Whitby [0947] 810703).**

WHITBY. "The Cottage", Howlet Hall, Sleights, Whitby. Situated up a short farm road between the villages of Sneaton and Ugglebarnby in the North Yorks Moors National Park, the cottage is three miles from Whitby with views of Abbey, moors and sea. Substantially built of local stone, it has a sheltered garden and is an excellent walking centre. It is comfortably furnished and accommodation comprises large lounge/diningroom, smaller snug with open or electric fire and TV. Three bedrooms upstairs with three single and one double bed. Cot. Bathroom, separate WC. Kitchenette with Calor gas cooker; immersion heater; walk in larder with fridge. Parking immediately outside cottage. Sorry, no pets. SAE, please, to **Mrs M. Weston, Tinkler Hall, Sleights, Whitby YO22 5HU (Whitby [0947] 810676).**

WHITBY. Mrs June Griffiths, Regent House, 7 Royal Crescent, Whitby YO21 3EJ (Whitby [0947] 602103). Five lovely self-contained flats with beautiful sea views and lifts to all floors. Situated on Royal Crescent in tall Victorian house. Each has modern well-equipped kitchen, bathroom, two family bedrooms, lounge with bed settee and dining area. TV and fridge. Accommodates eight. Cot and high chair. Small pet allowed at extra charge. Yards from cliff tops and sea. North Yorkshire moors three miles. Fully equipped. Linen may be hired. Golf, tennis, bathing nearby; trekking six miles. Shooting and river fishing (permits required). Electricity metered. Open all year. Off main road. Ideal holiday centre. Weekly terms on request. Reductions off season.

WHITBY. Modern self-contained holiday flats situated in main residential holiday area. Close to all main leisure amenities, shops and beach. Accommodating two to seven people in fully equipped flats with lounge/diningroom and TV; bedrooms with divan beds and Continental quilts, "extra blankets if needed". Cot and high chair. Bathroom and toilet. Fully equipped kitchen with cooker and fridge; immersion heater. Electric fires and electric slot meter. Pets allowed. Spare keys. Open Easter to November. Attended personally by proprietors guaranteeing cleanliness and good service. SAE to **Mrs O. M. Dixon, Camden House, 18 John Street, Whitby, North Yorkshire.**

WHITBY. Harbourside Flats, 7 Pier Road, Whitby. Two luxury holiday flats, recently modernised, situated on the harbourside of the picturesque old fishing town of Whitby. The properties, both accommodating seven people (one two-bedroom, the other three-bedroom), are spacious — lounge bay windows have panoramic views over the harbour; fully equipped kitchen; bathroom; immersion heater; electric fires; TV. Electricity by 50p meter. Children welcome, cot and high chair provided. Pets accepted free of charge. Guests to bring own linen. Whitby — the home of Captain Cook — offers ideal sandy beaches, leisure amenities, fishing trips, golf and tennis. Excellent location for touring North Yorkshire Moors National Park, unique coastal villages and many other places of local interest. Available Easter to September. Terms and further details on request — **Mrs S. Harland, High Leas, Glaisdale, Whitby YO21 2PX (Whitby [0947] 87255).**

Terms quoted in this publication may be subject to increase if rises in costs necessitate

West Yorkshire — SELF-CATERING

Sproxton Hall Farm Cottages
Helmsley, North Yorkshire

Winner of C.L.A. and C.P.R.E. Henley Award 1983. You can be assured of a warm personal welcome and the best in comfort and cleanliness at Sproxton Hall. We are justly proud of our five cottages which have been thoughtfully and tastefully converted from 18th century stone farm buildings, retaining originality whilst providing all modern facilities including colour TV, bed linen, laundry room, CH and log fires (sleeps 4-8). One cottage is suitable for the disabled. Enjoy peace, tranquillity and panoramic views, yet Helmsley is only 1½ miles away. Regret no dogs. Winter breaks/weekends. SAE for brochure to:

Mr and Mrs A. Wainwright, Sproxton Hall, Helmsley, York YO6 5EQ.
Tel. 0439 70225.

YORK
Self Catering Cottages

We are beautifully set in the surrounding countryside of York, whilst still being only 4 miles from the city centre. The converted farm buildings still have their original character and charm.

AA Listed . . . an ideal place to stay

Jack and Josie Hughes,
Copmanthorpe Grange, York YO2 3TN
Tel: 0904 84-318

MEMBER — Yorkshire and Humberside Tourist Board

YORK. 2 Wandale Cottage, Bulmer, York. This lovely cottage is situated in a quiet unspoilt village and is an ideal house from which to tour the Yorkshire Moors and Dales and the East Coast. Near Castle Howard. The historic city of York, with its Tudor houses and cobbled streets, is within easy driving distance. Trout fishing available. The cottage is available as self-catering accommodation all year. Accommodation for five in two double bedrooms (one with extra single bed); sittingroom (colour TV); bathroom, toilet; well-equipped electric kitchen. Meter for electricity. Everything supplied except linen. Children and pets welcome. Car essential — parking. Electric heating; open fires. SAE, please, to **Mrs J. Goodwill, Wandale Farm, Bulmer, York YO6 7BW (Whitwell-on-the-Hill) [065-381] 326).**

YORK. Mr R. Barry, White Lodge, Ellerton, York YO4 4PA (0757) 85297 or (0757) 703898. Accommodation comprises three double bedrooms. Ground floor bedroom has double bed and is next to the bathroom. First floor bedrooms each have one double and one single bed and are inter-connected, i.e., access to bedroom No. 3 is through bedroom No. 2. Stands at edge of small village surrounded by arable farmland. Delightful walks include banks of river Derwent and rural Pocklington Canal. York 12 miles and M62 14 miles. Electric cooking and heating. Children welcome but regret, no pets. Car essential — parking. Nearest shops four miles. Open all year. Weekly terms from £50 – £125. Fuller details may be obtained by ringing **Mr Barry.**

YORK. Sunset Cottages, Grimston Manor Farm, Gilling East, York. Working farm. Six beautiful cottages lovingly converted from the granaries of our family farm. Superbly situated in the heart of the Howardian Hills, on the outskirts of the National Park and only 17 miles north of the historic City of York — Herriot Country. With panoramic views, these warm and comfortable cottages retain their original mellow beams and interesting stonework while still providing all the modern comforts you rightfully expect in a well-designed self-catering cottage. Full central heating. Personally supervised by the resident owners Heather and Richard Kelsey. Sorry, no pets (sheep country). Please phone or write for brochure — **Mr and Mrs R. J. and J. H. Kelsey, Grimston Manor Farm, Gilling East, York YO6 4HR (Brandsby [03475] 654).**

SELF-CATERING   North Yorkshire   507

TERRINGTON HOLIDAY COTTAGES
NORTH YORKSHIRE

8 super, well-appointed stone-built Holiday Cottages. Recommended by Egon Ronay. AA Approved. Surrounded by picturesque lawns and flower beds. Situated in the centre of the unspoilt farming village of Terrington. Beautiful countryside. 14 miles N.E. of York, three miles from Castle Howard. Sleeps 2-6 people; illustrated brochure. SAE for full particulars to:

**Mrs. D. Goodrick, Rose Villa, Terrington, York YO6 4PP
(Tel. 065-384 268 or 370)**

YORK (North Yorks Moors). Mrs G. M. Wilson, Stonegrave Lodge, Stonegrave, York YO6 4LL (Nunnington [043-95] 257). Working farm. "The Cottage" is completely detached and stands in its own garden (mainly lawn), 100 yards from the farm and 400 yards from B1257. Panoramic views of the countryside from all rooms. This is a 160-acre mixed farm. The cottage has fitted carpets throughout. There are two double and one twin-bedded rooms, sleeping six. Cot. Bathroom, toilet. Sittingroom; kitchen-diner with electric cooker, fridge, work tops. No linen supplied. One mile from shops; 20 miles from sea. Pets by arrangement only. Car essential — parking. Open all year round. The district is full of glorious scenery, with many interesting villages and market towns such as Thirsk and Malton. Many abbeys and stately homes, etc., within a short drive. SAE, please, for terms.

YORK. Tea Pot Cottage, Meltonby, Pocklington, York. Tea Pot Cottage (the centre one of three) has lawned garden to front, and open views. Situated in Meltonby at the foot of the Yorkshire Wolds, it is near the owners' 170-acre farm. Ideal centre for historic York (13 miles), coast (30 miles), Forest Drives, Moors, Dales, Stately Homes, fishing, boating, country inns, horse riding. Pocklington (two-and-a-half miles) has excellent shopping facilities, supermarkets, cinema, bingo, heated swimming pool, gardens, museum, lily pond. Newly carpeted throughout, the cottage has two double bedrooms plus cot (if required); kitchen with dining area; lounge; bathroom, toilet. TV, immersion and economy water heaters, fridge, washer, automatic double oven, shaving point, etc. Electricity on 50p meter. Children, pets welcome. Garage — car essential. Open all year. SAE for terms to **Miss J. Smith, Fair View Farm, Meltonby, Pocklington, York YO4 2PN (Pocklington [07592] 3256 or 2042).**

YORK. Mrs R. C. Reed, Field House Farm, Bielby, York YO4 4JR (Melbourne [075-93] 386). Working farm. This spacious, traditional, but modernised, very clean, well-furnished farmhouse is on quiet country lane, half-mile from village, on a 210 acres family dairy farm. Near to Pocklington and few miles York. Beautiful ride to coast over the Yorkshire Wolds and within easy reach of the Moors, Dales and new Humber Bridge. Three double bedrooms (cot and high chair), bathroom, WC upstairs. Large sittingroom, colour TV. Diningroom; well-equipped kitchen with large fridge. All bed linen included (poly-cotton sheets). Visitors welcome to look round farm. Fresh milk available. Sorry, no dogs/cats. Telephone or SAE.

FARM HOLIDAY GUIDES LIMITED publish a large range of well-known accommodation guides. We will be happy to send you details or you can use the order form at the back of this book.

508 West Yorkshire SELF-CATERING

WEST YORKSHIRE

KEIGHLEY. Mrs W. Cocks, High Hob Cote Farm, Colne Road, Oakworth, Keighley BD22 0RW (Haworth [0535] 42376). Situated on the above 30 acre farm, a semi-detached 18th century weavers cottage, stone mullioned windows, curving stone staircase. Recently modernised, breakfast kitchen, gas cooker, fridge, immersion heater. Modern bathroom. Dining lounge with TV. One double, one twin bedroom, one single put-u-up. Bed linen provided. Three gas fires, electric fires. Small south facing garden. Dogs by arrangement. Enjoys magnificent panoramic views across fields to Haworth and Haworth Moors. Haworth, home of the Bronte family of "Wuthering Heights" fame (a museum), and the Worth Valley Steam Railway. Ten miles from Shipton, gateway to the beautiful Dales National Park. Open all year. Shops and Pub one mile.

WEST YORKSHIRE – LITERARY CONNECTIONS!
Head for the village of Haworth and sample some of the Bronte atmosphere. The parsonage is now a museum and well woth a visit. Make sure you also experience the adjacent moors. Also of interest in this county – Harlow Car Gardens, Shibden Hall and the French-style gardens at Bramham Park.

Don't go on holiday without a
Visitor's Guide

The BEST guidebook for your holiday

* Where to go, what to do and see
* Places of interest highlighted
* addresses, opening times etc

Chilterns
Cornwall & Isles of Scilly
Cotswolds
Devon
East Anglia
Hampshire & Isle of Wight
Kent
Lake District
Historic Places of Wales
North Wales and Snowdonia
Scottish Borders & Edinburgh
Guernsey, Alderney & Sark
Peak District
North York Moors, & Yorkshire Coast
Severn & Avon Valleys
Somerset & Dorset
Sussex
Yorkshire Dales
South & West Wales
Welsh Borders

only £4.50

From bookshops including W.H. Smith or direct from:

8 Station Street, Ashbourne, Derbyshire Tel: (0335) 44486

Moorland Publishing

The information in the entries in this guide is presented by the publishers in good faith and after the signed acceptance by advertisers that they will uphold the high standards associated with
FARM HOLIDAY GUIDES LIMITED. The publishers do not accept responsibility for any inaccuracies or omissions or any results thereof. Before making final holiday arrangements readers should confirm the prices and facilities directly with advertisers.

ISLES OF SCILLY

ST. MARY'S. Mrs R. C. May, Seaways Flower Farm, Porth Loo, St. Mary's TR21 0NF (Scillonia [0720] 22398). This chalet is situated in its own private surroundings with views of the harbour, adjacent to the island's nine-hole golf course and Porthloo Beach. Sleeping five, there are two bedrooms, one with twin beds and one with bunks and a single bed. Modern all-electric kitchen (cooker, fridge, heater over sink). Shower with toilet and washbasin. Cot, high chair for children who are welcome. Combined sitting/diningroom. Colour TV in each holiday home. Shops under one mile, sea 100 yards away. Pets by prior arrangement only. Parking. Groceries, milk delivered on request. Please send SAE for terms which exclude fuel. Linen supplied. Suitable for disabled guests. Motor launch trips from St. Mary's to neighbouring inhabited and uninhabited islands — St. Martin's, St. Agnes and Bryher, Tresco for gardens and fascinating "Valhalla," as well as Bishop Rock Lighthouse.

ISLE OF WIGHT

CARISBROOKE. Mrs Jane Cross, Alvington View, Calbourne Road, Carisbrooke PO30 5SR (0983) 527700). Alvington View is a smallholding set in open country with panoramic views of the Solent and surrounding countryside. Its central situation makes it an ideal touring base; half a mile out of Carisbrooke with its historic castle and church. A few goats, pigs, ducks, chickens and bantams are kept at Alvington View (with plenty of chicks and ducklings hatching out during summer), and there is a swimming pool in the garden for guests' use. The Brewhouse has been skilfully converted to provide a compact all-electric holiday flat, to sleep four. Family room with bed settee, breakfast bar, chairs, wardrobe, dressing table and black and white TV. Stair ladder to sleeping gallery with two single divan beds. Kitchenette has full-size fridge, Baby Belling cooker, sink, electric kettle, etc. Shower room with basin, WC suite and shower. Ample parking. No linen supplied. Terms include electricity. Further details on request.

TOTLAND BAY. 3 Seaview Cottages, Broadway, Totland Bay. This well modernised cosy old coastguard cottage holds the Farm Holiday Guide Diploma for the highest standard of accommodation. It is warm and popular throughout the year. Four days winter break — £20; a week in summer £129. Located close to two beaches in beautiful walking country near mainland links. It comprises lounge/dinette/kitchenette; two bedrooms (sleeping five); bathroom/toilet. Well furnished, fully heated, TV, selection of books and other considerations. An alternative larger cottage is also available at Cowes, Isle of Wight. **Mrs C. Pitts, 11 York Avenue, New Milton, Hampshire BH25 6BT (New Milton [0425] 615215).**

WROXALL. Nos 1 and 2. Span Cottages, Rew Lane, Wroxall. Span Cottages are a delightful pair of stone cottages built over 300 years ago. Quietly situated with a large garden, they enjoy rural views and provide all modern amenities, whilst retaining much of their character. Comfortably furnished and each equipped to a high standard, accommodation comprises kitchen, lounge, TV, diningroom, three double bedrooms (sleeps six), bathroom. Cot and high chair. Numerous footpaths provide lovely walks through the 500-acre farm. Two miles from the sea. They are set in some of the island's most beautiful scenery and are ideally situated for visiting the many attractions. Under personal supervision, they are available all year. Centrally heated and log fires. Terms and brochure on request. SAE, please, to **H. N. Butler (Farms) Ltd., Span Farm, Wroxall PO38 3AU (Isle of Wight [0983] 852419).**

CHANNEL ISLANDS

GUERNSEY. Misses K. O. and N. A. Dennis, Duvaux Farm, Duvaux Road, St. Sampsons, Guernsey (Guernsey [0481] 44022). A holiday home from home, ideally situated for beach jaunts and outings. This typical Guernsey farmhouse, occupied by the same family for hundreds of years, has a rare antique atmosphere and historical links with Guernsey City, Ohio, USA. Four double bedrooms; bathroom, inside and outside toilets; sittingroom and diningroom. Coal and electric heating. Cot and high chair can be hired. Sorry, no pets. Open from May to October. The owners, who live in the house, will provide the food for guests to cook their own Breakfast, but food for other meals must be bought and prepared as required. Terms on request.

SWALLOW FLATS
Les Clotures, L'Ancresse, Guernsey
Telephone: 0481 49633

Ten modern, fully equipped, self-catering flats sleep from 2-9 including children. Free car park. Close to sandy beaches, golf course, horse riding and marina. Charges include linen, colour TV, cot, high chair and children's bed if required. Please state number of adults and children in party and dates required.

LA COUTURE COTTAGES
La Couture, St. Peter's, Guernsey

3 fully furnished Cottages for 4-6 people. 2 double bedrooms (1 double bed – 2 singles) and double put-u-up in lounge. Fitted carpets. TV, parking. Situated on country farm.

Further details: Mr and Mrs J. C. Tostevin Telephone: (0481) 63232 after 6 pm

HELP IMPROVE BRITISH TOURIST STANDARDS

You are choosing holiday accommodation from our very popular FARM HOLIDAY GUIDES. Whether it be a hotel, guest house, farmhouse or self-catering accommodation, we think you will find it hospitable, comfortable and clean, and your host and hostess friendly and helpful.

Why not write and tell us about it?

As a recognition of the generally well-run and excellent holiday accommodation reviewed in our publications, we at FARM HOLIDAY GUIDES LIMITED present a diploma to proprietors who receive the highest recommendation from their guests who are also readers of our Guides. If you care to write to us praising the holiday you have booked through FARM HOLIDAY GUIDES – whether this be board, self-catering accommodation, a sporting or a caravan holiday, the content of your letter will be evaluated and the proprietors who reach our final list will be contacted.

The winning proprietor will receive an attractive framed diploma to display on his premises as recognition of a high standard of comfort, amenity and hospitality. FARM HOLIDAY GUIDES LIMITED offer this diploma as a contribution towards the improvement of standards in tourist accommodation in Britain. Help your excellent host or hostess to win it!

DIPLOMA
AWARDED BY
READERS
of
FARM HOLIDAY GUIDE
PUBLICATIONS LIMITED

TO..
FOR HOLIDAY ACCOMMODATION
of the HIGHEST STANDARD

AT..

ORDER NOW! *See Overleaf*

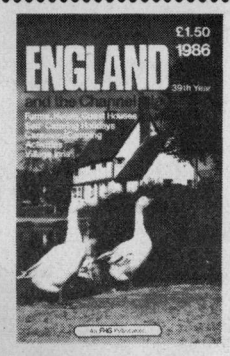

ONE FOR YOUR FRIEND

We hope you enjoy this Guide. Have you thought how useful a copy of this, or any of our Guides, might be to your friends? Any of these handsome Guides would make a useful gift at any time of the year. We will also send them abroad for you but we will have to charge separately for postage or freight costs. The inclusive cost of posting and packing the Guides to you or your friends in the UK is as follows:

No. of Copies

1986 HERITAGE BRITAIN — *Where to Visit, Where to Stay*   £1.80   ....
For selected Heritage properties and historic sites.

1986 FARM HOLIDAY GUIDE — ENGLAND   £2.00   ....
Farmhouses and other coast and country holiday accommodation in England, county by county. Board and Self-Catering. Colour Section.

1986 FARM HOLIDAY GUIDE — SCOTLAND   £1.10   ....
Farmhouses and other coast and country holiday accommodation in Scotland, county by county. Board and Self-Catering. Colour Section.

1986 FARM HOLIDAY GUIDE — WALES/IRELAND   £1.10   ....
Farmhouses and other coast and country holiday accommodation in Wales and Ireland, county by county. Board and Self-Catering.

1986 BRITAIN'S BEST HOLIDAYS — A QUICK REFERENCE GUIDE   £1.25   ....
A large range of all kinds of Board and Self-Catering all round Britain. Ideal for family and touring holidays. With symbols and colour.

1986 FHG SELF-CATERING AND FURNISHED HOLIDAYS   £1.25   ....
Self-Catering only, including caravans. Over a thousand addresses throughout Britain. Colour Section.

1986 ENGLAND'S BEST HOLIDAYS   £1.00   ....
Board and Self-Catering throughout England. A large selection to suit all tastes.

1986 SCOTLAND'S BEST HOLIDAYS   £1.00   ....
A full selection of Scotland's hospitality. Board and Self-Catering.

1986 HOLIDAYS IN WALES   £1.00   ....
Farms, hotels, guest houses, cottages, flats, caravans for Board or Self-Catering.

1986 CARAVANS AND CAMPING HOLIDAYS   £1.10   ....
Caravans for hire, Caravan Sites and night halts, camping sites. Colour Section.

1986 BED AND BREAKFAST STOPS   £1.10   ....
A large selection of overnight accommodation throughout Britain.

1986 ACTIVITY HOLIDAYS IN BRITAIN   95p   ....
Sporting and special interest holidays for adults and children.

1986 GETTING AROUND THE HIGHLANDS AND ISLANDS   £2.00   ....
Comprehensive timetables and other travel information.

**SEND YOUR ORDER AND PAYMENT TO: FARM HOLIDAY GUIDES LTD.
Abbey Mill Centre, Seedhill, Paisley PA1 1JN**

To: Mr, Mrs, Miss ....

Address ....

.... Post Code ....

I enclose cheque/postal order for ....

From: Signed ....

Address ....

.... Post Code ....

*Additional names and addresses can be sent on a separate sheet.
Remember to mark your choice. Postage included UK only.